DELPHI 3
SUPERBIBLE

**Paul Thurrott, Gary Brent,
Richard Bagdazian, Steve Tendon**

WAITE
GROUP
PRESS™

A Division of
Sams Publishing

Corte Madera, CA

PUBLISHER: Mitchell Waite
ASSOCIATE PUBLISHER: Charles Drucker

ACQUISITIONS EDITOR: Jill Pisoni

EDITORIAL DIRECTOR: John Crudo
PROJECT EDITOR: Kurt Stephan
DEVELOPMENTAL EDITOR: Harry Henderson
TECHNICAL REVIEWERS: Gary Frerking, Wayne Niddery
SOFTWARE SPECIALIST: Dan Scherf
COPY EDITORS: Merrilee Eggleston, Michelle Goodman, Ann Longknife/Creative Solutions

PRODUCTION DIRECTOR: Julianne Ososke
PRODUCTION MANAGER: Cecile Kaufman
PRODUCTION EDITOR: Kelsey McGee
SENIOR DESIGNER: Sestina Quarequio
DESIGNER: Karen Johnston
COVER DESIGN: Regan Honda
COVER ART: © 1996 Photodisk, Inc.
PRODUCTION: Jenaffer Brandt, Paula Lowell, Shawn Ring, Tim Tate, Mark Walchle

Printed in the United States of America
97 98 99 • 10 9 8 7 6 5 4 3 2 1

Library of Congress Cataloging-in-Publication Data
Delphi 3 SuperBible / Paul Thurrott . . . [et al.].
     p. cm.
   Includes index.
   ISBN 1-57169-027-1
   1. Delphi (Computer file) 2. Computer software--Development.
I. Thurrott, Paul B.
QA76.76.D47D47   1996   96-36399
005.265--DC20   CIP

Dedication

For my wife, Stephanie. Thanks so much.
—Paul Thurrott

To my father, Lawrence B. Brent. Remember the typewriter you gave me when I was a kid?
—Gary Brent

To Christina, who creates our memories.
To Meredith, Whitney, and Michael, the joy of our days.
And to an October full moon in a place called Kona.
—Richard Bagdazian

To the memory of my grandparents, Ingrid and Sven.
—Steve Tendon

About the Authors

Paul Thurrott is the Webmaster at Big Tent Media Labs, a publishing company in San Francisco, where he uses Microsoft Visual InterDev and SQL Server to create dynamic, data-driven Web sites. Paul is the author of several books, including titles about Windows 95, Windows NT 4.0, Visual Basic 3.0, 4.0, and VBScript, Excel for Windows 95, and other Windows-related technologies. Currently, he lives in Phoenix, AZ, with his wife Stephanie and their two bilingual cats, Fred and Barney.

Gary Brent is currently professor of computer information systems at Scottsdale Community College in Scottsdale, AZ. Gary programmed exclusively in (and later taught) C and C++ for nearly 10 years, until he encountered an early beta of Delphi 1.0. His conversion was immediate, reminiscent of the appearance of Turbo Pascal so many years earlier. Gary and his wife April also run a small company called Key Control (`www.keycontrol.com`), an Internet-based distributor of ultra-high security residential/commercial door locks (a Cold War spin-off technology) for do-it-your-selfers nationwide.

Richard Bagdazian is an electrical engineer currently working in the field of satellite communcations in the San Diego area. He designs digital signal processing software for satellite modems and writes about computer languages and the Internet in his free time. He also races triathlon events when time allows.

Steve Tendon is the owner of TWT ObjektExpert KB, a consulting firm based in Sweden that specializes in international Delphi application development. He began programming professionally in the early 1980s by writing assembly interfaces between C-language programs and hardware drivers. Between 1989 and 1991, he was technical director of Borland Italy, where he was in charge of in-house information system implementation, software localization, customer support, and sales engineering. He also co-authored *Borland C++ Object-Oriented Programming* and, more recently, *Delphi 2 Developers' Solutions* by Waite Group Press. Currently he works on custom software development in the areas of sales and marketing automation in Italy and banking systems in Switzerland, where he deploys object-oriented programming and database technology in client/server architectures. Of course, Delphi is his preferred development tool.

Table of Contents

PART I   **OVERVIEW** 1
CHAPTER 1   Getting Started 3
CHAPTER 2   VCL Basics 15

PART II   **OBJECTS** 27
CHAPTER 3   TObject 29
CHAPTER 4   TIniFile 35
CHAPTER 5   TThread 49
CHAPTER 6   TRegistry and TRegIniFile 57
CHAPTER 7   TList and TPopupList 75
CHAPTER 8   Exception and Its Descendents 89
CHAPTER 9   Introduction to Internet Controls 103

PART III   **PERSISTENT OBJECTS** 107
CHAPTER 10   TPersistent 109
CHAPTER 11   TClipboard 111
CHAPTER 12   TColumnTitle 123
CHAPTER 13   TControlScrollBar 131
CHAPTER 14   TIconOptions 137
CHAPTER 15   TListItem and TListItems 141
CHAPTER 16   TParaAttributes 161
CHAPTER 17   TPicture 167
CHAPTER 18   TTextAttributes 175
CHAPTER 19   TTreeNode and TTreeNodes 181
CHAPTER 20   TCanvas and Its Descendants 217
CHAPTER 21   TCollection, TCollectionItem, and Their Descendants . . .247
CHAPTER 22   TDataLink and Its Descendants 287
CHAPTER 23   TGraphicsObject and Its Descendants 305
CHAPTER 24   TGraphic and Its Descendants 317
CHAPTER 25   TStrings and Its Descendants 333

PART IV   **COMPONENTS** 377
CHAPTER 26   TComponent 379
CHAPTER 27   TApplication 387
CHAPTER 28   TDataSource 423
CHAPTER 29   TMenuItem 429
CHAPTER 30   TScreen 447
CHAPTER 31   TSession 457
CHAPTER 32   TTimer 473

CHAPTER 33	TMenu and Its Descendants	477
CHAPTER 34	TCommonDialog and Its Descendants	487
CHAPTER 35	TCustomImageList and Its Descendants	517
CHAPTER 36	TDataSet and Its Descendants	563
CHAPTER 37	TField and Its Descendants	649
CHAPTER 38	TControl	717

PART V — NONWINDOWED CONTROLS 753

CHAPTER 39	TGraphicControl	755
CHAPTER 40	TBevel	761
CHAPTER 41	TImage	767
CHAPTER 42	TPaintBox	775
CHAPTER 43	TShape	779
CHAPTER 44	TCustomLabel and Its Descendants	787
CHAPTER 45	TSpeedButton and Its Descendants	795
CHAPTER 46	TSplitter	807

PART VI — WINDOWED CONTROLS 813

CHAPTER 47	TWinControl	815
CHAPTER 48	TDBCtrlGrid	835
CHAPTER 49	THeaderControl	851
CHAPTER 50	TProgressBar	861
CHAPTER 51	TScrollBar	869
CHAPTER 52	TStatusBar	879
CHAPTER 53	TTabSheet	887
CHAPTER 54	TTrackBar	895
CHAPTER 55	TCustomComboBox and Its Descendants	909
CHAPTER 56	TCustomHotKey and THotKey	927
CHAPTER 57	TCustomListBox and Its Descendants	935
CHAPTER 58	TCustomListView and TListView	957
CHAPTER 59	TCustomTabControl and Its Descendants	997
CHAPTER 60	TCustomTreeView and TTreeView	1015
CHAPTER 61	TCustomUpDown and TUpDown	1039
CHAPTER 62	TScrollingWinControl and Its Descendants	1051
CHAPTER 63	TButtonControl and Its Descendants	1087
CHAPTER 64	TCustomEdit and Its Descendants	1115
CHAPTER 65	TCustomControl and Its Descendants	1149

APPENDIXES

A	Where to Go from Here	1195
B	Project CD	1197

Contents

PART I   OVERVIEW 1

CHAPTER 1   GETTING STARTED 3

About Delphi 3

What's New in Delphi 4

    Features Common to Each Edition 4

        32-Bit Optimizing Compiler 5

        Character Types 6

        `Currency` Type 7

        String Types 7

        `Variant` Type 8

        Data Modules 8

        Windows 95/NT and COM Support 8

        Enhanced IDE and Debugger 8

        Object Repository and Visual Form Inheritance 9

        Visual Component Library 9

        32-Bit Borland Database Engine 9

Converting Programs from 16-Bit to 32-Bit 9

    Windows 95 Common Controls 10

    Visual Basic Custom Controls (VBXs) 10

    New Type Sizes 10

    Windows Differences 11

Using This Book 11

    Part I: Overview 11

    Part II: Objects 11

    Part III: Persistent Objects 12

    Part IV: Components 12

    Part V: Nonwindowed Controls 12

    Part VI: Windowed Controls 12

    What's in a Chapter? 12

        Topic Discussion 13

        Summary Table 13

        Reference Entries 13

    Finding What You Need 13

Looking Up Complete Topics 13

Reviewing Delphi in Depth 14

CHAPTER 2   VCL BASICS 15

Programming with Objects 15

Pure and Hybrid Languages 15

OOP Concepts 16

Inheritance 17

Polymorphism 17

Encapsulation 17

Units and Classes 18

Class Visibility 19

Private 20

Protected 20

Public 20

Published 20

The Visual Component Library 21

Handling Events 22

Using Properties 22

Methods 23

Method Directives 23

`virtual` and `dynamic` 23

`override` 23

`abstract` 24

Run-Time Type Information 24

Using the Object Browser 25

Exploring the VCL on Your Own 26

PART II   OBJECTS 27

CHAPTER 3   `TObject` 29

CHAPTER 4   `TIniFile` 35

CHAPTER 5   `TThread` 49

CHAPTER 6   `TRegistry` AND `TRegIniFile` 57

Registry Differences 57

CHAPTER 7 **TList AND TPopupList** 75

TList 76

TPopupList 77

CHAPTER 8 **Exception AND ITS DESCENDANTS** 89

Writing Safe Programs 89

    try...except 90

    try...finally 90

Types of Exceptions 91

    EAbort 92

    EOutOfMemory 92

        EOutOfResources 92

    EInOutError 92

    EIntError 93

        EDivByZero 93

        ERangeError 93

        EIntOverflow 93

    EMathError 93

        EInvalidOp 93

        EZeroDivide 93

        EOverflow 93

        EUnderflow 93

    EInvalidPointer 93

    EInvalidCast 93

    EConvertError 94

    EAccessViolation 94

    EPrivilege 94

    EStackOverflow 94

    EControlC 94

    EVariantError 94

    EPropReadOnly 94

    EPropWriteOnly 94

    EExternalException 94

    EStreamError 95

        EFCreateError 95

        EFOpenError 95

    EResNotFound 95

    EListError 95

    EBitsError 95

    EStringListError 96

    EThread 96

    EPrinter 96

EMenuError 96
EInvalidOperation 96
EInvalidGraphic 96
EInvalidGraphicOperation 96
Exception Properties and Methods 96

CHAPTER 9   INTRODUCTION TO INTERNET CONTROLS 103
FTP 104
HTML 104
HTTP 104
NNTP 104
POP 105
SMTP 105
TCP 105
UDP 105

PART III   PERSISTENT OBJECTS 107
CHAPTER 10   TPersistent 109
CHAPTER 11   TClipboard 111
Delphi and the Clipboard 111
CHAPTER 12   TColumnTitle 123
CHAPTER 13   TControlScrollBar 131
CHAPTER 14   TIconOptions 137
CHAPTER 15   TListItem AND TListItems 141
TListItem 141
TListItems 153
CHAPTER 16   TParaAttributes 161
CHAPTER 17   TPicture 167
CHAPTER 18   TTextAttributes 175
CHAPTER 19   TTreeNode AND TTreeNodes .181
TTreeNodes 204
CHAPTER 20   TCanvas AND ITS DESCENDANTS 217
TMetaFileCanvas 219

TPrinterCanvas 220

CHAPTER 21   TCollection, TCollectionItem, AND THEIR DESCENDANTS 247

TCollection 247

TCollectionItem 248

TListColumns 249

TListColumn 249

THeaderSections 250

THeaderSection 250

TStatusPanels 251

TStatusPanel 252

TDBGridColumns 252

TColumn 253

Example Project 282

CHAPTER 22   TDataLink AND ITS DESCENDANTS 287

TDataLink 287

TTableDataLink 293

TFieldDataLink 293

TQueryDataLink 299

TNavDataLink 299

TDataSourceLink 299

TListSourceLink 300

TGridDataLink 300

TDBCtrlGridLink 304

CHAPTER 23   TGraphicsObject AND ITS DESCENDANTS 305

TGraphicsObject 305

TBrush 306

TPen 306

TFont 307

CHAPTER 24   TGraphic AND ITS DESCENDANTS 317

TGraphic 317

TIcon 318

TMetafile 319

TBitmap 319

CHAPTER 25   TStrings AND ITS DESCENDANTS 333

TStrings 333

TComboBoxStrings 336

THeaderStrings 336

TIndexFiles 337

TListBoxStrings 338

TMemoStrings 338

TOutlineStrings 339

TPageAccess 339

TRichEditStrings 339

TStringGridStrings 340

TStringList 340

TSubItems 341

TTabPageAccess 342

TTabStrings 342

TTreeStrings 343

Example Project 371

PART IV   COMPONENTS 377

CHAPTER 26   TComponent 379
Using Components 379

CHAPTER 27   TApplication 387

CHAPTER 28   TDataSource 423

CHAPTER 29   TMenuItem 429

CHAPTER 30   TScreen 447

CHAPTER 31   TSession 457

CHAPTER 32   TTimer 473

CHAPTER 33   TMenu AND ITS DESCENDANTS 477
Designing Menus 477

TMenu 477

TMainMenu 479

TPopupMenu 479

CHAPTER 34   TCommonDialog AND ITS DESCENDANTS 487
TCommonDialog 487

TColorDialog 489

TFindDialog 489

`TFontDialog` 490

`TOpenDialog` 491

    The Filter editor 492

`TPrintDialog` 493

`TPrinterSetupDialog` 494

`TReplaceDialog` 495

`TSaveDialog` 496

CHAPTER 35 `TCustomImageList` **AND ITS DESCENDANTS** 517

`TCustomImageList` 518

`TImageList` 520

`TGlyphList` 521

Example Project 559

CHAPTER 36 `TDataSet` **AND ITS DESCENDANTS** 563

`TDataSet` 563

`TDBDataSet` 646

`TTable` 646

`TStoredProc` 647

`TQuery` 647

CHAPTER 37 `TField` **AND ITS DESCENDANTS** 649

`TField` 649

    To Start the Fields Editor 651

    Creating Persistent Field Components 652

    Deleting Persistent Field Components 653

    Arranging the Order of Persistent Field Components 653

        To Change the Order of a Single Field: 653

        To Change the Order for a Block of Fields 654

        Defining New Persistent Field Components 654

    To Create a New Persistent Field Component 654

        Dialog Box Options 654

`TAutoIncField` 657

`TBCDField` 657

`TBinaryField` 658

`TBlobField` 658

`TBooleanField` 658

`TBytesField` 659

`TCurrencyField` 659

`TDateField` 659

TDateTimeField..659

TFloatField..659

TGraphicField..660

TIntegerField...660

TMemoField...660

TNumericField...660

TSmallIntField...661

TStringField..661

TTimeField..661

TVarBytesField..661

TWordField..661

CHAPTER 38 TControl 717

PART V   NONWINDOWED CONTROLS 753

CHAPTER 39 TGraphicControl 755

TGraphicControl 755

CHAPTER 40 TBevel 761

CHAPTER 41 TImage 767

CHAPTER 42 TPaintBox 775

CHAPTER 43 TShape 779

CHAPTER 44 TCustomLabel AND ITS DESCENDANTS 787

TDBText 790

TLabel 791

CHAPTER 45 TSpeedButton AND ITS DESCENDANTS 795

Creating Toolbars in Delphi 795

CHAPTER 46 TSplitter 807

PART VI   WINDOWED CONTROLS 813

CHAPTER 47 TWinControl 815

Windowed Controls 815

CHAPTER 48 TDBCtrlGrid 835

CHAPTER 49 THeaderControl 851

CHAPTER 50 TProgressBar 861

CHAPTER 51 TScrollBar 869

CHAPTER 52 TStatusBar 879

CHAPTER 53 TTabSheet 887

CHAPTER 54 TTrackBar 895

CHAPTER 55 TCustomComboBox AND ITS DESCENDANTS 909
TCustomComboBox 910
TComboBox 914
TDBComboBox 915

CHAPTER 56 TCustomHotKey AND THotKey 927
TCustomHotKey 927
THotKey 931

CHAPTER 57 TCustomListBox AND ITS DESCENDANTS 935
TCustomListBox 935
TDBListBox 939
TListBox 941

CHAPTER 58 TCustomListView AND TListView 957
TCustomListView 957
TListView 962

CHAPTER 59 TCustomTabControl AND ITS DESCENDANTS 997
TCustomTabControl 998
TPageControl 1002
TTabControl 1004

CHAPTER 60 TCustomTreeView AND TTreeView 1015
TCustomTreeView 1016
TTreeView 1020

CHAPTER 61 TCustomUpDown AND TUpDown 1039
TCustomUpDown 1040
TUpDown 1044

CHAPTER 62 TScrollingWinControl AND ITS DESCENDANTS 1051

`TScrollingWinControl` 1051
`TForm` 1055
    Programming MDI 1056

CHAPTER 63   `TButtonControl` AND ITS DESCENDANTS 1087

`TButtonControl` 1087
`TButton` 1087
`TBitBtn` 1091
`TCustomCheckBox` 1093
`TCheckBox` 1096
`TRadioButton` 1098

CHAPTER 64   `TCustomEdit` AND ITS DESCENDANTS 1115

`TCustomEdit` 1115
`TEdit` 1119
`TCustomMaskEdit` 1121
`TMaskEdit` 1121
`TCustomMemo` 1123
`TMemo` 1123
`TCustomRichEdit` 1125
`TRichEdit` 1125

CHAPTER 65   `TCustomControl` AND ITS DESCENDANTS 1149

`TCustomControl` 1149
`TMediaPlayer` 1153
`TCustomPanel` 1180
`TPanel` 1180
`TDBNavigator` 1184
`TCustomGroupBox` 1188
`TGroupBox` 1189
`TCustomRadioGroup` 1190
`TRadioGroup` 1191

APPENDIXES

A   Where to Go from Here 1195
B   Project CD 1197

Acknowledgments

The authors would like to thank Kurt Stephan of Waite Group Press for his patience and tireless dedication to this project. Kurt was a joy to work with and kept us on track for those many months. We would like to extend a special thanks to Sylvia "Cricket" Lutnes of the Delphi Deli (`http://www.intermid.com/delphi/`) for her support. Also, thanks to everyone who sent us email suggestions, including Katy Mulvey, Monico Moreno, Michael J. Pruitt, Bill Mogk, Shmuel Cohen, Nicholas Xanth, and the many others who took time to write.

   I would like to thank my wife Stephanie for giving up all the time it took to get this book completed and understanding the vampire-like schedule it required. I could never have done it without your support! I would also like to thank Steve "Croaker" Koskela for the late-night Duke Nukem 3D and Quake death matches that provided needed stress relief (and unneeded lost sleep). Now the rivalry can continue uninterrupted! Apologies to my family and friends back home in Boston, who wondered why I never visited during 1996: Mom and Dad, Jonathan and Cheryl, Nana, the Thurrott and Bianchi families, Chris Regan, Dave Abbott, and everyone else in the great Northeast. I'll be home soon! More apologies for those who were stuck with me in Phoenix: everyone in the McKiernan family, Gary, Steve, Brian Kelley, and, of course, Jeff Giles and Kerry Hawkins. I'll visit soon, really!

—Paul Thurrott

I want to especially acknowledge my wife April, daughter Alice, and son Alex, who had to accommodate their lives to the endless exigencies of this book-writing project.

—Gary Brent

I would like to thank all of the help and support I received from the great staff at Waite Group Press, especially Kurt Stephan and Kelsey McGee, who patiently and with good humor helped me bring this effort to completion. I also want to express my gratitude to my family for their support during the completion of this project.

—Richard Bagdazian

I would like to thank the whole team at Waite Group Press, and especially Kurt Stephan, for coordinating the whole effort. A special thanks to Gary Whizin at Borland for all times he has helped me with Delphi-related problems, and thus—indirectly—with the writing of this book.

—Steve Tendon

Introduction

Welcome to the *Delphi 3 SuperBible!* This book is the result of over a year and a half of hard work, long hours, and late nights. The effort was worth it, however, because our goal of cataloging Borland's excellent application framework, the Visual Component Library (VCL), is now largely accomplished. Every day, more and more programmers are discovering the richness and depth offered by this revolutionary product. Whether you are just beginning to use Delphi or are a seasoned veteran, we think you'll agree that a reference like this is long overdue.

About the Latest Version of Delphi

Delphi changed the RAD programming scene so completely and irreversibly when it was first introduced that it's sometimes hard to remember that we didn't always have this power at our fingertips. As Borland's financial situation grows shakier, it's important to remember that most of the innovations we take for granted in the programming community came from this little company in Scotts Valley, CA. The giant in Redmond is now flexing its muscles with an integrated suite of application and Web programming environments, and appears to have the advantage.

Or does it? Borland's revolutionary Delphi IDE is now showing up in its C++ compiler, making users wonder how Microsoft dares to call its competing product "Visual" C++. Borland is also preparing a Java environment based around the Delphi IDE, ensuring that the skills you develop with Delphi will be transferable to new languages if need be. This is the true nature of integration, and the real reason that Microsoft's tools will never really compete at a technical level.

Most importantly, Delphi's latest revision—to be named Delphi 3.0 or Delphi 97 (it seems to change daily as this is written)—is ready to hit the shelves, offering more features and ease of use than even Visual Basic can muster. At its heart is the powerful and familiar Object Pascal language, which makes VB syntax look painfully child-like. Yet, Object Pascal is far more readable than C, C++, or Java. New additions to Delphi widen the margin significantly. Package support has been added to the language specification, taking code sharing to a new level. The VCL class library now includes new Windows 95/Windows NT 4.0 controls like the splitter, toolbar, and more.

More importantly, COM and ActiveX object support has been added directly to the VCL, making Delphi the obvious choice for ActiveX control creation. You can even create ActiveX controls with VCL components, leveraging your knowledge of Delphi and opening new avenues of market exploitation. Web server applications can now be created with Delphi as well. The Delphi IDE has been improved to take advantage of recent Windows user interface changes and new design ideas. What this all adds up to is an important new release for the hundreds of thousands of Delphi programmers.

About This Book

Delphi 3 SuperBible, then, is for you, the Delphi developer. As a reference, it is an invaluable companion, meant to sit by your side as you code. While it would be impossible to cover every last property in the VCL, we have attempted to detail the vast majority of this class library, with an emphasis on the most commonly used components. This project began long ago as *Delphi 2 SuperBible,* but we quickly changed gears when faced with a new release of Delphi. As with any book written from beta code, there may be changes to the product that we could not foresee. Despite this, we are satisfied that we have created a reference that is far more useful—and useable—than Borland's own Reference Library Guide (RLG) because we have used the structure of the VCL itself as the structure of this very book. Additionally, we cover topics not included in the RLG and, more importantly, correct the many mistakes that appear there.

This book is divided into six parts, described as follows. (For more detailed information about the structure of this book, please refer to Chapter 1, "Getting Started.")

Part I, "Overview," provides a general introduction to Delphi and the Visual Component Library, with information about the new features in 32-bit versions of Delphi and an overview of the VCL framework.

Parts II through VI provide a reference to the VCL itself; these parts are organized around the structure of that object-oriented framework.

Part II, "Objects," covers `TObject` and its descendant branches such as `TThread`, `Exception`, and `TRegistry`.

Part III, "Persistent Objects," discusses `TPersistent` and its descendants, that branch of the VCL that deals with classes that can persist via storage media.

Part IV, "Components," describes `TComponent` and how the Delphi components that inherit its attributes are categorized.

Part V, "Nonwindowed Controls," deals with those controls that do not provide a handle and are therefore not part of their container's tab order.

Finally, Part VI, "Windowed Controls," deals with the most famous Windows controls such as status bars, progress bars, list views, and command buttons.

In addition, Appendix A, "Where to Go from Here," provides further valuable reference sources for Delphi programs, while Appendix B, "Project CD," describes the contents and use of the accompanying CD-ROM.

Delphi, This Book, and You

We believe that *Delphi 3 SuperBible* is an essential reference for every Delphi programmer, and we're interested in your feedback about the book. Please feel free to contact Paul Thurrott, care of Waite Group Press, if you have any suggestions or comments about this book. Together, we can contribute to the success of Delphi in the programming community and have fun doing it. Enjoy the book, and enjoy Delphi. You are taking part in a revolution.

PART I

Overview

GETTING STARTED

In February 1995, Borland introduced Delphi, and the world of programming hasn't been the same since. Delphi combines the power of a true object-oriented language with the convenience of a visual development environment. Microsoft's Visual Basic can be credited with popularizing the move toward visual development, but unfortunately, Visual Basic lacks the linguistic sophistication, object orientation, and efficiency of Delphi's Object Pascal.

Delphi 2, released in 1996, began to exploit the 32-bit power of Windows 95/NT, supporting such Win32 features as multithreading, ActiveX/OLE, and the Windows common controls.

Early 1997 brought Delphi 3, the premier 32-bit Rapid Application Development (RAD) environment, which you can use to create programs of comparable power to C++ applications with a fraction of the effort. In this chapter, you will find an overview of the important differences between earlier versions of Delphi 1.0 and the new 32-bit versions and learn how to use the *Delphi 3 SuperBible* as your one-stop reference. Remember that this book is a reference book, not a tutorial; Appendix A, "Where to Go from Here," includes a suggested reading list you may want to look over if you are also interested in tutorials.

About Delphi

Delphi began life as a revision to the venerable Borland Pascal product line. Early in the beta cycle, it became clear that Delphi was something special, and Borland decided to make a break with its other Pascal products and give Delphi its due as the company's premier development tool. The differences between Delphi and Borland Pascal are more than cosmetic; in addition to improving the underlying Object Pascal language, Delphi features a visual development environment that is similar to but more powerful than the Visual Basic Integrated Development Environment (IDE).

Delphi programs use an object-oriented framework called the Visual Component Library, or VCL. It is the VCL that really sets Delphi apart from the competition and brings RAD tools to the next level. Using object-oriented features like polymorphism, encapsulation, and inheritance, the Delphi VCL provides unparalleled control and power to the programmer. Refer to Chapter 2, "VCL Basics," for an overview of the Delphi VCL and how it applies object-oriented principles.

Like Visual Basic, Delphi supports the use of *components*—objects that can be placed, or painted, directly on the program's form window at design time. Programmers can extend the capabilities of Delphi by creating their own new components. These new components can inherit capabilities from existing components. If, for example, you like the default command button provided by Delphi but wish that it was sized differently, you can derive a new class based on the standard Delphi command button. All that needs to be changed is the default width and height. This button can then be integrated into the Delphi IDE, allowing you to use and share your new component with others.

Delphi can also use ActiveX controls, language-independent custom controls popular with C/C++ and Visual Basic programmers. There are a large number of these controls available from third-party vendors. Such controls are increasingly popular among Internet and Intranet programmers.

Previously, developers wishing to create custom controls (ActiveX or the older 16-bit VBXs) needed to use C or C++ in a decidedly nonvisual and unfriendly environment. Delphi removes many of the barriers that programmers face in other environments, be it the limitations in Visual Basic or the slow compile times and obfuscated code of Visual C++/MFC. For this reason, you may find yourself exploring areas that were previously inaccessible to you, like object-oriented programming and VCL component design.

The *Delphi 3 SuperBible* is a systematic, organized reference to the Delphi VCL, providing a variety of ways to quickly find the answers you need. This book was written with the object-oriented nature of the VCL in mind, describing the major VCL objects and their properties, methods, and events in their native, hierarchical format.

What's New in Delphi

If you are new to Delphi, you may want to skip ahead to the Using This Book section. Those familiar with earlier versions of Delphi may want to continue to read this section to discover the new features in Delphi. In the same way that the 16-bit Delphi offered a world of improvements over other programming environments, Delphi 2 and 3 offer a new paradigm for the 32-bit worlds of Windows 95 and Windows NT.

Delphi now comes in a variety of editions, from a low-cost starter edition to an advanced client/server edition. Each of these editions improves on the previous 16-bit version of Delphi by offering a wealth of features, including multithreading support, new datatypes, an enhanced IDE and debugger, Unicode support, and the ability to generate Windows 95 logo-compliant applications.

Features Common to Each Edition

The newer versions of Delphi have added a host of exciting new features. Most of these improvements are available in each edition of Delphi and are summarized in Table 1-1.

Table 1-1 New features in Delphi

Use This...	To Do This...
32-bit optimizing compiler	Create fast standalone executable files.
New character types	Create Unicode-compatible characters.
New Currency type	Access high-precision currency-based variables.
New string types	Implement virtually unlimited-length strings with Unicode support.
New Variant type	Facilitate dynamically changing datatypes for OLE automation.
Packages	Allow code sharing among applications (Delphi 3 only).
Data modules	Separate code for nonvisual components.
Windows 95/NT support	Develop 32-bit applications that adhere to the Windows Interface Style Guidelines.
Enhanced IDE and debugger	Quickly develop and debug your applications.
Object Repository	Reuse objects.
Visual form inheritance and form linking	Derive descendants from any form window.
Visual Component Library (VCL)	Create programs with an object-oriented application framework.
Interfaces	Support Common Object Model (COM) and ActiveX objects (Delphi 3 only).
32-bit Borland Database Engine (BDE)	Create powerful database applications.
Assertions	Enhance debugging and exception handling (Delphi 3 only).

32-Bit Optimizing Compiler

Delphi includes a 32-bit native-code optimizing compiler that boosts run-time executable speed dramatically while reducing the size of the generated executable file. This compiler is a native Win32 program that offers significant performance gains over Visual Basic–generated p-code interpretation. In the past, optimizing compilers required the programmer to experiment with various optimization techniques, checking each generated executable for performance gains. Delphi's optimizing compiler eliminates this need and makes RAD possible by using optimization techniques automatically. Optimizations are guaranteed to work correctly and will not change the meaning of the code you write. Table 1-2 summarizes the compiler optimizations used by the 32-bit Delphi compiler.

Table 1-2 Delphi optimizing compiler features and benefits

Optimization	Benefit
Call stack overhead elimination	If possible, function and procedure parameters are placed into CPU registers, making function and procedure calls very efficient.
Common sub-expression elimination	Code is reduced to its most compact and efficient form, allowing the programmer to write readable code without worrying about a performance penalty.
Loop induction variables	Speeds up access to arrays and strings within loops.
Register optimizations	Variables and parameters can be placed into CPU registers, speeding access to items that are frequently accessed.

The Delphi compiler shares its "back-end" engine with Borland's award-winning C++ compiler, paving the way for design-time C++/Delphi code sharing. Delphi can link C++ OBJ files directly into a Delphi application and can create OBJ files that can later be used in a C++ app. Previously, the only way to share code between C++ and Delphi was through the use of dynamic link libraries (DLLs) at run time.

In addition to the benefits of the 32-bit optimizing compiler, Delphi also includes a 32-bit optimizing linker that increases link speeds dramatically by caching units in memory so that they can be linked in RAM rather than on disk.

Because Windows 95 and Windows NT offer 32-bit, flat memory model architectures, there are virtually no memory barriers. Programmers used to the limitations of the 16-bit segmented memory model of Windows 3.1 will find 32-bit Delphi programming liberating. Many data structures like strings, arrays, and records can now be of virtually unlimited size.

Delphi offers several other compiler enhancements that make this mature product all the more easy to use. These features are summarized in Table 1-3.

Table 1-3 Other compiler enhancements

Compiler Enhancement	Benefit
COM/ActiveX support	Delphi programmers can create and inherit objects based on the Common Object Model, Microsoft's language-independent object model.
Open Tools API	Used for version control software and CASE development.
Single-line comments	Delphi now supports the C++-style // single-line comment.

Character Types

Delphi's support of Unicode has changed the way the compiler handles character types. Unicode is a double-byte character coding system that supports the symbols and characters used in all the world's languages. For backward compatibility, the ANSIChar type is equivalent to Delphi 1.0's 8-bit Char. WideChar is a 16-bit Unicode character. For compatibility with legacy code, Borland allows the use of Char, which defaults to ANSIChar. There are also new character pointer types, PANSIChar, PWideChar, and PChar, which point to ANSIChar, WideChar, and Char, respectively. Each of these pointers works in a similar manner, the only difference being the size of the object they reference. The new character types are summarized in Table 1-4.

Table 1-4 New character types in Delphi

This Character Type...	Does This...
ANSIChar	Provides compatibility with Delphi 1.0 char type, 8-bit.
Char	Defaults to ANSIChar.
WideChar	Contains a 16-bit Unicode character.

This Character Type...	Does This...
PANSIChar	Points to ANSIChar.
PChar	Points to Char.
PWideChar	Points to WideChar.

Currency *Type*

Delphi introduces a `Currency` type, which will be familiar to Visual Basic programmers. `Currency` behaves like a floating-point type but is stored as a 64-bit integer. It is fully compatible with other floating-point types and can be used in financial applications to handle monetary values with high precision.

String Types

Delphi supports a new, virtually unlimited length `String` type. For backward compatibility with Delphi 1.0, a 255-character string type is also supported, although the two types are toggled with a compiler directive. String types specific to Delphi 2 and 3 include `ShortString`, which has a maximum length of 255 `ANSIChar` (8-bit) characters. `ShortString`, referred to simply as a "short string," is analogous to the Delphi 1.0 `String`. `ANSIString`, or a "long string," is the new string type; it is of variable length and contains `ANSIChar`s. There is also a `WideString`, which is comprised of `WideChar`s. Otherwise, `WideString` is functionally equivalent to `ANSIString`.

Unlike the old Delphi 1.0 strings, Delphi's new long strings are null terminated, making them more compatible with Win32 API calls and code created with C/C++. For this reason, it is not necessary to perform the Delphi string-to-Windows API string conversions that hamper Delphi 1.0 users. Long strings are dynamically allocated, represented internally as a pointer to a string on the heap that is automatically dereferenced. For this reason, the Delphi 1.0 `PString` type should be avoided, although it is still possible to use it if you feel the need to juggle pointers yourself. Allocating memory for long strings now requires the use of the new `SetLength` procedure, which will properly allocate enough memory for a long string when its size changes.

Long strings are now reference counted, an internal mechanism that makes long string assignments occur much faster than short string assignments and allows Delphi to reallocate the memory used by a string when its reference count goes to zero.

The new string types are summarized in Table 1-5.

Table 1-5 New string types in Delphi

This String Type...	Does This...
ANSIString	Provides a dynamic "long string" with unlimited length.
ShortString	Provides a string of ANSIChars compatible with Delphi 1.0 String type.
String	Defaults to ANSIString.
WideString	Provides a string of WideChars functionally equivalent to ANSIString.

Variant *Type*

Delphi's **Variant** type was introduced primarily for OLE automation, allowing you to dynamically change a variable's type. OLE automation is a method that allows Windows applications to host other Windows applications. **Variant** is implemented as a 16-bit structure with embedded type information. A **Variant** can represent a string, an integer, or a floating-point value, and for the most part it can be used like any other variable. As you might expect, **Variant**s support typecasting and work with most operators. The type of a **Variant** variable is determined at run time.

Data Modules

A *data module* is a special type of form window that is designed to hold nonvisual components only. Used primarily for database controls, data modules appear similar to normal forms at design time but offer no sizing grid. Data module windows do not appear at run time.

Windows 95/NT and COM Support

Delphi conforms to the latest user interface guidelines as specified by Microsoft. It supports the creation of Windows custom controls, is capable of generating Windows 95/NT logo-compliant applications, and has full support for Automation and ActiveX controls. Automation allows Delphi applications to easily host and control applications like Word and Excel.

The entire Win32 API is accessible from Delphi—if it can be done in Windows 95 or Windows NT, it can be done with Delphi!

COM facilities supported by Delphi are summarized in Table 1-6.

Table 1-6 Delphi COM support

This COM Feature...	Allows You to Do This...
ActiveX controls	These controls can be installed and used just like standard VCL controls, allowing Delphi programmers to access the wealth of third-party ActiveX controls. You can even create new VCL components whose properties, methods, and events are descended from existing ActiveX controls.
Automation Controller	Control other applications such as Word and Excel.
Automation Server	Create in-process and local Automation servers, using the Automation Object Expert that does most of the work for you.

Delphi supports multithreading through the new **TThread** object, which can be easily accessed in the Object Repository. The VCL supports thread synchronization and local thread storage, which allows you to create and access variables unique to individual threads.

Enhanced IDE and Debugger

The integrated debugger includes multierror detection, descriptive messages, and hint and tip prompting, which points out potential coding errors like unused return values and variables. The multierror detection feature will create a list of compile errors instead of exiting on the first error. The error messages themselves have been made more descriptive and specific.

Delphi 3 introduced a gutter (sidebar) to the editor window so that it contains glyphs indicating the location of special code attributes such as break points.

Object Repository and Visual Form Inheritance

Delphi has always supported code and object reuse. This theme is best represented by the Object Repository, which allows you to store forms and other objects in a clearly defined way. The Object Repository is essentially an extensible container for object-oriented templates that can be used to create new objects. You access the Object Repository every time you select New from the File menu in Delphi. The resulting dialog box shows you the objects that are currently available.

If you have used older, 16-bit versions of Delphi, you are probably familiar with the fact that all forms derive from a single source—TForm. Starting with Delphi 2, however, new forms can be derived from any existing form, making them more consistent with the other objects in the VCL hierarchy. Derived forms will inherit the properties, methods, components, and code from the ancestor form, allowing the programmer to use a library of form templates that can easily be added to any project. When ancestor forms are changed, the changes automatically appear in descendant forms. The Delphi Object Repository stores predefined form templates that can be extended with forms of your own design.

Visual Component Library

The Visual Component Library (VCL), described in more detail in the next chapter, is an application framework consisting of dozens of object-oriented, 32-bit, reusable components. The Delphi VCL includes a full complement of Windows 95/NT common controls and the powerful collection of components offered by the original VCL. This includes such controls as property sheets, tree views, progress bars, track bars, rich edit controls, splitters, up/down controls, outlines, headers, and any other control you would expect to find in Windows 95 or NT.

32-Bit Borland Database Engine

The Borland Database Engine (BDE) supports Win32 features like long file names, multithreading, and the Windows 95 Registry. The Client Data Repository is used to store persistent data. Other features of the BDE include a new SQL Query Engine, named SQL queries called *views*, and simple transactions for Paradox and dBASE tables.

Converting Programs from 16-Bit to 32-Bit

Upgrading from Delphi 1.0 to Delphi 2 or 3 is generally easy; newer versions of Delphi are fully compatible with their 16-bit sibling. One of the benefits of an application framework like the VCL is that it abstracts the API for the programmer so that you don't need to deal with internal implementation details. While much has changed under the hood, all you will need to do to create a 32-bit version of an existing Delphi application is a simple recompile, with a few caveats. This section discusses the issues you face when porting to 32-bit versions of Delphi and the changes you may need to make.

Windows 95 Common Controls

In Delphi 1.0, Borland implemented several controls that were in use by various applications, but not part of the standard Windows API. When Microsoft introduced Windows 95, many of these controls, like property sheets (formerly known as tabbed dialogs) and tree views, became a standard part of the operating system. If your Delphi 1.0 program uses any of the controls listed in Table 1-7, you should consider changing them to a new Delphi 2/3 equivalent.

Table 1-7 Delphi 1.0 controls and the equivalent Delphi 2 and 3 controls

Delphi 1.0 Control	New Delphi Control
TMemo	TRichEdit
TGauge	TProgressBar
THeader	THeaderControl
TOutline	TTreeView
TSpinButton	TUpDown
TTabbedNotebook	TPageControl
TTabSet	TabControl

Please note that this book will not be covering the now obsolete and nonstandard Windows 3.x controls that were implemented in Delphi 1.0.

Visual Basic Custom Controls (VBXs)

VBXs are 16-bit controls that are being quickly superseded by more powerful, 32-bit, ActiveX control replacements. Since Delphi 1.0 only supported VBX 1.0 controls, it is unlikely that many Delphi programmers are using VBXs. In any event, we suggest using only 32-bit VCL components and ActiveX controls. VCL components usually provide performance superior to that of ActiveX controls, so ActiveX controls should only be used when an equivalent Delphi component is unavailable.

New Type Sizes

Delphi's dynamic long strings are a dramatic change from the Delphi 1.0 string, but surprisingly, no changes are needed to take advantage of this feature. Delphi long strings are backward compatible with the Delphi 1.0 string type and the standard null-terminated C-style string used in API calls. Just remember to use **SetLength** to allocate memory for a string in Delphi.

Code that relies on specific type sizes will need to be changed as well. For example, the **Integer** type in Delphi is 32-bit, not 16-bit as it was in Delphi 1.0. For compatibility with the 16-bit **Integer**, Delphi provides a **SmallInt** type.

Windows Differences

If your program uses Windows API calls at all, you will need to check each function against the Win32 API, looking for any changes that will affect its portability. In many cases, Win16 functions have ported over unscathed, but there are hundreds of Win16 API functions that have changed significantly or are no longer supported. Borland supplies Win32 API help files with Delphi that should aid you in researching the changes.

Delphi 1.0 run-time library (RTL) functions and exceptions that deal with the segmented memory model of Windows 3.x are no longer supported. Table 1-8 lists these functions and exceptions.

Table 1-8 Unsupported Delphi 1.0 RTL functions and exceptions

Delphi 1.0 RTL Functions That Are Now Obsolete

CSeg	PrefixSeg	Seg
DSeg	Ptr	SSeg
Ofs	PtrSeg	SPtr

Delphi 1.0 Exceptions Classes That Are Now Obsolete

EBreakpoint	EInvalidOpCode	ESingleStep
EFault	EPageFault	EStackFault
EGPFault	EProcessorException	

Using This Book

The *Delphi 3 SuperBible* consists of six parts, covering the essentials of Delphi's VCL. It also contains two appendices and a CD-ROM containing compiled projects from relevant chapters, and sample 32-bit components and tools. The following sections outline the contents of the book and CD-ROM.

Part I: Overview

Part I, "Overview," provides a quick look at Delphi, the new features in Delphi, and its Visual Component Library. Part I also addresses ways to use this book as an essential reference and explains how the Delphi VCL, an object-oriented class hierarchy, is organized and how you can best utilize its strengths and features. A quick overview of application frameworks is presented, culminating in the introduction of the Delphi VCL. The use of properties, methods, and events is discussed.

Part II: Objects

Part II begins your exploration of the VCL class hierarchy, starting with its most basic and abstract class, **TObject**, the common ancestor to all classes. In later chapters, you are introduced to the terminal descendants of **TObject**, that is, the classes that descend directly from `TObject` and have no descendants of their own. Finally, you will explore the exceptions that are implemented by Delphi and the ways they are handled.

Part III: Persistent Objects

Part III, "Persistent Objects," covers `TPersistent`, which is the largest branch descending from the `TObject` base. `TPersistent` is an abstract class that encapsulates those objects that can be stored on or retrieved from an external data storage device. Subsequent chapters in Part III discuss the descendants of `TPersistent`, which include `TCanvas`, `TCollection`, `TGraphicsObject`, `TGraphic`, and `TStrings`.

Part IV: Components

Part IV, "Components," discusses the primary descendant branch of `TPersistent`. `TComponent` is the abstract base class for all components in the VCL and the properties, methods, and events that it introduces. Later chapters cover the terminal descendants of `TComponent`, such as `TMenu`, `TCustomImageList`, `TDataSet`, and `TControl`. There are two types of controls: nonwindowed, covered in Part V, and windowed, covered in Part VI.

Part V: Nonwindowed Controls

Nonwindowed controls are those controls that do not have a window handle and cannot receive the input focus. `TGraphicControl` is the base class for all nonwindowed controls. This part explores the descendants of `TGraphicControl`, such as labels, speedbuttons, and other nonwindowed buttons.

Part VI: Windowed Controls

Part VI describes the various windowed controls, the largest set of controls in the Delphi VCL. `TWinControl` is the base class for all windowed controls. This part describes a wide range of controls, from headers and progress bars to scroll bars, status bars, and more. The windowed controls include `TComboBox`, `TCustomListBox`, `TCustomListView`, `TCustomUpDown`, `TScrollingWinControl`, `TButtonControl`, and `TCustomControl`.

What's in a Chapter?

Each chapter in Parts II–VI of the *Delphi 3 SuperBible* consists of three parts: a topic discussion, a summary table, and a section that describes properties, methods, and events introduced by the class that is being discussed.

Where a chapter describes a group of unrelated classes, the chapter is divided into sections, each of which consists of the three parts described above. This way, each class is described completely before the next class is introduced. If a chapter describes a group of related classes, the alphabetical listing of properties, methods, and events that are shared among the classes appears at the end of the chapter.

Topic Discussion

The beginning of each chapter introduces the topic with a discussion of its place in the VCL hierarchy and the services it provides. A general discussion of the practical application of the class in your own programs is provided with examples of its use in the Windows user interface where appropriate.

Summary Table

This alphabetical table lists the properties, methods, and events that are implemented and inherited by the current object. Properties, methods, and events that are inherited by the current object but not changed or extended in any way are covered in the chapters describing the ancestor classes for that object. The table includes entries that quickly refer you to the appropriate ancestor classes.

Reference Entries

The biggest section of each chapter consists of an alphabetical listing of the properties, methods, and events that are implemented by the current object. These entries correspond to the items shown in the table section of each chapter.

The alphabetical reference entries are designed to be concise yet thorough explanations. Each entry contains the following parts:

- *Name*. The name of the property, method, or event. The Table of Contents lists the entry by this name.

- *Objects Affected*. A list of the VCL objects that implement this item. In many cases, properties, methods, and events will be implemented by a number of different objects.

- *Purpose*. A short explanation describing the item. It answers the question *What is this used for?* Details on the item's use are provided later in the entry.

- *Declaration*. A template describing how the item is declared in Object Pascal code.

- *Parameters*. A listing, with definitions, of the parameters used in the methods.

- *Example Syntax*. A brief code listing illustrating how to use the item.

- *Description*. A look at the item with a discussion of its use, type, default value, and parameters, if any.

Finding What You Need

The *Delphi 3 SuperBible* provides many ways for you to quickly find the information you need. This section looks at the various ways you can use this reference as an effective information tool.

Looking Up Complete Topics

The index, located at the end of this book, provides a far more detailed list of the various elements discussed in this book. Some index entries will provide multiple page references, allowing you to explore the various places that certain elements are accessed throughout the VCL. If you are looking for a comprehensive listing of VCL elements covered by this book, the index is the place to look.

Reviewing Delphi in Depth

If you decide that you want to find out as much as possible about Delphi, we suggest that you browse the table of contents and look for topics that interest you. Remember that the VCL is set up as an object-oriented tree, with descendant classes inheriting behavior from their ancestors.

Chapter 2, "VCL Basics," is required reading for those who want to understand the Visual Component Library and how the various objects fit together in this hierarchical scheme. If you discover that more detail is needed for your understanding of the VCL or any of the objects it contains, you may want to consult the books described in Appendix A, "Where to Go from Here."

2

VCL BASICS

The Visual Component Library (VCL) is the core of Delphi, the first visual programming language with a fully integrated object-oriented framework. Whether you are an applications programmer or a component developer, learning the VCL and how it works is essential to your mastery of Delphi. Applications programmers need to be familiar with the properties, methods, and events that are available for the components they use. Component developers, in addition, require some knowledge of the inner workings of the VCL so that they can create new descendant components. This chapter will introduce the concepts behind object-oriented programming as they apply to Delphi and discuss the structure of Delphi's object-oriented framework—the VCL. It is not meant to be a thorough tutorial for beginners; however, many of the books listed in Appendix A, "Where to Go from Here," are tutorial in nature.

Programming with Objects

If you have experience with Visual Basic, you can think of Delphi as being a kind of "Visual Pascal." Beginning Delphi programmers can approach their new environment in much the same way as Visual Basic users do: Place an object on the form, resize it with the mouse, press the Run button, and—presto!—a real Windows program. At first glance, the Delphi programming environment seems suspiciously similar to that of Visual Basic, and, indeed, programmers can approach it in this way for many simple tasks, unaware of the power lurking inside Delphi. Eventually, though, an understanding of the way objects are implemented and used becomes crucial to taking advantage of Delphi's potential.

Pure and Hybrid Languages

Object-oriented languages can be divided into two groups—those that are considered "pure" OOP implementations like SmallTalk and Simula, and those that are hybrid languages like C++ and Delphi. Delphi's Object Pascal is an object-oriented extension of Pascal in the same way that C++ is an object-oriented extension of C. The goal of both Object Pascal and C++ is the same: They must run legacy code unaltered while offering the full benefits of object orientation. Though Pascal advocates may cringe at the thought, Delphi's use of OOP is based largely on the C++ model, which has proved very popular in recent years. In fact, hybrid languages like C++ and Delphi have been much more successful than pure OOP languages due largely to the fact that their base languages are so widely understood and used; C and Pascal programmers don't need to learn a whole new language when they decide to move on to OOP.

OOP Concepts

Object-oriented programming has long lacked a concise definition, although it can be thought of simply as this: An application created with an object-oriented language consists of objects. Each object has certain characteristics or *properties*, behaviors or *methods*, and *events* that it can respond to. A class is a *type*, a template or prototype that describes an object. An *object* is an *instance* of a class (a variable of the class type).

The code snippet in Listing 2-1 shows a simple Delphi program (with a few extraneous lines removed for clarity) that creates a single instance of a class. This code, which corresponds to an empty form, is generated for you automatically by Delphi when you start a new project.

Listing 2-1 Code for a basic Delphi form

```
unit Unit1;

interface

uses
  Windows, Messages, SysUtils, Classes, Graphics, Controls, Forms,
  Dialogs;

type
  TForm1 = class(TForm)
  end;

var
  Form1: TForm1;

implementation

end.
```

In Listing 2-1, Delphi creates a new class (datatype) called **TForm1**, which is derived from the class **TForm**:

```
type
  TForm1 = class(TForm)
  end;
```

If you were to read this in English, you might say, "I am declaring a new type, called **TForm1**, which is a kind of **TForm**."

To create an instance of this class, you must define a variable of type **TForm1**. This is done in the **var** section:

```
var
  Form1: TForm1;
```

This can be understood to mean "I want to define (create an instance in memory of) a variable—an object—of type `TForm1` called `Form1`." This is conceptually similar to defining an instance of a simpler native Pascal type like `Integer`:

```
var
  MyInteger: Integer;
```

Inheritance

Inheritance, the derivation of new types, occurs in even the simplest Delphi program and is one of the primary features of object-oriented programming. Inheritance is what enables the VCL to be a hierarchy. In Delphi, all classes ultimately derive from a single base class called `TObject`, with descendant classes inheriting attributes from ancestor classes while adding their own functionality. Typically, however, new Delphi classes will inherit from a class farther down the hierarchy so as to acquire more attributes than those found in `TObject`.

Class structures like the VCL have a parent-child relationship, where the ancestor class is typically referred to as the parent, or *base* class, and the descendant class, or *derived* class, is considered a child of that base class. Classes near the root of the hierarchy tend to be more abstract or generic, whereas classes farther from the root are more specialized and concrete.

Polymorphism

The attributes that descendant classes inherit from their parents can be used unchanged or can be modified as needed. The reason attributes are declared in ancestor classes is that they are shared by, or common to, a group of descendants. For example, `TObject`, the ancestor of all objects, contains a method (a Pascal procedure or function) called `Create`. All other classes inherit this method, but each class is free to implement a version of `Create` that is appropriate for that class.

An object-oriented feature called *polymorphism* makes it possible—and desirable— for the `Create` method to behave differently for each object that uses it. This feature allows you to access different objects in a similar manner, using a consistent interface. If you need to change the implementation of a property (one of the class's characteristics) or method, you can override it using polymorphism. This feature is heavily used throughout the VCL.

Encapsulation

Another basic feature of OOP, *encapsulation*, is concerned with keeping a class's properties and methods in the same block of code and dictates that the *interface* for a class be separated from the *implementation*. The interface is the part of the program that is exposed to the user (meaning, in this case, a programmer accessing your code), and the implementation is the part that is visible only to the programmer who wrote the code for the class. Delphi's Object Pascal takes this rather literally: Observe in Listing 2-1 the sections called interface and implementation. In that small example, there is no code in the implementation section, but this is typically where all the actual code for event handlers and methods would go. Encapsulation allows a programmer to access objects through their properties and methods without actually knowing how the details are manipulated internally.

Units and Classes

A *unit* is a Delphi source code file that consists of at least three parts: a unit statement, an interface section, and an implementation section. The *unit statement* is the first line of code, and it contains the name identifying the unit. In Listing 2-1, the unit statement looks like this:

```
unit Unit1;
```

When you save a unit for the first time, typically you will name the unit something a little more descriptive. If you were to save this unit with the name **LoanTable.pas**, for example, the unit statement in this unit would change to

```
unit LoanTable;
```

The *interface* section in a unit is used to contain information that is visible to, or can be shared with, other units in your program. Type, variable, constant, function, and procedure declarations may be placed in the interface section. Function and procedure *bodies* (the actual code) are never found in the interface section.

The *implementation* section follows the interface section and generally will consist of the actual code for the functions and procedures that were previously declared in the interface section. Any types, variables, constants, and methods that you do not want visible to other units can be declared here as well.

A unit can have an optional *initialization* section that is used to execute code once when the program is first loaded into memory. You can also optionally include a *finalization* section that executes when your application is closed. The general structure of a unit is shown in Listing 2-2.

Listing 2-2 Sections of a unit file

```
unit Unit1;

interface

uses <list of other units accessed by this unit>;

// type declarations that can be used by other units
type
  TForm1 = class(TForm)
  private
    { Private declarations }
  public
    { Public declarations }
  end;

// variables that can be used by other units
var
  Form1: TForm1;
```

```
implementation

// variables that are hidden to other units

// function and procedure bodies that were declared in
//   interface

initialization

// optional unit initialization

finalization

// optional unit finalization

end.
```

The sections of a unit file are summarized in Table 2-1.

Table 2-1 Sections of a unit file

Unit Section	Use it for...
interface	Declarations that can be seen by other units.
implementation	Method code and declarations that cannot be seen by other units.
initialization	Optional section for code that runs when the program is first loaded into memory.
finalization	Optional section for code that runs when the program is closed.

Units are the primary way that Delphi determines the *scope*, or visibility, of the identifiers in your program. Anything declared in the implementation section of a unit is local to that unit and cannot be seen or used by other units. The interface section, on the other hand, is the "face" that the unit presents to the outside world.

You may have noticed that unit files invariably have a **uses** clause right after the unit statement. This lists the various units that are accessed by the current unit. By default, the following files are listed in the **uses** clause when you start a new project:

```
Windows, Messages, SysUtils, Classes, Graphics, Controls, Forms, Dialogs;
```

The **uses** clause essentially gives your unit access to the interface sections of the units it lists.

Class Visibility

The different sections of a unit file are used to control the visibility of properties, methods, and events within the classes in your program. Though most class declarations occur within the interface section of a unit, you will frequently have some properties, methods, and events whose accessibility you wish to limit. Delphi supports various levels of access protection with the visibility specifiers private, protected, public, and published. If the type declaration for **TForm** in Listing 2-2 was expanded to show all of the available visibility specifiers, it would look like this:

```
TForm1 = class(TForm)
  private
    { Private declarations }
  protected
    { Protected declarations }
  public
    { Public declarations }
  published
    { Published declarations }
  end;
```

Private

This section is used to declare properties, methods, and events that will not be accessible from outside of the current unit. Descendant classes, however, can access private properties, methods, and events of their ancestors. Private properties, methods, and events are essentially public within the unit in which they are declared.

Protected

The protected section of a class declaration contains those properties, methods, and events that can be accessed by the class itself, its descendant classes, and other classes declared in the same unit, but *not* by code in other units.

Public

Public properties, methods, and events are accessible from anywhere in a program, regardless of whether the code is in the same unit as the declaration. All that is required for unit A to access the public properties, methods, and events of unit B is to have unit A include unit B's name in its **uses** clause.

Published

Published properties, methods, and events have the same scope as public properties, methods, and events but are accessible from the design-time interface and produce run-time type information (RTTI). Properties you see in the Object Inspector are declared in the published section. In fact, this is the primary purpose for the published specifier: Published properties are visually available to the programmer at design time. The default visibility for a class's properties, methods, or events is published, so any declarations directly below the class declaration in an unnamed section are published by default. In the form type declaration below, a command button has been added to the form. Its own declaration appears directly below the form declaration so it is implicitly published.

```
type
  TForm1 = class(TForm)
    Button1: TButton;
  end;
```

The use of these specifiers is summarized in Table 2-2.

Table 2-2 Class visibility specifiers

Modifier	Accessible from Anywhere in Same Unit?	Accessible from Other Units?	Accessible from Descendant Classes?	Accessible Through Design-Time Interface?	RTTI
private	Yes	No	Yes (not recommended)	No	No
protected	Yes	No	Yes	No	No
public	Yes	Yes	Yes	No	No
published	Yes	Yes	Yes	Yes	Yes

The Visual Component Library

This book is organized around the structure of the Visual Component Library. The VCL has five main branches, as shown in Figure 2-1.

Parts II-VI are dedicated to these five main branches: **TObject** itself (Part II: Objects), **TPersistent** (Part III: Persistent Objects), **TComponent** (Part IV: Components), **TGraphicControl** (Part V: Nonwindowed Controls), and **TWinControl** (Part VI: Windowed Controls).

The most widely used section of the tree is the **TComponent** branch, which implements *components*. Components are visible at design time and can be accessed from the Component Palette. They are the visual objects used by Delphi programmers at design time. Typically, component designers will create new components that descend from one of **TComponent**'s many children, inheriting the functionality of specific classes as needed.

Not all components remain visible at run time. Those that do are called *controls* and are descended from **TControl**, a direct descendant of **TComponent**. Farther down the tree, the windowed and non-windowed controls are those controls that encapsulate familiar Windows elements like command buttons, toolbar buttons, and labels. As you

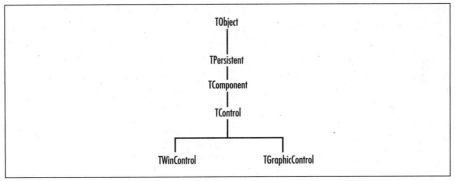

Figure 2-1 The root of the VCL tree and a portion of its most important branch, **TControl**

can see, classes that are found near the bottom of the tree are far more specific and functional than the abstract classes found near the top. This represents good object-oriented design, and many of the class structures in the VCL mimic this at different levels.

Handling Events

The overall goal of the VCL is to encapsulate those elements that a Windows programmer will need to create robust applications. Unlike other application frameworks such as Borland's Object Windows Library (OWL) and the Microsoft Foundation Classes (MFC), the VCL ties an OOP framework into a truly visual environment. Each time a component is selected from the Component Palette and placed on a form, an instance of that object is created in Object Pascal code. When you double-click the control on the form, its default *event handler*, a method, is displayed in the code window. Delphi creates the method declaration and an empty method body so you can concentrate on writing the code that executes when the event occurs. The declaration for the event handler is placed in the interface section of the current form's unit.

```
TForm1 = class(TForm)
  Button1: TButton;
  procedure Button1Click(Sender: TObject);
end;
```

The empty method body is placed in the implementation section:

```
procedure TForm1.Button1Click(Sender: TObject);
begin

end;
```

In the example above, the default event for a button is OnClick, and the default name used for the event handler implementation follows the syntax *ClassName.ComponentName* Click(Sender: TObject). This standard convention makes creating event handlers an easy task in Delphi.

If you wish to create an event handler for a nondefault event, a list of events for each component is available on the Events tab of the Object Inspector window. The TButton type, for example, allows you to handle events for single-clicks, double-clicks, drag-and-drop, key down and up, key-press, mouse down and up, and more.

Using Properties

Properties are special class attributes that allow you to determine or change the appearance, position, and behavior of an object. They are generally implemented at the TPersistent level, or lower, in the VCL tree. At design time, properties for the currently selected object can be found on the Properties tab of the Object Inspector window. At run time, properties can be checked and modified with Object Pascal code. In addition, many objects also have certain properties that can *only* be changed at run time (design-time properties can always be accessed at run time). Many of these run-time properties are read-only or write-only.

Internally, properties are implemented as fields or methods. Checking the value of a property will generally invoke a private or protected method of that class—in many ways, a property is a public interface to private data. This is, of course, transparent to the component user.

Methods

A *method* is simply a class member function or procedure—a function or procedure that is associated with an object. Functions return a value and can be used in expressions, while procedures do not return a value and are not used in expressions.

Method Directives

Delphi's Object Pascal uses a variety of directives to modify the scope and meaning of methods. These are especially prevalent throughout the VCL source. Unless you are writing your own components, you really don't need to worry about them too much, however. For advanced users, the most common method directives are discussed below.

virtual *and* dynamic

You will see the keywords `virtual` and `dynamic` throughout the VCL. They are used to create virtual methods, that is, those methods that are resolved at run time. By default, nonconstructor methods are statically bound when your program is compiled. The `virtual` and `dynamic` keywords override this behavior, allowing *dynamic*, or *late*, binding. The two directives differ only slightly; methods declared with `dynamic` require slightly less RAM than those declared with `virtual`, although they run a little slower. For purposes of this discussion, `virtual` and `dynamic` are the same thing.

Methods can be made virtual by adding the appropriate directive to the method declaration:

```
procedure SetIndex(Value: Integer); virtual;
procedure GetChildren(Proc: TGetChildProc); dynamic;
```

Virtual methods can be overridden by descendant classes. When a virtual method is called at run time, the type of the object calling the method determines which implementation of the method to run.

override

The `override` directive is used in a method declaration to override a virtual method in an ancestor class. When using override, the order and types of parameters of the method in the descendant class must match those found in the method in the ancestor class. For example, the following declaration overrides the `SetIndex` function shown above:

```
procedure SetIndex(Value: Integer); override;
```

abstract

An **abstract** method is a virtual method, usually found in an abstract base class, that lacks an implementation definition. In other words, an abstract method is not defined in the object in which it is declared—it is a "pure" virtual method. Abstract methods have to be overridden before they can be called; otherwise, a run-time error occurs and the program is terminated. You declare an abstract method using a virtual or dynamic directive, followed by the **abstract** directive:

```
function Get(Index: Integer): string; virtual; abstract;
```

Overriding an abstract method has the same requirements as overriding a **virtual** or **dynamic** function, although it is not possible to use **inherited** later. **Inherited** is a keyword placed in the implementation of a method in a descendant class used to execute the synonymous method in its immediate ancestor.

The method directives are summarized in Table 2-3.

Table 2-3 Common method directives found in the VCL

Method Directive	Use to...
virtual	Define a virtual method
dynamic	Define a virtual method
override	Override the behavior of a method in an ancestor class
abstract	Create the interface, but not the implementation, of a method

Run-Time Type Information

Objects in Delphi contain information about their own type and inheritance that can be accessed at run time. This is known as *run-time type information* (*RTTI*), and it allows you to query objects about their type and then act accordingly. This is particularly important in Delphi, since most event-handling methods take **TObject** as the **Sender** parameter so that the method can be used by any object. For example, the **OnClick** event handler for a command button could be called by various objects in your program, not just by a command button.

RTTI provides a new keyword, **is**, that identifies the type of an object at run time. In the case of the command button example, you might also have a toolbar button that calls the same method. In this case, the following code can be used to see whether the object that calls the method is a command button:

```
procedure TForm1.Button1Click(Sender: TObject);
begin
  // if the command button is pressed, just close the program
  if Sender is TButton then
    Close
  // otherwise, pop-up a dialog box and ask the user if he/she is sure
  else
  begin
    if Application.MessageBox('Really Close?', 'Are you sure?',
```

```
                    MB_YESNO) = IDYES then
    Close
  end
end;
```

RTTI is most often used to accomplish safe typecasting. Many Object Pascal and Delphi types cannot be legally typecast to otherwise valid types and will throw an exception if it is attempted. Once you have used **is** to determine whether an object is compatible with a specific typecast, the cast itself can be performed with the keyword **as**

```
with Sender as TButton do
  // ...
```

Using the Object Browser

One of the coolest ways to learn about the VCL is with the Object Browser, a Delphi IDE tool that allows you to explore the classes that are used in your programs. This tool is available from the Delphi IDE by choosing Browser from the View menu, although you will need to successfully compile your program before the Object Browser can be accessed. Individual objects in your program can be browsed by right-clicking them in the source code and then choosing Browse Symbol at Cursor from the pop-up menu as shown in Figure 2-2.

The Object Browser, shown in Figure 2-3, allows you to selectively display constants, methods, types, variables, and properties, their inheritance, and whether they are private, protected, public, or published. Virtual functions are also specially marked.

The Object Browser window is divided into two halves: the *Inspector pane*, which displays the VCL hierarchy with a standard tree view, and the *Details pane*, which is

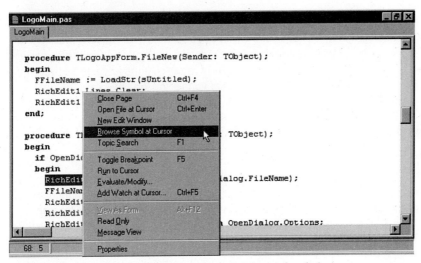

Figure 2-2 Launching the Object Browser with a right-click

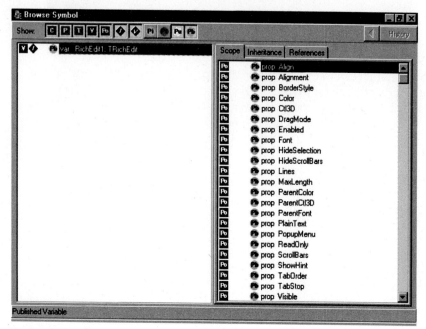

Figure 2-3 The Object Browser window

further subdivided into three pages: *Scope, Inheritance,* and *Reference.* The Scope page of the Details pane displays a list of those symbols that are defined in the unit that is being browsed. This pane is shown by default. The Inheritance page shows a tree view similar to the one in the Inspector pane that details the object currently being browsed. The last page, Reference, shows where the selected object is referenced in the source code.

The Object Browser window also has a useful *speedbar* (sort of a Borland-style toolbar) running along the top of the window that allows you to custom-tailor your viewing options. Browsing and display options are also configurable from the *speedmenu,* which is a pop-up menu that is activated by right-clicking anywhere in the Object Browser window. The speedmenu allows you to sort by object, unit, global type, or symbol.

Exploring the VCL on Your Own

The *Delphi 3 SuperBible* is a programmer's reference—this whirlwind tour of the hierarchy and its features is designed only as a quick overview. The very organization of this book is designed to drive home the way the VCL is structured, so you will increase your understanding of the VCL's design philosophy as you use the book. Also, the Delphi 3 SuperBible Help System, included on the CD, organizes the VCL classes in a standard help file format that you can reference as you use Delphi.

Enjoy the book!

PART II

Objects

3

TObject

TObject is the common ancestor of every class in Delphi, the root of the Visual Component Library. **TObject** is an abstract class, implementing only the most basic and generic of features that are universally shared by all objects in the VCL.

TObject is automatically used as the ancestor type when you create a new class in Delphi. Therefore, the following two code snippets have the same meaning:

```
type
  TNewObject = class
  end;
```

```
type
  TNewObject = class(TObject)
  end;
```

TObject declares a constructor and destructor (special methods that create and destroy objects), and implements type-information and message-handling methods. Because **TObject** is an abstract class, most of its methods are overridden by its descendants in the VCL. Typically, you will access descendant implementations of **Create**, the constructor, and **Free**, which safely calls the destructor **Destroy** for you.

Table 3-1 displays the general-purpose methods that are implemented by **TObject**. In general, only three of these are of interest to application developers: **Create**, **Destroy**, and **Free**.

Table 3-1 Methods implemented by TObject

Use or Set This...	To Do This...
ClassName	Get the name of an object's class.
ClassParent	Get the object's parent class.
ClassType	Get an object's actual type.
Create	Construct a new object.
DefaultHandler	This virtual function has no implementation—it does nothing at the TObject level.
Destroy	Destroy an object.

continued on next page

continued on next page

continued from previous page

Use or Set This...	To Do This...
Free	Destroy an object constructed with Create.
InheritsFrom	Determine whether the object is descended from a certain class.
InstanceSize	Determine the amount of memory allocated for an object.

ClassName METHOD

Objects Affected   All objects.

Purpose   The ClassName method returns the name of an object or class.

Declaration

```
class function ClassName: string;
```

Example Syntax

```
// Create a form with a single command button. When the button is
// clicked, the caption of Form1 changes to "TButton"
procedure TForm1.Button1Click(Sender: TObject);
begin
  Form1.Caption := Button1.ClassName;
end;
```

Description   ClassName returns a string containing the name of the current object's actual type. In the example above, Button1 is of type TButton, and that is the name that is returned by ClassName. If you derive a new type from another type and then use ClassName, it will return the name of the new type.

You will rarely need to get the name of an object's class. If you are trying to determine an object's *type* (as opposed to its type's *name*), use the is operator, discussed in Chapter 2, "VCL Basics."

ClassParent METHOD

Objects Affected   All objects.

Purpose   The ClassParent method returns the parent class of an object or a class.

Declaration

```
class function ClassParent: TClass;
```

Example Syntax

```
procedure TForm1.Button1Click(Sender: TObject);
var
  // Create a variable of type TClass
  MyParent: TClass;
```

```
begin
  // First, assign the class type of Button1 to MyParent
  MyParent := Button1.ClassType;
  // Next, use ClassParent to determine the parent class of MyParent
  MyParent := MyParent.ClassParent;
  // Finally, output the string with ClassName
  Form1.Caption := MyParent.ClassName;
end;
```

Description   ClassParent returns the immediate ancestor class of the current class. The return type of ClassParent is TClass, which is a direct descendant of TObject and is essentially the same as TObject, as it does not add any functionality to the base class. Typically, ClassParent is used to determine whether a particular object can be legally assigned to another object.

TObject.ClassParent will return Nil, since TObject has no parent class.

ClassParent rarely needs to be called by the application or component programmer, although it is used internally by the is and as operators and the InheritsFrom method (described later).

ClassType METHOD

Objects Affected   All objects.

Purpose   The ClassType method returns the class type of object.

Declaration

```
function ClassType: TClass;
```

Example Syntax

```
// When the button is clicked, the caption of Form1 changes to
// "TButton"
procedure TForm1.Button1Click(Sender: TObject);
begin
  Form1.Caption := Button1.ClassType.ClassName;
end;
```

Description   ClassType returns an object's actual type, not just its name as ClassName does. Unlike ClassInfo, ClassName, and ClassParent, ClassType operates on *objects* (class instances), not classes (object types).

ClassType returns information similar to that returned by the is operator. In fact, the is and as operators call ClassType themselves.

Create METHOD

Objects Affected   All objects.

Purpose   The Create method is the Object Pascal constructor.

Declaration

```
constructor Create;
```

Example Syntax

```
// Dynamically create a new object when the form is created and
// print the class type of the new object, TObject, in the form's
// caption
procedure TForm1.FormCreate(Sender: TObject);
var
  MyObject: TObject;
begin
  MyObject := TObject.Create;
  Form1.Caption := MyObject.ClassType.ClassName;
end;
```

Description

Create is used to construct an object by allocating memory for that object and initializing any object data. Create allocates and initializes the memory needed by the object it is constructing.

Every class in the VCL overrides or reimplements Create in some way. Objects that are instantiated with Create should be destroyed with Free.

Destroy METHOD

Objects Affected   All objects.

Purpose   The Destroy method is used to destroy an object.

Declaration

```
destructor Destroy;
```

Description   Destroy is the Delphi destructor. It is used to destroy an object, releasing the memory that was allocated to that object. Destroy is called by the Free method, which is the function you should use to destroy objects constructed with Create.

Free METHOD

Objects Affected   All objects.

Purpose   The Free method is used to destroy an object.

Declaration

```
procedure Free;
```

Example Syntax

```
// destroy the object AnObject
AnObject.Free;
```

Description   If you create an object, you should use **Free** to destroy that object and release the memory that was allocated to it. **Free** is guaranteed to be successful, even if the object is **NIL**, so you should always use **Free** instead of **Destroy**. **Free** actually calls **Destroy** itself, if the object you are attempting to destroy is not **NIL**.

InheritsFrom METHOD

Objects Affected   All objects.

Purpose   The **InheritsFrom** method determines whether the object is descended from another object type.

Declaration

```
class function InheritsFrom(AClass: TClass): Boolean;
```

Parameters

AClass   The parameter can be any class type.

Example Syntax

```
// Because TButton is a descendant of TWinControl, this event
// handler will change the form caption
procedure TForm1.Button1Click(Sender: TObject);
begin
  if (Sender.InheritsFrom(TWinControl)) then
    Form1.Caption := 'TButton descends from TWinControl';
end;
```

Description   **InheritsFrom** returns **True** if the object type specified by the *AClass* parameter is an ancestor of the object. If the object is not descended from the type specified by *AClass*, it will return **False**.

The **is** and **as** operators use **InheritsFrom** internally.

InstanceSize METHOD

Objects Affected   All objects.

Purpose   The **InstanceSize** method returns the amount of memory allocated for each instance of a given object type.

Declaration

```
class function InstanceSize: Word;
```

Description   **InstanceSize** returns the number of bytes required to hold each instance of the object type that calls the method. It is an internal function and is not typically used by developers. Use the **sizeof** function instead:

```
ButtonSize := sizeof(Button1);
```

InstanceSize is not virtual, so it cannot be overridden.

4

TIniFile

While Microsoft would no doubt like to banish INI files from Windows forever and force application developers to store information in the Registry, it is clear that INI files will be around for some time. INI files are simple text files with an `.INI` extension that are usually stored in the Windows directory. They are designed to store information about application programs, such as settings, configurations, window positions, and more. As Windows has become more popular and application support has grown, most users now have dozens of INI files littering their hard drive. Fortunately, they don't require much space and they are still a convenient way for you to store configuration options; so INI files can be a real time-saver.

If you are developing a large, complex application with many user-configurable settings, it would be better to access the Windows Registry via the `TRegistry` class rather than to rely on the vestigial INI files that are common in older versions of Windows. `TRegistry` is covered in Chapter 6, "`TRegistry` and `TRegIniFile`."

INI files are encapsulated by the `TIniFile` class, which is a direct, terminal descendant of `TObject`. To use the `TIniFile` class or any of its members, you must include `IniFiles` in the `uses` clause of the unit that will be accessing INI files.

INI files are divided into named *sections* that contain *identifiers*. Each identifier can be assigned a *value*; typically the value is a boolean, integer, or string. In Listing 4-1, a snippet from a typical `WIN.INI` file, the sections can be identified by the brackets surrounding the name of each section. `WIN.INI` is used only as an example; your application should normally maintain its own INI file.

Listing 4-1 A section of a typical `WIN.INI` file

```
[windows]
run=
NullPort=None
load=
device=LaserJet 5P,HPPCL5MS,LPT1:

[Desktop]
Wallpaper=(None)
```

continued on next page

continued from previous page

```
TileWallpaper=1
WallpaperStyle=0
Pattern=(None)

[Intl]
iCountry=1
ICurrDigits=2
iCurrency=0
iDate=0
iDigits=2
iLZero=1
iMeasure=1
iNegCurr=0
iTime=0
iTLZero=0
...
```

As you can see from this example, the identifiers are separated from their values by an equal sign, and take the form *identifier=value*. This expression is known as a *key*.

Figure 4-1 shows the derivation of `TIniFile`; Table 4-1 displays the properties and methods that are implemented by `TIniFile`.

Table 4-1 Properties and methods implemented by `TIniFile`

Use or Set This...	To Do This...	Inheritance
Create	Construct a `TIniFile` instance.	TObject
DeleteKey	Delete an INI file identifier and its value.	None
EraseSection	Erase an entire section in an INI file.	None
FileName	Get the encapsulated INI file name.	None
ReadBool	Retrieve a boolean value from an INI file.	None
ReadInteger	Retrieve an integer value from an INI file.	None
ReadSection	Retrieve identifier names from an INI file section.	None
ReadSections	Retrieve a list of the section names in the INI file.	None
ReadSectionValues	Retrieve the entire contents of an INI file section.	None
ReadString	Retrieve a string value from an INI file.	None
WriteBool	Write a boolean value to an INI file.	None
WriteInteger	Write an integer value to an INI file.	None
WriteString	Write a string value to an INI file.	None

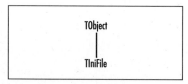

Figure 4-1 Derivation of `TIniFile`

> **IMPORTANT**
> TIniFile methods will attempt to locate the INI file in the Windows directory (usually C:\
> WINDOWS in Windows 95, or C:\WINNT in Windows NT). If you want to read or write to an INI file
> that is not located in the Windows directory, you will need to explicitly add the path to the name of the
> INI file when it is opened with Create.

Create METHOD

Objects Affected TIniFile

Purpose The Create method creates an instance of TIniFile that enables you to manipulate an INI file.

Declaration

```
constructor Create(const FileName: string);
```

Parameters

FileName The name of the INI file you wish to associate with the TIniFile object.

Example Syntax

```
procedure TForm1.FormCreate(Sender: TObject);
var
  MyIni: TIniFile;
begin
  // instantiate MyIni and assign it to an INI file
  MyIni := TIniFile.Create('TEST.INI');

  // *** Perform INI file processing here ***

  MyIni.Free;
end;
```

Description Create constructs a TIniFile object by allocating enough memory for the object. The single parameter, *FileName*, holds the Windows file name of the actual INI file. If no path is added to the file name, then your program will look in the Windows directory (usually C:\WINDOWS or C:\WINNT) for the file.

DeleteKey METHOD

Objects Affected TIniFile

Purpose The DeleteKey method deletes a key from the INI file.

Declaration

```
procedure DeleteKey(const Section, Ident: String);
```

Parameters

Section   The section of the INI file that contains the key.

Ident   The name of the identifier you are deleting.

Example Syntax

```
procedure TForm1.Button1Click(Sender: TObject);
var MyIni: TIniFile;
begin
  MyIni := TIniFile.Create('DELETE.INI');
  // Delete the key containing the Option1 identifier from the Main
  // section of the INI file
  MyIni.DeleteKey('Main', 'Option1');

  MyIni.Free;
end;
```

Description   DeleteKey erases the entire key, the identifier as well as its value.

EraseSection METHOD

Objects Affected   TIniFile

Purpose   The EraseSection method deletes a specific section in the INI file.

Declaration

```
procedure EraseSection(const Section: string);
```

Parameters

Section   The name of the section you wish to delete.

Example Syntax

```
// this procedure will open an INI file found in the Windows
// directory named TEST.INI and delete the section named
// Configuration
procedure TForm1.FormCreate(Sender: TObject);
// declare a variable of type TIniFile called MyIni
var
  MyIni: TIniFile;
begin
  // instantiate MyIni and assign it to an INI file
  MyIni := TIniFile.Create('TEST.INI');
  // Erase the section in TEST.INI called Configuration
  MyIni.EraseSection('Configuration');

  MyIni.Free;
end;
```

Description   EraseSection erases an entire section in an INI file. Section names are
denoted by brackets, so the section Configuration, used above, would
appear in the TEST.INI file as

```
[Configuration]
Key1
Key2
etc.
```

and continue to the next section name or the end of the file, whichever is
reached first.

FileName PROPERTY

Objects Affected	TIniFile
Purpose	The FileName method contains the file name encapsulated by the TIniFile object.
Declaration	

```
property FileName: string;
```

Example Syntax

```
// this procedure will print the file name of the INI
// file encapsulated by a TIniFile object
procedure TForm1.Button1Click(Sender: TObject);
var
  MyIni: TIniFile;
begin
  // instantiate MyIni and assign it to an INI file
  MyIni := TIniFile.Create('TEST.INI');
  // print the name of the INI file in the form's caption
  Form1.Caption := MyIni.FileName;

  MyIni.Free;
end;
```

Description	FileName is a run-time and read-only property that contains the name of the INI file encapsulated by an instance of TIniFile.

ReadBool PROPERTY

Objects Affected	TIniFile
Purpose	The ReadBool property gets a boolean value from an INI file.
Declaration	

```
function ReadBool(const Section, Ident: string; Default: Boolean):
Boolean;
```

Parameters

Section	The name of the section where the identifier is located.
Ident	The identifier you're attempting to read.
Default	The identifier's default value.

Example Syntax

```
// This procedure checks the TileWallpaper identifier of the Desktop
// section in your WIN.INI file. It then sets the caption of the
```

continued on next page

continued from previous page

```
// form, indicating whether the TileWallpaper option is on or off.
procedure TForm1.FormCreate(Sender: TObject);
var
  MyIni: TIniFile;
begin
  MyIni := TIniFile.Create('Win.Ini');
    if MyIni.ReadBool('Desktop', 'TileWallpaper', True) = True then
      Form1.Caption := 'Your desktop wallpaper is tiled'
    else
      Form1.Caption := 'Your desktop wallpaper is not tiled';

  MyIni.Free;
end;
```

Description   ReadBool retrieves a boolean value from an identifier in an INI file. In the example above, the TileWallPaper identifier of the [Desktop] section in WIN.INI is parsed, and the value it contains is returned. A value of 1 indicates True; 0 indicates False.

ReadBool is similar to ReadInteger and ReadString in that they all return values held by specific identifiers in an INI file.

ReadInteger METHOD

Objects Affected   TIniFile

Purpose   The ReadInteger method retrieves an integer value from an INI file.

Declaration

```
function ReadInteger(const Section, Ident: string; Default: Longint):
Longint;
```

Parameters

Section   The name of the section where the identifier is located.

Ident   The identifier you're attempting to read.

Default   The identifier's default value.

Example Syntax

```
// This procedure checks the iCountry identifier of the Intl
// section in your WIN.INI file. It then sets the caption of the
// form, indicating whether you are in the United States or not
procedure TForm1.FormCreate(Sender: TObject);
var
  MyIni: TIniFile;
begin
  MyIni := TIniFile.Create('win.ini');
    if MyIni.ReadInteger('Intl', 'iCountry', 1) = 1 then
      Form1.Caption := 'You are in the United States'
    else
      Form1.Caption := 'You are not in the United States';

  MyIni.Free;
end;
```

Description   ReadInteger retrieves an integer value from an identifier in an INI file. In the example above, your program checks **WIN.INI** for an identifier named **iCountry** in the **[Intl]** section. If the **iCountry** identifier is set to **1**, it indicates that your Control Panel Regional Settings are set to the United States configuration.

ReadInteger is similar to **ReadBool** and **ReadString** in that they all return values held by specific identifiers in an INI file.

ReadSection METHOD

Objects Affected   TIniFile

Purpose   The **ReadSection** method retrieves the names of all identifiers of a given section in an INI file and stores them in a strings object.

Declaration

```
procedure ReadSection (const Section: string; Strings: Tstrings);
```

Parameters

Section   The name of the section that is being read.

Strings   The string list where the values will be stored.

Example Syntax

```
// First, add a ListBox to your form. This procedure will print
// a list of the identifiers in the Desktop section of your WIN.INI
// file when the form is created
procedure TForm1.FormCreate(Sender: TObject);
var
  MyIni: TIniFile;
begin
  MyIni := TIniFile.Create('WIN.INI');
  MyIni.ReadSection('Desktop', ListBox1.Items);

  MyIni.Free;
end;
```

Description   ReadSection retrieves the names of the identifiers in a specific section of an INI file and places them in a strings object. This list can be placed directly in a component's string list (as in a list box's **Items** property) or placed in an independent string list.

ReadSection does not retrieve the *values* of the identifiers, it retrieves the *names* of the identifiers. **ReadSectionValues** can be used to retrieve the identifiers and the actual values.

In Figure 4-2, a typical INI file section is displayed using **ReadSection**.

Figure 4-2 The list box displays
the identifiers in the [Desktop]
section of your WIN.INI file

ReadSections METHOD

Objects Affected   TIniFile

Purpose   The ReadSections method copies all of the section names in the INI file to
a strings object.

Declaration

```
procedure ReadSections(Strings: Tstrings);
```

Parameters

Strings   The list of section names.

Example Syntax

```
// This event handler prints the names of the INI file sections
// in a list box when the button is clicked
procedure TForm1.Button1Click(Sender: TObject);
var
  MyIni: TIniFile;
begin
  ListBox1.Clear;

  MyIni := TIniFile.Create('test.ini');
  MyIni.ReadSections(ListBox1.Items);

  MyIni.Free;
end;
```

Description   A strings object is a list of strings used by components (like list boxes) that
need to manipulate many strings. ReadSections stores a list of the INI
file's section names in the *Strings* parameter. In the example code above,
this list is passed to the Items property of a list box, which is also type
TStrings.

ReadSectionValues METHOD

Objects Affected	TIniFile
Purpose	The ReadSectionValues method retrieves all of the keys from a given section of an INI file.
Declaration	

```
procedure ReadSectionValues(const Section: string; Strings: Tstrings);
```

Parameters

Section   The name of the section that is being read.

Strings   The string list where the identifiers and their values will be stored.

Example Syntax

```
// First, add a ListBox to your form. This procedure will print
// a list of the identifiers and their values in the Desktop section
// of your WIN.INI file when the form is created
procedure TForm1.FormCreate(Sender: TObject);
var
  MyIni: TIniFile;
begin
  MyIni := TIniFile.Create('WIN.INI');
  MyIni.ReadSectionValues('Desktop', ListBox1.Items);

  MyIni.Free;
end;
```

Description

ReadSectionValues retrieves all of the keys from a section of an INI file and stores them in a string object in the same way that they appear in the INI file:

identifier=value

In the example above, the entire list is displayed in a list box, as shown in Figure 4-3. It is possible to display single values by using the **Values** property of **TStrings**, or by copying the entire section into a string list and accessing each line by its index:

```
// In this example, WIN.INI's Desktop section is read into a
// string list and the list's first string is then printed in
// the form caption using its index.
procedure TForm1.FormCreate(Sender: TObject);
var
  MyIni: TIniFile;
  MyStringList: TStringList;
begin
  MyIni := TIniFile.Create('WIN.INI');
  // instantiate the string list
  MyStringList := TStringList.Create;
  // copy the section into the string list
  MyIni.ReadSectionValues('Desktop', MyStringList);
  // print the first string in the list in the form's caption
  Form1.Caption := MyStringList.Strings[0];
```

continued on next page

continued from previous page

```
            MyIni.Free;
            MyStringList.Free;
         end;
```

This is shown in Figure 4-4.

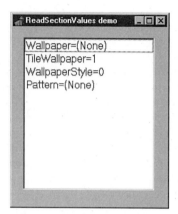

Figure 4-3   The list box displays the identifiers and their values in the [Desktop] section of your WIN.INI file.

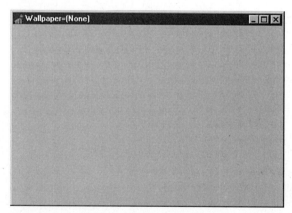

Figure 4-4   Getting an individual identifier and its value and printing it in the form's caption

ReadString Method

Objects Affected	TIniFile
Purpose	The ReadString method reads a string value from an identifier in a specific section of an INI file.

Declaration

```
function ReadString(const Section, Ident, Default: string): string;
```

Parameters

Section	The name of the section where the identifier is located.
Ident	The identifier you're attempting to read.
Default	The identifier's default value (returned if the identifier is not found).

Example Syntax

```
// This procedure checks the sCountry identifier of the Intl
// section in your WIN.INI file. It then sets the caption of the
// form to the sCountry identifier
procedure TForm1.FormCreate(Sender: TObject);
var
  MyIni: TIniFile;
begin
  MyIni := TIniFile.Create('Win.Ini');
  Form1.Caption := MyIni.ReadString('Intl', 'sCountry', 'no country
                                                          listed');
  // don't forget to destruct MyIni when you are done!
  MyIni.Free;
end;
```

Description

ReadString retrieves a string value from an identifier in an INI file. In the example above, your program retrieves an identifier named sCountry in the [Intl] section of your WIN.INI file and prints its value in the form's caption.

ReadString is similar to ReadBool and ReadInteger in that they all return values held by specific identifiers in an INI file.

WriteBool Method

Objects Affected	TIniFile
Purpose	The WriteBool method writes a boolean value to an identifier in a specific section of an INI file.

Declaration

```
procedure WriteBool(const Section, Ident: string; Value: Boolean);
```

Parameters

Section   The name of the section where the identifier is located.

Ident   The identifier you're attempting to write to.

Value   The value you wish to write to the identifier.

Example Syntax

```
// this procedure creates a new INI file named TEST.INI
// (if it doesn't already exit) and adds the boolean
// identifier SampleBooleanEntry with a value of True.
// If there is no identifier, that will be created as well
procedure TForm1.FormCreate(Sender: TObject);
var
  WriteIni: TIniFile;
begin
  WriteIni := TIniFile.Create('TEST.INI');
  WriteIni.WriteBool('Sample Section', 'SampleBooleanEntry', True);

  WriteIni.Free;
end;
```

Description WriteBool writes a boolean value, specified by the *Value* parameter, to an INI file. You specify the section and the identifier that the value will be written to with the *Section* and *Ident* parameters. If the section or identifier does not exist before the call to WriteBool, it will be created.

If you run the example above, you can open the newly created TEST.INI, found in your Windows directory, and the following lines will be present:

```
[Sample Section]
SampleBooleanEntry=1
```

WriteBool is used in a manner similar to WriteInteger and WriteString—the only real difference is the type of value that is being written.

WriteInteger METHOD

Objects Affected TIniFile

Purpose   The WriteBoolInteger method writes an integer value to an identifier in a specific section of an INI file.

Declaration

```
procedure WriteInteger(const Section, Ident: string; Value: Longint);
```

Parameters

Section   The name of the section where the identifier is located.

Ident   The identifier you're attempting to write to.

Value   The value you wish to write to the identifier.

Example Syntax

```
// this procedure creates a new INI file named TEST.INI
// (if it doesn't already exit) and adds the integer
// identifier SampleIntegerEntry with a value of 12024.
// If there is no identifier, that will be created as well
procedure TForm1.FormCreate(Sender: TObject);
var
  WriteIni: TIniFile;
begin
  WriteIni := TIniFile.Create('TEST.INI');
  WriteIni.WriteInteger('Sample Section', 'SampleIntegerEntry', 12024);

  WriteIni.Free;
end;
```

Description

WriteInteger writes an integer value to an INI file, where you specify the section and the identifier that the value will be written to. If the section or identifier does not exist before the call to WriteInteger, it will be created.

If you run the example above, you can open the newly created TEST.INI, found in your Windows directory, and the following lines will be present:

```
[Sample Section]
SampleIntegerEntry=12024
```

WriteInteger is used in a manner similar to WriteBool and WriteString—the only real difference is the type of value that is being written.

WriteString METHOD

Objects Affected   TIniFile

Purpose   The WriteString method writes a string value to an identifier in a specific section of an INI file.

Declaration

```
procedure WriteString(const Section, Ident, Value: string);
```

Parameters

Section   The name of the section where the identifier is located.

Ident   The identifier you're attempting to write to.

Value   The value you wish to write to the identifier.

Example Syntax

```
// this procedure creates a new INI file named TEST.INI
// (if it doesn't already exit) and adds the string
// identifier SampleStringEntry and a string value.
// If there is no identifier, that will be created as well
```

continued on next page

continued from previous page

```
procedure TForm1.FormCreate(Sender: TObject);
var
  WriteIni: TIniFile;
begin
  WriteIni := TIniFile.Create('TEST.INI');
  WriteIni.WriteString('Sample Section', 'SampleStringEntry',
          'this is an example of writing a string to an INI file');

  WriteIni.Free;
end;
```

Description

WriteString writes a string value to an INI file. You specify the section and the identifier to which the value will be written. If the section or identifier does not exist before the call to WriteString, it will be created.

If you run the example above, you can open the newly created TEST.INI, found in your Windows directory, and the following lines will be present:

```
[Sample Section]
SampleStringEntry=this is an example of writing a string to an INI file
```

WriteString is used in a manner similar to WriteBool and WriteInteger—the only real difference is the type of value that is being written.

5

TThread

Whenever you launch a program in Windows 95 and NT, it is called an *instance* of the program. When you begin working with threads, you will discover that an instance is known as a *process*. The process is composed of one or more *threads*, paths of execution through program code. Most traditional Windows programs are single-threaded processes; that is, they consist of only one thread.

Creating a program with more than a single thread is still fairly complex, even in Delphi, and is usually unnecessary. For the most part, operating system services and applications that extend the operating system—like Microsoft Office—utilize multithreading for complex tasks.

If you choose to delve into the world of multiple threads, you should be aware of the complexities and hazards involved. To fully exploit the power of multithreading in Delphi, you will need to resort to API and API-like calls. Fortunately, Delphi's Object Repository does provide an easy way to add *thread objects*—that is, objects of type `TThread`—into your applications. These objects represent threads of execution that you can utilize.

To add a thread object to an application, choose New from the File menu and then choose Thread Object from the Object Repository dialog that appears. This is shown in Figure 5-1.

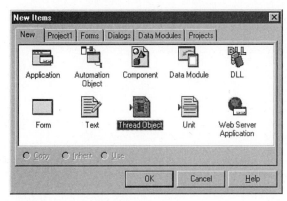

Figure 5-1 Object Repository

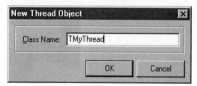

Figure 5-2   New Thread Object
dialog box

Delphi then prompts you for the name of the new thread object. The New Thread
dialog box is shown in Figure 5-2.

When you enter the name of your new object, Delphi creates a new unit containing
the declaration of a descendant class of **TThread**. This skeleton unit should resemble
Listing 5-1.

Listing 5-1 New thread unit

```
unit Unit2;

interface

uses
  Classes;

type
  TMyThread = class(TThread)
  private
    { Private declarations }
  protected
    procedure Execute; override;
  end;

implementation

{ Important: Methods and properties of objects in VCL can only be used in a
  method called using Synchronize, for example,

      Synchronize(UpdateCaption);

  and UpdateCaption could look like,

    procedure TMyThread.UpdateCaption;
    begin
      Form1.Caption := 'Updated in a thread';
    end; }

{ TMyThread }

procedure TMyThread.Execute;
begin
  { Place thread code here }
end;

end.
```

Once you have this new unit, you can add a new member object in the original unit and instantiate it with a call to its **Create** method, as shown in Listing 5-2.

Listing 5-2 Instantiating a new thread object

```
type
  TForm1 = class(TForm)
    procedure FormCreate(Sender: TObject);
  private
    { Private declarations }
  public
    { Public declarations }
    FMyThread: TMyThread;
  end;

var
  Form1: TForm1;

implementation

{$R *.DFM}

procedure TForm1.FormCreate(Sender: TObject);
begin
  FMyThread := TMyThread.Create(False);
end;
```

When you call the **Create** method, as in the above example, the **Execute** method of the new thread object is automatically executed. The skeleton of the **Execute** method is provided for you by the Object Repository, as shown in Listing 5-1. You can fill this method as you see fit.

Table 5-1 displays the properties, methods, and events implemented by **TThread**.

Table 5-1 Properties, methods, and events implemented by TThread

Use or Set This...	To Do This...	Inheritance
Create	Construct a new object.	None
Destroy	Destroy the object.	TObject
Free	Safely destroy the object.	TObject
FreeOnTerminate	Determine whether the programmer is responsible for destroying the thread object.	None
InheritsFrom	Determine whether the object is descended from a certain class.	TObject
InstanceSize	Determine the amount of memory allocated for the object.	TObject
OnTerminate	Handle the event that occurs when the thread terminates.	None
Priority	Determine the scheduling priority level of the thread.	None
Resume	Resume execution of the thread.	None
Suspend	Suspend execution of the thread.	None
Suspended	Determine whether the thread is suspended.	None
Terminate	Terminate execution of the thread.	None

Create METHOD

Objects Affected   TThread

Purpose   The `Create` method creates an instance of a thread object.

Declaration

```
constructor Create(CreateSuspended: Boolean);
```

Parameters

CreateSuspended   Determines whether the thread executes immediately upon creation.

Example Syntax

```
procedure TForm1.FormCreate(Sender: TObject);
begin
  FMyThread := TMyThread.Create(False);
end;
```

Description   If the *CreateSuspended* parameter is `True`, the new thread object is suspended after it is created. That is, its `Execute` method is not immediately invoked or called. If *CreateSuspended* is `False`, the thread's `Execute` method is immediately called.

FreeOnTerminate METHOD

Objects Affected   TThread

Purpose   The `FreeOnTerminate` method determines whether the programmer is responsible for destroying the thread object.

Declaration

```
property FreeOnTerminate: Boolean;
```

Example Syntax

```
FmyThread.FreeOnTerminate := True;
```

Description   If `FreeOnTerminate` is `True`, the VCL will automatically destroy the thread object for you when your thread is terminated. If `FreeOnTerminate` is `False`, you must manually destroy the thread. `FreeOnTerminate` is `False` by default.

OnTerminate EVENT

Objects Affected   TThread

Purpose   The `OnTerminate` event occurs when the thread terminates.

Declaration

```
property OnTerminate: TNotifyEvent;
```

Example Syntax

```
procedure TForm1.FormCreate(Sender: TObject);
begin
  FMyThread := TMyThread.Create(False);
  FMyThread.OnTerminate := ArnoldThread;
end;

procedure TForm1.ArnoldThread(Sender: TObject);
begin
  Label1.Caption := 'Hasta la vista, thread';
end;
```

Description   A thread terminates when the code in its **Execute** method concludes. If for some reason this point is not reached and the application terminates, the thread is automatically terminated at that point.

Priority PROPERTY

Objects Affected   TThread

Purpose   The **Priority** property specifies the thread's relative scheduling priority level.

Declaration

```
property Priority: TThreadPriority read GetPriority write SetPriority;
```

Example Syntax

```
procedure TForm1.FormCreate(Sender: TObject);
begin
  FMyThread := TMyThread.Create(True);
  FMyThread.Priority := tpIdle;
  FMyThread.Resume;
end;
```

Description   Windows schedules threads on a priority basis. The **Priority** property is type **TThreadPriority**, which is declared as

```
TThreadPriority = (tpIdle, tpLowest, tpLower, tpNormal, tpHigher, ⇐
tpHighest,
    tpTimeCritical);
```

The priority level is relative to the priority of the process (application). A value of **tpIdle** indicates that the thread is inactive. If **Priority** is **tpLowest** or **tpLower**, the thread will receive less CPU time than its process. If **Priority** is **tpHigher**, **tpHighest**, or **tpTimeCritical**, it will receive more CPU time than its process. If it uses **tpNormal**, it is the same priority level as its process and will receive equal CPU time. The default value is **tpNormal**.

Resume METHOD

Objects Affected	TThread
Purpose	The Resume method resumes execution of a suspended thread.
Declaration	

```
procedure Resume;
```

Example Syntax

```
procedure TForm1.Button1Click(Sender: TObject);
begin
  if FMyThread.Suspended then
  begin
    Button1.Caption := 'Suspend';
    FMyThread.Resume
  end
  else begin
    Button1.Caption := 'Resume';
    FMyThread.Suspend
  end
end;
```

Description   Resume is used to resume thread execution that was suspended with the Suspend method.

Suspend METHOD

Objects Affected	TThread
Purpose	The Suspend method suspends thread execution.
Declaration	

```
procedure Suspend;
```

Example Syntax

```
procedure TForm1.Button1Click(Sender: TObject);
begin
  if FMyThread.Suspended then
  begin
    Button1.Caption := 'Suspend';
    FMyThread.Resume
  end
  else begin
    Button1.Caption := 'Resume';
    FMyThread.Suspend
  end
end;
```

Description   Suspend pauses execution of the thread object. You can call Resume to resume thread execution.

Suspended PROPERTY

Objects Affected	TThread
Purpose	The **Suspended** property indicates whether a thread is suspended.
Declaration	

```
property Suspended: Boolean read FSuspended write SetSuspended;
```

Example Syntax

```
procedure TForm1.Button1Click(Sender: TObject);
begin
  if FMyThread.Suspended then
  begin
    Button1.Caption := 'Suspend';
    FMyThread.Resume
  end
  else begin
    Button1.Caption := 'Resume';
    FMyThread.Suspend
  end
end;
```

Description If **Suspended** is **True**, the thread object is currently suspended. If it is **False**, the thread is executing. Interestingly, you can use **Suspended** to suspend or resume a thread as well, by setting its value to **True** or **False**, respectively.

Terminate METHOD

Objects Affected	TThread
Purpose	The **Terminate** method terminates the thread object.
Declaration	

```
function Terminate: Integer;
```

Example Syntax

```
// ----------- thread unit -----------

procedure TMyThread.Execute;
begin
  { Place thread code here }
  while not Terminated do
    // add thread processing here
    ;
end;

// ----------- main unit -----------

procedure TForm1.Button2Click(Sender: TObject);
begin
  FMyThread.Terminate;
end;
```

Description The **Terminate** method informs your thread that it should terminate.

55

6

TRegistry AND TRegIniFile

The Windows Registry keeps track of information about the operating system and the various applications installed on the system. The Registry is a hierarchical database containing configuration information in specific formats that can be edited directly with the RegEdit program—shown in Figure 6-1—or modified by application programs. INI files haphazardly performed this function in earlier versions of Windows, though there are some similarities between INI files and the Registry that may help you understand how the Registry works. The Registry, however, is more sophisticated than the traditional INI file due to its organizational structure.

The Registry is divided into several major sections, such as `HKEY_CLASSES_ROOT` and `HKEY_CURRENT_USER`. These sections, or *Keys*, contain different categories of system information. When you create an application program, for example, you can register configuration values within the `SOFTWARE` subsection of the `HKEY_LOCAL_MACHINE` section. If you view this section with RegEdit, you will see the structure that companies use when storing data. Microsoft, Borland, and other companies create a company key, for example, and then an application key within it. This application stores configuration values. The values stored in a Key can take on any of a wide variety of useful data types, including string, currency, date, float, and boolean.

If it helps you to understand the Registry, you can compare Registry Keys with the familiar bracketed headings in an INI file.

Registry Differences

The Windows 95 and Windows NT Registries are structured somewhat differently. Before you access the Registry, you should determine which operating system you are running. You can do this with the Win32 API function `GetVersionEx`, as demonstrated in Listing 6-1.

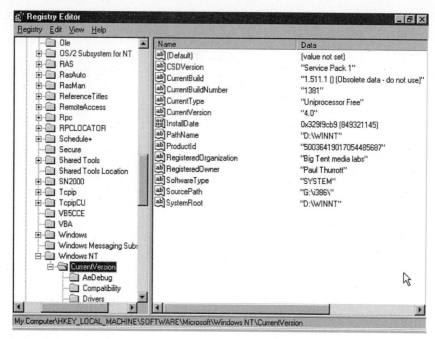

Figure 6-1   RegEdit

Listing 6-1 Determine the operating system before you access the Registry

```
var
  Form1: TForm1;
  MyVersionInfo: TOSVersionInfo;

implementation

{$R *.DFM}

procedure TForm1.FormCreate(Sender: TObject);
var
  MyReg: TRegistry;
  IsNT: Boolean;
begin
  MyReg := TRegistry.Create;
  MyReg.RootKey := HKEY_LOCAL_MACHINE;

  IsNT := False;

  // First, you must set the size of the dwOSVersionInfoSize
  // element in the OSVersionInfo record to the size of that type
  MyVersionInfo.dwOSVersionInfoSize := sizeof(TOSVERSIONINFO);

  // Call GetVersionEx to fill the MyVersionInfo record
  GetVersionEx(MyVersionInfo);
```

```
// Determine the OS
if MyVersionInfo.dwPlatformId = VER_PLATFORM_WIN32_WINDOWS then
  lblOSName.Caption := 'Windows 95';
if MyVersionInfo.dwPlatformId = VER_PLATFORM_WIN32_NT then
begin
  IsNT := True;
  lblOSName.Caption := 'Windows NT';
end;

// . . .
```

Once you have determined the operating system (in this case, Windows NT or Windows 95), you can access the Registry accordingly. As shown in Listing 6-2, some of the Registry paths and Keys in Windows NT and Windows 95 are different.

Listing 6-2 Access the proper Registry Key based on the operating system information obtained earlier

```
try
  if IsNT then
    if not MyReg.OpenKey
      ('\SOFTWARE\Microsoft\Windows NT\CurrentVersion', FALSE) then
    else lblVersionNumber.Caption := MyReg.ReadString('CurrentVersion')
  else
    if not MyReg.OpenKey
      ('\SOFTWARE\Microsoft\Windows\CurrentVersion', FALSE) then
    else lblVersionNumber.Caption := MyReg.ReadString('VersionNumber');
finally
end; // try..finally
```

Table 6-1 displays the properties and methods that are implemented by `TRegistry`.

Table 6-1 Properties and methods implemented by `TRegistry`

Use or Set This...	To Do This...	Inheritance
CloseKey	Close the current Key.	None
Create	Construct a new object.	TObject
CreateKey	Create a new Key in the Registry.	None
CurrentKey	Determine the name of the current Key.	None
CurrentPath	Determine the fully qualified hierarchical path of the current Key.	None
DeleteKey	Delete the specified Key.	None
DeleteValue	Delete a specified data value within the current Key.	None
Destroy	Destroy the object.	TObject
Free	Safely destroy the object.	TObject
GetDataInfo	Determine information about the data value of a Key in the Registry.	None
GetDataSize	Determine the length of the specified data value in the current Key.	None
GetDataType	Determine the type of data contained by a specified data value in the current Key.	None
GetKeyInfo	Determine information about the current Key.	None

continued on next page

continued from previous page

Use or Set This...	To Do This...	Inheritance
GetKeyNames	Obtain the names of all subkeys contained within the current Key.	None
GetValueNames	Obtain the names of all the data values contained by the current Key.	None
HasSubKeys	Determine whether the current Key has any subkeys.	None
InheritsFrom	Determine if the object is descended from a certain class.	TObject
InstanceSize	Determine the amount of memory allocated for the object.	TObject
KeyExists	Determine whether a specified Key exists in the Registry.	None
LazyWrite	Determine when the Registry is updated with new data.	None
OpenKey	Specify the current Key.	None
ReadBinaryData	Return the binary value from a data value associated with the current Key.	None
ReadBool	Return the boolean value from a data value associated with the current Key.	None
ReadCurrency	Return the currency value from a data value associated with the current Key.	None
ReadDate	Return the date value from a data value associated with the current Key.	None
ReadDateTime	Return the date/time value from a data value associated with the current Key.	None
ReadFloat	Return the floating-point value from a data value associated with the current Key.	None
ReadInteger	Return the integer value from a data value associated with the current Key.	None
ReadString	Return the string value from a data value associated with the current Key.	None
ReadTime	Return the time value from a data value associated with the current Key.	None
RenameValue	Rename a data value.	None
RootKey	Specify the Root Key for the Registry object.	None
ValueExists	Determine whether the specified data value exists.	None
WriteBinaryData	Write a new binary value to a data value associated with the current Key.	None
WriteBool	Write a new boolean value to a data value associated with the current Key.	None
WriteCurrency	Write a new currency value to a data value associated with the current Key.	None
WriteDate	Write a new date value to a data value associated with the current Key.	None
WriteDateTime	Write a new date/time value to a data value associated with the current Key.	None
WriteFloat	Write a floating-point new value to a data value associated with the current Key.	None
WriteInteger	Write a new integer value to a data value associated with the current Key.	None
WriteString	Write a new string value to a data value associated with the current Key.	None
WriteTime	Write a new time value to a data value associated with the current Key.	None

CloseKey METHOD

Objects Affected	TRegistry
Purpose	The CloseKey method closes the current Key.
Declaration	

```
procedure CloseKey;
```

Example Syntax

```
try
if IsNT then
  if not MyReg.OpenKey('\SOFTWARE\Microsoft\Windows NT\CurrentVersion',
                       FALSE) then
  else
    begin
      lblOrganization.Caption := MyReg.ReadString
                                 ('RegisteredOrganization');
      MyReg.CloseKey;
    end
finally
  MyReg.Free;
end; // try..finally
```

Description   When you close the Key, the value of the Key is written to the Registry. If no Key is open, `CloseKey` has no effect.

CreateKey METHOD

Objects Affected   `TRegistry`

Purpose   The `CreateKey` method creates a new Key in the Registry.

Declaration

```
function CreateKey(const Key: string): Boolean;
```

Parameters

Key   The name of the Key that is to be created.

Example Syntax

```
procedure TForm1.Button1Click(Sender: TObject);
begin
  MyReg := TRegistry.Create;
  MyReg.RootKey := HKEY_LOCAL_MACHINE;

  try
    if not MyReg.OpenKey('\SOFTWARE\', FALSE) then;
    if not MyReg.KeyExists('Thurrott') then
      MyReg.CreateKey('Thurrott');
    if not MyReg.OpenKey('\SOFTWARE\Thurrott', FALSE) then;

    MyReg.WriteString('Paul', 'a string data value');

    MyReg.CloseKey;
  finally
    MyReg.Free;
  end; // try..finally
end;
```

Description   If the Key you are creating already exists, `CreateKey` has no effect. If `CreateKey` was successful, it returns `True`. Otherwise, it returns `False`.

CurrentKey PROPERTY

Objects Affected	`TRegistry`
Purpose	The `CurrentKey` property contains the name of the current Key.
Declaration	

```
property CurrentKey: HKEY;
```

Example Syntax

```
procedure TForm1.Button1Click(Sender: TObject);
var MyTempKey: HKEY;
begin
  MyTempKey := MyReg.CurrentKey;
  // . . .
end;
```

Description	`CurrentKey` is run-time and read-only.

CurrentPath PROPERTY

Objects Affected	`TRegistry`
Purpose	The `CurrentPath` property contains the fully qualified hierarchical path of the current Key.
Declaration	

```
property CurrentPath: string;
```

Example Syntax

```
strPath := MyReg.CurrentPath;
```

Description	`CurrentPath` is run-time and read-only.

DeleteKey METHOD

Objects Affected	`TRegistry`
Purpose	The `DeleteKey` method deletes the specified Key.
Declaration	

```
function DeleteKey(const Key: string): Boolean;
```

Parameters	
Key	The name of the Key you wish to delete.

Example Syntax

```
procedure TForm1.Button2Click(Sender: TObject);
begin
  MyReg := TRegistry.Create;
  MyReg.RootKey := HKEY_LOCAL_MACHINE;

  try
    if not MyReg.OpenKey('\SOFTWARE\', FALSE) then;

    MyReg.DeleteKey('Thurrott');

    MyReg.CloseKey;
  finally
    MyReg.Free;
  end; // try..finally
end;
```

Description   DeleteKey deletes the Key whose name is specified by the *Key* argument.
                If the Key contains subkeys at any level, they will all be deleted. If the
                deletion is successful, the function returns True. Otherwise, DeleteKey
                returns False.

DeleteValue METHOD

Objects Affected   TRegistry

Purpose   The DeleteValue method deletes a specified data value within the current
                     Key.

Declaration

```
function DeleteValue(const Name: string): Boolean;
```

Parameters

Name   The name of the data value you wish to delete.

Example Syntax

```
procedure TForm1.Button2Click(Sender: TObject);
begin
  MyReg := TRegistry.Create;
  MyReg.RootKey := HKEY_LOCAL_MACHINE;

  try
    if not MyReg.OpenKey('\SOFTWARE\Thurrott', FALSE) then;

    MyReg.DeleteValue('Paul');

    MyReg.CloseKey;
  finally
    MyReg.Free;
  end; // try..finally
end;
```

Description   When you pass `DeleteValue` the valid name of a data value, it deletes the data value and its associated name from the current Key, and the function returns `True`. If the call is unsuccessful—if, for example, the data value doesn't exist—`DeleteValue` returns `False`.

`GetDataInfo` METHOD

Objects Affected   `TRegistry`

Purpose   The `GetDataInfo` method determines information about the data value of a Key in the Registry.

Declaration

```
function GetDataInfo(const ValueName: string;
                     var Value: TRegDataInfo): Boolean;
```

Parameters

ValueName   The name of the value.

Value   A record that will contain the information about the value.

Example Syntax

```
procedure TForm1.Button1Click(Sender: TObject);
var
  MyDataInfo: TRegDataInfo;
  MyString: string;
begin
  MyReg := TRegistry.Create;
  MyReg.RootKey := HKEY_LOCAL_MACHINE;

  if not MyReg.OpenKey('\SOFTWARE\Microsoft\Windows NT\CurrentVersion',
                       FALSE) then
    MyReg.GetDataInfo('RegisteredOrganization', MyDataInfo);
    Label1.Caption := MyReg.ReadString('RegisteredOrganization') ;

    // ...
end;
```

Description   When you need to find out the type of data and the size of that data contained by a data value in the current Key in the Registry, you can use the `GetDataInfo` method. The *ValueName* parameter identifies the Key you are querying. The *Value* parameter contains a record of type `TRegDataInfo`. This record contains two fields, `RegData` and `DataSize`:

```
TRegDataInfo = record
    RegData: TRegDataType;
    DataSize: Integer;
  end;
```

The `RegData` field is defined as

```
TRegDataType = (rdUnknown, rdString, rdExpandString,
                rdInteger, rdBinary);
```

When the method returns, you can use the value contained in the RegData field to determine what type of data the Key contains.

An easier way to get the data type of the data value in the current Key is to use GetDataType. You can also use GetDataSize to determine the size of the data more easily.

GetDataSize METHOD

Objects Affected	TRegistry
Purpose	The GetDataSize method returns the length of the specified data value in the current Key.
Declaration	

```
function GetDataSize(const ValueName: string): Integer;
```

Parameters

ValueName The name of the data value you are querying.

Example Syntax

```
procedure TForm1.Button1Click(Sender: TObject);
var MyDataInfo: TRegDataInfo;
    MyString: string;
begin
  MyReg := TRegistry.Create;
  MyReg.RootKey := HKEY_LOCAL_MACHINE;

  MyReg.OpenKey('\SOFTWARE\Microsoft\Windows NT\CurrentVersion',
            FALSE);

  Label5.Caption :=
        IntToStr(MyReg.GetDataSize('RegisteredOrganization'));

  // ...
end;
```

Description GetDataSize returns the size, in bytes, of the data value in the current Key specified by the *ValueName* parameter. If the data value is a string, GetDataSize will return an extra byte for the null terminator.

GetDataType METHOD

Objects Affected	TRegistry
Purpose	The GetDataType method returns the type of the data contained by a specified data value in the current Key.
Declaration	

```
function GetDataType(const ValueName: string): TRegDataType;
```

Parameters

ValueName   The name of the data value you are querying.

Example Syntax

```
procedure TForm1.Button1Click(Sender: TObject);
var MyDataInfo: TRegDataInfo;
    MyString: string;
begin
  MyReg := TRegistry.Create;
  MyReg.RootKey := HKEY_LOCAL_MACHINE;

  MyReg.OpenKey('\SOFTWARE\Microsoft\Windows NT\CurrentVersion', FALSE);

  MyDataInfo.RegData := MyReg.GetDataType('RegisteredOrganization');

  case MyDataInfo.RegData of
    rdUnknown: Label5.Caption := 'Unknown';
    rdString: Label5.Caption := 'String';
    rdExpandString: Label5.Caption := 'Expanded string';
    rdInteger: Label5.Caption := 'Integer';
    rdBinary: Label5.Caption := 'Binary';
  end;
  // ...
end;
```

Description   GetDataType returns the data type of the data value specified by the
                             ValueName parameter. The data type is of type **TRegDataType**, which is
                             defined as

```
TRegDataType = (rdUnknown, rdString, rdExpandString, rdInteger,
                rdBinary);
```

GetKeyInfo METHOD

Objects Affected   TRegistry

Purpose   The GetKeyInfo method returns information about the current Key.

Declaration

```
function GetKeyInfo(var Value: TRegKeyInfo): Boolean;
```

Parameters

Value   The **TRegKeyInfo** record that will hold information about the current Key.

Example Syntax

```
procedure TForm1.Button1Click(Sender: TObject);
var MyKeyInfo: TRegKeyInfo;
    MyString: string;
begin
  MyReg := TRegistry.Create;
  MyReg.RootKey := HKEY_LOCAL_MACHINE;

  MyReg.OpenKey('\SOFTWARE\Microsoft\Windows NT\CurrentVersion', FALSE);
```

```
    MyReg.GetKeyInfo(MyKeyInfo);
    ListBox1.Items.Add('NumSubKeys = ' + IntToStr(MyKeyInfo.NumSubKeys));
    ListBox1.Items.Add('MaxSubKeyLen = ' + ⇐
IntToStr(MyKeyInfo.MaxSubKeyLen));
    ListBox1.Items.Add('NumValues = ' + IntToStr(MyKeyInfo.NumValues));
    ListBox1.Items.Add('MaxValueLen = ' + IntToStr(MyKeyInfo.MaxValueLen));
end;
```

Description The *Value* parameter contains a record of type **TRegKeyInfo**, which is
filled with information about the current Key when the method is called.
TRegKeyInfo is declared as

```
TRegKeyInfo = record
    NumSubKeys: Integer;        // the number of sub-keys

    MaxSubKeyLen: Integer;      // the length of the longest sub-key name,⇐
                                   in bytes

    NumValues: Integer;         // the number of data values

    MaxValueLen: Integer;       // the length of the longest data value⇐
                                   name

    MaxDataLen: Integer;        // the size, in bytes, of the largest data⇐
                                   value

    FileTime: TFileTime;        // the time the value was last modified
end;
```

GetKeyNames METHOD

Objects Affected TRegistry

Purpose The **GetKeyNames** method returns a string list containing the names of all
subkeys contained within the current Key.

Declaration

```
procedure GetKeyNames(Strings: TStrings);
```

Parameters

Strings A list of strings containing the names of all the subkeys of the current Key.

Example Syntax

```
procedure TForm1.Button1Click(Sender: TObject);
var MyKeyInfo: TRegKeyInfo;
    MyString: string;
begin
  MyReg := TRegistry.Create;
  MyReg.RootKey := HKEY_LOCAL_MACHINE;

  MyReg.OpenKey('\SOFTWARE\Microsoft\Windows NT\CurrentVersion', FALSE);

  MyReg.GetKeyNames(ListBox1.Items);
end;
```

Description In the example above, a list box is filled with the names of the subkeys in
the current Key.

GetValueNames METHOD

Objects Affected	`TRegistry`
Purpose	The `GetValueNames` method fills a list of strings with the names of all the data values contained by the current Key.
Declaration	

```
procedure GetValueNames(Strings: TStrings);
```

Parameters

Strings   A list of strings containing the names of all the data values contained by the current Key.

Example Syntax

```
procedure TForm1.Button1Click(Sender: TObject);
var MyKeyInfo: TRegKeyInfo;
    MyString: string;
begin
  MyReg := TRegistry.Create;
  MyReg.RootKey := HKEY_LOCAL_MACHINE;

  MyReg.OpenKey('\SOFTWARE\Microsoft\Windows NT\CurrentVersion', FALSE);

  MyReg.GetValueNames(ListBox1.Items);
end;
```

Description   `GetValueNames` is similar to `GetKeyNames`, but provides the names of the data values associated with the subkeys in the current Key.

HasSubKeys METHOD

Objects Affected	`TRegistry`
Purpose	The `HasSubKeys` method determines whether the current Key has any subkeys.
Declaration	

```
function HasSubKeys: Boolean;
```

Example Syntax

```
procedure TForm1.Button1Click(Sender: TObject);
var MyKeyInfo: TRegKeyInfo;
    MyString: string;
begin
  MyReg := TRegistry.Create;
  MyReg.RootKey := HKEY_LOCAL_MACHINE;

  MyReg.OpenKey('\SOFTWARE\Microsoft\Windows NT\CurrentVersion', FALSE);
```

```
if MyReg.HasSubKeys then
  Label5.Caption := 'Yes, the current key has sub-keys'
else
  Label5.Caption := 'The current key has no sub-keys';
end;
```

Description   If the current Key has any subkeys, **HasSubKeys** returns **True**. Otherwise, it returns **False**.

KeyExists METHOD

Objects Affected   TRegistry

Purpose   The **KeyExists** method determines whether a specified Key exists in the Registry.

Declaration

```
function KeyExists(const Key: string): Boolean;
```

Parameters

Key   The name of the Key you are searching for.

Example Syntax

```
procedure TForm1.Button1Click(Sender: TObject);
var MyKeyInfo: TRegKeyInfo;
    MyString: string;
begin
  MyReg := TRegistry.Create;
  MyReg.RootKey := HKEY_LOCAL_MACHINE;

  MyReg.OpenKey('\SOFTWARE\Microsoft\Windows NT\CurrentVersion', FALSE);

  if MyReg.KeyExists('\SOFTWARE\Microsoft\Windows\Help') then
    // . . .
  else
    // . . .

end;
```

Description   The Key you query with **KeyExists** doesn't necessarily have to have any relationship to the current Key. If the Key exists, **KeyExists** returns **True**. Otherwise, it returns **False**.

LazyWrite PROPERTY

Objects Affected   TRegistry

Purpose   The **LazyWrite** property determines when the Registry is updated with new data.

Declaration

```
property LazyWrite: Boolean;
```

Description   LazyWrite is True by default, meaning that any changes you make to the Registry are not necessarily written immediately, but are written when the current Key is closed. Despite the small risk, you should leave this property to True because system performance will be degraded otherwise.

OpenKey METHOD

Objects Affected   TRegistry

Purpose   The OpenKey method specifies the current Key.

Declaration

```
function OpenKey(const Key: string; CanCreate: Boolean): Boolean;
```

Parameters

Key   The name of the Key you are trying to open.

CanCreate   Determines whether the Key is created if it does not already exist.

Example Syntax

```
var
  Form1: TForm1;
  MyReg: TRegistry;

implementation

{$R *.DFM}

procedure TForm1.FormCreate(Sender: TObject);
begin
  MyReg := TRegistry.Create;
  MyReg.RootKey := HKEY_LOCAL_MACHINE;

  try
    if not MyReg.OpenKey('\SOFTWARE\Microsoft\Windows\CurrentVersion',
                         FALSE) then
    // . . . registry processing here
  finally
    MyReg.Free;
  end; // try...finally

end;
```

Description   OpenKey attempts to open the Key specified by the *Key* parameter. If it exists, that Key becomes the current Key. If it does not exist, and the *CanCreate* parameter is True, the Key will be created, and it becomes the current Key. If *CanCreate* is False, the Key will not be created if it doesn't exist.

OpenKey is used in many of the examples in this chapter. The code snippet above demonstrates a reasonable skeleton for Registry access.

THE REGISTRY'S Read METHODS

Objects Affected	TRegistry
Purpose	The various Registry **Read** methods return the value from a data value associated with the current Key.
Declaration	

```
function ReadBinaryData(const Name: string; var Buffer;
                        BufSize: Integer): Integer;
function ReadBool(const Name: string): Boolean;
function ReadCurrency(const Name: string): Currency;
function ReadDate(const Name: string): TDateTime;
function ReadDateTime(const Name: string): TDateTime;
function ReadFloat(const Name: string): Double;
function ReadInteger(const Name: string): Integer;
function ReadString(const Name: string): string;
function ReadTime(const Name: string): TDateTime;
```

Parameters

Name	The name of the data value you are reading.
Buffer	The text buffer that will hold the binary data.
BufSize	The size of the buffer identified by *Buffer*.

Example Syntax

```
lblOrganization.Caption :=
            MyReg.ReadString('RegisteredOrganization');
```

Description The use of these functions is straightforward: If you know the datatype contained by a particular data value in a Key, you can use the appropriate **Read** method to extract the data. You can determine the datatype with GetDataType.

RenameValue METHOD

Objects Affected	TRegistry
Purpose	The **RenameValue** method renames a data value.
Declaration	

```
procedure RenameValue(const OldName, NewName: string);
```

Parameters

OldName	The existing name of the data value you wish to rename.
NewName	The new name.

Example Syntax

```
procedure TForm1.Button2Click(Sender: TObject);
begin
  MyReg := TRegistry.Create;
  MyReg.RootKey := HKEY_LOCAL_MACHINE;
```

```
try
   if not MyReg.OpenKey('\SOFTWARE\Thurrott', FALSE) then;

   MyReg.RenameValue('Paul', 'Steph');

   MyReg.CloseKey;
finally
   MyReg.Free;
end; // try..finally
end;
```

Description RenameValue renames the existing data value specified by the *OldName* parameter with the name specified by the *NewName* parameter. If the new name conflicts with an existing name, nothing happens. If a data value does not exist with that name, RenameValue does nothing. If the data identified by *OldName* is size 0, nothing happens.

RootKey PROPERTY

Objects Affected TRegistry

Purpose The RootKey property specifies the Root Key for the Registry object.

Declaration

```
property RootKey: HKEY;
```

Example Syntax

```
var
  Form1: TForm1;
  MyReg: TRegistry;

implementation

{$R *.DFM}

procedure TForm1.FormCreate(Sender: TObject);
begin
  MyReg := TRegistry.Create;
  MyReg.RootKey := HKEY_LOCAL_MACHINE;
  // . . .
```

Description By default, RootKey is set to HKEY_CURRENT_USER. To change the Root Key, set it to a new Key constant as in the above example.

ValueExists METHOD

Objects Affected TRegistry

Purpose The ValueExists method determines whether the specified data value exists.

Declaration

```
function ValueExists(const Name: string): Boolean;
```

Parameters

Name   The name of the data value you are querying.

Example Syntax

```
procedure TForm1.Button1Click(Sender: TObject);
var MyKeyInfo: TRegKeyInfo;
    MyString: string;
begin
  MyReg := TRegistry.Create;
  MyReg.RootKey := HKEY_LOCAL_MACHINE;

  MyReg.OpenKey('\SOFTWARE\Microsoft\Windows NT\CurrentVersion', FALSE);

  if MyReg.ValueExists('CSDVersion') then
    Label5.Caption := MyReg.ReadString('CSDVersion')
  else
    Label5.Caption := 'No Service Pack installed';
end;
```

Description   The `ValueExists` queries the data value identified by the *Name* parameter
to determine whether it exists. If the data value exists, ValueExists returns
`True`. Otherwise, it returns `False`. You should use `ValueExists` when you
wish to modify an existing Key's data value but don't want to create it if it
doesn't exist. Many Registry operations will add a Key or value by default
if it doesn't already exist.

THE REGISTRY'S Write METHODS

Objects Affected   `TRegistry`

Purpose   The various Registry `Write` methods write a new value to a data value
associated with the current Key.

Declaration

```
procedure WriteBinaryData(const Name: string; var Buffer;
                          BufSize: Integer);
procedure WriteBool(const Name: string; Value: Boolean);
procedure WriteCurrency(const Name: string; Value: Currency);
procedure WriteDate(const Name: string; Value: TDateTime);
procedure WriteDateTime(const Name: string; Value: TDateTime);
procedure WriteFloat(const Name: string; Value: Double);
procedure WriteInteger(const Name: string; Value: Integer);
procedure WriteString(const Name, Value: string);
procedure WriteTime(const Name: string; Value: TDateTime);
```

Parameters

Name   The name of the data value to which you are attempting to write.

Buffer   The text buffer that holds the binary data.

BufSize   The size of the buffer identified by *Buffer*.

Value   The value that will be written.

Example Syntax

```
procedure TForm1.Button1Click(Sender: TObject);
begin
  MyReg := TRegistry.Create;
  MyReg.RootKey := HKEY_LOCAL_MACHINE;

  try
    if not MyReg.OpenKey('\SOFTWARE\', FALSE) then;
    if not MyReg.KeyExists('Thurrott') then
      MyReg.CreateKey('Thurrott');
    if not MyReg.OpenKey('\SOFTWARE\Thurrott', FALSE) then;

    MyReg.WriteString('Paul', 'a string data value');

    MyReg.CloseKey;
  finally
    MyReg.Free;
  end; // try..finally
end;
```

Description   You can use the appropriate **Write** method to write data to a named data value.

7

TList AND TPopupList

Lists are used to maintain an index of objects of any class type. The index itself stores pointers to the objects and is dynamic—it can be resized at run time. Because of its ability to keep track of any object type, **TList** is flexible, but requires more programming than other VCL list classes that are designed to handle specific object types (such as **TStrings** and **TImageList**). **TList** should not be confused with full-scale collection classes or linked lists, because it does not handle memory allocation or deallocation for the objects it indexes. It is your responsibility as the programmer to handle these housekeeping chores yourself if you choose to use **TList**.

Though the internal operation of **TList** involves the extensive and ugly manipulation of pointers, Delphi often shields you from this implementation by providing convenient properties and methods to access your list. Some **TList** methods, however, take generic pointer types as parameters. Remember in these instances that named objects are implicitly pointers, so no further address manipulation is necessary. If you see a parameter of type **Pointer**, you can use it as if it were type **TObject**. In many ways, you can treat **TList** as an array of pointers, using the **Items** property to access individual list elements with subscript notation.

Another pointer issue you may run into is a result of **TList**'s use of generic pointers. You may need to typecast pointers returned by **TList** methods to the particular object you are indexing. For example, in the following code, a new object type is created and instances of those objects are organized in a list:

```
type
  TForm1 = class(TForm)
    ListBox1: TListBox;
    procedure FormCreate(Sender: TObject);
  end;

  TMyObject = class(TObject)
    MyValue: Integer;
  end;
```

continued on next page

continued from previous page

```
var
   Form1: TForm1;
   MyList: TList;
   MyObject1: TMyObject;
   MyObject2: TMyObject;

implementation

{$R *.DFM}

procedure TForm1.FormCreate(Sender: TObject);
var X, Y: integer;
begin
   MyList := TList.Create;
   MyObject1 := TMyObject.Create;
   MyObject2 := TMyObject.Create;

   MyList.Capacity := 10;

   MyObject1.MyValue := 1;
   MyList.Add(MyObject1);

   MyObject2.MyValue := 2;
   MyList.Add(MyObject2);
end;
```

To access data members of the objects pointed to by the list, you need to typecast the generic pointer maintained by the list to the appropriate type:

```
// Write the values of the list objects to the list box
for x := 0 to MyList.Count - 1 do

   ListBox1.Items.Add(IntToStr(TMyObject(MyList.Items[x]).MyValue));
```

This chapter discusses two list types: the generic **TList** and its descendant **TPopupList**. Figure 7-1 shows the lineage of **TList** and **TPopupList**.

TList

TList is the base class for lists. **TList** implements many methods and properties that can be used to manipulate the list, access and modify list items, and gather information about the list and its items.

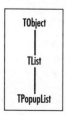

Figure 7-1   Lineage of **TList** and TPopupList

Table 7-1 displays the properties and methods that are implemented by TList.

Table 7-1 Properties and methods implemented by TList

Use or Set This...	To Do This...	Inheritance
Add	Add a new item to the end of the list.	None
Capacity	Determine the number of elements the list can hold.	None
Clear	Delete all the elements in the list.	None
Count	Determine the number of elements in the list.	None
Delete	Delete a list element by index number.	None
Destroy	Destroy the list.	TObject
Exchange	Exchange the position of two elements in the list.	None
Expand	Increase the capacity of the list.	None
First	Obtain a pointer to the first element in the list.	None
IndexOf	Determine the index number of an element in the list.	None
Insert	Add an element to the list.	None
Items	Specify an individual element in the list.	None
Last	Obtain a pointer to the last element in the list.	None
List	Use the actual array of pointers maintained by the list.	None
Move	Move an element to a new position in the list.	None
Pack	Remove any nil pointers in the list.	None
Remove	Delete an element from the list using a pointer.	None
Sort	Sort the elements in the list.	None

TList's properties and methods are described in the alphabetical section found at the end of this chapter.

TPopupList

TPopupList is a list that maintains the items you see in a pop-up menu. Though its Add and Remove methods are customized to deal with pop-up menu items, the conceptual actions of these methods are the same as they are for TList. Pop-up menus are covered in Chapter 33, "TMenu and Its Descendants." Table 7-2 displays the methods that are implemented by TPopupList.

Table 7-2 Methods implemented by TPopupList

Use or SetThis...	To Do This...	Inheritance
Add	Add an item to the end of the list of pop-up menu items.	TList
Remove	Remove an item from the list of pop-up menu items.	TList

Add Method

Objects Affected	TList, TPopupList
Purpose	The **Add** method adds a new item to the end of the list.
Declaration	
TList:	function Add(Item: Pointer): Integer;
TPopupList:	procedure Add(Popup: TPopupMenu);
Parameters	
Item	A pointer to the new item that is being added to the list.
Popup	The pop-up menu you wish to add to the pop-up list.

Example Syntax

```
// This procedure creates a new list and adds a new object
// to the list, printing its position in the list (0) as the
// caption to the form
procedure TForm1.FormCreate(Sender: TObject);
var
  MyList: TList;
  MyObject: TObject;
  Position: Integer;
begin
  // Create the list
  MyList := TList.Create;
  // Create an object and add it to the list
  MyObject := TObject.Create;
  Position := MyList.Add(MyObject);
  Form1.Caption := 'The position in the list is ' + IntToStr(Position);
  // Don't forget to free your objects
  MyObject.Free;
  MyList.Free;
end;
```

Description   Add returns the position (an integer) in the list where the new object is placed. The first item in a list is always position 0, so in the example above, the caption to the form will read "The position in the list is 0." The *Item* parameter is used to determine the object that is being placed in the list.

IMPORTANT

Add will not allocate memory for the actual object, but will merely insert the object's address into the index maintained by the list. If you wish to allocate memory for objects that will be added to the list, you must do so yourself.

Capacity PROPERTY

Objects Affected   TList and its descendants

Purpose   The Capacity property contains the number of elements a list can hold.

Declaration

```
property Capacity: Integer;
```

Example Syntax

```
procedure TForm1.FormCreate(Sender: TObject);
var
  MyList: TList;
begin
  // Create the list
  MyList := TList.Create;
  // Set the capacity of the list to 10
  MyList.Capacity := 10;

  // ... other processing here

  // Don't forget to free your list
  MyList.Free;
end;
```

Description   Capacity is a run-time only property that holds the *allocated* size of the list. This is different from the Count property, which contains the actual number of elements in the list. Delphi lists can dynamically size themselves up to 16,380 elements or to the limit of available memory, depending on which is reached first. If the element count in a list reaches the current capacity, the capacity is raised by 16, if possible.

Since a list is sized dynamically, you may think that you will never need to use the Capacity property. In most cases this is true, but if you know the exact number of elements you will be adding to a list, setting Capacity to the number of elements you will be using can save processing time.

Clear METHOD

Objects Affected   TList and its descendants

Purpose   The Clear method deletes all the elements in a list.

Declaration

```
procedure Clear;
```

Example Syntax

```
var
  Form1: TForm1;
  MyList: TList;

// ...
```

continued on next page

continued from previous page

```
// Create the list when the program starts
procedure TForm1.FormCreate(Sender: TObject);
begin
  MyList := TList.Create;
end;

// Free the list when the program ends
procedure TForm1.FormClose(Sender: TObject; var Action: TCloseAction);
begin
  MyList.Free;
end;

// If button one is pressed, add an element to the list
procedure TForm1.Button1Click(Sender: TObject);
begin
  MyList.Add(MyList);
  Form1.Caption := 'Number of Items in List = ' +
                   inttostr(MyList.Count);
end;

// If button two is pressed, clear the list
procedure TForm1.Button2Click(Sender: TObject);
begin
  MyList.Clear;
  Form1.Caption := 'Number of Items in List = ' +
                   inttostr(MyList.Count);
end;
```

IMPORTANT

Clear does not delete the actual objects pointed to by list index elements, it only deletes the pointers within the index. If you wish to delete the actual objects, you need to do so yourself.

Description   Use Clear to delete all the elements in a list. This also sets the Count and Capacity properties to 0, freeing the memory used by the list elements.

Count PROPERTY

Objects Affected   TList and its descendants

Purpose   The Count property contains the number of elements in the list.

Declaration

```
property Count: Integer read FCount write SetCount;
```

Example Syntax   Refer to the example code for Clear, above.

Description   Count is a run-time and read-only property that contains the number of elements in a list. A list with a Count value of 3 would have an element at indices 0, 1, and 2 in the list. This is the actual number of elements in use, not the number of elements allocated. The Capacity property contains the number of allocated elements.

Delete METHOD

Objects Affected	TList and its descendants
Purpose	The Delete property deletes a single element from the list.
Declaration	

```
procedure Delete(Index: Integer);
```

Parameters

Index The index of the element that will be deleted.

Example Syntax

```
procedure TForm1.FormCreate(Sender: TObject);
var
  x: integer;
  MyObject: TObject;
begin
  // Create the list and object
  MyList := TList.Create;
  MyObject := TObject.Create;
  // add 10 items to the list
  for x := 1 to 10 do MyList.Add(MyObject);
  // delete the second item in the list
  MyList.Delete(1);
  // ...
end;
```

Description Delete removes the element in the list determined by the *Index* parameter. Note that a list index starts with 0, so in the example above, a 1 is passed to Delete to remove the *second* item in the list. When an item is deleted from a list, the value of that index becomes nil. To remove the nils from a list, use Pack.

IMPORTANT

Delete does not physically remove the actual objects pointed to by list index elements, it only deletes the pointers within the index. If you wish to delete the actual objects and free the memory used by them, you need to do so yourself.

Exchange METHOD

Objects Affected	TList and its descendants
Purpose	The Exchange method exchanges the position of two list items.
Declaration	

```
procedure Exchange(Index1, Index2: Integer);
```

Parameters

Index1   The first item that is being exchanged.

Index2   The second item that is being exchanged.

Example Syntax

```
// Exchange the second and third elements in the list
// when Button1 is clicked
procedure TForm1.Button1Click(Sender: TObject);
begin
  MyList.Exchange(1,2);
end;
```

Description   Exchange literally exchanges the index position of two items in a list. Remember that lists are zero-based—in the example above, the second and third elements of the list are exchanged.

Expand METHOD

Objects Affected   TList and its descendants

Purpose   The Expand method increases the capacity of the list.

Declaration

```
function Expand: Tlist;
```

Example Syntax

```
// Expand the list when Button1 is clicked
procedure TForm1.Button1Click(Sender: TObject);
begin
  MyList.Expand;
end;
```

Description   Expand is used to increment the Capacity property of a list by predefined amounts: If the Capacity is more than 8, Expand will increase Capacity by 16. If Capacity is between 4 and 8, Expand will increase Capacity by 8. If Capacity is less than 4 when Expand is called, Capacity will be increased by 4.

The expanded list is returned by Expand.

If you wish to expand the list to a specific size, use the Capacity property.

First METHOD

Objects Affected   TList and its descendants

Purpose   First returns a pointer to the first element in the list.

Declaration

```
function First: Pointer;
```

Description   First is used to obtain a pointer to the first element in a list, or Items[0]. In general, you should be able to accomplish list tasks without directly using pointers: most of the TList methods allow you to use index values, which are easier to read and work with than pointers.

IndexOf METHOD

Objects Affected   TList and its descendants

Purpose   The IndexOf method returns the index of a specific item in the list.

Declaration

```
function IndexOf(Item: Pointer): Integer;
```

Parameters

Item   A pointer to the item in the list whose index you are obtaining.

Example Syntax

```
// Obtain the index of the object when Button1 is clicked
procedure TForm1.Button1Click(Sender: TObject);
begin
  MyList.IndexOf(MyObject);
end;
```

Description   IndexOf allows you to move from pointer to index notation while accessing the list. IndexOf will return the first index of the item in the list if it exists, or −1 if it is not in the list. Remember that list indices are zero-based, so the first element will have an index of 0.

Insert METHOD

Objects Affected   TList and its descendants

Purpose   The Insert method adds an item to the list.

Declaration

```
procedure Insert(Index: Integer; Item: Pointer);
```

Parameters

Index   The position in the list to insert *Item*.

Item   The item to insert at position *Index*.

Example Syntax

```
// This procedure will insert MyObject2 immediately after
// MyObject in the list MyList when Button1 is clicked.
procedure TForm1.Button1Click(Sender: TObject);
begin
  MyList.Insert(IndexOf(MyObject)+1, MyObject2);
end;
```

Description   Insert is used to add an item to a list at a specific index. The *Item* parameter specifies the object that will be placed into the list, and the *Index* parameter is used to set the location in the list that the item will be placed. When you add an item to the list with Insert, the Capacity and Count properties will expand to accommodate the new item.

If you wish to *replace* an item, use an assignment:

```
MyList.Items[0] := MyObject2;
```

In this example, the first element in the Items array is assigned to point to a new object. Remember that you may have to deallocate any objects that are no longer pointed to by your list. The TList class will not deallocate them for you.

Items PROPERTY

Objects Affected   TList and its descendants

Purpose   The Items property allows you to access an individual item in the list.

Declaration

```
property Items[Index: Integer]: Pointer;
```

Parameters

Index   The position of the item you are accessing.

Example Syntax

```
// This  procedure creates a new object, TNewObject, and
// assigns it to the first element of the list MyList.
procedure TForm1.Button1Click(Sender: TObject);
var
  MyNewObject: TObject;
begin
  MyNewObject := MyList.Items[0];
  // ...
end;
```

Description   Items is used to specify a particular item in a list, using the list index to determine which object you wish to retrieve. Items returns a pointer to the list item. Like most arrays created within the VCL, Items is zero-based. That is, the first element is referred to as Items[0], the second item is Items[1], and so on.

Last METHOD

Objects Affected   TList and its descendants

Purpose   The Last method returns a pointer to the last element in a list.

Declaration

```
function Last: Pointer;
```

Description

Last is used to obtain a pointer to the last element in a list, or Items[Count-1]. In general, you should be able to accomplish list tasks without directly using pointers: most of the TList methods allow you to use index values, which are easier to read and work with than pointers.

List PROPERTY

Objects Affected

TList and its descendants

Purpose

The List property contains the array of pointers that makes up a TList object.

Declaration

```
property List: PPointerList;
```

Example Syntax

```
// Obtain the index of the object when Button1 is clicked
procedure TForm1.Button1Click(Sender: TObject);
var
  MyNewObject: TObject;
begin
  // The following assignment is the same as
  // MyNewObject := MyList.Items[0];
  MyNewObject := MyList.List^[0]
end;
```

Description

List provides a legacy method for dereferencing item pointers in a list. The preferred method to access individual elements is to use the Items property, which dereferences the pointer for you. In general, you should be able to accomplish list tasks without directly using pointers: most of the TList methods allow you to use index values, which are easier to read and work with than pointers.

Move METHOD

Objects Affected

TList and its descendants

Purpose

The Move method moves an item to a new position in the list.

Declaration

```
procedure Move(CurIndex, NewIndex: Integer);
```

Parameters

CurIndex

The current index of the item you are moving.

NewIndex

The index to which you are moving the item.

Example Syntax

```
// Move the first element in the list to the
// end of the list when the button is clicked.
procedure TForm1.Button1Click(Sender: TObject);
begin
  MyList.Move(0, MyList.Count-1);
end;
```

Description

Move is used to move the element in a list identified by the *CurIndex* parameter to the position identified by the *NewIndex* parameter. When an item
in the list is moved, the other items are shifted appropriately to fill the
vacant space in the previously occupied position. No data is lost, and the
Count and Capacity properties remain unchanged.

Pack METHOD

Objects Affected   TList and its descendants

Purpose   The Pack method removes the nil pointers from a list.

Declaration

```
procedure Pack;
```

Example Syntax

```
// Pack the list MyList
procedure TForm1.Button1Click(Sender: TObject);
begin
  MyList.Pack;
end;
```

Description   Items that have been deleted with Delete or Remove point to nil. As a
result, a list that has been heavily manipulated may contain several nil
pointers that are wasting space and processing time. The Pack method
removes all of the nil pointers from a list and compresses the list so that
there are no empty spaces, conserving memory.

Remove METHOD

Objects Affected   TList, TPopupList

Purpose   The Remove method is used to delete an item from a list and return the
position of the item that was deleted.

Declaration

TList: `function Remove(Item: Pointer): Integer;`

TPopupList: `procedure Remove(Popup: TPopupMenu);`

Parameters

Item   The element you are deleting.

Popup   The pop-up menu you are removing from the pop-up list.

Example Syntax

```
// Remove MyObject from the list
procedure TForm1.Button1Click(Sender: TObject);
var
  x: Integer;
begin
  x := MyList.Remove(MyObject);
end;
```

Description

Remove deletes the element in the list that refers to the *Item* parameter; it does not delete the object the element is pointing to. When an item is deleted from a list, the value of that index becomes nil. To remove the nils from a list, use Pack. Remove is similar to Delete, although Delete requires that you know the element's position in the list before you can remove it. In fact, Remove uses Delete internally.

Sort METHOD

Objects Affected   TList and its descendants

Purpose   The Sort method sorts the index maintained by your list.

Declaration

```
procedure Sort(Compare: TListSortCompare);
```

Parameters

Compare   A function that performs compare routines for the sort.

Example Syntax

```
 function MySort(Item1, Item2: Pointer): Integer;

var
  Form1: TForm1;
  MyList: TList;
  MyObject1: TMyObject;
  MyObject2: TMyObject;
  // . . .

implementation

{$R *.DFM}

function MySort(Item1, Item2: Pointer): Integer;
begin
  if (TMyObject(Item1).MyValue) < (TMyObject(Item2).MyValue) then
    Result := -1
  else if (TMyObject(Item1).MyValue) > (TMyObject(Item2).MyValue) then
    Result := 1
  else Result := 0;
end;
```

```
procedure TForm1.FormCreate(Sender: TObject);
var X, Y: integer;
begin
  MyList := TList.Create;
  MyObject1 := TMyObject.Create;
  MyObject2 := TMyObject.Create;

  // . . .

  MyList.Sort(MySort);

  // After the list is sorted, place values in list box
  for x := 0 to MyList.Count - 1 do

    ListBox1.Items.Add(IntToStr(TMyObject(MyList.Items[x]).MyValue));
end;
```

Description

You are required to write your own `Compare` function that is used by `Sort` to determine how index elements should be ordered. `Sort` is type `TListSortCompare`, which is declared as

`TListSortCompare = function (Item1, Item2: Pointer): Integer;`

A function of type `TListSortCompare` should return a value less than zero if `Item1` should appear before `Item2` in sorted order, a value of 0 if `Item1` is the same as `Item2`, and a value greater than zero if `Item1` should appear after `Item2`.

Exception AND ITS DESCENDANTS

The error handling capabilities of Delphi are encapsulated by the `Exception` class. *Exception handling*, as Delphi's method of dealing with errors is known, frees you from having to write separate error-handling routines for every task your application performs. The various descendants of the `Exception` class encompass nearly all the errors that can occur in a Win32 environment. An exception object provides information about the type of error that occurred, causing the flow of execution in your program to temporarily stop if an exception is *raised*, or generated. Figure 8-1 shows the derivation of the `Exception` class.

Exception objects are automatically instantiated when an exception—the actual error—is raised and are destroyed when the exception is handled.

Writing Safe Programs

Delphi exceptions are designed to allow your program to respond in a graceful way to errors that occur at run time. Without exception handling, many errors can crash a program or even the entire operating environment. Win32 environments like Windows 95 and NT have exception handling built in, which normally allows these operating systems to recover from what were previously fatal errors. Delphi programs that generate an exception without a corresponding exception handler will spawn a dialog box that describes the exception that just occurred. While this is not particularly friendly to the user, it provides valuable feedback to the programmer and is still better than having the application simply crash.

Figure 8-1 Derivation of the `Exception` class

Unfortunately, there is no way for the compiler to anticipate which run-time errors can occur in your code. It cannot automatically incorporate customized exception handlers for you. That job falls into your hands, as the programmer, and you will need to analyze your code to determine where errors may occur.

try...except

Delphi's Object Pascal provides a special *protected* block of code that you can use for exception handling (don't confuse the term "protected" with the **protected** directive used to specify class member visibility). The basic format looks like the code in Listing 8-1.

Listing 8-1 Protected block of code used for exception handling

```
try
  // code that may cause an error
except
  on Exception do
    // exception-handling code block
end;
```

The **try** part of the **try-except** block shown above is protected, meaning that the exception code is guaranteed to execute if an error has occurred.

You may want to perform a more specific test in the **except** part of the **try-except** block to determine the type of exception that was raised. This can be accomplished by using a series of exception handlers denoted by the **on** and **do** directives, as shown in Listing 8-2.

Listing 8-2 Handling multiple exception types

```
try
  // code that may cause an error
except
  on EDivByZero do
    // exception-handling code block
  on EIntOverflow do
    // exception-handling code block
  on ERangeError do
    // exception-handling code block
end;
```

In Listing 8-2, the program can handle three specific types of exceptions with unique blocks of code.

try...finally

Although memory leakage due to unreleased resources is less of a problem in Win32 environments than it was in Windows 3.x, you should still perform resource exception handling to ensure that resources are properly freed. When freeing resources in Delphi, you can use the **try-finally** protected block, as shown in Listing 8-3.

Listing 8-3 Protected block of code used for resource exception handling

```
try
  // code that uses a resource
finally
  // code block to free the resource
end;
```

This way, if an exception occurs while using a particular resource, the `finally` part of the block is executed and the resource is guaranteed to be freed. In fact, the `finally` part of the block is executed regardless of whether an exception occurs.

Types of Exceptions

There are numerous descendants of `Exception`, each designed to handle a specific error. The descendants of `Exception` are summarized in Table 8-1.

Table 8-1 Exception classes

This Exception...	Is Raised When...	Inheritance
EAbort	You want to abort the current code block silently.	Exception
EAccessViolation	You attempt to access an invalid memory region.	Exception
EBitsError	A TBits object's Bits property is indexed improperly.	Exception
EClassNotFound		EFilerError
EControlC	CTRL-C is typed in a console application.	Exception
EConvertError	StrToInt or StrToFlt attempt to convert an illegal value.	Exception
EDivByZero	You attempt to divide an integer by zero.	EIntError
EExternalException	The exception code does not match a list of codes.	Exception
EFCreateError	There is an error during file creation.	EStreamError
EFOpenError	You attempt to open a file stream object that can't be opened.	EStreamError
EInOutError	Any type of file I/O error occurs.	Exception
EIntError	This exception is never actually raised.	Exception
EIntOverflow	An assignment to an integer is too large for the register.	EIntError
EInvalidCast	You attempt an illegal typecast with as.	Exception
EInvalidGraphic	You attempt to load an invalid graphic type into a picture.	Exception
EInvalidGraphicOperation	An illegal operation is attempted on a graphic.	Exception
EInvalidImage		EFilerError
EInvalidOp	A variety of floating-point errors occur.	EMathError
EInvalidOperation	A nonwindowed component does a windowed operation.	Exception
EInvalidPointer	You attempt an invalid pointer operation.	Exception
EListError	An error occurs with a list, string, or string list object.	Exception
EMathError	This exception is never directly raised.	Exception
EMenuError	A menu error occurs.	Exception

continued on next page

continued from previous page

This Exception...	Is Raised When...	Inheritance
EMethodNotFound		EFilerError
EOpenError	You attempt to open a file stream object that can't open.	EStreamError
EOutOfMemory	There isn't enough free memory to complete an operation.	Exception
EOutOfResources	This exception is not yet documented.	EOutOfMemory
EOverflow	A floating-point assignment is too large for the register.	EMathError
Eprinter	A printing error occurs.	Exception
Eprivilege	Your program executes an invalid CPU instruction.	Exception
EPropReadOnly	You attempt to write a read-only property.	Exception
EPropWriteOnly	You attempt to read a write-only property.	Exception
ERangeError	You attempt to assign an out-of-range value to an integer.	EIntError
EReadError		EFilerError
EResNotFound	The ReadComponentRes method cannot find a resource.	Exception
EStackOverflow	The current thread cannot dynamically resize.	Exception
EStreamError	A stream is read with LoadFromStream.	Exception
EStringListError	You refer to an item in a list outside the range of the list.	Exception
EThread		Exception
EUnderflow	A floating-point assignment is too small and is set to 0.	EMathError
EVariantError	An error with a variant type occurs.	Exception
EWriteError		EFilerError
EZeroDivide	You attempt to divide a floating-point number by zero.	EMathError

EAbort

EAbort is used when you want the current code block to abort but not open a message box. This "silent" exception allows your application to handle an exception behind the scenes.

The **Abort** function raises **EAbort** and should be used when you need to escape from a block of code.

EOutOfMemory

An **EOutOfMemory** object is instantiated when there isn't enough free memory to complete an operation that is requested by your application.

EOutOfResources

EOutOfResources is an undocumented child of **EOutOfMemory**.

EInOutError

EInOutError occurs when any type of file input/output error occurs. It holds the error code that is returned by the error that occurs.

EIntError

EIntError is the basic integer math exception. Its descendants can handle more specific integer math exceptions:

EDivByZero

This is the exception that is raised when you attempt to divide an integer by zero.

ERangeError

This integer math exception is raised when you try to assign a value to an integer that exceeds the range of that type.

EIntOverflow

Though it is likely that an ERangeError would occur first, this integer math exception is raised when an assignment to an integer is too large to fit in the register allocated for it, losing data. Since Delphi is now a 32-bit environment, normally you will not see this exception.

EMathError

EMathError is the base floating-point math exception class—its descendants encapsulate more specific floating-point errors:

EInvalidOp

This floating-point math exception class is raised under a variety of situations: the CPU encounters an invalid operation, an undefined instruction, a floating-point coprocessor stack overflow, or even more rarely, an undefined instruction.

EZeroDivide

EZeroDivide is a floating-point math exception class that is raised when you attempt to divide a floating-point number by zero.

EOverflow

This floating-point math exception occurs when a floating-point assignment is too large to fit into the register allocated for it, and data is lost. This will rarely happen in a 32-bit environment.

EUnderflow

EUnderflow is raised when a floating-point math operation produces a result that is too small to be represented as a floating-point value, so the result is set equal to zero.

EInvalidPointer

EInvalidPointer is raised when you attempt an invalid pointer operation.

EInvalidCast

EInvalidCast is raised when you attempt an illegal typecast using the **as** operator.

EConvertError

An `EConvertError` exception is raised if the functions `StrToInt` or `StrToFlt` attempt to convert an illegal value. For example, passing `'3.14'` to `StrToInt` would raise an `EConvertError`, because 3.14 is not a valid integer.

EAccessViolation

This exception is raised when you attempt to access an invalid region of memory. This can occur if you attempt to dereference a nil pointer or access a memory address that doesn't physically exist.

EPrivilege

This exception is raised if your program attempts to execute a CPU instruction that is reserved for a different processor privilege level. This is extremely rare.

EStackOverflow

The `EStackOverflow` exception is raised when the current thread cannot dynamically size itself anymore.

EControlC

This exception is only raised in console-mode applications and occurs when the user presses the CTRL-C key combination.

EVariantError

This exception can be raised for a variety of variant type–related issues: invalid variant typecast or operation, the system is unable to create the variant array, the variant is not an array, or an index of the variant is out of bounds.

EPropReadOnly

The `EPropReadOnly` exception is raised during OLE automation if you attempt to write to a read-only property.

EPropWriteOnly

The `EPropWriteOnly` exception is raised during OLE automation if you attempt to read a write-only property.

EExternalException

This exception is raised when the exception code that is detected does not match any of the following exception codes:

```
STATUS_INTEGER_DIVIDE_BY_ZERO
STATUS_ARRAY_BOUNDS_EXCEEDED
STATUS_FLOAT_OVERFLOW
```

```
STATUS_FLOAT_INEXACT_RESULT
STATUS_FLOAT_INVALID_OPERATION
STATUS_FLOAT_STACK_CHECK
STATUS_FLOAT_DIVIDE_BY_ZERO
STATUS_INTEGER_OVERFLOW
STATUS_FLOAT_UNDERFLOW
STATUS_FLOAT_DENORMAL_OPERAND
STATUS_ACCESS_VIOLATION
STATUS_PRIVILEGED_INSTRUCTION
STATUS_CONTROL_C_EXIT
STATUS_STACK_OVERFLOW
```

EStreamError

EStreamError is raised when an error occurs while a stream is being read with LoadFromStream.

EFCreateError

This exception is raised when there is an error during file creation. Errors include the new file attempting to overwrite a read-only file or attempting to use an invalid file name.

EFOpenError

This exception is raised when you attempt to open a file stream object whose corresponding file cannot be opened.

EResNotFound

This exception is raised when the ReadComponentRes method cannot find a specific resource in a resource file.

EListError

This exception is raised in response to various errors in lists, strings, and string list objects. Generally, this exception is raised when an attempt is made to access a member that is not within range of the list.

EListError can also occur if you attempt to insert a string into a sorted string list out of order.

If the Duplicates property of a string list object is set to dupError, then an EListError exception is raised if you attempt to add a duplicate item to the list.

EBitsError

This exception is raised when the index of the Bits property of a TBits object is less than zero or greater than or equal to its maximum size.

EStringListError

EStringListError is raised when you refer to an item in a list that is outside the range of the list.

EThread

This exception is not currently documented.

EPrinter

This exception is raised when a printing error occurs.

EMenuError

EMenuError is raised when an error occurs with your application's menu. One example of this would be an attempt to create a new menu item with the same identifier as an existing menu item.

EInvalidOperation

This exception is raised when a nonwindowed component (that is, a component without a window handle) attempts an operation that requires a window handle.

EInvalidGraphic

EInvalidGraphic is raised when you attempt to load a file that is not a valid graphic type into a picture. Valid graphic types include bitmaps, icons, metafiles, and others.

EInvalidGraphicOperation

This exception is raised when an illegal operation is attempted on a graphic.

Exception Properties and Methods

The Exception class has multiple constructor types, which allow exception objects to be created in a variety of ways. In addition, descendants of Exception implement some of their own specialized properties and methods. Table 8-2 displays the properties and methods that are implemented by the exception classes.

Table 8-2 Properties and methods implemented by Exception and its descendants

Use or Set This...	To Do This...	Inheritance
Create	Construct an exception object.	TObject
CreateFmt	Create a formatted message to display.	None
CreateFmtHelp	Same as CreateFmt but includes context-sensitive help ID.	None
CreateHelp	Create an exception object with a help context ID number.	None

Use or Set This...	To Do This...	Inheritance
CreateRes	Obtain the error string from a resource file.	None
CreateResFmt	Same as CreateRes, but with a formatted message display.	None
CreateResFmtHelp	Same as CreateResFmt but includes context-sensitive help ID.	None
CreateResHelp	Same as CreateRes, but with a context-sensitive help ID.	None
HelpContext	Contain the context-sensitive help ID number.	None
Message	Contain the error message.	None

Create METHOD

Objects Affected   All exceptions.

Purpose   The **Create** method is used to construct an exception object.

Declaration

```
constructor Create(const Msg: string);
```

Parameters

Msg   The message that is displayed when the exception is raised.

Description   **Create** is the default constructor for an exception object. Its only parameter, *Msg*, contains the message that is displayed when the exception occurs. The message is not formatted in any way.

Note that the message appears when you do not specify a handler for an exception.

CreateFmt METHOD

Objects Affected   All exceptions.

Purpose   The **CreateFmt** method is used to create an exception object with a formatted error message.

Declaration

```
constructor CreateFmt(const Msg: string; const Args: array of const);
```

Parameters

Msg   The message that is displayed when the exception is raised.

Args   An array of specifiers that determine how the message is formatted.

Description   Like **Create**, **CreateFmt** is used to construct an exception object. **CreateFmt** passes its parameters to the Object Pascal **Format** function, which is used to format the output of the error message.

CreateFmtHelp METHOD

Objects Affected	All exceptions.
Purpose	The `CreateFmtHelp` method is used to construct an exception object with a formatted error message and a help context ID.
Declaration	

```
constructor CreateFmtHelp(const Msg: string; const Args: array of
                           const; AHelpContext: Integer);
```

Parameters	
Msg	The message that is displayed when the exception is raised.
Args	An array of specifiers that determine how the message is formatted.
AHelpContext	The help context ID number.
Description	`CreateFmtHelp` combines the functionality of `CreateFmt` with the capability to link the exception with a help context ID number. It formats the text of the error message using the *Msg* and *Args* parameters as parameters of the Object Pascal `Format` function.

CreateHelp METHOD

Objects Affected	All exceptions.
Purpose	The `CreateHelp` method is used to construct an exception object that includes a help context ID.
Declaration	

```
constructor CreateHelp(const Msg: string; AHelpContext: Integer);
```

Parameters	
Msg	The message that is displayed when the exception is raised.
AHelpContext	The help context ID number.
Description	`CreateHelp` constructs an exception object and links it to a help context ID number.

CreateRes METHOD

Objects Affected	All exceptions.
Purpose	The `CreateRes` method constructs an exception object, using a string from a resource file as the error message.

Declaration

```
constructor CreateRes(Ident: Integer);
```

Parameters

Ident   The error message.

Description   `CreateRes` is similar to `Create`, but the string outputted in the error message is obtained from a Windows resource file.

CreateResFmt METHOD

Objects Affected   All exceptions.

Purpose   The `CreateResFmt` method constructs an exception object and displays a formatted error message that was obtained from a resource file.

Declaration

```
constructor CreateResFmt(Ident: Integer; const Args: array of const);
```

Parameters

Ident   The error message.

Args   An array of specifiers that determine how the message is formatted.

Description   `CreateResFmt` performs the same function as `CreateRes`—constructing an exception object whose error message is obtained from a resource file—and formats the error message using the Object Pascal `Format` function. The *Ident* and *Args* parameters are passed directly to `Format`.

CreateResFmtHelp METHOD

Objects Affected   All exceptions.

Purpose   The `CreateResFmtHelp` method constructs an exception object that displays a formatted error message that is obtained from a resource file and links the exception object to a help context ID.

Declaration

```
constructor Exception.CreateResFmtHelp(Ident: Integer;
                          const Args: array of const;
                          AHelpContext: Integer);
```

Parameters

Ident   The error message.

Args   An array of specifiers that determine how the message is formatted.

AHelpContext   The help context ID number.

Description	CreateResFmtHelp combines the functionality of CreateResFmt with the capability to link the exception object to a context help ID number. CreateResFmtHelp obtains its error message from a string in a standard Windows resource file, formats it with the Object Pascal Format function, and gives the exception object a help context ID number.

CreateResHelp METHOD

Objects Affected	All exceptions.
Purpose	The CreateResHelp method constructs an exception object with a context help ID whose error message is obtained from a resource file.
Declaration	

```
constructor CreateResHelp(Ident: Integer; AHelpContext: Integer);
```

Parameters	
Ident	The error message.
AHelpContext	The help context ID number.
Description	CreateResHelp constructs an exception object that includes a context help ID number. The error message that is displayed when the object is created is obtained from a standard Windows resource file.

HelpContext PROPERTY

Objects Affected	All exceptions.
Purpose	The HelpContext property holds the help context ID number for the exception object.
Declaration	

```
property HelpContext: Integer;
```

Description	Help context IDs are used to call context-sensitive help—each object in a Delphi program that needs this capability should have a unique help context ID number (unless you want that object to use the help context ID of its parent, in which case you can use 0 as the ID number).

Message PROPERTY

Objects Affected	All exceptions.
Purpose	The Message property contains informational text about the most recent exception.

Declaration

```
property Message: string;
```

Description   **Message** contains the string you see in the dialog box that appears by default when an exception occurs.

9

INTRODUCTION TO INTERNET CONTROLS

With the release of Delphi 3, Borland has adopted ActiveX/COM in a big way. The Delphi programming environment now makes it very easy to create Common Object Model (COM) objects such as ActiveX controls and automation objects in familiar Object Pascal. The COM programming paradigm is vast, however, and covering it properly would require a separate book of equal length to the one you now hold. By the time this book is released, there will be many COM and ActiveX programming titles available, and with the release of Visual Basic 5, it is likely that these books will cover the topic in a more general way than the C++ OLE/COM books of the past. Additionally, most Delphi programmers should have little problem converting C/C++ code to Object Pascal if need be.

This chapter, then, provides a brief overview of some of the more popular ActiveX Internet controls that come with Delphi 3. The Internet controls are thin wrappers around the ActiveX controls that Microsoft originally supplied in the Internet Control Pack (ICP). You can access them in the Delphi Integrated Development Environment (IDE) from the Internet tab of the Component Palette. Currently, these controls also ship with all of Microsoft's Windows programming language packages. They are designed to provide simple access to common Internet programming protocols, so that you can create applications that connect to the World Wide Web or to Internet e-mail services. Given the space constraints of this book, it is impossible to cover these controls—and other ActiveX/COM topics—adequately in a Delphi-specific way, so you should refer to the excellent online documentation that Microsoft has provided for these controls.

Delphi's Internet controls are summarized in Table 9-1.

Table 9-1 Delphi Internet controls

This Control...	Is Used to...
FTP	Transfer data between a remote and local machine.
HTML	Implement Web browsing.
HTTP	Directly retrieve HTTP documents.
NNTP	Connect to an Internet USENET news server.
POP	Access Internet mail servers using the POP3 protocol.
SMTP	Send Internet e-mail to SMTP mail servers.
TCP	Send data over the Internet in a low-level way.
UDP	Send and receive UDP data over the Internet.

FTP

The FTP control allows file and data transfer between a remote and local machine using File Transfer Protocol (FTP), one of the oldest and best-known Internet protocols. You can use the FTP control to easily connect to a remote machine and exchange data in both directions, perform file and directory parsing, and access the file size, attributes, name, or other fields on the remote server, regardless of the operating system it uses.

HTML

The HTML control lets you implement an HTML browser, with automatic network retrieval of HTML documents if required.

HTTP

The HTTP control implements the Hypertext Transfer Protocol (HTTP), based on the HTTP specification. HTTP defines a set of commands that determines how an HTTP client makes a connection, requests data, responds to the data, and then closes the connection. The HTTP control enables you to directly retrieve HTTP documents, but will not perform browsing or image processing functions. It can also retrieve Multipurpose Internet Mail Extensions (MIME) information about HTTP documents.

NNTP

The NNTP control allows you to connect to an Internet USENET news server, retrieve the list of available newsgroups and their descriptions, connect to a newsgroup, get lists of articles, and open articles in the newsgroup. This control implements the Network News Transfer Protocol (NNTP).

POP

The **POP** control provides access to Internet mail servers by implementing the Post Office Protocol (POP3). POP3 is the most popular mail protocol, and this control can retrieve mail from a UNIX or any other server that supports the POP3 protocol. The **POP** control can connect to a server, send user and password authentication information, retrieve user mailbox information, retrieve messages from the server, and delete messages from the server.

SMTP

The **SMTP** control provides access to Simple Mail Transport Protocol (SMTP) mail servers and e-mail. The **SMTP** control is typically used to send e-mail to an SMTP mail server.

TCP

The **TCP** control provides easy access to Transmission Control Protocol (TCP) network services. TCP takes information sent across a network and breaks it up into packets that are sent independently, increasing transfer speed. You can write client and server applications without understanding the details of TCP or needing to call low-level Winsock APIs. This control allows you to easily connect to a remote machine, exchange data, and monitor network activities.

UDP

The **UDP** control implements the Winsock User Datagram Protocol (UDP) for both client and server. The control is a communication point utilizing UDP network services. It can be used to send and retrieve UDP data. UDP is a lot simpler than TCP, because UDP doesn't require the overhead of packet synchronization. On the other hand, UDP is only well suited for sending small messages.

PART III

Persistent Objects

10

TPersistent

A *persistent object* is an object that can save to or load from a storage medium. In Delphi, persistent objects are encapsulated by **TPersistent**, an abstract base class for objects whose properties can be saved and loaded on a *stream*. Streams are used to represent a physical storage medium like a hard drive or RAM. They are used by **TPersistent** and its descendants to save information to disk. As a result, the use of streams is normally transparent to an application developer.

Figure 10-1 gives the ancestry of **TPersistent**, while Table 10-1 displays the methods that are implemented by **Tpersistent**.

Table 10-1 Methods implemented by **TPersistent**

Use or Set This...	To Do This...	Inheritance
Assign	Assign one persistent object to another.	None

Assign METHOD

Objects Affected   All persistent objects.

Purpose   The **Assign** method is used to assign one persistent object to another persistent object.

Figure 10-1   Ancestry of **TPersistent**

TObject
|
TPersistent

Declaration

```
procedure Assign(Source: TPersistent); virtual;
```

Parameters

Source

The persistent object that is being assigned to the current persistent object.

Example Syntax

```
// When the form loads, assign the picture used by Image1
// to Image2
procedure TForm1.FormCreate(Sender: TObject);
begin
 Image2.Picture.Assign(Image1.Picture);
end;
```

Description

Assign allows you to assign an object to another object of the same type. It is possible, in some instances, to assign objects of different but compatible types. For example, objects of type TBitmap, TIcon, and TMetafile can be assigned to a TPicture object.

Assign appears to have the same effect as an actual assignment operator, but the two are, in fact, quite different. The assignment operator is used to assign the value of one operand to the value of another. Assign, however, is used to assign an actual object reference to another object. In essence, the two objects become the same object.

11

TClipboard

TClipboard encapsulates the Windows clipboard, an area of memory that the operating system sets aside to temporarily store data. The user, or even your own application, can place and retrieve information there. The clipboard is designed to store almost any type of object, so one of the pieces of information that is stored with the object is its type, *clipboard format*. To access information stored in the clipboard, your application must know how to access the *type* of data that is held there; otherwise, it will be retrieved in a default format.

TIP
Information in the clipboard can be viewed with the Clipboard Viewer program, included with Windows.

The clipboard provides the simplest method that applications have to interchange data, because the user initiates the exchange. If the contents of the clipboard have changed and the user wishes to use a previously exchanged piece of data again, he or she will need to repeat the copy-and-paste process manually. The clipboard is present in all Windows operating systems and is accessible from the Edit menu of most applications—users now expect to be able to access the features of the clipboard from the applications they use. In fact, even Windows itself now uses standard copy-and-paste and cut-and-paste operations for many file operations.

Delphi and the Clipboard

Delphi's clipboard support stems from the TClipboard class, which in turn is used by many other classes, from TMemo and TEdit through methods such as CopyToClipboard and PasteFromClipboard. Delphi also implements a global Clipboard object, which is an instance of TClipboard, that encapsulates the actual Windows clipboard. The clipboard object's methods, described in this section, are used to perform standard clipboard tasks such as determining the type of data that is held in the clipboard and clearing the contents of the clipboard. Figure 11-1 gives the lineage of TClipboard. Table 11-1 displays all of the properties and methods that are implemented by TClipboard.

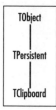

Figure 11-1 Lineage of
`TClipboard`

Table 11-1 Properties and methods implemented by `TClipboard`

Use or Set This...	To Do This...	Inheritance
Assign	Assign one persistent object to another.	TPersistent
AsText	Hold the text that is in the clipboard.	None
ClassName	Get the name of the object's class.	TObject
ClassParent	Get the object's parent class.	TObject
ClassType	Get the object's actual type.	TObject
Clear	Empty the contents of the clipboard.	None
Close	Close the clipboard object if it is open.	None
Create	Construct a new object.	TObject
Destroy	Destroy the object.	TObject
FormatCount	Determine how many formats the clipboard supports.	None
Formats	See the list of formats the clipboard supports.	None
Free	Safely destroy the object.	TObject
GetAsHandle	Return the data in the clipboard as a handle.	None
GetComponent	Paste a component from the clipboard.	None
GetTextBuf	Copy the clipboard contents to a buffer.	None
HasFormat	Determine if the data in the clipboard is compatible.	None
InheritsFrom	Determine if the object is descended from a certain class.	TObject
InstanceSize	Determine the amount of memory allocated for the object.	TObject
Open	Open the clipboard object, locking it for your use.	None
SetAsHandle	Place a handle to data into the clipboard.	None
SetComponent	Copy a component to the clipboard.	None
SetTextBuf	Copy text from a buffer to the clipboard.	None

IMPORTANT

You must include the file `clipbrd` in the uses clause of the unit that will be accessing clipboard methods and properties to use the global clipboard object.

Also, it may be helpful when testing programs that access the clipboard to have the clipboard viewer program running so that you can dynamically check the contents of the clipboard. In developing software that uses the clipboard, the clipboard viewer is a valuable "watch" tool.

AsText PROPERTY

Objects Affected	TClipboard
Purpose	The AsText property contains the text, if any, that is found in the clipboard.
Declaration	

```
property AsText: String;
```

Example Syntax

```
// Pressing Button1 will place some text in the clipboard.
procedure TForm1.Button1Click(Sender: TObject);
begin
  Clipboard.AsText := 'This text will be placed in the clipboard';
end;
```

Description   Using the clipboard to hold text is such a common operation that Delphi provides a single property that can both copy text into the clipboard and retrieve the contents of the clipboard, automatically treating the clipboard format as text. You can use AsText to place text in the clipboard, or you can assign the contents of the AsText property to any string:

```
Edit1.Text := Clipboard.AsText;
```

Clear METHOD

Objects Affected	TClipboard
Purpose	The Clear method is used to erase the contents of the clipboard.
Declaration	

```
procedure Clear;
```

Example Syntax

```
// Clear the clipboard when the button is pressed
procedure TForm1.Button1Click(Sender: TObject);
begin
  Clipboard.Clear;
end;
```

Description   Clear clears the contents of the clipboard. Delphi calls Clear automatically when the contents of the clipboard are changed, erasing the current data so that the new data can be written in its place. You can use Clear to erase the contents of the clipboard manually. For example, if a user of your application places a large amount of data on the clipboard, you may want to ask him or her if the clipboard should be erased when the application is closed.

Close METHOD

Objects Affected	TClipboard
Purpose	The Close method closes the clipboard if it is open.
Declaration	

```
procedure Close;
```

Example Syntax

```
procedure TForm1.Button1Click(Sender: TObject);
begin
  // obtain exclusive access to the clipboard
  Clipboard.Open;
  // copy a picture to the clipboard
  Clipboard.Assign(Image1.Picture);
  // ö other clipboard processing
  // make sure you close the clipboard when you are done.
  Clipboard.Close;
end;
```

Description

Close is used in conjunction with the Open method, which allows your application to temporarily have exclusive access to the clipboard. Close must be called the exact number of times that Open was called. Although Delphi will automatically close the clipboard when your application shuts down, you should make a habit of calling Close as soon as your program is done using the clipboard exclusively; this will ensure that other running applications will be able to access the clipboard.

FormatCount PROPERTY

Objects Affected	TClipboard
Purpose	The FormatCount property holds the number of formats that the clipboard currently supports.
Declaration	

```
property FormatCount: Integer;
```

Example Syntax

```
// Print the number of formats the clipboard
// currently supports.
procedure TForm1.Button1Click(Sender: TObject);
begin
  Edit1.Text := IntToStr(Clipboard.FormatCount);
end;
```

Description

FormatCount is a run-time, read-only property that holds the number of elements in the Formats property array, that is, the number of formats or datatypes that are currently supported by the clipboard. To view the list of formats, use the `Formats` property.

Formats PROPERTY

Objects Affected `TClipboard`

Purpose The `Formats` property is a list of the actual data formats currently supported by the clipboard.

Declaration

```
property Formats[Index: Integer]: Word;
```

Example Syntax

```
// List the formats supported by the clipboard
// in a list box.
procedure TForm1.Button1Click(Sender: TObject);
var x: Integer;
begin
  for x := 0 to Clipboard.FormatCount - 1 do
    ListBox1.Items.Add(IntToStr(Clipboard.Formats[x]));
end;
```

Description This run-time and read-only property contains a list of the data formats (types) that are supported by the clipboard. Each item that is placed in the clipboard can usually be accessed in a variety of formats, and this is the list that is maintained by `Formats`. The formats are represented by integer values. To find out if a particular format is available on the clipboard, use `HasFormat`.

Some of the common formats supported by the clipboard are listed in Table 11-2.

Table 11-2 Some of the common formats used by the clipboard

Format Number	Format Name
1	CF_TEXT
2	CF_BITMAP
3	CF_METAFILEPICT
4	CF_SYLK
5	CF_DIF
6	CF_TIFF
7	CF_OEMTEXT
8	CF_DIB
9	CF_PALETTE
10	CF_PENDATA

continued on next page

continued from previous page

Format Number	Format Name
11	CF_RIFF
12	CF_WAVE
13	CF_UNICODETEXT
14	CF_ENHMETAFILE
15	CF_HDROP

GetAsHandle METHOD

Objects Affected	TClipboard
Purpose	The GetAsHandle method returns the data in the clipboard as a Windows handle.
Declaration	

```
function GetAsHandle(Format: Word): THandle;
```

Parameters

Format   The format you would like to use to access the data in the clipboard.

Example Syntax

```
procedure TForm1.Button1Click(Sender: TObject);
var MyHandle: THandle;
begin
  ClipBoard.Open;
  try
    MyHandle := Clipboard.GetAsHandle(CF_TEXT);
    // . . . process the handle here
  finally
    // Remember to close the clipboard.
    Clipboard.Close;
  end;
end;
```

Description   GetAsHandle is used when you need to get a raw Windows handle to the data in the clipboard. Since the handle is only valid while the clipboard is open, you should copy the handle or do any necessary processing *before* calling TClipboard's Close method.

GetComponent METHOD

Objects Affected	TComponent
Purpose	The GetComponent method copies a Delphi component from the clipboard.

Declaration

```
function GetComponent(Owner, Parent: TComponent): TComponent;
```

Parameters

Owner   The component that becomes the owner of the retrieved component.

Parent   The component that becomes the parent of the retrieved component.

Example Syntax

```
procedure TForm1.Button1Click(Sender: TObject);
begin
  // Copy an image component to the Clipboard
  Clipboard.SetComponent(Image1);
  // Change the name of the component--no two components
  // can have the same name
  Image1.Name := '';
  // Get the image and place it in a group box
  Clipboard.GetComponent(Self, GroupBox1);
end;
```

Description   GetComponent retrieves a Delphi component from the clipboard that was copied there with SetComponent. The *Owner* and *Parent* parameters are used to change these properties for the copied component. They can be set to Nil, although Owner is usually set to the current form with Self.

Before you can copy a component from the clipboard, you must register it with the Classes unit using the RegisterClasses method. This can be done in the initialization section:

```
// Register the TImage class before you use SetComponent
// and GetComponent.
initialization
  RegisterClasses([TImage]);
```

GetTextBuf METHOD

Objects Affected   TClipboard

Purpose   The GetTextBuf method copies the text contents of the clipboard into a buffer.

Declaration

```
function GetTextBuf(Buffer: PChar; BufSize: Integer): Integer;
```

Parameters

Buffer   The name of the buffer.

BufSize   The size of the buffer.

Example Syntax

```
procedure TForm1.Button1Click(Sender: TObject);
var
  MyBuffer: PChar;
  MyBufferSize: Byte;
  MyString: String;
begin
  // Copy contents of the clipboard to the string
  MyString := Clipboard.AsText;
  // Set the length of the buffer to the length of
  // the string
  MyBufferSize := Length(MyString);
  // Create the buffer dynamically
  GetMem(MyBuffer, MyBufferSize);
  // Copy the contents of the clipboard to the buffer
  Clipboard.GetTextBuf(MyBuffer, MyBufferSize);
  // Copy buffer contents to Edit box to make
  // sure it worked
  Edit1.Text := MyBuffer;
  // Free the buffer.
  FreeMem(MyBuffer, MyBufferSize);
end;
```

Description

GetTextBuf retrieves the textual contents of the clipboard and copies as much of it as it can to a buffer, as specified by the *BufSize* parameter. The text in *Buffer* is a standard null-terminated string that can then be used in any normal string operations. Before copying to a buffer, you should determine the size needed to hold the text and allocate memory accordingly. In the example above, the size of the text is determined with the standard Length function.

HasFormat METHOD

Objects Affected TClipboard

Purpose The HasFormat method determines if the data in the clipboard can be accessed with a particular format.

Declaration

```
function HasFormat(Format: Word): Boolean;
```

Parameters

Format The format you would like to use.

Example Syntax

```
// This procedure will copy clipboard data to the
// edit box if it is text or output an error message
procedure TForm1.Button1Click(Sender: TObject);
begin
```

```
  if Clipboard.HasFormat(CF_TEXT) then
    Edit1.Text := Clipboard.AsText
  else
    MessageDlg('The data in the clipboard is not text.',
               mtInformation, [mbOK],0);
end;
```

Description   HasFormat is used to query the *data* in the clipboard to see if it supports the format specified by the *Format* parameter. HasFormat returns True if the data supports that format, or False if it does not. The basic formats supported by the clipboard are listed in Table 11-2, although user-defined formats can be created if needed.

Open METHOD

Objects Affected   TClipboard

Purpose   The Open method prevents other applications from changing the clipboard until you close it.

Declaration

```
procedure Open;
```

Example Syntax

```
procedure TForm1.Button1Click(Sender: TObject);
begin
  // Obtain exclusive access to the clipboard
  Clipboard.Open;
  // Copy a picture to the clipboard
  Clipboard.Assign(Image1.Picture);
  // ö other clipboard processing
  // Make sure you close the clipboard when you are done.
  Clipboard.Close;
end;
```

Description   You will need to call Open if you want *exclusive* access to the clipboard. Open prevents other applications from changing the clipboard while your application is using it. You must call Close once for every time you use Open, otherwise other applications will be unable to access the clipboard until your application closes.

SetAsHandle METHOD

Objects Affected   TClipboard

Purpose   The SetAsHandle method places a handle in the clipboard.

Declaration

```
procedure SetAsHandle(Format: Word; Value: THandle);
```

Parameters

Format   The format of the data.

Value   The handle that is being copied to the clipboard.

Example Syntax

```
// This is a rather low-level way of placing a Bitmap graphic
// into the clipboard using its handle
procedure TForm1.Button1Click(Sender: TObject);
begin
  Clipboard.SetAsHandle(CF_BITMAP, Image1.Picture.Bitmap.Handle);
end;
```

Description   SetAsHandle provides an API-style way to copy data to the clipboard
                            using handles. Typically, this type of clipboard activity is not necessary
                            from Delphi, but it does provide a way to copy data using a standard win-
                            dow handle. Refer also to the GetAsHandle method.

SetComponent METHOD

Objects Affected   TClipboard

Purpose   The SetComponent method copies a Delphi component to the clipboard.

Declaration

```
procedure SetComponent(Component: TComponent);
```

Parameters

Component   The name of the component you wish to copy to the clipboard.

Example Syntax

```
procedure TForm1.Button1Click(Sender: TObject);
begin
  // Copy an image component to the Clipboard
  Clipboard.SetComponent(Image1);
  // Change the name of the component--no two components
  // can have the same name
  Image1.Name := '';
  // Get the image and place it in a group box
  Clipboard.GetComponent(Self, GroupBox1);
end;
```

Description   SetComponent is used with GetComponent to copy components using the
                            clipboard. It is unlikely that the typical applications developer will ever
                            need to use these methods, although it is used by the Delphi Integrated
                            Development Environment (IDE) at design time.

SetTextBuf METHOD

Objects Affected   TClipboard

Purpose   The **SetTextBuf** method is used to copy text from a buffer to the clipboard.

Declaration

```
procedure SetTextBuf(Buffer: PChar);
```

Parameters

Buffer   The buffer whose text is being copied to the clipboard.

Example Syntax

```
// This procedure copies the contents of a buffer
// to the clipboard
procedure TForm1.Button1Click(Sender: TObject);
var
  MyBuffer: PChar;
  MyBufferSize: Byte;
begin
  MyBufferSize := Length(Edit1.Text) + 1;
  // Create the buffer dynamically
  GetMem(MyBuffer, MyBufferSize);
  // Write the text to the buffer
  Edit1.GetTextBuf(MyBuffer, MyBufferSize);
  // Copy the contents of the clipboard to the buffer
  Clipboard.SetTextBuf(MyBuffer);
  // Free the buffer.
  FreeMem(MyBuffer, MyBufferSize);
end;
```

Description   SetTextBuf is the companion to GetTextBuf—these methods offer the programmer a way to copy to and from the clipboard using a buffer. The text held in the *Buffer* parameter is a null-terminated string.

12

TColumnTitle

Column title objects, encapsulated by **TColumnTitle**, contain attribute information for column titles in a database grid. These attributes include such characteristics as color, font, and alignment. **TColumnTitle** objects can be created at design time with the Column Properties tab of the DBGrid Columns Editor, shown in Figure 12-1. They can also be modified at run time.

Database grids have a **Columns** property, which is a database grid column type (**TDBGridColumn** object). This object has an **Items** property, which in turn has a **Title** property that is of type **TColumnTitle**. This series of references can be written as

DBGrid name.Columns.Items[*Index number*].Title

Figure 12-2 shows the derivation of **TColumnTitle**. Table 12-1 displays the properties and methods that are implemented by **TColumnTitle**.

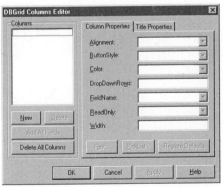

Figure 12-1   The DBGrid Columns Editor

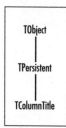

Figure 2-2 Derivation of `TColumnTitle`

Table 12-1 Properties and methods implemented by `TColumnTitle`

Use or Set This...	To Do This...	Inheritance
Alignment	Align the title caption.	None
Assign	Assign one persistent object to another.	TPersistent
Caption	Determine the caption of the column title.	None
ClassName	Get the name of the object's class.	TObject
ClassParent	Get the object's parent class.	TObject
ClassType	Get the object's actual type.	TObject
Color	Determine the background color of the column title.	None
Create	Construct a new column title object.	TObject
DefaultAlignment	Return the default alignment of the column title.	None
DefaultCaption	Return the default caption of the column title.	None
DefaultColor	Return the default color of the column title.	None
DefaultFont	Return the default font of the column title.	None
Destroy	Destroy the column title object.	TObject
Font	Determine the font used to display the caption.	None
Free	Safely destroy the object.	TObject
InheritsFrom	Determine if the object is descended from a certain class.	TObject
InstanceSize	Determine the amount of memory allocated for the object.	TObject
RestoreDefaults	Restore the column title to its default state.	None

Alignment PROPERTY

Objects Affected `TColumnTitle`

Purpose The `Alignment` property determines the alignment of text in a column title.

Declaration

```
property Alignment: TAlignment;
```

Example Syntax

```
// Center align all of the column titles
procedure TForm1.Button1Click(Sender: TObject);
var x: integer;
begin
  for x := 0 to DBGrid1.Columns.Count - 1 do
    DBGrid1.Columns.Items[x].Title.Alignment := taRightJustify
end;
```

Description

Alignment is of type TALignment, which can be set to the following possible values: taLeftJustify (left justification), taRightJustify (right justification), and taCenter (centered). The default value for Alignment is taLeftJustify.

Caption PROPERTY

Objects Affected   TColumnTitle

Purpose   The Caption property determines the string that appears as the column title caption.

Declaration

```
property Caption: string;
```

Example Syntax

```
procedure TForm1.Button1Click(Sender: TObject);
begin
  DBGrid1.Columns.Items[1].Title.Caption := 'Street Address';
end
```

Description   The Caption property labels the column title.

Color PROPERTY

Objects Affected   TColumnTitle

Purpose   The Color property determines the color of the column title.

Declaration

```
property Color: TColor;
```

Example Syntax

```
procedure TForm1.Button2Click(Sender: TObject);
begin
  DBGrid1.Columns.Items[1].Title.Color := clMaroon;
end
```

Description   The Color property changes the background color of the entire column title, not the font color of the text caption. Color is of type TColor. Some common colors include clAqua, clBlack, clBlue, clDkGray, clFuchsia, clGray, clGreen, clLime, clLtGray, clMaroon, clNavy, clOlive, clPurple, clRed, clSilver, clTeal, clWhite, and clYellow.

DefaultAlignment METHOD

Objects Affected TColumnTitle

Purpose The DefaultAlignment method returns the default alignment of a column title object.

Declaration

```
function DefaultAlignment: Talignment;
```

Example Syntax

```
// Right-align the column titles
procedure TForm1.Button3Click(Sender: TObject);
var x: Integer;
begin
  for x := 0 to DBGrid1.Columns.Count - 1 do
    // This will always be true, even if the alignment has changed
    if DBGrid1.Columns.Items[x].Title.DefaultAlignment = taLeftJustify
then
      DBGrid1.Columns.Items[x].Title.Alignment := taRightJustify;
end;
```

Description Column titles are left-aligned by default, although that can be changed by the programmer. DefaultAlignment is of type TALignment, which can be set to the following possible values: taLeftJustify (left justification), taRightJustify (right justification), and taCenter (centered).

DefaultAlignment is read-only. To actually set the alignment of a column title, use the Alignment property.

DefaultCaption METHOD

Objects Affected TColumnTitle

Purpose The DefaultCaption method returns the default caption for a column title.

Declaration

```
function DefaultCaption: string;
```

Example Syntax

```
// print out the default caption for any column title
procedure TForm1.Button1Click(Sender: TObject);
var Count: Integer;
begin
  Count := DBGrid1.Columns.Count;
  if (StrToInt(Edit1.Text) >= 0) and (StrToInt(Edit1.Text) < Count) then
    Label1.Caption :=
      DBGrid1.Columns.Items[StrToInt(Edit1.Text)].Title.DefaultCaption
  else Label1.Caption := 'Column title index out of bounds';
end;
```

Description	`DefaultCaption` returns the column title's default caption, that is, the caption as it was set at design time. If the title is changed during run time, `DefaultCaption` will still return the original title.

DefaultColor METHOD

Objects Affected	`TColumnTitle`
Purpose	The `DefaultColor` method returns the default color of a column title.
Declaration	

```
function DefaultColor: TColor;
```

Example Syntax	

```
// Change the color of the column title
procedure TForm1.Button1Click(Sender: TObject);
begin
  DBGrid1.Columns.Items[1].Title.Color := clRed;
end;

// . . .

// If the color has changed, set it back to the default color
procedure TForm1.Button2Click(Sender: TObject);
begin
  with DBGrid1.Columns.Items[1].Title do
    if Color <> DefaultColor then
      Color := DefaultColor;
end;
```

Description	`DefaultColor` is a read-only, run-time-only property that returns the column title's default background color, that is, the color as it was set at design time. If the title's background color is changed during run time, `DefaultColor` will still return the original background color.

DefaultFont METHOD

Objects Affected	`TColumnTitle`
Purpose	The `DefaultFont` method returns the default font of the column title.
Declaration	

```
function DefaultFont: TFont;
```

Example Syntax	

```
// Change the font properties for all column titles
procedure TForm1.Button1Click(Sender: TObject);
var x: Integer;
begin
  for x := 0 to DBGrid1.Columns.Count - 1 do
```

continued on next page

continued from previous page

```
      begin
        with DBGrid1.Columns.Items[x].Title do
        begin
          Color := clWhite;
          Font.Color := clBlue;
          Font.Name := 'Arial';
          Font.Size := 12;
          Font.Style := [fsBold] + [fsItalic];
        end;
      end;
  end;

  // Restore the font properties for all column titles
  procedure TForm1.Button2Click(Sender: TObject);
  var x: Integer;
  begin
    for x := 0 to DBGrid1.Columns.Count - 1 do
      with DBGrid1.Columns.Items[x].Title do
      begin
        Color := DefaultColor;
        if Font <> DefaultFont then
          Font := DefaultFont
      end;
  end;
```

Description DefaultFont is a read-only, run-time-only property that returns the column title's default font, that is, the font as it was set at design time. If the title font is changed during run time, DefaultFont will still return the original title font.

Font PROPERTY

Objects Affected TColumnTitle

Purpose The Font property determines what font is used to render the column title caption.

Declaration

```
property Font: TFont;
```

Example Syntax

```
// Change the font properties for all column titles
procedure TForm1.Button1Click(Sender: TObject);
var x: Integer;
begin
  for x := 0 to DBGrid1.Columns.Count - 1 do
  begin
    with DBGrid1.Columns.Items[x].Title do
    begin
      Color := clWhite;
      Font.Color := clBlue;
      Font.Name := 'Arial';
      Font.Size := 12;
      Font.Style := [fsBold] + [fsItalic];
```

```
            end;
          end;
        end;
```

Description   Font is of type **TFont**, which has properties for the font's color, name, height, pitch, size, and style.

RestoreDefaults METHOD

Objects Affected   TColumnTitle

Purpose   The **RestoreDefaults** method restores the caption, color, font, and alignment properties of the column title to their default values.

Declaration

```
procedure RestoreDefaults; virtual;
```

Example Syntax

```
// Restore the column titles to their original state
procedure TForm1.Button8Click(Sender: TObject);
var x: Integer;
begin
  for x := 0 to DBGrid1.Columns.Count - 1 do
    DBGrid1.Columns.Items[x].Title.RestoreDefaults;
end;
```

Description   RestoreDefaults uses the values contained in **DefaultCaption**, **DefaultColor**, **DefaultFont**, and **DefaultAlignment** to return the column title to its original state.

13

TControlScrollBar

TControlScrollBar objects are used by the HorzScrollBar and VertScrollBar properties of forms and scroll boxes to display the actual scroll bar that users can
manipulate. As a direct descendant of TPersistent, TControlScrollBar inherits all of
the properties and methods of its ancestors. Figure 13-1 shows the ancestry of
TControlScrollBar. Table 13-1 displays the properties that are unique to
TControlScrollBar.

IMPORTANT

Common usage and Microsoft terminology describe the "thumb" portion of a scroll bar as a *scroll box*.
Borland, however, uses the name scroll box to describe a Delphi control that allows you to create a
scrolling area on a form that is smaller than the entire form. For the purposes of this chapter, the
phrase "scroll box" refers to Borland's control.

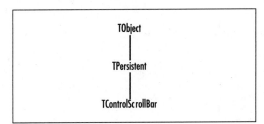

Figure 13-1 Ancestry of TControlScrollBar

Table 13-1 Properties and methods implemented by `TControlScrollBar`

Use or Set This...	To Do This...	Inheritance
Assign	Assign one persistent object to another.	TPersistent
ClassName	Get the name of the object's class.	TObject
ClassParent	Get the object's parent class.	TObject
ClassType	Get the object's actual type.	TObject
Create	Construct a new object.	TObject
Destroy	Destroy the object.	TObject
Free	Safely destroy the object.	TObject
Increment	Determine the number of units the thumb tab will move.	None
InheritsFrom	Determine whether the object is descended from a certain class.	TObject
InstanceSize	Determine the amount of memory allocated for the object.	TObject
Kind	Determine whether the form scroll bar is horizontal or vertical.	None
Margin	Determine the minimum distance from a control to the edge of the form.	None
Position	Determine the position of the scroll bar thumb.	None
Range	Determine the range of values that are possible while scrolling.	None
ScrollPos	Determine the current value of the `Position` property.	None
Visible	Determine whether the form scroll bar can be seen.	None

Increment PROPERTY

Objects Affected   `TControlScrollBar`

Purpose   The `Increment` property determines the number of units the scroll bar thumb will move when the user clicks a scroll bar arrow.

Declaration

```
property Increment: TScrollBarInc;
```

Example Syntax

```
procedure TForm1.FormCreate(Sender: TObject);
begin
  // Set the properties for the form's horizontal
  // scrollbar
  HorzScrollBar.Visible := True;
  HorzScrollBar.Range := ClientWidth * 2;
  HorzScrollBar.Increment := 20;
  HorzScrollBar.Position := 0;
end;
```

Description   `Increment` determines the size of the movement the scroll box makes when a scroll bar arrow is clicked.

The default value of **Increment** is **8**; it can be set to any integer value in the range of 1 to 32,767.

Kind PROPERTY

Objects Affected	TControlScrollBar
Purpose	The **Kind** property determines if a scroll bar is horizontal or vertical.
Declaration	

```
property Kind: TControlScrollBarKind;
```

Description   The **Kind** property of a **TControlScrollBar** is used internally—the **HorzScrollBar** property is always horizontal and **VertScrollBar** is always vertical. **Kind** can contain one of two values: **sbHorizontal** for horizontal, or **sbVertical** for vertical.

Margin PROPERTY

Objects Affected	TControlScrollBar
Purpose	The **Margin** property specifies the minimum distance you want controls to be from the edge of the form or scroll box they are contained within.
Declaration	

```
property Margin: Word;
```

Example Syntax

```
// If any controls get to within 20 pixels of the edge
// of the form a scroll bar will appear
procedure TForm1.FormCreate(Sender: TObject);
begin
  HorzScrollBar.Margin := 20;
  VertScrollBar.Margin := 20;
end;
```

Description   The **Margin** property allows you to set the minimum distance, in pixels, you want controls to be from the edge of their container. If controls (perhaps controls that are added at run time) appear closer to the edge, then a scroll bar will appear. Obviously, you can determine the position of many controls at design time, but this property allows you to handle those instances where controls are added at run time. The addition of such controls may require that scroll bars appear on the containing form so that the user can access them.

The default value of **Margin** is **0**.

Position PROPERTY

Objects Affected	`TControlScrollBar`
Purpose	The `Position` property determines the position of the scroll bar thumb.
Declaration	

```
property Position: Integer;
```

Example Syntax

```
procedure TForm1.FormCreate(Sender: TObject);
begin
  // Set the properties for the form's horizontal
  // scrollbar
  HorzScrollBar.Visible := True;
  HorzScrollBar.Range := ClientWidth * 2;
  HorzScrollBar.Increment := 10;
  // place the thumb in the middle of the scrollbar
  HorzScrollBar.Position := ClientWidth div 2;
  HorzScrollBar.Margin := 5;
end;
```

Description   `Position` allows you to read or set the position of the scroll bar thumb within the scroll bar. In the example above, the scroll bar thumb position is centered when the form is created.

Range PROPERTY

Objects Affected	`TControlScrollBar`
Purpose	The `Range` property contains the range of positional values that are possible within the scroll bar.
Declaration	

```
Property Range: Integer;
```

Example Syntax

```
procedure TForm1.FormCreate(Sender: TObject);
begin
  // Set the properties for the form's horizontal scroll
  // bar
  HorzScrollBar.Visible := True;
  // Set the range to twice the form's width
  HorzScrollBar.Range := ClientWidth * 2;
  HorzScrollBar.Increment := 10;
  HorzScrollBar.Margin := 5;
end;
```

Description   The value of `Range` determines how far the form scroll bar can scroll and the virtual size of the window it is contained within. If the value of `Range` is less than the width or height of the form (depending on whether `Range` applies to `HorzScrollBar` or `VertScrollBar`), then no scroll bar will appear.

Range can be set to any integer value, although the meaningful range is 1–32,767.

ScrollPos PROPERTY

Objects Affected	TControlScrollBar
Purpose	ScrollPos holds the current value of the Position property.
Declaration	

```
property ScrollPos: Integer;
```

Example Syntax

```
// This procedure will change the caption of the form if
// you click anywhere and the horizontal scroll bar position
// is over 200
procedure TForm1.FormClick(Sender: TObject);
begin
  If HorzScrollBar.ScrollPos > 200 then
    Form1.Caption := 'That's too far.';
end;
```

Description   ScrollPos is a run-time, read-only property that can be used to read the value of Position. ScrollPos can only be used to *get* the position of the thumb tab. If the scroll bar is not visible, ScrollPos will return 0.

Visible PROPERTY

Objects Affected	TControlScrollBar
Purpose	The Visible property determines whether the scroll bar is displayed.
Declaration	

```
property Visible: Boolean;
```

Example Syntax

```
procedure TForm1.FormCreate(Sender: TObject);
begin
  // Set the properties for the form's horizontal
  // scrollbar
  HorzScrollBar.Visible := True;
  HorzScrollBar.Range := ClientWidth * 2;
  HorzScrollBar.Increment := 20;
  HorzScrollBar.Position := 0;
end;
```

Description   If Visible is True, then the scroll bar is visible. If Visible is False, it is not visible.

The default value is True.

14

TIconOptions

The **TIconOptions** class, a property of **TListView**, stores information for icons that are displayed in the list view when the **ViewStyle** property is set to **vsIcon** (Large Icons view) or **vsSmallIcon** (Small Icons view).

Figure 14-1 shows the lineage of **TIconOptions**. Table 14-1 displays the properties and methods that are implemented by **TIconOptions**.

Table 14-1 Properties and methods implemented by *TIconOptions*

Use or Set This...	To Do This...	Inheritance
Arrangement	Determine how the icons are arranged in a list view.	None
Assign	Assign one persistent object to another.	TPersistent
AutoArrange	Determine whether the icons will automatically arrange.	None
ClassName	Get the name of the object's class.	TObject
ClassParent	Get the object's parent class.	TObject
ClassType	Get the object's actual type.	TObject
Create	Construct a new object.	TObject
Destroy	Destroy the object.	TObject
Free	Safely destroy the object.	TObject
InheritsFrom	Determine if the object is descended from a certain class.	TObject
InstanceSize	Determine the amount of memory allocated for the object.	TObject
WrapText	Determine whether the icon captions will wrap text.	None

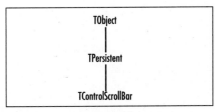

Figure 14-1 Lineage of **TIconOptions**

Arrangement PROPERTY

Objects Affected	TIconOptions
Purpose	The Arrangement property determines how the icons are arranged in the list view.
Declaration	

```
property Arrangement: TIconArrangement;
```

Example Syntax

```
// Construct a list view and its associated itemsö

// Clicking SpeedButton1 will arrange the icons
// along the top of the list view
procedure TForm1.SpeedButton1Click(Sender: TObject);
begin
  ListView1.IconOptions.Arrangement := iaTop;
end;

// Clicking SpeedButton1 will arrange the icons
// along the left of the list view
procedure TForm1.SpeedButton2Click(Sender: TObject);
begin
  ListView1.IconOptions.Arrangement := iaLeft;
end;
```

Description   Arrangement can contain one of two values: iaTop, for aligning the icons along the top edge of the list control, and iaLeft, which will arrange them along the left edge of the list control. The default arrangement is iaTop.

AutoArrange PROPERTY

Objects Affected	TIconOptions
Purpose	The AutoArrange property determines whether the icons in a list view will automatically arrange themselves if the list view resizes.
Declaration	

```
property AutoArrange: Boolean;
```

Example Syntax

```
// Automatically arrange the icons in the list view
procedure TForm1.FormCreate(Sender: TObject);
begin
  ListView1.IconOptions.AutoArrange := True;
end;
```

Description   AutoArrange is a boolean method that determines whether the icons in a list view will arrange themselves automatically if the list view is resized. It defaults to False.

WrapText PROPERTY

Objects Affected   TIconOptions

Purpose   The **WrapText** property determines whether the captions of icons in a list view will automatically text wrap.

Declaration

```
property WrapText: Boolean;
```

Example Syntax

```
procedure TForm1.FormCreate(Sender: TObject);
begin
  ListView1.IconOptions.WrapText := False;
end;
```

Description   If you would prefer the captions of an icon in a list view to wrap rather than display on one line when the width of the caption exceeds the width of the icon, set **WrapText** to **True**. **WrapText** is a boolean function that defaults to **True**. **WrapText** is used so that the icon captions do not over-write each other in the list view.

15

TListItem AND *TListItems*

This chapter documents the **TListItem** and **TListItems** classes, which maintain the individual items in a list view control.

TListItem

A list view item is a single element in a list view control. Individual list view items are encapsulated by the **TListItem** class, which holds a kind of "record" about each item in the list. List view items consist of two parts: some data and a caption. The actual list view control is discussed in Chapter 58, "**TCustomListView** and **TListView**." Most of your work with list views will occur at the **TListView** level. **TListItem** deals with the individual elements in the **Items** array of a **TListView** control. The **Items** array itself is of type **TListItems** (note the *s* at the end of the name), which is covered in the next section in this chapter.

Figure 15-1 shows the derivation of **TListItem** and **TListItems**. Table 15-1 displays the properties and methods that are implemented by **TListItem**.

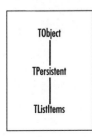

Figure 15-1
Derivation of **TListItem** and **TListItems**

Table 15-1 Properties and methods implemented by `TListItem`

Use or Set This...	To Do This...	Inheritance
Assign	Assign one persistent object to another.	TPersistent
CancelEdit	Cancel the editing of the list view item caption.	None
Caption	Determine the list view item's caption.	None
ClassName	Get the name of the object's class.	TObject
ClassParent	Get the object's parent class.	TObject
ClassType	Get the object's actual type.	TObject
Create	Construct a new object.	TObject
Cut	Determine whether the list view item is selected as part of a cut-and-paste operation.	None
Data	Determine what data is associated with a list view item.	None
Delete	Delete a list item.	None
Destroy	Destroy a list item object.	TObject
DropTarget	Determine whether the list item is a drop target.	None
EditCaption	Determine whether the list item's caption is being edited.	None
Focused	Determine whether the list item has the focus.	None
Free	Safely destroy the object.	TObject
Handle	Obtain a Windows handle to the list item.	None
ImageIndex	Determine which image is associated with the list item.	None
Index	Determine the index value of the list item in an `Items` array.	None
InheritsFrom	Determine whether the object is descended from a certain class.	TObject
InstanceSize	Determine the amount of memory allocated for the object.	TObject
ListView	Determine the name of the list view object containing the item.	None
MakeVisible	Make a list item partially or totally visible.	None
OverlayIndex	Determine which image is used as an overlay mask.	None
Owner	Indicate the owner of the list item.	None
Selected	Determine whether the list item is currently selected.	None
StateIndex	Determine which image will be displayed if state images are used.	None
SubItems	Determine the list of strings that can appear as subitems.	None
Update	Update a list item object by redrawing it.	None

`CancelEdit` METHOD

Objects Affected	TListItem
Purpose	The `CancelEdit` method cancels the editing of the list view item caption.
Declaration	

```
procedure CancelEdit;
```

Example Syntax

```
procedure TForm1.ListView1Editing(Sender: TObject; Item: TListItem;
  var AllowEdit: Boolean);
begin
  // Don't allow Item1's caption to be edited
  if ListView1.Selected = ListView1.Items[0] then
  begin
    ListView1.Items[0].CancelEdit;
    Application.MessageBox('Editing of this caption not allowed!',
                           'No editing allowed!', MB_OK)
  end
end;
```

Description   If the list view control itself is not read-only, you may want to use
CancelEdit to manually stop the user from editing the caption of an individual item in the control.

Caption PROPERTY

Objects Affected   TListItem

Purpose   The **Caption** property determines the caption of the list view item.

Declaration

```
property Caption: String;
```

Example Syntax

```
// Copy the text from Edit1 to the caption of
// the first item in the list view.
procedure TForm1.Button1Click(Sender: TObject);
begin
  ListView1.Items[0].Caption := Edit1.Text;
end;
```

Description   The **Caption** property is used to set or get the caption of a list view item.

Create METHOD

Objects Affected   TListItem

Purpose   The **Create** method is used to construct a new list item.

Declaration

```
constructor Create(AOwner: TListItems);
```

Parameters

AOwner   The owner of the list item, a **TListItems** (list of list items).

Example Syntax

```
var
  MyListItem: TListItem;
```

continued on next page

continued from previous page

```
. . .
// Create a new list view item when the form is
// created.
procedure TForm1.FormCreate(Sender: TObject);
begin
  MyListItem := TListItem.Create(ListView1.Items);
  // add list view processing here
  // . . .
end;
```

Description   Typically, you will add list view items to a list view control at design time using the ListView Items Editor, shown in Figure 15-2. Occasionally, however, you may need to create list view items dynamically (at run time). To do this, you must use the **Create** method, which modifies the standard **TPersistent** constructor to support features specific to **TListItem**. Remember to **Free** list item objects that you dynamically create.

Cut PROPERTY

Objects Affected   TListItem

Purpose   The **Cut** property determines whether the list view item is selected as part of a cut-and-paste operation.

Declaration

```
property Cut: Boolean;
```

Example Syntax

```
// Set the Cut and Paste state of the first list view item to False
ListView1.Items[0].Cut := False
```

Description   Cut is a run-time-only property. If **Cut** is **True**, the list view item is part of a cut-and-paste operation. If **Cut** is **False**, the list view item is not being cut. Typically, you will use **Cut** to test whether a particular list view is part of a cut-and-paste selection and then respond accordingly. While you could set **Cut** to **True** or **False** manually, you shouldn't normally need to do this.

Figure 15-2   The ListView Items Editor

Data PROPERTY

Objects Affected   TListItem

Purpose   The `Data` property determines the data that is associated with a list item object.

Declaration

```
property Data: Pointer;
```

Example Syntax

```
var
  Form1: TForm1;
  DataText: PChar;

implementation

{$R *.DFM}

procedure TForm1.FormCreate(Sender: TObject);
begin
  // . . .
  DataText := 'This is sample data text';
end;

// . . .

procedure TForm1.ListView1Enter(Sender: TObject);
var x: Integer;
begin
  // Set the data for all list view items
  for x := 0 to ListView1.Items.Count - 1 do
    ListView1.Items[x].Data := DataText;
end;
```

Description   `Data` is a pointer to the data structure that is associated with the list view item. Every application will have different needs with respect to the data that is associated with each item in a list view control. Since `Data` is a generic pointer, it can refer to any type of object. In the example code above, the `Data` pointer for each list view item refers to the same string. In your own applications, you can have the `Data` property point to different object types for each list view item.

Delete METHOD

Objects Affected   TListItem

Purpose   The `Delete` method is used to delete a list item.

Declaration

```
procedure Delete;
```

Example Syntax

```
// Delete the third item in the list when the
// button is clicked
procedure TForm1.Button1Click(Sender: TObject);
begin
  ListView1.Items[2].Delete;
end;
```

Description

Delete is used to delete an individual list item object. When the item is deleted, the list is redrawn to reflect the change. Internally, Delete uses the Free method to deallocate the memory associated with the item. This is the preferred method of destroying a list view item. Delphi will not automatically deallocate memory for any object pointed to by the Data property of the list view item. If you want to destroy that object, you must write code to do so yourself.

DropTarget PROPERTY

Objects Affected   TListItem

Purpose   The DropTarget property determines whether the list item is a drag-and-drop target.

Declaration

```
property DropTarget: Boolean;
```

Example Syntax

```
if ListView1.Items[0].DropTarget = True then
  Label1.Caption := 'The first list view item is the target';
```

Description   DropTarget is a run-time-only property. DropTarget is True if the list view item is the target of a drag-and-drop operation. It is False if the list view item is not a drag-and-drop target. Don't confuse this DropTarget property with the DropTarget property of the list view control itself; this property is used to answer the question, "Is this particular list view item the target of a drag-and-drop operation?" The DragDrop property of TListView answers the question, "Which list view item contained by the list view control is the target of a drag-and-drop operation?"

EditCaption METHOD

Objects Affected   TListItem

Purpose   The EditCaption property indicates whether the list item caption is currently being edited.

Declaration

```
function EditCaption: Boolean;
```

Example Syntax

```
// If the user edits the first list view item, disable the
// command button
procedure TForm1.ListView1Change(Sender: TObject; Item: TListItem;
  Change: TItemChange);
begin
  if ListView1.Items[0].EditCaption = True then
    Button1.Enabled := false;
end;
```

Description

The EditCaption property is set to True while the user is editing the caption of a list view item object. Otherwise, it is False.

Focused PROPERTY

Objects Affected   TListItem

Purpose   The Focused property indicates whether the list item object has the focus.

Declaration

```
property Focused: Boolean;
```

Example Syntax

```
procedure TForm1.ListView1Change(Sender: TObject; Item: TListItem;
  Change: TItemChange);
begin
  if ListView1.Items[0].Focused = True then
    Form1.Caption := 'The first list item has the focus'
  else Form1.Caption := 'Form1';
end;
```

Description

Only one list item in a list Items array can have the focus (although more than one item can be selected), and the Focused property holds a boolean value for each item. If the property is set to True, then that item has the focus. If it is False, then that item does not have the focus.

Handle PROPERTY

Objects Affected   TListItem

Purpose   Handle contains the Windows handle for a list item object.

Declaration

```
property Handle: HWND;
```

Example Syntax

```
var
  Form1: TForm1;
  ItemHandle: HWND;

procedure TForm1.FormCreate(Sender: TObject);
begin
```

continued on next page

continued from previous page

```
        ItemHandle := ListView1.Items[0].Handle;

        // . . .
    end;
```

Description   The `Handle` property contains a standard Windows `HWND` structure that can be used with API calls.

ImageIndex PROPERTY

Objects Affected   `TListItem`

Purpose   `ImageIndex` indicates which image in the associated image list is used for the list view item.

Declaration

```
property ImageIndex: Integer;
```

Example Syntax

```
// Change the image index value for the first list item
// to the fourth image in the image list that is associated
// with ListView1
procedure TForm1.Button1Click(Sender: TObject);
begin
  ListView1.Items[0].ImageIndex := 3;
end;
```

Description   An image list (containing an array of images) is associated with each list view control in your program. The `ImageIndex` property of a list view item associates an image from the image list with that list view item.

`ImageIndex` contains an integer. The index values of the image list, like the index value of the `Items` property of a list view control, start at zero.

Index PROPERTY

Objects Affected   `TListItem`

Purpose   The `Index` property contains the integer index value of the list item.

Declaration

```
property Index: Integer;
```

Example Syntax

```
procedure TForm1.SpeedButton1Click(Sender: TObject);
var x: integer;
begin
  x := 1;
  Form1.Caption := 'List view item '
                  + (IntToStr(ListView1.Selected.Index))
                  + ' is selected';
end;
```

Description   Because individual items in a **TListView** control are normally accessed by the **Items** array of the **TListView** control, it is unlikely that you will ever use **Index** directly. Remember that the index values of items in a list view control are zero-based; that is, the first item has an **Index** value of **0**, the second has a value of **1**, and so on.

ListView PROPERTY

Objects Affected   TListItem

Purpose   The **ListView** property contains the name of the list view object that the list item is a member of.

Declaration

```
property ListView: TCustomListView;
```

Example Syntax

```
procedure TForm1.Button1Click(Sender: TObject);
begin
  if ListView1.Items[0].ListView <> ListView1 then
    Form1.Caption := 'This program is hosed.'
  else
    Form1.Caption := 'Everything is OK.';
end;
```

Description   **ListView** is a run-time and read-only property that identifies the owner of the list view item. You do not normally need to access this property directly.

MakeVisible METHOD

Objects Affected   TListItem

Purpose   The **MakeVisible** method will make a list view item partially or totally visible.

Declaration

```
procedure MakeVisible(PartialOK: Boolean);
```

Parameters

PartialOK   Determines whether the list item must be totally visible.

Example Syntax

```
// Before running this program, ensure that ListView1 is
// only large enough to display one list item at a time.
// When the program is run, horizontal and vertical scroll
// bars will appear around the control. Clicking button 1
// causes the third list item to scroll into view.
procedure TForm1.Button1Click(Sender: TObject);
begin
  ListView1.Items[2].MakeVisible(False);
end;
```

Description
: MakeVisible ensures that a list item is partially or totally visible inside the list view control and will scroll the list view if necessary to view the item properly. If the *PartialOK* parameter is set to **True**, you are indicating that partial visibility is acceptable (meaning that a list item that is partially viewable will not scroll into place). If *PartialOK* is **False**, a partially visible or nonvisible item will scroll into the visible range of the list view control.

OverlayIndex PROPERTY

Objects Affected
: TListItem

Purpose
: The OverlayIndex property determines which image in the associated image list is used as an overlay mask.

Declaration

```
property OverlayIndex: Integer;
```

Example Syntax

```
// Set the overlay mask for the third item in the list view
// to the fourth image in its associated image list
procedure TForm1.Button1Click(Sender: TObject);
begin
   ListView1.Items[2].OverlayIndex := 3;
end;
```

Description
: An *overlay mask* is an image that is drawn over another image. In Windows 95, the little arrow image that is added to shortcut icons is an overlay mask—it is used to indicate that the icon is a shortcut.

In the case of a list view item, you could use an overlay mask for a variety of reasons—typical examples include a red X through an image to indicate that a particular item is unavailable, or a gray mesh image that will make an item look "grayed-out," also indicating that it is unavailable.

Owner PROPERTY

Objects Affected
: TListItem

Purpose
: The Owner property indicates the owner of the list item.

Declaration

```
property Owner: TListItems;
```

Example Syntax

```
procedure TForm1.ListView1Changing(Sender: TObject; Item: TListItem;
                    Change: TItemChange; var AllowChange: Boolean);
begin
   // Get the number of items in the list view using the Owner
   // property of the first list view item to access the Count
```

```
// property of the TListItems object that contains it.
lblNumItems.Caption := IntToStr(ListView1.Items[0].Owner.Count);

// Determine how many list view items are selected
lblNumSelItems.Caption := IntToStr(ListView1.SelCount);
end;
```

Description

It is unlikely that you will ever need to set the **Owner** property of a list item directly. If you are using a list view control, you will not need to set this property explicitly—it is done for you when list items are added at design time. If you need to create a list item dynamically at run time, the **Owner** property is set in the **Create** call. See **Create** for details.

Selected PROPERTY

Objects Affected   TListItem

Purpose   The **Selected** property indicates if the list item is currently selected.

Declaration

```
property Selected: Boolean;
```

Example Syntax

```
// Determine if the first list item is selected
// when the list view control is clicked
procedure TForm1.ListView1Click(Sender: TObject);
begin
  if ListView1.Items[0].Selected then
    Form1.Caption := 'the first item was selected'
  else Form1.Caption := 'Form1';
end;
```

Description

Typically, you will use the **Selected** property to test whether the list view item is selected. If **Selected** is **True**, that list view item is selected. If it is **False**, that list view item is not selected. It is possible for more than one list view item to be selected at a time. Note that a selected item will not necessarily have the focus.

StateIndex PROPERTY

Objects Affected   TListItem

Purpose   The **StateIndex** property determines which image in the associated state image array will be displayed if state images are used.

Declaration

```
property StateIndex: Integer;
```

Example Syntax

```
// Set the state image for the first item in the list view
// to the first image in its associated state image array
procedure TForm1.Button1Click(Sender: TObject);
begin
  ListView1.Items[0].StateIndex := 0;
end;
```

Description   This run-time-only property determines which image in the list view's associated state image array is used to display the item's status. This is traditionally an image that graphically displays some information about the current state of the item. If **StateIndex** is **–1**, no state image is drawn.

SubItems PROPERTY

Objects Affected   TListItem

Purpose   The **SubItems** property determines the list of strings that can appear as subitems of a list item.

Declaration

```
property SubItems: TStrings;
```

Example Syntax

```
// Add the text from the edit box to the list of
// sub-items for the first list item in ListView1
// when the button is clicked
procedure TForm1.Button1Click(Sender: TObject);
begin
  ListView1.Items[0].SubItems.Add(Edit1.Text);
end;
```

Description   **SubItems** can be added at run time with the **TStrings** method **Add**, or by clicking the New SubItem button in the ListView Items Editor dialog in the Delphi IDE.

Update METHOD

Objects Affected   TListItem

Purpose   The **Update** method is used to repaint a list item.

Declaration

```
procedure Update;
```

Example Syntax

```
// Update all of the list items
procedure TForm1.Button1Click(Sender: TObject);
var x: integer;
```

```
begin
  for x := 0 to ListView1.Items.Count - 1 do
    ListView1.Items[x].Update;
end;
```

Description   Update forces the system to repaint the list view item.

TListItems

TListItems is used to maintain a list of list view items that can be manipulated as if it were an array. The Items property of the TListView control is a TListItems object. Because the names are so similar, it is easy to confuse a TListItems object with a TListItem object; TListItems is the actual list, an array of TListItem objects, and the TListItem objects are the elements that make up the list. TListItems is technically not an array but rather contains an *array property*; this allows TListItems to conveniently use such array features as subscripted element access.

Table 15-2 displays the properties that are implemented by TListItems.

Table 15-2 Properties and methods implemented by TListItems

Use or Set This...	To Do This...	Inheritance
Add	Add a list item to a TListItems object.	None
Assign	Assign one persistent object to another.	TPersistent
BeginUpdate	Prevent the screen from updating when adding new list items.	None
ClassName	Get the name of the object's class.	TObject
ClassParent	Get the object's parent class.	TObject
ClassType	Get the object's actual type.	TObject
Clear	Delete all the list view items in the list.	None
Count	Determine the number of list items in a TListItems object.	None
Create	Create a new TListItems object.	TObject
Delete	Remove a list item from a TListItems object.	None
Destroy	Destroy the object.	TObject
EndUpdate	Allow normal screen draws to occur.	None
Free	Safely destroy the object.	TObject
Handle	Determine the handle to the TListItems object.	None
IndexOf	Determine the index of a specific list view item in the list.	None
InheritsFrom	Determine if the object is descended from a certain class.	TObject
Insert	Add a list item at a specific location in the list.	None
InstanceSize	Determine the amount of memory allocated for the object.	TObject
Item	Access an individual item in the list by its index position.	None
Owner	Determine the owner of the TListItems object.	None

Add METHOD

Objects Affected	TListItems
Purpose	The Add method is used to add a list view item to the TListItems object.
Declaration	

```
function Add: TListItem;
```

Example Syntax

```
var
  Form1: TForm1;
  MyItem: TListItem;
  // . . . other vars

implementation

// . . .

// Add a list item to the list view control
procedure TForm1.Button1Click(Sender: TObject);
begin
  MyItem := TListItem.Create(ListView1.Items);
  // Add properties to MyItem here.
  MyItem := ListView1.Items.Add;
end;
```

Description   Add is used to add a list item to the end of the list of list items maintained by the TListItems object.

You can use the BeginUpdate method when adding items to a list view object to prevent the screen from being updated until the addition is complete. See BeginUpdate for details.

BeginUpdate METHOD

Objects Affected	TListItems
Purpose	The BeginUpdate method prevents the screen from being updated while new list items are added to the TListItems object.
Declaration	

```
procedure BeginUpdate;
```

Example Syntax

```
// Add a list item to the list view control
procedure TForm1.Button1Click(Sender: TObject);
begin
  // Make sure the control isn't updated until the list item
  // is added.
  ListView1.Items.BeginUpdate;
  MyItem := TListItem.Create(ListView1.Items);
  // Add properties to MyItem here.
  MyItem := ListView1.Items.Add;
```

```
                    // Force the screen update when you are done
                    ListView1.Items.EndUpdate;
                 end;
```

Description   `BeginUpdate` prevents the list view control from being redrawn and the list view items from being re-indexed until the new item(s) are added or deleted. Since re-indexing and other list housekeeping incur processing overhead, it is better to momentarily defer such operations if multiple changes are being made to the list. When you are done adding items to or deleting items from the list view control, call `EndUpdate` so that the redraw and re-indexing can occur only once.

Clear METHOD

Objects Affected   `TListItems`

Purpose   The `Clear` method deletes all list view items maintained by the `TListItems` object.

Declaration

```
                 procedure Clear;
```

Example Syntax

```
                 ListView1.Items.Clear;
```

Description   You can call `Clear` if you need to remove every item in the list view control at once. Remember, if the `Data` properties of the individual list view items point to memory that you want to deallocate, you must do so yourself.

Count PROPERTY

Objects Affected   `TListItems`

Purpose   The `Count` property indicates the number of list view items in the `TListItems` object.

Declaration

```
                 property Count: Integer;
```

Example Syntax

```
                 // Update all of the list items
                 procedure TForm1.Button1Click(Sender: TObject);
                 var x: Integer;
                 begin
                   for x := 0 to ListView1.Items.Count - 1 do
                     ListView1.Items[x].Update;
                 end;
```

Description	Count is a read-only property that contains the number of elements (of type TListItem) in the list that is maintained by the TListItems object. Because the list of items in a TListItems object is indexed from zero, Count −1 is used in the preceding example so that the for loop processes the correct number of items.

Delete METHOD

Objects Affected	TListItems
Purpose	The Delete method is used to remove a single list item from the TListItems object.
Declaration	
	`procedure Delete(Index: Integer);`
Parameters	
Index	The index number of the list item you wish to delete.
Example Syntax	

```
// Delete the first item in the list view control
// when the button is pressed.
procedure TForm1.Button1Click(Sender: TObject);
begin
  ListView1.Items[0].Delete;
end;
```

Description	The Delete method is used to remove a TListItem object from the TListItems object—it uses the *Index* parameter to determine which object to remove. Remember that the items in a TListItems array are indexed from zero, so the first element is index 0, the second is index 1, and so forth.
	When an item is deleted from the TListItems list, the next item in the list, if any, assumes the index number of the deleted item. For example, if Items[0] is deleted, the item previously identified by Items[1] becomes Items[0]; subsequent items are also re-indexed in a similar manner.
	Remember, if the Data property of the list view item you are deleting points to memory that you want to deallocate, you must do so yourself.

EndUpdate METHOD

Objects Affected	TListItems
Purpose	The EndUpdate method allows normal redraw and reindexing activities to occur after they have been momentarily halted with BeginUpdate.

Declaration

```
procedure EndUpdate;
```

Example Syntax

```
// Add a list item to the list view control
procedure TForm1.Button1Click(Sender: TObject);
begin
  // Make sure the control isn't updated until the list item
  // is added.
  ListView1.Items.BeginUpdate;
  MyItem := TListItem.Create(ListView1.Items);
  // Add properties to MyItem here.
  MyItem := ListView1.Items.Add;
  // Force the screen update when you are done
  ListView1.Items.EndUpdate;
end;
```

Description

EndUpdate is always used in conjunction with BeginUpdate. BeginUpdate halts redraws and re-indexing for the list view control while items are added to the control. EndUpdate allows normal redraw and re-indexing processing to continue.

Handle PROPERTY

Objects Affected   TListItems

Purpose   The Handle property holds a standard Windows handle to the TListItems object.

Declaration

```
property Handle: HWND;
```

Example Syntax

```
var
  Form1: TForm1;
  MyHandle: HWND;
  // ... other vars

implementation

// ...

// get a handle to the Items list
procedure TForm1.FormCreate(Sender: TObject);
begin
  MyHandle := ListView1.Items.Handle;
end;
```

Description   Handle is useful if you need to access API calls that will need a handle to the TListItems object.

IndexOf METHOD

Objects Affected	`TListItems`
Purpose	The `IndexOf` method returns the index of a specific list view item in the list.
Declaration	

```
function IndexOf(Value: TListItem): Integer;
```

Parameters

Value   The list view item whose index you wish to obtain.

Example Syntax

```
procedure TForm1.SpeedButton1Click(Sender: TObject);
var x: integer;
begin
  x := 1;
  Form1.Caption := 'List view item '
                + (IntToStr(ListView1.Items.IndexOf(Selected)))
                + ' is selected';
end;
```

Description   `IndexOf` returns the integer index value of the list view item specified by the *Value* parameter.

Insert METHOD

Objects Affected	`TListItems`
Purpose	The `Insert` method is used to add a list view item at a specific location in the list.
Declaration	

```
function Insert(Index: Integer): TListItem;
```

Parameters

Index   The location in the list where you would like to insert a list item object.

Example Syntax

```
var
  Form1: TForm1;
  MyItem: TListItem;
  // ö other vars

implementation

// ö

// Add a list item to the list view control
// in the second position
```

```
procedure TForm1.Button1Click(Sender: TObject);
begin
  MyItem := TListItem.Create(ListView1.Items);
  MyItem := ListView1.Items.Insert(1);
  // Add properties to MyItem here.
  MyItem.Caption := 'Hello, world.';
end;
```

Description

Insert is similar to **Add** but allows you to specify the location in the list to place the new list view item. Remember that the list is zero-based, so the first list view item is **Items[0]**, the second is **Items[1]**, and so on. When you insert an item into the list at a particular index, all subsequent index values are incremented.

Item PROPERTY

Objects Affected

TListItems

Purpose

The Item property allows you to access an individual item in the list using its index value.

Declaration

```
property Item[Index: Integer];
```

Example Syntax

```
// This procedure using Item will do exactly the same thing. . .
procedure TForm1.ListView1Editing(Sender: TObject; Item: TListItem;
  var AllowEdit: Boolean);
begin
  // Don't allow Item1's caption to be edited
  if ListView1.Selected = ListView1.Items.Item[0] then
    ListView1.Items.Item[0].CancelEdit
end;

// . . . as this one using only the Items property of TListView
procedure TForm1.ListView1Editing(Sender: TObject; Item: TListItem;
  var AllowEdit: Boolean);
begin
  // Don't allow Item1's caption to be edited
  if ListView1.Selected = ListView1.Items[0] then
    ListView1.Items[0].CancelEdit
end;
```

Description

The Item property is the actual array property of the TListItems class that enables individual items in the list to be accessed using array notation. Normally there is no reason to explicitly use Item, because a more concise syntax is available: **MyListView.Items.Item[0]** is equivalent to **MyListView.Items[0]**.

Owner PROPERTY

Objects Affected   TListItems

Purpose   The Owner property refers to the object that owns the TListItems object.

Declaration

```
property Owner: TCustomListView;
```

Example Syntax

```
// Get the name of the list items object's owner
Label1.Caption := ListView1.Items.Owner.Name;
```

Description   Owner is a run-time, read-only property that refers to the list view control that owns the list items object.

16

TParaAttributes

The **TParaAttributes** class is used to hold information about paragraphs in a rich edit control. Paragraphs are separated by hard carriage returns. The *current paragraph* is defined as the paragraph that contains the insertion point. The rich edit control has a property called **Paragraph** that is of type **TParaAttributes**—this property describes the current paragraph. Rich edit controls are covered in Chapter 64, "**TCustomEdit** and Its Descendants."

Figure 16-1 shows the derivation of **TParaAttributes**. Table 16-1 displays the properties and methods that are implemented by **TParaAttributes**.

Table 16-1 Properties and methods implemented by `TParaAttributes`

Use or Set This...	To Do This...	Inheritance
Alignment	Specify the alignment attributes of the paragraph.	None
Assign	Assign one persistent object to another.	TPersistent
ClassName	Get the name of the object's class.	TObject
ClassParent	Get the object's parent class.	TObject
ClassType	Get the object's actual type.	TObject
Create	Create a new TParaAttributes object.	TObject
Destroy	Destroy the object.	TObject
FirstIndent	Determine the size of the paragraph's first indent.	None
Free	Safely destroy the object.	TObject
InheritsFrom	Determine if the object is descended from a certain class.	TObject
InstanceSize	Determine the amount of memory allocated for the object.	TObject
LeftIndent	Determine the size of the paragraph's left indentation.	None
Numbering	Determine whether the paragraph is a bulleted list.	None
RightIndent	Determine the size of the paragraph's right indentation.	None
Tab	Determine the absolute tab stop positions for the paragraph.	None
TabCount	Determine the number of tab stops in the paragraph.	None

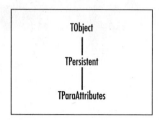

Figure 16-1 Derivation of TParaAttributes

Alignment PROPERTY

Objects Affected   TParaAttributes

Purpose   The Alignment property specifies the alignment attribute of the paragraph.

Declaration

```
property Alignment: TAlignment;
```

Example Syntax

```
// When an alignment button is clicked, the alignment
// is applied to the current paragraph
procedure TForm1.SpeedButton1Click(Sender: TObject);
begin
  RichEdit1.Paragraph.Alignment := taLeftJustify;
end;

procedure TForm1.SpeedButton2Click(Sender: TObject);
begin
  RichEdit1.Paragraph.Alignment := taCenter;
end;

procedure TForm1.SpeedButton3Click(Sender: TObject);
begin
  RichEdit1.Paragraph.Alignment := taRightJustify;
end;
```

Description   Alignment is a run-time-only property that is of type TAlignment. TAlignment is a set of alignment types; the possible values are taLeftJustify, taRightJustify, and taCenter. A rich edit control with three justification speedbuttons is shown in Figure 16-2.

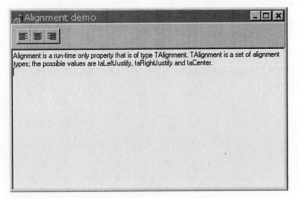

Figure 16-2 A rich edit control with three justification speedbuttons

FirstIndent PROPERTY

Objects Affected	TParaAttributes
Purpose	The FirstIndent property contains the size of the indent of the current paragraph's first line.
Declaration	

```
property FirstIndent: Longint;
```

Example Syntax

```
// Determine the current indent size when the button
// is clicked
procedure TForm1.Button1Click(Sender: TObject);
begin
  Label1.Caption := 'The indent of the current paragraph is ' +
    IntToStr(RichEdit1.Paragraph.FirstIndent) + ' pixels long.';
end;
```

Description   FirstIndent is a run-time-only property that determines the number of pixels of indentation for the first line of the current paragraph in a rich edit control. This is measured from the left edge of the client area of the rich edit control and does not account for any value in the LeftIndent property.

LeftIndent PROPERTY

Objects Affected   TParaAttributes

Purpose   The **LeftIndent** property contains the size of the left indentation of the current paragraph.

Declaration

```
property LeftIndent: Longint;
```

Example Syntax

```
// Determine the left indentation of the current paragraph when
// the button is clicked
procedure TForm1.Button1Click(Sender: TObject);
begin
  Label1.Caption := 'The left indentation of the current paragraph '
    + 'is ' + IntToStr(RichEdit1.Paragraph.LeftIndent)
    + ' pixels from the left side of the rich edit control.';
end;
```

Description   **LeftIndent** is a run-time-only property that measures the distance, in pixels, from the left edge of the rich edit control to the left margin of the current paragraph, exclusive of the first line (whose indentation is set with **FirstIndent**). If you decide to change the value of **LeftIndent**, you will probably want to change **FirstIndent** accordingly.

Numbering PROPERTY

Objects Affected   TParaAttributes

Purpose   The **Numbering** property determines whether the current paragraph is bulleted.

Declaration

```
property Numbering: TNumberingStyle;
```

Example Syntax

```
// Toggle Bulleting for the currently selected paragraph
procedure TForm1.SpeedButton4Click(Sender: TObject);
begin
  if RichEdit1.Paragraph.Numbering = nsNone then
    RichEdit1.Paragraph.Numbering := nsBullet
  else RichEdit1.Paragraph.Numbering := nsNone;
end;
```

Description   **Numbering** is type **TNumberingStyle**, which is defined as a set of two possible values: **nsNone** and **nsBullet**. If the **NumberingStyle** property of the current paragraph is set to **nsNone**, then it is not marked in any way. If it is set to **nsBullet**, bullet-style "numbering" is used and the paragraph is indented enough for the bullets.

RightIndent PROPERTY

Objects Affected   TParaAttributes

Purpose   The `RightIndent` property contains the size of the right indentation of the current paragraph.

Declaration

```
property RightIndent: LongInt;
```

Example Syntax

```
// Determine the right indentation of the current paragraph when
// the button is clicked
procedure TForm1.Button2Click(Sender: TObject);
begin
  Label1.Caption := 'The right indentation of the current paragraph '
    + 'is ' + IntToStr(RichEdit1.Paragraph.RightIndent)
    + ' pixels from the right side of the rich edit control.';
end;
```

Description   `RightIndent` determines the distance, in pixels, from the right margin of the current paragraph to the right edge of the rich edit control.

Tab PROPERTY

Objects Affected   TParaAttributes

Purpose   The `Tab` property contains an array of absolute tab stop positions.

Declaration

```
property Tab[Index: Byte];
```

Example Syntax

```
// Set the first tab stop in the paragraph to ten pixels
RichEdit1.Paragraph.Tab[0] := 10;
```

Description   `Tab` is an array of tab stop values that can be accessed by the index. The first tab stop has an index value of `0`. `Tab` can be used to change individual tab stop values for the current paragraph. The `Tab` values are measured in pixels, and are always relative to the left edge of the rich edit control.

TabCount PROPERTY

Objects Affected	TParaAttributes
Purpose	The TabCount property contains the number of tab stops in the current paragraph.
Declaration	

```
property TabCount: Integer;
```

Example Syntax

```
procedure TForm1.SpeedButton5Click(Sender: TObject);
begin
  Label1.Caption := IntToStr(RichEdit1.Paragraph.TabCount);
end;
```

Description   TabCount is a read-only property. To change a tab stop, use Tab.

17

TPicture

A picture object, encapsulated by **TPicture**, is a container for a **TGraphic** object, which in turn can be a bitmap, icon, metafile, or user-defined graphic. The **Graphic** property of **TPicture** indicates the type of graphic the picture object contains. Many of **TPicture**'s methods are polymorphic, allowing you to work with the different graphic types without having to specify graphic format–specific methods.

    TPicture objects are usually accessed through the **Picture** property of a **TImage** object. **Picture** is type **TPicture**.

    Figure 17-1 shows the ancestry of **TPicture**. Table 17-1 displays the properties, methods, and events that are implemented by **TPicture**.

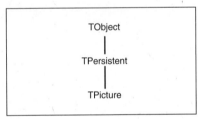

TObject

TPersistent

TPicture

Figure 17-1   Ancestry of **TPicture**

Table 17-1 Properties, methods, and events implemented by `TPicture`

Use or Set This...	To Do This...	Inheritance
Assign	Assign one persistent object to another.	TPersistent
Bitmap	Identify the bitmap graphic contained by the picture.	None
ClassName	Get the name of the object's class.	TObject
ClassParent	Get the object's parent class.	TObject
ClassType	Get the object's actual type.	TObject
Create	Construct a new object.	TObject
Destroy	Destroy the object.	TObject
Free	Safely destroy the object.	TObject
Graphic	Determine what type of graphic is contained by the picture object.	None
Height	Determine the height of the picture.	None
Icon	Identify the icon contained by the picture.	None
InheritsFrom	Determine if the object is descended from a certain class.	TObject
InstanceSize	Determine the amount of memory allocated for the object.	TObject
LoadFromFile	Load a graphic from disk.	None
Metafile	Identify the metafile graphic contained by the picture.	None
OnChange	Determine when the graphic is changed.	None
SaveToFile	Save a graphic image to disk.	None
Width	Determine the width of the picture.	None

`Bitmap` PROPERTY

Objects Affected   TPicture

Purpose   The `Bitmap` property identifies the bitmap graphic (if any) that is contained by the picture object.

Declaration

```
property Bitmap: TBitmap;
```

Example Syntax

```
// Load a bitmap into the first image control and
// copy it to the second image control
procedure TForm1.FormCreate(Sender: TObject);
begin
  Image1.Picture.LoadFromFile('C:\WINDOWS\CLOUDS.BMP');
  Image2.Picture.Bitmap := Image1.Picture.Bitmap;
end;
```

Description   If the `Graphic` property of the picture object indicates a bitmap graphic format, the `Bitmap` property contains the actual bitmap graphic contained by the picture object. In Figure 17-2, a bitmap is copied from one image to another using the `Bitmap` property.

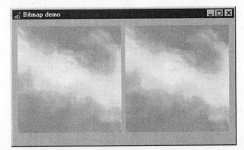

Figure 17-2 Copying the bitmap from one image to another

Graphic PROPERTY

Objects Affected	TPicture
Purpose	The Graphic property indicates what type (format) of graphic is contained by the picture object.
Declaration	

```
property Graphic: TGraphic;
```

Example Syntax

```
// Load a bitmap into the first image control and
// copy it to the second image control
procedure TForm1.FormCreate(Sender: TObject);
begin
  Image1.Picture.LoadFromFile('C:\WINDOWS\CLOUDS.BMP');
  Image2.Picture.Graphic := Image1.Picture.Graphic;
end;
```

Description   The Graphic property is type TGraphic, the base class for all graphic types in Delphi: TBitmap, TIcon, and TMetafile. The Graphic property of a TPicture object indicates the type of graphic that the TPicture object contains. Because TBitmap, TIcon, and TMetafile descend from TGraphic, the Graphic property can be used, as in the above example, when you can't be sure at run time with what type of graphic you are dealing.

Height PROPERTY

Objects Affected	TPicture
Purpose	The Height property determines the height of the picture object.
Declaration	

```
property Height: Integer;
```

Example Syntax

```
// Make the Image control the same size as the actual picture
// it contains
procedure TForm1.Button1Click(Sender: TObject);
begin
  Image1.Height := Image1.Picture.Height;
  Image1.Width := Image1.Picture.Width;
end;
```

Description `Height` is a read-only property that indicates the true height of the image contained by the `TPicture` object. The `Height` property of a `TImage` object, on the other hand, can be changed to cause the image to display in different sizes on the form. The `Height` and `Width` properties of `TPicture` are not valid if the graphic is a metafile, because metafiles are vector-based rather than raster graphics.

Icon PROPERTY

Objects Affected TPicture

Purpose The `Icon` property identifies the icon (if any) that is contained by the picture object.

Declaration

```
property Icon: TIcon;
```

Example Syntax

```
// Load the application's icon into the image
procedure TForm1.FormCreate(Sender: TObject);
begin
  Image1.Picture.Icon := Application.Icon;
end;
```

Description If the `Graphic` property of the picture object indicates an icon format, the `Icon` property contains the actual icon contained by the picture object.

LoadFromFile METHOD

Objects Affected TPicture

Purpose The `LoadFromFile` method replaces the graphic image in the picture object with one loaded from disk.

Declaration

```
procedure LoadFromFile(const Filename: String);
```

Parameters

Filename The name of the file you are loading into the picture.

Example Syntax

```
// Load a bitmap file into Image1
procedure TForm1.FormCreate(Sender: TObject);
begin
  Image1.Picture.LoadFromFile('C:\Windows\Red Blocks.bmp');
end;
```

Description   LoadFromFile loads a graphic image from disk into the picture object, using the *Filename* parameter to specify the file name of the graphic. To ensure that the image you load is displayed immediately, call the **Refresh** or **Repaint** method of the containing **Image** control.

Metafile PROPERTY

Objects Affected   TPicture

Purpose   The **Metafile** property identifies the metafile (if any) that is contained by the picture object.

Declaration

```
property Metafile: TMetafile;
```

Example Syntax

```
// Copy a metafile image to another image
procedure TForm1.FormCreate(Sender: TObject);
begin
  Image2.Picture.Metafile := Image1.Picture.Metafile;
end;
```

Description   If the **Graphic** property of the picture object indicates a normal or enhanced Windows metafile, the **Metafile** property identifies the actual metafile contained by the picture object.

Metafiles are denoted by the **.EMF** and **.WMF** extensions.

OnChange EVENT

Objects Affected   TPicture

Purpose   OnChange is triggered when a change has occurred to the picture object.

Declaration

```
property OnChange: TNotifyEvent;
```

Example Syntax

```
type
  TForm1 = class(TForm)
    Image1: TImage;
    Button3: TButton;
    Button4: TButton;
    procedure Button3Click(Sender: TObject);
```

continued on next page

continued from previous page

```
    procedure FormCreate(Sender: TObject);
    procedure Button4Click(Sender: TObject);

    // Added manually
    procedure OnChangePicture(Sender: TObject);
  private
    { Private declarations }
  public
    { Public declarations }
  end;

var
  Form1: TForm1;

implementation

{$R *.DFM}

// First, set the OnChange event handler for the
// Picture object in Image1 to the OnChangePicture
// procedure
procedure TForm1.FormCreate(Sender: TObject);
begin
  Image1.Picture.OnChange := OnChangePicture;
end;

// Every time a change occurs to the image contained by
// the TPicture object, refresh the image control so that
// the new image displays properly
procedure TForm1.OnChangePicture(Sender: TObject);
begin
  Image1.Refresh;
end;

// The following two event handlers load an image into
// the image control using the LoadFromFile method of
// its Picture property
procedure TForm1.Button3Click(Sender: TObject);
begin
  Image1.Picture.LoadFromFile('c:\windows\clouds.bmp');
end;

procedure TForm1.Button4Click(Sender: TObject);
begin
  Image1.Picture.LoadFromFile('d:\winnt\furry dog.bmp');
end;
```

Description   The **OnChange** event of a picture object is triggered when the graphic contained by the object is modified. One typical example of this, as illustrated by the code above, occurs when a new image is loaded from disk.

SaveToFile METHOD

Objects Affected	TPicture
Purpose	The SaveToFile method saves a graphic contained by a picture object to a file.
Declaration	

```
procedure SaveToFile(const Filename: String);
```

Parameters

Filename The file name to which you wish to save the graphic.

Example Syntax

```
// Save the graphic to disk
procedure TForm1.Button1Click(Sender: TObject);
begin
  Image1.Picture.SaveToFile('C:\Windows\Temp\My New Graphic.bmp');
end;
```

Description SaveToFile saves the graphic contained by the picture object to the file specified by the *Filename* parameter.

Width PROPERTY

Objects Affected	TPicture
Purpose	The Width property indicates the width of the picture object.
Declaration	

```
property Width: Integer;
```

Example Syntax

```
// Make the Image control the same size as the actual picture
// it contains
procedure TForm1.Button1Click(Sender: TObject);
begin
  Image1.Height := Image1.Picture.Height;
  Image1.Width := Image1.Picture.Width;
end;
```

Description Width is a read-only property that indicates the true width of the image contained by the TPicture object. The Width property of a TImage object, on the other hand, can be changed to cause the image to display in different sizes on the form. The Height and Width properties of TPicture are not valid if the graphic is a metafile, because metafiles are vector-based rather than raster graphics.

18

TTextAttributes

The **TTextAttributes** object is the type for two of **TRichEdit**'s properties:
DefAttributes and **SelAttributes**. **TTextAttributes** determines attributes such as
color, font size, and font style for these properties. **DefAttributes** describes the
default text style in the rich edit control, and **SelAttributes** describes the attributes
of selected text.

Figure 18-1 shows the lineage of **TTextAttributes**. Table 18-1 displays the properties that are implemented by **TTextAttributes**.

Table 18-1 Properties and methods implemented by `TTextAttributes`

Use or Set This...	To Do This...	Inheritance
Assign	Assign one persistent object to another.	TPersistent
ClassName	Get the name of the object's class.	TObject
ClassParent	Get the object's parent class.	TObject
ClassType	Get the object's actual type.	TObject
Color	Determine the color of text in a rich edit control.	None
ConsistentAttributes	Determine character formatting of text in a rich edit control.	None
Create	Construct a new object.	TObject
Destroy	Destroy the object.	TObject
Free	Safely destroy the object.	TObject
Height	Determine the horizontal size of text in a rich edit control.	None
InheritsFrom	Determine if the object is descended from a certain class.	TObject
InstanceSize	Determine the amount of memory allocated for the object.	TObject
Name	Determine the font used to display text.	None
Pitch	Determine the width of the text in a rich edit control.	None
Protected	Determine whether the text is read-only.	None
Size	Determine the point size of the text.	None
Style	Determine whether the text contains any styles.	None

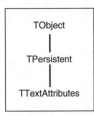

Figure 18-1 Lineage of `TTextAttributes`

Color PROPERTY

Objects Affected	`TTextAttributes`
Purpose	The `Color` property determines the color of text in a rich edit control.
Declaration	

```
property Color: TColor;
```

Example Syntax

```
// Change the color of all selected text to red
procedure TForm1.RichEdit1SelectionChange(Sender: TObject);
begin
  RichEdit1.SelAttributes.Color := clRed;
end;
```

Description   `Color` is of type `TColor`. Some examples of common color types include `clBlack` (black), `clGreen` (green), `clRed` (red), and `clWhite` (white).

ConsistentAttributes PROPERTY

Objects Affected	`TTextAttributes`
Purpose	The `ConsistentAttributes` property contains character formatting information for the selected text in a rich edit control.
Declaration	

```
property ConsistentAttributes: TConsistentAttributes;
```

Example Syntax

```
// Test to see if the selected text is consistently bold when the
// speed button is pressed. If the text is all bold, or none of the
// text is bold, it is consistent
procedure TForm1.SpeedButton6Click(Sender: TObject);
begin
  if caBold in RichEdit1.SelAttributes.ConsistentAttributes then
    Application.MessageBox(
    'The bold attribute is set consistently across the selection',
```

```
                        'Bold is consistent', MB_OK)
                      else
                        Application.MessageBox(
                        'The bold attribute is not set consistently across the selection',
                        'Bold is not consistent', MB_OK);
                      end;
```

Description ConsistentAttributes is a run-time, read-only property. You can use ConsistentAttributes with the SelAttributes property of the rich edit control to determine which attributes are consistent (the same) across the selected text. It does not set the text to any of those attributes. To do this, you would need to set the properties of SelAttributes to new values.

While you could use ConsistentAttributes with DefAttributes, this does not make sense, because the attributes of text that has yet to be entered are already consistent. You can change the default font characteristics that will be applied to newly entered text by adjusting the properties of DefAttributes.

ConsistentAttributes is type TConsistentAttributes, which is a set of the possible values shown in Table 18-2.

Table 18-2 Values supported by ConsistentAttributes

This Value...	Indicates...
caBold	That all characters in the selected text are bold or nonbold.
caColor	That the color of all characters in the selected text is the same.
caFace	That all characters in the selected text are of the same typeface.
caItalic	That all characters in the selected text are italic or nonitalic.
caSize	That the size of the font for all characters in the selected text is the same.
caStrikeout	That all characters in the selected text are struck out or not struck out.
caUnderline	That all characters in the selected text are underlined or not underlined.
caProtected	That all characters in the selected text are read-only or not read-only.

Height PROPERTY

Objects Affected TTextAttributes

Purpose The Height property determines the height of the font used to render text in the rich edit control.

Declaration

```
property Height;
```

Example Syntax

```
// Change height of selected text to 20 pixels
procedure TForm1.RichEdit1SelectionChange(Sender: TObject);
begin
  RichEdit1.SelAttributes.Height := 20;
end;
```

Description

`Height` is used to set or get the height, in pixels, of the font. With a rich edit control, you will typically be more concerned with a font's point size than with its height. You can determine the point size of the font with the `Size` property.

Name PROPERTY

Objects Affected   `TTextAttributes`

Purpose   The `Name` property indicates the name of the font used to render text in a rich edit control.

Declaration

```
property Name: TFontName;
```

Example Syntax

```
// Change font of selected text to Courier New
procedure TForm1.RichEdit1SelectionChange(Sender: TObject);
begin
  RichEdit1.SelAttributes.Name := 'courier new';
end;
```

Description   Do not confuse this `Name` property with the `Name` property used to identify components on your form. This property simply identifies the name of the font. Note that the specified font name must be 32 characters or less in length.

Pitch PROPERTY

Objects Affected   `TTextAttributes`

Purpose   The `Pitch` property determines the width of the characters in the font used to render text in a rich edit control.

Declaration

```
property Pitch: TFontPitch;
```

Example Syntax

```
// Change font of selected text to Courier New with a
// height of 12 and a fixed width pitch
procedure TForm1.RichEdit1SelectionChange(Sender: TObject);
```

```
begin
  RichEdit1.SelAttributes.Name := 'courier new';
  RichEdit1.SelAttributes.Height := 12;
  RichEdit1.SelAttributes.Pitch := fpDefault;
end;
```

Description Pitch can be set to one of three values: fpDefault, fpFixed, or fpVariable. Setting Pitch to fpDefault will cause the default pitch style to be used for the font specified in the Name property of the text. The fpFixed and fpVariable values can be used to explicitly set the pitch: a value of fpFixed causes each character in the font to have the same width, while a value of fpVariable allows different characters within a font to have unique widths. True Type fonts set to fpFixed will not be displayed as fixed width, and fixed width fonts cannot be made variable width, so you will typically only need to use fpDefault when you know the type of font that is being used.

The fpFixed and fpVariable values are most useful when you do not know what type of font is being used and you want to control how the text is displayed—provided it is a font that will allow you to do so.

The actual point size of the text is determined by the Size property.

Protected PROPERTY

Objects Affected TTextAttributes

Purpose The Protected property determines whether text in a rich edit control is read-only.

Declaration

```
property Protected: Boolean;
```

Example Syntax

```
// Do not allow selected text to be deleted
procedure TForm1.RichEdit1SelectionChange(Sender: TObject);
begin
  RichEdit1.SelAttributes.Protected := True;
end;
```

Description If the Protected property is set to True, the text is read-only and cannot be modified. If it is False, then the text can be modified.

Size PROPERTY

Objects Affected TTextAttributes

Purpose The Size property determines the point size of the font used to display text in a rich edit control.

Declaration

```
property Size: Integer;
```

Example Syntax

```
// Change point size of selected text to 18
procedure TForm1.RichEdit1SelectionChange(Sender: TObject);
begin
  RichEdit1.SelAttributes.Size := 18;
end;
```

Description

The `Size` property is used when you want to set the point size of text in a rich edit control. You can use the **Height** property when you need to specify a particular pixel height. The two properties are mutually exclusive—when you set the **Size** property, the **Height** property becomes −1. Likewise, if you set the **Height** property, the **Size** property becomes −1.

Style PROPERTY

Objects Affected TTextAttributes

Purpose The **Style** property determines whether the text in a rich edit control is bold, italic, underlined, struck out, or any combination of the four.

Declaration

```
property Style: TFontStyles;
```

Example Syntax

```
// Change style of selected text to bold and italic
procedure TForm1.RichEdit1SelectionChange(Sender: TObject);
begin
  RichEdit1.SelAttributes.Style := [fsBold] + [fsItalic];
end;
```

Description

Style is type **TFontStyles**, which is a set of the following values: **fsBold**, **fsItalic**, **fsUnderline**, and **fsStrikeout**. It can have multiple values specified at once. Note that since **TFontStyles** is a set, the style names must appear in brackets as they do in the above example.

19

TTreeNode AND TTreeNodes

A *tree node*, encapsulated by the **TTreeNode** class, is an individual element in a *tree view* control (type **TTreeView**). Tree node objects are grouped in a **TTreeNodes** object that maintains the list of the tree nodes that comprise the tree view control. **TTreeNodes** is covered later in this chapter; tree view controls are described in Chapter 60, "**TCustomTreeView** and **TTreeView**."

Generally, tree nodes are accessed by their index in the **Items** property of a tree view control. The **Items** property is a **TTreeNodes** object.

Figure 19-1 shows the derivation of **TTreeNodes** and **TTreeNode**. Table 19-1 displays the properties and methods that are implemented by **TTreeNode**.

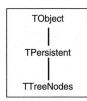

Figure 19-1 Derivation of
TTreeNodes and **TTreeNode**

Table 19-1 Properties and methods implemented by `TTreeNode`

Use or Set This...	To Do This...	Inheritance
AbsoluteIndex	Determine the index of the tree node.	None
AlphaSort	Sort the children of the tree node alphabetically.	None
Assign	Assign one persistent object to another.	TPersistent
ClassName	Get the name of the object's class.	TObject
ClassParent	Get the object's parent class.	TObject
ClassType	Get the object's actual type.	TObject
Collapse	Collapse the tree node.	None
Count	Retrieve the number of children contained by the tree node.	None
Create	Create a new tree node object.	TObject
Cut	Determine whether the tree node is selected as part of a cut-and-paste operation.	None
Data	Determine the external data associated with a tree node.	None
Delete	Delete a tree node from the list.	None
DeleteChildren	Delete all the children of a tree node.	None
Deleting	Indicate whether the tree node is being deleted.	None
Destroy	Destroy the object.	TObject
DropTarget	Determine whether the tree node is a drop target.	None
EditText	Begin in-place editing of the node's caption.	None
EndEdit	End the editing of a tree node caption.	None
Expand	Expand a tree node.	None
Expanded	Determine if the tree node is expanded.	None
Focused	Determine if the tree node has the focus.	None
Free	Safely destroy the object.	TObject
GetFirstChild	Retrieve the tree node's first child node.	None
GetLastChild	Retrieve the tree node's last child node.	None
GetNext	Retrieve the next tree node.	None
GetNextChild	Retrieve the next child node.	None
GetNextSibling	Retrieve the next sibling tree node.	None
GetNextVisible	Retrieve the next visible tree node.	None
GetPrev	Retrieve the previous tree node.	None
GetPrevChild	Retrieve the previous child node.	None
GetPrevSibling	Retrieve the previous sibling tree node.	None
Handle	Access API calls with the tree node.	None
HasAsParent	Determine if the specified node is a parent of the tree node.	None
HasChildren	Determine if the tree node has children.	None
ImageIndex	Contain the associated image index.	None
Index	Contain the index identity of the tree node.	None

Use or Set This...	To Do This...	Inheritance
IndexOf	Determine the position of a child node to the calling node relative to the other children of the calling node.	None
InheritsFrom	Determine if the object is descended from a certain class.	TObject
InstanceSize	Determine the amount of memory allocated for the object.	TObject
IsVisible	Determine whether the tree node is visible.	None
Item	Access the children of a tree node.	None
Level	Determine the level of the tree node within the tree view.	None
MakeVisible	Make the tree node visible.	None
MoveTo	Move the tree node to a new location.	None
OverlayIndex	Determine the image that will overlay itself on the tree node.	None
Parent	Determine the parent of the tree node.	None
SelectedIndex	Determine the image used when the tree node is selected.	None
StateIndex	Determine the image used to display the tree node.	None
Text	Set or retrieve the tree node's caption.	None
TreeView	Determine which tree view control owns the tree node.	None

AbsoluteIndex PROPERTY

Objects Affected   TTreeNode

Purpose   The **AbsoluteIndex** property determines the index of the tree node relative to the first tree node in the list.

Declaration

```
property AbsoluteIndex: Integer;
```

Example Syntax

```
// This allows you to enter an index value in Edit1
// and print out its absolute index value in Edit2
// when you click Button1
procedure TForm1.Button1Click(Sender: TObject);
begin
  Edit2.Text :=
IntToStr(TreeView1.Items[StrToInt(Edit1.Text)].AbsoluteIndex);
end;
```

Description   This run-time, read-only property contains the index of the current tree node relative to the first, or root, tree node, which is identified as index 0. Tree nodes are indexed sequentially starting with the root tree node.

A tree node with child nodes is indexed as one less than the absolute index value for its first child.

AlphaSort METHOD

Objects Affected	`TTreeNode`
Purpose	The `AlphaSort` method sorts the children of the tree node alphabetically by label.
Declaration	

```
function AlphaSort: Boolean;
```

Example Syntax

```
// Sort the children of the first node
procedure TForm1.Button1Click(Sender: TObject);
begin
  if (TreeView1.Items[0].AlphaSort) = True then
    Edit1.Text := 'Sort complete'
  else Edit1.Text := 'Sort unsuccessful';
end;
```

Description   `AlphaSort` only sorts the immediate children of the current tree node. If the sort is successful, `AlphaSort` returns `True`. Otherwise, it returns `False`. Figure 19-2 shows a tree view before being sorted. Figure 19-3 shows the tree view after sorting with AlphaSort.

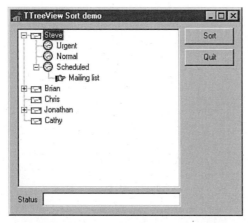

Figure 19-2   The tree view before sorting

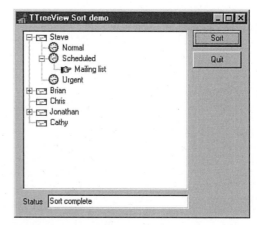

Figure 19-3   The tree view after sorting

Collapse METHOD

Objects Affected	TTreeNode
Purpose	The Collapse method collapses a tree node.
Declaration	

```
procedure Collapse(Recurse: Boolean);
```

Parameters

Recurse Set to True if you want the tree node's children to collapse as well. Otherwise, set to False.

Example Syntax

```
// Collapse the first node and all of its children
procedure TForm1.Button1Click(Sender: TObject);
begin
  TreeView1.Items[0].Collapse(True);
end;
```

Description When a tree node is collapsed, it "closes," hiding its children, if any. If the node does have children, a plus sign appears next to the tree node's icon. When a tree node with children is expanded, the plus sign becomes a minus sign.

The *Recurse* parameter determines if the children of the node should collapse as well. If *Recurse* is True, then all of the tree node's children will collapse. If *Recurse* is False, the children will be hidden as the node collapses but they will not themselves collapse—expanding the node will reveal the children in their previous, expanded state.

Count PROPERTY

Objects Affected	TTreeNode
Purpose	The Count property contains the number of the tree node's immediate children.
Declaration	

```
property Count: Integer;
```

Example Syntax

```
procedure TForm1.Button1Click(Sender: TObject);
begin
  Edit1.Text := IntToStr(TreeView1.Items[0].Count);
end;
```

Description Count will return the number of children directly located off a tree node. If any of those children have children of their own, they are not included in the value returned by Count.

Cut PROPERTY

Objects Affected	TTreeNode
Purpose	The Cut property determines whether the tree node is selected as part of a cut-and-paste operation.
Declaration	

```
property Cut: Boolean;
```

Example Syntax

```
// Set the Cut and Paste state of the first tree node item to False
TreeNode1.Items[0].Cut := False
```

Description Cut is a run-time-only property. If Cut is True, the tree node is part of a cut-and-paste operation. If Cut is False, the node is not being cut. Typically, you will use Cut to test whether a particular tree node is part of a cut-and-paste selection and then respond accordingly. While you could *set* Cut to True or False manually, you shouldn't normally need to do this.

Data PROPERTY

Objects Affected	TTreeNode
Purpose	The Data property determines the data that is associated with a tree node.
Declaration	

```
property Data: Pointer;
```

Example Syntax

```
var
  Form1: TForm1;
  MyData: PChar;

implementation

{$R *.DFM}

// Set the data property of the first tree node
// in TreeView1
procedure TForm1.FormCreate(Sender: TObject);
begin
  MyData := 'This is the first tree node';
  TreeView1.Items[0].Data := MyData;
end;

// If the first tree node is selected, display its
// data in the edit box
procedure TForm1.TreeView1Click(Sender: TObject);
begin
```

```
    If (TreeView1.Items[0].Selected) = True then
        Edit1.Text := String(TreeView1.Items[0].Data);
end;
```

Description
This run-time-only property points to data you would like to associate with a tree node object. Every application will have different needs with respect to the data that is associated with each node in a tree view control. Since **Data** is a generic pointer, it can refer to any type of object. In the example code above, the **Data** pointer for the first tree node refers to a string. You can have the **Data** property point to different object types for each node.

Delete METHOD

Objects Affected   TTreeNode

Purpose   The **Delete** method deletes the tree node.

Declaration

```
procedure Delete;
```

Example Syntax

```
// Delete the first tree node
procedure TForm1.Button1Click(Sender: TObject);
begin
    TreeView1.Items[0].Delete;
end;
```

Description
The tree node that calls this method is deleted. If the node has children, they are deleted as well.

DeleteChildren METHOD

Objects Affected   TTreeNode

Purpose   The **DeleteChildren** method deletes all of the tree node's children.

Declaration

```
procedure DeleteChildren;
```

Example Syntax

```
// Delete all of the first node's children
procedure TForm1.Button1Click(Sender: TObject);
begin
    TreeView1.Items[0].DeleteChildren;
end;
```

Description
DeleteChildren deletes all of the children and subchildren of the node calling it.

Deleting PROPERTY

Objects Affected	TTreeNode
Purpose	The `Deleting` property indicates whether the tree node is in the process of being deleted.
Declaration	

```
property Deleting: Boolean;
```

Example Syntax

```
// ... code to delete node here

  repeat
  until not TreeView1.Items[0].Deleting;

// ... continue processing here
```

Description   `Deleting` is a run-time, read-only property that is set to `True` when the tree node's `Destroy` method has been called and the node is about to be deleted. You may want to query this property if you want to ensure that certain processing does not commence until after deletion is complete.

DropTarget PROPERTY

Objects Affected	TTreeNode
Purpose	The `DropTarget` property determines whether the tree node is selected as a drag-and-drop target.
Declaration	

```
property DropTarget: Boolean;
```

Example Syntax

```
// Set the first tree node to a drop target
procedure TForm1.FormCreate(Sender: TObject);
begin
  TreeView1.Items[0].DropTarget := True;
end;
```

Description   This run-time-only property determines whether the tree node can be the target for a drag-and-drop operation. If the tree node is selected as a drag-and-drop target, the state of the node will indicate this by using an image from its associated state index list.

EditText METHOD

Objects Affected	TTreeNode
Purpose	The EditText method begins in-place editing of the tree node's caption.
Declaration	

```
function EditText: Boolean;
```

Example Syntax

```
// Start the editing of the selected tree node caption when the
// Ctrl+e key combination is typed
procedure TForm1.TreeView1KeyUp(Sender: TObject; var Key: Word;
  Shift: TShiftState);
begin
  if (Key = ord('e')) or (Key = ord('E')) and (Shift = [ssCtrl]) then
    TreeView1.Selected.EditText
end;
```

Description Typically, the caption of a tree node can be edited in-place by slowly clicking twice on the caption and typing in the new name for the tree node. EditText allows you to manually initiate the in-place editing of a tree node's caption immediately.

EndEdit METHOD

Objects Affected	TTreeNode
Purpose	The EndEdit method ends the editing of a tree node's caption.
Declaration	

```
procedure EndEdit(Cancel: Boolean);
```

Parameters

Cancel Determines whether the user can cancel the operation.

Example Syntax

```
// Roundabout way to not allowing the user to edit tree node
// captions
procedure TForm1.TreeView1Editing(Sender: TObject; Node: TTreeNode;
  var AllowEdit: Boolean);
begin
  TreeView1.Selected.EndEdit(True);
end;
```

Description Like EditText, EndEdit is a way to manually affect the editing of a tree node caption; in this case, the editing of the caption will immediately cease when EndEdit is called. Normally, users will end the edit themselves.

Expand METHOD

Objects Affected	TTreeNode
Purpose	The Expand method expands the current tree node.
Declaration	

```
procedure Expand(Recurse: Boolean);
```

Parameters

Recurse   Set to True if you want all children expanded as well.

Example Syntax

```
// Expand all of the nodes in TreeView1 when
// the button is clicked
procedure TForm1.Button1Click(Sender: TObject);
var x: Integer;
begin
  for x := 0 to TreeView1.Items.Count - 1 do
    TreeView1.Items[x].Expand(True);
end;
```

Description   The Expand method expands the tree node and sets the Expanded property to True. When a tree node is expanded, a minus sign will appear in the box next to the node's icon, indicating that the node can be collapsed. See Collapse for details.

The *Recurse* parameter should be set to True if you would like all of the node's children and subchildren to be expanded as well. Otherwise, set *Recurse* to False and only the node itself will expand.

Expanded PROPERTY

Objects Affected	TTreeNode
Purpose	The Expanded property determines whether the tree node is expanded.
Declaration	

```
property Expanded: Boolean;
```

Example Syntax

```
// Expand and collapse the first tree node as the
// button is clicked
procedure TForm1.ChangeButtonClick(Sender: TObject);
begin
  TreeView1.Items[0].Expanded := not TreeView1.Items[0].Expanded;
end;
```

Description   **Expanded** determines whether the node is expanded. Interestingly enough, you can also assign a **True** or **False** value to **Expanded**, causing the node to expand or collapse, respectively. This call does not expand or collapse the node's children. Following is a block of code functionally equivalent to—though less elegant than—the code in the example above:

```
procedure TForm1.Button4Click(Sender: TObject);
begin
  if TreeView1.Items[0].Expanded = True then
    TreeView1.Items[0].Expanded := False
  else TreeView1.Items[0].Expanded := True
end;
```

Focused PROPERTY

Objects Affected   **TTreeNode**

Purpose   The **Focused** property determines if the tree node has the focus.

Declaration

```
property Focused: Boolean;
```

Example Syntax

```
// Focus the first node when the form is created
procedure TForm1.FormCreate(Sender: TObject);
begin
  TreeView1.Items[0].Focused := True;
end;
```

Description   This run-time-only property determines if the tree node is focused, that is, surrounded by a bounding rectangle.

Only one node in a tree view can be focused at a time.

GetFirstChild METHOD

Objects Affected   **TTreeNode**

Purpose   The **GetFirstChild** method returns the first child of the tree node.

Declaration

```
function GetFirstChild: TTreeNode;
```

Example Syntax

```
// Expand the first node and its first child
procedure TForm1.Button1Click(Sender: TObject);
begin
  TreeView1.Items[0].Expanded := True;
  TreeView1.Items[0].GetFirstChild.Expanded := True;
end;
```

Description   If the tree node has no children, **GetFirstChild** returns **Nil**.

GetLastChild METHOD

Objects Affected	TTreeNode
Purpose	The GetLastChild method returns the last child of the tree node.
Declaration	

```
function GetLastChild: TTreeNode;
```

Example Syntax

```
// Expand the last child of the first tree node
procedure TForm1.Button1Click(Sender: TObject);
begin
  TreeView1.Items[0].GetLastChild.Expanded := True;
end;
```

Description

If the tree node has no children, GetLastChild returns Nil. GetLastChild works with the immediate children of the tree node, not subchildren.

GetNext METHOD

Objects Affected	TTreeNode
Purpose	The GetNext method returns the next tree node.
Declaration	

```
function GetNext: TTreeNode;
```

Example Syntax

```
// Expand the next node after the first node,
// regardless of whether it is a child node,
// a sibling node, or visible.
procedure TForm1.Button1Click(Sender: TObject);
begin
  TreeView1.Items[0].GetNext.Expanded := True;
end;
```

Description

GetNext returns the next tree node regardless of whether it is a child node, is a node at the same level in the tree, or is visible. If you start at the root node and make repeated calls to GetNext, you will systematically traverse each subbranch of the tree before proceeding to the next subbranch. To get the next node at the same level as the calling node, use GetNextSibling. If you would like to get the next visible node, use GetNextVisible. If you would like to get the next child node, use GetNextChild.

If the tree node is the last node in the tree view, GetNext returns Nil.

GetNextChild METHOD

Objects Affected	TTreeNode
Purpose	The GetNextChild method returns the next child node.
Declaration	

```
function GetNextChild(Value: TTreeNode): TTreeNode;
```

Parameters

Value   The tree node where the search begins.

Example Syntax

```
// A convoluted way to select the second child
// of the first tree node
procedure TForm1.Button1Click(Sender: TObject);
begin
  with TreeView1.Items[0] do
    GetNextChild(GetFirstChild).Selected := True;
end;
```

Description   GetNextChild uses the *Value* parameter to determine where to start searching—it returns the next child node after the node specified by the *Value* parameter. If there is no child tree node after *Value*, Nil is returned.

GetNextSibling METHOD

Objects Affected	TTreeNode
Purpose	The GetNextSibling method returns the next tree node that exists at the same level as the calling node.

Declaration

```
function GetNextSibling: TTreeNode;
```

Example Syntax

```
// Select the second tree node
procedure TForm1.Button1Click(Sender: TObject);
begin
  TreeView1.Items[0].GetNextSibling.Selected := True;
end;
```

Description   GetNextSibling returns the next tree node, even if it isn't visible. If there is no next sibling node, it will return Nil.

To retrieve the next node, regardless of its level in the tree hierarchy, use GetNext.

GetNextVisible METHOD

Objects Affected	TTreeNode
Purpose	The **GetNextVisible** method returns the next visible tree node.
Declaration	

```
function GetNextVisible: TTreeNode;
```

Example Syntax

```
// Select the next visible node after the first node.
// If the first node is expanded, it will select the
// first child node of the first node. Otherwise, the
// second node will be selected.
procedure TForm1.Button1Click(Sender: TObject);
begin
  TreeView1.Items[0].GetNextVisible.Selected := True;
end;
```

Description
A tree node is visible if its parent is expanded. **GetNextVisible** will return the next visible tree node, regardless of its level within the tree view. If there is no visible tree node after the calling tree node, **GetNextVisible** returns **Nil**.

GetPrev METHOD

Objects Affected	TTreeNode
Purpose	The **GetPrev** method returns the previous node.
Declaration	

```
function GetPrev: TTreeNode;
```

Example Syntax

```
// Select the node above the last node in the tree view. If
// the node above the last node is expanded, the last child
// of that node will be selected
procedure TForm1.Button1Click(Sender: TObject);
begin
  TreeView1.Items[TreeView1.Items.Count - 1].GetPrev.Selected := True;
end;
```

Description
GetPrev returns the previous node regardless of its level or whether it is visible. To return the previous visible node, use **GetPrevVisible**. To return the previous child node, use **GetPrevChild**.

GetPrevChild METHOD

Objects Affected	TTreeNode
Purpose	GetPrevChild returns the child node that precedes the calling node.
Declaration	

```
function GetPrevChild(Value: TTreeNode): TTreeNode;
```

Parameters

Value   The tree node where the search begins.

Example Syntax

```
// Select the first child of the last node in the tree view
procedure TForm1.Button1Click(Sender: TObject);
begin
  with TreeView1 do
    Items[0].GetPrevChild(Items[Items.Count - 1]).Selected := true;
end;
```

Description   GetPrevChild returns the previous child node before the node specified by the *Value* parameter. If there is no previous child node, GetPrevChild returns Nil.

GetPrevSibling METHOD

Objects Affected	TTreeNode
Purpose	The GetPrevSibling method returns the previous node at the same level as the current node.
Declaration	

```
function GetPrevSibling: TTreeNode;
```

Example Syntax

```
// Print the text from the previous node in Edit1
procedure TForm1.TreeView1Click(Sender: TObject);
begin
  if TreeView1.Selected = TreeView1.Items[0] then
    Edit1.Text := ''
  else
    Edit1.Text := TreeView1.Selected.GetPrevSibling.Text;
end;
```

Description   GetPrevSibling will return the node directly above the current node that is on the same level, regardless of whether it is visible. If there is no sibling node above the current node, GetPrevSibling returns Nil.

HandLe PROPERTY

Objects Affected	TTreeNode
Purpose	Handle contains the Windows handle for the tree node.
Declaration	

```
property Handle: HWND;
```

Example Syntax

```
procedure TForm1.FormCreate(Sender: TObject);
var MyHandle: HWND;
begin
  MyHandle := TreeView1.Items[0].Handle;

  // . . .
end;
```

Description   A tree node's handle is useful if you need to make API calls.

HasAsParent METHOD

Objects Affected	TTreeNode
Purpose	The HasAsParent method tests to see whether another node is the parent of the current node.
Declaration	

```
function HasAsParent(Value: TTreeNode): Boolean;
```

Parameters

Value   The node you are testing for parentage.

Example Syntax

```
// Determine whether the selected node is a child node
// of the first tree node
procedure TForm1.TreeView1Click(Sender: TObject);
begin
  if TreeView1.Selected.HasAsParent(TreeView1.Items[0]) = True then
    Edit1.Text := 'the current node is a child of the first node.'
  else Edit1.Text := '';
end;
```

Description   You use the HasAsParent method to test whether the node identified by
the *Value* is the parent of the current tree node.

HasChildren PROPERTY

Objects Affected	TTreeNode
Purpose	The HasChildren property tests whether the tree node has children.
Declaration	

```
property HasChildren: Boolean;
```

Example Syntax

```
// Expand and collapse nodes by single-clicking them
procedure TForm1.TreeView1Click(Sender: TObject);
begin
  if TreeView1.Selected.HasChildren = True
    and TreeView1.Selected.Expanded = False then
    TreeView1.Selected.Expanded := True
  else if TreeView1.Selected.HasChildren = True
    and TreeView1.Selected.Expanded = True then
    TreeView1.Selected.Expanded := False;
end;
```

Description This run-time-only property is **True** if the node has children and **False** if it does not.

ImageIndex PROPERTY

Objects Affected	TTreeNode
Purpose	The ImageIndex property indicates which image in the tree view's associated image list will be seen next to the tree node's caption.
Declaration	

```
property ImageIndex: Integer;
```

Example Syntax

```
// Change the image index for the first node
procedure TForm1.Button1Click(Sender: TObject);
begin
  TreeView1.Items[0].ImageIndex := 3;
end;
```

Description The image specified by this property is the image that will be displayed when the node is *not* selected. The associated image list is an array of images, specified by the **Images** property of the tree view control. Normally, you will pair the images in this list to the individual tree nodes at design time using the Tree View Items Editor, but you can modify the values at run time or associate an image with a tree node that you dynamically create.

Index PROPERTY

Objects Affected	TTreeNode
Purpose	The Index property indicates the index of the current tree node.
Declaration	

```
property Index: Integer;
```

Example Syntax

```
// Identify the current node
procedure TForm1.TreeView1Click(Sender: TObject);
begin
  Label1.Caption := 'The current node is ' +
    IntToStr(TreeView1.Selected.Index);
end;
```

Description

Index is a read-only property that identifies the tree node within its parent's Index array. Normally, you will access individual tree node objects in the Items property of a tree view control. The first tree node in the Items property has a value of 0.

IndexOf PROPERTY

Objects Affected	TTreeNode
Purpose	The IndexOf property returns the position of a child node to the calling node relative to the other children of the calling node.
Declaration	

```
function IndexOf(Value: TTreeNode): Integer;
```

Parameter

Value The node whose position is to be tested.

Example Syntax

```
// Determine whether the selected node is a child of the first node
procedure TForm1.Button4Click(Sender: TObject);
var
  x: Integer;
begin
  x := TreeView1.Items[0].IndexOf(TreeView1.Selected);
  if x = -1 then
    Label2.Caption :=
    'The selected node is not a child of the first node'
  else
    Label2.Caption :=
    'The selected node is child[' + IntToStr(x) + '] of the first node';
end;
```

Description	A parent node calls **IndexOf** and passes the node that is to be tested as the *Value* parameter. If the node identified by the *Value* parameter is not an immediate child of the calling node, **IndexOf** returns **–1**. If the node identified by *Value* is an immediate child of the calling node, **IndexOf** will return that child node's position within the group of children of the calling node, where the first child is **0**, the second is **1**, and so on.

IsVisible PROPERTY

Objects Affected	TTreeNode
Purpose	The **IsVisible** property indicates whether the tree node is visible.
Declaration	

```
property IsVisible: Boolean;
```

Example Syntax	

```
procedure TForm1.TreeView1Click(Sender: TObject);
begin
  if TreeView1.Items[0].IsVisible = True then
    Label1.Caption := 'The first tree node is visible';
end;
```

Description	This property is run-time and read-only. If **IsVisible** is **True**, the tree node is visible. If it is **False**, it is hidden by a collapsed node.

Item PROPERTY

Objects Affected	TTreeNode
Purpose	The **Item** property allows you to access the children of the tree node by index value.
Declaration	

```
property Item[Index: Integer]: TTreeNode;
```

Example Syntax	

```
// Change the caption titles for the first node's children
TreeView1.Items[0].Item[0].Text := 'Deferred';
TreeView1.Items[0].Item[1].Text := 'Immediate';
```

Description	**Item** is a run-time-only property. Each tree node maintains an array of its child nodes in which the first child node is **Item[0]**, the second is **Item[1]**, and so on. This property allows you to access these children.

Level PROPERTY

Objects Affected	TTreeNode
Purpose	The Level property indicates the level of the current tree node within the tree view control.
Declaration	

```
property Level: Integer;
```

Example Syntax

```
// Display the level of the current node
procedure TForm1.TreeView1Click(Sender: TObject);
begin
  Label1.Caption := IntToStr(TreeView1.Selected.Level);
end;
```

Description Level is run-time and read-only. The uppermost level is 0. The children of the nodes at level 0 are at level 1; their children are at level 2.

MakeVisible METHOD

Objects Affected	TTreeNode
Purpose	The MakeVisible method makes a tree node visible.
Declaration	

```
procedure MakeVisible;
```

Example Syntax

```
// Make the seventh tree node visible, expanding
// its parent if necessary
procedure TForm1.Button1Click(Sender: TObject);
begin
  TreeView1.Items[6].MakeVisible;
end;
```

Description MakeVisible will make a tree node that is the child of a collapsed node visible by expanding the parent node. If the tree node is already visible, MakeVisible has no effect.

MoveTo METHOD

Objects Affected	TTreeNode
Purpose	The MoveTo method moves a tree node to another location in the tree view.
Declaration	

```
procedure MoveTo(Destination: TTreeNode; Mode: TNodeAttachMode);
```

Parameters

Destination   The destination node for the move operation.

Mode   The method used to move the node.

Example Syntax

```
// Move the first tree node
procedure TForm1.Button1Click(Sender: TObject);
begin
  TreeView1.Items[0].MoveTo(TreeView1.Items[1], naInsert);
end;
```

Description   MoveTo moves the tree node to a new location, determined by the *Destination* parameter, reattaching itself to the tree using the method identified by the *Mode* parameter. The *Mode* parameter has the possible values listed in Table 19-2.

Table 19-2 Possible values of the *Mode* parameter

Use This...	To Do This...
naAdd	Add the node to the end of the tree view.
naAddFirst	Add the node at the beginning of the tree view.
naAddChild	Add the node as the last child of *Destination*.
naAddChildFirst	Add the node as the first child of *Destination*.
naInsert	Insert the node after *Destination* as a sibling.

OverlayIndex PROPERTY

Objects Affected   TTreeNode

Purpose   The OverlayIndex property determines the image that will act as an overlay mask for the tree node.

Declaration

```
property OverlayIndex: Integer;
```

Example Syntax

```
// Set the overlay index for all tree nodes
procedure TForm1.FormCreate(Sender: TObject);
var x: Integer;
begin
  for x := 0 to TreeView1.Items.Count - 1 do
    TreeView1.Items[x].OverlayIndex := 7;
end;
```

Description   This run-time-only property determines the image in the associated image list that will be used as an overlay mask for the tree node. An overlay mask is an image that is drawn over another image. In Windows 95, the little arrow image that is added to shortcut icons is an overlay mask—it is used to indicate that the icon is a shortcut. You might use an overlay mask on a tree node to indicate that it is no longer available, for example.

Parent PROPERTY

Objects Affected   TTreeNode

Purpose   The Parent property identifies the parent node of the current tree node.

Declaration

```
property Parent: TTreeNode;
```

Example Syntax

```
// Collapse the parent of the selected node when the tree view is
// right-clicked
procedure TForm1.TreeView1MouseUp(Sender: TObject; Button: TMouseButton;
  Shift: TShiftState; X, Y: Integer);
begin
  if Button = mbRight then
    if TreeView1.Selected.Parent <> nil then
      TreeView1.Selected.Parent.Collapse(True);
end;
```

Description   The parent of the current tree node is one level higher in the tree view hierarchy and is its immediate ancestor.

SelectedIndex PROPERTY

Objects Affected   TTreeNode

Purpose   The SelectedIndex property contains the index of the image to use when the node is selected.

Declaration

```
property SelectedIndex: Integer;
```

Example Syntax

```
// Set the selected index for all tree nodes
procedure TForm1.FormCreate(Sender: TObject);
var x: Integer;
begin
  for x := 0 to TreeView1.Items.Count - 1 do
    TreeView1.Items[x].SelectedIndex := 0;
end;
```

Description	The **SelectedIndex** property contains the index of the image, found in the tree view's associated image list, that will display when the tree node is selected. This property is run-time-only.

StateIndex PROPERTY

Objects Affected	TTreeNode
Purpose	The **StateIndex** property determines which image, if any, to use for the tree node.
Declaration	

```
property StateIndex: Integer;
```

Example Syntax	

```
// Don't display state images
procedure TForm1.FormCreate(Sender: TObject);
var x: Integer;
begin
  for x := 0 to TreeView1.Items.Count - 1 do
    TreeView1.Items[x].StateIndex := -1;
end;
```

Description	**StateIndex** determines the index of the image in the tree view's associated image list that is used to display the tree node. The main purpose of a tree node image is to indicate the state or status of the node, and not to uniquely identify the node. The image appears next to the tree node's caption, which is set with the **Text** property. If **StateIndex** is **-1**, no image is displayed.

Text PROPERTY

Objects Affected	TTreeNode
Purpose	The **Text** property determines the text caption that identifies the tree node.
Declaration	

```
property Text: String;
```

Example Syntax	

```
procedure TForm1.Button1Click(Sender: TObject);
begin
  TreeView1.Items[0].Text := Edit1.Text;
end;
```

Description	The **Text** property is used to label or identify the node.

TreeView PROPERTY

Objects Affected	TTreeNode
Purpose	The **TreeView** property identifies the owner of the tree node.
Declaration	

```
property TreeView: TCustomTreeView;
```

Example Syntax

```
MyNode.TreeView.FullCollapse;
```

Description — **TreeView** points to the tree view control that owns the tree node.

TTreeNodes

TTreeNodes is an object that maintains the list of tree nodes in a tree view control. Tree view controls have an **Items** property that is of type **TTreeNodes**, and it is through this property that you will most typically access the properties and methods of **TTreeNodes**.

Tree node objects are discussed in the previous section of this chapter; tree view controls are described in Chapter 60.

IMPORTANT

A **TTreeNode** object represents an individual tree node. A **TTreeNodes** object, on the other hand, collects all the nodes in the tree view into an arraylike structure.

Table 19-3 displays the properties and methods that are implemented by **TTreeNodes**.

Table 19-3 Properties and methods implemented by TTreeNodes

Use or Set This...	To Do This...	Inheritance
Add	Add a new tree node.	None
AddChild	Add a new child node to the current tree node.	None
AddChildFirst	Add a new child node to the current tree node.	None
AddChildObject	Add a new child node to the current tree node.	None
AddChildObjectFirst	Add a new child node to the current tree node.	None
AddFirst	Add a new tree node.	None
AddObject	Add a new tree node.	None
AddObjectFirst	Add a new tree node.	None
Assign	Assign one persistent object to another.	TPersistent
BeginUpdate	Temporarily suspend system redraws and updates.	None

Use or Set This...	To Do This...	Inheritance
ClassName	Get the name of the object's class.	TObject
ClassParent	Get the object's parent class.	TObject
ClassType	Get the object's actual type.	TObject
Clear	Destroy all of the tree nodes.	None
Count	Determine the number of tree nodes contained by the object.	None
Create	Create a new TTreeNodes object.	TPersistent
Delete	Delete a tree node.	None
Destroy	Destroy the object.	TObject
EndUpdate	Resume normal system redraws and updates.	None
Free	Safely destroy the object.	TObject
GetFirstNode	Retrieve the first node contained by the TTreeNodes object.	None
Handle	Use the TTreeNodes object with API calls.	None
InheritsFrom	Determine if the object is descended from a certain class.	TObject
Insert	Insert a new tree node object.	None
InsertObject	Insert a new tree node object.	None
InstanceSize	Determine the amount of memory allocated for the object.	TObject
Owner	Determine the owner of the tree node.	None

Add METHOD

Objects Affected TTreeNodes

Purpose The **Add** method adds a new tree node to the tree view.

Declaration

```
function Add(Node: TTreeNode; const S: string): TTreeNode;
```

Parameters

Node The tree node you would like to add.

S The text caption for the new node.

Example Syntax

```
var
  Form1: TForm1;
  MyNewNode: TTreeNode;

implementation

{$R *.DFM}

// Create a new tree node
procedure TForm1.FormCreate(Sender: TObject);
begin
  MyNewNode := TTreeNode.Create(TreeView1.Items);
end;
```

```
procedure TForm1.Button5Click(Sender: TObject);
begin
  TreeView1.Items.Add(MyNewNode, 'New tree node');
end;
```

Description

The **Add** method adds a tree node as the last node in the tree view. This node is added at the uppermost level of the tree. That is, it will not appear as a child of the last node in the list. The *Node* parameter specifies the node whose owner will contain the new node. The *S* parameter is used to specify the text caption that will identify the node.

Add is far more complex than it appears initially; it is designed to work in a variety of ways. In the above example, a tree node object is dynamically created and added to the tree view control. It is also possible to send *any* preexisting tree node, or **Nil**, as the first parameter of the **Add** function as in the following code snippets:

```
TreeView1.Items.Add(TreeView1.Items[0], 'New tree node');
TreeView1.Items.Add(TreeView1.Selected, 'New tree node');
TreeView1.Items.Add(nil, 'New tree node');
```

All of these lines will add a new tree node to the tree view control with a caption of "New tree node". Internally, **Add** allocates memory for its own copy of the node, which is then inserted into the tree.

AddChild METHOD

Objects Affected	TTreeNodes
Purpose	The **AddChild** method adds a tree node to the tree view as a child of a node you specify.
Declaration	

```
function AddChild(Node: TTreeNode; const S: string): TTreeNode;
```

Parameters

Node	The parent node of the new node.
S	The text caption for the new node.

Example Syntax

```
var
  Form1: TForm1;

implementation

{$R *.DFM}
```

```
// Add a new child node to the selected tree node
procedure TForm1.Button1Click(Sender: TObject);
begin
  TreeView1.Items.AddChild(TreeView1.Selected
                           'this is a new node');
end;

// Add a new child node to the selected tree node
// and add its associated data in one statement.
// This example uses the return type of AddChild,
// which is the address of the newly allocated node
procedure TForm1.Button2Click(Sender: TObject);
begin
  MyData := 'This is the data';
  TreeView1.Items.AddChild(TreeView1.Selected,
                           'this is a new node').Data := MyData;
end;
```

Description   AddChild adds a new child node to the node you specify with the *Node* parameter. The *s* parameter is used to specify the text caption that will identify the node.

> **WARNING**
> Delphi will not automatically allocate memory for the information pointed to by the Data property.

AddChildFirst METHOD

Objects Affected   TTreeNodes

Purpose   The AddChildFirst method adds a tree node to the tree view as the first child of a node you specify.

Declaration

```
function AddChildFirst(Node: TTreeNode; const S: string): TTreeNode;
```

Parameters

Node   The parent node of the new node.

S   The text caption for the new node.

Example Syntax

```
// Add the new node as the first child to the first tree node
procedure TForm1.Button1Click(Sender: TObject);
begin
  TreeView1.Items.AddChildFirst(TreeView1.Selected,
                                'New node');
end;
```

Description   This method works just like AddChild except that the node you insert is added as the first child of the tree node specified by the *Node* parameter. The *s* parameter is used to specify the text caption that will identify the node.

AddChildObject METHOD

Objects Affected	TTreeNodes
Purpose	AddChildObject adds a new child node that contains data to the tree view.
Declaration	

```
function AddChildObject(Node: TTreeNode; const S: string;
        Ptr: Pointer): TTreeNode;
```

Parameters

Node	The parent node of the new node.
S	The text caption for the new node.
Ptr	A pointer to the data that is associated with the new node.

Example Syntax

```
procedure TForm1.Button1Click(Sender: TObject);
begin
   TreeView1.Items.AddChildObject(TreeView1.Selected,
                'New Node', MyData);
end;
```

Description   AddChildObject is essentially the same as AddChild, with the added utility of extra data being attached to the new node. The *Ptr* parameter is a pointer to the data that is associated with the new node.

> **WARNING**
> Delphi will not automatically allocate memory for the information pointed to by the Data property.

AddChildObjectFirst METHOD

Objects Affected	TTreeNodes
Purpose	The AddChildObjectFirst method adds a tree node and its attached data to the tree view as the first child of a node you specify.
Declaration	

```
function AddChildObjectFirst(Node: TTreeNode; const S: string;
        Ptr: Pointer): TTreeNode;
```

Parameters

Node	The parent node of the new node.
S	The text caption for the new node.
Ptr	A pointer to the data that is associated with the new node.

Example Syntax

```
var
   Form1: TForm1;
   MyNewNode: TTreeNode;
   MyData: PChar;
```

```
implementation

{$R *.DFM}

procedure TForm1.FormCreate(Sender: TObject);
begin
  MyNewNode := TTreeNode.Create(TreeView1.Items);
  MyNewNode.Text := 'this is a new node';
  MyData := 'This is the data associated with the new node';
  MyNewNode.Data := MyData;
end;

procedure TForm1.Button1Click(Sender: TObject);
begin
  MyNewNode := TreeView1.Items.AddChildObjectFirst(TreeView1.Items[0],
            MyNewNode.Text, MyNewNode.Data);
end;
```

Description   AddChildObjectFirst is essentially the same as AddChildFirst, with the added functionality of having external data associated with the node you are adding. The *Ptr* parameter is a pointer to the data that is associated with the new node.

WARNING
Delphi will not automatically allocate memory for the information pointed to by the Data property.

AddFirst METHOD

Objects Affected   TTreeNodes

Purpose   The AddFirst method inserts a new node at the beginning of the current sibling group of the tree view.

Declaration

```
function AddFirst(Node: TTreeNode; const S: string): TTreeNode;
```

Parameters

Node   The node whose position will be occupied by the new node.

S   The text caption for the new node.

Example Syntax

```
var
  Form1: TForm1;
  MyNewNode: TTreeNode;

implementation

{$R *.DFM}
```

```
procedure TForm1.FormCreate(Sender: TObject);
begin
  MyNewNode := TTreeNode.Create(TreeView1.Items);
  MyNewNode.Text := 'this is a new node';
end;

// Add a new node at the beginning of the tree view
procedure TForm1.Button1Click(Sender: TObject);
begin
  MyNewNode := TreeView1.Items.AddFirst(TreeView1.Items[0],
           MyNewNode.Text);
end;
```

Description   AddFirst is used to insert a tree node at the beginning of the sibling group (subtree) that contains the node identified by the *Node* parameter. All other nodes in the subtree are moved down one position to accommodate the new node. The *S* parameter specifies the text caption that will identify the new node.

AddObject METHOD

Objects Affected   TTreeNodes

Purpose   The AddObject method inserts a tree node and its associated data at the end of the tree view control.

Declaration

```
function AddObject(Node: TTreeNode; const S: string;
         Ptr: Pointer): TTreeNode;
```

Parameters

Node   The node whose list you would like to add to.

S   The text caption for the new node.

Ptr   A pointer to the data that is associated with the new node.

Example Syntax

```
procedure TForm1.Button1Click(Sender: TObject);
begin
  TreeView1.Items.AddObject(TreeView1.Selected, 'New node',
                      MyData);
end;
```

Description   AddObject adds the new tree node to the end of the tree view that contains the node specified by the *Node* parameter. Note that tree nodes added with AddObject are associated with external data, specified by the *Ptr* parameter.

WARNING
Delphi will not automatically allocate memory for the information pointed to by the Data property.

AddObjectFirst METHOD

Objects Affected	TTreeNodes
Purpose	The `AddObjectFirst` method adds a tree node and its data to the beginning of a tree view.
Declaration	

```
function AddObjectFirst(Node: TTreeNode; const S: string;
      Ptr: Pointer): TTreeNode;
```

Parameters

Node	The node you would like to add.
S	The text caption for the new node.
Ptr	A pointer to the data that is associated with the new node.

Example Syntax

```
var
  Form1: TForm1;
  MyNewNode: TTreeNode;
  MyData: PChar;

implementation

{$R *.DFM}

procedure TForm1.FormCreate(Sender: TObject);
begin
  MyNewNode := TTreeNode.Create(TreeView1.Items);
  MyNewNode.Text := 'this is a new node';
  MyData := 'This is the data associated with the new node';
  MyNewNode.Data := MyData;
end;

procedure TForm1.Button1Click(Sender: TObject);
begin
  MyNewNode := TreeView1.Items.AddObjectFirst(TreeView1.Items[0],
             MyNewNode.Text, MyNewNode.Data);
end;
```

Description

`AddObjectFirst` is functionally equivalent to `AddFirst`, except that the tree node that is added is associated with external data, specified by the *Ptr* parameter. It is used to insert a tree node at the beginning of the sibling group (subtree) that contains the node identified by the *Node* parameter. All other nodes in the subtree are moved down one position to accommodate the new node. The *S* parameter specifies the text caption that will identify the new node.

WARNING
Delphi will not automatically allocate memory for the information pointed to by the `Data` property.

BeginUpdate METHOD

Objects Affected	TTreeNodes
Purpose	The BeginUpdate method prevents the system from updating the tree control while changes are made.
Declaration	

```
procedure BeginUpdate;
```

Example Syntax

```
// Prevent the tree view from being updated while a new
// tree node is added.
procedure TForm1.Button1Click(Sender: TObject);
begin
  TreeView1.Items.BeginUpdate;
  MyNewNode := TreeView1.Items.AddObjectFirst(TreeView1.Items[0],
          MyNewNode.Text, MyNewNode.Data);

  // other tree processing

  TreeView1.Items.EndUpdate;
end;
```

Description   BeginUpdate prevents Windows from updating or repainting the tree view control or reindexing the nodes until you call the **EndUpdate** method. This can be used if you need to make multiple changes to the tree and want to defer the repainting of the tree and the reindexing of the tree nodes. Be sure to call **EndUpdate** when you are done.

Clear METHOD

Objects Affected	TTreeNodes
Purpose	The Clear method deletes all the tree nodes in a **TTreeNodes** object.
Declaration	

```
procedure Clear;
```

Example Syntax

```
// Destroy all of the tree nodes
procedure TForm1.Button1Click(Sender: TObject);
begin
  TreeView1.Items.Clear;
end;
```

Description   Clear erases the contents of a tree view control, destroying all the tree nodes that are contained within it. Clear will not deallocate memory referred to by the **Data** properties of the tree nodes it is erasing.

Count PROPERTY

Objects Affected   `TTreeNodes`

Purpose   The `Count` property contains the number of tree nodes in a `TTreeNodes` object.

Declaration

```
property Count: Integer;
```

Example Syntax

```
// Determine the number of tree nodes in TreeView1
procedure TForm1.Button1Click(Sender: TObject);
begin
  Label1.Caption := IntToStr(TreeView1.Items.Count);
end;
```

Description   This run-time, read-only property contains the total number of tree nodes in a tree view control, including all children. Since the `Items` property of a tree view is like a zero-based array, valid index values range from `0` to `Count - 1`, as in the following code:

```
for x := 0 to TreeView1.Items.Count - 1 do
  // tree node processing
```

Delete METHOD

Objects Affected   `TTreeNodes`

Purpose   The `Delete` method removes a node from the `TTreeNodes` object.

Declaration

```
procedure Delete(Node: TTreeNode);
```

Parameters

Node   The node you wish to delete.

Example Syntax

```
// Delete the first node
procedure TForm1.Button1Click(Sender: TObject);
begin
  TreeView1.Items.Delete(TreeView1.Items[0]);
end;
```

Description   The *Node* parameter specifies the tree node you would like to delete. `Delete` will also remove any children of the node you are deleting but will not deallocate memory pointed to by the `Data` properties of deleted nodes.

EndUpdate METHOD

Objects Affected	`TTreeNodes`
Purpose	The `EndUpdate` method allows the system to begin updating the tree view normally.
Declaration	

```
procedure EndUpdate;
```

Example Syntax

```
// Prevent the tree view from being updated while a new
// tree node is added.
procedure TForm1.Button1Click(Sender: TObject);
begin
  TreeView1.Items.BeginUpdate;
  MyNewNode := TreeView1.Items.AddObjectFirst(TreeView1.Items[0],
              MyNewNode.Text, MyNewNode.Data);
  // other tree processing
  TreeView1.Items.EndUpdate;

end;
```

Description `EndUpdate` is used in conjunction with `BeginUpdate`. Where `BeginUpdate` prevents the system from updating the list view, `EndUpdate` is called to allow the system to resume normal reindexing and screen repainting.

GetFirstNode METHOD

Objects Affected	`TTreeNodes`
Purpose	The `GetFirstNode` method returns the first node contained by a `TTreeNodes` object.
Declaration	

```
function GetFirstNode: TTreeNode;
```

Example Syntax

```
// Print out the caption of the first node
procedure TForm1.Button1Click(Sender: TObject);
begin
  Label1.Caption := TreeView1.Items.GetFirstNode.Text;
end;
```

Description `GetFirstNode` returns the first tree node, a `TTreeNode` object, that is contained by the calling `TTreeNodes` object.

Handle PROPERTY

Objects Affected	`TTreeNodes`
Purpose	The `Handle` property contains a Windows handle to the `TTreeNodes` object.
Declaration	

```
property Handle: HWND;
```

Example Syntax

```
procedure TForm1.FormCreate(Sender: TObject);
begin
  MyHandle := TreeView1.Items.Handle;

  // . .
end;
```

Description	Handles are useful if you need to pass the `TTreeNodes` object to an API function call.

Insert METHOD

Objects Affected	`TTreeNodes`
Purpose	The `Insert` method inserts a new tree node at a specific position in the tree.
Declaration	

```
function Insert(Node: TTreeNode; const S: string): TTreeNode;
```

Parameters

Node	The tree node you are inserting the new node in front of.
S	The text caption for the new node.

Example Syntax

```
// Insert a new node at the position currently occupied by the
// selected node
procedure TForm1.Button8Click(Sender: TObject);
begin
  TreeView1.Items.Insert(TreeView1.Selected, 'New Node');
end;
```

Description	`Insert` can be used to place a new node anywhere in the tree view. When the new node is inserted, the nodes below it in the tree are repositioned and reindexed accordingly. The *Node* parameter specifies the node in whose position you will place the new node. The *S* parameter specifies the text caption that will identify the new node.

InsertObject METHOD

Objects Affected	TTreeNodes
Purpose	The InsertObject method inserts a new tree node and its associated data into a specific location in the tree.
Declaration	

```
function InsertObject(Node: TTreeNode; const S: string;
        Ptr: Pointer): TTreeNode;
```

Parameters

Node	The tree node you are inserting the new node in front of.
S	The text caption for the new node.
Ptr	The data that is associated with the new node.

Example Syntax

```
procedure TForm1.Button8Click(Sender: TObject);
begin
  TreeView1.Items.InsertObject(TreeView1.Selected, 'New Node', MyData);
end;
```

Description	InsertObject is functionally similar to Insert. The tree node object you are inserting with InsertObject includes associated data, however.

Owner PROPERTY

Objects Affected	TTreeNodes
Purpose	Owner contains the owner of the tree nodes object.
Declaration	

```
property Owner;
```

Description	The Owner of a TTreeNodes object is the tree view control in which it is contained.

20

TCanvas AND ITS DESCENDANTS

A *canvas object*, an instance of **TCanvas**, is a surface that you can draw to from your Delphi program. In Windows API parlance, it is a *DC*, or *device context*. Forms and many other components have a **Canvas** property, which is type **TCanvas**.

Canvas objects offer methods for drawing points, lines, shapes, and patterns. There is also a **Pen** property, which defines the drawing style, color, and drawing mode. If you wish to fill large areas with color or a pattern, **TCanvas** supplies a **Brush** property that defines these options. You can even render any of the available fonts onto a canvas, in a variety of point sizes and styles. The handle of a canvas is the *HDC*, or handle to a device context, that is used in many Win32 API calls.

Figure 20-1 gives the derivation of **TCanvas**. Table 20-1 displays the properties, methods, and events that are implemented by **Tcanvas**.

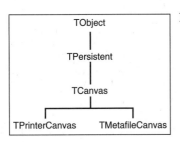

Figure 20-1 Derivation of **TCanvas**

217

Table 20-1 Properties, methods, and events implemented by `TCanvas`

Use or Set This...	To Do This...	Inheritance
Arc	Draw an arc on the canvas.	None
Assign	Assign one persistent object to another.	TPersistent
Brush	Determine the properties of the brush.	None
Chord	Draw a line across an ellipse.	None
ClassName	Get the name of the object's class.	TObject
ClassParent	Get the object's parent class.	TObject
ClassType	Get the object's actual type.	TObject
CopyMode	Determine how an image is copied to the canvas.	None
CopyRect	Copy a rectangular area from another canvas.	None
Create	Create a canvas object.	TObject
Destroy	Destroy the object.	TObject
Draw	Draw a graphic to the canvas.	None
DrawFocusRect	Draw a focus rectangle to the canvas.	None
Ellipse	Draw an ellipse to the canvas.	None
FillRect	Draw a filled rectangle on the canvas.	None
FloodFill	Flood fill an area of the canvas.	None
Font	Determine the font used to render text on the canvas.	None
FrameRect	Draw an unfilled rectangle on the canvas.	None
Free	Safely destroy the object.	TObject
Handle	Determine the HDC for the canvas object.	None
InheritsFrom	Determine if the object is descended from a certain class.	TObject
InstanceSize	Determine the amount of memory allocated for the object.	TObject
LineTo	Draw a line on the canvas.	None
MoveTo	Move the current pen position.	None
OnChange	This event occurs when the surface of the canvas has been modified.	None
OnChanging	This event occurs before the canvas is modified.	None
Pen	Determine the kind of pen the canvas will draw with.	None
PenPos	Determine the current location of the pen.	None
Pie	Draw a pie-shaped object.	None
Pixels	Access individual canvas pixels.	None
Polygon	Draw a polygon.	None
Polyline	Draw a series of connected lines.	None
Rectangle	Draw a filled rectangle.	None
Refresh	Refresh the canvas.	None
RoundRect	Draw a filled rectangle with rounded corners.	None
StretchDraw	Stretch an image to fit within a rectangle.	None
TextHeight	Determine the pixel height of text drawn to the canvas.	None

Use or Set This...	To Do This...	Inheritance
TextOut	Output text to the canvas.	None
TextRect	Determine the clipping rectangle for text on the canvas.	None
TextWidth	Determine the pixel width of text drawn to the canvas.	None

TCanvas has two specialized child classes that handle more specific canvas surfaces. These classes are summarized in Table 20-2.

Table 20-2 The children of TCanvas

Use This...	To Do This...
TMetafileCanvas	Access the canvas of metafile objects.
TPrinterCanvas	Access the canvas of the printer object.

TMetafileCanvas

The metafile canvas object, or **TMetafileCanvas**, is provided for programmers who need to create a metafile image dynamically. To create a metafile image, you must set the metafile's canvas properties first. When the metafile canvas object is destroyed, you can access the newly created metafile image normally. In Listing 20-1, a metafile image is dynamically created.

Listing 20-1 Dynamic creation of a metafile image with TMetafileCanvas

```
var
  Form1: TForm1;
  MyMeta: TMetafile;

implementation

{$R *.DFM}

procedure TForm1.FormCreate(Sender: TObject);
begin
  MyMeta := TMetafile.Create;
  with TMetafileCanvas.Create(MyMeta, 0) do
    Brush.Color := clBlue;
    Ellipse(0,0,150,75);
    Free;
    end;
  // draw the metafile image into the image control
  Image1.AutoSize := True;
  Image1.Picture.Metafile := MyMeta;
end;
```

Table 20-3 displays the methods that are implemented by TMetafileCanvas. These are in addition to the properties and methods it inherits from TCanvas (refer to Table 20-1).

Table 20-3 Methods implemented by TMetafileCanvas

Use or Set This...	To Do This...	Inheritance
Create	Construct a metafile canvas object.	TPersistent
Destroy	Destroy a metafile canvas object.	TPersistent

TPrinterCanvas

The printer canvas, of type TPrinterCanvas, is the surface area for the *printer object*, a globally accessible object of type TPrinter that can be used anytime your program needs to access a printer. TPrinterCanvas allows you to draw to the printer in the same way that you draw to other objects like forms and components. You access the surface area of a printer object through its Canvas property.

```
// Print Image1
procedure TForm1.Button1Click(Sender: TObject);
begin
  Printer.BeginDoc;
  Printer.Canvas.Draw(0, 0, Image1.Picture.Graphic);
  Printer.EndDoc;
end;
```

Note that you must include the file Printers in the uses clause of a unit that will be accessing the printer.

Table 20-4 displays the methods that are implemented by TPrinterCanvas. These are in addition to the properties and methods it inherits from TCanvas (refer to Table 20-1).

Table 20-4 Methods implemented by TPrinterCanvas

Use or Set This...	To Do This...	Inheritance
Create	Construct a printer canvas object.	TPersistent
CreateHandle	Create a handle to the printer canvas.	TPersistent

Arc METHOD

Objects Affected   All canvas objects.

Purpose   The **Arc** method draws an arc on the drawing surface.

Declaration

```
procedure Arc(X1, Y1, X2, Y2, X3, Y3, X4, Y4: Integer);
```

Parameters

X1   The starting x coordinate for the arc's bounding rectangle.

Y1   The starting y coordinate for the arc's bounding rectangle.

X2   The ending x coordinate for the arc's bounding rectangle.

Y2   The ending y coordinate for the arc's bounding rectangle.

X3   The x coordinate of the arc's starting point.

Y3   The y coordinate of the arc's starting point.

X4   The x coordinate of the arc's ending point.

Y4   The y coordinate of the arc's ending point.

Example Syntax

```
// Draw an arc
procedure TForm1.Button1Click(Sender: TObject);
begin
  Form1.Canvas.Arc(50,50,150,190,180,0,30,50);
end;
```

Description   The **Arc** method draws an arc to the canvas within the rectangle specified by the *X1*, *Y1*, *X2*, and *Y2* coordinates. The arc is drawn from the intersection of the ellipse edge along the line from the center of the ellipse to the *X1, Y2* starting point. The arc is drawn, counterclockwise, until it reaches the point where the edge of the ellipse intersects the line from the center of the ellipse to the *X4, Y4* ending point. Figure 20-2 shows a typical arc, drawn directly on the form's canvas.

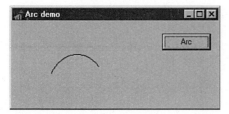

Figure 20-2 Drawing an arc on the form

Brush PROPERTY

Objects Affected	All canvas objects.
Purpose	The **Brush** property determines the color and pattern that will be used for paint fills.
Declaration	

```
property Brush: TBrush;
```

Example Syntax

```
procedure TForm1.FormCreate(Sender: TObject);
begin
  Image1.AutoSize := True;
  // Draw a hatched green circle on Image1
  Image1.Canvas.Brush.Color := clGreen;
  Image1.Canvas.Brush.Style := bsDiagCross;
  Image1.Canvas.Ellipse(0,0,100,100);
end;
```

Description   The **Brush** property determines the color and pattern that will be used when filling a solid shape like an ellipse or rectangle. It is type **TBrush**, a direct encapsulation of the Windows API brush resource. **TBrush** defines **Color** and **Style** properties, which are used by the **Brush** property to alter those settings.

Predefined color constants include identifiers that name common colors like **clAqua**, **clBlack**, and **clBlue**, as well as identifiers that refer to standard colors used by the system, such as **clActiveBorder**, **clActiveCaption**, and **clBackground**. If you need to define your own color, **TColor** objects are specified as 4-byte hexadecimal numbers, where the lower 3 bytes represent the RGB intensity values for the color and the high byte represents one of the three values shown in Table 20-5.

Table 20-5 Possible high-byte values for the Color property of Brush

High-Byte Value	Used to Do This...
$00	Use the system palette to obtain the closest possible color.
$01	Use the currently realized palette to obtain the closest possible color.
$02	Use the logical palette of the canvas handle (the DC) to obtain the closest possible color.

Style settings are **bsSolid**, **bsClear**, **bsCross**, **bsBDiagonal**, **bsDiagCross**, **bsHorizontal**, **bsVertical**, and **bsFDiagonal**.

Chord METHOD

Objects Affected	All canvas objects.
Purpose	The Chord method draws a line across an ellipse.
Declaration	

```
procedure Chord(X1, Y1, X2, Y2, X3, Y3, X4, Y4: Integer);
```

Parameters

X1	The starting x coordinate for the chord's bounding rectangle.
Y1	The starting y coordinate for the chord's bounding rectangle.
X2	The ending x coordinate for the chord's bounding rectangle.
Y2	The ending y coordinate for the chord's bounding rectangle.
X3	The starting x coordinate of the chord line.
Y3	The starting y coordinate of the chord line.
X4	The ending x coordinate of the chord line.
Y4	The ending y coordinate of the chord line.

Example Syntax

```
// Draw a chord
procedure TForm1.Button1Click(Sender: TObject);
begin
  Canvas.Chord(0, 0, 140, 100, 100, 0, 140, 150);
end;
```

Description   The Chord method is used to draw a line on the canvas connecting the points defined by *X3, Y3* and *X4, Y4* on an ellipse defined by the bounding rectangle whose origin can be found at *X1, Y1* and whose ending point can be found at *X2, Y2*. The Chord method is identical to Arc, except that it draws a straight line between the end points of the arc. The chord is filled with the color and style specified by the Brush property. Figure 20-3 shows a chord drawn on the form canvas.

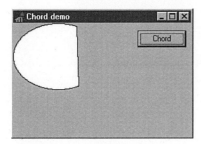

Figure 20-3 A chord

CopyMode PROPERTY

Objects Affected	All canvas objects.
Purpose	The CopyMode property determines how to copy an image from another canvas to its own drawing surface.
Declaration	

```
property CopyMode: TCopyMode;
```

Example Syntax

```
procedure TForm1.Button1Click(Sender: TObject);
begin
  Image2.Canvas.Brush.Style := bsCross;
  Image2.Canvas.CopyMode := cmMergeCopy;

  Image2.Canvas.Draw(0,0, Image1.Picture.Graphic);
end;
```

Description   CopyMode is of type TCopyMode, which is defined as a set of the possible values shown in Table 20-6.

Table 20-6 The possible values for CopyMode

Use This Copy Mode...	For This Effect...
cmBlackness	The output is all black.
cmDstInvert	The destination bitmap is inverted.
cmMergeCopy	ANDs the source bitmap with the destination brush style.
cmMergePaint	ORs the inverted source bitmap with the destination bitmap.
cmNotSrcCopy	Copies the inverted source bitmap to the destination.
cmNotSrcErase	Inverts the ORed combination of the destination and source bitmap.
cmPatCopy	XORs the destination brush style with the destination bitmap.
cmPatInvert	XORs the combination of the destination bitmap with the destination brush style.
cmPatPaint	First, the inverted source bitmap is ORed with the destination brush style. Then, the result of this operation is ORed with the destination bitmap.
cmSrcAnd	Combines pixels from the destination and source bitmaps by using the Boolean AND operator.
cmSrcCopy	Copies the source bitmap to the destination bitmap.
cmSrcErase	Inverts the destination bitmap and ORs the result with the source bitmap.
cmSrcInvert	XORs the destination and source bitmaps.
cmSrcPaint	ORs the destination and source bitmaps.
cmWhiteness	The output is all white.

The default copy mode is cmSrcCopy, which copies an image from the source canvas, overwriting any image that was previously contained in the destination canvas. Figure 20-4 shows an image merge-copied with a brush.

Figure 20-4 Merge-copying an image with a pattern

CopyRect METHOD

Objects Affected   All canvas objects.

Purpose   The CopyRect method copies a rectangular area on one canvas to another.

Declaration

```
procedure CopyRect(const Dest: TRect; Canvas: TCanvas;
    const Source: TRect);
```

Parameters

Dest   The destination rectangle.

Canvas   The source canvas.

Source   The source rectangle.

Example Syntax

```
// Copy the image from Image1 so that it covers the whole
// form drawing surface
procedure TForm1.Button1Click(Sender: TObject);
begin
  Form1.Canvas.CopyRect(Form1.Canvas.ClipRect, Image1.Canvas,
                        Image1.Canvas.ClipRect);
end;
```

Description   CopyRect copies the rectangular portion (the *Source* parameter) of the source canvas (the *Canvas* parameter) to the rectangular portion (*Dest*) of the destination canvas. If the source and destination rectangles are different sizes, the copied image will be stretched to fit the destination rectangle. In Figure 20-5, a bitmap image is copied to the form surface with CopyRect.

Figure 20-5 Result of copying a bitmap image to the form drawing surface

Draw METHOD

Objects Affected	All canvas objects.
Purpose	The `Draw` method draws a specified graphic to the canvas.
Declaration	

```
procedure Draw(X, Y: Integer; Graphic: TGraphic);
```

Parameters

X	The x coordinate of the draw location.
Y	The y coordinate of the draw location.
Graphic	The bitmap, icon, or metafile you wish to draw to the canvas.

Example Syntax

```
// Copy the graphic from Image1 to Image2
procedure TForm1.FormCreate(Sender: TObject);
begin
  Image2.Canvas.Draw(0, 0, Image1.Picture.Graphic);
end;
```

Description The `Draw` method draws the bitmap, icon, or metafile specified by the *Graphic* parameter to the canvas. The graphic is placed with its upper-left corner at the location specified by the *X* and *Y* parameters.

DrawFocusRect METHOD

Objects Affected	All canvas objects.
Purpose	The DrawFocusRect method draws a focus rectangle.
Declaration	

```
procedure DrawFocusRect(const Rect: TRect);
```

Parameters

Rect   The focus rectangle.

Example Syntax

```
procedure TForm1.Button1Click(Sender: TObject);
var
  MyRect: TRect;
begin
  MyRect.Left := 10;
  MyRect.Top := 10;
  MyRect.Right := 110;
  MyRect.Bottom := 110;
  Form1.Canvas.DrawFocusRect(MyRect);
end;
```

Description   The DrawFocusRect method is used internally by Delphi to draw focus rectangles around or on controls when they receive the input focus. Component writers can use this method to specify the focus rectangle that their component will receive.

DrawFocusRect is an XOR function, so calling it again after drawing the focus rectangle will erase the focus rectangle. Figure 20-6 shows a typical focus rectangle.

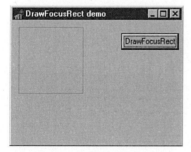

Figure 20-6   A focus rectangle

Ellipse METHOD

Objects Affected	All canvas objects.
Purpose	The Ellipse method draws an ellipse on the canvas.
Declaration	

```
procedure Ellipse(X1, Y1, X2, Y2: Integer);
```

Parameters

X1	The x coordinate of the top-left point of the ellipse's bounding rectangle.
Y1	The y coordinate of the top-left point of the ellipse's bounding rectangle.
X2	The x coordinate of the bottom-right point of the ellipse's bounding rectangle.
Y2	The y coordinate of the bottom-right point of the ellipse's bounding rectangle.

Example Syntax

```
procedure TForm1.FormCreate(Sender: TObject);
begin
  // Draw a white ellipse on the image control
  Image1.Canvas.Brush.Color := clWhite;
  Image1.Canvas.Ellipse(0,0,100,100);
end;
```

Description   Ellipse draws an ellipse in a bounding rectangle defined by the coordinates passed with its *X1*, *Y1*, *X2*, and *Y2* parameters.

The ellipse drawn is a circle when its bounding rectangle is a square.

FillRect METHOD

Objects Affected	All canvas objects.
Purpose	The FillRect method fills the specified rectangle with the color and pattern specified by the current brush.
Declaration	

```
procedure FillRect(const Rect: TRect);
```

Parameters

Rect	The rectangle that will be drawn with the current brush.

Example Syntax

```
// Draw a randomly sized and placed rectangle when the button is
// clicked.
procedure TForm1.Button1Click(Sender: TObject);
var
  MyRect: TRect;
  X1, X2, Y1, Y2: Integer;
begin
```

```
      Randomize;
      X1 := Random(Form1.Width);
      Y1 := Random(Form1.Height);
      X2 := Random(Form1.Width);
      Y2 := Random(Form1.Height);
      MyRect := Rect(X1, Y1, X2, Y2);
      Form1.Canvas.Brush.Color := clTeal;
      Form1.Canvas.FillRect(MyRect);
    end;
```

Description   FillRect draws a rectangle, specified by the *Rect* parameter, on the canvas using the color and pattern determined by the current brush. In the previous example, solid teal rectangles are drawn on the form's drawing surface every time the command button is clicked.

FloodFill Method

Objects Affected   All canvas objects.

Purpose   The FloodFill method paints an area of the canvas using the current brush.

Declaration

```
procedure FloodFill(X, Y: Integer; Color: TColor;
                    FillStyle: TFillStyle);
```

Parameters

X   The x coordinate of the location the flood fill is to start.

Y   The y coordinate of the location the flood fill is to start.

Color   The color to fill.

FillStyle   The style to use in the fill.

Example Syntax

```
// FloodFill the form
procedure TForm1.Button1Click(Sender: TObject);
begin
   Form1.Canvas.FloodFill(200, 60, clBlack, fsBorder);
end;
```

Description   The FloodFill method fills an area of the canvas, beginning at the point specified by the *X* and *Y* parameters, using the color specified by the *Color* parameter. The *FillStyle* parameter determines the way the flood fill proceeds. Possible values for *FillStyle* are fsBorder and fsSurface. A value of fsBorder causes the flood fill to continue in all directions until a border of the color specified by the *Color* parameter is reached. A value of fsSurface causes the flood fill to continue even if it reaches a border of the color specified by the *Color* parameter.

Font PROPERTY

Objects Affected   All canvas objects.

Purpose   The `Font` property determines the font that is used to display text on the canvas.

Declaration

```
property Font: TFont;
```

Example Syntax

```
procedure TForm1.FormCreate(Sender: TObject);
begin
  // Set the font properties for text that will be drawn on
  // the form surface
  Form1.Canvas.Font.Name := 'Arial';
  Form1.Canvas.Font.Size := 24;
  Form1.Canvas.Font.Style := [fsBold] + [fsItalic];
  Form1.Canvas.Font.Color := clBlack;
end;

procedure TForm1.Button1Click(Sender: TObject);
begin
  // Write text to the form canvas
  Form1.Canvas.TextOut(50,50, 'Hello, world');
end;
```

Description   `Font` is of type `TFont`, which describes the appearance of text by specifying various attributes of that text with properties like `Name`, `Size`, and `Style`.

`TFont` defines the appearance of text. Its properties are shown in Table 20-7.

Table 20-7 Properties of TFont

Use This TFont Property...	To Do This...	Type
Color	Specify the color of the text.	TColor
Name	Specify the name of the font used to render text.	TFontName
Size	Specify the point size of the font.	Integer
Style	Specify settings for bold, italic, underline, and strikeout.	TFontStyles

The `Color` property of `TFont` accepts color constant values like `clBlue`, `clWhite`, and so on, as well as system-specific color constants such as `clButtonFace` and `clWindow`. The `Name` property specifies the font manufacturer's name for the font; common examples include Arial and Times New Roman. `Style` is type `TFontStyles`, which is a set of rendering styles including `fsBold`, `fsItalic`, `fsUnderline`, and `fsStrikeout`. Since the `Style` settings are part of a set, remember that you must use set notation to specify styles for your font as in the previous example.

FrameRect METHOD

Objects Affected	All canvas objects.
Purpose	The `FrameRect` method draws an unfilled rectangle on the canvas.
Declaration	

```
procedure FrameRect(const Rect: TRect);
```

Parameters

Rect	The rectangle specifying the dimensions of the frame to draw.

Example Syntax

```
// Draw a frame rectangle using the current brush
procedure TForm1.Button1Click(Sender: TObject);
begin
  Canvas.FrameRect(Rect(10,10, 160, 160));
end;
```

Description   `FrameRect` draws an unfilled rectangle to the drawing surface using the current brush. To draw a filled rectangle, use the `FillRect` method.

In the code sample above, the `Rect` function is called to create the `TRect` record required by `FrameRect`.

Handle PROPERTY

Objects Affected	All canvas objects.
Purpose	The `Handle` property specifies a Windows handle to the canvas.
Declaration	

```
property Handle: HDC;
```

Example Syntax

```
// Use the form's canvas handle in an API call that requires
// an HDC parameter
procedure TForm1.Button1Click(Sender: TObject);
var PixelFormat: Integer;
begin
  // Get the index of the form's currently selected pixel format
  // using the Win32 API function GetPixelFormat
  PixelFormat := GetPixelFormat(Form1.Canvas.Handle);
  // . . .
end;
```

Description   The handle of a canvas object is the HDC, or handle to the device context, of the drawing surface. HDCs are used quite heavily in the Windows API, although they are not typically needed in Delphi programs.

LineTo METHOD

Objects Affected	All canvas objects.
Purpose	The LineTo method draws a line on the canvas.
Declaration	

```
procedure LineTo(X, Y: Integer);
```

Parameters

X	The x coordinate of the destination of the line.
Y	The y coordinate of the destination of the line.

Example Syntax

```
// Draw a line on the canvas
procedure TForm1.FormCreate(Sender: TObject);
begin
  Form1.Canvas.LineTo(100, 200);
end;
```

Description   LineTo draws a line from the current pen position to the point specified by the *X* and *Y* parameters. When the operation is complete, the current pen position is moved to *X, Y*. The current pen position is identified by the TCanvas PenPos property.

MoveTo METHOD

Objects Affected	All canvas objects.
Purpose	The MoveTo method moves the current pen position to a new location.
Declaration	

```
procedure MoveTo(X, Y: Integer);
```

Parameters

X	The x coordinate of the new pen position.
Y	The y coordinate of the new pen position.

Example Syntax

```
// Move the current pen position to the origin
procedure TForm1.FormCreate(Sender: TObject);
begin
  Form1.Canvas.MoveTo(0, 0);
end;
```

Description   MoveTo moves the current pen position to the point specified by the *X* and *Y* parameters. Nothing is drawn as the pen moves. The current pen position is specified by the PenPos property; MoveTo can be used to set this property to a new value.

OnChange EVENT

Objects Affected   All canvas objects.

Purpose   The `OnChange` event occurs when the surface of the canvas has been modified.

Declaration

```
property OnChange: TNotifyEvent;
```

Example Syntax

```
type
  TForm1 = class(TForm)
    Button1: TButton;
    Label1: TLabel;
    procedure FormCreate(Sender: TObject);
    procedure Button1Click(Sender: TObject);
  private
    { Private declarations }
  public
    { Public declarations }
  procedure CanvasChange(Sender: TObject);
  end;


var
  Form1: TForm1;

implementation

{$R *.DFM}

// This is the event handler set up by the programmer for
// Form1.Canvas.OnChange events
procedure TForm1.CanvasChange(Sender: TObject);
begin
  Form1.Caption := 'Canvas Changed';
end;

// Assign the OnChange event handler to the CanvasChange procedure
procedure TForm1.FormCreate(Sender: TObject);
begin
  Form1.Canvas.OnChange := Form1.CanvasChange;
end;

// Test OnChange
procedure TForm1.Button1Click(Sender: TObject);
begin
  Form1.Canvas.LineTo(100,100);
end;
```

Description   An `OnChange` event is triggered anytime the drawing surface of the canvas is modified. A `LineTo` or `Arc` method, for example, would trigger this event; a `MoveTo` or a change to the canvas font style would not.

You must create an event handler for the `OnChange` event yourself. In the example above, this is done with the `CanvasChange` procedure, which was manually added; you can name this procedure as you wish.

OnChanging EVENT

Objects Affected   All canvas objects.

Purpose   The `OnChanging` event is triggered before the canvas is modified.

Declaration

```
property OnChanging: TNotifyEvent;
```

Example Syntax

```
type
  TForm1 = class(TForm)
    Button1: TButton;
    procedure FormCreate(Sender: TObject);
    procedure Button1Click(Sender: TObject);
  private
    { Private declarations }
  public
    { Public declarations }
    procedure CanvasChanging(Sender: TObject);
  end;

var
  Form1: TForm1;

implementation

{$R *.DFM}

// This is the event handler set up by the programmer for
// Form1.Canvas.OnChange events
procedure TForm1.CanvasChanging(Sender: TObject);
begin
  Application.MessageBox('Form Canvas is about to change',
                        'OnChanging Event triggered', MB_OK);
end;

// Assign the OnChange event handler to the CanvasChange procedure
procedure TForm1.FormCreate(Sender: TObject);
begin
  Form1.Canvas.OnChanging := CanvasChanging;
end;

// Test OnChange
procedure TForm1.Button1Click(Sender: TObject);
begin
  Form1.Canvas.LineTo(100,100);
end;
```

Description
An `OnChanging` event is triggered whenever the drawing surface of the canvas is about to be modified; it occurs *before* the canvas is changed. Canvas methods that write to the drawing surface, like `Arc` and `LineTo`, would trigger this event; a `MoveTo` or a change to the canvas font style would not.

You must create an event handler for the `OnChanging` event yourself. In the example above, this is done with the `CanvasChanging` procedure, which was manually added; you can name this procedure as you wish.

Pen PROPERTY

Objects Affected All canvas objects.

Purpose The `Pen` property determines the attributes of the pen the canvas will use.

Declaration

```
property Pen: TPen;
```

Example Syntax

```
// Set the canvas pen attributes
procedure TForm1.FormCreate(Sender: TObject);
begin
  Form1.Canvas.Pen.Color := clWhite;
  Form1.Canvas.Pen.Style := psDot;
  Form1.Canvas.Pen.Width := 3;
  Form1.Canvas.Pen.Mode := pmCopy;
end;

// Draw a line using the new attributes
procedure TForm1.Button1Click(Sender: TObject);
begin
  Form1.Canvas.LineTo(300,200);
end;
```

Description
The pen is used to draw lines and shapes on the canvas. It is of type `TPen`, which has the properties `Color`, `Width`, `Style`, and `Mode` that allow you to set the attributes for the canvas pen. Table 20-8 briefly describes these properties.

Table 20-8 Properties of TPen

Use This TPen Property...	To Do This...	Type
Color	Specify the color of the text.	TColor
Mode	Specify the way the pen interacts with the pixels already on the drawing surface.	TPenMode
Style	Specify the style used by the pen to draw lines.	TPenStyle
Width	Specify the width, in pixels, of lines drawn by the pen.	Integer

The `Color` property of `TFont` accepts color constant values like `clBlue`, `clWhite`, and so on, as well as system-specific color constants such as `clButtonFace` and `clWindow`. The `Mode` property can be set to any of the possible values shown in Table 20-9.

Table 20-9 The values of the `Mode` property

Use This Mode...	So the Line Color...
pmBlack	Is always black.
pmCopy	Matches the color specified in the `Color` property.
pmMask	Combines the common colors of the pen and the drawing surface.
pmMaskNotPen	Combines the common colors of the drawing surface and the inverse of the pen.
pmMaskPenNot	Combines the common colors of the inverse of the drawing surface and the pen.
pmMerge	Combines the colors of the pen and the drawing surface.
pmMergeNotPen	Combines the colors of the drawing surface and the inverse of the pen.
pmMergePenNot	Combines the colors of the inverse of the drawing surface and the pen.
pmNop	Is unaffected by the colors in the drawing surface.
pmNot	Is the inverse of the drawing surface color.
pmNotCopy	Is the inverse of the pen color.
pmNotMask	Is the inverse of the effect caused by `pmMask`.
pmNotMerge	Is the inverse of the effect caused by `pmMerge`.
pmNotXor	Is the inverse of the effect caused by `pmXor`.
pmWhite	Is always white.
pmXor	Combines those colors that are different in the pen and the drawing surface.

The `Style` property can be set to one of the possible values shown in Table 20-10.

Table 20-10 The values of the `Style` property

Use This Style...	So the Lines Are Drawn...
psClear	As invisible marks.
psDash	As a series of dashes.
psDashDot	As alternating dashes and dots.
psDashDotDot	As a series of dash-dot-dot combinations.
psDot	As a series of dots.
psInsideFrame	Within the bounding rectangle of the drawing surface.
psSolid	As a solid line.

PenPos PROPERTY

Objects Affected	All canvas objects.
Purpose	The **PenPos** property describes the current location of the pen.
Declaration	

```
property PenPos: TPoint;
```

Example Syntax

```
// Move the pen position ten pixels right and ten pixels down
procedure TForm1.Button1Click(Sender: TObject);
begin
  Form1.Canvas.MoveTo(Form1.Canvas.PenPos.X + 10,
                      Form1.Canvas.PenPos.Y + 10);
  // . . .
end;
```

Description While **PenPos** is not a read-only property, it is suggested that you set the pen position with the **MoveTo** method and use **PenPos** to retrieve the pen position. **PenPos** is of type **TPoint**, which is a record of two integers, X and Y.

Pie METHOD

Objects Affected	All canvas objects.
Purpose	The **Pie** method draws a section of an ellipse and two radii, making a pie-wedge shape.
Declaration	

```
procedure Pie(X1, Y1, X2, Y2, X3, Y3, X4, Y4: Integer);
```

Parameters

X1	The x coordinate of the left corner of the ellipse's bounding rectangle.
Y1	The y coordinate of the left corner of the ellipse's bounding rectangle.
X2	The x coordinate of the right corner of the ellipse's bounding rectangle.
Y2	The y coordinate of the right corner of the ellipse's bounding rectangle.
X3	The x coordinate of the first radius line.
Y3	The y coordinate of the first radius line.
X4	The x coordinate of the second radius line.
Y4	The y coordinate of the second radius line.

Example Syntax

```
procedure TForm1.Button1Click(Sender: TObject);
begin
  Form1.Canvas.Pie(0, 0, 250, 250, 75, 10, 200, 75)
end;
```

Description	This method creates a filled ellipse with a pie wedge missing. This resembles a two-dimensional pie chart as shown in Figure 20-7.

Pixels PROPERTY

Objects Affected	All canvas objects.
Purpose	The **Pixels** property allows you to access the individual pixels on the canvas.
Declaration	

```
property Pixels[X, Y: Integer]: TColor;
```

Parameters

X	The x coordinate of the pixel.
Y	The y coordinate of the pixel.

Example Syntax

```
// Draw some dots on the canvas
procedure TForm1.Button1Click(Sender: TObject);
var
  x, x1, y1: Integer;
begin
  Randomize;
  for x := 1 to 100 do
  begin
    x1 := Random(Form1.ClientWidth);
    y1 := Random(Form1.ClientHeight);
    Form1.Canvas.Pixels[x1, y1] := clWhite
  end;
end;
```

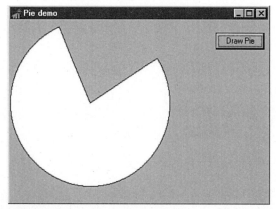

Figure 20-7   Drawing a pie

Description	**Pixels** contains the value of the color in the pixel located at the point specified by the *X* and *Y* array indices. You can both get and set pixels with this property.

Polygon METHOD

Objects Affected	All canvas objects.
Purpose	The **Polygon** method connects a series of points with lines and fills the shape with the current brush.
Declaration	

```
procedure Polygon(const Points: array of TPoint);
```

Parameters	
Points	An array of **TPoint** values that make up the polygon.
Example Syntax	

```
procedure TForm1.Button1Click(Sender: TObject);
begin
  Form1.Canvas.Brush.Color := clWhite;
  Form1.Canvas.Brush.Style := bsDiagCross;
  Form1.Canvas.Polygon([Point(6, 35), Point(22, 118),
    Point(200, 110), Point(210, 184), Point(110, 25)]);
end;
```

Description	The **Polygon** method connects the points passed to it by the *Points* parameters with lines, connecting the final point to the first point and filling the resulting shape, a polygon, with the current brush. Figure 20-8 shows a polygon drawn on a form window.

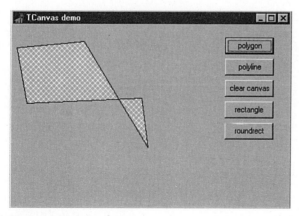

Figure 20-8 A polygon

Polyline METHOD

Objects Affected	All canvas objects.
Purpose	The `Polyline` method draws a series of connected lines on the canvas.
Declaration	

```
procedure Polyline(const Points: array of TPoint);
```

Parameters

Points   The array of `TPoint` values to connect to draw the line.

Example Syntax

```
procedure TForm1.Button1Click(Sender: TObject);
begin
  Form1.Canvas.Brush.Color := clWhite;
  Form1.Canvas.Brush.Style := bsDiagCross;
  Form1.Canvas.Polyline([Point(6, 35), Point(22, 118),
    Point(200, 110), Point(210, 184), Point(110, 25)]);
end;
```

Description   `Polyline` is similar to `Polygon` except that the final point is not connected to the first point and the resulting shape is not filled with the current brush. In the above example, the final point, **(110,25)**, is not connected to the first point. To draw an unfilled polygon similar to the example for the `Polygon` method, simply add the first point, **(6,35)**, again as the final point.

Rectangle METHOD

Objects Affected	All canvas objects.
Purpose	The `Rectangle` method draws a filled rectangle on the canvas.
Declaration	

```
procedure Rectangle(X1, Y1, X2, Y2: Integer);
```

Parameters

X1   The starting x coordinate of the rectangle.

Y1   The starting y coordinate of the rectangle.

X2   The ending x coordinate of the rectangle.

Y2   The ending y coordinate of the rectangle.

Example Syntax

```
procedure TForm1.Button1Click(Sender: TObject);
begin
  Form1.Canvas.Brush.Color := clPurple;
  Form1.Canvas.Brush.Style := bsSolid;
  Form1.Canvas.Rectangle(10, 10, 200, 200);
end;
```

Description	The `Rectangle` method draws a rectangle with one corner at the point specified by the *X1* and *Y1* parameters and the opposite diagonal corner at the point specified by the *X2* and *Y2* parameters. The rectangle frame is drawn with the current pen and filled using the current brush.

Refresh METHOD

Objects Affected	All canvas objects.
Purpose	The `Refresh` method erases the drawing surface of the canvas once the surface has been invalidated.
Declaration	

```
procedure Refresh;
```

Example Syntax

```
procedure TForm1.Button1Click(Sender: TObject);
begin
  Form1.Invalidate;
  Form1.Canvas.Refresh;
end;
```

Description	`Refresh` will clear only that area of the canvas marked as invalid. To ensure that the entire canvas is cleared, you must call the containing component's `Invalidate` method before calling `Refresh`. This has the same effect as calling the containing component's `Repaint` or `Refresh` method, so the following code snippets accomplish the same thing as the example code above:

```
Form1.Refresh;
```

and

```
Form1.Repaint;
```

Normally, you should use the containing component's `Refresh` method to erase its entire drawing surface.

RoundRect METHOD

Objects Affected	All canvas objects.
Purpose	The `RoundRect` method draws a rectangle with rounded corners on the canvas.
Declaration	

```
procedure RoundRect(X1, Y1, X2, Y2, X3, Y3: Integer);
```

Parameters

X1	The starting x coordinate of the rounded rectangle.
Y1	The starting y coordinate of the rounded rectangle.
X2	The ending x coordinate of the rounded rectangle.
Y2	The ending y coordinate of the rounded rectangle.
X3	The width of the ellipse that forms the corners.
Y3	The height of the ellipse that forms the corners.

Example Syntax

```
procedure TForm1.Button5Click(Sender: TObject);
begin
  Form1.Canvas.Brush.Color := clBlack;
  Form1.Canvas.Brush.Style := bsSolid;
  Form1.Canvas.RoundRect(10, 10, 200, 200, 20, 20);
end;
```

Description   Like the `Rectangle` method, `RoundRect` draws a filled rectangle on the canvas using the *X1*, *Y1*, *X2*, and *Y2* parameters. The corners of the `RoundRect` are rounded, using an ellipse whose width is specified by *X3* and whose height is specified by *Y3*.

StretchDraw METHOD

Objects Affected   All canvas objects.

Purpose   The `StretchDraw` method draws a graphic into a rectangle, stretching it to fit the size of the destination rectangle.

Declaration

```
procedure StretchDraw(const Rect: TRect; Graphic: TGraphic);
```

Parameters

Rect	The destination rectangle the graphic will be drawn to.
Graphic	The graphic to be drawn in the destination rectangle.

Example Syntax

```
// StretchDraw the graphic in Image1
procedure TForm1.Button1Click(Sender: TObject);
var MyRect: TRect;
begin
  MyRect := Rect(0, 0, 400, 400);
  Form1.Canvas.StretchDraw(MyRect, Image1.Picture.Graphic);
end;
```

Description   `StretchDraw` is used to resize the graphic image specified by the *Graphic* parameter so that it fits within a rectangle specified by the *Rect* parameter and then render it to the drawing surface. Figure 20-9 shows a bitmap image that's been stretched with `StretchDraw`.

Figure 20-9 Stretching a bitmap image

TextHeight METHOD

Objects Affected	All canvas objects.
Purpose	The **TextHeight** method returns the height of text that is to be drawn to the canvas.
Declaration	

```
function TextHeight(const Text: string): Integer;
```

Parameters

Text   The text to display on the canvas.

Example Syntax

```
// Determine the current height of text drawn to the form canvas
procedure TForm1.Button1Click(Sender: TObject);
begin
  Form1.Canvas.Font.Name := 'Arial';
  Form1.Canvas.Font.Size := 24;
  Form1.Caption := 'Canvas text is ' +
                   IntToStr(Form1.Canvas.TextHeight('Sample Text')) +
                   ' pixels in height';
end;
```

Description   The height value returned by **TextHeight** is an integer. It does not return the point size of the current font, but rather the height in pixels.

TextHeight is typically used to see if the specified text will fit on the canvas. See **TextWidth**.

TextOut METHOD

Objects Affected	All canvas objects.
Purpose	The `TextOut` method renders text on the canvas using the current font.
Declaration	

```
procedure TextOut(X, Y: Integer; const Text: string);
```

Parameters

X	The x coordinate of the upper-left position of the location where text is to be rendered.
Y	The y coordinate of the upper-left position of the location where text is to be rendered.
Text	The text to render.

Example Syntax

```
procedure TForm1.Button2Click(Sender: TObject);
begin
  Form1.Canvas.Font.Name := 'Arial';
  Form1.Canvas.Font.Size := 24;
  Form1.Canvas.Font.Style := [fsItalic];
  Form1.Canvas.TextOut(10, 10, 'This text is written on the canvas');
end;
```

Description	`TextOut` uses the attributes of the current font to render text at the location specified by the *X* and *Y* parameters on the drawing surface. The current font is specified by the `Font` property of the canvas.

TextRect METHOD

Objects Affected	All canvas objects.
Purpose	The `TextRect` method renders text using the current font inside of a clipping rectangle on the canvas.
Declaration	

```
procedure TextRect(Rect: TRect; X, Y: Integer; const Text: string);
```

Parameters

Rect	The clipping rectangle.
X	The x coordinate of the upper-left position of the location where text is to be rendered.
Y	The y coordinate of the upper-left position of the location where text is to be rendered.
Text	The text to render.

Example Syntax

```
procedure TForm1.Button3Click(Sender: TObject);
var MyRect: TRect;
begin
  MyRect := Rect(10, 10, 250, 100);
  Form1.Canvas.Font.Name := 'Arial';
  Form1.Canvas.Font.Size := 24;
  Form1.Canvas.Font.Style := [fsItalic];
  Form1.Canvas.TextRect(MyRect, 10, 10, 'This text is clipped');
end;
```

Description

TextRect is similar to TextOut except that the text is clipped by the rectangle specified by the *Rect* parameter. Any text that would be drawn outside of the clipping rectangle is not rendered. Compare the output of the above example with the output from the TextOut example.

TextWidth METHOD

Objects Affected   All canvas objects.

Purpose   The TextWidth method returns the width of text that is to be drawn to the canvas.

Declaration

```
function TextWidth(const Text: string): Integer;
```

Parameters

Text   The text you wish to display on the canvas.

Example Syntax

```
// Determine if the text can fit if drawn to the form canvas
procedure TForm1.Button4Click(Sender: TObject);
var MyString: String;
begin
  Form1.Canvas.Font.Name := 'Arial';
  Form1.Canvas.Font.Size := 24;
  MyString := 'Will it fit?';
  if Form1.Canvas.TextWidth(MyString) < Form1.ClientWidth then
    Form1.Canvas.TextOut(0, 0, MyString);
end;
```

Description

The width value returned from TextWidth is an integer. It returns the width, in pixels, of the text specified by the *Text* parameter.

Like TextHeight, TextWidth is typically used to see if the specified text will fit on the canvas.

21

TCollection, TCollectionItem, AND THEIR DESCENDANTS

TCollection and **TCollectionItem** are used to support the operation of certain Windows controls that are not native to the Windows environment and that maintain a list of items. A common example is the status bar, which typically has a number of indented regions capable of holding various text messages related to the current operating status of a given program. This is not a fundamental Windows control type in the way that a list box is, but is defined by the Delphi VCL. Similar examples are **TListColumns** and **TDBGridColumns** objects, which are used to support other controls in the Delphi VCL. Controls such as this, which are not native to Windows and which require the management of a list of objects, by convention should utilize the **TCollection** and **TCollectionItem** classes for the correct data organization and support. Figure 21-1 shows a graphical example of the VCL hierarchy related to the classes that will be discussed in this chapter.

TCollection

The **TCollection** class is similar to other classes defined in Delphi that manage lists of objects, namely **TList** and **TStrings**. The **TCollection** class is used to store objects of type **TCollectionItem**. **TCollection** is an abstract class and is not used directly. An example descendant class of **TCollection** is the **TStatusPanels** collection, which is embedded in the definition of the **TStatusBar** control.

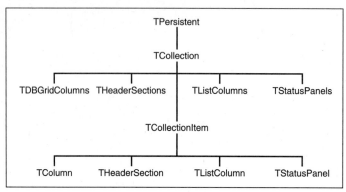

Figure 21-1 Hierarchy diagram of `TCollection` and `TCollectionItem` and descendant classes

Table 21-1 displays the properties and methods that are implemented by `TCollection`.

Table 21-1 Properties and methods implemented by `TCollection`

Use or Set This...	To Do This...	Inheritance
Add	Add new `TCollectionItem` object to list.	None
Assign	Copy contents of one `TPersistent` object to this `TCollection` object.	TPersistent
BeginUpdate	Start update operation.	None
Clear	Return `TCollection` to empty state.	None
Count	Return number of items in collection.	None
Create	Create new instance of `TCollection`.	None
Destroy	Delete instance of `TCollection`.	None
EndUpdate	Complete update operation.	None
FindItemID	Obtain `TCollectionItem` object reference with specified ID.	None
GetItem	Return indexed collection item.	None
Items	Provide access to collection items.	None

TCollectionItem

The `TCollectionItem` class is used to define the items that will be stored in each instance of `TCollection`. `TCollectionItem` is an abstract class that is not used directly. The definition of `TCollectionItem` is relatively simple and only implements a small set of members. The descendants of this class would typically define those internal properties that must be maintained in the collection to allow the control that owns the corresponding `TCollection` object to render the individual items from the collection correctly.

Table 21-2 displays the properties and methods that are implemented by TCollectionItem.

Table 21-2 Properties and methods implemented by TCollectionItem

Use or Set This...	To Do This...	Inheritance
Collection	Return or set owner TCollection object.	None
Create	Create new instance of TCollectionItem.	None
Destroy	Delete instance of TCollectionItem.	None
Index	Return or set item index value.	None
SetIndex	Specify index for collection item.	None

TListColumns

TListColumns is used by the TCustomListView class. The TCustomListView class is an abstract class that is the foundation used for the TListView type control. TListColumns inherits all of the properties and methods associated with the TCollection class and provides an additional Owner property.

Table 21-3 displays the properties and methods that are implemented by TListColumns.

Table 21-3 Properties and methods implemented by TListColumns

Use or Set This...	To Do This...	Inheritance
Add	Add new TListColumn object to collection.	TCollection
Create	Create new instance of TListColumns.	TCollection
Items	Retrieve or set the indexed TListColumns object in the collection.	TCollection
Owner	Retrieve TCustomListView that owns the collection.	None

TListColumn

This class is used to implement the individual objects that are stored in the TListColumns class. These form the individual objects that represent the column captions in the TCustomListView control descendants. This object stores a text string for the caption, a width type, and an alignment property for controlling the appearance of the column caption in the TCustomListView classes.

Table 21-4 displays the properties and methods that are implemented by TListColumn.

Table 21-4 Properties and methods implemented by TListColumn

Use or Set This...	To Do This...	Inheritance
Alignment	Specify how items should be justified. Use one of the following: taLeftJustify, taRightJustify, taCenter.	None
Assign	Copy contents of another TListColumn object to this instance of TListColumn.	TCollectionItem
Caption	Read or Write text string to use for caption.	None
Create	Create new instance of TListColumn.	TCollectionItem
Destroy	Free instance of TListColumn.	TCollectionItem
Width	Read or Write width of corresponding column.	None
WidthType	Determine how a list column is sized.	None

THeaderSections

The THeaderSections class contains the THeaderSection items defined by the THeaderSection class. It is used by the THeader Win95 control.

Table 21-5 displays the properties and methods that are implemented by THeaderSections.

Table 21-5 Properties and methods implemented by THeaderSections

Use or Set This...	To Do This...	Inheritance
Add	Add new THeaderSections object to collection.	TCollection
Create	Create new instance of THeaderSections.	TCollection
Items	Retrieve or set the indexed THeaderSections object in the collection.	TCollection

THeaderSection

This class is used to implement the individual objects that are stored in the THeaderSections class. These form the objects that represent the separate header sections contained in any THeader control. A THeaderSection can be one of two styles: either hsText or hsOwnerDraw. If the style for the section is set to hsOwnerDraw, the programmer must specify code in an OnSectionDraw event handler, which then renders whatever image is desired on the canvas of the section made available in the handler. Otherwise, the control uses a text string implemented in this class's private class member variables. The attributes associated with each THeaderSection and available by class methods are Text, Width, MinWidth, MaxWidth, Alignment, Style, and AllowClick.

Table 21-6 displays the properties and methods that are implemented by `THeaderSection`.

Table 21-6 Properties and methods implemented by `THeaderSection`

Use or Set This...	To Do This...	Inheritance
Alignment	Return or set alignment style of section (`taLeftJustify`, `taRightJustify`, `taCenter`).	None
AllowClick	Determine whether section should respond to click events by triggering `OnClick` handler.	None
Assign	Copy contents of another `THeaderSection` to current instance.	TCollectionItem
Create	Create new instance of `THeaderSection`.	TCollectionItem
Destroy	Release instance of `THeaderSection`.	TCollectionItem
Left	Return left-side coordinates of section.	None
MaxWidth	Specify maximum width in pixels of section.	None
MinWidth	Specify minimum width in pixels of section.	None
Right	Return right-side coordinates of section.	None
Style	Specify `hsText` or `hsOwnerDraw` style.	None
Text	Text used for `hsText` style sections.	None
Width	Set or obtain current section width.	None

TStatusPanels

The `TStatusPanels` class contains the `TStatusPanel` items defined by the `TStatusPanel` class.

Table 21-7 displays the properties and methods that are implemented by `TStatusPanels`.

Table 21-7 Properties and methods implemented by `TStatusPanels`

Use or Set This...	To Do This...	Inheritance
Add	Add new `TStatusPanel` object to collection.	TCollection
Create	Create new instance of `TStatusPanels`.	TCollection
Destroy	Delete instance of `TStatusPanels`.	TCollection
Items	Retrieve or set the indexed `TStatusPanel` object in the collection.	TCollection

TStatusPanel

This class is used to implement the individual objects stored in the **TStatusPanels** class. These form the objects that represent the separate panels contained in any **TStatus** control. A **TStatusPanel** can be one of two styles: either **hsText** or **hsOwnerDraw**. If the style for the section is set to **hsOwnerDraw**, the programmer must specify code in an **OnDrawPanel** event handler, which then renders whatever image is desired on the canvas of the panel made available in the handler. Otherwise, the control uses a text string implemented in this class's private class member variables. The attributes associated with each **TStatusPanel** and available by class methods are **Alignment**, **Bevel**, **Style**, **Text**, and **Width**.

Table 21-8 displays the properties and methods that are implemented by **TStatusPanel**.

Table 21-8 Properties and methods implemented by TStatusPanel

Use or Set This...	To Do This...	Inheritance
Alignment	Return alignment style of section (taLeftJustify, taRightJustify, taCenter).	None
Assign	Copy contents of another TStatusPanel to current instance.	TCollectionItem
Bevel	Specify whether Bevel is up or down.	None
Create	Create new instance of TStatusPanel.	TCollectionItem
Destroy	Release instance of TStatusPanel.	TCollectionItem
GetDisplayName	Obtain display name of TStatusPanel.	TCollectionItem
Style	Specify hsText or hsOwnerDraw style.	None
Text	Text used for hsText style sections.	None
Width	Set or obtain current section width.	None

TDBGridColumns

The **TDBGridColumns** class is used to hold a collection of **TColumn** objects that correspond to the columns in a **TDBGrid** component. Each **TDBGrid** component contains a **TDBGridColumns** object and makes it available to the programmer via the **Columns** property. The attributes of the **TColumn** objects contained in the **TDBGridColumns** is set up at design time using the Columns editor, which is available in the Object Inspector under **Columns** or from the Component Editor menu. At run time you can use the various **TDBGridColumn** methods to manipulate the columns contained in the component.

Table 21-9 contains the properties and methods defined by the **TDBGridColumns** class.

Table 21-9 Properties and methods implemented by TDBGridColumns

Use or Set This...	To Do This...	Inheritance
Add	Create new collection item.	TCollection
Create	Create new instance of TDBGridColumns.	TCollection
Destroy	Destroy instance of TDBGridColumns.	TCollection
Grid	Reference to the DBGrid control that owns this collection.	None
Items	Set or obtain individual TColumn objects in the collection.	None
RebuildColumns	Re-create columns in grid from fields in connected database.	None
RestoreDefaults	Return all columns to default state.	None
State	Set or obtain state of columns, either csDefault or csCustomized.	None

TColumn

The **TColumn** class defines the objects that are contained in the **TDBGridColumns** class. The **TColumn** class determines how a column in a **TDBGrid** should look. Various attributes are available to the programmer, such as color, font, width, and so forth.

Table 21-10 contains the properties and methods defined by the **TDBGridColumns** class.

Table 21-10 Properties and methods implemented by TColumn

Use or Set This...	To Do This...	Inheritance
Alignment	Set/obtain column alignment.	None
Assign	Copy contents of one TColumn object to another TColumn object.	TCollectionItem
AssignedValues	Return set of attributes that have been modified from default condition.	None
ButtonStyle	Set/obtain button style for column.	None
Color	Set/obtain color for column.	None
Create	Create new instance of TColumn.	TCollectionItem
CreateTitle	Create instance of TColumnTitle.	None
DefaultAlignment	Return alignment property of corresponding database field.	None
DefaultColor	Return color property of corresponding database field.	None
DefaultFont	Return TitleFont of TDBGrid object.	None
DefaultReadOnly	Return default ReadOnly setting.	None
DefaultWidth	Return default Width setting.	None
Destroy	Destroy instance of TColumn.	TCollectionItem

continued on next page

continued from previous page

Use or Set This...	To Do This...	Inheritance
DropDownRows	Set/obtain number of drop-down rows for combo boxes in TColumn object.	None
Field	Set/obtain corresponding field reference for TColumn object.	None
FieldName	Set/obtain corresponding field name for TColumn object.	None
Font	Set/obtain font in use by TColumn object.	None
GetGrid	Return TDBGrid reference that owns this TColumn object.	None
PickList	Set/obtain the items in the column pick list.	None
ReadOnly	Set/obtain the state of the ReadOnly attribute for the column.	None
RestoreDefaults	Return column settings to default.	None
Title	Set/obtain column title.	None
Width	Set/obtain column width.	None

Add METHOD

Objects Affected TCollection and all its descendants

Purpose Used to create a new element in a **TCollection** class.

Declaration

```
function Add: TCollectionItem;        {TCollection}
function Add: TColumn;        {TDBGridColumns}
function Add: THeaderSection;        {THeaderSections}
function Add: TListColumn;        {TListColumns}
function Add: TStatusPanel;        {TStatusPanels}
```

Example Syntax

```
procedure TForm1.FormCreate(Sender: TObject);
var
ths : THeaderSection;
begin
    ths := HeaderControl1.Sections.Add;
    ths.Text := 'hi';
end;
```

Description The above example uses the **Add** method to create a new section in a **THeader** control that is automatically added to the collection of other **THeaderSections** present in the **THeader** control. Then the newly created **Header** section's text value is set using the return value from the **Add** method to obtain a reference to the desired component. Note that the **Add** function returns an instance of the particular type of **TCollectionItem**, which the given **TCollection** class is the container for.

Alignment PROPERTY

Objects Affected   TStatusPanel, THeaderSection, TListColumn, TColumn

Purpose   Used to indicate the text justification used when text is displayed in the corresponding TCollectionItem object. Legal values are from the set [taLeftJustify, taRightJustify, taCenter].

Declaration

```
property Alignment:
```

Example Syntax

```
procedure TForm1.FormCreate(Sender: TObject);
var
ths : THeaderSection;
begin
    ths := HeaderControl1.Sections.Add;
    ths.Text := 'bar';
    ths.Alignment := taCenter;
end;
```

Description   The above example uses the Add method to create a new section in a THeader control similarly to the way it is created in the Add method description. After the text for the THeaderSection is set, the text is centered by setting the Alignment property to taCenter.

AllowClick PROPERTY

Objects Affected   THeaderSection

Purpose   Used to indicate whether or not a THeaderSection should respond to a mouse click. This property is a boolean that takes on True or False as legal values. If True, then the header section acts like a pushbutton and will cause the event handler OnSectionClick to be triggered when the mouse click takes place. If the property value is False, the header section will not depress when clicked nor will the event handler be triggered. Individual THeaderSections in the owning THeader control can be set independently either at design time using the component editor for THeader controls, or programmatically, using this property.

Declaration

```
property AllowClick
```

Example Syntax

```
procedure TForm1.FormCreate(Sender: TObject);
var
ths : THeaderSection;
```

continued on next page

continued from previous page

```
begin
    ths := HeaderControl1.Sections.Add;
    ths.Text := 'bar';
    ths.AllowClick:= false;
end;
```

Description   This example is similar to others in which a **THeader** control section is created. In this case, the **AllowClick** for the newly created **THeaderSection** is set to **False**.

Assign METHOD

Objects Affected   **TCollection** and all its descendants

Purpose   Used to copy the contents of one **TCollection** object to another. It is always possible to assign one object to another if the two objects are of the same type. If the two objects are not of the same type, then they have to "know" how to perform the assignment. The concept of knowing how to perform the assignment essentially means that the **Assign** method for the particular descendant of **TCollection** has been defined with knowledge of other potential objects that it might want to know how to handle. If the objects don't know how to perform the conversion, an **EConvertError** exception will be raised. In general, the complete internal state of the **TCollectionItem** objects in a **TCollection** are copied for this family of classes. That is to say, the **Assign** method iterates over each member of the **TCollectionItem** objects owned by the source **TCollection** object and copies them one by one into the destination **TCollectionItem**, expanding the **TCollectionItem** list as necessary.

Declaration

```
procedure Assign(Source: TPersistent); override;
```

Example Syntax

```
procedure TForm1.FormCreate(Sender: TObject);
var
ths1, ths2 : THeaderSection;
begin
    ths1 := HeaderControl1.Sections.Add; { add section to Header 1}
    ths1.Text := 'foo'; { set string value }
    ths1.AllowClick:= false; { disable click events }
    ths1 := HeaderControl1.Sections.Add; { add second section }
    ths1.Text := 'bar'; { set string value }
    ths1.AllowClick:= true; {enable click events }
    ths2.Assign(ths1); {perform copy operation }
end;
```

Description   In this example, the contents of one **THeader** control is copied into another one on the same form after the first **THeader** control is initialized with two sections containing the strings **'foo'** and **'bar'**, respectively.

AssignedValues PROPERTY

Objects Affected   TColumn

Purpose   Determines what properties of a **TColumn** object have been changed from the default settings. The property returns a value of type **TColumnValues**, which is defined as a set made up of the following values:

```
TColumnValue = (cvColor, cvWidth, cvFont, cvAlignment, cvReadOnly,
cvTitleColor, cvTitleCaption, cvTitleAlignment, cvTitleFont);
```

Declaration

```
property AssignedValues;
```

Example Syntax

```
procedure TForm1.Button1Click(Sender: TObject);
var
  theCols : TDBGridColumns;
  theCol : TColumn;
  theVals, theVals2 : TColumnValues;

begin
    theCols := DBGrid1.Columns;
    theCol := theCols.items[0];
    theVals := theCol.AssignedValues;
    theVals2 := theVals;
end;
```

Description   This example shows how to fetch the **AssignedValues** property from a **TDBGrid** component.

BeginUpdate METHOD

Objects Affected   TCollection and all its descendants

Purpose   Indicates that an internal update operation is beginning and can be used to inhibit refreshing of the control object until a matching **EndUpdate** call is issued. This method utilizes internal reference counts, which means that **BeginUpdate** calls and **EndUpdate** calls can be nested, and updating will be inhibited until a number of **EndUpdate** calls have been issued equal to the number of times the **BeginUpdate** method has been called.

Declaration

```
procedure BeginUpdate;
```

Example Syntax

```
procedure TMyCollection.Clear;
begin
  if FItems.Count > 0 then
```

continued on next page

continued from previous page

```
      begin
        BeginUpdate;
        try
          while FItems.Count > 0 do TCollectionItem(FItems.Last).Free;
        finally
          EndUpdate; // See EndUpdate description
        end;
      end;
    end;
```

Description   This example mimics the default processing that occurs for descendants of `TCollection` classes. In this case, the `BeginUpdate` method is called while the loop that releases the collection items executes. Then an `EndUpdate` call is issued, which allows screen updates to take place if necessary.

Bevel PROPERTY

Objects Affected   `TStatusPanel`

Purpose   Used to read or write the way the bevel should appear for a `TStatusPanel` in a `TStatusPanels` object. The individual `TStatusPanel` members of the `TStatusPanels` object can be set independently to one of the following values:

```
TStatusPanelBevel = (pbNone, pbLowered, pbRaised);
```

Declaration

```
property Bevel:
```

Example Syntax

```
procedure TForm1.Button1Click(Sender: TObject);
begin
  StatusBar1.Panels.Items[0].Bevel := pbRaised;
end;
```

Description   This example causes the first panel of a `StatusBar` control to be rendered with a raised bevel. After changing the bevel property, the `Panel` will be automatically redrawn. Figure 21-2 shows an example of the variations obtained with different settings of this property.

ButtonStyle PROPERTY

Objects Affected   `TColumn`

Purpose   Depending on how a `TColumn`'s field has been defined, the `ButtonStyle` property determines the different ways the user can choose values for that column, as described in Table 21-11.

Figure 21-2 Example of `Bevel` property
values for `TStatusPanel` objects

Table 21-11 Legal values for ButtonStyle property

ButtonStyle Value	Meaning
cbsAuto	If the column's field is a lookup field or has a pick list assigned to it, TDBGrid will show a combo box in the column, so the user can drop down the list to choose a value.
cbsEllipsis	The column will always show an ellipsis button that the user can click to choose a value. Clicking the ellipsis button triggers an OnEditButtonClick event.
cbsNone	Even if the column's field is a lookup field or has a pick list assigned to it, no combo box or ellipsis button is provided to let the user choose a value from a list.

Declaration

```
property ButtonStyle:
```

Example Syntax

```
procedure TForm1.Button1Click(Sender: TObject);
begin
  DBGrid1.Columns.Items[0].ButtonStyle := cbsEllipsis;
  DBGrid1.Refresh;
end;
```

Description

In this example, the **ButtonStyle** for a **DBGrid** column is set to
cbsEllipsis and the grid is refreshed. If the grid is connected to a database field, the cells in the column will display an ellipsis. The ellipsis style
is selected when the user is to be prompted to select an item from a finite
list provided by the database field the button is linked to.

Caption PROPERTY

Objects Affected	TListColumn
Purpose	Sets or obtains the Caption property of a TListColumn object.
Declaration	

```
property Caption: string read FCaption write SetCaption;
```

Example Syntax

```
procedure TForm1.Button1Click(Sender: TObject);
begin
     ListView1.Columns.Items[1].Caption := Edit1.Text;
end;
```

Description	This example copies the contents of an edit control into the second column's caption of a ListView control. Note that for a ListView control to display column captions, the ViewStyle must be set to vsReport and the ShowColumnHeaders property must be set to True.

Clear METHOD

Objects Affected	TCollection and all its descendants
Purpose	Removes all TCollectionItem objects from a TCollection object and returns the resources they may have consumed to the system.
Declaration	

```
procedure Clear;
```

Example Syntax

```
procedure TForm1.Button1Click(Sender: TObject);
begin
     ths1 := HeaderControl1.Sections.Clear; { remove all sections }
end;
```

Description	This example clears all sections from a Header control.

Collection PROPERTY

Objects Affected	TCollectionItem
Purpose	This property provides a reference to the TCollection object that the TCollectionItem object is a member of. Through the use of this property, methods that operate on TCollectionItem can gain access to the public properties and methods of the owner TCollection object. This property is of primary interest when constructing new components, and the only way to obtain access to the owning collection is through this property. It would

also be of use if a function or procedure accepted a `TCollectionItem` object as an argument and the function needed to modify some other aspect of the owning `TCollection` object in the course of operation.

Declaration

```
property Collection: TCollection read FCollection write SetCollection;
```

Example Syntax

```
procedure TMyCollectionItem.Transfer(dest:integer);
begin
  if (Collection.Items.Count > 0)  and
    (dest < Collection.Items.Count) then
  begin
    BeginUpdate;
    try
        {Perform a copy of current item to dest item
         in indexed Item list}
        Collection.Items[dest].Assign(Self);
    finally
      EndUpdate;
    end;
  end;
end;
```

Description

This hypothetical class example illustrates a transfer method in which the state of one `TCollectionItem` object is copied to another object in the `TCollectionItem` list by using the `Assign` method in conjunction with the use of the `Collection` property.

Color PROPERTY

Objects Affected   `TColumn`

Purpose   Allows the programmer to set or retrieve the value of the color associated with a `TDBGrid` column.

Declaration

```
property Color: TColor
```

Example Syntax

```
procedure TForm1.Button1Click(Sender: TObject);
begin
    DBGrid1.Columns.Items[0].Color := clRed;
end;
```

Description   This example changes the color of a column in a `DBGrid` control to red in response to a button click.

Count PROPERTY

Objects Affected	`TCollection` and all its descendants
Purpose	Returns the number of `TCollectionItem` objects contained in the `TCollection` object.
Declaration	

```
property Count: Integer read GetCount;        { TCollection , public}
```

Example Syntax

```
function TForm1.GridColumns: Integer;
begin
     Result := DBGrid1.Columns.Count;
end;
```

Description   This example defines a method that is part of a `Form` declaration and that returns the number of columns contained in a `DBGrid` object when the method is invoked.

Create METHOD

Objects Affected	`TCollection`, `TCollectionItem` and all their descendants
Purpose	This virtual method is available for all descendant classes of `TCollection` and `TCollectionItem` and is used to dynamically create new instances of the desired `TCollectionItem` type. In addition to actually creating the object, the `Create` method for descendants of `TCollectionItem` automatically appends the newly created object to the end of the current item list. The owning `TCollection` object is expected as an argument in all of the descendant `Create` override methods. This function would generally not be used directly, since the `Add` method for `TCollection` objects creates a new item at the end of the item list and returns a reference to the new `TCollectionItem` object as well. (See the `Add` method description.)
Declaration	

```
constructor Create(Collection: TCollection); virtual;
```

Example Syntax

```
procedure TForm1.Button1Click(Sender: TObject);
var
  ths:THeaderSection;
begin
     ths := THeaderSection.Create(HeaderControl.Sections);
     ths.text := 'hi';
end;
```

Description   This example uses the `Create` method of the `THeaderSection` class to create a new instance of a `THeaderSection` for a `Header` control already on a form (called **HeaderControl**). It passes the actual **THeaderSections** object as an argument that allows the operation to complete correctly. The new object is assigned to a temporary variable, and then the text associated with the section is assigned. Compare this to the description for the **Add** method. The **Add** method performs essentially the same operation with a slightly simpler syntax.

CreateTitle METHOD

Objects Affected   **TColumn**

Purpose   This is a protected method associated with the **TColumn** class that allows the creation of the column title object used by the column. The new **TColumnTitle** object is returned to the caller by the method. It performs the internal initialization required by the **TColumn** object appropriately.

Declaration

```
function CreateTitle: TColumnTitle;
```

Example Syntax

```
constructor TColumn.Create(Collection: TCollection);
var
  Grid: TCustomDBGrid;
begin
  Grid := nil;
  if Assigned(Collection) and (Collection is TDBGridColumns) then
    Grid := TDBGridColumns(Collection).Grid;
  if Assigned(Grid) then
    Grid.BeginLayout;
  try
    inherited Create(Collection);
    FDropDownRows := 7;
    FButtonStyle := cbsAuto;
    FFont := TFont.Create;
    FFont.Assign(DefaultFont);
    FFont.OnChange := FontChanged;
    FTitle := CreateTitle;
  finally
    if Assigned(Grid) then
      Grid.EndLayout;
  end;
end;
```

Description   This example illustrates the actual **TColumn.Create** method from the Delphi library. It uses the **CreateTitle** method to create the **FTitle** member variable for later use. It is unlikely you will ever need to use this method in your own work unless you are creating some new override of the **TColumn** class that would need to initialize the **FTitle** object in the same manner. In fact, the **CreateTitle** method can only be called from descendant classes of the **TColumn** class.

DefaultAlignment METHOD

Objects Affected	TColumn
Purpose	DefaultAlignment is a function that returns the default alignment of the data contained in a TColumn object. If the TColumn object has a field object associated with it, DefaultAlignment returns its Alignment property; otherwise, it returns taLeftJustify.
Declaration	
	`function DefaultAlignment: TAlignment;` `{ TColumn public}`
Example Syntax	

```
procedure TForm1.Button1Click(Sender: TObject);
var
da:TAlignment;
begin
    da := DBGrid1.Columns.Items[0].DefaultAlignment;
end;
```

Description	This example demonstrates how to access the DefaultAlignment property of a particular Column in a DBGrid object.

DefaultColor METHOD

Objects Affected	TColumn
Purpose	This function returns the default color associated with a TColumn object. This is the same as the Color property of the underlying TDBGrid object.
Declaration	
	`function DefaultColor: TColor;`
Example Syntax	

```
procedure TForm1.Button1Click(Sender: TObject);
var
dc:TColor;
begin
    dc := DBGrid1.Columns.Items[0].DefaultColor;
end;
```

Description	This example demonstrates how to access the DefaultColor property of a particular column in a DBGrid object.

DefaultFont METHOD

Objects Affected	TColumn
Purpose	This function returns the default font associated with a TColumn object. This is the same as the TitleFont property of the underlying TDBGrid object.
Declaration	

```
function DefaultFont: TFont;        { TColumn public}
```

Example Syntax

```
procedure TForm1.Button1Click(Sender: TObject);
var
df:TFont;
begin
      df := DBGrid1.Columns.Items[0].DefaultFont;
end;
```

Description	This example demonstrates how to access the DefaultFont property of a particular column in a DBGrid object.

DefaultReadOnly METHOD

Objects Affected	TColumn
Purpose	This function returns the DefaultreadOnly property associated with a TColumn object. By default this value is False.
Declaration	

```
function DefaultReadOnly: Boolean;
```

Example Syntax

```
procedure TForm1.Button1Click(Sender: TObject);
var
dro:Boolean;
begin
      dro := DBGrid1.Columns.Items[0].DefaultReadOnly;
end;
```

Description	This example demonstrates how to access the DefaultReadOnly property of a particular column in a DBGrid object.

DefaultWidth METHOD

Objects Affected	`TColumn`

Purpose   Returns the default width of a `TColumn` object. If the column is assigned to a field that was created using the Fields Editor, its `DisplayWidth` property is used to calculate the width in pixels. If the grid has a title row and the width of the column title is bigger than that of `DisplayWidth`, the title width becomes the default column width.

Declaration

```
function DefaultWidth: Integer;        { TColumn public}
```

Example Syntax

```
procedure TForm1.Button1Click(Sender: TObject);
var
dw:Integer;
begin
      dw := DBGrid1.Columns.Items[0].DefaultWidth;
end;
```

Description   This example demonstrates how to access the `DefaultWidth` property of a particular column in a `DBGrid` object.

Destroy METHOD

Objects Affected	`TCollection`, `TCollectionItem`, and all their descendants

Purpose   Used to return an object and all internal resources to the run-time environment.

Declaration

```
destructor Destroy;
```

Example Syntax

```
procedure TForm1.Button1Click(Sender: TObject);
var
ta:TColor;
begin
      HeaderControl1.Sections.Items[1].Destroy
end;
```

Description   This example illustrates how to remove a section from a `THeaderControl` object by using the `Destroy` method. The `Destroy` method, in addition to returning the particular `TCollectionItem` resources to the run-time environment, also unhooks the item from the collection to which it belongs.

DropDownRows PROPERTY

Objects Affected   TColumn

Purpose   Used to set or obtain the maximum number of rows that should be displayed in a drop-down list appearing in a **TColumn** object. The default is set to **7**.

Declaration

```
property DropDownRows: Integer:
```

Example Syntax

```
procedure TForm1.Button1Click(Sender: TObject);
var
ddr:Integer;
begin
    ddr := DBGrid1.Columns.Items[0].DropDownRows;
    ddr := ddr + 1;
    DBGrid1.Columns.Items[0].DropDownRows := ddr;
end;
```

Description   In this example, the value for **DropDownRows** for the first column in a **DBGrid** control is incremented by one.

EndUpdate METHOD

Objects Affected   TCollection and all its descendants

Purpose   Works in conjunction with the **BeginUpdate** method. Each time the **EndUpdate** method is called, an internal reference count is decremented. If this change causes the reference count to become zero, then the display will be refreshed if necessary; otherwise, no action is taken. During the time between the first call to **BeginUpdate** and the last call to **EndUpdate**, no drawing of the particular object will be performed; thus, this routine can be used to eliminate flicker in a component due to redrawing a control when it is not desired. For further information, see the **BeginUpdate** description.

Declaration

```
procedure EndUpdate;        { TCollection , public}
```

Example Syntax   Refer to the **BeginUpdate** section for an example of how to use this method and for a description of the syntax.

FIELD PROPERTY

Objects Affected	TColumn
Purpose	Used to set or retrieve the underlying TField object associated with a TColumn object of a TDBGrid control. TField is an abstract class; an instance of one of the descendant classes of TField will be returned in actual use. See Chapter 37, "TField and Its Descendants," for more information on the TField class.
Declaration	

```
property Field: TField:
```

Example Syntax

```
procedure TForm1.Button1Click(Sender: TObject);
var
  theField:TField;
begin
    theField := DBGrid1.Columns.Items[0].Field;
end;
```

Description Here the field associated with the first column in a DBGrid control is assigned to a variable in preparation for further activity involving the information contained in the field.

FieldName PROPERTY

Objects Affected	TColumn
Purpose	Sets or retrieves the name of the field associated with the TColumn object of a TDBGrid control.
Declaration	

```
property FieldName: string:
```

Example Syntax

```
procedure TForm1.Button1Click(Sender: TObject);
var
  theFieldName:string;
begin
    theFieldName := DBGrid1.Columns.Items[0].FieldName;
end;
```

Description Here the field name associated with the first column of the DBGrid control is retrieved.

FindItemID METHOD

Objects Affected	`TCollection` and all its descendants
Purpose	Obtains a reference to a specific member of the `TCollection` that is identified by an integer identifier previously assigned to the corresponding `TCollectionItem` object.
Declaration	

```
function FindItemID(ID: Integer): TCollectionItem;
```

Example Syntax

```
procedure TForm1.StatusBar1DrawPanel(StatusBar: TStatusBar;
  Panel: TStatusPanel; const Rect: TRect);
var
  tempPanel:TStatusPanel;
  Bitmap1:TBitmap;
begin

  Bitmap1 := TBitmap.Create;
  tempPanel := TStatusPanel(StatusBar.Panels.FindItemId(2));

  // this could also be written equivalently as:
  // tempPanel := StatusBar.Panels[2];

  if(Panel = tempPanel) then
    Bitmap1.LoadFromFile('c:\windows\tartan.bmp');

  // draw two versions of the bitmaps to ensure that we cover
  // the whole area of the panel canvas.
  StatusBar.Canvas.Draw(Rect.Left,Rect.Top, Bitmap1);
  StatusBar.Canvas.Draw(Rect.Left+Bitmap1.Width,Rect.Top, Bitmap1);

  Bitmap1.Free;

end;
```

Description   In this example code the `FindItemID` function is used in place of an array access, but the effect is the same, since the items in a collection receive an internal identifier that is equivalent to the corresponding item's array index.

Font PROPERTY

Objects Affected	`TColumn`
Purpose	Sets or retrieves the `TFont` object associated with a `TColumn` object of a `TDBGrid` control.
Declaration	

```
property Font: TFont;
```

Example Syntax

```
procedure TForm1.Button1Click(Sender: TObject);
var
font:TFont;
begin
     font := DBGrid1.Columns.Items[0].Font;
end;
```

Description   The font associated with the first column of a DBGrid control is retrieved
for additional operations.

GetDisplayName METHOD

Objects Affected   TStatusPanel

Purpose   Obtains an internal name representation for the TStatusPanel object. This
will either be the text contained in the status panel, or the class identifier
string 'TStatusPanel' if the text string for the particular TStatusPanel
object text string is empty.

Declaration

```
function GetDisplayName: string;
```

Example Syntax

```
procedure TForm1.StatusBar1DrawPanel(StatusBar: TStatusBar;
  Panel: TStatusPanel; const Rect: TRect);
var
  Bitmap1: TBitmap;
  tempPanel:TStatusPanel;
begin
  // perform the drawing desired on TStatusPanel
  // This is called for every panel whenever the
  // System determines that the panels need to be
  // redrawn. Primarily this occurs when the form
  // is resized or becomes topmost after having been
  // covered by another form.
  Bitmap1 := TBitmap.Create; // working bitmap object

// The following conditionals determine which of the
// three panels on the status bar is being redrawn and
// then load the appropriate graphic for that panel.

// See Chapter 21 of the Delphi 3.0 SuperBible for a discussion
// of an alternative method of accessing individual TCollectionItems
// of a TCollection using FindItemID function

  if(Panel = StatusBar.Panels[0]) then
    begin
    Bitmap1.LoadFromFile('c:\windows\Tartan.bmp');
    StatusBar.Panels[0].Text := 'one';
    Edit1.Text := StatusBar.Panels[0].GetDisplayName;
    end
  else if(Panel = StatusBar.Panels[1]) then
    begin
```

```
        Bitmap1.LoadFromFile('c:\windows\Marble.bmp');
        Edit2.Text := StatusBar.Panels[1].GetDisplayName;
        end
     else if(Panel = StatusBar.Panels[2]) then
        begin
        Bitmap1.LoadFromFile('c:\windows\Metal Links.bmp');
        Edit3.Text := StatusBar.Panels[2].GetDisplayName;
        end;

   // draw two versions of the bitmaps to ensure that we cover
   // the whole area of the panel canvas.
   StatusBar1.Canvas.Draw(Rect.Left,Rect.Top, Bitmap1);
   StatusBar1.Canvas.Draw(Rect.Left+Bitmap1.Width,Rect.Top, Bitmap1);

     Bitmap1.Free;
   end;
```

Description   This example is taken from the project example and illustrates the use of the `GetDisplayName` function. In the case when the `DrawPanel` method is invoked for panel `0`, the text of the corresponding panel is assigned a value of `'1'`, which is returned by the `GetDisplayName` method and in turn placed into the `Edit1` component. The other two cases have not had a string assigned, and so as a result the `GetDisplayName` will return `'TStatusPanel'`, which is what will appear in the other two edit controls.

GetGrid METHOD

Objects Affected   `TColumn`

Purpose   Used to obtain a reference to the `TDBGrid` control to which the `TColumn` object belongs. This provides a hook to all of the public methods and properties associated with a `TDBGrid` component. Note that this is a protected method and is exposed publicly by the `Grid` property.

Declaration

```
function GetGrid; TDBCustomGrid;
```

Example Syntax

```
procedure TMyColumn.copy(index:integer);
var
     theGrid:TDBGrid;
begin
     theGrid:= GetGrid;
     Assign(theGrid.Columns.Items[index]);
end;
```

Description   This method copies the contents of the column indicated by the value of the index variable into the object for which this method is invoked. Note that this is a member function of a class derived from `TColumn` called `TMyColumn`.

GetItem METHOD

Objects Affected	TCollection and all its descendants
Purpose	This protected method is used by all descendants of TCollection to obtain a reference to a particular item in the TCollection item list. This method is exposed publicly via the Items property. Note that it is generally overridden by the descendant class to return an object of the appropriate type.

Declaration

```
function GetItem(Index: Integer): TCollectionItem;
```

Example Syntax

```
function TMyHeaderSections.GetSectionWidth(index:integer): integer;
var
    theWidth:integer;
begin
    Result := GetItem(index).Width;
end;
```

Description	This method for a hypothetical class derived from THeaderSections uses the GetItem method to obtain a reference to the specified section, then returns the Width property for that section.

Grid PROPERTY

Objects Affected	TDBGridColumns
Purpose	This property is used to gain access to the TDBGrid object to which the TDBGridColumns object belongs. It is read-only. It returns an object of the same type as the GetGrid method returns.

Declaration

```
property Grid: TDBGrid;
```

Example Syntax

```
procedure TForm1.XferColumn(theColumn:TColumn; index:integer);
var
    theGrid:TDBGrid;
begin
    theGrid := theColumn.Grid;
    theGrid.Columns.Items[index].Assign(theColumn);
end;
```

Description	This procedure accepts a Source column contained in some unknown TDBGrid component and obtains the TDBGrid object using the Grid property of the TColumn object. Then the destination is copied from the source by using the Assign method to copy from theColumn, which is the source

column, to the indicated destination column, which is specified by index value. Once `theGrid` is determined, it is possible to index back into the correct `TColumn` object through the mechanism illustrated in this example.

Index PROPERTY

Objects Affected   `TCollectionItem`

Purpose   This property provides read and write access to the `Index` value associated with the underlying `TCollectionItem` object. Note that if a write is performed to this property that changes the value, the order of the items owned by the `TCollection` will change by performing a move of the current `TCollectionItem` object to the specified new index value. No change takes place if a write of index value is out of bounds.

Declaration

```
property Index:
```

Example Syntax

```
procedure TForm1.Button1Click(Sender: TObject);
var
  i,c:integer;
  s:string;
  res:integer;
begin
  s:= edit1.text;
  c:= HeaderControl1.Sections.Count;
  res := -1;
  for i:= 0 to c-1 do
  begin
     if s = HeaderControl1.Sections.Items[i].text then
        HeaderControl1.Sections.Items[i].index := 0;
  end;
end;
```

Description   This example scans through a `THeaderControl` section list checking to see if the contents of any of the header sections match the string contained in an edit control located on the form. If a match occurs, then the `Index` property is used to fetch the index value for the particular header section item, which is assigned a new value of `0`. This has the effect of moving the header section that matches the edit control to the top of the list.

Items PROPERTY

Objects Affected   `TCollection` and all its descendants

Purpose   This property allows indexed access to the items owned by the `TCollection` class descendant. This property will return a type of object determined by the class to which the `Items` property belongs. You can also use this property to change the object an indexed item refers to. This is, in fact, used by the **Assign** method when **TCollection** objects are copied from one **TCollectionItem** list to another. For example, the **Items** property for **TStatusPanels** will return a type of **TStatusPanel**, and so on. See the declaration below for the actual types returned. If the index value used to refer to the specific item is out of bounds, an **EListError** exception will be raised.

Declaration

TDBGridColumns

```
property Items[Index: Integer]: TColumn
```

THeaderSections

```
property Items[Index: Integer]: THeaderSection
```

TListColumns

```
property Items[Index: Integer]: TListColumn
```

TStatusPanels

```
property Items[Index: Integer]: TStatusPanel
```

Example Syntax

```
procedure TForm1.Button1Click(Sender: TObject);
begin
     ListView1.Columns.Items[1].Caption := Edit1.Text;
end;
```

Description   This example uses the **Items** property to access a particular column element of a **ListView** control to change its caption. In general when accessing the items array of a visual control object, the order of the object references will appear like this:

```
VisualControl.TCollection_ObjectReference.Items[n]
```

Left PROPERTY

Objects Affected   THeaderSection

Purpose   Used to obtain the location of the left edge of a **THeaderSection** object in a **THeader** control. The value of this property is computed by adding up the widths of all the preceding **THeaderSection** objects in the collection to which the specified **THeaderSection** belongs. The value is expressed in pixels.

Declaration

```
property Left: Integer;
```

Example Syntax

```
procedure TForm1.Button1Click(Sender: TObject);
var
    l:integer;
begin
    l := HeaderControl1.Sections.Items[1].Left
end;
```

Description   This example retrieves the left edge coordinate of a specific
THeaderSection object from a **HeaderControl** object.

MaxWidth PROPERTY

Objects Affected   **THeaderSection**

Purpose   Used to obtain the maximum string length a **THeaderSection** object in a
THeader control can contain. The default value for this is **10000**, unless
changed by the programmer.

Declaration

```
property MaxWidth: Integer;
```

Example Syntax

```
procedure TForm1.Button1Click(Sender: TObject);
var
    l:integer;
begin
    l := HeaderControl1.Sections.Items[1].MaxWidth
end;
```

Description   This example retrieves the **MaxWidth** property of a specific
THeaderSection object from a **HeaderControl** object.

MinWidth PROPERTY

Objects Affected   **THeaderSection**

Purpose   Used to obtain the smallest possible string length associated with a
THeaderSection object in a **THeader** control. The default value for this is
0, unless changed by the programmer.

Declaration

```
property MinWidth: Integer;
```

Example Syntax

```
procedure TForm1.Button1Click(Sender: TObject);
var
    l:integer;
begin
    l := HeaderControl1.Sections.Items[1].MinWidth
end;
```

| Description | This example retrieves the `MinWidth` property of a specific `THeaderSection` object from a `HeaderControl` object. |

Owner PROPERTY

| Objects Affected | `TListColumns` |
| Purpose | Used to obtain the `TListView` component that owns the particular `TListColumn` object referred to in the call. By the use of this property, the programmer can gain access to the public and published properties of the owning `TListView` component from any particular `TListColumn` object. |

Declaration

```
property Owner: TCustomListView;
```

Example Syntax

```
procedure TForm1.XferCol(theListCol:TListColumn; index:integer);
var
    theListView:TListView;
begin
    theListView := theListCol.Owner;
    theListView.Columns.Items[index].Assign(theListCol);
end;
```

| Description | This example is similar in design to the example presented for the `Grid` property but applicable to `TListColumn` components. The `Owner` property is used to obtain the particular `TListView` component that owns the *theListCol* parameter, and then the indexed `TListCol` is assigned accordingly. |

PickList PROPERTY

| Objects Affected | `TColumn` |
| Purpose | This property provides access to the pick list associated with a `TColumn` if a pick list has been defined in the form of a list of strings stored in a `TStrings` object. If no pick list has been defined, an empty `TStrings` object is returned. |

Declaration

```
property PickList: TStrings;
```

Example Syntax

```
procedure TForm1.Button1Click(Sender: TObject);
var
  sl:TStrings;
begin
    sl := DBGrid1.Columns.Items[0].PickList;
end;
```

Description   This example retrieves the string list associated with a `PickList` for a `TColumn` object of a `TDBGrid` component, if defined. If there is no pick list defined for the `TColumn` object, then an empty list is returned. Even though the generic `TStrings` type object is returned by the property, this is an abstract class, and the actual class type returned by the `PickList` property is a `TStringList` type object.

ReadOnly PROPERTY

Objects Affected   `TColumn`

Purpose   Used to set or retrieve the value of the `ReadOnly` state of a `TColumn` object. If `True`, then the contents of the `TColumn` object cannot be changed.

Declaration

```
property ReadOnly: Boolean;
```

Example Syntax

```
procedure TForm1.Button1Click(Sender: TObject);
var
  ro:boolean;
begin
    sl := DBGrid1.Columns.Items[0].ReadOnly;
end;
```

Description   This example retrieves the read-only state of a `TColumn` object.

RebuildColumns METHOD

Objects Affected   `TDBGridColumns`

Purpose   This procedure is used to cause the `TDBGridColumns` object to be rebuilt according to the fields available in the database to which the underlying `TDBGrid` object is connected.

Declaration

```
procedure RebuildColumns;
```

Example Syntax

```
procedure TForm1.Button1Click(Sender: TObject);
begin
    DBGrid1.Columns.RebuildColumns;
end;
```

Description   This example rebuilds the columns contained in a `TDBGrid` component by invoking the `RebuildColumns` method.

RestoreDefaults METHOD

Objects Affected	`TColumn`, `TDBGridColumns`
Purpose	This method is used to cause the default values for a particular column or all columns to be retrieved from the underlying database. If `RestoreDefaults` is called on a `TColumn` object, then only that particular column will be restored. If `RestoreDefaults` is called on a `TDBGridColumns` object, then all columns will be restored.
Declaration	

```
procedure RestoreDefaults;
```

Example Syntax	

```
procedure TForm1.Button1Click(Sender: TObject);
begin
     DBGrid1.Columns.RestoreDefaults;
end;
```

Description	This method is used to restore all default conditions to the columns contained in a `TDBGrid` component.

Right PROPERTY

Objects Affected	`THeaderSection`
Purpose	Used to obtain the location of the right-edge of a `THeaderSection` object in a `THeader` control. The value is expressed in pixels.
Declaration	

```
property Right: Integer;
```

Example Syntax	

```
procedure TForm1.Button1Click(Sender: TObject);
var
   r:integer;
begin
   r := HeaderControl1.Sections.Items[1].Right
end;
```

Description	This example retrieves the right-edge coordinate of a specific `THeaderSection` object from a `HeaderControl` object.

SetIndex METHOD

Objects Affected	`TCollectionItem` and all its descendants
Purpose	This protected method provides the ability to write the index value to a particular `TCollectionItem` object. When this value causes a change to

the existing value, a move is performed on the underlying object, position-ing it at the appropriate place in the TCollectionItem list. If the specified index is out of bounds, an EListError exception will be raised. Additionally, this is a virtual method that may be overridden by descendant classes if necessary.

Declaration

```
procedure SetIndex(Value: Integer);
```

Example Syntax

```
TMyHeaderSection.MoveSection(dest:integer)
begin
      SetIndex(dest);
end
```

Description

In this example, a method is defined for a class derived from THeaderSection called TMyHeaderSection. The new method, called MoveSection, utilizes the SetIndex method of TCollectionItem objects to change the index value of the object, which in turn causes the header section to be moved if the value changes from the original.

State PROPERTY

Objects Affected   TDBGridColumns

Purpose   This property is used to read or write the state of the columns owned by a TDBGridColumns object. The legal values for this property are either csDefault or csCustomized. The meanings of these values are shown in Table 21-12.

Table 21-12 Definition of TDBGridColumnsState

State Value	State Definition
csCustomized	The grid's column objects are persistent, which means that they're separate from the dataset's field properties. (You can make changes to persistent columns without affecting any of the corresponding fields.)
csDefault	The grid's column objects are the default column objects created using the properties of the dataset's field objects. Changes you make to the column objects are reflected in the field objects, and vice versa.

Declaration

```
property State: TDBGridColumnsState;
```

Style PROPERTY

Objects Affected   THeaderSection, TStatusPanel

Purpose   Used to determine whether or not a **THeaderSection** or **TStatusPanel** is a normal text-based object or an owner-draw object. In the case of the **THeaderSection**, the legal values are either **hsText** or **hsOwnerDraw**, while for a **TStatusPanel** the values can be either **psText** or **psOwnerDraw**. If either object is specified as owner draw, then the programmer determines what appears when the **OnDrawPanel** or **OnDrawSection** handlers are triggered by performing the desired drawing functions at that time.

Declaration

```
property Style: THeaderSectionStyle;

property Style: TStatusPanelStyle
```

Example Syntax   Refer to the example project listed at the end of the chapter for an example of the use of the **Style** property.

Text PROPERTY

Objects Affected   THeaderSection, TStatusPanel

Purpose   Used to specify what text should appear in either of the two object classes to which this method pertains. The style must be either **hsText** or **psText** for **THeaderSection** and **TStatusPanel**, respectively, for the text to be displayed. This property is readable and writable.

Declaration

```
property Text: string;
```

Example Syntax

```
procedure TForm1.FormCreate(Sender: TObject);
var
ths : THeaderSection;
begin
    ths := HeaderControl1.Sections.Add;
    ths.Text := 'hi';
end;
```

Description   The above example illustrates a way to set the text that appears in a **HeaderControl** section at run time via the use of the **Text** property.

Title PROPERTY

Objects Affected TColumn

Purpose This property is used to specify or obtain the title object associated with a TColumn object appearing in a TDBGrid object. This object is of the type TColumnTitle and contains information regarding the Font used to render the title as well as the title text.

Declaration

```
property Title: TColumnTitle;
```

Example Syntax

```
procedure TForm1.Button1Click(Sender: TObject);
begin
    DBGrid1.Columns.Column[0].Title.Caption := 'hi';
    DBGrid1.Columns.Column[0].Title.Font := 'arial';

end;
```

Description In the above example, the title caption and font are modified programmatically by accessing properties exposed by the Title property of a particular column in a DBGrid component.

Width PROPERTY

Objects Affected THeaderSection, TStatusPanel, TColumn, TListColumn

Purpose Used to determine the width (in pixels) of the particular object referenced by the method when it is called. This property is readable and writable.

Declaration

```
property Width: Integer
```

Example Syntax

```
procedure TForm1.Button1Click(Sender: TObject);
var
   w:integer;
begin
   w := HeaderControl1.Sections.Items[1].width
end;
```

Description This example retrieves the width of a specific THeaderSection object from a HeaderControl component.

WidthType PROPERTY

Objects Affected	`TListColumn`
Purpose	This property is available at run time and is a read-only property. If `WidthType` returns `ColumnTextWidth`, then the column header is sized automatically to fit the text contained in the columns. If `WidthType` returns `ColumnHeaderWidth`, then the column header is sized automatically to fit the text in the column header. If `WidthType` is zero or greater, the column header width will be the `WidthType` value in pixels. The list view must have its `ShowColumnHeaders` property set, and its `ViewStyle` property must be `vsReport` to see column headers. To set the column width or to have the column automatically sized, use the `Width` property.
Declaration	

```
property WidthType: TWidth
```

Example Syntax

```
procedure TForm1.FormCreate(Sender: TObject);
var
tw:TWidth;
begin
    tw := ListView1.Columns[0].WidthType;
end;
```

Description	This example retrieves the `WidthType` property from a `ListView Column` at form creation time. The returned value can be either `ColumnTextWidth`, `ColumnHeaderWidth`, or a numeric value. `ColumnTextWidth` and `ColumnHeaderWidth` are constant values defined in the `COMCTRLS` unit.

Example Project

The following example project illustrates some simple concepts related to the use of the `TCollection` and `TCollectionItem` classes. With minor variations, the concepts applied in this example to the `TStatusBar` component are applicable to other descendants of `TCollection` as well. The project shows how to create a status bar control that implements owner-draw capability and how to draw something different on each of the defined panels in the status bar. This is performed by iterating over the `TStatusPanels` members that are `TStatusPanel` objects.

Here is what the code looks like:

```
unit Ch21;

interface

uses
  Windows, Messages, SysUtils, Classes, Graphics, Controls, Forms, Dialogs,
  ComCtrls;
```

```
type
  TForm1 = class(TForm)
    StatusBar1: TStatusBar;

{ Note that we will do some of our work when the the FormResize handler is executed. The
StatusBar1DrawPanel handler is called by Delphi when one of the
panels in the TStatusBar control needs to be drawn and it has the
psOwnerDraw style selected. }

    procedure FormResize(Sender: TObject);
    procedure FormCreate(Sender: TObject);
    procedure StatusBar1DrawPanel(StatusBar: TStatusBar;
      Panel: TStatusPanel; const Rect: TRect);
  private
    { Private declarations }
    //None
  public
    { Public declarations }
    //None
  end;

var
  Form1: TForm1;

implementation

{$R *.DFM}

procedure TForm1.FormResize(Sender: TObject);
var
i,j,k:integer;

begin
  i := StatusBar1.Panels.Count; // obtain count of panels
  k := StatusBar1.Width; // compute total width of status bar
  for j:=0 to i-1 do
  begin
    //Divide the status bar into equal width segments
    //every time the form is resized.
    StatusBar1.Panels[j].Width := k div i;
  end
end;

procedure TForm1.FormCreate(Sender: TObject);
var
 i,j:integer;
begin
// Set every panel in the StatusBar to be OwnerDraw style.
    i := StatusBar1.Panels.Count;
    for j:=0 to i-1 do
        StatusBar1.Panels[j].Style := psOwnerDraw;
end;

procedure TForm1.StatusBar1DrawPanel(StatusBar: TStatusBar;
  Panel: TStatusPanel; const Rect: TRect);
var
  Bitmap1: TBitmap;
  tempPanel:TStatusPanel;
```

continued on next page

continued from previous page

```
begin
   // perform the drawing desired on TStatusPanel
   // This is called for every panel whenever the
   // System determines that the panels need to be
   // redrawn. Primarily this occurs when the form
   // is resized or becomes topmost after having been
   // covered by another form.
   Bitmap1 := TBitmap.Create; // working bitmap object

// The following conditionals determine which of the
// three panels on the status bar is being redrawn and
// then load the appropriate graphic for that panel.

// See Chapter 21 of the Delphi 3.0 SuperBible for a discussion
// of an alternative method of accessing individual TCollectionItems
// of a TCollection using FindItemID function.

   if(Panel = StatusBar.Panels[0]) then
      begin
      Bitmap1.LoadFromFile('c:\windows\Tartan.bmp');
      StatusBar.Panels[0].Text := 'one';
      Edit1.Text := StatusBar.Panels[0].GetDisplayName;
      end
   else if(Panel = StatusBar.Panels[1]) then
      begin
      Bitmap1.LoadFromFile('c:\windows\Marble.bmp');
      Edit2.Text := StatusBar.Panels[1].GetDisplayName;
      end
   else if(Panel = StatusBar.Panels[2]) then
      begin
      Bitmap1.LoadFromFile('c:\windows\Metal Links.bmp');
      Edit3.Text := StatusBar.Panels[2].GetDisplayName;
      end;

// draw two versions of the bitmaps to ensure that we cover
// the whole area of the panel canvas.
StatusBar1.Canvas.Draw(Rect.Left,Rect.Top, Bitmap1);
StatusBar1.Canvas.Draw(Rect.Left+Bitmap1.Width,Rect.Top, Bitmap1);

   Bitmap1.Free;
end;

end.
```

Only a couple of handlers are required to implement the functionality of this example. The **StatusBar** control is set up with three panels when it is placed on the main form. To illustrate iterating over the **TStatusPanels** collection, different graphics are drawn on the panels. To implement owner-draw **StatusBar** panels, the style of each panel needs to be set to **psOwnerDraw**. This could be done in the Component Editor, but it is done in the **FormCreate** handler to illustrate an iteration over the **TStatusPanels** set to set the **Style** property appropriately.

Another iteration over the **TStatusPanels** members occurs in the **FormResize** handler in which the width of the **TStatusPanel** objects is set to be equal in size and take up the complete status bar regardless of whatever size the form is set to by the user during a resize operation.

In the last example, the **StatusBar1DrawPanel** handler illustrates how to implement the owner-draw technique for **TStatusPanel** objects. In this case Delphi performs the iteration automatically for any panel that has the property set to **psOwnerDraw**. Some panels might be and some might not be owner-draw in general; however, in this case all the panels are set to **psOwnerDraw** style in the **FormCreate** handler. Thus, the **StatusBar1DrawPanel** handler will be called three times, with the parameters set appropriately for each panel. The handler illustrates how to determine which of the three panels is drawn by comparing the *StatusBar* parameter to one of the members of the **TStatusPanels** collection. When they match, you have found the panel that needs to be updated. Once the desired panel has been located, the appropriate bitmap graphic is loaded from disk and drawn on the panel. Note that the graphic is drawn twice in a way that ensures that the whole panel is covered with the desired graphic. Note that an alternative routine, **StretchDraw**, could be used, but with the bitmap graphics selected for this example, the results don't look very good. The image in Figure 21-3 illustrates the results of running the program.

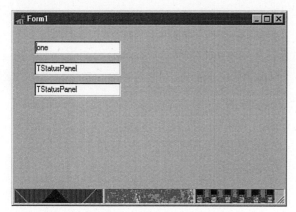

Figure 21-3 Results of running Chapter 21 example code

22

TDataLink AND ITS DESCENDANTS

The **TDataLink** class plays a fundamental role in providing data awareness to data-aware components. It literally constitutes a conduit between a data-aware component and the **TDataSet** that acts as the data-aware component's data source.

Neither **TDataLink** nor its descendants are available on Delphi's Component Palette. They derive from **TPersistent** rather than from **TComponent**. Application programmers will never be concerned with **TDataLink**, but if you're a component builder, then **TDataLink** is essential if you want to build data-aware components. When you're implementing a data-aware component, the most typical scenario is the following: The data-aware component will have a private or protected variable declared as a **TDataLink** or one of its descendants. That variable is initialized in the data-aware component's constructor, where an appropriate **TDataLink** object is created and assigned to the variable. (In the constructor you will also assign appropriate event handler procedures to the **TDataLink**'s event handler fields, if applicable. Naturally, you must also remember to undo the whole setup in the data-aware component's destructor.)

There are basically two kinds of data links: one that represents a whole record (or a set of records) in the underlying **TDataSet**, and one that represents a specific field in the current record of the underlying **TDataSet**. Naturally, the first kind is used for implementing data-aware components that interact with whole records (like **TDBGrid**), while the second kind is used for implementing data-aware components that represent only a single field (like **TDBEdit**).

TDataLink

The **TDataLink** class is the base class for all data links. Figure 22-1 shows the derivation of **TDataLink** and its descendants. Table 22-1 shows properties and methods that are implemented by **TDataLink**.

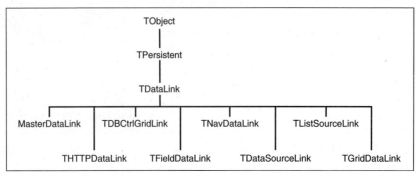

Figure 22-1 Derivation of `TDataLink` and its descendants

Table 22-1 Properties and methods implemented by `TDataLink`

Use or Set This...	To Do This...	Inheritance
Active	Inquire whether the TDataLink is active or not.	None
ActiveRecord	Set/get the TDataLink's active record.	None
BufferCount	Set/get the number of record buffers of the TDataLink.	None
DataSet	Get the TDataSet of the associated DataSource.	None
DataSource	Set/get the TDataLink's associated TDataSource.	None
DataSourceFixed	Check the validity of the TDataLink's DataSource.	None
Edit	Put the associated TDataSource in edit mode.	None
Editing	Inquire whether associated TDataSource is in editing state.	None
ReadOnly	Set/get the TDataLink's ReadOnly status.	None
RecordCount	Find the number of records in the associated dataset.	None
UpdateRecord	Update the current record.	None

Active PROPERTY

Objects Affected `TDataLink`

Purpose The **Active** property inquires as to whether the **TDataLink** is active or not.

Declaration

```
property Active: Boolean;
```

Example Syntax

```
if not DataLink.Active then
  exit;
```

Description   The `Active` property is a run-time, read-only property. The property will be `True` when the `TDataLink`'s `DataSource` is defined, and the `DataSource`'s dataset is not in the `dsInactive` state.

ActiveRecord PROPERTY

Objects Affected   `TDataLink`

Purpose   The `ActiveRecord` property sets or gets the `TDataLink`'s active record.

Declaration

```
property ActiveRecord: Integer;
```

Example Syntax

```
procedure MyDBMultiRecordControl.IterateThroughRecords;
var
  CurrentActive: Integer;
begin
  CurrentActive := FDataLink.ActiveRecord;
  { process all records here; then restore active one. }
  FDataLink.ActiveRecord := CurrentActive;
end;
```

Description   The `ActiveRecord` property will return the buffer index of the `TDataLink`'s active record, with respect to associated `TDataSet`'s active record, unless the associated `TDataSet` is in `dsSetKey` state, in which case it will return `0`.

You can successfully set this property only if the associated `TDataSet` is not in the `dsSetKey` state. When you set this property, the associated `TDataSet`'s active record is changed accordingly.

BufferCount PROPERTY

Objects Affected   `TDataLink`

Purpose   The `BufferCount` property sets or gets the number of record buffers associated with the `TDataLink`.

Declaration

```
property BufferCount: Integer;
```

Example Syntax

```
with FDataLink do for I := 0 to Pred( BufferCount ) do
begin
{ Process each buffered record here }
end;
```

Description   A `TDataLink` can represent a connection to more than one record. For instance, when a gridlike data-aware control is involved, the `TDataLink` will need a number of record buffers that is at least equal to the number of visible rows in the grid.

The **BufferCount** property is initialized to the value of **1** when the **TDataLink** is initially created. If you explicitly set the **BufferCount** property, and the **TDataLink** is active, then its internal range of acceptable record indexes will be updated accordingly.

DataSet PROPERTY

Objects Affected	TDataLink
Purpose	The **DataSet** property gets the **TDataSet** of the associated **DataSource**.
Declaration	

```
property DataSet: TDataSet;
```

Example Syntax

```
DataLink.DataSet.Open;
```

Description   The **TDataLink**'s **DataSet** property is a run-time, read-only property returning the **TDataSet** of the **TDataLink**'s **DataSource** property. Note that if the **TDataLink**'s **DataSource** property is not assigned, then the **DataSet** property will evaluate to **Nil**.

DataSource PROPERTY

Objects Affected	TDataLink
Purpose	The **DataSource** property sets or gets the **TDataLink**'s associated **TDataSource**.
Declaration	

```
property DataSource: TDataSource;
```

Example Syntax

```
DataLink.DataSource := TheDataSource;
```

Description   The **TDataLink**'s **DataSource** property represents the **TDataSource** that is associated with the **TDataLink**; typically, it will correspond to a **DataSource** property of a data-aware component. The **TDataLink**'s **DataSource** property is usually assigned a value in the write procedure of the corresponding data-aware component's **DataSource** property.

Note that because **TDataLink**'s **DataSource** property is a component reference, it is vital for the data-aware component to override the **Notification** method (defined as a virtual method in **TComponent**) and therein set the associated **TDataLink**'s **DataSource** property to **Nil** whenever the actual **TDataSource** component is removed from the form at design time (that is, the **Notification** operation parameter is equal to **opRemove**).

DataSourceFixed PROPERTY

Objects Affected	TDataLink
Purpose	The DataSourceFixed property checks the validity of the TDataLink's DataSource.
Declaration	

```
property DataSourceFixed: Boolean;
```

Example Syntax

```
if DataLink.DataSourceFixed then
raise EDatabaseError.Create( 'Datasource changed.' );
```

Description
The DataSourceFixed property is a boolean property indicating whether or not the TDataLink's DataSource property has been assigned a valid value.

Edit METHOD

Objects Affected	TDataLink
Purpose	The Edit method puts the associated TDataSource in edit mode.
Declaration	

```
function Edit: Boolean;
```

Example Syntax

```
if not DataLink.Edit then
raise EDatabaseError.Create( 'Cannot edit data.' );
```

Description
The TDataLink's Edit method will simply invoke the same method on its associated TDataSource component, if there is one. If the TDataLink has its ReadOnly property set to True, then the method will not do anything.

Editing PROPERTY

Objects Affected	TDataLink
Purpose	The Editing property inquires as to whether an associated TDataSource component is in editing state.
Declaration	

```
property Editing: Boolean;
```

Example Syntax

```
if not DataLink.Editing then exit;
```

Description   The `Editing` property is a run-time, read-only property. It will return `True` if all three of the following conditions exist: (1) there is a `TDataSource` component assigned to the `DataSource` property, (2) the component's state is `dsEdit`, `dsInsert`, or `dsSetKey`, and (3) the `TDataLink`'s `ReadOnly` property is `False`.

ReadOnly PROPERTY

Objects Affected   `TDataLink`

Purpose   The `ReadOnly` property sets or gets the `TDataLink`'s `ReadOnly` status.

Declaration

```
property ReadOnly: Boolean;
```

Example Syntax

```
if not DataLink.ReadOnly then
DataLink.Edit;
```

Description   The `TDataLink`'s `ReadOnly` property determines whether the data delivered can be changed or not. This property usually surfaces as a `ReadOnly` property in the `TDataLink`'s associated data-aware components; in other words, data-aware components don't really contain a `ReadOnly` property, but simply set or get the `ReadOnly` property of their `TDataLink` component.

RecordCount PROPERTY

Objects Affected   `TDataLink`

Purpose   The `RecordCount` property finds the number of records in the associated dataset.

Declaration

```
property RecordCount: Integer;
```

Example Syntax

```
if DataLink.RecordCount = 0 then
raise EDatabaseError.Create( 'No records to edit.' );
```

Description   The `RecordCount` property is a run-time, read-only property. It will report the number of records currently present in the `TDataSet` associated with the `TDataLink`. Note that if the `TDataSet` is in `dsSetKey` state, then this property will always evaluate to `1`. Also, if the `TDataSet`'s number of records is larger than the number of buffers available in the `TDataSet`, then the property will be equal to the number of buffers.

UpdateRecord METHOD

Objects Affected	TDataLink
Purpose	The UpdateRecord method updates the current record.
Declaration	

```
procedure UpdateRecord;
```

Example Syntax

```
FDataLink.UpdateRecord;
```

Description The UpdateRecord of the TDataLink component will call the TDataLink's UpdateData method. The UpdateData method is a protected virtual method in the TDataLink class, implemented as an empty method. This setup will allow components derived from TDataLink (such as TFieldDataLink) to implement their own versions of the UpdateData that will be called indirectly through a call to the UpdateRecord method.

The UpdateRecord method of the TDataLink will be called by the UpdateRecord method of its associated DataSet. Its purpose is that of giving the TDataLink (or more precisely, a descendant of TDataLink) a chance to update the data in the underlying record.

TTableDataLink

The TTableDataLink is a direct derivative of TDataLink. It differs from TDataLink in that it will maintain a private reference to a TTable. The only notable difference is that it has a redefined constructor that accepts a TTable parameter.

TFieldDataLink

The purpose of a TFieldDataLink is to connect its associated data source to a specific field in a dataset. In fact, the most significant feature that a TFieldDataLink adds to those of its TDataLink ancestor is the Field property, a reference to a TField. All other additions are there to support the capability of linking to that field.

Notice that any data-aware component that represents the value of a single field in a dataset will have to maintain an internal (usually private) reference to a TFieldDataLink. Symmetrically, the TFieldDataLink is able to refer to its associated data-aware component via its Control property. In this way, a data-aware component is knowledgeable about its associated TFieldDataLink, and vice versa. Table 22-2 gives the properties, methods, and events that are implemented by TFieldDataLink.

Table 22-2 Properties, methods, and events implemented by `TFieldDataLink`

Use or Set This...	To Do This...	Inheritance
CanModify	Check to see whether the underlying field can be modified.	None
Control	Refer to the `TFieldDataLink`'s associated data-aware component.	None
Edit	Edit the data in the underlying dataset's field.	None
Editing	Inquire as to whether the associated data source is being edited.	None
Field	Access the `TFieldDataLink`'s associated `TField` object.	None
FieldName	Set or get the field name of the associated `TField` object.	None
Modified	Mark the `TFieldDataLink` as modified.	None
OnActiveChange	React to changes of the `Active` property.	None
OnDataChange	React to changes in the associated dataset's data.	None
OnEditingChange	React to changes of editing states.	None
OnUpdateData	React when changes to the data in the data-aware component need to be transferred back to the underlying record.	None
Reset	Reset the data in the `TFieldDataLink`.	None

CanModify PROPERTY

Objects Affected   `TFieldDataLink`

Purpose   The `CanModify` property checks to see whether the underlying field can be modified.

Declaration

```
property CanModify: Boolean;
```

Example Syntax

```
if FieldDataLink.CanModify then
Text := FieldDataLink.Field.Text;
```

Description   The `CanModify` property is a run-time, read-only property that reports `True` when all of the following conditions exist: (1) the inherited `ReadOnly` property is `False`, (2) the `TFieldDataLink` contains an assigned reference to a `TField`, and (3) the referenced `TField`'s `CanModify` property is `True`.

Control PROPERTY

Objects Affected   `TFieldDataLink`

Purpose   The `Control` property refers to the `TFieldDataLink`'s associated data-aware component.

Declaration

```
property Control: TWinControl;
```

Example Syntax	

```
if Assigned( FieldDataLink.Control ) then
FieldDataLink.Control.SetFocus;
```

Description   The `Control` property refers to the `TWinControl` (that is, the data-aware component) that created the `TFieldDataLink`. Note that the `TFieldDataLink`'s `Control` property is usually initialized in the constructor of the associated data-aware component. Internally, the property is used to set focus on the associated data-aware component as necessary.

Edit METHOD

Objects Affected   `TFieldDataLink`

Purpose   The `Edit` method edits the data in the underlying dataset's associated field.

Declaration

```
function Edit: Boolean;
```

Example Syntax

```
if not FieldDataLink.Edit then
raise EDatabaseError.Create( 'Cannot edit data.' );
```

Description   The `TFieldDataLink`'s `Edit` method will check to see whether the `CanModify` property allows for editing, and in that case it will call the inherited `TDataLink`'s `Edit` method. Note that the method will return a boolean equivalent to the actual value of the `Editing` property.

Editing PROPERTY

Objects Affected   `TFieldDataLink`

Purpose   The `Editing` property inquires as to whether the associated data source is being edited.

Declaration

```
property Editing: Boolean;
```

Example Syntax

```
if not FieldDataLink.Editing then exit;
```

Description   The `Editing` property is a run-time, read-only property. It will return `True` if the inherited `TDataLink`'s `Editing` property is `True` and the `CanModify` property is also `True`.

Field PROPERTY

Objects Affected	`TFieldDataLink`
Purpose	The `Field` property accesses the `TFieldDataLink`'s associated `TField` object.
Declaration	

```
property Field: TField;
```

Example Syntax

```
Text := FieldDataLink.Field.DisplayText;
```

Description

The `Field` property is a run-time, read-only property that maintains a reference to the `TField` object associated with the `TFieldDataLink`. The `Field` property of the `TFieldDataLink` is usually set indirectly, by assigning a field name to a data-aware component's `DataField` property. When the `DataField` property of a data-aware control is being set, what really happens behind the scenes is that the string representing the field name is assigned to the `FieldName` property of the data-aware component's associated `TFieldDataLink`. (Note that this kind of data-aware component does not even have a private variable for managing and referencing its associated field; it simply delegates the task of keeping track of the associated field to its `TFieldDataLink` object.)

When the `TFieldDataLink`'s `FieldName` property is being assigned a value, the `TFieldDataLink` will call its private `UpdateField` procedure, where the current value of the `Field` property is first cleared (that is, assigned a `Nil`); then, if the data link is active and the given field name is not empty, the `TFieldDataLink`'s `Field` property will be assigned the `TField` reference returned by calling `FieldByName` (and specifying the given field name) on the dataset of the associated data source.

FieldName PROPERTY

Objects Affected	`TFieldDataLink`
Purpose	The `FieldName` property sets or gets the field name of associated `TField` object.
Declaration	

```
property FieldName: string;
```

Example Syntax

```
FieldDataLink.FieldName := 'CUSTOMER_ID';
```

Description   The `FieldName` property is a string that keeps track of the name of the field associated with the **TFieldDataLink**. When the property is set, it will also determine the **TField** reference returned by the **TFieldDataLink's** `Field` property.

Modified METHOD

Objects Affected   TFieldDataLink

Purpose   The `Modified` method marks the **TFieldDataLink** as modified.

Declaration

```
procedure Modified;
```

Example Syntax

```
FieldDataLink.Modified;
```

Description   The `Modified` method will simply set to **True** the **TFieldDataLink's** private `FModified` boolean variable. The modified state determines whether or not the **OnUpdateData** event is triggered when there is a record change.

OnActiveChange EVENT

Objects Affected   TFieldDataLink

Purpose   The `OnActiveChange` event reacts to changes of the **Active** property.

Declaration

```
property OnActiveChange: TNotifyEvent
```

Example Syntax

```
FFieldDataLink.OnActiveChange := ActiveChange;
```

Description   The `OnActiveChange` event of a **TFieldDataLink** is triggered anytime the **Active** property is changed. Since the **TFieldDataLink** is never visible at design time, the only way to assign an event handler procedure to the **OnActiveChange** event is by doing so in code. Typically you will do this in the constructor of the data-aware component associated with the **TFieldDataLink**.

OnDataChange EVENT

Objects Affected	`TFieldDataLink`
Purpose	The `OnDataChange` event reacts to changes in the associated dataset's data.
Declaration	

```
property OnDataChange: TNotifyEvent
```

Example Syntax

```
FieldDataLink.OnDataChange := DataChange;
```

Description
The `OnDataChange` event is triggered anytime the data underlying the `TFieldDataLink` changes. The event is also triggered when the `Field` property is changed, or when the associated dataset changes. Because the `TFieldDataLink` is never visible at design time, the only way to assign an event handler procedure to the `OnActiveChange` event is by doing so in code. Typically you will do this in the constructor of the data-aware component associated with the `TFieldDataLink`.

OnEditingChange EVENT

Objects Affected	`TFieldDataLink`
Purpose	The `OnEditingChange` event reacts to changes of editing states.
Declaration	

```
property OnEditingChange: TNotifyEvent
```

Example Syntax

```
FieldDataLink.OnEditingChange := EditingChange;
```

Description
The `OnEditingChange` event is triggered anytime there is a change in the `TFieldDataLink`'s `Editing` property. Since the `TFieldDataLink` is never visible at design time, the only way to assign an event handler procedure to the `OnEditingChange` event is by doing so in code. Typically you will do this in the constructor of the data-aware component associated with the `TFieldDataLink`.

OnUpdateData EVENT

Objects Affected	`TFieldDataLink`
Purpose	The `OnUpdateData` event reacts when changes to the data in the data-aware component need to be transferred back to the underlying record.
Declaration	

```
property OnUpdateData: TNotifyEvent
```

Example Syntax

```
FDataLink.OnUpdateData := UpdateData;
```

Description   The `OnUpdateData` event is triggered when the inherited `UpdateRecord` method is called. In practice, you will assign an appropriate event handler procedure to this event if you need to transfer data back from the data-aware component to the underlying database field. Because the `TFieldDataLink` is never visible at design time, the only way to assign an event handler procedure to the `OnUpdateData` event is by doing so in code. Typically you will do this in the constructor of the data-aware component associated with the `TFieldDataLink`.

Reset METHOD

Objects Affected   `TFieldDataLink`

Purpose   The `Reset` method resets the data in the `TFieldDataLink`.

Declaration

```
procedure Reset;
```

Example Syntax

```
FieldDataLink.Reset;
```

Description   The `Reset` method will invoke the `OnDataChange` event handler procedure (if one is assigned) and set the modified state to `False`.

TQueryDataLink

The `TQueryDataLink` is a direct derivative of `TDataLink`. The only notable difference (with respect to `TDataLink`) is that it will maintain a private reference to a `TQuery`; therefore, it has a redefined constructor that accepts a `TQuery` parameter.

TNavDataLink

The `TNavDataLink` is a direct derivative of `TDataLink`. The only notable difference (with respect to `TDataLink`) is that it will maintain a private reference to a `TDBNavigator`; therefore, it has a redefined constructor that accepts a `TDBNavigator` parameter.

TDataSourceLink

The `TDataSourceLink` is a direct derivative of `TDataLink`. It differs from `TDataLink` in that it will maintain a private reference to a `TDBLookupControl` and that it overrides the (protected) `ActiveChanged` and `RecordChanged` methods. The `TDataSourceLink` is used by `TDBLookupControl` components; the internal reference to the associated `TDBLookupControl` component is set in the constructor of the `TDBLookupControl` component itself.

TListSourceLink

The **TListSourceLink** is a direct derivative of **TDataLink**. It differs from **TDataLink** in that it will maintain a private reference to a **TDBLookupControl**, and that it overrides the (protected) **ActiveChanged** and **RecordChanged** methods. The **TListSourceLink** is used by **TDBLookupControl** components; the internal reference to the associated **TDBLookupControl** component is set in the constructor of the **TDBLookupControl** component itself.

TGridDataLink

The **TGridDataLink** is used internally to support data-aware grids. A **TGridDataLink** is used by a **TDBGrid**; more precisely, it is used by **TCustomDBGrid**, which is **TDBGrid's** direct ancestor. By deriving from **TCustomDBGrid**, you can define your own kind of data-aware grid and take advantage of the data-linking capabilities of the associated **TGridDataLink**.

TCustomDBGrid maintains a private reference (**FDataLink**) to a **TGridDataLink**; symmetrically, the corresponding **TGridDataLink** maintains a private reference (**FGrid**) to the **TCustomDBGrid**. These cross-references are set up in the constructor of **TCustomDBGrid**, which will create the **TGridDataLink** and assign it to its private reference. When the **TGridDataLink** is created, its constructor expects to receive in its sole parameter a reference to a **TCustomDBGrid**: the **TCustomDBGrid** that is creating the **TGridDataLink**. (This means that the constructor of **TCustomDBGrid** will call **TGridDataLink's** constructor and pass *Self* as a parameter.)

The **TGridDataLink** manages an internal private array (**FFieldMap**) that keeps track of how fields in the associated **TDataSet** are to be mapped onto the columns of the **TCustomDBGrid**. Table 22-3 shows the properties and methods that are implemented by **TGridDataLink**.

Table 22-3 Properties and methods implemented by `TGridDataLink`

Use or Set This...	To Do This...	Inheritance
AddMapping	Map a field in the dataset to a column in the grid.	None
ClearMapping	Clear the mapping between dataset fields and grid columns.	None
DefaultFields	Determine whether all of the dataset's default fields are available.	None
FieldCount	Report the number of fields in the underlying field map.	None
Fields	Shows array of TFields mapped to by the field map.	None
Modified	Flag the TGridDataLink's data as modified.	None
Reset	Reset the data in the TGridDataLink.	None
SparseMap	Report whether grid columns have custom layout or default layout.	None

AddMapping METHOD

Objects Affected	`TGridDataLink`
Purpose	The `AddMapping` method maps a `TField` in the associated `TDataSet` to a column in the `TCustomDBGrid`.
Declaration	

```
function AddMapping(const FieldName: string): Boolean;
```

Parameters

FieldName   The name of a field.

Example Syntax

```
for I := 0 to FColumns.Count-1 do
  GridDataLink.AddMapping(FColumns[I].FieldName);
```

Description   The `AddMapping` method will map the associated `TDataSet`'s field identified by the *FieldName* parameter onto a column in the calling `TCustomDBGrid`. The way the field is mapped depends on the `SparseMap` flag; if it is `True` (that is, the Fields Editor has been used to define the column layout), the field is sought for with a `FindField` on the `TDataSet`. If it is `False` (that is, the default fields are used), then it is sought for with a `FieldByName` on the `TDataSet`.

Once the `TField` has been successfully obtained from the `TDataSet`, space is allocated for it in an internal field map. The internal field map is an array corresponding to the columns in the associated `TCustomDBGrid`; each entry of this array will be assigned the `Index` of the `TField` in the corresponding `TDataSet`. If the `TField` was not retrieved, then the corresponding entry in the field map array will be set to −1.

ClearMapping METHOD

Objects Affected	`TGridDataLink`
Purpose	The `ClearMapping` method clears the mapping between dataset fields and grid columns.
Declaration	

```
procedure ClearMapping;
```

Example Syntax

```
GridDataLink.ClearMapping;
```

Description   The `ClearMapping` method will simply clear the mapping array between the fields in the `TGridDataLink`'s associated `TDataSet` and the columns in the `TCustomDBGrid`.

DefaultFields PROPERTY

Objects Affected	`TGridDataLink`
Purpose	The `DefaultFields` property reports as to whether all of the dataset's default fields are available in the `TGridDataLink`.
Declaration	

```
property DefaultFields: Boolean;
```

Example Syntax

```
if (not FDataLink.Active) and (FDatalink.DefaultFields) then
FColumns.Clear;
```

Description The `DefaultFields` property is a run-time, read-only property that reports as to whether the associated `TDataSet` is using its default fields. Note, however, that if this is the case and the `SparseMap` property is `True`, then `DefaultFields` will report `False` if any of the field map entries are not defined for the corresponding field (that is, the fields have been destroyed or are no longer in the field map).

FieldCount PROPERTY

Objects Affected	`TGridDataLink`
Purpose	The `FieldCount` property reports the number of fields in the underlying field map.
Declaration	

```
property FieldCount: Integer;
```

Example Syntax

```
with GridDataLink do for I := 0 to Pred( FieldCount ) do
begin
Fields[ I ].Visible := True;
end;
```

Description The `FieldCount` property is a run-time, read-only property that reports how many fields are present in the `TGridDataLink`'s field map.

Fields PROPERTY

Objects Affected	`TGridDataLink`
Purpose	The `Fields` property is an array of `TField`s mapped to by the field map.
Declaration	

```
property Fields[I: Integer]: TField;
```

Example Syntax

```
with GridDataLink do for I := O to Pred( FieldCount ) do
begin
Fields[ I ].Visible := True;
end;
```

Description The **Fields** array property will return the **TField** object corresponding to
the Ith column in the **TCustomDBGrid**, where **I** is the index into the array.

Modified METHOD

Objects Affected TGridDataLink

Purpose The **Modified** method flags the **TGridDataLink**'s data as modified.

Declaration

```
procedure Modified;
```

Example Syntax

```
FieldDataLink.Modified;
```

Description The **Modified** method will simply set to **True** the **TGridDataLink**'s private
modified state variable.

Reset METHOD

Objects Affected TGridDataLink

Purpose The **Reset** method resets the data in the **TGridDataLink**.

Declaration

```
procedure Reset;
```

Example Syntax

```
GridDataLink.Reset;
```

Description The **Reset** method will reset the data in the **TGridDataLink** (for instance,
when the user edits data in a grid and then presses the [ESC] key).

SparseMap PROPERTY

Objects Affected TGridDataLink

Purpose The **SparseMap** property reports whether grid columns have custom layout
or default layout.

Declaration

```
property SparseMap: Boolean;
```

Example Syntax

```
with GridDataLink do if SparseMap then
for I := 0 to Pred( FieldCount ) do
begin
Fields[ I ].Visible := True;
end;
```

Description

The `SparseMap` flag property will report `True` if the Fields Editor has been used to define the column layout of the associated `DataSet`; it will report `False` if the default fields are used. The property is associated with the `TCustomDBGrid` by the `TGridDataLink`. If the `State` property of the `TCustomDBGrid`'s `Column`'s collection is `csCustomized`, then the `SparseMap` flag will be `True`; otherwise, it will be `False`.

TDBCtrlGridLink

The `TDBCtrlGridLink` is a direct derivative of `TDataLink`. It differs from `TDataLink` in that it will maintain a private reference to a `TDBCtrlGrid` and in that it overrides the protected `ActiveChanged` and `DataSetChanged` methods. The `TDBCtrlGridLink` is used by `TDBCtrlPanel` components; the internal reference to the associated `TDBCtrlPanel` component is set in the constructor of the `TDBCtrlPanel` component itself. Note that a `TDBCtrlPanel` is the fundamental building block with which `TDBCtrlGrid`s are constructed.

23

TGraphicsObject
AND ITS DESCENDANTS

Delphi's support for graphics is quite rich with low-level classes devoted to drawing surfaces and graphic objects and higher-level classes encompassing bitmaps, icons, and other graphic types. *Graphics objects* encapsulate Windows Graphics Device Interface (GDI) objects like pens, brushes, and fonts.

TGraphicsObject

`TGraphicsObject` is the abstract base class for all graphics objects. It is a direct descendant of `TPersistent`. As it is an abstract class, you will not typically create an instance of `TGraphicsObject`, although you will often directly access its children: `TBrush`, `TPen`, and `TFont`.

Figure 23-1 shows the `TGraphicsObject` branch of the VCL. Table 23-1 displays the properties, methods, and events that are implemented by `TGraphicsObject`.

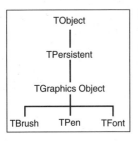

Figure 23-1 The `TGraphicsObject` branch of the VCL

Table 23-1 Properties, methods, and events implemented by `TGraphicsObject`

Use or Set This...	To Do This...	Inheritance
Assign	Assign one persistent object to another.	TPersistent
ClassName	Get the name of the object's class.	TObject
ClassParent	Get the object's parent class.	TObject
ClassType	Get the object's actual type.	TObject
Create	Construct a new object.	TObject
Destroy	Destroy the object.	TObject
Free	Safely destroy the object.	TObject
InheritsFrom	Determine if the object is descended from a certain class.	TObject
InstanceSize	Determine the amount of memory allocated for the object.	TObject
OnChange	Specify an event handler for the change event.	None

TBrush

`TBrush` is used to *fill* the drawing surface of a window or a shape with a color or pattern. It encapsulates the Windows GDI `HBRUSH`.

Table 23-2 displays the properties and methods that are implemented by `TBrush`. These are in addition to the properties and methods it inherits from `TGraphicsObject` (refer to Table 23-1).

Table 23-2 Properties and methods implemented by `TBrush`

Use or Set This...	To Do This...	Inheritance
Assign	Assign one brush object to another.	TPersistent
Bitmap	Determine the 8×8 bitmap that is used to fill windows and shapes.	None
Color	Determine the color of the brush.	None
Create	Create a new brush object.	TPersistent
Destroy	Destroy a brush object.	TPersistent
Handle	Determine the Windows handle to the brush object.	None
Style	Determine the style used to fill windows and shapes.	None

TPen

`TPen` encapsulates the Windows GDI `HPEN`. It is used to draw lines on a canvas.

Table 23-3 displays the properties and methods that are implemented by `TPen`. These are in addition to the properties and methods it inherits from `TGraphicsObject` (refer to Table 23-1).

Table 23-3 Properties and methods implemented by TPen

Use or Set This...	To Do This...	Inheritance
Assign	Assign one pen object to another.	TPersistent
Color	Determine the color used to draw lines on a canvas.	None
Create	Create a new pen object.	TPersistent
Destroy	Destroy a pen object.	TPersistent
Handle	Determine the Windows handle to the pen object.	None
Mode	Determine the drawing mode used to draw lines on a canvas.	None
Style	Determine the style used to draw lines on a canvas.	None
Width	Determine the width of the pen point.	None

TFont

TFont encapsulates the Windows GDI **HFONT**. Font objects determine the font that is used to draw text on a canvas, or on any control that uses a font. The font object can set styles, size, and other qualities for the text that is displayed.

Table 23-4 displays the properties and methods that are implemented by **TFont**. These are in addition to the properties and methods it inherits from **TGraphicsObject** (refer to Table 23-1).

Table 23-4 Properties and methods implemented by TFont

Use or Set This...	To Do This...	Inheritance
Assign	Assign one font object to another.	TPersistent
Color	Determine the color used when displaying text.	None
Create	Create a new font object.	TPersistent
Destroy	Destroy a font object.	TPersistent
Handle	Determine the Windows handle to the font object.	None
Height	Determine the height, in pixels, of the font object.	None
Name	Determine which font is used to display text.	None
Pitch	Determine the width, in pixels, of the font object.	None
Size	Determine the point size used to display text.	None
Style	Determine the style of the font object.	None

Bitmap PROPERTY

Objects Affected   TBrush

Purpose   The `Bitmap` property determines the graphic that is used by the brush to paint patterns.

Declaration

```
property Bitmap: TBitmap;
```

Example Syntax

```
// Create a pie chart that is filled with a custom bitmap
procedure TForm1.Button1Click(Sender: TObject);
begin
  Image1.Picture.Bitmap.LoadFromFile('mypattern.bmp');
  Form1.Canvas.Brush.Bitmap := Image1.Picture.Bitmap;
  Form1.Canvas.Pie(0, 0, 250, 250, 75, 10, 200, 75);
end;
```

Description   This run-time-only property determines the bitmap, which must be 8×8 pixels in size, that is used by the brush when it paints on a surface. You can use this bitmap to create patterns and special effects. The `Bitmap` property is actually a *reference* to a **TBitmap** object, not an actual bitmap, so the reference is **Nil** until an actual bitmap is assigned to the brush. You must explicitly destroy the bitmap with **Free** when you are done using it, since the brush will not do so for you. In Figure 23-2, a brush is used to paint images on a form.

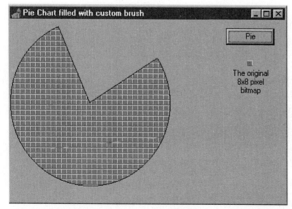

Figure 23-2   Painting with a bitmap brush

Color PROPERTY

Objects Affected	TBrush, TPen, TFont
Purpose	The Color property determines the color of the graphics object.
Declaration	

```
property Color: TColor;
```

Example Syntax

```
procedure TForm1.Button1Click(Sender: TObject);
var MyString: String;
begin
  MyString := 'Demonstration of font color';

  Label1.Font.Color := clRed;
  Label1.Caption := MyString;

  Label2.Font.Color := clGreen;
  Label2.Caption := MyString;

  Label3.Font.Color := clBlue;
  Label3.Caption := MyString;
end;
```

Description   Color is of type TColor. Some typical colors include constants like clAqua, clBlack, and clBlue, and system color constants like clButtonFace and clWindow.

Handle PROPERTY

Objects Affected	TBrush, TPen, TFont
Purpose	The Handle property holds a handle for a brush, pen, or font object.
Declaration	

TBrush

```
property Handle: HBrush;
```

TPen

```
property Handle: HPen;
```

TFont

```
property Handle: HFont;
```

Example Syntax

```
procedure TForm1.FormCreate(Sender: TObject);
var FontHandle: HFont;
begin
  FontHandle := Canvas.Font.Handle;
  // . . .
  // use the handle in API calls where needed
end;
```

Description   Handles are typically used in Win32 API calls. GDI functions often require a handle to a graphics object.

Height PROPERTY

Objects Affected   TFont

Purpose   The Height property contains the height of a font object.

Declaration

```
property Height: Integer;
```

Example Syntax

```
procedure TForm1.Button1Click(Sender: TObject);
begin
  Canvas.Font.Height := 24;
  Canvas.TextOut(10,10, 'Hello, world');
end;
```

Description   The value contained in the Height property represents the height of the font object in pixels. If you wish to use a specific point size, you should set the Size property. Height is useful when you want to see if text will fit in a specific area—you can test the size of the output area against the size of the font and change the font size as necessary.

Mode PROPERTY

Objects Affected   TPen

Purpose   The Mode property describes the drawing mode used to draw lines on the canvas.

Declaration

```
property Mode: TPenMode;
```

Example Syntax

```
procedure TForm1.Button1Click(Sender: TObject);
begin
  Canvas.LineTo(100,100);
  Canvas.Pen.Mode := pmWhite;
  Canvas.LineTo(200,0);
end;
```

Description	**Mode** is of type **TPenMode**. The **Mode** property can be set to any of the possible values shown in Table 23-5. A pen mode change is illustrated in Figure 23-3.

Table 23-5 Values of the Mode property

Use This Mode...	So the Line Color...
pmBlack	Is always black.
pmCopy	Matches the color specified in the Color property.
pmMask	Combines the common colors of the pen and the drawing surface.
pmMaskNotPen	Combines the common colors of the drawing surface and the inverse of the pen.
pmMaskPenNot	Combines the common colors of the inverse of the drawing surface and the pen.
pmMerge	Combines the colors of the pen and the drawing surface.
pmMergeNotPen	Combines the colors of the drawing surface and the inverse of the pen.
pmMergePenNot	Combines the colors of the inverse of the drawing surface and the pen.
pmNop	Is unaffected by the colors in the drawing surface.
pmNot	Is the inverse of the drawing surface color.
pmNotCopy	Is the inverse of the pen color.
pmNotMask	Is the inverse of the effect caused by pmMask.
pmNotMerge	Is the inverse of the effect caused by pmMerge.
pmNotXor	Is the inverse of the effect caused by pmXor.
pmWhite	Is always white.
pmXor	Combines those colors that are different in the pen and the drawing surface.

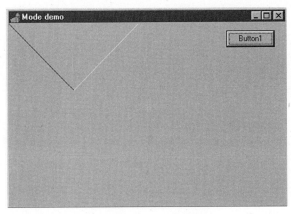

Figure 23-3   Changing the pen mode

Name PROPERTY

Objects Affected	TFont
Purpose	The Name property contains the manufacturer's name for the font.
Declaration	

```
property Name: TFontName;
```

Example Syntax

```
procedure TForm1.Button1Click(Sender: TObject);
begin
  Canvas.Font.Size := 18;
  Canvas.Font.Name := 'Arial';
  Canvas.TextOut(10, 10, 'Arial');
  Canvas.Font.Name := 'Times New Roman';
  Canvas.TextOut(10, 50, 'Times New Roman');
  Canvas.Font.Name := 'Courier New';
  Canvas.TextOut(10, 90, 'Courier New');
end;
```

Description   You can use any font that is installed on the current system. Most
                Windows 95 and NT 4.0 systems will have fonts like Arial, Times New
                Roman, System, and Courier New installed. Don't confuse this Name prop-
                erty with the Name property used by controls (that is, instances of
                TControl and its descendants); the TFont Name property does not identify
                the TFont object but rather specifies the name used by the system to label
                a particular font.

OnChange EVENT

Objects Affected	All graphics objects
Purpose	The OnChange event occurs when the graphics object changes.
Declaration	

```
property OnChange: TNotifyEvent;
```

Example Syntax

```
// . . .
type
  TForm1 = class(TForm)
    Button1: TButton;
    procedure Button1Click(Sender: TObject);
    procedure FormCreate(Sender: TObject);
    procedure FontChanged(Sender: TObject);
  private
    { Private declarations }
  public
    { Public declarations }
  end;

var
  Form1: TForm1;
```

```
    // other vars

implementation

{$R *.DFM}

procedure TForm1.Button1Click(Sender: TObject);
begin
  Canvas.Font.Name := 'Arial';
  Canvas.TextOut(10, 10, 'Arial');
end;

procedure TForm1.FontChanged(Sender: TObject);
begin
  Canvas.Font.Size := 24;
  // other processing
end;

procedure TForm1.FormCreate(Sender: TObject);
begin
  Canvas.Font.OnChange := FontChanged;
end;
```

Description

The `OnChange` event can be used to perform any special processing you wish to occur when a graphics object changes. For example, changing the name, size, or height property of a font object will cause this event to trigger.

In the example above, the procedure `FontChanged` is assigned as the event handler for the `OnChange` event for the canvas font. Anytime a change is made to the canvas font, the `FontChanged` procedure will execute.

Pitch PROPERTY

Objects Affected   `TFont`

Purpose   The `Pitch` property determines the width of the font object.

Declaration

```
property Pitch: TFontPitch;
```

Example Syntax

```
if Form1.Canvas.Pitch = fpFixed then
  Form1.Canvas.TextOut(10, 10, 'Font is fixed-width');
```

Description   `Pitch` can be set to one of three values: `fpDefault`, `fpFixed`, or `fpVariable`. Using `fpDefault` as the `Pitch` value will cause the default pitch style to be used for the font. The `fpFixed` and `fpVariable` values can be used to explicitly set the pitch; a value of `fpFixed` causes each character in the font to have the same width, while a value of `fpVariable` allows different characters within a font to have unique widths. TrueType fonts set to `fpFixed` will not be displayed as fixed width and fixed width fonts cannot be made variable width, so you will typically only need to use `fpDefault` when you know the type of font that is being used.

Size PROPERTY

Objects Affected	TFont
Purpose	The Size property determines the point size of a font object.
Declaration	

```
property Size: Integer;
```

Example Syntax

```
procedure TForm1.Button1Click(Sender: TObject);
begin
  Canvas.Font.Name := 'Arial';
  // set the point size to 24
  Canvas.Font.Size := 24;
  Canvas.TextOut(10, 10, 'Arial 24 point');
end;
```

Description   When dealing with Windows fonts, the measurement system used is typically point size. If you need to ensure that the font fits within a specified area, you can manipulate the Height and Pitch properties.

Setting the Size property causes Height to change to a negative value. Likewise, setting the Height property sets Size to a negative value.

Style PROPERTY

Objects Affected	TBrush, TPen, TFont
Purpose	The Style property determines the style used by the graphics object.
Declaration	

TBrush

```
property Style: TBrushStyle;
```

TPen

```
property Style: TPenStyle;
```

TFont

```
property Style: TFontStyles;
```

Example Syntax

```
procedure TForm1.Button1Click(Sender: TObject);
begin
  Canvas.Brush.Style := bsCross;
  Canvas.FillRect(Rect(10,10, 100,100));

  Canvas.Pen.Style := psDot;
  Canvas.MoveTo(200,10);
```

```
Canvas.LineTo(200,200);

Canvas.Font.Style := [fsBold] + [fsItalic];
Canvas.TextOut(10, 150, 'Bold, italic text');
end;
```

Description   For brush objects, **Style** determines the pattern used for filling window canvases and shapes as shown in Figure 23-4. **TBrushStyle** contains the styles shown in Table 23-6.

Table 23-6 TBrushStyle values

Use This Style...	So the Fill Is Painted...
bsBDiagonal	As diagonal lines rising to the right
bsClear	As the same color as the drawing surface
bsCross	As crosshatched lines
bsDiagCross	As diagonally crosshatched lines
bsFDiagonal	As diagonal lines rising to the left
bsHorizontal	As horizontal lines
bsSolid	As a solid color
bsVertical	As vertical lines

For pen objects, **Style** determines the style used to draw lines. **TPenStyle** contains the values shown in Table 23-7.

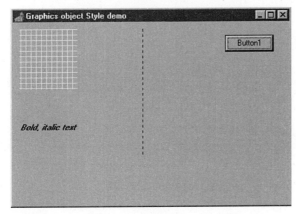

Figure 23-4   Using styles with graphics objects

Table 23-7 TPenStyle values

Use This Style...	So the Lines Are Drawn...
psClear	As invisible marks
psDash	As a series of dashes
psDashDot	As alternating dashes and dots
psDashDotDot	As a series of dash-dot-dot combinations
psDot	As a series of dots
psInsideFrame	Within the bounding rectangle of the drawing surface
psSolid	As a solid line

The Style property for the font object determines whether the font is bold, italic, underlined, struck out, or any combination of the four. Acceptable values include those shown in Table 23-8.

Table 23-8 TFontStyle values

Use This Style...	So the Font Appears...
fsBold	Boldfaced
fsItalic	Italic
fsStrikeOut	Struck out (there is a line running through the text)
fsUnderline	Underlined

Width PROPERTY

Objects Affected   TPen

Purpose   The Width property determines the width of the line drawn by a pen object.

Declaration

```
property Width: Integer;
```

Example Syntax

```
procedure TForm1.Button1Click(Sender: TObject);
begin
  Canvas.Pen.Width := 10;
  Canvas.LineTo(200,200);
end;
```

Description   Width is measured in pixels and determines the space in both the x and y directions that a single pen point will occupy.

24

TGraphic AND ITS DESCENDANTS

TGraphic and its descendants encapsulate common Windows graphic entities like bitmaps, icons, and metafiles. As descendants of **TPersistent**, these objects can be read from and saved to disk.

TGraphic

TGraphic is the abstract base class for all graphic objects in Delphi. As such, you will not typically create an instance of **TGraphic**, but will use one of its more specific descendants: **TMetafile**, **TBitmap**, or **TIcon**. Do not confuse graphic objects with *graphics* objects, that is, those objects that descend from **TGraphicsObject**.

One of the more common ways to access graphic objects is through the **Picture** property of an image control. **Picture** is of type **TPicture**, which is a container for any type of graphic object. Most of the examples in this chapter access the graphic objects through a **TPicture** container in an image control.

Figure 24-1 shows the **TGraphic** branch of the VCL. Table 24-1 displays the properties, methods, and events that are implemented by **TGraphic**.

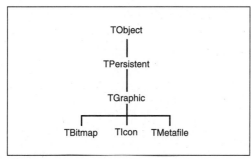

Figure 24-1   The **TGraphic** branch of the VCL

Table 24-1 Properties, methods, and events implemented by `TGraphic`

Use or Set This...	To Do This...	Inheritance
Assign	Assign one persistent object to another.	TPersistent
ClassName	Get the name of the object's class.	TObject
ClassParent	Get the object's parent class.	TObject
ClassType	Get the object's actual type.	TObject
Create	Construct a new object.	TObject
Destroy	Destroy the object.	TObject
Empty	Determine whether the graphic object is empty.	None
Free	Safely destroy the object.	TObject
Height	Determine the height of the graphic object.	None
InheritsFrom	Determine if the object is descended from a certain class.	TObject
InstanceSize	Determine the amount of memory allocated for the object.	TObject
LoadFromClipboardFormat	This is an abstract, virtual method.	None
LoadFromFile	Load a graphic object from disk.	None
Modified	Determine if the graphic object was changed.	None
OnChange	Determine the event handler for the Change event.	None
SaveToClipboardFormat	This is an abstract, virtual method.	None
SaveToFile	Save a graphic object to disk.	None
Width	Determine the width of a graphic object.	None

TIcon

`TIcon`, an icon object, is the Delphi encapsulation of the Windows **HICON** structure.
`Icon` objects represent *icons*, a common and familiar object to any user of Windows.
An icon is essentially a bitmap picture that is masked so that areas of the icon appear
transparent. For this reason, icons, unlike bitmaps and metafiles, are often not rectangular in shape (at least not to the eye; internally, of course, they are rectangular).

Icons are a pervasive Windows user-interface tool used to represent objects on the
desktop, files, folders, and drives in Explorer.

Table 24-2 displays the properties and methods that are implemented by `TIcon`.
These are in addition to the properties and methods it inherits from `TGraphic` (refer to
Table 24-1).

Table 24-2 Properties and methods implemented by `TIcon`

Use or Set This...	To Do This...	Inheritance
Assign	Assign an icon to another icon.	TPersistent
Create	Create a new icon object.	TPersistent

Use or Set This...	To Do This...	Inheritance
Destroy	Destroy an icon object.	TPersistent
Handle	Use the Windows handle to an icon object.	None

TMetafile

The **TMetafile** object encapsulates the Win32 Enhanced Metafile graphic, which provides backward compatibility with the Windows 3.1 metafile. Enhanced metafiles typically are stored with an **.EMF** extension; standard metafiles are saved with **.WMF**. In either case, a metafile is a device independent graphic whose structure is largely composed of a series of Graphics Device Interface (GDI) functions that explain how the graphic should be drawn. Metafiles are slower than bitmaps, but they can be scaled to a wide range of sizes without a loss in quality.

Great things were expected of metafiles when Windows was first introduced, but they have been largely displaced by bitmaps as the graphic type of choice.

Table 24-3 displays the properties and methods that are implemented by **TMetafile**. These are in addition to the properties and methods it inherits from **TGraphic** (refer to Table 24-1).

Table 24-3 Properties and methods implemented by T M e t a f i l e

Use or Set This...	To Do This...	Inheritance
Assign	Assign one metafile graphic to another.	TPersistent
Create	Create a new metafile object.	TObject
CreatedBy	Determine the author, or creator, of the metafile.	None
Description	Hold text describing the metafile graphic.	None
Destroy	Destroy a metafile object.	TObject
Enhanced	Determine whether a metafile is enhanced.	None
Handle	Determine the Windows handle to the metafile.	None
LoadFromClipboardFormat	Load the metafile from the clipboard.	None
MMHeight	Determine the metafile height in 0.01mm units.	None
MMWidth	Determine the metafile width in 0.01mm units.	None
Palette	Describe the palette of the metafile graphic.	None
SaveToClipboardFormat	Save the metafile to the clipboard.	None
SaveToFile	Save the metafile to disk.	None

TBitmap

The **TBitmap** class encapsulates the Windows API **HBITMAP**. Bitmaps are, by far, the most common graphic type found in Windows and are normally stored with a **.BMP** extension. **TBitmap** also encapsulates **HPALETTE** through its **Palette** property and realizes palettes automatically for you. See **Palette** for details.

The structure of a bitmap is composed of a header that describes the image's resolution (dimensions), a palette, and a data array that describes the image. This internal structure is largely hidden from the Delphi programmer, who can easily access bitmaps at a relatively high level.

Table 24-4 displays the properties and methods that are implemented by TBitmap. These are in addition to the properties and methods it inherits from TGraphic (refer to Table 24-1).

Table 24-4 Properties and methods implemented by TBitmap

Use or Set This...	To Do This...	Inheritance
Assign	Assign one bitmap graphic to another.	TPersistent
Canvas	Use the drawing surface of the bitmap.	None
Create	Create a new bitmap graphic.	TObject
Destroy	Destroy a bitmap graphic.	TObject
Handle	Determine the Windows handle to the bitmap.	None
IgnorePalette	Determine whether a bitmap palette is realized.	None
LoadFromClipboardFormat	Load a bitmap from the clipboard.	None
Monochrome	Determine whether a bitmap is monochrome.	None
Palette	Access the palette of the bitmap graphic.	None
SaveToClipboardFormat	Save a bitmap to the clipboard.	None

Canvas PROPERTY

Objects Affected TBitmap

Purpose The Canvas property determines the drawing surface of the bitmap image.

Declaration

```
property Canvas: TCanvas;
```

Example Syntax

```
procedure TForm1.Button1Click(Sender: TObject);
begin
  // draw a white border around the bitmap
  Image1.Picture.Bitmap.Canvas.Pen.Color := clWhite;
  Image1.Picture.Bitmap.Canvas.FrameRect
                    (Rect(0, 0, Image1.Width, Image1.Height));
end;
```

Description This property allows you to modify the image associated with the bitmap object, as shown in Figure 24-2. Canvas properties, methods, and events are described in Chapter 20, "TCanvas and Its Descendants."

Figure 24-2 A rectangle border
drawn to a bitmap canvas

CreatedBy PROPERTY

Objects Affected	TMetafile
Purpose	The CreatedBy property indicates the author of the metafile.
Declaration	

```
property CreatedBy: String;
```

Example Syntax

```
// Output the name of the metafile creator
procedure TForm1.btnAuthorClick(Sender: TObject);
begin
  Label1.Caption := MyMeta.CreatedBy;
end;
```

Description   Metafile graphics contain embedded textual information about the graphic
itself and the author of the graphic. The CreatedBy property is a string
that holds the name of the person who created the metafile. It is a run-
time, read-only property.

Description PROPERTY

Objects Affected	TMetafile
Purpose	The Description property contains information about the metafile graphic.
Declaration	

```
property Description: String;
```

Example Syntax

```
procedure TForm1.btnDescriptionClick(Sender: TObject);
begin
  Label1.Caption := MyMeta.Description;
end;
```

Description   Metafile graphics contain embedded textual information about the graphic itself and the author of the graphic. The `Description` property is a string that contains some comment-like information about the metafile. It is a run-time, read-only property.

Empty PROPERTY

Objects Affected   `TGraphic` and its descendants.

Purpose   The `Empty` property indicates whether the graphic object actually contains a graphic image.

Declaration

```
property Empty: Boolean;
```

Example Syntax

```
procedure TForm1.Button1Click(Sender: TObject);
begin
  If Image1.Picture.Bitmap.Empty then
    Image1.Picture.LoadFromFile('c:\windows\forest.bmp');
end;
```

Description   `Empty` is a read-only property that returns `True` if the graphic object does not contain a graphic, and `False` if it does.

Enhanced PROPERTY

Objects Affected   `TMetafile`

Purpose   The `Enhanced` property determines whether the metafile is enhanced.

Declaration

```
property Enhanced: Boolean;
```

Example Syntax

```
procedure TForm1.btnEnhancedClick(Sender: TObject);
begin
  if MyMeta.Enhanced = True then
    Label1.Caption := 'Enhanced metafile'
  else Label1.Caption := 'Normal metafile';
end;
```

Description   This run-time-only property determines how a metafile graphic is stored to disk. The default value is `True`, which indicates that the metafile is an enhanced Win32 metafile with a three-letter extension of `.EMF`. If `Enhanced` is `False`, the metafile is stored as a normal Windows 3.1–style metafile. You should use enhanced metafiles unless backward compatibility with 16-bit applications that use the metafile is required.

Handle PROPERTY

Objects Affected	`TIcon`, `TMetafile`, `TBitmap`
Purpose	The `Handle` property contains the Windows handle to the graphic object.
Declaration	

`TIcon`

```
property Handle: HICON;
```

`TMetafile`

```
property Handle: HENHMETAFILE;
```

`TBitmap`

```
property Handle: HBITMAP;
```

Example Syntax

```
procedure TForm1.FormCreate(Sender: TObject);
var BHandle: HBITMAP;
begin
  BHandle := Image1.Picture.Bitmap.Handle;
  // call any API functions that need the handle...
end;
```

Description   A handle is useful if the object needs to be passed as a parameter to an API function call. Many GDI calls require the handle to a graphic object.

Height PROPERTY

Objects Affected	`TGraphic` and its descendants.
Purpose	The `Height` property contains the height of the graphic object.
Declaration	

```
property Height: Integer;
```

Example Syntax

```
Image1.Height := MyPicture.Bitmap.Height;
Image1.Width := MyPicture.Bitmap.Width;
```

Description   `Height` is the vertical measurement of the object, in pixels. Normally, when you are displaying a graphic object in an image control, you will manipulate the display of the object through the properties and methods of the image control. While it is possible to change the `Height` and `Width` properties of the `TGraphic` object, it normally doesn't make sense to do so and may well lead to unexpected results.

IgnorePalette PROPERTY

Objects Affected   TBitmap

Purpose   The IgnorePalette property determines whether a bitmap's palette is realized.

Declaration

```
property IgnorePalette: Boolean;
```

Example Syntax

```
procedure TForm1.FormCreate(Sender: TObject);
begin
  // Ensure that the palette is realized
  Image1.Picture.Bitmap.IgnorePalette := False;
  Image1.Picture.Bitmap.LoadFromFile('c:\graphics\dragon.bmp');
end;
```

Description   If IgnorePalette is set to True, the bitmap will not realize its palette when it is drawn. If it is set to False, it will realize its palette. When a palette is *realized*, it is matched to the system palette—any colors that do not match are mapped to the closest possible color. This is the way that high-color images are displayed on low-color displays. There will be a loss in image quality if you do not allow the palette to realize, although it will load faster because it will not require the overhead of palette mapping.

The default value for IgnorePalette is False.

LoadFromClipboardFormat METHOD

Objects Affected   TGraphic and its descendants.

Purpose   The LoadFromClipboardFormat method loads a graphic object from the clipboard.

Declaration

TGraphic

```
procedure LoadFromClipboardFormat(AFormat: Word; AData: THandle;
                           APalette: HPALETTE); virtual; abstract;
```

Descendants of TGraphic

```
procedure LoadFromClipboardFormat(AFormat: Word; AData: THandle;
                           APalette: HPALETTE); override;
```

Parameters

AFormat   A Windows-registered clipboard format.

AData   The actual graphic data of the graphic.

APalette   The palette for the graphic.

Example Syntax

```
var
  Form1: TForm1;
  MyClipboardFormat: Word;
  MyHandle: HWND;
  MyPalette: HPalette;

implementation

{$R *.DFM}

// Load a bitmap into Image1 and save it to the clipboard
procedure TForm1.FormCreate(Sender: TObject);
begin
  MyHandle := Image1.Picture.Bitmap.Handle;
  Image1.Picture.Bitmap.LoadFromFile('C:\WINDOWS\CLOUDS.BMP');
  MyPalette := Image1.Picture.Bitmap.Palette;
  with Image1.Picture.Bitmap do
    SaveToClipboardFormat(MyClipboardFormat, MyHandle, MyPalette);
end;

// Copy the image from the clipboard to the second image
procedure TForm1.Button1Click(Sender: TObject);
begin
  with Image2.Picture.Bitmap do
    LoadFromClipboardFormat(MyClipboardFormat, MyHandle, MyPalette);
end;
```

Description

LoadFromClipboardFormat replaces the image in the graphic object with one loaded from the clipboard. The clipboard image must have been copied to the clipboard format with the SaveToClipboardFormat method and previously registered as a valid clipboard format. Predefined types like TBitmap are automatically registered with the Clipboard for you.

See Chapter 11, "TClipboard," for more general information about the clipboard.

LoadFromFile METHOD

Objects Affected TGraphic and its descendants.

Purpose The LoadFromFile method loads a graphic from disk into the current graphic object.

Declaration

```
procedure LoadFromFile(const Filename: string); virtual;
```

Parameters

Filename The file name of the graphic you wish to load.

Example Syntax

```
// load a bitmap graphic when the form is created
procedure TForm1.FormCreate(Sender: TObject);
begin
  Image1.Picture.LoadFromFile('c:\windows\clouds.bmp');
end;
```

Description	`LoadFromFile` loads a compatible type of graphic into a graphic object— that is, bitmap objects can load bitmaps, icon objects can load icons. The `Picture` property of an `Image` control is of type `TGraphic`, so it can load any of the graphic object formats from disk.

MMHeight PROPERTY

Objects Affected	TMetafile
Purpose	The `MMHeight` property contains the height of the metafile object.
Declaration	

```
property MMHeight: Integer
```

Example Syntax	

```
procedure TForm1.FormCreate(Sender: TObject);
begin
  MyMeta := TMetaFile.Create;
  Label1.Caption := IntToStr(MyMeta.MMHeight);
end;
```

Description	The native measurement scale for a metafile graphic object is 0.01 millimeter units—`MMHeight` is the height of a metafile measured in these units. The `MMHeight` and `MMWidth` properties allow you to get or set the dimensions of a metafile graphic object within normal pixel-based screen coordinates.

MMWidth PROPERTY

Objects Affected	TMetafile
Purpose	The `MMWidth` property contains the width of the metafile object.
Declaration	

```
property MMWidth: Integer;
```

Example Syntax	

```
procedure TForm1.FormCreate(Sender: TObject);
begin
  MyMeta := TMetaFile.Create;
  MyMeta.MMHeight := 5000;
  MyMeta.MMWidth := 5000;
end;
```

Description	`MMWidth` is the width of a metafile measured in its native measurement scale of 0.01 millimeter units—`MMHeight` is the height of a metafile measured in these units. The `MMHeight` and `MMWidth` properties allow you to get or set the dimensions of a metafile graphic object within normal pixel-based screen coordinates.

Modified PROPERTY

Objects Affected   `TGraphic` and its descendants.

Purpose   The `Modified` property indicates whether the graphic object has been changed.

Declaration

```
property Modified: Boolean;
```

Example Syntax

```
procedure TForm1.FormCreate(Sender: TObject);
begin
  // Draw a white border around the bitmap
  Image1.Picture.Bitmap.Canvas.Pen.Color := clWhite;
  Image1.Picture.Bitmap.Canvas.FrameRect
              (Rect(0, 0, Image1.Width, Image1.Height));
end;

// If the image is modified, save it to the current directory
// with the name 'Cheryl.bmp'
procedure TForm1.FormDestroy(Sender: TObject);
begin
  If Image1.Picture.Bitmap.Modified = True then
    If Application.MessageBox('Bitmap changed, do you wish to save it',
                           'Bitmap changed', mb_YesNo) = IDYES then
      Image1.Picture.Bitmap.SaveToFile('Cheryl.bmp');
end;
```

Description   If `Modified` is `True`, the graphic object has been modified since you loaded or created it. If it is `False`, it hasn't been changed.

Monochrome PROPERTY

Objects Affected   `TBitmap`

Purpose   The `Monochrome` property determines whether the bitmap is a monochrome bitmap.

Declaration

```
property Monochrome: Boolean;
```

Example Syntax

```
procedure TForm1.Button1Click(Sender: TObject);
begin
  if Image1.Picture.Bitmap.Monochrome = False then
    ProcessBitmap;
  else if Application.MessageBox('Bitmap is monochrome. Load another?',
                           'Monochrome bitmap', mb_YesNo) = IDYES then
    // load another bitmap and continue. . .
end;
```

Description A monochrome bitmap has only two colors. They can be any two colors, not just black and white. If `Monochrome` returns `True`, the bitmap is monochrome. If it returns `False`, it is not a monochrome bitmap.

OnChange EVENT

Objects Affected `TGraphic` and its descendants.

Purpose The `OnChange` event specifies which event handler will run when a graphic object is changed.

Declaration

```
property OnChange: TNotifyEvent;
```

Example Syntax

```
type
  TForm1 = class(TForm)
    Image1: TImage;
    Button1: TButton;
    procedure FormCreate(Sender: TObject);
    procedure Button1Click(Sender: TObject);
    // Added to handle bitmap OnChange events
    procedure BitmapChange(Sender: TObject);
  private
    { Private declarations }
  public
    { Public declarations }
  end;

var
  Form1: TForm1;

implementation

{$R *.DFM}

// This procedure was manually created and could be named
// anything
procedure TForm1.BitmapChange(Sender: TObject);
begin
  Form1.Caption := 'Bitmap changed';
end;

// Set the OnChange event to an event handler procedure
procedure TForm1.FormCreate(Sender: TObject);
begin
  Image1.Picture.Bitmap.OnChange := BitmapChange;
end;

// Change the bitmap to test the event handler
procedure TForm1.Button1Click(Sender: TObject);
begin
  Image1.Picture.Bitmap.Canvas.FrameRect(Rect(10, 10, 50, 50));
end;
```

Description   The `OnChange` event determines the event handler that will execute when the graphic object is modified. In the above example, the event handler `BitmapChange` is assigned to the `OnChange` event at run time. To test the event handling procedure, a rectangle is drawn on the bitmap. When the change is detected, a message is output.

`Palette` PROPERTY

Objects Affected   `TMetafile, TBitmap`

Purpose   The `Palette` property determines the set of colors that make up a metafile or bitmap graphic.

Declaration

```
property Palette: HPALETTE;
```

Description   The `Palette` property encapsulates the Windows API `HPALETTE` structure. It is essentially an array of colors in which each element in the array is a structure of separate bytes for each RGB value and a flags byte that determines how the colors are to be matched with the system palette. Typically, you will not need to modify the `Palette` entries directly—although `Palette` can be used in conjunction with the API function `CreatePalette`.

The foreground application in Windows maps its palette to the system palette—if there aren't enough colors in the system palette to display the colors needed by the foreground application, the system will convert those colors to the closest possible in the system palette. Again, this is something that happens transparently. Accessing individual palette entries is beyond the scope of this book.

`SaveToClipboardFormat` METHOD

Objects Affected   `TGraphic` and its descendants.

Purpose   The `SaveToClipboardFormat` method copies a graphic object to the clipboard.

Declaration

`TGraphic`

```
procedure SaveToClipboardFormat(var AFormat: Word; var AData: THandle;
          var APalette: HPALETTE); virtual; abstract;
```

Descendants of `TGraphic`

```
procedure SaveToClipboardFormat(var Format: Word; var Data: THandle;
                                var APalette: HPALETTE); override;
```

Parameters

AFormat   A Windows-registered clipboard format.

AData   The actual graphic data of the graphic.

APalette   The palette for the graphic.

Example Syntax

```
var
  Form1: TForm1;
  MyClipboardFormat: Word;
  MyHandle: HWND;
  MyPalette: HPalette;

implementation

{$R *.DFM}

// Load a bitmap into Image1 and save it to the clipboard
procedure TForm1.FormCreate(Sender: TObject);
begin
  MyHandle := Image1.Picture.Bitmap.Handle;
  Image1.Picture.Bitmap.LoadFromFile('C:\WINDOWS\CLOUDS.BMP');
  MyPalette := Image1.Picture.Bitmap.Palette;
  with Image1.Picture.Bitmap do
    SaveToClipboardFormat(MyClipboardFormat, MyHandle, MyPalette);
end;

// Copy the image from the clipboard to the second image
procedure TForm1.Button1Click(Sender: TObject);
begin
  with Image2.Picture.Bitmap do
    LoadFromClipboardFormat(MyClipboardFormat, MyHandle, MyPalette);
end;
```

Description   Before you can save an object to the clipboard, it must be compatible with a clipboard format—all of the descendants of `TGraphic` are clipboard format compatible. See Chapter 11, "`TClipboard`," for general information about the clipboard.

SaveToFile METHOD

Objects Affected   `TGraphic` and its descendants.

Purpose   The `SaveToFile` method copies a graphic object to disk.

Declaration

`TGraphic`

```
procedure SaveToFile(const Filename: string); virtual;
```

Descendants of `TGraphic`

```
procedure SaveToFile(const Filename: String); override;
```

Parameters

Filename   The name of the file that will contain the graphic on disk.

Example Syntax

```
var
  Form1: TForm1;
  FileName: String;

implementation

{$R *.DFM}

procedure TForm1.FormCreate(Sender: TObject);
begin
  FileName := 'Durango Ski Trip.bmp';
  Image1.Picture.LoadFromFile(FileName);
end;

procedure TForm1.FormClose(Sender: TObject; var Action: TCloseAction);
begin
  Image1.Picture.SaveToFile(FileName);
end;
```

Description   SaveToFile writes the graphic object to the file specified by the *Filename* parameter. If the file already exists, SaveToFile will overwrite it.

Width PROPERTY

Objects Affected   TGraphic and its descendants.

Purpose   The Width property indicates the width of the graphic object.

Declaration

```
property Width: Integer
```

Example Syntax

```
Image1.Height := MyPicture.Bitmap.Height;
Image1.Width := MyPicture.Bitmap.Width;
```

Description   The width of a graphic object is measured in pixels.

25

TStrings AND ITS DESCENDANTS

This chapter discusses the `TStrings` class and the classes that directly descend from `TStrings`. Figure 25-1 illustrates the relationship of `TStrings` to the overall VCL hierarchy and to the descendant classes that will be discussed in this chapter.

TStrings

The `TStrings` class is an abstract class type that is generally not used directly but supports the creation of descendant classes that operate on string data. The most general descendant of `TStrings` is `TStringList`, which is used for most generic string operations. This chapter will look in some detail at the `TStrings` class, then cover all the other descendant classes of `TStrings`.

Even though the class is named `TStrings`, it is designed to perform a more general class of operations than just string manipulation. In fact, the class doesn't operate on strings at all, but rather on collections of strings. In that sense `TStrings` is an abstract container class, and all classes that descend from it provide the implementational details that allow the methods defined in `TStrings` to do their work. Frequently an argument of type `TStrings` is specified just so the function can operate polymorphically on the different descendants of `TStrings`. One of the more interesting and potentially useful features of `TStrings` is that it can function as an association list or dictionary in which the various string entries act as key names that can be used to retrieve any object by name.

Each string entry in `TStrings` derivative classes is capable of holding not only a string, but also a reference to any Delphi object. This feature is what allows descendants of the `TStrings` class to function as elementary symbol tables if required. This is often used with various controls to provide a mechanism to support owner-draw capabilities, in which case the object reference points to a bitmap image to be drawn in conjunction with the text that appears in a list of some sort. The most fundamental

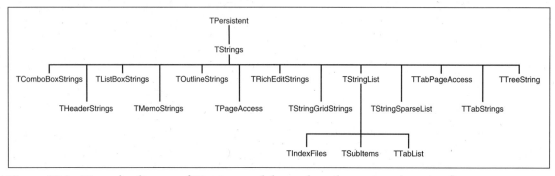

Figure 25-1 Hierarchy diagram of `TStrings` and descendant classes

derivative class of `TStrings` is `TStringList`. This class overrides all the necessary `TStrings` virtual functions to implement the desired behavior of a list of strings capable of storing objects. If you take the time to study the `TStrings` and `TStringList` classes in depth, you will gain a much better understanding of some of the neat things that can be performed with this useful family of classes.

Here is what the public `TStrings` class declaration looks like. Note the large number of virtual functions, which is a clue that much of the detail work will be fleshed out by other descendant classes.

```
TStrings = class(TPersistent)
  .
  .
  .
public
    function Add(const S: string): Integer; virtual;
    function AddObject(const S: string; AObject: TObject): Integer; virtual;
    procedure AddStrings(Strings: TStrings); virtual;
    procedure Assign(Source: TPersistent); override;
    procedure BeginUpdate;
    procedure Clear; virtual; abstract;        procedure Delete(Index: Integer); virtual; ⇐
abstract;
    procedure EndUpdate;
    function Equals(Strings: TStrings): Boolean;
    procedure Exchange(Index1, Index2: Integer); virtual;
    function GetText: PChar; virtual;
    function IndexOf(const S: string): Integer; virtual;
    function IndexOfName(const Name: string): Integer;
    function IndexOfObject(AObject: TObject): Integer;
    procedure Insert(Index: Integer; const S: string); virtual; abstract;
    procedure InsertObject(Index: Integer; const S: string;AObject: TObject);
    procedure LoadFromFile(const FileName: string);
    procedure LoadFromStream(Stream: TStream); virtual;
    procedure Move(CurIndex, NewIndex: Integer); virtual;
    procedure SaveToFile(const FileName: string);
    procedure SaveToStream(Stream: TStream); virtual;
    procedure SetText(Text: PChar); virtual;
    property Capacity: Integer;
    property CommaText: string;
```

```
    property Count: Integer;
    property Names[Index: Integer]: string;
    property Objects[Index: Integer]: TObject;
    property Values[const Name: string]: string;
    property Strings[Index: Integer]: string;
    property Text: string;
end;
```

Table 25-1 shows the properties that are implemented by `TStrings`.

Table 25-1 Properties implemented by `TStrings`

Use or Set This...	To Do This...	Inheritance
Add	Append new string to end of list.	None
AddObject	Add new string and object to end of list.	None
AddStrings	Copy strings and object refs from one `TStrings` object to tail of another `TStrings` object.	None
Assign	Make contents of one `TStrings` object equal to another `TStrings` object.	TPersistent
BeginUpdate	Indicate that the `TStrings` object is being updated.	None
Capacity	Indicate number of `Strings` the `TString` object is capable of holding without requiring expansion.	None
Clear	Initialize to empty internal state.	None
Count	Return size of list.	None
Delete	Remove an entry from list by index number.	None
EndUpdate	Indicate that the `TStrings` object has completed the update operation.	None
Equals	Compare two `TStrings` objects for equality.	None
Exchange	Swap two `TStrings` list entries with each other.	None
GetText	Return all strings contained in the list items in a single `PChar` array.	None
IndexOf	Return numeric entry of list element matching string argument.	None
IndexOfName	Return the `Index` of the name part of a string that is of the form `Name=Value`.	None
IndexOfObject	Return numeric entry of list element matching object reference argument.	None
Insert	Insert new string at specified location in list.	None
InsertObject	Insert new string and object ref in list at specified location.	None
LoadFromFile	Load string data into list from specified disk file.	None
LoadFromStream	Load string data into list from specified stream object.	None
Move	Move list element from one location to another in the list.	None

continued on next page

continued from previous page

Use or Set This...	To Do This...	Inheritance
Names	Return the name part of a string at the Index position in the string list when the form is Name=Value.	None
Objects	Return object at specified index location.	None
SaveToFile	Save all string data to a disk file.	None
SaveToStream	Save all string data to a specified stream.	None
SetText	Specify list elements from a PChar array.	None
Strings	Access strings at indexed locations.	None
Text	Get or set the contents of the TStrings component. Individual items are separated by a carriage return/line feed (#13#10) sequence.	None
Values	Read or write indexed Property values.	None

TComboBoxStrings

The TComboBoxStrings class is utilized by all the control classes that descend from TCustomComboBox. This includes TComboBox, TDriveComboBox, TFilterComboBox, and TDBComboBox. The methods defined specifically by this descendant of TStrings work in conjunction with the Windows combo box control to provide the Delphi programmer with the functionality that would be expected of any of the classes that descend from TStrings. TComboBoxStrings is similar in function to the TListBoxStrings class, except that the underlying Windows control is the combo box instead of the list box.

Table 25-2 shows the methods that are implemented by TComboBoxStrings.

Table 25-2 Methods implemented by TComboBoxStrings

Use or Set This...	To Do This...	Inheritance
Add	Add item to end of list.	TStrings
Clear	Remove all entries from the list.	TStrings
Delete	Delete a specified entry.	TStrings
Insert	Insert an entry at a specified location, pushing all entries down one.	TStrings

THeaderStrings

The THeaderStrings class is defined for use by the THeader component and corresponds to the Sections property of the THeader component. That is, the Sections property of the **THeader** component is of type **THeaderStrings**. The size and contents of the **THeaderStrings** list in large part determine what appears in the **THeader** component when it is displayed on the parent form.

Table 25-3 shows the methods that are implemented by **THeaderStrings**.

Table 25-3 Methods implemented by **THeaderStrings**

Use or Set This...	To Do This...	Inheritance
Assign	Copy any TStrings descendant object into THeaderStrings object.	TStrings
Clear	Remove all entries from the list.	TStrings
Create	Create a new instance of THeaderStrings and initialize list.	Tobject
Delete	Delete item from string list.	TStrings
Destroy	Destroy object instance.	TObject
Insert	Add new item at indexed location.	TStrings

TIndexFiles

The **TIndexFiles** class is used by the **TTable** class, which is concerned with database management. Since **TIndexFiles** is used to manage internal data structures owned by the **TTable** instance, it is unlikely that you will need to deal with this class directly, unless, of course, you actually get involved in writing your own version or descendant of **TTable**.

Table 25-4 shows the methods that are implemented by **TIndexFiles**.

Table 25-4 Methods implemented by **TIndexFiles**

Use or Set This...	To Do This...	Inheritance
Add	Add a new IndexFile to the list and cause it to be opened for use by the owning TTable object.	TStrings
Clear	Close all index files, then remove all entries from the list.	TStrings
Create	Create a new instance of TIndexFiles and initialize internal TTable structures associated with its use.	TStrings
Delete	Close the associated index file and delete the indexed item from the string list.	TStrings
Insert	Add new file name item at indexed location and open it for use with the owning TTable object.	TStrings

TListBoxStrings

The **TListBoxStrings** class is used by the **TCustomListBox** class to manage the actual list of items presented by the classes that descend from **TCustomListBox**. These are the **TListBox** and the **TFileListBox** classes. Note that every one of the methods defined for this class is an override of a virtual function defined in **TStrings**. These functions are designed internally to interact in such a way as to fetch or store the requested information from the corresponding Windows control. This is different from the **TStringList**, which creates and maintains the required storage for the list items on its own. In this case Delphi relies on behavior provided by the Windows internals for the corresponding functionality.

Table 25-5 shows the methods that are implemented by **TListBoxStrings**.

Table 25-5 Methods implemented by TListBoxStrings

Use or Set This...	To Do This...	Inheritance
Add	Add item to end of list.	TStrings
Clear	Remove all entries from the list.	TStrings
Delete	Delete a specified entry.	TStrings
Insert	Insert an entry at a specified location, pushing all entries down one.	TStrings

TMemoStrings

The **TMemoStrings** class provides a string list–based interface to the standard Windows edit control. The separate lines of an edit control are mapped into the individual items in the string list. Note that there is no provision with this class definition for the storage and retrieval of object references as there are for the **TListBoxStrings** and **TComboBoxStrings** classes, since in general an edit box is intended to hold textual information only.

Table 25-6 shows the methods implemented by **TMemoStrings**.

Table 25-6 Methods implemented by TMemoStrings

Use or Set This...	To Do This...	Inheritance
Clear	Remove all entries from the list.	TStrings
Delete	Delete a specified entry.	TStrings
Insert	Insert an entry at a specified location, pushing all entries down one.	TStrings
LoadFromStream	Load text contents of memo box from TStream object.	TStrings
SaveToStream	Save text contents of memo box to TStream object.	TPersistent

TOutlineStrings

The **TOutlineStrings** provides the string storage class used by the **TOutline** component.

Table 25-7 shows the methods implemented by **TOutlineStrings**.

Table 25-7 Methods implemented by TOutlineStrings

Use or Set This...	To Do This...	Inheritance
Add	Add item to end of list.	TStrings
Clear	Remove all items from list.	TStrings
Delete	Delete indexed item from list.	TStrings
GetObject	Retrieve object contained at indexed list item.	TStrings
Insert	Insert item into list.	TStrings
PutObject	Place object into indexed TOutline list item.	TStrings

TPageAccess

The **TPageAccess** class is utilized by the Notebook control to store the names of the pages associated with the Notebook contents.

Table 25-8 shows the methods implemented by **TPageAccess**.

Table 25-8 Methods implemented by TPageAccess

Use or Set This...	To Do This...	Inheritance
Clear	Remove all entries from the list.	TStrings
Create	Create a new instance of TPageAccess and initialize list.	TObject
Delete	Delete item from string list.	TStrings
Insert	Add new item at indexed location.	TStrings
Move	Move an item from one location to another in the string list.	TStrings

TRichEditStrings

The **TRichEditStrings** class is used to provide access to the lines of text contained in a **TRichEdit** control. The corresponding **TRichEditStrings** component is obtained from the **Lines** property of the associated **TRichEdit** control. For additional information related to the **TRichEdit** control, refer to Table 25-9 and to Chapter 64, "**TCustomEdit** and Its Descendants."

Table 25-9 Methods implemented by `TRichEditStrings`

Use or Set This...	To Do This...	Inheritance
AddStrings	Add the contents of another descendant of `TStrings` to the `TRichEditStrings` object.	TStrings
Clear	Remove all lines from the list.	TStrings
Delete	Delete a specific line from the list control.	TStrings
Insert	Add new line at indexed location.	TStrings
LoadFromFile	Load the list from a file.	TStrings
LoadFromStream	Load the list from a stream.	TStrings
SaveToFile	Save the list to a file.	TStrings
SaveToStream	Save the list to a stream.	TStrings
PlainText	Boolean property used to determine whether `TRichEditStrings` contains lines of text only (read/write).	None

TStringGridStrings

The **TStringGridStrings** is used by the **TStringGrid** to provide the basic storage class for the strings contained in the cells of the **TStringGrid** component. The **TStringGrid** object provides indexed member properties **Cols** and **Rows**, which return references to objects of type **TStringGridStrings**. Using this technique, you can obtain a string list representing either the rows or columns of a **TStringGrid** component and manipulate the contents as you would any other **TStrings** descendant.

Table 25-10 shows the methods that are implemented by **TStringGridStrings**.

Table 25-10 Methods implemented by `TStringGridStrings`

Use or Set This...	To Do This...	Inheritance
Assign	Copy contents of one `TStrings` descendant type into the `TStringGridStrings` array.	TStrings
Create	Create a new instance of type `TStringGridStrings`.	TObject

TStringList

The **TStringList** class is the most general descendant class of **TStrings** and provides a rich collection of operations to allow generalized list management of the contents. Many of the functions are overrides of the abstract virtual methods defined by the **TStrings** class. This is the class to use when you need to manage string lists or string/object associations independently of any other components or controls.

Table 25-11 shows the methods and event handlers that are implemented by **TStringList**.

Table 25-11 Methods, properties, and event handlers implemented by **TStringList**

Use or Set This...	To Do This...	Inheritance
Add	Conditionally add new string to end of list (see Duplicates).	TStrings
Clear	Remove all items from the list.	TStrings
Create	Create new TStringList object (class constructor).	TObject
Delete	Delete entry at location and destroy string stored there.	TStrings
Destroy	Destroy the TStringList object (class destructor).	TObject
Duplicates	Specify how the list is to handle duplicate entries.	TStrings
Exchange	Swap two list members.	TStrings
Find	Return index of specified string if found in list (used for sorted lists).	None
IndexOf	Return index of specified string in list.	TStrings
Insert	Insert new string item at specified location, pushing all other entries down.	TStrings
OnChange	Executed after change occurs in list.	TStrings
OnChanging	Executed as change in list is starting.	TStrings
Sort	Sort the list using the QuickSort algorithm.	None
Sorted	Obtain whether the list is sorted or not.	None

TSubItems

The **TSubItems** class allows access to the strings that appear as subitems to the list items in the List View control that is encapsulated in the **TListView** component. You should refer to the discussion of the **TListView** component in Chapter 58, "**TCustomListView** and **TListView**" to gain a better understanding of when **TSubItems** comes into use. To add a new subitem, use the **TSubItem**'s **Add** method. **TSubItems** are only visible when the owning **TListView** component's **ViewStyle** property is set to **vsReport**.

Table 25-12 shows the properties that are implemented by **TSubItems**.

Table 25-12 Properties implemented by TSubItems

Use or Set This...	To Do This...	Inheritance
Add	Add new string to end of list.	TStrings
Create	Create a new instance of type TSubItems.	TStrings
Insert	Insert new string item at specified location, pushing all other entries down.	TStrings
Handle	Obtain handle of corresponding Win95 object.	None
Owner	Obtain reference to the TListItem that owns the TSubView string list.	None

TTabPageAccess

The **TTabPageAccess** object is used to maintain the list of **TTabPages** for a **TPageControl** (**TTabbedNotebook** in Delphi 1.0) component. The corresponding **TTabPageAccess** object is obtained via the **Pages** property of the owning **TPageControl** component. The string list represents the individual pages of the **TPageControl**. For more information, you should refer to the description of the **TPageControl** component in Chapter 59, "**TCustomTabControl** and Its Descendants." Table 25-13 shows the properties implemented by **TTabPageAccess**.

Table 25-13 Properties implemented by TTabPageAccess

Use or Set This...	To Do This...	Inheritance
Clear	Remove all contents from the list.	TStrings
Create	Create a new instance of type TTabPageAccess.	TObject
Delete	Remove indexed item from the list.	Tstrings
GetPageAt	Obtain reference to the TTabPage that owns the TTabPageAccess string list.	None
Insert	Insert new string item at specified location, pushing all other entries down.	TStrings
Move	Move item from one location to another in the string list.	TStrings

TTabStrings

The **TTabStrings** class defines the string list class used internally by the **TCustomTabControl** and the **TTabControl** class for the management of the tab information used by those components. For additional information on **TCustomTabControl** and **TTabControl**, refer to Chapter 59.

Table 25-14 shows the methods that are implemented by **TTabStrings**.

Table 25-14 Methods implemented by TTabStrings

Use or Set This...	To Do This...	Inheritance
Clear	Remove all contents from the list.	TStrings
Delete	Remove indexed item from the list.	TStrings
Insert	Insert new string item at specified location, pushing all other entries down.	TStrings

TTreeStrings

The **TTreeStrings** class is used to maintain the list of strings managed by the **TCustomTreeView** class and its descendants. It is unlikely that you will need to interact directly with **TTreeStrings**; you would more likely utilize the methods provided by the **TCustomTreeView** class and its descendants when working with these classes. For additional information related to the **TCustomTreeView** class and its descendant classes, refer to Chapter 60, "**TCustomTreeView** and **TTreeView**."

Table 25-15 shows the methods that are implemented by **TTreeStrings**.

Table 25-15 Methods implemented by **TTreeStrings**

Use or Set This...	To Do This...	Inheritance
Add	Add a new string to the **TTreeStrings** list.	TStrings
Clear	Remove all contents from the list.	TStrings
Create	Create a new instance of type **TTreeStrings**, passing a **TTreeNodes** as the Owner.	TObject
Delete	Remove indexed item from the list.	TStrings
Insert	Insert new string item at specified location, pushing all other entries down.	TStrings
Owner	Obtain reference to the **TTreeNodes** that owns the **TTreeStrings** string list.	None

Add METHOD

Objects Affected TComboBoxStrings, TIndexFiles, TListBoxStrings, TOutlineStrings, TStringList, TStrings, TSubItems, TTreeStrings

Purpose The **Add** method is used by the above classes to add a string to the end of the selected **TStrings** descendant. The corresponding object reference is set to **Nil**. The new item's position in the list is returned to the caller. The first element of the list is **0**.

Declaration

```
function Add(const S: string): Integer
```

Example Syntax

```
procedure TForm1.Button1Click(Sender: TObject);
var
  loc: Integer;
begin
  loc := ListBox1.Items.Add('New item');
  theStringList.Add('New item');
  Label1.Caption := IntToStr(loc);
end;
```

Description   In this example, a form contains a pushbutton, a label, and a list box. The form declaration also contains a variable of type `TStringList`, which has been created at form creation. When the pushbutton is clicked, the string `'New item'` is appended to the end of the string list owned by the list box. The string list is obtained from a list box via the use of the `Items` property, then the `Add` method is used to add to the string list. The call to `Add` returns a positional value indicating the location where the string was placed. This integer value is then converted to a string and placed in the label on the form.

AddObject METHOD

Objects Affected   `TStrings` and all its descendants

Purpose   The `AddObject` method is used to add a string and an object reference to the end of the selected `TStrings` descendant. The new item's position in the list is returned to the caller. The first element of the list is `0`.

Declaration

```
function AddObject(const S: string; AObject: TObject): Integer;
```

Example Syntax

```
procedure TForm1.Button1Click(Sender: TObject);
var
  loc: Integer;
begin
  loc := ListBox1.Items.AddObject('New item',Sender);
  theStringList.AddObject('New item',Sender);
  Label1.Caption := IntToStr(loc);
end;
```

Description   In this example, a form contains a pushbutton, a label, and a list box. The form declaration also contains a variable of type `TStringList`, which has been created at form creation. When the pushbutton is clicked, the string `'New item'` is appended to the end of the string list owned by the list box, and the sender object is also stored with the string item. The string list is obtained from a list box via the use of the `Items` property, then the `Add` method is used to add to the string list. The call to `Add` returns a positional value indicating the location where the string was placed. This integer value is then converted to a string and placed in the label on the form.

AddStrings METHOD

Objects Affected   `TStrings` and all its descendants

Purpose   The `AddStrings` method is used to add a group of strings collectively to the end of a `TStrings` descendant object. The argument accepts an object of type `TStrings` and appends all items in that string list to the end of the object whose `AddStrings` method is being invoked. The **Object** references of the new items are copied along with the list.

Declaration

```
procedure AddStrings(Strings: TStrings);
```

Example Syntax

```
procedure TForm1.Button1Click(Sender: TSender);
var
  FileStrings: TStringList;
begin
  FileStrings.LoadFromFile('ListStrs.TXT');
  ListBox1.Items.AddStrings(FileStrings);
finally
  FileStrings.Free;
end;
```

Description

This code reads the contents of a file into a **TStrings** object and uses **AddStrings** to append it to the end of a **TListBox** control.

Assign METHOD

Objects Affected   **TStrings** and all its descendants

Purpose   The **Assign** method assigns one object to another if the objects know how. **TStrings** descendants know how to assign from one to another in general. Note that this is a "deep copy," in which the information contained in one list is replicated and is used to replace any prior contents in the original list. If the original list is empty to start with, the information is just duplicated via the **Assign** operation. If the two objects do not know how to convert from one to another, an **EConvertError** exception will be raised.

Declaration

```
procedure Assign(Source: TPersistent);
```

Example Syntax

```
procedure TForm1.Button1Click(Sender: TSender);
var
  FileStrings: TStringList;
begin
  FileStrings.LoadFromFile('ListStrs.TXT');
  ListBox1.Items.Assign(FileStrings);
  FileStrings.Add('New list item');
  ListBox2.Items.Assign(FileStrings);
finally
  FileStrings.Free;
end;
```

Description   The example code assigns a string list read from a file to two separate list boxes, making a change in-between the two assignment operations to illustrate that a deep copy is performed rather than just a referential copy.

BeginUpdate METHOD

Objects Affected   TStrings and all its descendants

Purpose   The BeginUpdate method is used to prevent screen updates when changes are being made to visual component descendants of TStrings such as TComboBox, TListBox, TOutline, and so on. In the case of TStringList, this routine indirectly causes the OnChanging handler to be triggered if it has been assigned. Note that calls to BeginUpdate may be nested and that an equal number of EndUpdate calls must be made to match every previous call to BeginUpdate to allow screen updates. BeginUpdate and EndUpdate maintain an internal reference counter to manage this mechanism.

Declaration

```
procedure BeginUpdate;
```

Example Syntax

```
procedure TForm1.Button1Click(Sender: TSender);
var
   FileStrings: TStringList;
begin

   FileStrings.LoadFromFile('ListStrs.TXT');
   ListBox1.BeginUpdate;
   ListBox2.BeginUpdate;
   ListBox1.Items.Assign(FileStrings);
   FileStrings.Add('New list item');
   ListBox2.Items.Assign(FileStrings);
   ListBox1.EndUpdate;
   ListBox2.EndUpdate;
finally
   FileStrings.Free;
end;
```

Description   The example code is similar to the previous Assign example. The difference involves the use of the BeginUpdate method to prevent Windows from updating either list box until both have been updated. The call to EndUpdate signals Windows that it is now okay to redraw the controls.

Capacity PROPERTY

Objects Affected   TStrings and all its descendants

Purpose   The Capacity property is used to find out how many strings the TString object is capable of storing in its current state without requiring additional elements to be added. It is not a measure of how many strings are currently valid in the **TString** object, since there may be some unoccupied cells in the internal memory used by the object.

Declaration

```
property Capacity: Integer;
```

Example Syntax

```
function TForm1.GetStringCapacity(str: TString);
begin
    Result := str.Capacity;
end;
```

Description   This example function obtains the capacity of a supplied **TString** object and returns it to the caller.

Clear METHOD

Objects Affected   **TStrings** and all its descendants

Purpose   The **Clear** method is used to remove all entries from a string list and return it to the empty state. It does not delete or free any associated object references that have been saved in the list.

Declaration

```
procedure Clear;
```

Example Syntax

```
procedure TForm1.Button1Click(Sender: TSender);
begin
  ListBox1.Items.Clear;
end;
```

Description   This example procedure invokes the **Clear** method to remove all items from a list box. When this method is invoked on the string classes associated with visual controls (via the **Items** property), the control will be redrawn after the **Clear** operation is performed.

CommaText PROPERTY

Objects Affected   **TStrings** and all its descendants

Purpose   The **CommaText** property retrieves and sets the contents of the string list in a style known as system data format (SDF). The string returned contains each string in the string list separated by commas. If any of the member strings contain spaces, commas, or quotes, the individual string will be quoted as well. For example, if the string list contains the following strings:

```
Hel,,lo 1
thi""s 2
is 3
a test4
```

`CommaText` will return

`"Hel,,lo 1","thi""""s 2","is 3","a test4"`

When assigning `CommaText` to a `TStrings` object, the string is interpreted as SDF formatted text also. When making assignments using SDF format, strings are separated by commas, spaces, #10, #13, and #0, and delimited by double quotes. For example, suppose `CommaText` is set to

`"Hel,,lo 1","Thi""""s 2",is 3,"a test4"`

The string list will then contain

```
Hel,,lo 1
Thi""s 2
is
3
a test4
```

Declaration

```
property CommaText: string;
```

Example Syntax

```
procedure TForm1.Button1Click(Sender: TSender);
var
  pos: Integer;
begin
  ListBox1.Items.Clear;
  ListBox1.Items.CommaText = 'This,is,a,test';;
end;
```

Description This example assigns the contents of the list box in response to a button click after first clearing it.

Count PROPERTY

Objects Affected TStrings and all its descendants

Purpose The Count property returns the number of items contained in a list.

Declaration

```
property Count: Integer...;
```

Example Syntax

```
TMyListBox = class(TListBox)
  .
  .
  .
```

```
function TMyListBox.HowMany: Integer;
begin
   Result := Count;
end;
```

Description   This example is for a method called **HowMany** for a new hypothetical class derived from **TListBox**. The method simply returns the number of items in the list by retrieving the **Count** property and assigning it to the result of the function.

Create METHOD

Objects Affected   TStrings and all its descendants

Purpose   The **Create** method performs internal initialization required by the descendant class.

Declaration

TStrings, TStringList

```
Constructor Create;
```

> **NOTE**
> Any classes not listed below inherit Create from TObject and use this form.

TIndexFiles

```
Constructor Create(AOwner: Ttable);
```

TPageAccess

```
Constructor Create(APageList: TList; ANotebook: Tnotebook);
```

TStringsGridStrings

```
Constructor Create(AGrid: TStringsGrid; AIndex: Longint);
```

TSubItems

```
Constructor Create(AOwner: TListItem);
```

TTabPageAccess

```
Constructor Create(APageList: TList; ANotebook: TTabbedNotebook);
```

TTreeStrings

```
Constructor Create(AOwner: TTreeNodes);
```

Example Syntax

```
unit Unit1;

interface

uses
  SysUtils, WinTypes, WinProcs, Messages, Classes, Graphics, Controls,
  Forms, Dialogs;

type
  TForm1 = class(TForm)
    procedure FormCreate(Sender: TObject);
  private
    { Private declarations }
    FStrList: TStringList;
  public
    { Public declarations }
  end;

var
  Form1: TForm1;

implementation

{$R *.DFM}

procedure TForm1.FormCreate(Sender: TObject);
begin
    FStrList := TStringList.Create;
end;

procedure TForm1.FormDestroy(Sender: TObject);
begin
    FStrList.Free;
end;

end.
```

Description   This example illustrates a complete form-based unit that has a variable of type **TStringList** as a private member. During the **FormCreate** handler execution, the **FStrList** variable is created using the **Create** method of the **TStringList** class. During the **FormDestroy** handler execution, the **FStrList** variable is freed. This automatically calls the **Destroy** method as long as the **FStrList** is valid (see **Destroy** method).

Delete METHOD

Objects Affected   **TStrings** and all its descendants

Purpose   The **Delete** method is used to remove a particular string item from the string list. This method automatically disposes of the storage required to contain the string at the specified location; however, it doesn't do anything with an object reference if the string list item contains a valid object reference. Thus, care must be exercised if a list holding objects in addition to strings is used to avoid memory leaks.

Declaration

```
procedure Delete(Index: Integer); virtual; abstract;
```

Example Syntax

```
procedure TForm1.Button1Click(Sender: TSender);
var
  pos: Integer;
begin
  pos := StrToInt(text1.text);
  if (pos >=0) and (pos < ListBox1.Items.Count) then
    ListBox1.Items.Delete(pos);
end;
```

Description

This example converts the value of a text box to an integer value and then checks to see if the resulting value obtained is in bounds of the list item count. If so, it then calls upon the **Delete** method to remove the particular item specified.

Destroy METHOD

Objects Affected	**TStrings** and all its descendants
Purpose	The **Destroy** method is used to clear all entries from a string list and return appropriate resources to the system.

Declaration

```
destructor Destroy; override;
```

Example Syntax	Refer to **Create** method above for an example of how to dispose of a **TStrings** descendant object.
Description	Note that in the example syntax under **Create**, the code makes use of a call to **Free**. This is the generally accepted way to actually dispose of a dynamically created object at run time in Delphi. **Free** internally makes a call to **Destroy** for a given class if it determines that it is safe to do so. Delphi documentation recommends against calling **Destroy** directly.

Duplicates PROPERTY

Objects Affected	**TStringList**
Purpose	The **Duplicates** property is used to determine how sorted lists should handle the situation when duplicate values are added to the list. If a **TStringList** object is not sorted (see **Sorted** property) this property is ignored. Table 25-16 lists the possible values to which the **Duplicates** property can be set.

Table 25-16 TStringList.Duplicate property legal values

Value	Meaning
dupAccept	Duplicate strings can be added to a sorted string list.
dupError	Adding a duplicate string results in an EListError exception.
dupIgnore	Attempts to add a duplicate string to a sorted string list are ignored.

Declaration

```
property Duplicates: TDuplicates read FDuplicates write Fduplicates;
```

Example Syntax

```
procedure TForm1.FormCreate(Sender: TSender);
begin
  FMyStrings:=TStringList.Create;
  FMyStrings.Sorted := true;
  FMyStrings.Duplicates := dupIgnore;
end;
```

Description

In this example a TStringList form variable is created in the FormCreate routine. Then the Sorted property is set to True and the Duplicates property is set to dupIgnore, which has the effect of not allowing any duplicates to occur in the string list.

EndUpdate METHOD

Objects Affected   TStrings and all its descendants

Purpose   The EndUpdate method is used to re-enable screen updates of controls that contain TStrings descendant classes after corresponding calls to BeginUpdate. Note that calls to BeginUpdate may be nested and that an equal number of EndUpdate calls must be made to match every previous call to BeginUpdate to allow screen updates. BeginUpdate and EndUpdate maintain an internal reference counter to manage this mechanism.

Declaration

```
procedure EndUpdate;
```

Example Syntax   Refer to BeginUpdate earlier in chapter.

Description   Refer to BeginUpdate earlier in chapter.

Equals METHOD

Objects Affected   TStrings and all its descendants

Purpose   The Equals method is used to determine whether two string lists contain the same textual information and are of the same length.

Declaration

```
function Equals(Strings: TStrings): Boolean;
```

Example Syntax

```
function TForm1.AreListsEqual: Boolean;
begin
  Result := ListBox1.Items.Equals(TStrings(ListBox2.Items));
end;
```

Description

This example performs a test on two list boxes to determine whether they contain the same information and returns **True** if they are equal in length and the strings in each list element match. If either criterion is violated, the method returns **False**.

Exchange METHOD

Objects Affected   **TStrings** and all its descendants

Purpose   The **Exchange** method swaps two string list elements. The string and its associated object reference are exchanged as a unit.

Declaration

```
procedure Exchange(Index1, Index2: Integer); virtual;
```

Example Syntax

```
function TForm1.DoExch(i,j:integer): Boolean;
begin
  if (i>0) and (j>0) and (i<ListBox1.Items.Count) and⇐
(j<ListBox1.ItemsCount)
  then begin
      ListBox1.Items.Exchange(i,j);
      Result := true;
      end
  else begin
      Result := false;
  end;
end;
```

Description   This example accepts two indices, which indicate which two elements of a list box are to be exchanged. First, the example checks to ensure that the passed parameters are in bounds for the **ListBox1** component, then it calls the **Exchange** method to actually perform the desired operation.

Find METHOD

Objects Affected   **TStringList**

Purpose   The **Find** method is used to determine whether a given string value is stored at any of the locations in the string list.

Declaration

```
function Find(const S: string; var Index: Integer): Boolean; virtual;
```

Example Syntax

```
procedure TForm1.SomeMethod;
var
  i:boolean;
  pos:integer;
begin
  .
  .

  i:= theStringList.Find('apple', pos);
  .
  .

end;
```

Description   A code fragment is shown in this example in which a `TStringList` variable (assumed to be declared in the form declarations) is scanned for the occurrence of the string `'apple'`. If successful, the position in the list will be placed into the integer variable **pos** and the function will return **True**. If `'apple'` is not found in the string list, the function will return **False** and **pos** will be undefined.

GetObject METHOD

Objects Affected   `TOutlineStrings`

Purpose   The `GetObject` method is publicly exposed only in the `TOutlineStrings` class and is used to obtain the object reference located at a specified location in the string list. This method will return a pointer to the object associated with the indexed `TOutlineStrings` entry if one exists, or else it will return **Nil**.

Declaration

```
function GetObject(Index: Integer): TObject;
```

Example Syntax

```
function TForm1.SomeMethod(ind:integer):Pointer ;
begin
   Result:= mOutlineStrings.GetObject(ind);
end;
```

Description   In this example a call is made to `GetObject` to obtain a pointer to the object associated with the indexed item in the `TOutlineStrings` object `mOutlineStrings`.

GetPageAt METHOD

Objects Affected   TTabPageAccess

Purpose   The GetPageAt method is publicly exposed only in the **TTabPageAccess** class and is used to obtain the **TTabPage** object located at a specified location in the string list. This method will return the **TTabPage** object associated with the indexed **TTabPage** entry if one exists, or else it will return **Nil**.

Declaration

```
function GetPageAt(Index: Integer): TTabPage;
```

Example Syntax

```
function TForm1.SomeMethod(ind:integer):TTabPage ;
begin
   Result:= mTabObj.GetPageAt(ind);
end;
```

Description   In this example a call is made to **GetPageAt** to obtain the **TTabPage** associated with the indexed item in the **TTabPage** object **mTabObj**.

Handle PROPERTY

Objects Affected   TSubItems

Purpose   The **Handle** property returns a Win95 handle for the **TSubItems** object to the user.

Declaration

```
property Handle: HWND;
```

Example Syntax

```
procedure TForm1.getSubItemHandle;
begin
   .
   .
   mSubItemHwnd := mSubItems.Handle;
end;
```

Description   This function retrieves the handle of a private **mSubItems** class variable previously assigned and assigns that handle to the class variable called **mSubItemHwnd**.

IndexOf METHOD

Objects Affected	TStrings and all its descendants
Purpose	This method accepts a string as an argument and determines whether the string is contained in the string list. It returns an integer indicating the position of the string in the list, or −1 if the string argument is not found in the list.
Declaration	

```
function IndexOf(const S: string): Integer;
```

Example Syntax

```
function TForm1.IsStringInListBox(theList:TListBox; theString:string):
integer;
begin
    Result := theList.Items.IndexOf(theString);
end;
```

Description This example accepts a TListBox argument that contains the string list to be scanned, and a string argument that is the string to search for. The function then uses the IndexOf method to determine whether the passed string is contained in the supplied TListBox object.

IndexOfName METHOD

Objects Affected	TStrings and all its descendants
Purpose	This method accepts a string as an argument and determines whether the string is contained in the string list where the contents of the items are in the form

```
<Name>=<Value>
```

It returns an integer indicating the position of the entry with the indicated name in the list, or −1 if the string argument is not found in the name list.

Declaration

```
function IndexOfName(const S: string): Integer;
```

Example Syntax

```
function TForm1.IsNameInList(theList:TStrings; theString:string):⇐
integer;
begin
    Result := theList.Items.IndexOfName(theString);
end;
```

Description This example accepts as an argument any descendant of TStrings that contains the <Name>=<Value> list pairs to be scanned, and a string argument that is the name to be matched. The function then uses the IndexOfName method to determine whether the passed string is contained in the supplied TStrings object. Note that this particular example illustrates how to declare a function that accepts any of the descendant classes of TStrings.

IndexOfObject METHOD

Objects Affected   TStrings and all its descendants

Purpose   This method searches a string list to determine whether a supplied object reference is contained in the string list, and if so, returns the index of the list entry containing the same reference, or returns −1 if the object is not found in the list.

Declaration

```
function IndexOfObject(AObject: TObject): Integer;
```

Example Syntax

```
function TForm1.IsStringInListBox(theList:TListBox; theObj:TObject):
integer;
begin
    Result := theList.Items.IndexOfObject(theObj);
end;
```

Description   This example accepts a TListBox argument that contains the string list to be scanned, and a TObject type argument that is the object to search for. The function then uses the IndexOfObject method to determine whether the passed TObject is contained in the supplied TListBox object. The argument theObj could be any type of Delphi object that would have been typecast to type TObject when the function was called.

Insert METHOD

Objects Affected   TStrings and all its descendants

Purpose   This method accepts an index value and a string as arguments. The method shifts the item contained in the list at the specified location and all items that follow in the list to the next higher indexed location in the list. It then inserts the newly supplied string into the list item location specified in the Index argument.

Note that if an insertion is made more than one item beyond the last list entry, an EListError exception will be raised. In the case of string lists associated with visual controls such as TListBox.Items, insertion of more than one item beyond the last entry will be ignored without raising an exception.

Declaration

```
procedure Insert(Index: Integer; const S: string); virtual; abstract;
```

Example Syntax

```
procedure TForm1.Button1Click(Sender: TObject);
var
i:integer;
ts:TStrings;
tsx:TStringList;
begin
 tsx := TStringList.Create;
 tsx.Add('A');
 tsx.Add('B');
 tsx.Insert(1,'C');
 ListBox1.Items.Assign(tsx);
 tsx.free;
end;
```

Description   In this example a form is created that contains a single list box and a pushbutton. When the button is pressed, an instance of **TStringList** is created and two items are added to the list: **'A'** and **'B'**. Then the **Insert** function is used to add a third item between the original two items. The resulting string is then assigned to the **ListBox** items. Finally, the temporary **TStringList** is freed.

InsertObject METHOD

Objects Affected   TStrings and all its descendants

Purpose   This method performs a function similar to that of the **Insert** method described above, except that in addition to inserting a string at a specified location, it also allows the caller to pass an object reference, which is stored in the list at the specified location along with the string data.

Declaration

```
procedure InsertObject(Index: Integer; const S: string;AObject: Tobject);
```

Example Syntax

```
procedure TForm1.FormCreate(Sender: TObject);
var
i:integer;
ts:TStrings;
tsx:TStringList;
begin
 tsx := TStringList.Create;
 tsx.InsertObject(0,'A',nil);
 tsx.InsertObject(1,'B',nil);
 tsx.InsertObject(2,'C',nil);
 ListBox1.Items.Assign(tsx);
 tsx.free;
end;
```

Description   This example is similar to the one shown earlier in **Insert**. The difference is that **InsertObject** is used to add strings sequentially to the list and also to set the object reference of each entry to **Nil**. (This is actually done by default in the

Insert method.) Note also that the calling procedure is FormCreate, where it would make more sense to see a list box being initialized. This might be done in preparing the list for later owner-draw operations where the object references would be changed to bitmaps.

LoadFromFile METHOD

Objects Affected TStrings and all its descendants

Purpose This method is used to restore a string list from a disk file that was created using the SaveToFile method on a TStrings descendant class object. If the specified file cannot be found, the procedure will raise an EFOpenError exception.

Declaration

```
procedure LoadFromFile(const FileName: string);
```

Example Syntax

```
procedure TForm1.Button1Click(Sender: TObject);
begin
    ListBox1.Items.LoadFromFile('foo.bar');
end;
```

Description This example loads the string items associated with a ListBox on a form from a file 'foo.bar', which was saved previously using SaveToFile. ListBox2 will automatically be refreshed once the new data has been loaded.

LoadFromStream METHOD

Objects Affected TStrings and all its descendants

Purpose This method is used to restore, from an existing stream, a string list that was created using the SaveToStream method on a TStrings descendant class object.

Declaration

```
procedure LoadFromStream(Stream: TStream); virtual;
```

Example Syntax

```
procedure TForm1.Button1Click(Sender: TObject);
begin
    ListBox1.Items.LoadFromStream(listStream);
end;
```

Description This example loads the string items associated with a TListBox on a form from a stream called textStream, which was loaded with text data previously using SaveToStream. The TListBox object named ListBox1 will automatically be refreshed once the new data has been loaded.

Move METHOD

Objects Affected	TStrings and all its descendants
Purpose	This method is used to move one item in the string list to another location in the same string list. The first parameter passed is the index of the item that will be moved. The second parameter is the index that the item to be moved will occupy after the move is performed. If an out of bounds index is specified, an EListError exception is raised.
Declaration	

```
procedure Move(CurIndex, NewIndex: Integer); virtual;
```

Example Syntax

```
procedure TForm1.Button1Click(Sender: TObject);
begin
    ListBox1.Items.Move(1,3);
end;
```

Description	This example implements the actual move operation in response to a button click on a form that contains a list box object.

Names PROPERTY

Objects Affected	TStrings and all its descendants
Purpose	This property provides access to a structured string list in which individual items in the string list are assumed to have the form Name=Value.
	When reading the Names property, the caller specifies the index of the TString Name=Value pair to be retrieved. This property is read only. If a particular element is not already in the list, the property will return an empty string.
Declaration	

```
property Names[Index: Integer]: string
```

Example Syntax

```
function getName(st:TString; i:index):string;
begin
    Result := st.Names[i];
end;
```

Description	This example illustrates the syntax used to access names associated with Name=Value pairs that can be stored in TString objects. (See also the description for the Values property.)

Objects PROPERTY

Objects Affected	`TStrings` and all its descendants
Purpose	`Objects` is an indexed property that is used to access the object reference values stored in string list items. It provides both read and write access to the object associated with each entry of the string list. If an object has never been specified for a string list item, retrieving the object will return `Nil` as the object reference; otherwise, the property will return or accept objects of type `TObject`. Typecasting can be used to store a specific object as type `TObject` rather than as its original type, and on read operations, a type-safe typecast can convert the returned `TObject` back to its original class type. One important use of string list objects is to support owner-draw functionality for graphical controls that work with string lists. This includes `TListBox`, `TComboBox`, and so on. For more information regarding the implementation of owner-draw controls, refer to the Delphi online help system.

Declaration

```
property Objects[Index: Integer]: TObject ...;
```

Example Syntax

```
procedure TForm1.Button1Click(Sender: TObject);
begin
     ListBox1.Items.Objects[1] := Sender;
end;
```

Description   This example illustrates the syntax used to access string list objects. Specifically, the `Sender` passed into the procedure when it is executed is stored in the first element of the list's object value.

OnChange EVENT

Objects Affected	`TStringList`
Purpose	`OnChange` is an event handler that is called after a change has been made to an object of type `TStringList`. It is used to perform programmed actions in response to changes in the list, if required.

Declaration

```
property OnChange: TNotifyEvent read FOnChange write FOnChange;
```

Example Syntax

```
unit Unit1;

interface
```

continued on next page

continued from previous page

```
uses
  SysUtils, WinTypes, WinProcs, Messages, Classes, Graphics, Controls,
  Forms, Dialogs, StdCtrls;

type
  TForm1 = class(TForm)
    ListBox1: TListBox;
    procedure FormCreate(Sender: TObject);
  private
    { Private declarations }
    procedure ListBoxUpdate(Sender: TObject);
  public
    { Public declarations }
    theStringList:TStringList;
  end;

var
  Form1: TForm1;

implementation

{$R *.DFM}

procedure TForm1.FormCreate(Sender: TObject);
begin
  theStringList := TStringList.Create;
  theStringList.OnChange := ListBoxUpdate;
  theStringList.Add('hi');
  theStringList.free;
end;

procedure TForm1.ListBoxUpdate(Sender: TObject);
begin
    ListBox1.Items.Assign(TStrings(theStringList));
end;

end.
```

Description

The previous example code illustrates the method by which the OnChange handler can be used for TStringList objects. Since the TStringList is not a visual component in the same way that a list box, or combo box is, there is no visual way to program the OnChange handler for a TStringList object as there is when components are selected on a form and events made visible in the Property editor. However, the OnChange handler can be specified in code, and the previous example illustrates the method to do so. Note that the ListBoxUpdate method is declared to be functionally similar to a standard Delphi event handler. To connect the handler to the TStringList, assign the procedure to the OnChange property as shown in the FormCreate method above. In the above example, the form variable theStringList is created at run time, and then the OnChange handler is assigned. Finally, an item is added to theStringList, which in turn causes the OnChange event handler to execute. In this example, the OnChange handler simply assigns theStringList to ListBox1, a component on the form, which in turn causes the information in **theStringList** to appear in **ListBox1** when the form is created. After the string manipulation is completed, **theStringList** is freed to return the string data to the system, since it is no longer needed.

OnChanging EVENT

Objects Affected   TStringList

Purpose   OnChanging is an event handler that is called before a change has been made to an object of type **TStringList**. It is used to perform programmed actions prior to changes in the list, if required.

Declaration

```
property OnChanging: TNotifyEvent read FOnChanging write FOnChanging;
```

Example Syntax

```
unit Unit1;

interface

uses
  SysUtils, WinTypes, WinProcs, Messages, Classes, Graphics, Controls,
  Forms, Dialogs, StdCtrls;

type
  TForm1 = class(TForm)
    ListBox1: TListBox;
    procedure FormCreate(Sender: TObject);
  private
    { Private declarations }
    procedure ListBoxUpdate(Sender: TObject);
    procedure ListBoxFix(Sender:TObject);
  public
    { Public declarations }
    theStringList:TStringList;
  end;

var
  Form1: TForm1;

implementation

{$R *.DFM}

procedure TForm1.FormCreate(Sender: TObject);
begin
  theStringList := TStringList.Create;
  theStringList.Add('hi');
  theStringList.Add('there');
  theStringList.Add('you');
  theStringList.Add('all');
  theStringList.OnChanging := ListBoxFix;
```

continued on next page

continued from previous page

```
        theStringList.OnChange := ListBoxUpdate;
        theStringList.Add('hi');
        theStringList.free;
end;

procedure TForm1.ListBoxFix(Sender: TObject);
begin
        ListBox1.Items.Add('OnChanging');
end;

procedure TForm1.ListBoxUpdate(Sender: TObject);
begin
        ListBox1.Items.AddStrings(TStrings(theStringList));
end;

end.
```

Description   The example for OnChanging is similar to the example for OnChange, with the addition of a handler for the OnChanging event. This handler will be called prior to the actual Add of the string 'hi' to the list. When run, the following sequence of events occurs:

1. The MainForm Form1 is created.

2. During the FormCreate handler for Form1, theStringList is created.

3. theStringList is initialized with the string list ('hi', 'there', 'you', 'all').

4. theStringList event handlers are set to the desired procedures.

5. theStringList is modified by using the Add method.

6. The Add method invokes the OnChanging handler, which adds the string 'OnChanging' to the list box (not theStringList).

7. The string 'hi' is added to theStringList (not ListBox1).

8. The OnChange handler is called by the Add method, which is programmed to copy theStringList into the ListBox.

9. Control returns to the FormCreate event handler.

Owner PROPERTY

Objects Affected   TSubItems, TTreeStrings

Purpose   This property, available in the two classes shown above, allows the user to access the object that owns the corresponding string list. This can be useful for manipulating other properties of the owner object in response to changing conditions related to the string list. This property is read-only.

Declaration

TSubItems

```
property Owner: TListItem;
```

TTreeStrings

```
property Owner TTreeNodes;
```

Example Syntax

```
procedure TForm1.Button1Click(Sender: TObject);
var
  theTreeNodes: TTreeNodes;
begin
    theTreeNodes := mTreeStrings.Owner;
end;
```

Description

This procedure copies the owner of a private **TTreeStrings** type class variable into the local variable called **theTreeNodes**.

PlainText PROPERTY

Objects Affected   TRichEditStrings

Purpose   The **PlainText** property is used to control whether the **TRichEditStrings** class object treats text as plain text or rich text. The default is **False**. This property is useful when saving files or loading files to or from an RTF format or a text format. Simple file conversions are possible with proper use of this control.

Declaration

```
property PlainText: Boolean;
```

Example Syntax

```
procedure TForm1.Button1Click(Sender: TObject);
var
  theEdiTStrings:TRichEdiTStrings;
  oldState:Boolean;
begin
    theEdiTStrings := RichEditControl1.Lines;
    oldState := theEdiTStrings.PlainText;
    theEdiTStrings.PlainText := true;
    theEdiTStrings.SaveToFile('savefile.txt');
    theEdiTStrings.PlainText := oldState;
end;
```

Description   This example obtains the **TRichEditStrings** object for a **TRichEdit** control and saves the state of the **PlainText** variable in a temporary variable, then sets the

PlainText property to True in preparation for saving the file to a file intended for use as a plain ASCII text file. The SaveToFile method is used to save theEditStrings to a file called 'savefile.txt'. Finally, the original value of PlainText is restored into the PlainText property of the string list.

PutObject METHOD

Objects Affected	TOutlineStrings
Purpose	This method is exposed publicly only in the TOutlineStrings class and is used to set the object reference located at a specified location in the string list. Most of the other TStrings descendants use the indexed property known as Objects to provide both read and write access to the objects in the list. In fact, this can also be done with the TOutlineStrings class, so it was actually unnecessary to make the PutOwner and GetOwner methods public. They should probably have been made protected, as are all other descendants of TStrings.
Declaration	

```
procedure PutObject(Index: Integer; AObject: TObject);
```

Example Syntax	

```
function TForm1.setOutlineObj(theOutline:TOutline; i:Integer;⇐
theObj:TObject): Boolean;
begin

  if (i<theOutline.Items.Count) and (i>=0) then
     begin
        theOutline.Items.PutObject(i,theObj);
        publicPutObject := true;
     end
  else
     publicPutObject := false;
end;
```

Description	In this example a function is declared that first checks to see whether the index passed by the caller is in the legal bounds for the TOutline list, and if so calls PutObject to save the object provided by the caller at the desired location. It then sets the boolean return value to True. If the list index is out of bounds, the function returns False.

SaveToFile METHOD

Objects Affected	TStrings and all its descendants
Purpose	This method is used to save the string values contained in any of the descendant classes of TStrings to a specified disk file (see the LoadFromFile method described above).

Declaration

```
procedure SaveToFile(const FileName: string);
```

Example Syntax

```
procedure TForm1.Button2Click(Sender: TObject);
begin
    ListBox1.Items.SaveToFile('foo.bar');
end;
```

Description   This example saves the string items associated with a **ListBox** on a form into a file called **'foo.bar'**. Later, these strings can be retrieved using the **LoadFromFile** method.

SaveToStream METHOD

Objects Affected   **TStrings** and all its descendants

Purpose   This method is used to save a string list into an existing stream.

Declaration

```
procedure SaveToStream(Stream: TStream); virtual;
```

Example Syntax

```
procedure TForm1.Button1Click(Sender: TObject);
begin
    ListBox1.Items.SaveToStream(listStream);
end;
```

Description   This example saves the string items associated with a **ListBox** on a form into a stream called list**Stream** for later recall using **LoadFromStream**.

SetText METHOD

Objects Affected   **TStrings** and all its descendants

Purpose   This method is a virtual method defined in class **TStrings**. The default behavior is to accept a **PChar** object (null-terminated string) that contains each string element separated by a carriage-return/line-feed sequence and copy those items into the string list. Before the strings are copied into the list, it is first cleared of any previous information.

Declaration

```
procedure SetText(Text: PChar); virtual;
```

Example Syntax

```
procedure TForm1.FormCreate(Sender: TObject);
var
```

continued on next page

continued from previous page

```
        ts:string;
        tc:array[0..256] of char;
begin

    ts := format('%s'+#13#10+'%s'+#13#10+'%s'+#13#10+'%s'+#13#10,
                ['this','is','a','test']);
    StrPCopy(tc,ts);
    ListBox1.Items.SetText(tc);

end;
```

Description
This example uses the format function to create a string containing the individual list elements to be placed into a **ListBox** component on a form at form creation. After the format function creates the desired string of data, the **StrPCopy** function is used to convert the Pascal string into an array of **char** type that is suitable for use with the **SetText** method. This **PChar** string is then passed to the **SetText** method, which copies the items from the original string into separate list items prior to displaying the form.

Sort METHOD

Objects Affected TStringList

Purpose
This method is a virtual procedure provided in **TStringList** to provide the user with the ability to sort the items stored in a **TStringList** object or descendant class object. The default behavior for **TStringList** and its descendants is to trigger the execution of the **OnChanging** event handler if it is assigned, then execute a **QuickSort** algorithm on the string list items, then trigger the execution of the **OnChange** event handler. If you use this method directly, be aware that it will not on its own change the state of the **Sorted** property for the **TStringList** object. (See **Sorted** property below for more information.)

Declaration

```
procedure Sort; virtual;
```

Example Syntax

```
procedure TForm1.Button1Click(Sender: TObject);
var
  ts:TStringList;
begin
  ts := TStringList.create;
  ts.Assign(TStrings(Memo1.Lines));
  ts.Sort;
  Memo1.Lines.Assign(ts);
  ts.free;
end;
```

Description   This example illustrates a way to perform a sort operation on the contents of a memo control, since the control doesn't support one directly. A temporary string list is created, then the contents of the memo control are copied to the string list. The string list is sorted, then the resulting string list is returned to the memo control. Finally, the temporary string list is freed.

Sorted PROPERTY

Objects Affected   `TStringList`

Purpose   `Sorted` is a boolean property indicating whether or not a `TStringList` object is sorted. This property operates in conjunction with the `Sort` method for the `TStringList` class. When this property is set to `True` by the user, the `Sort` method is called automatically and the `TStringList` object is sorted as described under the `Sort` method above. Then the `Sorted` property is set to a value of `True`. If the property is set to a value of `False`, that is the only operation performed. When this property is read, it simply returns the value stored internally by the last write operation to the property.

Declaration

```
property Sorted: Boolean read FSorted write SetSorted;
```

Example Syntax

```
procedure TForm1.Button1Click(Sender: TObject);
var
  ts:TStringList;
begin
  ts := TStringList.create;
  ts.Assign(TStrings(Memo1.Lines));
  ts.Sorted := true;
  Memo1.Lines.Assign(ts);
  ts.free;
end;
```

Description   This example is similar to the example shown for the `Sort` method, with the exception that the `Sorted` property is used to perform the sort operation instead of using the `Sort` method directly. This has the added benefit that the internal value for the `Sorted` property will be properly maintained.

Strings PROPERTY

Objects Affected   `TStrings` and all its descendants

Purpose   This property allows the user to gain access to the strings stored in a `TStrings` descendant class by using indexed array notation.

Declaration

```
property Strings[Index: Integer]: string ...;
```

Example Syntax

```
procedure TForm1.Button1Click(Sender: TObject);
var
  ts:TStringList;
  s1,s2:string;
begin
  ts := TStringList.create;
  ts.Assign(TStrings(Memo1.Lines));
  s1 := ts.Strings[0];
  s2 := ts.Strings[ts.Count-1];
  ts.Strings[ts.Count-1] := s1;
  ts.Strings[0] := s2;
  Memo1.Lines.Assign(ts);
  ts.free;
end;
```

Description   This example uses the `Strings` property to interchange the first and last items contained in a memo control.

Text PROPERTY

Objects Affected   `TStrings` and all its descendants

Purpose   This property provides access to the string contained in the `TString` object.

Declaration

```
property Text: string ...;
```

Example Syntax

```
function getString(sl:TString): string;
   Result := sl.text;
end;
```

Description   This simple example extracts the string contained in any `TString` descendant class and returns it to the caller.

Values PROPERTY

Objects Affected   `TStrings` and all its descendants

Purpose   This property provides access to a structured string list in which individual items in the string list are assumed to have the form `Name=Value`.

When reading the `Values` property, the caller specifies the name of the value to be retrieved, and when writing, the caller specifies the name of the property to be written to the string list. If a particular name is not already in the list, a new item will be added to the end of the string list. If the named value is not found during a read operation, the property will return an empty string.

Declaration

```
property Values[const Name: string]: string ...;
```

Example Syntax

```
procedure TForm1.Button1Click(Sender: TObject);
var
  pl:TStringList;
  s1:string;
  i,c:integer;
begin
  pl := TStringList.create;
  c := ListBox1.Items.Count-1;
  for i:= 0 to c do
  begin
    s1:=format('file%0d',[i]);
    pl.Values[s1] := ListBox1.Items[i];
  end;
  pl.SaveToFile('foo.bar');
  pl.free;
end;

procedure TForm1.FormCreate(Sender: TObject);
begin
  ListBox1.Items.Clear;
  ListBox1.Items.Add('This.dat');
  ListBox1.Items.Add('Is.dat');
  ListBox1.Items.Add('A.dat');
  ListBox1.Items.Add('Test.dat');
end;
```

Description

In this example code a list box component is initialized with some hypothetical file names. Then in response to a click on a pushbutton located on the same form, the contents of the list box are copied to a **TStringList** object using a format function call to generate a name to be associated with each value retrieved from the list box. After the **For** loop is completed, which copies the contents of the list box to the values array, a call to **SaveToFile** is performed on the **TStringList** object. Finally, the **TStringList** object is freed. The file that was saved via the **SaveToFile** call contains the following information:

```
file0=This.dat
file1=Is.dat
file2=A.dat
file3=Test.dat
```

Example Project

In the following example project you will investigate the use of **TStringList** and other **TStrings** descendants to get a feel for how the various parts of the string classes work.

There is a great deal of commonality among the various derived string class types, owing to the fact that they all share a common parent class in TStrings. Thus, other than specific behavior determined by the override methods, most of the other TStrings methods apply to all classes in a similar manner, and once you have mastered the generalities of the TStrings class, you will be able to extend that understanding to the derived classes as a whole. More importantly, most of the override functions are written in such a way as to allow more or less functional equivalence among the different TStrings descendants. One thing to remember is that any components that utilize string information as part of the display maintain their string values in classes derived from the TStrings class. Therefore; if you are designing a wild new custom control, you would do well to study the implementation of some of the standard Delphi controls to get a feel for how the controls and the string classes interact. In the example that follows, you will derive a new string class that descends from TStringList. If you remember, the TStringList class implements a sort method, but the direction is always ascending. You will add a new method to the new class that will allow you to perform descending order sorts (the reverse of ascending order). Then you will use the new class to implement a simple program that allows you to open a text file for viewing, perform optional sort operations, and save if desired.

The form contains a Memo control and a number of buttons for control of the sort operations you will program. The corresponding code unit implementing the program is shown here:

```
unit Fview;

interface

uses
  SysUtils, WinTypes, WinProcs, Messages, Classes, Graphics, Controls,
  Forms, Dialogs, StdCtrls, ExtCtrls, Menus;

type
  TForm1 = class(TForm)
    Bevel1: TBevel;
    Memo1: TMemo;
    MainMenu1: TMainMenu;
    File1: TMenuItem;
    Open1: TMenuItem;
    N1: TMenuItem;
    Save1: TMenuItem;
    SaveAs1: TMenuItem;
    N2: TMenuItem;
    Exit1: TMenuItem;
    Panel1: TPanel;
    Button1: TButton;
    RadioButton1: TRadioButton;
    RadioButton2: TRadioButton;
    OpenDialog1: TOpenDialog;
    SaveDialog1: TSaveDialog;
    procedure Open1Click(Sender: TObject);
    procedure Save1Click(Sender: TObject);
    procedure SaveAs1Click(Sender: TObject);
    procedure RadioButton1Click(Sender: TObject);
```

```
      procedure RadioButton2Click(Sender: TObject);
      procedure Button1Click(Sender: TObject);
      procedure FormCreate(Sender: TObject);
      procedure Exit1Click(Sender: TObject);
   private
      { Private declarations }
      sortMode:boolean; { true for up, false for down }
   public
      { Public declarations }
   end;

   { New StringList class supporting bi-directional sorts}
   TNewStringList = class(TStringList)
   public
      procedure Sortup; { method to sort ascending order }
      procedure Sortdn; { method to sort descending order }
      procedure Reverse; { method to reverse order of strings in list }
   end;


var
   Form1: TForm1;

implementation

{$R *.DFM}

procedure TForm1.Open1Click(Sender: TObject);
begin
   { call upon standard OpenDialog for assistance in retrieving desired file }
   if OpenDialog1.Execute then
   begin
      Memo1.Lines.LoadfromFile(OpenDialog1.FileName); {Load memo from file}
      SaveDialog1.Filename := OpenDialog1.FileName; {Set name for save}
      Caption := OpenDialog1.FileName; {Set form caption}
   end;
end;

procedure TForm1.Save1Click(Sender: TObject);
begin
   Memo1.Lines.SaveToFile(SaveDialog1.FileName); {Save memo to file}
end;

procedure TForm1.SaveAs1Click(Sender: TObject);
begin
   if SaveDialog1.Execute then { let user pick new name for save }
   begin
      Memo1.Lines.SaveToFile(SaveDialog1.FileName); { save to new name }
      Caption := SaveDialog1.FileName; { set new caption on form }
      OpenDialog1.FileName := Caption; { Set new name in Open Dialog }
   end;
end;

{ definition of functions and procedures for
  new string class }

procedure TNewStringList.Sortup;
```

continued on next page

continued from previous page

```
begin
     Sorted := true; { simply set the Sorted property from TStringList}
end;

procedure TNewStringList.Sortdn;
begin
     Sorted := true; { set the Sorted property to sort ascending}
     Reverse; { then call Reverse to reverse the order of the string list }
end;

procedure TNewStringList.Reverse;
var
  i:integer;
  lc:integer;
begin
  lc := Count div 2; { this is the number of exchanges we must perform }
  for i:= 0 to lc-1 do
  begin
     exchange(i,Count-1-i); {exchange from the outside in, simple eh? }
  end;
end;

procedure TForm1.RadioButton1Click(Sender: TObject);
begin
  sortMode := true; { record change in sortMode }
end;

procedure TForm1.RadioButton2Click(Sender: TObject);
begin
   sortMode := false; { record change in sortMode }
end;

procedure TForm1.Button1Click(Sender: TObject);
var
ts : TNewStringList;
begin
   if sortMode = true then
     begin
          ts := TNewStringList.Create; { create new instance of string list }
          ts.assign(Memo1.Lines); { copy memo contents to the string list }
          ts.Sortup; { sort ascending }
          Memo1.Lines.Assign(ts); { re assign results of sort to memo }
          ts.free; { release working string object }
     end
   else
     begin
          ts := TNewStringList.Create;
          ts.assign(Memo1.Lines);
          ts.Sortdn; { only difference for descending is this call }
          Memo1.Lines.Assign(ts);
          ts.free;
     end;
end;

procedure TForm1.FormCreate(Sender: TObject);
begin
 { initialize appropriately }
```

```
  RadioButton1.Checked := true;
  RadioButton1Click(Sender); { force to up mode initially }
end;

procedure TForm1.Exit1Click(Sender: TObject);
begin
 halt; { exit program }
end;

end.
```

The first thing of interest to note is the declaration of a new class type called `TNewStringList`. This new class will inherit all of its behavior from the `TStringList` class and add three new procedures. The procedures are called `Sortup`, `Sortdn`, and `Reverse`. The `Sortup` procedure simply sets the `Sorted` property to `True`, which as you will remember automatically causes the `Sort` method to be invoked on the list when set to `True`. The `Sortdn` procedure does the same thing initially to get the contents of the string into ascending sort order, then it calls upon the procedure `Reverse` to reverse the order of the strings. `Reverse` operates by using the `TStringList` method exchange to swap entries in the list appropriately. The `TForm1.Button1Click` method actually performs the sort operation desired by inspecting a form global variable called `sortMode`, which is set initially to `True` when the form is created, and modified every time one of the radio buttons is pressed. The Open and Save menu entries perform their operations with the help of the Delphi built-in dialogs and then use string methods to load from the selected file or save to the selected file. Since this program is intended to be a sort utility, the memo box is programmed to be read-only so that the only changes that can be made are the results of the sort operation. You can refer to the program listing for more comments.

PART *IV*

Components

26

TComponent

Components are the heart of the VCL, and **TComponent** is the base class for all components. A direct descendant of **TPersistent**, **TComponent** inherits all of the properties, methods, and events that are provided by **TObject** and **TPersistent**. Components have the ability to *own* other components—every time you drop a component onto the form at design time, for example, that component is automatically owned by the form. This means that destroying the form will automatically destroy the component, freeing you from the hassle of determining how every object in your program is destroyed.

Components, which can be visual or nonvisual, can appear on the Component Palette in the Delphi Integrated Development Environment (IDE) and can be saved as part of a form (DFM) file by the Delphi IDE. The Component Palette is shown in Figure 26-1.

Many *nonvisual components* derive directly from **TComponent**. **TTimer** is a typical example, although there are others in the VCL, like **TSession** and **TApplication**. *Visual components* derive from **TControl** and are known simply as *controls*. The **TControl** class is described in Chapter 38, "**TControl**," and the two major types of controls are covered in Part V, "Nonwindowed Controls" and Part VI, "Windowed Controls."

Using Components

Most of the properties and methods made available by **TComponent** are used internally by Delphi and will not need to be accessed by the applications programmer. The *Form Designer* in the Delphi IDE uses the component properties and methods to manage components at design time. Developers of VCL or ActiveX controls will want to

Figure 26-1   The Component Palette

acquaint themselves with these properties and methods so that their components will interact properly with the Delphi IDE.

The properties and methods described here represent only the base functionality of components—as classes descend further from TComponent, they implement more powerful features that are specific to the needs of those classes.

Figure 26-2 shows the derivation of TComponent. Table 26-1 displays the properties and methods that are implemented by TComponent.

Table 26-1 Properties and methods implemented by TComponent

Use or Set This...	Type	To Do This...	Inheritance
Assign	Method	Assign one persistent object to another.	TPersistent
ClassName	Method	Get the name of the object's class.	TObject
ClassParent	Method	Get the object's parent class.	TObject
ClassType	Method	Get the object's actual type.	TObject
ComponentCount	Property	Determine the number of owned components.	None
ComponentIndex	Property	The index of the component in its owner's Components list.	None
Components	Property	Determine the list of owned components.	None
ComponentState	Property	Determine the state of the current component.	None
Create	Method	Create a new component.	TObject
Destroy	Method	Destroy the component.	TObject
DestroyComponents	Method	Destroy all of the components owned by the component.	None
Destroying	Method	Notify the component that it is being destroyed.	None
FindComponent	Method	Find a component in the Components array list.	None
Free	Method	Safely destroy the object.	TObject
InheritsFrom	Method	Determine if the object is descended from a certain class.	TObject
InstanceSize	Method	Determine the amount of memory allocated for the object.	TObject
Name	Property	Determine the name of the component.	None
Owner	Property	Determine the owner of the component.	None
Tag	Property	Store an additional integer value with the component.	None

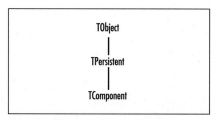

Figure 26-2 Derivation of TComponent

ComponentCount PROPERTY

Objects Affected	All components
Purpose	The ComponentCount property lists the number of components owned by the current component.
Declaration	

```
property ComponentCount: Integer;
```

Example Syntax

```
procedure TForm1.Button1Click(Sender: TObject);
var x: Integer;
begin
  x := Form1.ComponentCount;
  Label1.Caption := IntToStr(x);
end;
```

Description This run-time, read-only property indicates the number of components that are owned by the component. When you place components on a form at design time, the form (which is itself a component) becomes that component's **Owner**. The **Components** property lists the components owned by the current component.

ComponentIndex PROPERTY

Objects Affected	All components
Purpose	The ComponentIndex property indicates the position of the current component within its owner's **Components** list.
Declaration	

```
property ComponentIndex: Integer;
```

Example Syntax

```
procedure TForm1.Button1Click(Sender: TObject);
begin
  Label1.Caption := IntToStr(RadioButton3.ComponentIndex);
end;
```

Description Every component maintains a zero-based array of its owned components, which can be accessed with the **Components** property. The **ComponentIndex** property lists the position of a component within its owner's **Components** array. This property is run-time and read-only.

Components PROPERTY

Objects Affected	All components
Purpose	The `Components` property is an array of components that is owned by the current component.
Declaration	

```
property Components[Index: Integer]: TComponent;
```

Example Syntax

```
// Indirectly access the check boxes owned by the
// form and check them all
procedure TForm1.Button3Click(Sender: TObject);
var x: Integer;
begin
  for x := 0 to Form1.ComponentCount -1 do
    if Form1.Components[x] is TCheckBox then
      TCheckBox(Form1.Components[x]).Checked := True;
end;
```

Description   `Components` is a run-time, read-only property that can be used to indirectly access any of the components that are owned by a component, assuming you know the index of the component. Typically, it is easier to access components directly, but you may need to use this method if you are dynamically creating many components at run time. Since the `Components` array is zero-based, the first component is index **0**, the second is index **1**, and so forth.

ComponentState PROPERTY

Objects Affected	All components
Purpose	The `ComponentState` property describes the state of the component.
Declaration	

```
property ComponentState: TComponentState;
```

Description   `ComponentState` is a run-time, read-only property that is type `TComponentState`, which is declared as

```
TComponentState = set of (csLoading, csReading, csWriting, csDestroying,⇐
csDesigning, csAncestor, csUpdating, csFixups);
```

`TComponentState` is a set of flags that can be combined to derive the component state. Some common flags include

`csDesigning`	The Delphi environment is in design mode, so the component can be edited.
`csReading`	The component is reading its property values from a stream.
`csWriting`	The component is writing its property values to a stream.

Components use the `ComponentState` property internally to ensure that certain actions can be performed. You will not usually need to directly access `ComponentState`.

DestroyComponents METHOD

Objects Affected	All components
Purpose	The `DestroyComponents` method destroys all of the components owned by the current component.
Declaration	

```
procedure DestroyComponents;
```

Description   `DestroyComponents` is called by the `Destroy` method after it first calls `Destroying`. Unless you are designing a component, you will not normally need to access `DestroyComponents` directly.

Destroying METHOD

Objects Affected	All components
Purpose	The `Destroying` method notifies the component that it is being destroyed.
Declaration	

```
procedure Destroying;
```

Description   `Destroying` notifies the current component of its imminent destruction by setting the `csDestroying` flag in its `ComponentState` property (unless a last-minute `msgPardon` message is generated by the global `TGovernor` object). Then it calls the `Destroying` method for every component owned by the current component. Calling `Destroying` is the first action taken by a component's `Destroy` method.

You will not normally need to access `Destroying` directly.

FindComponent METHOD

Objects Affected	All components
Purpose	The `FindComponent` method will find the specified component in the `Components` array of the current component.
Declaration	

```
function FindComponent(const AName: string): TComponent;
```

Parameters

AName   The name of the component you are trying to obtain.

Example Syntax

```
// Use FindComponent to obtain another pointer
// to CheckBox1
procedure TForm1.Button4Click(Sender: TObject);
var MyComponent: TComponent;
begin
  MyComponent := FindComponent('CheckBox1');
  TCheckBox(MyComponent).Checked := True;
end;
```

Description   The string you pass to FindComponent is the Name of the component you are trying to find, like "Edit1", "Label1", or "MyButton". FindComponent will return the component, if it exists. Otherwise, it returns Nil.

Name PROPERTY

Objects Affected   All components

Purpose   The Name property contains the name of the component.

Declaration

```
property Name: TComponentName;
```

Description   Name is the identifier that is used in Delphi source code and the design environment to access the component. Delphi provides rather boring default names for components you add at design time, like "Form1", "Form2", and so on. You may change these as you wish.

When dynamically creating a component, you name the component in a var section of the source code, as shown in Listing 26-1.

Listing 26-1 Dynamically creating a button control

```
var
  Form2: TForm2;
  MyButton: Tbutton;        // the Name property is MyButton

implementation

{$R *.DFM}

procedure TForm1.FormCreate(Sender: TObject);
begin
  MyButton := TButton.Create(Self);
  MyButton.Parent := Form1;
  MyButton.Height := 32;
  MyButton.Width := 40;
  MyButton.Caption := 'Hi';
  // set other button properties as needed
end;
```

> **WARNING**
> Do not change the names of design-time-created components at run time. Delphi keeps track of the methods and event handlers for components that are added at design time, and changing the name of the component while the program is running will lead to some nasty crashes.

Owner PROPERTY

Objects Affected	All components
Purpose	The `Owner` property designates the owner of the current component.
Declaration	

```
property Owner: TComponent;
```

Example Syntax

```
// Passing Self to Create makes the form the Owner of MyButton
MyButton := TButton.Create(Self);
```

Description A form is the owner of all components that are on it. When the owner of a component is destroyed and its memory is freed, that component is destroyed as well, and its memory is also freed. Owning a component is not the same as being the parent of a component. *Controls* (which are descendants of `TComponent`) have a `Parent` property that indicates the *visual container* for the component, not the owner. Visual containers like panels contain other controls, but they do not own them. Contained controls are still owned by the form. See Chapter 38, "`TControl`," for details on `TControl`.

When creating components dynamically, the `Owner` property is set by the `Create` method as in the above example. Components created at design time have their `Owner` property set to the current form.

`Owner` is a run-time-only property.

Tag PROPERTY

Objects Affected	All components
Purpose	The `Tag` property is used to store a user-defined long integer value with the component.
Declaration	

```
property Tag: Longint;
```

Example Syntax

```
procedure TForm1.Button5Click(Sender: TObject);
begin
  if Button5.Tag = 1 then
  begin
    Button5.Tag := 0;
    Button5.Caption := 'Begin'
  end
  else begin
    Button5.Tag := 1;
    Button5.Caption := 'End'
  end
end;
```

Description

Tag allows you to store a long integer value with your component that you may use as you see fit. Its use is strictly optional.

27

TApplication

The **TApplication** component encapsulates your entire application program. Delphi automatically creates an object of type **TApplication**, named **Application**, every time your program is run. The **Application** object is actually just a window with a standard API **WndProc** procedure, but the Delphi VCL hides the ugly API-level calls such a structure requires and allows you to program your application within Windows at a higher level. The window for the **Application** object is essentially hidden and is separate from the form window that provides a user interface for your program. This is the reason a Delphi application can have a different name in its taskbar icon than in its main form's caption: the *application's* title appears in the taskbar icon. You may want to make the application title the same as your form's caption; this can be done from the Application tab of the Project Options dialog box shown in Figure 27-1.

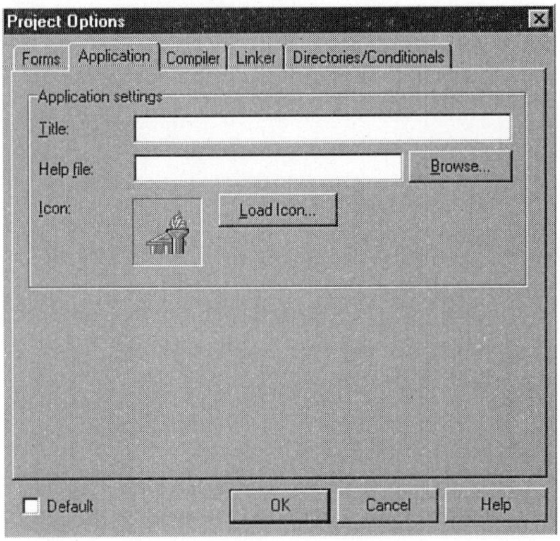

Figure 27-1   Application options

This dialog box allows you to easily set three of **TApplication**'s properties from the Integrated Development Environment (IDE). Because the **Application** object is global to your program, its properties and methods, such as the often-used **MessageBox** method and **Icon** property, are available from anywhere in your code.

Typically, application developers will not need to use most of **TApplication**'s properties, methods, and events, although component writers and other advanced programmers may want to access some of its more esoteric internals like the **DialogHandle/HookMainWindow** combination, which allows you to use non-Delphi dialog boxes in your Delphi program.

TApplication is not available at design time in the Object Inspector, but the automatic creation of the **Application** object can be seen by viewing the source code for the project (DPR) file; select Project Source from the View menu in the Delphi IDE. The code shown in Listing 27-1 will appear in a new, unchanged project.

Listing 27-1 Source code for a new Delphi project

```
program Project1;

uses
  Forms,
  Unit1 in 'Unit1.pas' {Form1};

{$R *.RES}

begin
  Application.Initialize;
  Application.CreateForm(TForm1, Form1);
  Application.Run;
end.
```

These three **Application** methods, described in this section, are executed every time your application runs.

Figure 27-2 shows the ancestry of **TApplication**. Table 27-1 displays the properties, methods, and events that are implemented by **TApplication**.

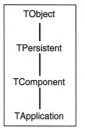

Figure 27-2 Ancestry of **TApplication**

Table 27-1 Properties, methods, and events implemented by TApplication

Use or Set This...	To Do This...	Inheritance
Active	Determine whether the application is the active application.	None
Assign	Assign one persistent object to another.	TPersistent
BringToFront	Bring your application to the front of all windows.	None
ClassName	Get the name of the object's class.	TObject
ClassParent	Get the object's parent class.	TObject
ClassType	Get the object's actual type.	TObject
ComponentCount	Determine the number of owned components.	TComponent
ComponentIndex	Determine the index of the component in its owner's Components list.	TComponent
Components	Determine the list of owned components.	TComponent
ComponentState	Determine the state of the current component.	TComponent
Create	Create a new component.	TObject
CreateForm	Create a new form window.	None
Destroy	Destroy the component.	TObject
DestroyComponents	Destroy all of the components owned by the component.	TComponent
Destroying	Notify the component that it is being destroyed.	TComponent
ExeName	Determine the executable file name of your application.	None
FindComponent	Find a component in the Components array list.	TComponent
Free	Safely destroy the object.	TObject
Handle	Contain a handle to your application window.	None
HelpCommand	Access any of the commands in the Windows Help API.	None
HelpContext	Open Windows Help and display a specific screen.	None
HelpFile	Determine the name of the Help file your application uses.	None
HelpJump	Launch Windows Help at a specific page.	None
HintColor	Determine the color of your application's hint windows.	None
HintHidePause	Determine the amount of time hints display.	None
HintPause	Determine the amount of time before hints display.	None
HintShortPause	Determine the amount of time before a hint redisplays.	None
Icon	Determine the icon associated with your application.	None
InheritsFrom	Determine whether the object is descended from a certain class.	TObject
Initialize	Normally, the first method called by your application.	None
InstanceSize	Determine the amount of memory allocated for the object.	TObject
MainForm	Determine your application's main form.	None
MessageBox	Display a message box.	None
Minimize	Minimize all of the windows in your application.	None
Name	Determine the name of the component.	TComponent
OnActivate	Perform processing when the application is activated.	None
OnDeactivate	Perform processing when the application is deactivated.	None

continued on next page

continued from previous page

Use or Set This...	To Do This...	Inheritance
OnException	Perform processing when an exception occurs.	None
OnHelp	Perform processing when the application calls Help.	None
OnHint	Perform processing when a hint appears.	None
OnIdle	Perform processing when the application is idle.	None
OnMessage	Occurs when the application receives a message.	None
OnMinimize	Perform processing when the application is minimized.	None
OnRestore	Perform processing when the application is restored.	None
OnShowHint	Perform processing before a hint appears.	None
Owner	Determine the owner of the component.	TComponent
Restore	Restore your application to its previous size.	None
Run	Run your application.	None
ShowHint	Enable hints for your application.	None
ShowMainForm	Determine whether the main form is displayed.	None
Tag	Store an additional integer value with the component.	TComponent
Terminate	Terminate your application.	None
Title	Determine your application's title.	None

Active PROPERTY

Objects Affected   TApplication

Purpose   The **Active** property indicates whether the application is the active application.

Declaration

```
property Active: Boolean;
```

Example Syntax

```
// Place a timer on the form, and change its interval property
// to 100
procedure TForm1.Timer1Timer(Sender: TObject);
begin
  If Application.Active = True then
    Form1.Caption := 'Application is active'
  else Form1.Caption := 'Application is inactive';
end;
```

Description   **Active** is a run-time, read-only property that returns **True** when the application is active and has the focus. It returns **False** otherwise.

In the example above, the form title changes as the form is made active and inactive. This can be best demonstrated with several windows open on the Desktop, so you can observe the form caption changing as you deselect and reselect your window.

BringToFront METHOD

Objects Affected	TApplication
Purpose	The BringToFront method brings your application's main form window to the logical "front" of other windows on the Windows Desktop.
Declaration	

```
procedure BringToFront;
```

Example Syntax

```
// Rather annoying example that forces your window
// to the front
procedure TForm1.Timer1Timer(Sender: TObject);
begin
  if Application.Active = False then
    Application.BringToFront;
end;
```

Description

The Windows Desktop has a z-order that determines the logical placement of windows "above" and "below" other windows. This z-order lets windows appear as if they overlap and determines the current, focused window. BringToFront brings your application's main form window to the top of the z-order, which gives it the focus, makes it active, and makes it appear above all other windows on the Desktop.

CreateForm METHOD

Objects Affected	TApplication
Purpose	The CreateForm method creates a new form.
Declaration	

```
procedure CreateForm(InstanceClass: TComponentClass; var Reference);
```

Parameters

InstanceClass	The type of form to create.
Reference	The variable that is assigned to the new form.

Example Syntax

```
// Project source - use View|Project Source from the IDE
program Project1;

uses
  Forms,
  Unit1 in 'Unit1.pas' {Form1};

{$R *.RES}

begin
  Application.Initialize;
  Application.CreateForm(TForm1, Form1);
  Application.Run;
end.
```

Description	CreateForm creates a new form of the type specified by the *InstanceClass* parameter and assigns it to the variable specified by the *Reference* parameter. The **Application** object owns the newly created form.
	CreateForm is called at least once in the project source code, and will be called for every form your program contains. It is called automatically by Delphi—you will not need to manually call this method yourself.

ExeName PROPERTY

Objects Affected	TApplication
Purpose	The **ExeName** property contains the path and file name of your application's executable file.
Declaration	

```
property ExeName: string;
```

Example Syntax	

```
procedure TForm1.Button1Click(Sender: TObject);
begin
  Label1.Caption := Application.ExeName;
end;
```

Description	ExeName is a run-time, read-only property that contains the fully qualified file name of your application's executable. The output of **ExeName** is shown in Figure 27-3.

Handle PROPERTY

Objects Affected	TApplication
Purpose	The **Handle** property contains a handle to your application window.
Declaration	

```
property Handle: HWND;
```

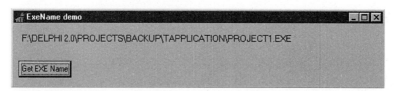

Figure 27-3 Output of the **ExeName** demo

Description   The `Handle` property is useful if you need to process an API call that requires a window handle. You will not normally need to access the `Application Handle` property yourself. Note that this is a handle to the invisible **application** window and not to the main form window. To get a handle to the main form window, use the `Handle` property of that `TForm` object.

HelpCommand METHOD

Objects Affected   `TApplication`

Purpose   `HelpCommand` allows you to access any of the commands in the Windows Help API.

Declaration

```
function HelpCommand(Command: Integer; Data: Longint): Boolean;
```

Parameters

Command   The Windows Help API command you wish to call.

Data   Data that needs to be passed to the Help command.

Example Syntax

```
// Load Windows Help
procedure TForm1.mnuWindowsHelpClick(Sender: TObject);
begin
  Application.HelpFile := 'winhelp.hlp';
  Application.HelpCommand(HELP_FINDER, 0);
end;
```

Description   The `HelpCommand` method starts the Windows Help file, **WINHELP.EXE**, and passes it the command specified by the *Command* parameter and additional data specified by the *Data* parameter. This is shown in Figure 27-4.

The command you send specifies the type of help you are requesting. The *Data* you send depends on which command you request. While a full explanation of the Windows Help system is beyond the scope of this book, the following table lists some of the possible commands and data values that can be passed to `HelpCommand`:

Figure 27-4 Loading Windows Help from your application

Command Value	Data Value	Does This...
HELP_COMMAND	The address of a string that contains a Help macro to execute, or a series of Help macros separated by semicolons.	Executes a Help macro or set of macros.
HELP_CONTENTS	Ignored—set to 0.	This command is provided for compatibility with pre-4.0 Help engines. 32-bit applications should use the HELP_FINDER command instead.
HELP_CONTEXT	The context identifier for the topic.	Displays the topic identified by the *Data* value.
HELP_CONTEXTPOPUP	The context identifier for the topic.	Creates a pop-up window that displays the topic specified by the *Data* value.
HELP_FINDER	Ignored—set to 0.	Displays a version 4.0 Help Topics dialog box.
HELP_FORCEFILE	Ignored—set to 0.	Used to ensure that WinHelp is displaying the correct Help file. If it isn't, the correct Help file is loaded.
HELP_HELPONHELP	Ignored—set to 0.	Displays Help on using Windows Help.
HELP_INDEX	Ignored—set to 0.	This command is for backward compatibility with pre-4.0 Help engines. New applications should use HELP_FINDER instead. Used to display the Help Index.
HELP_KEY	Address of the keyword string.	Displays the topic identified by the keyword whose address is passed by *Data*.
HELP_PARTIALKEY	Address of the keyword string.	Displays the topic identified by the keyword whose address is passed by *Data* if there is an exact match. If there is more than one match, the Index tab is displayed.

Command Value	Data Value	Does This...
HELP_QUIT	Ignored—set to 0.	Closes the Help application if no other applications have asked for Help.
HELP_SETCONTENTS	The context identifier for the Contents topic.	Specifies the topic that is displayed when the user clicks the Contents button.
HELP_SETINDEX	The context identifier for the index topic.	Specifies the keyword table that will be displayed in the Index.

Delphi 2.0 includes the Microsoft Help Workshop and some other utility programs to help you create Help files for your own applications. See the Delphi documentation for details.

HelpContext METHOD

Objects Affected   TApplication

Purpose   The **HelpContext** method opens Windows Help and displays the specified screen.

Declaration

```
function HelpContext(Context: THelpContext): Boolean;
```

Parameters

Context   The Help Context ID number.

Example Syntax

```
procedure TForm1.mnuHelpClick(Sender: TObject);
begin
  Application.HelpFile := 'my_apps_help.hlp';
  Application.HelpContext(11);
end;
```

Description   Before you call **HelpContext**, you must ensure that **Application**'s **HelpFile** property is set to a valid Help file. **HelpContext** will open the Help file specified by the **HelpFile** property and load the screen specified by the *Context* parameter. **HelpContext** is of type **THelpContext**, which is simply an integer—Help context ID values are defined within the Help file and can be associated with interface elements (like command buttons) through that control's **HelpContext** property.

Creating Help files is beyond the scope of this book. Please refer to the Microsoft Help Workshop (included with Delphi) and its Help Author's Guide for details on designing context-sensitive Help.

HelpFile PROPERTY

Objects Affected	TApplication
Purpose	The HelpFile property specifies the name of the Help file your application uses.
Declaration	

```
property HelpFile: string;
```

Example Syntax

```
// Load Windows Help
procedure TForm1.mnuWindowsHelpClick(Sender: TObject);
begin
  Application.HelpFile := 'winhelp.hlp';
  Application.HelpCommand(HELP_FINDER, 0);
end;
```

Description   HelpFile is a run-time-only property that defaults to a null string. If you attempt to call Help methods like HelpContext without first setting HelpFile to a valid file name, the attempt will be ignored by your application.

HelpJump METHOD

Objects Affected	TApplication
Purpose	The HelpJump method opens a specific page of Windows Help.
Declaration	

```
function HelpJump(const JumpID: string): Boolean;
```

Parameters

JumpID   The context string contained in the page you wish to jump to.

Example Syntax

```
procedure TForm1.mnuGotoHelpClick(Sender: TObject);
begin
  Application.HelpFile := 'my_apps_help.hlp';
  Application.HelpJump(hlpMyIdentifier);
end;
```

Description   The HelpJump method launches the Windows Help application, WINHELP.EXE, and opens the page that contains the context string specified by the *JumpID* parameter. HelpJump returns True if Application's HelpFile property contains a valid Help file reference, and False if it does not.

Creating Help systems and assigning context identifier strings is beyond the scope of this chapter. Please refer to the Microsoft Help Workshop (included with Delphi) and its Help Author's Guide for details on designing context-sensitive Help.

HintColor PROPERTY

Objects Affected	TApplication
Purpose	The HintColor property determines the color of the tooltip windows that appear in your application.
Declaration	

```
property HintColor: TColor;
```

Example Syntax

```
procedure TForm1.FormCreate(Sender: TObject);
begin
  Application.HintColor := clAqua;
  Form1.Hint := 'The HintColor demo program';
  Form1.ShowHint := True;
end;
```

Description HintColor determines the background color of the tooltip windows used by your application and can be set to any color supported by your system. Some common colors include clBlack, clWhite, clYellow, clCaption, and clWindow. HintColor is a run-time-only property. Tooltips are generally accessible with the Hint property of various components.

HintHidePause PROPERTY

Objects Affected	TApplication
Purpose	The HintHidePause property determines the amount of time tooltips will display if the mouse pointer is not moved away from the object displaying the tooltip.
Declaration	

```
property HintHidePause: Integer;
```

Example Syntax

```
procedure TForm1.FormCreate(Sender: TObject);
begin
  // Set the HintHidePause to 5 seconds
  Application.HintHidePause := 5000;
end;
```

Description By default, tooltips will display for 2500 milliseconds, or 2.5 seconds, before the tooltip will disappear. You can use this run-time-only property to modify this behavior; the unit of time it uses is milliseconds. Tooltips are generally accessible with the Hint property of various components.

HintPause PROPERTY

Objects Affected	TApplication
Purpose	The HintPause property specifies the amount of time that passes before a tooltip is displayed.
Declaration	

```
property HintPause: Integer;
```

Example Syntax

```
procedure TForm1.FormCreate(Sender: TObject);
begin
  // Set the HintHidePause to 5 seconds
  Application.HintHidePause := 5000;
  // Set the HintPause to 1 second
  Application.HintPause := 1000;
end;
```

Description When you mouse over a component that will display a tooltip, there is a slight pause before the tooltip appears. The length of the pause is determined by the HintPause method and is measured in milliseconds. The default pause is 800 milliseconds. Tooltips are generally accessible with the Hint property of various components.

HintShortPause PROPERTY

Objects Affected	TApplication
Purpose	The HintShortPause property determines the amount of time a tooltip will pause before redisplaying.
Declaration	

```
property HintShortPause: Integer;
```

Example Syntax

```
procedure TForm1.FormCreate(Sender: TObject);
begin
  // Set the HintPause to 1 second
  Application.HintPause := 1000;
  // Set the HintShortPause to 1/10th of a second
  Application.HintShortPause := 100;
end;
```

Description HintShortPause is used to keep tooltips from rapidly redisplaying as the user moves the mouse over a sequence of components with associated tooltips. It determines the length of time a tooltip will wait before it redisplays itself—that is, if the tooltip has already displayed recently and the mouse pointer is once again moved over the component, HintShortPause will determine the time delay that occurs before the tooltip is redisplayed.

This run-time-only property's pause time is measured in milliseconds—the default value is 50 ms. Tooltips are generally accessible with the `Hint` property of various components.

Icon PROPERTY

Objects Affected   TApplication

Purpose   The `Icon` property determines the icon that represents your application.

Declaration

```
property Icon: TIcon;
```

Example Syntax

```
procedure TForm1.FormCreate(Sender: TObject);
begin
  // Set the application icon
  Application.Icon.LoadFromFile(
                'f:\Delphi 2.0\Images\Icons\Earth.ico');
end;
```

Description   The `Icon` property for an application appears in the application's taskbar window button, as the title bar icon on the application's main form, and as the icon for the application in file browsers like Windows Explorer and My Computer. Although the `Icon` property for your application can be set with code, as in the above example, it should be set from the Application tab of the Project Options dialog box, as shown in Figure 27-5. If you don't change the icon in Project Options, you will get the default Delphi "torch" icon for your application when you view it in the Shell.

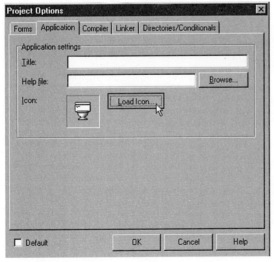

Figure 27-5   Changing the `Icon` in Project Options

Initialize METHOD

Objects Affected   TApplication

Purpose   The `Initialize` method is normally the first method called by your application.

Declaration

```
procedure Initialize;
```

Example Syntax

```
program Project1;

uses
  Forms,
  Unit1 in 'Unit1.pas' {Form1};

{$R *.RES}

begin
  Application.Initialize;
  Application.Title := 'Delphi TApplication Demo Program';
  Application.CreateForm(TForm1, Form1);
  Application.Run;
end.
```

Description   `Initialize` is added to your project source automatically when you create a new Delphi application project. Unless your program is an OLE automation server, you may delete the line of code that calls `Initialize`, as it does nothing. For OLE automation servers, `Initialize` registers your OLE automation server class with the system registry.

An OLE automation server is an application or DLL that exports OLE objects to OLE automation clients.

MainForm PROPERTY

Objects Affected   TApplication

Purpose   The `MainForm` property indicates which form is the main form for an application.

Declaration

```
property MainForm: TForm;
```

Description   `MainForm` is a run-time, read-only property. The main form is the form that is first created as your application executes—when the main form is closed, the application is destroyed. In the project source code shown in Listing 27-2, the first form that is created is `Form1`, so it is the main form.

Listing 27-2 An application with two forms. `Form1` *is the main form.*

```
program Project1;

uses
  Forms,
  Unit1 in 'Unit1.pas' {Form1},
  Unit2 in 'Unit2.pas' {Form2};

{$R *.RES}

begin
  Application.Initialize;
  Application.Title := 'MainForm Demo Program';
  Application.CreateForm(TForm1, Form1);
  Application.CreateForm(TForm2, Form2);
  Application.Run;
end.
```

If you would like to set another form to be the main form (say, `Form2` in Listing 27-2), this can be set from the Forms page of the Project Options dialog box, shown in Figure 27-6.

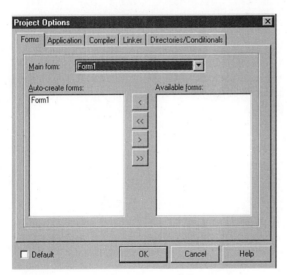

Figure 27-6 The Forms page of the Project Options dialog box

MessageBox METHOD

Objects Affected	`TApplication`
Purpose	The `MessageBox` method displays a dialog box with a message and one or more buttons.
Declaration	

```
function MessageBox(Text, Caption: PChar; Flags: Word): Integer;
```

Parameters

Text	The message that appears in the dialog.
Caption	The dialog's caption.
Flags	Content and behavior specifiers. See the following table for possible values.

Example Syntax

```
// Close the application
procedure TForm1.mnuFileQuitClick(Sender: TObject);
begin
  if Application.MessageBox('Do you really want to quit?', 'Quit?',
          MB_YESNO + MB_ICONHAND) = IDYES then
    Close;
end;
```

Description `MessageBox` is one of the most commonly used methods of `TApplication`. It encapsulates the Windows API `MessageBox` function. Anyone who uses Windows has seen a `MessageBox`, and, it seems, anyone who has programmed with Delphi or Visual Basic has created them as well. A typical message box is shown in Figure 27-7.

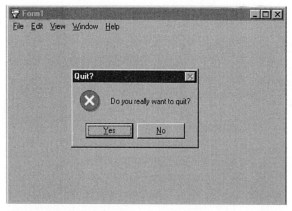

Figure 27-7 `MessageBox` with Yes and No buttons and an icon

The *Flags* value can be a combination of the following possible values:

Flag	Windows 95 or Windows NT?	Effect
MB_ABORTRETRYIGNORE	Both	Three command buttons are present: Abort, Retry, and Ignore.
MB_APPLMODAL	Both	The message box is modal to the application; that is, the user must click one of its buttons before returning to another window in the application. MB_APPLMODAL is set by default, although this behavior can be changed with MB_SYSTEMMODAL or MB_TASKMODAL.
MB_DEFAULT_DESKTOP_ONLY	Both	The message box must appear on the default desktop, which is the desktop that the user logs on to.
MB_DEFBUTTON1	Both	The first button in the message box is the default button. It is set to this button by default.
MB_DEFBUTTON2	Both	The second button in the message box is the default button.
MB_DEFBUTTON3	Both	The third button in the message box is the default button.
MB_DEFBUTTON4	Both	The fourth button in the message box is the default button.
MB_HELP	Both	Adds a Help button to the message box that can trigger a Help event when F1 is pressed or the button is clicked.
MB_ICONASTERISK	Both	Same as MB_ICONINFORMATION.
MB_ICONERROR	Both	Same as MB_ICONHAND.
MB_ICONEXCLAMATION	Both	An exclamation point icon appears.
MB_ICONHAND	Both	Same as MB_ICONSTOP.
MB_ICONINFORMATION	Both	A lowercase i icon appears.
MB_ICONQUESTION	Both	A question mark icon appears.
MB_ICONSTOP	Both	A red X icon appears.
MB_ICONWARNING	Both	Same as MB_ICONEXPLANATION.
MB_OK	Both	The message box has one button, labeled OK.
MB_OKCANCEL	Both	The message box has two buttons, labeled OK and Cancel.
MB_RETRYCANCEL	Both	The message box has two buttons, labeled Retry and Cancel.
MB_RIGHT	Windows 95	The text in the message box is right-justified.
MB_RTLREADING	Windows 95	Displays the text in the message box in right-to-left format for Hebrew and Arabic systems.
MB_SERVICE_NOTIFICATION	Windows NT	Allows the message box to display on the active desktop even if no users are logged on.
MB_SETFOREGROUND	Both	The message box becomes the foreground window.
MB_SYSTEMMODAL	Both	This type of message box prevents the user from completing any other tasks until it is closed. This flag should be reserved for extremely important messages; it is not suggested that you use this normally.
MB_TASKMODAL	Both	Same as MB_APPLMODAL.
MB_YESNO	Both	The message box has two buttons, labeled Yes and No.
MB_YESNOCANCEL	Both	The message box has three buttons, labeled Yes, No, and Cancel.

The Delphi **MessageBox** method supports numerous return types, as outlined in the following table:

Named Return Value	Integer Return Value	Has This Effect...
	0	There wasn't enough memory to display the message box.
IDABORT	3	The user chose the Abort button.
IDCANCEL	2	The user chose the Cancel button.
IDIGNORE	5	The user chose the Ignore button.
IDNO	7	The user chose the No button.
IDOK	1	The user chose the OK button.
IDRETRY	4	The user chose the Retry button.
IDYES	6	The user chose the Yes button.

Minimize METHOD

Objects Affected	TApplication
Purpose	The **Minimize** method minimizes your application to a taskbar button.
Declaration	

```
procedure Minimize;
```

Example Syntax

```
procedure TForm1.mnuMinimizeClick(Sender: TObject);
begin
  Application.Minimize;
end;
```

Description	**Minimize** will minimize every window that belongs to your application and is currently displayed.

OnActivate EVENT

Objects Affected	TApplication
Purpose	The **OnActivate** event occurs when your application becomes active.
Declaration	

```
property OnActivate: TNotifyEvent;
```

Example Syntax

```
unit Unit1;

interface

uses
  Windows, Messages, SysUtils, Classes, Graphics, Controls, Forms,
  Dialogs;
```

```
type
  TForm1 = class(TForm)
    procedure FormCreate(Sender: TObject);
    // add these function declarations manually
    procedure AppActivate(Sender: TObject);
    procedure AppDeactivate(Sender: TObject);
  private
    { Private declarations }
  public
    { Public declarations }
  end;

var
  Form1: TForm1;

implementation

{$R *.DFM}

procedure TForm1.FormCreate(Sender: TObject);
begin
  // determine which methods will handle OnActivate
  // and OnDeactivate
  Application.OnActivate := AppActivate;
  Application.OnDeactivate := AppDeactivate;
end;

// Add this event handler manually
procedure TForm1.AppActivate(Sender: TObject);
begin
  // Perform task here that you want to happen every
  // time the application is activated.
end;

// Add this event handler manually
procedure TForm1.AppDeactivate(Sender: TObject);
begin
  // Perform task here that you want to happen every
  // time the application is deactivated.
end;

end.
```

Description

The OnActivate event occurs when your application receives the focus. Because TApplication objects are not available from the Object Inspector, you need to manually create event handlers for Application events. In the example code above, the OnActivate event is assigned to the AppActivate method, which is manually created by the programmer. Inside the body of the AppActivate method, any tasks that need to be completed each time the application is activated can be added.

OnDeactivate EVENT

Objects Affected	TApplication
Purpose	The OnDeactivate event occurs when your application loses focus.
Declaration	

```
property OnDeactivate: TNotifyEvent;
```

Example Syntax

```
unit Unit1;

interface

uses
  Windows, Messages, SysUtils, Classes, Graphics, Controls, Forms,
  Dialogs;

type
  TForm1 = class(TForm)
    procedure FormCreate(Sender: TObject);
    // add these function declarations manually
    procedure AppActivate(Sender: TObject);
    procedure AppDeactivate(Sender: TObject);
  private
    { Private declarations }
  public
    { Public declarations }
  end;

var
  Form1: TForm1;

implementation

{$R *.DFM}

procedure TForm1.FormCreate(Sender: TObject);
begin
  // determine which methods will handle OnActivate
  // and OnDeactivate
  Application.OnActivate := AppActivate;
  Application.OnDeactivate := AppDeactivate;
end;

// Add this event handler manually
procedure TForm1.AppActivate(Sender: TObject);
begin
  // Perform task here that you want to happen every
  // time the application is activated.
end;

// Add this event handler manually
procedure TForm1.AppDeactivate(Sender: TObject);
begin
  // Perform task here that you want to happen every
  // time the application is deactivated.
```

```
        end;

        end.
```

Description   OnDeactivate allows you to perform tasks before your application is deac-
               tivated. Because TApplication objects are not available from the Object
               Inspector, you need to manually create event handlers for Application
               events. In the code listing above, the OnDeactivate event is assigned to
               the AppDeactivate method, which is manually created by the program-
               mer. The event handler for OnDeactivate can perform any tasks that need
               to be completed before the application loses focus.

OnException EVENT

Objects Affected   TApplication

Purpose   The OnException event occurs when an unhandled exception occurs in
                    your application.

Declaration

```
property OnException: TExceptionEvent;
```

Example Syntax

```
unit Unit1;

interface

uses
  Windows, Messages, SysUtils, Classes, Graphics, Controls, Forms,
  Dialogs,StdCtrls;

type
  TForm1 = class(TForm)
    Button1: TButton;
    Label1: TLabel;
    procedure FormCreate(Sender: TObject);
    procedure AppException(Sender: TObject; E: Exception);
    procedure Button1Click(Sender: TObject);
  private
    { Private declarations }
  public
    { Public declarations }
  end;

var
  Form1: TForm1;
  X: Integer;

implementation

{$R *.DFM}

procedure TForm1.FormCreate(Sender: TObject);
begin
```

continued on next page

continued from previous page

```
      Application.OnException := AppException;
      X := 100;
      Label1.Caption := IntToStr(X);
end;

procedure TForm1.AppException(Sender: TObject; E: Exception);
begin
  if Sender = Button1 then
    X := 0;
end;

procedure TForm1.Button1Click(Sender: TObject);
var Y: Integer;
begin
  Y := 0;
  try
    X := X div Y;
  except
    on ERangeError do
      X := 0;
  end;
end;
```

Description   OnException is similar to a global **else** for exceptions—if you do not explicitly handle an exception, the OnException event will be triggered by the HandleException method. By default, HandleException calls ShowException, which displays a message box describing the exception. If you prefer to change this behavior, you may add a handler for the OnException event.

TExceptionEvent, which is OnException's type, is declared as

```
TExceptionEvent = procedure (Sender: TObject; E:⇐
Exception) of object;
```

The *Sender* parameter identifies the object that raised the exception, and the *E* parameter is the exception message.

OnHelp EVENT

Objects Affected   TApplication

Purpose   The OnHelp event occurs when your application receives a user request for help.

Declaration

```
property OnHelp: THelpEvent;
```

Description   The HelpContext and HelpJump methods trigger OnHelp. If you would like to perform certain tasks every time Help is invoked, you can create an event handler for the OnHelp event.

OnHint EVENT

Objects Affected   TApplication

Purpose   OnHint occurs when the mouse pointer is positioned over a component whose **Hint** property contains a valid string.

Declaration

```
property OnHint: TNotifyEvent;
```

Example Syntax

```
unit Unit1;

interface

uses
  Windows, Messages, SysUtils, Classes, Graphics, Controls, Forms,
Dialogs,
  Buttons, ExtCtrls, ComCtrls;

type
  TForm1 = class(TForm)
    StatusBar1: TStatusBar;
    Panel1: TPanel;
    SpeedButton1: TSpeedButton;
    SpeedButton2: TSpeedButton;
    SpeedButton3: TSpeedButton;
    SpeedButton4: TSpeedButton;
    SpeedButton5: TSpeedButton;
    procedure FormCreate(Sender: TObject);
  private
    { Private declarations }
  public
    // manually added handler for the OnHint event
    procedure HandleHints(Sender: TObject);
  end;

var
  Form1: TForm1;

implementation

{$R *.DFM}

// Set the OnHint event to be handled by HandleHints
procedure TForm1.FormCreate(Sender: TObject);
begin
  Application.OnHint := HandleHints;
end;

// When an OnHint event occurs, display the hint in
// the status bar
procedure TForm1.HandleHints(Sender: TObject);
begin
  StatusBar1.SimpleText := Application.Hint;
end;
```

Description   For the `OnHint` event to occur, the component attempting to trigger the event must have a string other than `''` contained in its `Hint` property. You can handle the `OnHint` event to perform any tasks you wish to have happen when this event occurs. Figure 27-8 shows hints displaying in the status bar.

Typically, applications will handle this event to display the `Hint` text or additional Help information in the form's status bar, as in the above example.

OnIdle EVENT

Objects Affected   TApplication

Purpose   The `OnIdle` event occurs when the application is idle.

Declaration

```
property OnIdle: TIdleEvent;
```

Example Syntax

```
unit Unit1;

interface

uses
  Windows, Messages, SysUtils, Classes, Graphics, Controls, Forms,
  Dialogs, ComCtrls, StdCtrls;

type
  TForm1 = class(TForm)
    StatusBar1: TStatusBar;
    procedure FormCreate(Sender: TObject);
  private
    { Private declarations }
```

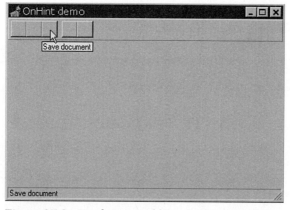

Figure 27-8   Display control hints in the status bar

```
public
  procedure Waiting(Sender: TObject; var Done: Boolean);
end;

var
  Form1: TForm1;

implementation

{$R *.DFM}

// Setup an OnIdle event handler
procedure TForm1.FormCreate(Sender: TObject);
begin
  Application.OnIdle := Waiting;
end;

// The handler for OnIdle events
procedure TForm1.Waiting(Sender: TObject; var Done: Boolean);
begin
  StatusBar1.SimplePanel := True;
  StatusBar1.SimpleText := 'OK!  Let''s get going!';
  Done := True;
end;
```

Description

You can add an event handler for the **OnIdle** event if you'd like to do some processing while the application is idle. **TIdleEvent**, which is the type of **OnIdle**, is declared as

```
TIdleEvent = procedure (Sender: TObject; var Done:⇐
Boolean) of object;
```

The *Done* parameter defaults to **True**, which means that your application is waiting for Windows messages. While the *Done* parameter is **False**, your application will not process Windows messages.

Use **OnIdle** with caution; most applications will not need to handle this event.

OnMessage EVENT

Objects Affected   TApplication

Purpose   The **OnMessage** event is triggered when your application receives a Windows message.

Declaration

```
property OnMessage: TMessageEvent;
```

Example Syntax

```
unit Unit1;

interface
```

continued on next page

continued from previous page

```
uses
  Windows, Messages, SysUtils, Classes, Graphics, Controls, Forms,
  Dialogs, StdCtrls, ComCtrls;

type
  TForm1 = class(TForm)
    ListBox1: TListBox;
    procedure FormCreate(Sender: TObject);
  private
    { Private declarations }
  public
    procedure MessageHandler(var Msg: TMsg; var Handled: Boolean);
  end;

var
  Form1: TForm1;

implementation

{$R *.DFM}

// Determine the handler for OnMessage
procedure TForm1.FormCreate(Sender: TObject);
begin
  Application.OnMessage := MessageHandler;
end;

// The OnMessage event handler
procedure TForm1.MessageHandler(var Msg: TMsg; var Handled: Boolean);
begin
  ListBox1.Items.Add('message received');
  if ListBox1.Items.Count > 15 then
    ListBox1.Clear;
end;

end.
```

Description

You can create a handler for the **OnMessage** event if you wish to respond to specific messages in a particular way. Most messages are automatically handled or routed for you by Delphi, but this event allows you to handle messages in an API-style way. In Figure 27-9, Windows messages are intercepted and displayed in a list box.

In the example above, a text string is output every time the window receives a message. Move your mouse over the window and watch the flurry of messages that is sent to the window.

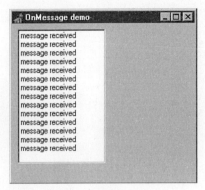

Figure 27-9 Intercepting
Windows messages

OnMinimize EVENT

Objects Affected	TApplication
Purpose	The OnMinimize event occurs when your application is minimized.
Declaration	

```
property OnMinimize: TNotifyEvent;
```

Example Syntax

```
unit Unit1;

interface

uses
  Windows, Messages, SysUtils, Classes, Graphics, Controls, Forms,
Dialogs;

type
  TForm1 = class(TForm)
    procedure FormCreate(Sender: TObject);
  private
    { Private declarations }
  public
    // manually added method declarations
    procedure MinimizeHandler(Sender: TObject);
    procedure RestoreApp(Sender: TObject);
  end;

var
  Form1: TForm1;

implementation

{$R *.DFM}

// Set custom handlers for the OnMinimize and OnRestore events
```

continued on next page

continued from previous page

```
                    procedure TForm1.FormCreate(Sender: TObject);
                    begin
                      Application.Title := 'My application';
                      Application.OnMinimize := MinimizeHandler;
                      Application.OnRestore := RestoreApp;
                    end;

                    // Change the app title when the app is minimized
                    procedure TForm1.MinimizeHandler(Sender: TObject);
                    begin
                      Application.Title := 'Minimized!';
                    end;

                    // Change the app title back when it is restored
                    procedure TForm1.RestoreApp(Sender: TObject);
                    begin
                      Application.Title := 'My application';
                    end;

                    end.
```

Description   Like other TApplication events, you can add a custom handler to OnMinimize when you want to perform certain tasks when the application is minimized. The OnMinimize event is triggered when your application is minimized because the Minimize method is called or the minimize window button in the application's main form is clicked. In Figure 27-10, the application's title is changed when the application is minimized.

OnRestore EVENT

Objects Affected   TApplication

Purpose   The OnRestore event is triggered when a minimized application is restored.

Declaration

```
                    property OnRestore: TNotifyEvent;
```

Example Syntax

```
                    unit Unit1;

                    interface

                    uses
                      Windows, Messages, SysUtils, Classes, Graphics, Controls, Forms,
                    Dialogs;

                    type
                      TForm1 = class(TForm)
```

Figure 27-10 Changing the application title when it minimizes

```
      procedure FormCreate(Sender: TObject);
    private
      { Private declarations }
    public
      // manually added method declarations
      procedure MinimizeHandler(Sender: TObject);
      procedure RestoreApp(Sender: TObject);
    end;

var
  Form1: TForm1;

implementation

{$R *.DFM}

// Set custom handlers for the OnMinimize and OnRestore events
procedure TForm1.FormCreate(Sender: TObject);
begin
  Application.Title := 'My application';
  Application.OnMinimize := MinimizeHandler;
  Application.OnRestore := RestoreApp;
end;

// Change the app title when the app is minimized
procedure TForm1.MinimizeHandler(Sender: TObject);
begin
  Application.Title := 'Minimized!';
end;

// Change the app title back when it is restored
procedure TForm1.RestoreApp(Sender: TObject);
begin
  Application.Title := 'My application';
end;

end
```

Description   Like other **TApplication** events, you can handle the **OnRestore** event when you want a certain block of code to execute when your application restores.

OnShowHint EVENT

Objects Affected   TApplication

Purpose   The **OnShowHint** event occurs when your application is about to show a tooltip.

Declaration

```
property OnShowHint: TShowHintEvent;
```

Example Syntax

```
unit Unit1;

interface

uses
  Windows, Messages, SysUtils, Classes, Graphics, Controls, Forms,
  Dialogs, Buttons, ExtCtrls, ComCtrls;

type
  TForm1 = class(TForm)
    StatusBar1: TStatusBar;
    Panel1: TPanel;
    SpeedButton1: TSpeedButton;
    SpeedButton2: TSpeedButton;
    SpeedButton3: TSpeedButton;
    SpeedButton4: TSpeedButton;
    SpeedButton5: TSpeedButton;
    procedure FormCreate(Sender: TObject);
  private
    { Private declarations }
  public
    procedure HandleHints(Sender: TObject);
    procedure DoBeforeHint(var HintStr: string; var CanShow: Boolean;
                           var HintInfo: THintInfo);
  end;

var
  Form1: TForm1;

implementation

{$R *.DFM}

procedure TForm1.FormCreate(Sender: TObject);
begin
  Application.OnHint := HandleHints;
  Application.OnShowHint := DoBeforeHint;
  Application.Hint := 'Hello, world';
end;

procedure TForm1.HandleHints(Sender: TObject);
begin
  StatusBar1.SimpleText := Application.Hint;
end;

procedure TForm1.DoBeforeHint(var HintStr: string;
                              var CanShow:  Boolean;
                              var HintInfo: THintInfo);
begin
  // If the hint is for the Abort button, display it in red
  if HintInfo.HintControl = SpeedButton5 then
    HintInfo.HintColor := clRed;
end;

end.
```

Description   OnShowHint occurs before the tooltip is shown, so handling this event allows you to change the behavior of the tooltip before it displays. OnShowHint is of type TShowHintEvent, which is declared as

```
TShowHintEvent = procedure (var HintStr: string; var⇐
CanShow:
Boolean;
                            var HintInfo: THintInfo) of object;
```

The TShowHintEvent type is a pointer that points to a method that displays a tooltip for a control. The text of the tooltip is specified by the *HintStr* parameter. If the *CanShow* parameter is True, the tooltip can display. If it is False, it cannot display. The *HintInfo* parameter is of type THintInfo, a Pascal record with the following type declaration:

```
THintInfo = record
  HintControl: TControl;
  HintPos: TPoint;
  HintMaxWidth: Integer;
  HintColor: TColor;
  CursorRect: TRect;
  CursorPos: TPoint;
end;
```

The fields in THintInfo determine the attributes of the tooltip.

The example program, listed above, is the same as the example for OnHint, modified to handle the OnShowHint method. One of the speedbuttons in the toolbar has an Abort glyph, and a tooltip that reads "Abort! Abort!" If this button is moused over, the tooltip will be displayed in a red window, not the standard yellow.

Restore METHOD

Objects Affected   TApplication

Purpose   The Restore method restores a minimized application.

Declaration

```
procedure Restore;
```

Example Syntax

```
unit Unit1;

interface

uses
  Windows, Messages, SysUtils, Classes, Graphics, Controls, Forms,
  Dialogs, StdCtrls, ExtCtrls;
```

continued on next page

continued from previous page

```
type
  TForm1 = class(TForm)
    Edit1: TEdit;
    procedure FormCreate(Sender: TObject);
  private
    { Private declarations }
  public
    // Manually added function declaration
    procedure MinApp(Sender: TObject);
  end;

var
  Form1: TForm1;

implementation

{$R *.DFM}

// Handle the OnMinimize event
procedure TForm1.FormCreate(Sender: TObject);
begin
  Application.OnMinimize := MinApp;
end;

// If the Edit box is not filled in, restore the
// application window when the user tries to minimize it
procedure TForm1.MinApp(Sender: TObject);
begin
  if Edit1.Text = '' then
  begin
    Application.Restore;
    Application.MessageBox('You must fill in the edit field first!',
                          'Restore Demo', MB_OK);
  end
end;

end.
```

Description   The **Restore** method can be used to restore your main form to its previous size (before it was minimized).

Run METHOD

Objects Affected   TApplication

Purpose   The **Run** method executes your application.

Declaration

```
procedure Run;
```

Example Syntax

```
program Project1;

uses
  Forms,
  Unit1 in 'Unit1.pas' {Form1};
```

```
{$R *.RES}

begin
  Application.Initialize;
  Application.CreateForm(TForm1, Form1);
  Application.Run;
end.
```

Description   The Run method is called automatically for every Delphi program, usually as the last statement in the project source code.

ShowHint PROPERTY

Objects Affected   TApplication

Purpose   ShowHint determines whether tooltips are enabled for the entire application.

Declaration

```
property ShowHint: Boolean;
```

Example Syntax

```
procedure TForm1.Button1Click(Sender: TObject);
begin
  If Button1.Caption = 'No hints!' then
  begin
    Button1.Caption := 'Use hints!';
    Application.ShowHint := True;
  end
  else begin
    Button1.Caption := 'No hints!';
    Application.ShowHint := False;
  end
end;
```

Description   This run-time-only property is set to True if tooltips are enabled at the application level. This is the default value. If ShowHint is False, all tooltips are disabled in the application.

Even if tooltips are enabled for the application, individual controls like forms and buttons can override this application-wide setting with their own individual ShowHint properties. If the Application ShowHint is set to True, but the main form's ShowHint is set to False, tooltips will not display.

ShowMainForm PROPERTY

Objects Affected   TApplication

Purpose   The ShowMainForm property determines whether your application displays its main form when it starts up.

Declaration

```
property ShowMainForm: Boolean;
```

Example Syntax

```
// Do not show a window as the program runs
procedure TForm1.FormCreate(Sender: TObject);
begin
  Application.ShowMainForm := False;
end;
```

Description

ShowMainForm defaults to True, which displays the main form when your application starts. If you do not want the main form to display, set ShowMainForm to False. Note that applications "hidden" with ShowMainForm still display a button on the taskbar.

Terminate METHOD

Objects Affected	TApplication
Purpose	The Terminate method terminates your application.
Declaration	

```
procedure Terminate;
```

Example Syntax

```
procedure TForm1.mnuTerminateClick(Sender: TObject);
begin
  if MessageBox(Form1.Handle, 'Really Terminate?', 'Terminate?',
        MB_OKCANCEL) = IDOK then
    Application.Terminate
end;
```

Description

Terminate frees all the memory occupied by the objects in your application and terminates the application. Normally, you do not need to call Terminate; the main form's Close method can be used to close your application.

Title PROPERTY

Objects Affected	TApplication
Purpose	The Title property determines the text that identifies your application in its taskbar button.
Declaration	

```
property Title: string;
```

Example Syntax

```
procedure TForm1.FormCreate(Sender: TObject);
begin
```

```
    Application.Title := 'Chris--Travel Expense Report';
    Form1.Caption := Application.Title;
end;
```

Description   The `Title` property can have a name that is different from the main form's caption, which is why the form and its taskbar button will often have different captions. Your application's title can be set with the `Title` property or from the IDE by choosing the Application page from Project Options.

The default name for your application is the name you give your project (PRJ) file. If you do not rename it, your application will be called `PROJECT1`.

28

TDataSource

A data source component, an instance of **TDataSource**, interfaces a *dataset* component to data-aware controls like database grids (that is, objects of type **TDBGrid**). The dataset component is attached to your data source object with the **DataSet** property—data-aware controls are attached with the **DataSource** property. You will typically attach one only data source to each dataset, but it is possible to connect as many data sources as you require.

The **TDataSource** component is available from the Data Access tab of the Component Palette. The properties, methods, and events of **TDataSource** are therefore most easily modified with the Object Inspector.

Figure 28-1 shows the derivation of **TDataSource**. Table 28-1 displays the properties, methods, and events that are implemented by **TDataSource**.

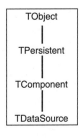

Figure 28-1 Derivation of
TDataSource

Table 28-1 Properties, methods, and events implemented by `TDataSource`

Use or Set This...	To Do This...	Inheritance
AutoEdit	Determine whether connected data-aware controls autoedit.	None
Create	Create a new data source object.	TComponent
DataSet	Specify the dataset that supplies data to the data source.	None
Destroy	Destroy a data source object.	TComponent
Edit	Call the associated dataset's `Edit` method.	None
Enabled	Determine whether a connected data source is updated.	None
IsLinkedTo	Determine whether the data source is linked to a dataset.	None
OnDataChange	Handle the event that occurs when data changes.	None
OnStateChange	Handle the event that occurs when the state changes.	None
OnUpdateData	Handle the event that occurs when data is about to update.	None
State	Determine the state of the attached dataset.	None

AutoEdit PROPERTY

Objects Affected TDataSource

Purpose The `AutoEdit` property determines whether a data-aware control connected to the data source automatically places the current record into Edit mode if the user begins typing.

Declaration

```
property AutoEdit: Boolean;
```

Example Syntax

```
procedure TForm1.FormCreate(Sender: TObject);
begin
DataSource1.AutoEdit := False;
end;
```

Description By default, `AutoEdit` is `True`, which allows the user to modify the data in the record. If you would like to prevent the data from being modified, set `AutoEdit` to `False`.

DataSet PROPERTY

Objects Affected TDataSource

Purpose The `DataSet` property specifies the dataset component that is supplying data to the data source.

Declaration

```
property DataSet: TDataSet;
```

Example Syntax

```
procedure TForm1.FormCreate(Sender: TObject);
begin
  DataSource1.DataSet := Table1;
end;
```

Description

The DataSet property can be set to a TTable, TQuery, or TStoreProc object. Like most properties, methods, and events implemented by TDataSource, DataSet is usually set at design time with the Object Inspector.

Edit METHOD

Objects Affected   TDataSource

Purpose   The Edit method calls the associated dataset's Edit method.

Declaration

```
procedure Edit;
```

Description   AutoEdit must be True and State must be dsBrowse before Edit will call the dataset's Edit method. The dataset's Edit method puts the current record in Edit mode and prepares it for change.

Enabled PROPERTY

Objects Affected   TDataSource

Purpose   The Enabled property determines whether data-aware controls connected to the data source are updated when the current record in the dataset is edited.

Declaration

```
property Enabled: Boolean;
```

Example Syntax

```
// Jump forward ten records when the button is pressed and disable
// the table display
procedure TForm1.Button1Click(Sender: TObject);
var X: Integer;
begin
  DataSource1.Enabled := False;
  for X := 1 to 10 do
    Table1.Next;
end;

// Re-enable the table display
procedure TForm1.Button2Click(Sender: TObject);
begin
  DataSource1.Enabled := True;
end;
```

Description While `Enabled` is `False`, the display of connected data-aware controls is disabled, allowing you to modify the controls without the effect being visible. When `Enabled` is set to `True`, each change is visible. If changes are made while `Enabled` is `False`, and then `Enabled` is set to `True`, the control will update at that time.

IsLinkedTo METHOD

Objects Affected `TDataSource`

Purpose The `IsLinkedTo` method determines whether the data source is linked to the specified dataset.

Declaration

```
function IsLinkedTo(DataSet: TDataSet): Boolean;
```

Parameters

DataSet The dataset you are testing.

Example Syntax

```
procedure TForm1.btnLinkClick(Sender: TObject);
begin
  if DataSource1.IsLinkedTo(Table1) = False then
    DataSource1.DataSet := Table1;
end;
```

Description If the data source is linked to the dataset specified by the *DataSet* parameter, `IsLinkedTo` returns `True`. If it is not, `IsLinkedTo` returns `False`.

OnDataChange EVENT

Objects Affected `TDataSource`

Purpose The `OnDataChange` event occurs when the data changes.

Declaration

```
property OnDataChange: TDataChangeEvent;
```

Example Syntax

```
// The default event handler for OnDataChange events
procedure TForm1.DataSource1DataChange(Sender: TObject; Field: TField);
begin
  // add any processing you wish to occur when the data has changed
end;
```

Description `OnDataChange` can be triggered by the data source's `State` property changing from `dsInactive` or when the connected data-aware component notifies the data source that a change has occurred. This change can be any of the following: the user has scrolled to a new record, a field has been modified, or the content or layout has changed.

OnDataChange is of type `TDataChangeEvent`, which is declared as

```
TDataChangeEvent = procedure(Sender: TObject; Field: TField)⇐
of object;
```

The *Sender* parameter is the object that triggered the event. The *Field* parameter is the field where the change occurred.

OnStateChange EVENT

Objects Affected	TDataSource
Purpose	The OnStateChange event occurs when the State property changes.
Declaration	

```
property OnStateChange: TNotifyEvent;
```

Example Syntax

```
// The default event handler for OnStateChange
procedure TForm1.DataSource1StateChange(Sender: TObject);
begin
// add any processing you wish to occur when the state has changed
end;
```

Description Adding an event handler for the OnStateChange allows your program to react to state changes. The State property determines the state of the data source, which will have the same value as the connected dataset control unless Enabled is False or the DataSet property is not assigned.

OnUpdateData EVENT

Objects Affected	TDataSource
Purpose	The OnUpdateData event occurs when a connected dataset notifies all data-aware controls connected to the data source that data is about to be updated.
Declaration	

```
property OnUpdateData: TNotifyEvent;
```

Example Syntax

```
// Default event handler for the OnUpdateData event
procedure TForm1.DataSource1UpdateData(Sender: TObject);
begin
  // add any processing you wish to occur when
end;
```

Description OnUpdateData is triggered by a dataset's Post or UpdateRecord methods. Handling the OnUpdateData event allows your program to react to data updates.

State PROPERTY

Objects Affected	`TDataSource`
Purpose	The `State` property duplicates the value of the attached dataset's `State` property.
Declaration	

```
property State: TDataSetState;
```

Description   `State` is of type `TDataSetState`, and can have one of the following possible values:

Value	Means This...
dsBrowse	The user is navigating between records.
dsCalcFields	Field values are being calculated.
dsEdit	The user is editing a record.
dsInactive	The dataset is not open.
dsInsert	The user is inserting or appending a new record.
dsSetKey	The user is setting key values by changing fields for finding records or setting a range.

State has the same value as the `State` property of the associated dataset, except when `Enabled` is `False` or when the dataset has not been assigned a value. In these cases, `State` will be `dsInactive`.

29

TMenuItem

The **TMenuItem** class encapsulates *menu items*, the individual items that make up a menu. A menu item typically appears as a text caption that describes its function—it can be checked or bulleted to indicate that it is enabled, or grayed out to indicate that it is disabled.

TMenuItem is used to represent the so-called main menu items that appear on an application bar as well as the items that appear within each drop-down menu and each pop-up menu. A *menu*—that is, a menu bar and all the items it contains—is encapsulated by the **TMenu** class and its descendants and is covered in Chapter 33, "**TMenu** and Its Descendants." Menus are one of the earliest user interface paradigms that Microsoft implemented in Windows, and they continue in Windows 95 and NT 4.0 largely unchanged from the days of Windows 1.0.

Figure 29-1 shows the lineage of **TMenuItem**. Table 29-1 displays the properties, methods, and events that are implemented by **TMenuItem**.

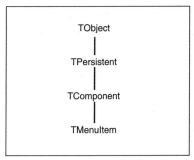

TObject

|

TPersistent

|

TComponent

|

TMenuItem

Figure 29-1 Lineage of **TMenuItem**

Table 29-1 Properties, methods, and events implemented by `TMenuItem`

Use or Set This...	To Do This...	Inheritance
ComponentCount	Determine the number of owned components.	TComponent
ComponentIndex	Determine the index of the component in its owner's `Components` list.	TComponent
Components	Determine the list of owned components.	TComponent
ComponentState	Determine the state of the current component.	TComponent
Create	Create a new component.	TObject
Destroy	Destroy the component.	TObject
DestroyComponents	Destroy all the components owned by the component.	TComponent
Destroying	Notify the component that it is being destroyed.	TComponent
FindComponent	Find a component in the `Components` array list.	TComponent
Free	Safely destroy the object.	TObject
InheritsFrom	Determine if the object is descended from a certain class.	TObject
InstanceSize	Determine the amount of memory allocated for the object.	TObject
Name	Determine the name of the component.	TComponent
Owner	Determine the owner of the component.	TComponent
Add	Add a new menu item to the bottom of a menu.	None
Break	Break a long menu into columns.	None
Caption	Determine the caption of the menu item.	None
Checked	Determine whether the menu item is checked.	None
Click	Simulate a mouse click on the menu item.	None
Count	Determine the number of subitems the menu item has.	None
Default	Determine whether the menu item is the default menu item.	None
Delete	Delete a menu item.	None
Enabled	Determine if the menu item is enabled or disabled (grayed out).	None
GroupIndex	Determine how menus are merged.	None
Handle	Obtain a Windows handle to the menu item.	None
HelpContext	Determine the menu item's help context ID.	None
IndexOf	Determine the position of the menu item within its menu.	None
Insert	Insert a new menu at a specified position.	None
Items	Determine the submenu item that resides at a particular position.	None
MenuIndex	Determine the index of the menu item within its parent menu.	None
OnClick	Handle the method that occurs when the user clicks the menu item.	None
Parent	Determine the parent of the menu item.	None
RadioItem	Determine whether a checked menu item is bulleted.	None
Remove	Remove the menu item.	None
ShortCut	Determine the keystroke shortcut to the menu item.	None
Visible	Determine whether the menu item is visible.	None

Add METHOD

Objects Affected	TMenuItem
Purpose	The **Add** method adds the menu item to the end of a menu.
Declaration	

```
procedure Add(Item: TMenuItem);
```

Parameters	
Item	The menu item you want to add to the menu.
Example Syntax	

```
procedure TForm1.mnuAddMenuItemClick(Sender: TObject);
var MyNewMenuItem: TMenuItem;
begin
  MyNewMenuItem := TMenuItem.Create(Self);
  MyNewMenuItem.Caption := 'Added at run-time';
  mnuFile.Add(MyNewMenuItem);
end;
```

Description	If you can add your menu item at design time, it is easier to do so using the Menu Designer. Sometimes, however, you will need to dynamically add menu items at run time. The menu item you are adding becomes the last menu item in the submenu that begins with the menu item that called **Add**. If the current menu item is a menu title in the main menu bar, the new item will appear as the bottom item in the current item's menu. If the menu item is in a drop-down or pop-up menu, the new item appears as the last item in the submenu of the current menu. If no submenu previously existed, one is created.

Break PROPERTY

Objects Affected	TMenuItem
Purpose	The **Break** property determines whether the menu is divided into columns.
Declaration	

```
property Break: TMenuBreak;
```

Example Syntax	

```
procedure TForm1.mnuDivideMenuHorizontallyClick(Sender: TObject);
begin
  mnuSave.Break := mbBarBreak;
end;
```

Description	The menu in Figure 29-2 is divided vertically with the **Break** property. Please note that multicolumn menus are discouraged and not normally used. The **Break** property can be set to three possible values:

mbBarBreak	The menu is broken into two columns starting after the menu item that calls **Break**, and a bar separates the two columns.
mbBreak	The menu is broken into two columns starting after the menu item that calls **Break**.
mbNone	The menu is not divided.
	The default value is **mbNone**.

Caption PROPERTY

Objects Affected	TMenuItem
Purpose	The **Caption** property contains the text string that displays as the menu item caption.
Declaration	

```
property Caption: string;
```

Example Syntax

```
// Change the menu caption each time it is clicked
procedure TForm1.mnuContextClick(Sender: TObject);
begin
  if mnuContext.Caption = '&Enable Context Switching' then
  begin
    mnuContext.Caption := '&Disable Context Switching';
    DoContextSwitch(1)
  end
  else begin
    mnuContext.Caption := '&Enable Context Switching';
    DoContextSwitch(0)
  end
end;
```

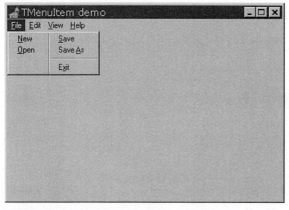

Figure 29-2 Dividing a menu vertically

Description   You can add an ampersand (**&**) to the menu item caption to assign a hotkey (access key) that will activate the **OnClick** event. This will place an underline beneath the character immediately following the ampersand. For example, assigning the string **'&File'** to a menu item **Caption** property would display as <u>F</u>ile when the menu is opened.

Checked PROPERTY

Objects Affected   TMenuItem

Purpose   The **Checked** property determines whether the menu choice is active or selected.

Declaration

```
property Checked: Boolean;
```

Example Syntax

```
procedure TForm1.mnuTurboModeClick(Sender: TObject);
begin
  if mnuTurboMode.Checked = True then
  begin
    mnuTurboMode.Checked := False;
    Timer1.Interval := 500
  end
  else begin
    mnuTurboMode.Checked := True;
    Timer1.Interval := 1000
  end
end;
```

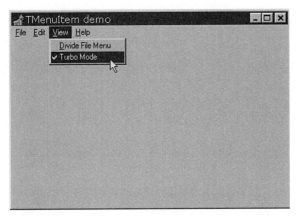

Figure 29-3   A checked menu item

Description   If `Checked` is set to `True`, then a check mark graphic appears next to the menu item, as shown in Figure 29-3. A checked menu item indicates whether the feature represented by the menu choice is active, or selected. If `Checked` is `False`, there is no check mark, indicating the menu item is not selected.

To change the check mark to a bulletlike dot, use the `RadioItem` property.

Click METHOD

Objects Affected   TMenuItem

Purpose   The `Click` method is used to simulate a menu item `OnClick` event.

Declaration

```
procedure Click; virtual;
```

Example Syntax

```
// Use the speedbuttons on the toolbar to launch menu OnClick
// event handlers
procedure TForm1.spbNewClick(Sender: TObject);
begin
  mnuNew.Click;
end;

procedure TForm1.spbOpenClick(Sender: TObject);
begin
  mnuOpen.Click;
end;

procedure TForm1.spbSaveAsClick(Sender: TObject);
begin
  mnuSaveAs.Click;
end;

. . .
```

Description   You can use the `Click` method to force an `OnClick` event—the result is the same as if the user had clicked the menu item.

Count PROPERTY

Objects Affected   TMenuItem

Purpose   The `Count` property contains the number of subitems contained by a menu item.

Declaration

```
property Count: Integer;
```

Example Syntax

```
// Divide the File menu (mnuFile) by calculating the number of menu
// items in the menu: this is nice if you have a menu whose item count
// can change at run-time
procedure TForm1.mnuCalcMenuDivideClick(Sender: TObject);
var X: Integer;
begin
  // First, get the amount of items in the menu and divide it by 2
  X := mnuFile.Count div 2;
  // Then, Break the menu vertically so that half of the menu items
  // are on each side
  mnuFile.Items[X].Break := mbBarBreak;
end;
```

Description

If your menu has no subitems below it, the Count for that menu item is 0. If the menu item has subitems, Count will equal the number of subitems. A File menu with New, Open, Save, Save As, Close, and Exit submenu items will have a Count of 6, for example.

Note that every menu item has a Count property, not just the top-level menu items.

Default PROPERTY

Objects Affected   TMenuItem

Purpose   The Default property determines if the menu item is the default menu item for the menu that contains it.

Declaration

```
property Default: Boolean;
```

Example Syntax

```
procedure TForm1.FormCreate(Sender: TObject);
begin
  // Set default menu items
  mnuNew.Default := True;
  mnuTurboMode.Default := True;
end;
```

Description

Using a default menu item is a little-known and little-used feature of Windows menus. When you set a menu item's Default property to True, the item is displayed in bold text, as shown in Figure 29-4. Double-clicking the menu title that contains the default menu item causes that menu item's OnClick event handler to execute. The default value for Default is False.

Since this menu feature is almost never used, it is suggested that you don't implement it in your applications—it will probably just confuse the user.

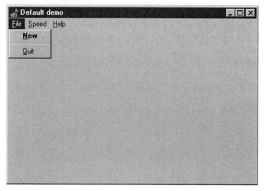

Figure 29-4 A default menu item displays with bold text

Delete METHOD

Objects Affected TMenuItem

Purpose The Delete method removes the specified subitem from the menu.

Declaration

```
procedure Delete(Index: Integer);
```

Parameters

Index The index number of the submenu item you wish to delete.

Example Syntax

```
// Remove the 'Turbo Mode' menu item
procedure TForm1.mnuDeleteItemClick(Sender: TObject);
begin
  if mnuEdit.Items[3].Caption = '&Turbo Mode' then
    mnuEdit.Delete(3);
end;
```

Description Delete will delete the subitem specified by the *Index* parameter. The subitems of a menu item are contained in an array that is accessed through the Items property—this array is zero-based, so the first subitem is Items[0], the second is Items[1], and so on. If the subitem you are deleting has subitems of its own, they are deleted as well.

Enabled PROPERTY

Objects Affected TMenuItem

Purpose The Enabled property determines whether the menu item will react to mouse, keyboard, and timer events.

Declaration

```
property Enabled: Boolean;
```

Example Syntax

```
procedure TForm1.FormCreate(Sender: TObject);
begin
  // Disable menu items until they are needed
  mnuSave.Enabled := False;
  mnuSaveAs.Enabled := False;
end;
```

Description

If the **Enabled** property of a menu item is **True**, the menu item appears normally in the menu and reacts to mouse, keyboard, and timer events. If it is set to **False**, the caption is grayed out, indicating that it is disabled, and it will not respond to events. The default value is **True**.

GroupIndex PROPERTY

Objects Affected   TMenuItem

Purpose

The **GroupIndex** property determines the position of a menu item within a group and determines how menus are merged.

Declaration

```
property GroupIndex: Byte;
```

Description

Each menu item has a **GroupIndex** property, available in the Object Inspector, that is set to **0** by default. Changing the value of **GroupIndex** affects the way menus are *inserted* and *replaced*.

You can insert a menu from a child form into the menu on your application's main form by setting the **GroupIndex** property of one or more menu items in the child form to a value that is greater than the **GroupIndex** value for the menu items on the main form. The menu items are inserted *in order*—that is, a menu item with a **GroupIndex** property of **2** would be inserted between menu items with the values of **1** and **3** in the main form. If any menu items in the child form have the same **GroupIndex** value as a menu item in the form, the menu item from the child form will *replace* the menu item in the main form. If more than one of the menu items on the child form has the same **GroupIndex** value as all of the menu items on the main form, the entire menu from the child form replaces the entire menu from the main form as they are merged.

To merge menus, use the **Merge** method.

Handle PROPERTY

Objects Affected	TMenuItem
Purpose	The Handle property contains a handle to the menu item.
Declaration	

```
property Handle: HMENU;
```

Description	A Handle to a menu item is useful if you need to call a Win32 API function that requires a menu handle.

HelpContext PROPERTY

Objects Affected	TMenuItem
Purpose	The HelpContext property contains a context number used to call Help.
Declaration	

```
property HelpContext: THelpContext;
```

Example Syntax

```
procedure TForm1.FormCreate(Sender: TObject);
begin
  // Set context numbers
  mnuHelpApp.HelpContext := 13;
  mnuHelpWin.HelpContext := 14;
  mnuHelpToDo.HelpContext := 16;
end;
```

Description	Each Help screen in your application can have a unique context number that can be associated with onscreen elements in your program like buttons and menu items. If the menu item is selected and the user presses F1, the proper screen will appear when Help loads.
	To inherit the HelpContext value of the menu item's parent, set its HelpContext property to 0.

IndexOf METHOD

Objects Affected	TMenuItem
Purpose	The IndexOf method contains the position of the menu item within its parent's Items array.
Declaration	

```
function IndexOf(Item: TMenuItem): Integer;
```

Parameters	
Item	The menu item whose position you wish to detect.

Example Syntax

```
// Remove the 'Turbo Mode' menu item.
// Compare this example with the example for Items
procedure TForm1.mnuDeleteItemClick(Sender: TObject);
begin
  if mnuEdit.IndexOf(mnuTurboMode) = 3 then
    mnuEdit.Delete(3);
end;
```

Description   IndexOf returns the position of the menu item in its parent's zero-based Items array where the first menu item is 0, the second is 1, and so on.

Insert METHOD

Objects Affected   TMenuItem

Purpose   The Insert method inserts a menu item at a specified location in the menu.

Declaration

```
procedure Insert(Index: Integer; Item: TMenuItem);
```

Parameters

Index   The position where the menu item will be inserted.

Item   The menu item to insert.

Example Syntax

```
// Dynamically create new menu items using the text from an edit
// box as the caption for the menu item.
procedure TForm1.Button1Click(Sender: TObject);
var MyItem: TMenuItem;
begin
  if Edit1.Text <> '' then
  begin
    MyItem := TMenuItem.Create(Self);
    MyItem.Caption := Edit1.Text;
    // Add other properties, methods, and events for the
    // menu item here
    mnuPrograms.Insert(mnuPrograms.Count, MyItem);
    Edit1.Text := '';
  end
end;
```

Description   The Insert method is used to insert menu items as subitems to an existing menu item specified by the *Item* parameter. The *Index* parameter indicates the position the new menu item will have in the array of menu items it is joining.

Items PROPERTY

Objects Affected	TMenuItem
Purpose	The Items property is an array of subitems to the current menu item.
Declaration	

```
property Items[Index: Integer]: TMenuItem;
```

Example Syntax

```
// Remove the 'Turbo Mode' menu item
procedure TForm1.mnuDeleteItemClick(Sender: TObject);
begin
  if mnuEdit.Items[3].Caption = '&Turbo Mode' then
    mnuEdit.Delete(3);
end;
```

Description   Each top-level menu item and any menu item with subitems lists the menu items below it in its Items property. Items allows you to access subitems by their position in a zero-based array, so that the first subitem is represented by Items[0], the second by Items[1], and so on.

MenuIndex PROPERTY

Objects Affected	TMenuItem
Purpose	The MenuIndex property contains the value of that menu item within its parent's Items array.
Declaration	

```
property MenuIndex: Integer;
```

Example Syntax

```
// If selected, display the Cut menu item first, then Copy
procedure TForm1.CutthenCopy1Click(Sender: TObject);
begin
  Cut1.MenuIndex := 0;
end;

// If selected, display the Copy menu item first, then Cut
procedure TForm1.CopythenCopy1Click(Sender: TObject);
begin
  Copy1.MenuIndex := 0;
end;
```

Description   The MenuIndex property represents a menu item's position within the menu. If you change its MenuIndex property, the menu item will move within the menu. A menu item with a MenuIndex of 0 is the first menu item in the submenu (or menu); if the MenuIndex is 1, it is the second menu item, and so forth.

OnClick EVENT

Objects Affected	TMenuItem
Purpose	The OnClick event occurs when the user clicks the menu item.
Declaration	

```
property OnClick: TNotifyEvent;
```

Example Syntax

```
// Determine the OnClick event handler for the Paste1 menu item
procedure TForm1.FormCreate(Sender: TObject);
begin
  Paste1.OnClick := PasteIt;
end;
```

Description   The OnClick event occurs in the following situations:

- The user clicks the menu item.
- The user types the hotkey combination for that menu item.
- The user uses the keyboard to navigate the menu and presses ENTER when the menu item is selected.
- The Click method is called.

The OnClick event triggers the event handler that contains code that executes when the menu item is clicked.

While it is possible to assign event handlers from Object Pascal code as in the above example, it is easier to use the Events tab of the Object Inspector to do so at design time if your menu item is not dynamically created.

Parent PROPERTY

Objects Affected	TMenuItem
Purpose	The Parent property contains a reference to the menu item's parent.
Declaration	

```
property Parent: TMenuItem;
```

Example Syntax

```
// Delete the menu item with a user-defined procedure
procedure TForm1.DeleteItem(Sender: TObject);
begin
  if TMenuItem(Sender).Parent = mnuPrograms then
    mnuPrograms.Delete(mnuPrograms.IndexOf(TMenuItem(Sender)));
end;
```

Description   Parent is a read-only property that identifies a menu item's parent. The parent of a menu item is another menu item.

RadioItem PROPERTY

Objects Affected   TMenuItem

Purpose   The RadioItem property determines whether checked menu items appear with a check mark graphic or a round, bullet-style dot graphic.

Declaration

```
property RadioItem: Boolean;
```

Example Syntax

```
// Check the Page View menu item with a bullet, deselect the
// other view menu items and run the user-defined SetPageView
// procedure
procedure TForm1.PageView1Click(Sender: TObject);
begin
  PageView1.Checked := True;
  LargeIcon1.Checked := False;
  SmallIcon1.Checked := False;
  List1.Checked := False;
  Details1.Checked := False;
  Page1.RadioItem := True;
  SetPageView;
end;
```

Description   If a menu item's RadioItem property is set to True, and the menu item is checked, then the graphic that indicates that it is selected will be a round, bullet-style dot. This is shown in Figure 29-5. If RadioItem is False, the standard check mark graphic is used.

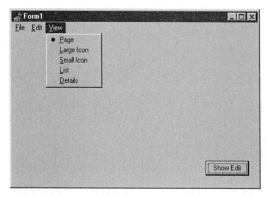

Figure 29-5   Using RadioItem to make bulleted menu items

Remove METHOD

Objects Affected	TMenuItem
Purpose	The Remove method deletes the specified menu item.
Declaration	

```
procedure Remove(Item: TMenuItem);
```

Parameters

Item   The menu item you wish to remove.

Example Syntax

```
procedure TForm1.ShowEdit1Click(Sender: TObject);
begin
  Edit1.Remove(Cut1);
  Edit1.Remove(Copy1);
  Edit1.Remove(Paste1);
  Edit1.Visible := False;
end;
```

Description   Remove deletes the menu item specified by the *Item* parameter from the menu. When a menu item is removed, each of the menu items below it moves up a position in the Items property of its parent. If the menu item has a submenu, the submenu and the items in it are also removed.

ShortCut PROPERTY

Objects Affected	TMenuItem
Purpose	The ShortCut property determines the keystroke shortcut that can be used to activate the menu item's OnClick event.

Declaration

```
property ShortCut: TShortCut;
```

Example Syntax

```
procedure TForm1.FormCreate(Sender: TObject);
begin
  Cut1.ShortCut := ShortCut(Word('X'), [ssCtrl]);
  Copy1.ShortCut := ShortCut(Word('C'), [ssCtrl]);
  Paste1.ShortCut := ShortCut(Word('V'), [ssCtrl]);
end;
```

Description   Menu item shortcuts appear to the right of the menu item's caption and indicate the keystrokes that will activate that menu item's OnClick event. This is shown in Figure 29-6.

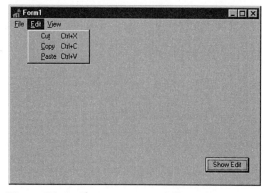

Figure 29-6 Shortcuts on an Edit menu

It is easier to create shortcuts—also known as *accelerator keys*—at design time within the Object Inspector, but if you are dynamically creating menu items, they can be assigned at run time as well with the global `ShortCut` function.

The `ShortCut` function is declared as

```
function ShortCut(Key: Word; Shift: TShiftState): TShortCut;
```

If the shortcut you wish to create is CTRL-C, then the shortcut definition would look like this:

```
Copy1.ShortCut := ShortCut(Word('X'), [ssCtrl]);
```

The first parameter, *Key*, will be the trailing letter in your shortcut, cast to a `Word`. In this case, the key is an X. The *Shift* parameter represents the special key you will be holding down while you press a key and is declared as

```
TShiftState = set of
      (ssShift, ssAlt, ssCtrl, ssLeft, ssRight, ssMiddle, ssDouble);
```

where `ssShift` represents the SHIFT key, `ssAlt` represents the ALT key, and so on.

Visible PROPERTY

Objects Affected `TMenuItem`

Purpose The `Visible` property determines whether the menu item is visible onscreen.

Declaration

```
property Visible: Boolean;
```

Example Syntax

```
procedure TForm1.ShowEdit1Click(Sender: TObject);
begin
  Edit1.Remove(Cut1);
  Edit1.Remove(Copy1);
  Edit1.Remove(Paste1);
  Edit1.Visible := False;
end;
```

Description

If Visible is True, the menu item appears onscreen. If it is False, the menu item does not appear onscreen. The default value for Visible is True.

30

TScreen

The **TScreen** class encapsulates the screen that your application runs within. Delphi automatically creates a global object named **Screen**, which is of type **TScreen**, for every application you create, allowing you to change the cursor and access screen information like width and height.

Since **Screen** is available in every Delphi program, you will not usually need to create **TScreen** objects of your own. **TScreen** is not available at design time, so all of its properties and methods are run-time-only.

Figure 30-1 gives the derivation of **TScreen**. Table 30-1 displays the properties, methods, and events that are implemented by **TScreen**.

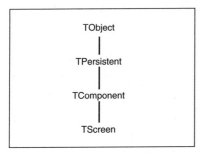

TObject
|
TPersistent
|
TComponent
|
TScreen

Figure 30-1 Derivation of **TScreen**

Table 30-1 Properties, methods, and events implemented by `TScreen`

Use or Set This...	Type	To Do This...	Inheritance
ActiveControl	Property	Determine the active control.	None
ActiveForm	Property	Determine the active form.	None
ComponentCount	Property	Determine the number of owned components.	TComponent
ComponentIndex	Property	Determine the index of the component in its owner's `Components` list.	TComponent
Components	Property	Determine the list of owned components.	TComponent
ComponentState	Property	Determine the state of the current component.	TComponent
Create	Method	Create a new component.	TObject
Cursor	Property	Determine the graphic used to display the mouse cursor.	None
Cursors	Property	Access the list of possible cursors.	None
Destroy	Method	Destroy the component.	TObject
DestroyComponents	Method	Destroy all the components owned by the component.	TComponent
Destroying	Method	Notify the component that it is being destroyed.	TComponent
FindComponent	Method	Find a component in the `Components` array list.	TComponent
Fonts	Property	Determine the available fonts.	None
FormCount	Property	Determine the number of forms displayed onscreen.	None
Forms	Property	Access a form by its position in a list of forms.	None
Free	Method	Safely destroy the object.	TObject
Height	Property	Determine the height of the screen.	None
InheritsFrom	Method	Determine if the object is descended from a certain class.	TObject
InstanceSize	Method	Determine the amount of memory allocated for the object.	TObject
Name	Property	Determine the name of the component.	TComponent
OnActiveControlChange	Event	Handle the event that occurs when the active control changes.	None
OnActiveFormChange	Event	Handle the event that occurs when the active form changes.	None
Owner	Property	Determine the owner of the component.	TComponent
Tag	Property	Store an additional integer value with the component.	TComponent
Width	Property	Determine the width of the screen.	None

ActiveControl PROPERTY

Objects Affected TScreen

Purpose The `ActiveControl` property determines which control has the focus.

Declaration

```
property ActiveControl: TWinControl;
```

Example Syntax

```
// Create a form with many controls, change the Interval property
// of the Timer to 500--every time a control is selected, the
```

```
// Form Caption changes to indicate which control has the focus
procedure TForm1.Timer1Timer(Sender: TObject);
begin
  Form1.Caption := Screen.ActiveControl.Name;
end;
```

Description ActiveControl indicates which control has the focus—only one control on the entire screen can have the focus. If the control is outside your application, you will not be able to access it—ActiveControl is essentially confined to your application.

ActiveForm PROPERTY

Objects Affected TScreen

Purpose The ActiveForm property indicates which form window is the active form window.

Declaration

```
property ActiveForm: TForm;
```

Example Syntax

```
// Create a program with two forms—Show Form2 by
// clicking a button on the first form. This method
// will put the name of the active form on Form 2's
// caption
procedure TForm2.Timer1Timer(Sender: TObject);
begin
  Form2.Caption := Screen.ActiveForm.Name;
end;
```

Description This read-only property indicates which form has the focus.

Cursor PROPERTY

Objects Affected TScreen

Purpose The Cursor property determines the cursor shape.

Declaration

```
property Cursor: TCursor;
```

Example Syntax

```
procedure TForm1.FormCreate(Sender: TObject);
begin
  Screen.Cursor := crUpArrow;
end;
```

Description Changing TScreen's Cursor property will change the cursor shape as it passes over the client area of your application, as shown in Figure 30-2.

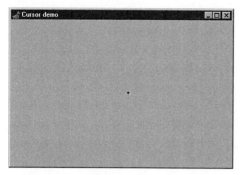

Figure 30-2 Changing the cursor shape

Cursor is of type TCursor, which can have any of the following possible values: crArrow, crCross, crDefault, crDrag, crHourglass, crHSplit, crIBeam, crNoDrop, crSize, crSizeNESW, crSizeNS, crSizeNWSE, crSizeWE, crUpArrow, or crVSplit.

To restore the cursor to the "normal" arrow cursor, set Cursor to crDefault.

Cursors PROPERTY

Objects Affected   TScreen

Purpose   The Cursors property is the array of cursors available to your application.

Declaration

```
property Cursors[Index: Integer]: HCURSOR;
```

Example Syntax

```
implementation

{$R *.DFM}

const
  crMyArrow = 1;

procedure TForm1.FormCreate(Sender: TObject);
begin
  Screen.Cursors[crMyArrow] := LoadCursor(HInstance, 'MYARROW');
  Cursor := crMyArrow;
end;
```

Description   The main purpose of Cursors is to allow you to add custom cursors to your application. The predefined set of global cursors, defined by TCursor and shown in Table 30-2, occupies positions 0 through −17 in the array.

Table 30-2 Predefined elements in the Cursors array

Cursor	Value	Cursor	Value
crDefault	0	crSizeWE	-9
crNone	-1	crUpArrow	-10
crArrow	-2	crHourglass	-11
crCross	-3	crDrag	-12
crIBeam	-4	crNoDrop	-13
crSize	-5	crHSplit	-14
crSizeNESW	-6	crVSplit	-15
crSizeNS	-7	crMultiDrag	-16
crSizeNWSE	-8	crSQLWait	-17

To create your own cursor, use Delphi's Image Editor program to draw the cursor, declare a constant in your source code to represent your cursor's position in the Cursors array, and use the Windows API function LoadCursor to make the cursor resource available to your application. LoadCursor is declared as

```
HCURSOR LoadCursor(
    HINSTANCE  hInstance,           // handle of application instance
    LPCTSTR  lpCursorName           // name string or cursor resource
identifier
    );
```

where lpCursorName should be set to the name you gave your new cursor resource. This procedure is outlined in the code sample above.

Fonts PROPERTY

Objects Affected   TScreen

Purpose   The Fonts property contains a list of fonts that are available to your application.

Declaration

```
property Fonts: TStrings;
```

Example Syntax

```
// Display all of the available fonts
procedure TForm1.FormCreate(Sender: TObject);
begin
  ListBox1.Sorted := True;
  ListBox1.Items := Screen.Fonts;
end;
```

Description   Fonts is a read-only property that contains a list of the fonts that are supported by the screen and are, therefore, accessible to your application. You can use the Fonts property to determine if a font is available, and then determine which font to use based on what is available.

FormCount PROPERTY

Objects Affected   TScreen

Purpose   The FormCount property contains the number of forms that your application currently has visible on the screen.

Declaration

```
property FormCount: Integer;
```

Example Syntax

```
// Get form count
procedure TForm1.Button1Click(Sender: TObject);
begin
  Label1.Caption := 'There is/are ' + IntToStr(Screen.FormCount) +
                    ' form(s) on the screen.';
end;
```

Description   FormCount is a read-only property.

Forms PROPERTY

Objects Affected   TScreen

Purpose   The Forms property is an array of the forms that are available to display.

Declaration

```
property Forms[Index: Integer]: TForm;
```

Example Syntax

```
procedure TForm1.Button1Click(Sender: TObject);
begin
  Screen.Forms[0].Caption := 'Using the Forms array';
end;
```

Description   Each form that your application creates is given a position in the Forms array. The first form that is created is Forms[0], the second is Forms[1], and so on. Forms allows you to access each form in your application by its Index value.

Height PROPERTY

Objects Affected   TScreen

Purpose   The Height property contains the height of the screen.

Declaration

```
property Height: Integer;
```

Example Syntax

```
procedure TfrmScreenInfo.FormCreate(Sender: TObject);
begin
  lblWidth.Caption := IntToStr(Screen.Width);
  lblHeight.Caption := IntToStr(Screen.Height);
  lblPixelsPerInch.Caption := IntToStr(Screen.PixelsPerInch);
end;
```

Description

This read-only property contains the vertical size of the screen, measured in pixels. Note that Windows 95/NT 4.0 screen heights and/or widths include the space taken up by the taskbar, which is just another window.

OnActiveControlChange EVENT

Objects Affected   TScreen

Purpose   The OnActiveControlChange event occurs when the focus of the screen changes from one control to another.

Declaration

```
property OnActiveControlChange: TNotifyEvent;
```

Example Syntax

```
unit Unit1;

interface

uses
  Windows, Messages, SysUtils, Classes, Graphics, Controls, Forms,
  Dialogs, StdCtrls, ExtCtrls;

type
  TForm1 = class(TForm)
    RadioGroup1: TRadioGroup;
    RadioButton1: TRadioButton;
    RadioButton2: TRadioButton;
    RadioButton3: TRadioButton;
    CheckBox1: TCheckBox;
    CheckBox2: TCheckBox;
    Button1: TButton;
    Button2: TButton;
    procedure FormCreate(Sender: TObject);
  private
    { Private declarations }
  public
    // Manually added method declaration
    procedure FocusChanged(Sender: TObject);
  end;
```

continued on next page

continued from previous page

```
var
  Form1: TForm1;

implementation

{$R *.DFM}

// Create an event handler for OnActiveControlChange
procedure TForm1.FormCreate(Sender: TObject);
begin
  Screen.OnActiveControlChange := FocusChanged;
end;

// Respond to OnActiveControlChange events
procedure TForm1.FocusChanged(Sender: TObject);
begin
  if Screen.ActiveControl = Button2 then
      Button1.Enabled := False
    else Button1.Enabled := True
end;

end.
```

Description   You can create an event handler for the `OnActiveControlChange` event if you wish to perform some processing each time this event occurs. When the `OnActiveControlChange` event is triggered, the value of the `Screen`'s `ActiveControl` property changes to the control that is receiving the focus.

OnActiveFormChange EVENT

Objects Affected   `TScreen`

Purpose   The `OnActiveFormChange` occurs just before the active form changes.

Declaration

```
property OnActiveFormChange: TNotifyEvent;
```

Example Syntax

```
unit Unit1;

interface

uses
  Windows, Messages, SysUtils, Classes, Graphics, Controls, Forms,
Dialogs,
  StdCtrls, ExtCtrls;

type
  TForm1 = class(TForm)
    RadioGroup1: TRadioGroup;
    RadioButton1: TRadioButton;
    RadioButton2: TRadioButton;
    RadioButton3: TRadioButton;
    CheckBox1: TCheckBox;
    CheckBox2: TCheckBox;
    Button1: TButton;
```

```
      Button2: TButton;
      Label1: TLabel;
      procedure FormCreate(Sender: TObject);
      procedure Button1Click(Sender: TObject);
    private
      { Private declarations }
    public
      procedure FormChanged(Sender: TObject);
    end;

var
  Form1: TForm1;

implementation

uses Unit2;

{$R *.DFM}

// Create an event handler for OnActiveFormChange
procedure TForm1.FormCreate(Sender: TObject);
begin
  Screen.OnActiveFormChange := FormChanged;
end;

// Handle the OnActiveFormChange event
procedure TForm1.FormChanged(Sender: TObject);
begin
  Label1.Caption := 'Active Form is ' + Screen.ActiveForm.Name;
end;

// Show Form2 when the button is pressed
procedure TForm1.Button1Click(Sender: TObject);
begin
  Form2.Show;
end;

end.
```

Description   You can create an event handler for the `OnActiveFormChange` if you need any processing to occur before every active form change.

Width PROPERTY

Objects Affected   `TScreen`

Purpose   The `Width` property contains the width of the screen.

Declaration

```
property Width: Integer;
```

Example Syntax

```
procedure TfrmScreenInfo.FormCreate(Sender: TObject);
begin
  lblWidth.Caption := IntToStr(Screen.Width);
  lblHeight.Caption := IntToStr(Screen.Height);
  lblPixelsPerInch.Caption := IntToStr(Screen.PixelsPerInch);
end;
```

Description   This read-only property contains the horizontal size of the screen, measured in pixels. Note that Windows 95/NT 4.0 screen widths and/or heights include the space taken up by the taskbar, which is just another window, not part of the screen.

31

TSession

A session object, or instance of **TSession**, provides global control over the database connections in your application. Every time your application runs, a default **TSession** component named **Session** is created so you won't need to explicitly create a session object unless you are creating a multithreaded database application. In that case, you can select the Session icon from the Component Palette to add another session object.

When we refer to a session, we are implicitly referring to a BDE session.

WARNING

At the time of this writing, the Borland documention and online help incorrectly state that Delphi automatically creates a session object called Sessions each time your application runs. Actually, Sessions is of type TSessionList, which is a container for multiple session objects. TSessionList objects are used in multithreaded database applications that need to access the same database more than once at the same time. The use of TSessionList is an advanced topic beyond the scope of this book.

Figure 31-1 shows the ancestry of **TSession**. Table 31-1 displays the properties, methods, and events that are implemented by **TSession**.

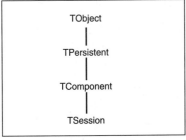

Figure 31-1 Ancestry of **TSession**

Table 31-1 Properties, methods, and events implemented by `TSession`

Use or Set This...	To Do This...	Inheritance
Active	Determine whether the session is active.	None
AddAlias	Create a new alias for a database in the current session.	None
AddPassword	Add a password to the session.	None
AddStandardAlias	Create a new alias to a standard database in the session.	None
Assign	Assign one persistent object to another.	TPersistent
ClassName	Get the name of the object's class.	TObject
ClassParent	Get the object's parent class.	TObject
ClassType	Get the object's actual type.	TObject
Close	Close the session.	None
ComponentCount	Determines the number of owned components.	TComponent
ComponentIndex	The index of the component in its owner's `Components` list.	TComponent
Components	Determine the list of owned components.	TComponent
ComponentState	Determine the state of the current component.	TComponent
ConfigMode	Determine whether the run-time alias is global or local.	None
Create	Create a new component.	TObject
Databases	Use the active databases as an array.	None
DeleteAlias	Delete an alias.	None
Destroy	Destroy the component.	TObject
DestroyComponents	Destroy all of the components owned by the component.	TComponent
Destroying	Notify the component that it is being destroyed.	TComponent
DropConnections	Drop all inactive database and dataset connections.	None
FindComponent	Find a component in the `Components` array list.	TComponent
FindDatabase	Attempt to find a database component.	None
Free	Safely destroy the object.	TObject
GetAliasDriverName	Get the name of the BDE driver for a specified alias.	None
GetAliasNames	Get a list of all defined BDE alias names.	None
GetAliasParams	Get a list of the parameters to an alias.	None
GetDatabaseNames	Get a list of alias names.	None
GetDriverNames	Get a list of driver names.	None
GetDriverParams	Get a list of parameters to a specified driver.	None
GetPassword	Trigger the `OnPassword` event.	None
InheritsFrom	Determine if the object is descended from a certain class.	TObject
InstanceSize	Determine the amount of memory allocated for the object.	TObject
KeepConnections	Determine whether temporary databases will maintain connections when no tables are open.	None
Name	Determine the name of the component.	TComponent
OnPassword	Handle the event that occurs when a password is required.	None
OnStartup	Handle the event that occurs before a session starts.	None

Use or Set This...	To Do This...	Inheritance
Open	Open a new session.	None
Owner	Determine the owner of the component.	TComponent
PrivateDir	Determine the directory where temporary files are kept.	None
RemoveAllPasswords	Delete all of the previously entered passwords.	None
RemovePassword	Remove a specified password from a list of passwords.	None
SaveConfigFile	Save the BDE configuration file.	None
SessionName	Determine the name of the current session.	None
Tag	Store an additional integer value with the component.	TComponent

Active PROPERTY

Objects Affected	TSession
Purpose	The **Active** property determines whether the session is active.
Declaration	

```
property Active: Boolean;
```

Description Set **Active** to **True** to start the session and make it the current session. This is equivalent to calling the **Open** method. Setting the session's **Active** property to **False** will close the session and is equivalent to calling the **Close** method.

You cannot set the **Active** property of the default session to **False** at design time. Although you can do so at run time, it is not recommended and will likely throw an exception.

AddAlias METHOD

Objects Affected	TSession
Purpose	The **AddAlias** property creates and adds a new alias for a database in the current session.
Declaration	

```
procedure AddAlias(const Name, Driver: string; List: Tstrings);
```

Parameters

Name The name of the alias you are creating.

Driver The BDE driver to use.

List A list of parameters to pass to the driver, represented as a list of strings.

Description	AddAlias creates a new alias with the name passed by the *Name* parameter. The *Driver* parameter determines the type of database driver to use and can be any of the following values: STANDARD (for dBASE and Paradox), ORACLE, SYBASE, INFORMIX, or INTERBASE. The *List* parameter is a list of strings that act as parameters to the alias. An Alias is usually defined by the BDE Configuration Utility or the Alias Manager in the Database Desktop. Aliases appear in the IDE in the database Name property for a table, query, or stored procedure object.

AddPassword METHOD

Objects Affected	TSession
Purpose	AddPassword adds a password to the session.
Declaration	

```
procedure AddPassword(const Password: string);
```

Parameter	
Password	The password you are adding to the session.
Example Syntax	

```
procedure TForm1.FormCreate(Sender: TObject);
begin
  Session.Active := True;
  Session.AddPassword('PBT1029');
end;
```

Description	The password you are adding to the session is valid for use with Paradox tables that require a password; adds your new password to the list of existing passwords for the session.

AddStandardAlias METHOD

Objects Affected	TSession
Purpose	The AddStandardAlias method creates and adds a new alias to a standard database in the current session.
Declaration	

```
procedure AddStandardAlias(const Name, Path, DefaultDriver: string);
```

Parameters	
Name	The name of the alias you are adding.
Path	The directory name where the database is stored.
DefaultDriver	The table type to use. Can be PARADOX, DBASE, or ASCIIDRV.

Example Syntax

```
procedure TForm1.FormCreate(Sender: TObject);
begin
  Session.AddStandardAlias('MyCountryList',
         'f:\delphi 2.0\demos\data\country.db', '');
end;
```

Description   AddStandardAlias creates a new alias with the name passed by the *Name* parameter. The *DefaultDriver* parameter determines the type of database driver to use and can be any of the following values: STANDARD (for dBASE and Paradox), ORACLE, SYBASE, INFORMIX, or INTERBASE. The *List* parameter is a list of strings that act as parameters to the alias. An Alias is usually defined by the BDE Configuration Utility or the Alias Manager in the Database Desktop. Aliases appear in the IDE in the database Name property for a table, query, or stored procedure object.

Close METHOD

Objects Affected	TSession
Purpose	The Close method closes the current session.
Declaration	

```
procedure Close;
```

Description   Close has the same effect as setting the Active property to False.

ConfigMode PROPERTY

Objects Affected	TSession
Purpose	The ConfigMode property determines whether run-time aliases are global or local.

Declaration

```
property ConfigMode: TConfigMode;
```

Example Syntax

```
procedure TForm1.FormCreate(Sender: TObject);
begin
  Session.ConfigMode := cmAll;
end;
```

Description   ConfigMode is a run-time-only property that affects aliases created at run time with AddAlias or AddStandardAlias. It is of type TConfigMode, and can be set to one the following possible values:

Use This Value...	To Do This...
cmPersistent	Aliases you add at run time are global. GetAliasNames will return only global aliases.
cmSession	Aliases you add at run time are local and can't be saved. GetAliasNames will return only local aliases.
cmAll	Aliases you add at run time are global. GetAliasNames will return global and local aliases.

Global aliases can be made permanent by calling the `SaveConfigFile` method whereas local aliases are lost when the session is closed.

Databases PROPERTY

Objects Affected	TSession
Purpose	The `Databases` property is an array of the active databases associated with the session.
Declaration	

```
property Databases[Index: Integer]: TDatabase;
```

Example Syntax

```
// Close all databases
procedure TForm1.btnCloseClick(Sender: TObject);
var x: Integer;
begin
  if Application.MessageBox('Close all Databases?', 'Close all',
                           MB_YESNO) = ID_YES then
    for x := 0 to Session.DatabaseCount - 1 do
      Session.Databases[x].Close;
end;
```

Description   `Databases` can be used to iterate through all the active databases and to perform actions that you would like to occur in every database. Note that `Databases` is a zero-based array; so the first database is `Databases[0]`, the second is `Databases[1]`, and so on.

DeleteAlias METHOD

Objects Affected	TSession
Purpose	The `DeleteAlias` method removes an alias.
Declaration	

```
procedure DeleteAlias(const Name: string);
```

Parameter	
Name	The name of the alias you would like to remove.

Example Syntax

```
procedure TForm1.btnCloseClick(Sender: TObject);
var x: Integer;
begin
  if Application.MessageBox('Close all Databases?', 'Close all',
  MB_YESNO) = ID_YES then
    for x := 0 to Session.DatabaseCount - 1 do
      Session.Databases[x].Close;
    Session.DeleteAlias('MyAlias');
end;
```

Description

A permanent alias will be reactivated every time your application runs unless you call the **SaveConfigFile** immediately after deleting it.

DropConnections METHOD

Objects Affected   TSession

Purpose   **DropConnections** drops all inactive databases and datasets.

Declaration

```
procedure DropConnections;
```

Example Syntax

```
procedure TForm1.btnDropConnsClick(Sender: TObject);
begin
  Session.DropConnections;
end;
```

Description

Normally, temporary database components keep their connections open even when they're not in use so they do not need to reconnect every time a dataset component is opened. The **KeepConnections** property determines this default behavior. If **KeepConnections** is set to **True**, and you wish to close all inactive database connections, you can call **DropConnections**.

FindDatabase METHOD

Objects Affected   TSession

Purpose   The **FindDatabase** method attempts to find a database component.

Declaration

```
function FindDatabase(const DatabaseName: string): TDatabase;
```

Parameter

DatabaseName   The name of the database you are trying to find.

Example Syntax

```
procedure TForm1.btnFindDataClick(Sender: TObject);
begin
  TmpData := Session.FindDatabase('MY_CLIENTS');
end;
```

Description   FindDatabase attempts to find a database that is an instance of **TDatabase** in the **Databases** array whose name matches the **DatabaseName** parameter. If the database is found, it is returned. Otherwise, **FindDatabase** returns **Nil**.

GetAliasDriverName METHOD

Objects Affected   TSession

Purpose   The **GetAliasDriverName** method returns the name of the BDE driver for a specified alias.

Declaration

```
function GetAliasDriverName(const AliasName: string): string;
```

Parameter

AliasName   The name of the alias whose driver name you are retrieving.

Description   The name returned by **GetAliasDriverName** depends on the type of driver the alias uses, although standard aliases for Paradox and dBASE return **STANDARD**.

GetAliasNames METHOD

Objects Affected   TSession

Purpose   The **GetAliasNames** method returns a list of all defined DBE alias names.

Declaration

```
procedure GetAliasNames(List: TStrings);
```

Parameter

List   A string list that will contain the list of alias names.

Description   **GetAliasNames** clears the contents of the *List* parameter and fills it with a list of the names of all defined BDE alias names.

GetAliasParams METHOD

Objects Affected	TSession
Purpose	The `GetAliasParams` method retrieves the list of parameters to a specified alias.
Declaration	

```
procedure GetAliasParams(const AliasName: string; List: TStrings);
```

Parameter	
AliasName	The name of the alias whose parameters you are trying to retrieve.
List	A string list that will contain the list of parameters.
Description	`GetAliasNames` clears the string list passed in the *List* parameter and fills it with the list of parameters to the alias specified by the *AliasName* parameter.

GetDatabaseNames METHOD

Objects Affected	TSession
Purpose	The `GetDatabaseNames` method retrieves the names of all aliases.
Declaration	

```
procedure GetDatabaseNames(List: TStrings);
```

Parameter	
List	A string list to hold the list of aliases.
Description	`GetDatabaseNames` clears the list passed by the *List* parameter and fills it with the list of names of all BDE and application-specific aliases.

GetDriverNames METHOD

Objects Affected	TSession
Purpose	The `GetDriverNames` method retrieves the list of currently installed BDE drivers.
Declaration	

```
procedure GetDriverNames(List: TStrings);
```

Parameter	
List	A string list to contain the list of currently installed BDE drivers.

Description | GetDriverNames clears the string list specified by the *List* parameter and fills it with the list of BDE drivers that are currently installed. Standard drivers, that is, Paradox and dBASE drivers, are not included in this list as they are handled by the standard driver.

GetDriverParams METHOD

Objects Affected | TSession

Purpose | The GetDriverParams method retrieves the default parameters to the specified driver name.

Declaration

```
procedure GetDriverParams(const DriverName: string; List: TStrings);
```

Parameter

DriverName | The name of the driver whose parameters you are obtaining.

List | A string list to hold the list of parameters.

Description | GetDriverParams clears the list passed by the *List* parameter and fills it with the default parameters to the driver specified by the *DriverName* parameter.

Note that the dBASE and Paradox standard driver has only one parameter, *PATH=*. SQL drivers, which are beyond the scope of this book, will have varying numbers of parameters.

GetPassword METHOD

Objects Affected | TSession

Purpose | The GetPassword method triggers the OnPassword event handler if it exists or displays the default password dialog box.

Declaration

```
function GetPassword: Boolean;
```

Example Syntax

```
procedure TForm3.btnGetPasswordClick(Sender: TObject);
begin
  Session.GetPassword;
end;
```

Description | GetPassword either triggers the OnPassword event or displays the default password dialog box if you haven't handled OnPassword. The default password dialog, shown in Figure 31-2, returns True if the OK button is clicked or False if the Cancel button is clicked.

Figure 31-2 The default password
dialog box

KeepConnections PROPERTY

Objects Affected	TSession
Purpose	The KeepConnections property determines whether temporary database components will maintain database connections when no tables in the database are open.
Declaration	

```
property KeepConnections: Boolean;
```

Example Syntax

```
procedure TForm1.FormCreate(Sender: TObject);
begin
  Session.KeepConnections := False;
end;
```

Description The default value for KeepConnections is True, which keeps database connections open. If KeepConnections is False, your application will disconnect database connections when there are no open tables. If you would like to explicity close a temporary database, you can call the DropConnections method.

OnPassword EVENT

Objects Affected	TSession
Purpose	The OnPassword event is triggered when a Paradox table is opened and the BDE detects that the application does not have sufficient access.
Declaration	

```
property OnPassword: TPasswordEvent;
```

Example Syntax

```
// Handle the OnPassword event
procedure TForm1.FormCreate(Sender: TObject);
begin
  Session.OnPassword := HandlePassword;
end;

// An example OnPassword event handler shell
procedure TForm1.HandlePassword(Sender: TObject;
                                var Continue: Boolean);
begin
  // Add code to process password here
end;
```

Description

The OnPassword event can be handled with a custom event handler, but the default password dialog box is usually sufficient. This default dialog will appear if you do not handle the OnPassword event explicitly. OnPassword is of type TPasswordEvent which is declared as:

```
TPasswordEvent = procedure(Sender: TObject; var Continue: Boolean);
```

where Continue determines whether the caller should make further attempts to access the database. If there are additional passwords, set Continue to True. If there are not, set it to False.

OnStartUp EVENT

Objects Affected   TSession

Purpose   The OnStartup event is triggered before the session becomes active.

Declaration

```
property OnStartup: TNotifyEvent;
```

Example Syntax

```
unit Unit3;

interface

uses
  SysUtils, Windows, Messages, Classes, Graphics, Controls,
  StdCtrls, Forms, DBCtrls, DB, Mask, ExtCtrls;

type
  TForm1 = class(TForm)
    procedure FormCreate(Sender: TObject);
  private
    { private declarations }
  public
    procedure DoStartup(Sender: TObject);
  end;

var
  Form1: TForm1;
```

```
implementation

{$R *.DFM}

// Determine the event handler for OnStartup
procedure TForm3.FormCreate(Sender: TObject);
begin
  Session.OnStartup := DoStartUp;
end;

// Event handler for OnStartup
procedure TForm3.DoStartup(Sender: TObject);
begin
  Session.PrivateDir := 'c:\windows\temp';
end;
```

Description Create an event handler for **OnStartup** if you need to perform any processing before the session becomes active.

Open METHOD

Objects Affected   TSession

Purpose   The **Open** method opens the session and makes it the active session.

Declaration

```
procedure Open;
```

Description   **Open** has the same effect as setting the **Active** property.

PrivateDir PROPERTY

Objects Affected   TSession

Purpose   The **PrivateDir** property specifies the directory to store temporary files.

Declaration

```
property PrivateDir: string;
```

Example Syntax

```
// Event handler for OnStartup
procedure TForm3.DoStartup(Sender: TObject);
begin
  Session.PrivateDir := 'c:\windows\temp';
end;
```

Description   **PrivateDir** is a run-time-only property that allows you to specify the directory your application uses to store temporary files.

RemoveAllPasswords METHOD

Objects Affected	TSession
Purpose	The RemoveAllPasswords method deletes all the previously entered passwords.
Declaration	

```
procedure RemoveAllPasswords;
```

Description	RemoveAllPasswords only affects Paradox databases.

RemovePassword METHOD

Objects Affected	TSession
Purpose	The RemovePassword method removes a specified password from the list of known passwords.
Declaration	

```
procedure RemovePassword(const Password: string);
```

Parameter	
Password	The password you would like to remove.
Description	RemovePassword only affects Paradox databases.

SaveConfigFile METHOD

Objects Affected	TSession
Purpose	The SaveConfigFile method writes the DBE configuration file to disk.
Declaration	

```
procedure SaveConfigFile;
```

Description	Use SaveConfigFile to permanently save any configuration changes you made.

SessionName PROPERTY

Objects Affected	TSession
Purpose	The SessionName property contains the name of the current session.
Declaration	

```
property SessionName: string;
```

Example Syntax

```
procedure TForm3.FormCreate(Sender: TObject);
begin
  Session.OnStartup := DoStartUp;
  Session.SessionName := 'ClientDatabase';
  // . . .
end;
```

Description   If you are going to be using multiple sessions in your application, be sure to name your sessions so their purpose is clear.

TTimer

Timer objects, instances of the **TTimer** class, allow you to trigger events at specified intervals. Though timer intervals can be specified in milliseconds, the timer is only approximate and can be drastically affected by other processing in your system. Timer objects are available from the Component Palette and appear on the System page, shown in Figure 32-1. Since the timer is available at design time, you will likely set most of its properties there.

Figure 32-2 shows the derivation of **TTimer**. Table 32-1 displays the properties, methods, and events implemented by **TTimer**.

Figure 32-1 The System tab of the Component Palette

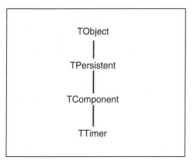

Figure 32-2 Derivation of **TTimer**

Table 32-1 Properties, methods, and events that are implemented by `TTimer`

Use or Set This...	To Do This...	Inheritance
Assign	Assign one persistent object to another.	TPersistent
ClassName	Get the name of the object's class.	TObject
ClassParent	Get the object's parent class.	TObject
ClassType	Get the object's actual type.	TObject
ComponentCount	Determine the number of owned components.	TComponent
ComponentIndex	The index of the component in its owner's `Components` list.	TComponent
Components	Determine the list of owned components.	TComponent
ComponentState	Determine the state of the current component.	TComponent
Create	Create a new component.	TObject
Destroy	Destroy the component.	TObject
DestroyComponents	Destroy all of the components owned by the component.	TComponent
Destroying	Notify the component that it is being destroyed.	TComponent
Enabled	Determine whether the timer is enabled.	None
FindComponent	Find a component in the `Components` array list.	TComponent
Free	Safely destroy the object.	TObject
InheritsFrom	Determine if the object is descended from a certain class.	TObject
InstanceSize	Determine the amount of memory allocated for the object.	TObject
Interval	Determine the interval for `OnTimer` events to occur.	None
Name	Determine the name of the component.	TComponent
OnTimer	Handle the event that occurs when the interval passes.	None
Owner	Determine the owner of the component.	TComponent
Tag	Store an additional integer value with the component.	TComponent

Enabled PROPERTY

Objects Affected	TTimer
Purpose	The **Enabled** property determines whether the **Timer** is enabled.
Declaration	

```
property Enabled: Boolean;
```

Example Syntax

```
procedure TForm1.FormCreate(Sender: TObject);
begin
  Timer1.Enabled := True;
  // Set timer interval to 5 seconds
  Timer1.Interval := 5000;
end;
```

Description   If `Enabled` is `True`, `Timer` events will be generated. If it is `False`, `Timer` events are not generated. The default value for `Enabled` is `True`.

Interval PROPERTY

Objects Affected   `TTimer`

Purpose   The `Interval` property determines the length of time that will pass between successive `OnTimer` events.

Declaration

```
property Interval: Cardinal;
```

Example Syntax

```
procedure TForm1.FormCreate(Sender: TObject);
begin
  Timer1.Enabled := True;
  // Set timer interval to 5 seconds
  Timer1.Interval := 5000;
end;
```

Description   `Interval` is measured in milliseconds. The default value is `1000` (or 1 second), although you can set it to any valid unsigned integral value. If you set `Interval` to `0`, no `OnTimer` events will occur.

OnTimer EVENT

Objects Affected   `TTimer`

Purpose   The `OnTimer` event occurs when the `Timer`'s interval passes.

Declaration

```
property OnTimer: TNotifyEvent;
```

Example Syntax

```
var
  Form1: TForm1;
  Counter: Integer;

// . . .

// default OnTimer event handler
procedure TForm1.Timer1Timer(Sender: TObject);
begin
  inc(Counter);
  Label1.Caption := Counter;
end;
```

Description   You create an event handler for the `OnTimer` event to cause code to execute at specific time intervals determined by the `Interval` property. `OnTimer` is available from the Object Inspector in the Delphi IDE.

33

TMenu AND ITS DESCENDANTS

Everyone who uses Windows is familiar with menus—one of the most common user interface elements found in any graphical computer environment. A *menu* is simply a list of choices the user can select with a mouse. The current Delphi VCL offers great support for Windows menus with a base abstract class `TMenu` and its more functional children `TMainMenu` and `TPopupMenu`. `TMainMenu` encapsulates the *drop-down menu*, the menu that drops down from a window's menu bar. `TPopupMenu` encapsulates *pop-up menus*, those menus that appear over an object when it is right-clicked and which contain choices contextually relevant to that object. Both types of menus have the same elements, or items, which are abstracted by the `TMenuItem.` class, covered in Chapter 29.

Designing Menus

Delphi's IDE includes an integrated Menu Designer which can be invoked by double-clicking a main menu or pop-up menu component placed on a form. The Menu Designer, shown in Figure 33-1, allows you to edit menus and their properties, methods, and events.

TMenu

The `TMenu` class is an abstract base class for all menu objects. It provides the base functionality for menu operations used by `TMainMenu` and `TPopupMenu`. You will never create an object of type `TMenu`, but you will access its properties and methods through its descendant classes.

Regardless of the type, menus are designed to list commands for the user to choose from. The list of choices is held in the `Items` property, which is an array of menu item objects. Menu items are the individual commands that can be chosen—they are essentially contained by the menu.

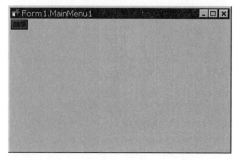

Figure 33-1 Editing a menu with the
Menu Designer

Figure 33-2 shows the TMenu branch of the VCL. Table 33-1 displays the properties and methods implemented by TMenu.

Table 33-1 Properties and methods implemented by TMenu

Use or Set This...	To Do This...	Inheritance
Assign	Assign one persistent object to another.	TPersistent
ClassName	Get the name of the object's class.	TObject
ClassParent	Get the object's parent class.	TObject
ClassType	Get the object's actual type.	TObject
ComponentCount	Determine the number of owned components.	TComponent
ComponentIndex	The index of the component in its owner's Components list.	TComponent
Components	Determine the list of owned components.	TComponent
ComponentState	Determine the state of the current component.	TComponent
Create	Create a new component.	TObject
Destroy	Destroy the component.	TObject
DestroyComponents	Destroy all of the components owned by the component.	TComponent
Destroying	Notify the component that it is being destroyed.	TComponent
FindComponent	Find a component in the Components array list.	TComponent
FindItem	Find a menu item.	None
Free	Safely destroy the object.	TObject
Handle	Obtain an HMENU to your menu.	None
InheritsFrom	Determine if the object is descended from a certain class.	TObject
InstanceSize	Determine the amount of memory allocated for the object.	TObject
Name	Determine the name of the component.	TComponent
Owner	Determine the owner of the component.	TComponent
Tag	Store an additional integer value with the component.	TComponent

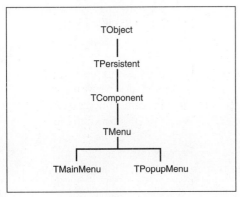

Figure 33-2 The TMenu branch of the VCL

TMainMenu

Drop-down menus and their menu bars are encapsulated by the TMainMenu class, a direct descendant of TMenu. A drop-down menu, sometimes called a main menu, can be added to your application by choosing the MainMenu component from the Standard page of the Component Palette in the IDE.

Table 33-2 displays the properties, methods, and events that are implemented by TMainMenu. These are in addition to the properties and methods it inherits from TMenu (refer to Table 33-1).

Table 33-2 Properties and methods implemented by TMainMenu

Use or Set This...	To Do This...	Inheritance
AutoMerge	Automatically merge menus in a SDI application.	None
Merge	Merge two menus in a SDI application.	None
Unmerge	Unmerge two menus that were joined with Merge.	None

TPopupMenu

Pop-up menus began appearing in Microsoft Office 4.x for Windows 3.1 and were such a hit that Microsoft decided to add them to their operating systems. Windows 95 and Windows NT 4.0 natively support pop-up menus, or context menus, for most objects in the environment. Pop-up menus are designed to show the user what commands or operations are available with any object, be it an icon on the desktop, the taskbar, or any other onscreen element. They are typically invoked with the right mouse button and appear at the cursor position so the user doesn't need to move the mouse to a menu bar or toolbar. Since pop-up menus are displayed only when the user *wants* to see them, they do not normally take up any screen space. In an object-based environment like Windows, the pop-up menu is a valuable tool when the user isn't sure what operations are available to a particular object. This leads to the familiar refrain that began with Office 4.x: "If you don't know what it does, just right-click it."

Menu items in a pop-up menu should affect the object that is right-clicked, whereas drop-down menus usually contain commands that are global to the application. Like drop-down menus, pop-up menus can cascade to submenus if necessary. A typical example of this is the desktop pop-up menu in Windows 95, shown in Figure 33-3.

Table 33-3 displays the properties, methods, and events implemented by TPopupMenu. These are in addition to the properties and methods it inherits from TMenu (refer to Table 33-1).

Table 33-3 Properties, methods, and events implemented by TPopupMenu

Use or Set This...	To Do This...	Inheritance
Alignment	Determine the way the pop-up is aligned.	None
AutoPopup	Determine if the pop-up appears if a control is right-clicked.	None
Create	Create a new pop-up menu.	TObject
Destroy	Destroy a pop-up menu.	TObject
HelpContext	Determine the help context ID for the pop-up menu.	None
OnPopup	Handle the event that occurs when the pop-up appears.	None
Popup	Display the pop-up menu at a specific screen location.	None
PopupComponent	Determine what component caused the pop-up to appear.	None

Alignment PROPERTY

Objects Affected   TPopupMenu

Purpose   The Alignment property determines where the pop-up menu appears in relation to the mouse pointer.

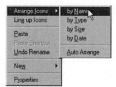

Figure 33-3   A cascading pop-up menu in Windows 95

Declaration

```
property Alignment: TPopupAlignment;
```

Example Syntax

```
// Right-align the pop-up menu
procedure TForm1.FormCreate(Sender: TObject);
begin
  PopupMenu1.Alignment := paRight;
end;
```

Description

Alignment is of type TPopupAlignment, and can be set to one of the following three possible values:

paLeft	The pop-up menu appears with its top-left corner under the mouse pointer.
paCenter	The pop-up menu appears with the top of the menu centered under the mouse pointer.
paRight	The pop-up menu appears with its top-right corner under the mouse pointer.

The default value for Alignment is paLeft.

AutoMerge PROPERTY

Objects Affected   TMainMenu

Purpose   The AutoMerge property determines how the drop-down menus in SDI applications merge.

Declaration

```
property AutoMerge: Boolean;
```

Example Syntax

```
procedure TForm1.FormCreate(Sender: TObject);
begin
  MainMenu1.AutoMerge := False;
end;

// . . .

procedure TForm2.FormCreate(Sender: TObject);
begin
  MainMenu1.AutoMerge := True;
end;
```

Description   The AutoMerge property determines whether the drop-down menus in an SDI application's secondary forms merge with the drop-down menu in the main form when the application runs. For the menus to merge, the AutoMerge property of each menu *except* the main form's must be set to True—the AutoMerge property of the drop-down menu for the main form should remain False. The way that menu's merge is determined by the TMenuItem GroupIndex property.

MDI applications perform menu merging automatically so you will not need to set the `AutoMerge` property explicitly. For either type of application, SDI or MDI, the default value of `AutoMerge` is `False`.

AutoPopup PROPERTY

Objects Affected   TPopupMenu

Purpose   The `AutoPopup` property determines whether the pop-up menu appears when the user right-clicks a component that uses the pop-up menu.

Declaration

```
property AutoPopup: Boolean;
```

Example Syntax

```
// 'Disable Pop-ups' menu item disables pop-up menus
procedure TForm1.DisablePopups1Click(Sender: TObject);
begin
  PopupMenu1.AutoPopup := False;
  EnablePopups1.Enabled := True;
  DisablePopups1.Enabled := False;
end;

// 'Enable Pop-ups' menu item enables pop-up menus
procedure TForm1.EnablePopups1Click(Sender: TObject);
begin
  PopupMenu1.AutoPopup := True;
  DisablePopups1.Enabled := True;
  EnablePopups1.Enabled := False;
end;
```

Description   Components for which you want to use a particular pop-up menu, set their `PopupMenu` property to the name of the pop-up menu. The `AutoPopUp` property determines whether that pop-up menu appears when the user right-clicks the component. The default value is `True`, which causes the pop-up menu to appear when the component is right-clicked. If `AutoPopup` is set to `False`, the pop-up menu will not appear when the component is right-clicked, although you can call the `Popup` method to active it manually.

FindItem METHOD

Objects Affected   All menu objects

Purpose   The `FindItem` method finds the menu item that has a property matching that specified in the method call.

Declaration

```
function FindItem(Value: Integer; Kind: TFindItemKind): TMenuItem;
```

Parameters

Value
The value of a menu handle, menu command, or menu shortcut used by the menu item you are trying to find.

Kind
Determines if you are searching with a menu handle, menu command, or menu shortcut (see below).

Description
FindItem searches for a particular menu item contained in the menu that has a menu handle, menu command, or menu shortcut matching the value passed by the *Value* parameter. The *Kind* parameter, which is of TFindItemKind, determines the type of the value you are searching for and can be one of the following possible values:

If Kind Is..	You Are Searching for This Type...
fkCommand	The value parameter is a menu command number.
fkHandle	The value parameter is a menu handle.
fkShortCut	The value parameter is a menu shortcut.

Handle PROPERTY

Objects Affected
All menu objects

Purpose
The Handle property contains a Windows handle to the menu.

Declaration

```
property Handle: HMENU;
```

Description
Menu handles are often required for API calls although most Windows menu functionality is encapsulated by the methods and properties of the various VCL menu classes.

HelpContext PROPERTY

Objects Affected
TPopupMenu

Purpose
The HelpContext property determines which screen in Help will appear if F1 is pressed while the pop-up menu is open.

Declaration

```
property HelpContext: THelpContext;
```

Example Syntax

```
procedure TForm1.FormCreate(Sender: TObject);
begin
  EnablePopups1.Enabled := False;
  PopupMenu1.HelpContext := 13;
end;
```

Description   If you set `HelpContext` to `0`, it will use the `HelpContext` value of the pop-up menu's parent (the form) and open that help screen.

Merge METHOD

Objects Affected   `TMainMenu`

Purpose   The `Merge` method merges the drop-down menu of the main form with the drop-down menu of one of its child forms in an SDI application.

Declaration

```
procedure Merge(Menu: TMainMenu);
```

Parameter

Menu   The menu to merge with the current menu.

Example Syntax

```
procedure TForm2.FormCreate(Sender: TObject);
begin
  Form1.MainMenu1.Merge(Form2.MainMenu1);
end;
```

Description   If your application has two forms with menus, their menus can be merged into one menu on the main form. `Merge` works only with SDI applications; MDI applications automatically merge menus. The *Menu* parameter specifies the menu that will be merged with the menu on the main form.

The `GroupIndex` property of `TMenuItem` determines how the menu items of the two menus are merged. The menus can also be merged automatically when the second menu appears by setting the `AutoMerge` property of the second form to `True`.

OnPopup EVENT

Objects Affected   `TPopupMenu`

Purpose   The `OnPopup` event occurs when the pop-up menu appears.

Declaration

```
property OnPopup: TNotifyEvent;
```

Example Syntax

```
// The default event-handler for OnPopup
procedure TForm1.PopupMenu1Popup(Sender: TObject);
begin

end;
```

Description   You can create a handler for the `OnPopup` event if you need to perform some processing every time that event occurs. `OnPopup` is triggered by the user right-clicking an object that uses a pop-up menu or when the **Popup** method is invoked.

Popup METHOD

Objects Affected	TPopupMenu
Purpose	The **Popup** method displays a pop-up menu at a specific screen location.
Declaration	

```
procedure Popup(X, Y: Integer); virtual;
```

Parameter

X   The x coordinate of the location onscreen where the pop-up menu will appear.

Y   The y coordinate of the location onscreen where the pop-up menu will appear.

Example Syntax

```
// Show the pop-up menu if the client area of the form is double-
// clicked
procedure TForm1.FormDblClick(Sender: TObject);
begin
  PopupMenu1.Popup(Form1.Top,Form1.Left);
end;
```

Description   **Popup** displays the pop-up menu at the screen location specified by the *X* and *Y* parameters. The x and y screen coordinates are measured in pixels.

PopupComponent PROPERTY

Objects Affected	TPopupMenu
Purpose	The **PopupComponent** property indicates which component caused the pop-up menu to appear.
Declaration	

```
property PopupComponent: TComponent;
```

Example Syntax

```
// Three Bitbtns use PopupMenu1 as their pop-up menu. PopupMenu1
// has a menu item, 'Properties'. This event handler determines
// which button was right-clicked to display the pop-up menu.
procedure TForm1.popPropertiesClick(Sender: TObject);
begin
  If PopupMenu1.PopupComponent = BitBtn1 then
    Application.MessageBox('BitBtn 1',
                           'Properties', MB_OK);
  If PopupMenu1.PopupComponent = BitBtn2 then
    Application.MessageBox('BitBtn 2',
```

continued on next page

continued from previous page

```
                                        'Properties', MB_OK);
        If PopupMenu1.PopupComponent = BitBtn3 then
          Application.MessageBox('BitBtn 3',
                                    'Properties', MB_OK);
    end
```

Description   This run-time-only property can be used to determine which component displayed the pop-up menu when the same menu is used for multiple components.

Unmerge METHOD

Objects Affected   TMainMenu

Purpose   The Unmerge method reverses the merging of two menus that were previously combined with **Merge**.

Declaration

```
procedure Unmerge(Menu: TMainMenu);
```

Parameter

Menu   The menu you wish to unmerge from the current form's drop-down menu.

Example Syntax

```
procedure TForm2.FormDestroy(Sender: TObject);
begin
  Form1.MainMenu1.Unmerge(Form2.MainMenu1);
end;
```

Description   Unmerge will reverse the merging of two menus in an SDI application. The *Menu* parameter specifies the menu that was merged with the current menu and now needs to be unmerged.

34

TCommonDialog
AND ITS DESCENDANTS

One of the design goals for Windows is that it offers a standardized user interface that the user can rely on. Menus and toolbars in application programs are meant to be similar enough so the user is not confused and is not forced to learn a new set of interface conventions for each new application. Another area of standardization in Windows is the use of *common dialog boxes*, a set of dialog boxes supported directly by the operating system and made available to any application. When the Windows user interface changed from Windows/NT 3.x to the Explorer shell used in Windows 95 and NT 4.0, the common dialog boxes were improved to handle long file names and offer usability improvements over their obsolete predecessors. By using the Windows common dialog boxes, you will not need to reinvent the wheel and can offer your users the consistent, standardized interface they expect.

Delphi encapsulates the Windows common dialog boxes with the abstract `TCommonDialog` class and its descendants.

TCommonDialog

`TCommonDialog` is the abstract base class for Delphi's implementation of the Windows common dialog boxes. Delphi-created common dialogs are components that directly represent the standard Windows common dialogs available to all application developers.

`TCommonDialog` provides base functionality for all common dialog boxes. You will not normally derive new descendants from `TCommonDialog`, as it is designed specifically to encapsulate the Windows common dialog boxes, not generic dialog boxes. Developers wishing to create a customized dialog box should use a standard Delphi form instead.

Figure 34-1 shows the `TCommonDialog` branch of the VCL. Table 34-1 displays the properties and methods implemented by `TCommonDialog`.

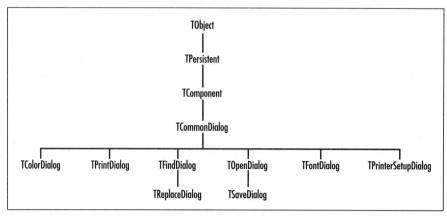

Figure 34-1 The TCommonDialog branch of the VCL

Table 34-1 Properties and methods implemented by TCommonDialog

Use or Set This...	To Do This...	Inheritance
Assign	Assign one persistent object to another.	TPersistent
ClassName	Get the name of the object's class.	TObject
ClassParent	Get the object's parent class.	TObject
ClassType	Get the object's actual type.	TObject
ComponentCount	Determine the number of owned components.	TComponent
ComponentIndex	The index of the component in its owner's Components list.	TComponent
Components	Determine the list of owned components.	TComponent
ComponentState	Determine the state of the current component.	TComponent
Create	Create a new component.	TObject
Ctl3D	Display the dialog box with a 3D or 2D effect.	None
Destroy	Destroy the component.	TObject
DestroyComponents	Destroy all of the components owned by the component.	TComponent
Destroying	Notify the component that it is being destroyed.	TComponent
FindComponent	Find a component in the Components array list.	TComponent
Free	Safely destroy the object.	TObject
HelpContext	Determine the Help context ID number for the dialog box.	None
InheritsFrom	Determine if the object is descended from a certain class.	TObject
InstanceSize	Determine the amount of memory allocated for the object.	TObject
Name	Determine the name of the component.	TComponent
Owner	Determine the owner of the component.	TComponent
Tag	Store an additional integer value with the component.	TComponent

TColorDialog

The TColorDialog class encapsulates the Color dialog box, shown in Figure 34-2.

The Color dialog box allows the user to select a color from a palette of colors. It can be used to set the color of any component that has a Color property and, in fact, holds the color selected by the user in its own Color property.

Table 34-2 displays the properties and methods implemented by TColorDialog. These are in addition to the properties and methods it inherits from TCommonDialog (refer to Table 34-1).

Table 34-2 Properties and methods implemented by TColorDialog

Use or Set This...	To Do This...	Inheritance
Color	Retrieve the color returned by the Color dialog box.	None
Create	Create a new Color dialog box.	TObject
Ctl3D	Display the Color dialog box with a 3D or 2D effect.	TCommonDialog
CustomColors	Determine whether the Custom colors section is displayed.	None
Destroy	Destroy the Color dialog box.	TObject
Execute	Open the Color dialog box.	None
Options	Determine the options that are available to the Color dialog box.	None

TFindDialog

The TFindDialog class creates a standard Find dialog box, used to find text in a file. The Find dialog has a FindText property that contains the text you are searching for

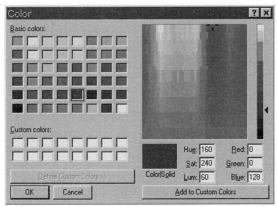

Figure 34-2 The Color dialog box

Figure 34-3 The Find dialog box

and can handle the event that occurs when the text is found with the `OnFind` event. The Find dialog box is shown in Figure 34-3.

    `TReplaceDialog`, described below, is a direct descendant of `TFindDialog` and therefore inherits all the properties and methods implemented by `TFindDialog`, shown in Table 34-3. These are in addition to the properties and methods it inherits from `TCommonDialog` (refer to Table 34-1).

Table 34-3 Properties, methods, and events implemented by `TFindDialog` and `TReplaceDialog`

Use or Set This...	To Do This...	Inheritance
`Create`	Create a new Find or Replace dialog box.	`TObject`
`Destroy`	Destroy the Find or Replace dialog box.	`TObject`
`Execute`	Open the Find or Replace dialog box.	None
`FindText`	Determine the text the user is trying to find or replace.	None
`Handle`	Obtain a Windows handle to the dialog box.	None
`Left`	Determine the x-coordinate position where the dialog box appears.	None
`OnFind`	Handle the event that occurs when the `FindText` text is found.	None
`Options`	Determine what options are available to the dialog box.	None
`Position`	Determine the position the dialog box appears at onscreen.	None
`Top`	Determine the y-coordinate position where the dialog box appears.	None

TFontDialog

Font dialog boxes are encapsulated by the `TFontDialog` class. Font dialog boxes allow the user to select a font and set the style of that font. The font that the user selected is contained in the `Font` property. A Font dialog box is shown in Figure 34-4.

    The Font dialog box can be used to set the font for any component that has a `Font` property.

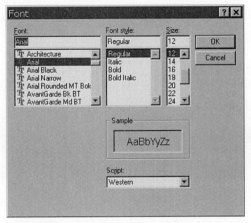

Figure 34-4   The Font dialog box

Table 34-4 displays the properties, methods, and events implemented by
TFontDialog. These are in addition to the properties and methods it inherits from
TCommonDialog (refer to Table 34-1).

Table 34-4 Properties, methods, and events implemented by TFontDialog

Use or Set This...	To Do This...	Inheritance
Create	Create a new Font dialog box.	TObject
Destroy	Destroy the Font dialog box.	TObject
Device	Determine what device the returned font will affect.	None
Execute	Open the Font dialog box.	None
Font	Determine which font was returned by the Font dialog box.	None
MaxFontSize	Set the maximum font size allowed in the Font dialog box.	None
MinFontSize	Set the minimum font size allowed in the Font dialog box.	None
OnApply	Handle the event that occurs when the Apply button is clicked.	None
Options	Determine what options are available to the Font dialog box.	None

TOpenDialog

The Open dialog box allows the user to specify a file in the Windows namespace to
open. The file name chosen by the user is contained by the FileName property. The
TOpenDialog class encapsulates the Windows Open dialog box, shown in Figure 34-5.

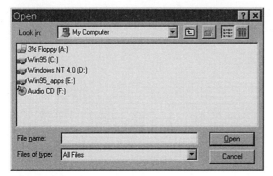

Figure 34-5 The Open dialog box

The Filter Editor

The Delphi IDE includes a Filter editor that allows you to define filters for the Open and Save dialogs boxes. A *filter* is a set of file name specifications that determine what types of files the dialog is going to show. For example, when you choose Open from the File menu in the Delphi IDE, the Open dialog box that appears uses a default filter that displays only Delphi files; that is, files that are identified as ***.pas** and ***.dpr**.

The Filter editor, shown in Figure 34-6, can be accessed by doubling-clicking the **Filter** property field in the Object Inspector when an Open dialog or Save dialog is selected. See the **Filter** property entry for details.

TSaveDialog, described below, is a direct descendant of **TOpenDialog** and therefore inherits all the properties and methods implemented by **TOpenDialog**. These are displayed in Table 34-5 and are in addition to the properties and methods it inherits from **TCommonDialog** (refer to Table 34-1).

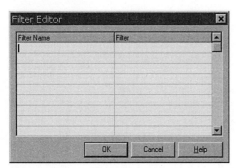

Figure 34-6 The Filter editor

Table 34-5 Properties and methods implemented by TOpenDialog and TSaveDialog

Use or Set This...	To Do This...	Inheritance
Create	Create a new Open or Save dialog box.	TObject
DefaultExt	Determine the default extension for files in the dialog box.	None
Destroy	Destroy the Open or Save dialog box.	TObject
Execute	Open the Open or Save dialog box.	None
FileName	Determine what file name was returned by the dialog box.	None
Files	Determine the files returned by a dialog box with multi-select.	None
Filter	Determine the filter or filters used by the dialog box.	None
FilterIndex	Determine the default filter used when the dialog box opens.	None
InitialDir	Determine the directory displayed in the dialog box when opened.	None
Options	Determine what options are available to the dialog box.	None
Title	Determine the caption in the title bar of the dialog box.	None

TPrintDialog

TPrintDialog encapsulates the standard Print dialog box shown in Figure 34-7.

The Print dialog box allows the user to print a document and specify settings like the target printer and the number of copies to print. The Print dialog box also includes a Setup button that, when clicked, opens a Printer Setup dialog, encapsulated by TPrinterSetupDialog.

Table 34-6 displays the properties and methods implemented by TPrintDialog. These are in addition to the properties and methods it inherits from TCommonDialog (refer to Table 34-1).

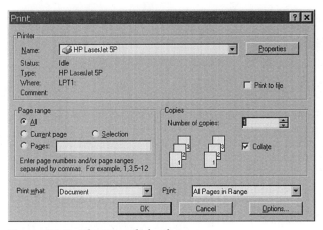

Figure 34-7 The Print dialog box

Table 34-6 Properties and methods implemented by `TPrintDialog`

Use or Set This...	To Do This...	Inheritance
Collate	Determine whether the print job is collated.	None
Copies	Determine the number of copies to print.	None
Execute	Open the Print dialog box.	None
FromPage	Determine the "from" part of the print range.	None
MaxPage	Determine the largest page number you will allow the user to print.	None
MinPage	Determine the smallest page number you will allow the user to print.	None
Options	Determine what options are available to the Print dialog box.	None
PrintRange	Determine the type of print range used to print a file.	None
PrintToFile	Determine whether the print job is printed to a file or a printer.	None
ToPage	Determine the "to" part of the print range.	None

TPrinterSetupDialog

The Printer Setup dialog is invoked when the Setup button on a Print dialog box is clicked. It is encapsulated by the **TPrinterSetupDialog** class, and allows the user to set printer properties, determine the layout of the printed pages, and the paper size and source. The Printer Setup dialog box is shown in Figure 34-8.

You do not need to have a Printer Setup dialog box component on your form to use it in your program. If the user clicks the Setup button on a Print dialog box, Delphi creates one automatically. Since this dialog box interacts with the system at a low level, it is not necessary to write any support routines. The only method you can directly access is **Execute**, which opens the dialog box.

Figure 34-8   The Printer Setup dialog box

Table 34-7 displays the method implemented by **TPrinterSetupDialog**. These are in addition to the properties and methods it inherits from **TCommonDialog** (refer to Table 34-1).

Table 34-7 Method implemented by TPrinterSetupDialog

Use or Set This...	To Do This...	Inheritance
Execute	Open the Printer Setup dialog box.	None

TReplaceDialog

The Replace dialog box, shown in Figure 34-9, allows the user to replace text with a specified string. The **ReplaceText** property contains the text that will replace the found text.

The Replace dialog box is encapsulated by the **TReplaceDialog** class.

> **NOTE**
> TReplaceDialog is a direct descendant of TFindDialog, so the properties and methods used by TFindDialog are applicable to TReplaceDialog as well.

Table 34-8 displays the properties, methods, and events implemented by **TReplaceDialog**. These are in addition to the properties and methods it inherits from **TCommonDialog** (refer to Table 34-1) and **TFindDialog** (refer to Table 34-3).

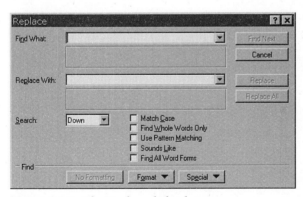

Figure 34-9   The Replace dialog box

Table 34-8 Properties, methods, and events implemented by `TReplaceDialog`

Use or Set This...	To Do This...	Inheritance
Create	Create a Replace dialog box.	TObject
OnReplace	Handle the event that occurs when the user replaces text.	None
ReplaceText	The text to replace the text held in `FindText`.	None

TSaveDialog

The Save As dialog box is encapsulated by `TSaveDialog` and allows the user to save a file to disk. The Save As dialog box is shown in Figure 34-10.

You can specify `filter` for the Save As dialog box, as described in the description of `TOpenDialog`, previously, and the entry for the `Filter` property later in this chapter.

> **NOTE**
> `TSaveDialog` is a direct descendant of `TOpenDialog`, so the properties and methods used by `TOpenDialog` are applicable to `TSaveDialog` as well.

Table 34-9 displays the method implemented by `TSaveDialog`. This is in addition to the properties and methods it inherits from `TCommonDialog` (refer to Table 34-1).

Table 34-9 Method implemented by `TSaveDialog`

Use or Set This...	To Do This...	Inheritance
Execute	Open the Save dialog box.	None

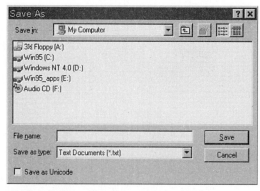

Figure 34-10 The Save As dialog box

Collate PROPERTY

Objects Affected	TPrintDialog
Purpose	The **Collate** property determines whether the Collate check box on the Print dialog box is checked.
Declaration	

```
property Collate: Boolean;
```

Example Syntax

```
procedure TForm1.sbPrintClick(Sender: TObject);
begin
  PrintDialog1.Collate := True;
  PrintDialog1.Execute;
end;
```

Description   If **Collate** is **True**, then the Collate check box is checked when the Print dialog box is opened and collating is enabled. If **Collate** is **False**, the Collate check box is not checked and collating is not used. The default setting is **False**, although the user can always check the Collate check box to enable collating.

Color PROPERTY

Objects Affected	TColorDialog
Purpose	The **Color** property determines which color was chosen in the Color dialog box.
Declaration	

```
property Color: TColor;
```

Example Syntax

```
// Change the color of the selected text when the user chooses
// a color from the Color dialog box
procedure TForm1.sbColorClick(Sender: TObject);
begin
  ColorDialog1.Execute;
  RichEdit1.SelAttributes.Color := ColorDialog1.Color;
end;
```

Description   When the user selects a color in the Color dialog box, the **Color** property is set to that new color value.

Copies PROPERTY

Objects Affected	`TPrintDialog`
Purpose	The `Copies` property determines the number that appears in the Number of copies spin box.
Declaration	

```
property Copies: Integer;
```

Example Syntax

```
// Retrieve the number of copies that were printed...
procedure TForm1.sbPrintClick(Sender: TObject);
begin
  PrintDialog1.Execute;
  NumCopies := PrintDialog1.Copies;
end;
```

Description   The `Copies` property can be set to determine the default value that will appear in the **Number of copies** up-down control on the Printer dialog box. The default value is **1**.

Ctl3D PROPERTY

Objects Affected	All common dialogs
Purpose	The `Ctl3D` property determines whether the common dialog box has a three-dimensional or two-dimensional look.
Declaration	

```
TCommonDialog:
property Ctl3D: Boolean;
TColorDialog:
property Ctl3D default False;
```

Example Syntax

```
procedure TForm1.sbFontClick(Sender: TObject);
begin
  FontDialog1.Ctl3D := True;
  if FontDialog1.Execute = True then
  begin
    RichEdit1.SelAttributes.Name := FontDialog1.Font.Name;
    RichEdit1.SelAttributes.Size := FontDialog1.Font.Size;
    RichEdit1.SelAttributes.Style := FontDialog1.Font.Style;
    RichEdit1.SelAttributes.Color := FontDialog1.Font.Color;
  end
end;
```

Description   If `Ctl3D` is set to `True`, the common dialog box has a three-dimensional look consistent with most Windows user-interface elements. If `Ctl3D` is `False`, the common dialog box will display with a flat, 2D look.

CustomColors PROPERTY

Objects Affected	TColorDialog
Purpose	The **CustomColors** determine which custom colors are available in the Color dialog box.
Declaration	

```
property CustomColors: TStrings;
```

Example Syntax

```
procedure TForm1.sbColorClick(Sender: TObject);
var x: Integer;
begin
  ColorDialog1.CustomColors := strCustomColors;
  ColorDialog1.Execute;
  RichEdit1.SelAttributes.Color := ColorDialog1.Color;
  strCustomColors := ColorDialog1.CustomColors;
  // Save strCustomColors to the registry or an INI file
  // when the program exits ...
end;
```

Description   CustomColors holds a list of strings. Each string follows the format ColorX=HexValue where ColorX is one of 16 custom colors, ColorA through ColorP, and HexValue is a 6-digit hexadecimal value that represents the RGB values that make up the color. Using this scheme, FFFFFF would be pure white and 000000 would be pure black. To assign the color black to ColorC, use the following string:

ColorC=000000

You should save the list of custom colors every time the Color dialog box is closed so the user can access any custom colors he/she might have set while using the dialog box. The Custom color portion of the Color dialog box is opened by pressing the Define Custom Colors button. The Color dialog box then expands.

DefaultExt PROPERTY

Objects Affected	TOpenDialog, TSaveDialog
Purpose	The **DefaultExt** property specifies the extension automatically added to the filename entered in the File Name edit box if the user doesn't add it manually.
Declaration	

```
property DefaultExt: string;
```

Example Syntax

```
procedure TForm1.FileOpen(Sender: TObject);
begin
  OpenDialog1.DefaultExt := 'RTF';
  OpenDialog1.Execute;
end;
```

Description   If the user adds an extension to the end of the file name he/she is opening or saving, the default extension specified by **DefaultExt** is ignored. If **DefaultExt** is not set and the user enters a file name without an extension, no extension is used.

In Windows 3.1, file name extensions had to be 3 characters in length, in accordance with the 8.3 file-naming restriction. This is no longer the case—extensions like **html** and **text** are now possible. Because multiple periods (.) are now allowed in file names, the extension of a file name is now defined as the text following the last period in the file name. A file named **This.Is.My.File.text** uses *text* as its extension.

Device PROPERTY

Objects Affected   TFontDialog

Purpose   The **Device** property represents the rendering device that is affected by the font returned by the Font dialog box.

Declaration

```
property Device: TFontDialogDevice;
```

Example Syntax

```
procedure TForm1.sbFontClick(Sender: TObject);
begin
  FontDialog1.Device := fdBoth;
  if FontDialog1.Execute = True then
    // . . .
end;
```

Description   Fonts chosen with a Font dialog box can affect two devices: the screen or the printer—they can also affect both. Font is of type **TFontDialogDevice**, which can have one of the following possible values:

Use This Value...	To Affect This Device...
fdBoth	Both the printer and the screen
FdPrinter	The printer
FdScreen	The screen

Execute METHOD

Objects Affected	TColorDialog, TFindDialog, TFontDialog, TOpenDialog, TPrintDialog, TPrinterSetupDialog, TSaveDialog, TReplaceDialog
Purpose	The Execute method is used to open a common dialog box.

Declaration

TPrinterSetupDialog

```
procedure Execute;
```

All others

```
function Execute: Boolean;
```

Example Syntax

```
// Open the Find dialog box in the screen's upper left corner
procedure TForm1.sbFindClick(Sender: TObject);
begin
  FindDialog1.Left := 0;
  FindDialog1.Top := 0;
  FindDialog1.Execute;
end;

// Open the Color dialog box
procedure TForm1.sbColorClick(Sender: TObject);
var x: Integer;
begin
  if ColorDialog1.Execute = True then
  begin
   RichEdit1.SelAttributes.Color := ColorDialog1.Color;
    strCustomColors := ColorDialog1.CustomColors;
  end;
end;
```

Description   Execute displays the common dialog box and returns True if the user closes the dialog box by clicking the OK command button. If the user clicks Cancel or closes the dialog box by choosing Close from the System menu, Execute returns False. You can use the return value of Execute to determine which block of code to run when the dialog box is closed, as in the above example.

The Execute method for TPrinterSetupDialog does not return a value, but it is handled automatically by the system.

FileName PROPERTY

Objects Affected	TOpenDialog, TSaveDialog
Purpose	The FileName property specifies the file name that appears in the File name edit box.

Declaration

```
property FileName: TFileName;
```

Example Syntax

```
procedure TForm1.FileOpen(Sender: TObject);
begin
  if OpenDialog1.Execute then
  begin
    RichEdit1.Lines.LoadFromFile(OpenDialog1.FileName);
    // MyFileName is a private variable of type String
    MyFileName := OpenDialog1.FileName;
    // . . .
  end;
end;
```

Description   You can set `FileName` to the name of a valid file before the dialog opens if you wish to have that file name appear in the File name edit box. When the user closes the dialog box by clicking OK, the file name that appears in the File name edit box is assigned to the `FileName` property. It is possible for the file name specified by `FileName` to contain the full path in addition to the file name. If the file name specified in the File name edit box does not exist, and the user opens or saves it, then a new file is created with that name.

`Files` PROPERTY

Objects Affected   TOpenDialog, TSaveDialog

Purpose   The `Files` property contains a list of file names that can be opened or saved at the same time.

Declaration

```
property Files: TStrings;
```

Example Syntax

```
// Use an Open dialog box to allow the user to select multiple
// files and list those file in the rich edit control
procedure TForm1.sbGetFileClick(Sender: TObject);
begin
  GetFilesDialog.Options := [ofAllowMultiSelect];
  GetFilesDialog.Filter := 'All files|*.*';
  if GetFilesDialog.Execute then
    RichEdit1.Lines := OpenDialog1.Files;
end;
```

Description   This run-time, read-only property allows the user to open or save multiple files simultaneously if the `ofAllowMultiSelect` bits of the `Options` property are set to `True`. The list of file names is assigned to the `FileName` property if the dialog box is closed by user clicking the OK command button.

Filter PROPERTY

Objects Affected	`TOpenDialog, TSaveDialog`
Purpose	The `Filter` property specifies a list of file name masks that are used in an Open or Save dialog box to determine which types of files the dialog box will display.
Declaration	

```
property Filter: string;
```

Example Syntax

```
// Open a text markup file
procedure TForm1.FileOpen(Sender: TObject);
begin
  OpenDialog1.Filter :=
          'Markup files (*.htm, *.html, *.sgml)|*.HTM;*.HTML;*.SGML';
  if OpenDialog1.Execute then
  begin
    RichEdit1.Lines.LoadFromFile(OpenDialog1.FileName);
    FFileName := OpenDialog1.FileName;
    RichEdit1.SetFocus;
    RichEdit1.Modified := False
  end
end;
```

Description   `Filters` are created by assigning a text string to the `Filter` property. The string can specify a single file type:

```
OpenDialog1.Filter := 'All files|*.*'
```

or multiple file types using a semicolon as a separator:

```
OpenDialog1.Filter := 'Markup files|*.HTM;*.HTML;*.SGML';
```

You can also specify multiple filters in one line, separating each filter by a | character:

```
OpenDialog1.Filter :=
        'Text files|*.TXT;*.TEXT|HTML files|*.HTM;*.HTML'
```

Although you can assign filters for the dialog box at run time, it is easier to use the Filter editor at design time to assign them all at once. To activate the Filter editor, make sure that the Open or Save dialog box component is selected, and double-click its `Filter` property field in the Object Inspector.

FilterIndex PROPERTY

Objects Affected	`TOpenDialog, TSaveDialog`
Purpose	The `FilterIndex` property determines which filter displays in the List files of type drop-down list box when the dialog box opens.

Declaration

```
property FilterIndex: Integer;
```

Example Syntax

```
procedure TForm1.FileOpen(Sender: TObject);
begin
  OpenDialog1.FilterIndex := 2;
  if OpenDialog1.Execute then
    // . . .
end;
```

Description   The list of filters is indexed by 1, starting at 1, so the first filter is **1**, the second is **2**, and so on. The default is **1**. Also, see **Filters**.

FindText PROPERTY

Objects Affected	TFindDialog, TReplaceDialog
Purpose	The FindText property contains the text you are searching for.

Declaration

```
property FindText: string;
```

Declaration

```
procedure TForm1.btnFindClick(Sender: TObject);
begin
  FindDialog1.FindText := 'Delphi';
  FindDialog1.Execute;
end;
```

Description   If the dialog box is a Replace dialog box, the **FindText** property represents the text you are going to replace with the text in the **ReplaceText** property.

Font PROPERTY

Objects Affected	TFontDialog
Purpose	The Font property contains the font returned by the Font dialog box.

Declaration

```
property Font: TFont;
```

Example Syntax

```
procedure TForm1.sbFontClick(Sender: TObject);
begin
  if FontDialog1.Execute = True then
```

```
begin
  RichEdit1.SelAttributes.Name := FontDialog1.Font.Name;
  RichEdit1.SelAttributes.Size := FontDialog1.Font.Size;
  RichEdit1.SelAttributes.Style := FontDialog1.Font.Style;
  RichEdit1.SelAttributes.Color := FontDialog1.Font.Color;
end
end;
```

Description   If you specify a font in the Font property before opening the Font dialog box with Execute, then that font will be the selected font when the dialog box appears.

FromPage PROPERTY

Objects Affected   TPrintDialog

Purpose   The FromPage property determines the first page the print job will start printing.

Declaration

```
property FromPage: Integer;
```

Description   The default value is 1, and the user can manually change the value by editing the From edit box in the Print range section of the Print dialog box.

Handle PROPERTY

Objects Affected   TFindDialog, TReplaceDialog

Purpose   The Handle property contains a Windows handle to the dialog box.

Declaration

```
property Handle: HWnd;
```

Description   Handle is provided for the Find and Replace dialog boxes in case you need to call an API function that requires a handle to the dialog box (which is a window).

HelpContext PROPERTY

Objects Affected   All common dialogs

Purpose   The HelpContext property determines which screen in Help will appear if [F1] is pressed.

Declaration

```
property HelpContext: THelpContext;
```

Example Syntax

```
procedure TForm1.FormCreate(Sender: TObject);
begin
  // . . .
  ColorDialog1.HelpContext := 13;
end;
```

Description If you set `HelpContext` to `0`, it will use the `HelpContext` value of the common dialog's parent (the form) and open that help screen.

InitialDir PROPERTY

Objects Affected `TOpenDialog`, `TSaveDialog`

Purpose The `InitialDir` property contains a string specifying the directory that should be displayed when the dialog box appears.

Declaration

```
property InitialDir: string;
```

Example Syntax

```
procedure TForm1.FileOpen(Sender: TObject);
begin
  OpenDialog1.InitialDir := 'C:\WINDOWS\';
  if OpenDialog1.Execute then
    // . . .
end;
```

Description If `InitialDir` is not specified, the dialog box will open in the directory that the executable resides in or the directory that was last specified in the previous Open or Save dialog box.

Left PROPERTY

Objects Affected `TFindDialog`, `TReplaceDialog`

Purpose The `Left` property determines the x-coordinate of the screen position where the dialog box should appear.

Declaration

```
property Left: Integer;
```

Example Syntax

```
// Open the Find dialog box in the screen's upper left corner
procedure TForm1.sbFindClick(Sender: TObject);
begin
  FindDialog1.Left := 0;
  FindDialog1.Top := 0;
  FindDialog1.Execute;
end;
```

Description	The `Left` and `Top` properties determine the position of the dialog box when it appears, using the coordinate system of the screen, measured in pixels. `Left` is only available at run time. The system determines the default position of the dialog unless you specify `Top` and `Left` values explicitly. Setting the `Left` and `Top` properties has the same effect as setting the `Position` property.

MaxFontSize PROPERTY

Objects Affected	`TFontDialog`
Purpose	The `MaxFontSize` property determines the largest point size available in the Font dialog box.
Declaration	

```
property MaxFontSize: Integer;
```

Description	You can use the `MaxFontSize` property to limit the size of fonts available to the user as long as the `Options` property of the Font dialog box has the `fdLimitSize` value enabled. Otherwise, `MaxFontSize` will have no effect. The default value is `0`, which does not limit the maximum font size.

MaxPage PROPERTY

Objects Affected	`TPrintDialog`
Purpose	The `MaxPage` property specifies the highest page number that the user can print.
Declaration	

```
property MaxPage: Integer;
```

Description	If `MaxPage` is set and the user tries to select a *to* page that is higher than `MaxPage`, a warning dialog box will automatically be generated. `MaxPage` will have no effect unless the `Options` property set includes the `poPageNums` value. The default value is `0`, which does not set a limit.

MinFontSize PROPERTY

Objects Affected	`TFontDialog`
Purpose	The `MinFontSize` property determines the smallest point size available to fonts in the Font dialog box.
Declaration	

```
property MinFontSize: Integer;
```

Description   Specify a `MinFontSize` value to limit the size of fonts available to the user. For `MinFontSize` to work, **the** `Options` property of the Font dialog box must have the `fdLimitSize` value enabled. Otherwise, **`MaxFontSize`** will have no effect. The default value is **0**, which does not limit the minimum font size.

MinPage PROPERTY

Objects Affected   `TPrintDialog`

Purpose   The `MinPage` property determines the smallest page number the user can print.

Declaration

```
property MinPage: Integer;
```

Description   If `MinPage` is set and the user tries to select a *from* page that is lower than `MinPage`, a warning dialog box will automatically be generated. `MinPage` has no effect unless the `Options` property set includes the `poPageNums` value. The default value is **0**, which does not set a lower limit.

OnApply EVENT

Objects Affected   `TFontDialog`

Purpose   The `OnApply` event occurs when the `Apply` button in a Font dialog box is clicked.

Declaration

```
property OnApply: TFDApplyEvent;
```

Example Syntax

```
// The default event handler for OnApply
procedure TForm1.FontDialog1Apply(Sender: TObject; Wnd: Integer);
begin
  // . . .
end;
```

Description   The Apply button won't appear in the Font dialog box unless you handle the `OnApply` event. While you can manually specify an event handler for the `OnApply` event in Object Pascal code, it is available from the Events page of the Object Inspector at design time.

OnFind EVENT

Objects Affected	TFindDialog, TReplaceDialog
Purpose	The OnFind event occurs when the Find Next button is clicked in a Find or Replace dialog box.
Declaration	

```
property OnFind: TNotifyEvent;
```

Example Syntax

```
type
  TForm1 = class(TForm)
    FindDialog1: TFindDialog;
    procedure FormCreate(Sender: TObject);
    // . . .
  public
    procedure TextFound(Sender: TObject);
  end;

procedure TForm1.FormCreate(Sender: TObject);
begin
  FindDialog1.OnFind := TextFound;
end;

procedure TForm1.TextFound(Sender: TObject);
begin
  // Enter code to handle the OnFind event
end;
```

Description Handle the OnFind event to process a block of code when the Find Next button is clicked.

OnReplace EVENT

Objects Affected	TReplaceDialog
Purpose	The OnReplace event occurs when the Replace or Replace All button is clicked in a Replace dialog box.
Declaration	

```
property OnReplace: TNotifyEvent;
```

Example Syntax

```
type
  TForm1 = class(TForm)
    ReplaceDialog1: TReplaceDialog;
    procedure FormCreate(Sender: TObject);
    // . . .
```

continued on next page

continued from previous page

```
      public
        procedure ReplaceText (Sender: TObject);
      end;

procedure TForm1.FormCreate(Sender: TObject);
begin
  ReplaceDialog1.OnReplace := ReplaceText;
end;

procedure TForm1.ReplaceText(Sender: TObject);
begin
  if frReplaceAll in ReplaceDialog1.Options then
    // handle it here
  else if frReplaceAll in ReplaceDialog1.Options then
    // handle it here
end;
```

Description Handle the `OnReplace` event to specify the code that executes when text needs to be replaced. In the event handler for `OnReplace`, you will need to find out which button, Replace or Replace All, triggered the event. This is done by checking the `frReplace` and `frReplaceAll` values in the replace dialog's `Options` property to determine which button was clicked.

`Options` PROPERTY

Objects Affected `TColorDialog`, `TFindDialog`, `TFontDialog`, `TOpenDialog`, `TPrintDialog`, `TSaveDialog`, `TReplaceDialog`

Purpose The `Options` property contains a set of options that determines how the dialog box behaves. The `Options` property is specific to each common dialog box type.

Declaration

`TColorDialog`

```
property Options: TColorDialogOptions;
```

`TFindDialog` and `TReplaceDialog`

```
property Options: TFindOptions;
```

`TFontDialog`

```
property Options: TFontDialogOptions;
```

`TOpenDialog` and `TSaveDialog`

```
property Options: TOpenOptions;
```

`TPrintDialog`

```
property Options: TPrintDialogOptions;
```

Example Syntax

```
procedure TForm1.FormCreate(Sender: TObject);
begin
  OpenDialog1.Options := [ofReadOnly, ofShareAware];
end;
```

Description

TColorDialog   The Color dialog Options property is a set that can contain a combination of the following possible values:

Set This Value...	To Do This...
cdFullOpen	Display the Custom Colors section when the Color dialog box opens.
cdPreventFullOpen	Disable the Create Custom Colors command button in the Color dialog box.
cdShowHelp	Add a Help button to the Color dialog box.

The default value is [ ], an empty set, which sets all these values to False.

TFindDialog and   The Find and Replace dialog box Options property is a set that can
TReplaceDialog   contain a combination of the following possible values:

Set This Value...	To Do This...
frDisableMatchCase	Dim the Match Case check box so users cannot check it. When set to False, users can check the Match Case check box.
frDisableUpDown	Dim the Direction Up and Down buttons so the user cannot select either. When set to False, users can select one of them. This option only affects the Find dialog box.
frDisableWholeWord	Dim the Match Whole Word check box so the user cannot select it. Set it to False if you want users to be able to check the check box.
frDown	Select the Down button in the dialog box and set the the search direction to *down*. If frDown is set to False, the Up button is selected and the search direction is *up*.
frFindNext	This flag is set when the user clicks the Find Next button—you should search for the string in the FindText property when this occurs. See OnFind.
frHideMatchCase	Make the Match Case check box non-visible. Set it to False to make the Match Case check box visible.
frHideWholeWord	Make the Match Whole Word check box non-visible. Set it to False to make the Match Whole Word check box visible.
frHideUpDown	Make the Direction Up and Down buttons non-visible. Set it to False to make the Direction Up and Down buttons visible. This option only affects the Find dialog box.
frMatchCase	Check the Match Case check box. Set it to False to uncheck the Match Case check box.
frReplace	This option is set by the system, indicating that your application should replace the current occurrence of the FindText string with the ReplaceText string. This option applies only to the Replace dialog box.
frReplaceAll	This option is set by the system, indicating that your application should replace all occurrences of the FindText string with the ReplaceText string. This option applies only to the Replace dialog box.
frShowHelp	Display a Help button in the dialog box. Set frShowHelp to False if you do not wish to display a Help button.
frWholeWord	Check the Match Whole Word check box in the dialog box.

The default value is [frDown] which indicates that only the frDown option is enabled.

| TFontDialog | The Font dialog Options property is a set that can contain a combination of the following possible values: |

Set This Value...	To Do This...
fdAnsiOnly	Allow the user to select only those fonts that use the Windows character set.
fdEffects	Enable the Effects check boxes and the Color list box in the Font dialog box. The Effects check boxes are used to specify strikeout or underlined text and the Color list box is used to select the font's color. Set to False if you do not want the Effects check boxes and Color list box to be visible.
fdFixedPitchOnly	Display only monospaced fonts in the Font combo box.
fdForceFontExist	Trigger an error message dialog box if the user enters an invalid font name in the Font combo box and clicks OK.
fdLimitSize	Limit the number of fonts available in the dialog box by allowing the MinFontSize and MaxFontSize properties to have effect.
fdNoFaceSel	Do not diplay a selected font name in the Font combo box.
fdNoOEMFonts	Display only non-vector fonts in the Font combo box.
fdScalableOnly	Display only scalable fonts in the Font combo box.
fdNoSimulations	Display actual fonts in the Font combo box, not GDI font simulations.
fdNoSizeSel	Do not display a selected size in the Size combo box.
fdNoStyleSel	Do not display a selected style in the Style combo box.
fdNoVectorFonts	Same as fdNoOEMFonts.
fdShowHelp	Display a Help button in the dialog box.
fdTrueTypeOnly	Display only TrueType fonts in the Font list box.
fdWysiwyg	Display only fonts that are available to both the printer and the screen in the Font combo box.

The default value is [fdEffects] which indicates that only the fdEffects option is enabled.

| TOpenDialog and TSaveDialog | The Open and Save dialog Options property is a set that can contain a combination of the following possible values: |

Set This Value...	To Do This...
ofAllowMultiSelect	Allow the user to select more than one file in the File Name list box.
ofCreatePrompt	Display an error message box if the user enters a file name that doesn't exist in the File Name edit box and clicks OK.
ofExtensionDifferent	This option is set automatically when the file name returned from the dialog box has a different extension than the default file extension as specified by the DefaultExt property. Although you can set ofExtensionDifferent at design time in the Object Inspector, it has no meaning.
ofFileMustExist	Display a message box if the user enters a file name that doesn't exist in the File Name edit box and then clicks OK.
ofHideReadOnly	Hide the Read Only check box.
ofNoChangeDir	Set the current directory to the previous current directory, ignoring any directory changes the user may have made while using the dialog box.

ofNoReadOnlyReturn	Display message box informing the user when a selected file is read-only.
ofNoTestFileCreate	Don't check for write protection, a full disk, an open drive door, or network protection when saving the file. This option applies only when the user wants to save a file on a create-no-modify network share point.
ofNoValidate	Do not prevent the user from entering invalid characters in a file name. If ofNoValidate is set to False and the user enters invalid characters in a file name in the File Name edit box, a message box appears informing the user the filename contains invalid characters.
ofOverwritePrompt	Display a message box if the user attempts to save a file that already exists. The message box will allow the user to overwrite the file if desired.
ofReadOnly	Check the Read Only check box.
ofPathMustExist	Allow the user to type only existing path names as part of the file name in the File Name edit box. If the user enters an invalid path name, a message box appears informing the user.
ofShareAware	Ignore all sharing errors and return the name of the selected file anyway. If ofShareAware is set to False, a sharing violation results in a message box informing the user of the problem.
ofShowHelp	Display a Help button in the dialog box.

The default value is [ ], an empty set, meaning that all these options are disabled.

TPrintDialog	The Print dialog Options property is a set that can contain a combination of the following possible values:

Set This Value...	To Do This...
poHelp	Display a Help button in the dialog box.
poPageNums	Enable the Pages radio button and the user can specify a range of pages to print.
poPrintToFile	Display a Print to File check box in the dialog box, allowing the user to print to a file rather than to a printer.
poSelection	Enable the Selection radio button so the user can choose to print selected text.
poWarning	A warning message appears when the user clicks OK if no printer is installed.
poDisablePrintToFile	Dim the Print to File check box when the dialog box appears if poPrintToFile is also True. If poPrintToFile is False, poDisablePrintToFile has no effect because the dialog box won't have a Print To File check box.

The default value is [ ], an empty set, indicating that all these options are disabled.

Position PROPERTY

Objects Affected	TFindDialog, TReplaceDialog
Purpose	The Position property determines the onscreen coordinates where the dialog box will appear.
Declaration	

```
property Position: TPoint;
```

Example Syntax

```
procedure TForm1.sbFindClick(Sender: TObject);
begin
  FindDialog1.Position := Point(0,0);
  FindDialog1.Execute;
end;
```

Description   Setting the `Position` property for a Find or Replace dialog box is function-ally equivalent to setting the `Top` and `Left` properties.

PrintRange PROPERTY

Objects Affected   TPrintDialog

Purpose   The `PrintRange` property determines the print range used to print a file.

Declaration

```
property PrintRange: TPrintRange;
```

Description   `PrintRange` is valid if the `poSelection` value is set in the `Options` property—otherwise, setting `PrintRange` will have no effect and every time the user prints, all pages will print. `PrintRange` is of type `TPrintRange`, which can be set to one of the following possible values:

Use This Value...	To Print This Range of Pages...
prAllPages	Print all pages of the print job. Setting the `PrintRange` value to `prAllPages` at design time selects the All Pages radio button when the Print dialog box first appears.
prSelection	Print only selected text. Setting the `PrintRange` value to `prSelection` at design time selects the Selection radio button when the Print dialog box first appears.
prPageNums	Print a range of pages to print specified by the user. Setting the `PrintRange` value to `prPageNum` at design time selects the Pages radio button when the Print dialog box first appears, allowing the user to specify a range of page numbers to print. Valid page number ranges can be set with the `MinPage` and `MaxPage` properties.

The default value is `prAllPages`.

PrintToFile PROPERTY

Objects Affected   TPrintDialog

Purpose   The `PrintToFile` property determines whether the Print To File check box is checked.

Declaration

```
property PrintToFile: Boolean;
```

Example Syntax

```
procedure TForm1.sbPrintClick(Sender: TObject);
begin
  PrintDialog1.Options := [poPrintToFile];
  PrintDialog1.PrintToFile := True;
  if PrintDialog1.Execute = True then
    // . . .
end;
```

Description

If `PrintToFile` is `True`, the user has selected the Print To File check box and the print job will print to a file. If it is `False`, the print job will print to a printer. You can set the `PrintToFile` property before the dialog box is opened if you wish to have the Print To File check box checked by default. The default value is `False`.

The Print To File check box will appear only if the `poPrintToFile` value is set in the Print dialog box `Option` property.

ReplaceText PROPERTY

Objects Affected   `TPrinterSetupDialog`

Purpose   The `ReplaceText` property contains the string that will replace text specified in the `FindText` property when the `FindText` string is found in a text search.

Declaration

```
property ReplaceText: string;
```

Description   The `ReplaceText` property is filled when the user enters text into the Replace with edit box in a Replace dialog box.

Title PROPERTY

Objects Affected   `TOpenDialog`, `TSaveDialog`

Purpose   The `Title` property determines the caption that appears in the dialog box title bar.

Declaration

```
property Title: string;
```

Example Syntax

```
procedure TForm1.FileSaveAs(Sender: TObject);
begin
  SaveDialog1.Title := 'Save As';
  if SaveDialog1.Execute then
    // . . .
end;
```

Top PROPERTY

Objects Affected	`TFindDialog`, `TReplaceDialog`
Purpose	The `Top` property determines the y-coordinate of the position onscreen where the Find or Replace dialog box will appear.
Declaration	

```
property Top: Integer;
```

Example Syntax

```
// Open the Find dialog box in the screen's upper left corner
procedure TForm1.sbFindClick(Sender: TObject);
begin
  FindDialog1.Left := 0;
  FindDialog1.Top := 0;
  FindDialog1.Execute;
end;
```

Description   The `Left` and `Top` properties determine the position of the dialog box when it appears, using the coordinate system of the *screen*, measured in pixels. `Top` is available only at run time. The system determines the default position of the dialog unless you specify `Top` and `Left` values explicitly.

Setting the `Left` and `Top` properties has the same effect as setting the `Position` property.

ToPage PROPERTY

Objects Affected	`TPrintDialog`
Purpose	The `ToPage` property determines the last page printed in a print job.
Declaration	

```
property ToPage: Integer;
```

Description   The `ToPage` property contains the value that was entered in the *to* edit box of the Print range section of the dialog box.

35

TCustomImageList
AND ITS DESCENDANTS

TCustomImageList is an abstract class from which two principle classes are derived: **TImageList** and **TGlyphList**. The inheritance hierarchy appears in Figure 35-1.

We will discuss the functionality of **TCustomImageList** first, then investigate those properties exposed by the **TImageList** component, finally concluding with a discussion of the **TGlyphList** class.

In general the **TCustomImageList** group of classes are used as containers for a group of graphic images. The classes are capable of holding a large number of same-sized images. These images default to 16 pixels on an edge, which makes them suitable for use as icon images. It is possible to store other sized images as well by specifying alternate sizes with a specialized create method. As with most container classes, the individual items contained in the class are accessed via an indexed property. The **TCustomImageList** class is abstract and not used directly. The **TImageList** component is used and directly descends from **TCustomImageList**. The images contained in a **TImageList** can be prestored for use in applications where quick recall of images is desired without the overhead of reading them in from disk. This is the primary purpose of the **TGlyphList** class and is used internally by the **TSpeedButton**

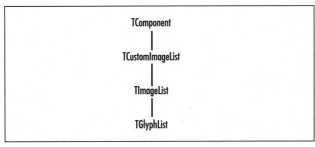

Figure 35-1 **TCustomImageList** and descendant hierarchy

component. We will only discuss those things which distinguish a `TGlyphList` from a `TImageList` in this chapter. For more information about the `TSpeedButton` component, see Chapter 45, "`TSpeedButton` and Its Descendants."

HELPFUL INFORMATION

A new feature supported by Windows 95 (and Windows NT) is the image list. According to the definition supplied by Borland:

"An image list is a collection of same-sized images, each of which can be referred to by its index. Image lists are used to efficiently manage large sets of icons or bitmaps. All images in an image list are contained in a single, wide bitmap in screen device format. An image list may also include a monochrome bitmap that contains masks used to draw images transparently (icon style)." The `TCustomImageList` class and its descendants actually encapsulate the interface to this new Windows internal data structure. In many instances a `mask` object is referred to. The *mask* is a monochrome bitmap of the same size as the image bitmap which is combined in such a way that any non-zero pixels in the bitmap allow the corresponding pixel in the image to be drawn. A zero pixel in the mask indicates that the pixel from the background is used when the image is drawn on the particular canvas involved.

TCustomImageList

The `TCustomImageList` class is similar to other classes defined in Delphi which manage lists of objects, namely `TList` and `TStrings`. The `TCustomImageList` class is used to store one or more images defined to be of the same size. The size of the images is defined when the particular instance is created. `TCustomImageList` is an abstract class not used directly. Many of the functions make reference to a group of enumerated types, which are shown in Listing 35-1 for reference.

Listing 35-1 Enumerated types used by `TCustomImageList` *and descendant classes*

```
TDrawingStyle = (dsFocus, dsSelected, dsNormal, dsTransparent);
TImageType = (itImage, itMask);
TResType = (rtBitmap, rtCursor, rtIcon);
TOverlay = 0..3;
TLoadResource = (lrDefaultColor, lrDefaultSize, lrFromFile, lrMap3DColors, lrTransparent, lrMonoChrome);
TLoadResources = set of TLoadResource;
```

Table 35-1 displays the properties, methods, and events implemented by `TCustomImageList`.

Table 35-1 Properties, methods, and events implemented by `TCustomImageList`.

Use or Set This..	To Do This...	Inheritance
Add	Add an image and mask to the list.	None
AddIcon	Add an icon to the list.	None
AddImages	Add images from another `TCustomImageList` to the current object.	None

Use or Set This..	To Do This...	Inheritance
AddMasked	Add image to the list and specify color for generating mask.	None
Assign	Perform deep copy of images from another TCustomImageList control to the current object.	TPersistent
BeginDrag	Begin a dragging operation on current TCustomImageList object.	None
Clear	Remove image list from internal storage and release resources.	None
Count	Return number of images stored in list.	None
Create	Default constructor TComponent.	TComponent
CreateSize	Alternate constructor.	None
Delete	Delete a particular image from the list	
	Destructor TComponent.	None
Destroy		
DragCursor	Determine which TCursor is to be used when dragging is performed on control.	None
Dragging	Determine whether or not the image list component is being dragged.	None
DragLock	Associate image with a component being dragged.	None
DragMove	Move drag image to specified location.	None
DragUnlock	Remove association between drag image and a window.	None
Draw	Draw indexed image onto specified canvas.	None
DrawOverlay	Draw an image and overlay onto specified canvas.	None
EndDrag	Terminate drag operation.	None
FileLoad	Load bitmap, cursor, or icon from named file, specify transparent color.	None
GetBitmap	Fetch indexed image as bitmap.	None
GetHotSpot	Get hotspot associated with current drag image.	None
GetIcon	Fetch indexed image as icon.	None
GetImageBitmap	Obtain handle to a bitmap containing all images.	None
GetInstRes	Get an image resource and add it to the image list.	None
GetMaskBitmap	Obtain handle to a bitmap containing all masks.	None
GetResource	Load specified resource from file.	None
Handle	Obtain handle for use with Windows API functions.	None
HandleAllocated	Determine if handle has been created for image list.	None
HideDragImage	Hide drag image if it was previously visible.	None
Insert	Insert bitmap and mask after location specified.	None
InsertIcon	Insert icon after location specified.	None
InsertMasked	Insert bitmap after location specified and create mask from specified color.	None
Move	Move image from one index to another.	None

continued on next page

continued from previous page

Use or Set This..	To Do This...	Inheritance
Overlay	Make image at specified location usable as overlay.	None
RegisterChanges	Specify object to be notified when image list is changed.	None
Replace	Replace image at specified location with new image and mask.	None
ReplaceIcon	Replace icon at specified location with new image and mask.	None
ReplaceMasked	Replace image at specified location with new image using specified color for generating mask.	None
ResourceLoad	Load image from named resource and use specified color for generating mask.	None
ResInstLoad	Get an image resource and add it to the image list.	None
SetDragImage	Specify indexed image to be used when control is being used for drag-and-drop.	None
ShowDragImage	Show current drag image if it was previously hidden.	None
UnRegisterChanges	Remove linkage to object receiving change notification on list changes.	None

TImageList

The TImageList class defines a component available from the Win95 page of the standard Component Palette in Delphi 3. The main distinction between the TImageList component and the parent TCustomImageList class is that a number of protected properties are exposed and published by this class, which makes them available in the Object Inspector when one of these components is used.

The additional properties, methods, and events published by this component are shown in Table 35-2.

Table 35-2 Properties, methods, and events implemented by TImageList

Use or Set This..	To Do This...	Inheritance
AllocBy	Specify growth increment.	None
BkColor	Specify background color.	None
BlendColor	Specify foreground color.	None
DrawingStyle	Specify drawing method for images.	None
Height	Set image height for stored images.	None
ImageType	Specify whether to use image or mask for drawing.	None
Masked	Determine whether list contains transparent or non-transparent images.	TCustomImageList
OnChange	Method to execute on changes.	TCustomImageList
ShareImages	Determine whether image handle is destroyed when list is destroyed.	TCustomImageList
Width	Set image width for stored images .	TCustomImageList

TGlyphList

The **TGlyphList** class is used internally by the **TSpeedButton** component for the storage of images which that component uses. A few additional methods and properties are defined by this class, which make it suitable for the needs of the **TSpeedButton** component. The main distinction between the **TListImage** class and the **TGlyphList** class is that deleted entries are recycled automatically by the **add related** method. If a particular image is deleted from the glyph images, the internals of the **TGlyphList** take note of the deleted entry. Upon the next call to add the unused entry, **TGlyphList** is utilized for the new glyph image. The changes in methods for this class are modifications of the standard **TListImage** methods to provide this additional level of complexity which is not supported by the **TImageList** class.

These additional properties and methods are described in Table 35-3.

Table 35-3 Properties and methods implemented by **TGlyphList**

Use or Set This..	To Do This...	Inheritance
Add	Add new glyph image.	TCustomImageList
AddMasked	Add new glyph image using specified color for mask.	TCustomImageList
Count	Obtain number of active glyphs in list.	TCustomImageList
Create	Constructor.	TCustomImageList
Delete	Remove image from glyph list.	TCustomImageList
Destroy	Destructor.	TCustomImageList

Be aware that properties protected in **TCustomImageList** and published in **TImageList** will only be available externally to the component in classes derived from **TImageList** or which explicitly mark them as published. This is why a property like **ShareImages** is shown as descending from **TCustomImageList** in the **TImageList** component even though that particular property is not visible externally in **TCustomImageList** since it is declared as a protected property there. If you derive a new class from **TCustomImageList**, check to see that the desired properties are correctly specified as published if they are intended to be accessible by the user.

Add METHOD

Objects Affected   **TCustomImageList, TImageList, TGlyphList**

Purpose   This method is used to add an image and a mask to the end of the image list contained in the object. The method returns an index value indicating the position that the new image occupies in the image list. This function will automatically cause the image list to grow as required to hold additional images as they are added. In the case of the **TGlyphList**, the **Add** method will reuse index locations previously vacated by the use of the

Delete method. It will return the appropriate index value, unlike the **TCustomImageList** and **TImageList** classes, which always add to the end of the list regardless of whether or not a previous image has been deleted.

Declaration

```
function Add(Image, Mask: TBitmap): Integer;
```

Example Syntax

```
procedure TForm1.Button1Click(Sender: TObject);
var
    theBits:TBitmap;
    theMask:TBitmap;
begin
    theBits := TBitmap.Create;
    theMask := TBitmap.Create;
    theBits.Height := 32;
    theBits.Width := 32;
    theMask.Height := 32;
    theMask.Width := 32;

    theMask.LoadFromFile('MASK.BMP');
    theBits.LoadFromFile('SPIN1.BMP');

    ImageList1.Clear;
    ImageList1.Add(theBits,theMask);
    ImageList1.Draw(Form1.Canvas,0,200,0);

    theMask.Destroy;
    theBits.Destroy;


end;
```

Description

In this example, two **TBitmap**s are created to contain the appropriate bitmap information to be displayed. The two bitmaps—called **theBits** and **theMask** respectively—are sized by setting the **Height** and **Width** properties to 32 on a side. Then the desired bitmaps are loaded from disk. These bitmap images were created with the Delphi Image Editor available from the Tools menu on the main menu bar in Delphi. The **ImageList** is cleared using the **Clear** method, then the image and the mask are added to the **ImageList** object. The **Draw** method is used to draw the desired image on the canvas associated with the form which contains the **ImageList** component. Last, the **TIcon** object is destroyed.

AddIcon METHOD

Objects Affected   **TCustomImageList, TImageList**

Purpose   This method is used to copy an instance of **TIcon** to the end of the image list. If the image list's masked property is **True**, then the mask associated with the `TIcon` supplied will be copied in addition to the `TIcon` bitmap. Otherwise, just the `TIcon` bitmap will be copied to the end of the image.

Declaration

```
function AddIcon(Image: TIcon): Integer;
```

Example Syntax

```
procedure TForm1.Button1Click(Sender: TObject);
var
    theIcon:TIcon;
begin
    theIcon := TIcon.Create;

    theIcon.LoadFromFile('SPIN1.ICO');

    ImageList1.Clear;
    ImageList1.AddIcon(theIcon);

    ImageList1.Draw(Form1.Canvas,0,200,0);

    theIcon.Destroy;

end;
```

Description

This example creates an instance of a `TIcon` object to be used with the `AddIcon` method. After the `TIcon` is created and assigned to the `theIcon` object, the actual icon is loaded from a disk file called `SPIN1.ICO`. After the icon has been loaded from disk, the icon is actually added to the end of the icon list after it is cleared using the `Clear` method. The `Draw` method is used to draw the desired image on the canvas associated with the form which contains the `ImageList` component. Last, the `TIcon` object is destroyed.

AddImages METHOD

Objects Affected   `TCustomImageList, TImageList`

Purpose   This method is used to copy the contents of one image list to the end of another image list. The destination list will automatically be enlarged as required to hold the additional images contained in the source image list.

Declaration

```
procedure AddImages(Value: TCustomImageList);
```

Example Syntax

```
procedure TForm1.Button1Click(Sender: TObject);
var
    theBits:TBitmap;
    theMask:TBitmap;
begin
    theBits := TBitmap.Create;
```

continued on next page

continued from previous page

```
theMask := TBitmap.Create;
theBits.Height := 32;
theBits.Width := 32;
theMask.Height := 32;
theMask.Width := 32;
theMask.LoadFromFile('c:\temp\MASK.BMP');

theBits.LoadFromFile('c:\temp\SPIN1.BMP');
ImageList1.Add(theBits,theMask);

theBits.LoadFromFile('c:\temp\SPIN2.BMP');
ImageList1.Add(theBits,theMask);

theBits.LoadFromFile('c:\temp\SPIN3.BMP');
ImageList1.Add(theBits,theMask);

theBits.LoadFromFile('c:\temp\SPIN4.BMP');
ImageList1.Add(theBits,theMask);

ImageList2.Clear;

// The next line illustrates the use of the AddImages method
ImageList2.AddImages(ImageList1);

ImageList2.Draw(Form1.Canvas,0,200,0);
ImageList2.Draw(Form1.Canvas,64,200,1);
ImageList2.Draw(Form1.Canvas,128,200,2);
ImageList2.Draw(Form1.Canvas,192,200,3);

theMask.Destroy;
theBits.Destroy;

end;
```

Description   This example illustrates the use of the **AddImages** method by loading a set of images and a corresponding mask in from disk, then using the **AddImages** method to append the images from **ImageList1** to **ImageList2**. After the four images have been transferred to the second image list component, the images that were just copied are rendered on the **Form1** canvas using the **Draw** method to place them in a row near the left edge of the form. Finally, the **mask** and **bitmap** objects are destroyed.

AddMasked METHOD

Objects Affected   TCustomImageList, TImageList, TGlyphList

Purpose   The **AddMasked** method is similar to the **Add** method except that the mask is automatically created by the function. A mask is created in which any pixels in the image supplied to the call that match the *MaskColor* argument in value are used to set the corresponding pixel in the mask image. This has the effect of causing those pixels in the original image that match the *MaskColor* to be drawn transparently while the rest of the image is drawn normally.

Declaration

```
function AddMasked(Image: TBitmap; MaskColor: TColor): Integer;
```

Example Syntax

```
procedure TForm1.Button1Click(Sender: TObject);
var
    theBits:TBitmap;
begin
    theBits := TBitmap.Create;
    theBits.Height := 32;
    theBits.Width := 32;

    theBits.LoadFromFile('SPINM.BMP');
    ImageList1.AddMasked(theBits,theBits.Canvas.Pixels[0,0]);

    ImageList1.Draw(Form1.Canvas,0,200,0);

    theBits.Destroy;
end;
```

Description

This example illustrates the use of the **AddMasked** method to automatically mask out a portion of an image when rendered via the **Draw** method. In this example, the bitmap is loaded from a file and directly added to the image list using the **AddMasked** method. Note that the second parameter in the call to **AddMasked** makes reference to one of the pixels in the icon, namely the upper-left pixel in the bitmap image. Passing this upper-left pixel value to the **AddMasked** routine causes all pixels that have the value of that pixel to be masked out when the image is rendered.

AllocBy PROPERTY

Objects Affected   TCustomImageList, TImageList

Purpose   This property is used to determine how many image locations are added to the image list each time the list must grow due to additions. The default value is 4.

Declaration

```
property AllocBy: Integer;
```

Example Syntax

```
    .
    .
ImageList1.AllocBy := 4;
    .
    .
```

Description   This code fragment demonstrates the setting of the **AllocBy** property of a particular **ImageList** object. Internal storage for images in this **TImageList** component will be expanded by four images each time more space is required to hold additional images.

Assign METHOD

Objects Affected	TCustomImageList, TImageList
Purpose	The `Assign` method is used to copy the contents of one TCustomImageList descendant to another. The `Assign` method performs a deep copy in which the contents are duplicated during the copy process.

Declaration

```
procedure Assign(Source: TPersistent); override;
```

Example Syntax

```
procedure TForm1.Button1Click(Sender: TObject);
var
    theBits:TBitmap;
    theMask:TBitmap;
begin
    theBits := TBitmap.Create;
    theMask := TBitmap.Create;
    theBits.Height := 32;
    theBits.Width := 32;
    theMask.Height := 32;
    theMask.Width := 32;
...//note: you will need to change the paths in the following
    // lines to work on another machine.
    theMask.LoadFromFile('c:\temp\MASK.BMP');

    theBits.LoadFromFile('c:\temp\SPIN1.BMP');
    ImageList1.Add(theBits,theMask);

    theBits.LoadFromFile('c:\temp\SPIN2.BMP');
    ImageList1.Add(theBits,theMask);

    theBits.LoadFromFile('c:\temp\SPIN3.BMP');
    ImageList1.Add(theBits,theMask);

    theBits.LoadFromFile('c:\temp\SPIN4.BMP');
    ImageList1.Add(theBits,theMask);

    // The next line illustrates the use of the Assign method
    ImageList2.Assign(ImageList1);

    ImageList2.Draw(Form1.Canvas,0,200,0);
    ImageList2.Draw(Form1.Canvas,64,200,1);
    ImageList2.Draw(Form1.Canvas,128,200,2);
    ImageList2.Draw(Form1.Canvas,192,200,3);

    theMask.Destroy;
    theBits.Destroy;

end;
```

Description	This example illustrates the use of the `Assign` method by loading a set of images and a corresponding mask in from disk, then using the `Assign` method to copy the images from **ImageList1** to **ImageList2**. After the four images have been transferred to the second image list component, the

images that were just copied are rendered on the **Form1** canvas using the **Draw** method to place them in a row near the left edge of the form. Finally, the **mask** and **bitmap** objects are destroyed.

BeginDrag METHOD

Objects Affected   TCustomImageList, TImageList

Purpose   The **BeginDrag** method provides a way to associate one of the images contained in the image list with a window via that window's **HWND** property. The image is drawn at the location specified by the *X* and *Y* values. The image associated with the indicated window is selected by the ***Index*** parameter. The function returns **True** if it was successful.

Declaration

```
function BeginDrag(Window: HWND; X, Y: Integer): Boolean;
```

Example Syntax

```
procedure TForm1.FormMouseDown(Sender: TObject; Button: TMouseButton;
  Shift: TShiftState; X, Y: Integer);
begin
   ImageList1.BeginDrag(Form1.Handle,X,Y);
end;
```

Description   This example is taken from the **DragDem.dpr** project on the project CD-ROM for this chapter. This demonstration project illustrates how to use the **ImageList** object to support the dragging of an image within a given window. The call to **BeginDrag** accepts the handle for the window that will act as a clipping region for the image being dragged. The *X* and *Y* arguments mark the location to place the image to be dragged. Through the use of this method, the cursor can be effectively changed during a drag operation. The call to **BeginDrag** contains a call internally to **DragImage**, which selects image 0 from the image list to be used in the drag operation and sets pixel [0,0] (the upper-left pixel) as the hot spot for the drag image. If you want to use another image from the list, or set a different hot spot, you will need to use the **DragLock** method. For more information on using the drag operations, see the **DragMove** and the **EndDrag** method descriptions.

BkColor PROPERTY

Objects Affected   TCustomImageList, TImageList

Purpose   The **BkColor** property is used to determine which background color to use when drawing an image. A value of **clNone** indicates there is no background color (the image is drawn transparently) while a value of **clDefault** indicates that the background color of the image list should be used when drawing.

Declaration

```
property BkColor;
```

Example Syntax

```
ImageList1.BkColor := clNavy;
```

Description   Masked regions are drawn with the color value specified by **BkColor**. Thus, in the above example, the region surrounding the central region of the image is colored with navy blue, as shown in Figure 35-2. This property has no effect on images being dragged, since masked regions are always drawn transparently. The following figure illustrates four bitmap images drawn with a mask region set to cover the region surrounding the central circular area. Four separate renderings are drawn with the background colors set to **clNavy**, **clMaroon**, **clAqua**, and **clFuchsia**, respectively.

BlendColor PROPERTY

Objects Affected   **TCustomImageList, TImageList**

Purpose   The **BlendColor** property is used to determine which foreground color to use when an image is rendered. A value of **clNone** indicates that there is no blend color, whereas **clDefault** indicates that the system highlight color should be used for the foreground color.

Declaration

```
property BlendColor;
```

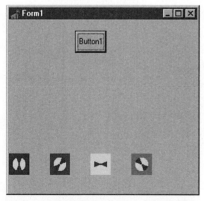

Figure 35-2   Illustration of masked region with **BkColor** set to **clNavy**

Example Syntax

```
    .
    .
ImageList1.BlendColor := clFuchsia;
    .
    .
```

Description

The **BlendColor** property operates in conjuction with the **DrawingStyle** parameter as follows. If the masked image **DrawingStyle** is set to **dsFocused**, then those regions in the image not masked out will be blended 75% from the original image and 25% **BlendColor**. If the masked image **DrawingStyle** is set to **dsSelected**, then the blending will be 50% original image and 50% **BlendColor**. If the image is not masked, or the **DrawingStyle** is not one of the two styles mentioned, this property will have no effect on the image.

Clear METHOD

Objects Affected	**TCustomImageList**, **TImageList**
Purpose	This method is used to remove all images from the image list and return it to an empty condition.
Declaration	

```
procedure Clear;
```

Example Syntax	See the example for the **Add** method.
Description	See the description for the **Add** method.

Count PROPERTY

Objects Affected	**TCustomImageList**, **TImageList**, **TGlyphList**
Purpose	This property is used to provide a count of the actual number of images present in the image list.
Declaration	

```
property Count: Integer
```

Example Syntax

```
function TForm1.Images(theImgLst:TImageList): Integer;
var
    imageCount:Integer;
begin
    imageCount := theImgLst.Count;
end;
```

Description

This property returns the number of images contained in an image list which is passed as a parameter to the function.

Create METHOD

Objects Affected	TCustomImageList, TImageList, TGlyphList
Purpose	This method is the object constructor for the **TCustomImageList** components and their descendants. In the case of **TCustomImageList** and **TImageList**, the first form is used as shown in the Declaration section below. This is the standard form for a Delphi component. The second form of **Create** is utilized by the **TGlyphList**, which allows two arguments indicating the size for the images to be specified at object creation time. Note that, in the first case shown below, the image size is defaulted to 16 pixels on each side.

Declaration

```
constructor Create(AOwner: TComponent); override; {TCustomImageList, ⇐
TImageList}
constructor Create(AWidth, AHeight: Integer); {TGlyphList}
```

Example Syntax

```
procedure TForm1.Button1Click(Sender: TObject);
var
    tempImgLst:TImageList;

begin

    tempImgLst := TImageList.Create(Form1);

    tempImgList.Assign(ImageList1);
{
.
.intermediate steps
.
.}

....tempImgList.Clear;
    tempImgList.Free; { return temporary image list to system }

end;
```

Description	This example illustrates how to create an image list dynamically at run time. Note that the list resources are cleared and released using the **Clear** method and the **Free** method when the image list is no longer needed.

CreateSize METHOD

Objects Affected	TCustomImageList, TImageList
Purpose	The **CreateSize** method is an alternative constructor method and can be used to create an instance of **TCustomImageList** or **TImageList** in which the image size differs from the default value of 16×16.

Declaration

```
constructor CreateSize(AWidth, AHeight: Integer);
```

Example Syntax

```
procedure TForm1.Button1Click(Sender: TObject);
var
    tempImgLst:TImageList;

begin

    tempImgLst := TImageList.CreateSize(32,32);

    tempImgList.Assign(ImageList1);
{
.
.intermediate steps
.
.}

....tempImgList.Clear;
    tempImgList.Free; { return temporary image list to system }

end;
```

Description

This example illustrates how to create an image list dynamically at run time using the **CreateSize** method. In this example the image list will be capable of holding images of 32×32 pixels, which is large enough to contain icon-sized images. Note that the list resources are cleared and released using the **Clear** method and the **Free** method when the image list is no longer needed.

Delete METHOD

Objects Affected TCustomImageList, TImageList, TGlyphList

Purpose Used to delete a particular image from an image list.

Declaration

```
procedure Delete(Index: Integer);
```

Example Syntax

```
procedure TForm1.Button1Click(Sender: TObject);
var
    theBits:TBitmap;
    theMask:TBitmap;
begin
    theBits := TBitmap.Create;
    theMask := TBitmap.Create;
    theBits.Height := 32;
    theBits.Width := 32;
    theMask.Height := 32;
    theMask.Width := 32;
```

continued on next page

continued from previous page

```
            theMask.LoadFromFile('c:\temp\MASK.BMP');

            theBits.LoadFromFile('c:\temp\SPIN1.BMP');
            ImageList1.Add(theBits,theMask);

            theBits.LoadFromFile('c:\temp\SPIN2.BMP');
            ImageList1.Add(theBits,theMask);

            theBits.LoadFromFile('c:\temp\SPIN3.BMP');
            ImageList1.Add(theBits,theMask);

            theBits.LoadFromFile('c:\temp\SPIN4.BMP');
            ImageList1.Add(theBits,theMask);

            { The next line illustrates the use of the Assign method}
            ImageList2.Assign(ImageList1);

            ImageList2.Delete(1);

            ImageList2.Draw(Form1.Canvas,0,200,0);
            ImageList2.Draw(Form1.Canvas,64,200,1);
            ImageList2.Draw(Form1.Canvas,128,200,2);

            theMask.Destroy;
            theBits.Destroy;

        end;
```

Description   This example is similar to the example for the **Assign** method. There is an additional call to the **Delete** method to cause the removal of the image at location 1 in the image list. Thus, only three images are available for rendering on the form canvas since there are only three calls to the **Draw** method.

Destroy METHOD

Objects Affected   TCustomImageList, TImageList, TGlyphList

Purpose   Standard object destructor. Used to return object and internal resources to the Delphi run-time system. The **Destroy** method correctly returns all system resources utilized by the component. In addition, if changes have been registered with the image list when it is destroyed, they will automatically be un-registered so that dangling references are not left intact.

Declaration

```
destructor Destroy; override;
```

Example Syntax   See example for **Create** method.

Description   See description for **Create** method.

DragCursor PROPERTY

Objects Affected   `TCustomImageList, TImageList`

Purpose   Used to indicate what the mouse cursor should look like when the cursor hot spot is located on a control that can accept an object being dragged. The legal values are shown in Table 35-4.

Table 35-4 List of legal DragCursor property values

DragCursor values

crDefault	crSizeNESW	crHourglass
crArrow	crSizeNS	crDrag
crCross	crSizeNWSE	crNoDrop
crIBeam	crSizeWE	crHSplit
crSize	crUpArrow	crVSplit

Declaration

```
property DragCursor: TCursor
```

Example Syntax

```
procedure TForm1.FormMouseDown(Sender: TObject; Button: TMouseButton;
  Shift: TShiftState; X, Y: Integer);
begin
    ImageList1.SetDragImage(0,15,15);
    ImageList1.BeginDrag(Form1.Handle,X,Y);
    ImageList1.ShowDragImage;
    ImageList1.DragCursor := crDrag; {added to change cursor image}
end;
```

Description   This example is modified from the `BeginDrag` example in which an additional call to the `DragCursor` method is made. The call to `DragCursor` has the effect of causing one of the standard cursors from the previous list to be placed at the hot spot defined by the `SetDragImage` method.

Dragging PROPERTY

Objects Affected   `TCustomImageList, TImageList`

Purpose   The `Dragging` property indicates whether a control is being dragged. If the value of `Dragging` is `True`, the control is being dragged. If the value of `Dragging` is `False`, the control is not being dragged.

Declaration

```
property Dragging: Boolean {read only}
```

Example Syntax   See `DragMove` example.

Description   See `DragMove` description.

DragLock METHOD

Objects Affected   TCustomImageList, TImageList

Purpose   The `DragLock` method is used to associate the specified image with the given window handle. The indexed image is drawn at the position given by the parameters *XPos* and *YPos* while the window is in Drag mode. The method returns `True` if successful.

Declaration

```
function DragLock(Window: HWND; XPos, YPos: Integer): Boolean;
```

Example Syntax

```
procedure TForm1.FormMouseDown(Sender: TObject; Button: TMouseButton;
  Shift: TShiftState; X, Y: Integer);
begin
    ImageList1.SetDragImage(0,15,15);
    ImageList1.DragLock(Form1.Handle,X,Y);
    ImageList1.ShowDragImage;
end;
```

Description   This example illustrates the use of the `DragLock` method to associate an image with a window at the onset of a dragging operation. Note that similar operations are performed internally by the `BeginDrag` method. Generally, the combination of three calls shown above could be replaced by a single call to `BeginDrag`, although it is more limited in capability. (See the description for `BeginDrag` previously in this chapter.)

DragMove METHOD

Objects Affected   TCustomImageList, TImageList

Purpose   The `DragMove` method is used to move the drag image to a new position specified by *X* and *Y* within its currently associated window while the window is in Drag mode. The drag image is that image selected by the initial `DragLock` method call. It returns `True` if successful.

Declaration

```
function DragMove(X, Y: Integer): Boolean;
```

Example Syntax

```
procedure TForm1.FormMouseMove(Sender: TObject; Shift: TShiftState; X,
  Y: Integer);
begin
    if ImageList1.Dragging then
        ImageList1.DragMove(X,Y);
end;
```

Description
This example illustrates the use of the `DragMove` method to cause the drag image location to be updated with changes in mouse movement across the form involved. Refer to the `DragDemo` project on the distribution disk for working code related to the use of `DragMove`.

DragUnlock METHOD

Objects Affected
TCustomImageList, TImageList

Purpose
The `DragUnlock` method terminates the association between the drag image and a window originally selected by a previous call to `DragLock`. This method directly deals with the Windows NT/95 support for image lists, but doesn't update internal states of the image list component. As a result, `DragUnlock` should only be used in combination with `DragLock`. If a call is made to `BeginDrag`, followed by a call to `DragUnlock` to terminate a drag operation, the image list component can be left in an inappropriate state.

Declaration

```
procedure DragUnlock;
```

Example Syntax

```
procedure TForm1.FormMouseUp(Sender: TObject; Button: TMouseButton;
  Shift: TShiftState; X, Y: Integer);
begin
    ImageList1.DragUnlock;
end;
```

Description
This example shows the use of the `DragUnlock` method to terminate a dragging operation on a window.

Draw METHOD

Objects Affected
TCustomImageList, TImageList

Purpose
The `Draw` method is used to draw the specified image as indicated by the value of *Index* on a canvas specified by the *Canvas* parameter. The upper-left corner of the image is drawn at the location specified by the *XLoc* and *YLoc* parameters.

Declaration

```
procedure Draw(Canvas: TCanvas; X, Y, Index: Integer);
```

Example Syntax
See the example for the **Add** method.

Description
See the description for the **Add** method.

DrawingStyle PROPERTY

Objects Affected	TCustomImageList, TImageList
Purpose	The DrawingStyle property specifies the style to be used when the ImageList is drawing an image. These are the possible values:

Value	Meaning
dsFocus	Draws the image blending 25% with the system highlight color. This only affects image lists that contain masks.
dsSelected	Draws the image blending 50% with the system highlight color. This only affects image lists that contain masks.
dsNormal	Draws the image using the color specified in the BkColor property. If the BkColor is clNone, then the image is drawn transparently using the mask.
dsTransparent	Draws using the mask regardless of the BkColor setting.

Declaration

```
property DrawingStyle;
```

Example Syntax

```
    .
    .
    .    ImageList1.DrawingStyle := dsSelected;
```

Description

This property is used to determine the appearance of an image when it is rendered on a canvas. Figure 35-3 illustrates the effect the different settings have with the BkColor property set to clNavy and the BlendColor property set to clFuchsia. The four renderings of the spinner icon are drawn with the DrawingStyle property set to dsFocus, dsSelected, dsNormal, and dsTransparent, respectively from left to right.

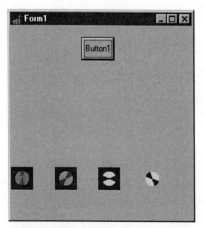

Figure 35-3 Effect of DrawingStyle settings

DrawOverlay METHOD

Objects Affected	`TCustomImageList, TImageList`
Purpose	The `DrawOverlay` method is used to draw an image and an overlay onto the specified canvas. To use an image as an overlay, the `Overlay` method must be called for the image first. (See `Overlay` description.)

Declaration

```
procedure DrawOverlay(Canvas: TCanvas; X, Y: Integer; ImageIndex:⇐
Integer; Overlay: TOverlay);
```

Example Syntax

```
procedure TForm1.Button1Click(Sender: TObject);
var
    theBits:TBitmap;
    theMask:TBitmap;
begin
    theBits := TBitmap.Create;
    theMask := TBitmap.Create;
    theBits.Height := 32;
    theBits.Width := 32;
    theMask.Height := 32;
    theMask.Width := 32;
    theMask.LoadFromFile('MASK.BMP');

    theBits.LoadFromFile('SPIN1.BMP');
    ImageList1.Add(theBits,theMask);

    theBits.LoadFromFile('OVLY1.BMP');
    ImageList1.AddMasked(theBits,theBits.Canvas.Pixels[0,0]);

    ImageList1.Overlay(1,0);
    ImageList1.DrawOverlay(Form1.Canvas,128,200,0,0);

    theMask.Destroy;
    theBits.Destroy;

end;
```

Description

This example loads two images from disk and adds them to the specified image list component. The second image is set up as an overlay image to be referenced as overlay 0. Finally, the images are combined using the `DrawOverlay` method in which the first image is drawn at specified coordinates, then the second image is placed on top of the first image at the same location. Figure 35-4 shows the results of running the above code. Note the overlay of the elliptical region over the top of the spin wheel in the center of the image.

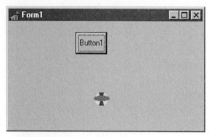

Figure 35-4 Example of use of the `DrawOverlay` method

EndDrag METHOD

Objects Affected	`TCustomImageList`, `TImageList`
Purpose	The `EndDrag` method is used to unconditionally terminate a drag operation. If the *Drop* parameter is `True`, the object being dragged is dropped. If the *Drop* parameter is `False`, the object is not dropped and dragging is canceled. Note that this particular implementation of `EndDrag`, unlike some other class implementations of `EndDrag` in the VCL component library, accepts no parameters.

Declaration

```
function EndDrag: Boolean;
```

Example Syntax

```
procedure TForm1.FormMouseUp(Sender: TObject; Button: TMouseButton;
  Shift: TShiftState; X, Y: Integer);
begin
   ImageList1.HideDragImage;
   ImageList1.EndDrag;
end;
```

Description   This is the preferred method to terminate a dragging operation with an image list component since it not only calls `DragUnlock` internally, but it also correctly manages the internal state variables of the image list that work in conjunction with other dragging operations. This method should always be paired with a `BeginDrag` call, which internally makes the appropriate call to the `DragLock` method.

FileLoad METHOD

Objects Affected	`TCustomImageList`, `TImageList`
Purpose	The `FileLoad` method is used to load a file of type `TResType` into the image list. *MaskColor* is used to set the transparent color for the images in the file. The possible values for *ResType* are `rtBitmap`, `rtIcon`, or

rtCursor. The name is a string representing the desired file that contains the image of the type specified by the *ResType* argument. *MaskColor* specifies the value of the color in the specified image file that will be masked when the image is rendered.

Declaration

```
function FileLoad(ResType: TResType; Name: string; MaskColor: TColor):⇐
Boolean;
```

Example Syntax

```
procedure TForm1.Button1Click(Sender: TObject);
begin

    ImageList1.FileLoad(rtBitmap,'Spin1.Bmp',RGB(0,0,0));
    ImageList1.FileLoad(rtBitmap,'Spin2.Bmp',RGB(0,0,0));
    ImageList1.FileLoad(rtBitmap,'Spin3.Bmp',RGB(0,0,0));
    ImageList1.FileLoad(rtBitmap,'Spin4.Bmp',RGB(0,0,0));

    ImageList1.Draw(Form1.Canvas,0,200,0);
    ImageList1.Draw(Form1.Canvas,64,200,1);
    ImageList1.Draw(Form1.Canvas,128,200,2);
    ImageList1.Draw(Form1.Canvas,192,200,3);

end;
```

Description

This example uses the FileLoad method to retrieve some bitmap images from disk directly into the image list. Compare this to the Add method. In this case, however, you can only mask a single color as a result of the load. Thus, if you intend to use this method with images that must be masked, you should pick a unique color to be placed in the image where you want the masking to take place or, if you don't want any masking to take place, pick a color that doesn't appear in the image when you make the call to FileLoad.

GetBitmap METHOD

Objects Affected	TCustomImageList, TImageList
Purpose	The GetBitmap method is used to return the image specified by the *Index* parameter as a bitmap into the specified TBitmap object (the *Image* parameter).

Declaration

```
procedure GetBitmap(Index: Integer; Image: TBitmap);
```

Example Syntax

```
procedure TForm1.Button1Click(Sender: TObject);
var
    aBitmap:TBitmap;
begin
```

continued on next page

continued from previous page

```
        aBitmap := TBitmap.Create;
        aBitmap.Height := 32;
        aBitmap.Width := 32;

        ImageList1.FileLoad(rtBitmap,'Spin1.Bmp',RGB(0,0,0));
        ImageList1.GetBitmap(0,aBitmap);
        aBitmap.SaveToFile('temp.bmp');
    end;
```

Description

This example demonstrates the use of the `GetBitmap` method to retrieve an image bitmap from the image list component and save it to a file. This bitmap can then be used elsewhere.

GetHotSpot METHOD

Objects Affected TCustomImageList, TImageList

Purpose The `GetHotSpot` method is used to obtain the location of the hot spot in the current drag image.

Declaration

```
function GetHotSpot: TPoint;
```

Example Syntax

```
procedure TForm1.FormMouseMove(Sender: TObject; Shift: TShiftState; X,
  Y: Integer);
var
   theHotSpot:TPoint;
begin
    if ImageList1.Dragging then
    begin
        ImageList1.DragMove(X,Y);
        theHotSpot :=ImageList1.GetHotSpot;
    end;
end;
```

Description

This method obtains the location of the hot spot of the drag image specified when the `DragLock` method was called to start the drag operation. Note that if `DragLock` was actually invoked indirectly via a call to `BeginDrag`, then the hot spot will be set to [0,0] automatically. The hot spot might be used to position a component correctly at the end of a drag operation by offsetting the position of the object being dragged by adding the location of the hot spot to the final *X, Y* location of the drag image.

GetIcon METHOD

Objects Affected TCustomImageList, TImageList

Purpose The `GetIcon` method is used to return the image indicated by the *Index* parameter as an icon into the provided *TIcon* parameter.

Declaration

```
procedure GetIcon(Index: Integer; Image: TIcon);
```

Example Syntax

```
procedure TForm1.Button1Click(Sender: TObject);
var
    anIcon:TIcon;
begin

    anIcon := TBitmap.Create;
    anIcon.Height := 32;
    anIcon.Width := 32;

    ImageList1.FileLoad(rtBitmap,'Spin1.Bmp',RGB(0,0,0));
    ImageList1.GetIcon(0,anIcon);
    anIcon.SaveToFile('temp.ico');
end;
```

Description

This example demonstrates the use of the `GetIcon` method to retrieve an icon image from the image list component and save it to a file. This icon file can then be used elsewhere.

GetImageBitmap METHOD

Objects Affected	`TCustomImageList`, `TImageList`
Purpose	The `GetImageBitmap` method is used to obtain a handle to a bitmap containing all the images in the `ImageList`.

Declaration

```
function GetImageBitmap: HBITMAP;
```

Example Syntax

```
procedure TForm1.Button1Click(Sender: TObject);
var
    theIcon:TIcon;
begin
    theIcon := TIcon.Create;
    ImageList1.FileLoad(rtBitmap,'Spin1.Bmp',RGB(0,0,0));
    ImageList1.GetIcon(0,theIcon);
    theIcon.SaveToFile('Spinx.ico');
    theIcon.Destroy;
end;
```

Description

This method effectively converts a bitmap to an icon image by using `FileLoad` with a type of `rtBitmap` specified to load a bitmap image, then using `GetIcon` to retrieve the image just loaded as an `Icon` type image, then finally saving the icon to disk using the `SaveToFile` method of the `TIcon` class.

GetInstRes METHOD

Objects Affected	All descendants of `TCustomImageList`
Purpose	The `GetInstRes` method is used to add an image to the image list by using a resource identifier to fetch the desired image resource from the application resource pool.

Declaration

```
function GetInstRes( Instance: THandle;  ResType: TResType; Name:
string;              Width: Integer; LoadFlags: TLoadResources;
MaskColor: TColor):  Boolean;
```

Example Syntax

```
function ResLoad(Rt: TResType; Name: string; Mc: TColor; w:integer):
Boolean;
begin
  Result := GetInstRes(MainInstance, Rt, Name, Width, [], Mc);
end;
```

Description   This function returns `True` if the resource of type `Rt` and name *Name* is found in the `MainInstance` resource pool. If found, the corresponding image is added to the image list. The `TResType` is defined as follows:
`TResType = (rtBitmap, rtCursor, rtIcon);`

GetMaskBitmap METHOD

Objects Affected	TCustomImageList, TImageList
Purpose	The `GetMaskBitmap` method is used to obtain a handle to a bitmap containing all the masks for images in the `ImageList`.

Declaration

```
function GetMaskBitmap: HBITMAP;
```

Example Syntax

```
procedure TForm1.Button1Click(Sender: TObject);
var
   theBits:HBITMAP;
begin
   ImageList1.FileLoad(rtBitmap,'Spin1.Bmp',RGB(0,0,0));
   theBits := ImageList1.GetMaskBitmap;
end;
```

Description   This method demonstrates the use of the `GetMaskBitmap` to fetch the handle to the bitmap images used internally by the `TCustomImageList` descendants. This bitmap represents the actual bitmap of the masks associated with each image in the image list. This method might be used with various Windows 95 API functions that expect a handle to a bitmap as an argument.

GetResource **Method**

Objects Affected   TCustomImageList, TImageList

Purpose   The GetResource method is used to load an image specified by the *Name* parameter, with the specified *ResType*, and *MaskColor* into the ImageList using the specified *LoadFlags*. The possible values for the *LoadFlags* parameter are listed in Table 35-2.

Value	Meaning
LrNone	No specific resource flags.
LrDefaultColor	Use the color format of the display.
LrDefaultSize	Use system metrics for height and width if the *Width* parameter to GetResource is 0. If the *Width* parameter is 0 and this option is not specified for cursors and icons, the resource's width and height will be used.
LrFromFile	Loads the resource from the specified file.
LrMap3DColors	Replaces the image's gray shades with the 3D window colors.
LrTransparent	Replaces the color table entry for the first pixel of the resource with the default window color (COLOR_WINDOW). This applies only to images with color tables.
LrMonoChrome	Loads the resource as black and white.

Declaration

```
function GetResource(ResType: TResType; Name: string; Width: Integer;
LoadFlags: TLoadResources; MaskColor: TColor): Boolean;
```

Example Syntax

```
procedure TForm1.Button1Click(Sender: TObject);
var
    Res:boolean;
begin
    Res := ImageList1.GetResource(rtBitmap, FName, FWidth, [lrFromFile],
RGB(0,0,0));
end;
```

Description   This example is used to load a resource into the image list. In this case, since *rtBitmap* is specified, the function will expect that the *FName* will be the name of a bitmap resource, and since the load flag is specified as [lrFromFile], the resource will be fetched from the file name contained in the *FName* parameter which, in this case, is assumed to be a variable declared in the **Form** declaration section under the private or public section and would have been specified elsewhere, as would *FWidth*. The specification of RGB(0,0,0) for the mask color indicates that all black pixels in the image should be masked.

Handle PROPERTY

Objects Affected TCustomImageList, TImageList

Purpose The **Handle** property returns a handle to the Windows **ImageList** object so it can be used with various Windows API functions that might require it. If no **Handle** exists at the time this property is read, one is created automatically.

Declaration

```
property Handle: HImageList read GetHandle write SetHandle;
```

Example Syntax

```
procedure TForm1.Button1Click(Sender: TObject);
var
   Res:boolean;
   Image:TIcon;
begin
   Image := TIcon.Create;
   Res := Image.LoadFromFile('Foo.Bar');
   if Res = True then
      Res := ImageList_AddIcon(ImageList1.Handle, Image.Handle);
   Image.free;
end;
```

Description This example illustrates the use of the **Handle** property with a direct call to a Windows 95 internal API function. In this case, a call to **ImageList_AddIcon** requires a handle to an **ImageList** object as an argument. This is an example of the kind of things that are done extensively in the actual controls unit that defines the behavior of the **TCustomImageList** descendants.

HandleAllocated METHOD

Objects Affected TCustomImageList, TImageList

Purpose The **HandleAllocated** method returns **True** if a window handle for the control exists. If no window handle exists, **HandleAllocated** returns **False**. This call neither creates nor destroys the control handle.

Declaration

```
function HandleAllocated: Boolean;
```

Example Syntax

```
procedure TForm1.Button1Click(Sender: TObject);
var
   Res:boolean;
   Image:TIcon;
begin
   if ImageList1.HandleAllocated = False then
   begin
      Image := TIcon.Create;
```

```
        Res := Image.LoadFromFile('Foo.Bar');
        if Res = True then
            Res := ImageList_AddIcon(ImageList1.Handle, Image.Handle);
        Image.free;
    end;
end;
```

Description This example makes a query to **HandleAllocated** to determine if the image list has been initialized as desired. If no **ImageList** handle is associated with the control internally, then the image list must be initialized and the appropriate action is taken.

Height PROPERTY

Objects Affected	TCustomImageList, TImageList
Purpose	This property is used to read or write the height of images stored in the **ImageList** component. If the value is changed by a write operation from a previous value, the **ImageList** object will be cleared automatically.
Declaration	

```
property Height;
```

Example Syntax	See **Add** method syntax example.
Description	See **Add** method description.

HideDragImage Method

Objects Affected	TCustomImageList, TImageList
Purpose	This method causes the **DragImage** to be made invisible if it is visible.
Declaration	

```
procedure HideDragImage;
```

Example Syntax	See **EndDrag** method.
Description	See **EndDrag** method.

ImageType PROPERTY

Objects Affected	TCustomImageList, TImageList
Purpose	The **ImageType** property determines whether the image list will use the image or the associated image mask when drawing. The possible values are **itImage** or **itMask**.
Declaration	

```
property ImageType;
```

Example Syntax

```
procedure TForm1.Button1Click(Sender: TObject);
var
   theBits:TBitmap;
   theMask:TBitmap;
begin
   theBits := TBitmap.Create;
   theMask := TBitmap.Create;
   theBits.Height := 32;
   theBits.Width := 32;
   theMask.Height := 32;
   theMask.Width := 32;

   theMask.LoadFromFile('MASK.BMP');
   theBits.LoadFromFile('SPIN1.BMP');

   ImageList1.Clear;
   ImageList1.Add(theBits,theMask);
   ImageList1.ImageType := itMask;
   ImageList1.Draw(Form1.Canvas,0,200,0);

   theMask.Destroy;
   theBits.Destroy;

end;
```

Description   This example is similar to the example presented for the **Add** method with the modification that the **ImageType** property is set to **itMask** to cause the corresponding image mask to be drawn when the **Draw** method is called.

Insert METHOD

Objects Affected   TCustomImageList, TImageList

Purpose   This method is used to insert a new image and mask at the location specified by index in the list. If an image already occupies the specified location, then it will be pushed down one location in the list, as will all other images that follow the insertion point.

Declaration

```
procedure Insert(Index: Integer; Image, Mask: TBitmap);
```

Example Syntax

```
procedure TForm1.Button1Click(Sender: TObject);
var
   theBits:TBitmap;
   theMask:TBitmap;
begin
   theBits := TBitmap.Create;
   theMask := TBitmap.Create;
   theBits.Height := 32;
   theBits.Width := 32;
   theMask.Height := 32;
   theMask.Width := 32;
   theMask.LoadFromFile('MASK.BMP');
```

```
theBits.LoadFromFile('SPIN1.BMP');
ImageList1.Add(theBits,theMask);

theBits.LoadFromFile('SPIN2.BMP');
ImageList1.Add(theBits,theMask);

theBits.LoadFromFile('SPIN3.BMP');
ImageList1.Add(theBits,theMask);

ImageList2.Clear;

{ The next line illustrates the use of the Assign method}
ImageList2.Assign(ImageList1);

theBits.LoadFromFile('SPIN4.BMP');
ImageList2.Insert(2,theBits,theMask);

ImageList2.Draw(Form1.Canvas,0,200,0);
ImageList2.Draw(Form1.Canvas,64,200,1);
ImageList2.Draw(Form1.Canvas,128,200,2);
ImageList2.Draw(Form1.Canvas,192,200,3);

theMask.Destroy;
theBits.Destroy;

end;
```

Description   This example demonstrates the use of the **Insert** method to place an image and a mask at a specified location in an image list. A number of images are loaded from disk. Then that image list is assigned to another image list, then, before the images are drawn, a final image is added at location 2 in the second image list.

InsertIcon METHOD

Objects Affected   TCustomImageList, TImageList

Purpose   This method is used to insert a new icon at the location specified by the index in the list. If an image already occupies the specified location, then it will be pushed down by one location in the list as will all other images that follow the insertion point.

Declaration

```
procedure InsertIcon(Index: Integer; Image: TIcon);
```

Example Syntax

```
procedure TForm1.Button1Click(Sender: TObject);
var
    theIcon:TIcon;
begin
    theIcon := TIcon.Create;

    theIcon.LoadFromFile('SPIN1.ICO');

    ImageList1.Clear;
```

continued on next page

continued from previous page

```
                        ImageList1.AddIcon(theIcon);

                ...theIcon.LoadFromFile('SPIN2.ICO');
                        ImageList1.InsertIcon(0,theIcon);

                        ImageList1.Draw(Form1.Canvas,0,200,0);
                        ImageList1.Draw(Form1.Canvas,64,200,1);

                        theIcon.Destroy;

                end;
```

Description   Initially an icon is added to an empty image list, then a second icon is
                       loaded from disk and inserted at the head of the image list, causing it to
                       have index 0 and the first icon to assume an index value of 1.

InsertMasked METHOD

Objects Affected   `TCustomImageList, TImageList`

Purpose   This method is used to insert a new image at the location specified by the
                       index in the list. The new image will have a corresponding mask created in
                       which the mask pixel values are determined by the pixels in the specified
                       image that match the *MaskColor* parameter. If an image already occupies
                       the specified location, then it will be pushed down by one location in the
                       list as will all other images that follow the insertion point.

Declaration

```
procedure InsertMasked(Index: Integer; Image: TBitmap; ⇐
MaskColor: TColor);
```

Example Syntax

```
procedure TForm1.Button1Click(Sender: TObject);
var
    theBits:TBitmap;
begin
    theBits := TBitmap.Create;
    theBits.Height := 32;
    theBits.Width := 32;

    theBits.LoadFromFile('SPINM.BMP');
    ImageList1.AddMasked(theBits,theBits.Canvas.Pixels[0,0]);

...theBits.LoadFromFile('SPIN1.BMP');
    ImageList1.InsertMasked(0,theBits,theBits.Canvas.Pixels[0,0]);

    ImageList1.Draw(Form1.Canvas,0,200,0);
    ImageList1.Draw(Form1.Canvas,64,200,1);

    theBits.Destroy;
end;
```

Description	Initially an image is added to an empty image list, then a second image is loaded from disk and inserted at the head of the image list, causing it to have index 0 and the first icon to assume an index value of 1. Both of the images use the upper-left corner pixel value as the color used to generate the accompanying mask.

Masked PROPERTY

Object Affected	`TCustomImageList`, `TImageList`
Purpose	This property returns a value of `True` if the image list contains transparent images or a value of `False` if the image list contains nontransparent images.
Declaration	

```
property Masked;
```

Example Syntax	

```
procedure TForm1.Button1Click(Sender: TObject);
var
   imt : TImageType;
begin
   imt := ImageList1.ImageType;
   if ImageList1.Masked = True then
      ImageList1.ImageType := itMask;
   ImageList1.Draw(Form1.Canvas,0,200,0);
   ImageList1.ImageType := imt;
   end;
end;
```

Description	This example queries the value of the `Masked` property and if it is `True` sets the value of the `ImageType` to `itMasked` (see description of `ImageType` property), then draws the image `ImageType` at location 0 in the image list. This will cause the mask to be drawn instead of the image. Then the method returns the value of `ImageType` to the original value.

Move METHOD

Objects Affected	`TCustomImageList`, `TImageList`
Purpose	The `Move` method is used to move an image at a specified location to another location in the image list.
Declaration	

```
procedure Move(CurIndex, NewIndex: Integer);
```

Example Syntax	

```
procedure TForm1.Button1Click(Sender: TObject);
var
```

continued on next page

continued from previous page

```
                theBits:TBitmap;
                theMask:TBitmap;
            begin
                theBits := TBitmap.Create;
                theMask := TBitmap.Create;
                theBits.Height := 32;
                theBits.Width := 32;
                theMask.Height := 32;
                theMask.Width := 32;

                ImageList1.Clear;
                theMask.LoadFromFile('MASK.BMP');

                theBits.LoadFromFile('SPIN1.BMP');
                ImageList1.Add(theBits,theMask);
                theBits.LoadFromFile('SPIN2.BMP');
                ImageList1.Add(theBits,theMask);
                theBits.LoadFromFile('SPIN3.BMP');
                ImageList1.Add(theBits,theMask);
                ImageList1.Move(1,2);

                ImageList1.Draw(Form1.Canvas,0,200,0);
                ImageList1.Draw(Form1.Canvas,100,200,1);
                ImageList1.Draw(Form1.Canvas,200,200,2);

                theMask.Destroy;
                theBits.Destroy;


            end;
```

Description This example demonstrates the use of the **Move** method to reorder the contents of the image list. In this example three images are loaded from disk, then the middle image is moved to the beginning of the list, causing the final order of image files to be **SPIN2.BMP**, **SPIN1.BMP**, **SPIN3.BMP**.

OnChange EVENT

Objects Affected TCustomImageList, TImageList

Purpose The OnChange event handler is called anytime a change is made to the internal state of the image list component. Within this event handler, you can perform any actions that might be necessary when image list changes take place. You should never make changes to the image list itself within this event handler or an event cascade can take place, causing an infinite loop to be generated.

Overlay METHOD

Objects Affected TCustomImageList, TImageList

Purpose   The **Overlay** method is used to make the image located at **ImageIndex** usable as an overlay image. It is referenced as an overlay image by using the **Overlay** value (0...3) provided.

Declaration

```
function Overlay(ImageIndex: Integer; Overlay: TOverlay): Boolean;
```

Example Syntax   See the **DrawOverlay** example syntax for a method that uses the **Overlay** method.

Description   See the **DrawOverlay** description for further information.

RegisterChanges Method

Objects Affected   **TCustomImageList, TImageList**

Purpose   The **RegisterChanges** method is called by an object that wants to be informed when changes occur in the image list. The **TChangeLink**'s **OnChange** event will be called whenever a change in the image list occurs. This effectively allows another control to hook the image list component so that any changes that take place in the image control cause the **OnChange** event handler of the requestor to be invoked.

Declaration

```
procedure RegisterChanges(Value: TChangeLink);
```

Example Syntax

```
unit rchng;

interface

uses
  Windows, Messages, SysUtils, Classes, Graphics, Controls, Forms,
Dialogs,  ComCtrls, StdCtrls;

type
  TForm1 = class(TForm)
    ListView1: TListView;
    ImageList1: TImageList;
    Button1: TButton;
    procedure FormCreate(Sender: TObject);
    procedure Button1Click(Sender: TObject);
    procedure FormDestroy(Sender: TObject);
  private
    { Private declarations }
    theChangeLink:TChangeLink;
    procedure theChangeLinkChange(Sender :TObject);
  public
    { Public declarations }
  end;
```

continued on next page

continued from previous page

```
var
  Form1: TForm1;

implementation

{$R *.DFM}

procedure TForm1.FormCreate(Sender: TObject);
var
   theBits:TBitmap;
begin
  theBits := TBitmap.create;
  theBits.Height := 32;
  theBits.Width := 32;
  theBits.LoadFromFile('Spin1.bmp');
  ImageList1.Height := 32;
  ImageList1.Width := 32;
  ImageList1.AddMasked(theBits,theBits.Canvas.Pixels[0,0]);
  ListView1.LargeImages := ImageList1;
  theChangeLink := TChangeLink.Create;
  theChangeLink.OnChange := theChangeLinkChange;
  ImageList1.RegisterChanges(theChangeLink);
  theBits.free;
end;

procedure TForm1.Button1Click(Sender: TObject);
var
   theBits:TBitmap;
begin
  theBits := TBitmap.create;
  theBits.Height := 32;
  theBits.Width := 32;
  theBits.LoadFromFile('Spin2.bmp');

  ImageList1.ReplaceMasked(0,theBits,theBits.Canvas.Pixels[0,0]);
  theBits.Free;
end;

procedure TForm1.theChangeLinkChange(Sender :TObject);
begin
  ListView1.Font.Color := clRed;
end;

procedure TForm1.FormDestroy(Sender: TObject);
begin
   ImageList1.UnRegisterChanges(theChangeLink);
   theChangeLink.free;
end;

end.
```

Description   Because the **RegisterChanges** and **UnRegisterChanges** methods involve some complex programming, a complete example program is presented here to illustrate how one can register a change routine to be called any time a change takes place in an image list. In this project, a form was created that contained an image list component and a list view component.

The list view component has one item installed at design time. Notice that in the form declaration there is an object called `theChangeLink` declared with type `TChangeLink`. This is an object type that is used with the `RegisterChange` method. The `TChangeLink` object has an `OnChange` event handler that must be assigned to a procedure that is to be invoked any time the image list detects a change has occurred. That is the purpose of the procedure called `theChangeLinkChange` in the declaration section.

During the form creation process, a number of preparatory steps are performed. An image is added to the image list, and the `LargeIcons` property of the `ListView` is assigned to the image list. Most importantly, the `theChangeLink` object is created and the `theChangeLink.OnChange` event handler is assigned to the `theChangeLinkChange` procedure. Finally the `RegisterChanges` method of the image list is called with `theChangeLink` specified as the object to be notified when image list changes occur.

At this point the program displays the main form, which shows the `ListView` object with the image list image [0] displayed, along with the first item in the `ListView`, as shown in Figure 35-5.

When the pushbutton is depressed, a new image is loaded and is used to replace the original image in the image list. This causes a change to take place in the image list. Because a change handler has been registered with the `ImageList`, the `theChangeListChange` routine is invoked automatically. If you take a look at the `theChangeListChange` procedure in the unit you will see that it changes the color of the list view font to `clRed`. This, in fact, does take place in response to the press of the pushbutton. Figure 35-6 shows the result.

Last, when the program is terminating and the form is destroyed, the change handler is unlinked from the image list, then the `TChangeLink` object is freed as normal for dynamically created objects.

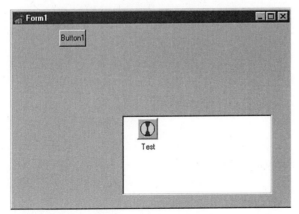

Figure 35-5 Example image prior to button push

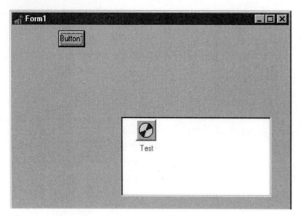

Figure 35-6 Example image after button push

If you would like to play around with this example, it is located on the distribution disk.

Replace METHOD

Objects Affected	TCustomImageList, TImageList
Purpose	The Replace method is used to replace an image and mask at a specified index location in the image list.
Declaration	

```
procedure Replace(Index: Integer; Image, Mask: TBitmap);
```

Example Syntax

```
procedure TForm1.Button1Click(Sender: TObject);
var
   theBits:TBitmap;
   theMask:TBitmap;
begin
   theBits := TBitmap.create;
   theBits.Height := 32;
   theBits.Width := 32;
   theMask := TBitmap.create;
   theMask.Height := 32;
   theMask.Width := 32;

   theBits.LoadFromFile('Spin2.bmp');
   theMask.LoadFromFile('SpinM.bmp');

   ImageList1.Replace(0,theBits,theMask);

   theBits.Free;
   theMask.Free;
end;
```

Description

This example illustrates the use of the `Replace` method to cause the image located at a specified index in the image list to be overwritten with another image and mask. This code obtains an image and corresponding mask from disk, then uses `Replace` to select image 0 for replacement.

ReplaceIcon METHOD

Objects Affected `TCustomImageList, TImageList`

Purpose The `ReplaceIcon` method is used to replace an icon at a specified index location in the image list.

Declaration

```
procedure ReplaceIcon(Index: Integer; Image: TIcon);
```

Example Syntax

```
procedure TForm1.Button1Click(Sender: TObject);
var
    theIcon:TIcon;
begin
    theIcon := TIcon.create;

    theIcon.LoadFromFile('Spin2.ico');

    ImageList1.ReplaceIcon(0,theIcon);

    theIcon.Free;
end
```

Description This example illustrates the use of the `ReplaceIcon` method to cause the image located at a specified index in the image list to be overwritten with another icon. This code obtains an icon from disk, then uses `ReplaceIcon` to select icon 0 for replacement.

ReplaceMasked METHOD

Objects Affected `TCustomImageList, TImageList`

Purpose The `ReplaceMasked` method is used to replace an image and mask at a specified index location in the image list. The mask inserted at the specified location is created by matching pixels in the *NewImage TBitmap* object to the *MaskColor* and setting the mask so that those pixels that match will be transparent when rendered.

Declaration

```
procedure ReplaceMasked(Index: Integer; NewImage: TBitmap; MaskColor:⇐
TColor);
```

Example Syntax

```
procedure TForm1.Button1Click(Sender: TObject);
var
    theBits:TBitmap;
begin
    theBits := TBitmap.create;
    theBits.Height := 32;
    theBits.Width := 32;

    theBits.LoadFromFile('Spin2.bmp');

    ImageList1.ReplaceMasked(0,theBits,theBits.Canvas.Pixels[0,0]);

    theBits.Free;
end;
```

Description   This example illustrates the use of the `ReplaceMasked` method to cause the image located at a specified index in the image list to be overwritten with another image and mask derived from the image pixels which match the upper-left corner of the bitmap itself. This code obtains an image from disk then uses `ReplaceMasked` to select image 0 for replacement.

ResInstLoad METHOD

Objects Affected   All descendants of `TCustomImageList`

Purpose   The `ResInstLoad` function is used to load an image resource from the main instance resource pool and add it to the end of the image list.

Declaration

```
function ResInstLoad(Instance: THandle; ResType: TResType; Name: string;
    MaskColor: TColor): Boolean;
```

Example Syntax

```
procedure LoadIcon(theImageList:TImageList;Name:string)
begin
    theImageList.ResInstLoad(MainInstance, rtIcon,
Name,RGB(255,255,255));
end;
```

Description   This example simplifies the loading of an icon image into an image list by the use of the `ResInstLoad` method. A `TImageList` object is supplied and the named resource is fetched from the main application resource pool with a white mask color specified. This function differs from the following method in that a handle to any application can be supplied as an argument to `ResInstLoad`.

ResourceLoad METHOD

Objects Affected   `TCustomImageList, TImageList`

Purpose	The `ResourceLoad` method is used to load a resource of type `TResType` into the `ImageList`. The *MaskColor* parameter is used to create the mask for the resulting image.
Declaration	

```
function ResourceLoad(ResType: TResType; Name: string;  MaskColor:
TColor): Boolean;
```

Example Syntax	This method is functionally the same as the `GetResource` method with an empty set specified for the *LoadFlags* parameter. (See `GetResource` for more information).
Description	See `GetResource` for more information.

SetDragImage METHOD

Objects Affected	`TCustomImageList, TImageList`
Purpose	The `SetDragImage` method is used to set the image specified by *Index* within the image list to be shown when the image list is being used for drag-and-drop. The hot spot of the image is determined by the value of *HotSpotX* and the value of *HotSpotY*.
Declaration	

```
function SetDragImage(Index, HotSpotX, HotSpotY: Integer): Boolean;
```

Example Syntax	See the `DragCursor` example syntax for a method that uses the `SetDragImage` method.
Description	See the `DragCursor` description.

ShareImages PROPERTY

Objects Affected	`TCustomImageList, TImageList`
Purpose	The `ShareImages` property is used to determine if the image list should destroy its handle when the image list is destroyed. If the property value is `True`, the handle will not be destroyed when the control is destroyed, and vice versa.
Declaration	

```
property ShareImages;
```

Example Syntax

```
procedure TForm1.Button1Click(Sender: TObject);
var
    tempImageList:TImageList;
begin
    ImageList1.FileLoad(rtBitmap,'Spin1.Bmp',RGB(0,0,0));
```

continued on next page

continued from previous page

```
            ImageList1.FileLoad(rtBitmap,'Spin2.Bmp',RGB(0,0,0));

            tempImageList := TImageList.Create;
            tempImageList.ShareImages := true;
            tempImageList.Handle := ImageList1.Handle;
        ...tempImageList.Draw(Form1.Canvas,0,200,0);
        ...tempImageList.free;

            ImageList1.Draw(Form1.Canvas,64,200,0);

        end;
```

Description   This example creates a temporary image list object dynamically, then assigns the image list handle of the newly created object to be equal to the handle of a previously initialized image list. The temporary image list is used to render an image, then it is deleted. Since the temporary image list `ShareImages` property was set to a value of `True`, when it is freed, the actual image bitmap is not destroyed and the original image list can still be used normally. This allows for certain special situations where different image list objects could share the same basic image bitmap, but have other internal settings different from each other, thus conserving memory utilization. In the case of Delphi 3, which runs under Windows 95, this may not be of much importance since memory limitations are not generally a problem.

ShowDragImage METHOD

Objects Affected   TCustomImageList, TImageList

Purpose   The `ShowDragImage` method will cause the current drag image to be displayed if it was previously hidden.

Declaration

```
procedure ShowDragImage;
```

Example Syntax   See the `DragCursor` method for an example that uses the `ShowDragImage` method.

Description   See the `DragCursor` description.

UnRegisterChanges METHOD

Objects Affected   TCustomImageList, TImageList

Purpose   The `UnRegisterChanges` method is used to unhook an `OnChange` event handler from the image list component, which was originally specified by a call to the `RegisterChanges` method. The *Value* parameter specifies which particular hook should be broken, as there can be more than one hook in existence at any particular time.

Declaration

```
procedure UnRegisterChanges(Value: TChangeLink);
```

Example Syntax   See the **RegisterChanges** example for more details.

Description   See the **RegisterChanges** example for more details.

Width PROPERTY

Objects Affected   **TCustomImageList, TImageList**

Purpose   This property is used to read or write the width of images stored in the **ImageList** component. If the value is changed by a write operation from a previous value, the **ImageList** object will be cleared automatically.

Declaration

```
property Width;
```

Example Syntax   See the **Add** method syntax example.

Description   See the **Add** method description.

Example Project

The example project for this chapter illustrates elementary use of the **TImageList** component to render some successive icon images that might be used to animate a spinning progress icon. In this example, however, the successive images are drawn sequentially next to each other so that they can be seen here. (It would be tough to get animation down on paper!) The form used for the project is shown in Figure 35-7.

Note that the form contains a **TImageList** component, a pushbutton which activates the code to be illustrated. The results of pressing the pushbutton in the program are shown in Figure 35-8. Note that this project also serves as a basis for some of the

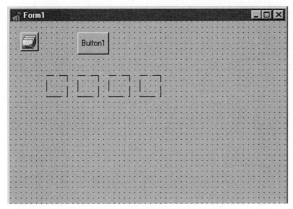

Figure 35-7   Form design for example project

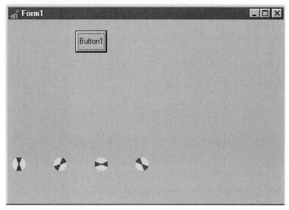

Figure 35-8 Results of pressing the pushbutton
while program is running

figures that appeared earlier in the chapter. If you wanted to experiment, for example
with DrawingStyle or BkColor, it would be easy to modify this program, which is
what was done to generate the figures which appeared above.

Listing 35-2 shows the code for the project:

Listing 35-2 Example project code listing

```
unit TILDemo;

interface

uses
  Windows, Messages, SysUtils, Classes, Graphics, Controls, Forms, Dialogs,
  StdCtrls, ExtCtrls;

type
  TForm1 = class(TForm)
    ImageList1: TImageList;
    Button1: TButton;
    procedure Button1Click(Sender: TObject);
  private
    { Private declarations }
  public
    { Public declarations }
  end;

var
  Form1: TForm1;

implementation

{$R *.DFM}

procedure TForm1.Button1Click(Sender: TObject);
var
```

```
    theBits:TBitmap;
    theMask:TBitmap;
begin
    theBits := TBitmap.Create;
    theMask := TBitmap.Create;
    theBits.Height := 32;
    theBits.Width := 32;
    theMask.Height := 32;
    theMask.Width := 32;
    theMask.LoadFromFile('MASK.BMP');

    theBits.LoadFromFile('SPIN1.BMP');
    ImageList1.Add(theBits,theMask);

    theBits.LoadFromFile('SPIN2.BMP');
    ImageList1.Add(theBits,theMask);

    theBits.LoadFromFile('SPIN3.BMP');
    ImageList1.Add(theBits,theMask);

    theBits.LoadFromFile('SPIN4.BMP');
    ImageList1.Add(theBits,theMask);

    ImageList1.Draw(Form1.Canvas,0,200,0);
    ImageList1.Draw(Form1.Canvas,64,200,1);
    ImageList1.Draw(Form1.Canvas,128,200,2);
    ImageList1.Draw(Form1.Canvas,192,200,3);

    theMask.Destroy;
    theBits.Destroy;

end;
```

When the button is pressed, the `Button1Click` handler is invoked by Delphi, which then performs the following operations. Two bitmaps are created, one to hold the desired bitmap images that will be read in from disk and one to hold the mask which will also be read in from disk. After the bitmap objects are created, the sizes are specified to match the images that will be read in from disk via a call to `LoadFromFile`—once for the image mask, and once for each separate image that will make up the animation sequence. After the `Mask` is read in, four images are loaded and added to the `ImageList` component, which then becomes the image repository used for later recall. Finally, after the bitmaps have been added to the `ImageList`, the `Draw` method of the `TImageList` component is used to render the animation sequence on the form at suitable locations for viewing. If this had been an actual animation, the images could have been drawn at the same location with a time delay between renderings to cause the animation effect. Last, after the images are rendered, the bitmap objects, which were dynamically created, are destroyed.

36

TDataSet AND ITS DESCENDANTS

Delphi's database access capabilities are provided through the **TDataSet** class. **TDataSet**, as the name suggests, represents sets of data as rows in a table, and provides both relational and navigational data access. **TDataSet** defines all fundamental record navigation and editing functions. A **TDBDataSet**, derived directly from **TDataSet**, represents datasets that are actually connected to a BDE (Borland Database Engine) database. Finally, **TDBDataSet** yields **TTable**, **TStoredProc**, and **TQuery**, the non-visual data access components found on the component palette.

> **IMPORTANT**
> The TDBDataSet, TTable, TStoredProc, and TQuery reference sections were omitted from this edition. For coverage of these, please refer to Borland's Reference Library Guide (RLG).

TDataSet

TDataSet encapsulates the relational concept of a set of data, which can more easily be thought of as a set of rows in a table. In a relational database, relations can roughly be thought of as tables. In more precise terms, a relation can be *represented* by a table (although the converse is not necessarily true). However, such a table must have certain properties, the foremost being that all rows contained in it must be unique. The **TDataSet** class is somewhat relaxed on these points, since it really is a wrapper around the BDE functionalities that let you interface with a number of different physical databases, from low-end desktop databases (like Paradox and dBASE) to high-end SQL database servers (like Oracle, Informix, and so on). Some of these databases are more (or less) relational than others. Therefore, the **TDataSet** class must allow for the broadest definition: It simply is a collection of rows in a table.

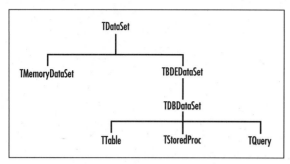

Figure 36-1 TDataSet branch of the VCL

The most significant functionality found in the **TDataSet** is given by methods and events letting you interact or control interaction with the underlying set of data.

Figure 36-1 shows the **TDataSet** branch of the VCL. Table 36-1 illustrates properties, methods, and events implemented by **TDataSet**.

Table 36-1 Properties, methods, and events implemented by TDataSet

Use or Set This. . .	To Do This. . .	Inheritance
Active	Get or set the TDataset's state.	None
ActiveBuffer	Access the TDataSet's active buffer.	None
AfterCancel	Custom processing after canceling a record edit.	None
AfterClose	Custom processing after the TDataSet's closing.	None
AfterDelete	Custom processing after deleting a record.	None
AfterEdit	Custom processing after entering edit mode.	None
AfterInsert	Custom processing after inserting a new record.	None
AfterOpen	Custom processing after opening the TDataSet.	None
AfterPost	Custom processing after posting a record edit.	None
Append	Append a new empty record at the end of the TDataSet.	None
AppendRecord	Append a new record giving some or all field values.	None
ApplyUpdates	Write to the database any changes to cached data.	None
AutoCalcFields	Establish to calculated fields automatically or not.	None
BOF	Check if at beginning of TDataSet.	None
BeforeCancel	Custom processing before canceling a record edit.	None
BeforeClose	Custom processing before closing the TDataSet.	None
BeforeDelete	Custom processing before deleting a record.	None
BeforeEdit	Custom processing before editing a record.	None
BeforeInsert	Custom processing before inserting a record.	None
BeforeOpen	Custom processing before opening a TDataSet.	None
BeforePost	Custom processing before posting a record.	None
Bookmark	Tag a record for easy retrieval.	None

Use or Set This. . .	To Do This. . .	Inheritance
CachedUpdates	Enable/disable cached updates.	None
CanModify	Check whether the TDataSet can be modified.	None
Cancel	Cancel the record editing.	None
CancelUpdates	Cancel pending cached updates.	None
CheckBrowseMode	Make sure TDataSet is in Browse mode.	None
ClearFields	Initialize the record buffer.	None
Close	Close the TDataSet.	None
CommitUpdates	Commit to the database any changes to cached data.	None
ControlsDisabled	Check if associated data-aware components are disabled.	None
CursorPosChanged	Notify that the BDE cursor's position has changed.	None
DataSource	Reference the TDataSet's master DataSource.	None
DefaultFields	Indicates whether the TDataSet has default fields or not.	None
Delete	Delete the current record.	None
DisableControls	Temporarily disable display update of associated data-aware components.	None
Edit	Activate Edit mode on the current record.	None
EnableControls	Enable display update of associated data-aware components.	None
EOF	Check if at end of TDataSet.	None
ExpIndex	Indicate whether index is a dBASE expression index.	None
FetchAll	Force a re-read of the entire result set of a query.	None
FieldByName	Retrieve a TField associated with a database field.	None
FieldCount	Retrieve the number of fields in the TDataSet.	None
FieldDefs	Retrieve the array of field definitions in the TDataSet.	None
FieldValues	Work with the array property of field values as variants.	None
Fields	Work with the array of TFields in the TDataSet.	None
Filter	Define a record filter expression.	None
FilterOptions	Set a filter's options.	None
Filtered	Activate/deactivate a filter.	None
FindField	Retrieve a TField associated with a database field.	None
FindFirst	Find the first record matching the filter criteria.	None
FindLast	Find the last record matching the filter criteria.	None
FindNext	Find the next record matching the filter criteria	None
FindPrior	Find the prior record matching the filter criteria.	None
First	Get to the first record of the TDataSet.	None
Found	Check whether there was a matching record.	None
FreeBookmark	Free a bookmark on the TDataSet.	None
GetBookmark	Set a bookmark on the TDataSet's current record.	None
GetCurrentRecord	Retrieve the TDataSet's current record into a memory buffer.	None
GetFieldList	Get a list of field objects given the physical field names.	None
GetFieldNames	Get a list of the physical field names in the TDataSet.	None
GotoBookmark	Go to a given bookmark.	None

continued on next page

continued from previous page

Use or Set This. . .	To Do This. . .	Inheritance
Handle	Access the BDE cursor handle associated with the TDataSet.	None
Insert	Go into insert mode and insert a new record.	None
InsertRecord	Insert a new record giving some or all field values.	None
IsLinkedTo	Inquire whether the TDataSet is linked to given data source.	None
KeySize	Retrieve the TDataSet's key size in bytes.	None
Last	Go to the last record in the TDataSet.	None
Locale	Retrieve a TDataSet's language driver.	None
Locate	Locate a record according to given field values.	None
Lookup	Look up specific fields according to given field values.	None
Modified	Check whether the record's data has been modified.	None
MoveBy	Move by a given number of records forward or backwards in the TDataSet.	None
Next	Go to the next record of the TDataSet.	None
OnCalcFields	Compute calculated field in the TDataSet.	None
OnDeleteError	Detect record deletion errors.	None
OnEditError	Detect record editing errors.	None
OnFilterRecord	Create custom record filtering.	None
OnNewRecord	Custom processing when inserting a new record.	None
OnPostError	Detect record posting errors.	None
OnServerYield	Cancel a long running query.	None
OnUpdateError	Detect errors when updating a record.	None
OnUpdateRecord	Custom processing when updating a record with cached updates.	None
Open	Open the TDataSet.	None
Post	Post a new or a modified record to the TDataSet.	None
Prior	Go to the prior record in the TDataSet.	None
RecNo	Retrieve the current record's record number.	None
RecordCount	Retrieve the number of records in the TDataSet.	None
RecordSize	Retrieve the record's footprint size in bytes.	None
Refresh	Re-read data from the database.	None
Resync	Resynchronize all records.	None
RevertRecord	Discard changes to current record with cached updates.	None
SetDetailFields	Set the TDataSet's key values given a list of master key field objects.	None
SetFields	Set some or all field values in the current record.	None
State	Retrieve the TDataSet's current state.	None
UpdateCursorPos	Update the TDataSet's cursor position.	None
UpdateObject	Control the TDataSet's associated cached updates SQL statements.	None
UpdateRecord	Notify data sources that a record update is about to be posted.	None
UpdateRecordTypes	Control the type of records updated via cached updates.	None
UpdateStatus	Inquire about the status of cached updates.	None
UpdatesPending	Inquire whether there are any pending cached updates.	None

Active PROPERTY

Objects Affected	TDataSet
Purpose	The `Active` property holds the current state of the `TDataSet`.
Declaration	

```
property Active: Boolean
```

Example Syntax

```
// The ActiveSpeedButton will toggle the CustomerTable on and off.
procedure TTDataSetTestForm.ActiveSpeedButtonClick(Sender: TObject);
begin
 CustomerTable.Active := Not CustomerTable.Active;
end;
```

Description   `Active` reports whether the `TDataSet` is open or not. By assigning a boolean to `Active`, you can change the state of `TDataSet`. You can use the `Open` or the `Close` methods to achieve the same result.

ActiveBuffer METHOD

Objects Affected	TDataSet
Purpose	The `ActiveBuffer` method returns a pointer to the currently active record buffer.
Declaration	

```
function ActiveBuffer: PChar;
```

Example Syntax

```
// Make a copy of the current record via ActiveBuffer.
procedure TTDataSetTestForm.ActiveBufferSpeedButtonClick(Sender: ⇐
TObject);
var
  TemporaryRecordCopy: PChar;
begin
  // Allocate memory.
  TemporaryRecordCopy := AllocMem( CustomerTable.RecordSize );
  try
    // Copy the current record to the temporary buffer
    Move
    (
      CustomerTable.ActiveBuffer^,
      TemporaryRecordCopy^,
      CustomerTable.RecordSize
    );
    // Here you can use temporary copy in some way...
    // ...for instance to insert a duplicate record into the table.
    CustomerTable.Append;
    Move
```

continued on next page

567

continued from previous page

```
      (
        TemporaryRecordCopy^,
        CustomerTable.ActiveBuffer^,
        CustomerTable.RecordSize
      );
      CustomerTable.FieldByName( 'CustNo' ).AsInteger := GetNewCustNo;
    finally
      // Free temporary copy
      FreeMem( TemporaryRecordCopy, CustomerTable.RecordSize );
    end;
  end;
```

Description The **TDataSet** object maintains a list of buffers. At any moment, one of these buffers is designated as the *active* buffer. The **ActiveBuffer** method returns a pointer to the currently active buffer of the **TDataSet**, such as a pointer to the in-memory copy (field by field) of the current record in the **TDataSet**.

AfterCancel EVENT

Objects Affected TDataSet

Purpose The **AfterCancel** event can refer to an event handler procedure in which you specify custom processing to perform after canceling a record edit.

Declaration

```
Type
  TDataSetNotifyEvent = procedure(DataSet: TDataSet) of object;

property AfterCancel: TDataSetNotifyEvent;
```

Example Syntax

```
// Assign or Deassign AfterCancel event handler according to
// corresponding check box.
procedure TTDataSetTestForm.AfterCancelCheckBoxClick(Sender: TObject);
begin
  if AfterCancelCheckBox.Checked
  then CustomerTable.AfterCancel := CustomerTableAfterCancel
  else CustomerTable.AfterCancel := Nil;
end;

// AfterCancel event handler procedure.
procedure TTDataSetTestForm.CustomerTableAfterCancel(DataSet: TDataSet);
begin
  MessageBeep( MB_ICONEXCLAMATION );
  MessageDlg( 'Changes were cancelled.', mtWarning, [ mbOK ], 0 );
end;
```

Description The **AfterCancel** event of a **TDataSet** is triggered when the insertion of new data or the editing of existing data is canceled in any way, either by the user's interaction or by the code invoking the **Cancel** method of the **TDataSet**.

AfterClose EVENT

Objects Affected	`TDataSet`
Purpose	The `AfterClose` event can refer to an event handler procedure in which you can specify custom processing to perform after closing the `TDataSet`.
Declaration	

```
Type
  TDataSetNotifyEvent = procedure(DataSet: TDataSet) of object;

property AfterClose: TDataSetNotifyEvent;
```

Example Syntax

```
// Assign or Deassign AfterClose event handler according to
// corresponding check box.
procedure TTDataSetTestForm.AfterCloseCheckBoxClick(Sender: TObject);
begin
  if AfterCloseCheckBox.Checked
  then CustomerTable.AfterClose := CustomerTableAfterClose
  else CustomerTable.AfterClose := Nil;
end;

// AfterClose event handler procedure.
procedure TTDataSetTestForm.CustomerTableAfterClose(DataSet: TDataSet);
begin
  MessageBeep( MB_ICONEXCLAMATION );
  MessageDlg( 'Dataset was closed.', mtWarning, [ mbOK ], 0 );
end;
```

Description
The `AfterClose` event of a `TDataSet` is triggered when the `TDataSet` closes, either by the user's interaction or by the code invoking the `Close` method of the `TDataSet`.

AfterDelete EVENT

Objects Affected	`TDataSet`
Purpose	The `AfterDelete` event can refer to an event handler procedure in which you can specify custom processing to perform after deleting the current record in the `TDataSet`.
Declaration	

```
Type
  TDataSetNotifyEvent = procedure(DataSet: TDataSet) of object;

property AfterDelete: TDataSetNotifyEvent;
```

Example Syntax

```
// Assign or Deassign AfterDelete event handler according to
// corresponding check box.
```

continued on next page

continued from previous page

```
procedure TTDataSetTestForm.AfterDeleteCheckBoxClick(Sender: TObject);
begin
  if AfterDeleteCheckBox.Checked
  then CustomerTable.AfterDelete := CustomerTableAfterDelete
  else CustomerTable.AfterDelete := Nil;
end;

// AfterDelete event handler procedure.
procedure TTDataSetTestForm.CustomerTableAfterDelete(DataSet: TDataSet);
begin
  Refresh;
  MessageBeep( MB_ICONEXCLAMATION );
  MessageDlg( 'Record was deleted.', mtWarning, [ mbOK ], 0 );
end;
```

Description
The **AfterDelete** event of a **TDataSet** is triggered whenever the current record is deleted from **TDataSet**, either by the user's interaction or by the code invoking the **Delete** method of the **TDataSet**. When **AfterDelete** is triggered, the original record has already been deleted. You can define your own event handler procedure in order to take special action whenever a deletion occurs (for instance, writing a log for auditing purposes).

AfterEdit EVENT

Objects Affected   TDataSet

Purpose
The **AfterEdit** event can refer to an event handler procedure in which you can specify custom processing to perform as soon as the **TDataSet** enters Edit mode.

Declaration

```
Type
  TDataSetNotifyEvent = procedure(DataSet: TDataSet) of object;

property AfterEdit: TDataSetNotifyEvent;
```

Example Syntax

```
// Assign or Deassign AfterEdit event handler according to
// corresponding check box.
procedure TTDataSetTestForm.AfterEditCheckBoxClick(Sender: TObject);
begin
  if AfterEditCheckBox.Checked
  then CustomerTable.AfterEdit := CustomerTableAfterEdit
  else CustomerTable.AfterEdit := Nil;
end;

// AfterEdit event handler procedure.
procedure TTDataSetTestForm.CustomerTableAfterEdit(DataSet: TDataSet);
begin
  MessageBeep( MB_ICONEXCLAMATION );
  MessageDlg( 'You can now edit the current record.',
    mtWarning, [ mbOK ], 0 );
end;
```

Description   The `AfterEdit` event of a `TDataSet` is triggered whenever the `TDataSet`
enters Edit mode, either by the user's interaction or by the code invoking
the `Edit` method of the `TDataSet`. When `AfterEdit` is triggered, the original record has not yet been changed by the user's editing actions—only the
state of the `TDataSet` has been changed.

AfterInsert EVENT

Objects Affected   `TDataSet`

Purpose   The `AfterInsert` event can refer to an event handler procedure in which
you specify custom processing to perform after inserting a new record.

Declaration

```
Type
  TDataSetNotifyEvent = procedure(DataSet: TDataSet) of object;

property AfterInsert: TDataSetNotifyEvent;

Example Syntax
// Assign or Deassign AfterInsert event handler according to
// corresponding check box.
procedure TTDataSetTestForm.AfterInsertCheckBoxClick(Sender: TObject);
begin
  if AfterInsertCheckBox.Checked
  then CustomerTable.AfterInsert := CustomerTableAfterInsert
  else CustomerTable.AfterInsert := Nil;
end;

// AfterInsert event handler procedure.
procedure TTDataSetTestForm.CustomerTableAfterInsert(DataSet: TDataSet);
begin
  MessageBeep( MB_ICONEXCLAMATION );
  MessageDlg( 'A new record is available.', mtWarning, [ mbOK ], 0 );
end;
```

Description   The `AfterInsert` event of a `TDataSet` is triggered whenever the `TDataSet`
enters Insert mode, either by the user's interaction or by the code invoking
the `Insert` or `Append` method of the `TDataSet`. Once `AfterInsert` is triggered, the new record is accessible to your code.

AfterOpen EVENT

Objects Affected   `TDataSet`

Purpose   The `AfterOpen` event refers to an event handler procedure in which you
specify custom processing to perform after opening the `TDataSet`.

Declaration

```
Type
  TDataSetNotifyEvent = procedure(DataSet: TDataSet) of object;

property AfterOpen: TDataSetNotifyEvent;
```

Example Syntax

```
// Assign or Deassign AfterOpen event handler according to
// corresponding check box.
procedure TTDataSetTestForm.AfterOpenCheckBoxClick(Sender: TObject);
begin
 if AfterOpenCheckBox.Checked
 then CustomerTable.AfterOpen := CustomerTableAfterOpen
 else CustomerTable.AfterOpen := Nil;
end;

// AfterOpen event handler procedure.
procedure TTDataSetTestForm.CustomerTableAfterOpen(DataSet: TDataSet);
begin
  MessageBeep( MB_ICONEXCLAMATION );
  MessageDlg( 'Dataset is open.', mtWarning, [ mbOK ], 0 );
end;
```

Description   The **AfterOpen** event of a **TDataSet** is triggered whenever the **TDataSet** is opened, either by invoking the **Open** method of the **TDataSet** or by setting the its **Active** property to **True**.

AfterPost EVENT

Objects Affected   **TDataSet**

Purpose   The **AfterPost** event refers to an event handler procedure in which you specify custom processing to perform after posting a record edit.

Declaration

```
Type
  TDataSetNotifyEvent = procedure(DataSet: TDataSet) of object;

property AfterPost: TDataSetNotifyEvent;
```

Example Syntax

```
// Assign or Deassign AfterPost event handler according to
// corresponding check box.
procedure TTDataSetTestForm.AfterPostCheckBoxClick(Sender: TObject);
begin
 if AfterPostCheckBox.Checked
 then CustomerTable.AfterPost := CustomerTableAfterPost
 else CustomerTable.AfterPost := Nil;
end;

// AfterPost event handler procedure.
procedure TTDataSetTestForm.CustomerTableAfterPost(DataSet: TDataSet);
begin
  MessageBeep( MB_ICONEXCLAMATION );
  MessageDlg( 'Changes were posted.', mtWarning, [ mbOK ], 0 );
end;
```

Description   The **AfterPost** event of a **TDataSet** is triggered whenever the changes (insertions or edits) to the current record are accepted by calling the **Post**

method of the **TDataSet**. Typically, you use this method to implement any special processing after a record has been posted. For instance, you might want to write a log file for auditing purposes, or update some visible element of the user interface to inform the user that the post was successful. If the validity checks don't hold, you can prevent the record from being posted by raising an exception.

Append METHOD

Objects Affected	TDataSet
Purpose	The Append method will add a new empty record at the end of the TDataSet.
Declaration	

```
procedure Append;
```

Example Syntax

```
// Append a new empty record at the end of the TDataSet.
procedure TTDataSetTestForm.AppendSpeedButtonClick(Sender: TObject);
begin
   CustomerTable.Append;
end;
```

Description

Append opens a new empty record at the end of the **TDataSet**. Note that the method works only on **TDataSets** returning a modifiable live result set. If that is not the case, an exception is raised. The **TDataSet** must be open for the **Insert** method to work, otherwise an exception is raised.

The method will first call **CheckBrowseMode** and check the modify flag. Next, if a **BeforeInsert** event handler procedure is assigned, it will be called. The new record is then created and initialized. The record count of the **TDataSet** is updated, and the **BOF** property is set to **False**.

The state of the **TDataSet** is then set to **dsInsert**. If there is an **OnNewRecord** event handler procedure, it will be called. If the **OnNewRecord** event handler procedure raises an exception, the append aborts, the state returns to **dsBrowse**, the **TDataSet** resynchronizes to its previous position, and the exception is re-raised. If there was no **OnNewRecord** event handler procedure, or if it executed without raising any exceptions, then the **Modified** property is initialized to **False**. Finally, if there is an **AfterInsert** event handler procedure assigned, it will be called.

Note that for indexed tables, when you post the new record created with the **Append** method, it is placed in the correct location in the table, based on the table's index. This is also known as the *record fly-away effect*. Keep in mind that this might cause current data-aware components, including data grids, to change in unexpected ways. As a general rule of thumb, you should refresh and reposition the **TDataSet** after posting a *new* record. (Obviously, if no index is used, the record will keep its position.)

AppendRecord METHOD

Objects Affected	TDataSet
Purpose	The **AppendRecord** method will add a new record to the end of the table, given some or all field values.
Declaration	

```
procedure AppendRecord(const Values: array of const);
```

Parameters

Values Array of constant values that can be converted to the datatypes of the corresponding fields in the **TDataSet**.

Example Syntax

```
// Demonstrate usage of AppendRecord.
procedure TTDataSetTestForm.AppendRecordSpeedButtonClick(Sender: ⇐
TObject);
var
  NewCustNo:      LongInt;
  CompanyName:    String;
  AddressLine1:   String;
  AddressLine2:   String;
  City:           String;
  State:          String;
  Zip:            String;
  Country:        String;
  InputCaption:   String;

begin
  NewCustNo      := GetNewCustNo;
  InputCaption   := 'New Customer ' + IntToStr( NewCustNo );
  CompanyName    := InputBox( InputCaption, 'Company?',    '' );
  AddressLine1   := InputBox( InputCaption, 'Address 1?', '' );
  AddressLine2   := InputBox( InputCaption, 'Address 2?', '' );
  City           := InputBox( InputCaption, 'City?',       '' );
  State          := InputBox( InputCaption, 'State?',      '' );
  Zip            := InputBox( InputCaption, 'Zip Code?',  '' );
  Country        := InputBox( InputCaption, 'Country?',   '' );

  CustomerTable.AppendRecord
  (
    [
      NewCustNo,
      CompanyName,
      AddressLine1,
      AddressLine2,
      City,
      State,
      Zip,
      Country
    ]
```

```
  );
end;

// Note that GetNewCustNo is a support function.
// It could be defined like this:

// Support function to get the next available record number.
//    NOTE: Multiuser issues are not taken into accout!
function TTDataSetTestForm.GetNewCustNo: LongInt;
var
  MaxCustNoQuery: TQuery;
begin
  Result := 0;
  MaxCustNoQuery := TQuery.Create( Nil );
  try
    with MaxCustNoQuery do
    begin
      DatabaseName := 'DBDEMOS';
      Sql.Clear;
      Sql.Add( 'SELECT MAX( CUSTNO ) FROM CUSTOMER' );
      Open;
      if not Fields[ 0 ].isNull then
      begin
        Result := Succ( Fields[ 0 ].AsInteger );
      end;
      Close;
    end;
  finally
    MaxCustNoQuery.Free;
  end;
end;
```

Description

The **AppendRecord** method will add a new record at the end of the **TDataSet**. The method takes an array of constant values as a parameter. Each value in the array parameter is sequentially assigned to the **TFields** in the **TDataSet**. If there are less values in the array than fields in the **TDataSet**, the remaining fields are assigned a **NULL** value. If there are more values in the array than fields in the **TDataSet**, a run-time List Index Out of Bounds error is generated. To skip any values, you can use the reserved word **Nil**.

The method works only on **TDataSet** returning a modifiable live result set. If that is not the case, an exception is raised. The **TDataSet** must be open for the **Insert** method to work, otherwise an exception is raised.

The method first calls **CheckBrowseMode** and checks the modify flag. If a **BeforeInsert** event handler procedure is assigned, it is called. The new record is then created and initialized, and the state of the **TDataSet** is set to **dsInsert**.

If there is an **OnNewRecord** event handler procedure, it will be called. If there is an **AfterInsert** event handler procedure assigned, it will be called. The field values are then copied to the actual record buffer. If there is a **BeforePost** event handler procedure, it will be called. The new record is then posted.

If any of the `OnNewRecord`, `AfterInsert`, or `BeforePost` event handler procedures raise an exception, the insertion aborts, all field buffers are freed, the state returns to `dsBrowse`, the `TDataSet` is resynchronized to its previous position, and the exception is re-raised.

If there were no event handler procedures, or if they executed without raising exceptions, the `TDataSet` is resynchronized. Finally, if there is an `AfterInsert` event handler procedure assigned, it will be called.

Note that for indexed tables, after executing the `AppendRecord` method, the new record is placed in the correct location in the table, based on the table's index. This is also known as the record fly-away effect. Keep in mind that this might cause current data-aware components, including data grids, to change in unexpected ways. As a general rule of thumb, you should refresh and reposition the `TDataSet` after posting a *new* record. (Obviously, if no index is used, the record will keep its position.)

`ApplyUpdates` Method

Objects Affected	`TDataSet`
Purpose	The `ApplyUpdates` method writes to the database any pending changes to cached data.
Declaration	

```
procedure ApplyUpdates;
```

Example Syntax

```
// Invoke ApplyUpdates only if CachedUpdates is true.
procedure TTDataSetTestForm.ApplyUpdatesSpeedButtonClick(Sender: ⇐
TObject);
begin
  with CustomerTable do
  begin
    if CachedUpdates then
    begin
      ApplyUpdates;
    end;
  end;
end;
```

Description

When using cached updates, the `ApplyUpdates` method writes to the database any changes made to cached data. Any inserts, deletes, or modifications made since the last `ApplyUpdates` are sent in a batch to the database.

In terms of transaction processing, the `ApplyUpdates` method corresponds to the first phase of a two-phase commit. All changes in the cache are applied to the underlying data. Unless you're in a single user environment, the `ApplyUpdates` method should always be called within a transaction to allow for proper error recovery. (Note that explicit transaction management is not illustrated in the above sample code fragment.)

In general, after a successful `ApplyUpdates` call, you should eventually call the `CommitUpdates` method, which corresponds to the second phase of the two-phase commit.

In practice, you can avoid calling `ApplyUpdates` on single `TDataSets` altogether by calling the equivalent `ApplyUpdates` method of the `TDataBase` object to which the `TDataSet` belongs, since it will call `ApplyUpdates` and `CommitUpdates` within a proper transaction.

AutoCalcFields PROPERTY

Objects Affected	`TDataSet`
Purpose	The `AutoCalcFields` property determines whether or not the `OnCalcFields` event is called automatically.
Declaration	

```
property AutoCalcFields: Boolean
```

Description   `AutoCalc` is set to `True` by default when a `TDataSet` is created. When `AutoCalc` is `False`, the `OnCalcFields` event is triggered only when `TDataSet` reads a record from the database. When `AutoCalc` is `True`, the `OnCalcFields` event is triggered for each edit performed on any field in the record (besides being triggered when the record is read from the database). Note that whenever `AutoCalc` is set to `True`, you should not modify the `TDataSet` within its `OnCalcFields` event handler procedure, since that leads to recursion. However, when you do have calculated fields, you will most likely want the property to be `True`, since any changes the user performs interactively will update any dependent calculated values.

BOF PROPERTY

Objects Affected	`TDataSet`
Purpose	The `BOF` property evaluates to `True` if the current cursor position is at the beginning of the `TDataSet`.
Declaration	

```
property BOF: Boolean;
```

Example Syntax

```
// Check if TDataSet is empty.
procedure TTDataSetTestForm.EofBofSpeedButtonClick(Sender: TObject);
begin
```

continued on next page

continued from previous page

```
    with CustomerTable do
    begin
      if BOF and EOF then
      begin
        MessageBeep( MB_ICONEXCLAMATION );
        MessageDlg( 'The table is empty.', mtWarning, [ mbOK ], 0 );
      end;
    end;
end;
```

Description

BOF shows whether the current record is the first one in the TDataSet. This property is read-only and available only at run time. Since the TDataSet in a multiuser database environment is in a constant state of change, the definition of being first has to be restricted to well-defined and specific states of the TDataSet. BOF will report True only when the TDataSet is first opened, immediately after calling the First method, or if a call to the Prior method fails because the current record is already the first one in the TDataSet.

Note, as shown in the sample code fragment above, you can use BOF in conjunction with the EOF property to easily test whether a TDataSet is empty or not. Also notice that the test will work even if the set has only one record, since only one of the two conditions will be True, depending on the direction of the last navigational movement (Next or Previous).

BeforeCancel EVENT

Objects Affected   TDataSet

Purpose   The BeforeCancel event refers to an event handler procedure in which you can specify custom processing to perform before a record edit is cancelled.

Declaration

```
Type
  TDataSetNotifyEvent = procedure(DataSet: TDataSet) of object;

property BeforeCancel: TDataSetNotifyEvent;
```

Example Syntax

```
// Assign or Deassign BeforeCancel event handler according to
// corresponding check box.
procedure TTDataSetTestForm.BeforeCancelCheckBoxClick(Sender: TObject);
begin
  if BeforeCancelCheckBox.Checked
  then CustomerTable.BeforeCancel := CustomerTableBeforeCancel
  else CustomerTable.BeforeCancel := Nil;
end;

// BeforeCancel event handler procedure.
procedure TTDataSetTestForm.CustomerTableBeforeCancel(DataSet: TDataSet);
```

```
begin
  MessageBeep( MB_ICONQUESTION );
  if MessageDlg ( 'Are you sure you want to cancel?',
              mtConfirmation,
              [mbYes, mbNo],
              0 ) <> mrYes then
  begin
    // Raise silent exception to prevent cancel from being performed.
    Abort;
  end;
end;
```

Description

The **BeforeCancel** event of a **TDataSet** is triggered just before performing the cancellation of any changes made to the current record, either by the user's interaction or by the code invoking the **Cancel** method of the **TDataSet**. If you raise an exception in the **BeforeCancel** event handler procedure, you can inhibit the cancellation. The above code shows a typical usage of this technique: Whenever a cancellation is about to be performed, you can ask the user to confirm. If the user does not want to cancel all edits, you raise a silent exception in order to not perform the cancel and preserve all edits made in the meantime.

BeforeClose EVENT

Objects Affected   TDataSet

Purpose   The **BeforeClose** event refers to an event handler procedure in which you can specify custom processing to perform before the **TDataSet** is closed.

Declaration

```
Type
  TDataSetNotifyEvent = procedure(DataSet: TDataSet) of object;

property BeforeClose: TDataSetNotifyEvent;
```

Example Syntax

```
// Assign or Deassign BeforeClose event handler according to
// corresponding check box.
procedure TTDataSetTestForm.BeforeCloseCheckBoxClick(Sender: TObject);
begin
  if BeforeCloseCheckBox.Checked
  then CustomerTable.BeforeClose := CustomerTableBeforeClose
  else CustomerTable.BeforeClose := Nil;
end;

// BeforeCancel event handler procedure.
procedure TTDataSetTestForm.CustomerTableBeforeClose(DataSet: TDataSet);
begin
  MessageBeep( MB_ICONQUESTION );
  if MessageDlg ( 'Are you sure you want to close the data set?',
              mtConfirmation,
              [mbYes, mbNo],
```

continued on next page

continued from previous page

```
                              O ) <> mrYes then
    begin
      // Raise silent exception to prevent close from being performed.
      Abort;
    end;
  end;
```

Description   The **BeforeClose** event of a **TDataSet** is triggered just before it is closed, either by the user's interaction or by the code invoking the **Close** method of the **TDataSet**. If you raise an exception in the **BeforeClose** event handler procedure, you can inhibit the closing of the **TDataSet**.

BeforeDelete Event

Objects Affected   TDataSet

Purpose   The **BeforeDelete** event refers to an event handler procedure in which you can specify custom processing to perform before a record is deleted.

Declaration

```
Type
  TDataSetNotifyEvent = procedure(DataSet: TDataSet) of object;

property BeforeDelete: TDataSetNotifyEvent;
```

Example Syntax

```
// Assign or Deassign BeforeDelete event handler according to
// corresponding check box.
procedure TTDataSetTestForm.BeforeDeleteCheckBoxClick(Sender: TObject);
begin
  if BeforeDeleteCheckBox.Checked
  then CustomerTable.BeforeDelete := CustomerTableBeforeDelete
  else CustomerTable.BeforeDelete := Nil;
end;

// BeforeDelete event handler procedure.
procedure TTDataSetTestForm.CustomerTableBeforeDelete(DataSet: TDataSet);
begin
  {
    NOTE: If you have a TDBGrid or a TDBNavigator connected to this
    TDataset, beware that the functionality implemented in this
    example might be duplicated by the Options.dgConfirmDelete
    property of the TDBGrid, or the ConfirmDelete property of the
    TDBNavigator.
  }
  MessageBeep( MB_ICONQUESTION );
  if MessageDlg ( 'Are you sure you want to delete this record?',
                   mtConfirmation,
                   [mbYes, mbNo],
                   O ) <> mrYes then
  begin
    // Raise silent exception to prevent delete from being performed.
    Abort;
  end;
end;
```

Description   The `BeforeDelete` event of a `TDataSet` is triggered just before performing the deletion of the current record, either by the user's interaction or by the code invoking the `Delete` method of the `TDataSet`. If you raise an exception in the `BeforeDelete` event handler procedure, you can prevent the current record from being deleted.

BeforeEdit EVENT

Objects Affected   `TDataSet`

Purpose   The `BeforeEdit` event refers to an event handler procedure in which you can specify custom processing to perform before beginning a record edit.

Declaration

```
Type
  TDataSetNotifyEvent = procedure(DataSet: TDataSet) of object;

property BeforeEdit: TDataSetNotifyEvent;
```

Example Syntax

```
procedure TTDataSetTestForm.BeforeEditCheckBoxClick(Sender: TObject);
begin
  if BeforeEditCheckBox.Checked
  then CustomerTable.BeforeEdit := CustomerTableBeforeEdit
  else CustomerTable.BeforeEdit := Nil;
end;

// BeforeEdit event handler procedure.
procedure TTDataSetTestForm.CustomerTableBeforeEdit(DataSet: TDataSet);
begin
  MessageBeep( MB_ICONQUESTION );
  if MessageDlg ( 'Are you sure you want to edit the current record?',
                  mtConfirmation,
                  [mbYes, mbNo],
                  0 ) <> mrYes then
  begin
    // Raise silent exception to prevent edit from being performed.
    Abort;
  end;
end;
```

Description   The `BeforeEdit` event of a `TDataSet` is triggered just before entering the Edit mode of the current record, either by the user's interaction or by the code invoking the `Edit` method of the `TDataSet`. If you raise an exception in the `BeforeEdit` event handler procedure, you can prevent the current record from being edited. You might want to do this to prevent the user from editing the current record, for instance, because in the event handler procedure code you have verified that he or she does not have sufficient rights to do so.

BeforeInsert Event

Objects Affected	TDataSet
Purpose	The **BeforeInsert** event refers to an event handler procedure in which you can specify custom processing to perform before inserting a new empty record.
Declaration	

```
Type
   TDataSetNotifyEvent = procedure(DataSet: TDataSet) of object;

property BeforeInsert: TDataSetNotifyEvent;
```

Example Syntax

```
// Assign or Deassign BeforeInsert event handler according to
// corresponding check box.
procedure TTDataSetTestForm.BeforeInsertCheckBoxClick(Sender: TObject);
begin
   if BeforeInsertCheckBox.Checked
   then CustomerTable.BeforeInsert := CustomerTableBeforeInsert
   else CustomerTable.BeforeInsert := Nil;
end;

// BeforeInsert event handler procedure.
procedure TTDataSetTestForm.CustomerTableBeforeInsert(DataSet: TDataSet);
begin
   MessageBeep( MB_ICONQUESTION );
   if MessageDlg ( 'Are you sure you want to insert a new record?',
                   mtConfirmation,
                   [mbYes, mbNo],
                   0 ) <> mrYes then
   begin
     // Raise silent exception to prevent close from being performed.
     Abort;
   end;
end;
```

Description

The **BeforeInsert** event of a **TDataSet** is triggered just before a new record is inserted, either by the user's interaction or by the code invoking the **Insert** or **Append** method of the **TDataSet**. If you raise an exception in the **BeforeInsert** event handler procedure, you can inhibit the insertion of a new record.

Note that in the context of the BDE (Borland Database Engine), *inserting* a record means creating a new empty record in the BDE's record buffer. The new record will then be filled by the user's actions, usually by filling in data-aware controls. (It could also be populated by your coding the appropriate actions in Object Pascal.) Only when the user is done and requests the record to be *posted,* is the new record actually written out of the underlying database table.

The previous example code is somewhat contrived because it explicitly asks the user whether he or she wants to insert the record or not. However, in a **BeforeInsert** event handler procedure you will most likely test for some condition, and, if it is not met, you will raise an exception in order to prevent the action from happening. You could test, for instance, whether some business logic is verified or not.

BeforeOpen EVENT

Objects Affected **TDataSet**

Purpose The **BeforeOpen** event refers to an event handler procedure in which you can specify custom processing to perform before a **TDataSet** is opened.

Declaration

```
Type
  TDataSetNotifyEvent = procedure(DataSet: TDataSet) of object;

property BeforeOpen: TDataSetNotifyEvent;
```

Example Syntax

```
// Assign or Deassign BeforeOpen event handler according to
// corresponding check box.
procedure TTDataSetTestForm.BeforeOpenCheckBoxClick(Sender: TObject);
begin
 if BeforeOpenCheckBox.Checked
 then CustomerTable.BeforeOpen := CustomerTableBeforeOpen
 else CustomerTable.BeforeOpen := Nil;
end;

// BeforeOpen event handler procedure.
procedure TTDataSetTestForm.CustomerTableBeforeOpen(DataSet: TDataSet);
begin
  MessageBeep( MB_ICONQUESTION );
  if MessageDlg ( 'Are you sure you want to open the dataset?',
                  mtConfirmation,
                  [mbYes, mbNo],
                  0 ) <> mrYes then
  begin
    // Raise silent exception to prevent close from being performed.
    Abort;
  end;
end;
```

Description The **BeforeOpen** event of a **TDataSet** is triggered just before performing the opening of the **TDataSet**, either by the user's interaction or by the code invoking the **Open** method of the **TDataSet**. If you raise an exception in the **BeforeOpen** event handler procedure, you can inhibit the opening of the **TDataSet**.

The above example code is somewhat contrived because it explicitly asks the user whether he or she wants to open the dataset. However, in a

583

BeforeOpen event handler procedure you will most likely test for some condition, and, if it is not met, you will raise an exception in order to prevent the action from happening. You could test, for instance, whether some business logic is verified or not.

BeforePost EVENT

Objects Affected   TDataSet

Purpose   The **BeforePost** event refers to an event handler procedure in which you can specify custom processing to perform before a record edit is posted to the underlying database table.

Declaration

```
Type
    TDataSetNotifyEvent = procedure(DataSet: TDataSet) of object;

property BeforePost: TDataSetNotifyEvent;
```

Example Syntax

```
// Assign or Deassign BeforePost event handler according to
// corresponding check box.
procedure TTDataSetTestForm.BeforePostCheckBoxClick(Sender: TObject);
begin
 if BeforePostCheckBox.Checked
 then CustomerTable.BeforePost := CustomerTableBeforePost
 else CustomerTable.BeforePost := Nil;
end;

// BeforePost event handler procedure.
procedure TTDataSetTestForm.CustomerTableBeforePost(DataSet: TDataSet);
begin
  MessageBeep( MB_ICONQUESTION );
  if MessageDlg ( 'Does the current record pass all validation ⇐
criteria?',
                  mtConfirmation,
                  [mbYes, mbNo],
                  0 ) <> mrYes then
  begin
    // Raise silent exception to prevent close from being performed.
    Abort;
  end;
end;
```

Description   The **BeforePost** event of a **TDataSet** is triggered just before the posting of any changes made to the current record, either by the user's interaction or by the code invoking the **Post** method of the **TDataSet**. A **Post** can also be generated implicitly by moving off the current record (again by the user's interaction or by call to **TDataSet** methods such as **Next**, **Prior**, and so on). By raising an exception in the **BeforePost** event handler procedure, you can inhibit the posting.

A typical usage of the **BeforePost** event handler procedure is implementing record-wide validation rules. If the record does not pass the validation rule, an exception is raised and the invalid record will not be accepted.

Another typical usage of the **BeforePost** event handler is copying the results of calculated fields to shadow result fields in the same (or different) datasets. This usage stems from the fact that during the recalculation (for example, when the state of **TDataSet** is **dsCalcFields**) you cannot assign to field values without firing a recursive (endless) call to the **OnCalcFields** event handler.

Bookmark PROPERTY

Objects Affected	**TDataSet**
Purpose	The **Bookmark** property allows you to access the current record's internal bookmark string.
Declaration	

```
type
  TBookmarkStr = String;

property Bookmark: TBookmarkStr;
```

Description	The **Bookmark** property of a **TDataSet** will return a string used internally by Delphi to represent the bookmark for the current record. By assigning another bookmark string to this property, you will move the cursor's position to the corresponding record. You should not manipulate bookmarks strings directly. Instead, use the **GetBookmark**, **GotoBookmark**, and **FreeBookmark** methods.

CachedUpdates PROPERTY

Objects Affected	**TDataSet**
Purpose	The **CachedUpdates** boolean property is used to enable or disable cached updates.
Declaration	

```
property CachedUpdates: Boolean;
```

Example Syntax

```
// Toggle CachedUpdates on and off.
procedure TTDataSetTestForm.CachedUpdatesSpeedButtonClick(Sender: ⇐
TObject);
begin
  CustomerTable.CachedUpdates := Not CustomerTable.CachedUpdates;
```

continued on next page

continued from previous page

```
                        StatusBar.SimpleText :=
                          Format
                          (
                            'CachedUpdates = %d',
                            [Integer(CustomerTable.CachedUpdates)]
                          );
                        end;
```

Description   The CachedUpdates property toggles the cached update mode on and off.
When cached updates are enabled, any changes you make on the
TDataSet will be stored in memory, instead of being written onto disk. By
invoking ApplyUpdates, all pending changes will be written onto disk at
the same time. If there are any pending updates, you will discard all of
them by setting the CachedUpdates property to False.

CanModify PROPERTY

Objects Affected   TDataSet

Purpose   The CanModify boolean property is used to check whether or not the
TDataSet can be modified.

Declaration

```
property CanModify: Boolean;
```

Example Syntax

```
// If Customer table can be modified then enter edit mode,
// otherwise raise an exception.
procedure TTDataSetTestForm.CanModifySpeedButtonClick(Sender: TObject);
begin
  if not CustomerTable.CanModify then
  begin
    raise EDataBaseError.Create( 'Table cannot be modified' );
  end;
  CustomerTable.Edit;
end;
```

Description   CanModify is a read-only, run-time property that reports whether the
TDataSet can be modified or not. If CanModify returns True, it means you
can successfully invoke the Insert or Edit methods of the TDataSet. In
order to actually change the data in the TDataSet, a True CanModify property is a necessary condition, although it might not be sufficient. Even if a
TDataSet accepts changes to its data, it is not guaranteed that the underlying database provides sufficient access privileges for the changes to get
through. Such access privileges are determined by the underlying database's security options, and usually depend on how the current user
logged into the database (that is, typed in his or her username/password
combination).

When the **TDataSet** is represented by a **TTable** component, the **CanModify** property usually is the negation of the **ReadOnly** property of the **TTable**. In other words, you can modify a table's data only if you have complete read and write access to it.

When the **TDataSet** is represented by a **TQuery** component, the **CanModify** property corresponds to the setting of the **RequestLive** property of the **TQuery**. In other words, the query must return a live result set.

If the **TDataSet** is represented by a **TQuery** that is not a live result set **CanModify** can still be **True** provided that **CachedUpdates** is **True**, and either a **TUpdateSql** component is referenced in the **UpdateObject** property of the **TQuery**, or an event handler is assigned to the **OnUpdateRecord** of the **TQuery**.

Cancel METHOD

Objects Affected	TDataSet
Purpose	The Cancel method will undo any edits performed on the current record.
Declaration	

```
procedure Cancel;
```

Example Syntax

```
// Disregard any changes and return to Browse mode.
procedure TTDataSetTestForm.CancelSpeedButtonClick(Sender: TObject);
begin
  CustomerTable.Cancel;
end;
```

Description

The **Cancel** method will disregard any changes made to the current record and return the **TDataSet** to Browse mode. By invoking this method, you also call indirectly the **BeforeCancel** and **AfterCancel** event handler procedures if they are assigned. (Therefore, if there is a **BeforeCancel** event handler procedure assigned, it will be executed. Keep in mind that the **BeforeCancel** event handler procedure can possibly prevent the cancel action, simply by raising an exception. Refer to the description of the **BeforeCancel** event for more information.)

Note that the **Cancel** method will disregard the changes made to the current record only. If you are using cached updates and want to cancel the whole batch of pending edits, then you should set the **CachedUpdates** property to **False**, or invoke the **CancelUpdates** method. If you are using explicit transactions to control changes over multiple **TDataSets**, you can use the **Rollback** method of the **TDatabase** to cancel all modifications made to the database since the last call to **StartTransaction**.

CancelUpdates METHOD

Objects Affected	TDataSet
Purpose	The CancelUpdates method will undo any pending cached updates.
Declaration	

```
procedure CancelUpdates;
```

Example Syntax

```
// Invoke CancelUpdates only if CachedUpdates is true.
procedure TTDataSetTestForm.CancelUpdatesSpeedButtonClick(Sender: ⇐
TObject);
begin
  with CustomerTable do
  begin
    if CachedUpdates then
    begin
      CancelUpdates;
    end;
  end;
end;
```

Description The CancelUpdates method will disregard all pending cached updates. The operation will clear the cache and restore the **TDataSet** to the state it was in when opened, when the **CachedUpdates** were first enabled, or when the last **ApplyUpdates** occurred successfully.

CheckBrowseMode METHOD

Objects Affected	TDataSet
Purpose	The CheckBrowseMode method will ensure that the TDataSet is in Browse mode.
Declaration	

```
procedure CheckBrowseMode;
```

Example Syntax

```
// CheckBrowseMode will put the CustomerTable in Browse mode.
procedure TTDataSetTestForm.CheckBrowseModeSpeedButtonClick(
  Sender: TObject);
begin
  CustomerTable.CheckBrowseMode;
end;
```

Description The CheckBrowseMode method ensures that the **TDataSet** is in Browse mode. Typically, you call this method if you need to perform any action requiring the **TDataSet** be in Browse mode (for instance, when moving the record cursor). However, you will almost never need to call this method directly, since all **TDataSet** methods that need it (such as **First**, **Next**, and so on) already call **CheckBrowseMode** for you. The only time you will have to call **CheckBrowseMode** directly is when you interact directly with the BDE.

When **CheckBrowseMode** is called, if the **TDataSet** is not open, an **EDatabaseError** exception is raised. If the **TDataSet** is in Insert or Edit mode and there are pending changes, the current record will be posted. If there are no pending changes, the editing will be canceled. If the **TDataSet** is in SetKey mode, any pending changes will be posted.

ClearFields METHOD

Objects Affected	**TDataSet** and associated **TField** objects
Purpose	The **ClearFields** method will initialize the record buffer.
Declaration	

```
procedure ClearFields;
```

Example Syntax

```
// Initialize the current record with NULL or default values.
procedure TTDataSetTestForm.ClearFieldsSpeedButtonClick(Sender: TObject);
begin
  CustomerTable.ClearFields;
end;
```

Description   The **ClearFields** method will initialize the record buffer. After its execution the record buffer will contain blank fields (according to their datatypes). If the underlying database table is a Paradox table and has associated default values with some of the fields, then default values will be used to initialize them. If the **TDataSet** is not in Edit, Insert, or SetKey mode, an **EDatabaseError** exception will be raised.

Close METHOD

Objects Affected	**TDataSet**
Purpose	The **Close** method will close the **TDataSet**.
Declaration	

```
procedure Close;
```

Example Syntax

```
// Close the TDataSet.
procedure TTDataSetTestForm.CloseSpeedButtonClick(Sender: TObject);
begin
  CustomerTable.Close;
end;
```

Description   The `Close` method will close the `TDataSet`. It is the equivalent of setting its `Active` property to `False`. Note that by invoking this method, you also indirectly call the `BeforeClose` and `AfterClose` event handler procedures if they are assigned. If the `TDataSet` is in Edit or Insert mode when you call the `Close` method, any pending changes will not be posted automatically. To ensure no changes get lost, you should define a `BeforeClose` event handler procedure that will make the post explicitly.

CommitUpdates METHOD

Objects Affected   `TDataSet`

Purpose   The `CommitUpdates` method will commit to the database any changes to cached data.

Declaration

```
procedure CommitUpdates;
```

Example Syntax

```
// Invoke CommitUpdates only if CachedUpdates is true.
procedure TTDataSetTestForm.CommitUpdatesSpeedButtonClick(Sender: ⇐
TObject);
begin
  with CustomerTable do
  begin
    if CachedUpdates then
    begin
      CommitUpdates;
    end;
  end;
end;
```

Description   When using `CachedUpdates`, the `ApplyUpdates` method writes to the database any changes made to cached data. Any inserts, deletes, or modifications made since the last `ApplyUpdates` are sent in a batch to the database. After a successful call to `ApplyUpdates`, you should eventually call the `CommitUpdates` method to permanently store the changes in the database.

In terms of transaction processing, the `ApplyUpdates` method corresponds to the first phase of a two-phase commit, and the `CommitUpdates` corresponds to the second phase.

With `ApplyUpdates`, all changes in the cache are applied to the underlying data. Unless you're in a single user environment, the `ApplyUpdates` method should always be called within a transaction to allow for proper error recovery. (Note that explicit transaction management is not illustrated in the above sample code fragment.)

In practice, you can avoid calling `ApplyUpdates`/`CommitUpdates` on single `TDataSets` altogether by calling the equivalent `ApplyUpdates` method of the **TDataBase** object to which the **TDataSet** belongs, since it will call **ApplyUpdates** and **CommitUpdates** within a proper transaction.

ControlsDisabled METHOD

Objects Affected   **TDataSet** and associated data-aware components

Purpose   The **ControlsDisabled** method checks if associated data-aware components are disabled.

Declaration

```
function ControlsDisabled: Boolean;
```

Example Syntax

```
// If associated data-aware controls are disabled,
// then make sure to enable them.
procedure TTDataSetTestForm.ControlsDisabledSpeedButtonClick(
  Sender: TObject);
begin
  with CustomerTable do
  begin
    while ControlsDisabled do
    begin
      EnableControls;
    end;
  end;
end;
```

Description   The **ControlsDisabled** method reports whether there have been calls to **DisableControls** without a matching call to **EnableControls**. Since there can be multiple calls to **DisableControls** (maintained with a count by the **TDataSet**), a code fragment like the one shown above makes sure any unmatched **DisableControls** call has a matching call to **EnableControls**.

CursorPosChanged METHOD

Objects Affected   **TDataSet**

Purpose   The **CursorPosChanged** method notifies the system that the BDE cursor's position has changed.

Declaration

```
procedure CursorPosChanged;
```

Example Syntax

```
// Position current cursor to end of table.
procedure TTDataSetTestForm.CursorPosChangedSpeedButtonClick(
  Sender: TObject);
```

continued on next page

continued from previous page

```
begin
  Check( DbiSetToEnd( CustomerTable.Handle ));
  CustomerTable.CursorPosChanged;
  CustomerTable.Resync( [] );
end;
```

Description   When you make direct calls to the BDE via the `Handle` property and such calls change the BDE cursor's position (in turn changing the current record), you must call `CursorPosChanged` immediately after calling the BDE in order to inform the `TDataSet`. This procedure resets an internal index, the integer `FCurrentRecord` private variable, to the default value of −1. The `FCurrentRecord` is an index into the array of record buffers maintained by the `TDataSet`. A value of −1 in `FCurrentRecord` means the `TDataSet` does not know which buffer in the array represents the current record; however, subsequent operations will resynchronize.

DataSource PROPERTY

Objects Affected   TDataSet

Purpose   The `DataSource` property is a reference to the master data source of the `TDataSet`, if there is one.

Declaration

```
property DataSource: TDataSource
```

Description   In a `TDataSet` the `DataSource` property is a read-only property, and it will always contain the value of `Nil`. In the derived classes `TTable` and `TQuery`, the `DataSource` property is redefined, and it represents the master data source controlling the `TDataSet`. There can be multiple levels of controlling masters, and it is possible to iterate through all these levels simply by traversing the data source links. The highest level master, which is not a detail of any other `TDataSet`, has its `MasterSource` or `DataSource` property set to `Nil`.

By having the `DataSource` property of the `TDataSet` always return a `Nil` and redefining it in `TTable` and `TQuery`, the VCL ensures that only `TTables` and `TQueries` will have controlling master data sources. Any other kind of `TDataSet` (like `TStoredProc`) will always be without a controlling master data source by definition.

DefaultFields PROPERTY

Objects Affected   TDataSet

Purpose   The `DefaultFields` property indicates whether or not the `TDataSet` has default fields.

Declaration

```
property DefaultFields: Boolean;
```

Example Syntax

```
// if Fields Editor was used...
if not CustomerTable.DefaultFields then
begin
  //...process custom field names here
end;
```

Description

The `DefaultFields` property is a run-time, read-only property. It indicates whether the Fields list of the `TDataSet` contains its default fields (`True`), or whether it was built by the programmer via the Fields Editor (`False`).

Delete METHOD

Objects Affected   `TDataSet`

Purpose   The `Delete` method will delete the current record from the `TDataSet`.

Declaration

```
procedure Delete;
```

Example Syntax

```
// Delete the current record from the TDataSet.
procedure TTDataSetTestForm.DeleteSpeedButtonClick(Sender: TObject);
begin
  CustomerTable.Delete:
end;
```

Description

The `Delete` method will delete the current record from the `TDataSet`. It will work only on a `TDataSet` that returns a live result set. The `TDataSet` must be open for `Delete` to work, otherwise an exception is raised. An exception will also be raised if the `TDataSet` is empty. If the `TDataSet` is in Insert or SetKey mode, then `Delete` is equivalent to `Cancel`.

In all other cases, if there is a `BeforeDelete` event handler procedure assigned, then it will be called. The current record will then be deleted. If the deletion is successful, the `TDataSet` is placed in Browse mode and the next record becomes the new current record, unless the current record was the last record, in which case the previous record becomes current. Finally, if there is an `AfterDelete` event handler procedure assigned, it will be called.

If the deletion is not successful, an exception is raised. If there is an `OnDeleteError` event handler procedure assigned, it is called and the exception handed over to it. If there is no `OnDeleteError` event handler, the exception is passed over to the default application exception handler.

DisableControls METHOD

Objects Affected	TDataSet
Purpose	The DisableControls method will temporarily disable display updates of associated data-aware components.
Declaration	

```
procedure DisableControls;
```

Example Syntax

```
// Disable the update of associated data-aware components.
procedure TTDataSetTestForm.DisableControlsSpeedButtonClick(
  Sender: TObject);
begin
  CustomerTable.DisableControls;
end;
```

Description

The DisableControls method will temporarily disconnect the TDataSet from any associated TDataSource components, which means all associated data-aware components will not be updated to show any changes made to the TDataSet in the meantime. Typically, DisableControls is used in conjunction with the EnableControls method that does just the opposite: It re-establishes the connection with the associated TDataSource components. In between the two calls you will usually perform some time-consuming operation, like scanning through all the records of the TDataSet. By not having to update the screen display at each iteration, you can improve performance and let all processing take place behind the scenes, without the user actually seeing what is going on.

Note that DisableControls can be called several times, and each call must have a matching EnableControls. The TDataSet keeps a count of all calls. You can use the ControlsDisabled method to test if there are any unmatched calls to DisableControls.

Edit METHOD

Objects Affected	TDataSet
Purpose	The Edit method activates Edit mode on the current record of the TDataSet.
Declaration	

```
procedure Edit;
```

Example Syntax

```
// Edit the current record in the TDataSet.
procedure TTDataSetTestForm.EditSpeedButtonClick(Sender: TObject);
begin
```

```
  CustomerTable.Edit;
end;
```

Description The `Edit` method will edit the current record in the `TDataSet`. It will work only on a `TDataSet` that returns a modifiable live result set. If that is not the case, an exception is raised. The `TDataSet` must be open for the `Edit` method to work, otherwise an exception is raised. If the `TDataSet` is already in Edit or Insert mode, no further action is taken. If the `TDataSet` is empty when `Edit` is invoked, the call is equivalent to calling the `Insert` method of the `TDataSet`.

In all other cases, executing the `Edit` method first calls `CheckBrowseMode` and checks the `CanModify` flag. Next, if a `BeforeEdit` event handler procedure is assigned, it is called. The current record is then read anew from the table and locked with a BDE WRITELOCK, which allows other users to read the record, but prevents them from updating or placing other locks on it. If the locking is successful, the `TDataSet` will recalculate its calculated fields (if any) and finally activate Edit mode. If the `TDataSet` is referenced in any `TDataSource` objects and any of them have their `OnDataChange` event handler procedure assigned, they are called. Finally, if the `TDataSet` has its `AfterEdit` event handler procedure assigned, it is called.

If the record locking is not successful, an exception is raised. If there is an `OnEditError` event handler procedure assigned, it is called and the exception handed over to it. If there is no `OnEditError` event handler, the exception is passed over to the default application exception handler.

EnableControls METHOD

Objects Affected `TDataSet`

Purpose The `EnableControls` method enables display updates of associated data-aware components.

Declaration

```
procedure EnableControls;
```

Example Syntax

```
// Enable the update of associated data-aware components.
procedure TTDataSetTestForm.DisableControlsSpeedButtonClick(
  Sender: TObject);
begin
  CustomerTable.EnableControls;
end;
```

Description The `EnableControls` method reconnects the `TDataSet` from any associated `TDataSource` components disconnected with a call to `DisableControls`. In turn, this means all associated data-aware components are updated again to show any changes that might have occurred to the **TDataSet** while it was disconnected. Typically, **EnableControls** is used in conjunction with the method **DisableControls**, which does just the opposite. In between the two calls you will usually perform some time-consuming operation, like scanning through all the records of the **TDataSet**.

Note that **DisableControls** can be called several times, and each call must have a matching **EnableControls**. The **TDataSet** keeps a count of all calls. You can use the **ControlsDisabled** method to test for any unmatched calls to **DisableControls**, and call **EnableControls** the required number of times to truly re-establish the connection.

EOF PROPERTY

Objects Affected   TDataSet

Purpose   The **EOF** property evaluates to **True** if the current cursor position is at the at the end of the **TDataSet**.

Declaration

```
property EOF: Boolean;
```

Example Syntax

```
// Check if TDataSet is empty.
procedure TTDataSetTestForm.EofBofSpeedButtonClick(Sender: TObject);
begin
  with CustomerTable do
  begin
    if BOF and EOF then
    begin
      MessageBeep( MB_ICONEXCLAMATION );
      MessageDlg( 'The table is empty.', mtWarning, [ mbOK ], 0 );
    end;
  end;
end;
```

Description   EOF shows whether the current record is the last one in the **TDataSet**. This property is read-only and available only at run time. Since the **TDataSet** in a multiuser database environment is in a constant state of change, the definition of being last must be restricted to well-defined and specific states of the **TDataSet**. EOF will report **True** only when the **TDataSet** is first opened and is empty, immediately after calling the **Last** method, or a call to the **Next** method fails because the current record is already the last one in the **TDataSet**.

Note, as shown in the sample code fragment above, you can easily test whether a **TDataSet** is empty or not by using **BOF** in conjunction with the **EOF** property.

ExpIndex PROPERTY

Objects Affected	`TDataSet`
Purpose	The `ExpIndex` boolean property indicates whether an index is a dBASE expression index.
Declaration	

```
property ExpIndex: Boolean;
```

Description	The `ExpIndex` property is a run-time, read-only property set to `True` if the index is an expression index. It is supported for dBASE only.

FetchALL METHOD

Objects Affected	`TDataSet`
Purpose	The `FetchAll` method forces a re-read of the entire result set of a server-based query.
Declaration	

```
procedure FetchAll;
```

Description	The `FetchAll` method, when used with a query against a server database, forces the server to release all intermediate locks and reads the entire result set. The method will perform its actions only if the `TDataSet` is not at its last row. In this case, it will first make a call to `CheckBrowseMode`, then reposition the cursor at the end of the result set, and update the current record position accordingly.

FieldByName METHOD

Objects Affected	`TDataSet`
Purpose	The `FieldByName` method returns a `TField` associated with a given database field.
Declaration	

```
function FieldByName(const FieldName: string): TField;
```

Parameters	
FieldName	· Name of the physical database field.
Example Syntax	

```
{...}
CustomerTable.FieldByName( 'CustNo' ).AsInteger := GetNewCustNo;
{...}
```

Description   The `FieldByName` method returns the `TField` object (in the Fields array of the `TDataSet`), the `FieldName` property which is equal to the field name given as parameter. The `FieldByName` method is really a shortcut for calling the `FindField` method. While the `FindField` method returns `Nil` if the specified field cannot be found, the `FieldByName` method raises an exception. This protects your code from running against any changes in the table's field structure. If the table's field name changes, your code will no longer run. Also, the `FieldByName` method protects the application from any changes in the physical order of the fields in the `TDataSet`, which, for instance, is not the case if you access the `TFields` objects by using the Fields array directly.

The `FieldByName` method is most typically used with the returned value property or conversion properties of `TField`, such as `AsInteger`, `AsString`, and so on.

Notice that the code fragment listed in the Example Syntax section is taken from the Example Syntax of the `ActiveBuffer`. For a more complete listing, refer back to the `ActiveBuffer` section.

`FieldCount` PROPERTY

Objects Affected   `TDataSet`

Purpose   The `FieldCount` property contains the number of fields in the `TDataSet`.

Declaration

```
property FieldCount: Integer;
```

Example Syntax

```
// Transfer the current record from the source table
// to the destination table.
procedure TTDataSetTestForm.TransferRecord(
  SourceTable, DestinationTable: TTable
);
var
  i: Integer;
begin
  { Assume SourceTable and DestinationTable have the
    same structure, and that all fields can be
    read and written as strings.
    Make a field-by-field copy. }
  DestinationTable.Append;
  for i := 0 to Pred(SourceTable.FieldCount) do
  begin
    DestinationTable.Fields[ i ].AsString :=
      SourceTable.Fields[ i ].AsString;
  end;
end;
```

Description The `FieldCount` property is a run-time, read-only property that indicates the number of fields present in the `TDataSet`. Notice that the number of fields in the `TDataSet` may not be the same as the number of fields in the physical table, since you might use the Fields Editor to remove original fields and add calculated fields. (In the above code fragment, it is assumed the Fields Editor has not been used. You can programmatically check for this condition by checking the `DefaultFields` property.)

`FieldDefs` PROPERTY

Objects Affected TDataSet

Purpose The `FieldDefs` property is an array of field definitions.

Declaration

```
property FieldDefs: TFieldDefs;
```

Example Syntax

```
procedure TCreateTableForm.FormCreate(Sender: TObject);
begin
  { Create the StructureTable on disk. StructureTable is
    a TTable object on the form.}
  with StructureTable do
  begin
    DatabaseName := Session.PrivateDir;
    TableName    := tbStructure;
    TableType    := ttParadox;

    { Define the structure of the temporary structure table. }
    with FieldDefs do
    begin
      Clear;
      Add('Field Name', ftString,   31,  true  );
      Add('Type',       ftString,   18,  true  );
      Add('Size',       ftSmallint,  0,  false );
      Add('Dec',        ftSmallint,  0,  false );
      Add('Key',        ftBoolean,   0,  false );
      Add('Order',      ftSmallint,  0,  true  );
    end;

    { Define the structure table's indexes. }
    with IndexDefs do
    begin
      Add( inUniqueName, stFieldName, [ixPrimary, ixUnique] );
      Add( inFieldOrder, stOrder,     [ixUnique]            );
    end;

    { Create the table }
    CreateTable;

    { Display the table according to ascending values of the
      Order field. }
```

continued on next page

continued from previous page

```
              IndexName := inFieldOrder;

          end;

          { Finally open the table }
          StructureTable.Open;

      end;
```

Description   The `FieldDefs` property is available at run time only. It is an array of field definitions. You can use it either to retrieve information about the fields in an existing `TDataSet`, or to describe the structure of a table you intend to create programmatically (as illustrated in the above code fragment).

FieldValues PROPERTY

Objects Affected   `TDataSet`

Purpose   The `FieldValues` array property is an array of all field values as variants.

Declaration

```
property FieldValues[const FieldName: string]: Variant; default;
```

Example Syntax

```
// FieldValue property.
procedure TTDataSetTestForm.FieldValueSpeedButtonClick(Sender: TObject);
var
  TaxPayer: Variant;
  VarArrayIndex, LowBound, HighBound: Integer;
  TheMessage: String;
begin
  if CustomerTable[ 'TaxRate' ] <> 0 then
  begin
    TheMessage := 'Remember that taxes apply for:';
    TaxPayer := ⇐
CustomerTable['Company;Addr1;Addr2;City;State;Zip;Country'];
    LowBound := VarArrayLowBound( TaxPayer, 1 );
    HighBound := VarArrayHighBound( TaxPayer, 1 );
    for VarArrayIndex := LowBound to HighBound do
    begin
      TheMessage := TheMessage + #13#10 + TaxPayer[ VarArrayIndex ];
    end;
    MessageBeep( $FFFF );
    ShowMessage( TheMessage );
  end;
end;
```

Description   The `FieldValues` property is an array property that evaluates to a `Variant` containing the value of one or more fields in the `TDataSet`. The array property can be indexed by a string indicating the name of a field in the

TDataSet, or by a semicolon-separated list of field names in the TDataSet. In the first case, the resulting Variant contains a value compatible with the type of the field indicated. In the second case, the resulting Variants is an array of Variants corresponding to the single fields in the list. Notice that the property is the default array property for TDataSets. This allows you to use the shortcut of not writing FieldValues when referring to it. (In other words, CustomerTable.FieldValues['State'] can also be written as CustomerTable['State'], as in the example code.)

Fields PROPERTY

Objects Affected	TDataSet
Purpose	The Fields array property is an array of TFields in the TDataSet.
Declaration	

```
property Fields[Index: Integer]: TField;
```

Example Syntax

```
// Convert all non calculated/non lookup string fields to upper case.
procedure TTDataSetTestForm.FieldsSpeedButtonClick(Sender: TObject);
var
  FieldIndex: Integer;
begin
  with CustomerTable do
    if State in [dsInsert, dsEdit] then
      for FieldIndex := 0 to Pred( FieldCount ) do
        if Fields[ FieldIndex ] is TStringField then
          with Fields[ FieldIndex ] as TStringField do
            if (not Calculated) and (not Lookup) then
              Value := UpperCase( Value );
end;
```

Description

The Fields array property is a run-time property listing all TField objects associated with the TDataSet, either implicitly or explicitly, with the Editor of Fields. The index is an integer number ranging from 0 to FieldCount -1.

Filter PROPERTY

Objects Affected	TDataSet
Purpose	The Filter property is used to define a record filter expression.
Declaration	

```
property Filter: string;
```

Example Syntax

```
// Toggle filtering by State field on and off.
procedure TTDataSetTestForm.FilterSpeedButtonClick(Sender: TObject);
var
  FilterState: String;
begin
  with CustomerTable do
  begin
    if not Filtered then
    begin
      InputQuery( 'Define Filter', 'By which State?', FilterState );
      Filter := '[State] = ''' + FilterState + '''';
      FilterOptions := [foCaseInsensitive];
      Filtered := True;
    end
    else
    begin
      Filtered := False;
    end;
  end;
end;
```

Description

The `Filter` property is used to define a filter expression. A *filter expression* is a boolean expression that compares fields to other fields or literal values using the ordinary comparison operators (<, >, >=, <=, =, and <>). If the field names contain spaces, you must enclose them in square brackets; otherwise, square brackets are optional. You can combine several comparisons with the AND, OR, and NOT operators, and use parentheses to enforce the correct order of evaluation. For instance, you could express a compound condition like this:

```
Filter :=
  '([State] = ''' + FilterState + ''') AND ([City]= ''Kapaa Kauai'')';
```

The filtered expression will be used when the `Filtered` property of the `TDataSet` is set to `True`. When that happens, the `TDataSet` actually shows only those records meeting the criteria specified with the filter expression in the `Filter` property. Filters are conceptually similar to queries, although less powerful (especially if the conditions span several tables). Filters are also less efficient than real queries since they don't actually restrict the number of records present in the `TDataSet`, only the number of *visible* records. The main advantage of filters is the result set is always a *live* one (provided, of course, that the original unfiltered `TDataSet` was a live one).

If you cannot express the filtering criteria by the `Filter` property's filter expression, you can resort to defining the `OnFilterRecord` event handler, which defines the most complex filtering criteria by expressing them in Object Pascal code. Refer to the `OnFilterRecord` event for more information on this technique.

FilterOptions PROPERTY

Objects Affected	`TDataSet`
Purpose	The `FilterOptions` property defines whether the filter is case sensitive or not, and whether partial matches are allowed.
Declaration	

```
property FilterOptions: TFilterOptions;
```

Description   The `FilterOptions` property is a set of `TFilterOption`, which is defined as an enumeration of filter options. In terms of type declarations, Delphi defines the following:

```
type
  TFilterOption = (foCaseInsensitive, foNoPartialCompare);
  TFilterOptions = set of TFilterOption;
```

If the `FilterOptions` property contains `foCaseInsensitive`, the filter is applied regardless of the case in the fields tested for matching. If the `FilterOptions` property contains `foNoPartialCompare`, the matches must be exact; otherwise they can be partial. (For an example code segment, see the example for the `Filter` property.)

Filtered PROPERTY

Objects Affected	`TDataSet`
Purpose	The `Filtered` boolean property is used to activate or deactivate a filter.
Declaration	

```
property Filtered: Boolean;
```

Example Syntax

```
// See the example for the Filter property.
// See the example for the OnFilterRecord event handler.
```

Description   The `Filtered` boolean property determines whether filtering is active or not. When filtering is active, the `Filter` property is taken into account for restricting the number of records visible in the `TDataSet`. In addition, the `OnFilterRecord` event handler is fired once for every record retrieved by the `TDataSet`. Note that filtering is enforced in addition to any other restrictions, like those given by ranges or master/detail relationships.

FindField METHOD

Objects Affected	TDataSet
Purpose	The FindField method retrieves a TField associated with a given database field.

Declaration

```
function FindField(const FieldName: string): TField;
```

Parameters

FieldName   Name of the physical database field.

Example Syntax

```
// Retrieve a field's data type.
procedure TTDataSetTestForm.FindFieldSpeedButtonClick(Sender: TObject);
var
  TheFieldName: String;
  TheField: TField;
  TheDataType: String;
begin
  InputQuery( 'Field Type Inquiry', 'Which field?', TheFieldName );
  TheField := CustomerTable.FindField( TheFieldName );
  if TheField = Nil then
  begin
    // Note: this unit's uses clause must reference:
    //       Db       for accessing the DBErrorFmt procedure, and
    //       DbConsts for accessing the SFieldNotFound error code.
    DBErrorFmt(SFieldNotFound, [TheFieldName]);
  end

  else
  begin
    case TheField.DataType of
      ftUnknown   : TheDataType := 'Unknown or undetermined';
      ftString    : TheDataType := 'Character or string field';
      ftSmallint  : TheDataType := '16-bit integer field';
      ftInteger   : TheDataType := '32-bit integer field';
      ftWord      : TheDataType := '16-bit unsigned integer field';
      ftBoolean   : TheDataType := 'Boolean field';
      ftFloat     : TheDataType := 'Floating-point numeric field';
      ftCurrency  : TheDataType := 'Money field';
      ftBCD       : TheDataType := 'Binary-Coded Decimal field';
      ftDate      : TheDataType := 'Date field';
      ftTime      : TheDataType := 'Time field';
      ftDateTime  : TheDataType := 'Date and time field';
      ftBytes     : TheDataType :=
                       'Fixed number of bytes (binary storage)';
      ftVarBytes  : TheDataType :=
                       'Variable number of bytes (binary storage)';
      ftAutoInc   : TheDataType :=
                       'Autoincrementing 32-bit integer counter field';
      ftBlob      : TheDataType := 'Binary Large Object field';
```

```
                  ftMemo      : TheDataType := 'Text memo field';
                  ftGraphic   : TheDataType := 'Bitmap field';
                  ftFmtMemo   : TheDataType := 'Formatted text memo field';
                  ftParadoxOle : TheDataType := 'Paradox OLE field';
                  ftDBaseOle  : TheDataType := 'dBASE OLE field';
                  ftTypedBinary: TheDataType := 'Typed binary field';
                end;
                ShowMessage( 'The [' + TheFieldName + '] field is of type:' +
                            #13#10 + TheDataType + '.'
                );
              end;
            end;
```

Description

The `FindField` method will return the `TField` object (in the Fields array of the `TDataSet`) whose `FieldName` property is equal to the field name given as parameter. If the field is not found, then `Nil` is returned.

Notice that the `FieldByName` method is a convenient wrapper method around `FindField`. The advantage of `FieldByName` is that it raises an exception if the specified field is not found, and lets you write more robust code, should the underlying table structure be changed (with fields being renamed or removed). You can use `FindField` when you don't want the exception to be raised and know how to treat the case when the field is not found (or you wish to raise a different exception yourself).

FindFirst, FindLast, FindNext, AND FindPrior METHODS

Objects Affected   `TDataSet`

Purpose   The `FindFirst`, `FindLast`, `FindNext`, and `FindPrior` methods will find, respectively, the first, last, next, or prior record matching the filter criteria.

Declaration

```
function FindFirst: Boolean;
function FindLast: Boolean;
function FindNext: Boolean;
function FindPrior: Boolean;
```

Example Syntax

```
// Report number of records in filtered set.
procedure TTDataSetTestForm.FindFirstNextSpeedButtonClick(
  Sender: TObject);
var
  NumberOfRecords : Integer;
begin
  NumberOfRecords := 0;
  with CustomerTable do
    if FindFirst then
      repeat Inc( NumberOfRecords );
      until not FindNext;
```

continued on next page

continued from previous page

```
      ShowMessage( IntToStr( NumberOfRecords ) +
        ' record(s) in Filtered set.'
      );
    end;
```

Description   The **FindFirst**, **FindLast**, **FindNext**, and **FindPrior** methods allow you to navigate through a filtered **TDataSet**, in which the filtering criteria are provided either by a filter expression specified in the **Filter** property of the **TDataSet**, or by an **OnFilterRecord** event handler. Note that the filter does not have to be active (in other words, the **Filter** property does not have to be **True**) for these methods to work. Therefore, you can use them effectively even on the *unfiltered* **TDataSet**.

(By the way, this is why in the above code fragment, the **NumberOfRecords** variable is computed by scanning through the filtered set. With this technique, you will always know exactly how many records are in the filtered set. Alternatively, you could use the **RecordCount** property, but *only* if at that moment the filter is truly active. With the given code, you will find the number of records in the filtered set even if the filter is not active.)

All four of these methods return a boolean, which is **True** when a record matching the given filter is found. If the record is found, it becomes the current record of the **TDataSet**.

First METHOD

Objects Affected   TDataSet

Purpose   The **First** method moves the cursor position to the first record of the TDataSet.

Declaration

```
procedure First;
```

Example Syntax

```
{ ... }
var
  CurrentCustomerBookmark: TBookmark;
begin
  { ... }
  { Scan through all records in result set. }
  with CustomerTable do
  begin
    DisableControls;
    CurrentCustomerBookmark := GetBookmark;
    try
      First;
```

```
            While not Eof do
            begin
              { ... here you would code any further record processing... }
              Next;
            end;
          finally
            GotoBookmark( CurrentCustomerBookmark );
            EnableControls;
            FreeBookmark( CurrentCustomerBookmark );
          end;
          { ... }
```

Description

The `First` method makes the first record of the `TDataSet` the current record. The method takes into account any range and filter that might be defined on the `TDataSet`. Note that before actually making the move to the first record, the method makes a call to `CheckBrowseMode`. If there are any pending changes in the current record, they will be posted prior to making the move.

You can use the method to position the current record of the `TDataSet` according to the user's interactive actions or to programmatically control navigation through all records in the `TDataSet`. For instance, you can initialize a record scanning loop, as shown in the above sample code fragment.

Found PROPERTY

Objects Affected   TDataSet

Purpose

The `Found` boolean property reports whether there is a matching record after using a navigation method.

Declaration

```
property Found: Boolean;
```

Example Syntax

```
procedure TTDataSetTestForm.FoundSpeedButtonClick(Sender: TObject);
var
  NumberOfRecords : Integer;
begin
  NumberofRecords := 0;
  with CustomerTable do if FindFirst then while Found do
  begin
    Inc( NumberOfRecords );
    FindNext;
  end;
  ShowMessage( IntToStr( NumberOfRecords ) +
               ' record(s) in Filtered set.' );
end;
```

Description The **Found** property is a run-time, read-only boolean property. It will be **True** if the last call to the **FindFirst**, **FindLast**, **FindNext**, or **FindPrior** methods was successful. Note that the example code is an alternative way of writing the same sample code given for the **FindFirst** method.

FreeBookmark METHOD

Objects Affected TDataSet, TBookmark
Purpose The **FreeBookmark** method releases a given bookmark on the **TDataSet**.
Declaration

```
procedure FreeBookmark(Bookmark: TBookmark);
```

Parameters
Bookmark The bookmark initially obtained by calling the **GetBookmark** method.
Description The **FreeBookmark** method releases a bookmark previously created by calling the **GetBookmark** method. The method expects a *Bookmark* as its sole parameter. For an example of how to use this method, refer to the example code given for the **First** method.

GetBookmark METHOD

Objects Affected TDataSet, TBookmark
Purpose The **GetBookmark** method creates a bookmark on the current record of the **TDataSet**.
Declaration

```
function GetBookmark: TBookmark;
```

Description The **GetBookmark** method creates a bookmark on the current record of the **TDataSet**. The bookmark is the method's return value, which is of the **TBookmark** type. Typically, you store the returned bookmark in a **TBookmark** variable, and eventually use it in a call to **GotoBookmark** to return to the original record.

Internally, a **TBookmark** is nothing but a pointer to a block of memory capable of holding information about the current position of the cursor of the **TDataSet**. The size of this block of memory is handled internally by the BDE, and it differs depending on the kind of database tables you use. Once you have finished using a bookmark, you must always make a call to the **FreeBookmark** method to ensure that the block of memory consumed by the bookmark is released properly.

Sometimes a bookmark cannot be used reliably. In such cases, the bookmark is said to be unstable. You can determine whether or not a bookmark is stable by examining the **bBookMarkStable** property returned by **DbiGetCursorProps**, available in the BDE unit. If a bookmark is stable, it is guaranteed that the cursor can be repositioned on the original record; if the bookmark is unstable, the cursor may be in an unexpected position. The type of table involved greatly affects the bookmark's stability. For dBASE tables, the bookmark is always stable. For Paradox tables, the bookmark is stable only if the table has a primary key. For SQL tables, the bookmark is stable only if the table has a unique index or unique row identifier.

For an example of how to use this method, refer to the example code given for the **First** method.

GetCurrentRecord METHOD

Objects Affected	TDataSet
Purpose	The GetCurrentRecord method retrieves the current record of the TDataSet into a given memory buffer.
Declaration	

```
function GetCurrentRecord(Buffer: PChar): Boolean;
```

Parameters

Buffer Pointer to a buffer.

Example Syntax

```
var
  RecordBuffer: PChar;
begin
  // Allocate memory.
  RecordBuffer := AllocMem( CustomerTable.RecordSize );
  try
    if CustomerTable.GetCurrentRecord( RecordBuffer ) then
    begin
      { ... do your own processing on the RecordBuffer here ... }
    end;
  finally
    FreeMem( RecordBuffer, CustomerTable.RecordSize );
  end;
end;
```

Description The **GetCurrentRecord** method retrieves the current record from the **TDataSet** into a memory buffer large enough to contain the whole record. Memory management of the buffer is your responsibility, so you must remember to release it once you are done using it.

GetFieldList METHOD

Objects Affected	`TDataSet`
Purpose	The `GetFieldList` method retrieves a list of field objects given their physical field names.

Declaration

```
procedure GetFieldList(List: TList; const FieldNames: string);
```

Parameters

List	A list object to which field objects will be added.
FieldNames	A semicolon-separated list of physical field names of `TDataSet`.

Example Syntax

```
var
  AddressFields: TList;
  i: Integer;
begin
  AddressFields := TList.Create;
  try
    CustomerTable.GetFieldList(
      AddressFields,
      'Company;Addr1;Addr2;City;State;Zip;Country'
    );
    { ...  process AddressFields here ...}
  finally
    AddressFields.Free;
  end;
end;
```

Description The `GetFieldList` method will add to a list object new field objects corresponding to the `TDataSet`'s physical fields indicated in the `FieldName` string. Memory management of the `List` object is your responsibility. Typically, you would use this method to gain access to a specified subset of fields in the `TDataSet`, for instance, the key fields or some logically related fields (such as the address fields in the above code segment). Since the method loads field objects into the `List` parameter, you will most likely access each item in the list by a loop, typecast it to a `TField`, and use `TField` properties and methods to perform any further processing.

GetFieldNames METHOD

Objects Affected	`TDataSet`
Purpose	The `GetFieldNames` method will get the list of the physical field names in the `TDataSet`.

Declaration

```
procedure GetFieldNames(List: TStrings);
```

Parameters

List   String list that will receive all field names.

Example Syntax

```
procedure TTDataSetTestForm.GetFieldNamesSpeedButtonClick(Sender: ⇐
TObject);
begin
  CustomerTable.GetFieldNames( TheListBox.Items );
end;
```

Description   The `GetFieldNames` method adds the names of all fields in the **TDataSet**
to a string list. You are responsible for creating and releasing the string list.
The string list is cleared before the field names are added to it.

GotoBookmark METHOD

Objects Affected   **TDataSet**

Purpose   The `GotoBookmark` method will position the record cursor on a given
bookmark.

Declaration

```
procedure GotoBookmark(Bookmark: TBookmark);
```

Parameters

Bookmark   The bookmark initially obtained by calling the **GetBookmark** method.

Example Syntax

```
{ ... }
var
  CurrentCustomerBookmark: TBookmark;
begin
  { ... }
  { Scan through all records in result set. }
  with CustomerTable do
  begin
    DisableControls;
    CurrentCustomerBookmark := GetBookmark;
    try
      First;
      While not Eof do
      begin
        { ... here you would code any further record processing... }
        Next;
      end;
```

continued on next page

continued from previous page

```
  finally
    GotoBookmark( CurrentCustomerBookmark );
    EnableControls;
    FreeBookmark( CurrentCustomerBookmark );
  end;
  { ... }
```

Description   The `GotoBookmark` method positions the record cursor on the given book-mark. The bookmark passed in the method's parameter must be set prior to calling this method (by calling the `GetBookmark` method). The parameter can also be `Nil`, in which case no movement is performed.

Handle PROPERTY

Objects Affected   TDataSet

Purpose   The `Handle` property returns the BDE cursor handle associated with the TDataSet.

Declaration

```
property Handle: HDBICur;
```

Example Syntax

```
// Get cursor properties associated with CustomerTable.
// Note that the BDE unit must be in the uses statement
// for the following to work.
procedure TTDataSetTestForm.HandleSpeedButtonClick(Sender: TObject);
var
  CustomerTableProperty: CURProps;
begin
  with CustomerTable do
  begin
    Check( DbiGetCursorProps( Handle, CustomerTableProperty ));
    { ... use the cursor properties here ... }
  end;
end;
```

Description   The `Handle` property is a run-time, read-only property. It represents the so-called cursor handle associated with the **TDataSet**. A *cursor handle* is the basic data structure used by the BDE to manipulate tables and query result sets. By using the cursor handle, you will be able to make direct calls to the BDE.

Insert METHOD

Objects Affected   TDataSet

Purpose   The `Insert` method puts the **TDataSet** in Insert mode and inserts a new empty record into it.

Declaration

```
procedure Insert;
```

Example Syntax

```
// Insert a new empty record into the TDataSet.
procedure TTDataSetTestForm.InsertSpeedButtonClick(Sender: TObject);
begin
  CustomerTable.Insert;
end;
```

Description

The `Insert` method opens a new empty record at the current cursor position of the **TDataSet**. Note that the method will work only on a **TDataSet** returning a modifiable live result set. If that is not the case, an exception is raised. The **TDataSet** must be open for the `Insert` method to work, otherwise an exception is raised.

The method first calls `CheckBrowseMode` and checks the modify flag. Next, if a `BeforeInsert` event handler procedure is assigned, it is called. The new record is then created and initialized. Any bookmarks that may be affected by the insertion are adjusted. The record count of the **TDataSet** is also updated.

The state of the **TDataSet** is then set to `dsInsert`. If there is an `OnNewRecord` event handler procedure, it is called. If the `OnNewRecord` event handler procedure raises an exception, the insertion aborts, the state returns to `dsBrowse`, the **TDataSet** is resynchronized to its previous position, and the exception is re-raised. If there was no `OnNewRecord` event handler procedure, or if it executed without raising any exceptions, the `Modified` property of the **TDataSet** is initialized to `False`. Finally, if there is an `AfterInsert` event handler procedure assigned, it is called.

Note that for indexed tables, when you post the new record created with the `Insert` methods, it is placed in the correct location in the table, based on the index. This is also known as the record fly-away effect. Keep in mind that this might cause current data-aware components, including data grids, to change in unexpected ways. As a general rule of thumb, you should refresh and reposition the **TDataSet** after posting a *new* record. (Obviously, if no index is used, the record will keep its position).

InsertRecord METHOD

Objects Affected `TDataSet`

Purpose The `InsertRecord` method will insert a new record given some or all of its field values.

Declaration

```
procedure InsertRecord(const Values: array of const);
```

Parameters

Values   An array of constant values that can be converted to the datatypes of the corresponding fields in the `TDataSet`.

Example Syntax

```
// Demonstrate usage of InsertRecord.
procedure TTDataSetTestForm.InsertRecordSpeedButtonClick(Sender: ⇐
TObject);
var
  NewCustNo:        LongInt;
  CompanyName:      String;
  AddressLine1:     String;
  AddressLine2:     String;
  City:             String;
  State:            String;
  Zip:              String;
  Country:          String;
  InputCaption:     String;

begin
  NewCustNo     := GetNewCustNo;
  InputCaption  := 'New Customer ' + IntToStr( NewCustNo );
  CompanyName   := InputBox( InputCaption, 'Company?',   '' );
  AddressLine1  := InputBox( InputCaption, 'Address 1?', '' );
  AddressLine2  := InputBox( InputCaption, 'Address 2?', '' );
  City          := InputBox( InputCaption, 'City?',      '' );
  State         := InputBox( InputCaption, 'State?',     '' );
  Zip           := InputBox( InputCaption, 'Zip Code?',  '' );
  Country       := InputBox( InputCaption, 'Country?',   '' );

  CustomerTable.InsertRecord
  (
    [
      NewCustNo,
      CompanyName,
      AddressLine1,
      AddressLine2,
      City,
      State,
      Zip,
      Country
    ]
  );
end;

// Note that GetNewCustNo is a support function.
// It could be defined like this:

// Support function to get the next available record number.
//     NOTE: Multiuser issues are not taken into account!
function TTDataSetTestForm.GetNewCustNo: LongInt;
var
  MaxCustNoQuery: TQuery;
begin
  Result := 0;
```

```
     MaxCustNoQuery := TQuery.Create( Nil );
     try
       with MaxCustNoQuery do
       begin
         DatabaseName := 'DBDEMOS';
         Sql.Clear;
         Sql.Add( 'SELECT MAX( CUSTNO ) FROM CUSTOMER' );
         Open;
         if not Fields[ 0 ].isNull then
         begin
           Result := Succ( Fields[ 0 ].AsInteger );
         end;
         Close;
       end;
     finally
       MaxCustNoQuery.Free;
     end;
   end;
```

Description

The **InsertRecord** method will insert a new record at the current position of the **TDataSet**. The method takes as a parameter an array of constant values. Each value in the array parameter is sequentially assigned to the **TFields** in the **TDataSet**. If there are less values in the array than fields in the **TDataSet**, remaining fields are assigned a **NULL** value. If there are more values in the array than fields in the **TDataSet**, a run-time List Index Out of Bounds error is generated. To skip any values, you can use the reserved word **Nil**.

The method works only on **TDataSets** returning a live result set that can be modified. If that is not the case, an exception is raised. The **TDataSet** must be open for the **Insert** method to work, otherwise, an exception is raised.

The method first calls **CheckBrowseMode** and checks the modify flag. Next, if a **BeforeInsert** event handler procedure is assigned, it is called. The new record is then created and initialized, and the state of the **TDataSet** is set to **dsInsert**.

If there is an **OnNewRecord** event handler procedure, it is called. If there is an **AfterInsert** event handler procedure assigned, it is called. The field values are then copied to the actual record buffer. If there is a **BeforePost** event handler procedure, it is called. The new record is then posted.

If any of the **OnNewRecord**, **AfterInsert**, or **BeforePost** event handler procedures raise an exception, the insertion aborts, all field buffers are freed, the state returns to **dsBrowse**, the **TDataSet** is resynchronized to its previous position, and the exception is re-raised.

If there were no event handler procedures or if they executed without raising exceptions, the **TDataSet** is resynchronized. Finally, if there is an **AfterInsert** event handler procedure assigned, it is called.

Note that for indexed tables, after executing the **InsertRecord** method, the new record is placed in the correct location in the table, based on the table's index. This is also known as the record fly-away effect. Keep in mind that this might cause current data-aware components, including data grids, to change in unexpected ways. As a general rule of thumb, you should refresh and reposition the **TDataSet** after posting a *new* record. (Obviously, if no index is used, the record will keep its position.)

IsLinkedTo METHOD

Objects Affected TDataSet

Purpose The **IsLinkedTo** method inquires whether the **TDataSet** is linked to a given data source.

Declaration

```
function IsLinkedTo(DataSource: TDataSource): Boolean;
```

Parameters

DataSource Target data source being inquired about.

Example Syntax

```
{ ... }
if CustomerTable.IsLinkedTo( OrdersDataSource ) then
{ ... }
```

Description The **IsLinkedTo** method reports **True** if the **TDataSet** is in some way (directly or indirectly) linked to (or, is a master dataset of) a given data source.

KeySize PROPERTY

Objects Affected TDataSet

Purpose The **KeySize** property will report the key size in bytes of the **TDataSet**.

Declaration

```
property KeySize: Word;
```

Example Syntax

```
// The following is extracted from the VCL source code:
// Reproduced by permission Borland International, Inc.
function TTable.GotoKey: Boolean;
var
  KeyBuffer: PKeyBuffer;
  IndexBuffer, RecBuffer: PChar;
```

```
      UseKey: Boolean;
    begin
      CheckBrowseMode;
      CursorPosChanged;
      KeyBuffer := GetKeyBuffer(kiLookup);
      IndexBuffer := AllocMem(KeySize);
      try
        RecBuffer := PChar(KeyBuffer) + SizeOf(TKeyBuffer);
        UseKey := DbiExtractKey(Handle, RecBuffer, IndexBuffer) = 0;
        if UseKey then RecBuffer := IndexBuffer;
        Result := DbiGetRecordForKey(Handle, UseKey,
          KeyBuffer^.FieldCount, 0, RecBuffer, nil) = 0;
        if Result then Resync([rmExact, rmCenter]);
      finally
        FreeMem(IndexBuffer, KeySize);
      end;
    end;
```

Description The **KeySize** property is a run-time, read-only property indicating the size in bytes of the currently active index. It is used almost exclusively when making direct calls to the BDE.

Last METHOD

Objects Affected TDataSet

Purpose The **Last** method moves the record cursor to the last record of the TDataSet.

Declaration

```
procedure Last;
```

Example Syntax

```
{ ... }
var
  CurrentCustomerBookmark: TBookmark;
begin
  { ... }
  { Scan through all records in result set in reverse order. }
  with CustomerTable do
  begin
    DisableControls;
    CurrentCustomerBookmark := GetBookmark;
    try
      Last;
      While not Bof do
      begin
        { ... here you would code any further record processing... }
        Prior;
      end;
    finally
      { reposition cursor on original record and re-enable controls }
```

continued on next page

continued from previous page

```
        GotoBookmark( CurrentCustomerBookmark );
        EnableControls;
        FreeBookmark( CurrentCustomerBookmark );
      end;
      { ... }
```

Description   The `Last` method makes the last record of the `TDataSet` the current record. The method takes into account any range and filter that might be defined on the `TDataSet`. Note that before actually making the move to the last record, the method makes a call to `CheckBrowseMode`. Therefore, if there are any pending changes in the current record, they will be posted before making the move.

You can use the method to position the current record of the `TDataSet` according to the user's interactive actions, or to programmatically control navigation through all records in the `TDataSet`, for instance, initializing a record scanning loop, as shown in the above sample code fragment.

Locale PROPERTY

Objects Affected   `TDataSet`

Purpose   The `Locale` property retrieves a language driver of the `TDataSet`.

Declaration

```
property Locale: TLocale;
```

Description   The `Locale` property of the `TDataSet` is a run-time, read-only property. It is actually a pointer (the `TLocale` type) to the BDE structure representing the language driver associated with the `TDataSet`. You need to access this function only if you intend to make direct calls to the BDE, typically by calling the `AnsiToNative` function or the `NativeToAnsi` procedure in the DB.PAS unit.

A language driver associated with the `TDataSet` has the same lifespan as the `TDataSet` itself. The language driver specifies a particular primary (or native) character set, as well as a country/language-dependent set of rules for character manipulation (such as sorting, uppercasing, lowercasing, and alphabetizing). A language driver also determines the character translation mapping between its primary character set and the ANSI code page, when necessary.

Locate METHOD

Objects Affected   `TDataSet`

Purpose   The `Locate` method will find a record with the given field values.

Declaration

```
function Locate(const KeyFields: string; const KeyValues: Variant;
      Options: TLocateOptions): Boolean;
```

Parameters

KeyFields   A semicolon-separated list of fields.

KeyValues   Variant of values being sought.

Options   Search options.

Example Syntax

```
procedure TTDataSetTestForm.LocateButtonSpeedButtonClick(Sender: ⇐
TObject);
var
  KeyFields: String;
  KeyValues: Variant;
  Options: TLocateOptions;
begin
  KeyFields := 'State;Company';
  KeyValues := VarArrayOf( [ 'CA', 'Underwater' ] );
  Options := [loCaseInsensitive, loPartialKey];
  // Locate "Underwater Sports Co." in "CA"
  if CustomerTable.Locate(KeyFields, KeyValues, Options) then
  begin
    { ... process found record here ... }
  end;
end;
```

Description

The `Locate` method will find a record in the **TDataSet** by matching provided criteria. The first parameter, **KeyFields**, is a semicolon-separated list of fields to be examined. The second parameter, **KeyValues**, is a variant indicating the single field value to match if only one field was given in **KeyFields**. If more than one field was given, then **KeyValues** is a variant array holding, field by field, the values to be found. The last parameter, **Options**, is a set of **TLocateOptions**. You can indicate whether the search should be case insensitive or not, and whether partial matches are allowed on any single field. If the search is successful, the method returns **True**.

Lookup METHOD

Objects Affected   TDataSet

Purpose   The `Lookup` method will look up specific fields according to given field values.

Declaration

```
function Lookup(const KeyFields: string; const KeyValues: Variant;
      const ResultFields: string): Variant;
```

Parameters

KeyFields   A semicolon-separated list of fields.

KeyValues   Variant of values being sought.

ResultFields   A semicolon-separated list of fields to be retrieved.

Example Syntax

```
procedure TTDataSetTestForm.LookupSpeedButtonClick(Sender: TObject);
var
  KeyFields: String;
  KeyValues: Variant;
  ResultFields: String;
  ResultVariant: Variant;
  VarArrayIndex, LowBound, HighBound: Integer;
  TheMessage: String;
begin
  KeyFields := 'State;Company';
  KeyValues := VarArrayOf( [ 'CA', 'Underwater Sports Co.' ] );
  ResultFields := 'Company;Addr1;Addr2;City;State;Zip;Country';
  // Lookup "Underwater Sports Co." in "CA"
  ResultVariant := CustomerTable.Lookup(
    KeyFields,
    KeyValues,
    ResultFields
  );
  if not VarIsNull( ResultVariant ) then
  begin
    TheMessage := 'A lookup match was found for:';
    LowBound := VarArrayLowBound( ResultVariant, 1 );
    HighBound := VarArrayHighBound( ResultVariant, 1 );
    for VarArrayIndex := LowBound to HighBound do
      TheMessage := TheMessage
        + #13#10 + ResultVariant[ VarArrayIndex ];
  end
  else
  begin
    TheMessage := 'No lookup match found.';
  end;
  MessageBeep( $FFFF );
  ShowMessage( TheMessage );
end;
```

Description   The **Lookup** method works almost like the **Locate** method. While the
                     Locate method actually positions the **TDataSet** on the record matching
                     the specified search criteria, the **Lookup** method returns a variant with the
                     specified fields read from the matching record. The **Lookup** method will
                     never move the current record cursor to another one.

                     The first parameter, *KeyFields*, is a semicolon-separated list of fields to be
                     examined. The second parameter, **KeyValues**, is a variant indicating the
                     single field value to match if only one field was given in *KeyFields*. If
                     more than one field was given in *KeyFields*, then **KeyValues** is a variant
                     array holding, field by field, the values to be found. The last parameter,

ResultFields, is a semicolon-separated list of the names of the fields to be retrieved from the matching record. The actual lookup will be performed with a case-sensitive search in which no partial matches are allowed on any single field. If the search is successful, the method will return a variant containing the specified field's value (or a variant array containing the multiple specified fields' values) from the matching record. If the search is not successful, a **NULL** variant is returned. (Do not confuse the **NULL** variant with the **Nil** pointer; you can test for **NULL** variants with the **VarIsNull** variant support routine.)

Modified PROPERTY

Objects Affected	TDataSet
Purpose	The **Modified** boolean property will report whether the record's data has been modified.
Declaration	

```
property Modified: Boolean;
```

Example Syntax

```
{...}
with CustomerTable do
begin
  if (State in [dsEdit]) and (Modified) then
  begin
      { Current record is being edited and has been modified }
      { Perform any special processing here }
  end;
end;
{...}
```

Description	The **Modified** property is a run-time, read-only property that evaluates to **True** whenever there are pending changes in the record's data. The property will eventually be reset to **False** with a call to the **Cancel** or the **Post** method.

MoveBy METHOD

Objects Affected	TDataSet
Purpose	The **MoveBy** method will move the current record cursor forward or backward in the **TDataSet** by a given number of records.
Declaration	

```
function MoveBy(Distance: Integer): Integer;
```

Parameters

Distance   The number of records by which to move.

Example Syntax

```
{ ... }
CustomerTable.MoveBy( -5 );
{ ... }
```

Description The `MoveBy` method will move the cursor of the `TDataSet` by the given number of records (`Distance`) forward or backward. If the parameter is negative, there will be a backward move; if positive, a forward move. If the number is zero, no move is performed. If the move extends beyond the beginning or end of the `TDataSet`, it stops there. The method will return the number of records by which the cursor was actually moved. Note that before making the move, the method makes a call to `CheckBrowseMode`. Therefore, if there are any pending changes in the current record, they will be posted prior to making the move (even if the distance is zero).

Next METHOD

Objects Affected `TDataSet`

Purpose The `Next` method moves the record cursor to the next record of the `TDataSet`.

Declaration

```
procedure Next;
```

Example Syntax

```
{ ... }
var
  CurrentCustomerBookmark: TBookmark;
begin
  { ... }
  { Scan through all records in result set. }
  with CustomerTable do
  begin
    DisableControls;
    CurrentCustomerBookmark := GetBookmark;
    try
      First;
      While not Eof do
      begin
        { ... here you would code any further record processing... }
        Next;
      end;
    finally
      GotoBookmark( CurrentCustomerBookmark );
      EnableControls;
```

```
      FreeBookmark( CurrentCustomerBookmark );
   end;
   { ... }
```

Description

The `Next` method makes the next record of the `TDataSet` the current record. The method takes into account any range and filter that might be defined on the `TDataSet`. Note that before actually moving to the next record, the method calls to `CheckBrowseMode`. If there are any pending changes in the current record, they will be posted prior to moving. If the cursor happens to be on the last record, the method will not move it.

You can use the method to position the current record of the `TDataSet` according to the user's interactive actions, or to programmatically control navigation through all records in the `TDataSet`; for instance, to iterate through a record scanning loop, as shown in the above sample code fragment.

OnCalcFields EVENT

Objects Affected   `TDataSet`

Purpose

The `OnCalcFields` event refers to an event handler procedure in which you can specify custom processing for determining the values of any calculated field in the `TDataSet`.

Declaration

```
Type
  TDataSetNotifyEvent = procedure(DataSet: TDataSet) of object;

property OnCalcFields: TDataSetNotifyEvent;
```

Example Syntax

```
// Assign or Deassign OnCalcFields event handler according to
// corresponding check box.
procedure TTDataSetTestForm.OnCalcFieldsCheckBoxClick(Sender: TObject);
begin
   if OnCalcFieldsCheckBox.Checked
   then CustomerTable.OnCalcFields := CustomerTableCalcFields
   else CustomerTable.OnCalcFields := Nil;
end;

// OnCalcFields event handler procedure.
procedure TTDataSetTestForm.CustomerTableCalcFields(DataSet: TDataSet);
begin
   // Note: that CustomerTableDaysSinceLastInvoice is a calculated
   // TFloatField added to the CustomerTable with the Fields Editor.
   if not CustomerTableLastInvoiceDate.isNull then
      CustomerTableDaysSinceLastInvoice.Value :=
         Int( Date - CustomerTableLastInvoiceDate.Value );
end;
```

Description   The `OnCalcFields` event of a `TDataSet` is triggered whenever a record is read from the database. The `OnCalcFields` event will also be triggered whenever a noncalculated field is modified interactively by the user (such as when the `TDataSet` is in the `Edit` or `Insert` state) and its `AutoCalcFields` property is `True`.

Note that during the execution of the `OnCalcFields` event handler procedure, the `TDataSet` state is set to `CalcFields`. While the `TDataSet` is in the `CalcFields` state, you should not change the values of calculated fields. Be aware that if any noncalculated field of the `TDataSet` (or even any field of its linked `TDataSet`s) is modified during the execution of the `OnCalcFields` event handler procedure, you could possibly fall into an infinite recursion loop.

If the `OnCalcFields` event handler procedure needs to refer to fields in other `TDataSet`s, the very first call to it (during the form's creation process) might not work properly if the `TDataSet` referred to isn't already created. To make sure all `TDataSet`s are created in the correct order (the `TDataSet`s referred to most often should come first), you can use the File | Creation menu command of the Form Designer in order to establish the desired creation order.

Naturally, before referring to calculated fields inside the `OnCalcFields` event handler procedure, you must use the Fields Editor to create them.

OnDeleteError EVENT

Objects Affected   `TDataSet`

Purpose   The `OnDeleteError` event refers to an event handler procedure to perform whenever record deletion errors are detected.

Declaration

```
type
  TDataAction = (daFail, daAbort, daRetry);
  TDataSetErrorEvent = procedure(DataSet: TDataSet;
                                 E: EDatabaseError;
                                 var Action: TDataAction) of object;

property OnDeleteError: TDataSetErrorEvent;
```

Example Syntax

```
procedure TTDataSetTestForm.OnDeleteErrorCheckBoxClick(Sender: TObject);
begin
  if OnDeleteErrorCheckBox.Checked
  then CustomerTable.OnDeleteError := CustomerTableDeleteError
  else CustomerTable.OnDeleteError := Nil;
end;
```

```
procedure TTDataSetTestForm.CustomerTableDeleteError(DataSet: TDataSet;
  E: EDatabaseError; var Action: TDataAction);
var
  I: Integer;
begin
  // if the error is a database engine error, then
  // scan through the engine's error stack, starting from
  // the top of the stack down to the bottom.
  if (E is EDBEngineError) then with (E as EDBEngineError) do
    for I := Pred( ErrorCount ) downto 0 do with Errors[ I ] do
      // Check if the current stack entry is the one you want.
      // Note that the DBIERR_DETAILRECORDSEXIST constant is
      // declared in the BDE unit.
      if Errorcode = DBIERR_DETAILRECORDSEXIST then
      begin
        // If it is, give a message, set the error action,
        // and break out of the loop;
        MessageBeep( $FFFF );
        MessageDlg('Customer has orders. Cannot delete.',
          mtWarning, [mbOK], 0);
        Action := daAbort;
        break;
      end;
end;
```

Description

The OnDeleteError event is triggered if a call to the Delete method of the TDataSet did not succeed due to some error. If you define an event handler procedure for the OnDeleteError, it will have three parameters. The first parameter identifies the TDataSet, the second is an EDatabaseError exception object describing the error, and the third is an Action data control parameter passed by reference. The Action parameter determines if and how you intend to perform custom error handling. You can assign one of three possible values to the Action parameter: daFail, daAbort, and daRetry. The daFail data action re-raises the original exception and passes it over to the ordinary exception handling system. It is the default value for the Action parameter. The daAbort data action raises an EAbort silent exception. The daRetry data action will try once again to perform the delete operation. Note that if any errors are encountered during a retry, the OnDeleteError event handler is called again.

OnEditError EVENT

Objects Affected   TDataSet

Purpose   The OnEditError event refers to an event handler procedure in which you can specify custom processing to perform when record edit errors are detected.

Declaration

```
type
  TDataAction = (daFail, daAbort, daRetry);
  TDataSetErrorEvent = procedure(DataSet: TDataSet;
                                 E: EDatabaseError;
                                 var Action: TDataAction) of object;

property OnEditError: TDataSetErrorEvent;
```

Example Syntax

```
// Assign or Deassign OnEditError event handler according to
// corresponding check box.
procedure TTDataSetTestForm.OnEditErrorCheckBoxClick(Sender: TObject);
begin
  if OnEditErrorCheckBox.Checked
  then CustomerTable.OnEditError := CustomerTableEditError
  else CustomerTable.OnEditError := Nil;
end;

procedure TTDataSetTestForm.CustomerTableEditError(DataSet: TDataSet;
  E: EDatabaseError; var Action: TDataAction);
var
  I: Integer;
begin
  // if the error is a database engine error, then
  // scan through the engine's error stack, starting from
  // the top of the stack down to the bottom.
  if (E is EDBEngineError) then with (E as EDBEngineError) do
    for I := Pred( ErrorCount ) downto 0 do with Errors[ I ] do
      // Check if the current stack entry is the one you want.
      // The DBIERR_LOCKED constant is declared in the BDE unit.
      if Errorcode = DBIERR_LOCKED then
      begin
        // If it is, give a message, set the error action,
        // and break out of the loop;
        MessageBeep( $FFFF );
        if MessageDlg('Record is locked by another user. Retry?',
          mtConfirmation, [mbYes, mbNo], 0) = mrYes
        then Action := daRetry
        else Action := daAbort;
        break;
      end;
end;
```

Description

The **OnEditError** event is triggered if a call to the **Edit** method of the **TDataSet** did not succeed due to some error. If you define an event handler procedure for the **OnEditError**, it will have three parameters. The first parameter identifies the **TDataSet**, the second is an **EDatabaseError** exception object describing the error, and the third is an *Action* data control parameter passed by reference. The *Action* parameter determines if and how you intend to perform custom error handling. You can assign one of three possible values to the *Action* parameter: **daFail**, **daAbort**, and daRetry. The daFail data action re-raises the original exception and passes it to the ordinary exception handling system. It is the default value for the Action parameter. The daAbort data action raises an EAbort silent exception. The daRetry data action will try once again to perform the operation. Note that if any errors are encountered during a retry, the OnEditError event handler is called again.

OnFilterRecord EVENT

Objects Affected TDataSet

Purpose The OnFilterRecord event refers to an event handler procedure in which you can specify custom processing to perform for filtering records.

Declaration

```
Type
  TFilterRecordEvent = procedure(DataSet: TDataSet;
                                  var Accept: Boolean) of object;

property OnFilterRecord: TFilterRecordEvent;
```

Example Syntax

```
// Assign or Deassign OnFilterRecord event handler according to
// corresponding check box.
procedure TTDataSetTestForm.OnFilterRecordCheckBoxClick(Sender: TObject);
begin
  if OnFilterRecordCheckBox.Checked
  then CustomerTable.OnFilterRecord := CustomerTableFilterRecord
  else CustomerTable.OnFilterRecord := Nil;
end;

// OnFilterRecord event handler.
procedure TTDataSetTestForm.CustomerTableFilterRecord(DataSet: TDataSet;
  var Accept: Boolean);
begin
  Accept := Not CustomerTableAddr2.IsNull;
end;
```

Description The OnFilterRecord event handler is called whenever record filtering is enabled (the Filtered property is set to True, or there are calls to the FindFirst, FindLast, FindNext, or FindPrior methods). You express any filtering condition by coding the OnFilterRecord event handler procedure and setting the *Accept* parameter (passed by reference) to True or False according to whether the condition is met or not. The event is triggered once for every record read into the TDataSet. Notice that if there are any filtering expressions defined with the Filter property, the filtering condition expressed by the OnFilterRecord event handler procedure is assessed *after* applying the filtering condition. You can therefore combine ordinary filtering expressions with the `OnFilterRecord` event handler procedure. In practice it is as though the two conditions are joined with a logical AND.

Keep in mind that since the `OnFilterRecord` handler procedure is called once for each record read into the `TDataSet`, you should keep the event as short and efficient as possible to minimize possible performance degradation.

OnNewRecord EVENT

Objects Affected   `TDataSet`

Purpose   The `OnNewRecord` event refers to an event handler procedure in which you can specify custom processing to perform when inserting a new record.

Declaration

```
Type
  TDataSetNotifyEvent = procedure(DataSet: TDataSet) of object;

property OnNewRecord: TDataSetNotifyEvent;
```

Example Syntax

```
// Assign or Deassign OnNewRecord event handler according to
// corresponding check box.
procedure TTDataSetTestForm.OnNewRecordCheckBoxClick(Sender: TObject);
begin
  if OnNewRecordCheckBox.Checked
  then CustomerTable.OnNewRecord := CustomerTableNewRecord
  else CustomerTable.OnNewRecord := Nil;
end;

// OnNewRecord event handler.
// Initializes the Country field with the native country name which
// is fetched from the Windows' system registry.
// For instance, if your system is configured for Italy, then
// the string "Italia" will be assigned to the country field.
procedure TTDataSetTestForm.CustomerTableNewRecord(DataSet: TDataSet);
var
  DefaultLCID: LCID;
begin
  DefaultLCID := GetSystemDefaultLCID;
  CustomerTableCountry.Value := GetLocaleStr( DefaultLCID,
                                              LOCALE_SNATIVECTRYNAME,
                                              '' );
end;
```

Description   The `OnNewRecord` event is triggered any time a new record is inserted into the `TDataSet` (for instance, by a call to the `Insert`, `Append`, `InsertRecord`, or `AppendRecord` methods). The `OnNewRecord` event takes place after the `BeforeInsert` event and before the `AfterInsert` event. In the case of a call to the `InsertRecord` or `AppendRecord` method, the event happens before any values (given as parameters to those methods) are actually assigned to the `TDataSet` fields of the `TDataSet`.

An `OnNewRecord` event handler procedure is most typically used to initialize a record before the user's input. For instance, assigning new key values or setting up default field values are tasks that can be performed in the `OnNewRecord` event handler procedure. Note that although database servers usually let you define default value constraints for any field in the database's tables, you can take advantage of the `OnNewRecord` event handler procedure to initialize fields with values depending on the user's local settings. (For instance, in the Example Syntax code segment above, the user's native country name is assigned to the table's `Country` field.) Note that the `Modified` property of the `TDataSet` is set to `False` after the `OnNewRecord` event, and any subsequent change to its field values will set the `Modified` property to `True`. Therefore, you can safely use the `OnNewRecord` event handler procedure to assign values to the fields of the `TDataSet`, and still rely on the `Modified` flag to report only changes made directly by the user's interactions.

OnPostError EVENT

Objects Affected   TDataSet

Purpose   The `OnPostError` event refers to an event handler procedure in which you can specify custom processing to perform whenever record posting errors are detected.

Declaration

```
type
  TDataAction = (daFail, daAbort, daRetry);
  TDataSetErrorEvent = procedure(DataSet: TDataSet;
                                 E: EDatabaseError;
                                 var Action: TDataAction) of object;

property OnPostError: TDataSetErrorEvent;
```

Example Syntax

```
// Assign or Deassign OnPostError event handler according to
// corresponding check box.
procedure TTDataSetTestForm.OnPostErrorCheckBoxClick(Sender: TObject);
begin
  if OnPostErrorCheckBox.Checked
  then CustomerTable.OnPostError := CustomerTablePostError
  else CustomerTable.OnPostError := Nil;
end;
```

continued on next page

continued from previous page

```
procedure TTDataSetTestForm.CustomerTablePostError(DataSet: TDataSet;
  E: EDatabaseError; var Action: TDataAction);
var
  I: Integer;
begin
  // if the error is a database engine error, then
  // scan through the engine's error stack, starting from
  // the top of the stack down to the bottom.
  if (E is EDBEngineError) then with (E as EDBEngineError) do
    for I := Pred( ErrorCount ) downto 0 do with Errors[ I ] do
      // Check if the current stack entry is the one you want.
      // The DBIERR_KEYVIOL constant is declared in the BDE unit.
      if Errorcode = DBIERR_KEYVIOL then
      begin
        // If it is, give a message, set the error action,
        // and break out of the loop;
        MessageBeep( $FFFF );
        MessageDlg('Duplicate Customer No. Assign a different one.',
          mtWarning, [mbOK], 0);
        Action := daAbort;
        break;
      end;
end;
```

Description

The OnPostError event is triggered if a call to the Post method of the TDataSet does not succeed due to some error. If you define an event handler procedure for the OnPostError, it will have three parameters. The first parameter identifies the TDataSet, the second is an EDatabaseError exception object describing the error, and the third is an Action data control parameter passed by reference. The Action parameter determines if and how you intend to perform custom error handling. You can assign one of three possible values to the Action parameter: daFail, daAbort, and daRetry. The daFail data action re-raises the original exception and passes it over to the ordinary exception handling system; it is the default value for the Action parameter. The daAbort data action raises an EAbort silent exception. The daRetry data action will try once again to perform the operation. Note that if any errors are encountered during a retry, the OnPostError event handler is called again.

OnServerYield EVENT

Objects Affected   TDataSet

Purpose   The OnServerYield event refers to an event handler procedure in which you can specify custom processing to perform a BDE callback procedure to be called periodically during a long running query.

Declaration

```
Type
  TOnServerYieldEvent = procedure(DataSet: TDataSet;
                                 var AbortQuery: Boolean) of object;

property OnServerYield: TOnServerYieldEvent
```

Example Syntax

```
// Assign or Deassign OnServerYield event handler according to
// corresponding check box.
procedure TTDataSetTestForm.OnServerYieldCheckBoxClick(Sender: TObject);
begin
  if OnServerYieldCheckBox.Checked
  then OrdersQuery.OnServerYield := OrdersQueryServerYield
  else OrdersQuery.OnServerYield := Nil;
end;

procedure TTDataSetTestForm.OrdersQueryServerYield(DataSet: TDataSet;
  var AbortQuery: Boolean);
begin
  if not TimeOutTimer.Enabled then
  begin
    AbortQuery := True;
  end;
end;
```

Description

The OnServerYield event is triggered by the BDE while querying the TDataSet on the database. In practice, the OnServerYield event handler procedure you write becomes a BDE callback function, which is then called periodically by the database engine. The purpose of the OnServerYield event is to let you cancel a long-running query. In order to do so, you just need to set the AbortQuery *var* parameter of the event handler procedure to True. Notice that you should not open or query any TDataSet during the OnServerYield event, and in general, you are not allowed to make any BDE API calls.

OnUpdateError EVENT

Objects Affected   TDataSet

Purpose   The OnUpdateError event refers to an event handler procedure in which you can specify custom processing to perform when record update errors are detected.

Declaration

```
type
  TUpdateKind = (ukModify, ukInsert, ukDelete);
  TUpdateAction = (uaFail, uaAbort, uaSkip, uaRetry, uaApplied);
```

continued on next page

continued from previous page

```
TUpdateErrorEvent = procedure(DataSet: TDataSet;
                              E: EDatabaseError;
                              UpdateKind: TUpdateKind;
                              var UpdateAction: TUpdateAction
                              ) of object;

property OnUpdateError: TUpdateErrorEvent;
```

Example Syntax

```
// Assign or Deassign OnUpdateError event handler according to
// corresponding check box.
procedure TTDataSetTestForm.OnUpdateErrorCheckBoxClick(Sender: TObject);
begin
  if OnUpdateErrorCheckBox.Checked
  then CustomerTable.OnUpdateError := CustomerTableUpdateError
  else CustomerTable.OnUpdateError := Nil;
end;
```

Description

The OnUpdateError event is triggered if a call to the ApplyUpdates of the TDataSet method does not succeed due to some error. If you define an event handler procedure for the OnPostError, it will have four parameters. The first parameter identifies the TDataSet, the second is an EDatabaseError exception object describing the error, the third indicates the kind of update causing the problem, and the fourth is a **var** UpdateAction control parameter by which you can conclude any custom error handling set up in the event handler procedure.

The *UpdateKind* parameter can be ukModify, ukInsert, or ukDelete. These values indicate, respectively, the problematic update was a modification of an existing record, an insertion of a new record, or the deletion of an existing record.

You can assign one of five possible values to the *UpdateAction* parameter: uaFail, uaAbort, uaSkip, uaRetry, and uaApplied. The uaFail update action re-raises the original exception and passes it over to the ordinary exception handling system. It is the default value for the *UpdateAction* parameter. The uaAbort update action aborts the cached updated and raises an EAbort silent exception. The uaSkip update action skips the current update and proceeds with the remaining ones. The uaRetry update action tries once again to perform the update operation for the current record. Note that if any errors are encountered during a retry, the OnUpdateError event handler is called again. Finally, the uaApplied update action signals the update was successfully applied with the OnUpdateError event handler procedure.

OnUpdateRecord EVENT

Objects Affected   `TDataSet`

Purpose   The `OnUpdateRecord` event refers to an event handler procedure in which you can specify custom processing to perform when a record is updated through cached updates.

Declaration

```
type
  TUpdateKind = (ukModify, ukInsert, ukDelete);
  TUpdateAction = (uaFail, uaAbort, uaSkip, uaRetry, uaApplied);
  TUpdateRecordEvent = procedure(DataSet: TDataSet;
                                 UpdateKind: TUpdateKind;
                                 var UpdateAction: TUpdateAction
                                 ) of object;

property OnUpdateRecord: TUpdateRecordEvent;
```

Example Syntax

```
// Assign or Deassign OnUpdateRecord event handler according to
// corresponding check box.
procedure TTDataSetTestForm.OnUpdateRecordCheckBoxClick(Sender: TObject);
begin
  if OnUpdateRecordCheckBox.Checked
  then CustomerTable.OnUpdateRecord := CustomerTableUpdateRecord
  else CustomerTable.OnUpdateRecord := Nil;
end;
```

Description   The `OnUpdateRecord` event is triggered whenever a call to the `ApplyUpdates` method of the `TDataSet` occurs. By defining an `OnUpdateRecord` event handler, you can take care of implementing your own updates in Object Pascal. Alternatively, if you have assigned a `TUpdateSql` component to the `UpdateObject` property of the `TDataSet`, you call its `Apply` method and express the update by the SQL statement of the `TUpdateSql`. Note that if both the `OnUpdateRecord` event and the `UpdateObject` are assigned, the `Apply` method of the `UpdateObject` is not called implicitly by Delphi. If you need its operations, you must invoke the `Apply` method explicitly from within the `OnUpdateRecord` event handler procedure. (On the other hand, if an `UpdateObject` has been assigned but there's no `OnUpdateRecord` event handler procedure, the `Apply` method of the `UpdateObject` is called automatically.)

The `OnUpdateRecord` event handler procedure has three parameters. The first parameter identifies the `TDataSet`, the second indicates the kind of update being performed, and the third is a **var** *UpdateAction* control parameter by which you can conclude any custom update handling set up in the event handler procedure.

The *UpdateKind* parameter can be **ukModify, ukInsert, ukDelete**. These values indicate, respectively, that the update was a modification of an existing record, an insertion of a new record, or the deletion of an existing record.

You can assign one out of five possible values to the *UpdateAction* parameter: **uaFail, uaAbort, uaSkip, uaRetry,** and **uaApplied**. The **uaFail** update action raises an exception and passes it over to the ordinary exception handling system. It is the default value for the **UpdateAction** parameter. The **uaAbort** update action aborts the cached update. The **uaSkip** update action skips the current update and proceeds with the remaining ones. The **uaRetry** update action tries once again to perform the update operation for the current record. Note that if any errors are encountered during a retry, the **OnUpdateError** event handler is called. Finally, the **uaApplied** update action signals that the update was successfully applied with the **OnUpdateError** event handler procedure.

Open METHOD

Objects Affected	TDataSet
Purpose	The Open method will open the TDataSet.
Declaration	

```
procedure Open;
```

Example Syntax

```
// Open the customer table.
procedure TTDataSetTestForm.OpenSpeedButtonClick(Sender: TObject);
begin
  CustomerTable.Open;
end;
```

Description   The **Open** method will close the **TDataSet**. It is the equivalent of setting its **Active** property to **True**. Note that by invoking this method you also indirectly call the **BeforeOpen** and **AfterOpen** event handler procedures, if they are assigned.

Note that if the **TDataSet** is a **TQuery**, you can only use the **Open** method if it returns a result set. Otherwise you should call the **ExecSql** of the **TQuery** method instead. Likewise, if the **TDataSet** is a **TStoredProc**, you can only use the **Open** method if it returns a result set. If the stored procedure returns a single row, you should use the **ExecProc** of the **TStoredProc** method instead.

Post METHOD

Objects Affected   TDataSet

Purpose   The **Post** method writes out a new or modified record to the underlying database table of the **TDataSet**.

Declaration

```
procedure Post;
```

Example Syntax

```
// Post pending record changes.
procedure TTDataSetTestForm.PostSpeedButtonClick(Sender: TObject);
begin
  CustomerTable.Post;
end;
```

Description   The **Post** method writes to the **TDataSet** any pending changes the user might have performed interactively (or you might have done programmatically) to the current record, after an initial call to the **Insert**, **Append**, or **Edit** methods. If the **TDataSet** is not in **dsEdit**, **dsInsert**, **dsSetKey** modes, an exception is raised.

If the **TDataSet** is in **dsSetKey** mode, the **Post** method writes the changes to the search key buffer and returns the **TDataSet** to **dsBrowse** mode.

If the **TDataSet** is in **dsEdit** or **dsInsert** mode, the method first checks if there are any required fields in the **TDataSets**. If there are and they do not contain appropriate values, an exception is raised. If all required fields are assigned and if there is a **BeforePost** event handler procedure, that procedure is called. The cursor position is then updated, and the record is actually posted to the underlying **TDataSet**. All buffers used for keeping the field changes are freed, the mode of the **TDataSet** is reset to **dsBrowse**, and the record is resynchronized. Finally, if there is an **AfterPost** event handler procedure assigned, it is called.

Prior METHOD

Objects Affected   TDataSet

Purpose   The **Prior** method moves the record cursor to the prior record of the **TDataSet**.

Declaration

```
procedure Prior;
```

Example Syntax

```
{ ... }
var
  CurrentCustomerBookmark: TBookmark;
begin
  { ... }
  { Scan through all records in result set in reverse order. }
  with CustomerTable do
  begin
    DisableControls;
    CurrentCustomerBookmark := GetBookmark;
    try
      Last;
      While not Bof do
      begin
        { ... here you would code any further record processing... }
        Prior;
      end;
    finally
      GotoBookmark( CurrentCustomerBookmark );
      EnableControls;
      FreeBookmark( CurrentCustomerBookmark );
    end;
  { ... }
```

Description

The `Prior` method makes the prior record of the `TDataSet` the current record. The method takes into account any range and filter that might be defined on the `TDataSet`. Note that before actually making the move to the prior record, the method makes a call to `CheckBrowseMode`. Therefore, if there are any pending changes in the current record, they will be posted before moving. If the cursor is on the first record, the method will not move it.

You can use the method to position the current record of the `TDataSet` according to the user's interactive actions, or to programmatically control navigation through all records in the `TDataSet`. For instance, you can iterate through a record scanning loop, as shown in the above sample code fragment.

RecNo PROPERTY

Objects Affected   `TDataSet`

Purpose   The `RecNo` property retrieves the number of the current record.

Declaration

```
property RecNo: Longint;
```

Description   The `RecNo` property is a run-time, read-only property that returns the current record's sequential number within the `TDataSet`. Note that this property is significant only for Paradox and dBASE tables; for SQL tables, the property will always return -1.

RecordCount PROPERTY

Objects Affected	TDataSet
Purpose	The RecordCount property retrieves the number of records in the TDataSet.
Declaration	

```
property RecordCount: Longint;
```

Description	The RecordCount property is a run-time, read-only property that reports how many records are currently in the **TDataSet**. The number returned by the property may be affected by the capabilities of the database server. If there are any active filters associated with the **TDataSet**, or if there are any active ranges declared on it, the results may be affected. In the case of Paradox tables, if a range is active, the record count is the number of records in the range. In the case of dBASE tables, the record count is always the total number of records in the table, and any range limitation is not taken into account.

RecordSize PROPERTY

Objects Affected	TDataSet
Purpose	The RecordSize property retrieves the record's footprint size in bytes.
Declaration	

```
property RecordSize: Word;
```

Example Syntax

```
// Make a copy of the current record via ActiveBuffer.
procedure TTDataSetTestForm.ActiveBufferSpeedButtonClick(Sender: ⇐
TObject);
var
  TemporaryRecordCopy: PChar;
begin
  // Allocate memory.
  TemporaryRecordCopy := AllocMem( CustomerTable.RecordSize );
  try
    // Copy the current record to the temporary buffer
    Move
    (
      CustomerTable.ActiveBuffer^,
      TemporaryRecordCopy^,
      CustomerTable.RecordSize
    );
    // Here you can use temporary copy in some way...
    // ...for instance to insert a duplicate record into the table.
    CustomerTable.Append;
    Move
```

continued on next page

continued from previous page

```
    (
      TemporaryRecordCopy^,
      CustomerTable.ActiveBuffer^,
      CustomerTable.RecordSize
    );
    CustomerTable.FieldByName( 'CustNo' ).AsInteger := GetNewCustNo;
  finally
    // Free temporary copy
    FreeMem( TemporaryRecordCopy, CustomerTable.RecordSize );
  end;
end;
```

Description   The RecordSize property is a run-time, read-only property that reports how many bytes are needed to host an in-memory record buffer. The property is typically used when allocating memory for a record buffer.

Refresh METHOD

Objects Affected   TDataSet

Purpose   The Refresh method will re-read data from the database.

Declaration

```
procedure Refresh;
```

Example Syntax

```
{...}
CustomerTable.Refresh;
{...}
```

Description   The Refresh method will reread the whole TDataSet. You need to call Refresh if you change the TDataSet programmatically, or if some other process changes the data currently displayed or used by your application. By calling the Refresh method, you ensure all data-aware controls present the most recent data and all calculated fields are computed with the most recent data. If the TDataSet is a TTable, then you can call the Refresh method only if the underlying table has a unique index. If the TDataSet is a TQuery, then you can call the method only if it is a live query on local tables like those in Paradox or dBASE. (Note that you can otherwise reread the whole result set of a TQuery simply by closing and reopening it).

A call to the Refresh method ensures the data is current at the time of the call. You can periodically use Refresh to ensure current data. You can also use record locking to prevent other users from updating records being modified in your application.

> **NOTE**
> If you are using a Paradox table, you can implement more sophisticated refresh strategies by registering a BDE callback of the type cbTABLECHANGED. This will allow the BDE to notify your application that the table's underlying data was actually modified by a remote user, since the callback will be called whenever a data change is detected.

Resync METHOD

Objects Affected	TDataSet
Purpose	The Resync method will resynchronize all records.
Declaration	

```
Type
  TResyncMode = set of (rmExact, rmCenter);

procedure Resync(Mode: TResyncMode);
```

Example Syntax

```
{ ... }
CustomerTable.Resync( [rmExact, rmCenter] );
{ ... }
```

Description

The Resync method will resynchronize all records in the TDataSet. The Resync method is used at the end of any series of operations that might have changed the contents of the TDataSet. Ordinarily, you don't need to call the Resync method yourself, since all methods that need record resynchronization (like Post, Insert, Append, Cancel, and so on) already do so. However, you might need to invoke an explicit Resync if you interact with the TDataSet at the BDE level.

The method's execution can be controlled through its *Mode* parameter. The *Mode* parameter is a set that can contain up to two values: rmExact and rmCenter.

If rmExact is specified, the current record is reread from the TDataSet.

If rmExact is not specified, the method will check if there are records available before and after the current one. If so, all buffers will be cleared, a data change event will be issued, and the method simply exits.

If rmExact is specified, or rmExact is not specified and there are no records available before and after the current one, execution will continue by checking if the rmCenter mode is specified. If it is specified, the current record is repositioned to the middle of the TDataSet; otherwise, it is left on the active record.

Finally, all records before and after the current one are reread and a data change event is issued.

RevertRecord METHOD

Objects Affected	TDataSet
Purpose	The RevertRecord method discards changes to the current record with cached updates.
Declaration	

```
procedure RevertRecord;
```

Example Syntax

```
procedure TTDataSetTestForm.RevertRecordSpeedButtonClick(Sender: ⇐
TObject);
begin
  with CustomerTable do
  begin
    if CachedUpdates then
    begin
      RevertRecord;
    end;
  end;
end;
```

Description   The RevertRecord method is used when cached updates are in effect. By calling this method, you restore the current record to its original unmodified state. If the record was not changed in any way, the call has no effect. Note that you can control what kind of record edits are affected by setting the UpdateRecordTypes appropriately.

SetDetailFields METHOD

Objects Affected	TDataSet
Purpose	The SetDetailFields method sets the key values of the TDataSet given a list of master key field objects.
Declaration	

```
procedure SetDetailFields(MasterFields: TList);
```

Parameters

MasterFields   A list of master field objects.

Example Syntax

```
procedure TTDataSetTestForm.SetDetailFieldsSpeedButtonClick(
  Sender: TObject);
var
  MasterFieldList: TList ;
begin
  MasterFieldList := TList.Create;
  try
    MasterFieldList.Add( CustomerTableCustNo );
```

```
      with OrdersTable do
      begin
        IndexFieldNames := 'CustNo';
        SetDetailFields( MasterFieldList );
        GotoKey;
      end;
    finally
      MasterFieldList.Free;
    end;
end;
```

Description The `SetDetailFields` method is a shorthand method for putting the
`TDataSet` into the `dsSetKey` state and assigning key values according to
the values of the `TField` objects given in the method's `TList` parameter.
Note that the number of `TFields` in the `TList` parameter must equal the
number of fields in the currently active index of the `TDataSet`. If the given
list of key values contains more items than the currently active index's
number of fields, then a Field Index Out of Range exception is raised.

SetFields METHOD

Objects Affected `TDataSet`

Purpose The `SetFields` method will set some or all field values in the current
record.

Declaration

```
procedure SetFields(const Values: array of const);
```

Parameters

Value An array of constant values that can be converted to the datatypes of the
corresponding fields in the `TDataSet`.

Example Syntax

```
{ ... }
CustomerTable.SetFields(
  [123456, 'Borland International, Inc. ']
);

{ ... }
```

Description The `SetFields` method takes an array of constant values as a parameter.
Each value in the array parameter is sequentially assigned to the `TFields`
in the `TDataSet` (note that if you have used the fields editor to add,
remove, or change the order of fields, that's the order considered). If there
are fewer values in the array than fields in the `TDataSet`, the remaining
fields are left unchanged. If there are more values in the array than fields
in the `TDataSet`, a run-time List Index Out of Bounds exception is raised.
To skip any values, you can use the reserved keyword `<NIL>` (they will
keep their previous values, if any, or receive their default values, if any). To
assign a `NULL` value, use the `<NULL>` reserved keyword.

Obviously the method will work only on **TDataSets** returning a live result set that can be modified. If that is not the case, an exception is raised. The **TDataSet** must be in **dsInsert** or **dsEdit** mode for the method to work, otherwise an exception is raised.

State PROPERTY

Objects Affected	TDataSet
Purpose	The **State** property will retrieve the current state of the **TDataSet**.
Declaration	

```
type
  TDataSetState = (dsInactive, dsBrowse, dsEdit, dsInsert,
                   dsSetKey, dsCalcFields, dsUpdateNew,
                   dsUpdateOld, dsFilter);

  property State: TDataSetState;
```

Example Syntax

```
// Enable or Disable speed button according to DataSet's state.
procedure TTDataSetTestForm.CustomerDataSourceStateChange(Sender: ⇐
TObject);
begin
  with CustomerDataSource do if Dataset <> nil then
    PostSpeedButton.Enabled := Dataset.State in [dsInsert, dsEdit];
end;
```

Description   The **State** property is a run-time, read-only property that holds the current state of the **TDataSet**. The state of a **TDataSet** is defined in terms of the **TDataSetState** type, a set containing the following values, as shown in Table 36-2.

Table 36-2 Values of the State property method

Value	Description
dsInactive	TDataSet is not open.
dsBrowse	Navigating between records.
dsEdit	Editing a record.
dsInsert	Inserting or appending a new record.
dsSetKey	Setting key values by manipulating fields for finding records or setting a range.
dsCalcFields	Calculating calculated field values.
dsUpdateNew	Internal state; used when accessing a field's NewValue property.
dsUpdateOld	Internal state; used when accessing a field's OldValue property.
dsFilter	TDataSet is processing an OnFilterRecord event.

UpdateCursorPos METHOD

Objects Affected	TDataSet
Purpose	The UpdateCursorPos method will update the cursor position of the TDataSet.
Declaration	

```
procedure UpdateCursorPos;
```

Example Syntax

```
{...}
with CustomerTable do
begin
  { Following two BDE calls will fetch all records in the dataset }
  Check(DbiSetToEnd(Handle));
  Check(DbiGetPriorRecord(FHandle, dbiNoLock, nil, nil));
  UpdateCursorPos;
end;
```

Description

The UpdateCursorPos method will reposition the BDE cursor of the TDataSet to its current position. You should not need to call this method directly. This method is useful only if you make direct calls to the BDE in which the internal cursor is moved off its original position. By calling the UpdateCursorPos method, you ensure the internal cursor is again pointing to the current position of the TDataSet.

UpdateObject PROPERTY

Objects Affected	TDataSet
Purpose	The UpdateObject property controls the associated cached updates SQL statements of the TDataSet.
Declaration	

```
property UpdateObject: TDataSetUpdateObject;
```

Example Syntax

```
procedure TTDataSetTestForm.CustomerTableUpdateRecord(DataSet: TDataSet;
  UpdateKind: TUpdateKind; var UpdateAction: TUpdateAction);
begin
  with DataSet.UpdateObject as TUpdateSql do Apply( UpdateKind );
end;
```

Description

The UpdateObject property of a TDataSet can reference a TUpdateSql component. You can perform the actions of the TUpdateSql component explicitly by calling its Apply method from within an OnUpdateRecord event handler. However, if there is no OnUpdateRecord event handler, the

Apply method of the `TUpdateSql` component referenced by the `UpdateObject` property of the `TDataSet` is called automatically by Delphi (provided cached updates are in effect).

UpdateRecord METHOD

Objects Affected   `TDataSet`

Purpose   The `UpdateRecord` method notifies data sources that a record update is about to be posted.

Declaration

```
procedure UpdateRecord;
```

Example Syntax

```
procedure TTDataSetTestForm.UpdateRecordSpeedButtonClick(Sender: ⇐
TObject);
begin
  CustomerTable.UpdateRecord;
end;
```

Description   The `UpdateRecord` method notifies any `TDataSource` component that the current record has been updated with new data. In practice, the method notifies all data-aware controls connected to the data source of the pending update, letting them change their associated fields to the currently displayed values. `UpdateRecord` calls the `OnUpdateData` event handler procedure of the `TDataSet`, if one is assigned. Note that by calling this method, the underlying record is updated, although it is not posted.

UpdateRecordTypes PROPERTY

Objects Affected   `TDataSet`

Purpose   The `UpdateRecordTypes` property controls the type of records updated via cached updates.

Declaration

```
type
  TUpdateRecordTypes = set of (rtModified, rtInserted,
                               rtDeleted, rtUnModified);

property UpdateRecordTypes: TUpdateRecordTypes;
```

Example Syntax

```
{...}
with CustomerTable do
begin
  UpdateRecordTypes := [];
```

```
      Include( UpdateRecordTypes, rtDeleted );
      {...}
    end;
```

Description   The `UpdateRecordTypes` property is a set indicating what types of records are affected by cached updates. By default, it is assigned the set `[rtModified, rtInserted, rtUnModified]`. The contents of the set assigned to the `UpdateRecordTypes` directly determine what records are visible, much like a range or a filter. For instance, by assigning the set `[rtDeleted]`, only deleted records are visible (which is useful to undelete records via a call to `RevertRecord`). By assigning the set `[rtInserted]`, only the newly inserted records are visible.

UpdateStatus METHOD

Objects Affected	`TDataSet`
Purpose	The `UpdateStatus` method inquires about the status of cached updates.
Declaration	

```
Type
  TUpdateStatus = (usUnmodified, usModified, usInserted, usDeleted);

function UpdateStatus: TUpdateStatus;
```

Description   The `UpdateStatus` method is useful only when cached updates are enabled. The method returns a `TUpdateStatus` enumerated type, reporting the most recent update applied to the current record. The return value can be one of the following: `usUnmodified`, `usModified`, `usInserted`, `usDeleted`. Initially, all records are in the `usUnModified` status. Subsequent changes alter the update status accordingly. Note that when (and only when) the update status is `usModified`, you can use the `OldValue` property of each field to access its previous value.

UpdatesPending PROPERTY

Objects Affected	`TDataSet`
Purpose	The `UpdatesPending` property inquires whether there are any pending cached updates.
Declaration	

```
property UpdatesPending: Boolean
```

Description   The `UpdatesPending` property is a run-time, read-only property that evaluates to `True` if there are any pending cached updates.

TDBDataSet

```
//Declarations
function CheckOpen(Status: DBIResult): Boolean;
property Database: TDatabase read FDatabase;
property DBHandle: HDBIDB read GetDBHandle;
property DBLocale: TLocale read GetDBLocale;
property DBSession: TSession read GetDBSession;
property DatabaseName: string read FDatabaseName write SetDatabaseName;
property SessionName: string read FSessionName write SetSessionName;
```

TTable

```
// Declarations
constructor Create(AOwner: TComponent); override;
destructor Destroy; override;
function BatchMove(ASource: TDataSet; AMode: TBatchMode): Longint;
procedure AddIndex(const Name, Fields: string; Options: TIndexOptions);
procedure ApplyRange;
procedure CancelRange;
procedure CloseIndexFile(const IndexFileName: string);
procedure CreateTable;
procedure DeleteIndex(const Name: string);
procedure DeleteTable;
procedure EditKey;
procedure EditRangeEnd;
procedure EditRangeStart;
procedure EmptyTable;
function FindKey(const KeyValues: array of const): Boolean;
procedure FindNearest(const KeyValues: array of const);
procedure GetIndexNames(List: TStrings);
procedure GotoCurrent(Table: TTable);
function GotoKey: Boolean;
procedure GotoNearest;
procedure LockTable(LockType: TLockType);
procedure OpenIndexFile(const IndexName: string);
procedure RenameTable(const NewTableName: string);
procedure SetKey;
procedure SetRange(const StartValues, EndValues: array of const);
procedure SetRangeEnd;
procedure SetRangeStart;
procedure UnlockTable(LockType: TLockType);
property IndexDefs: TIndexDefs read FIndexDefs;
property IndexFieldCount: Integer read GetIndexFieldCount;
property IndexFields[Index: Integer]: TField read GetIndexField write SetIndexField;
property KeyExclusive: Boolean read GetKeyExclusive write SetKeyExclusive;
property KeyFieldCount: Integer read GetKeyFieldCount write SetKeyFieldCount;
  published
property Exclusive: Boolean read FExclusive write SetExclusive default False;
property IndexFieldNames: string read GetIndexFieldNames write SetIndexFieldNames;
property IndexFiles: TStrings read FIndexFiles write SetIndexFiles;
property IndexName: string read GetIndexName write SetIndexName;
property MasterFields: string read GetMasterFields write SetMasterFields;
property MasterSource: TDataSource read GetDataSource write SetDataSource;
property ReadOnly: Boolean read FReadOnly write SetReadOnly default False;
property TableName: TFileName read FTableName write SetTableName;
```

```
property TableType: TTableType read FTableType write SetTableType default ttDefault;
property UpdateMode;
property UpdateObject;
```

TStoredProc

```
//Declarations
constructor Create(AOwner: TComponent); override;
destructor Destroy; override;
procedure CopyParams(Value: TParams);
function DescriptionsAvailable: Boolean;
procedure ExecProc;
function ParamByName(const Value: string): TParam;
procedure Prepare;
procedure GetResults;
procedure UnPrepare;
property ParamCount: Word read GetParamsCount;
property StmtHandle: HDBIStmt read FStmtHandle;
property Prepared: Boolean read FPrepared write SetPrepare;
  published
property StoredProcName: string read FProcName write SetProcName;
property Overload: Word read FOverload write SetOverload default 0;
property Params: TParams read FParams write SetParamsList;
property ParamBindMode: TParamBindMode read FBindMode write FBindMode default pbByName;
property UpdateObject;
```

TQuery

```
//Declarations
constructor Create(AOwner: TComponent); override;
destructor Destroy; override;
procedure ExecSQL;
function ParamByName(const Value: string): TParam;
procedure Prepare;
procedure UnPrepare;
property Prepared: Boolean read FPrepared write SetPrepare;
property ParamCount: Word read GetParamsCount;
property Local: Boolean read FLocal;
property StmtHandle: HDBIStmt read FStmtHandle;
property Text: string read FText;
property RowsAffected: Integer read GetRowsAffected;
property SQLBinary: PChar read FSQLBinary write FSQLBinary;
  published
property Constrained: Boolean read FConstrained write FConstrained default False;
property DataSource: TDataSource read GetDataSource write SetDataSource;
property Params: TParams read FParams write SetParamsList;
property ParamCheck: Boolean read FParamCheck write FParamCheck default True;
property RequestLive: Boolean read FRequestLive write FRequestLive default False;
property SQL: TStrings read FSQL write SetQuery;
property UniDirectional: Boolean read FUniDirectional write FUniDirectional default False;
property UpdateMode;
property UpdateObject;
```

37

TField AND ITS DESCENDANTS

TField is an abstract class from which all field related classes are derived. Figure 37-1 shows the hierarchical relationship of the TField class and its related descendants.

TField

TField objects represent individual columns in datasets. In programming for Delphi, you never use a TField component directly since TField is an abstract class. You use one of the descendant field components that corresponds to the type of data found in the corresponding column from the underlying dataset component. (Refer to Chapter 36, "TDataSet and Its Descendants" for more detailed information regarding TDataSet classes). As you can see in Figure 37-1, there is a large number of descendants of TField. These descendants share most properties and methods and differ only in a small number of details usually appropriate for the datatype being represented by the TField descendant class. This section will list those methods and properties shared by all descendants of TField. Later sections will detail the specific differences.

TField components are not visible at either design time or run time. They are associated with dataset components and provide the hook that data-aware components can use to access information in a dataset column.

Every time a dataset is opened either at run time or design time, Delphi, in conjunction with the Borland Database Engine (BDE), determines the number of columns in the table or query and creates one TField component appropriate to the data contained in those columns.

The appearance of the data in the data-aware components is, to a large extent, controlled by properties associated with the TField descendant object.

The TField class also provides an OnChange event handler that is invoked as a result of editing changes on a particular field.

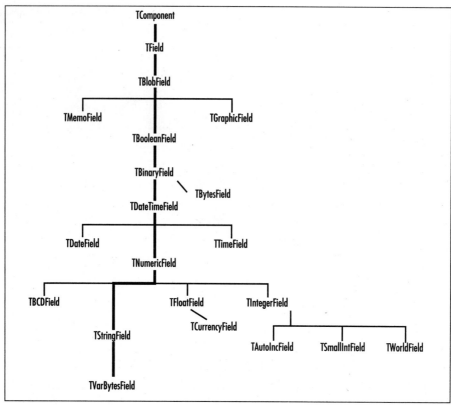

Figure 37-1 TField and its descendant hierarchy

There are actually two methods by which field components are created. The first and simplest is called dynamic generation. In this case, every time a dataset is opened, either at design time or run time, Delphi interrogates the dataset and creates the appropriate number of TField descendant types in which the descendant type is determined by the underlying dataset column. This set of TField components will automatically be adjusted properly if the underlying dataset structure changes such that the available TField components correspond in a one-to-one fashion with the columns of the underlying dataset. In this case, the program uses an indirect Lookup method to obtain the data from the dataset, so that even if the data structure of the dataset changes, the correct column will still be referenced. The persistent field list is the underlying dataset structure, so changes to the available TField components correspond in a one-to-one fashion with the columns of the dataset.

This mechanism can present a problem to the run-time environment. If, after a program has been compiled into an executable, the underlying dataset changes, it is likely the program will make errors in accessing the data since it will have made assumptions regarding the order in which the underlying data would be presented by the dataset when the program was compiled.

Borland has provided a solution to this problem by providing the concept of persistent field lists. This second method of specifying dataset `TField` components uses the fields stored in the program for use at run time and will provide proper data management on your behalf. If, by chance, a referenced column is deleted from the underlying dataset or the datatype of that column changes, the program will generate an exception instead of trying to run the program against a faulty data reference.

Other useful features gained through the use of persistent field lists are

■ the ability to define calculated fields that are computed from other fields in the dataset.

■ the ability to define lookup fields that are computed based on fields from other datasets.

■ the ability to modify field component display and editing properties instead of using the values assigned by the dynamically created field component.

■ typesafe data access. Exceptions are generated in the case of an error.

The following discussion describes the use of the Fields editor and its basic capabilities. For further information you should refer to the Delphi Online Help.

The Fields editor enables you to create, delete, arrange, and define persistent field components associated with a dataset.

To Start the Fields Editor

1. Double-click the dataset component, or

2. Select the component, right-click to invoke the speedmenu, then choose Fields editor.

The Fields editor contains a title bar, navigator buttons, and a list box, as shown in Figure 37-2.

The title bar of the Fields editor displays both the name of the data module or form containing the dataset, and the name of the dataset itself. So the title bar would contain `FormName.DatasetName`.

A set of navigation buttons enables you to navigate the fields in the dataset. If the dataset is not active or is empty, then the navigation buttons are dimmed.

The list box displays the names of the field components for the dataset. For a new dataset, the list is empty because the field components for the dataset are dynamic, not persistent. If you invoke the Fields editor for a dataset that already has persistent field components, you see the field component names in the list box.

Figure 37-2 The Fields editor

Creating Persistent Field Components

To create a persistent field component for a dataset:

1. Right-click the Fields editor list box.

2. Choose Add Fields from the speedmenu. The Add Fields dialog box appears.

The Add Fields dialog box appears as shown in Figure 37-3.

Figure 37-3 The Add Fields dialog box

The Available fields list box displays all fields in the dataset that do not have persistent field components. Select the fields for which you want to create persistent field components, and click OK.

This will add the selected field to the Fields editor list box. Fields in the Fields editor list box are persistent. If the dataset is active and there are persistent fields defined, the Next and Last navigation buttons above the list box are enabled.

After you have assigned persistent fields in this manner, Delphi will no longer create dynamic field components for every column in the underlying database, but will only create persistent components for the fields you specify.

Each time you open the dataset, Delphi verifies that each noncalculated persistent field exists or can be created from data in the database. If it cannot, Delphi raises an exception, warning you that the field is not valid, and does not open the dataset.

Deleting Persistent Field Components

Deleting a persistent field component is useful for accessing a subset of available columns in a table, and for defining your own persistent fields to replace a column in a table. To remove one or more persistent field components for a dataset:

1. Select the field(s) to remove in the Fields editor list box.

2. Press DELETE.

> **NOTE**
> You can also delete selected fields by invoking the speedmenu and choosing DELETE.

Fields you remove are no longer available to the program and cannot be displayed by data-aware controls. You can always re-create persistent field components that you delete by accident, but any changes previously made to the properties or events are lost.

> **NOTE**
> If you remove all persistent field components for a dataset, then Delphi will generate dynamic field components for every column in the database table underlying the dataset as it would if you had never created a persistent field list with the Fields editor.

Arranging the Order of Persistent Field Components

The order in which persistent field components are listed in the Fields editor list box is the default order in which the fields appear in a data-aware grid component. You can change field order by dragging and dropping fields in the list box.

To Change the Order of a Single Field

1. Select the field.

2. Drag it to a new location.

You can also select the field, and use Ctrl-Up and Ctrl-Dn to move the field to a new location in the list.

To Change the Order for a Block of Fields

1. Select the fields.

2. Drag them to their new location.

If you select a non-contiguous set of fields and drag them to a new location, they will be inserted as a contiguous block. Within the block, the order of fields to one another does not change.

Defining New Persistent Field Components

You can create new persistent fields as additions to or replacements of the other persistent fields in a dataset. Three types of persistent fields can be created with the Fields editor.

1. Data fields, which usually replace existing fields, are based on columns in the table or a query underlying a dataset.

2. Calculated fields, which display values calculated at run time by a dataset's `OnCalcFields` event handler.

3. Lookup fields, which retrieve values from a specified dataset at run time based on search criteria you specify.

The data contained in these fields at run time are not retained because they are temporary. The physical structure of the table and data underlying the dataset are not changed in any way.

To Create a New Persistent Field Component

1. Right-click the Fields editor list box.

2. Choose New field from the speedmenu.

The New Field dialog box appears and is shown in Figure 37-4.

Dialog Box Options

The New Field dialog box contains three group boxes: Field properties, Field type, and Lookup definition.

Field Type Radio Group Box

The Field type radio group box enables you to specify the type of new field component to create. The default type the first time you open the New Field dialog box in a session is Data. If you choose Lookup, the Dataset and Source Fields edit boxes in the Lookup definition group box are enabled. The Lookup definition group box is only used to create lookup fields.

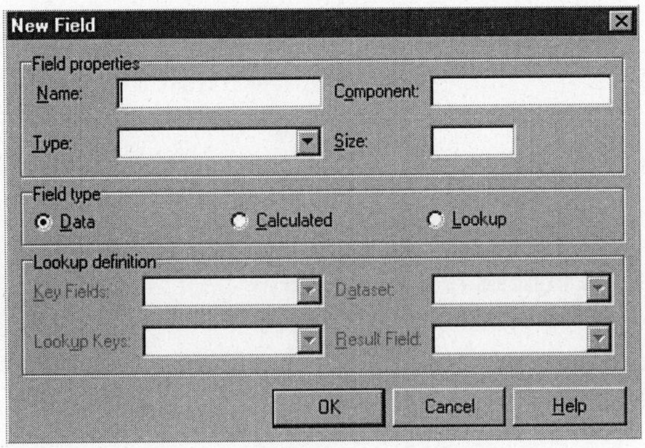

Figure 37-4 The New Field dialog box

Field Properties Group Box

The Field properties group box enables you to enter general field component information. Enter the component's field name in the Name edit box. The name you enter here corresponds to the field component's `FieldName` property. Delphi uses this name to build a component name in the Component edit box. The name that appears in the Component edit box corresponds to the field component's `Name` property and is only provided for informational purposes (`Name` contains the identifier by which you refer to the field component in your source code). Delphi discards anything you enter directly in the Component edit box.

Type Combo Box

The Type combo box in the Field properties group enables you to specify the field component's datatype. You must supply a datatype for any new field component you create. For example, to display floating point currency values in a field, select Currency from the drop-down list. The Size edit box enables you to specify the maximum number of characters that can be displayed or entered in a string-based field or the size of the `Bytes` and `VarBytes` fields. For all other datatypes, size is meaningless.

The `TField` class defines a large number of properties defined in Table 37-1.

Table 37-1 TField properties summary

Use or Set This...	To Do This...	Inheritance
Alignment	Control text alignment of field.	None
AsBoolean	Interpret `string` field as boolean.	None
AsCurrency	Interpret various fields as `Currency`.	None
AsDateTime	Intepret `TStringField` as `Date` and `Time`.	None
AsFloat	Interpret various `TField` components as floating point.	None
AsInteger	Interpret various `TField` components as integer.	None

continued on next page

continued from previous page

Use or Set This...	To Do This...	Inheritance
Assign	Copy contents of one field to another.	TPersistent
AssignValue	Copy argument to TField value.	None
AsString	Interpret various TField components as a string.	None
AsVariant	Interpret any TField component as a variant.	None
AttributeSet	Determine attributes associated with TField object.	None
Calculated	Indicate whether or not field is calculated at run time.	None
CanModify	Indicate whether field is writable or not.	None
Clear	Erase contents of field (and underlying dataset entry).	None
Create	Create instance of TField (rarely used).	TComponent
DataSet	Return reference to TDataSet object underlying the field.	None
DataSize	Return size of memory required to store the field.	None
DataType	Return field type of associated field.	None
Destroy	Destructor for TField component.	TComponent
DisplayLabel	Obtain column heading or field name of field component.	None
DisplayName	Obtain field name of field component.	None
DisplayText	Obtain string used for field component when displayed.	None
DisplayWidth	Obtain number of characters required to display field.	None
EditMask	Determine how field should be displayed.	None
EditMaskPtr	Obtain pointer to edit mask property of a string.	None
FieldKind	Determine if field is from dataset, calculated, or lookup type.	None
FieldName	Determine field name in physical dataset underlying field.	None
FieldNo	Obtain ordinal value for associated field in dataset.	None
FocusControl	Set focus to data-aware component using field.	None
GetData	Get untranslated data from field.	None
Index	Determine a field's order in underlying dataset.	None
IsBlob	Determine whether a field contains a BLOB object.	None
IsIndexField	Determine whether a field is indexed or not.	None
IsNull	Return True if field value is NULL.	None
IsValidChar	Return True if character passed is accepted by field.	None
KeyFields	Determine which fields are used by lookup fields in a dataset.	None
Lookup	Determine whether a field is a lookup field.	None
LookupCache	Determine whether a lookup field is cached.	None
LookupDataSet	Determine table used by lookup fields.	None
LookupKeyFields	Identify fields in lookup dataset used by lookup field.	None
LookupList	Obtain a TLookupList object for a lookup field list containing the lookup field.	None
LookupResultField	Identify field in lookup dataset to be copied to lookup field.	None
NewValue	Determine current value of field.	None
Offset	Determine the virtual offset of the data field.	None

Use or Set This...	To Do This...	Inheritance
OldValue	Obtain original value of field before changes.	None
OnChange	Perform action whenever a field is changed.	None
OnGetText	Perform action whenever Text or DisplayText is read.	None
OnSetText	Perform action whenever Text is changed.	None
OnValidate	Perform special validation when a field is modified.	None
ReadOnly	Specify that a field should be read-only or not.	None
RefreshLookupList	Reload a lookup list into a field.	None
Required	Set to True to require non-nil field values.	None
ServerCalcField	Determine whether a field is calculated by the database server.	None
SetData	Assign raw data to field.	None
SetFieldType	Specify field type for field .	None
Size	Determine size of field stored in database.	None
Text	Obtain string data displayed in data-aware component.	None
Validate	Cause the OnValidate handler to be triggered if one is assigned using supplied data as the test value.	None
ValidChars	Read or write the characters that can be accepted by the field.	None
Value	Obtain actual value of data in field.	None
Visible	Determine whether field can be displayed in TDBGrid component.	None

TAutoIncField

TAutoIncField represents a field of a record in a dataset. It is represented as a binary value with a range from -2,147,483,648 to 2,147,483,647. Use TAutoIncField for auto-incrementing fields that hold large, signed whole numbers.

Set the DisplayFormat property to control the formatting of the field for display purposes, and the EditFormat property for editing purposes. Use the Value property to access or change the current field value. Set the MinValue or the MaxValue property to limit the smallest or largest value permitted in a field.

TBCDField

A TBCDField represents a field of a record in a dataset. It is represented as a Binary Coded Decimal (BCD) value. Use TBCDField for a floating-point number with a fixed number of digits following the decimal point. The range depends on the number of digits after the decimal point since the accuracy is 18 digits.

Set the DisplayFormat property to control the formatting of the field for display purposes, and the EditFormat property for editing purposes. Set the Size property to define the number of BCD digits following the decimal point. Use the Value property to access or change the current field value. This class publishes a property called Currency that is used to indicate whether the field contains a currency value. Note also that the public variable called FCurrency is accessible. This is somewhat nonstandard in that it is unusual for a class to expose private variables in this manner in Delphi. If you choose to modify this variable directly, do so with caution as there could be unexpected side effects of doing so. The `Currency` property actually passes the control to an internal procedure to write this value. Note also that there is a public function in `TBCDField` called `SetCurrency`. This accepts a single boolean type argument which allows the user to set the property using a function invocation as well. Borland may have done this to provide enhanced performance or to allow a nonstandard use of this class. This class also makes an internal variable public called `TCheckRange` that is boolean and is used to indicate that the object should check the field value to be in a range which is bounded by the other public variables called `FMaxValue` and `FMinValue` and which are `Currency` type objects. Again note that these are internal variables which are made public in deviation from normal Delphi practices for components.

TBinaryField

A `TBinaryField` component represents a field of a record in a dataset. It is represented by a value consisting of an arbitrary set of bytes with indefinite size.

Use the `Assign` method to copy values from another field to a `TBinaryField`.

TBlobField

The `TBlobField` component represents a field of a record in a dataset. It is capable of containing a value consisting of an arbitrary set of bytes of indefinite size.

Use the `Assign` method to copy values from another field to a `TBlobField`. Use the `LoadFromFile` method to load a field's contents from a file. Use the `LoadFromStream` method to load a field from a stream. Use the `SaveToFile` method to write a field's contents to a file. Use the `SaveToStream` method to write a field's contents to a stream.

`TBlobField` defines a published property called `BlobType` which is used to determine the type of `BLOB` contained in the field. It can be assigned to one of the following types defined in the DB unit, which are denoted by the enumerated constant type called `TBlobType` in the `DBTables` unit.

Listing 37-1 Valid settings for `BlobType` property

```
[ftBlob, ftMemo, ftGraphic, ftFmtMemo, ftParadoxOle, ftDBaseOle, ftTypedBinary]
```

TBooleanField

A `TBooleanField` component represents a field of a record in a dataset. A `Boolean` field is either `True` or `False`, but the display string in a data-aware control can be varied.

Set the `DisplayValues` property to control the formatting of the field for display purposes or input recognition. Use the `Value` property to access or change the current field value.

TBytesField

A **TBytesField** component represents a field of a record in a dataset. It is represented by a value consisting of an array of 16 bytes. It is directly descended from the **TBinaryField** object.

Use the **Assign** method to copy values from another field to a **TBytesField**.

TCurrencyField

A **TCurrencyField** component represents a field of a record in a dataset. It is represented as a binary value with a range from (positive or negative) 5.0 * 10E-324 to 1.7 * 10E+308. It has an accuracy of 15 to 16 digits. Use **TCurrencyField** for fields that hold currency values.

Set the **DisplayFormat** property to control the formatting of the field for display purposes, and the **EditFormat** property for editing purposes. Use the **Value** property to access or change the current field value.

This class publishes a property called **Currency** used to indicate whether the field actually contains a currency value and defaults to **True**.

TDateField

A **TDateField** component is an indirect descendant of **TComponent**. It represents a field of a record in dataset. It represents a value consisting of a date.

Set the **DisplayFormat** property to control the formatting of the field for display purposes, and the **EditFormat** property for editing purposes. Use the **Value** property to access or change the current field value.

TDateTimeField

A **TDateTimeField** component is an indirect descendant of **TComponent**. It represents a field of a record in a dataset. It represents a value consisting of a date and time.

Set the **DisplayFormat** property to control the formatting of the field for display purposes, and the **EditFormat** property for editing purposes. Use the **Value** property to access or change the current field value.

This class publishes a property called **DisplayFormat** that is used to contain a text string that indicates how the field should be displayed. See its description later in the chapter for an example.

TFloatField

The **TFloatField** component represents a field of a record in a dataset. It is represented as a binary value with a range from (positive or negative) 5.0 * 10E-324 to 1.7 * 10E+308. It has an accuracy of 15 to 16 digits. Use **TFloatField** for fields that hold floating-point numbers.

Set the **DisplayFormat** property to control the formatting of the field for display purposes and the **EditFormat** property for editing purposes. Use the **Value** property to access or change the current field value. This class publishes a property called Currency that is used to indicate whether the field contains a value representing currency.

The TFloatField publishes a property called Precision which is used to determine how many digits after the decimal place should be used when displaying the value in a field.

TGraphicField

A TGraphicField component represents a field of a record represented by a value consisting of an arbitrary set of bytes with indefinite size. The bytes should correspond to graphics data.

Use the Assign method to transfer another component to a TGraphicField. Use the LoadFromFile method to load a field's contents from a file. Use the LoadFromStream method to load a field from a stream. Use the SaveToFile method to write a field's contents to a file. Use the SaveToStream method to write a field's contents to a stream.

TIntegerField

TIntegerField represents a field of a record in a dataset. It is represented as a binary value with a range from -2,147,483,648 to 2,147,483,647. Use TIntegerField for fields that hold large, signed whole numbers.

Set the DisplayFormat property to control the formatting of the field for display purposes and the EditFormat property for editing purposes. Use the Value property to access or change the current field value. Set the MinValue or the MaxValue property to limit the smallest or largest value permitted in a field.

TMemoField

A TMemoField component represents a field of a record in a dataset. It is represented by a value consisting of an arbitrary set of bytes with indefinite size. The bytes should correspond to text data.

Use the Assign method to transfer another component to a TMemoField. Use the LoadFromFile method to load a field's contents from a file. Use the LoadFromStream method to load a field from a stream. Use the SaveToFile method to write a field's contents to a file. Use the SaveToStream method to write a field's contents to a stream.

The class also publishes a property called Transliterate that determines whether translations to and from the respective locales of the Source and Destination properties will be done. Transliterate is True by default.

TNumericField

TNumericField is an abstract class that is never used directly. Any numeric field will descend from this class. This class publishes a property called DisplayFormat that is used to contain a text string that indicates how the field should be displayed. See its description later in this chapter for an example.

TSmallIntField

A `TSmallIntField` component represents a field of a record in a dataset. It is represented as a binary value with a range from -32,768 to 32,767. Use `TSmallIntField` for fields that hold signed whole numbers.

Set the `DisplayFormat` property to control the formatting of the field for display purposes and the `EditFormat` property for editing purposes. Use the `Value` property to access or change the current field value. Set the `MinValue` or the `MaxValue` property to limit the smallest or largest value permitted in a field.

TStringField

A `TStringField` component represents a field of a record in a dataset. A field of `TStringField` is physically stored as a sequence of up to 255 characters. Use `TStringField` for fields that contain text, such as names and addresses.

Use the `Value` property to access or change the current field value. The class also publishes a property called `Transliterate` that determines whether translations to and from the respective locales of the `Source` and `Destination` properties will be done. `Transliterate` is `True` by default.

TTimeField

A `TTimeField` component represents a field of a record in a dataset. It represents a value consisting of a time.

Set the `DisplayFormat` property to control the formatting of the field for display purposes and the `EditFormat` property for editing purposes. Use the `Value` property to access or change the current field value.

TVarBytesField

A `TVarBytesField` component represents a field of a record represented by a value consisting of an arbitrary set of up to 65,535 bytes. The first two bytes are a binary value defining the actual length.

Use the `Assign` method to copy values from another field to a `TVarBytesField`.

TWordField

A `TWordField` component represents a field of a record in a dataset. It is represented as a binary value with a range from 0 to 65,535. Use `TWordField` for fields that hold unsigned whole numbers.

Set the `DisplayFormat` property to control the formatting of the field for display purposes and the `EditFormat` property for editing purposes. Use the `Value` property to access or change the current field value. Set the `MinValue` or the `MaxValue` property to limit the smallest or largest value permitted in a field.

Alignment Property

Objects Affected	TField, TNumericField
Purpose	Control text alignment of field using TAlignment type. TAlignment is an enumerated constant that can be set to one of the following choices: taLeftJustify, taRightJustify, or taCenter.

Declaration

TField

```
property Alignment: TAlignment
```

TNumericField

```
property Alignment: TAlignment default taRightJustify;
```

Example Syntax

```
function Tflddlg.demAlignment(theField:TField):string;
var
  tempStr:string;
begin

try

  case theField.Alignment of

   taLeftJustify:
      tempStr := 'Left Justify';
   taRightJustify:
      tempStr := 'Right Justify';
   taCenter:
      tempStr := 'Center';
  end;

  Result := theField.Name + '.Alignment =' + tempStr;
except
  on E:EDataBaseError do
     Result := E.Message;
end;


end;
```

Description	This example function uses the value of the **Alignment** property in a case statement to generate the appropriate output string based on the value of the field alignment property value.

AsBoolean Property

Objects Affected	All descendant classes of **TField**
Purpose	Interpret **String** field as boolean.

Declaration

```
property AsBoolean: Boolean
```

Example Syntax

```
function Tflddlg.demAsBoolean(theField:TField):string;
var
   tempStr:string;
begin

try
if theField.AsBoolean = true then
   tempStr := 'True'
else
   tempStr := 'False';

Result := theField.Name + '.AsBoolean =' + tempStr;

except
   on E:EConvertError do
      Result := theField.Name +'.AsBoolean '+ E.Message;
   on E:EDataBaseError do
      Result := E.Message;
end;

end;
```

Description

This example function uses the value of the **AsBoolean** property to generate the appropriate output string based on the value of the field boolean property value. The function result is set depending on the value of the boolean result. Only string-based fields can be interpreted as boolean. Since this function accepts a generic **TField** argument, it would be possible to pass one of the **TNumericField** descendant classes, which would cause an error in this case. Because of this, the routine is protected by an exception handler invoked whenever there is a conversion error. In this case, the message associated with the exception is returned as the function value rather than **True** or **False**.

AsCurrency PROPERTY

Objects Affected   All descendant classes of **TField**

Purpose   Interpret various Fields as **Currency**.

Declaration

```
property AsCurrency: Currency
```

Example Syntax

```
function Tflddlg.demAsCurrency(theField:TField):string;
var
   tempStr:string;
   currval:Currency;
begin

try
```

continued on next page

continued from previous page

```
        currval := theField.AsCurrency;
        Str(Currval,tempStr);

        Result := theField.Name + '.AsCurrency =' + tempStr;

    except
      on E:EConvertError do
         Result := theField.Name +'.AsCurrency '+ E.Message;

      on E:EDataBaseError do
         Result := E.Message;
    end;

    end;
```

Description   This example function uses the value of the **AsCurrency** property to generate the appropriate output string based on the value of the field **AsCurrency** property value. The currency value returned is converted to a string that is then returned to the caller with descriptive text. To protect against conversion errors, the routine contains an exception handler that is invoked whenever there is a database conversion error.

AsDateTime Property

Objects Affected   All descendant classes of **TField**

Purpose   Interpret **TStringField** as **Date** and **Time**.

Declaration

```
property AsDateTime: TDateTime
```

Example Syntax

```
function Tflddlg.demAsDateTime(theField:TField):string;
var
  tempStr:string;
  thedt: TDateTime;
begin

try
thedt := theField.AsDateTime;

Result := theField.Name + '.AsDateTime =' + DateToStr(thedt);

except
  on E:EConvertError do
     Result := theField.Name +'.AsDateTime '+ E.Message;
  on E:EDataBaseError do
     Result := E.Message;
end;

end;
```

Description   This example function uses the value of the **AsDateTime** property to generate the appropriate output string based on the value of the field **AsDateTime** property value. The **DateTime** value returned is converted to a string that is then returned to the caller with descriptive text. To protect against conversion errors, the routine contains an exception handler that is invoked whenever there is a database conversion error.

AsFloat PROPERTY

Objects Affected	All descendant classes of **TField**
Purpose	Interpret various **TField** components as floating point.
Declaration	

```
property AsFloat: Double
```

Example Syntax

```
function Tflddlg.demAsFloat(theField:TField):string;
var
  tempStr:string;
  fval:double;
begin

try

fval := theField.AsFloat;

Result := theField.Name + '.AsFloat =' + FloatToStr(fval);

except
   on E:EConvertError do
      Result := theField.Name +'.AsFLoat '+ E.Message;
   on E:EDataBaseError do
      Result := E.Message;
end;

end;
```

Description   This example function uses the value of the **AsFloat** property to generate the appropriate output string based on the value of the field **AsFloat** property value. The float value returned is converted to a string that is then returned to the caller with descriptive text. To protect against conversion errors, the routine contains an exception handler that is invoked whenever there is a database conversion error.

AsInteger PROPERTY

Objects Affected	All descendant classes of **TField**
Purpose	Interpret various **TField** components as integer.
Declaration	

```
property AsInteger: Longint
```

Example Syntax

```
function Tflddlg.demAsInteger(theField:TField):string;
var
  tempStr:string;
  ival:integer;
begin

try

ival := theField.asInteger;

Result := theField.Name + '.AsInteger =' + IntToStr(ival);

except
   on E:EConvertError do
      Result := theField.Name +'.AsInteger '+ E.Message;
   on E:EDataBaseError do
      Result := E.Message;
end;

end;
```

Description   This example function uses the value of the **AsInteger** property to generate the appropriate output string based on the value of the field **AsInteger**
property value. The integer value returned is converted to a string that is
then returned to the caller with descriptive text. To protect against conversion errors, the routine contains an exception handler that is invoked
whenever there is a database conversion error.

Assign METHOD

Objects Affected   All descendant classes of **TField**

Purpose   Copy contents of one field to another.

Declaration

```
procedure Assign(Source: TPersistent); override;
```

Example Syntax

```
procedure Tflddlg.demAssign(theField1,theField2:TField);
var
tvr:TVarRec;
newval:integer;
begin
    theField2.DataSet.Edit;
    theField2.Assign(theField1);
    theField2.DataSet.Post;
    close;
end;
```

Description   This example uses the **Assign** method to assign the value of a field called
theField1 to the value of another field called **theField2**, which are supplied as parameters to this particular method. After the dataset is updated
via the **Post** operation, the dialog is closed using the **Close** method and
control returns to the original form with the appropriate fields updated.

AssignValue METHOD

Objects Affected	All descendant classes of TField
Purpose	Copy argument to TField value.
Declaration	

```
procedure AssignValue(const Value: TVarRec);
```

Example Syntax

```
procedure Tflddlg.demAssignVal(theField:TField);
var
tvr:TVarRec;
newval:integer;
begin
    tvr.VType := vtInteger;
    newval := StrToInt(Memo1.lines[0]);
    tvr.VInteger := newval;
    theField.DataSet.Edit;
    theField.AssignValue(tvr);
    theField.DataSet.Post;
    close;
end;
```

Description   This example uses the AssignValue method to set the field value through the use of a TVarRec. This allows the function to accept any of a number of datatypes that can be represented by the TVarRec object. The first line of a memo field is converted to an integer representation. Then the appropriate fields of the TVarRec object are set up to contain an integer value. Next, the dataset is placed into edit mode and the AssignValue method is used to change the selected field to the desired value. Finally, the dataset is updated via the Post method and taken out of edit mode.

AsString PROPERTY

Objects Affected	All descendant classes of TField
Purpose	Interpret various TField components as a string.
Declaration	

```
property AsString: string
```

Example Syntax

```
function Tflddlg.demAsString(theField:TField):string;
var
  tempStr:string;
begin

try
tempStr := theField.AsString;

Result := theField.Name + '.AsString =' + tempStr;
```

continued on next page

continued from previous page

```
except
   on E:EConvertError do
      Result := theField.Name +'.AsString '+ E.Message;
   on E:EDataBaseError do
      Result := E.Message;
end;

end;
```

Description   This example function uses the value of the **AsString** property to generate the appropriate output string based on the value of the field **AsString** property value. The string obtained is then returned to the caller with descriptive text. To protect against conversion errors, the routine contains an exception handler that is invoked whenever there is a database conversion error.

AsVariant PROPERTY

Objects Affected   All descendant classes of **TField**

Purpose   Interpret any **TField** component as a variant.

Declaration

```
property AsVariant: Variant
```

Example Syntax

```
function Tflddlg.demAsVariant(theField:TField):string;
var
   tempStr:string;
   theVar:variant;

begin

try

theVar := theField.asVariant;

Result := theField.Name + '.AsVariant =' + theVar;

except
   on E:EConvertError do
      Result := theField.Name +'.AsVariant '+ E.Message;
   on E:EDataBaseError do
      Result := E.Message;
end;

end;
```

Description   This example function uses the value of the **AsVariant** property to generate the appropriate output string based on the value of the field **AsVariant** property value. The variant value returned is converted to a string that is then returned to the caller with descriptive text. To protect against conversion errors, the routine contains an exception handler that is invoked whenever there is a database conversion error.

AttributeSet PROPERTY

Objects Affected	All descendant classes of `TField`
Purpose	Used to determine the attributes associated with a `TField` object.
Declaration	

```
property AttributeSet: string
```

Example Syntax

```
function Tflddlg.demAttributeSet(theField:TField):string;
var
   tempStr:string;
begin

try

tempStr := theField.AttributeSet;

Result := theField.Name + '.AttributeSet =' + tempStr;

except
   on E:EConvertError do
       Result := theField.Name +' '+ E.Message;
   on E:EDataBaseError do
       Result := E.Message;
end;

end;
```

Description

This example function uses the value of the `AttributeSet` property to generate the appropriate output string based on the value of the `AttributeSet`. The string value obtained is returned to the caller with descriptive text. To protect against conversion errors, the routine contains an exception handler that is invoked whenever there is a database conversion error.

BlobType PROPERTY

Objects Affected	`TBlobField`
Purpose	Used to determine the type of object contained in the `BLOB` field.
Declaration	

```
property BlobType: TBlobType;

Note that the possible value of TBlobType are:
[ftBlob, ftMemo, ftGraphic, ftFmtMemo, ftParadoxOle, ftDBaseOle,
ftTypedBinary]
```

Example Syntax

```
procedure Tflddlg.demSetBlobType(theField:TBlobField, btype: TBlobType);
begin
```

continued on next page

continued from previous page

```
try

    theField.BlobType := btype;

except
    on E:EConvertError do
        Result := theField.Name +' '+ E.Message;
    on E:EDataBaseError do
        Result := E.Message;
end;

end;
```

Description   This example procedure demonstrates a method to set the `BlobType` property of a `TBlobField` object.

Calculated PROPERTY

Objects Affected   All descendant classes of `TField`

Purpose   Indicate whether or not field is calculated at run time.

Declaration

```
property Calculated: Boolean
```

Example Syntax

```
function Tflddlg.demCalculated(theField:TField):string;
var
    tempStr:string;
    cval:boolean;
begin

try

cval := theField.Calculated;

if (cval = true) then
    tempStr := 'True'
else
    tempStr := 'False';

Result := theField.Name + '.Calculated =' + tempStr;

except
    on E:EConvertError do
        Result := theField.Name +' '+ E.Message;
    on E:EDataBaseError do
        Result := E.Message;
end;

end;
```

Description   This example function uses the value of the `Calculated` property to generate the appropriate output string based on the value of `Calculated`. The boolean value obtained is converted to a value of `True` or `False`, which is then returned to the caller with descriptive text. To protect against conversion errors, the routine contains an exception handler that is invoked whenever there is a database conversion error.

CanModify PROPERTY

Objects Affected	All descendant classes of `TField`
Purpose	Indicates whether field is writable or not.
Declaration	

```
property CanModify: Boolean
```

Example Syntax

```
function Tflddlg.demCanModify(theField:TField):string;
var
  tempStr:string;
begin

try

if theField.CanModify = true then
   tempStr := 'True'
else
   tempStr := 'False';

Result := theField.Name + '.CanModify =' + tempStr;

except
   on E:EConvertError do
      Result := theField.Name +' '+ E.Message;
   on E:EDataBaseError do
      Result := E.Message;
end;

end;
```

Description   This example function uses the value of the `CanModify` property to generate the appropriate output string based on the value of the `CanModify` property. The boolean value obtained is converted to a value of `True` or `False` that is then returned to the caller with descriptive text. To protect against conversion errors, the routine contains an exception handler that is invoked whenever there is a database conversion error.

CheckRange PROPERTY

Objects Affected	`TBCDField`
Purpose	Indicates whether field should check for values within limits prior to updating.

Declaration

```
property CheckRange: Boolean
```

Example Syntax

```
function Tflddlg.demCheckRange(theField:TField):string;
var
  tempStr:string;
begin

try

if theField.CheckRange = true then
   tempStr := 'True'
else
   tempStr := 'False';

Result := theField.Name + '.CheckRange =' + tempStr;

except
   on E:EConvertError do
      Result := theField.Name +' '+ E.Message;
   on E:EDataBaseError do
      Result := E.Message;
end;

end;
```

Description
This example function uses the value of the `CheckRange` property to generate the appropriate output string based on the value of the `CheckRange` property. The boolean value obtained is converted to a value of `True` or `False` that is then returned to the caller with descriptive text. To protect against conversion errors, the routine contains an exception handler that is invoked whenever there is a database conversion error. Note that this property could be accessed directly via the `FCheckRange` public variable in the `TBCDField` class.

Clear METHOD

Objects Affected All descendant classes of `TField`

Purpose Erase contents of field (and underlying dataset entry).

Declaration

```
procedure Clear; virtual;
```

Example Syntax See `Create` example syntax.

Description See `Create` description.

Create CONSTRUCTOR

Objects Affected	All descendant classes of **TField**.
Purpose	Create instance of **TField** (rarely used).
Declaration	

```
constructor Create(AOwner: TComponent); override;
```

Example Syntax

```
procedure Tflddlg.demDynCreate(theField:TField);
var
    tempField:TField;
    tempFieldClass : TFieldClass;
    tempDataSet: TDataSet;
    tft:TFieldType;

begin
    tft := theField.DataType; { determine field type }

    {use helper function to obtain field class ref}
    tempFieldClass := GetFieldClass(tft);

    { obtain field data set passed in }
    tempDataSet := theField.DataSet;

    { dynamically create the field }
    tempField:=tempFieldClass.Create(tempDataSet);
    tempField.Clear;
    try

      tempField.FieldName := theField.FieldName; { set field name }
      tempField.Size := theField.Size; { set size }
      tempField.Required := theField.Required; { set required prop }
      tempField.SetFieldType(tft); { set field type for new field }
      tempField.DataSet := tempDataSet; { assign data set }
    except
      tempField.destroy; { eliminate the field if error }
    end;
end;

{ this function returns a field class type when passed a TFieldType con-
stant value }
function Tflddlg.GetFieldClass(tft:TFieldType): TFieldClass;
const
  FieldClasses: array[TFieldType] of TFieldClass = (
    nil,                 { ftUnknown }
    TStringField,        { ftString }
    TSmallintField,      { ftSmallint }
    TIntegerField,       { ftInteger }
    TWordField,          { ftWord }
    TBooleanField,       { ftBoolean }
    TFloatField,         { ftFloat }
    TCurrencyField,      { ftCurrency }
    TBCDField,           { ftBCD }
    TDateField,          { ftDate }
    TTimeField,          { ftTime }
    TDateTimeField,      { ftDateTime }
```

continued on next page

continued from previous page

```
          TBytesField,        { ftBytes }
          TVarBytesField,     { ftVarBytes }
          TAutoIncField,      { ftAutoInc }
          TBlobField,         { ftBlob }
          TMemoField,         { ftMemo }
          TGraphicField,      { ftGraphic }
          TBlobField,         { ftFmtMemo }
          TBlobField,         { ftParadoxOle }
          TBlobField,         { ftDBaseOle }
          TBlobField);        { ftTypedBinary }
begin
  Result := FieldClasses[tft];
end;
```

Description   This example demonstrates the method used to dynamically create an instance of a **TField** type object. It is unlikely that you will ever need to actually perform this operation in normal use of Delphi: The creation and manipulation of **TField** objects is automatically performed with appropriate use of the Fields editor when you use a **TTable** component on a form. Note that this code will not operate correctly if the database that you are connecting the field to is already open. However, for completeness, an example is shown illustrating the dynamic creation of a **TField** object.

Currency PROPERTY

Objects Affected   TBCDField, TCurrencyField, TFloatField

Purpose   Used to indicate whether the particular field contains a value representing a currency.

Declaration

`TBCDField, TFloatField`

```
property Currency:Boolean;
(can also be accessed via FCurrency variable directly in class
TBCDField).
```

`TCurrencyField`

```
property Currency:Boolean; default True;
```

Example Syntax

```
procedure Tflddlg.demCurrencySet(theField:TBCDField, cv:Boolean);
begin

try

theField.Currency := cv;

except
  on E:EDataBaseError do
     Result := E.Message;
end;

end;
```

Description	This procedure sets the value of the **Currency** property according to the boolean value passed in as an argument. If any error occurs, an exception will be thrown.

DataSet PROPERTY

Objects Affected All descendant classes of **TField**

Purpose Return reference to **TDataSet** object underlying the field.

Declaration

```
property DataSet: TDataSet
```

Example Syntax

```
function Tflddlg.demDataSet(theField:TField):string;
var
  tempStr:string;
  tds:TDataSet;
begin

try

tds := theField.DataSet;

Result := theField.Name + '.DataSet =' + tds.Name;

except
   on E:EDataBaseError do
       Result := E.Message;
end;

end;
```

Description This function uses the field **DataSet** property to obtain a reference to the **DataSet** that underlies the field definition. The name of the **DataSet** is then fetched and combined with descriptive text that is returned to the caller. Database errors are trapped via an exception.

DataSize PROPERTY

Objects Affected All descendant classes of **TField**

Purpose Return size of memory required to store the field.

Declaration

```
property DataSize: Word
```

Example Syntax

```
function Tflddlg.demDataSize(theField:TField):string;
var
  tempStr:string;
  tds:integer;
```

continued on next page

continued from previous page

```
begin

try

tds := theField.DataSize;
Result := theField.Name + '.DataSize =' + IntToStr(tds);

except
   on E:EDataBaseError do
      Result := E.Message;
end;

end;
```

Description   This function retrieves the `DataSize` property for the supplied field and converts it to a string and combines it with descriptive text that is then returned to the caller. Database errors are trapped via an exception.

DataType PROPERTY

Objects Affected All descendant classes of `TField`

Purpose   Return field type of associated field.

Declaration

```
property DataType: TFieldType
```

Example Syntax

```
function Tflddlg.demDataType(theField:TField):string;
var
  tempStr:string;
  tft: TFieldType;
  tfts:string;
begin

try

tft := theField.DataType;

case tft of
  ftUnknown:
     tfts := 'ftUnknown';
  ftString:
     tfts := 'ftString';
  ftSmallint:
     tfts := 'ftSmallint';
  ftInteger:
     tfts := 'ftInteger';
  ftWord:
     tfts := 'ftWord';
  ftBoolean:
     tfts := 'ftBoolean';
  ftFloat:
     tfts := 'ftFloat';
  ftCurrency:
```

```
              tfts := 'ftCurrency';
          ftBCD:
              tfts := 'ftBCD';
          ftDate:
              tfts := 'ftDate';
          ftTime:
              tfts := 'ftTime';
          ftDateTime:
              tfts := 'ftDateTime';
          ftBytes:
              tfts := 'ftBytes';
          ftVarBytes:
              tfts := 'ftVarBytes';
          ftAutoInc:
              tfts := 'ftAutoInc';
          ftBlob:
              tfts := 'ftBlob';
          ftMemo:
              tfts := 'ftMemo';
          ftGraphic:
              tfts := 'ftGraphic';
          ftFmtMemo:
              tfts := 'ftFmtMemo';
          ftParadoxOle:
              tfts := 'ftParadoxOle';
          ftDBaseOle:
              tfts := 'ftDBaseOle';
          ftTypedBinary:
              tfts := 'ftTypedDinary';
      end;

      Result := theField.Name + '.DataType =' + tfts;

      except
        on E:EDataBaseError do
            Result := E.Message;
      end;

      end;
```

Description   This function retrieves the **DataType** property for the supplied field and uses a case statement to convert the **TFieldType** result to a string. It then combines it with descriptive text that is then returned to the caller. Database errors are trapped via an exception.

Destroy DESTRUCTOR

Objects Affected	All descendant classes of **TField**
Purpose	Destructor for **TField** component.
Declaration	

```
destructor Destroy; override; { rarely used }
```

Example Syntax	See **Create** example syntax.
Description	See **Create** description.

DisplayFormat PROPERTY

Objects Affected   TDateField, TDateTimeField, TIntegerField, TSmallIntField, TTimeField, TWordField, TBCDField, TCurrencyField, TFloatField components

Purpose   Determine the DisplayFormat to be used for the field.

Declaration

```
published DisplayFormat: string
```

Example Syntax

```
procedure Tflddlg.demDisplayFormat(theField:TField, fs:string);
begin

try

theField.DisplayFormat := fs;

except
   on E:EDataBaseError do
      Result := E.Message;
end;

end;
```

Description   The DisplayFormat property is used to format the value of the field for display purposes. For TIntegerField, TSmallIntField, and TWordField, formatting is performed by the FloatToTextFmt library function. If DisplayFormat has not been assigned a string, the value is formatted by Str. If the field type is TDateField, TDateTimeField, or TTimeField, formatting is performed by DateTimeToStr. If DisplayFormat is not assigned a string, the value is formatted according to the default Windows specifications in the [International] section of the WIN.INI file.

If the field type is TBCDField, TCurrencyField, or TFloatField, formatting is performed by FloatToTextFmt. If DisplayFormat is not assigned a string, the value is formatted according to the value of the Currency property.

DisplayLabel PROPERTY

Objects Affected   All descendant classes of TField

Purpose   Obtain column heading or field name of field component.

Declaration

```
property DisplayLabel: string
```

Example Syntax

```
function Tflddlg.demDisplayLabel(theField:TField):string;
var
  tempStr:string;
begin

try

tempStr := theField.DisplayLabel;

Result := theField.Name + '.DisplayLabel =' + tempStr;

except
   on E:EDataBaseError do
      Result := E.Message;
end;

end;
```

Description

This function obtains the `DisplayLabel` property for the supplied field and returns it to the caller with descriptive text added. Database errors are trapped via an exception.

DisplayName PROPERTY

Objects Affected All descendant classes of `TField`

Purpose Obtain field name of field component.

Declaration

```
property DisplayName: string
```

Example Syntax

```
function Tflddlg.demDisplayName(theField:TField):string;
var
  tempStr:string;
begin

try

tempStr := theField.DisplayName;

Result := theField.Name + '.DisplayName =' + tempStr;

except
   on E:EDataBaseError do
      Result := E.Message;
end;

end;
```

Description

This function obtains the `DisplayName` property for the supplied field and returns it to the caller with descriptive text added. Database errors are trapped via an exception.

DisplayText PROPERTY

Objects Affected	All descendant classes of `TField`
Purpose	Obtain string used for field component when displayed.
Declaration	

```
property DisplayText: string
```

Example Syntax

```
function Tflddlg.demDisplayText(theField:TField):string;
var
  tempStr:string;
begin

try

tempStr := theField.DisplayText;

Result := theField.Name + '.DisplayText =' + tempStr;

except
  on E:EDataBaseError do
     Result := E.Message;
end;

end;
```

Description	This function obtains the `DisplayText` property for the supplied field and returns it to the caller with descriptive text added. Database errors are trapped via an exception.

DisplayValues PROPERTY

Objects Affected	`TBooleanField` component
Purpose	`DisplayValues` controls the manner in which the `TBooleanField` is translated to and from display format. You can use any pair of phrases you want, separated by a semicolon. For example, `t;f` for true and false, or `Y;N` as another possibility. If one phrase is omitted, no text is displayed and a data-aware control with no text assigns the corresponding value to the field. The default value is `True;False`.
Declaration	

```
property DisplayValues: string
```

Example Syntax

```
procedure Tflddlg.demDisplayValues(theField:TBooleanField);
begin

try

theField.DisplayValues:= 'Foo;Bar';
```

```
except
   on E:EDataBaseError do
      Result := E.Message;
end;

end;
```

Description   This function will cause **'Foo'** to be displayed when the field is **True** in a data-aware control and **'Bar'** to be displayed in the data control when the field is **False**.

DisplayWidth PROPERTY

Objects Affected   All descendant classes of **TField**

Purpose   Obtain number of characters required to display field.

Declaration

```
property DisplayWidth: Integer
```

Example Syntax

```
function Tflddlg.demDisplayWidth(theField:TField):string;
var
   tempStr:string;
   wid: integer;
begin

try

wid := theField.DisplayWidth;

Result := theField.Name + '.DisplayWidth =' + IntToStr(wid);

except
   on E:EDataBaseError do
      Result := E.Message;
end;

end;
```

Description   This function obtains the **DisplayWidth** property for the supplied field, converts the width to a string, and returns it to the caller with descriptive text added. Database errors are trapped via an exception.

EditFormat PROPERTY

Objects Affected   TBCDField, TCurrencyField, TFloatField, TIntegerField, TSmallIntField, TWordField components

Purpose   The **EditFormat** property is used to format the value of the field for display purposes when the field is being edited. For **TIntegerField**,

TSmallIntField, and TWordField, formatting is performed by
FloatToTextFmt library function. If DisplayFormat has not been assigned
a string, the value is formatted by Str. If the field type is TDateField,
TDateTimeField, or TTimeField, formatting is performed by
DateTimeToStr. If DisplayFormat is not assigned a string, the value is for-
matted according to the default Windows specifications in the
[International] section of the WIN.INI file.If the field type is TBCDField,
TCurrencyField, or TFloatField, formatting is performed by
FloatToTextFmt. If DisplayFormat is not assigned a string, the value is
formatted according to the value of the Currency property.

Declaration

```
property EditFormat: string;
```

Example Syntax

```
procedure Tflddlg.demEditFormat(theField:TField, fs:string);
begin

try

theField.EditFormat := fs;

except
   on E:EDataBaseError do
      Result := E.Message;
end;

end;
```

Description   This procedure sets the desired EditFormat as passed by the caller.

EditMask PROPERTY

Objects Affected   All descendant classes of TField

Purpose   Determine how field should be displayed.

Declaration

```
property EditMask: string
```

Example Syntax

```
function Tflddlg.demEditMask(theField:TField):string;
var
   tempStr:string;
begin

try

tempStr := theField.EditMask;

Result := theField.Name + '.EditMask =' + tempStr;
```

```
except
   on E:EDataBaseError do
      Result := E.Message;
end;

end;
```

Description This function obtains the `EditMask` property for the supplied field and returns it to the caller with descriptive text added. Database errors are trapped via an exception.

EditMaskPtr PROPERTY

Objects Affected   All descendant classes of `TField`

Purpose   Obtain pointer to `EditMask` property of a string.

Declaration

```
property EditMaskPtr: string
```

Example Syntax

```
function Tflddlg.demEditMaskPtr(theField:TField):string;
var
  tempStr:string;
begin

try

tempStr := theField.EditMaskPtr;

Result := theField.Name + '.EditMaskPtr =' + tempStr;

except
   on E:EDataBaseError do
      Result := E.Message;
end;

end;
```

Description This function obtains the `EditMaskPtr` property for the supplied field, which is a string type result and returns it to the caller with descriptive text added. Database errors are trapped via an exception.

FieldKind PROPERTY

Objects Affected   All descendant classes of `TField`.

Purpose   Determine whether field is from dataset, calculated, or lookup type.

Declaration

```
property FieldKind: TFieldKind
```

Example Syntax

```
function Tflddlg.demFieldKind(theField:TField):string;
var
  tempStr:string;
  fk : TFieldKind;
  fks:string;
begin

try

fk := theField.FieldKind;

case fk of
  fkData:
    fks := 'fkData';
  fkCalculated:
    fks := 'fkCalculated';
  fkLookup:
    fks := 'fkLookup';
end;

Result := theField.Name + '.FieldKind =' + fks;

except
  on E:EDataBaseError do
    Result := E.Message;
end;

end;
```

Description
This function uses the **FieldKind** property of the supplied field to classify the field and create an appropriate return message to the caller. Database errors are trapped via exception handling.

FieldName PROPERTY

Objects Affected   All descendant classes of **TField**

Purpose   Determine field name in physical dataset underlying field.

Declaration

```
property FieldName: string
```

Example Syntax

```
function Tflddlg.demFieldName(theField:TField):string;
var
  tempStr:string;

begin

try

tempStr := theField.FieldName;

Result := theField.Name + '.FieldName =' + tempStr;
```

```
except
   on E:EDataBaseError do
      Result := E.Message;
end;

end;
```

Description This function retrieves the `FieldName` property of the supplied field and uses it to generate an appropriate return message to the caller. Database errors are trapped via exception handling.

FieldNo PROPERTY

Objects Affected All descendant classes of `TField`

Purpose Obtain ordinal value for associated field in dataset.

Declaration

```
property FieldNo: Integer
```

Example Syntax

```
function Tflddlg.demFieldNo(theField:TField):string;
var
  tempStr:string;
  fn:integer;
begin

try

fn := theField.FieldNo;

Result := theField.Name + '.FieldNo =' + IntToStr(fn);

except
   on E:EDataBaseError do
      Result := E.Message;
end;

end;
```

Description The `Retrieve` function retrieves the `FieldNo` property of the supplied field and uses it to generate an appropriate return message, which contains the field number converted to a string, to the caller. Database errors are trapped via exception handling.

FocusControl METHOD

Objects Affected All descendant classes of `TField`

Purpose Set focus to data-aware component using field.

Declaration

```
procedure FocusControl;
```

Example Syntax

```
procedure Tflddlg.demSetFocus(theField:TField);
begin
   close;
   theField.FocusControl;
end;
```

Description   This example uses focus control in a hypothetical dialog. The **Close** function dismisses the dialog that invoked the call and to which the **demSetFocus** method is a member. Then after the close has taken place and control has returned to the original form that contains the data-aware component associated with the field in question, the call to **FocusControl** moves the active keyboard focus to the first form control associated with the **TField** object passed as an argument. See the example syntax for actual use of this method.

GetData FUNCTION

Objects Affected   All descendant classes of **TField**

Purpose   Get untranslated data from field.

Declaration

```
function GetData(Buffer: Pointer): Boolean;
```

Example Syntax

```
procedure Tflddlg.demMisc(theField:TField);
var
   theBuff:PChar;
   fsize:integer;
   tchar:char;
begin
   fsize := theField.Size+1; { get field size }
   GetMem(theBuff,fsize); { get buffer }
   theField.GetData(theBuff); { get copy of raw data }
   tchar := theBuff[1]; { get second char in buffer }
   if theField.IsValidChar(tchar) = true then
   begin
      { only do this if second char in original string is
         valid char for field, which it should be since we
         got it from the field in the first place ! }

      theField.DataSet.Edit; { place data base into edit mode }
      theField.SetData(theBuff+1); { modify data }
      theField.DataSet.Post; { update data base and leave edit }
   end;

end;
```

Description   This example illustrates the use of the **GetMem** function to obtain a copy of the field contents exactly as stored by the field object. The information is copied to the supplied buffer exactly as stored by the datatype that the field represents. This function also demonstrates syntax for the use of the **IsValidChar** and **SetData** methods.

Index PROPERTY

Objects Affected	All descendant classes of **TField**
Purpose	Determine a field's order in the underlying dataset.
Declaration	

```
property Index: Integer
```

Example Syntax

```
function Tflddlg.demIndex(theField:TField):string;
var
  tempStr:string;
  fn:integer;
begin

try

fn := theField.Index;

Result := theField.Name + '.Index =' + IntToStr(fn);

except
   on E:EDataBaseError do
      Result := E.Message;
end;

end;
```

Description This function retrieves the **Index** property of the supplied field and uses it to generate an appropriate return message, which contains the field index number converted to a string, to the caller. Database errors are trapped via exception handling.

IsBlob FUNCTION

Objects Affected	All descendant classes of **TField**
Purpose	Determine whether a field contains a **BLOB** object.
Declaration	

```
property IsBlob: Boolean
```

Example Syntax

```
function Tflddlg.demIsBlobField(theField:TField):string;
var
  tempStr:string;
  fn:boolean;
begin

try

fn := theField.IsBlob;
```

continued on next page

continued from previous page

```
if fn = true then
   tempStr := 'Yes'
else
   tempStr := 'No';

Result := theField.Name + '.IsBlob =' + tempStr;

except
   on E:EDataBaseError do
      Result := E.Message;
end;

end;
```

Description   This function determines whether or not the field supplied by the caller is a **BLOB** field and returns a string indicating the result to the caller. Database errors are trapped via exception handling.

IsIndexField FUNCTION

Objects Affected   All descendant classes of **TField**

Purpose   Determine whether a field is indexed or not.

Declaration

```
property IsIndexField: Boolean
```

Example Syntax

```
function Tflddlg.demIsIndexField(theField:TField):string;
var
  tempStr:string;
  fn:boolean;
begin

try

fn := theField.IsIndexField;

if fn = true then
   tempStr := 'Yes'
else
   tempStr := 'No';

Result := theField.Name + '.IsIndexField =' + tempStr;

except
   on E:EDataBaseError do
      Result := E.Message;
end;

end;
```

Description   This function determines whether or not the field supplied by the caller is an indexed field and returns a string indicating the result to the caller. Database errors are trapped via exception handling.

I s N u l l PROPERTY

Objects Affected   All descendant classes of **TField**

Purpose   Return **True** if field value is NULL.

Declaration

```
property IsNull: Boolean
```

Example Syntax

```
function Tflddlg.demIsNull(theField:TField):string;
var
  tempStr:string;
  fn:boolean;
begin

try

fn := theField.IsNull;

if fn = true then
   tempStr := 'Yes'
else
   tempStr := 'No';

Result := theField.Name + '.IsNull =' + tempStr;

except
   on E:EDataBaseError do
      Result := E.Message;
end;

end;
```

Description   This function determines whether or not the field supplied by the caller is a NULL pointer field and returns a string indicating the result to the caller. Database errors are trapped via exception handling.

I s V a l i d C h a r FUNCTION

Objects Affected   All descendant classes of **TField**

Purpose   Return **True** if character passed is accepted by the field.

Declaration

```
function IsValidChar(InputChar: Char): Boolean; virtual;
```

Example Syntax   See **GetData** example syntax.

Description   See **GetData** description.

KeyFields PROPERTY

Objects Affected	All descendant classes of TField
Purpose	Determine which fields are used by lookup fields in a dataset.
Declaration	

```
property KeyFields: string
```

Example Syntax

```
function Tflddlg.demKeyFields(theField:TField):string;
var
  tempStr:string;
begin

try

tempStr := theField.KeyFields;

Result := theField.Name + '.KeyFields =' + tempStr;

except
   on E:EDataBaseError do
      Result := E.Message;
end;

end;
```

Description This function obtains the key field names for the specified lookup field and returns a string indicating the result to the caller. Database errors are trapped via exception handling.

LoadFromFile FUNCTION

Objects Affected	TBlobField, TGraphicField, TMemoField
Purpose	Used to load one of the above named components with the contents of a specified file. In the case of TGraphicField and TMemoField, the named file should have been saved originally by the SaveToFile method or the SaveToStream method.
Declaration	

```
procedure LoadFromFile(const FileName:string);
```

Example Syntax

```
procedure Tflddlg.demLoadFromFile(theField:TGraphicField; fn:string);
begin

try

theField.LoadFromFile(fn);

except
```

```
        on E:EDataBaseError do
            Result := E.Message;
    end;

    end;
```

Description   This function loads a file into a **TGraphicField**.

LoadFromStream FUNCTION

Objects Affected   **TBlobField, TGraphicField, TMemoField**

Purpose   Used to load one of the above named components from a specified **TStream** object. In the case of **TGraphicField** and **TMemoField**, the stream should have been saved originally by the **SaveToFile** method or the **SaveToStream** method.

Declaration

```
procedure LoadFromStream(Stream:TStream);
```

Example Syntax

```
procedure Tflddlg.demLoadFromStream(theField:TGraphicField; fn:TStream);
begin

try

theField.LoadFromStream(fn);

except
    on E:EDataBaseError do
        Result := E.Message;
end;

end;
```

Description   This function loads a file into a **TGraphicField**.

Lookup PROPERTY

Objects Affected   All descendant classes of **TField**

Purpose   Determine whether a field is a lookup field.

Declaration

```
property Lookup: Boolean
```

Example Syntax

```
function Tflddlg.demLookup(theField:TField):string;
var
  tempStr:string;
  fn:boolean;
```

continued on next page

continued from previous page

```
begin

try

fn := theField.Lookup;

if fn = true then
   tempStr := 'Yes'
else
   tempStr := 'No';

Result := theField.Name + '.Lookup =' + tempStr;

except
   on E:EDataBaseError do
      Result := E.Message;
end;

end;
```

Description   This function determines whether or not a field is a lookup field type and returns a message indicating the result to the caller. Database errors are trapped via an exception handler.

LookupCache PROPERTY

Objects Affected   All descendant classes of `TField`

Purpose   Determine whether a lookup field uses a cache to store its contents.

Declaration

```
property LookupCache: Boolean
```

Example Syntax

```
function Tflddlg.demLookupCache(theField:TField):string;
var
  tempStr:string;
  fn:boolean;
begin

try

fn := theField.LookupCache;

if fn = true then
   tempStr := 'Yes'
else
   tempStr := 'No';

Result := theField.Name + '.LookupCache =' + tempStr;

except
   on E:EDataBaseError do
      Result := E.Message;
end;

end;
```

Description
Even though this property is published at the **TField** level, it only has use in conjunction with lookup fields. It is used to determine whether a cache is in use with a lookup field and results in better performance for those field types.

LookupDataSet PROPERTY

Objects Affected
All descendant classes of **TField**

Purpose
Determine table used by lookup fields.

Declaration

```
property LookupDataSet: TDataSet
```

Example Syntax

```
function Tflddlg.demLookupDataSet(theField:TField):string;
var
  tempStr:string;
  fn:integer;
  tds:TDataSet;
begin

try

if theField.Lookup = true then
   tds := theField.LookupDataSet
else
   tds := nil;

if tds <> nil then
   Result := theField.Name + '.LookupDataSet =' + tds.name
else
   Result := theField.Name + '.LookupDataSet is not defined.';

except
   on E:EDataBaseError do
      Result := E.Message;
end;

end;
```

Description
This function determines if a field is a **Lookup** field. If so, it then determines the **Lookup** dataset underlying the **Lookup** field, and obtains the name of the **Lookup** dataset name which is then returned to the caller. Database errors are trapped via an exception handler.

LookupKeyFields FUNCTION

Objects Affected
All descendant classes of **TField**

Purpose
Identify fields in **Lookup** dataset used by lookup field.

Declaration

```
property LookupKeyFields: string
```

Example Syntax

```
function Tflddlg.demLookupKeyFields(theField:TField):string;
var
  tempStr:string;
  fn:integer;

begin

try

if theField.Lookup = true then
   tempStr := theField.LookupKeyFields
else
   tempStr := '';

if tempStr <> '' then
   Result := theField.Name + '.LookupKeyFields =' + tempStr
else
   Result := theField.Name + '.LookupKeyFields are not defined.';

except
   on E:EDataBaseError do
      Result := E.Message;
end;

end;
```

Description

This function determines the key fields for a lookup field. It then returns the resulting string to the caller with some additional descriptive text. Database errors are trapped via an exception handler.

LookupList FUNCTION

Objects Affected   All descendant classes of `TField`

Purpose   Obtain the information contained in a lookup field in a single data structure of type `TLookupList`.

Declaration

```
property LookupList: TLookupList; {read only}
```

Example Syntax

```
function Tflddlg.demLookupList(theField:TField,key:Variant):Variant;
var
  tempStr:string;
  fn:integer;
  ll:TLookupList;
begin

try

  ll := theField.LookupList;
  Result := ll.ValueOfKey(key);
```

```
except
   on E:EDataBaseError do
      Result := E.Message;
end;

end;
```

Description   This function finds the value object associated with a given key variant object supplied by the caller and returns that value to the caller. Database errors are trapped via an exception handler.

LookupResultFieLd FUNCTION

Objects Affected   All descendant classes of **TFieLd**

Purpose   Identify field in **Lookup** dataset to be copied to lookup field.

Declaration

```
property LookupResultField: string
```

Example Syntax

```
function TflddLg.demLookupResultField(theField:TField):string;
var
   tempStr:string;
   fn:integer;

begin

try

if theField.Lookup = true then
   tempStr := theField.LookupResultField
else
   tempStr := '';

if tempStr <> '' then
   Result := theField.Name + '.LookupResultField =' + tempStr
else
   Result := theField.Name + '.LookupResultField is not defined.';

except
   on E:EDataBaseError do
      Result := E.Message;
end;

end;
```

Description   This function fetches the value of the **LookupResultFieLd** if the supplied field is a **Lookup** type and creates an appropriate result string that is passed back to the function caller. Database errors are trapped via exception handling.

MaxValue FUNCTION

Objects Affected   TBCDField, TCurrencyField, TFloatField, TIntegerField, TSmallintField, TWordField

Purpose   Determine the maximum numeric value allowable to the field types shown above.

Declaration
TBCDField

```
property MaxValue: Currency;
```

TFloatField, TCurrencyField

```
property MaxValue:Double;
```

TIntegerField, TSmallintField, TWordField

```
property MaxValue:LongInt;
```

Example Syntax

```
procedure Tflddlg.demSetMaxValue(theField:TFloatField; mv:double);
begin

theField.MaxValue := mv;

end;
```

Description   This procedure sets the maximum value property of the supplied **TFloatField**. Note that this property value can also be accessed directly via the class variable **FMaxValue**, which is publicly declared in **TBCDField**, but not in the other classes. This is a deviation from normal object-oriented practice and is not the preferred way of accessing class properties. If the field is assigned a value that is greater than the maximum value, an exception will be raised.

MinValue FUNCTION

Objects Affected   TBCDField, TCurrencyField, TFloatField, TIntegerField, TSmallintField, TWordField

Purpose   Determine the minimum numeric value allowable the field types shown above.

Declaration
TBCDField

```
property MinValue: Currency;
```

TFloatField, TCurrencyField

```
property MinValue:Double;
```

TIntegerField, TSmallintField, TWordField

```
property MinValue:LongInt;
```

Example Syntax

```
procedure Tflddlg.demSetMinValue(theField:TFloatField; mv:double);
begin

theField.MinValue := mv;

end;
```

Description
This procedure sets the minimum value property of the supplied **TFloatField**. Note that this property value can also be accessed directly via the class variable **FMaxValue**, which is publicly declared in **TBCDField**, but not in the other classes. This is a deviation from normal object-oriented practice and is not the preferred way of accessing class properties. If the field is assigned a value that is less than the minimum value, an exception will be raised.

NewValue PROPERTY

Objects Affected   All descendant classes of **TField**

Purpose   Determine current value of field.

Declaration

```
property NewValue: Variant
```

Example Syntax

```
function Tflddlg.demNewValue(theField:TField):string;
var
  nv:variant;
begin

try

nv := theField.NewValue;

Result := theField.Name + '.NewValue =' + nv;

except
   on E:EDataBaseError do
      Result := E.Message;
end;

end;
```

Description
This function obtains the new value for the supplied field, which is the value for the field after the latest editing change has been completed. Database errors are trapped via an exception handler.

Offset FUNCTION

Objects Affected	All descendant classes of `TField`
Purpose	Obtain the virtual offset of a field.
Declaration	

```
property Offset: Word;
```

Example Syntax

```
function Tflddlg.demGetOffset(theField:TField):word;
var
  ov:word;
begin

try

ov := theField.Offset;

Result := theField.Name + '.OldValue =' + inttostr(ov);

except
   on E:EDataBaseError do
       Result := E.Message;
end;

end;
```

Description This function obtains the virtual offset of a field relative to the table in which it belongs. This can be useful for the storage of field contents in stream objects to allow a particular field to be found in a stream when used in conjunction with the `Size` property.

OldValue PROPERTY

Objects Affected	All descendant classes of `TField`
Purpose	Obtain original value of field before changes.
Declaration	

```
property OldValue: Variant
```

Example Syntax

```
function Tflddlg.demOldValue(theField:TField):string;
var
  ov:variant;
begin

try

ov := theField.OldValue;

Result := theField.Name + '.OldValue =' + ov;
```

```
except
   on E:EDataBaseError do
      Result := E.Message;
end;

end;
```

Description   This function obtains the old value for the supplied field, which is the value for the field before any editing changes have been completed. Database errors are trapped via an exception handler.

OnChange EVENT

Objects Affected   All descendant classes of `TField`

Purpose   Perform actions whenever a field is changed.

Declaration

```
TFieldNotifyEvent = procedure(Sender: TField) of object;
property OnChange: TFieldNotifyEvent;
```

Example Syntax

```
procedure CheckVal(theField:TField)
var
   tval:double;
begin
   tval := theField.AsFloat;
   if tval < 0.0 then
     tval := 0.0;
   theField.Value := tval;
end;
   .
   .
   .
TPosField.OnChange := CheckVal;
   .
   .
   .
```

Description   `OnChange` is invoked when the contents of the field are changed. If a data-aware control is linked to the field on a form, the `OnChange` handler is not invoked until the control attempts to store the changes into the current record. Note that the `TFieldNotifyEvent` defines a procedure type that accepts a `TField` object as argument. The `TField` object that is changing will be passed as an argument to the user-supplied procedure. This means that any public or published method or property of the `TField` involved will be available to the procedure. The above example illustrates the definition of a procedure that checks to make sure the value of a field is positive and, if not, forces the value of that field to zero. It then shows the syntax used to assign the procedure to a particular `TField` object.

OnGetText EVENT

Objects Affected   All descendant classes of `TField`

Purpose   Perform action whenever `Text` or `DisplayText` is read.

Declaration

```
TFieldGetTextEvent = procedure(Sender: TField; var Text: string;
DisplayText: Boolean) of object;
property OnGetText: TFieldGetTextEvent
```

Example Syntax

```
procedure GetText(Sender: TField; var Text: string; DisplayText: Boolean)
begin
  Text := LowerCase(Text);
end;
    .
    .
    .

SomeTextField.OnGetText := GetText;
    .
    .
    .
```

Description   The `OnGetText` event is invoked when the `DisplayText` or `Text` properties are referenced. The `DisplayText` parameter indicates whether the event should supply the text in display format or in edit format for the `Text` property. This could allow the user to change internal data for a field depending on whether or not `DisplayText` was `True` or `False` or to perform some appropriate formatting prior to retrieving the field text from the component.

If `OnGetText` has been assigned a method, the event handler will perform any conversion required to display the value. If you assign a method to this property, you can take any special actions required by the event.

OnSetText EVENT

Objects Affected   All descendant classes of `TField`

Purpose   Perform action whenever `Text` or `DisplayText` is read.

Declaration

```
TFieldSetTextEvent = procedure(Sender: TField; Text: string) of object;
property OnSetText: TFieldSetTextEvent
```

Example Syntax

```
procedure SetText(Sender:TMemoField; Text: string)
var
   tv:Variant;
begin
  tv:= UpperCase(Text);
  Sender.Value := tv;
```

```
end;
    .
    .
    .
SomeTextField.OnSetText := SetText;
    .
    .
    .
```

Description   The `OnSetText` event is invoked when the `Text` property is referenced.
This method overrides the default processing when a value is assigned to a
`TField` descendant and allows the user to perform whatever manipula-
tions might be desired on the text value written to the field. In this
example, the `OnSetText` handler causes the text to be converted to uppercase prior to sending it to the `TTextField` component.

OnValidate EVENT

Objects Affected   All descendant classes of `TField`

Purpose   Perform special validation when a field is modified.

Declaration

```
TFieldNotifyEvent = procedure(Sender: TField) of object;
property OnValidate: TFieldNotifyEvent
```

Example Syntax

```
procedure myValidate(Sender:TField)
var
   tv:double;
begin
   tv:= Sender.Value; // fetch field value
   if tv > Sender.MaxValue then
      tv := Sender.MaxValue
   else if tv < Sender.MinValue then
      tv := Sender.MinValue;
   Sender.Value := tv;
end;
    .
    .
    .
SomeTextField.OnValidate := myValidate;
    .
    .
    .
```

Description   The `OnValidate` event is invoked when a field is changed. If a data-aware
control is linked to the field, changes in the control do not activate
`OnValidate` until the control attempts to store the results of those changes
into the current record. By assigning a method to this property, you can
perform any special validation required for the field. The
`TFieldNotifyEvent` type points to a method that handles the validation of
data in a field or handles the changing of data in a field.

Precision PROPERTY

Objects Affected	`TBCDField`, `TCurrencyField`, `TFloatField` components
Purpose	Used in conjunction with formatting the numeric field types shown above.
Declaration	

```
property Precision: Integer;
```

Example Syntax

```
procedure Tflddlg.demSetPrecision(theField:TFloatField, p:integer);
begin

theField.precision := p;
end;
```

Description   The example sets the precision to the value passed in **p** which represents the number of digits to which the numeric value should be formatted before rounding begins. The property defaults to a value of **15**.

ReadOnly PROPERTY

Objects Affected	All descendant classes of `TField`
Purpose	Specify that a field should be read-only or not.
Declaration	

```
property ReadOnly: Boolean
```

Example Syntax

```
function Tflddlg.demReadOnly(theField:TField):string;
var
  tempStr:string;
  ro:boolean;
begin

try

ro := theField.ReadOnly;

if ro = true then
   tempStr := 'true'
else
   tempStr := 'false';

Result := theField.Name + '.ReadOnly =' + tempStr;

except
  on E:EDataBaseError do
     Result := E.Message;
end;

end;
```

Description | This function determines whether a field is read-only via the **ReadOnly** property, then formats an appropriate result string that indicates the state of the **ReadOnly** property. Any database errors are trapped via exception handling.

RefreshLookupList METHOD

Objects Affected | All descendant classes of **TField**

Purpose | Cause a lookup field to refresh its contents from the underlying data source.

Declaration

```
procedure RefreshLookupList;
```

Example Syntax

```
function Tflddlg.demRefreshList(theField:TField):string;
begin

try

  theField.RefreshLookupList;

except
  on E:EDataBaseError do
      Result := E.Message;
end;

end;
```

Description | This function applies to lookup fields and causes them to refresh their contents from the underlying data source if the underlying **TLookupList** data object associated with the field is defined (see **LookupList** property).

Required PROPERTY

Objects Affected | All descendant classes of **TField**

Purpose | Set to **True** to require non-nil field values.

Declaration

```
property Required: Boolean
```

Example Syntax

```
function Tflddlg.demRequired(theField:TField):string;
var
  tempStr:string;
  rq:boolean;
begin

try

rq := theField.Required;
```

continued on next page

continued from previous page

```
if rq = true then
   tempStr := 'true'
else
   tempStr := 'false';

Result := theField.Name + '.Required =' + tempStr;

except
   on E:EDataBaseError do
      Result := E.Message;
end;

end;
```

Description This function determines whether a field is required (must be non-null) via the `Required` property, then formats an appropriate result string that indicates the state of the `Required` property. Any database errors are trapped via exception handling.

SaveToFile METHOD

Objects Affected `TBlobField`, `TGraphicField`, `TMemoField`

Purpose Used to save the contents of one of the above named components to a specified file. This function should be used in conjunction with `LoadFromFile` for `TGraphicField` and `TMemoField`.

Declaration

```
procedure SaveToFile(const FileName:string);
```

Example Syntax

```
procedure Tflddlg.demSaveToFile(theField:TGraphicField; fn:string);
begin

try

theField.SaveToFile(fn);

except
   on E:EDataBaseError do
      Result := E.Message;
end;

end;
```

Description This function saves the contents of a `TGraphicField` into a specified disk file.

SaveToStream METHOD

Objects Affected	TBlobField, TGraphicField, TMemoField
Purpose	Used to save the contents of one of the above named components to a specified stream object. This function should be used in conjunction with LoadFromStream for TGraphicField and TMemoField.
Declaration	

```
procedure SaveToStream(stream:TStream);
```

Example Syntax

```
procedure Tflddlg.demSaveToStream(theField:TGraphicField; s:TStream);
begin

try

theField.SaveToStream(s);

except
   on E:EDataBaseError do
      Result := E.Message;
end;

end;
```

Description   This function saves the contents of a TGraphicField into a specified
TStream object.

ServerCalcField PROPERTY

Objects Affected	All descendant classes of TField
Purpose	Determine whether a field is calculated by the server.
Declaration	

```
property ServerCalcField: Boolean
```

Example Syntax

```
function Tflddlg.demServerCalc(theField:TField):string;
var
  tempStr:string;
  rq:boolean;
begin

try

rq := theField.ServerCalcField;

if rq = true then
   tempStr := 'true'
else
   tempStr := 'false';

Result := theField.Name + '.Required =' + tempStr;
```

continued on next page

continued from previous page

```
except
    on E:EDataBaseError do
        Result := E.Message;
end;

end;
```

Description   This function determines whether a field is calculated by the database server supporting the underlying database.

SetCurrency METHOD

Objects Affected   `TBCDField` component

Purpose   This method performs the equivalent function of the `Currency` property in the `TBCDField` component.

Declaration

```
procedure SetCurrency(isCurrency:Boolean);
```

Example Syntax

```
procedure Tflddlg.demSetCurrency(theField:TBCDField, cv:Boolean);
begin

try

theField.SetCurrency(cv);

except
    on E:EDataBaseError do
        Result := E.Message;
end;

end;
```

Description   This procedure sets the value of the `Currency` property according to the boolean value passed in as an argument. If any error occurs, an exception will be thrown.

SetData METHOD

Objects Affected   All descendant classes of `TField`

Purpose   Assign raw data to field.

Declaration

```
procedure SetData(Buffer: Pointer);
```

Example Syntax   See `GetData` example syntax.

Description   See `GetData` description.

SetFieldType METHOD

Objects Affected	All descendant classes of `TField`, `TBlobField`
Purpose	Specify field type for field.
Declaration	

```
procedure SetFieldType(Value: TFieldType); virtual;
```

Example Syntax	See `Create` example syntax.
Description	See `Create` description.

Size PROPERTY

Objects Affected	All descendant classes of `TField`,
Purpose	Determine size of field stored in database.
Declaration	

TField

```
property Size: Word; //no default
```

TBCDField

```
property Size: Word; //default 4
```

TBinaryField

```
property Size: Word; //default 16
```

TBlobField

```
property Size: Word; //default 0
```

TStringField

```
property Size: Word; //default 20
```

Example Syntax

```
function Tflddlg.demSize(theField:TField):string;
var
  tempStr:string;
  sz:integer;
begin

try

sz := theField.Size;

Result := theField.Name + '.Size =' + IntToStr(sz);

except
  on E:EDataBaseError do
    Result := E.Message;
end;

end;
```

Description   This function obtains the size of the field in bytes stored in the supplied field object. It then converts the result to a string and returns the size along with descriptive text to the caller. Database errors are trapped via exception handling.

Text PROPERTY

Objects Affected   All descendant classes of `TField`

Purpose   Obtain string data displayed in data-aware component.

Declaration

```
property Text: string
```

Example Syntax

```
function Tflddlg.demText(theField:TField):string;
var
  tempStr:string;
begin

try

tempStr := theField.Text;

Result := theField.Name + '.Text =' + tempStr;

except
   on E:EDataBaseError do
      Result := E.Message;
end;

end;
```

Description   This function obtains the current text display associated with the field and returns it together with descriptive text to the caller.

Transliterate PROPERTY

Objects Affected   `TMemoField`, `TStringField` component

Purpose   The `Transliterate` property controls whether translations to and from the tables underlying the fields and the corresponding data-aware component will be performed. `Transliterate` is `True` by default.

Declaration

```
property Transliterate: Boolean;
```

Example Syntax

```
procedure Tflddlg.demNoTranslit(theField:TField);
begin
```

```
theField.Transliterate := false;

end;
```

Description   This function turns off transliteration for the specified field.

Validate PROPERTY

Objects Affected   All descendant classes of `TField`

Purpose   Cause the `OnValidate` handler to be triggered if one is assigned to the field object.

Declaration

```
procedure Validate(Buffer:Pointer);
```

Example Syntax

```
procedure Tflddlg.demValidateString(theField:TField,str:PChar);
begin

theField.Validate(str);

end;
```

Description   This procedure assigns the data contained in `Str` to an internal variable and causes the `OnValidate` handler to be called if one is defined for the field. It is then the responsibility of the `OnValidate` handler to determine whether the contents of the pointer argument are valid in the context of the field and take action if necessary.

ValidChars PROPERTY

Objects Affected   All descendants of `TField`

Purpose   The `ValidChars` property is used to set or obtain the set of characters that are acceptable for storage in the corresponding field.

Declaration

```
property ValidChars: TFieldChars;
```

Example Syntax

```
procedure Tflddlg.demSetValid(theField:TField, charset:TFieldChars);
begin

theField.ValidChars := charset;

end;
```

Description   This function sets the acceptable character set for the field supplied in the call. See `Validate`.

Value PROPERTY

Objects Affected   All descendant classes of `TField`

Purpose   This property is only available at run time. `Value` represents the actual data in a `TField`. `Value` can be used to read data directly from and write data directly to a `TField`.

Declaration

`TField`

```
property Value: Variant
```

`TStringField, TBlobField`

```
property Value: string;
```

`TAutoIncField, TIntegerField, TSmallintField, TWordField`

```
property Value: Longint;
```

`TBCDField, TCurrencyField, TFloatField`

```
property Value: Double;
```

`TBooleanField`

```
property Value: Boolean;
```

`TDateField, TDateTimeField, TTimeField`

```
property Value: TDateTime
```

Example Syntax

```
function Tflddlg.demValue(theField:TField):string;
var
  v:variant;
begin

try

v := theField.Value;

Result := theField.Name + '.Value =' + v;

except
  on E:EDataBaseError do
     Result := E.Message;
end;

end;
```

Description   This function demonstrates the retrieval of a field value by the use of a `Variant` type variable. The result of the `Value` property is converted to a string and returned with descriptive text to the caller. Database errors are trapped via exception handling.

Visible PROPERTY

Objects Affected   All descendant classes of **TField**

Purpose   Determine whether field can be displayed in **TDBGrid** component.

Declaration

```
property Visible: Boolean
```

Example Syntax

```
function Tflddlg.demVisible(theField:TField):string;
var
  tempStr:string;
  vis:boolean;
begin

try

vis := theField.Visible;

if vis = true then
   tempStr := 'true'
else
   tempStr := 'false';

Result := theField.Name + '.Visible =' + tempStr;

except
   on E:EDataBaseError do
      Result := E.Message;
end;

end;
```

Description   This function determines whether or not a field is visible by inspecting the **Visible** property value associated with the **TField** object. An appropriate string is created and returned to the caller. Any database errors are trapped via exception handling.

Example Project   This example demonstrates the use of many of the routines shown previously as examples. Initially, a simple database table was created using the Borland Database Desktop that came with Delphi 2.0. After the table was created and the fields defined, the Database wizard was used to incorporate the desired data table into the example project. The project was set up to use a separate database handling unit.

After the database was set up, a dialog form was created that displays the names of the fields available in the underlying dataset and allows the user to select one of the fields from the list box in the dialog.

Once one of the fields has been selected, the Examine button can be pressed. Doing so will cause the program to execute most of the above listed sample functions to investigate various properties associated with the selected field. Some fields are not compatible with all properties, which is why all of the earlier examples contain exception handlers. This example is available on the disk that came with this book. The key portions of code are illustrated here.

The event handler for the pushbutton that appears in Figure 37-3 is shown in Listing 37-2. As you can see, it executes a typical dialog startup sequence. The dialog displayed as a result of the execution of this code is the dialog that is displayed in Figure 37-4.

Listing 37-2 Field properties pushbutton event handler

```
procedure Tptrkr_f.Button1Click(Sender: TObject);
var
theDialog: Tflddlg;
begin

theDialog := Tflddlg.create(Self);
theDialog.showModal;
theDialog.free;
end;
```

Rather than show all the modules in the demonstration program, we'll show just enough to give you the idea of what the dialog performs in response to the push of one of the selector pushbuttons in the following listings.

At form creation time, the list box is initialized as shown in Listing 37-3.

Listing 37-3 Tflddlg form creation handler

```
procedure Tflddlg.FormCreate(Sender: TObject);
var
    i,fcnt:integer;
begin
    ListBox1.Clear;

    { now fill the list box with the names of
    the fields in the data table we are using
    in this project }

    fcnt := DataModule2.Table1.FieldCount;
    for i := 0 to fcnt-1 do
      with DataModule2.Table1 do
        if Fields[i].Name <> '' then
          ListBox1.Items.AddObject(Fields[i].Name,Fields[i]);

end;
```

At this point the list box is filled with text that provides the names of the fields in the underlying dataset, which is **DataModule2**, located elsewhere in the project. In addition to the names of the fields, a reference to the field itself is saved in the list box by using the **AddObject** method of the list box. This makes it easy to associate a list item with a dataset field later on.

When the first button marked Examine is clicked on the dialog, the code shown in Listing 37-4 is executed.

Listing 37-4 Event handler for **TFlddlg** *dialog Examine pushbutton*

```
procedure Tflddlg.Button1Click(Sender: TObject);
var
   i,fcnt:integer;
   ind:integer;
begin
   fcnt := ListBox1.items.count;
   ind := -1;

   {find selected field}
   for i := 0 to fcnt-1 do
     if( ListBox1.Selected[i] = true) then
     begin
          ind := i;
          break;
     end;

   if(ind >= 0) then
   begin
     { a field was selected so interrogate the data base field }
     theField := TField(ListBox1.items.Objects[ind]);
     interrogateField(theField);
   end

end;
```

When the Examine button is pressed, the code in Listing 37-4 performs a scan of the entries in **ListBox1** looking for a selected item. If one is found, the program breaks out of the **For** loop and proceeds to the test for **(ind >= 0)**. This will only be **True** if a selected item was found. If one was found, then the desired dataset field is fetched from the object field of the selected list item using the **Objects** method, and this field reference is passed to the **interrogateField** routine. The **interrogateField** procedure is shown in Listing 37-5.

Listing 37-5 **interrogateField** *method*

```
procedure Tflddlg.interrogateField(theField:TField);
var
   resStr:string;
   tempStr:string;
begin

{
here is where we can put the code that demonstrates
the use of the various TField properties and methods
}

Memo1.lines.Add(demAlignment(theField));
Memo1.lines.Add(demAsBoolean(theField));

Memo1.lines.Add(demAlignment(theField));
Memo1.lines.Add(demAsBoolean(theField));
Memo1.lines.Add(demAsCurrency(theField));
Memo1.lines.Add(demAsDateTime(theField));
Memo1.lines.Add(demAsFloat(theField));
```

continued on next page

continued from previous page

```
Memo1.lines.Add(demAsInteger(theField));
Memo1.lines.Add(demAsString(theField));
Memo1.lines.Add(demAsVariant(theField));
Memo1.lines.Add(demAttributeSet(theField));
Memo1.lines.Add(demBDECalcField(theField));
Memo1.lines.Add(demCalculated(theField));
Memo1.lines.Add(demCanModify(theField));

    .
    .
    .

end;
```

This function performs actions repeatedly that take the following form:

```
"Memo1.lines.Add(demAlignment(theField));".
```

This line invokes the function **demAlignment** with the argument **theField**, which was obtained from the **ListBox** objects information. The function **demAlignment** returns a formatted string that is then added to the end of the **Memo1** string list. Listing 37-6 shows the **demAlignment** function, which is typical of all of the methods for obtaining field information from the requested field.

Listing 37-6 Example of field method function `demAlignment`

```
function Tflddlg.demAlignment(theField:TField):string;
var
   tempStr:string;
begin

try

  case theField.Alignment of

   taLeftJustify:
      tempStr := 'Left Justify';
   taRightJustify:
      tempStr := 'Right Justify';
   taCenter:
      tempStr := 'Center';
  end;

  Result := theField.Name + '.Alignment =' + tempStr;
except
   on E:EDataBaseError do
      Result := E.Message;
end;


end;
```

This method fetches the alignment information for the field by invoking **theField.Alignment** as part of a case statement. The appropriate branch in the case statement is taken, which serves to generate the appropriate portion of the output string to be returned to the caller—in this case, a string that indicates how the field is aligned. Some additional information is combined with the string and set to the

Result of the function. Additionally note that the dataset field access is protected by an exception block to trap any **database error** exceptions that might occur. This is a particularly good thing to do with dataset interactions to trap errors at the earliest possible time. All the functions used to generate information in this example program follow much the same pattern to access dataset field information. For additional examples see the distribution disk for the Chapter 37, "**TFieLd** and Its Descendants," example project and associated code.

38

TControl

TControl is the abstract base class for all controls in the Delphi VCL. Controls are components that are visible at run time. Most common user interface elements in Windows are implemented by Delphi as controls, such as command buttons, panels, tree views, and menus.

TControl provides the base functionality of all visual components, with properties to determine size and position, the caption or text that the user sees on the control, and more. As such, **TControl** provides only those attributes that are common to all controls and is not very useful itself. You would not normally create an instance of **TControl**.

Figure 38-1 shows the lineage of **TControl**. Table 38-1 displays the properties, methods, and events implemented by **Tcontrol**.

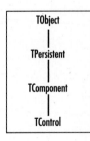

Figure 38-1   Lineage of **TControl**

Table 38-1 Properties, methods, and events implemented by `TControl`

Use or Set This...	To Do This...	Inheritance
Align	Determine how the control is aligned within its parent.	None
Assign	Assign one persistent object to another.	TPersistent
BeginDrag	Begin a manual drag operation.	None
BoundsRect	Determine the boundary rectangle occupied by the control.	None
BringToFront	Bring the control to the front of the z-order.	None
Caption	Label the control with a text string.	None
ClassName	Get the name of the object's class.	TObject
ClassParent	Get the object's parent class.	TObject
ClassType	Get the object's actual type.	TObject
ClientHeight	Determine the control's client height.	None
ClientOrigin	Determine the upper-left position of the control's client area.	None
ClientRect	Determine the rectangle occupied by the control's client area.	None
ClientToScreen	Convert control (local) coordinates to screen coordinates.	None
ClientWidth	Determine the width of the control's client area.	None
Color	Determine the color of the control.	None
ComponentCount	Determine the number of owned components.	TComponent
ComponentIndex	The index of the component in its owner's `Components` list.	TComponent
Components	Determine the list of owned components.	TComponent
ComponentState	Determine the state of the current component.	TComponent
ControlState	Determine the state of the control at any given time.	None
ControlStyle	Determine what attributes are present in the control.	None
Create	Create a new component.	TObject
Cursor	Determine what image is used for the cursor over the control.	None
Destroy	Destroy the component.	TObject
DestroyComponents	Destroy all of the components owned by the component.	TComponent
Destroying	Notify the component that it is being destroyed.	TComponent
DragCursor	Determine the shape of the mouse cursor as it drags an object over the control.	None
Dragging	Determine whether the control is being dragged.	None
DragMode	Determine the drag-and-drop behavior of the control.	None
Enabled	Determine whether the control is enabled.	None
EndDrag	End or cancel a manual drag operation.	None
FindComponent	Find a component in the `Components` array list.	TComponent
Font	Determine the font used to render text on the control.	None
Free	Safely destroy the object.	TObject
GetTextBuf	Copy the text of the control into a buffer.	None
GetTextLen	Get the length of the text of the control.	None
Height	Determine the height of the control.	None
Hide	Make the control invisible.	None

Use or Set This...	To Do This...	Inheritance
Hint	Determine the text that displays in a tooltip for the control.	None
InheritsFrom	Determine if the object is descended from a certain class.	TObject
InstanceSize	Determine the amount of memory allocated for the object.	TObject
Invalidate	Force the control to be repainted as soon as possible.	None
Left	Determine the left edge of the control within its container.	None
Name	Determine the name of the component.	TComponent
OnClick	Handle the event that occurs when a mouse button is clicked.	None
OnDblClick	Handle the event that occurs when a mouse button is double-clicked.	None
OnDragDrop	Handle the event that occurs when an object is dropped on the control.	None
OnDragOver	Handle the event that occurs when an object is dragged over the control.	None
OnEndDrag	Handle the event that occurs when a drag-and-drop operation is cancelled.	None
OnMouseDown	Handle the event that occurs when a mouse button is held down and not immediately released.	None
OnMouseMove	Handle the event that occurs when the cursor moves over the control.	None
OnMouseUp	Handle the event that occurs when a mouse button is released.	None
OnStartDrag	Handle the event that occurs when a drag-and-drop operation is started.	None
Owner	Determine the owner of the component.	TComponent
Parent	Determine the parent, or container, of the control.	None
ParentColor	Determine whether the control's parent's Color information is used.	None
ParentFont	Determine whether the control's parent's Font information is used.	None
ParentShowHint	Determine whether the control's parent's ShowHint information is used.	None
PopupMenu	Determine which pop-up menu is associated with the control.	None
Refresh	Erase the control and repaint it.	None
Repaint	Repaint the control.	None
ScreenToClient	Convert screen coordinates to client (control) coordinates.	None
SendToBack	Send the control to the end of the z-order.	None
SetBounds	Determine the coordinates of the control's bounding rectangle.	None
SetTextBuf	Set the text of the control to the text in a buffer.	None
Show	Make the control visible.	None
ShowHint	Enable tooltips for the control.	None
Tag	Store an additional integer value with the component.	TComponent
Text	Access the changeable text on the control.	None
Top	Determine the upper edge of the control.	None
Update	Update is called automatically by Refresh.	None
Visible	Make the control visible.	None
Width	Determine the width of the control.	None

Align PROPERTY

Objects Affected	All controls
Purpose	The Align property determines how the control is aligned within its parent (visual container).
Declaration	

```
property Align: TAlign;
```

Example Syntax

```
procedure TForm1.FormCreate(Sender: TObject);
begin
  TreeView1.Align := alLeft;
  // . . .
end;
```

Description   Align is of type TAlign, and can be set to any of the following possible values:

Use This Value...	To Do This...
alBottom	Move the control to the bottom of its parent and resize it to fill the width of the parent. This value only affects the width of the control—the height is not changed.
alClient	Resize the control to fill the parent's client area.
alLeft	Move the control to the left side of the parent and resize it to fill the height of the parent. This value only affects the height of the control—the width is not changed.
alNone	Keep the control where you placed it in the parent. The default value is alNone.
alRight	Move the control to the right side of the parent and resize it to fill the height of the parent. This value only affects the height of the control—the width is not changed.
alTop	Move the control to the top of the parent and resize it to fill the width of the parent. This value only affects the width of the control—the height is not changed.

The default Align value for THeaderControl is alTop; for TStatusBar the default is alBottom. See Figure 38-2. For all other controls, the default is alNone.

BeginDrag METHOD

Objects Affected	All controls
Purpose	BeginDrag starts the process of dragging a control when the manual drag mode for the control is enabled.
Declaration	

```
procedure BeginDrag(Immediate: Boolean);
```

Parameters

Immediate   Determines the shape of the cursor and when dragging begins.

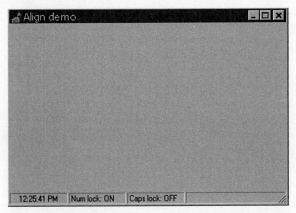

Figure 38-2 A status bar is aligned to the bottom of
the form by default.

Description
The *Immediate* parameter determines when the dragging will begin. If
Immediate is **True**, dragging begins immediately and the mouse cursor
changes to the cursor specified by the **DragCursor** property. If *Immediate*
is **False**, the mouse cursor will not be changed and dragging begins when
the mouse cursor is moved more than five pixels away. The **BeginDrag** and
EndDrag methods are used when the control's **DragMode** property is set to
dmManual.

BoundsRect PROPERTY

Objects Affected   All controls

Purpose   The **BoundsRect** property indicates the bounding rectangle of the control.

Declaration

```
property BoundsRect: TRect;
```

Description   The **BoundsRect** property contains a bounding rectangle that describes the
area of the control's parent. The coordinates of the rectangle are given in
the parent's coordinate system.

BringToFront METHOD

Objects Affected   All controls

Purpose   The **BringToFront** method changes the control's z-order to bring it to the
front of all other controls.

Declaration

```
procedure BringToFront;
```

Example Syntax

```
procedure TForm1.Button2Click(Sender: TObject);
begin
   Button1.BringToFront;
end;
```

Description Windowed and non-windowed controls have different sets of z-orders. Every windowed control on a form exists within the same z-order set, and every non-windowed control exists within a separate z-order set. All windowed controls on a form exist within a single z-order set and all non-windowed controls exist within another z-order set. Windowed controls always appear *above* nonwindowed controls, so a nonwindowed control that is behind a windowed control cannot use **BringToFront** to appear above that windowed control.

Caption PROPERTY

Objects Affected All controls

Purpose The **Caption** property determines the text string used to label the control.

Declaration

```
property Caption: TCaption;
```

Example Syntax

```
procedure TForm1.FormCreate(Sender: TObject);
begin
   Form1.Caption := 'Delphi Explorer';
   Button1.Caption := 'OK';
   Button2.Caption := 'Cancel';
   Label1.Caption := 'Captions are relatively static';
end;
```

Description Although you can change the caption, it is rarely changed at run time. Controls that allow the user to edit text displayed in the control will implement the **Text** property instead of **Caption**, since **Caption** is not user-editable.

Caption is type **TCaption**, which is simply a standard string.

ClientHeight PROPERTY

Objects Affected All controls

Purpose The **ClientHeight** property contains the height of the control's client area.

Declaration

```
property ClientHeight: Integer;
```

Example Syntax

```
procedure TForm1.FormCreate(Sender: TObject);
var
  X, Y: Integer;
begin
  X := Form1.ClientWidth;
  Y := Form1.ClientHeight;
  // . . .
end;
```

Description   ClientHeight is a run-time-only property for all controls other than
forms. It is measured in pixels. Most controls have the same value for
Height as ClientHeight, although forms, for example, consider the client
area to be the area within the form's frame.

ClientOrigin PROPERTY

Objects Affected   All controls

Purpose   The ClientOrigin property contains the top left coordinate of the client
area of the control.

Declaration

```
property ClientOrigin: TPoint;
```

Example Syntax

```
procedure TForm1.FormCreate(Sender: TObject);
var OriginPoint: TPoint;
begin
  OriginPoint := Form1.ClientOrigin;
end;
```

Description   ClientOrigin holds the X,Y coordinate of the top left pixel of the control's
client area, measured in the screen's coordinates.

ClientRect PROPERTY

Objects Affected   All controls

Purpose   The ClientRect property holds the dimensions of the control's client area.

Declaration

```
property ClietntRect: TRect;
```

Example Syntax

```
procedure TForm1.Button1Click(Sender: TObject);
begin
  Form1.Canvas.Brush.Color := clBlue;
  Form1.Canvas.FillRect(Form1.ClientRect);
end;
```

| Description | ClientRect is a run-time, read-only property that holds the top, left, bottom, and right pixel location of the control's client area within a TRect structure where the top and left pixels are 0 and the bottom and right pixels indicate the height and width. |

ClientToScreen METHOD

Objects Affected	All controls
Purpose	The ClientToScreen method converts a specified point on the control from the control's coordinate system to screen coordinates.
Declaration	

```
function ClientToScreen(const Point: TPoint): TPoint;
```

Parameters	
Point	The point you wish to convert to global coordinates.
Example Syntax	

```
procedure TForm1.FormCreate(Sender: TObject);
var
  ButtonPos: TPoint;
begin
  ButtonPos := Button1.ClientToScreen(Point(Button1.Left,Button1.Top));
  // . . .
end;
```

| Description | ClientToScreen can be used to access the coordinates of the control as screen coordinates. |

ClientWidth PROPERTY

Objects Affected	All controls
Purpose	The ClientWidth property contains the width of the control's client area.
Declaration	

```
property ClientWidth: Integer;
```

| Example Syntax | |

```
procedure TForm1.FormCreate(Sender: TObject);
var
  X, Y: Integer;
  begin
  X := Form1.ClientWidth;
  Y := Form1.ClientHeight;
  // . . .
end;
```

| Description | ClientWidth is a run-time-only property for all controls other than forms that represent the horizontal size, in pixels, of the client area of the control. For most controls, ClientWidth will be the same as Width. Forms, |

however, consider the client area to be everything within the form's frame: the `ClientWidth` of the form will be less than the `Width` of the form.

Color PROPERTY

Objects Affected	All controls
Purpose	The `Color` property determines the color of the control.
Declaration	

```
property Color: TColor;
```

Description	You can use the `Color` property to get or set the color of the control. If the control's `ParentColor` property is `True`, the control will automatically inherit the color of its parent control. You can override this behavior by manually assigning a value to the control's `Color` property. `Color` is type `TColor`, which defines many color constants such as `clBlack`, `clWhite`, `clTeal`, `clActiveCaption`, and `clInactiveBorder`. Check the Delphi help for a detailed list of color values.

ControlState PROPERTY

Objects Affected	All controls
Purpose	The `ControlState` property queries the state of the control at run time.
Declaration	

```
property ControlState: TControlState;
```

Description	`ControlState` indicates the condition of the control at that exact time at run time. It is of type `TControlState` which is a set of flags. `ControlState` can be set to a combination of the following values:

This Flag...	Indicates That...
csAlignmentNeeded	The control needs to be realigned when alignment is enabled.
csClicked	The left mouse button was clicked and not released. This flag is only set if the `ControlStyle` property contains the `csClickEvents` flag.
csCreating	The control or its owner is being created.
csFocusing	The application is about to give the control focus.
csLButtonDown	The left mouse button was clicked and not released. This flag is set for mouse-down events.
csPalette	The control has a palette that needs to be realized.
csReadingState	The control is reading its state from a stream.

ControlStyle PROPERTY

Objects Affected	All controls
Purpose	ControlStyle indicates which attributes are activated for that control.
Declaration	

```
property ControlStyle: TControlStyle;
```

Description   The styles possible in **ControlStyle** are less likely to change than the flags in **ControlState**, which are constantly fluctuating. **ControlStyle** is of type **TControlStyle** which is a set of the following possible values:

This Flag...	Indicates That...
csAcceptsControls	The control accepts any controls dropped on it at design time and becomes the parent of those controls.
csCaptureMouse	The control captures mouse events.
csClickEvents	The control can receive and respond to mouse clicks.
csDoubleClicks	The control can receive and respond to double-click messages. Otherwise, double-clicks are processed as single-clicks.
csFixedHeight	The height of the control is fixed and cannot change.
csFixedWidth	The width of the control is fixed and cannot change.
csFramed	The control has a frame.
csOpaque	The control hides any items behind it.
csSetCaption	The control changes its caption to match the Name property unless Caption has been previously set.

Cursor PROPERTY

Objects Affected	All controls
Purpose	The Cursor property determines which image is used to display the mouse pointer as it passes over the control.
Declaration	

```
property Cursor: TCursor;
```

Example Syntax

```
procedure TForm1.FormCreate(Sender: TObject);
begin
  Button1.Cursor := crCross;
  Panel1.Cursor := crArrow;
end;
```

Description   Cursor is of type TCursor, which defines the standard mouse pointer (or cursor) types available to the Delphi programmer. Some common cursor types include crDefault, crCross, crBeam, and crHourGlass.

DragCursor PROPERTY

Objects Affected	All controls
Purpose	The **DragCursor** property determines the shape of the mouse pointer as it drags an object over the control.
Declaration	

```
property DragCursor: TCursor;
```

Example Syntax

```
// Change the cursor shape if an object is dragged over the panel
procedure TForm1.Panel1DragOver(Sender, Source: TObject; X, Y: Integer;
  State: TDragState; var Accept: Boolean);
begin
  Panel1.DragCursor := crDrag;
end;
```

Description   You must first set the control to accept dropped objects before **DragCursor** will take effect. This is actually very simple: All you need to do is handle one of the drag-and-drop events such as **OnDragOver** as in the above example.

Dragging METHOD

Objects Affected	All controls
Purpose	The **Dragging** method indicates whether a control is being dragged.
Declaration	

```
function Dragging: Boolean;
```

Example Syntax

```
// Change the color of the form if one of the color wells (images)
// is dragged
procedure TForm1.FormDragOver(Sender, Source: TObject; X, Y: Integer;
                              State: TDragState; var Accept: Boolean);
begin
  if Image1.Dragging then
    Color := clRed
  else if Image2.Dragging then
    Color := clGreen
  else if Image3.Dragging then
    Color := clBlue;
end;
```

Description   If the control is being dragged, **Dragging** returns **True**. Otherwise, it returns **False**.

DragMode PROPERTY

Objects Affected   All controls

Purpose   The **DragMode** property determines the drag-and-drop behavior of the control.

Declaration

```
property DragMode: TDragMode
```

Example Syntax

```
procedure TForm1.FormCreate(Sender: TObject);
begin
  // . . .

  Form1.DragMode := dmAutomatic;
  Panel1.DragMode := dmAutomatic;
end;
```

Description   DragMode is type **TDragMode** which defines two possible drag modes: **dmAutomatic** and **dmManual**. If **DragMode** is set to **dmAutomatic**, the control can be dragged at any time by clicking and dragging it with the mouse pointer. If **DragMode** is **dmManual**, the control cannot be dragged until the **BeginDrag** method is called.

Enabled PROPERTY

Objects Affected   All controls

Purpose   The **Enabled** property determines whether the control responds to the mouse or keyboard, or to **Timer** events.

Declaration

```
property Enabled: Boolean;
```

Description   If the **Enabled** property is **True**, the control will respond to user input with the mouse and keyboard, and will respond to **Timer** events. If **Enabled** is **False**, the control appears dimmed—or disabled—and will not respond to mouse, keyboard, or **Timer** events. Typically, controls are disabled when the function they perform makes no sense given current conditions.

EndDrag METHOD

Objects Affected   All controls

Purpose   The **EndDrag** method stops the controls from being dragged further.

Declaration

```
procedure EndDrag(Drop: Boolean);
```

Parameters

Drop   Determines whether the dragged object is dropped.

Description   If the *Drop* parameter is `True`, the control is dropped. If *Drop* is `False`, the
                            control is not dropped and the drag operation is canceled.

Font PROPERTY

Objects Affected   All controls

Purpose   The `Font` property determines the font used to render text on the control.

Declaration

```
property Font: TFont;
```

Example Syntax

```
with Form1.Font do
  begin
    Size := 12;
    Name := 'Arial';
    Color := clGreen;
    Style := [fsBold];
  end;
```

Description   The `Font` property allows you to set the various font attributes for the
                            `Text` or `Caption` property of the control. These attributes include `Color`,
                            `Name`, `Size`, and `Style`.

GetTextBuf METHOD

Objects Affected   All controls

Purpose   The `GetTextBuf` method gets the text contained by the control and copies
                            it into a buffer.

Declaration

```
function GetTextBuf(Buffer: PChar; BufSize: Integer): Integer;
```

Parameters

Buffer   The buffer that will receive the text.

BufSize   The size of the buffer.

Example Syntax

```
procedure TForm1.Button2Click(Sender: TObject);
var
  MyBuffer: PChar;
  MyBufSize: Integer;
begin
  MyBufSize := Button1.GetTextLen;
  Button1.GetTextBuf(MyBuffer, MyBufSize);
  StatusBar1.SetTextBuf(MyBuffer);
end;
```

Description   GetTextBuf takes the text from the control and copies it as a null-terminated string into the buffer specified by *Buffer*. The *BufSize* parameter indicates the size of the buffer, which should be set with GetTextLen before GetTextBuf is called.

The text that is copied to the buffer is automatically copied as a null-terminated string.

GetTextLen METHOD

Objects Affected   All controls

Purpose   The GetTextLen method retrieves the size of the control's text.

Declaration

```
function GetTextLen: Integer;
```

Example Syntax

```
procedure TForm1.Button2Click(Sender: TObject);
var
  MyBuffer: PChar;
  MyBufSize: Integer;
begin
  MyBufSize := Button1.GetTextLen;
  Button1.GetTextBuf(MyBuffer, MyBufSize);
  StatusBar1.SetTextBuf(MyBuffer);
end;
```

Description   GetTextLen is typically used right before a call to GetTextBuf so that the buffer can be sized properly. Use GetTextLen instead of string-specific functions like Length.

Height PROPERTY

Objects Affected   All controls

Purpose   The Height property contains the vertical size of the control.

Declaration

```
property Height: Integer;
```

Example Syntax

```
procedure TForm1.FormPaint(Sender: TObject);
begin
  Panel1.Top := 10;
  Panel1.Left := 10;
  Panel1.Height := Form1.ClientHeight - 20;
  Panel1.Width := Form1.ClientWidth - 20;
end;
```

Description   Height is measured in pixels, and indicates the height of the control.

Hide METHOD

Objects Affected	All controls
Purpose	The **Hide** method makes a control invisible.
Declaration	

```
procedure Hide;
```

Example Syntax

```
// If the "Hide menus" menu item is clicked, hide the
// forms menus but make the "Show menu" button visible
// so the user can turn the menu on again if necessary
procedure TForm1.mnuHideMenu1Click(Sender: TObject);
begin
  btnHideMenu.Hide;
  Form1.Menu := nil;
end;

// If the "Show menu" button is clicked, hide the
// button and show the form's main menu
procedure TForm1.btnShowMenuClick(Sender: TObject);
begin
  Form1.Menu := MainMenu1;
  btnHideMenu.Hide;
end;
```

Description   **Hide** sets the control's **Visible** property to **False**, making the control invisible.

Hint PROPERTY

Objects Affected	All controls
Purpose	The **Hint** property contains the text that will appear in a tooltip window when the cursor lingers over the control.
Declaration	

```
property Hint: string;
```

Example Syntax

```
type
  TForm1 = class(TForm)
    btnHide: TButton;
    StatusBar1: TStatusBar;
    procedure FormCreate(Sender: TObject);
  private
    { Private declarations }
  public
    { Public declarations }
    procedure DoHint(Sender: TObject);
  end;

var
```

continued on next page

continued from previous page

```
        Form1: TForm1;

implementation

{$R *.DFM}

// Enable short and long hints for the button and set the
// OnHint handler for the application to the DoHint procedure,
// which was created by the programmer
procedure TForm1.FormCreate(Sender: TObject);
begin
  btnHideMenu.Hint := 'Enable menus|Click here to enable menus';
  Application.OnHint := Form1.DoHint;
end;

// Output the long hint in the status bar
procedure TForm1.DoHint(Sender: TObject);
begin
  StatusBar1.SimpleText := GetLongHint(Button1.Hint);
end;
```

Description

For the **Hint** text to appear in the tooltip, the **ShowHint** property for the control of the form that contains it must be set to **True**. If **ShowHint** is **True** for the form and the control, but the control's **Hint** property is not set, the tooltip will display the **Hint** text for the control's parent (which may be the form).

In the above example, some extended syntax is used for the button tooltip. A **Hint** string can optionally be composed of two parts: a *short hint*, displayed as the standard tooltip, and a *long hint* which the programmer can choose to display in some other area of the form, such as a status bar. The short hint and the long hint are separated by a pipe (|) character. The **OnHint** method of the **Application** object is used to determine how the long hint is displayed.

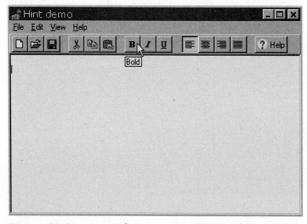

Figure 38-3 A **Hint** shown in a tooltip window

Invalidate METHOD

Objects Affected   All controls

Purpose   The `Invalidate` method forces the control to repaint itself.

Declaration

```
procedure Invalidate; virtual;
```

Example Syntax

```
procedure TForm1.Button1Click(Sender: TObject);
begin
  // Invalidate the form so that it can be repainted
  Form1.Invalidate;
  Form1.Canvas.Repaint;
end;
```

Description   When `Invalidate` is called, the control is repainted as soon as possible. `Invalidate` is called by `Refresh`.

Left PROPERTY

Objects Affected   All controls

Purpose   The `Left` property contains the horizontal coordinate of the left edge of the control.

Declaration

```
property Left: Integer;
```

Example Syntax

```
procedure TForm1.FormPaint(Sender: TObject);
begin
  Panel1.Top := 10;
  Panel1.Left := 10;
  Panel1.Height := Form1.ClientHeight - 20;
  Panel1.Width := Form1.ClientWidth - 20;
end;
```

Description   The `Left` property uses the coordinate system of its container. It indicates how many pixels the left edge of the control is from the left edge of its container. The `Left` property for a form is measured using screen coordinates.

OnClick EVENT

Objects Affected   All controls

Purpose   The `OnClick` event is triggered when the control is clicked with the mouse pointer.

Declaration

```
property OnClick: TNotifyEvent;
```

Example Syntax

```
type
  TForm1 = class(TForm)
    Button1: TButton;
    procedure MyClickHandler(Sender: TObject);
  end;

var
  Form1: TForm1;

implementation

{$R *.DFM}

// An OnClick event handler
procedure TForm1.MyClickHandler(Sender: TObject);
begin
  Button1.Height := Button1.Height + 5;
  Button1.Width := Button1.Width + 5;
end;

// Specify MyClickHandler as the OnClick event handler for
// Button1
procedure TForm1.FormCreate(Sender: TObject);
begin
  Button1.OnClick := MyClickHandler;
end;
```

Description   A control is clicked when the user moves the mouse pointer over the control and presses the primary mouse button. The OnClick event can also be triggered by other related actions such as the user pressing the Space bar while a button or check box has the focus. This is one of the most common events used in Delphi applications (and Windows in general).

Although the sample code above sets the event handler for a button's OnClick event to a procedure at run time, you will typically be able to do this by selecting the OnClick event for a control in the Object Inspector at design time.

OnDblClick EVENT

Objects Affected   All controls

Purpose   The OnDblClick event occurs when the control is double-clicked.

Declaration

```
property OnDblClick: TNotifyEvent
```

Example Syntax

```
type
  TForm1 = class(TForm)
```

```
    Button1: TButton;
    procedure MyDblClickHandler(Sender: TObject);
  end;

var
  Form1: TForm1;

implementation

{$R *.DFM}

// An OnDblClick event handler
procedure TForm1.MyDblClickHandler(Sender: TObject);
begin
Application.MessageBox('The form was double-clicked',
                         'Form event', MB_OK);
end;

// Specify MyClickHandler as the OnDblClick event handler for
// Button1
procedure TForm1.FormCreate(Sender: TObject);
begin
  Form1.OnDblClick := MyDblClickHandler;
end;
```

Description

The OnDblClick event occurs when the user double-clicks the mouse while the mouse pointer is over the control.

Although the sample code above sets the event handler for a button's OnDblClick event to a procedure at run time, you will typically be able to do this by selecting the OnDblClick event for a control in the Object Inspector at design time.

OnDragDrop EVENT

Objects Affected   All controls

Purpose   The OnDragDrop event occurs when a dragged object is dropped on the control.

Declaration

```
property OnDragDrop: TDragDropEvent
```

Example Syntax

```
type
  TForm1 = class(TForm)
    Panel1: TPanel;
    Image1: TImage;
    procedure MyDragDrop(Sender, Source: TObject; X, Y: Integer);
    procedure MyDragOver(Sender, Source: TObject; X, Y: Integer;
              State: TDragState; var Accept: Boolean);
  private
    { Private declarations }
  public
    { Public declarations }
```

continued on next page

continued from previous page

```
        end;

    var
      Form1: TForm1;

    implementation

    {$R *.DFM}
    procedure TForm1.MyDragDrop(Sender, Source: TObject; X, Y: Integer);
    begin
      if Source is TImage then
      begin
        TImage(Source).Parent := Panel1;
        TImage(Source).Left := X;
        TImage(Source).Top := Y;
      end;
    end;

    procedure TForm1.MyDragOver(Sender, Source: TObject; X, Y: Integer;
      State: TDragState; var Accept: Boolean);
    begin
      if Source is TImage then
        begin
          TImage(Source).DragCursor := crCross;
          Accept := True;
        end;
    end;

    procedure TForm1.FormCreate(Sender: TObject);
    begin
      Panel1.OnDragDrop := Form1.MyDragDrop;
      Panel1.OnDragOver := Form1.MyDragOver;
    end;
```

Description

The `OnDragDrop` event occurs when the user drops an object that is being dragged onto the control. The **Sender** parameter identifies the control that is receiving the dropped object. The **Source** parameter specifies the object being dropped. The *X* and *Y* parameters specify the coordinates of the drop location, using the **Sender** control's coordinate system.

Although the sample code above sets the event handler for a button's `OnDragDrop` event to a procedure at run time, you will typically be able to do this by selecting the `OnDragDrop` event for a control in the Object Inspector at design time.

OnDragOver EVENT

Objects Affected   All controls

Purpose   The `OnDragOver` event occurs when an object is dragged over the control.

Declaration

```
property OnDragOver: TDragOverEvent;
```

Example Syntax

```
type
  TForm1 = class(TForm)
    Panel1: TPanel;
    Image1: TImage;
    procedure MyDragDrop(Sender, Source: TObject; X, Y: Integer);
    procedure MyDragOver(Sender, Source: TObject; X, Y: Integer;
              State: TDragState; var Accept: Boolean);
  private
    { Private declarations }
  public
    { Public declarations }
  end;

var
  Form1: TForm1;

implementation

{$R *.DFM}
procedure TForm1.MyDragDrop(Sender, Source: TObject; X, Y: Integer);
begin
  if Source is TImage then
  begin
    TImage(Source).Parent := Panel1;
    TImage(Source).Left := X;
    TImage(Source).Top := Y;
  end;
end;

procedure TForm1.MyDragOver(Sender, Source: TObject; X, Y: Integer;
  State: TDragState; var Accept: Boolean);
begin
  if Source is TImage then
    begin
      TImage(Source).DragCursor := crCross;
      Accept := True;
    end;
end;

procedure TForm1.FormCreate(Sender: TObject);
begin
  Panel1.OnDragDrop := Form1.MyDragDrop;
  Panel1.OnDragOver := Form1.MyDragOver;
end;
```

Description

The OnDragOver event occurs when the user drags an object over the control. The *Sender* parameter identifies the control. The *Source* parameter specifies the object being dragged. The *X* and *Y* parameters specify the coordinates of the object's current location, using the *Sender* control's coordinate system. The *Accept* parameter determines whether the control will allow the dragged object to be dropped upon it. If *Accept* is set to True, as in the above example, the *Sender* control will accept the object. If *Accept* is False, it will not accept the object.

Although the sample code above sets the event handler for a button's OnDragOver event to a procedure at run time, you will typically be able to do this by selecting the `OnDragOver` event for a control in the Object Inspector at design time.

OnEndDrag EVENT

Objects Affected	All controls
Purpose	The `OnEndDrag` event occurs when a drag-and-drop operation is ended.
Declaration	

```
property OnEndDrag: TEndDragEvent;
```

Example Syntax

```
type
  TForm1 = class(TForm)
    Panel1: TPanel;
    Image1: TImage;
    procedure MyEndDrag(Sender, Target: TObject; X, Y: Integer);
  private
    { Private declarations }
  public
    { Public declarations }
  end;

var
  Form1: TForm1;

implementation

{$R *.DFM}

procedure TForm1.FormCreate(Sender: TObject);
begin
  Image1.OnEndDrag := Form1.MyEndDrag;
end;

procedure TForm1.MyEndDrag(Sender, Target: TObject; X, Y: Integer);
begin
  if Target is TPanel then
    StatusBar1.Panels[1].Text := 'Drag ended on panel.'
  else
    StatusBar1.Panels[1].Text := 'Drag did not end on panel.';
end;
```

Description

A drag-and-drop operation can end when a receiving control accepts the dropped object or when the user cancels the operation. The *Sender* parameter is the object being dragged. The *Target* parameter is the control that is under the mouse pointer and the dragged object when the drag-and-drop operation has ended. *X* and *Y* identify the current location of the dragged object using the *Target* control's coordinate system.

Although the sample code above sets the event handler for a button's `OnEndDrag` event to a procedure at run time, you will typically be able to do this by selecting the **OnEndDrag** event for a control in the Object Inspector at design time.

OnMouseDown EVENT

Objects Affected   All controls

Purpose   The `OnMouseDown` event occurs when a mouse button is pressed down over the control.

Declaration

```
property OnMouseDown: TMouseEvent;
```

Example Syntax

```
type
  TForm1 = class(TForm)
    procedure MyMouseDown(Sender: TObject; Button: TMouseButton;
                          Shift: TShiftState; X, Y: Integer);
  private
    { Private declarations }
  public
    { Public declarations }
  end;

var
  Form1: TForm1;

implementation

{$R *.DFM}

procedure TForm1.FormCreate(Sender: TObject);
begin
  Form1.OnMouseDown := Form1.MyMouseDown;
end;

procedure TForm1.MyMouseDown(Sender: TObject; Button: TMouseButton;
  Shift: TShiftState; X, Y: Integer);
begin
  StatusBar1.Panels[0].Text := 'MouseDown on Form: ' + IntToStr(X) + ',⇐
' + IntToStr(Y);
end;
```

Description   The *Sender* parameter refers to the control that is under the mouse pointer when the button is pressed. The *Button* parameter indicates which mouse button was used. It is type **TMouseButton**, which can take on one of the following values: **mbLeft**, **mbMiddle**, or **mbRight**. The *Shift* parameter indicates whether a modifier key was held down when the mouse button was pressed. The *Shift* parameter can be any combination from the following set: **ssAlt**, **ssCtrl**, **ssDouble**, **ssLeft**, **ssMiddle**, **ssRight**, and **ssShift**. If no modifier key was pressed, *Shift* will be set to []. The *X* and *Y* parameters indicate the position of the mouse pointer when the button was pressed, using the coordinate system of the *Sender* control.

Although the sample code above sets the event handler for a button's **OnMouseDown** event to a procedure at run time, you will typically be able to do this by selecting the **OnMouseDown** event for a control in the Object Inspector at design time.

OnMouseMove EVENT

Objects Affected   All controls

Purpose   The **OnMouseMove** event occurs when the mouse pointer moves over the control.

Declaration

```
property OnMouseMove: TMouseMoveEvent;
```

Example Syntax

```
type
  TForm1 = class(TForm)
    StatusBar1: TStatusBar;
    procedure MyMouseMove(Sender: TObject; Shift: TShiftState; X, Y:
Integer);
  private
    { Private declarations }
  public
    { Public declarations }
  end;

var
  Form1: TForm1;

implementation

{$R *.DFM}

procedure TForm1.FormCreate(Sender: TObject);
begin
  Form1.OnMouseMove := Form1.MyMouseMove;
end;

procedure TForm1.MyMouseMove(Sender: TObject; Shift: TShiftState;⇐
                             X, Y: Integer);
begin
 StatusBar1.Panels[2].Text := 'MouseMove on Form: ' + IntToStr(X) + ', '
+ IntToStr(Y);
end;
```

Description   OnMouseMove events are continuously generated as the mouse pointer passes over each control. A mouse button does not need to be pressed for this event to occur. The *Sender* parameter indicates which control the mouse pointer is over. The *Shift* parameter can be any combination from the following set: ssAlt, ssCtrl, ssDouble, ssLeft, ssMiddle, ssRight, and ssShift. If no modifier key was pressed, *Shift* will be set to []. The *X* and *Y* parameters indicate the position of the mouse pointer when the event was triggered, using the coordinate system of the *Sender* control.

Although the sample code above sets the event handler for a button's OnMouseMove event to a procedure at run time, you will typically be able to do this by selecting the OnMouseMove event for a control in the Object Inspector at design time.

OnMouseUp EVENT

Objects Affected   All controls

Purpose   The OnMouseUp event occurs when a mouse button is released.

Declaration

```
property OnMouseUp: TMouseEvent;
```

Example Syntax

```
type
  TForm1 = class(TForm)
    StatusBar1: TStatusBar;
    procedure MyMouseUp(Sender: TObject; Button: TMouseButton;
      Shift: TShiftState; X, Y: Integer);
  private
    { Private declarations }
  public
    { Public declarations }
  end;

var
  Form1: TForm1;

implementation

{$R *.DFM}

procedure TForm1.FormCreate(Sender: TObject);
begin
  Form1.OnMouseUp := Form1.MyMouseUp;
end;

procedure TForm1.MyMouseUp(Sender: TObject; Button: TMouseButton;
  Shift: TShiftState; X, Y: Integer);
begin
 StatusBar1.Panels[0].Text := 'MouseUp on Form: ' + IntToStr(X) + ', '⇐
+ IntToStr(Y);
end;
```

Description   This event will occur whenever a mouse button is clicked, but can be more useful than `OnClick` because it provides information about which button was clicked, the modifier key that was pressed, if any, and the coordinates of the mouse pointer at the time the button was released. The *Sender* parameter indicates which control the mouse pointer is over when a mouse button is released. The *Shift* parameter can be any combination from the following set: `ssAlt`, `ssCtrl`, `ssDouble`, `ssLeft`, `ssMiddle`, `ssRight`, and `ssShift`. If no modifier key was pressed, *Shift* will be set to []. The *Button* parameter indicates which mouse button was released. It can be one of the following: `mbLeft`, `mbMiddle`, or `mbRight`. The *X* and *Y* parameters indicate the position of the mouse pointer when the button was released, using the coordinate system of the *Sender* control.

Although the sample code above sets the event handler for a button's `OnMouseUp` event to a procedure at run time, you will typically be able to do this by selecting the `OnMouseUp` event for a control in the Object Inspector at design time.

OnStartDrag EVENT

Objects Affected   All controls

Purpose   The `OnStartDrag` event occurs at the beginning of a drag-and-drop operation involving the control.

Declaration

```
property OnStartDrag: TStartDragEvent;
```

Example Syntax

```
type
  TForm1 = class(TForm)
    StatusBar1: TStatusBar;
    procedure MyStartDrag(Sender: TObject;
      var DragObject: TDragObject);
  private
    { Private declarations }
  public
    { Public declarations }
  end;

var
  Form1: TForm1;

implementation

{$R *.DFM}

procedure TForm1.FormCreate(Sender: TObject);
begin
  Image1.OnStartDrag := Form1.MyStartDrag;
end;
```

```
procedure TForm1.MyStartDrag(Sender: TObject;
  var DragObject: TDragObject);
begin
 StatusBar1.Panels[1].Text := 'Drag Started.'
end;
```

Description

The `OnStartDrag` event is triggered when the user starts dragging the control by positioning the mouse pointer on the control and holding the button down. The *Sender* parameter represents the object being dragged and the *DragObject* parameter specifies the target of the drag-and-drop operation.

Although the sample code above sets the event handler for a button's `OnStartDrag` event to a procedure at run time, you will typically be able to do this by selecting the `OnStartDrag` event for a control in the Object Inspector at design time.

Parent PROPERTY

Objects Affected All controls

Purpose The `Parent` property indicates the parent (visual container) of the control.

Declaration

```
property Parent: TWinControl;
```

Example Syntax

```
// . . .
var
  Form1: TForm1;
  MyButton: TButton;

implementation

{$R *.DFM}

// Dynamically create a button when the form is created
procedure TForm1.FormCreate(Sender: TObject);
begin
  MyButton := TButton.Create(Self);
  MyButton.Parent := Form1;
  with MyButton do
  begin
    Left := 10;
    Top := 10;
    Width := 36;
    Height := 36;
    Caption := 'Click';
    OnClick := Button1Click;
    // other properties, methods, and event handlers here
  end
end;
```

Description   The parent of a control is the windowed control that visually contains the control. The control is automatically destroyed when its parent is destroyed.

ParentColor PROPERTY

Objects Affected   All controls

Purpose   The `ParentColor` property determines whether the control uses its parent's `Color` information.

Declaration

```
property ParentColor: Boolean;
```

Example Syntax

```
procedure TForm1.FormCreate(Sender: TObject);
begin
  Panel1.ParentColor := True;
  Panel1.ParenFont := False;
  Panel1.ShowHint := False;
end;
```

Description   If `ParentColor` is `True`, the control will use the information in its parent's `Color` property to determine its own color attribute. If `ParentColor` is `False`, the control uses the value in its own `Color` property to determine its color.

ParentFont PROPERTY

Objects Affected   All controls

Purpose   The `ParentFont` property determines whether the control uses its parent's `Font` information.

Declaration

```
property ParentFont: Boolean;
```

Example Syntax

```
procedure TForm1.FormCreate(Sender: TObject);
begin
  Panel1.ParentColor := True;
  Panel1.ParentFont := False;
  Panel1.ShowHint := False;
end;
```

Description   If `ParentFont` is `True`, the control will use the information in its parent's `Font` property to determine its own font attributes. If `ParentFont` is `False`, the control uses the value in its own `Font` property to determine its font attributes.

ParentShowHint PROPERTY

Objects Affected	All controls
Purpose	The `ParentShowHint` property determines whether the control uses its parent's `ShowHint` property to display a tooltip.
Declaration	

```
property ParentShowHint: Boolean;
```

Example Syntax

```
procedure TForm1.FormCreate(Sender: TObject);
begin
  Panel1.ParentColor := True;
  Panel1.ParenFont := False;
  Panel1.ShowHint := False;
end;
```

Description   If `ParentShowHint` is `True`, the control will use the information in its parent's `ShowHint` property to determine whether it displays a tooltip. If `ParentShowHint` is `False`, the control uses the value in its own `ShowHint` property to determine whether to display a tooltip.

PopupMenu PROPERTY

Objects Affected	All controls
Purpose	The `PopupMenu` property determines which pop-up menu is displayed when the control is right-clicked.
Declaration	

```
property PopupMenu: TPopupMenu;
```

Example Syntax

```
procedure TForm1.FormCreate(Sender: TObject);
begin
  Form1.PopupMenu := PopupMenu1;

  // . . .
end;

// Exit the application when the Exit pop-up menu item is clicked
procedure TForm1.PopUpExitClick(Sender: TObject);
begin
  Close;
end;
```

Description   The user can open the pop-up menu associated with the control by right-clicking the control with the mouse. You can programmatically cause the pop-up to appear by calling the pop-up menu's `Popup` method. Refer to Chapter 33, "**TMenu** and Its Descendants," for details on **TPopupMenu**.

Refresh METHOD

Objects Affected	All controls
Purpose	The `Refresh` method erases the control's image and repaints the control.
Declaration	

```
procedure Refresh;
```

Example Syntax

```
procedure TForm1.mnuRefreshClick(Sender: TObject);
begin
  Form1.Refresh;
end;
```

Description	`Refresh` uses `Invalidate` and `Update` to refresh the control. It can be used if the display becomes cluttered with garbage.

Repaint METHOD

Objects Affected	All controls
Purpose	The `Repaint` method forces the control to repaint itself.
Declaration	

```
procedure Repaint; virtual;
```

Description	`Repaint` is similar to `Refresh` except that it does not erase its image first. To erase the control first and then repaint it, use `Refresh`.

ScreenToClient METHOD

Objects Affected	All controls
Purpose	The `ScreenToClient` method converts screen coordinates to the control's coordinate system.
Declaration	

```
function ScreenToClient(const Point: TPoint): TPoint;
```

Parameters	
Point	The X- and Y-coordinates you would like to convert to the control's coordinates.
Description	You can use the `ClientToScreen` and `ScreenToClient` methods together to convert coordinates from one control to another control's coordinate system. For example, to convert `Panel1`'s coordinates to the `Form`'s coordinates, you could use:

```
MyPoint := Form1.ScreenToClient(Panel1.ClientToScreen(MyPoint));
```

ScreenToClient is a simple wrapper around the API ScreenToClient function.

SendToBack METHOD

Objects Affected   All controls

Purpose   The SendToBack method places the control *behind* all other controls in the container control.

Declaration

```
procedure SendToBack;
```

Example Syntax

```
// Send the button behind the Panel
procedure TForm1.Button1Click(Sender: TObject);
begin
  Button1.SendToBack;
end;
```

Description   Windowed and non-windowed controls have different sets of z-orders. Every windowed control on a form exists within the same z-order set, and every non-windowed control exists within a separate z-order set. All windowed controls on a form exist within a single z-order set and all non-windowed controls exist within another z-order set. Windowed controls always appear *above* non-windowed controls, so a windowed control that is in front of a non-windowed control cannot use SendToBack to appear below that non-windowed control.

SetBounds METHOD

Objects Affected   All controls

Purpose   The SetBounds method sets the Left, Top, Width, and Height properties of the control.

Declaration

```
procedure SetBounds(ALeft, ATop, AWidth, AHeight: Integer); virtual;
```

Parameters

ALeft   The new value for the control's Left property.

ATop   The new value for the control's Top property.

AWidth   The new value for the control's Width property.

AHeight   The new value for the control's Height property.

Example Syntax

```
// Have the panel resize with the form
procedure TForm1.FormResize(Sender: TObject);
begin
  Panel1.SetBounds(10, 10, Form1.ClientWidth - 20,
                   Form1.ClientHeight - 20);
end;
```

Description   SetBounds allows you to set all the control's bounding properties together at once. This forces the control to repaint only once, whereas the individual calls would force a repaint for each setting.

SetTextBuf METHOD

Objects Affected   All controls

Purpose   The SetTextBuf method copies the text from a buffer to a control's text.

Declaration

```
procedure SetTextBuf(Buffer: PChar);
```

Parameters

Buffer   The buffer containing the text you are copying to the control.

Example Syntax

```
procedure TForm1.Button2Click(Sender: TObject);
var
  MyBuffer: PChar;
  MyBufSize: Integer;
begin
  MyBufSize := Button1.GetTextLen;
  Button1.GetTextBuf(MyBuffer, MyBufSize);
  StatusBar1.SetTextBuf(MyBuffer);
end;
```

Description   Buffer must point to a null-terminated string.

Show METHOD

Objects Affected   All controls

Purpose   The Show method makes the control visible.

Declaration

```
procedure Show;
```

Example Syntax

```
// If the "Hide Menus" menu item is clicked, hide the menus
// and show the "Show Menus" button
procedure TForm1.HideMenu1Click(Sender: TObject);
begin
```

```
    btnShowMenu.Show;
    Form1.Menu := nil;
  end;
```

Description   Show sets the control's Visible property to True. If the control is a form and the form is obscured, Show will also call BringToFront.

ShowHint PROPERTY

Objects Affected   All controls

Purpose   The ShowHint property determines whether the control displays a tooltip.

Declaration

```
property ShowHint: Boolean;
```

Example Syntax

```
procedure TForm1.FormPaint(Sender: TObject);
begin
  btnHideMenu.ShowHint := True;
  btnHideMenu.Hint := 'Click here to enable menus';
end;
```

Description   If ShowHint is set to True, then a tooltip containing the text in the Hint property is shown if the mouse cursor lingers over the control. If ShowHint is False, and the ParentShowHint property is False, no tooltip is displayed. If ShowHint is False, and ParentShowHint is True, the tooltip will display based on the parent's ShowHint property. If the parent's ShowHint is True, the tooltip appears. Otherwise, it does not appear.

The default value for ShowHint is False.

Text PROPERTY

Objects Affected   All controls

Purpose   The Text property determines the user-editable text that appears within the control.

Declaration

```
property Text: TCaption;
```

Example Syntax

```
procedure TForm1.FormCreate(Sender: TObject);
begin
  Edit1.Text := '';
  Edit2.Text := 'Your name here';
end;

// . . .

procedure TForm1.MyEndDrag(Sender, Target: TObject; X, Y: Integer);
```

```
begin
  if Target is TPanel then
    StatusBar1.Panels[1].Text := 'Drag ended on panel.'
  else
    StatusBar1.Panels[1].Text := 'Drag did not end on panel.';
end;
```

Description Although you can change a control's **Text** programmatically at run time, this is rarely done. Controls that do not allow the user to edit text displayed in the control will implement the **Caption** property instead of **Text**, since **Caption** is not user-editable.

Text is type **TCaption**, which is simply a standard string.

Top PROPERTY

Objects Affected All controls

Purpose The **Top** property determines the vertical coordinate of the top left corner of the control.

Declaration

```
property Top: Integer;
```

Example Syntax

```
procedure TForm1.FormPaint(Sender: TObject);
begin
  Panel1.Top := 10;
  Panel1.Left := 10;
  Panel1.Height := Form1.ClientHeight - 20;
  Panel1.Width := Form1.ClientWidth - 20;
end;
```

Description **Top** is a run-time-only property that uses the coordinate system of its container. It indicates how many pixels the top edge of the control is from the top edge of its container. The **Top** property for a form is measured in screen coordinates.

Update METHOD

Objects Affected All controls

Purpose The **Update** method processes any pending **Paint** messages.

Declaration

```
procedure Update; virtual;
```

Description **Update** calls the Windows API function **UpdateWindow**. It is automatically called by **Refresh**.

Visible PROPERTY

Objects Affected	All controls
Purpose	The Visible property determines whether the control is visible.
Declaration	

```
property Visible: Boolean;
```

Example Syntax

```
// If the "Show Menus" button is clicked, show the menus
// and hide the button
procedure TForm1.btnHideMenuClick(Sender: TObject);
begin
  Form1.Menu := MainMenu1;
  btnShowMenu.Visible := False;
end;
```

Description If Visible is True, the control is visible. If Visible is False, the control is invisible, although you can still set the control's properties and call its methods.

Width PROPERTY

Objects Affected	All controls
Purpose	The Width property contains the width of the control.
Declaration	

```
property Width: Integer;
```

Example Syntax

```
procedure TForm1.FormPaint(Sender: TObject);
begin
  Panel1.Top := 10;
  Panel1.Left := 10;
  Panel1.Height := Form1.ClientHeight - 20;
  Panel1.Width := Form1.ClientWidth - 20;
end;
```

Description Width is measured in pixels and indicates the horizontal size of the control. You change the Width property to change the width of the control at run time.

PART V

Nonwindowed Controls

39

TGraphicControl

Graphic controls are encapsulated by **TGraphicControl** and its descendants. They are those controls that cannot receive the input focus or be the parents of other controls. Graphic controls are sometimes called *nonwindowed controls* because they do not have window handles and therefore consume fewer resources than *windowed controls*. Windowed controls are encapsulated by **TWinControl** and its descendants and are covered in Part VI, Windowed Controls.

While the necessity of conserving system resources is not as compelling in the Win32 world as it was with Windows 3.x, the architecture of Windows 95 is close enough to its 16-bit predecessors that you should still consider the effect your program has on its environment. In addition to the reduced resource requirements, graphic controls repaint far faster than windowed controls do, so they should be used wherever possible. If your application requires a toolbar, for example, Delphi's speed-buttons are a better solution than using standard command buttons or bitmap buttons.

TGraphicControl

TGraphicControl is the parent of all graphic controls. It inherits all the properties, methods, and events of **TControl** and adds a property and a method that access its drawing surface. Figure 39-1 gives the ancestry of **TGraphicControl**. Table 39-1 displays the properties, methods, and events that are implemented by **TGraphicControl**.

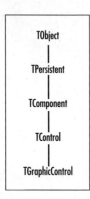

Figure 39-1 Ancestry of `TGraphicControl`

TObject

TPersistent

TComponent

TControl

TGraphicControl

Table 39-1 Properties, methods, and events implemented by `TGraphicControl`

Use or Set This...	To Do This...	Inheritance
Align	Determine how the control is aligned within its parent.	TControl
Assign	Assign one persistent object to another.	TPersistent
BeginDrag	Begin a manual drag operation.	TControl
BoundsRect	Determine the boundary rectangle occupied by the control.	TControl
BringToFront	Bring the control to the front of the z-order.	TControl
Canvas	Access the graphic control's drawing surface.	None
Caption	Label the control with a text string.	TControl
ClassName	Get the name of the object's class.	TObject
ClassParent	Get the object's parent class.	TObject
ClassType	Get the object's actual type.	TObject
ClientHeight	Determine the control's client height.	TControl
ClientOrigin	Determine the upper-left position of the control's client area.	TControl
ClientRect	Determine the rectangle occupied by the control's client area.	TControl
ClientToScreen	Convert control (local) coordinates to screen coordinates.	TControl
ClientWidth	Determine the width of the control's client area.	TControl
ComponentCount	Determine the number of owned components.	TComponent
ComponentIndex	Determine the index of the component in its owner's `Components` list.	TComponent
Components	Determine the list of owned components.	TComponent
ComponentState	Determine the state of the current component.	TComponent
ControlState	Determine the state of the control at any given time.	TControl
ControlStyle	Determine what attributes are present in the control.	TControl
Create	Create a new component.	TObject
Cursor	Determine what image is used for the cursor over the control.	TControl
Destroy	Destroy the component.	TObject

Use or Set This...	To Do This...	Inheritance
DestroyComponents	Destroy all the components owned by the component.	TComponent
Destroying	Notify the component that it is being destroyed.	TComponent
DragCursor	Determine the shape of the mouse cursor as it drags an object over the control.	TControl
Dragging	Determine whether the control is being dragged.	TControl
DragMode	Determine the drag-and-drop behavior of the control.	TControl
Enabled	Determine whether the control is enabled.	TControl
EndDrag	End or cancel a manual drag operation.	TControl
FindComponent	Find a component in the Components array list.	TComponent
Font	Determine the font used to render text on the control.	TControl
Free	Safely destroy the object.	TObject
GetTextBuf	Copy the text of the control into a buffer.	TControl
GetTextLen	Get the length of the text of the control.	TControl
Height	Determine the height of the control.	TControl
Hide	Make the control invisible.	TControl
Hint	Determine the text that displays in a tooltip for the control.	TControl
InheritsFrom	Determine if the object is descended from a certain class.	TObject
InstanceSize	Determine the amount of memory allocated for the object.	TObject
Invalidate	Force the control to be repainted as soon as possible.	TControl
Left	Determine the left edge of the control within its container.	TControl
Name	Determine the name of the component.	TComponent
OnClick	Handle the event that occurs when a mouse button is clicked.	TControl
OnDblClick	Handle the event that occurs when a mouse button is double-clicked.	TControl
OnDragDrop	Handle the event that occurs when an object is dropped on the control.	TControl
OnDragOver	Handle the event that occurs when an object is dragged over the control.	TControl
OnEndDrag	Handle the event that occurs when a drag-and-drop operation is cancelled.	TControl
OnMouseDown	Handle the event that occurs when a mouse button is held down and not immediately released.	TControl
OnMouseMove	Handle the event that occurs when the cursor moves over the control.	TControl
OnMouseUp	Handle the event that occurs when a mouse button is released.	TControl
OnStartDrag	Handle the event that occurs when a drag-and-drop operation is started.	TControl
Owner	Determine the owner of the component.	TComponent
Parent	Determine the parent, or container, of the control.	TControl
ParentColor	Determine whether the control's parent's Color information is used.	TControl
ParentFont	Determine whether the control's parent's Font information is used.	TControl
ParentShowHint	Determine whether the control's parent's ShowHint information is used.	TControl
PopupMenu	Determine which pop-up menu is associated with the control.	TControl
Refresh	Erase the control and repaint it.	TControl
Repaint	Repaint the control.	TControl

continued on next page

continued from previous page

Use or Set This...	To Do This...	Inheritance
ScreenToClient	Convert screen coordinates to client (control) coordinates.	TControl
SendToBack	Send the control to the end of the z-order.	TControl
SetBounds	Determine the coordinates of the control's bounding rectangle.	TControl
SetTextBuf	Set the text of the control to the text in a buffer.	TControl
Show	Make the control visible.	TControl
ShowHint	Enable tooltips for the control.	TControl
Tag	Store an additional integer value with the component.	TComponent
Text	Access the changeable text on the control.	TControl
Top	Determine the upper edge of the control.	TControl
Update	Update is called automatically by Refresh.	TControl
Visible	Make the control visible.	TControl
Width	Determine the width of the control.	TControl

Canvas PROPERTY

Objects Affected   TGraphicControl

Purpose   The **Canvas** property allows you to access the drawing surface of the graphic control.

Declaration

```
property Canvas: TCanvas;
```

Example Syntax

```
// Place a command button, an image control, and a Color dialog
// on the form. Add this OnClick event handler to the button
procedure TForm1.Button1Click(Sender: TObject);
begin
  If ColorDialog1.Execute = True then
  begin
    Image1.Canvas.Brush.Color := ColorDialog1.Color;
    Image1.Canvas.Brush.Style := bsSolid;
    Image1.Canvas.Floodfill(100, 100, ColorDialog1.Color, fsBorder);
  end
end;
```

Description   Canvas allows you to access the control's drawing surface, that is, the area on the control where you can draw or paint images. In Figure 39-2, an image control is colored by accessing the **FloodFill** property of its canvas.

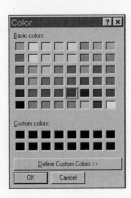

Figure 39-2 Coloring an image control with its canvas

40

TBevel

The **TBevel** class allows you to put beveled rectangular areas, frames, or lines onto a form. They have a chiseled, 3D look and are typically used to contain other controls, setting them off visually in an aesthetically pleasing or functional way. They can appear to be raised over the surface of the form or sunken below it, depending on the **Style** property. The **Shape** property is used to determine the shape the bevel displays.

You will typically encounter bevels when they are used as parts of **TPanel** objects. A sample panel is shown in Figure 40-1.

Figure 40-2 gives the ancestry of **TBevel**. Table 40-1 displays the properties, methods, and events that are implemented by **TBevel**.

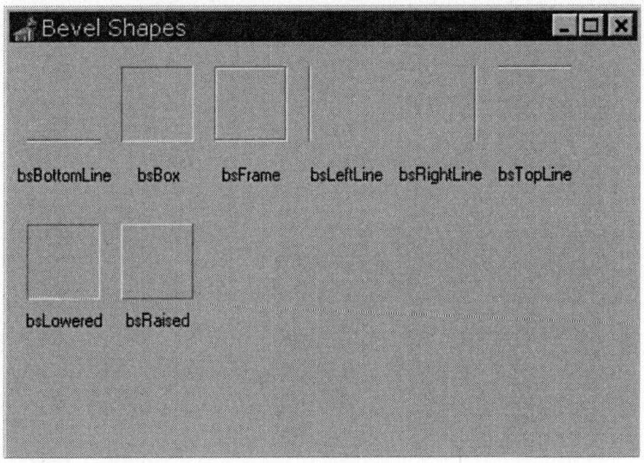

Figure 40-1 Bevel controls

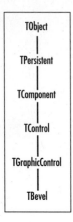

Figure 40-2 Ancestry of TBevel

TObject
|
TPersistent
|
TComponent
|
TControl
|
TGraphicControl
|
TBevel

Table 40-1 Properties, methods, and events implemented by TBevel

Use or Set This...	To Do This...	Inheritance
Align	Determine how the control is aligned within its parent.	TControl
Assign	Assign one persistent object to another.	TPersistent
BeginDrag	Begin a manual drag operation.	TControl
BoundsRect	Determine the boundary rectangle occupied by the control.	TControl
BringToFront	Bring the control to the front of the z-order.	TControl
Canvas	Access the graphic control's drawing surface.	TGraphicControl
Caption	Label the control with a text string.	TControl
ClassName	Get the name of the object's class.	TObject
ClassParent	Get the object's parent class.	TObject
ClassType	Get the object's actual type.	TObject
ClientHeight	Determine the control's client height.	TControl
ClientOrigin	Determine the upper-left position of the control's client area.	TControl
ClientRect	Determine the rectangle occupied by the control's client area.	TControl
ClientToScreen	Convert control (local) coordinates to screen coordinates.	TControl
ClientWidth	Determine the width of the control's client area.	TControl
Color		TControl
ComponentCount	Determine the number of owned components.	TComponent
ComponentIndex	Determine the index of the component in its owner's Components list.	TComponent
Components	Determine the list of owned components.	TComponent
ComponentState	Determine the state of the current component.	TComponent
ControlState	Determine the state of the control at any given time.	TControl
ControlStyle	Determine what attributes are present in the control.	TControl

Use or Set This...	To Do This...	Inheritance
Create	Create a new component.	TObject
Cursor	Determine what image is used for the cursor over the control.	TControl
Destroy	Destroy the component.	TObject
DestroyComponents	Destroy all the components owned by the component.	TComponent
Destroying	Notify the component that it is being destroyed.	TComponent
DragCursor	Determine the shape of the mouse cursor as it drags an object over the control.	TControl
Dragging	Determine whether the control is being dragged.	TControl
DragMode	Determine the drag-and-drop behavior of the control.	TControl
Enabled	Determine whether the control is enabled.	TControl
EndDrag	End or cancel a manual drag operation.	TControl
FindComponent	Find a component in the Components array list.	TComponent
Font	Determine the font used to render text on the control.	TControl
Free	Safely destroy the object.	TObject
GetTextBuf	Copy the text of the control into a buffer.	TControl
GetTextLen	Get the length of the text of the control.	TControl
Height	Determine the height of the control.	TControl
Hide	Make the control invisible.	TControl
Hint	Determine the text that displays in a tooltip for the control.	TControl
InheritsFrom	Determine if the object is descended from a certain class.	TObject
InstanceSize	Determine the amount of memory allocated for the object.	TObject
Invalidate	Force the control to be repainted as soon as possible.	TControl
Left	Determine the left edge of the control within its container.	TControl
Name	Determine the name of the component.	TComponent
OnClick	Handle the event that occurs when a mouse button is clicked.	TControl
OnDblClick	Handle the event that occurs when a mouse button is double-clicked.	TControl
OnDragDrop	Handle the event that occurs when an object is dropped on the control.	TControl
OnDragOver	Handle the event that occurs when an object is dragged over the control.	TControl
OnEndDrag	Handle the event that occurs when a drag-and-drop operation is cancelled.	TControl
OnMouseDown	Handle the event that occurs when a mouse button is held down and not immediately released.	TControl
OnMouseMove	Handle the event that occurs when the cursor moves over the control.	TControl
OnMouseUp	Handle the event that occurs when a mouse button is released.	TControl
OnStartDrag	Handle the event that occurs when a drag-and-drop operation is started.	TControl
Owner	Determine the owner of the component.	TComponent
Paint	Render the image of a graphic control.	TGraphicControl

continued on next page

continued from previous page

Use or Set This...	To Do This...	Inheritance
Parent	Determine the parent, or container, of the control.	TControl
ParentColor	Determine whether the control's parent's Color information is used.	TControl
ParentFont	Determine whether the control's parent's Font information is used.	TControl
ParentShowHint	Determine whether the control's parent's ShowHint information is used.	TControl
PopupMenu	Determine which pop-up menu is associated with the control.	TControl
Refresh	Erase the control and repaint it.	TControl
Repaint	Repaint the control.	TControl
ScreenToClient	Convert screen coordinates to client (control) coordinates.	TControl
SendToBack	Send the control to the end of the z-order.	TControl
SetBounds	Determine the coordinates of the control's bounding rectangle.	TControl
SetTextBuf	Set the text of the control to the text in a buffer.	TControl
Shape	Determine whether the bevel is a line, a rectangle, or a frame.	None
Show	Make the control visible.	TControl
ShowHint	Determine whether the bevel will show a tooltip.	TControl
Style	Determine if the bevel appears raised or lowered.	None
Tag	Store an additional integer value with the component.	TComponent
Text	Access the changeable text on the control.	TControl
Top	Determine the upper edge of the control.	TControl
Update	Update is called automatically by Refresh.	TControl
Visible	Make the control visible.	TControl
Width	Determine the width of the control.	TControl

Shape PROPERTY

Objects Affected	TBevel
Purpose	The Shape property determines the shape used by the bevel.
Declaration	

```
property Shape: TBevelShape;
```

Example Syntax

```
procedure TForm1.FormCreate(Sender: TObject);
begin
  Bevel1.Shape := bsBox;
  Bevel1.Style := bsRaised;
  // . . .
end;
```

Description	Shape is of type TBevelShape, and can be set to any of the following possible values:

Set This Value...	To Use This Shape...
bsBottomLine	A line at the bottom of the bevel control
bsBox	A box shape
bsFrame	A frame shape
bsLeftLine	A line at the left side of the bevel control
bsRightLine	A line at the right side of the bevel control
bsTopLine	A line at the top of the bevel control

Figure 40-3 shows each of the possible shapes the bevel can use.

Style PROPERTY

Objects Affected	TBevel
Purpose	The Style property determines the style used by the bevel.
Declaration	

```
property Style: TBevelStyle;
```

Example Syntax

```
procedure TForm1.FormCreate(Sender: TObject);
begin
  Bevel1.Shape := bsBox;
  Bevel1.Style := bsRaised;
  // . . .
end;
```

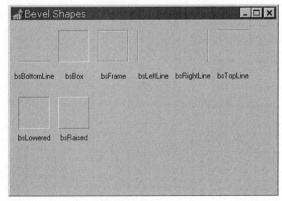

Figure 40-3 Bevel shapes

Description   Style determines whether the bevel style is lowered or raised. The possible values are bsLowered and bsRaised. If Style is bsLowered, the bevel appears lowered. If it is bsRaised, it appears to be raised above the surface of its container.

41

TImage

Image controls, defined as instances of **TImage**, are used to display graphic images, like bitmaps, metafiles, and icons. Image controls are essentially invisible containers for the actual graphics and are typically used directly on the surface of a form. Image controls support many operations such as stretching the image to fit the control, or resizing the image control so it fits the image.

Figure 41-1 shows the ancestry of **TImage**. Table 41-1 displays the properties, methods, and events implemented by **TImage**.

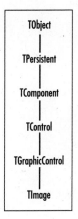

Figure 41-1 Ancestry of **TImage**

Table 41-1 Properties, methods, and events implemented by `TImage`

Use or Set This...	To Do This...	Inheritance
Align	Determine how the control is aligned within its parent.	TControl
Assign	Assign one persistent object to another.	TPersistent
AutoSize	Determine whether the image control automatically resizes to match the size of the image it contains.	
BeginDrag	Begin a manual drag operation.	TControl
BoundsRect	Determine the boundary rectangle occupied by the control.	TControl
BringToFront	Bring the control to the front of the z-order.	TControl
Canvas	Access the graphic control's drawing surface.	TGraphicControl
Caption	Label the control with a text string.	TControl
Center	Determine whether the contained image is centered in the image control.	None
ClassName	Get the name of the object's class.	TObject
ClassParent	Get the object's parent class.	TObject
ClassType	Get the object's actual type.	TObject
ClientHeight	Determine the control's client height.	TControl
ClientOrigin	Determine the upper-left position of the control's client area.	TControl
ClientRect	Determine the rectangle occupied by the control's client area.	TControl
ClientToScreen	Convert control (local) coordinates to screen coordinates.	TControl
ClientWidth	Determine the width of the control's client area.	TControl
Color	Determine the color of the control.	Tcontrol
ComponentCount	Determine the number of owned components.	TComponent
ComponentIndex	The index of the component in its owner's `Components` list.	TComponent
Components	Determine the list of owned components.	TComponent
ComponentState	Determine the state of the current component.	TComponent
ControlState	Determine the state of the control at any given time.	TControl
ControlStyle	Determine what attributes are present in the control.	TControl
Create	Create a new component.	TObject
Cursor	Determine what image is used for the cursor over the control.	TControl
Destroy	Destroy the component.	TObject
DestroyComponents	Destroy all of the components owned by the component.	TComponent
Destroying	Notify the component that it is being destroyed.	TComponent
DragCursor	Determine the shape of the mouse cursor as it drags an object over the control.	TControl
DragCursor	Determine the shape of the mouse pointer as it passes over the image control, dragging an object.	TControl
Dragging	Determine whether the control is being dragged.	TControl
DragMode	Determine the image control's drag-and-drop behavior.	TControl
Enabled	Determine whether the image control is enabled.	TControl

Use or Set This...	To Do This...	Inheritance
EndDrag	End or cancel a manual drag operation.	TControl
FindComponent	Find a component in the Components array list.	TComponent
Font	Determine the font used to render text on the control.	TControl
Free	Safely destroy the object.	TObject
GetTextBuf	Copy the text of the control into a buffer.	TControl
GetTextLen	Get the length of the text of the control.	TControl
Height	Determine the height of the control.	TControl
Hide	Make the control invisible.	TControl
Hint	Determine the text that displays in a tooltip for the control.	TControl
InheritsFrom	Determine if the object is descended from a certain class.	TObject
InstanceSize	Determine the amount of memory allocated for the object.	TObject
Invalidate	Force the control to be repainted as soon as possible.	TControl
Left	Determine the left edge of the control within its container.	TControl
Name	Determine the name of the component.	TComponent
OnClick	Handle the event that occurs when the image control is clicked.	TControl
OnDblClick	Handle the event that occurs when the image control is double-clicked.	TControl
OnDragDrop	Handle the event that occurs when an object is dropped on the image control.	TControl
OnDragOver	Handle the event that occurs when an object is dragged over the image control.	TControl
OnEndDrag	Handle the event that occurs when an object's drag operation is cancel'led or ended over the image control.	TControl
OnMouseDown	Handle the event that occurs when a mouse button is held down and not immediately released.	TControl
OnMouseMove	Handle the event that occurs when the mouse pointer moves over the image control.	TControl
OnMouseUp	Handle the event that occurs when the mouse button is released while the mouse pointer is over the image control.	TControl
OnStartDrag	Handle the event that occurs when a drag operation is begun over the image control.	TControl
Owner	Determine the owner of the component.	TComponent
Paint	Render the image of a graphic control.	TGraphicControl
Parent	Determine the parent, or container, of the control.	TControl
ParentColor	Determine whether the control's parent's Color information is used.	TControl
ParentFont	Determine whether the control's parent's Font information is used.	TControl
ParentShowHint	Determine whether the control's parent's ShowHint information is used.	TControl
Picture	Determine the image that is contained by the image control.	None
PopupMenu	Determine which pop-up menu is associated with the control.	TControl

continued on next page

continued from previous page

Use or Set This...	To Do This...	Inheritance
Refresh	Erase the control and repaint it.	TControl
Repaint	Repaint the control.	TControl
ScreenToClient	Convert screen coordinates to client (control) coordinates.	TControl
SendToBack	Send the control to the end of the z-order.	TControl
SetBounds	Determine the coordinates of the control's bounding rectangle.	TControl
SetTextBuf	Set the text of the control to the text in a buffer.	TControl
Show	Make the control visible.	TControl
ShowHint	Determine whether tooltips are enabled.	TControl
Stretch	Determine whether the contained image is stretched to match the size of the image control.	None
Tag	Store an additional integer value with the component.	TComponent
Text	Access the changeable text on the control.	TControl
Top	Determine the upper edge of the control.	TControl
Update	Update is called automatically by Refresh.	TControl
Visible	Determine whether the image control is visible.	TControl
Width	Determine the width of the control.	TControl

AutoSize PROPERTY

Objects Affected	TImage
Purpose	The AutoSize property determines whether the image control resizes itself to match the size of the image it contains.
Declaration	

```
property AutoSize: Boolean;
```

Example Syntax

```
procedure TForm1.FormCreate(Sender: TObject);
begin
  Image1.AutoSize := False;
  Image2.AutoSize := True;
end;
```

Description If AutoSize is True, then the image control will size itself to match the size of the image it contains. The image data itself is contained within the Picture property. If AutoSize is False, the image control will not resize when an image is loaded; if the image is larger than the image control, only a portion of the image will display. The default value is False.

If **AutoSize** is set to **True** after the image is loaded, it will not have any effect; if you want the image control to size to fit the image it is containing, you must set **AutoSize** to **True** before the image is loaded.

To resize an image to fit an image control, use the **Stretch** property.

See Figure 41-4.

Center PROPERTY

Objects Affected	**TImage**
Purpose	The **Center** property determines whether an image is centered within the image control.
Declaration	

```
property Center: Boolean;
```

Example Syntax

```
procedure TForm1.FormCreate(Sender: TObject);
begin
  Image1.Center := True;
  Image2.Center := False;
end;
```

Description   If **Center** is **True**, the image is centered within the image control. If **Center** is **False**, the image is aligned with the top-left corner of the image control. The default value for **Center** is **True**. See Figure 41-3.

Figure 41-2   Image controls with different **AutoSize** values

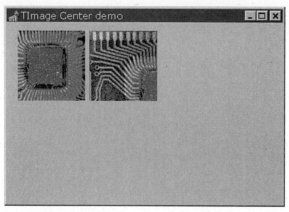

Figure 41-3 Centered and uncentered images

Picture PROPERTY

Objects Affected   TImage

Purpose   The `Picture` property determines the image that appears within the image control.

Declaration

```
property Picture: TPicture;
```

Example Syntax

```
procedure TForm1.FormCreate(Sender: TObject);
begin
  Image1.Top := 10;
  Image1.Left := 10;
  Image1.Width := Form1.ClientWidth - 20;
  Image1.Height := Form1.ClientHeight - 20;
  Image1.AutoSize := False;
  Image1.Stretch := True;
  Image1.Picture.LoadFromFile('c:\windows\clouds.bmp');
end;

procedure TForm1.FormResize(Sender: TObject);
begin
  Image1.Width := Form1.ClientWidth - 20;
  Image1.Height := Form1.ClientHeight - 20;
end;
```

Description   `Picture` is of type `TPicture`, which means that it can be a bitmap image, a metafile image, or an icon.

Stretch PROPERTY

Objects Affected   TImage

Purpose   The **Stretch** property determines whether the bitmap or metafile contained by the image control resizes to fit the image control.

Declaration

```
property Stretch: Boolean;
```

Example Syntax

```
procedure TForm1.FormCreate(Sender: TObject);
begin
  Image1.Top := 10;
  Image1.Left := 10;
  Image1.Width := Form1.ClientWidth - 20;
  Image1.Height := Form1.ClientHeight - 20;
  Image1.AutoSize := False;
  Image1.Stretch := True;
  Image1.Picture.LoadFromFile('c:\windows\clouds.bmp');
end;

procedure TForm1.FormResize(Sender: TObject);
begin
  Image1.Width := Form1.ClientWidth - 20;
  Image1.Height := Form1.ClientHeight - 20;
end;
```

Description   If **Stretch** is **True**, and the image contained by the image control is a bitmap or metafile, then the image will resize to match the size of the image control. This is shown in Figure 41-4. If **Stretch** is **False**, the image will load with its normal size. **Stretch** has no effect on icons. The default value for **Stretch** is **False**.

Figure 41-4   Stretching a bitmap to fit the image control

42

TPaintBox

A paint box control provides a rectangular area on the form where drawing and painting operations can occur. The paint box control is useful if you want to limit the form's drawing surface to a smaller area than the full-form background.

Figure 42-1 shows the derivation of **TPaintBox**. Table 42-1 displays the properties, methods, and events implemented by **TPaintBox**.

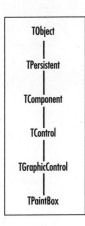

Figure 42-1 Derivation of **TPaintBox**

Table 42-1 Properties, methods, and events implemented by `TPaintBox`

Use or Set This...	To Do This...	Inheritance
Align	Determine how the control is aligned within its parent.	TControl
Assign	Assign one persistent object to another.	TPersistent
BeginDrag	Begin a manual drag operation.	TControl
BoundsRect	Determine the boundary rectangle occupied by the control.	TControl
BringToFront	Bring the control to the front of the z-order.	TControl
Canvas	Access the drawing surface of the paint box.	TControl
Caption	Label the control with a text string.	TControl
ClassName	Get the name of the object's class.	TObject
ClassParent	Get the object's parent class.	TObject
ClassType	Get the object's actual type.	TObject
ClientHeight	Determine the control's client height.	TControl
ClientOrigin	Determine the upper-left position of the control's client area.	TControl
ClientRect	Determine the rectangle occupied by the control's client area.	TControl
ClientToScreen	Convert control (local) coordinates to screen coordinates.	TControl
ClientWidth	Determine the width of the control's client area.	TControl
Color	Determine the color used by the paint box.	TControl
ComponentCount	Determine the number of owned components.	TComponent
ComponentIndex	The index of the component in its owner's `Components` list.	TComponent
Components	Determine the list of owned components.	TComponent
ComponentState	Determine the state of the current component.	TComponent
ControlState	Determine the state of the control at any given time.	TControl
ControlStyle	Determine what attributes are present in the control.	TControl
Create	Create a new component.	TObject
Cursor	Determine what image is used for the cursor over the control.	TControl
Destroy	Destroy the component.	TObject
DestroyComponents	Destroy all of the components owned by the component.	TComponent
Destroying	Notify the component that it is being destroyed.	TComponent
DragCursor	Determine the shape of the cursor as it drags an object over the control.	TControl
DragCursor	Determine the shape of the mouse cursor as it drags an object over the control.	TControl
Dragging	Determine whether the control is being dragged.	TControl
DragMode	Determine the drag-and-drop behavior of the control.	TControl
Enabled	Determine whether the paint box is enabled.	TControl
EndDrag	End or cancel a manual drag operation.	TControl
FindComponent	Find a component in the `Components` array list.	TComponent
Font	Determine the font used to render text on the paint box.	TControl
Free	Safely destroy the object.	TObject
GetTextBuf	Copy the text of the control into a buffer.	TControl
GetTextLen	Get the length of the text of the control.	TControl
Height	Determine the height of the control.	TControl

Use or Set This...	To Do This...	Inheritance
Hide	Make the control invisible.	TControl
Hint	Determine the text that displays in a tooltip for the control.	TControl
InheritsFrom	Determine if the object is descended from a certain class.	TObject
InstanceSize	Determine the amount of memory allocated for the object.	TObject
Invalidate	Force the control to be repainted as soon as possible.	TControl
Left	Determine the left edge of the control within its container.	TControl
Name	Determine the name of the component.	TComponent
OnClick	Handle the event that occurs when the paint box is clicked.	TControl
OnDblClick	Handle the event that occurs when the paint box is double-clicked.	TControl
OnDragDrop	Handle the event that occurs when an object is dropped on the paint box.	TControl
OnDragOver	Handle the event that occurs when an object is dragged over the paint box.	TControl
OnEndDrag	Handle the event that occurs when a drag operation is completed over the paint box.	TControl
OnMouseDown	Handle the event that occurs when the mouse is clicked but the mouse button is not released over the paint box.	TControl
OnMouseMove	Handle the event that occurs when the mouse pointer moves over the paint box.	TControl
OnMouseUp	Handle the event that occurs when the mouse button is released over the paint box.	TControl
OnStartDrag	Handle the event that occurs when a drag-and-drop operation starts over the paint box.	TControl
Owner	Determine the owner of the component.	TComponent
Paint	Render the image of a graphic control.	TGraphicControl
Parent	Determine the parent, or container, of the control.	TControl
ParentColor	Determine whether the paint box derives Color information from its parent.	TControl
ParentFont	Determine whether the paint box derives Font information from its parent.	TControl
ParentShowHint	Determine whether the paint box uses its own ShowHint.	TControl
PopupMenu	Determine which pop-up menu is associated with the control.	TControl
Refresh	Erase the control and repaint it.	TControl
Repaint	Repaint the control.	TControl
ScreenToClient	Convert screen coordinates to client (control) coordinates.	TControl
SendToBack	Send the control to the end of the z-order.	TControl
SetBounds	Determine the coordinates of the control's bounding rectangle.	TControl
SetTextBuf	Set the text of the control to the text in a buffer.	TControl
Show	Make the control visible.	TControl
ShowHint	Determine whether the paint box should use tooltips.	TControl
Tag	Store an additional integer value with the component.	TComponent
Text	Access the changeable text on the control.	TControl
Top	Determine the upper edge of the control.	TControl
Update	Update is called automatically by Refresh.	TControl
Visible	Determine whether the paint box is visible.	TControl
Width	Determine the width of the control.	TControl

43

TShape

The **TShape** class lets you display a simple geometric shape on a form. The shape of the **TShape** object is determined, strangely, by the **Shape** property, which allows the object to display as a circle, ellipse, rectangle, rounded rectangle, square, or rounded square.

When dealing with the width and height of a shape, remember that these properties correspond to the underlying rectangle of the shape, even if it appears as a circle or an ellipse. The height of a circle, for example, would be its height at the widest horizontal position.

Figure 43-1 gives the derivation of **TShape**. Table 43-1 displays the properties, methods, and events implemented by **TShape**.

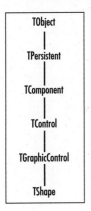

Figure 43-1 Derivation of **TShape**

Table 43-1 Properties, methods, and events implemented by TShape

Use or Set This...	To Do This...	Inheritance
Align	Determine how the control is aligned within its parent.	TControl
Assign	Assign one persistent object to another.	TPersistent
BeginDrag	Begin a manual drag operation.	TControl
BoundsRect	Determine the boundary rectangle occupied by the control.	TControl
BringToFront	Bring the control to the front of the z-order.	TControl
Brush	Determine the color and pattern used to fill the shape.	None
Canvas	Access the graphic control's drawing surface.	TGraphicControl
Caption	Label the control with a text string.	TControl
ClassName	Get the name of the object's class.	TObject
ClassParent	Get the object's parent class.	TObject
ClassType	Get the object's actual type.	TObject
ClientHeight	Determine the control's client height.	TControl
ClientOrigin	Determine the upper-left position of the control's client area.	TControl
ClientRect	Determine the rectangle occupied by the control's client area.	TControl
ClientToScreen	Convert control (local) coordinates to screen coordinates.	TControl
ClientWidth	Determine the width of the control's client area.	TControl
Color	Determine the background color of the control.	TControl
ComponentCount	Determine the number of owned components.	TComponent
ComponentIndex	The index of the component in its owner's Components list.	TComponent
Components	Determine the list of owned components.	TComponent
ComponentState	Determine the state of the current component.	TComponent
ControlState	Determine the state of the control at any given time.	TControl
ControlStyle	Determine what attributes are present in the control.	TControl
Create	Create a new component.	TObject
Cursor	Determine what image is used for the cursor over the control.	TControl
Destroy	Destroy the component.	TObject
DestroyComponents	Destroy all of the components owned by the component.	TComponent
Destroying	Notify the component that it is being destroyed.	TComponent
DragCursor	Determine the shape of the mouse cursor as it drags an object over the control.	TControl
DragCursor	Determine the shape of the mouse pointer as it drags an object over the shape.	TControl
Dragging	Determine whether the control is being dragged.	TControl
DragMode	Determine the drag-and-drop behavior of the control.	TControl
Enabled	Determine whether the shape is enabled.	TControl
EndDrag	End or cancel a manual drag operation.	TControl
FindComponent	Find a component in the Components array list.	TComponent
Font	Determine the font used to render text on the control.	TControl

Use or Set This...	To Do This...	Inheritance
Free	Safely destroy the object.	TObject
GetTextBuf	Copy the text of the control into a buffer.	TControl
GetTextLen	Get the length of the text of the control.	TControl
Height	Determine the height of the control.	TControl
Hide	Make the control invisible.	TControl
Hint	Determine the text that displays in a tooltip for the control.	TControl
InheritsFrom	Determine if the object is descended from a certain class.	TObject
InstanceSize	Determine the amount of memory allocated for the object.	TObject
Invalidate	Force the control to be repainted as soon as possible.	TControl
Left	Determine the left edge of the control within its container.	TControl
Name	Determine the name of the component.	TComponent
OnClick	Handle the event that occurs when a mouse button is clicked.	TControl
OnDblClick	Handle the event that occurs when a mouse button is double-clicked.	TControl
OnDragDrop	Handle the event that occurs when an object is dropped on the control.	TControl
OnDragDrop	Handle the event that occurs when an object is dropped on the shape.	
OnDragOver	Handle the event that occurs when an object is dragged over the control.	TControl
OnDragOver	Handle the event that occurs when an object is dragged over the shape.	
OnEndDrag	Handle the event that occurs when a drag-and-drop operation is cancelled.	TControl
OnEndDrag	Handle the event that occurs when a drag-and-drop operation is cancelled over the shape.	TControl
OnMouseDown	Handle the event that occurs when a mouse button is held down and not immediately released.	TControl
OnMouseDown	Handle the event that occurs when the mouse is clicked over the shape and the mouse button is not released.	TControl
OnMouseMove	Handle the event that occurs when the cursor moves over the control.	TControl
OnMouseMove	Handle the event that occurs when the mouse pointer passes over the shape.	TControl
OnMouseUp	Handle the event that occurs when a mouse button is released.	TControl
OnStartDrag	Handle the event that occurs when a drag-and-drop operation is started.	TControl
OnStartDrag	Handle the event that occurs when a drag-and-drop operation is started over the shape.	TControl
Owner	Determine the owner of the component.	TComponent
Paint	Render the image of a graphic control.	TGraphicControl
Parent	Determine the parent, or container, of the control.	TControl
ParentColor	Determine whether the Color information of the control's parent is used.	TControl
ParentFont	Determine whether the Font information of the control's parent is used.	TControl
ParentShowHint	Determine whether the shape uses the parent's ShowHint property.	TControl

continued on next page

continued from previous page

Use or Set This...	To Do This...	Inheritance
Pen	Determine the kind of pen used to draw lines and outlines on the shape's drawing surface.	None
PopupMenu	Determine which pop-up menu is associated with the control.	TControl
Refresh	Erase the control and repaint it.	TControl
Repaint	Repaint the control.	TControl
ScreenToClient	Convert screen coordinates to client (control) coordinates.	TControl
SendToBack	Send the control to the end of the z-order.	TControl
SetBounds	Determine the coordinates of the control's bounding rectangle.	TControl
SetTextBuf	Set the text of the control to the text in a buffer.	TControl
Shape	Determine the shape of the shape object.	None
Show	Make the control visible.	TControl
ShowHint	Determine whether to show tooltips.	TControl
StyleChanged	Force the shape to repaint.	None
Tag	Store an additional integer value with the component.	TComponent
Text	Access the changeable text on the control.	TControl
Top	Determine the upper edge of the control.	TControl
Update	Update is called automatically by Refresh.	TControl
Visible	Determine whether the shape is visible.	TControl
Width	Determine the width of the control.	TControl

Brush PROPERTY

Objects Affected	TShape
Purpose	The Brush property determines the color and pattern used to fill the shape object.
Declaration	

```
property Brush: TBrush;
```

Example Syntax

```
procedure TForm1.FormCreate(Sender: TObject);
begin
  Shape1.Brush.Color := clRed;
  Shape1.Brush.Style := bsSolid;
  Shape2.Brush.Color := clWhite;
  Shape2.Brush.Style := bsCross;
  Shape3.Brush.Color := clBlue;
  Shape3.Brush.Style := bsDiagCross;
end;
```

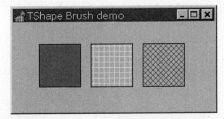

Figure 43-2 Filling shapes with colors
and patterns

Description   Brush is a **TBrush** object. Basically, **TBrush** lets you specify the pattern it
uses with its **Style** property and the color it uses with its **Color** property.
If you would like **Brush** to fill using a bitmap image, you can specify a
value for its **Bitmap** property. **TBrush** is covered in Chapter 23,
"**TGraphicsObject** and Its Descendants."

Pen PROPERTY

Objects Affected   TShape

Purpose   The **Pen** property determines the kind of pen used to draw lines and outlines on the shape object's canvas.

Declaration

```
property Pen: TPen;
```

Example Syntax

```
procedure TForm1.FormCreate(Sender: TObject);
begin
  Shape1.Pen.Color := clGreen;
  Shape1.Pen.Width := 5;
end;
```

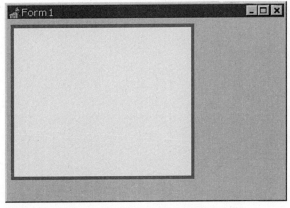

Figure 43-3 A shape with a thick green border

Description	Pen is of type TPen, which is covered in Chapter 23.

Shape PROPERTY

Objects Affected	TShape
Purpose	The Shape property determines the shape of the Shape object.
Declaration	

```
property Shape: TShapeType;
```

Example Syntax

```
procedure TForm1.FormCreate(Sender: TObject);
begin
  Shape1.Shape := stCircle;
  Shape2.Shape := stEllipse;
  Shape3.Shape := stRectangle;
  Shape4.Shape := stRoundRect;
  Shape5.Shape := stRoundSquare;
  Shape6.Shape := stSquare;
end;
```

Description	Shape can be one of the following possible values:

Use This Value...	To Get This Shape...
stCircle	Circle
stEllipse	Ellipse
stRectangle	Rectangle
stRoundRect	A rectangle with rounded corners
stRoundSquare	A square with rounded corners
stSquare	Square

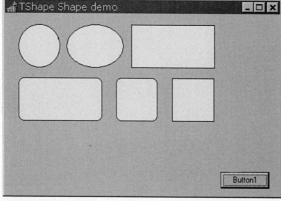

Figure 43-4 The possible shapes

StyleChanged METHOD

Objects Affected	TShape
Purpose	The StyleChanged method forces a repaint of the shape object.
Declaration	

```
procedure StyleChanged(Sender: TObject);
```

Table 43-2 Parameters of the StyleChanged method

Argument	Description
Sender	Can be any valid object—it has no effect on the method.

Example Syntax

```
// Shape1 is a circle. When the button is clicked, it
// is changed to a rectangle and repainted.
procedure TForm1.btnRepaintShape1Click(Sender: TObject);
begin
  Shape1.Shape := stRectangle;
  Shape1.StyleChanged(Self);
end;
```

Description   StyleChanged calls Invalidate to force a repaint of the shape object.

44

TCustomLabel
AND ITS DESCENDANTS

Labels are used to display text on a form. **TCustomLabel** and its descendants provide this functionality for your Delphi programs, creating text labels that cannot be edited or selected by the user.

TCustomLabel is the abstract base class for Delphi labels, providing the base functionality for its children to publish and use. You will never create instances of **TCustomLabel**, but will typically use its children **TDBText** and **TLabel**, available from Delphi's Component Palette. **TCustomLabel** inherits many properties and methods from **TGraphicControl** and overrides the **Canvas** property and the **Create** method, although they are not conceptually different from their ancestors.

Figure 44-1 shows the **TCustomLabel** branch of the VCL. Table 44-1 displays the properties, methods, and events implemented by **TCustomLabel**.

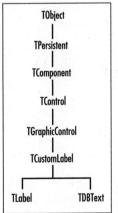

Figure 44-1 The **TCustomLabel** branch of the VCL

TObject
|
TPersistent
|
TComponent
|
TControl
|
TGraphicControl
|
TCustomLabel
|
TLabel   TDBText

Table 44-1 Properties, methods, and events implemented by `TCustomLabel`

Use or Set This...	To Do This...	Inheritance
Align	Determine how the control is aligned within its parent.	TControl
Assign	Assign one persistent object to another.	TPersistent
BeginDrag	Begin a manual drag operation.	TControl
BoundsRect	Determine the boundary rectangle occupied by the control.	TControl
BringToFront	Bring the control to the front of the z-order.	TControl
Canvas	Access the graphic control's drawing surface.	TGraphicControl
Caption	Label the control with a text string.	TControl
ClassName	Get the name of the object's class.	TObject
ClassParent	Get the object's parent class.	TObject
ClassType	Get the object's actual type.	TObject
ClientHeight	Determine the control's client height.	TControl
ClientOrigin	Determine the upper-left position of the control's client area.	TControl
ClientRect	Determine the rectangle occupied by the control's client area.	TControl
ClientToScreen	Convert control (local) coordinates to screen coordinates.	TControl
ClientWidth	Determine the width of the control's client area.	TControl
Color	Determine the background color of the control.	TControl
ComponentCount	Determine the number of owned components.	TComponent
ComponentIndex	The index of the component in its owner's `Components` list.	TComponent
Components	Determine the list of owned components.	TComponent
ComponentState	Determine the state of the current component.	TComponent
ControlState	Determine the state of the control at any given time.	TControl
ControlStyle	Determine what attributes are present in the control.	TControl
Create	Create a new component.	TObject
Cursor	Determine what image is used for the cursor over the control.	TControl
Destroy	Destroy the component.	TObject
DestroyComponents	Destroy all the components owned by the component.	TComponent
Destroying	Notify the component it is being destroyed.	TComponent
DragCursor	Determine the shape of the mouse cursor as it drags an object over the control.	TControl
Dragging	Determine whether the control is being dragged.	TControl
DragMode	Determine the drag-and-drop behavior of the control.	TControl
Enabled	Determine whether the control is enabled.	TControl
EndDrag	End or cancel a manual drag operation.	TControl
FindComponent	Find a component in the `Components` array list.	TComponent
Font	Determine the font used to render text on the control.	TControl
Free	Safely destroy the object.	TObject
GetTextBuf	Copy the text of the control into a buffer.	TControl
GetTextLen	Get the length of the control's text.	TControl

Use or Set This...	To Do This...	Inheritance
Height	Determine the height of the control.	TControl
Hide	Make the control invisible.	TControl
Hint	Determine the text that displays in a tooltip for the control.	TControl
InheritsFrom	Determine if the object is descended from a certain class.	TObject
InstanceSize	Determine the amount of memory allocated for the object.	TObject
Invalidate	Force the control to be repainted as soon as possible.	TControl
Left	Determine the left edge of the control within its container.	TControl
Name	Determine the name of the component.	TComponent
OnClick	Handle the event that occurs when a mouse button is clicked.	TControl
OnDblClick	Handle the event that occurs when a mouse button is double-clicked.	TControl
OnDragDrop	Handle the event that occurs when an object is dropped on the control.	TControl
OnDragOver	Handle the event that occurs when an object is dragged over the control.	TControl
OnEndDrag	Handle the event that occurs when a drag-and-drop operation is cancelled.	TControl
OnMouseDown	Handle the event that occurs when a mouse button is held down and not immediately released.	TControl
OnMouseMove	Handle the event that occurs when the cursor moves over the control.	TControl
OnMouseUp	Handle the event that occurs when a mouse button is released.	TControl
OnStartDrag	Handle the event that occurs when a drag-and-drop operation is started.	TControl
Owner	Determine the owner of the component.	TComponent
Paint	Render the image of a graphic control.	TGraphicControl
Parent	Determine the parent, or container, of the control.	TControl
ParentColor	Determine whether the Color information of the control's parent is used.	TControl
ParentFont	Determine whether the Font information of the control's parent is used.	TControl
ParentShowHint	Determine whether the ShowHint information control's parent is used.	TControl
PopupMenu	Determine which pop-up menu is associated with the control.	TControl
Refresh	Erase the control and repaint it.	TControl
Repaint	Repaint the control.	TControl
ScreenToClient	Convert screen coordinates to client (control) coordinates.	TControl
SendToBack	Send the control to the end of the z-order.	TControl
SetBounds	Determine the coordinates of the control's bounding rectangle.	TControl

continued on next page

continued from previous page

Use or Set This...	To Do This...	Inheritance
SetTextBuf	Set the text of the control to the text in a buffer.	TControl
Show	Make the control visible.	TControl
ShowHint	Enable tooltips for the control.	TControl
Tag	Store an additional integer value with the component.	TComponent
Text	Access the changeable text on the control.	TControl
Top	Determine the upper edge of the control.	TControl
Update	Update is called automatically by Refresh.	TControl
Visible	Determine whether the control is visible.	TControl
Width	Determine the width of the control.	TControl

TDBText

TDBText objects, or database text labels, are data-aware controls that display text on a form. Database text labels are used to display the contents of a field in the current record of a dataset (a TDataSet object) that the user cannot modify. See Chapter 35, "TCustomImageList and Its Descendants," for information on datasets.

Database text labels are *data-aware*; you do not need to explicitly handle OnChange events for the dataset that contains the data you are displaying. As the field in the current record changes, the database text label updates its text.

TDBText is available on the Data Controls page of the Component Palette.

Table 44-2 displays the properties, methods, and events implemented by TDBText. These are in addition to the properties and methods it inherits from TCustomLabel (refer to Table 44-1).

Table 44-2 Properties, methods, and events implemented by TDBText

Use or Set This...	To Do This...	Inheritance
Align	Determine how the label is aligned within its container.	TControl
Alignment	Determine how the text caption is aligned within the label.	TControl
AutoSize	Determine whether the label resizes to the width of its caption.	TControl
Color	Determine the background color of the label.	TControl
Create	Create a new database text label.	TComponent
DataField	Determine which field is used to obtain the data to display.	None
DataSource	Determine the dataset the label gets the data to display.	None
Destroy	Destroy the database text label.	TComponent
DragCursor	Determine the shape of the cursor as it drags an object over the database text label.	TControl
DragMode	Determine the label's drag-and-drop behavior.	TControl

Use or Set This...	To Do This...	Inheritance
Enabled	Determine whether the label is enabled.	TControl
Field	Determine the field to which the label is linked.	TControl
Font	Determine the font used to display text in the label.	TControl
OnClick	Handle the event that occurs when the label is clicked.	TControl
OnDblClick	Handle the event that occurs when the label is double-clicked.	TControl
OnDragDrop	Handle the event that occurs when an object is dropped on the label.	TControl
OnDragOver	Handle the event that occurs when an object is dragged over the label.	TControl
OnEndDrag	Handle the event that occurs when a drag-and-drop operation is cancelled over the label.	TControl
OnMouseDown	Handle the event that occurs when the mouse is clicked over the label and the mouse button is not released.	TControl
OnMouseMove	Handle the event that occurs when the mouse is moved over the label.	TControl
OnMouseUp	Handle the event that occurs when the mouse button is released while the mouse pointer is over the label.	TControl
OnStartDrag	Handle the event that occurs when a drag-and-drop operation is started over the label.	TControl
ParentColor	Determine whether the background color of the label's parent is used for the label.	TControl
ParentFont	Determine whether the label uses its parent's font.	TControl
ParentShowHint	Determine whether the label uses its parent's ShowHint property to determine whether to display a tooltip.	TControl
PopupMenu	Determine which pop-up menu is associated with the label.	TControl
ShowHint	Determine whether the label should display a tooltip.	TControl
Transparent	Determine whether the label is transparent.	TControl
Visible	Determine whether the label is visible.	TControl
WordWrap	Determine whether the text caption of the label wraps.	TControl

TLabel

TLabel objects, known simply as *labels*, are used to output read-only text on a form. Labels are typically used to label other controls that do not have built-in caption properties, like edit boxes, scroll bars, list boxes, and track bars.

TLabel is available on the Standard page of the Component Palette.

Table 44-3 displays the properties, methods, and events implemented by TLabel. These are in addition to the properties and methods it inherits from TCustomLabel (refer to Table 44-1).

Table 44-3 Properties, methods, and events implemented by `TLabel`

Use or Set This...	To Do This...	Inheritance
Align	Determine how the label is aligned within its container.	TControl
Alignment	Determine how the text caption is aligned within the label.	TControl
AutoSize	Determine whether the label resizes to the width of its caption.	TControl
Caption	Determine the text used for the label's caption.	TControl
Color	Determine the background color of the label.	TControl
DragCursor	Determine the shape of the cursor as it drags an object over the database text label.	TControl
DragMode	Determine the label's drag-and-drop behavior.	TControl
Enabled	Determine whether the label is enabled.	TControl
FocusControl	Link the label with another control so a user typing the label's accelerator character will enable the other control.	TControl
Font	Determine the font used to display text in the label.	TControl
OnClick	Handle the event that occurs when the label is clicked.	TControl
OnDblClick	Handle the event that occurs when the label is double-clicked.	TControl
OnDragDrop	Handle the event that occurs when an object is dropped on the label.	TControl
OnDragOver	Handle the event that occurs when an object is dragged over the label.	TControl
OnEndDrag	Handle the event that occurs when a drag-and-drop operation is cancelled over the label.	TControl
OnMouseDown	Handle the event that occurs when the mouse is clicked over the label and the mouse button is not released.	TControl
OnMouseMove	Handle the event that occurs when the mouse is moved over the label.	TControl
OnMouseUp	Handle the event that occurs when the mouse button is released while the mouse pointer is over the label.	TControl
OnStartDrag	Handle the event that occurs when a drag-and-drop operation is started over the label.	TControl
ParentColor	Determine whether the background color of the label's parent is used for the label.	TControl
ParentFont	Determine whether the label uses its parent's font.	TControl
ParentShowHint	Determine whether the label uses its parent's ShowHint property to determine whether to display a tooltip.	TControl
PopupMenu	Determine which pop-up menu is associated with the label.	TControl
ShowAccelChar	Determine whether an ampersand in the caption of the label appears as an underline to indicate the accelerator character, or as an actual ampersand.	TControl
ShowHint	Determine whether the label should display a tooltip.	TControl
Transparent	Determine whether the label is transparent.	TControl
Visible	Determine whether the label is visible.	TControl
WordWrap	Determine whether the text caption of the label wraps.	TControl

DataField PROPERTY

Objects Affected	TDBText
Purpose	DataField identifies the field from which it displays data.
Declaration	

```
property DataField: string;
```

Description   The DataField property specifies the field in the current record from which it gets its data. The dataset containing the field is specified by a data source (that is, a TDataSource component) in the DataSource property of that dataset.

DataSource PROPERTY

Objects Affected	TDBText
Purpose	The DataSource property specifies the data source for the database text label.
Declaration	

```
property DataSource: TDataSource;
```

Example Syntax

```
procedure TForm1.FormCreate(Sender: TObject);
begin
  DBText1.DataSource := DataSource1;
  DBText2.DataSource := DataSource1;
end;
```

Description   The DataSource property specifies where the component gets the data to display as a label. Since the database text label is data-aware, the text displayed by the label is dynamic and will change as the field in the current record changes. DataSource is of type TDataSource, a data source component identifying the dataset in which the data is found. Refer to Chapter 27, "TDataSource" and Chapter 35, "TDataSet" for more information.

TSpeedButton AND ITS DESCENDANTS

Speedbuttons are nonwindowed controls that don't directly encapsulate anything in the Windows API. As nonwindowed buttons, they can be used in areas where the overhead of windowed buttons is undesirable. Speedbuttons are often used by Delphi programmers to create toolbars, as you will see below. The **TSpeedButton** class enables you to create buttons with glyphs and/or captions similar to bitmap buttons (**TBitBtn** objects), although they take up fewer resources and cannot receive the input focus. **TBitBtn** is covered in Chapter 63, "**TButtonControl** and Its Descendants."

Creating Toolbars in Delphi

One of the few user interface elements Delphi 2 doesn't support directly is the *toolbar*. Toolbar support was, however, added to Delphi 3. A toolbar contains a row of unlabeled buttons identified by the graphic on its face, or by viewing its tooltip. Many Windows applications, such as Explorer and Word for Windows, have toolbars, and programming environments like Visual C++ and Visual Basic support them natively. Fortunately, you can create toolbars in Delphi with a panel control and a collection of speedbuttons. Figure 45-1 shows a typical toolbar.

To implement a toolbar in Delphi 2, create a menu (if needed) and place a panel on the form. Set its **Align** property to **Top**. Then, add the speedbuttons you need and space them as necessary. Typically, if your application has a menu, the buttons on the toolbar will duplicate the functionality of menu items like Open, Save, and New. Because of this, you can have the **OnClick** event handlers for the speedbuttons call the **OnClick** event handlers for the menu items whose functionality they are duplicating:

Figure 45-1   A toolbar

Listing 45-1 A speedbutton event handler that calls a menu item event handler

```
procedure TForm1.sbNewClick(Sender: TObject);
begin
  // Call the OnClick handler for the New menu item, sending
  // the speed button as the Sender parameter
  New1Click(sbNew);
end;
```

Figure 45-2 shows a simple toolbar created with Delphi:

Figure 45-3 shows the TSpeedButton branch of the VCL. Table 45-1 displays the properties, methods, and events implemented by TSpeedButton.

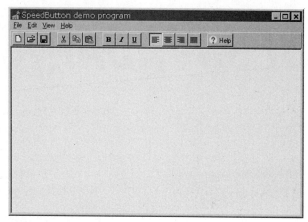

Figure 45-2 A Delphi toolbar

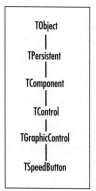

Figure 45-3 The TSpeedButton branch of the VCL

Table 45-1 Properties, methods, and events implemented by `TSpeedButton`

Use or Set This...	To Do This...	Inheritance
Align	Determine how the control is aligned within its parent.	TControl
AllowAllUp	Determine whether grouped buttons can all be unselected.	None
Assign	Assign one persistent object to another.	TPersistent
BeginDrag	Begin a manual drag operation.	TControl
BoundsRect	Determine the boundary rectangle occupied by the control.	TControl
BringToFront	Bring the control to the front of the z-order.	TControl
Canvas	Access the graphic control's drawing surface.	TGraphicControl
Caption	Determine the text that appears on the face of the button.	TControl
ClassName	Get the name of the object's class.	TObject
ClassParent	Get the object's parent class.	TObject
ClassType	Get the object's actual type.	TObject
Click	Simulate an `OnClick` event.	TControl
ClientHeight	Determine the control's client height.	TControl
ClientOrigin	Determine the upper-left position of the control's client area.	TControl
ClientRect	Determine the rectangle occupied by the control's client area.	TControl
ClientToScreen	Convert control (local) coordinates to screen coordinates.	TControl
ClientWidth	Determine the width of the control's client area.	TControl
Color	Determine the background color of the control.	TControl
ComponentCount	Determines the number of owned components.	TComponent
ComponentIndex	The index of the component in its owner's `Components` list.	TComponent
Components	Determine the list of owned components.	TComponent
ComponentState	Determine the state of the current component.	TComponent
ControlState	Determine the state of the control at any given time.	TControl
ControlStyle	Determine what attributes are present in the control.	TControl
Create	Create a new component.	TObject
Cursor	Determine what image is used for the cursor over the control.	TControl
Destroy	Destroy the component.	TObject
DestroyComponents	Destroy all of the components owned by the component.	TComponent
Destroying	Notify the component that it is being destroyed.	TComponent
Down	Determine whether the button is selected.	None
DragCursor	Determine the shape of the mouse cursor as it drags an object over the control.	TControl
Dragging	Determine whether the control is being dragged.	TControl
DragMode	Determine the drag-and-drop behavior of the control.	TControl
Enabled	Determine whether the button is enabled.	TControl
EndDrag	End or cancel a manual drag operation.	TControl
FindComponent	Find a component in the `Components` array list.	TComponent

continued on next page

continued from previous page

Use or Set This...	To Do This...	Inheritance
Font	Determine the font used to render text on the control.	TControl
Free	Safely destroy the object.	TObject
GetTextBuf	Copy the text of the control into a buffer.	TControl
GetTextLen	Get the length of the text of the control.	TControl
Glyph	Determine the image or images used on the button.	None
GroupIndex	Determine which group, if any, the button is a member of.	None
Height	Determine the height of the control.	TControl
Hide	Make the control invisible.	TControl
Hint	Determine the text that displays in a tooltip for the control.	TControl
InheritsFrom	Determine if the object is descended from a certain class.	TObject
InstanceSize	Determine the amount of memory allocated for the object.	TObject
Invalidate	Force the control to be repainted as soon as possible.	TControl
Layout	Determine where the glyph appears on the button face.	None
Left	Determine the left edge of the control within its container.	TControl
Margin	Determine the width between the glyph and the button edge.	None
Name	Determine the name of the component.	TComponent
NumGlyphs	Determine how many images the glyph uses.	None
OnClick	Specify what happens when the button is clicked.	TControl
OnDblClick	Specify what happens when the button is double-clicked.	TControl
OnDragDrop	Handle the event that occurs when an object is dropped on the control.	TControl
OnDragOver	Handle the event that occurs when an object is dragged over the control.	TControl
OnEndDrag	Handle the event that occurs when a drag-and-drop operation is cancelled.	TControl
OnMouseDown	Specify what happens when the button is clicked and the mouse button is not released.	TControl
OnMouseMove	Handle the event that occurs when the cursor moves over the control.	TControl
OnMouseUp	Handle the event that occurs when a mouse button is released.	TControl
OnStartDrag	Handle the event that occurs when a drag-and-drop operation is started.	TControl
Owner	Determine the owner of the component.	TComponent
Paint	Render the image of a graphic control.	TGraphicControl
Parent	Determine the parent, or container, of the control.	TControl
ParentColor	Determine whether the Color information of the control's parent is used.	TControl
ParentFont	Determine whether the Font information of the control's parent is used.	TControl
ParentShowHint	Determine whether the button uses its parent's ShowHint.	TControl
PopupMenu	Determine which pop-up menu is associated with the control.	TControl
Refresh	Erase the control and repaint it.	TControl

Use or Set This...	To Do This...	Inheritance
Repaint	Repaint the control.	TControl
ScreenToClient	Convert screen coordinates to client (control) coordinates.	TControl
SendToBack	Send the control to the end of the z-order.	TControl
SetBounds	Determine the coordinates of the control's bounding rectangle.	TControl
SetTextBuf	Set the text of the control to the text in a buffer.	TControl
Show	Make the control visible.	TControl
ShowHint	Determine whether to show a tooltip.	TControl
Spacing	Determine how the caption and glyph appear on the button.	None
Tag	Store an additional integer value with the component.	TComponent
Text	Access the changeable text on the control.	TControl
Top	Determine the upper edge of the control.	TControl
Update	Update is called automatically by Refresh.	TControl
Visible	Determine whether the button is visible.	TControl
Visible	Determine whether the control is visible.	TControl
Width	Determine the width of the control.	TControl

AllowAllUp PROPERTY

Objects Affected   TSpeedButton

Purpose   AllowAllUp determines whether grouped speedbuttons can be unselected at the same time.

Declaration

```
property AllowAllUp: Boolean;
```

Example Syntax

```
procedure TForm1.FormCreate(Sender: TObject);
begin
  sbBold.GroupIndex := 13;
  sbItalic.GroupIndex := 14;
  sbUnderline.GroupIndex := 15;

  sbBold.AllowAllUp := True;
  sbItalic.AllowAllUp := True;
  sbUnderline.AllowAllUp := True;

  // . . .
end;
```

Description

To group speedbuttons, set their `GroupIndex` property to a non-zero value. If the `AllowAllUp` property is set to `True`, all the buttons in that group can be unselected at the same time. An unselected speedbutton is in the *up state*, that is, it appears as if it is not pressed down. If `AllowAllUp` is `False`, one of the buttons in the group must always be selected, and it can only be unselected by clicking on one of the other buttons in the group. The speedbutton currently selected will have a `True` value in its `Down` property. If you change the `AllowAllUp` property of any button in a group, the property automatically changes for all other buttons within the group.

You can also use a single button in its own group to mimic a check box by setting its `AllowAllUp` property to `True`. To do this, set its `GroupIndex` property to a unique value. The button will stay down when clicked and return to the up state when clicked again. The Bold, Italic, and Underline buttons in the toolbar of Microsoft Word exhibit this behavior. The example code above shows how to implement it in your own programs.

The default value for `AllowAllUp` is `False`.

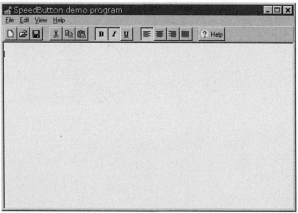

Figure 45-4   The Bold, Italic, and Underline buttons work independently of each other

Down PROPERTY

Objects Affected	TSpeedButton
Purpose	The Down property determines whether the speedbutton is selected.
Declaration	

```
property Down: Boolean;
```

Example Syntax

```
procedure TForm1.FormCreate(Sender: TObject);
begin
  // . . .

  // Put the text alignment buttons in the same group
  sbAlignLeft.GroupIndex := 1;
  sbCenter.GroupIndex := 1;
  sbAlignRight.GroupIndex := 1;
  sbJustify.GroupIndex := 1;

  // Use left align by default
  sbAlignLeft.Down := True;
end;
```

Description Speedbuttons are selected when clicked (in the down state, or position) and unselected when not, that is, when they are in the up state. The Down property determines whether the speedbutton is selected and returns True if it is, False if not. Down can be used to display a speedbutton in the selected state when it first appears. If you have grouped speedbuttons with GroupIndex, you may want one of them to be selected initially.

Glyph PROPERTY

Objects Affected	TSpeedButton
Purpose	The Glyph property specifies the bitmap graphic that will appear on the speedbutton.
Declaration	

```
property Glyph: TBitmap;
```

Example Syntax

```
procedure TForm1.FormCreate(Sender: TObject);
begin
  // . . .
```

```
sbAlignLeft.Glyph.LoadFromFile('alignleft.bmp');
sbCenter.Glyph.LoadFromFile('center.bmp');
sbAlignRight.Glyph.LoadFromFile('alignright.bmp');
sbJustify.Glyph.LoadFromFile('justify.bmp');

// . . .
end;
```

Description   While you can certainly load bitmaps from a disk at run time as in the example above, it is easiest to specify the glyph at design time. The bitmap image you use as a speedbutton glyph can have up to four images. Each image will display at a specific time, based on the state of the speed-button:

Image Position	Button State
1	Up—the image displayed when the button is in its normal position.
2	Disabled—the image displayed when the button is not currently enabled.
3	Clicked—the image displayed when the button is being clicked by the mouse pointer.
4	Down—the image displayed when the button remains selected and stays down.

If you do not supply more than a single image, Delphi uses the image as the up state image and will attempt to represent the other states by altering that image somewhat for each. The images that Borland includes in the `Delphi 2.0/Images/Buttons` directory have two images each, an **Up** image and a **Disabled** image. Use the `NumGlyphs` property to specify the number of glyphs in the bitmap used for the glyph.

GroupIndex PROPERTY

Objects Affected   TSpeedButton

Purpose   The `GroupIndex` property specifies the group of which the speedbutton is a member.

Declaration

```
property GroupIndex: Integer;
```

Example Syntax

```
procedure TForm1.FormCreate(Sender: TObject);
begin
  // . . .
```

```
// Group the text alignment buttons together
sbAlignLeft.GroupIndex := 1;
sbCenter.GroupIndex := 1;
sbAlignRight.GroupIndex := 1;
sbJustify.GroupIndex := 1;

// . . .
end;
```

Description By default, a speedbutton is not grouped and its `GroupIndex` property is set to zero. By specifying a `GroupIndex` value for a speedbutton, you are including it in a group of one or more speedbuttons. Speedbuttons are grouped so they can automatically work together—if one speedbutton in a group is selected, the others are automatically unselected. This saves you the labor of manually implementing this mutually exclusive behavior yourself.

Layout PROPERTY

Objects Affected `TSpeedButton`

Purpose The `Layout` property determines where the speedbutton's glyph appears within the button.

Declaration

```
property Layout: TButtonLayout;
```

Example Syntax

```
sbJustify.Glyph.LoadFromFile('justify.bmp');
sbJustify.Layout := blGlyphRight;
```

Description `Layout` is of the type `TButtonLayout`, which can be set to one of the following possible values:

Use This Value...	To Place the Glyph...
`blGlyphBottom`	At the bottom of the speedbutton.
`blGlyphLeft`	At the left side of the speedbutton.
`blGlyphRight`	At the right side of the speedbutton.
`blGlyphTop`	At the top of the speedbutton.

The default value is `blGlyphLeft`.

`Margin` PROPERTY

Objects Affected	`TSpeedButton`
Purpose	The `Margin` property determines the gap between the speedbutton's glyph and the edge of the button.
Declaration	

```
property Margin: Integer;
```

Example Syntax

```
sbHelp.Margin := 1;
```

Description	The `Margin` property is a pixel measurement of the space between the glyph and the edge of the button. The default value is **–1**, which centers the glyph and the text caption on the face of the speedbutton.

`NumGlyphs` PROPERTY

Objects Affected	`TSpeedButton`
Purpose	The `NumGlyphs` property specifies the number of images in the bitmap specified by the `Glyph` property.
Declaration	

```
property NumGlyphs: TNumGlyphs;
```

Example Syntax

```
procedure TForm1.FormCreate(Sender: TObject);
begin
  // . . .

  sbHelp.Glyph.LoadFromFile('f:\Delphi 2.0\Images\Buttons\help.bmp');
  sbHelp.NumGlyphs := 2;

  // . . .
end;
```

Description	If you are using a bitmap with multiple glyph images, you must specify this in the `NumGlyphs` property. The maximum number of images is four. The images must all be the same width and height, as well as next to each other horizontally in the bitmap. Refer to the `Glyph` property for information about how Delphi uses each image in the bitmap.
	The default value for `NumGlyphs` is **1**.

Spacing PROPERTY

Objects Affected   TSpeedButton

Purpose   The **Spacing** property determines where the glyph and caption appear on the face of the speedbutton.

Declaration

```
property Spacing: Integer;
```

Example Syntax

```
procedure TForm1.FormCreate(Sender: TObject);
begin
  // . . .

  sbHelp.Glyph.LoadFromFile('f:\Delphi 2.0\Images\Buttons\help.bmp');
  sbHelp.NumGlyphs := 2;
  sbHelp.Caption := 'Help';
  sbHelp.Spacing := -1;
end;
```

Description   If **Spacing** is a positive value, it specifies the number of pixels between the glyph and the caption. The default value for **Spacing** is **4** pixels. If **Spacing** is **0**, there is no space between them. If **Spacing** is **-1**, the caption is centered between the glyph and the right edge of the button.

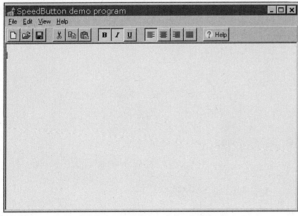

Figure 45-5   A speedbutton with a caption

46

TSplitter

The splitter control became a standard feature of the operating system with the introduction of Windows 95. It acts to divide the client area of its container (typically a form or panel) into resizable sections called *panes*. The most famous example of this is the Windows Explorer, which uses a splitter control, as shown in Figure 46-1, to separate the All Folders tree view and the Contents list view. Note that `TSplitter`, which encapsulates the splitter control, is only available in Delphi 3.

Figure 46-2 shows the derivation of `TSplitter`. Table 46-1 displays the properties and methods implemented by `TSplitter`.

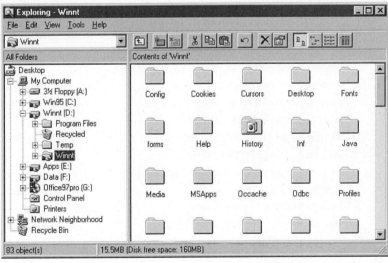

Figure 46-1   Windows Explorer uses a splitter control

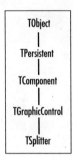

Figure 46-2 Derivation of `TSplitter`

TObject
|
TPersistent
|
TComponent
|
TGraphicControl
|
TSplitter

Table 46-1 Properties and methods implemented by `TSplitter`

Use or Set This...	To Do This...	Inheritance
Align	Determine how the control is aligned within its parent.	TControl
Assign	Assign one persistent object to another.	TPersistent
BeginDrag	Begin a manual drag operation.	TControl
Beveled	Determines whether the splitter displays with beveled edges.	None
BoundsRect	Determine the boundary rectangle occupied by the control.	TControl
BringToFront	Bring the control to the front of the z-order.	TControl
Canvas	Access the graphic control's drawing surface.	TGraphicControl
Caption	Label the control with a text string.	TControl
ClassName	Get the name of the object's class.	TObject
ClassParent	Get the object's parent class.	TObject
ClassType	Get the object's actual type.	TObject
ClientHeight	Determine the control's client height.	TControl
ClientOrigin	Determine the upper-left position of the control's client area.	TControl
ClientRect	Determine the rectangle occupied by the control's client area.	TControl
ClientToScreen	Convert control (local) coordinates to screen coordinates.	TControl
ClientWidth	Determine the width of the control's client area.	TControl
Color	Determine the background color of the control.	TControl
ComponentCount	Determine the number of owned components.	TComponent
ComponentIndex	The index of the component in its owner's `Components` list.	TComponent
Components	Determine the list of owned components.	TComponent
ComponentState	Determine the state of the current component.	TComponent
ControlState	Determine the state of the control at any given time.	TControl
ControlStyle	Determine what attributes are present in the control.	TControl
Create	Create a new component.	TObject
Cursor	Determine what image is used for the cursor over the control.	TControl
Destroy	Destroy the component.	TObject
DestroyComponents	Destroy all the components owned by the component.	TComponent
Destroying	Notify the component that it is being destroyed.	TComponent

Use or Set This...	To Do This...	Inheritance
DragCursor	Determine the shape of the mouse cursor as it drags an object over the control.	TControl
Dragging	Determine whether the control is being dragged.	TControl
DragMode	Determine the drag-and-drop behavior of the control.	TControl
Enabled	Determine whether the control is enabled.	TControl
EndDrag	End or cancel a manual drag operation.	TControl
FindComponent	Find a component in the Components array list.	TComponent
Font	Determine the font used to render text on the control.	TControl
Free	Safely destroy the object.	TObject
GetTextBuf	Copy the text of the control into a buffer.	TControl
GetTextLen	Get the length of the text of the control.	TControl
Height	Determine the height of the control.	TControl
Hide	Make the control invisible.	TControl
Hint	Determine the text that displays in a tooltip for the control.	TControl
InheritsFrom	Determine if the object is descended from a certain class.	TObject
InstanceSize	Determine the amount of memory allocated for the object.	TObject
Invalidate	Force the control to be repainted as soon as possible.	TControl
Left	Determine the left edge of the control within its container.	TControl
MinSize	Specify the minimum distance between the splitter and the container edge to which it is aligned.	None
Name	Determine the name of the component.	TComponent
OnClick	Handle the event that occurs when a mouse button is clicked.	TControl
OnDblClick	Handle the event that occurs when a mouse button is double-clicked.	TControl
OnDragDrop	Handle the event that occurs when an object is dropped on the control.	TControl
OnDragOver	Handle the event that occurs when an object is dragged over the control.	TControl
OnEndDrag	Handle the event that occurs when a drag-and-drop operation is cancelled.	TControl
OnMouseDown	Handle the event that occurs when a mouse button is held down and not immediately released.	TControl
OnMouseMove	Handle the event that occurs when the cursor moves over the control.	TControl
OnMouseUp	Handle the event that occurs when a mouse button is released.	TControl
OnMoved	Handle the event that occurs when the user is done dragging the splitter.	None
OnStartDrag	Handle the event that occurs when a drag-and-drop operation is started.	TControl
Owner	Determine the owner of the component.	TComponent
Paint	Render the image of a graphic control.	TGraphicControl
Parent	Determine the parent, or container, of the control.	TControl
ParentColor	Determine whether the Color information of the the control's parent is used.	TControl
ParentFont	Determine whether the Font information of the the control's parent is used.	TControl
ParentShowHint	Determine whether the ShowHint information of the the control's parent is used.	TControl
PopupMenu	Determine which pop-up menu is associated with the control.	TControl

continued on next page

continued from previous page

Use or Set This...	To Do This...	Inheritance
Refresh	Erase the control and repaint it.	TControl
Repaint	Repaint the control.	TControl
ScreenToClient	Convert screen coordinates to client (control) coordinates.	TControl
SendToBack	Send the control to the end of the z-order.	TControl
SetBounds	Determine the coordinates of the control's bounding rectangle.	TControl
SetTextBuf	Set the text of the control to the text in a buffer.	TControl
Show	Make the control visible.	TControl
ShowHint	Enable tooltips for the control.	TControl
Tag	Store an additional integer value with the component.	TComponent
Text	Access the changeable text on the control.	TControl
Top	Determine the upper edge of the control.	TControl
Update	Update is called automatically by Refresh.	TControl
Visible	Determine whether the control is visible.	TControl
Width	Determine the width of the control.	TControl

Beveled PROPERTY

Objects Affected	TSplitter
Purpose	The Beveled property determines whether the splitter displays with beveled edges.
Declaration	

```
property Beveled: Boolean;
```

Example Syntax	

```
Splitter1.Beveled := False;
```

Description	If Beveled is True, the splitter displays with beveled edges. Otherwise, it is flat. The default value is True.

MinSize PROPERTY

Objects Affected	TSplitter
Purpose	The MinSize property specifies the minimum distance between the splitter and the container edge to which it is aligned.
Declaration	

```
property MinSize: NaturalNumber;
```

Example Syntax

```
Splitter1.MinSize := 150;
```

Description

Normally, a splitter is aligned to an edge of its container. In the case of an Explorer-like application, for example, the splitter is aligned to the left edge of the window, but a tree view control resides between it and the edge. Here, the `MinSize` value would determine the minimum width of the tree view control because it is sandwiched between the left edge of the window and the splitter.

`MinSize` is measured in pixels, and the default value is **30**.

OnMoved EVENT

Objects Affected   `TSplitter`

Purpose   The `OnMoved` event occurs when the user is done dragging the splitter.

Declaration

```
property OnMoved: TnotifyEvent;
```

Example Syntax

```
procedure TForm1.Splitter1Moved(Sender: TObject);
begin
  HeaderControl2.Sections[0].Width := Panel1.Width;
  HeaderControl1.Sections[0].Width := Panel2.Width;
end;
```

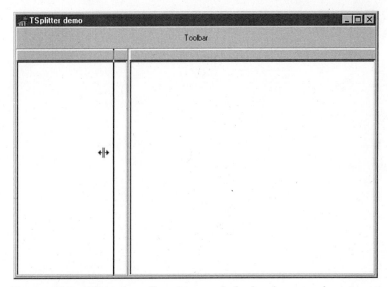

Figure 46-3   When the splitter is moved, the header controls resize accordingly

Description   You should handle the OnMoved event when you need code to execute
every time the splitter's position changes.

PART VI

Windowed Controls

47

TWinControl

TWinControl is the abstract base class for all *windowed controls*, those controls that can obtain the focus and have a window handle. Windowed controls are essentially windows designed for specific tasks, like command buttons, edit boxes, and scroll bars. **TWinControl** represents the final, and largest, branch of the VCL tree—most of the controls Delphi programmers are familiar with belong to its descendant branches.

Windowed Controls

Windowed controls have three primary attributes distinguishing them from nonwindowed controls. They can receive the *input focus*, meaning they are in the *tab order* of controls on the form surface. Nonwindowed controls cannot receive the input focus. Windowed controls are capable of containing other controls, that is, they can be the *parents* of other controls. Although this feature is not always exploited, it is critical to the organization of complex Windows programs. Finally, windowed controls have a Windows handle. A *handle* is essential a reference number identifying a resource in Windows (and can be used like a pointer in Windows 3.x). Handles are most often used in Win32 API calls and are occasionally needed by ordinary Delphi programmers.

Figure 47-1 gives the ancestry of **TWinControl**. Table 47-1 displays the properties, methods, and events implemented by **TWinControl**.

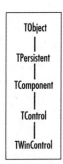

Figure 47-1   Ancestry of
TWinControl

TObject
|
TPersistent
|
TComponent
|
TControl
|
TWinControl

Table 47-1 Properties, methods, and events implemented by `TWinControl`

Use or Set This...	To Do This...	Inheritance
Align	Determine how the control is aligned within its parent.	TControl
Assign	Assign one persistent object to another.	TPersistent
BeginDrag	Begin a manual drag operation.	TControl
BoundsRect	Determine the boundary rectangle occupied by the control.	TControl
BringToFront	Bring the control to the front of the z-order.	TControl
Brush	Determine the color and pattern used for the windowed control background.	TComponent
CanFocus	Determine whether the windowed control can receive the focus.	None
Caption	Label the control with a text string.	TControl
ClassName	Get the name of the object's class.	TObject
ClassParent	Get the object's parent class.	TObject
ClassType	Get the object's actual type.	TObject
ClientHeight	Determine the control's client height.	TControl
ClientOrigin	Determine the upper-left position of the control's client area.	TControl
ClientRect	Determine the rectangle occupied by the control's client area.	TControl
ClientToScreen	Convert control (local) coordinates to screen coordinates.	TControl
ClientWidth	Determine the width of the control's client area.	TControl
ComponentCount	Determine the number of owned components.	TComponent
ComponentIndex	The index of the component in its owner's Components list.	TComponent
Components	Determine the list of owned components.	TComponent
ComponentState	Determine the state of the current component.	TComponent
ContainsControl	Determine whether the specified control is contained by the windowed control.	None
ControlAtPos	The control contained at a specified position.	None
ControlCount	Determine the number of controls contained by the windowed control.	None
Controls	Access the controls contained by the windowed control using their positions in an array.	None
ControlState	Determine the state of the control at any given time.	TControl
ControlStyle	Determine what attributes are present in the control.	TControl
Create	Create a new component.	TObject
Ctl3D	Determine whether the windowed control displays in 3D.	None
Cursor	Determine what image is used for the cursor over the control.	TControl
Destroy	Destroy the component.	TObject
DestroyComponents	Destroy all of the components owned by the component.	TComponent
Destroying	Notify the component that it is being destroyed.	TComponent
DragCursor	Determine the shape of the mouse cursor as it drags an object over the control.	TControl
Dragging	Determine whether the control is being dragged.	TControl
DragMode	Determine the drag-and-drop behavior of the control.	TControl
Enabled	Determine whether the control is enabled.	TControl
EndDrag	End or cancel a manual drag operation.	TControl

Use or Set This...	To Do This...	Inheritance
FindComponent	Find a component in the Components array list.	TComponent
Focused	Determine whether the windowed control has the focus.	TControl
Font	Determine the font used to render text on the control.	TControl
Free	Safely destroy the object.	TObject
GetTextBuf	Copy the text of the control into a buffer.	TControl
GetTextLen	Get the length of the text of the control.	TControl
Handle	Obtain a handle to the windowed control.	TComponent
HandleAllocated	Determine if a handle is allocated for the windowed control.	None
Height	Determine the height of the control.	TControl
HelpContext	Determine the help context ID of the windowed control.	TComponent
Hide	Make the control invisible.	TControl
Hint	Determine the text that displays in a tooltip for the control.	TControl
InheritsFrom	Determine if the object is descended from a certain class.	TObject
InsertControl	Insert a control into the windowed control's Controls array.	None
InstanceSize	Determine the amount of memory allocated for the object.	TObject
Invalidate	Force the control to be repainted as soon as possible.	TControl
Left	Determine the left edge of the control within its container.	TControl
Name	Determine the name of the component.	TComponent
OnClick	Handle the event that occurs when a mouse button is clicked.	TControl
OnDblClick	Handle the event that occurs when a mouse button is double-clicked.	TControl
OnDragDrop	Handle the event that occurs when an object is dropped on the control.	TControl
OnDragOver	Handle the event that occurs when an object is dragged over the control.	TControl
OnEndDrag	Handle the event that occurs when a drag-and-drop operation is cancelled.	TControl
OnEnter	Handle the event that occurs when the windowed control receives the focus.	None
OnExit	Handle the event that occurs when the windowed control loses the focus.	None
OnKeyDown	Handle the event that occurs when a key is pressed down and not immediately released while the windowed control has the focus.	None
OnKeyPress	Handle the event that occurs when a key is pressed while the windowed control has the focus.	None
OnKeyUp	Handle the event that occurs when a key is released while the windowed control has the focus.	None
OnMouseDown	Handle the event that occurs when a mouse button is held down and not immediately released.	TControl
OnMouseMove	Handle the event that occurs when the cursor moves over the control.	TControl
OnMouseUp	Handle the event that occurs when a mouse button is released.	TControl
OnStartDrag	Handle the event that occurs when a drag-and-drop operation is started.	TControl
Owner	Determine the owner of the component.	TComponent
Parent	Determine the parent, or container, of the control.	TControl

continued on next page

continued from previous page

Use or Set This...	To Do This...	Inheritance
ParentColor	Determine whether the Color information of the control's parent is used.	TControl
ParentCtl3D	Determine whether the windowed control uses its parent's Ctl3D settings.	None
ParentFont	Determine whether the control's parent's Font information is used.	TControl
ParentShowHint	Determine whether the control's parent's ShowHint information is used.	TControl
PopupMenu	Determine which pop-up menu is associated with the control.	TControl
Refresh	Erase the control and repaint it.	TControl
RemoveControl	Remove the specified control from the windowed control's Controls array.	None
Repaint	Repaint the control.	TControl
ScaleBy	Resize the windowed control.	None
ScreenToClient	Convert screen coordinates to client (control) coordinates.	TControl
SendToBack	Send the control to the end of the z-order.	TControl
SetBounds	Determine the coordinates of the control's bounding rectangle.	TControl
SetFocus	Set the focus to the windowed control.	None
SetTextBuf	Set the text of the control to the text in a buffer.	TControl
Show	Make the control visible.	TControl
ShowHint	Enable tooltips for the control.	TControl
Showing	Determine whether the windowed control is currently showing onscreen.	TComponent
TabOrder	Determine the tab order of the windowed control.	None
TabStop	Determine whether the windowed control is in the tab order.	None
Tag	Store an additional integer value with the component.	TComponent
Text	Access the changeable text on the control.	TControl
Top	Determine the upper edge of the control.	TControl
Update	Called automatically by Refresh.	TControl
Visible	Make the control visible.	TControl
Width	Determine the width of the control.	TControl

ContainsControl METHOD

Objects Affected All windowed controls

Purpose The ContainsControl method indicates whether the specified control is contained within the windowed control. See Figure 47-2.

Declaration

```
function ContainsControl(Control: TControl): Boolean;
```

Parameters

Control The control that may or may not be contained by the windowed control.

Example Syntax

```
type
  TForm1 = class(TForm)
    Panel1: TPanel;
    Button1: TButton;
    Button2: TButton;
    Label1: TLabel;
    procedure Button1Click(Sender: TObject);
    procedure Button2Click(Sender: TObject);
    // added by hand
    procedure Contained(Sender: TButton);
  end;

var
  Form1: TForm1;

implementation

{$R *.DFM}

procedure TForm1.Contained(Sender: TButton);
begin
  if Panel1.ContainsControl(Sender) = True then
    Label1.Caption := 'the button is contained by the panel'
  else Label1.Caption := 'the button is not contained by the panel';
end;

procedure TForm1.Button1Click(Sender: TObject);
begin
  Contained(Button1);
end;

procedure TForm1.Button2Click(Sender: TObject);
begin
  Contained(Button2);
end;
```

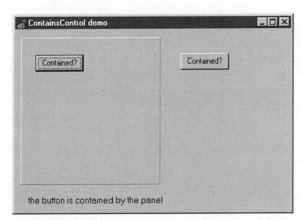

Figure 47-2   Test to see if the button is contained by the panel

Description   If `ContainsControl` returns `True`, the control specified by the *Control* parameter is contained within the windowed control. If `ContainsControl` returns `False`, it is not contained by the windowed control.

ControlAtPos METHOD

Objects Affected   All windowed controls

Purpose   `ControlAtPos` returns the child control found at the specified position of the windowed control.

Declaration

```
function ControlAtPos(const Pos: TPoint;

                      AllowDisabled: Boolean):TControl;
```

Parameters

Pos   The location you are testing within the windowed control.

AllowDisabled   Determines whether disabled controls are included in the search.

Example Syntax

```
procedure TForm1.FormMouseMove(Sender: TObject; Shift: TShiftState;

                               X, Y: Integer);
begin
  if ControlAtPos(Point(X,Y), False) = Image1 then
    Label1.Caption := 'Image1 is under the mouse'
  else Label1.Caption := '';
end;
```

Description   `ControlAtPos` determines whether a control exists at the position specified by the `Pos` parameter. If a control is found there, the name of the control is returned. If a control is not found, `Nil` is returned. If `AllowDisabled` is `True`, a disabled control can be returned; otherwise a disabled control found there will return `Nil`.

ControlCount PROPERTY

Objects Affected   All windowed controls

Purpose   `ControlCount` contains the number of controls in the windowed control.

Declaration

```
property ControlCount: Integer;
```

Example Syntax

```
procedure TForm1.FormCreate(Sender: TObject);
begin
  Label1.Caption := 'The form contains ' + IntToStr(Form1.ControlCount)
                    + ' controls';
```

```
      Label2.Caption := 'The panel contains ' + IntToStr(Panel1.ControlCount)
                        + ' controls';
    end;
```

Description   `ControlCount` is a run-time, read-only property containing the number of controls in the windowed control. To access the individual contained controls, use the `Controls` property shown in Figure 47-3.

Controls METHOD

Objects Affected   All windowed controls

Purpose   `Controls` is an array of the controls contained by the windowed control.

Declaration

```
property Controls[Index: Integer];
```

Example Syntax

```
procedure TForm1.FormCreate(Sender: TObject);
var x: Integer;
begin
  cbUseAdvancedOptions.Checked := False;
  for x := 0 to GroupBox1.ControlCount - 1 do
    GroupBox1.Controls[x].Enabled := False;
end;

procedure TForm1.cbUseAdvancedOptionsClick(Sender: TObject);
var x: Integer;
begin
  if cbUseAdvancedOptions.Checked = True then
    for x := 0 to GroupBox1.ControlCount - 1 do
      GroupBox1.Controls[x].Enabled := True
  else for x := 0 to GroupBox1.ControlCount - 1 do
      GroupBox1.Controls[x].Enabled := False;
end;
```

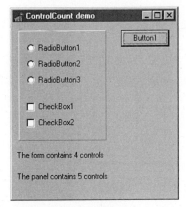

Figure 47-3   Using `ControlCountControls` Property

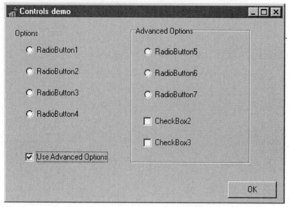

Figure 47-4 Using the `Controls` array to disable and enable child controls

Description   `Controls` can be used when it is convenient to refer to a windowed control's children by their numerical position in an array, rather than by name. In Figure 47-4, all the controls on a group box are disabled if the proper option is chosen. `Controls` is a zero-based array, so the first element is `Controls[0]`, the second is `Controls[1]`, and so on.

Ctl3D PROPERTY

Objects Affected   All windowed controls

Purpose   The `Ctl3D` property determines whether the windowed control displays in a 3D style.

Declaration

```
property Ctl3D: Boolean;
```

Example Syntax

```
procedure TForm1.FormCreate(Sender: TObject);
begin
  Form1.Ctl3D := True;
  Panel1.ParentCtl3D := True;


  // . . .

end;
```

Description   If the `Ctl3D` property is `True`, the windowed control displays with a 3D look. If it is `False`, it displays in a flat, 2D look. The default value is `True`.

HandleAllocated METHOD

Objects Affected	All windowed controls
Purpose	HandleAllocated determines whether a handle to the windowed control exists.
Declaration	

```
function HandleAllocated: Boolean;
```

Example Syntax

```
procedure TForm1.Button1Click(Sender: TObject);
begin
  if Form1.HandleAllocated = True then
    Label1.Caption := 'there is a handle allocated for the form'
  else Label1.Caption := 'there is no handle allocated for the form';
end;
```

Description   If HandleAllocated returns True, a handle has been allocated to the windowed control. If it is False, no handle has been allocated. If you use the Handle property of a windowed control directly, a handle is automatically allocated. So HandleAllocated can be used when you want to determine if there is a handle without actually creating one.

InsertControl METHOD

Objects Affected	All windowed controls
Purpose	InsertControl makes the specified control a child of the windowed control.
Declaration	

```
procedure InsertControl(AControl: TControl);
```

Parameters

AControl   The control that will become a child of the windowed control.

Example Syntax

```
// Create a new radio button and add it to the group box
procedure TForm1.btnInsertClick(Sender: TObject);
begin
  RadioButton4 := TRadioButton.Create(Self);
  RadioButton4.Caption := 'RadioButton4';
  GroupBox1.InsertControl(RadioButton4);
  RadioButton4.Enabled := True;
  RadioButton4.Left := 28;
  RadioButton4.Top := 122;
end;
```

Description   InsertControl inserts the control specified by the *AControl* parameter into the Controls array of the windowed control, making it a child of the windowed control.

OnEnter EVENT

Objects Affected   All windowed controls

Purpose   The OnEnter event occurs when the windowed control receives the focus.

Declaration

```
property OnEnter: TNotifyEvent;
```

Example Syntax

```
type
  TForm1 = class(TForm)
    Button1: TButton;
    Button2: TButton;
    GroupBox1: TGroupBox;
    Label1: TLabel;
    Label2: TLabel;
    Label3: TLabel;
    Label4: TLabel;
    Label5: TLabel;
    procedure FormCreate(Sender: TObject);
    procedure MyEnterHandler(Sender: TObject);
  private
    { Private declarations }
  public
    { Public declarations }
  end;

var
  Form1: TForm1;

implementation

{$R *.DFM}

procedure TForm1.FormCreate(Sender: TObject);
begin
  Button1.OnEnter := MyEnterHandler;
  Button2.OnEnter := MyEnterHandler;
end;

procedure TForm1.MyEnterHandler(Sender: TObject);
begin
  Label1.Caption := TButton(Sender).Name +
                       ' received the focus';
end;
```

Description   You can handle the OnEnter event to perform certain processing when the windowed control receives the focus.

Although the sample code above sets the handler for this event to a procedure at run time, you can typically do this by selecting the OnEnter event for a windowed control in the Object Inspector at design time.

OnExit EVENT

Objects Affected   All windowed controls

Purpose   The OnExit event occurs when the windowed control loses the focus.

Declaration

```
property OnExit: TNotifyEvent;
```

Example Syntax

```
type
  TForm1 = class(TForm)
    Button1: TButton;
    Button2: TButton;
    GroupBox1: TGroupBox;
    Label1: TLabel;
    Label2: TLabel;
    Label3: TLabel;
    Label4: TLabel;
    Label5: TLabel;
    procedure FormCreate(Sender: TObject);
    procedure MyExitHandler(Sender: TObject);
  private
    { Private declarations }
  public
    { Public declarations }
  end;

var
  Form1: TForm1;

implementation

{$R *.DFM}

procedure TForm1.FormCreate(Sender: TObject);
begin
  Button1.OnExit := MyExitHandler;
  Button2.OnExit := MyExitHandler;
end;

procedure TForm1.MyExitHandler(Sender: TObject);
begin
  Label2.Caption := TButton(Sender).Name +
                    ' lost the focus';
end;
```

Description   You can handle the OnExit event to perform certain processing when the windowed control loses the focus.

Although the sample code above sets the handler for this event to a procedure at run time, you can typically do this by selecting the OnExit event for a windowed control in the Object Inspector at design time.

OnKeyDown EVENT

Objects Affected   All windowed controls

Purpose   The OnKeyDown event occurs when any key is pressed down while the windowed control has the focus.

Declaration

```
property OnKeyDown: TKeyEvent;
```

Example Syntax

```
type
  TForm1 = class(TForm)
    Button1: TButton;
    Button2: TButton;
    GroupBox1: TGroupBox;
    Label1: TLabel;
    Label2: TLabel;
    Label3: TLabel;
    Label4: TLabel;
    Label5: TLabel;
    procedure FormCreate(Sender: TObject);
    procedure MyKeyDownHandler(Sender: TObject; var Key: Word;
      Shift: TShiftState);
  private
    { Private declarations }
  public
    { Public declarations }
  end;

var
  Form1: TForm1;

implementation

{$R *.DFM}

procedure TForm1.FormCreate(Sender: TObject);
begin
  Button1.OnKeyDown := MyKeyDownHandler;
  Button2.OnKeyDown := MyKeyDownHandler;
end;

procedure TForm1.MyKeyDownHandler(Sender: TObject; var Key: Word; Shift:
TShiftState);
begin
  Label3.Caption := Chr(Key) + ' key down at'  + TButton(Sender).Name;
end;
```

Description

The OnKeyDown event occurs whenever a key is pressed while the windowed control is focused. OnKeyDown responds to all keys, including (SHIFT), (ALT), and (CTRL). It also handles combination key presses, such as (CTRL)-(A). The *Key* parameter specifies which key was pressed. Use the Chr function to convert it to a character, as in the above example. The *Shift* parameter indicates which modifier keys or mouse buttons are held down when the event occurs. *Shift* is type TShiftState, which can assume any combination of these possible values: ssAlt, ssCtrl, ssDouble, (both mouse buttons), ssLeft (left mouse button), ssMiddle (middle mouse button), or ssShift.

Although the sample code above sets the handler for this event to a procedure at run time, you can typically do this by selecting the OnKeyDown event for a windowed control in the Object Inspector at design time.

OnKeyPress EVENT

Objects Affected All windowed controls

Purpose The OnKeyPress event occurs when a key is pressed while the windowed control has the focus.

Declaration

```
property OnKeyPress: TKeyPressEvent;
```

Example Syntax

```
type
  TForm1 = class(TForm)
    Button1: TButton;
    Button2: TButton;
    GroupBox1: TGroupBox;
    Label1: TLabel;
    Label2: TLabel;
    Label3: TLabel;
    Label4: TLabel;
    Label5: TLabel;
    procedure FormCreate(Sender: TObject);
    procedure MyKeyPressHandler(Sender: TObject; var Key: Char);
  private
    { Private declarations }
  public
    { Public declarations }
  end;

var
  Form1: TForm1;

implementation
```

```
{$R *.DFM}

procedure TForm1.FormCreate(Sender: TObject);
begin
  Button1.OnKeyPress := MyKeyPressHandler;
  Button2.OnKeyPress := MyKeyPressHandler;
end;

procedure TForm1.MyKeyPressHandler(Sender: TObject; var Key: Char);
begin
  Label4.Caption := 'Key press at'  + TButton(Sender).Name;
end;
```

Description

OnKeyPress occurs when a single key is pressed. Unlike OnKeyDown or OnKeyUp, OnKeyPress will not indicate which modifier keys or mouse buttons were simultaneously pressed when the event occurs. The *Key* parameter indicates which key was pressed.

Although the sample code above sets the handler for this event to a procedure at run time, you can typically do this by selecting the OnKeyPress event for a windowed control in the Object Inspector at design time.

OnKeyUp EVENT

Objects Affected   All windowed controls

Purpose   The OnKeyUp event occurs when a key is released while the windowed control has the focus.

Declaration

```
property OnKeyUp: TKeyEvent;
```

Example Syntax

```
type
  TForm1 = class(TForm)
    Button1: TButton;
    Button2: TButton;
    GroupBox1: TGroupBox;
    Label1: TLabel;
    Label2: TLabel;
    Label3: TLabel;
    Label4: TLabel;
    Label5: TLabel;
    procedure FormCreate(Sender: TObject);
    procedure MyKeyUpHandler(Sender: TObject; var Key: Word;
      Shift: TShiftState);
  private
    { Private declarations }
  public
    { Public declarations }
  end;

var
  Form1: TForm1;
```

```
implementation

{$R *.DFM}

procedure TForm1.FormCreate(Sender: TObject);
begin
  Button1.OnKeyUp := MyKeyUpHandler;
  Button2.OnKeyUp := MyKeyUpHandler;
end;

procedure TForm1.MyKeyUpHandler(Sender: TObject; var Key: Word; Shift:
TShiftState);
begin
  Label5.Caption := 'Key up at'  + TButton(Sender).Name;
end;
```

Description

The **OnKeyUp** event occurs whenever a key is pressed while the windowed control is focused. **OnKeyUp** responds to all keys, including SHIFT, ALT, and CTRL. It also handles combination key presses, such as CTRL-X. The *Key* parameter specifies which key was pressed. Use the **Chr** function to convert it to a character, as in the above example. The *Shift* parameter indicates which modifier keys or mouse buttons are held down when the event occurs. *Shift* is type **TShiftState**, which can assume any combination of these possible values: **ssAlt**, **ssCtrl**, **ssDouble** (both mouse buttons), **ssLeft** (left mouse button), **ssMiddle** (middle mouse button), or **ssShift**.

Although the sample code above sets the handler for this event to a procedure at run time, you can typically do this by selecting the **OnKeyUp** event for a windowed control in the Object Inspector at design time.

ParentCtl3D PROPERTY

Objects Affected   All windowed controls

Purpose   The **ParentCtl3D** property determines whether the windowed control uses its parent's **Ctl3D** property.

Declaration

```
property ParentCtl3D: Boolean;
```

Example Syntax

```
procedure TForm1.FormCreate(Sender: TObject);
begin
  Form1.Ctl3D := True;
  Panel1.ParentCtl3D := True;

  // . . .
end;
```

Description   If **ParentCtl3D** is **True**, the windowed control uses the value in its parent's **Ctl3D** property to determine how to display itself. If **ParentCtl3D** is

False, the windowed control uses its own Ctl3D property for this decision.

RemoveControl Method

Objects Affected	All windowed controls
Purpose	RemoveControl terminates the parent-child relationship between the windowed control and the specified control.
Declaration	

```
procedure RemoveControl(AControl: TControl);
```

Parameters

AControl   The control being removed from the parent-child relationship with the windowed control.

Example Syntax

```
procedure TForm1.btnRemoveClick(Sender: TObject);
begin
  if RadioButton3.Parent = Panel1 then
  begin
    Panel1.RemoveControl(RadioButton3);
    RadioButton3.Parent := Form1;
    RadioButton3.Top := 120;
    RadioButton3.Left := 180;
  end
end;

procedure TForm1.btnParentClick(Sender: TObject);
begin
  Label1.Caption := RadioButton3.Parent.Name;
end;
```

Description   RemoveControl removes the control specified by the *AControl* parameter from the windowed control's Controls array. In effect, this terminates the parent-child relationship the two controls previously held, and the parent of the control becomes undefined. So the control is no longer displayed unless you explicitly reset its Parent property.

ScaleBy Method

Objects Affected	All windowed controls
Purpose	The ScaleBy method scales a control to a percentage of its original size. See Figure 47-5.
Declaration	

```
procedure ScaleBy(M, D: Integer);
```

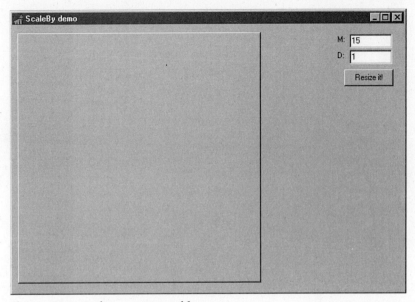

Figure 47-5 Scaling a command button

Parameters

M   The multiplier of the fraction by which the control is scaled.

D   The divisor of the fraction by which the control is scaled.

Example Syntax

```
procedure TForm1.FormCreate(Sender: TObject);
begin
  Edit1.Text := '1';
  Edit2.Text := '1';
end;

procedure TForm1.Button1Click(Sender: TObject);
var
  x, y: Integer;
begin
  X := StrToInt(Edit1.Text);
  Y := StrToInt(Edit2.Text);
  Button2.ScaleBy(X,Y);
end;

procedure TForm1.Edit2KeyPress(Sender: TObject; var Key: Char);
begin
  if Key = #13 then Button1Click(Self);
end;

procedure TForm1.Edit1KeyPress(Sender: TObject; var Key: Char);
begin
  if Key = #13 then Button1Click(Self);
end;
```

continued on next page

continued from previous page

```
procedure TForm1.Button2Click(Sender: TObject);
begin
  Button2.Width := 25;
  Button2.Height := 25;
end;
```

Description   ScaleBy scales the windowed control, using the *M* parameter as the multiplier and the *D* parameter as the divisor in the fraction the control is scaled by. For example, if you set *M* to **50** and *D* to **100**, the control is scaled by 50/100, or to 50 percent of its original size. To scale the control up (making it larger), specify an *M* parameter larger than the *D* parameter.

SetFocus METHOD

Objects Affected   All windowed controls

Purpose   The SetFocus method gives the focus to the windowed control.

Declaration

```
procedure SetFocus; virtual;
```

Example Syntax

```
procedure TForm1.Button2Click(Sender: TObject);
begin
  Edit3.SetFocus;
end;
```

Description   SetFocus sets the focus to the windowed control or, in the case of a form, to the form's active control.

TabOrder PROPERTY

Objects Affected   All windowed controls

Purpose   The TabOrder property determines the windowed control's position in its parent's tab order.

Declaration

```
property TabOrder: TTabOrder;
```

Example Syntax

```
procedure TForm1.FormCreate(Sender: TObject);
begin
  Button1.TabOrder := 0;
  Button2.TabOrder := 1;
end;
```

Description	When controls are placed on a form or other container at design time, the tab order is set so each control is ordered as it is created. When a user runs your program, he or she can press the TAB key to cycle through the different windowed controls present. If you want to explicitly change the tab order of the windowed controls in your program, you can use the TabOrder property. The first control in the tab order has a value of 0, the next has a value of 1, and so on. Changing the tab order for one control will change the tab order of other controls, if necessary, because each control must have a unique TabOrder value.

The control with a TabOrder value of 0 is the active control on the form when the form is created. If the TabStop property is False, the TabOrder property has no meaning.

TabStop PROPERTY

Objects Affected	All windowed controls
Purpose	The TabStop property determines whether the user can tab to the windowed control.
Declaration	

```
property TabStop: Boolean;
```

Example Syntax	

```
// Place five buttons on the form and rename Button5 'btnTabStop'.
// This program will show the effect of setting the TabStop
// property of one of the buttons to False.
procedure TForm1.FormCreate(Sender: TObject);
begin
  // remove btnTabStop from the tab order
  btnTabStop.TabStop := False;
end;

procedure TForm1.btnTabStopClick(Sender: TObject);
begin
  if Button2.TabStop  = True then
  begin
    Button2.TabStop := False;
    Label1.Caption := 'Button2 is not a tab stop'
  end
  else begin
    Button2.TabStop := True;
    Label1.Caption := 'Button2 is a tab stop'
  end
end;
```

Description	If TabStop is True, the windowed control is part of the tab order and the user can press the TAB to focus the control. If TabStop is False, the windowed control is not part of the tab order and cannot be focused with the TAB key.

TDBCtrlGrid

The *database control grid*, an instance of **TDBCtrlGrid**, displays multiple fields within record panels that can be organized as columns and rows. The database control grid is used to view database fields in a more aesthetically pleasing way than a standard database grid (**TDBGrid**). Database control grids can contain data-aware controls such as **TDBText**, **TDBEdit**, **TDBComboBox**, **TDBCheckBox**, **TDBLookupListBox**, and **TDBLookupComboBox** objects. You place these data-aware controls on the active panel of the database grid control, and the organization you create in it is used for each panel in the control.

The easiest way to understand how the database control grid works is to see one in action. Figure 48-1 shows a database control grid with one visible panel.

Figure 48-2 shows the same program with three vertically visible panels. It is possible to specify horizontal orientation as well, using the **Orientation** property. It is also possible to view the panels in a spreadsheet-like fashion with rows and columns. You can specify values for **RowCount** and **ColCount** to determine the layout of your database control grid.

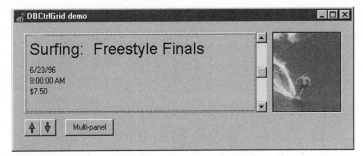

Figure 48-1 A one-panel database control grid

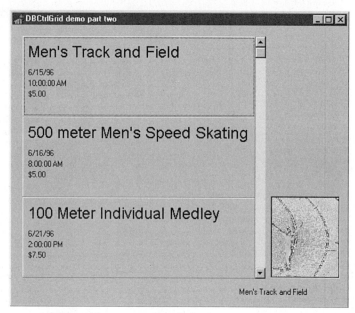

Figure 48-2   The same program with a three-panel database control grid

Figure 48-3 gives the ancestry of **TDBCtrlGrid**. Table 48-1 displays the properties, methods, and events implemented by **TDBCtrlGrid**.

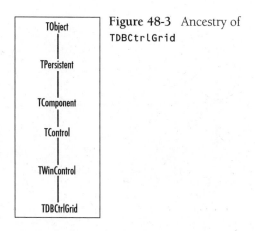

Figure 48-3   Ancestry of **TDBCtrlGrid**

Table 48-1 Properties, methods, and events implemented by `TDBCtrlGrid`

Use or Set This...	To Do This...	Inheritance
Align	Determine how the control is aligned within its parent.	TControl
AllowDelete	Determine whether the user can delete the current record.	
AllowInsert	Determine whether the user can insert and append new records into the database control grid.	
Assign	Assign one persistent object to another.	TPersistent
BeginDrag	Begin a manual drag operation.	TControl
BoundsRect	Determine the boundary rectangle occupied by the control.	TControl
BringToFront	Bring the control to the front of the z-order.	TControl
Brush	Determine the color and pattern used for the windowed control background.	TComponent
CanFocus	Determine whether the windowed control can receive the focus.	TWinControl
Canvas	Access the drawing surface of the database control grid.	TComponent
Caption	Label the control with a text string.	TControl
ClassName	Get the name of the object's class.	TObject
ClassParent	Get the object's parent class.	TObject
ClassType	Get the object's actual type.	TObject
ClientHeight	Determine the control's client height.	TControl
ClientOrigin	Determine the upper-left position of the control's client area.	TControl
ClientRect	Determine the rectangle occupied by the control's client area.	TControl
ClientToScreen	Convert control (local) coordinates to screen coordinates.	TControl
ClientWidth	Determine the width of the control's client area.	TControl
ColCount	Determines the number of columns visible in the database control grid.	None
Color	Determine the color of the windowed control.	TControl
ComponentCount	Determines the number of owned components.	TComponent
ComponentIndex	The index of the component in its owner's `Components` list	TComponent
Components	Determine the list of owned components.	TComponent
ComponentState	Determine the state of the current component.	TComponent
ContainsControl	Determine whether the specified control is contained by the windowed control.	TWinControl
ControlAtPos	Determine the control contained at a specified position.	TWinControl
ControlCount	Determine the number of controls contained by the windowed control.	TWinControl
Controls	Access the controls contained by the windowed control using their positions in an array.	TWinControl
ControlState	Determine the state of the control at any given time.	TControl
ControlStyle	Determine what attributes are present in the control.	TControl
Create	Create a new component.	TObject
Ctl3D	Determine whether the windowed control displays in 3D.	TWinControl
Cursor	Determine what image is used for the cursor over the control.	TControl
DataSource	Determine the source of the data displayed.	None
Destroy	Destroy the component.	TObject

continued on next page

continued from previous page

Use or Set This...	To Do This...	Inheritance
DestroyComponents	Destroy all the components owned by the component.	TComponent
Destroying	Notify the component that it is being destroyed.	TComponent
DoKey	Simulate a key press.	None
DragCursor	Determine the shape of the mouse cursor as it drags an object over the control.	TControl
DragCursor	Determine the shape of the mouse cursor when the database control grid will accept a dragged object.	TWinControl
Dragging	Determine whether the control is being dragged.	TControl
DragMode	Determine the drag-and-drop behavior of the control.	TControl
EditMode	Determine whether the user is editing the current record.	None
Enabled	Determine whether the control is enabled.	TControl
EndDrag	End or cancel a manual drag operation.	TControl
FindComponent	Find a component in the Components array list.	TComponent
Focused	Determine whether the windowed control has the focus.	TControl
Font	Determine the font used to render text on the control.	TControl
Free	Safely destroy the object.	TObject
GetTabOrderList	Create a list of controls that can receive the focus.	TWinControl
GetTextBuf	Copy the text of the control into a buffer.	TControl
GetTextLen	Get the length of the control's text.	TControl
Handle	Obtain a handle to the windowed control.	TComponent
HandleAllocated	Determine if a handle is allocated for the windowed control.	TWinControl
Height	Determine the height of the control.	TControl
HelpContext	Determine the help context ID of the windowed control.	TComponent
Hide	Make the control invisible.	TControl
Hint	Determine the text that displays in a tooltip for the control.	TControl
InheritsFrom	Determine if the object is descended from a certain class.	TObject
InsertControl	Insert a control into the windowed control's Controls array.	TWinControl
InstanceSize	Determine the amount of memory allocated for the object.	TObject
Invalidate	Force the control to be repainted as soon as possible.	TControl
Left	Determine the left edge of the control within its container.	TControl
Name	Determine the name of the component.	TComponent
OnClick	Handle the event that occurs when the control is clicked.	TControl
OnDblClick	Handle the event that occurs when the control is double-clicked.	TControl
OnDragDrop	Handle the event that occurs when an object is dropped on the control.	TControl
OnDragOver	Handle the event that occurs when an object is dragged over the control.	TControl
OnEndDrag	Handle the event that occurs when a drag operation ends over the control.	TControl
OnEnter	Handle the event that occurs when the windowed control receives the focus.	TWinControl
OnExit	Handle the event that occurs when the windowed control loses the focus.	TWinControl
OnKeyDown	Handle the event that occurs when a key is pressed down and not immediately released while the windowed control has the focus.	TWinControl

Use or Set This...	To Do This...	Inheritance
OnKeyPress	Handle the event that occurs when a key is pressed while the windowed control has the focus.	TWinControl
OnKeyUp	Handle the event that occurs when a key is released while the windowed control has the focus.	TWinControl
OnMouseDown	Handle the event that occurs when a mouse button is held down and not immediately released.	TControl
OnMouseMove	Handle the event that occurs when the cursor moves over the control.	TControl
OnMouseUp	Handle the event that occurs when a mouse button is released.	TControl
OnPaintPanel	Handle the event that occurs when a grid is displayed.	None
OnStartDrag	Handle the event that occurs when a drag-and-drop operation is started.	TControl
Orientation	Determine how multiple records will wrap within the grid.	None
Owner	Determine the owner of the component.	TComponent
PanelBorder	Determine the type of border drawn around the database control grid.	None
PanelCount	Determine the number of panels visible in the grid.	
PanelHeight	Determine the height of each panel in the grid.	None
PanelIndex	Determine which panel is the current panel.	None
PanelWidth	Determine the width of each panel in the grid.	None
Parent	Determine the parent, or container, of the control.	TControl
ParentColor	Determine whether the Color information of the control's parent's used.	TControl
ParentCtl3D	Determine whether the windowed control uses its parent's Ctl3D settings.	TWinControl
ParentFont	Determine whether the Font information of the control's parent's used.	TControl
ParentShowHint	Determine whether the ShowHint information of the control's parent's used.	TControl
PopupMenu	Determine which pop-up menu is associated with the control.	TControl
Refresh	Erase the control and repaint it.	TControl
RemoveControl	Remove the specified control from the windowed control's Controls array.	TWinControl
Repaint	Repaint the control.	TControl
RowCount	Determine the number of rows visible.	None
ScaleBy	Resize the windowed control.	TWinControl
ScreenToClient	Convert screen coordinates to client (control) coordinates.	TControl
SendToBack	Send the control to the end of the z-order.	TControl
SetBounds	Determine the coordinates of the control's bounding rectangle.	TControl
SetFocus	Set the focus to the windowed control.	TWinControl
SetTextBuf	Set the text of the control to the text in a buffer.	TControl
Show	Make the control visible.	TControl
ShowFocus	Determine whether a focus rectangle is drawn in the panel around the current record.	None
ShowHint	Enable tooltips for the control.	TControl
Showing	Determine whether the windowed control is currently showing onscreen.	TComponent
TabOrder	Determine the position of the control within its parent's tab order.	TWinControl
TabOrder	Determine the tab order of the windowed control.	TWinControl
TabStop	Determine whether the windowed control is in the tab order of its parent.	TWinControl

continued on next page

continued from previous page

Use or Set This...	To Do This...	Inheritance
TabStop	Determine whether the control is a tab stop.	TWinControl
Tag	Store an additional integer value with the component.	TComponent
Text	Access the changeable text on the control.	TControl
Top	Determine the upper edge of the control.	TControl
Update	Is called automatically by Refresh.	TControl
Visible	Make the control visible.	TControl
Width	Determine the width of the control.	TControl

AllowDelete PROPERTY

Objects Affected TDBCtrlGrid

Purpose AllowDelete determines whether the user can delete the current record.

Declaration

```
property AllowDelete: Boolean;
```

Example Syntax

```
procedure TForm1.FormCreate(Sender: TObject);
begin
  DBCtrlGrid1.AllowDelete := False;
  // . . .
end;
```

Description If AllowDelete is True, the user can delete the current record by typing
CTRL-DELETE. If AllowDelete is False, the user cannot delete the current
record in this fashion, although the attatched dataset's Delete method can
still be used to delete records. AllowDelete is True by default.

AllowInsert PROPERTY

Objects Affected TDBCtrlGrid

Purpose AllowInsert determines whether the user can insert and append new
records into the database control grid.

Declaration

```
property AllowInsert: Boolean;
```

Example Syntax

```
procedure TForm1.FormCreate(Sender: TObject);
begin
  DBCtrlGrid1.AllowDelete := False;
  DBCtrlGrid1.AllowInsert := False;
  // . . .
end;
```

Description   If `AllowInsert` is `True`, the user can insert a new record by pressing INSERT or append a record by typing CTRL-INSERT. If `AllowInsert` is `False`, the user will be unable to insert or append new records, although he or she can still call the attached dataset's `Insert` or `Append` methods to do so. The default value for `AllowInsert` is `True`.

ColCount PROPERTY

Objects Affected   TDBCtrlGrid

Purpose   The `ColCount` property determines the number of columns visible in the database control grid.

Declaration

```
property ColCount: Integer;
```

Example Syntax

```
procedure TForm2.FormCreate(Sender: TObject);
begin
  DBCtrlGrid1.ColCount := 1;
  DBCtrlGrid1.RowCount := 3;
end;
```

Description   When you change the value of `ColCount` at run time, the database control grid resizes itself automatically, multiplying the `PanelWidth` by the `ColCount` value to determine the new control size.

DataSource PROPERTY

Objects Affected   TDBCtrlGrid

Purpose   The `DataSource` property determines the source of the data displayed by the database control grid.

Declaration

```
property DataSource: TDataSource;
```

Example Syntax

```
procedure TForm1.FormCreate(Sender: TObject);
begin
  // . . .

  DBCtrlGrid1.DataSource := DataSource1;

  // . . .
end;
```

Description   The data source control specified by `DataSource` will be connected to a dataset (a table or query) through its `DataSet` property. By making these connections at design time, you can work with live data in the Delphi 3 IDE.

DoKey Method

Objects Affected	`TDBCtrlGrid`
Purpose	The `DoKey` method simulates a key-press.
Declaration	

```
procedure DoKey(Key: TDBCtrlGridKey);
```

Table 48-2 Parameters of the DoKey method

Argument	Description
Key	The key-press you are simulating.

Example Syntax

```
procedure TForm1.sbUpClick(Sender: TObject);
begin
  DBCtrlGrid1.DoKey(gkUp);
end;

procedure TForm1.sbDownClick(Sender: TObject);
begin
  DBCtrlGrid1.DoKey(gkDown);
end;
```

Description DoKey simulates a key-press to the database grid control, so it should be used in the handler for the **OnKeyPress** event. **Key** is of type **TDBCtrlGridKey**, so the following possible values can be sent as a parameter to **DoKey**:

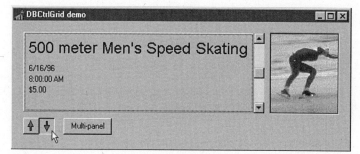

Figure 48-4 Using speedbuttons to scroll the database control grid

Use This Value...	To Do This...
gkAppend	Append a new record if AllowInsert is True.
gkCancel	Cancel any pending changes to the current record.
gkDelete	Delete the current record if AllowDelete is True.
gkDown	Move to the next row, scrolling if necessary. The next record becomes the current record.
gkEditMode	Toggle EditMode. If EditMode is True, the user is editing the current record.
gkEnd	Move to the last record in the database control grid.
gkHome	Move to the first record in the database control grid.
gkInsert	Insert a new record if AllowInsert is True.
gkLeft	Move one column to the left, scrolling if necessary.
gkNextTab	Move the focus to the next control in the application's tab order.
gkNull	Does nothing.
gkPageDown	Move to the next panel.
gkPageUp	Move to the previous panel.
gkPriorTab	Move the focus to the previous control in the application's tab order.
gkRight	Move one column to the right, scrolling if necessary.
gkScrollDown	Make the record in the next row the current record without scrolling the control.
gkScrollUp	Make the record in the previous row the current record without scrolling the control.
gkUp	Move to the previous row, scrolling if necessary.

EditMode PROPERTY

Objects Affected	TDBCtrlGrid
Purpose	Determine whether the user is editing the current record.
Declaration	

```
property EditMode: Boolean;
```

Description	EditMode is a run-time only property. The user can toggle EditMode by pressing F2 or ENTER.

OnPaintPanel EVENT

Objects Affected	TDBCtrlGrid
Purpose	The OnPaintPanel event occurs before a panel's grid is displayed.
Declaration	

```
property OnPaintPanel: TPaintPanelEvent;
```

Example Syntax

```
// . . .
type
  TForm2 = class(TForm)
    DBCtrlGrid1: TDBCtrlGrid;
    DBText2: TDBText;
    DBText3: TDBText;
    DBText4: TDBText;
    DataSource1: TDataSource;
    Table1: TTable;
    DBImage1: TDBImage;
    dbeTitle: TDBEdit;
    DBEdit1: TDBEdit;
    procedure FormCreate(Sender: TObject);
  private
    { Private declarations }
  public
    // Handler for DBCtrlGrid's OnPaintPanel event -- added manually
    procedure UpdatePanelInfo(DBCtrlGrid: TDBCtrlGrid; Index: Integer);
  end;

var
  Form2: TForm2;

implementation

{$R *.DFM}

// Event handler for DBCtrlGrid1.OnPaintPanel
// When the current panel is repainted (usually as the user
// scrolls through the grid, set the text for DBEdit1 (which
// is used as a caption for the image to the text in dbeTitle
// Since Form2 displays a multi-panel grid, this makes it
// clear which panel goes with the image
procedure TForm2.UpdatePanelInfo(DBCtrlGrid: TDBCtrlGrid;
                                    Index: Integer);
begin
  DBEdit1.Text := dbeTitle.Text;
end;

procedure TForm2.FormCreate(Sender: TObject);
begin
  DBCtrlGrid1.OnPaintPanel := UpdatePanelInfo;

  DBCtrlGrid1.ColCount := 1;
  DBCtrlGrid1.RowCount := 3;
end;

// . . .
```

Description

You can handle the `OnPaintPanel` if you need to perform specific processing each time the controls in the visible panel(s) are displayed. `OnPaintPanel` is of type `TPainPanelEvent`, which is defined as:

```
TPaintPanelEvent = procedure(DBCtrlGrid: TDBCtrlGrid;
                               Index: Integer) of object;
```

The *DBCtrlGrid* parameter indicates which grid will be painted, and the *Index* parameter specifies the panel in the grid that needs painting.

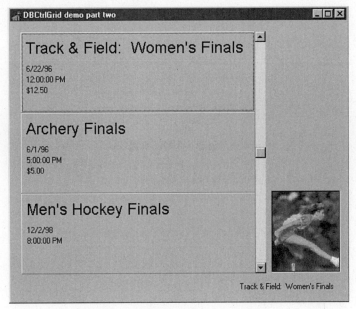

Figure 48-5 Handling the `OnPaintPanel` to keep the image caption aligned with the current record

Orientation PROPERTY

Objects Affected   `TDBCtrlGrid`

Purpose   The `Orientation` property determines how multiple records will wrap within the grid.

Declaration

```
property Orientation: TDBCtrlGridOrientation;
```

Example Syntax

```
procedure TForm2.FormCreate(Sender: TObject);
begin
  // . . .
  DBCtrlGrid1.Orientation := goVertical;

  DBCtrlGrid1.ColCount := 1;
  DBCtrlGrid1.RowCount := 3;
end;
```

Description   `Orientation` is type `TDBCtrlGridOrientation`, which defines two possible values, `goVertical` and `goHorizontal`. If `Orientation` is set to `goVertical`, the panels in the grid will display from the upper-left, down the left column, then across the columns from left to right. If `Orientation` is set to `goHorizontal`, the panels will display from the upper-left, across the top row, then down rows from top to bottom. The database control grid shown in Figure 48-2 has a vertical orientation.

PanelBorder PROPERTY

Objects Affected	TDBCtrlGrid
Purpose	The PanelBorder property determines the type of border drawn around the database control grid.
Declaration	

```
property PanelBorder: TDBCtrlGridBorder;
```

Example Syntax

```
procedure TForm1.FormCreate(Sender: TObject);
begin
  DBCtrlGrid1.PanelBorder := gbNone;
  DBCtrlGrid1.ShowFocus := False;

  DBCtrlGrid1.AllowDelete := False;
  DBCtrlGrid1.AllowInsert := False;

  // . . .
end;
```

Description   PanelBorder is of type TDBCtrlGridBorder, which defines two border types, gbNone and gbRaised. If PanelBorder is set to gbNone, there is no border drawn around the database grid control. If PanelBorder is set to gbRaised, a raised 3D border is drawn. The default is bgRaised.

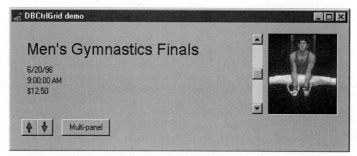

Figure 48-6   The database control grid with no panel border

PanelCount PROPERTY

Objects Affected	TDBCtrlGrid
Purpose	The PanelCount property contains the number of panels visible in the grid.
Declaration	

```
property PanelCount: Integer;
```

Description	PanelCount is a run-time, read-only property.

PanelHeight PROPERTY

Objects Affected	TDBCtrlGrid
Purpose	The PanelHeight property determines the height of each panel in the grid.
Declaration	

```
property PanelHeight: Integer;
```

Example Syntax

```
procedure TForm1.FormCreate(Sender: TObject);
begin
  DBCtrlGrid1.Height := 120;
  DBCtrlGrid1.Width := 375;
  // . . .
end;
```

Description	If you change the PanelHeight property at run time, the grid automatically resizes itself to fit the new height.

PanelIndex PROPERTY

Objects Affected	TDBCtrlGrid
Purpose	The PanelIndex property specifies which panel is current.
Declaration	

```
property PanelIndex: Integer;
```

Description	The panels in a database control grid are organized in a zero-based set, so the first panel would be 0, the second panel would be 1, and so on. Setting the PanelIndex to a valid value makes that panel the current panel.

PanelWidth PROPERTY

Objects Affected	TDBCtrlGrid
Purpose	The PanelWidth property determines the width of each panel in the grid.
Declaration	

```
property PanelWidth: Integer;
```

Example Syntax

```
procedure TForm1.FormCreate(Sender: TObject);
begin
  DBCtrlGrid1.Height := 120;
  DBCtrlGrid1.Width := 375;
  // . . .
end;
```

Description   If you change the PanelWidth property at run time, the grid automatically resizes itself to fit the new width.

RowCount PROPERTY

Objects Affected	TDBCtrlGrid
Purpose	The RowCount property determines the number of rows visible in the database control grid.
Declaration	

```
property RowCount: Integer;
```

Example Syntax

```
procedure TForm2.FormCreate(Sender: TObject);
begin
  DBCtrlGrid1.ColCount := 1;
  DBCtrlGrid1.RowCount := 3;
end;
```

Description   When you change the value of RowCount at run time, the database control grid resizes itself automatically, multiplying the PanelHeight by the RowCount value to determine the new control size.

ShowFocus PROPERTY

Objects Affected	TDBCtrlGrid
Purpose	ShowFocus determines whether a focus rectangle is drawn in the panel around the current record.
Declaration	

```
property ShowFocus: Boolean;
```

Example Syntax

```
procedure TForm1.FormCreate(Sender: TObject);
begin
  // do not show border or focus rectangle
  DBCtrlGrid1.PanelBorder := gbNone;
  DBCtrlGrid1.ShowFocus := False;

  // . . .
end;
```

Description

If ShowFocus is True, a focus rectangle is drawn in the panel around the current record. If ShowFocus is False, no focus rectangle is drawn.

49

THeaderControl

The *header control*, also known as the *column heading control*, is a common control that was introduced with Windows 95. It is encapsulated by **THeaderControl** and used to display a heading above columns of text. The header control can be divided into sections, each with its own caption and/or graphic to provide a heading for multiple columns. The header control is used in the details view of Windows Explorer, where clicking the header sections determines how the list view is sorted. This is shown in Figure 49-1.

Header sections can be resized by the user by clicking a divider that separates two sections and dragging the mouse.

Figure 49-2 shows the derivation of **THeaderControl**. Table 49-1 displays the properties, methods, and events implemented by **THeaderControl**.

HeaderControl demo	☒
Name	Relationship
David and Deb Abbott	friends
Lou and Jean Bianchi	family
Steve and Kim Cords	friends
Lisa Flanagan	friend
Jeff Giles and Kerry Hawkins	friends
Mary Ellen Krug	friend
Patrick Lally	friend
Paul and Sharon McKiernan	family
Beth McKiernan	family
Lori McKiernan	family
Jill McKiernan	family
Chris Regan	friend
Ron Raye	friend
Tabb and Marilyn Sheridan	family
John and Beverly Thurrott	family
Cheryl Thurrott	family
Jonathan Thurrott	family
Doris Thurrott	family
George and Jackie Thurrott	family
Wayne and Valerie Thurrott	family
Suzanne Thurrott	family
Lou and Laura Trubiano	friends
Karen Viera	friend
Joseph and Thelma White	family
Cathy White	family
Joseph and Missy White	family

Figure 49-1 Windows Explorer details view uses the header control

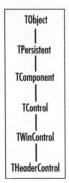

TObject
|
TPersistent
|
TComponent
|
TControl
|
TWinControl
|
THeaderControl

Figure 49-2 Derivation of
THeaderControl

Table 49-1 Properties, methods, and events implemented by THeaderControl

Use or Set This...	To Do This...	Inheritance
Align	Determine how the control is aligned within its parent.	TControl
Assign	Assign one persistent object to another.	TPersistent
BeginDrag	Begin a manual drag operation.	TControl
BoundsRect	Determine the boundary rectangle occupied by the control.	TControl
BringToFront	Bring the control to the front of the z-order.	TControl
Brush	Determine the color and pattern used for the windowed control background.	TComponent
CanFocus	Determine whether the windowed control can receive the focus.	TWinControl
Canvas	Access the drawing surface of the header control.	TControl
Caption	Label the control with a text string.	TControl
ClassName	Get the name of the object's class.	TObject
ClassParent	Get the object's parent class.	TObject
ClassType	Get the object's actual type.	TObject
ClientHeight	Determine the control's client height.	TControl
ClientOrigin	Determine the upper-left position of the control's client area.	TControl
ClientRect	Determine the rectangle occupied by the control's client area.	TControl
ClientToScreen	Convert control (local) coordinates to screen coordinates.	TControl
ClientWidth	Determine the width of the control's client area.	TControl
Color	Determine the color of the windowed control.	TControl
ComponentCount	Determine the number of owned components.	TComponent
ComponentIndex	The index of the component in its owner's Components list.	TComponent
Components	Determine the list of owned components.	TComponent
ComponentState	Determine the state of the current component.	TComponent
ContainsControl	Determine whether the specified control is contained by windowed control.	TWinControl
ControlAtPos	Determine the control contained at a specified position.	TWinControl
ControlCount	Determine the number of controls contained by the windowed control.	TWinControl

Use or Set This...	To Do This...	Inheritance
Controls	Access the controls contained by the windowed control using their positions in an array.	TWinControl
ControlState	Determine the state of the control at any given time.	TControl
ControlStyle	Determine what attributes are present in the control.	TControl
Create	Create a new component.	TObject
Ctl3D	Determine whether the windowed control displays in 3D.	TWinControl
Cursor	Determine what image is used for the cursor over the control.	TControl
Destroy	Destroy the component.	TObject
DestroyComponents	Destroy all the components owned by the component.	TComponent
Destroying	Notify the component that it is being destroyed.	TComponent
DragCursor	Determine the shape of the mouse cursor as it drags an object over the control.	TControl
Dragging	Determine whether the control is being dragged.	TControl
DragMode	Determine the drag-and-drop behavior of the control.	TControl
Enabled	Determine whether the control is enabled.	TControl
EndDrag	End or cancel a manual drag operation.	TControl
FindComponent	Find a component in the Components array list.	TComponent
Focused	Determine whether the windowed control has the focus.	TControl
Font	Determine the font used to render text on the control.	TControl
Free	Safely destroy the object.	TObject
GetTextBuf	Copy the text of the control into a buffer.	TControl
GetTextLen	Get the length of the text of the control.	TControl
Handle	Obtain a handle to the windowed control.	TComponent
HandleAllocated	Determine if a handle is allocated for the windowed control.	TWinControl
Height	Determine the height of the control.	TControl
HelpContext	Determine the help context ID of the windowed control.	TComponent
Hide	Make the control invisible.	TControl
Hint	Determine the text that displays in a tooltip for the control.	TControl
InheritsFrom	Determine if the object is descended from a certain class.	TObject
InsertControl	Insert a control into the windowed control's Controls array.	TWinControl
InstanceSize	Determine the amount of memory allocated for the object.	TObject
Invalidate	Force the control to be repainted as soon as possible.	TControl
Left	Determine the left edge of the control within its container.	TControl
Name	Determine the name of the component.	TComponent
OnClick	Handle the event that occurs when a mouse button is clicked.	TControl
OnDblClick	Handle the event that occurs when a mouse button is double-clicked.	TControl
OnDragDrop	Handle the event that occurs when an object is dropped on the header control.	TControl
OnDragOver	Handle the event that occurs when an object is dragged over the header control.	None
OnDrawSection	Handle the event that occurs when a section of the header control needs to be redisplayed.	None

continued on next page

continued from previous page

Use or Set This...	To Do This...	Inheritance
OnEndDrag	Handle the event that occurs when a drag-and-drop operation ends over the control.	TControl
OnEnter	Handle the event that occurs when the windowed control receives the focus.	TWinControl
OnExit	Handle the event that occurs when the windowed control loses the focus.	TWinControl
OnKeyDown	Handle the event that occurs when a key is pressed down and not immediately released while the windowed control has the focus.	TWinControl
OnKeyPress	Handle the event that occurs when a key is pressed while the windowed control has the focus.	TWinControl
OnKeyUp	Handle the event that occurs when a key is released while the windowed control has the focus.	TWinControl
OnMouseDown	Handle the event that occurs when a mouse button is held down and not immediately released.	TControl
OnMouseMove	Handle the event that occurs when the mouse pointer moves over the control.	TControl
OnMouseUp	Handle the event that occurs when the mouse button is released.	TControl
OnResize	Handle the event that occurs when the header is resized.	None
OnSectionClick	Handle the event that occurs when one of the header sections is clicked.	None
OnSectionResize	Handle the event that occurs when one of the header sections is resized.	None
OnSectionTrack	Handle the event that occurs when a divider is dragged.	None
OnStartDrag	Handle the event that occurs when a drag-and-drop operation is started.	TControl
Owner	Determine the owner of the component.	TComponent
Parent	Determine the parent, or container, of the control.	TControl
ParentColor	Determine whether the control uses its parent's Color information.	TControl
ParentCtl3D	Determine whether the windowed control uses its parent's Ctl3D settings.	TWinControl
ParentFont	Determine whether the control uses its parent's Font information.	TControl
ParentShowHint	Determine whether the control uses its parent's ShowHint to determine whether to show tooltips.	TControl
PopupMenu	Determine which pop-up menu is associated with the control.	TControl
Refresh	Erase the control and repaint it.	TControl
RemoveControl	Remove the specified control from the windowed control's Controls array.	TWinControl
Repaint	Repaint the control.	TControl
ScaleBy	Resize the windowed control.	TWinControl
ScreenToClient	Convert screen coordinates to client (control) coordinates.	TControl
Sections	Determine the sections present in the control.	None
SendToBack	Send the control to the end of the z-order.	TControl
SetBounds	Determine the coordinates of the control's bounding rectangle.	TControl
SetFocus	Set the focus to the windowed control.	TWinControl
SetTextBuf	Set the text of the control to the text in a buffer.	TControl
Show	Make the control visible.	TControl
ShowHint	Determine whether to show tooltips.	TControl

Use or Set This...	To Do This...	Inheritance
Showing	Determine whether the windowed control is currently showing onscreen.	TComponent
TabOrder	Determine the tab order of the windowed control.	TWinControl
TabStop	Determine whether the windowed control is in the TWinControl.	TWinControl
Tag	Store an additional integer value with the component.	TComponent
Text	Access the changeable text on the control.	TControl
Top	Determine the upper edge of the control.	TControl
Update	Automatically called by Refresh.	TControl
Visible	Determine whether the control is visible.	TControl
Width	Determine the width of the control.	TControl

OnDrawSection EVENT

Objects Affected   THeaderControl

Purpose   The OnDrawSection event occurs when a header control section needs to be redisplayed.

Declaration

```
property OnDrawSection: TDrawSectionEvent;
```

Description   OnDrawSection occurs when the user resizes or selects a section, but only if the HeaderSection Style property is set to hsOwnerDraw. You can handle the OnDrawSection event if you prefer to redraw the header section's caption and graphic manually.

OnResize EVENT

Objects Affected   THeaderControl

Purpose   The OnResize event occurs when the header control is resized.

Declaration

```
property OnResize: TNotifyEvent;
```

Description   The OnResize event will not occur if the Align property of the header control is alNone. Otherwise, it can occur when the form is resized if the header control needs resizing and redrawing. You can handle the OnResize event if you need to perform processing when the header control is resized.

OnSectionClick EVENT

Objects Affected	THeaderControl
Purpose	The OnSectionClick event occurs when a header section is clicked.
Declaration	

```
property OnSectionClick: TSectionNotifyEvent;
```

Example Syntax

```
procedure TForm1.HeaderControl1SectionClick(HeaderControl: THeaderControl;
  Section: THeaderSection);
begin
  // If the 'Name' section is clicked, change the font
  if Section = HeaderControl1.Sections[0] then
    if RichEdit1.Font.Name = 'MS Sans Serif' then
    begin
      RichEdit1.Font.Name := 'Times New Roman';
      RichEdit2.Font.Name := 'Times New Roman'
    end
    else begin
      RichEdit1.Font.Name := 'MS Sans Serif';
      RichEdit2.Font.Name := 'MS Sans Serif'
    end
  else
  // Otherwise, the 'Relationship' section was clicked change
  // the point size
  if RichEdit1.Font.Size = 8 then
    begin
      RichEdit1.Font.Size := 12;
      RichEdit2.Font.Size := 12
    end
    else begin
      RichEdit1.Font.Size := 8;
      RichEdit2.Font.Size := 8
    end
end;
```

Description

If the AllowClick property of a header section is set to True, mouse clicks on that section will trigger an OnSectionClick event as shown in Figure 49-3 for the header control. OnSectionClick is type TSectionNotifyEvent, which is defined as:

```
TSectionNotifyEvent = procedure (HeaderControl: THeaderControl;
                                 Section: THeaderSection) of object;
```

The HeaderControl parameter specifies the header control affected, and the Section parameter specifies the actual header section clicked.

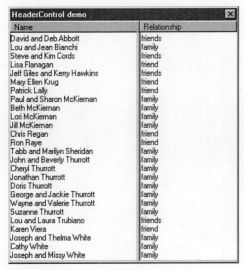

Figure 49-3 Changing the rich edit boxes'
font and point size with header control
`OnSectionClick` events

OnSectionResize EVENT

Objects Affected	`THeaderControl`
Purpose	The `OnSectionResize` event occurs when a header section is resized.
Declaration	

```
property OnSectionResize: TSectionNotifyEvent;
```

Example Syntax

```
procedure TForm1.HeaderControl1SectionResize(HeaderControl:
                         THeaderControl; Section: THeaderSection);
begin
  RichEdit2.Left := HeaderControl1.Sections[0].Width;
  RichEdit2.Width := HeaderControl1.Sections[1].Width;
  RichEdit1.Width := HeaderControl1.Sections[0].Width;
end;
```

Description   Header sections are resized when the user selects the divider between two
sections, as in Figure 49-4, and drags it with the mouse. If you need to
process code, you can handle this event whenever a header section is
resized.

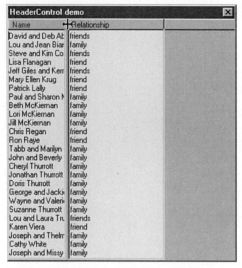

Figure 49-4 This handler for `OnSection-`
`Resize` resizes the rich edit boxes as the
header control section is resized

OnSectionTrack EVENT

Objects Affected   `THeaderControl`

Purpose   The `OnSectionTrack` event occurs when a header section is resized.

Declaration

```
property OnSectionTrack: TSectionTrackEvent;
```

Example Syntax

```
procedure TForm1.HeaderControl1SectionTrack(HeaderControl: THeaderControl;
                           Section: THeaderSection; Width: Integer;
                           State: TSectionTrackState);
begin
  // When resizing begins, change the background color of
  // both rich edit boxes yellow
  if State = tsTrackBegin then
  begin
    RichEdit1.Color := clYellow;
    RichEdit2.Color := clYellow
  end
  // When resizing is finished, return them to their original color
  else if State = tsTrackEnd then
  begin
    RichEdit1.Color := clWindow;
    RichEdit2.Color := clWindow
  end
end;
```

Description Like `OnSectionResize`, `OnSectionTrack` occurs when a header section is resized, but it allows you to handle three possible states. This state is passed to the `OnSectionResize` event handler, which is type `TSectionTrackEvent`, in its *State* parameter:

```
TSectionTrackEvent = procedure (HeaderControl: THeaderControl;
                                Section: THeaderSection;
                                Width: Integer;
                                State: TSectionTrackState) of object;
```

The three states are described in the following table:

Table 49-2 Possible values of the *State* parameter

Check for This State...	To Execute Code When...
tsTrackBegin	The divider is about to be dragged.
tsTrackEnd	The divider has been dragged.
tsTrackMove	The divider is being dragged.

By checking the *State* parameter, you can have code execute when the divider is about to be dragged, while it is being dragged, or after the drag is complete.

Sections PROPERTY

Objects Affected THeaderControl

Purpose The `Sections` property contains a list of the header sections contained by the header control.

Declaration

```
property Sections: THeaderSections;
```

Example Syntax

```
procedure TForm1.HeaderControl1SectionResize(HeaderControl:
                                THeaderControl; Section: THeaderSection);
begin
  RichEdit2.Left := HeaderControl1.Sections[0].Width;
  RichEdit2.Width := HeaderControl1.Sections[1].Width;
  RichEdit1.Width := HeaderControl1.Sections[0].Width;
end;
```

Description Header control sections can be accessed using array notation, as in the above example. The first section is `Sections[0]`, the next is `Sections[1]`, and so on.

50

TProgressBar

The *progress bar*, encapsulated by the **TProgressBar** class in Delphi 2, is a graphical bar that shows the progress of a lengthy operation. A progress bar is a horizontal rectangle that fills with colored boxes, from left to right, as the operation occurs. The length of the colored boxes in the progress bar indicates the percentage of completion of the operation. A typical progress bar is shown in Figure 50-1.

Typically, progress bars will be accompanied by a text label displaying the actual percentage. This must be added separately, as **TProgressBar** does not support a **Caption** or **Text** property. Progress bars provide general visual feedback and are typically used in a dialog box, not the main form window of your application.

Figure 50-2 shows the derivation of **TProgressBar**. Table 50-5 displays the properties, methods, and events implemented by **TProgressBar**.

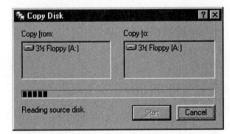

Figure 50-1   A progress bar used in the Windows Copy Disk dialog box

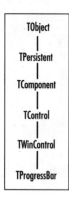

TObject
|
TPersistent
|
TComponent
|
TControl
|
TWinControl
|
TProgressBar

Figure 50-2 Derivation of `TProgressBar`

Table 50-1 Properties, methods, and events implemented by `TProgressBar`

Use or Set This...	To Do This...	Inheritance
Align	Determine how the control is aligned within its container.	TControl
Assign	Assign one persistent object to another.	TPersistent
BeginDrag	Begin a manual drag operation.	TControl
BoundsRect	Determine the boundary rectangle occupied by the control.	TControl
BringToFront	Bring the control to the front of the z-order.	TControl
Brush	Determine the color and pattern used for the windowed control background.	TComponent
CanFocus	Determine whether the windowed control can receive the focus.	TWinControl
Caption	Label the control with a text string.	TControl
ClassName	Get the name of the object's class.	TObject
ClassParent	Get the object's parent class.	TObject
ClassType	Get the object's actual type.	TObject
ClientHeight	Determine the control's client height.	TControl
ClientOrigin	Determine the upper-left position of the control's client area.	TControl
ClientRect	Determine the rectangle occupied by the control's client area.	TControl
ClientToScreen	Convert control (local) coordinates to screen coordinates.	TControl
ClientWidth	Determine the width of the control's client area.	TControl
Color	Determine the color of the windowed control.	TControl
ComponentCount	Determine the number of owned components.	TComponent
ComponentIndex	The index of the component in its owner's `Components` list.	TComponent
Components	Determine the list of owned components.	TComponent
ComponentState	Determine the state of the current component.	TComponent
ContainsControl	Determine whether the specified control is contained by windowed control.	TWinControl
ControlAtPos	Determine the control contained at a specified position.	TWinControl
ControlCount	Determine the number of controls contained by the windowed control.	TWinControl
Controls	Access the controls contained by the windowed control using their positions in an array.	TWinControl

Use or Set This...	To Do This...	Inheritance
ControlState	Determine the state of the control at any given time.	TControl
ControlStyle	Determine what attributes are present in the control.	TControl
Create	Create a new component.	TObject
Ctl3D	Determine whether the windowed control displays in 3D.	TWinControl
Cursor	Determine what image is used for the cursor over the control.	TControl
Destroy	Destroy the component.	TObject
DestroyComponents	Destroy all of the components owned by the component.	TComponent
Destroying	Notify the component that it is being destroyed.	TComponent
DragCursor	Determine the shape of the mouse cursor as it drags an object over the control.	TControl
Dragging	Determine whether the control is being dragged.	TControl
DragMode	Determine the drag-and-drop behavior of the control.	TControl
Enabled	Determine whether the control is enabled.	TControl
EndDrag	End or cancel a manual drag operation.	TControl
FindComponent	Find a component in the Components array list.	TComponent
Focused	Determine whether the windowed control has the focus.	TControl
Font	Determine the font used to render text on the control.	TControl
Free	Safely destroy the object.	TObject
GetTextBuf	Copy the text of the control into a buffer.	TControl
GetTextLen	Get the length of the text of the control.	TControl
Handle	Obtain a handle to the windowed control.	TComponent
HandleAllocated	Determine if a handle is allocated for the windowed control.	TWinControl
Height	Determine the height of the control.	TControl
HelpContext	Determine the help context ID of the windowed control.	TComponent
Hide	Make the control invisible.	TControl
Hint	Determine the text that displays in a tooltip for the control.	TControl
InheritsFrom	Determine if the object is descended from a certain class.	TObject
InsertControl	Insert a control into the windowed control's Controls array.	TWinControl
InstanceSize	Determine the amount of memory allocated for the object.	TObject
Invalidate	Force the control to be repainted as soon as possible.	TControl
Left	Determine the left edge of the control within its container.	TControl
Max	Determine the maximum value of the range of the progress bar.	None
Min	Determine the minimum value of the range of the progress bar.	None
Name	Determine the name of the component.	TComponent
OnClick	Handle the event that occurs when a mouse button is clicked.	TControl
OnDblClick	Handle the event that occurs when a mouse button is double-clicked.	TControl
OnDragDrop	Handle the event that occurs when an object is dropped on the control.	TControl
OnDragDrop	Handle the event that occurs when an object is dropped on the progress bar.	TControl
OnDragOver	Handle the event that occurs when an object is dragged over the control.	TControl
OnEndDrag	Handle the event that occurs when a drag-and-drop operation is cancelled.	TControl

continued on next page

continued from previous page

Use or Set This...	To Do This...	Inheritance
OnEnter	Handle the event that occurs when the windowed control receives the focus.	TWinControl
OnExit	Handle the event that occurs when the windowed control loses the focus.	TWinControl
OnKeyDown	Handle the event that occurs when a key is pressed down and not immediately released while the windowed control has the focus.	TWinControl
OnKeyPress	Handle the event that occurs when a key is pressed while the windowed control has the focus.	TWinControl
OnKeyUp	Handle the event that occurs when a key is released while the windowed control has the focus.	TWinControl
OnMouseDown	Handle the event that occurs when a mouse button is held down and not immediately released.	TControl
OnMouseMove	Handle the event that occurs when the mouse pointer passes over the control.	TControl
OnMouseUp	Handle the event that occurs when a mouse button is released.	TControl
OnStartDrag	Handle the event that occurs when a drag-and-drop operation is started.	TControl
Owner	Determine the owner of the component.	TComponent
Parent	Determine the parent, or container, of the control.	TControl
ParentColor	Determine whether the Color information of the control's parent is used.	TControl
ParentCtl3D	Determine whether the windowed control uses its parent's Ctl3D settings.	TWinControl
ParentFont	Determine whether the Font information of the control's parent is used.	TControl
ParentShowHint	Determine whether the ShowHint information of the control's parent is used.	TControl
PopupMenu	Determine which pop-up menu is associated with the control.	TControl
Position	Determine the current position of the progress bar.	None
Refresh	Erase the control and repaint it.	TControl
RemoveControl	Remove the specified control from the windowed control's Controls array.	TWinControl
Repaint	Repaint the control.	TControl
ScaleBy	Resize the windowed control.	TWinControl
ScreenToClient	Convert screen coordinates to client (control) coordinates.	TControl
SendToBack	Send the control to the end of the z-order.	TControl
SetBounds	Determine the coordinates of the control's bounding rectangle.	TControl
SetFocus	Set the focus to the windowed control.	TWinControl
SetTextBuf	Set the text of the control to the text in a buffer.	TControl
Show	Make the control visible.	TControl
ShowHint	Determine whether to show a tooltip.	TControl
Showing	Determine whether the windowed control is currently showing on screen.	TComponent
Step	Determine the amount Position will increase when the StepIt method is called.	None
StepBy	Increment Position by a specified amount.	None
StepIt	Increment Position by the amount specified by Step.	None
TabOrder	Determine the tab order of the windowed control.	TWinControl

Use or Set This...	To Do This...	Inheritance
TabStop	Determine whether the windowed control is in the tab order.	TWinControl
Tag	Store an additional integer value with the component.	TComponent
Text	Access the changeable text on the control.	TControl
Top	Determine the upper edge of the control.	TControl
Update	Update is called automatically by Refresh.	TControl
Visible	Make the control visible.	TControl
Width	Determine the width of the control.	TControl

Many of the properties and methods implemented by **TProgressBar** use the type **TProgressRange**, which is defined as:

```
TProgressRange = 0..65535;
```

Max PROPERTY

Objects Affected TProgressBar

Purpose The **Max** property defines the maximum value of the progress bar range.

Declaration

```
property Max: TProgressRange;
```

Example Syntax

```
procedure TForm1.FormCreate(Sender: TObject);
begin
  ProgressBar1.Min := 1;
  ProgressBar1.Max := 100;
  ProgressBar1.Step := 1;
end;
```

Description The **Max** and **Min** properties determine the range of the progress bar. **Max** and **Min** are used by Delphi to create a sub-range within the range of possible **Position** values (0...65535).

Min PROPERTY

Objects Affected TProgressBar

Purpose The **Min** property defines the minimum value of the progress bar range.

Declaration

```
property Min: TProgressRange;
```

Example Syntax

```
procedure TForm1.FormCreate(Sender: TObject);
begin
  ProgressBar1.Min := 1;
  ProgressBar1.Max := 100;
  ProgressBar1.Step := 1;
end;
```

Description   The Max and Min properties determine the range of the progress bar. Max and Min are used by Delphi to create a sub-range within the range of possible Position values (0...65535).

Position PROPERTY

Objects Affected   TProgressBar

Purpose   The Position property determines the position of the progress bar.

Declaration

```
property Position: TProgressRange;
```

Example Syntax

```
procedure TForm1.btnStartClick(Sender: TObject);
begin
  // step the progress bar through the operation
  // . . .
  // when done, clear the progress bar
  ProgressBar1.Position := 0;
end;
```

Description   Position determines the current amount that is complete as a value existing within the range of possible values for the progress bar. The range is determined by the Min and Max properties. If Min is 0, Max is 10, and Position is 2, the progress bar will indicate that the operation is 20 percent done.

Step PROPERTY

Objects Affected   TProgressBar

Purpose   The Step property determines the amount the position increases each time the progress bar increases.

Declaration

```
property Step: TProgressRange;
```

Example Syntax

```
procedure TForm1.FormCreate(Sender: TObject);
begin
  ProgressBar1.Min := 1;
  ProgressBar1.Max := 100;
  ProgressBar1.Step := 1;
end;
```

Description

The `Position` property is incremented by the value held by `Step` each time the `StepIt` method is called.

StepBy METHOD

Objects Affected TProgressBar

Purpose

The `StepBy` property increments the position of the progress bar by a specified value.

Declaration

```
procedure StepBy(Delta: TProgressRange);
```

Parameters

Delta

The amount to increment `Position`.

Example Syntax

```
procedure TForm1.btnStartClick(Sender: TObject);
begin
  if btnStart.Caption = 'Start' then
  begin
    btnStart.Caption := 'Cancel';
    // process operation
    // . . .
  end
  else if btnStart.Caption = 'Cancel' then
  begin
    ProgressBar1.StepBy(ProgressBar1.Max - ProgressBar1.Position);
    Application.MessageBox('Cancelled', 'Progress Cancelled', MB_OK);
    ProgressBar1.Position := 0;
    btnStart.Caption := 'Start';
  end;
end;
```

Description

`StepBy` is a run-time-only property that increments `Position` by the value passed by the *Delta* parameter.

StepIt METHOD

Objects Affected TProgressBar

Purpose The `StepIt` method increments the position of the progress bar.

Declaration

```
procedure StepIt;
```

Example Syntax

```
procedure TForm1.btnStartClick(Sender: TObject);
begin
  if btnStart.Caption = 'Start' then
  begin
    btnStart.Caption := 'Cancel';
    // process operation . . .
    ProgressBar1.StepIt;
  end
  // handle else case
end;
```

Description

StepIt increments the Position property by the value held in the Step property.

51

TScrollBar

Scroll bars, like menus and windows themselves, have been a part of GUI computing from the very beginning. `TScrollBar` encapsulates the Windows scroll bar, which is used to scroll through information when the window or control containing it is not large enough to display all the information at once. Scroll bars can be horizontally or vertically oriented and consist of a rectangular shaft terminated at either end by *scroll bar arrows*. A *scroll box*, contained in the scroll bar shaft, indicates the distance the visible information is from the top or left edge of the information (depending on what type of scroll bar you use). The size of the scroll box can grow larger or smaller to indicate the proportion of the information currently visible.

Scroll bars can be manipulated by clicking the scroll bar arrows, clicking the scroll bar shaft, or dragging the scroll box.

Figure 51-1 shows the lineage of `TScrollBar`. Table 51-1 displays the properties, methods, and events implemented by `TScrollBar`.

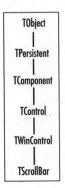

Figure 51-1   Lineage of `TScrollBar`

TObject
|
TPersistent
|
TComponent
|
TControl
|
TWinControl
|
TScrollBar

Table 51-1 Properties, methods, and events implemented by TScrollBar

Use or Set This...	To Do This...	Inheritance
Align	Determine how the control is aligned within its parent.	TControl
Assign	Assign one persistent object to another.	TPersistent
BeginDrag	Begin a manual drag operation.	TControl
BoundsRect	Determine the boundary rectangle occupied by the control.	TControl
BringToFront	Bring the control to the front of the z-order.	TControl
Brush	Determine the color and pattern used for the windowed control background.	TComponent
CanFocus	Determine whether the windowed control can receive the focus.	TWinControl
Caption	Label the control with a text string.	TControl
ClassName	Get the name of the object's class.	TObject
ClassParent	Get the object's parent class.	TObject
ClassType	Get the object's actual type.	TObject
ClientHeight	Determine the control's client height.	TControl
ClientOrigin	Determine the upper-left position of the control's client area.	TControl
ClientRect	Determine the rectangle occupied by the control's client area.	TControl
ClientToScreen	Convert control (local) coordinates to screen coordinates.	TControl
ClientWidth	Determine the width of the control's client area.	TControl
Color	Determine the color of the windowed control.	TControl
ComponentCount	Determine the number of owned components.	TComponent
ComponentIndex	The index of the component in its owner's Components list.	TComponent
Components	Determine the list of owned components.	TComponent
ComponentState	Determine the state of the current component.	TComponent
ContainsControl	Determine whether the specified control is contained by the windowed control.	TWinControl
ControlAtPos	Determine the control contained at a specified position.	TWinControl
ControlCount	Determine the number of controls contained by the windowed control.	TWinControl
Controls	Access the controls contained by the windowed control using their positions in an array.	TWinControl
ControlState	Determine the state of the control at any given time.	TControl
ControlStyle	Determine what attributes are present in the control.	TControl
Create	Create a new component.	TObject
Ctl3D	Determine whether the windowed control displays in 3D.	TWinControl
Cursor	Determine what image is used for the cursor over the control.	TControl
Destroy	Destroy the component.	TObject
DestroyComponents	Destroy all the components owned by the component.	TComponent
Destroying	Notify the component that it is being destroyed.	TComponent
DragCursor	Determine the shape of the mouse cursor as it drags an object over the control.	TControl
Dragging	Determine whether the control is being dragged.	TControl
DragMode	Determine the drag-and-drop behavior of the control.	TControl

Use or Set This...	To Do This...	Inheritance
Enabled	Determine whether the control is enabled.	TControl
EndDrag	End or cancel a manual drag operation.	TControl
FindComponent	Find a component in the Components array list.	TComponent
Focused	Determine whether the windowed control has the focus.	TControl
Font	Determine the font used to render text on the control.	TControl
Free	Safely destroy the object.	TObject
GetTextBuf	Copy the text of the control into a buffer.	TControl
GetTextLen	Get the length of the text of the control.	TControl
Handle	Obtain a handle to the windowed control.	TComponent
HandleAllocated	Determine if a handle is allocated for the windowed control.	TWinControl
Height	Determine the height of the control.	TControl
HelpContext	Determine the help context ID of the windowed control.	TComponent
Hide	Make the control invisible.	TControl
Hint	Determine the text that displays in a tooltip for the control.	TControl
InheritsFrom	Determine if the object is descended from a certain class.	TObject
InsertControl	Insert a control into the windowed control's Controls array.	TWinControl
InstanceSize	Determine the amount of memory allocated for the object.	TObject
Invalidate	Force the control to be repainted as soon as possible.	TControl
Kind	Determine if the scroll bar is horizontal or vertical.	None
LargeChange	Determine how far the scroll box moves when the scroll bar shaft is clicked.	None
Left	Determine the left edge of the control within its container.	TControl
Max	Determine the maximum value in the range of the scroll bar.	None
Min	Determine the minimum value in the range of the scroll bar.	None
Name	Determine the name of the component.	TComponent
OnChange	Handle the event that occurs when the scroll bar position is changed.	TControl
OnClick	Handle the event that occurs when a mouse button is clicked.	TControl
OnDblClick	Handle the event that occurs when a mouse button is double-clicked.	TControl
OnDragDrop	Handle the event that occurs when an object is dropped on the control.	TControl
OnDragOver	Handle the event that occurs when an object is dragged over the control.	TControl
OnEndDrag	Handle the event that occurs when a drag-and-drop operation is cancelled.	TControl
OnEnter	Handle the event that occurs when the scroll bar gets the focus.	TControl
OnEnter	Handle the event that occurs when the windowed control receives the focus.	TWinControl
OnExit	Handle the event that occurs when the windowed control loses the focus.	TWinControl
OnKeyDown	Handle the event that occurs when a key is pressed down and not immediately released while the windowed control has the focus.	TWinControl
OnKeyPress	Handle the event that occurs when a key is pressed while the windowed control has the focus.	TWinControl
OnKeyUp	Handle the event that occurs when a key is released while the windowed control has the focus.	TWinControl

continued on next page

continued from previous page

Use or Set This...	To Do This...	Inheritance
OnMouseDown	Handle the event that occurs when a mouse button is held down and not immediately released.	TControl
OnMouseMove	Handle the event that occurs when the cursor moves over the control.	TControl
OnMouseUp	Handle the event that occurs when a mouse button is released.	TControl
OnScroll	Handle the event that occurs when the user uses the scroll bar.	None
OnStartDrag	Handle the event that occurs when a drag-and-drop operation is started.	TControl
Owner	Determine the owner of the component.	TComponent
Parent	Determine the parent, or container, of the control.	TControl
ParentColor	Determine whether the Color information of the control's parent is used.	TControl
ParentCtl3D	Determine whether the windowed control uses its parent's Ctl3D settings.	TWinControl
ParentFont	Determine whether the Font information of the control's parent is used.	TControl
ParentShowHint	Determine whether the ShowHint information of the control's parent is used.	TControl
PopupMenu	Determine which pop-up menu is associated with the control.	TControl
Position	Determine the current position of the scroll bar.	None
Refresh	Erase the control and repaint it.	TControl
RemoveControl	Remove the specified control from the windowed control's Controls array.	TWinControl
Repaint	Repaint the control.	TControl
ScaleBy	Resize the windowed control.	TWinControl
ScreenToClient	Convert screen coordinates to client (control) coordinates.	TControl
SendToBack	Send the control to the end of the z-order.	TControl
SetBounds	Determine the coordinates of the control's bounding rectangle.	TControl
SetFocus	Set the focus to the windowed control.	TWinControl
SetParams	Set the Position, Min, and Max properties.	None
SetTextBuf	Set the text of the control to the text in a buffer.	TControl
Show	Make the control visible.	TControl
ShowHint	Determine whether to display a tooltip.	TControl
Showing	Determine whether the windowed control is currently showing onscreen.	TComponent
SmallChange	Determine how far the scroll box moves when the scroll bar arrows are clicked.	None
TabOrder	Determine the tab order of the windowed control.	TWinControl
TabStop	Determine whether the scroll bar is a tab stop.	TControl
Tag	Store an additional integer value with the component.	TComponent
Text	Access the changeable text on the control.	TControl
Top	Determine the upper edge of the control.	TControl
Update	Is called automatically by Refresh.	TControl
Visible	Determine whether the scroll bar is visible.	TControl
Width	Determine the width of the control.	TControl

Kind PROPERTY

Objects Affected	TScrollBar
Purpose	The Kind property determines if the scroll bar is horizontal or vertical.
Declaration	

```
property Kind: TScrollBarKind;
```

Example Syntax

```
ScrollBar1.Kind := sbHorizontal;
```

Description   Kind can have one of two possible values: **sbHorizontal** for horizontal scroll bars, or **sbVertical** for vertical scroll bars.

LargeChange PROPERTY

Objects Affected	TScrollBar
Purpose	The LargeChange property determines how far the scroll box moves when the user clicks the scroll bar shaft or presses PgUp or PgDn while the scroll bar is active.
Declaration	

```
property LargeChange: TScrollBarInc;
```

Example Syntax

```
procedure TForm1.FormCreate(Sender: TObject);
begin
  scrollHoriz.Max := 1000;
  scrollHoriz.Min := 0;
  scrollHoriz.LargeChange := 100;
  scrollHoriz.SmallChange := 10;
  scrollHoriz.Position := 0;
end;
```

Description   The default value for **LargeChange** is 1. The size of the change depends on the **Max** and **Min** values. In the above example, clicking the scroll bar shaft would cause the scroll box to move 1/10th of the distance across the scroll bar.

Max PROPERTY

Objects Affected	TScrollBar
Purpose	The Max property determines the maximum position of the scroll box.
Declaration	

```
property Max: Integer;
```

Example Syntax

```
procedure TForm1.FormCreate(Sender: TObject);
begin
  scrollHoriz.Max := 1000;
  scrollHoriz.Min := 0;
  scrollHoriz.LargeChange := 100;
  scrollHoriz.SmallChange := 10;
  scrollHoriz.Position := 0;
  // . . .
end;
```

Description

The `Max` and `Min` properties represent the range of positions within the scroll bar. The position of the scroll box is determined by the `Position` property. The default value for `Max` is 100.

Min PROPERTY

Objects Affected	TScrollBar
Purpose	The `Min` property determines the minimum position of the scroll box.
Declaration	

```
property Min: Integer;
```

Example Syntax

```
procedure TForm1.FormCreate(Sender: TObject);
begin
  scrollHoriz.Max := 1000;
  scrollHoriz.Min := 0;
  scrollHoriz.LargeChange := 100;
  scrollHoriz.SmallChange := 10;
  scrollHoriz.Position := 0;
  // . . .
end;
```

Description

The `Min` and `Max` properties represent the range of positions within the scroll bar. The position of the scroll box is determined by the `Position` property. The default value for `Min` is 0.

OnScroll EVENT

Objects Affected	TScrollBar
Purpose	The `OnScroll` event occurs when the scroll bar is used.
Declaration	

```
property OnScroll: TScrollEvent;
```

Example Syntax

```
procedure TForm1.scrollHorizScroll(Sender: TObject;
  ScrollCode: TScrollCode; var ScrollPos: Integer);
begin
  lblPosition.Caption := IntToStr(scrollHoriz.Position);
```

```
          case ScrollCode of
            scBottom:    lblScrollEvent.Caption :=
                         'Scroll box moved to left-most position';
            scLineDown:  lblScrollEvent.Caption :=
                         'Right scroll bar arrow clicked';
            scLineUp:    lblScrollEvent.Caption :=
                         'Left scroll bar arrow clicked';
            scPageDown:  lblScrollEvent.Caption :=
                         'Scroll bar shafted clicked to the right of scroll box';
            scPageUp:    lblScrollEvent.Caption :=
                         'Scroll bar shafted clicked to the left of scroll box';
            scPosition:  lblScrollEvent.Caption :=
                         'User moved the scroll box and released it';
            scTop:       lblScrollEvent.Caption :=
                         'Scroll box moved to the right-most position';
            scTrack:     lblScrollEvent.Caption :=
                         'User now moving the scroll box';
          end;
        end;
```

Description   OnScroll is type TScrollEvent. TScrollEvent is declared as

```
TScrollEvent = procedure(Sender: TObject; ScrollCode: TScrollCode;
                         var ScrollPos: Integer) of object;
```

in which the *ScrollCode* parameter can be any of those in Table 51-2.

Figure 51-2 shows the scroll bar demo programs that display scroll codes.

Table 51-2 Scroll codes and their meanings

Scroll Code	Means This...
scBottom	The user moved the scroll box to the bottom or far right of the scroll bar.
scEndScroll	The user has finished moving the scroll box.
scLineDown	The user clicked the bottom or right scroll bar arrow or pressed the ⊡ key.
scLineUp	The user clicked the top or left scroll bar arrow or pressed the ⊡ key.
scPageDown	The user clicked the scroll bar shaft to the right of the scroll box or pressed PgDn.
scPageUp	The user clicked the scroll bar shaft to the left of the scroll box or pressed PgUp.
scPosition	The user moved the scroll box and released it.
scTop	The user moved the scroll box to the top or far left of the scroll bar.
scTrack	The user is now moving the scroll box.

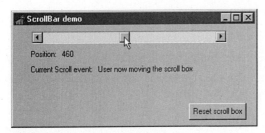

Figure 51-2   The ScrollBar demo program
displays scroll codes

The `ScrollPos` parameter specifies the position of the scroll box.

You can handle the `OnScroll` event when you wish to respond to changes to the scroll bar.

Position PROPERTY

Objects Affected	`TScrollBar`
Purpose	The `Position` property determines the position of the scroll box within the scroll bar.
Declaration	

```
property Position: Integer;
```

Example Syntax

```
procedure TForm1.FormCreate(Sender: TObject);
begin
  scrollHoriz.Max := 1000;
  scrollHoriz.Min := 0;
  scrollHoriz.LargeChange := 100;
  scrollHoriz.SmallChange := 10;
  scrollHoriz.Position := 0;
  // . . .
end;
```

Description

The range of values possible for `Position` are determined by the `Min` and `Max` properties. The default value for `Position` is 0. When the user accesses the scroll bar, the position of the scroll box changes and the value in the `Position` property is updated. You can manually change the position of the scroll box by setting `Position` to a new value.

SetParams METHOD

Objects Affected	`TScrollBar`
Purpose	`SetParams` sets the scroll box position and the range of the scroll bar at the same time.
Declaration	

```
procedure SetParams(APosition, AMin, AMax: Integer);
```

Parameters

`APosition`	The position in which you want the scroll box to be placed.
`AMin`	The minimum value of the range of values possible for the scroll box.
`AMax`	The maximum value of the range of value possible for the scroll box.

Example Syntax

```
procedure TForm1.Button1Click(Sender: TObject);
begin
  ScrollBar1.SetParams(0, 0, 1000);
  lblPosition.Caption := IntToStr(ScrollBar1.Position);
  lblScrollEvent.Caption := 'Scroll box reset';
end;
```

Description

The SetParams method allows you to set the value of the Position, Min, and Max properties with one call.

SmallChange PROPERTY

Objects Affected   TScrollBar

Purpose

The SmallChange property determines how far the scroll box moves when the user clicks a scroll bar arrow or presses one of the arrow keys when the scroll bar is active.

Declaration

```
property SmallChange: TScrollBarInc;
```

Example Syntax

```
procedure TForm1.FormCreate(Sender: TObject);
begin
  scrollHoriz.Max := 1000;
  scrollHoriz.Min := 0;
  scrollHoriz.LargeChange := 100;
  scrollHoriz.SmallChange := 10;
  scrollHoriz.Position := 0;
  // . . .
end;
```

Description

The default value of SmallChange is 1. The size of the change depends on the Max and Min values. In the above example, clicking a scroll bar arrow makes the scroll box move 10/1000th of the full distance across the scroll bar (an increment of 10).

52

TStatusBar

A *status bar* is a control that is typically aligned along the bottom of an application's primary window. It displays state information about the contents of the window or the keyboard, or any other contextual information like the current menu item or toolbar button. Status bars almost always display read-only information.

If the window it resides in is resizable, the status bar can contain a size grip at its right edge. The size grip, shown in Figure 52-1, makes it clear to the user that the window can be resized.

Delphi exposes the Windows status bar through the VCL with the **TStatusBar** class. A **TStatusBar** object can have a single panel or multiple panels. A single-paneled status bar uses the **SimpleText** property to output text in a manner similar to controls with a **Caption** property. If you wish to use multiple panels, the **SimplePanel** property can be set to **False**, and each panel can set its own **Text** property.

Figure 52-2 gives the ancestry of **TStatusBar**. Table 52-1 displays the properties, methods, and events implemented by **TStatusBar**.

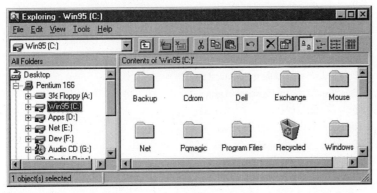

Figure 52-1   The Windows Explorer program has a multi-paneled status bar with a size grip

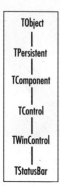

Figure 52-2 Ancestry of `TStatusBar`

TObject
|
TPersistent
|
TComponent
|
TControl
|
TWinControl
|
TStatusBar

Table 52-1 Properties, methods, and events implemented by `TStatusBar`

Use or Set This...	To Do This...	Inheritance
Align	Determine how the control is aligned within its parent.	TControl
Assign	Assign one persistent object to another.	TPersistent
BeginDrag	Begin a manual drag operation.	TControl
BoundsRect	Determine the boundary rectangle occupied by the control.	TControl
BringToFront	Bring the control to the front of the z-order.	TControl
Brush	Determine the color and pattern used for the windowed control background.	TComponent
CanFocus	Determine whether the windowed control can receive the focus.	TWinControl
Canvas	Access the drawing surface of the status bar.	TControl
Caption	Label the control with a text string.	TControl
ClassName	Get the name of the object's class.	TObject
ClassParent	Get the object's parent class.	TObject
ClassType	Get the object's actual type.	TObject
ClientHeight	Determine the control's client height.	TControl
ClientOrigin	Determine the upper-left position of the control's client area.	TControl
ClientRect	Determine the rectangle occupied by the control's client area.	TControl
ClientToScreen	Convert control (local) coordinates to screen coordinates.	TControl
ClientWidth	Determine the width of the control's client area.	TControl
Color	Determine the color of the windowed control.	TControl
ComponentCount	Determine the number of owned components.	TComponent
ComponentIndex	The index of the component in its owner's Components list.	TComponent
Components	Determine the list of owned components.	TComponent
ComponentState	Determine the state of the current component.	TComponent
ContainsControl	Determine whether the specified control is contained by the windowed control.	TWinControl
ControlAtPos	Determine the control contained at a specified position.	TWinControl
ControlCount	Determine the number of controls contained by the windowed control.	TWinControl

Use or Set This...	To Do This...	Inheritance
Controls	Access the controls contained by the windowed control using their positions in an array.	TWinControl
ControlState	Determine the state of the control at any given time.	TControl
ControlStyle	Determine what attributes are present in the control.	TControl
Create	Create a new component.	TObject
Ctl3D	Determine whether the windowed control displays in 3D.	TWinControl
Cursor	Determine what image is used for the cursor over the control.	TControl
Destroy	Destroy the component.	TObject
DestroyComponents	Destroy all the components owned by the component.	TComponent
Destroying	Notify the component that it is being destroyed.	TComponent
DragCursor	Determine the shape of the mouse cursor as it drags an object over the control.	TControl
DragCursor	Determine the shape of the mouse pointer when it drops an accepted object on the status bar.	TControl
Dragging	Determine whether the control is being dragged.	TControl
DragMode	Determine the drag-and-drop behavior of the control.	TControl
Enabled	Determine whether the control is enabled.	TControl
EndDrag	End or cancel a manual drag operation.	TControl
FindComponent	Find a component in the Components array list.	TComponent
Focused	Determine whether the windowed control has the focus.	TControl
Font	Determine the font used to render text on the control.	TControl
Free	Safely destroy the object.	TObject
GetTextBuf	Copy the text of the control into a buffer.	TControl
GetTextLen	Get the length of the text of the control.	TControl
Handle	Obtain a handle to the windowed control.	TComponent
HandleAllocated	Determine if a handle is allocated for the windowed control.	TWinControl
Height	Determine the height of the control.	TControl
HelpContext	Determine the help context ID of the windowed control.	TComponent
Hide	Make the control invisible.	TControl
Hint	Determine the text that displays in a tooltip for the control.	TControl
InheritsFrom	Determine if the object is descended from a certain class.	TObject
InsertControl	Insert a control into the windowed control's Controls array.	TWinControl
InstanceSize	Determine the amount of memory allocated for the object.	TObject
Invalidate	Force the control to be repainted as soon as possible.	TControl
Left	Determine the left edge of the control within its container.	TControl
Name	Determine the name of the component.	TComponent
OnClick	Handle the event that occurs when a mouse button is clicked.	TControl
OnDblClick	Handle the event that occurs when a mouse button is double-clicked.	TControl
OnDragDrop	Handle the event that occurs when an object is dropped on the control.	TControl
OnDragOver	Handle the event that occurs when an object is dragged over the control.	TControl

continued on next page

881

continued from previous page

Use or Set This...	To Do This...	Inheritance
OnEndDrag	Handle the event that occurs when a drag-and-drop operation is cancelled.	TControl
OnEnter	Handle the event that occurs when the windowed control receives the focus.	TWinControl
OnExit	Handle the event that occurs when the windowed control loses the focus.	TWinControl
OnKeyDown	Handle the event that occurs when a key is pressed down and not immediately released while the windowed control has the focus.	TWinControl
OnKeyPress	Handle the event that occurs when a key is pressed while the windowed control has the focus.	TWinControl
OnKeyUp	Handle the event that occurs when a key is released while the windowed control has the focus.	TWinControl
OnMouseDown	Handle the event that occurs when a mouse button is held down and not immediately released.	TControl
OnMouseMove	Handle the event that occurs when the cursor moves over the control.	TControl
OnMouseUp	Handle the event that occurs when a mouse button is released.	TControl
OnResize	Handle the event that occurs when the status bar is resized.	TControl
OnStartDrag	Handle the event that occurs when a drag-and-drop operation is started.	TControl
Owner	Determine the owner of the component.	TComponent
Panels	Access the panels that exist on the status bar.	None
Parent	Determine the parent, or container, of the control.	TControl
ParentColor	Determine whether the Color information of the control's parent is used.	TControl
ParentCtl3D	Determine whether the windowed control uses its parent's Ctl3D settings.	TWinControl
ParentFont	Determine whether the Font information of the control's parent is used.	TControl
ParentShowHint	Determine whether the ShowHint information of the control's parent is used.	TControl
PopupMenu	Determine which pop-up menu is associated with the control.	TControl
Refresh	Erase the control and repaint it.	TControl
RemoveControl	Remove the specified control from the windowed control's Controls array.	TWinControl
Repaint	Repaint the control.	TControl
ScaleBy	Resize the windowed control.	TWinControl
ScreenToClient	Convert screen coordinates to client (control) coordinates.	TControl
SendToBack	Send the control to the end of the z-order.	TControl
SetBounds	Determine the coordinates of the control's bounding rectangle.	TControl
SetFocus	Set the focus to the windowed control.	TWinControl
SetTextBuf	Set the text of the control to the text in a buffer.	TControl
Show	Make the control visible.	TControl
ShowHint	Determine whether to display a tooltip.	TControl
Showing	Determine whether the windowed control is currently showing onscreen.	TComponent
SimplePanel	Determine whether the status bar has multiple panels.	None
SimpleText	Obtain the text that will appear in the status bar if it has only one panel.	None
SizeGrip	Determine whether the status bar has a size grip.	None
TabOrder	Determine the tab order of the windowed control.	TWinControl

Use or Set This...	To Do This...	Inheritance
TabStop	Determine whether the windowed control is in the tab order.	TWinControl
Tag	Store an additional integer value with the component.	TComponent
Text	Access the changeable text on the control.	TControl
Top	Determine the upper edge of the control.	TControl
Update	Called automatically by Refresh.	TControl
Visible	Determine whether the status bar is visible.	TControl
Width	Determine the width of the control.	TControl

Panels PROPERTY

Objects Affected   TStatusBar

Purpose   The Panels property is a collection of status bar panels.

Declaration

```
property Panels: TStatusPanels;
```

Example Syntax

```
procedure TForm1.Timer1Timer(Sender: TObject);
begin
  // Get the time
  StatusBar1.Panels[0].Text := TimeToStr(Time);

  // Use the Win32 API function GetKeyState to determine whether
  // the Num Lock key is pressed
  if GetKeyState(VK_NUMLOCK) = 1 then
    StatusBar1.Panels[1].Text := 'Num lock: ON'
  else
    StatusBar1.Panels[1].Text := 'Num lock: OFF';

  // Use the Win32 API function GetKeyState to determine whether
  // the Caps Lock key is pressed
  if GetKeyState(VK_CAPITAL) = 1 then
    StatusBar1.Panels[2].Text := 'Caps lock: ON'
  else
    StatusBar1.Panels[2].Text := 'Caps lock: OFF';
end;
```

Description   The Panels property lets you access the panels in the status bar as items in a zero-based array, where the first item is Panels[0], the next is Panels[1], and so on. Figure 52-3 shows a multi-panel status bar. You can edit the panels in a status bar at design time from the Delphi IDE using the StatusBar Panels Editor, shown in Figure 52-4. To activate the StatusBar Panels Editor, double-click the Panels value in the Object Inspector window.

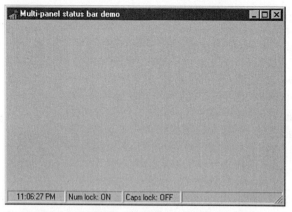

Figure 52-3 Accessing multiple panels in a status bar

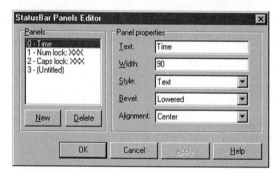

Figure 52-4 The StatusBar Panels Editor

SimplePanel PROPERTY

Objects Affected   TStatusBar

Purpose   The SimplePanel property determines whether the status bar supports multiple panels.

Declaration

```
property SimplePanel: Boolean;
```

Example Syntax

```
procedure TForm1.FormCreate(Sender: TObject);
begin
  StatusBar1.SimplePanel := True;
  StatusBar1.SimpleText := TimeToStr(Time);
  StatusBar1.SizeGrip := False;
end;
```

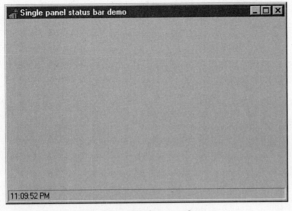

Figure 52-5 A single-panel status bar

Description   If `SimplePanel` is `True`, the status bar has only one panel, and its text can be set with the `SimpleText` property. Figure 52-5 shows a single-panel status bar. If `SimplePanel` is `False`, the status bar supports multiple panels, and the text of each panel is set with the `Text` property of each individual panel. See `Panels` for an example of setting the `Text` property of each. The default value is `False`.

SimpleText PROPERTY

Objects Affected   `TStatusBar`

Purpose   `SimpleText` contains the text appearing in a single-panel status bar.

Declaration

```
property SimpleText: string;
```

Example Syntax

```
procedure TForm1.FormCreate(Sender: TObject);
begin
  StatusBar1.SimplePanel := True;
  StatusBar1.SimpleText := TimeToStr(Time);
  StatusBar1.SizeGrip := False;
end;
```

Description   If the `SimplePanel` property is `True`, the text contained by `SimpleText` will appear in the status bar. To set the text of panels in a multi-panel status bar, use the `Text` property for each.

SizeGrip PROPERTY

Objects Affected	TStatusBar
Purpose	The SizeGrip property determines whether the status bar contains a size grip.
Declaration	

```
property SizeGrip: Boolean;
```

Example Syntax

```
StatusBar1.SizeGrip := False;
```

Description   If SizeGrip is True, a size grip appears at the right corner of the status bar (assuming the status bar is bottom-aligned). If SizeGrip is False, no size grip appears. If the Align property of the StatusBar is alTop or alBottom, SizeGrip is True by default; otherwise it is False.

53

TTabSheet

Tab sheets represent the individual pages in a *page control*, a major element in the new property sheet dialog boxes introduced with Windows 95. Property sheets provide a consistent way for dialog boxes to contain a lot of information in a relatively small space by providing virtual pages the user can select. The Display Properties dialog, shown in Figure 53-1, is an example of a common property sheet available in Windows 95.

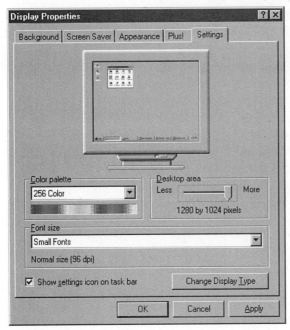

Figure 53-1 The Display Properties dialog

Tab sheets, also known simply as *pages*, are encapsulated by the **TTabSheet** class. **TPageControl**, covered in Chapter 59, "**TCustomTabControl** and Its Descendants," maintains its individual pages with a **Pages** property, a zero-based array of **TTabSheet** objects. Typically, you will access individual tab sheets through the **Pages** property of their **TPageControl** container.

It is easiest to add pages to a page control at design time by placing a page control on a form and right-clicking it. In the pop-up menu that appears, choose New Page. This is shown in Figure 53-2.

Figure 53-3 shows the ancestry of **TTabSheet**. Table 53-1 displays the properties, methods, and events that are implemented by **TTabSheet**.

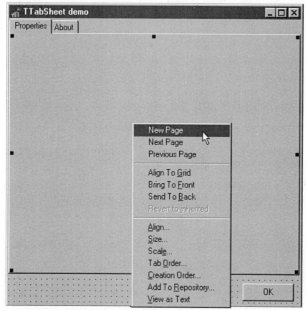

Figure 53-2 Add a new tab sheet to a page control

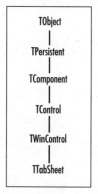

Figure 53-3 Ancestry of **TTabSheet**

Table 53-1 Properties, methods, and events that are implemented by TTabSheet

Use or Set This...	To Do This...	Inheritance
Align	Determine how the control is aligned within its parent.	TControl
Assign	Assign one persistent object to another.	TPersistent
BeginDrag	Begin a manual drag operation.	TControl
BoundsRect	Determine the boundary rectangle occupied by the control.	TControl
BringToFront	Bring the control to the front of the z-order.	TControl
Brush	Determine the color and pattern used for the windowed control background.	TComponent
CanFocus	Determine whether the windowed control can receive the focus.	TWinControl
Caption	Label the control with a text string.	TControl
ClassName	Get the name of the object's class.	TObject
ClassParent	Get the object's parent class.	TObject
ClassType	Get the object's actual type.	TObject
ClientHeight	Determine the control's client height.	TControl
ClientOrigin	Determine the upper left position of the control's client area.	TControl
ClientRect	Determine the rectangle occupied by the control's client area.	TControl
ClientToScreen	Convert control (local) coordinates to screen coordinates.	TControl
ClientWidth	Determine the width of the control's client area.	TControl
Color	Determine the color of the windowed control.	TControl
ComponentCount	Determines the number of owned components.	TComponent
ComponentIndex	The index of the component in its owner's Components list.	TComponent
Components	Determine the list of owned components.	TComponent
ComponentState	Determine the state of the current component.	TComponent
ContainsControl	Determine whether the specified control is contained by windowed control.	TWinControl
ControlAtPos	Determine the control contained at a specified position.	TWinControl
ControlCount	Determine the number of controls contained by the windowed control.	TWinControl
Controls	Access the controls contained by the windowed control using their positions in an array.	TWinControl
ControlState	Determine the state of the control at any given time.	TControl
ControlStyle	Determine what attributes are present in the control.	TControl
Create	Create a new component.	TObject
Ctl3D	Determine whether the windowed control displays in 3D.	TWinControl
Cursor	Determine what image is used for the cursor over the control.	TControl
Destroy	Destroy the component.	TObject
DestroyComponents	Destroy all of the components owned by the component.	TComponent
Destroying	Notify the component that it is being destroyed.	TComponent
DragCursor	Determine the shape of the mouse cursor as it drags an object over the control.	TControl
Dragging	Determine whether the control is being dragged.	TControl

continued on next page

continued from previous page

Use or Set This...	To Do This...	Inheritance
DragMode	Determine the drag-and-drop behavior of the control.	TControl
Enabled	Determine whether the control is enabled.	TControl
EndDrag	End or cancel a manual drag operation.	TControl
FindComponent	Find a component in the Components array list.	TComponent
Focused	Determine whether the windowed control has the focus.	TControl
Font	Determine the font used to render text on the control.	TControl
Free	Safely destroy the object.	TObject
GetTextBuf	Copy the text of the control into a buffer.	TControl
GetTextLen	Get the length of the text of the control.	TControl
Handle	Obtain a handle to the windowed control.	TComponent
HandleAllocated	Determine if a handle is allocated for the windowed control.	TWinControl
Height	Determine the height of the control.	TControl
HelpContext	Determine the help context ID of the windowed control.	TComponent
Hide	Make the control invisible.	TControl
Hint	Determine the text that displays in a tooltip for the control.	TControl
InheritsFrom	Determine if the object is descended from a certain class.	TObject
InsertControl	Insert a control into the windowed control's Controls array.	TWinControl
InstanceSize	Determine the amount of memory allocated for the object.	TObject
Invalidate	Force the control to be repainted as soon as possible.	TControl
Left	Determine the left edge of the control within its container.	TControl
Name	Determine the name of the component.	TComponent
OnClick	Handle the event that occurs when a mouse button is clicked.	TControl
OnDblClick	Handle the event that occurs when a mouse button is double-clicked.	TControl
OnDragDrop	Handle the event that occurs when an object is dropped on the control.	TControl
OnDragOver	Handle the event that occurs when an object is dragged over the control.	TControl
OnEndDrag	Handle the event that occurs when a drag-and-drop operation is cancelled.	TControl
OnEnter	Handle the event that occurs when the windowed control receives the focus.	TWinControl
OnExit	Handle the event that occurs when the windowed control loses the focus.	TWinControl
OnKeyDown	Handle the event that occurs when a key is pressed down and not immediately released while the windowed control has the focus.	TWinControl
OnKeyPress	Handle the event that occurs when a key is pressed while the windowed control has the focus.	TWinControl
OnKeyUp	Handle the event that occurs when a key is released while the windowed control has the focus.	TWinControl
OnMouseDown	Handle the event that occurs when a mouse button is held down and not immediately released.	TControl

Use or Set This...	To Do This...	Inheritance
OnMouseMove	Handle the event that occurs when the cursor moves over the control.	TControl
OnMouseUp	Handle the event that occurs when a mouse button is released.	TControl
OnStartDrag	Handle the event that occurs when a drag-and-drop operation is started.	TControl
Owner	Determine the owner of the component.	TComponent
PageControl	Determine the page control that contains the tab sheet.	None
PageIndex	Determine the index number of the tab sheet within the parent page control's Pages array.	None
Parent	Determine the parent, or container, of the control.	TControl
ParentColor	Determine whether the control's parent's Color information is used.	TControl
ParentCtl3D	Determine whether the windowed control uses its parent's Ctl3D settings.	TWinControl
ParentFont	Determine whether the tab sheet uses its parent's font information.	TControl
ParentShowHint	Determine whether the control's parent's ShowHint information is used.	TControl
PopupMenu	Determine which pop-up menu is associated with the control.	TControl
Refresh	Erase the control and repaint it.	TControl
RemoveControl	Remove the specified control from the windowed control's Controls array.	TWinControl
Repaint	Repaint the control.	TControl
ScaleBy	Resize the windowed control.	TWinControl
ScreenToClient	Convert screen coordinates to client (control) coordinates.	TControl
SendToBack	Send the control to the end of the z-order.	TControl
SetBounds	Determine the coordinates of the control's bounding rectangle.	TControl
SetFocus	Set the focus to the windowed control.	TWinControl
SetTextBuf	Set the text of the control to the text in a buffer.	TControl
Show	Make the control visible.	TControl
ShowHint	Determine whether to display a tooltip.	TControl
Showing	Determine whether the windowed control is currently showing on screen.	TComponent
TabIndex	Determine the position of the tab sheet in its parent's array of visible pages.	TWinControl
TabOrder	Determine the tab order of the windowed control.	TWinControl
TabStop	Determine whether the windowed control is in the tab order.	TWinControl
TabVisible	Determine whether the tab sheet's tab is visible in its page control container.	None
Tag	Store an additional integer value with the component.	TComponent
Text	Access the changeable text on the control.	TControl
Top	Determine the upper edge of the control.	TControl
Update	Update is called automatically by Refresh.	TControl
Visible	Determine whether the control is visible.	TControl
Width	Determine the width of the control.	TControl

PageControl METHOD

Objects Affected	TTabSheet
Purpose	The **PageControl** property identifies the name of the page control that contains the tab sheet.
Declaration	

```
property PageControl: TPageControl;
```

Description	PageControl is a run-time-only property.

PageIndex PROPERTY

Objects Affected	TTabSheet
Purpose	The **PageIndex** property contains the index value of the tab sheet.
Declaration	

```
property PageIndex: Integer;
```

Description	The index of a tab sheet represents it position in the **Pages** property of its page control container. **Pages** is a zero-based array, so the first tab sheet will be **Pages[0]**, the second is **Pages[1]**, and so on.

TabVisible PROPERTY

Objects Affected	TTabSheet
Purpose	The **TabVisible** property determines whether the tab sheet is visible.
Declaration	

```
property TabVisible: Boolean;
```

Example Syntax

```
// Show property sheet with only the properties page visible
procedure TMainForm.Openproperties1Click(Sender: TObject);
begin
  Form1.TabSheet1.TabVisible := True;
  Form1.TabSheet2.TabVisible := False;
  Form1.ShowModal;
end;

// Show property sheet with only the about page visible
procedure TMainForm.Aboutthisprogram1Click(Sender: TObject);
begin
  Form1.TabSheet1.TabVisible := False;
  Form1.TabSheet2.TabVisible := True;
  Form1.ShowModal;
end;
```

```
// Show property sheet with both pages visible
procedure TMainForm.OpenBoth1Click(Sender: TObject);
begin
  Form1.TabSheet1.TabVisible := True;
  Form1.TabSheet2.TabVisible := True;
  Form1.ShowModal;
end;
```

Description   If **TabVisible** is **True**, the tab sheet is visible. If **TabVisible** is **False**, the tab sheet is not visible. **TabVisible** is **True** by default.

54

TTrackBar

The Delphi VCL encapsulates the Windows *track bar* control, also known as a *slider*, with the **TTrackBar** class. A track bar is used for setting or changing values within a range. Typical uses for a track bar include volume control, graphic resolution range, and brightness control. A track bar consists of a thin horizontal bar with tick marks below it indicating the range of values. A slider moves along the bar, indicating the current value of the track bar. The Desktop area section of the Settings page on the Display Properties dialog, shown in Figure 54-1, uses a track bar control to indicate the possible display resolutions available in your Windows setup.

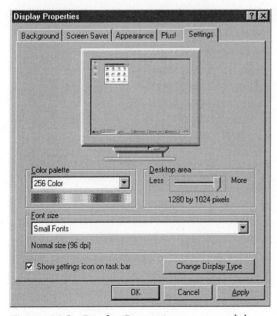

Figure 54-1 Display Properties uses a track bar to let the user specify the desired resolution

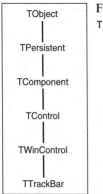

Figure 54-2 Derivation of
`TTrackBar`

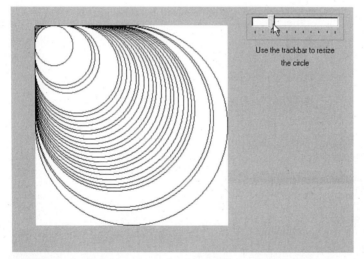

Figure 54-3 The `TTrackBar` demo used for many of the
examples in this section

The track bar is typically manipulated with the mouse: You can drag the slider or
click on the bar to the right or left of it. You can also move the slider using [PgUp], [PgDn],
and the arrow keys on the keyboard, though this is rarely used.

Figure 54-2 shows the derivation of `TTrackBar` and Figure 54-3 shows the
`TTrackBar` demo used for many examples in this section. Table 54-1 displays the
properties, methods, and events implemented by `TTrackBar`.

Table 54-1 Properties, methods, and events implemented by `TTrackBar`

Use or Set This...	To Do This...	Inheritance
Align	Determine how the control is aligned within its parent.	TControl
Assign	Assign one persistent object to another.	TPersistent

Use or Set This...	To Do This...	Inheritance
BeginDrag	Begin a manual drag operation.	TControl
BoundsRect	Determine the boundary rectangle occupied by the control.	TControl
BringToFront	Bring the control to the front of the z-order.	TControl
Brush	Determine the color and pattern used for the windowed control background.	TComponent
CanFocus	Determine whether the windowed control can receive the focus.	TWinControl
Caption	Label the control with a text string.	TControl
ClassName	Get the name of the object's class.	TObject
ClassParent	Get the object's parent class.	TObject
ClassType	Get the object's actual type.	TObject
ClientHeight	Determine the control's client height.	TControl
ClientOrigin	Determine the upper-left position of the control's client area.	TControl
ClientRect	Determine the rectangle occupied by the control's client area.	TControl
ClientToScreen	Convert control (local) coordinates to screen coordinates.	TControl
ClientWidth	Determine the width of the control's client area.	TControl
Color	Determine the color of the windowed control.	TControl
ComponentCount	Determine the number of owned components.	TComponent
ComponentIndex	Determine the index of the component in its owner's Components list.	TComponent
Components	Determine the list of owned components.	TComponent
ComponentState	Determine the state of the current component.	TComponent
ContainsControl	Determine whether the specified control is contained by the windowed control.	TWinControl
ControlAtPos	Determine the control contained at a specified position.	TWinControl
ControlCount	Determine the number of controls contained by the windowed control.	TWinControl
Controls	Access the controls contained by the windowed control using their positions in an array.	TWinControl
ControlState	Determine the state of the control at any given time.	TControl
ControlStyle	Determine what attributes are present in the control.	TControl
Create	Create a new component.	TObject
Ctl3D	Determine whether the windowed control displays in 3D.	TWinControl
Cursor	Determine what image is used for the cursor over the control.	TControl
Destroy	Destroy the component.	TObject
DestroyComponents	Destroy all of the components owned by the component.	TComponent
Destroying	Notify the component that it is being destroyed.	TComponent
DragCursor	Determine the shape of the mouse cursor as it drags an object over the control.	TControl
Dragging	Determine whether the control is being dragged.	TControl
DragMode	Determine the drag-and-drop behavior of the control.	TControl
Enabled	Determine whether the control is enabled.	TControl
EndDrag	End or cancel a manual drag operation.	TControl
FindComponent	Find a component in the Components array list.	TComponent
Focused	Determine whether the windowed control has the focus.	TControl
Font	Determine the font used to render text on the control.	TControl

continued on next page

continued from previous page

Use or Set This...	To Do This...	Inheritance
Free	Safely destroy the object.	TObject
Frequency	Determine how often tick marks appear on the track bar.	None
GetTextBuf	Copy the text of the control into a buffer.	TControl
GetTextLen	Get the length of the text of the control.	TControl
Handle	Obtain a handle to the windowed control.	TComponent
HandleAllocated	Determine whether a handle is allocated for the windowed control.	TWinControl
Height	Determine the height of the control.	TControl
HelpContext	Determine the help context ID of the windowed control.	TComponent
Hide	Make the control invisible.	TControl
Hint	Determine the text that displays in a tooltip for the control.	TControl
InheritsFrom	Determine whether the object is descended from a certain class.	TObject
InsertControl	Insert a control into the windowed control's Controls array.	TWinControl
InstanceSize	Determine the amount of memory allocated for the object	TObject
Invalidate	Force the control to be repainted as soon as possible.	TControl
Left	Determine the left edge of the control within its container.	TControl
LineSize	Determine the number of ticks the slider is moved when the user presses an arrow key.	None
Max	Determine the maximum value in the range of possible track bar values.	None
Min	Determine the mimimum value in the range of possible track bar values.	None
Name	Determine the name of the component.	TComponent
OnChange	Handle the event that occurs when the track bar position changes.	TControl
OnClick	Handle the event that occurs when a mouse button is clicked.	TControl
OnDblClick	Handle the event that occurs when a mouse button is double-clicked.	TControl
OnDragDrop	Handle the event that occurs when an object is dropped on the control.	TControl
OnDragOver	Handle the event that occurs when an object is dragged over the control.	TControl
OnEndDrag	Handle the event that occurs when a drag-and-drop operation is cancelled.	TControl
OnEnter	Handle the event that occurs when the windowed control receives the focus.	TWinControl
OnExit	Handle the event that occurs when the windowed control loses the focus.	TWinControl
OnKeyDown	Handle the event that occurs when a key is pressed down and not immediately released while the windowed control has the focus.	TWinControl
OnKeyPress	Handle the event that occurs when a key is pressed while the windowed control has the focus.	TWinControl
OnKeyUp	Handle the event that occurs when a key is released while the windowed control has the focus.	TWinControl
OnMouseDown	Handle the event that occurs when a mouse button is held down and not immediately released.	TControl
OnMouseMove	Handle the event that occurs when the cursor moves over the control.	TControl
OnMouseUp	Handle the event that occurs when a mouse button is released.	TControl

Use or Set This...	To Do This...	Inheritance
OnStartDrag	Handle the event that occurs when a drag-and-drop operation is started.	TControl
Orientation	Determine whether the track bar is horizontal or vertical.	None
Owner	Determine the owner of the component.	TComponent
PageSize	Determine the number of ticks the slider is moved when the PgUp and PgDn keys are pressed.	None
Parent	Determine the parent, or container, of the control.	TControl
ParentColor	Determine whether the Color information of the control's parent is used.	TControl
ParentCtl3D	Determine whether the windowed control uses its parent's Ctl3D settings.	TWinControl
ParentFont	Determine whether the Font information of the control's parent is used.	TControl
ParentShowHint	Determine whether the ShowHint information of the control's parent is used.	TControl
PopupMenu	Determine which pop-up menu is associated with the control.	TControl
Position	Determine the current position of the slider.	None
Refresh	Erase the control and repaint it.	TControl
RemoveControl	Remove the specified control from the windowed control's Controls array.	TWinControl
Repaint	Repaint the control.	TControl
ScaleBy	Resize the windowed control.	TWinControl
ScreenToClient	Convert screen coordinates to client (control) coordinates.	TControl
SelEnd	Determine the end point for a selected range.	None
SelStart	Determine the start point for a selected range.	None
SendToBack	Send the control to the end of the z-order.	TControl
SetBounds	Determine the coordinates of the control's bounding rectangle.	TControl
SetFocus	Set the focus to the windowed control.	TWinControl
SetTextBuf	Set the text of the control to the text in a buffer.	TControl
SetTick	Place a tick at a specified point on the track bar.	None
Show	Make the control visible.	TControl
ShowHint	Determine whether to display a tooltip.	TControl
Showing	Determine whether the windowed control is currently showing onscreen.	TComponent
TabOrder	Determine the tab order of the windowed control.	TWinControl
TabStop	Determine whether the windowed control is in the tab order.	TWinControl
Tag	Store an additional integer value with the component.	TComponent
Text	Access the changeable text on the control.	TControl
TickMarks	Determine where the tick marks are placed on the track bar.	None
TickStyle	Determine the tick mark style.	None
Top	Determine the upper edge of the control.	TControl
Update	Called automatically by Refresh.	TControl
Visible	Determine whether the control is visible.	TControl
Width	Determine the width of the control.	TControl

Frequency PROPERTY

Objects Affected	TTrackBar
Purpose	The Frequency property determines the frequency of tick marks below the slider bar.
Declaration	

```
property Frequency: Integer;
```

Example Syntax

```
procedure TForm1.FormCreate(Sender: TObject);
begin
  TrackBar1.Orientation := trHorizontal;
  TrackBar1.Min := 0;
  TrackBar1.Max := 300;
  TrackBar1.TickStyle := tsAuto;
  TrackBar1.Frequency := 30;
  TrackBar1.LineSize := 30;
  TrackBar1.PageSize := 2;
  TrackBar1.Position := 150;

  TrackBar1Change(Self);
end;

procedure TForm1.TrackBar1Change(Sender: TObject);
begin
  Image1.Canvas.Ellipse(0, 0, TrackBar1.Position, TrackBar1.Position);
end;
```

Description For the Frequency property to be used, the **TickMarks** property must be set to **tsAuto**. If the **Frequency** is set to **5**, there is one tick mark for every five values in the range, as specified by the **Min** and **Max** properties. In the example above, there is one tick mark for every 30 values in the range, which is 300. In that case, there are 11 tick marks total (there is one tick mark for zero).

LineSize PROPERTY

Objects Affected	TTrackBar
Purpose	The LineSize property determines how far the slider will move when you press the arrow keys on the keyboard.
Declaration	

```
property LineSize: Integer;
```

Example Syntax

```
procedure TForm1.FormCreate(Sender: TObject);
begin
  TrackBar1.Orientation := trHorizontal;
  TrackBar1.Min := 0;
```

```
      TrackBar1.Max := 300;
      TrackBar1.TickStyle := tsAuto;
      TrackBar1.Frequency := 30;
      TrackBar1.LineSize := 30;
      TrackBar1.PageSize := 2;
      TrackBar1.Position := 150;

      TrackBar1Change(Self);
    end;

    procedure TForm1.TrackBar1Change(Sender: TObject);
    begin
      Image1.Canvas.Ellipse(0, 0, TrackBar1.Position, TrackBar1.Position);
    end;
```

Description   The up and left arrow keys will decrement the value of **Position** and move the slider up or left. The down and right arrow keys will increment **Position** and move the slider down or right, depending on its orientation. Use the **LineSize** property to determine the size of the change when the ⬆ and ⬇ keys are pressed.

Max PROPERTY

Objects Affected   TTrackBar

Purpose   The **Max** property determines the maximum value of the slider.

Declaration

```
    property Max: Integer;
```

Example Syntax

```
    procedure TForm1.FormCreate(Sender: TObject);
    begin
      TrackBar1.Orientation := trHorizontal;
      TrackBar1.Min := 0;
      TrackBar1.Max := 300;
      TrackBar1.TickStyle := tsAuto;
      TrackBar1.Frequency := 30;
      TrackBar1.LineSize := 30;
      TrackBar1.PageSize := 2;
      TrackBar1.Position := 150;

      TrackBar1Change(Self);
    end;

    procedure TForm1.TrackBar1Change(Sender: TObject);
    begin
      Image1.Canvas.Ellipse(0, 0, TrackBar1.Position, TrackBar1.Position);
    end;
```

Description   The range of values possible with the track bar is determined by the **Min** and **Max** properties. The current position of the slider is determined with the **Position** property.

Min PROPERTY

Objects Affected	TTrackBar
Purpose	The Min property determines the minimum value of the slider.
Declaration	

```
property Min: Integer;
```

Example Syntax

```
procedure TForm1.FormCreate(Sender: TObject);
begin
  TrackBar1.Orientation := trHorizontal;
  TrackBar1.Min := 0;
  TrackBar1.Max := 300;
  TrackBar1.TickStyle := tsAuto;
  TrackBar1.Frequency := 30;
  TrackBar1.LineSize := 30;
  TrackBar1.PageSize := 2;
  TrackBar1.Position := 150;

  TrackBar1Change(Self);
end;

procedure TForm1.TrackBar1Change(Sender: TObject);
begin
  Image1.Canvas.Ellipse(0, 0, TrackBar1.Position, TrackBar1.Position);
end;
```

Description The range of values possible with the track bar is determined by the Min and Max properties. The current position of the slider is determined with the Position property.

Orientation PROPERTY

Objects Affected	TTrackBar
Purpose	Orientation determines whether the track bar is vertical or horizontal.
Declaration	

```
property Orientation: TTrackBarOrientation;
```

Example Syntax

```
procedure TForm1.FormCreate(Sender: TObject);
begin
  TrackBar1.Orientation := trHorizontal;
  TrackBar1.Min := 0;
  TrackBar1.Max := 300;
  TrackBar1.TickStyle := tsAuto;
  TrackBar1.Frequency := 30;
  TrackBar1.LineSize := 30;
  TrackBar1.PageSize := 2;
  TrackBar1.Position := 150;

  TrackBar1Change(Self);
```

```
end;

procedure TForm1.TrackBar1Change(Sender: TObject);
begin
  Image1.Canvas.Ellipse(0, 0, TrackBar1.Position, TrackBar1.Position);
end;
```

Description Orientation is type TTrackBarOrientation and can be set to one of the following possible values: trHorizontal for a horizontal track bar, or trVertical for a vertical track bar. Most track bars are horizontal. The default value is trHorizontal.

> **WARNING**
> At the time of this writing, Borland's documentation incorrectly identifies the possible TTrackBarOrientation values as tbHorizontal and tbVertical. The correct values are trHorizontal and trVertical.

PageSize PROPERTY

Objects Affected TTrackBar

Purpose The PageSize property determines how far the slider will move when you press [PgUp] or [PgDn].

Declaration

```
property PageSize: Integer;
```

Example Syntax

```
procedure TForm1.FormCreate(Sender: TObject);
begin
  TrackBar1.Orientation := trHorizontal;
  TrackBar1.Min := 0;
  TrackBar1.Max := 300;
  TrackBar1.TickStyle := tsAuto;
  TrackBar1.Frequency := 30;
  TrackBar1.LineSize := 30;
  TrackBar1.PageSize := 2;
  TrackBar1.Position := 150;

  TrackBar1Change(Self);
end;

procedure TForm1.TrackBar1Change(Sender: TObject);
begin
  Image1.Canvas.Ellipse(0, 0, TrackBar1.Position, TrackBar1.Position);
end;
```

Description Pressing [PgUp] will decrement the value of Position and move the slider up or left. Pressing [PgDn] will increment Position and move the slider down or right, depending on its orientation. Use the PageSize property to determine the size of the change when the arrow keys on the keyboard are pressed.

Position PROPERTY

Objects Affected	TTrackBar
Purpose	The `Position` property indicates the current position of the slider.
Declaration	

```
property Position: Integer;
```

Example Syntax

```
procedure TForm1.FormCreate(Sender: TObject);
begin
  TrackBar1.Orientation := trHorizontal;
  TrackBar1.Min := 0;
  TrackBar1.Max := 300;
  TrackBar1.TickStyle := tsAuto;
  TrackBar1.Frequency := 30;
  TrackBar1.LineSize := 30;
  TrackBar1.PageSize := 2;
  TrackBar1.Position := 150;

  TrackBar1Change(Self);
end;

procedure TForm1.TrackBar1Change(Sender: TObject);
begin
  Image1.Canvas.Ellipse(0, 0, TrackBar1.Position, TrackBar1.Position);
end;
```

Description

The `Position` property contains a value within the range specified by the `Min` and `Max` properties, indicating the current position of the slider. You can increment or decrement `Position` in a variety of ways: move the slider with the mouse; click the bar to either side of the mouse; press PgUp, PgDn, or one of the arrow keys; or change `Position` directly with Object Pascal code. In the example above, the `Position` property is set when the form is created so the slider appears in the middle of the track bar.

SelEnd PROPERTY

Objects Affected	TTrackBar
Purpose	`SelEnd` specifies the end of the selected range within the full range of the track bar.
Declaration	

```
property SelEnd: Integer;
```

Example Syntax

```
procedure TForm1.FormCreate(Sender: TObject);
begin
```

```
    TrackBar1.TickStyle := tsManual;
    TrackBar1.Min := 0;
    TrackBar1.Max := 100;
    TrackBar1.SelStart := 25;
    TrackBar1.SelEnd := 75;
    TrackBar1.TickMarks := tmBottomRight;
end;

procedure TForm1.TrackBar1Change(Sender: TObject);
begin
    Label1.Caption := IntToStr(TrackBar1.Position);
end;
```

Description   SelStart and SelEnd highlight a selected range within the track bar using the system highlight color. The starting and ending points of the selection range are marked with triangular ticks instead of the standard vertical dash. See Figure 54-4, in the entry for SelStart, for an illustration of a selection range.

SelStart PROPERTY

Objects Affected   TTrackBar

Purpose   SelStart specifies the start of the selected range within the full range of the track bar.

Declaration

```
property SelStart: Integer;
```

Example Syntax

```
procedure TForm1.FormCreate(Sender: TObject);
begin
    TrackBar1.TickStyle := tsManual;
    TrackBar1.Min := 0;
    TrackBar1.Max := 100;
    TrackBar1.SelStart := 25;
    TrackBar1.SelEnd := 75;
    TrackBar1.TickMarks := tmBottomRight;
end;

procedure TForm1.TrackBar1Change(Sender: TObject);
begin
    Label1.Caption := IntToStr(TrackBar1.Position);
end;
```

Description   SelStart and SelEnd highlight a selected range within the track bar using the system highlight color. The starting and ending points of the selection range are marked with triangular ticks instead of the standard vertical dash. Figure 54-4 illustrates this selection range.

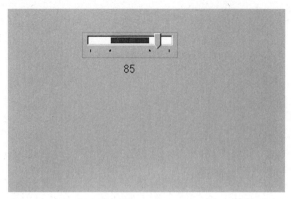

Figure 54-4 A selection range in a track bar control

SetTick METHOD

Objects Affected	TTrackBar
Purpose	SetTick sets a tick at any position within the range of the slider.
Declaration	

```
procedure SetTick(Value: Integer);
```

Parameters	
Value	The location within the range of the slider to draw a tick.
Example Syntax	

```
procedure TForm1.FormCreate(Sender: TObject);
begin
  TrackBar1.TickStyle := tsManual;
  TrackBar1.Min := 0;
  TrackBar1.Max := 100;
  TrackBar1.TickMarks := tmBottomRight;
  TrackBar1.SetTick(50);
end;
```

Description SetTick is a write-only method. TickStyle must be set to tsManual for SetTick to have any effect.

TickMarks PROPERTY

Objects Affected	TTrackBar
Purpose	TickMarks determines the position of the tick marks on the track bar.
Declaration	

```
property TickMarks: TTickMark;
```

Example Syntax

```
procedure TForm1.FormCreate(Sender: TObject);
begin
  TrackBar1.TickStyle := tsManual;
  TrackBar1.Min := 0;
  TrackBar1.Max := 100;
  TrackBar1.TickMarks := tmBottomRight;
  TrackBar1.SetTick(50);
end;
```

Description   TickMarks is type TTickMark and can be set to any of the following possible values:

This Value...	Has This Effect...
tmBoth	Tick marks appear on both sides of the track bar.
tmBottomRight	Tick marks appear on the bottom (of horizontal track bars) or the right (of vertical track bars).
tmTopLeft	Tick marks appear on either the top (of horizontal track bars) or the left (of vertical track bars).

The default value is tmBottomRight.

TickStyle PROPERTY

Objects Affected   TTrackBar

Purpose   The TickStyle property determines the style of the tick marks on the track bar.

Declaration

```
property TickStyle: TTickStyle;
```

Example Syntax

```
procedure TForm1.FormCreate(Sender: TObject);
begin
  TrackBar1.Orientation := trHorizontal;
  TrackBar1.Min := 0;
  TrackBar1.Max := 300;
  TrackBar1.TickStyle := tsAuto;
  TrackBar1.Frequency := 30;
  TrackBar1.LineSize := 30;
  TrackBar1.PageSize := 2;
  TrackBar1.Position := 150;

  TrackBar1Change(Self);
end;

procedure TForm1.TrackBar1Change(Sender: TObject);
begin
  Image1.Canvas.Ellipse(0, 0, TrackBar1.Position, TrackBar1.Position);
end;
```

Description   TickStyle is type TTickStyle and can be set to one of the following possible values to customize the appearance of tick marks on the track bar:

This Style...	Does This...
tsAuto	Displays tick marks automatically for each increment in the range.
tsManual	Displays a tick mark at either end of the track bar. Use SetTick to set ticks at any other position.
tsNone	Displays no tick marks.

The default value for TickStyle is tsAuto.

55

TCustomComboBox
AND ITS DESCENDANTS

A *combo box* combines an edit box with a list box. A variation of this, the drop-down list box, combines an edit box with a drop-down list box. Delphi supports both styles of combo boxes, but you must manually add a list box to the control to create a standard combo box. In either style, a combo box enables the user to make a choice from a list, or type a choice into the edit box. The different combo box styles are described more fully in the Styles entry later in this chapter. Figure 55-1 shows a standard combo box; Figure 55-2 shows a drop-down combo box.

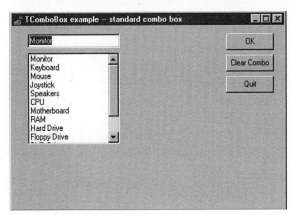

Figure 55-1 A combo box

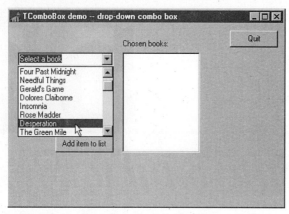

Figure 55-2 A drop-down combo box

TCustomComboBox

TCustomComboBox is the abstract base class for all combo box controls in Delphi, offering only base functionality. **TCustomComboBox** has several descendants, including **TComboBox**, **TDBComboBox**, **TDriveComboBox**, and **TFilterComboBox**.

OBSOLETE CONTROLS

TDriveComboBox and **TFilterComboBox** are obsolete in Windows 95/NT and are offered for backward compatibility only. For this reason, they are not covered in the *Delphi 3 SuperBible*. The functionality of these controls is duplicated and surpassed by the new common dialog boxes, covered in Chapter 34, "**TCommonDialog** and Its Descendants."

Figure 55-3 shows the **TCustomComboBox** branch of the VCL. Table 55-1 displays the properties, methods, and events implemented by **TCustomComboBox**.

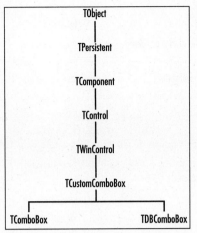

Figure 55-3 The `TCustomComboBox` branch of the VCL

Table 55-1 Properties, methods, and events implemented by `TCustomComboBox`

Use or Set This...	To Do This...	Inheritance
Align	Determine how the control is aligned within its parent.	TControl
Assign	Assign one persistent object to another.	TPersistent
BeginDrag	Begin a manual drag operation.	TControl
BoundsRect	Determine the boundary rectangle occupied by the control.	TControl
BringToFront	Bring the control to the front of the z-order.	TControl
Brush	Determine the color and pattern used for the windowed control background.	TComponent
CanFocus	Determine whether the windowed control can receive the focus.	TWinControl
Canvas	Access the drawing surface of the combo box.	TComponent
Caption	Label the control with a text string.	TControl
ClassName	Get the name of the object's class.	TObject
ClassParent	Get the object's parent class.	TObject
ClassType	Get the object's actual type.	TObject
Clear	Clear the edit portion of the combo box.	None
ClientHeight	Determine the control's client height.	TControl
ClientOrigin	Determine the upper-left position of the control's client area.	TControl
ClientRect	Determine the rectangle occupied by the control's client area.	TControl
ClientToScreen	Convert control (local) coordinates to screen coordinates.	TControl
ClientWidth	Determine the width of the control's client area.	TControl
Color	Determine the color of the windowed control.	TControl
ComponentCount	Determine the number of owned components.	TComponent
ComponentIndex	The index of the component in its owner's `Components` list.	TComponent
Components	Determine the list of owned components.	TComponent
ComponentState	Determine the state of the current component.	TComponent

continued on next page

continued from previous page

Use or Set This...	To Do This...	Inheritance
ContainsControl	Determine whether the specified control is contained by the windowed control.	TWinControl
ControlAtPos	Determine the control contained at a specified position.	TWinControl
ControlCount	Determine the number of controls contained by the windowed control.	TWinControl
Controls	Access the controls contained by the windowed control using their positions in an array.	TWinControl
ControlState	Determine the state of the control at any given time.	TControl
ControlStyle	Determine what attributes are present in the control.	TControl
Create	Create a new component.	TObject
Ctl3D	Determine whether the windowed control displays in 3D.	TWinControl
Cursor	Determine what image is used for the cursor over the control.	TControl
Destroy	Destroy the component.	TObject
DestroyComponents	Destroy all the components owned by the component.	TComponent
Destroying	Notify the component that it is being destroyed.	TComponent
DragCursor	Determine the shape of the mouse cursor as it drags an object over the control.	TControl
Dragging	Determine whether the control is being dragged.	TControl
DragMode	Determine the drag-and-drop behavior of the control.	TControl
DroppedDown	Determine whether the combo box list is open.	**None**
Enabled	Determine whether the control is enabled.	TControl
EndDrag	End or cancel a manual drag operation.	TControl
FindComponent	Find a component in the Components array list.	TComponent
Focused	Determine whether the windowed control has the focus.	TControl
Font	Determine the font used to render text on the control.	TControl
Free	Safely destroy the object.	TObject
GetTextBuf	Copy the text of the control into a buffer.	TControl
GetTextLen	Get the length of the text of the control.	TControl
Handle	Obtain a handle to the windowed control.	TComponent
HandleAllocated	Determine if a handle is allocated for the windowed control.	TWinControl
Height	Determine the height of the control.	TControl
HelpContext	Determine the help context ID of the windowed control.	TComponent
Hide	Make the control invisible.	TControl
Hint	Determine the text that displays in a tooltip for the control.	TControl
InheritsFrom	Determine if the object is descended from a certain class.	TObject
InsertControl	Insert a control into the windowed control's Controls array.	TWinControl
InstanceSize	Determine the amount of memory allocated for the object.	TObject
Invalidate	Force the control to be repainted as soon as possible.	TControl
ItemIndex	Determine the position of the current combo box item.	**None**
Items	Determine the strings displayed in the combo box list.	**None**
Left	Determine the left edge of the control within its container.	TControl
Name	Determine the name of the component.	TComponent
OnClick	Handle the event that occurs when a mouse button is clicked.	TControl
OnDblClick	Handle the event that occurs when a mouse button is double-clicked.	TControl

Use or Set This...	To Do This...	Inheritance
OnDragDrop	Handle the event that occurs when an object is dropped on the control.	TControl
OnDragOver	Handle the event that occurs when an object is dragged over the control.	TControl
OnEndDrag	Handle the event that occurs when a drag-and-drop operation is cancelled.	TControl
OnEnter	Handle the event that occurs when the windowed control receives the focus.	TWinControl
OnExit	Handle the event that occurs when the windowed control loses the focus.	TWinControl
OnKeyDown	Handle the event that occurs when a key is pressed down and not immediately released while the windowed control has the focus.	TWinControl
OnKeyPress	Handle the event that occurs when a key is pressed while the windowed control has the focus.	TWinControl
OnKeyUp	Handle the event that occurs when a key is released while the windowed control has the focus.	TWinControl
OnMouseDown	Handle the event that occurs when a mouse button is held down and not immediately released.	TControl
OnMouseMove	Handle the event that occurs when the cursor moves over the control.	TControl
OnMouseUp	Handle the event that occurs when a mouse button is released.	TControl
OnStartDrag	Handle the event that occurs when a drag-and-drop operation is started.	TControl
Owner	Determine the owner of the component.	TComponent
Parent	Determine the parent, or container, of the control.	TControl
ParentColor	Determine whether the Color information of the control's parent is used.	TControl
ParentCtl3D	Determine whether the windowed control uses its parent's Ctl3D settings.	TWinControl
ParentFont	Determine whether the Font information of the control's parent is used.	TControl
ParentShowHint	Determine whether the ShowHint information of the control's parent is used.	TControl
PopupMenu	Determine which pop-up menu is associated with the control.	TControl
Refresh	Erase the control and repaint it.	TControl
RemoveControl	Remove the specified control from the windowed control's Controls array.	TWinControl
Repaint	Repaint the control.	TControl
ScaleBy	Resize the windowed control.	TWinControl
ScreenToClient	Convert screen coordinates to client (control) coordinates.	TControl
SendToBack	Send the control to the end of the z-order.	TControl
SetBounds	Determine the coordinates of the control's bounding rectangle.	TControl
SetFocus	Set the focus to the windowed control.	TWinControl
SetTextBuf	Set the text of the control to the text in a buffer.	TControl
Show	Make the control visible.	TControl
ShowHint	Enable tooltips for the control.	TControl
Showing	Determine whether the windowed control is currently showing onscreen.	TComponent
TabOrder	Determine the tab order of the windowed control.	TWinControl
TabStop	Determine whether the windowed control is in the tab order.	TWinControl
Tag	Store an additional integer value with the component.	TComponent
Text	Access the changeable text on the control.	TControl
Top	Determine the upper edge of the control.	TControl

TComboBox

TComboBox encapsulates the standard Windows combo box and drop-down combo box. Combo boxes allow the user to select a choice from the list or enter it in the edit box. The drop-down combo box requires less space onscreen when it is not being used.

Table 55-2 displays the properties, methods, and events implemented by TComboBox. These are in addition to the properties and methods it inherits from TCustomComboBox (refer to Table 55-1).

Table 55-2 Properties, methods, and events implemented by TComboBox

Use or Set This...	To Do This...	Inheritance
Color	Determine the color of the edit area and drop-down list.	TControl
Ctl3D	Determine whether the combo box is displayed in 3D.	TControl
DragCursor	Determine the shape of the cursor if it drags an object over the combo box.	TControl
DragMode	Determine the drag-and-drop behavior of the combo box.	TControl
DropDownCount	Determine the length of the drop-down list.	None
Enabled	Determine whether the combo box is enabled.	TControl
Font	Determine the font used to display text in the combo box.	TControl
ItemHeight	Determine the height of each item in the string list.	None
Items	Determine the list of strings displayed by the drop-down list.	TCustomComboBox
MaxLength	Determine the maximum number of characters the user can enter in the edit area of the combo box.	TControl
OnChange	Handle the event that occurs when the text in the edit area is changed.	TControl
OnClick	Handle the event that occurs when the combo box is clicked.	TControl
OnDblClick	Handle the event that occurs when the combo box is double-clicked.	TControl
OnDragDrop	Handle the event that occurs when an object is dropped on the combo box.	TControl
OnDragOver	Handle the event that occurs when an object is dragged over the combo box.	TControl
OnDrawItem	Handle the event that occurs when an item in an owner-draw combo box needs to be redisplayed.	None
OnDropDown	Handle the event that occurs when the drop-down list in the combo box is displayed.	None
OnEndDrag	Handle the event that occurs when a drag-and-drop operation is cancelled.	TControl
OnEnter	Handle the event that occurs when the combo box receives the focus.	TControl
OnExit	Handle the event that occurs when the combo box loses the focus.	TControl
OnKeyDown	Handle the event that occurs when a key is pressed down and not released.	TControl
OnKeyPress	Handle the event that occurs when a key is pressed.	TControl
OnKeyUp	Handle the event that occurs when a key is released.	TControl
OnMeasureItem	Handle the event that occurs when a item in an owner-draw combo box with a variable style needs to be redisplayed.	None
OnStartDrag	Handle the event that occurs when a drag-and-drop operation is started.	TControl
ParentColor	Determine whether to use the parent's Color information.	TControl
ParentCtl3D	Determine whether to use the parent's Ctl3D information.	TControl

Use or Set This...	To Do This...	Inheritance
ParentFont	Determine whether to use the parent's Font information.	TControl
ParentShowHint	Determine whether to use the parent's ShowHint property to determine whether to display tooltips.	TControl
PopupMenu	Determine which pop-up menu is associated with the combo box.	TControl
ShowHint	Determine whether to display a tooltip.	TControl
Sorted	Determine whether the string list displayed in the combo box is sorted.	None
Style	Determine how the combo box displays the items in its list.	None
TabOrder	Determine whether the combo box is in its parent's tab order.	TCustomComboBox
TabStop	Determine whether the combo box is a tab stop.	TControl
Text	Determine the text that appears in the combo box edit area.	TControl
Visible	Determine whether the combo box is visible.	TControl

TDBComboBox

A database combo box is created with the **TDBComboBox** class. It is a data-aware combo box that allows the user to update fields by choosing a value from its list or by entering a value.

Table 55-3 displays the properties, methods, and events implemented by **TDBComboBox**. These are in addition to the properties and methods it inherits from **TCustomComboBox** (refer to Table 55-1).

Table 55-3 Properties, methods, and events implemented by TDBComboBox

Use or Set This..	To Do This...	Inheritance
Color	Determine the background color used for the the edit area and list.	TControl
Create	Create a new database combo box.	TComponent
Ctl3D	Determine whether the combo box displays in 3D.	TControl
DataField	Determine the field the combo box uses to obtain the data to display.	None
DataSource	Determine the data source of the combo box.	None
Destroy	Destroy the combo box.	TComponent
DragCursor	Determine the shape of the mouse pointer as it drags an object over the combo box.	TControl
DragMode	Determine the drag-and-drop behavior of the combo box.	TControl
DropDownCount	Determine the number of items that display in the drop-down list portion of the combo box.	None
Enabled	Determine whether the combo box is enabled.	TControl
Field	Determine which field the combo box is attatched to.	None
Font	Determine the font used to display text in the combo box.	TControl
ItemHeight	Determine the height of each item in the drop-down list.	None
Items	Determine the strings contained in the combo box string list.	TCustomComboBox
OnChange	Handle the event that occurs when the contents of the combo box are changed.	TControl

continued on next page

continued from previous page

OnClick	Handle the event that occurs when the combo is clicked.	TControl
OnDblClick	Handle the event that occurs when the combo box is double-clicked.	TControl
OnDragDrop	Handle the event that occurs when an object is dropped on the combo box.	TControl
OnDragOver	Handle the event that occurs when an object is dragged over the combo box.	TControl
OnDrawItem	Handle the event that occurs when an item in an owner-draw combo box needs to be redisplayed.	None
OnDropDown	Handle the event that occurs when the drop-down list is displayed.	TControl
OnEndDrag	Handle the event that occurs when a drag-and-drop operation is cancelled.	TControl
OnEnter	Handle the event that occurs when the combo box receives the focus.	TControl
OnExit	Handle the event that occurs when the combo box loses the focus.	TControl
OnKeyDown	Handle the event that occurs when a key is pressed and not released.	TControl
OnKeyPress	Handle the event that occurs when a key is pressed.	TControl
OnKeyUp	Handle the event that occurs when a key is released.	TControl
OnMeasureItem	Handle the event that occurs when an item in an owner-draw combo box with a variable style needs to be redrawn.	None
OnStartDrag	Handle the event that occurs when a drag operation begins over the combo box.	TControl
ParentColor	Determine whether to use the parent's Color information.	TControl
ParentCtl3D	Determine whether to use the parent's Ctl3D information.	TControl
ParentFont	Determine whether to use the parent's Font information.	TControl
ParentShowHint	Determine whether to use the parent's ShowHint property to determine whether to display a tooltip.	TControl
PopupMenu	Determine which pop-up menu is associated with the combo box.	TControl
ReadOnly	Determine whether the user can edit the contents of the combo box.	None
ShowHint	Determine whether to display a tooltip.	TControl
Sorted	Determine whether the string list displayed in the combo box is sorted.	None
Style	Determine whether the combo box displays items in its list.	None
TabOrder	Determine whether the combo box is in its parent's tab order.	TControl
TabStop	Determine whether the combo box is a tab stop.	TControl
Text	Determine the text to display in the combo box edit area.	TControl
Visible	Determine whether the combo box is visible.	TControl

Clear METHOD

Objects Affected	All combo boxes
Purpose	The Clear method erases any text in the edit area of the combo box.
Declaration	

```
procedure Clear; override;
```

Example Syntax

```
ComboBox1.Clear;
```

Description   If the text in the combo box exists in the Items list, `Clear` does not remove the Items list entry, it just erases the text from the edit area.

DataField PROPERTY

Objects Affected   TDBComboBox

Purpose   The `DataField` property determines which field the database combo box uses to display its text.

Declaration

```
property DataField: string;
```

Example Syntax

```
procedure TForm1.FormCreate(Sender: TObject);
begin
  Table1.DatabaseName := 'DBDEMOS';
  DataSource1.DataSet := Table1;
  DBComboBox1.DataSource := DataSource1;
  DBComboBox1.DataField := 'Common_Name';
  // . . .
end;
```

Description   The field referenced by the database combo box is contained in the data source specified by the `DataSource` property.

DataSource PROPERTY

Objects Affected   TDBComboBox

Purpose   The `DataSource` property specifies the data source for the database combo box.

Declaration

```
property DataSource: TDataSource;
```

Example Syntax

```
procedure TForm1.FormCreate(Sender: TObject);
begin
  Table1.DatabaseName := 'DBDEMOS';
  DataSource1.DataSet := Table1;
  DBComboBox1.DataSource := DataSource1;
  DBComboBox1.DataField := 'Common_Name';
  // . . .
end;
```

Description   `DataSource` contains the name of a table or query providing data to the database combo box.

DropDownCount PROPERTY

Objects Affected All combo boxes

Purpose The `DropDownCount` property determines the number of strings visible at a time in the drop-down list.

Declaration

```
property DropDownCount: Integer;
```

Example Syntax

```
procedure TForm1.FormCreate(Sender: TObject);
begin
  // . . .
  ComboBox1.DropDownCount := 5;
  // . . .
end;
```

Description If the value held in the `Count` property of `Items` is greater than `DropDownCount`, scroll bars automatically appear on the drop-down list so the user can scroll through all the available choices in the string list. If the string list is shorter than `DropDownCount`, the size of the drop-down list shrinks to accommodate the list. The default value is 8.

DroppedDown PROPERTY

Objects Affected All combo boxes

Purpose The `DroppedDown` property determines whether the combo box list is dropped down.

Declaration

```
property DroppedDown: Boolean;
```

Example Syntax

```
procedure TForm1.FormCreate(Sender: TObject);
begin
  Cost := 0;
  ComboBox1.Text := 'Select a book';
  // Open the combo box when the program starts
  ComboBox1.DroppedDown := True;
  // . . .
end;
```

Description If `DroppedDown` is `True`, the combo box drop-down list is visible. If `DroppedDown` is `False`, the combo box drop-down list is closed. The default value for `DroppedDown` is `False`.

If you need to handle the event occurring when the combo box is dropped down, Delphi provides an `OnDropDown` event.

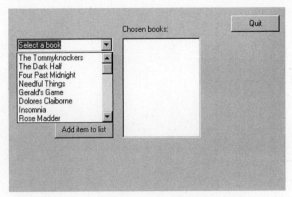

Figure 55-4 Open the combo box when the
program starts

Field PROPERTY

Objects Affected   T D B C o m b o B o x

Purpose   The **Field** property specifies the field to which the database combo box is
connected.

Declaration

```
property Field: TField;
```

Example Syntax

```
procedure TForm1.FormCreate(Sender: TObject);
begin
  Table1.DatabaseName := 'DBDEMOS';
  DataSource1.DataSet := Table1;
  DBComboBox1.DataSource := DataSource1;
  DBComboBox1.DataField := 'Common_Name';
  Label1.Caption := DBComboBox1.Field.DisplayName;
end;
```

Description   **Field** is a run-time, read-only property that lets you access the properties
and methods of the field to which the database combo box is connected.

Figure 55-5 The field display name
is used for the label caption

ItemHeight Property

Objects Affected	TComboBox, TDBComboBox
Purpose	ItemHeight determines the height of items in the drop-down list when the combo box style is set to csOwnerDrawFixed.
Declaration	

```
property ItemHeight: Integer;
```

Example Syntax

```
procedure TForm1.FormCreate(Sender: TObject);
begin
  ComboBox1.Style := csOwnerDrawFixed;
  ComboBox1.ItemHeight := 24;
end;
```

Description   ItemHeight is the height, in pixels, of the items in the drop-down list portion of the combo box when its Style property is set to csOwnerDrawFixed. If Style is not csOwnerDrawFixed, ItemHeight is ignored.

ItemIndex Property

Objects Affected	All combo boxes
Purpose	The ItemIndex property contains the position of the combo box's current item in the combo box Items array.
Declaration	

```
property ItemIndex: Integer;
```

Example Syntax

```
procedure TForm1.ComboBox1Change(Sender: TObject);
var x: Integer;
begin
  if ComboBox1.Text = '' then
  begin
    x := 0;
    Label1.Caption := 'Select a book'
  end
  else begin
  x := ComboBox1.ItemIndex;
  Label1.Caption := 'Book ' + IntToStr(x) + ' of ' +
    IntToStr(ComboBox1.Items.Count)
  end
end;
```

Description   If no item is selected in the combo box, the value of `ItemIndex` is -1. Otherwise, `ItemIndex` specifies the positional value of the selected item. The first item in the list has an `ItemIndex` of 0, the second is 1, and so on.

Items PROPERTY

Objects Affected   All combo boxes

Purpose   `Items` is the array of strings appearing in the combo box.

Declaration

```
property Items: TStrings;
```

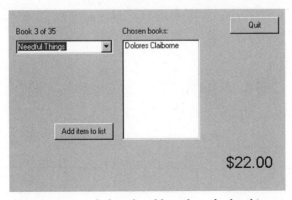

Figure 55-6   Label updated based on the book's position in a list

Example Syntax

```
procedure TForm1.ComboBox1Change(Sender: TObject);
var x: Integer;
begin
  if ComboBox1.Text = '' then
  begin
    x := 0;
    Label1.Caption := 'Select a book'
  end
  else begin
  x := ComboBox1.ItemIndex;
  Label1.Caption := 'Book ' + IntToStr(x) + ' of ' +
    IntToStr(ComboBox1.Items.Count)
  end
end;
```

Description
Items is type TStrings, so you can use any of the standard TStrings methods to insert, add, delete, or move a string in the array Items contains. See Chapter 25, "TStrings and Its Descendants," for details. Items lets you access the individual strings in the combo box by their position within the list.

OnDropDown Event

Objects Affected   TComboBox, TDBComboBox

Purpose   The OnDropDown event lets you handle the event occurring when the drop-down list in the combo box is displayed.

Declaration

```
property OnDropDown: TNotifyEvent;
```

Example Syntax

```
procedure TForm1.ComboBox1DropDown(Sender: TObject);
begin
  // Default event handler for OnDropDown
end;
```

Description   The OnDropDown event is triggered when the user opens a drop-down combo box.

OnDrawItem Event

Objects Affected   TComboBox, TDBComboBox

Purpose   The OnDrawItem event occurs when an item in an owner-draw combo box needs to be redisplayed.

Declaration

```
property OnDrawItem: TDrawItemEvent;
```

Description	Owner-draw combo boxes have the `Style` property set to `csOwnerDrawFixed` or `csOwnerDrawVariable`. The `OnDrawItem` event occurs, for example, when the combo box list is scrolled or when an item in the list is selected. `OnDrawItem` is type `TDrawItemEvent`, which is declared as

```
TDrawItemEvent = procedure(Control: TWinControl; Index: Integer;
              Rect: TRect; State: TOwnerDrawState) of object;
```

where *Control* is a reference to the combo box containing the item that needs to be redrawn, *Index* is the item's `ItemIndex` value, *Rect* is the rectangular area in which to draw, and *State* is the state of the item. The area of the *Rect* parameter is determined by the `Style` of the combo box: If `Style` is `csOwnerDrawFixed`, the `ItemHeight` property determines the height of the rectangle; if `Style` is `csOwnerDrawVariable`, the `OnMeasureItem` event handler determines the height of the rectangle. The *State* parameter is type `TOwnerDrawState`, which is declared as:

```
TOwnerDrawState = set of (odSelected, odGrayed, odDisabled, odChecked,
            odFocused);
```

OnMeasureItem EVENT

Objects Affected	`TComboBox`, `TDBComboBox`
Purpose	The `OnMeasureItem` event occurs when an owner-draw combo box with a variable style needs to redraw an item.
Declaration	

```
property OnMeasureItem: TMeasureItemEvent;
```

Description	If the `Style` property of the combo box is set to `csOwnerDrawVariable`, the `OnMeasureItem` event occurs when an item in the list needs to be redrawn. `OnMeasureItem` is declared as:

```
TMeasureItemEvent = procedure(Control: TWinControl; Index: Integer;
                var Height: Integer) of object;
```

Control is the combo box with the item that needs to be redrawn, *Index* is the `ItemIndex` value for the item, and *Height* is the pixel height of the rectangular area that needs to be redrawn. After `OnMeasureItem` is processed, the `OnDrawItem` event occurs.

ReadOnly PROPERTY

Objects Affected	`TDBComboBox`
Purpose	The `ReadOnly` property determines if the user can edit the contents of the edit area.

Declaration

```
property ReadOnly: Boolean;
```

Example Syntax

```
procedure TForm1.FormCreate(Sender: TObject);
begin
  Table1.DatabaseName := 'DBDEMOS';
  DataSource1.DataSet := Table1;
  DBComboBox1.DataSource := DataSource1;
  DBComboBox1.ReadOnly := True;
end;
```

Description

If ReadOnly is set to True, the user cannot edit the text appearing in the edit area of the database combo box. If ReadOnly is False, the user can change the text if the data set is in edit mode. Since a database combo box is data-aware, changing the text of the control affects the value of the field in the current record connected to the combo box. The default value is False.

Sorted PROPERTY

Objects Affected
TComboBox, TDBComboBox

Purpose
The Sorted property determines whether the items in the combo box are listed alphabetically.

Declaration

```
property Sorted: Boolean;
```

Example Syntax

```
procedure TForm1.FormCreate(Sender: TObject);
begin
  ComboBox1.Sorted := True;
  // . . .
end;
```

Description

If Sorted is True, the list of strings determined by Items is sorted alphabetically. If Sorted is False, the items are unsorted and display in the order created. If an item is added to the list when Sorted is True, it is automatically placed in its correct alphabetical position. Otherwise, it is placed at the end of the list of strings.

Style PROPERTY

Objects Affected
TComboBox, TDBComboBox

Purpose
The Style property determines whether the combo box is a drop-down or standard combo box.

Declaration

```
property Style: TComboBoxStyle;
```

Example Syntax

```
procedure TForm1.FormCreate(Sender: TObject);
begin
  ComboBox1.Style := csSimple;
  ListBox1.Items := ComboBox1.Items;
  ComboBox1.Text := ListBox1.Items[0];
end;
```

Description

Style is type TComboBoxStyle, which is declared as:

```
TComboBoxStyle = (csDropDown, csSimple, csDropDownList,
                  csOwnerDrawFixed, csOwnerDrawVariable);
```

The styles allowed by the Style property define the appearance and behavior of the combo box and are summarized below:

Use This Style...	To Do This...
csDropDown	Create a combo box with a drop-down list and an edit box.
csDropDownList	Create a combo box with a drop-down list. There is no attached edit box, so the user will not be able to add items to the list or edit items.
csOwnerDrawFixed	Create a combo box with fixed-height list items, as specified by the ItemHeight property.
csOwnerDrawVariable	Create a combo box with items that can be of varying height.
csSimple	Create a standard combo box with an edit box but no list. This type of combo box will need to be linked to a list box to create a true Win32-style combo box.

56

TCustomHotKey AND THotKey

Hotkeys, also known as *shortcut keys* and *accelerator keys*, let the user emulate common operations by pressing a key combination on the keyboard. Pressing CTRL-V for example, has the same effect in many programs (and in the operating system itself) as choosing Paste from a menu. Most hotkeys are combinations of two simultaneous key presses. Hotkeys are also case-insensitive, so CTRL-v has the same effect as CTRL-V.

Delphi has two classes, an abstract parent **TCustomHotKey** and its child **THotKey**, which provide a visual control the user can manipulate to change hotkeys. Typically, this control is used in a configuration dialog your application provides so the user can change hotkeys associated with particular actions.

TCustomHotKey

TCustomHotKey is the abstract base class for **THotKey** and provides no specific functionality the application programmer can use.

Figure 56-1 shows the ancestry of **THotKey** and **TCustomHotKey**. Table 56-1 displays the methods implemented by **TCustomHotKey**.

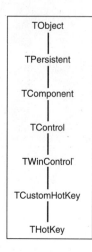

Figure 56-1 Ancestry of `THotKey`
and `TCustomHotKey`

TObject

TPersistent

TComponent

TControl

TWinControl

TCustomHotKey

THotKey

Table 56-1 Methods implemented by `TCustomHotKey`

Use or Set This...	To Do This...	Inheritance
Align	Determine how the control is aligned within its parent.	TControl
Assign	Assign one persistent object to another.	TPersistent
BeginDrag	Begin a manual drag operation.	TControl
BoundsRect	Determine the boundary rectangle occupied by the control.	TControl
BringToFront	Bring the control to the front of the z-order.	TControl
Brush	Determine the color and pattern used for the windowed control background.	TComponent
CanFocus	Determine whether the windowed control can receive the focus.	TWinControl
Caption	Label the control with a text string.	TControl
ClassName	Get the name of the object's class.	TObject
ClassParent	Get the object's parent class.	TObject
ClassType	Get the object's actual type.	TObject
ClientHeight	Determine the control's client height.	TControl
ClientOrigin	Determine the upper-left position of the control's client area.	TControl
ClientRect	Determine the rectangle occupied by the control's client area.	TControl
ClientToScreen	Convert control (local) coordinates to screen coordinates.	TControl
ClientWidth	Determine the width of the control's client area.	TControl
Color	Determine the color of the windowed control.	TControl
ComponentCount	Determine the number of owned components.	TComponent
ComponentIndex	Determine the index of the component in its owner's Components list.	TComponent
Components	Determine the list of owned components.	TComponent
ComponentState	Determine the state of the current component.	TComponent
ContainsControl	Determine whether the specified control is contained by the windowed control.	TWinControl
ControlAtPos	Determine the control contained at a specified position.	TWinControl

Use or Set This...	To Do This...	Inheritance
ControlCount	Determine the number of controls contained by the windowed control.	TWinControl
Controls	Access the controls contained by the windowed control using their positions in an array.	TWinControl
ControlState	Determine the state of the control at any given time.	TControl
ControlStyle	Determine what attributes are present in the control.	TControl
Create	Create a new component.	TObject
Ctl3D	Determine whether the windowed control displays in 3D.	TWinControl
Cursor	Determine what image is used for the cursor over the control.	TControl
Destroy	Destroy the component.	TObject
DestroyComponents	Destroy all the components owned by the component.	TComponent
Destroying	Notify the component that it is being destroyed.	TComponent
DragCursor	Determine the shape of the mouse cursor as it drags an object over the control.	TControl
Dragging	Determine whether the control is being dragged.	TControl
DragMode	Determine the drag-and-drop behavior of the control.	TControl
Enabled	Determine whether the control is enabled.	TControl
EndDrag	End or cancel a manual drag operation.	TControl
FindComponent	Find a component in the Components array list.	TComponent
Focused	Determine whether the windowed control has the focus.	TControl
Font	Determine the font used to render text on the control.	TControl
Free	Safely destroy the object.	TObject
GetTextBuf	Copy the text of the control into a buffer.	TControl
GetTextLen	Get the length of the text of the control.	TControl
Handle	Obtain a handle to the windowed control.	TComponent
HandleAllocated	Determine if a handle is allocated for the windowed control.	TWinControl
Height	Determine the height of the control.	TControl
HelpContext	Determine the help context ID of the windowed control.	TComponent
Hide	Make the control invisible.	TControl
Hint	Determine the text that displays in a tooltip for the control.	TControl
InheritsFrom	Determine if the object is descended from a certain class.	TObject
InsertControl	Insert a control into the windowed control's Controls array.	TWinControl
InstanceSize	Determine the amount of memory allocated for the object.	TObject
Invalidate	Force the control to be repainted as soon as possible.	TControl
Left	Determine the left edge of the control within its container.	TControl
Name	Determine the name of the component.	TComponent
OnClick	Handle the event that occurs when a mouse button is clicked.	TControl
OnDblClick	Handle the event that occurs when a mouse button is double-clicked.	TControl
OnDragDrop	Handle the event that occurs when an object is dropped on the control.	TControl
OnDragOver	Handle the event that occurs when an object is dragged over the control.	TControl
OnEndDrag	Handle the event that occurs when a drag-and-drop operation is cancelled.	TControl
OnEnter	Handle the event that occurs when the windowed control receives the focus.	TWinControl

continued on next page

continued from previous page

Use or Set This...	To Do This...	Inheritance
OnExit	Handle the event that occurs when the windowed control loses the focus.	TWinControl
OnKeyDown	Handle the event that occurs when a key is pressed down and not immediately released while the windowed control has the focus.	TWinControl
OnKeyPress	Handle the event that occurs when a key is pressed while the windowed control has the focus.	TWinControl
OnKeyUp	Handle the event that occurs when a key is released while the windowed control has the focus.	TWinControl
OnMouseDown	Handle the event that occurs when a mouse button is held down and not immediately released.	TControl
OnMouseMove	Handle the event that occurs when the cursor moves over the control.	TControl
OnMouseUp	Handle the event that occurs when a mouse button is released.	TControl
OnStartDrag	Handle the event that occurs when a drag-and-drop operation is started.	TControl
Owner	Determine the owner of the component.	TComponent
Parent	Determine the parent, or container, of the control.	TControl
ParentColor	Determine whether the Color information of the control's parent is used.	TControl
ParentCtl3D	Determine whether the windowed control uses its parent's Ctl3D settings.	TWinControl
ParentFont	Determine whether the control's parent's Font information of the control's parent is used.	TControl
ParentShowHint	Determine whether the control's parent's ShowHint information of the control's parent is used.	TControl
PopupMenu	Determine which pop-up menu is associated with the control.	TControl
Refresh	Erase the control and repaint it.	TControl
RemoveControl	Remove the specified control from the windowed control's Controls array.	TWinControl
Repaint	Repaint the control.	TControl
ScaleBy	Resize the windowed control.	TWinControl
ScreenToClient	Convert screen coordinates to client (control) coordinates.	TControl
SendToBack	Send the control to the end of the z-order.	TControl
SetBounds	Determine the coordinates of the control's bounding rectangle.	TControl
SetFocus	Set the focus to the windowed control.	TWinControl
SetTextBuf	Set the text of the control to the text in a buffer.	TControl
Show	Make the control visible.	TControl
ShowHint	Enable tooltips for the control.	TControl
Showing	Determine whether the windowed control is currently showing onscreen.	TComponent
TabOrder	Determine the tab order of the windowed control.	TWinControl
TabStop	Determine whether the windowed control is in the tab order.	TWinControl
Tag	Store an additional integer value with the component.	TComponent

Use or Set This...	To Do This...	Inheritance
Text	Access the changeable text on the control.	TControl
Top	Determine the upper edge of the control.	TControl
Update	Called automatically by Refresh.	TControl
Visible	Determine whether the control is visible.	TControl
Width	Determine the width of the control.	TControl

THotKey

THotKey is a visual component that lets the user change hotkeys at run time. While a hotkey component has the focus, the user can type in a key combination, typically consisting of a modifier key such as (ALT), (CTRL), or (SHIFT) and another key, which can be any character, function, or arrow key. The hotkey control is associated with another control by assigning its HotKey property (not to be confused with the hotkey's own HotKey property, which holds the key combination).

If you are familiar with Microsoft Word, you may have seen the Customize dialog box that lets you, among other things, customize the hotkeys used by Word. This is shown in Figure 56-2.

Table 56-2 displays the properties, methods, and events implemented by THotKey. These are in addition to the properties and methods it inherits from TCustomHotKey (refer to Table 56-1).

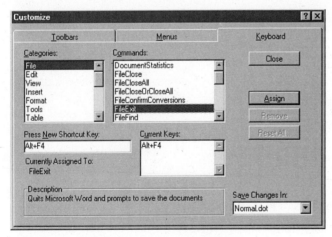

Figure 56-2 A hotkey control in Word lets you customize shortcuts

Table 56-2 Properties, methods, and events implemented by THotKey

Use or Set This...	To Do This...	Inheritance
AutoSize	Determine whether the hotkey control should size itself to the text it contains.	TControl
Enabled	Determine whether the hotkey control is enabled.	TControl
Hint	Determine the tooltip that appears.	TControl
HotKey	Determine the hotkey combination contained by the control.	None
InvalidKeys	Determine which keys are invalid.	None
Modifiers	Determine which modifier keys are allowed by the control.	None
OnEnter	Handle the event that occurs when the control receives the focus.	TControl
OnExit	Handle the event that occurs when the control loses the the focus.	TControl
OnMouseDown	Handle the event that occurs when the mouse button is pressed but not released.	TControl
OnMouseMove	Handle the event that occurs when the mouse pointer moves.	TControl
OnMouseUp	Handle the event that occurs when the mouse button is released.	TControl
ParentShowHint	Determine whether to use the parent's ShowHint property to determine whether to display a tooltip.	TControl
PopupMenu	Determine which pop-up menu is associated with the control.	TControl
ShowHint	Determine whether to display a tooltip.	TControl
TabOrder	Determine the control's position in its parent's tab order.	TControl
TabStop	Determine whether the control is a tab stop.	TControl
Visible	Determine whether the hotkey control is visible.	TControl

HotKey PROPERTY

Objects Affected	THotKey
Purpose	The HotKey property contains the key combination used by the hotkey control.
Declaration	

```
property HotKey: TShortCut;
```

Example Syntax

```
procedure TForm1.btnApplyClick(Sender: TObject);
begin
  mnuCut.ShortCut := HotKey1.HotKey;
  mnuCopy.ShortCut := HotKey2.HotKey;
  mnuPaste.ShortCut := HotKey3.HotKey;
end;
```

Description

HotKey is type TShortCut, which is declared as:

```
TShortCut = Low(Word) .. High(Word);
```

Typically, you assign hotkeys from the IDE, using the Object Inspector.

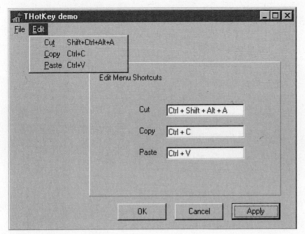

Figure 56-3 When the Apply button is pressed, the hotkeys are assigned to the menu items

InvalidKeys PROPERTY

Objects Affected   THotKey

Purpose   The **InvalidKeys** property defines those keys that will not be accepted as input to the hotkey control.

Declaration

```
property InvalidKeys: THKInvalidKeys;
```

Example Syntax

```
procedure TForm1.FormCreate(Sender: TObject);
begin
  mnuCut.ShortCut := HotKey1.HotKey;
  mnuCopy.ShortCut := HotKey2.HotKey;
  mnuPaste.ShortCut := HotKey3.HotKey;

  HotKey1.InvalidKeys := HotKey1.InvalidKeys + [hcShiftCtrl];
  HotKey2.InvalidKeys := HotKey1.InvalidKeys;
  HotKey3.InvalidKeys := HotKey1.InvalidKeys;
end;
```

Description   **InvalidKeys** is used to omit undesirable key-presses from the range of values possible with the hotkey control. **InvalidKeys** is type **THKInvalidKeys**, which is declared as a set of **THKInvalidKey**:

```
THKInvalidKeys = set of THKInvalidKey;
. . .
THKInvalidKey = (hcNone, hcShift, hcCtrl, hcAlt, hcShiftCtrl,
                 hcShiftAlt, hcCtrlAlt, hcShiftCtrlAlt);
```

InvalidKeys can be set to any combination of elements in the **THKInvalidKey** set. Here are the possible values:

This key...	Has this effect...
hcNone	Unmodified keys are invalid.
hcShift	The SHIFT key is invalid.
hcCtrl	The CTRL key is invalid.
hcAlt	The ALT key is invalid.
hcShiftCtrl	The SHIFT–CTRL key combination is invalid.
hcShiftAlt	The SHIFT–ALT key combination is invalid.
hcCtrlAlt	The CTRL–ALT key combination is invalid.
hcShiftCtrlAlt	The SHIFT–CTRL–ALT key combination is invalid.

The default value is [hcNone] + [hcShift].

Modifiers PROPERTY

Objects Affected THotKey

Purpose The Modifiers property determines which modifier keys are valid.

Declaration

```
property Modifiers: THKModifiers;
```

Example Syntax

```
HotKey1.Modifiers := [hkAlt] + [hkCtrl];
```

Description Modifier keys include SHIFT, CTRL, and ALT. Modifiers is type
THKModifiers, which is declared as a set of THKModifier:

```
THKModifiers = set of THKModifier;
. . .
THKModifier = (hkShift, hkCtrl, hkAlt, hkExt);
```

The default value is hkAlt.

57

TCustomListBox
AND ITS DESCENDANTS

A *list box* presents a list of choices to the user. Typically, the list is a collection of related items from which the user can select. List boxes allow for multiple item selection. Common uses for list boxes in Windows include font, point size, and color lists. List box items can be sorted alphabetically or placed into the list by the programmer in any order. As with other Delphi collection entities, the list box offers facilities for adding and removing list items, and determining which item or items are currently selected.

If you choose to implement a list box, shown in Figure 57-1, in your Delphi application, add a descriptive text label to identify its use. Typically, the text label is located along the top edge of the list box and disabled if the list box is disabled. The list box should be wide enough to accommodate the text in the list it displays, if possible.

TCustomListBox

Delphi encapsulates the Windows list box control within the abstract base class **TCustomListBox** and its descendants, **TListBox**, **TDBListBox**, **TDirectoryListBox**, and **TFileListBox**. **TCustomListBox** adds base functionality to the list box family.

> **OBSOLETE CONTROLS**
>
> TDirectoryListBox and TFileListBox are obsolete in Windows 95 and Windows NT and are offered for backward compatibility only. Therefore, they are not covered in the *Delphi 3 SuperBible*. The functionality of these controls is duplicated and surpassed by the new common dialog boxes, covered in Chapter 20, "TCanvas and Its Descendants."

Figure 57-2 shows the **TCustomListBox** branch of the VCL. Table 57-1 displays the properties, methods, and events implemented by **TCustomListBox**.

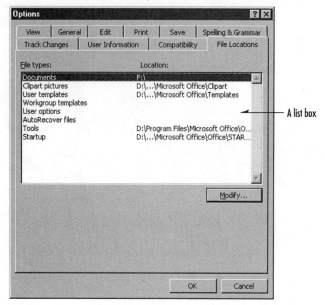

Figure 57-1 A list box

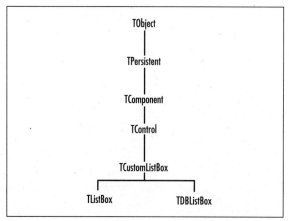

Figure 57-2 The `TCustomListBox` branch of the VCL

Table 57-1 Properties, methods, and events implemented by `TCustomListBox`

Use or Set This...	To Do This...	Inheritance
Align	Determine how the control is aligned within its parent.	TControl
Assign	Assign one persistent object to another.	TPersistent
BeginDrag	Begin a manual drag operation.	TControl
BoundsRect	Determine the boundary rectangle occupied by the control box.	TControl

Use or Set This...	To Do This...	Inheritance
BringToFront	Bring the control to the front of the z-order.	TControl
Brush	Determine the color and pattern used for the windowed control background.	TComponent
CanFocus	Determine whether the windowed control can receive the focus.	TWinControl
Canvas	Access the drawing surface of the list box.	TControl
Caption	Label the control with a text string.	TControl
ClassName	Get the name of the object's class.	TObject
ClassParent	Get the object's parent class.	TObject
ClassType	Get the object's actual type.	TObject
Clear	Delete all the items in the list box.	None
ClientHeight	Determine the control's client height.	TControl
ClientOrigin	Determine the upper-left position of the control's client area.	TControl
ClientRect	Determine the rectangle occupied by the control's client area.	TControl
ClientToScreen	Convert control (local) coordinates to screen coordinates.	TControl
ClientWidth	Determine the width of the control's client area.	TControl
Color	Determine the color of the windowed control.	TControl
ComponentCount	Determine the number of owned components.	TComponent
ComponentIndex	Determine the index of the component in its owner's Components list.	TComponent
Components	Determine the list of owned components.	TComponent
ComponentState	Determine the state of the current component.	TComponent
ContainsControl	Determine whether the specified control is contained by the windowed control.	TWinControl
ControlAtPos	Determine the control contained at a specified position.	TWinControl
ControlCount	Determine the number of controls contained by the windowed control.	TWinControl
Controls	Access the controls contained by the windowed control using their positions in an array.	TWinControl
ControlState	Determine the state of the control at any given time.	TControl
ControlStyle	Determine what attributes are present in the control.	TControl
Create	Create a new component.	TObject
Ctl3D	Determine whether the windowed control displays in 3D.	TWinControl
Cursor	Determine what image is used for the cursor over the control.	TControl
Destroy	Destroy the component.	TObject
DestroyComponents	Destroy all the components owned by the component.	TComponent
Destroying	Notify the component that it is being destroyed.	TComponent
DragCursor	Determine the shape of the mouse cursor as it drags an object over the control.	TControl
Dragging	Determine whether the control is being dragged.	TControl
DragMode	Determine the drag-and-drop behavior of the control.	TControl
Enabled	Determine whether the control is enabled.	TControl
EndDrag	End or cancel a manual drag operation.	TControl

continued on next page

continued from previous page

Use or Set This...	To Do This...	Inheritance
FindComponent	Find a component in the Components array list.	TComponent
Focused	Determine whether the windowed control has the focus.	TControl
Font	Determine the font used to render text on the control.	TControl
Free	Safely destroy the object.	TObject
GetTextBuf	Copy the text of the control into a buffer.	TControl
GetTextLen	Get the length of the text of the control.	TControl
Handle	Obtain a handle to the windowed control.	TComponent
HandleAllocated	Determine whether a handle is allocated for the windowed control.	TWinControl
Height	Determine the height of the control.	TControl
HelpContext	Determine the help context ID of the windowed control.	TComponent
Hide	Make the control invisible.	TControl
Hint	Determine the text that displays in a tooltip for the control.	TControl
InheritsFrom	Determine whether the object is descended from a certain class.	TObject
InsertControl	Insert a control into the windowed control's Controls array.	TWinControl
InstanceSize	Determine the amount of memory allocated for the object.	TObject
Invalidate	Force the control to be repainted as soon as possible.	TControl
ItemAtPos	Determine which item is at the specified position.	None
ItemIndex	Determine the index value of the selected item in the list box.	None
ItemRect	Return the rectangle that borders the specified item in the list.	None
Items	Determine the list of strings that appears in the list box.	None
Left	Determine the left edge of the control within its container.	TControl
Name	Determine the name of the component.	TComponent
OnClick	Handle the event that occurs when a mouse button is clicked.	TControl
OnDblClick	Handle the event that occurs when a mouse button is double-clicked.	TControl
OnDragDrop	Handle the event that occurs when an object is dropped on the control.	TControl
OnDragOver	Handle the event that occurs when an object is dragged over the control.	TControl
OnEndDrag	Handle the event that occurs when a drag-and-drop operation is cancelled.	TControl
OnEnter	Handle the event that occurs when the windowed control receives the focus.	TWinControl
OnExit	Handle the event that occurs when the windowed control loses the focus.	TWinControl
OnKeyDown	Handle the event that occurs when a key is pressed down and not immediately released while the windowed control has the focus.	TWinControl
OnKeyPress	Handle the event that occurs when a key is pressed while the windowed control has the focus.	TWinControl
OnKeyUp	Handle the event that occurs when a key is released while the windowed control has the focus.	TWinControl
OnMouseDown	Handle the event that occurs when a mouse button is held down and not immediately released.	TControl
OnMouseMove	Handle the event that occurs when the cursor moves over the control.	TControl
OnMouseUp	Handle the event that occurs when a mouse button is released.	TControl

Use or Set This...	To Do This...	Inheritance
OnStartDrag	Handle the event that occurs when a drag-and-drop operation is started.	TControl
Owner	Determine the owner of the component.	TComponent
Parent	Determine the parent, or container, of the control.	TControl
ParentColor	Determine whether the Color information of the control's parent is used.	TControl
ParentCtl3D	Determine whether the windowed control uses its parent's Ctl3D settings.	TWinControl
ParentFont	Determine whether the Font information of the control's parent is used.	TControl
ParentShowHint	Determine whether the ShowHint information of the control's parent is used.	TControl
PopupMenu	Determine which pop-up menu is associated with the control.	TControl
Refresh	Erase the control and repaint it.	TControl
RemoveControl	Remove the specified control from the windowed control's Controls array.	TWinControl
Repaint	Repaint the control.	TControl
ScaleBy	Resize the windowed control.	TWinControl
ScreenToClient	Convert screen coordinates to client (control) coordinates.	TControl
SelCount	Determine the number of selected items in the list box.	None
Selected	Determine whether the specified item is selected.	None
SendToBack	Send the control to the end of the z-order.	TControl
SetBounds	Determine the coordinates of the control's bounding rectangle.	TControl
SetFocus	Set the focus to the windowed control.	TWinControl
SetTextBuf	Set the text of the control to the text in a buffer.	TControl
Show	Make the control visible.	TControl
ShowHint	Enable tooltips for the control.	TControl
Showing	Determine whether the windowed control is currently showing onscreen.	TComponent
Sorted	Determine whether the items in the list box are sorted alphabetically.	None
TabOrder	Determine the tab order of the windowed control.	TWinControl
TabStop	Determine whether the windowed control is in the tab order.	TWinControl
Tag	Store an additional integer value with the component.	TComponent
Text	Access the changeable text on the control.	TControl
Top	Determine the upper edge of the control.	TControl
TopIndex	Determine which item will display at the top of the list box.	None
Update	Called automatically by Refresh.	TControl
Visible	Determine whether the control is visible.	TControl
Width	Determine the width of the control.	TControl

TDBListBox

TDBListBox is a data-aware version of TListBox, the standard Delphi list box control. The database list box adds DataSource and DataField properties to link it with a data source and a specific field in the dataset from which it gets its data. It also has a ReadOnly property that determines whether the user edits the current record by editing the contents of the list box.

Table 57-2 displays the properties, methods, and events implemented by
`TDBListBox`. This is in addition to the properties, methods, and events this class inherits from `TCustomListBox`.

Table 57-2 Properties, methods, and events implemented by `TDBListBox`

Use or Set This...	To Do This...	Inheritance
Align	Determine how the list box is aligned with its container.	TControl
BorderStyle	Determine whether the list box has a border.	None
Color	Determine the background color of the list box.	TControl
Create	Create a new database list box.	TComponent
Ctl3D	Determine whether the list box displays in 3D.	TControl
DataField	Determine the field from which the list box gets its data.	None
DataSource	Determine the list box data source.	None
Destroy	Destroy the database list box.	TComponent
DragCursor	Determine the shape of the cursor as it passes over the the control.	TControl
DragMode	Determine the drag-and-drop behavior of the list box.	TControl
Enabled	Determine whether the list box is enabled.	TControl
Font	Determine the font used to display text in the list box.	TControl
ItemHeight	Determine the height of an item in the list box if the list box style is `lbOwnerDrawFixed`.	TControl
Items	Access the list of strings displayed in the list box.	TControl
OnClick	Handle the event that occurs when the mouse is clicked.	TControl
OnDblClick	Handle the event that occurs when the mouse is double-clicked.	TControl
OnDragDrop	Handle the event that occurs when an object is dropped on the list box.	TControl
OnDragOver	Handle the event that occurs when an object is dragged over the list box.	TControl
OnEndDrag	Handle the event that occurs when a drag-and-drop operation is cancelled.	TControl
OnEnter	Handle the event that occurs when the list box receives the focus.	TControl
OnExit	Handle the event that occurs when the list box loses the focus.	TControl
OnKeyDown	Handle the event that occurs when a key is pressed and held down.	TControl
OnKeyPress	Handle the event that occurs when a key is pressed.	TControl
OnKeyUp	Handle the event that occurs when a key is released.	TControl
OnMeasureItem	Handle the event that occurs when an item in an owner-draw list box with a variable style needs to be redisplayed.	None
OnMouseDown	Handle the event that occurs when the mouse button is clicked and not released.	TControl
OnMouseMove	Handle the event that occurs when the mouse pointer moves over the list box.	TControl
OnMouseUp	Handle the event that occurs when the mouse button is released.	TControl
OnStartDrag	Handle the event that occurs when a drag-and-drop operation is started.	TControl
ParentColor	Determine whether the list box uses its parent's `Color` information.	TControl

Use or Set This...	To Do This...	Inheritance
ParentCtl3D	Determine whether the list box uses its parent's Ctl3D information.	TControl
ParentFont	Determine whether the list box uses its parent's Font information.	TControl
ParentShowHint	Determine whether the list box uses its parent's ShowHint information.	TControl
PopupMenu	Determine which pop-up menu is attached to the list box	TControl
ReadOnly	Determine whether the user can edit the items in the list.	None
ShowHint	Determine whether the list box displays a tooltip.	TControl
Style	Determine whether the list box is a standard or owner-draw style list box.	TControl
TabOrder	Determine whether the list box's position is in its parent's tab order.	Tcontrol
TabStop	Determine whether the list box is a tab stop.	TControl
Visible	Determine whether the list box is visible.	TControl

TListBox

TListBox is the Delphi implementation of the Windows list box. The **TListBox** component is available from the Standard tab of the main Delphi window in the IDE. A Delphi list box can have a visible border using the **BorderStyle** property, can have a variety of selection attributes determined by **MultiSelect** and **ExtendedSelect**, and can be sorted alphabetically by setting the **Sorted** property to **True**.

Table 57-3 displays the properties, methods, and events implemented by **TListBox**. This is in addition to the properties, methods, and events this class inherits from **TCustomListBox**.

Table 57-3 Properties, methods, and events implemented by TListBox

Use or Set This..	To Do This...	Inheritance
Align	Determine how the list box is aligned with its container.	TControl
BorderStyle	Determine whether the list box has a border.	None
Color	Determine the background color of the list box.	TControl
Create	Create a new list box.	TComponent
Ctl3D	Determine whether the list box displays in 3D.	TControl
DragCursor	Determine the shape of the cursor as it passes over the the control.	TControl
DragMode	Determine the drag-and-drop behavior of the list box.	TControl
Enabled	Determine whether the list box is enabled.	TControl
ExtendedSelect	Determine whether the user can select a range of items.	None
ItemHeight	Determine the height of an item in the list box if the list box style is lbOwnerDrawFixed.	TControl
Items	Access the list of strings that are displayed in the list box.	TControl
MultiSelect	Determine whether the user can select more than one item from the list.	None
OnClick	Handle the event that occurs when the mouse is clicked.	TControl

continued on next page

continued from previous page

Use or Set This..	To Do This...	Inheritance
OnDblClick	Handle the event that occurs when the mouse is double-clicked.	TControl
OnDragDrop	Handle the event that occurs when an object is dropped on the list box.	TControl
OnDragOver	Handle the event that occurs when an object is dragged over the list box.	TControl
OnEndDrag	Handle the event that occurs when a drag-and-drop operation is cancelled.	TControl
OnEnter	Handle the event that occurs when the list box receives the focus.	TControl
OnExit	Handle the event that occurs when the list box loses the focus.	TControl
OnKeyDown	Handle the event that occurs when a key is pressed and held down.	TControl
OnKeyPress	Handle the event that occurs when a key is pressed.	TControl
OnKeyUp	Handle the event that occurs when a key is released.	TControl
OnMeasureItem	Handle the event that occurs when an item in an owner-draw list box with a variable style needs to be redisplayed.	None
OnMouseDown	Handle the event that occurs when the mouse button is clicked and not released.	TControl
OnMouseMove	Handle the event that occurs when the mouse pointer moves over the list box.	TControl
OnMouseUp	Handle the event that occurs when the mouse button is released.	TControl
OnStartDrag	Handle the event that occurs when a drag-and-drop operation is started.	TControl
ParentColor	Determine whether the list box uses its parent's Color information.	TControl
ParentCtl3D	Determine whether the list box uses its parent's Ctl3D information.	TControl
ParentFont	Determine whether the list box uses its parent's Font information.	TControl
ParentShowHint	Determine whether the list box uses its parent's ShowHint information.	TControl
PopupMenu	Determine which pop-up menu is attached to the list box.	TControl
ShowHint	Determine if the list box displays a tooltip.	TControl
Style	Determine whether the list box is a standard or owner-draw style list box.	TControl
TabOrder	Determine whether the list box's position is in its parent's tab order.	TControl
TabStop	Determine whether the list box is a tab stop.	TControl
Visible	Determine whether the list box is visible.	TControl

BorderStyle PROPERTY

Objects Affected All list boxes

Purpose The BorderStyle property determines whether the list box has a border.

Declaration

```
property BorderStyle: TBorderStyle;
```

Example Syntax

```
procedure TForm1.FormCreate(Sender: TObject);
begin
  ListBox2.Sorted := True;
  ListBox1.BorderStyle := bsNone;
  ListBox2.BorderStyle := bsNone;
end;
```

Description

BorderStyle is type TBorderStyle, which is declared as

```
TBorderStyle = bsNone..bsSingle;
```

If BorderStyle is set to bsNone, as in Figure 57-3, the list box does not have a border. If BorderStyle is bsSingle, a single-pixel line is drawn around the list box.

Clear METHOD

Objects Affected   All list boxes

Purpose   The Clear method deletes all the text in the list box.

Declaration

```
procedure Clear;
```

Example Syntax

```
procedure TForm1.btnClearClick(Sender: TObject);
begin
  ListBox2.Clear;
end;
```

Description   Clear removes every string from the Items string list and erases all the text in the list box.

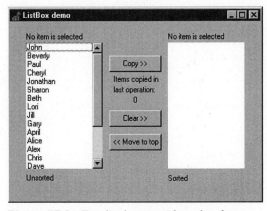

Figure 57-3   Two list boxes with no borders

DataField PROPERTY

Objects Affected	TDBListBox
Purpose	The DataField property determines which field the database list box uses for its display data.
Declaration	

```
property DataField: string;
```

Example Syntax

```
procedure TForm1.FormCreate(Sender: TObject);
begin
  Table1.DatabaseName := 'DBDEMOS';
  Table1.TableName := 'COUNTRY.DB';
  DataSource1.DataSet := Table1;
  DBListBox1.DataSource := DataSource1;
  DBListBox1.DataField := Name;
end;
```

Description The field identified by DataField is located in the data source component specified by the DataSource property.

DataSource PROPERTY

Objects Affected	TDBListBox
Purpose	The DataSource property specifies the data source of the database list box.
Declaration	

```
property DataSource: TDataSource;
```

Example Syntax

```
procedure TForm1.FormCreate(Sender: TObject);
begin
  Table1.DatabaseName := 'DBDEMOS';
  Table1.TableName := 'COUNTRY.DB';
  DataSource1.DataSet := Table1;
  DBListBox1.DataSource := DataSource1;
  DBListBox1.DataField := Name;
end;
```

Description DataSource determines where the database list box gets its data and specifies a TDataSource component that is linked to a dataset containing the data. The dataset can be a table or query.

ExtendedSelect PROPERTY

Objects Affected   All list boxes

Purpose   The **ExtendedSelect** property determines whether the user can select a range of items in the list box.

Declaration

```
property ExtendedSelect: Boolean;
```

Example Syntax

```
procedure TForm1.FormCreate(Sender: TObject);
begin
  // . . .

  // Allow multiple- and range-selections
  ListBox1.ExtendedSelect := True;
  ListBox1.MultiSelect := True;
end;
```

Description   If **MultiSelect** is **False**, the setting for **ExtendedSelect** has no effect. If both **MultiSelect** and **ExtendedSelect** are **True**, the user can select a range of items in the list box by clicking the first item, then clicking the last item while holding down the (SHIFT) key, or by (CTRL)-clicking multiple, unordered items. If **MultiSelect** is **True** and **ExtendedSelect** is **False**, the (CTRL) and (SHIFT) keys work as the (CTRL) key would if **ExtendedSelect** was **True**: The user can (CTRL)-click or (SHIFT)-click multiple, unordered items, but not a whole range of items. See Figure 57-4.

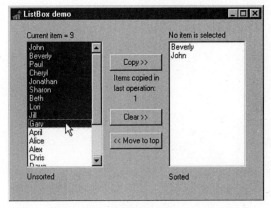

Figure 57-4   Selecting multiple items in the list box with the mouse pointer and the (SHIFT) key

IntegralHeight PROPERTY

Objects Affected	All list boxes
Purpose	The `IntegralHeight` property determines whether the height of the list box changes slightly to show the last viewable item completely.
Declaration	

```
property IntegralHeight: Boolean;
```

Example Syntax

```
ListBox1.IntegralHeight := False;
```

Description

If `IntegralHeight` is `False`, the list box displays using the height set with the `Height` property. If `IntegralHeight` is `True`, the list box resizes vertically if needed, so its last viewable item is not clipped. This is most clearly demonstrated with an illustration. In Figure 57-5 below, the list box on the left partially obscures the last viewable item—its `IntegralHeight` is `False`. The list box on the right, which has an `IntegralHeight` value of `True`, has resized slightly so it only displays complete items.

> **NOTE**
> If the `Style` property of the list box is set to `LbOwnerDrawVariable`, the `IntegralHeight` property has no effect.

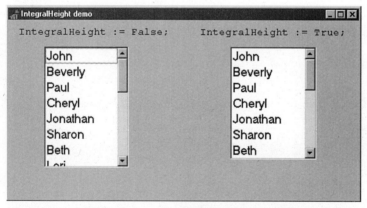

Figure 57-5 The list box on the right has `IntegralHeight` set to `True`; otherwise, the two list boxes are identical

ItemAtPos METHOD

Objects Affected	All list boxes
Purpose	The **ItemAtPos** method returns the index of the list box item located at the specified coordinates.
Declaration	

```
function ItemAtPos(Pos: TPoint; Existing: Boolean): Integer;
```

Parameters

Pos   The coordinates of the item to be returned.

Existing   Determines the value returned if no item is found at that position.

Example Syntax

```
procedure TForm1.ListBox1MouseUp(Sender: TObject; Button: TMouseButton;
                                 Shift: TShiftState; X, Y: Integer);
var
  ItemText: PChar;
  ItemPos: Integer;
begin
  ItemPos := ListBox1.ItemAtPos(Point(X, Y), True);
  if ItemPos = -1 then ItemText := 'no item was selected'
  else
      ItemText := PChar(ListBox1.Items[ItemPos]);
  if Button = mbRight then
    Application.MessageBox(ItemText, 'Right click', IDOK);
end;
```

Description   **ItemAtPos** returns the position of the item found at the coordinate position specified by the *Pos* parameter. See Figure 57-6. The *Existing* parameter determines what value to return if no item is found at *Pos*. If

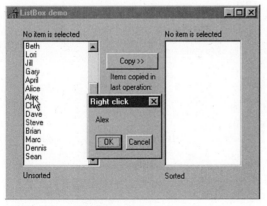

Figure 57-6 Right-clicking the list box returns the item at that position

Existing is True, ItemPos returns −1. If *Existing* is False, ItemPos returns the value of Items.Count, which is the same as adding 1 to the positional value of the last item in the list.

ItemHeight PROPERTY

Objects Affected	All list boxes
Purpose	The ItemHeight property specifies the height of items in pixels in an owner-draw list box.
Declaration	

```
property ItemHeight: Integer;
```

Example Syntax

```
ListBox1.ItemHeight := 15;
```

Description   ItemHeight is used to change the height of items in an owner-draw list box. It has no effect unless the Style property of the list box is set to lbOwnerDrawFixed. That is, if the Style property is lbStandard or lbOwnerDrawVariable, ItemHeight is ignored.

ItemIndex PROPERTY

Objects Affected	All list boxes
Purpose	The ItemIndex property is the positional value of the selected item in the list box.
Declaration	

```
property ItemIndex: Integer;
```

Example Syntax

```
procedure TForm1.ListBox1Click(Sender: TObject);
begin
  lblListItem1.Caption := 'Current item = '  +
                      IntToStr(ListBox1.ItemIndex);
end;
```

Description   ItemIndex is a run-time-only property containing the positional value of the currently selected item in the list box. If you want to select a specific list box item at run time, set the value of ItemIndex to that item's index number, with 0 the first item in the list, 1 the second, and so on. Figure 57-7 shows the current item's index with a label.

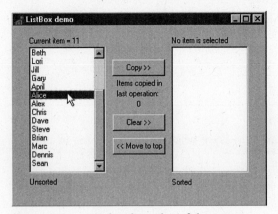

Figure 57-7 Display the index of the current
item with a label

ItemRect METHOD

Objects Affected	All list boxes
Purpose	The **ItemRect** method returns the rectangle surrounding the specified item in the list box.
Declaration	

```
function ItemRect(Index: Integer): TRect;
```

Parameters

Index   The index of the string in the list box string list you are specifying.

Example Syntax

```
procedure TForm1.ListBox2MouseUp(Sender: TObject; Button: TMouseButton;
                               Shift: TShiftState; X, Y: Integer);
var
  MyRect: TRect;
  ItemPos: Integer;
begin
  if Button = mbRight then
  begin
    ItemPos := ListBox2.ItemAtPos(Point(X,Y), True);
    if ItemPos <> -1 then
    begin
      MyRect := ListBox2.ItemRect(ItemPos);
      ListBox2.Canvas.Brush.Color := clGreen;
      ListBox2.Canvas.FrameRect(MyRect);
    end
  end
end;
```

Description   ItemRect returns the rectangle surrounding the item specified by the *Index* parameter. See Figure 57-8. *Index* represents the item's position in the string list the list box displays.

Items PROPERTY

Objects Affected   All list boxes

Purpose   The Items property contains the list of strings appearing in the list box.

Declaration

```
property Items: TStrings;
```

Example Syntax

```
procedure TForm1.btnCopyClick(Sender: TObject);
var x: Integer;
begin
  for x := 0 to ListBox1.Items.Count - 1 do
    if ListBox1.Selected[x] = True then
      ListBox2.Items.Add(ListBox1.Items[x]);
end;
```

Description   Items is type TStrings, which is used to maintain a list of strings within a VCL control. The string list is zero-based, so the first item is Items[0], the second is Items[1], and so on. You can use TString methods such as Add, Append, Delete, Exchange, Insert, and Move to manipulate the strings in Items. See Chapter 25, "TStrings and Its Descendants," for details on TStrings and its properties and methods.

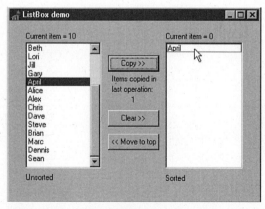

Figure 57-8   Right-clicking an item in the list box draws a green frame around the item

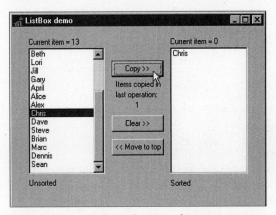

Figure 57-9 Clicking the Copy button copies the selected list box item to the other list box

MultiSelect PROPERTY

Objects Affected	All list boxes
Purpose	The MultiSelect property determines whether the user can select more than one item at a time in the list box.
Declaration	

```
property MultiSelect: Boolean;
```

Example Syntax

```
procedure TForm1.FormCreate(Sender: TObject);
begin
  // . . .

  // Allow multiple- and range-selections
  ListBox1.ExtendedSelect := True;
  ListBox1.MultiSelect := True;
end;
```

Description   If MultiSelect is True, the user can select more than one item at a time from the list box. If MultiSelect is False, the user cannot select multiple items from the list box. MultiSelect also works in conjunction with the ExtendedSelect property. Refer to the ExtendedSelect entry for details.

OnMeasureItem EVENT

Objects Affected	All list boxes
Purpose	The OnMeasureItem event occurs when an item in an owner-draw list box with a variable style needs to be redrawn.

Declaration

```
property OnMeasureItem: TMeasureItemEvent;
```

Example Syntax

```
// Standard event handler for OnMeasureItem
procedure TForm1.ListBox2MeasureItem(Control: TWinControl;
                   Index: Integer; var Height: Integer);
begin

end;
```

Description

If the list box `Style` is `lbOwnerDrawVariable`, the `OnMeasureItem` event occurs when an item in `Style` needs to be redrawn. `OnMeasureItem` is type `TMeasureItemEvent`, which is declared as:

```
TMeasureItemEvent = procedure(Control: TWinControl; Index: Integer;
                   var Height: Integer) of object;
```

The `Control` parameter identifies the list box. `Index` specifies the index of the list box item that needs to be redrawn, and `Height` specifies the height of the item that needs to be redrawn.

ReadOnly PROPERTY

Objects Affected TDBListBox

Purpose The `ReadOnly` property determines if the user can edit the contents of the database list box.

Declaration

```
property ReadOnly: Boolean;
```

Example Syntax

```
DBListBox1.ReadOnly := False;
```

Description

If `ReadOnly` is `True`, the user cannot edit the contents of the database list box. In this mode, the list box is used to simply display the field data. If `ReadOnly` is `False`, the user can edit the contents and, as a result, edit the value of the field in the current record if the dataset is in edit mode.

The default value is `True`.

SelCount PROPERTY

Objects Affected All list boxes

Purpose The `SelCount` property contains the number of list box items currently selected.

Declaration

```
property SelCount: Integer;
```

Example Syntax

```
procedure TForm1.btnCopyClick(Sender: TObject);
var x: Integer;
begin
  for x := 0 to ListBox1.Items.Count - 1 do
    if ListBox1.Selected[x] = True then
      ListBox2.Items.Add(ListBox1.Items[x]);
  // update the label that details the number of
  // items copied...
  Label5.Caption := IntToStr(ListBox1.SelCount);
end;
```

Description

There can be more than one item selected in a list box if the **MultiSelect** property is set to **True**. Otherwise, **SelCount** can be **1** if one item is selected, or **0** if no items are selected.

Selected PROPERTY

Objects Affected   All list boxes

Purpose   The **Selected** property determines whether the specified item is currently selected.

Declaration

```
property Selected[Index: Integer]: Boolean;
```

Example Syntax

```
procedure TForm1.btnCopyClick(Sender: TObject);
var x: Integer;
begin
  for x := 0 to ListBox1.Items.Count - 1 do
    if ListBox1.Selected[x] = True then
      ListBox2.Items.Add(ListBox1.Items[x]);
  // . . .
end;
```

Description

The *Index* parameter is used to specify the item based on its index value in the **Items** property. If the item specified by *Index* is selected, **Selected** returns **True**. Otherwise, **Selected** returns **False**. If more than one item is selected in the list box, you can loop through the items and text each one, as in the example above.

Sorted PROPERTY

Objects Affected All list boxes

Purpose The `Sorted` property determines whether the items in the list box are sorted alphabetically.

Declaration

```
property Sorted: Boolean;
```

Example Syntax

```
procedure TForm1.FormCreate(Sender: TObject);
begin
  ListBox1.Sorted := False;
  ListBox2.Sorted := True;

  // Allow multiple- and range-selections
  ListBox1.ExtendedSelect := True;
  ListBox1.MultiSelect := True;

  ListBox1.IntegralHeight := False;
end;
```

Description If `Sorted` is set to `True`, the items are always sorted alphabetically. When sorting is enabled for a list box and items are added to it, they are automatically placed into the list in alphabetical order. If `Sorted` is `False`, the items in the list box appear in the order they were added to it. The default value is `False`.

TopIndex PROPERTY

Objects Affected All list boxes

Purpose The `TopIndex` property determines which item appears at the top of the list box.

Declaration

```
property TopIndex: Integer;
```

Example Syntax

```
procedure TForm1.btnMoveItemToTopClick(Sender: TObject);
var x: Integer;
begin
  for x := 0 to ListBox1.Items.Count - 1 do
    if ListBox1.Selected[x] = True then
      ListBox1.TopIndex := x;
end;
```

Description   TopIndex does not re-sort the list box. Rather, it moves the whole list up
or down within the list box client area, so the specified item appears near
the top of the list box window. This is especially useful if you have a list
box containing numerous items, and you want to move an item that's near
the middle of the list to the top of the list box's viewable client area. For
example, you may want to create a list of fonts in which the list is scrolled
so the current font is displayed at the top of the list box.

58

TCustomListView AND TListView

List view controls are among the new custom controls introduced with Windows 95. *List views* contain a collection of related items consisting of an icon, caption, and optional 32-bit data value. The most obvious example of a list view, shown in Figure 58-1, is the Windows Explorer: The right pane of Explorer is a list view control. In Explorer, the optional data associated with each item is a pointer to the path of the program executed if you double-click its icon.

List view controls are not confined to browsing your hard drive, however. List views can also be used to display any type of information lending itself to their organizational strengths. The list view offers four *view styles:* Large Icon view, Small Icon view, List view, and Details view. These view styles can be set with the `ViewStyle` property. Details view (called Report view by Borland for some reason) adds column headers displaying optional descriptive captions to the control.

List view controls also offer several different item alignment options, sorting capability, drag-and-drop facilities, and the ability to let the user edit individual item captions. As with tree view controls, the items in a list view control can display an additional graphic next to their standard icon to indicate state. A check box or circle with a line through it, for example, may indicate that an item is available, unavailable, or ready for a user action.

The `TCustomListView` and `TListView` classes encapsulate the list view control for Delphi programmers. The individual items in a list view control are encapsulated by `TListItem`, which is covered in Chapter 15, "`TListItem` and `TListItems`."

TCustomListView

`TCustomListView` is the abstract base class for list views in Delphi. It offers the basic functionality needed to implement the `TListView` class. You will need to create instances of `TCustomListView`.

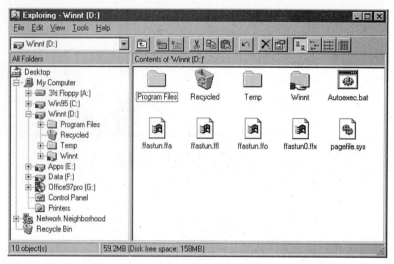

Figure 58-1 A list view is used in Windows Explorer

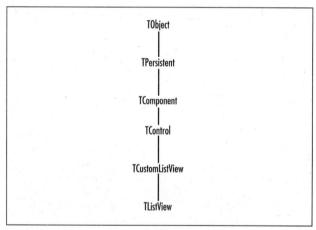

Figure 58-2 Ancestry of `TCustomListView` and `TListView`

Figure 58-2 shows the ancestry of `TCustomListView` and `TListView`. Table 58-1 displays the properties, methods, and events implemented by `TCustomListView`.

Table 58-1 Properties, methods, and events implemented by `TCustomListView`

Use or Set This...	To Do This...	Inheritance
Align	Determine how the control is aligned within its parent.	TControl
AllocBy	Allocate memory for a number of items at one time.	None
AlphaSort	Sort the list view items alphabetically.	None

Use or Set This...	To Do This...	Inheritance
Arrange	Arrange the list view items in preset ways.	None
Assign	Assign one persistent object to another.	TPersistent
BeginDrag	Begin a manual drag operation.	TControl
BoundingRect	Retrieve the bounding rectangle of the list view.	None
BoundsRect	Determine the boundary rectangle occupied by the control.	TControl
BringToFront	Bring the control to the front of the z-order.	TControl
Brush	Determine the color and pattern used for the windowed control background.	TComponent
CanFocus	Determine whether the windowed control can receive the focus.	TWinControl
Caption	Label the control with a text string.	TControl
ClassName	Get the name of the object's class.	TObject
ClassParent	Get the object's parent class.	TObject
ClassType	Get the object's actual type.	TObject
ClientHeight	Determine the control's client height.	TControl
ClientOrigin	Determine the upper-left position of the control's client area.	TControl
ClientRect	Determine the rectangle occupied by the control's client area.	TControl
ClientToScreen	Convert control (local) coordinates to screen coordinates.	TControl
ClientWidth	Determine the width of the control's client area.	TControl
Color	Determine the color of the windowed control.	TControl
ColumnClick	Determine whether column headings will respond to mouse clicks.	None
Columns	Access the list view columns.	None
ComponentCount	Determine the number of owned components.	TComponent
ComponentIndex	Determine the index of the component in its owner's Components list.	TComponent
Components	Determine the list of owned components.	TComponent
ComponentState	Determine the state of the current component.	TComponent
ContainsControl	Determine whether the specified control is contained by the windowed control.	TWinControl
ControlAtPos	Determine the control contained at a specified position.	TWinControl
ControlCount	Determine the number of controls contained by the windowed control.	TWinControl
Controls	Access the controls contained by the windowed control using their positions in an array.	TWinControl
ControlState	Determine the state of the control at any given time.	TControl
ControlStyle	Determine what attributes are present in the control.	TControl
Create	Create a new component.	TObject
Ctl3D	Determine whether the windowed control displays in 3D.	TWinControl
Cursor	Determine what image is used for the cursor over the control.	TControl
CustomSort	Sort the list view items using custom criteria.	None
Destroy	Destroy the component.	TObject
DestroyComponents	Destroy all the components owned by the component.	TComponent
Destroying	Notify the component that it is being destroyed.	TComponent
DragCursor	Determine the shape of the mouse cursor as it drags an object over the control.	TControl

continued on next page

continued from previous page

Use or Set This...	To Do This...	Inheritance
Dragging	Determine whether the control is being dragged.	TControl
DragMode	Determine the drag-and-drop behavior of the control.	TControl
DropTarget	Determine which item in the list view control is the target of a drag-and-drop operation.	None
Enabled	Determine whether the control is enabled.	TControl
EndDrag	End or cancel a manual drag operation.	TControl
FindCaption	Search for a list view item with the specified caption.	None
FindComponent	Find a component in the Components array list.	TComponent
FindData	Search for a list view item with the specified data.	None
Focused	Determine whether the windowed control has the focus.	TControl
Font	Determine the font used to render text on the control.	TControl
Free	Safely destroy the object.	TObject
GetItemAt	Retrieve the list view item at the specified position.	None
GetNearestItem	Retrieve the list view item that is closest to a specified point.	None
GetNextItem	Retrieve the next list view item given a starting item, a direction, and a state criteria.	None
GetTextBuf	Copy the text of the control into a buffer.	TControl
GetTextLen	Get the length of the text of the control.	TControl
Handle	Obtain a handle to the windowed control.	TComponent
HandleAllocated	Determine if a handle is allocated for the windowed control.	TWinControl
Height	Determine the height of the control.	TControl
HelpContext	Determine the help context ID of the windowed control.	TComponent
Hide	Make the control invisible.	TControl
Hint	Determine the text that displays in a tooltip for the control.	TControl
IconOptions	Determine the list view control icon options.	None
InheritsFrom	Determine if the object is descended from a certain class.	TObject
InsertControl	Insert a control into the windowed control's Controls array.	TWinControl
InstanceSize	Determine the amount of memory allocated for the object.	TObject
Invalidate	Force the control to be repainted as soon as possible.	TControl
IsEditing	Determine whether a list view item is being edited.	None
ItemFocused	Determine which list view item has the focus.	None
Items	Access the list view items in the list view control.	None
LargeImages	Determine the image list that contains the images used to display when the view style is vsIcon.	None
Left	Determine the left edge of the control within its container.	TControl
MultiSelect	Determine whether the user can select multiple items.	None
Name	Determine the name of the component.	TComponent
OnChange	Handle the event that occurs when an item in the list view changes.	None

Use or Set This...	To Do This...	Inheritance
OnChanging	Handle the event that occurs when a change is about to happen in the list view control.	None
OnClick	Handle the event that occurs when a mouse button is clicked.	TControl
OnColumnClick	Handle the event that occurs when a column heading is clicked.	None
OnCompare	Handle the event that occurs when the list view is sorted.	None
OnDblClick	Handle the event that occurs when a mouse button is double-clicked.	TControl
OnDeletion	Handle the event that occurs when a list view item is deleted.	None
OnDragDrop	Handle the event that occurs when an object is dropped on the control.	TControl
OnDragOver	Handle the event that occurs when an object is dragged over the control.	TControl
OnEdited	Handle the event that occurs when a list view item is edited.	None
OnEditing	Handle the event that occurs when a list view item is being edited.	None
OnEndDrag	Handle the event that occurs when a drag-and-drop operation is cancelled.	TControl
OnEnter	Handle the event that occurs when the windowed control receives the focus.	TWinControl
OnExit	Handle the event that occurs when the windowed control loses the focus.	TWinControl
OnInsert	Handle the event that occurs when an item is inserted in the list view.	None
OnKeyDown	Handle the event that occurs when a key is pressed down and not immediately released while the windowed control has the focus.	TWinControl
OnKeyPress	Handle the event that occurs when a key is pressed while the windowed control has the focus.	TWinControl
OnKeyUp	Handle the event that occurs when a key is released while the windowed control has the focus.	TWinControl
OnMouseDown	Handle the event that occurs when a mouse button is held down and not immediately released.	TControl
OnMouseMove	Handle the event that occurs when the cursor moves over the control.	TControl
OnMouseUp	Handle the event that occurs when a mouse button is released.	TControl
OnStartDrag	Handle the event that occurs when a drag-and-drop operation is started.	TControl
Owner	Determine the owner of the component.	TComponent
Parent	Determine the parent, or container, of the control.	TControl
ParentColor	Determine whether the Color information of the control's parent is used.	TControl
ParentCtl3D	Determine whether the windowed control uses its parent's Ctl3D settings.	TWinControl
ParentFont	Determine whether the Font information of the control's parent is used.	TControl
ParentShowHint	Determine whether the ShowHint information of the control's parent is used.	TControl
PopupMenu	Determine which pop-up menu is associated with the control.	TControl
ReadOnly	Determine whether the items in the list view control can be edited by the user.	None
Refresh	Erase the control and repaint it.	TControl
RemoveControl	Remove the specified control from the windowed control's Controls array.	TWinControl
Repaint	Repaint the control.	TControl
ScaleBy	Resize the windowed control.	TWinControl
ScreenToClient	Convert screen coordinates to client (control) coordinates.	TControl

continued on next page

continued from previous page

Use or Set This...	To Do This...	Inheritance
Scroll	Scroll the contents of the list view control.	None
SelCount	Determine how many list view items are selected.	None
Selected	Determine which list view item is selected.	None
SendToBack	Send the control to the end of the z-order.	TControl
SetBounds	Determine the coordinates of the control's bounding rectangle.	TControl
SetFocus	Set the focus to the windowed control.	TWinControl
SetTextBuf	Set the text of the control to the text in a buffer.	TControl
Show	Make the control visible.	TControl
ShowColumnHeaders	Determine whether to display the column headers.	None
ShowHint	Enable tooltips for the control.	TControl
Showing	Determine whether the windowed control is currently showing onscreen.	TComponent
SmallImages	Determine which image list contains the images used to display icons in small icon view.	None
SortType	Determine how the list view items are sorted.	None
StateImages	Determine which image list contains the state images used by the items in the list view.	None
StringWidth	Determine the pixel length of a string if it appears as the caption of an item in the list view control.	None
TabOrder	Determine the tab order of the windowed control.	TWinControl
TabStop	Determine whether the windowed control is in the tab order.	TWinControl
Tag	Store an additional integer value with the component.	TComponent
Text	Access the changeable text on the control.	TControl
Top	Determine the upper edge of the control.	TControl
Update	Called automatically by Refresh.	TControl
UpdateItems	Redraw a range of list view items.	None
ViewOrigin	Determine the origin of the list view control.	None
Visible	Determine whether the control is visible.	TControl
VisibleRowCount	Determine the number of visible rows in the list view.	None
Width	Determine the width of the control.	TControl

TListView

TListView encapsulates the Windows list view control. It has properties and methods
enabling you to manipulate list view items and determine the view style, item alignment options, and properties of the column headers, if visible.

TListView controls are available in the Delphi IDE from the Win95 tab of the
Component Palette.

Table 58-2 displays the properties, methods, and events implemented by
`TListView`. This is in addition to the properties, methods, and events this class inherits from `TCustomListView`.

Table 58-2 Properties, methods, and events implemented by `TListView`

Use or Set This...	To Do This...	Inheritance
Align	Determine how the list view aligns with its parent.	TControl
AllocBy	Allocate memory for a number of items at one time.	TCustomListView
BorderStyle	Determine whether the list view control has a border.	TControl
Color	Determine the color of the list view control.	TControl
ColumnClick	Determine whether column headings will respond to mouse clicks.	TCustomListView
Columns	Access the list view columns.	TCustomListView
Ctl3D	Determine whether the list view control displays with a 3D style.	TControl
DragCursor	Determine the shape of the mouse pointer as it drags an object over the list view control.	TControl
DragMode	Determine the drag-and-drop behavior of the list view control.	TControl
Font	Determine the font used to render text in the list view control.	TControl
IconOptions	Determine the list view control icon options.	TCustomListView
Items	Access the list view items in the list view control.	TCustomListView
LargeImages	Determine the image list that contains the images used to display when the view style is vsIcon.	TCustomListView
MultiSelect	Determine whether the user can select multiple items.	TCustomListView
OnChange	Handle the event that occurs when an item in the list view changes.	TCustomListView
OnChanging	Handle the event that occurs when a change is about to happen in the list view control.	TCustomListView
OnClick	Handle the event that occurs when the mouse is clicked.	TControl
OnColumnClick	Handle the event that occurs when a column heading is clicked.	TCustomListView
OnCompare	Handle the event that occurs when the list view is sorted.	TCustomListView
OnDblClick	Handle the event that occurs when the mouse is double-clicked.	TControl
OnDeletion	Handle the event that occurs when a list view item is deleted.	TCustomListView
OnDragDrop	Handle the event that occurs when an object is dropped on the list view control.	TControl
OnDragOver	Handle the event that occurs when an object is dragged over the list view control.	TControl
OnEdited	Handle the event that occurs when a list view item is edited.	TCustomListView
OnEditing	Handle the event that occurs when a list view item is being edited.	TCustomListView
OnEndDrag	Handle the event that occurs when a drag-and-drop operation is cancelled over the list view.	TControl
OnEnter	Handle the event that occurs when the list view control receives the focus.	TControl
OnExit	Handle the event that occurs when the list view control loses the focus.	TControl

continued on next page

continued from previous page

Use or Set This...	To Do This...	Inheritance
OnInsert	Handle the event that occurs when an item is inserted in the list view.	TCustomListView
OnKeyDown	Handle the event that occurs when a key is pressed and not released.	TControl
OnKeyPress	Handle the event that occurs when a key is pressed.	TControl
OnKeyUp	Handle the event that occurs when a key is released.	TControl
OnMouseDown	Handle the event that occurs when the mouse button is pressed down.	TControl
OnMouseMove	Handle the event that occurs when the mouse pointer moves over the list view.	TControl
OnMouseUp	Handle the event that occurs when the mouse button is released.	TControl
OnStartDrag	Handle the event that occurs when the user begins dragging the control.	TControl
ParentShowHint	Determine whether the list view uses its parent's ShowHint property to determine whether to display a tooltip.	TControl
PopupMenu	Determine which pop-up menu is associated with the list view control.	TControl
ReadOnly	Determine whether the items in the list view control can be edited by the user.	TCustomListView
ShowColumnHeaders	Determine whether to display the column headers.	TCustomListView
ShowHint	Determine whether the list view control should display a tooltip.	TControl
SmallImages	Determine which image list contains the images used to display icons in small icon view.	TCustomListView
SortType	Determine how the list view items are sorted.	TCustomListView
StateImages	Determine which image list contains the state images used by the items in the list view.	TCustomListView
TabOrder	Determine the list view's position in its parent's tab order.	TControl
TabStop	Determine whether the list view is a tab stop.	TControl
ViewStyle	Determine the origin of the list view control.	TCustomListView
Visible	Determine whether the list view is visible.	TControl

ALLocBy PROPERTY

Objects Affected   All list view controls

Purpose   The AllocBy property enables you to allocate memory for multiple list view items in a single call, rather than having the system allocate memory every time an item is added.

Declaration

```
property AllocBy: Integer;
```

Example Syntax

```
procedure TForm1.AddTenMoreItems1Click(Sender: TObject);
var
  AListItem: TListItem;
  x: integer;
begin
  // Add ten more list view items.  Since the number of
  // items being added is fairly large, AllocBy is called
  // first so that the list view doesn't need to allocate
  // RAM every time an item is added.
  AListItem := TListItem.Create(ListView1.Items);
  ListView1.AllocBy := 10;
  for x := 1 to 10 do
  begin
    AListItem := ListView1.Items.Add;
    AListItem.Caption := 'New Item ' + IntToStr(x);
    AListItem.ImageIndex := x - 1;
  end
end;
```

Description

You should use **AllocBy** when you are adding a large number of items to the list view. This simplifies your code and prevents memory fragmentation. The value of **AllocBy** should be set to the number of items you will add to the list view control.

AlphaSort METHOD

Objects Affected

All list view controls

Purpose

The **AlphaSort** method sorts all the list view items alphabetically.

Declaration

```
function AlphaSort: Boolean;
```

Example Syntax

```
procedure TForm1.SortItemsAlphabetically1Click(Sender: TObject);
begin
  // Sort the items in the list view alphabetically
  if ListView1.AlphaSort = False then
    Application.MessageBox('Sorry, alphabetical sort did not work',
                           'No can do!', ID_OK);
end;
```

Description

AlphaSort returns **True** if the alphabetical sort was a success, **False** if not.

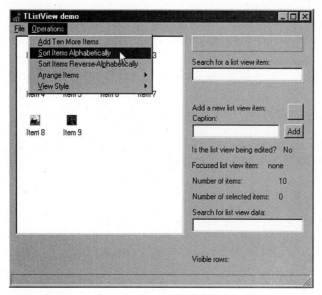

Figure 58-3 Sorting the list view alphabetically

Arrange METHOD

Objects Affected   All list view controls

Purpose   The **Arrange** method arranges the items in a list view control when the Icon or Small Icon view style is used.

Declaration

```
procedure Arrange(Code: TListArrangement);
```

Parameters

Code   Determines how the items will be arranged. See the chart below for details.

Example Syntax

```
procedure TForm1.Bottom1Click(Sender: TObject);
begin
  ListView1.Arrange(arAlignBottom);
end;

procedure TForm1.Left1Click(Sender: TObject);
begin
  ListView1.Arrange(arAlignLeft);
end;

procedure TForm1.Right1Click(Sender: TObject);
begin
  ListView1.Arrange(arAlignRight);
end;
```

```
procedure TForm1.Top1Click(Sender: TObject);
begin
  ListView1.Arrange(arAlignTop);
end;

procedure TForm1.Default1Click(Sender: TObject);
begin
  ListView1.Arrange(arDefault);
end;

procedure TForm1.ToGridPosition1Click(Sender: TObject);
begin
  ListView1.Arrange(arSnapToGrid);
end;
```

Description

The `Arrange` method arranges the items in the list view as specified by the *Code* parameter. *Code* is type **TListArrangement**, which is declared as

```
TListArrangement = (arAlignBottom, arAlignLeft, arAlignRight,
                     arAlignTop, arDefault, arSnapToGrid);
```

Code can be set to any of the following values:

Use This Code...	To Do This...
arAlignBottom	Align the list view items along the bottom edge of the list view control.
arAlignLeft	Align the list view items along the left edge of the list view control.
arAlignRight	Align the list view items along the right edge of the list view control.
arAlignTop	Align the list view items along the top edge of the list view control.
arDefault	Align the list view items according to the `Arrangement` property of `IconOptions`.
arSnapToGrid	Align the list view items to the nearest grid position.

`Arrange` has no effect unless the the `ViewStyle` property of the list view control is set to `vsIcon` or `vsSmallIcon`.

BoundingRect PROPERTY

Objects Affected   All list view controls

Purpose   The `BoundingRect` property obtains the bounding rectangle of the list view control's client area.

Declaration

```
property BoundingRect: TRect;
```

Example Syntax

```
MyRect := ListView1.BoundingRect;
```

Description   The `ViewStyle` property of the list view control must be set to `vsIcon` or `vsSmallIcon` for `BoundingRect` to have any effect.

Column PROPERTY

Objects Affected	All list view controls
Purpose	The Column property identifies the column with the specified index value.
Declaration	

```
property Column[Index: Integer]: TListColumn;
```

Example Syntax

```
procedure TForm1.FormCreate(Sender: TObject);
begin
  ListView1.Column[1].Width := 75;
  ListView1.Column[2].Width := 75;
end;
```

Description   Columns appear only when the list view ViewStyle property is set to vsReport. Column is used when you want to access column items by their index value. Column represents the whole column (not just the column heading) and is type TListColumn, which is declared as

```
TListColumn = class(TCollectionItem)
public
  constructor Create(Collection: TCollection); override;
  destructor Destroy; override;
  procedure Assign(Source: TPersistent); override;
  property WidthType: TWidth;
published
  property Alignment: TAlignment;
  property Caption: string;
  property Width: TWidth default 50;
end;
```

ColumnClick PROPERTY

Objects Affected	All list view controls
Purpose	The ColumnClick property determines whether a list view column heading responds to mouse clicks.
Declaration	

```
property ColumnClick: Boolean;
```

Example Syntax

```
procedure TForm1.FormCreate(Sender: TObject);
begin
  // . . .
  ListView1.ColumnClick := True;
  ListView1.ShowColumnHeaders := True;
end;
```

Description   Columns and column headings are displayed when the `ViewStyle` property is set to `vsReport` and the `ShowColumnHeadings` property is `True`. The column heading is a panel that typically displays a caption identifying the items collected in the column beneath it. Set `ColumnClick` to `True` if you want the column headings to respond to mouse clicks. Use the `OnColumnClick` event to respond to column heading mouse clicks. Set `ColumnClick` to `False` to disable this feature. The default value is `True`.

Columns PROPERTY

Objects Affected   All list view controls

Purpose   The `Columns` property contains the list view columns.

Declaration

```
property Columns: TListColumns;
```

Example Syntax

```
procedure TForm1.FormCreate(Sender: TObject);
begin
  // This code has the same effect as the Column example
  ListView1.Columns.Items[1].Width := 75;
  ListView1.Columns.Items[2].Width := 75;
end;
```

Description   The column of a list view control is optional and only visible if the `ViewStyle` property is `vsReport` and the `ShowColumnHeadings` property is `True`. Columns are type `TListColumns`, which is declared as

```
TListColumns = class(TCollection)
public
  constructor Create(AOwner: TCustomListView);
  function Add: TListColumn;
  property Owner: TCustomListView;
  property Items[Index: Integer]: TListColumn;
end;
```

Individual items in a list column object are type `TListColumn`. `TListColumn` is described in the listing for the `Column` property.

Although you can add column items at run time, Delphi provides a ListView Items Editor that enables you to do this at design time. This dialog box is shown in Figure 58-4.

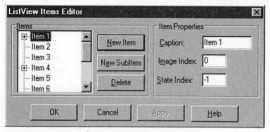

Figure 58-4 The ListView Items Editor
dialog box

CustomSort METHOD

Objects Affected   All list view controls

Purpose   The `CustomSort` method enables you to sort the items in a list view control based on programmer-defined criteria.

Declaration

```
function CustomSort(SortProc: TLVCompare; lParam: Longint): Boolean;
```

Parameters

SortProc   The address of the callback function to be called.

lParam   Optional data to be sent to the callback function.

Example Syntax

```
// callback function declaration
function MyCustomSort(Item1, Item2: TListItem; ParamSort: Integer):
                      Integer; stdcall;

// . . .

// callback function implementation
function MyCustomSort(Item1, Item2: TListItem; ParamSort: Integer):
                      Integer; stdcall;
begin
  // compare the two strings, reverse the result
  Result := -lstrcmp(PChar(TListItem(Item1).Caption),
                     PChar(TListItem(Item2).Caption));
end;

// . . .

// Call the callback function to reverse sort the list view items
procedure TForm1.SortItemsReverseAlphabetically1Click(Sender: TObject);
begin
  ListView1.CustomSort(@MyCustomSort, 0);
end;
```

Description

The `AlphaSort` method enables you to sort list view items alphabetically, but if any other type of sorting is needed, the `CustomSort` method can be used instead. `CustomSort` requires you to write a *callback function* that performs the comparison to be used as the sorting basis. The `SortProc` parameter contains the address of this callback function (using Object Pascal @ notation). The *lParam* parameter can contain an optional 32-bit integer value. If you do not need to use *lParam*, just set it to 0.

The example code listed above sorts the list view items in reverse alphabetical order. First, you need to write the declaration and implementation for the function that will be called when `CustomSort` is called. In the example above, this function is `MyCustomSort`. The callback function can have any name, but it must take the following form:

```
function FuncName(Item1, Item2: TListItem; ParamSort: Integer):
         Integer; stdcall;
```

The *Item1* and *Item2* parameters are the two list view items being compared. `ParamSort` is the optional value passed by *lParam*. If the first item should be sorted before the second item, the callback function returns a negative value. If the first item should be sorted after the second item, it returns a positive value. If the two items are identical, the callback function returns 0.

DropTarget PROPERTY

Objects Affected   All list view controls

Purpose   The `DropTarget` property returns the item in the list view that is a target of a drag-and-drop operation.

Declaration

```
property DropTarget: TListItem;
```

Example Syntax

```
// Accept drag and drop operation if the object being dragged is
// another list view item
procedure TForm1.ListView1DragOver(Sender, Source: TObject;
                                   X, Y: Integer; State: TDragState;
                                   var Accept: Boolean);
begin
  If Sender is TListItem then
    Accept := True;
end;

// Handle the drag and drop by printing which list view item
// is the target of the operation
procedure TForm1.ListView1DragDrop(Sender, Source: TObject;
                                   X, Y: Integer);
```

continued on next page

continued from previous page

```
                var MyListItem: TListItem;
                begin
                  MyListItem := TListItem.Create(ListView1.Items);
                  MyListItem := ListView1.DropTarget;
                  if MyListItem = nil then
                    Label1.Caption := 'No drop target'
                  else
                    Label1.Caption := MyListItem.Caption + ' is the drag target';
                end;
```

Description If no item in the list view control is the target of a drag-and-drop operation, **DropTarget** returns **Nil**. (See Figure 58-5.)

FindCaption METHOD

Objects Affected All list view controls

Purpose The **FindCaption** method searches the items in a list view control for one that matches the specified caption and criteria.

Declaration

```
function FindCaption(StartIndex: Integer; Value: string;
                     Partial, Inclusive, Wrap: Boolean): TListItem;
```

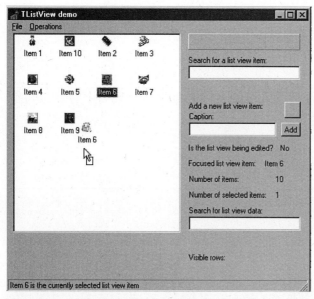

Figure 58-5 Dragging-and-dropping a list view item

Parameters

StartIndex	The list view item the search begins with.
Value	The caption to search for.
Partial	Determines whether a partial match will result in a successful search.
Inclusive	Determines whether to include the list view item specified by *StartIndex* in the search.
Wrap	Determines whether the search will wrap to the beginning of the list if no match is found.

Example Syntax

```
// This procedure makes use of an edit box the user can use to enter
// a list item caption to search for. When Enter is pressed, the
// FindCaption method determines if the text in the edit box matches
// the caption of any list view items. If it does, the caption of that
// is printed to a label. If it does not, the caption "No item was
// found" is printed.
procedure TForm1.Edit1KeyPress(Sender: TObject; var Key: Char);
var
   MyListItem: TListItem;
   x: Integer;
begin
   // if the Enter key is pressed...
   if Key = #13 then
   begin
     MyListItem := TListItem.Create(ListView1.Items);
     MyListItem := ListView1.FindCaption(0, Edit1.Text, False,
                                          True, False);
     if MyListItem = nil then
     begin
        MyListItem := TListItem.Create(ListView1.Items);
        MyListItem.Caption := 'No item';
     end;
     lblSearchResult.Caption := MyListItem.Caption + ' was found'
   end
end;
```

Description

FindCaption searches through the list view items contained by the list view control for an item with the caption the *Value* parameter specifies. (See Figure 58-6.) The search begins with the list view item specified by the *StartIndex* parameter, continuing until it finds a match or reaches the end of the items list. The *StartIndex* parameter is an integer value representing the item's position in the list view **Items** array. The *Partial* parameter determines whether the string the *Value* parameter contains can make a partial match. If *Partial* is **True**, a partial match will succeed. If it is **False**, a partial match will fail.

The *Inclusive* parameter determines whether the *StartIndex* item is included in the search: If it is **True**, it is included. If *Inclusive* is **False**, the item specified by *StartIndex* is not included in the search. The *Wrap*

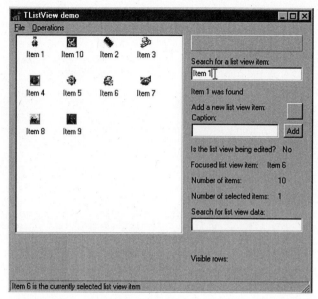

Figure 58-6 Using `FindCaption` to search for a list view item

parameter determines if the search continues to the front of the list when the list's end has been reached without making a match. If *Wrap* is `True`, the search continues from the beginning of the list, until reaching the item before the one that began the search. If *Wrap* is `False`, the search ends when the list end is reached.

FindData METHOD

Objects Affected	All list view controls
Purpose	The `FindData` method searches for a list view item with the specified data.
Declaration	

```
function FindData(StartIndex: Integer; Value: Pointer;
                  Inclusive, Wrap: Boolean): TListItem;
```

Parameters

StartIndex	The list view item at which the search begins.
Value	A pointer to the data to search for.
Inclusive	Determines whether the item specified by *StartIndex* is included in the search.
Wrap	Determines whether the search should wrap to the beginning of the list items if it reaches the list end without making a match.

Example Syntax

```
var
  Form1: TForm1;
  DataText: PChar;

// . . .

procedure TForm1.FormCreate(Sender: TObject);
begin
  DataText := 'This is test data';
end;

// When the list view is entered, set the data field of the list
// view items to the data text
procedure TForm1.ListView1Enter(Sender: TObject);
var x: Integer;
begin
  for x := 0 to ListView1.Items.Count - 1 do
    ListView1.Items[x].Data := DataText;
end;

// Search to see if the text in the edit box matches the
// list view item data
procedure TForm1.Edit3KeyPress(Sender: TObject; var Key: Char);
var AListItem: TListItem;
begin
  AListItem := TListItem.Create(ListView1.Items);
  if Key = #13 then
  begin
    AListItem := ListView1.FindData(0, DataText, True, False);
    if AListItem <> nil then
      lblDataFound.Caption := 'The first item with that data is '
                              + AListItem.Caption
    else lblDataFound.Caption := 'no item found with that data';
  end
end;
```

Description

The **TListItem Data** property is a pointer to optional data you want to associate with the item.

FindData searches through the list of list view items, beginning with the one specified by the *StartIndex* parameter, for an item whose **Data** property matches the data to which the *Value* parameter points. If the *Inclusive* parameter is **True**, the item *StartIndex* specifies is included in the search. If *Inclusive* is **False**, the *StartIndex* item is not included in the search. If the search starts at an item other than the first and the end of the list is reached with no match made, *Wrap* can determine whether to continue searching from the beginning of the list again. If *Wrap* is **True**, the search wraps to the beginnning of the list. If it is **False**, the search ends at the list end.

GetItemAt METHOD

Objects Affected	All list view controls
Purpose	The GetItemAt method returns the list view item found at the specified position.
Declaration	

```
function GetItemAt(X, Y: Integer): TListItem;
```

Parameters

X	The horizontal coordinate of the position you are checking.
Y	The vertical coordinate of the position you are checking.

Example Syntax

```
// When the right mouse button is clicked within the list view control,
// GetItemAt checks to see if there is a list view item at that
// position and displays a message box accordingly.
procedure TForm1.ListView1MouseUp(Sender: TObject;
        Button: TMouseButton; Shift: TShiftState; X, Y: Integer);
var
  MyListItem: TListItem;
  TempString: String;
begin
  if Button = mbRight then
  begin
    MyListItem := TListItem.Create(ListView1.Items);
    MyListItem := ListView1.GetItemAt(X, Y);
    if MyListItem <> nil then
    begin
      TempString := MyListItem.Caption + ' found';
      Application.MessageBox(PChar(TempString),
                            'List View Item Found', MB_OK);
    end
    else
      // MyListItem is nil
      Application.MessageBox('There is no list view item there',
                            'No List View Item Found', MB_OK);
  end
end;
```

Description	GetItemAt returns the list view item found at the position specified by the *X* and *Y* parameters, using the coordinate system of the list view control. If no item is found at that position, Nil is returned.

GetNearestItem METHOD

Objects Affected	All list view controls
Purpose	The GetNearestItem method returns the list view item closest to a specified point.

Declaration

```
function GetNearestItem(Point: TPoint; Direction: TSearchDirection):
                       TListItem;
```

Parameters

Point   The point within the list view at which the search begins.

Direction   The direction to search.

Example Syntax

```
// When the right mouse button is clicked within the list view control,
// GetNearestItem checks to see which list view item is closest to
// the position that was clicked and displays a message box
// accordingly.
procedure TForm1.ListView1MouseUp(Sender: TObject;
        Button: TMouseButton; Shift: TShiftState; X, Y: Integer);
var
  MyListItem: TListItem;
  TempString: String;
begin
  if Button = mbRight then
  begin
    MyListItem := TListItem.Create(ListView1.Items);
    MyListItem := ListView1.GetNearestItem(Point(X,Y), sdAll);
    TempString := MyListItem.Caption + 'is the closest item';
    Application.MessageBox(PChar(TempString),
                'And the closest list view item is...', MB_OK);
  end
end;
```

Description

GetNearestItem searches for the list view item closest to the point specified by the *Point* parameter, using the coordinate system of the list view
control. It searches in the direction specified by *Direction*, which is type
TSearchDirection. **TSearchDirection** is declared as:

```
TSearchDirection = (sdLeft, sdRight, sdAbove, sdBelow, sdAll);
```

where the possible values have the following meanings:

Use This Direction...	To Search...
sdAbove	Above the specified list item.
sdAll	By index. GetNearestItem searches for the next item in the list view Items array.
sdBelow	Below the specified list item.
sdLeft	To the left of the specified list item.
sdRight	To the right of the specified list item.

The default value is sdAll.

CHAPTER 58

GetNextItem METHOD

Objects Affected	All list view controls
Purpose	The `GetNextItem` method searches for the next list view item given a starting item, direction, and state criteria.
Declaration	

```
function GetNextItem(StartItem: TListItem; Direction: TSearchDirection;
                     States: TItemStates): TListItem;
```

Parameters

StartItem	The list item with which the search begins.
Direction	The direction to search.
States	The state of the list view item for which you are searching.

Example Syntax

```
// When the right mouse button is clicked within the list view control,
// GetItemAt checks to see if a list view item was clicked. If an
// item was clicked, GetNextItem finds the next item and displays a
// message box accordingly.
procedure TForm1.ListView1MouseUp(Sender: TObject; Button: TMouseButton;
  Shift: TShiftState; X, Y: Integer);
var
  MyListItem,
  MyNextListItem: TListItem;
  TempString: String;
begin
  if Button = mbRight then
  begin
    MyListItem := TListItem.Create(ListView1.Items);
    // First, the item at the mouse pointer position
    MyListItem := ListView1.GetItemAt(X, Y);

    // If the mouse pointer clicked a list view item, proceed
    if MyListItem <> nil then
    begin
      MyNextListItem := TListItem.Create(ListView1.Items);
      MyNextListItem.Caption := 'No item';
      // Check to see if the item that was right-clicked is the last
      // item.  If it is, there is no "next" item.
      if MyListItem <> ListView1.Items[ListView1.Items.Count - 1] then
        MyNextListItem := ListView1.GetNextItem(MyListItem, sdAll,
                                                [isNone])
      else
        MyNextListItem.Caption := 'No item';

      TempString := MyNextListItem.Caption + ' is the next item';
      Application.MessageBox(PChar(TempString),
                     'And the next list view item is...', MB_OK);
    end
  end
end;
```

Description	GetNextItem searches for the next list view item, beginning its search at the list view item specified by the *StartItem* parameter. It searches in the direction specified by the *Direction* parameter. *Direction* is type TSearchDirection, which is described in the preceding entry (for the GetNearestItem method). It has the following possible values: **sdLeft**, **sdRight**, **sdAbove**, **sdBelow**, and **sdAll**. You can specify the state of the list view item to search for, using the *States* parameter, which is type TItemStates. TItemStates is declared as

```
function GetNextItem(StartItem: TListItem; Direction: TSearchDirection;
                     States: TItemStates): TListItem;
```

in which its possible values have the following meanings:

Use This Value...	To Search for a List View Item That Is...
isCut	Marked for a cut and paste operation.
isDropHilited	A drag-and-drop target.
isFocused	Focused.
isNone	In its default state.
isSelected	Selected.

IconOptions PROPERTY

Objects Affected	All list view controls
Purpose	The IconOptions property contains list view item icon options.
Declaration	

```
property IconOptions: TIconOptions;
```

Example Syntax	

```
procedure TForm1.FormCreate(Sender: TObject);
begin
  ListView1.IconOptions.Arrangement := iaTop;
  ListView1.IconOptions.AutoArrange := True;
  ListView1.IconOptions.WrapText := True;
end;
```

Description	IconOptions is type TIconOptions, which is declared as

```
TIconOptions = class(TPersistent)
  public
    constructor Create(AOwner: TCustomListView);
  published
    property Arrangement: TIconArrangement;
    property AutoArrange: Boolean;
    property WrapText: Boolean default True;
  end;
```

IconOptions has three properties determining the arrangement of the list view item icons in the list view control: Arrangement, AutoArrange, and WrapText. The Arrangement property is type TIconArrangement and can be set to iaTop (aligned to the top of the control) or iaLeft (aligned to the left edge of the control). The default value for Arrangement is iaTop.

The AutoArrange property determines whether the icons automatically arrange themselves when the control is modified. If the AutoArrange property is True, the item icons in the list view arrange themselves automatically. If it is False, the icons do not automatically arrange. AutoArrange is False by default.

The WrapText property determines whether the icon captions wrap if they exceed the width of the icon. If WrapText is True, the captions wrap. If it is False, the captions do not wrap. The default value is True.

IsEditing METHOD

Objects Affected All list view controls

Purpose The IsEditing method determines whether a list view item is currently being edited.

Declaration

```
function IsEditing: Boolean;
```

Example Syntax

```
procedure TForm1.Timer1Timer(Sender: TObject);
begin
  if ListView1.IsEditing then
    lblEditing.Caption := 'Yes'
  else lblEditing.Caption := 'No';
end;
```

Description If a list view item is being edited when IsEditing is called, it returns True. Otherwise, it returns False. In Figure 58-7, IsEditing returns True when the caption of a list view item is edited.

ItemFocused PROPERTY

Objects Affected All list view controls

Purpose The ItemFocused property specifies the list view item with the focus.

Declaration

```
property ItemFocused: TListItem;
```

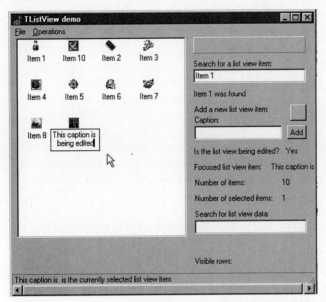

Figure 58-7 Editing the caption of a list view item causes
IsEditing to return **True**

Example Syntax

```
// Print the caption of the focused list view item
procedure TForm1.ListView1Changing(Sender: TObject; Item: TListItem;
                    Change: TItemChange; var AllowChange: Boolean);
var x: Integer;
begin
  for x := 0 to ListView1.Items.Count - 1 do
    if ListView1.Items[x].Focused = True then
      lblFocused.Caption := ListView1.ItemFocused.Caption;
end;
```

Description   **ItemFocused** is a run-time only property containing the list view item that
currently has the focus in the list view control. You can also get and set the
focus to a particular item with **ItemFocused**. If no item has the focus,
ItemFocused is **Nil**.

Items PROPERTY

Objects Affected   All list view controls

Purpose   The **Items** property is a container for the list view items in the list view
control.

Declaration

```
property Items: TListItems;
```

Example Syntax

```
procedure TForm1.ListView1Changing(Sender: TObject; Item: TListItem;
  Change: TItemChange; var AllowChange: Boolean);
var x: Integer;
begin
  for x := 0 to ListView1.Items.Count - 1 do
    if ListView1.Items[x].Focused = True then
      lblFocused.Caption := ListView1.ItemFocused.Caption;
end;
```

Description

Items contains the items in the list view and enables you to access them as elements in an array, in which the first element is Items[0], the second is Items[1], and so on. Items is type TListItems, which is declared as

```
TListItems = class(TPersistent)
  public
    constructor Create(AOwner: TCustomListView);
    destructor Destroy; override;
    function Add: TListItem;
    procedure Assign(Source: TPersistent); override;
    procedure BeginUpdate;
    procedure Clear;
    procedure Delete(Index: Integer);
    procedure EndUpdate;
    function IndexOf(Value: TListItem): Integer;
    function Insert(Index: Integer): TListItem;
    property Count: Integer;
    property Handle: HWND;
    property Item[Index: Integer]: TListItem;
    property Owner: TCustomListView;
  end;
```

The properties and methods of TListItems enable you to insert and delete individual items to the list, determine the number of items in the list, and clear the entire list at once. TListItems is covered in Chapter 15.

LargeImages PROPERTY

Objects Affected   All list view controls

Purpose   The LargeImages property determines where the list view gets the icons to display when its view style is vsIcon.

Declaration

```
property LargeImages: TImageList;
```

Example Syntax

```
procedure TForm1.FormCreate(Sender: TObject);
begin
  ListView1.LargeImages := ImageList1;
  ListView1.SmallImages := ImageList2;
  ListView1.StateImages := ImageList3;
end;
```

Description   **LargeImages** determines which image list control contains the graphics used to display the list view items when the list view control's **ViewStyle** property is set to **vsIcon**. Image lists can contain a number of different bitmap images.

MultiSelect PROPERTY

Objects Affected   All list view controls

Purpose   The **MultiSelect** property determines whether the user can select more than one list view item at a time.

Declaration

```
property MultiSelect: Boolean;
```

Example Syntax

```
ListView1.MultiSelect := True;
```

Description   If **MultiSelect** is **True**, the user can select multiple list view items at once. If it is **False**, only one list view item can be selected at a time. The default value is **False**.

OnChange EVENT

Objects Affected   All list view controls

Purpose   The **OnChange** event occurs when an item in the list view changes.

Declaration

```
property OnChange: TLVChangeEvent;
```

Example Syntax

```
// This is the standard event handler for OnChange
procedure TForm1.ListView1Change(Sender: TObject; Item: TListItem;
                                 Change: TItemChange);
begin
  // add code here
end;
```

Description   Changes that trigger an **OnChange** event include a selection change, or a state, image, or caption change. Handle the **OnChange** event when you need to do processing whenever a list view change occurs. **OnChange** is type **TLVChangeEvent**, which is declared as

```
TLVChangeEvent = procedure (Sender: TObject; Item: TListItem;
                            Change: TItemChange) of object;
```

OnChange and **OnChanging** are similar; however, **OnChanging** enables you to process code before a change occurs.

OnChanging EVENT

Objects Affected   All list view controls

Purpose   The OnChanging event occurs when a change is about to happen in the list view control.

Declaration

```
property OnChanging: TLVChangingEvent;
```

Example Syntax

```
// This is a standard handler for the OnChanging event
procedure TForm1.ListView1Changing(Sender: TObject; Item: TListItem;
                        Change: TItemChange; var AllowChange: Boolean);
var x: Integer;
begin
  for x := 0 to ListView1.Items.Count - 1 do
    if ListView1.Items[x].Focused = True then
      lblFocused.Caption := ListView1.ItemFocused.Caption;

  lblNumSelItems.Caption := IntToStr(ListView1.SelCount);

  if ListView1.Selected <> nil then
  begin
    StatusBar1.SimpleText := ListView1.Selected.Caption +
                             ' is the currently selected list view item'
  end
  else
    StatusBar1.SimpleText := '';
end;
```

Description   The OnChanging event is triggered by a change of selection from one list view item to another, or by a change in item state, image, or caption. OnChanging is type **TLVChangingEvent**, which is declared as

```
TLVChangingEvent = procedure (Sender: TObject; Item: TListItem;
                        Change: TItemChange) of object;
```

OnChanging and OnChange are similar; however, OnChange is triggered *after* the change occurs.

OnColumnClick EVENT

Objects Affected   All list view controls

Purpose   The OnColumnClick event occurs when the user clicks on a column header in the list view.

Declaration

```
property OnColumnClick: TLVColumnClickEvent;
```

Example Syntax

```
// This is a standard handler for the OnColumnClick event
procedure TForm1.ListView1ColumnClick(Sender: TObject;
                                      Column: TListColumn);
begin
  If Column = ListView1.Column[0] then
    ListView1.AlphaSort;
end;
```

Description

Column headers are visible if the **ViewStyle** property is **vsReport**, which puts the list view control into **Details** view. The **ColumnClick** property must be **True** for the **OnColumnClick** event to occur. In the example above, the items in the list view are sorted alphabetically.

OnCompare EVENT

Objects Affected   All list view controls

Purpose   The **OnCompare** event occurs whenever a pair of items in the list view control are compared as part of a sorting process.

Declaration

```
property OnCompare: TLVCompareEvent;
```

Example Syntax

```
// This is the standard handler for the OnCompare event
procedure TForm1.ListView1Compare(Sender: TObject;
                Item1, Item2: TListItem;
                Data: Integer; var Compare: Integer);
begin
  // Add code here
end;
```

Description   **OnCompare** is type **TLVCompareEvent** which is declared as

```
TLVCompareEvent = procedure(Sender: TObject; Item1, Item2: TListItem;
                Data: Integer; var Compare: Integer) of object;
```

You should handle this event if you need to do specific processing when the list view control is sorted.

OnDeletion EVENT

Objects Affected   All list view controls

Purpose   The **OnDeletion** event occurs when an item is deleted from the list view control.

Declaration

```
property OnDeletion: TLVDeletedEvent;
```

Example Syntax

```
// This is the standard handler for the OnDeletion event
procedure TForm1.ListView1Deletion(Sender: TObject; Item: TListItem);
begin
  // Add code here
end;
```

Description OnDeletion occurs when an item is deleted from the list view, so you should handle this event if you need to process any code at that time. OnDeletion is type TLVDeletedEvent, which is declared as

```
TLVDeletedEvent = procedure (Sender: TObject; Item: TListItem)
                  of object;
```

OnEdited EVENT

Objects Affected All list view controls

Purpose The OnEdited event occurs after the caption of a list view item has been edited.

Declaration

```
property OnEdited: TLVEditedEvent;
```

Example Syntax

```
// This is the default handler for the OnEdited event
procedure TForm1.ListView1Edited(Sender: TObject; Item: TListItem;
  var S: string);
begin
  // Add code here
end;
```

Description You should handle the OnEdited event if you need to process code after the caption of a list view item has been edited. OnEdited is type TLVEditedEvent, which is declared as

```
TLVEditedEvent = procedure (Sender: TObject; Item: TListItem;
                            var S: string) of object;
```

OnEdited will not occur if the ReadOnly property of the list view control is True.

OnEditing EVENT

Objects Affected All list view controls

Purpose The OnEditing event occurs when the caption of a list view item is being edited by the user.

Declaration

```
property OnEditing: TLVEditingEvent;
```

Example Syntax

```
// This is the default handler for the OnEdited event
procedure TForm1.ListView1Editing(Sender: TObject; Item: TListItem;
  var AllowEdit: Boolean);
begin
  // Add code here
end;
```

Description

You should handle OnEditing if you need to process code when the user begins editing the caption of a list view item. OnEditing is type TLVEditingEvent, which is declared as

```
TLVEditingEvent = procedure (Sender: TObject; Item: TListItem;
                              var AllowEdit: Boolean) of object;
```

OnEdited will not occur if the ReadOnly property of the list view control is True.

OnInsert EVENT

Objects Affected   All list view controls

Purpose   The OnInsert event occurs when a new list view item is inserted in the list view control.

Declaration

```
property OnInsert: TLVDeletedEvent;
```

Example Syntax

```
// This is the standard handler for the OnInsert event
procedure TForm1.ListView1Insert(Sender: TObject; Item: TListItem);
begin
  // Add code here
end;
```

Description   OnInsert is type TLVDeletedEvent, which is declared as

```
TLVDeletedEvent = procedure (Sender: TObject; Item: TListItem)
                    of object;
```

You should handle the OnInsert event if you need to process code every time a list view item is inserted into the list view control.

ReadOnly PROPERTY

Objects Affected   All list view controls

Purpose   The ReadOnly property determines whether the items in the list view control can be edited.

Declaration

```
property ReadOnly: Boolean;
```

Example Syntax

```
procedure TForm1.FormCreate(Sender: TObject);
begin
  ListView1.ReadOnly := True;
end;
```

Description   If ReadOnly is True, the items in the list view control cannot be modified. If ReadOnly is False, they can be changed by the user. The default value is False.

Scroll METHOD

Objects Affected   All list view controls

Purpose   The Scroll method scrolls the items in the list view for a specified distance.

Declaration

```
procedure Scroll(DX, DY: Integer);
```

Parameters

DX   The number of pixels to scroll the list view items horizontally.

DY   The number of pixels to scroll the list view items vertically.

Example Syntax

```
ListView1.Scroll(0, 25);
```

Description   The *DX* and *DY* parameters specify the distance, in pixels, to scroll the contents of the list view control in the horizontal and vertical directions. If *DX* is positive, the list items move left. If *DY* is positive, the items move up.

You will not normally need to manually scroll list view items this way because standard scrolling functionality is provided by the control.

SelCount PROPERTY

Objects Affected   All list view controls

Purpose   The SelCount property contains the number of selected items.

Declaration

```
property SelCount: Integer;
```

Example Syntax

```
// Print the number of list view items that are currently selected
procedure TForm1.ListView1Changing(Sender: TObject; Item: TListItem;
  Change: TItemChange; var AllowChange: Boolean);
begin
  lblNumSelItems.Caption := IntToStr(ListView1.SelCount);
end;
```

Description   SelCount is a run-time-only property containing the number of list view items currently selected. If MultiSelect is True, more than one item can be selected at a time.

Selected PROPERTY

Objects Affected   All list view controls

Purpose   The Selected property specifies which list view item is currently selected.

Declaration

```
property Selected: TListItem;
```

Example Syntax

```
// Print the name of the currently selected list view item in the
// status bar
procedure TForm1.ListView1Changing(Sender: TObject; Item: TListItem;
  Change: TItemChange; var AllowChange: Boolean);
begin
  if ListView1.Selected <> nil then
    StatusBar1.SimpleText := ListView1.Selected.Caption +
                        ' is the currently selected list view item'
  else StatusBar1.SimpleText := '';
end;
```

Description   Selected is a run-time-only property containing the list view item currently selected in the list view control. You can get and set the selected list view item with this property.

ShowColumnHeaders PROPERTY

Objects Affected   All list view controls

Purpose   The ShowColumnHeaders property determines whether to display the column headers above the columns in the list view while in Report view.

Declaration

```
property ShowColumnHeaders: Boolean;
```

Example Syntax

```
procedure TForm1.FormCreate(Sender: TObject);
begin
  // . . .
  ListView1.ColumnClick := True;
  ListView1.ShowColumnHeaders := True;
end;
```

Description Column headers are the gray panels that display above the columns in a list view control when it is in `Report` view. A column header typically contains a caption describing the objects it lists. To display the list view control in `Report` view, set the `ViewStyle` property to `vsReport`.

SmallImages PROPERTY

Objects Affected All list view controls

Purpose The `SmallImages` property determines where the list view gets the icons to display when its view style is `vsSmallIcon`.

Declaration

```
property SmallImages: TImageList;
```

Example Syntax

```
procedure TForm1.FormCreate(Sender: TObject);
begin
  ListView1.LargeImages := ImageList1;
  ListView1.SmallImages := ImageList2;
  ListView1.StateImages := ImageList3;
end;
```

Description `SmallImages` determines which image list control contains the graphics used to display the list view items when the list view control's `ViewStyle` property is set to `vsSmallIcon`. Image lists can contain a number of different bitmap images.

SortType PROPERTY

Objects Affected All list view controls

Purpose The `SortType` property determines if and how the items in the list view control are sorted.

Declaration

```
property SortType: TSortType;
```

Example Syntax

```
procedure TForm1.FormCreate(Sender: TObject);
begin
```

```
    ListView1.SortType := stBoth;
end;
```

Description   The `SortType` property is type **TSortType**, which defines the possible values for determining how a list view control is sorted. **TSortType** is declared as

```
TSortType = (stNone, stData, stText, stBoth);
```

Use This Value...	To Do This...
stBoth	Sort the items when either the data object or the item caption is changed.
stData	Sort the items when the data object is changed.
stNone	Do not sort the items.
stText	Sort the items when the item caption is changed.

The default value is **nsNone**.

IMPORTANT
Once you sort the items in a list view control, there is no way to return to the previous arrangement, unless it was already sorted in some way.

StateImages PROPERTY

Objects Affected   All list view controls

Purpose   The **StateImages** property determines which image list component is the source of state images for the items in the list view control.

Declaration

```
property StateImages: TImageList;
```

Example Syntax

```
procedure TForm1.FormCreate(Sender: TObject);
begin
  ListView1.LargeImages := ImageList1;
  ListView1.SmallImages := ImageList2;
  ListView1.StateImages := ImageList3;
end;

procedure TForm1.ListView1DblClick(Sender: TObject);
begin
  if ListView1.Selected <> nil then
    if ListView1.Selected.StateIndex = -1 then
      ListView1.Selected.StateIndex := 0
    else ListView1.Selected.StateIndex := -1;
end;
```

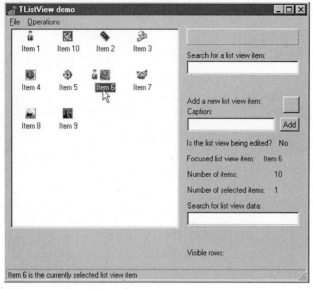

Figure 58-8 Double-clicking the list view item displays the state image associated with it

Description **StateImages** determines which image list control is the source for the state images the list view items use. A *state image* appears to the left of the item's normal icon. In Windows, the little arrow you see on shortcut icons is a state image. They can appear as solid bitmaps or as masks. In Figure 58-8, the state image used for all the items is a red check mark.

StringWidth METHOD

Objects Affected All list view controls

Purpose The **StringWidth** method returns the width of a string (in pixels) if it was rendered using the list view's current font.

Declaration

```
function StringWidth(S: string): Integer;
```

Parameters

S The string whose width you wish to test.

Example Syntax

```
// Add a new list view item to the list view control. An edit box
// allows the user to enter a caption for the item.  If the caption
// will render at wider than 50 pixels, the program prompts the user
// for a shorter caption.
```

```
procedure TForm1.SpeedButton1Click(Sender: TObject);
var
  AListItem: TListItem;
begin
  AListItem := TListItem.Create(ListView1.Items);
  if Edit2.Text <> '' then
    if ListView1.StringWidth(Edit2.Text) <= 50 then
    begin
      AListItem := ListView1.Items.Add;
      AListItem.Caption := Edit2.Text;
      Edit2.Text := '';
    end
    else begin
      Application.MessageBox('Caption is too long...please reenter',
                            'Enter a new caption', MB_OK);
      Edit2.Text := '';
    end
end;
```

Description   **StringWidth** can be used to calculate the pixel width of a caption for a new list view item before rendering it (see Figure 58-9), so you can determine whether it will wrap, be cut off, or display properly. You can also use it to automatically size the width of columns in **Report** view to the length of the widest string displayed.

UpdateItems METHOD

Objects Affected   All list view controls

Purpose   The **UpdateItems** method forces a redraw of items in the list view control.

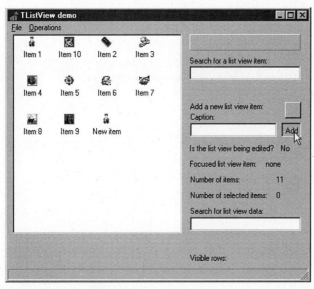

Figure 58-9 Adding items to the list view control

Declaration

```
procedure UpdateItems(FirstIndex, LastIndex: Integer);
```

Parameters

FirstIndex   The first list view item that needs to be redrawn.

LastIndex   The last list view item that needs to be redrawn.

Example Syntax

```
procedure TForm1.ToGridPosition1Click(Sender: TObject);
begin
  ListView1.Arrange(arSnapToGrid);
  // redraw all items
  ListView1.UpdateItems(0, ListView1.Items.Count - 1);
end;
```

Description   UpdateItems redraws the range of list view items, beginning with the item specified by the *FirstIndex* parameter and ending with the item specified by the *LastIndex* parameter. Remember that the range of list view items is zero-based, so the first item is item 0, the second is item 1, and so on.

ViewOrigin PROPERTY

Objects Affected   All list view controls

Purpose   The ViewOrigin property returns the point at the upper-left of the list view control.

Declaration

```
property ViewOrigin: TPoint;
```

Example Syntax

```
Example Syntax
// Print out the origin of the list view control
procedure TForm1.SpeedButton2Click(Sender: TObject);
begin
  Edit1.Text :=
    IntToStr(ListView1.ViewOrigin.X) + ',' +
    IntToStr(ListView1.ViewOrigin.Y);
end;
```

Description   ViewOrigin is a run-time, read-only property returning the origin of the list view's client area when the list view's ViewStyle property is set to vsIcon or vsSmallIcon. If ViewStyle is vsList or vsReport, ViewOrigin returns a garbage value.

VisibleRowCount PROPERTY

Objects Affected   All list view controls

Purpose   The `VisibleRowCount` property contains the number of visible rows in the list view control.

Declaration

```
property VisibleRowCount: Integer;
```

Example Syntax

```
procedure TForm1.DetailsReport1Click(Sender: TObject);
begin
  ListView1.ViewStyle := vsReport;
  lblVisibleRows.Caption := IntToStr(ListView1.VisibleRowCount);
end;
```

Description   `VisibleRowCount` is a run-time, read-only property containing the number of rows the list view can show completely without scrolling. `VisibleRowCount` applies only to the **vsList** and **vsReport** view styles. If `ViewStyle` is **vsIcon** or **vsSmallIcon**, `VisibleRowCount` is 0.

59

TCustomTab-Control AND ITS DESCENDANTS

TCustomTabControl and its descendants, TPageControl and TTabControl, let you implement property sheets and similar tabbed dialog boxes with Delphi. *Property sheets* are dialog boxes normally used to display the properties of an object and let the user change them. Windows uses property sheets extensively—almost any object you right-click contains a Properties item in the resulting pop-up menu. Selecting this item causes the object's property sheet to appear. One common property sheet is Display properties, which can be reached by right-clicking the Windows desktop.

As shown in Figure 59-1, property sheets contain one or more *pages* that can be accessed by selecting the appropriate *tab*. This interface was first implemented in Microsoft Office for Windows 3.x and proved so popular that Microsoft made it a standard common control. The TPageControl class encapsulates the page container and tab portion of the property sheet within Delphi. A similar but less capable control, called a tab control, is encapsulated by the TTabControl class. TTabControl does not offer the range of capabilities TPageControl does, and is more generic. Individual pages contained in the page or tab controls are called *tab sheets* and are type TTabSheet.

In addition to a page control and the tab sheets it contains, most property sheets contain command buttons that let you accept, apply, or cancel any property changes the user makes. These buttons are typically labeled OK, Cancel, and Apply. Clicking OK or Cancel should close the dialog box. If the user clicks Apply, any changes he or she has made to the properties of the object should be applied immediately. In the case of a read-only property sheet, a single OK button is used.

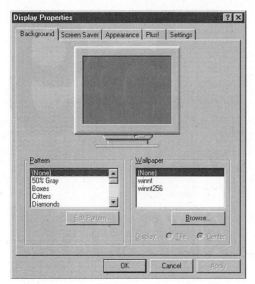

Figure 59-1 The Display Properties dialog

OBSOLETE CONTROLS

Delphi includes the `TTabbedNotebook`, `TNotebook`, and `TTabSet` controls for backward compatibility with Windows 3.x–Based applications. These controls are obsolete and should not be used in Windows 95 and NT applications. Therefore, they are not covered in this book. Use `TPageControl` or `TTabControl` instead.

TCustomTabControl

`TCustomTabControl` offers the basic functionality implemented by `TTabControl` and `TPageControl`. It is an abstract base class with protected properties, methods, and events inherited and published by its children. You will not need to create instances of `TCustomTabControl`.

Figure 59-2 displays the `TCustomTabControl` branch of the VCL. Table 59-1 displays the properties, methods, and events implemented by `TCustomTabControl`.

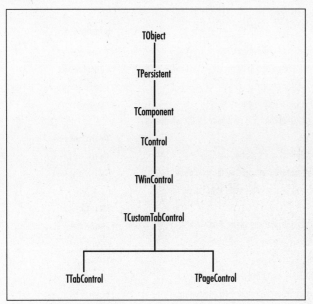

Figure 59-2 The `TCustomTabControl` branch of the VCL

Table 59-1 Properties, methods, and events implemented by `TCustomTabControl`

Use or Set This...	To Do This...	Inheritance
Align	Determine how the control is aligned within its parent.	TControl
Assign	Assign one persistent object to another.	TPersistent
BeginDrag	Begin a manual drag operation.	TControl
BoundsRect	Determine the boundary rectangle occupied by the control.	TControl
BringToFront	Bring the control to the front of the z-order.	TControl
Brush	Determine the color and pattern used for the windowed control background.	TComponent
CanFocus	Determine whether the windowed control can receive the focus.	TWinControl
Caption	Label the control with a text string.	TControl
ClassName	Get the name of the object's class.	TObject
ClassParent	Get the object's parent class.	TObject
ClassType	Get the object's actual type.	TObject
ClientHeight	Determine the control's client height.	TControl
ClientOrigin	Determine the upper-left position of the control's client area.	TControl
ClientRect	Determine the rectangle occupied by the control's client area.	TControl
ClientToScreen	Convert control (local) coordinates to screen coordinates.	TControl
ClientWidth	Determine the width of the control's client area.	TControl
Color	Determine the color of the windowed control.	TControl

continued on next page

continued from previous page

Use or Set This...	To Do This...	Inheritance
ComponentCount	Determine the number of owned components.	TComponent
ComponentIndex	Determine the index of the component in its owner's Components list.	TComponent
Components	Determine the list of owned components.	TComponent
ComponentState	Determine the state of the current component.	TComponent
ContainsControl	Determine whether the specified control is contained by the windowed control.	TWinControl
ControlAtPos	Determine the control contained at a specified position.	TWinControl
ControlCount	Determine the number of controls contained by the windowed control.	TWinControl
Controls	Access the controls contained by the windowed control using their positions in an array.	TWinControl
ControlState	Determine the state of the control at any given time.	TControl
ControlStyle	Determine what attributes are present in the control.	TControl
Create	Create a new component.	TObject
Ctl3D	Determine whether the windowed control displays in 3D.	TWinControl
Cursor	Determine what image is used for the cursor over the control.	TControl
Destroy	Destroy the component.	TObject
DestroyComponents	Destroy all the components owned by the component.	TComponent
Destroying	Notify the component that it is being destroyed.	TComponent
DragCursor	Determine the shape of the mouse cursor as it drags an object over the control.	TControl
Dragging	Determine whether the control is being dragged.	TControl
DragMode	Determine the drag-and-drop behavior of the control.	TControl
Enabled	Determine whether the control is enabled.	TControl
EndDrag	End or cancel a manual drag operation.	TControl
FindComponent	Find a component in the Components array list.	TComponent
Focused	Determine whether the windowed control has the focus.	TControl
Font	Determine the font used to render text on the control.	TControl
Free	Safely destroy the object.	TObject
GetTextBuf	Copy the text of the control into a buffer.	TControl
GetTextLen	Get the length of the text of the control.	TControl
Handle	Obtain a handle to the windowed control.	TComponent
HandleAllocated	Determine if a handle is allocated for the windowed control.	TWinControl
Height	Determine the height of the control.	TControl
HelpContext	Determine the help context ID of the windowed control.	TComponent
Hide	Make the control invisible.	TControl
Hint	Determine the text that displays in a tooltip for the control.	TControl
InheritsFrom	Determine if the object is descended from a certain class.	TObject
InsertControl	Insert a control into the windowed control's Controls array.	TWinControl
InstanceSize	Determine the amount of memory allocated for the object.	TObject

Use or Set This...	To Do This...	Inheritance
Invalidate	Force the control to be repainted as soon as possible.	TControl
Left	Determine the left edge of the control within its container.	TControl
Name	Determine the name of the component.	TComponent
OnClick	Handle the event that occurs when a mouse button is clicked.	TControl
OnDblClick	Handle the event that occurs when a mouse button is double-clicked.	TControl
OnDragDrop	Handle the event that occurs when an object is dropped on the control.	TControl
OnDragOver	Handle the event that occurs when an object is dragged over the control.	TControl
OnEndDrag	Handle the event that occurs when a drag-and-drop operation is cancelled.	TControl
OnEnter	Handle the event that occurs when the windowed control receives the focus.	TWinControl
OnExit	Handle the event that occurs when the windowed control loses the focus.	TWinControl
OnKeyDown	Handle the event that occurs when a key is pressed down and not immediately released while the windowed control has the focus.	TWinControl
OnKeyPress	Handle the event that occurs when a key is pressed while the windowed control has the focus.	TWinControl
OnKeyUp	Handle the event that occurs when a key is released while the windowed control has the focus.	TWinControl
OnMouseDown	Handle the event that occurs when a mouse button is held down and not immediately released.	TControl
OnMouseMove	Handle the event that occurs when the cursor moves over the control.	TControl
OnMouseUp	Handle the event that occurs when a mouse button is released.	TControl
OnStartDrag	Handle the event that occurs when a drag-and-drop operation is started.	TControl
Owner	Determine the owner of the component.	TComponent
Parent	Determine the parent, or container, of the control.	TControl
ParentColor	Determine whether the Color information of the control's parent is used.	TControl
ParentCtl3D	Determine whether the windowed control uses its parent's Ctl3D settings.	TWinControl
ParentFont	Determine whether the Font information of the control's parent is used.	TControl
ParentShowHint	Determine whether the ShowHint information of the control's parent is used.	TControl
PopupMenu	Determine which pop-up menu is associated with the control.	TControl
Refresh	Erase the control and repaint it.	TControl
RemoveControl	Remove the specified control from the windowed control's Controls array.	TWinControl
Repaint	Repaint the control.	TControl
ScaleBy	Resize the windowed control.	TWinControl
ScreenToClient	Convert screen coordinates to client (control) coordinates.	TControl
SendToBack	Send the control to the end of the z-order.	TControl

continued on next page

continued from previous page

Use or Set This...	To Do This...	Inheritance
SetBounds	Determine the coordinates of the control's bounding rectangle.	TControl
SetFocus	Set the focus to the windowed control.	TWinControl
SetTextBuf	Set the text of the control to the text in a buffer.	TControl
Show	Make the control visible.	TControl
ShowHint	Enable tooltips for the control.	TControl
Showing	Determine whether the windowed control is currently showing onscreen.	TComponent
TabOrder	Determine the tab order of the windowed control.	TWinControl
TabStop	Determine whether the windowed control is in the tab order.	TWinControl
Tag	Store an additional integer value with the component.	TComponent
Text	Access the changeable text on the control.	TControl
Top	Determine the upper edge of the control.	TControl
Update	Called automatically by Refresh.	TControl
Visible	Determine whether the control is visible.	TControl
Width	Determine the width of the control.	TControl

TPageControl

TPageControl is used to create property sheets with Delphi. Each page in a property sheet represents an individual dialog box of information. Using TPageControl, you can contain the information of several dialog boxes in an area no larger than a single dialog box. The user clicks on tabs to select the page he or she wants to view. Property sheets are typically modeless—that is, the focus can be directed back to other windows in the application.

Adding pages to the page control in the Delphi IDE is not obvious—you cannot access the Pages property from the Object Inspector at design time. To add a page to the page control, right-click the control and choose New Page from the resulting pop-up menu as shown in Figure 59-3.

As Figure 59-3 demonstrates, you can also navigate between the existing pages using this pop-up menu.

The properties and methods implemented by TPageControl enable you to set or get the active page, go to the next or previous page, access pages by index value, and count the number of contained pages. Individual pages in a page control can contain any control you place on a standard window or dialog box. Since property sheets are everywhere in Windows, plenty of good design examples exist.

Table 59-2 displays the properties, methods, and events implemented by TPageControl.

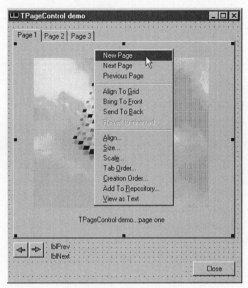

Figure 59-3 Adding a page to the page control

Table 59-2 Properties, methods, and events implemented by `TPageControl`, in addition to those introduced by `TCustomTabControl`

Use or Set This..	To Do This...	Inheritance
`ActivePage`	Determine which page is the active page.	None
`Align`	Align the page control within its container.	TComponent
`Create`	Create a new page control.	TCustomTabControl
`Destroy`	Destroy the page control.	TCustomTabControl
`DragCursor`	Determine the shape of the cursor as it passes over the page control.	TComponent
`DragMode`	Determine the drag-and-drop behavior of the page control.	TComponent
`Enabled`	Determine whether the page control is enabled.	TComponent
`FindNextPage`	Search for the next page in the page control.	None
`Font`	Determine which font is used to render text in the page control.	TComponent
`MultiLine`	Determine whether the tabs in the page control are displayed in multiple rows.	None
`OnChange`	Handle the event that occurs when a page is activated.	TComponent
`OnChanging`	Handle the event that occurs before a page is activated.	TComponent
`OnDragDrop`	Handle the event that occurs when an object is dropped on the page control.	TComponent
`OnDragOver`	Handle the event that occurs when an object is dragged over the page control.	TComponent

continued on next page

continued from previous page

Use or Set This..	To Do This...	Inheritance
OnEndDrag	Handle the event that occurs when a drag-and-drop operation is cancelled.	TComponent
OnEnter	Handle the event that occurs when the page control receives the focus.	TComponent
OnExit	Handle the event that occurs when the page control loses the focus.	TComponent
OnMouseDown	Handle the event that occurs when a mouse button is pressed and not released.	TComponent
OnMouseMove	Handle the event that occurs when the mouse pointer moves over the page control.	TComponent
OnMouseUp	Handle the event that occurs when a mouse button is released.	TComponent
OnStartDrag	Handle the event that occurs when a drag-and-drop operation is started.	TComponent
PageCount	Determine the number of pages contained by the page control.	None
Pages	Access the individual pages in the page control.	None
ParentFont	Determine whether the page control derives its Font information from its parent.	TComponent
ParentShowHint	Determine whether the page control derives its ShowHint information from its parent.	TComponent
PopupMenu	Determine which pop-up menu is associated with the page control.	TComponent
SelectNextPage	Activate the next or previous page.	None
ShowHint	Determine whether the page control displays a tooltip.	TComponent
TabHeight	Determine the height of the tabs in the page control.	None
TabOrder	Determine the position of the page control within its parent's tab order.	TComponent
TabStop	Determine whether the page control is a tab stop.	TComponent
TabWidth	Determine the width of the tabs in the page control.	None
Visible	Determine whether the page control is visible.	TComponent

TTabControl

Tab controls resemble notebook dividers and are conceptually similar to page controls. Both offer a tab interface to a series of pages of information within a dialog box. Technically, **TTabControl** and **TPageControl** exist at the same level of the VCL hierarchy—both are children of **TCustomTabControl**. But tab controls are more generic than page controls and do not offer the same level of features within Delphi. For this reason, it is suggested you use page controls when implementing property sheets as they are much easier to work with. Most of the tab control features are accessible only at run time and not easily modified from the Delphi IDE.

Table 59-3 displays the properties, methods, and events implemented by **TTabControl**.

Table 59-3 Properties, methods, and events implemented by `TTabControl`, in addition to those introduced by `TCustomTabControl`

Use or Set This..	To Do This...	Inheritance
Align	Determine how the tab control aligns within its container.	TComponent
DisplayRect	Determine the size and position of the tab control client area.	None
DragCursor	Determine the shape of the mouse pointer as it moves over the tab control.	TComponent
DragMode	Determine the drag-and-drop behavior of the tab control.	TComponent
Enabled	Determine whether the tab control is enabled.	TComponent
Font	Determine the font used to render text in the tab control.	TComponent
MultiLine	Determine whether the tabs in the tab control are displayed in multiple rows.	None
OnChange	Handle the event that occurs when a page is activated.	TComponent
OnChanging	Handle the event that occurs when a page is about to be activated.	TComponent
OnDragDrop	Handle the event that occurs when an object is dropped on the tab control.	TComponent
OnDragOver	Handle the event that occurs when an object is dragged over the tab control.	TComponent
OnEndDrag	Handle the event that occurs when a drag-and-drop operation is completed.	TComponent
OnEnter	Handle the event that occurs when the tab control receives the focus.	TComponent
OnExit	Handle the event that occurs when the tab control loses the focus.	TComponent
OnMouseDown	Handle the event that occurs when a mouse button is pressed and not released.	TComponent
OnMouseMove	Handle the event that occurs when the mouse pointer moves over the tab control.	TComponent
OnMouseUp	Handle the event that occurs when a mouse button is released.	TComponent
OnStartDrag	Handle the event that occurs when a drag-and-drop operation is started.	TComponent
ParentFont	Determine whether the tab control uses its parent's `Font` information.	TComponent
ParentShowHint	Determine whether the tab control uses its parent's tooltip information.	TComponent
PopupMenu	Determine which pop-up menu is associated with the tab control.	TComponent
ShowHint	Determine whether the tab control displays a tooltip.	TComponent
TabHeight	Determine the height of the tabs in the tab control.	None
TabOrder	Determine the position of the tab control within its parent's tab order.	TComponent
Tabs	Access the string list that contains the captions of each tab in the tab control.	None
TabStop	Determine whether the tab control is a tab stop.	TComponent
TabWidth	Determine the width of the tabs in the tab control.	None
Visible	Determine whether the tab control is visible.	TComponent

ActivePage PROPERTY

Objects Affected	TPageControl
Purpose	The ActivePage property specifies the top page in the page control.
Declaration	

```
property ActivePage: TTabSheet;
```

Example Syntax

```
// Print the caption of the current page in a label
procedure TForm2.PageControl1Change(Sender: TObject);
begin
  lblActivePage.Caption := 'The current page is ' +
                PageControl1.ActivePage.Caption;
end;

procedure TForm2.FormCreate(Sender: TObject);
begin
  PageControl1Change(Self);
end;
```

Description

ActivatePage enables you to activate a specific page, or *tab sheet*, by assigning it to the property. In the example above, **ActivePage** is used to find out which page is currently active so its caption can be printed in a label. See Figure 59-4.

ActivePage activates visible pages only. To activate nonvisible pages, use FindNextPage.

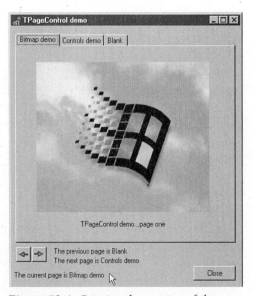

Figure 59-4 Printing the caption of the current page in a label

DisplayRect PROPERTY

Objects Affected	TTabControl
Purpose	The DisplayRect property contains the size of the tab control client area.
Declaration	

```
property DisplayRect: TRect;
```

Example Syntax

```
procedure TForm3.FormCreate(Sender: TObject);
begin
  Label2.Caption := IntToStr(TabControl1.DisplayRect.Top);
  Label3.Caption := IntToStr(TabControl1.DisplayRect.Left);
  Label4.Caption := IntToStr(TabControl1.DisplayRect.Bottom);
  Label5.Caption := IntToStr(TabControl1.DisplayRect.Right);
end;
```

Description   DisplayRect is a rectangle describing the client area of the tab control in pixel measurements. It contains the top, left, width, and height coordinates of the client area, as shown in Figure 59-5.

FindNextPage METHOD

Objects Affected	TPageControl
Purpose	The FindNextPage method returns the next page in the page control.

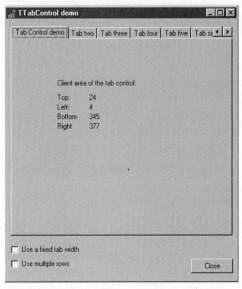

Figure 59-5 Displaying the coordinates of the tab control client area display rectangle

Declaration

```
function FindNextPage(CurPage: TTabSheet;
                      GoForward, CheckTabVisible: Boolean): TTabSheet;
```

Parameters

CurPage   The page in the page control in which the search begins.

GoForward   Determines whether to search forward or backward through the list of pages.

CheckTabVisible   Searches for visible pages only.

Example Syntax

```
procedure TForm2.PageControl1Change(Sender: TObject);
begin
  // Find the previous page
  lblPrev.Caption := 'The previous page is ' +
         PageControl1.FindNextPage(PageControl1.ActivePage,
         False, False).Caption;

  // Find the next page
  lblNext.Caption := 'The next page is ' +
         PageControl1.FindNextPage(PageControl1.ActivePage,
         True, False).Caption;
end;

procedure TForm2.FormCreate(Sender: TObject);
begin
  PageControl1Change(Self);
end;
```

Description   FindNextPage searches through the tab sheets (or pages) in the page control, beginning with the page specified by the *CurPage* parameter. If *GoForward* is True, the search progresses forward through the list of pages. If *GoForward* is False, the search progresses backward from the start page. The *CheckTabVisible* parameter determines whether the search includes pages not visible. Set the TabVisible property of a tab sheet to False to make it invisible. If *CheckTabVisible* is True, only visible pages are searched. If it is False, nonvisible pages are searched as well.

Since FindNextPage finds nonvisible pages, this is the first step toward activating such a page—the ActivePage property only activates visible pages.

MultiLine PROPERTY

Objects Affected   TPageControl, TTabControl

Purpose   The MultiLine property determines whether the tabs in the control display as multiple rows or a single row.

Declaration

```
property MultiLine: Boolean;
```

Example Syntax

```
// Toggle multiple tab rows in the tab control with a check box
procedure TForm3.cbMultipleRowsClick(Sender: TObject);
begin
  If cbMultipleRows.Checked = True then
    TabControl1.MultiLine := True
  else TabControl1.MultiLine := False;
end;
```

Description

The tabs in a page control or tab control normally display in a single row. By setting **MultiLine** to **True**, you can display the tabs in multiple rows, as in Figure 59-6.

The number of rows depends on the value of the **TabWidth** property. **MultiLine** is **False** by default. If the number of tabs in the control is too great to display in a single row and **MultiLine** is **False**, an **UpDown** control appears at the right end of the tab row so you can scroll through the tabs.

PageCount PROPERTY

Objects Affected   TPageControl

Purpose   The **PageCount** property contains the number of tab sheets in the page control.

Declaration

```
property PageCount: Integer;
```

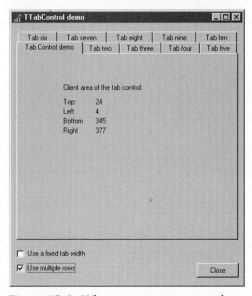

Figure 59-6 When **MultiLine** is **True**, the tabs can be stacked in multiple rows

Example Syntax

```
AnInteger := PageControl1.PageCount;
```

Description   `PageCount` is a run-time, read-only property.

Pages PROPERTY

Objects Affected   `TPageControl`

Purpose   The `Pages` property contains the pages in the page control.

Declaration

```
property Pages[Index: Integer]: TTabSheet;
```

Example Syntax

```
procedure TForm2.FormCreate(Sender: TObject);
begin
  PageControl1.Pages[0].Caption := 'Bitmap demo';
  PageControl1.Pages[1].Caption := 'Controls demo';
  PageControl1.Pages[2].Caption := 'Blank';
end;
```

Description   `Pages` is a run-time, read-only property enabling you to access the pages
in the page control by index value, in which the first page is `Pages[0]`, the
second page is `Pages[1]`, and so on. You should use `Pages` when you need
to access a page by its index value.

SelectNextPage METHOD

Objects Affected   `TPageControl`

Purpose   The `SelectNextPage` method activates the previous or next page.

Declaration

```
procedure SelectNextPage(GoForward: Boolean);
```

Parameters

GoForward   Determines whether to activate the previous or next page.

Example Syntax

```
procedure TForm2.sbPrevClick(Sender: TObject);
begin
  PageControl1.SelectNextPage(False);
end;

procedure TForm2.sbNextClick(Sender: TObject);
begin
    PageControl1.SelectNextPage(True);
end;
```

| Description | If the *GoForward* parameter is `True`, `SelectNextPage` activates the next visible page. If it is `False`, `SelectNextPage` activates the first visible page preceding the currently active page. See Figure 59-7. |

Tabs PROPERTY

Objects Affected	`TTabControl`
Purpose	The `Tabs` property is a list of the strings used to form tab captions.
Declaration	

```
property Tabs: TStrings;
```

| Example Syntax | |

```
TabControl1.Tabs[0] := 'Tab Control demo';
```

| Description | Each time a string is added to `Tabs`, a new tab is created with that caption. You can edit the Tabs string list from the Delphi IDE using the String list editor, as shown in Figure 59-8. |

You can edit the tab captions at run time by changing the value of the strings in the list, using index notation where the first tab is `Tabs[0]`, the second is `Tabs[1]`, and so on.

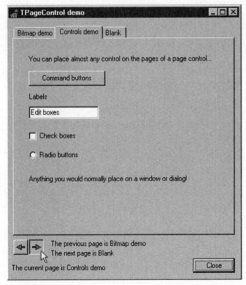

Figure 59-7 The Forward and Back speedbuttons cycle through the available pages using `SelectNextPage`

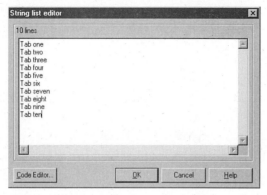

Figure 59-8 Using the String list editor to edit the Tabs string list

TabHeight PROPERTY

Objects Affected	TPageControl, TTabControl
Purpose	The TabHeight property determines the height of tabs displayed by a page control or tab control.
Declaration	

```
property TabHeight: Smallint;
```

Example Syntax

```
TabControl1.TabHeight := 15;
```

Description If TabHeight is 0, the tabs automatically size themselves vertically to fit the height of the caption they need to display. You can specify a TabHeight if you wish to make all the tabs taller or shorter than normal.

TabWidth PROPERTY

Objects Affected	TPageControl, TTabControl
Purpose	The TabWidth property determines the width of tabs displayed by a page control or tab control. See Figure 59-9.
Declaration	

```
property TabWidth: SmallInt;
```

Example Syntax

```
// Use a check box to determine whether to use a fixed tab width
procedure TForm3.cbFixedTabWidthClick(Sender: TObject);
begin
  If cbFixedTabWidth.Checked = True then
    TabControl1.TabWidth := 75
  else TabControl1.TabWidth := 0;
end;
```

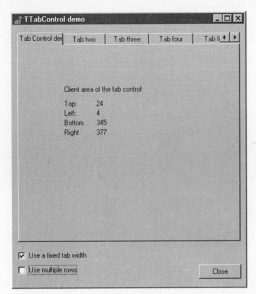

Figure 59-9 A fixed tab width can create awkward caption runovers

Description   If `TabWidth` is 0, the tabs automatically size themselves to fit the caption they need to display. Specifying a `TabWidth` value manually sets all the tabs to the same width.

60
TCustomTreeView
AND TTreeView

The tree view control was introduced with Windows 95 as a common control and central element in the Windows Explorer. *Tree views* display a list of hierarchical items in which each item consists of a caption and, optionally, a small icon. The All Folders pane in Windows Explorer (see Figure 60-1) is a tree view control that enables you to navigate the Windows namespace.

The top object, or node, in the tree view is called the *root item*. The root item is the *parent* of all items in the hierarchy. *Child items* cascade off the root item and other parent items and are indented for emphasis. Optional lines connect the various items in the tree view, indicating their relationship. Also, each level of the hierarchy can be

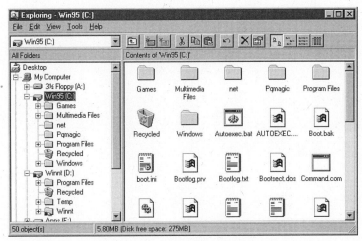

Figure 60-1   The All Folders pane in Explorer is a tree view control

collapsed and expanded as needed, using a small button resembling a plus (+) or minus sign (-). An item with a plus sign next to it can be expanded. When a minus sign appears, the user can collapse that level.

You should consider what information you need to display before using a tree view control. Tree views are designed to display information that lends itself to hierarchical organization. Obviously, file manager–type programs can benefit from the inclusion of a tree view control—file systems are, by nature, logical and hierarchical. The Delphi VCL is a hierarchical list of classes, and the examples in this chapter use a tree view control to display its structure.

In addition to optional icons that can appear next to the item labels, tree view items support *state images*. A state image, like a check mark or cross-out, is designed to give a visual clue to the item's state.

Delphi implements the tree view control with the abstract base class `TCustomTreeView` and its child `TTreeView`. `TTreeView` supports the full range of tree view capabilities available to all Win32 programmers.

TCustomTreeView

`TCustomTreeView` is the abstract base class for `TTreeView`. You will never need to create an instance of `TCustomTreeView`.

Figure 60-2 shows the `TCustomTreeView` branch of the VCL. Table 60-1 displays the properties, methods, and events implemented by `TCustomTreeView`.

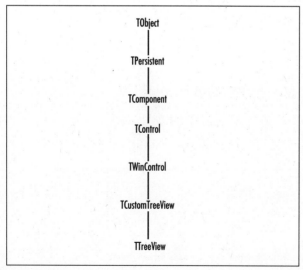

TObject

TPersistent

TComponent

TControl

TWinControl

TCustomTreeView

TTreeView

Figure 60-2 The `TCustomTreeView` branch of the VCL

Table 60-1 Properties, methods, and events implemented by `TCustomTreeView`

Use or Set This...	To Do This...	Inheritance
Align	Determine how the control is aligned within its parent.	TControl
AlphaSort	Sort the tree nodes alphabetically.	None
Assign	Assign one persistent object to another.	TPersistent
BeginDrag	Begin a manual drag operation.	TControl
BoundsRect	Determine the boundary rectangle occupied by the control.	TControl
BringToFront	Bring the control to the front of the z-order.	TControl
Brush	Determine the color and pattern used for the windowed control background.	TComponent
CanFocus	Determine whether the windowed control can receive the focus.	TWinControl
Caption	Label the control with a text string.	TControl
ClassName	Get the name of the object's class.	TObject
ClassParent	Get the object's parent class.	TObject
ClassType	Get the object's actual type.	TObject
ClientHeight	Determine the control's client height.	TControl
ClientOrigin	Determine the upper-left position of the control's client area.	TControl
ClientRect	Determine the rectangle occupied by the control's client area.	TControl
ClientToScreen	Convert control (local) coordinates to screen coordinates.	TControl
ClientWidth	Determine the width of the control's client area.	TControl
Color	Determine the color of the windowed control.	TControl
ComponentCount	Determine the number of owned components.	TComponent
ComponentIndex	Determine the index of the component in its owner's `Components` list.	TComponent
Components	Determine the list of owned components.	TComponent
ComponentState	Determine the state of the current component.	TComponent
ContainsControl	Determine whether the specified control is contained by the windowed control.	TWinControl
ControlAtPos	Determine the control contained at a specified position.	TWinControl
ControlCount	Determine the number of controls contained by the windowed control.	TWinControl
Controls	Access the controls contained by the windowed control using their positions in an array.	TWinControl
ControlState	Determine the state of the control at any given time.	TControl
ControlStyle	Determine what attributes are present in the control.	TControl
Create	Create a new component.	TObject
Ctl3D	Determine whether the windowed control displays in 3D.	TWinControl
Cursor	Determine what image is used for the cursor over the control.	TControl
Destroy	Destroy the component.	TObject
DestroyComponents	Destroy all the components owned by the component.	TComponent
Destroying	Notify the component that it is being destroyed.	TComponent

continued on next page

CHAPTER 60

continued from previous page

Use or Set This...	To Do This...	Inheritance
DragCursor	Determine the shape of the mouse cursor as it drags an object over the control.	TControl
Dragging	Determine whether the control is being dragged.	TControl
DragMode	Determine the drag-and-drop behavior of the control.	TControl
Enabled	Determine whether the control is enabled.	TControl
EndDrag	End or cancel a manual drag operation.	TControl
FindComponent	Find a component in the Components array list.	TComponent
Focused	Determine whether the windowed control has the focus.	TControl
Font	Determine the font used to render text on the control.	TControl
Free	Safely destroy the object.	TObject
FullCollapse	Collapse all the nodes in the tree view.	None
FullExpand	Expand all the nodes in the tree view.	None
GetHitTestInfoAt	Retrieve information about a specific point within the tree view control.	None
GetNodeAt	Retrieve the node at a specific location.	None
GetTextBuf	Copy the text of the control into a buffer.	TControl
GetTextLen	Get the length of the text of the control.	TControl
Handle	Obtain a handle to the windowed control.	TComponent
HandleAllocated	Determine if a handle is allocated for the windowed control.	TWinControl
Height	Determine the height of the control.	TControl
HelpContext	Determine the help context ID of the windowed control.	TComponent
Hide	Make the control invisible.	TControl
Hint	Determine the text that displays in a tooltip for the control.	TControl
InheritsFrom	Determine if the object is descended from a certain class.	TObject
InsertControl	Insert a control into the windowed control's Controls array.	TWinControl
InstanceSize	Determine the amount of memory allocated for the object.	TObject
Invalidate	Force the control to be repainted as soon as possible.	TControl
IsEditing	Determine whether the user is editing a node caption.	None
Left	Determine the left edge of the control within its container.	TControl
Name	Determine the name of the component.	TComponent
OnClick	Handle the event that occurs when a mouse button is clicked.	TControl
OnDblClick	Handle the event that occurs when a mouse button is double-clicked.	TControl
OnDragDrop	Handle the event that occurs when an object is dropped on the control.	TControl
OnDragOver	Handle the event that occurs when an object is dragged over the control.	TControl
OnEndDrag	Handle the event that occurs when a drag-and-drop operation is cancelled.	TControl
OnEnter	Handle the event that occurs when the windowed control receives the focus.	TWinControl
OnExit	Handle the event that occurs when the windowed control loses the focus.	TWinControl
OnKeyDown	Handle the event that occurs when a key is pressed down and not immediately released while the windowed control has the focus.	TWinControl

Use or Set This...	To Do This...	Inheritance
OnKeyPress	Handle the event that occurs when a key is pressed while the windowed control has the focus.	TWinControl
OnKeyUp	Handle the event that occurs when a key is released while the windowed control has the focus.	TWinControl
OnMouseDown	Handle the event that occurs when a mouse button is held down and not immediately released.	TControl
OnMouseMove	Handle the event that occurs when the cursor moves over the control.	TControl
OnMouseUp	Handle the event that occurs when a mouse button is released.	TControl
OnStartDrag	Handle the event that occurs when a drag-and-drop operation is started.	TControl
Owner	Determine the owner of the component.	TComponent
Parent	Determine the parent, or container, of the control.	TControl
ParentColor	Determine whether the Color information of the control's parent is used.	TControl
ParentCtl3D	Determine whether the windowed control uses its parent's Ctl3D settings.	TWinControl
ParentFont	Determine whether the Font information of the control's parent is used.	TControl
ParentShowHint	Determine whether the ShowHint information of the control's parent is used.	TControl
PopupMenu	Determine which pop-up menu is associated with the control.	TControl
Refresh	Erase the control and repaint it.	TControl
RemoveControl	Remove the specified control from the windowed control's Controls array.	TWinControl
Repaint	Repaint the control.	TControl
ScaleBy	Resize the windowed control.	TWinControl
ScreenToClient	Convert screen coordinates to client (control) coordinates.	TControl
SendToBack	Send the control to the end of the z-order.	TControl
SetBounds	Determine the coordinates of the control's bounding rectangle.	TControl
SetFocus	Set the focus to the windowed control.	TWinControl
SetTextBuf	Set the text of the control to the text in a buffer.	TControl
Show	Make the control visible.	TControl
ShowHint	Enable tooltips for the control.	TControl
Showing	Determine whether the windowed control is currently showing onscreen.	TComponent
TabOrder	Determine the tab order of the windowed control.	TWinControl
TabStop	Determine whether the windowed control is in the tab order.	TWinControl
Tag	Store an additional integer value with the component.	TComponent
Text	Access the changeable text on the control.	TControl
.Top	Determine the upper edge of the control.	TControl
Update	Called automatically by Refresh.	TControl
Visible	Determine whether the control is visible.	TControl
Width	Determine the width of the control.	TControl

TTreeView

Delphi encapsulates the Windows tree view custom control with **TTreeView**.
TTreeView is available from the Win95 tab of the Component Palette in the Delphi
IDE.

Individual items in a tree view are called *tree nodes*, which are encapsulated in
Delphi by the **TTreeNode** class. **TTreeNode** is discussed in Chapter 19.

Table 60-2 displays the properties, methods, and events implemented by
TTreeView.

Table 60-2 Properties, methods, and events implemented by TTreeView, in addition to those introduced by TCustomTreeView

Use or Set This...	To Do This...	Inheritance
Align	Determine how the tree view control is aligned within its container.	TComponent
BorderStyle	Determine whether the tree view has a border.	TComponent
Color	Determine the color of the tree view control.	TComponent
Ctl3D	Determine whether the tree view displays in a 3D style.	TComponent
DragCursor	Determine the shape of the mouse pointer as it passes over the tree view control.	TComponent
DragMode	Determine the drag-and-drop behavior of the tree view control.	TComponent
Enabled	Determine whether the tree view is enabled.	TComponent
Font	Determine the font used to render text in the tree view control.	TComponent
HideSelection	Determine whether a selected tree node loses its selection if the focus shifts to another control.	None
Images	Determine which image list contains the images used to display tree node icons.	None
Indent	Determine the width each child node is indented.	None
Items	Access the tree nodes contained by the tree view.	None
OnChanging	Handle the event that occurs when the selection changes from one node to another.	None
OnClick	Handle the event that occurs when the tree view is clicked.	TComponent
OnCollapsed	Handle the event that occurs when a tree node is collapsed.	None
OnCollapsing	Handle the event that occurs when a tree node is about to collapse.	None
OnCompare	Handle the event that occurs when the tree view is sorted.	None
OnDblClick	Handle the event that occurs when the tree view is double-clicked.	TComponent
OnDeletion	Handle the event that occurs when a tree node is deleted.	None
OnDragDrop	Handle the event that occurs when an object is dropped on the tree view.	TComponent
OnDragOver	Handle the event that occurs when an object is dragged over the tree view.	TComponent
OnEdited	Handle the event that occurs when the caption of a tree node has been edited.	None
OnEditing	Handle the event that occurs when the caption of a tree node is about to be edited.	None

Use or Set This...	To Do This...	Inheritance
OnEndDrag	Handle the event that occurs when a drag-and-drop operation is cancelled.	TComponent
OnEnter	Handle the event that occurs when the tree view receives the focus.	TComponent
OnExit	Handle the event that occurs when the tree view loses the focus.	TComponent
OnExpanded	Handle the event that occurs when a node in the tree view has been expanded.	None
OnExpanding	Handle the event that occurs when a node in the tree view is about to be expanded.	None
OnGetImageIndex	Handle the event that occurs when the ImageIndex property of a tree node is queried by the tree view.	None
OnGetSelectedIndex	Handle the event that occurs when the SelectedIndex property of a tree node is queried by the tree view control.	None
OnKeyDown	Handle the event that occurs when a key is pressed and not released.	TComponent
OnKeyPress	Handle the event that occurs when a key is pressed.	TComponent
OnKeyUp	Handle the event that occurs when a key is released.	TComponent
OnMouseDown	Handle the event that occurs when a mouse button is clicked.	TComponent
OnMouseMove	Handle the event that occurs when the mouse pointer is moved over the tree view.	TComponent
OnMouseUp	Handle the event that occurs when the mouse button is released.	TComponent
OnStartDrag	Handle the event that occurs when a drag-and-drop operation begins.	TComponent
ParentColor	Determine whether the tree view uses its parent's Color information.	TComponent
ParentCtl3D	Determine whether the tree view uses its parent's Ctl3D information.	TComponent
ParentFont	Determine whether the tree view uses its parent's Font information.	TComponent
ParentShowHint	Determine whether the tree view uses its parent's ShowHint information.	TComponent
PopupMenu	Determine which pop-up menu is associated with the tree view.	TComponent
ReadOnly	Determine whether the tree node captions can be edited by the user.	None
ShowButtons	Determine whether the tree view control displays the plus (+) and minus (-) buttons.	None
ShowHint	Determine whether the tree view displays a tooltip.	TComponent
ShowLines	Determine whether the tree view displays lines connecting parent nodes with their child nodes.	None
ShowRoot	Determine whether the root nodes are connected to lines and buttons.	None
SortType	Determine how the tree view nodes are sorted.	None
StateImages	Determine which image list contains the state images for the tree view.	None
TabOrder	Determine the position of the tree view within its parent's tab order.	TComponent
TabStop	Determine whether the tree view is a tab stop.	TComponent
Visible	Determine whether the tree view is visible.	TComponent

AlphaSort METHOD

Objects Affected	All tree view controls
Purpose	The `AlphaSort` method sorts all the items in the tree view control.
Declaration	

```
function AlphaSort: Boolean;
```

Example Syntax

```
// Sort the tree view items when the program starts
procedure TForm1.FormCreate(Sender: TObject);
begin
  if TreeView1.AlphaSort <> True then
    Application.MessageBox('The tree view could not be sorted',
                          'Not sorted', MB_OK);
end;
```

Description `AlphaSorts` sorts all the items in the tree view control alphabetically by each item's caption. Items are sorted within their hierarchical level; sorting will not destroy the structure of the tree. If `AlphaSort` was successful, it returns `True`.

FullCollapse METHOD

Objects Affected	All tree view controls
Purpose	The `FullCollapse` method collapses each level in the tree view so only the root is visible.

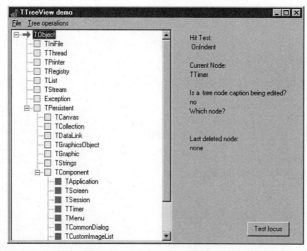

Figure 60-3 The sorted tree view

Declaration

```
procedure FullCollapse;
```

Example Syntax

```
procedure TForm1.CollapseAll1Click(Sender: TObject);
begin
  TreeView1.FullCollapse;
end;
```

Description   FullCollapse collapses every level in the tree view—not just the root level. In contrast, if the user manually collapsed the root while child items were expanded and then re-expanded the root, the previously expanded child levels would still have been visible. FullCollapse collapses expanded child items, as well as the root level.

FullExpand METHOD

Objects Affected   All tree view controls

Purpose   The FullExpand method expands all levels in the tree view hierarchy.

Declaration

```
procedure FullExpand;
```

Example Syntax

```
procedure TForm1.ExpandAll1Click(Sender: TObject);
begin
  TreeView1.FullExpand;
end;
```

Description   When FullExpand is called, every level in the tree view hierarchy expands, exposing all the items in the tree view.

GetHitTestInfoAt METHOD

Objects Affected   All tree view controls

Purpose   The GetHitTestInfoAt retrieves information about a specific point within the tree view.

Declaration

```
function GetHitTestInfoAt(X, Y: Integer): THitTests;
```

Parameters

X   The horizontal coordinate of the point you wish to test.

Y   The vertical coordinate of the point you wish to test.

Example Syntax

```
// This handler checks all of the possible hit values and prints
// the ones that are occurring in a label caption
procedure TForm1.TreeView1MouseDown(Sender: TObject;
                                    Button: TMouseButton;
                                    Shift: TShiftState; X, Y: Integer);
var
  AHit: THitTests;
begin
  lblHitTest.Caption := '';
  AHit := TreeView1.GetHitTestInfoAt(X,Y);
  if htAbove in AHit then
    lblHitTest.Caption := lblHitTest.Caption + ' Above';
  if htBelow in AHit then
    lblHitTest.Caption := lblHitTest.Caption + ' Below';
  if htNowhere in AHit then
    lblHitTest.Caption := lblHitTest.Caption + ' Nowhere';
  if htOnItem in AHit then
    lblHitTest.Caption := lblHitTest.Caption + ' OnItem';
  if htOnButton in AHit then
    lblHitTest.Caption := lblHitTest.Caption + ' OnButton';
  if htOnIcon in AHit then
    lblHitTest.Caption := lblHitTest.Caption + ' OnIcon';
  if htOnIndent in AHit then
    lblHitTest.Caption := lblHitTest.Caption + ' OnIndent';
  if htOnLabel in AHit then
    lblHitTest.Caption := lblHitTest.Caption + ' OnLabel';
  if htOnRight in AHit then
    lblHitTest.Caption := lblHitTest.Caption + ' OnRight';
  if htOnStateIcon in AHit then
    lblHitTest.Caption := lblHitTest.Caption + ' OnStateIcon';
  if htToRight in AHit then
    lblHitTest.Caption := lblHitTest.Caption + ' ToRight';
  if htToLeft in AHit then
    lblHitTest.Caption := lblHitTest.Caption + ' ToLeft';
end;
```

Description

GetHitTestInfoAt is best used with the mouse pointer position to determine where the pointer is in the tree view at any given time. It is type THitTests, which defines a set of possible values. The return value of GetHitTestInfoAt, shown in Figure 6-4, can be one or more of the following:

This Value...	Indicates That the Point Is...
htAbove	Above the tree view client area.
htBelow	Below the tree view client area.
htNowhere	In the the tree view client area, but over empty space below the last item.
htOnButton	On the + or - button associated with an item.
htOnIcon	On the bitmap associated with an item.
htOnIndent	On an indentation.
htOnItem	On the bitmap or caption associated with an item.
htOnLabel	On the caption associated with an item.
htOnRight	To the right of an item.

This Value...	Indicates That the Point Is...
htOnStateIcon	On the state image for an item in a user-defined state.
htToLeft	To the left of the tree view control client area.
htToRight	To the right of the tree view client area.

In the preceding example syntax, `GetHitTestInfoAt` uses the coordinates of the mouse pointer when it clicks the surface of the tree view control as its input. The results are displayed in a label control.

GetNodeAt METHOD

Objects Affected	All tree view controls
Purpose	The `GetNodeAt` method returns the tree node found at a specified point.
Declaration	

```
function GetNodeAt(X, Y: Integer): TTreeNode;
```

Parameters

X   The horizontal coordinate of the point you wish to test.

Y   The vertical coordinate of the point you wish to test.

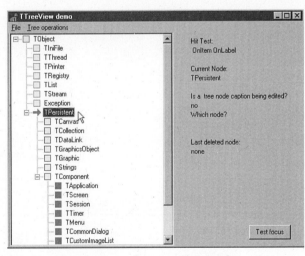

Figure 60-4 Retrieving hit test values with `GetHitTestInfoAt`

Example Syntax

```
// Print out the caption of the currently selected node every time
// the mouse is clicked within the tree view control
procedure TForm1.TreeView1Click(Sender: TObject);
var
  MousePos: TPoint;
  ANode: TTreeNode;
begin
  if GetCursorPos(MousePos) = True then
  begin
    ANode := TTreeNode.Create(TreeView1.Items);
    MousePos := ScreenToClient(MousePos);
    ANode := TreeView1.GetNodeAt(MousePos.X, MousePos.Y);
    if ANode = nil then
      lblCurrNode.Caption := 'none'
    else
      lblCurrNode.Caption := ANode.Text
  end
end;
```

Description

The *X* and *Y* parameters specify the point within the coordinate system of the tree view control you are testing. If a tree node exists at that position, it is returned by GetNodeAt. Otherwise, it returns Nil.

HideSelection PROPERTY

Objects Affected   All tree view controls

Purpose   The HideSelection property determines whether a selected tree node retains its selection if the focus shifts to another control.

Declaration

```
property HideSelection: Boolean;
```

Example Syntax

```
procedure TForm1.FormCreate(Sender: TObject);
begin
// Keep node captions highlighted if the focus shifts to
// another control
  TreeView1.HideSelection := False;
end;
```

Description   If HideSelection is True, the selected tree node loses its focus rectangle when the focus switches to another control. If it is False, the node retains its focus rectangle even when the tree view loses the focus. The default value is True.

Images PROPERTY

Objects Affected   All tree view controls

Purpose   The Images property determines which image list control contains the images for displaying the tree node icons.

Declaration

```
property Images: TImageList;
```

Example Syntax

```
TreeView1.Images := ImageList1;
```

Description   You can assign images to the tree nodes at design time by double-clicking the **Items** property in the Object Inspector, which brings up the TreeView Items Editor. See **Items** for details.

Indent PROPERTY

Objects Affected   All tree view controls

Purpose   The **Indent** property determines the amount a list of child items is indented from its parent when the node is expanded.

Declaration

```
property Indent: Integer;
```

Example Syntax

```
TreeView1.Indent := 10;
```

Description   Child items are indented relative to their parent. The **Indent** property holds the amount each child item is indented. **Indent** is measured in pixels. The default value is **9**.

IsEditing METHOD

Objects Affected   All tree view controls

Purpose   The **IsEditing** method indicates whether a tree node caption is currently being edited by the user.

Declaration

```
function IsEditing: Boolean;
```

Example Syntax

```
procedure TForm1.Timer1Timer(Sender: TObject);
begin
  if TreeView1.IsEditing = True then
    lblIsEditing.Caption := 'yes'
  else lblIsEditing.Caption := 'no';
end;
```

Description   If the caption of a tree node is being edited, **IsEditing** returns **True**. If the caption of a tree node is not being edited, **IsEditing** returns **False**. Otherwise, **IsEditing** returns **0xFB**.

Items PROPERTY

Objects Affected All tree view controls

Purpose The **Items** property contains the individual items, or nodes, appearing in the tree view control.

Declaration

```
property Items: TTreeNodes;
```

Example Syntax

```
procedure TForm1.FormCreate(Sender: TObject);
var x: Integer;
begin
  TreeView1.StateImages := ImageList1;

  // set the StateIndex for each node in the tree view
  for x := 0 to TreeView1.Items.Count - 1 do
    TreeView1.Items[x].StateIndex := -1;
end;
```

Description **Items** enables you to access the tree nodes by their index value, with the first node being **Items[0]**, the second **Items[1]**, and so on. **Items** is type **TTreeNodes**, which is covered in Chapter 19. At design time, you can add, remove, and modify items with the TreeView Items Editor, as shown in Figure 60-5.

The TreeView Items Editor also enables you to assign a caption, image, selection image, and state image to each item.

OnChanging EVENT

Objects Affected All tree view controls

Purpose The **OnChanging** event occurs when the selection is about to change from one node to another in the tree view.

Declaration

```
property OnChanging: TTVChangingEvent;
```

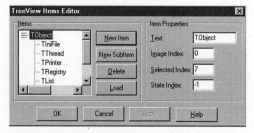

Figure 60-5 The TreeView Items Editor

Example Syntax

```
// This is the standard handler for the OnChanging event
procedure TForm1.TreeView1Changing(Sender: TObject; Node: TTreeNode;
                                    var AllowChange: Boolean);
begin
  // Add code here
end;
```

Description OnChanging is type **TTVChangingEvent**, which is declared as

```
TTVChangingEvent = procedure(Sender: TObject; Node: TTreeNode;
                             var AllowChange: Boolean) of object;
```

The **Node** parameter specifies the node being selected. The **AllowChange** parameter determines whether the selection change is permitted. If **AllowChange** is **False**, the change is not permitted. If **AllowChange** is **True**, the change is permitted.

OnCollapsed EVENT

Objects Affected All tree view controls

Purpose The OnCollapsed event occurs when a node has been collapsed.

Declaration

```
property OnCollapsed: TTVExpandedEvent;
```

Example Syntax

```
// This is the standard handler for the OnCollapsed event
procedure TForm1.TreeView1Collapsed(Sender: TObject; Node: TTreeNode);
begin
  // Add code here
end;
```

Description OnCollapsed occurs after a node is collapsed. It is type **TTVExpandedEvent**, which is declared as

```
TTVExpandedEvent = procedure(Sender: TObject; Node: TTreeNode) of
                                                            object;
```

OnCollapsing EVENT

Objects Affected All tree view controls

Purpose The OnCollapsing event occurs when a node is about to collapse.

Declaration

```
property OnCollapsing: TTVCollapsingEvent;
```

Example Syntax

```
// This is the standard handler for the OnCollapsing event
procedure TForm1.TreeView1Collapsing(Sender: TObject; Node: TTreeNode;
                                       var AllowCollapse: Boolean);
begin
  // Add code here
end;
```

Description

OnCollapsing is type TTVCollapsingEvent, which is declared as

```
TTVCollapsingEvent = procedure(Sender: TObject; Node: TTreeNode;
                        var AllowCollapse: Boolean) of object;
```

OnCompare EVENT

Objects Affected	All tree view controls
Purpose	The OnCompare event occurs when the tree view is sorted.
Declaration	

```
property OnCompare: TTVCompareEvent;
```

Example Syntax

```
// This is the standard handler for the OnCompare event
procedure TForm1.TreeView1Compare(Sender: TObject;
                               Node1, Node2: TTreeNode;
                               Data: Integer; var Compare: Integer);
begin
  // Add code here
end;
```

Description

OnCompare is type TTVCompareEvent, which is declared as

```
TTVCompareEvent = procedure(Sender: TObject; Node1, Node2: TTreeNode;
                         Data: Integer; var Compare: Integer) of object;
```

OnDeletion EVENT

Objects Affected	All tree view controls
Purpose	The OnDeletion event occurs when a node is deleted.
Declaration	

```
property OnDeletion: TTVExpandedEvent;
```

Example Syntax

```
// This is the standard handler for the OnDeletion event
// This method runs when a node is deleted
procedure TForm1.TreeView1Deletion(Sender: TObject; Node: TTreeNode);
begin
  lblDeleted.Caption := TreeView1.Selected.Text;
end;
```

```
// Delete the selected node when this menu item is chosen
procedure TForm1.DeleteCurrentNode1Click(Sender: TObject);
begin
   TreeView1.Selected.Delete;
end;
```

Description   OnDeletion is type TTVExpandedEvent, which is declared as:

```
TTVExpandedEvent = procedure(Sender: TObject; Node: TTreeNode)
                       of object;
```

OnEdited EVENT

Objects Affected   All tree view controls

Purpose   The OnEdited event occurs after a node caption is edited by the user.

Declaration

```
property OnEdited: TTVEditedEvent;
```

Example Syntax

```
// This is the standard handler for the OnEdited event
procedure TForm1.TreeView1Edited(Sender: TObject; Node: TTreeNode;
  var S: string);
begin
  // Add code here
end;
```

Description   OnEdited occurs after the text of the node caption has been edited by the user. It is type TTVEditedEvent, which is declared as

```
TTVEditedEvent = procedure(Sender: TObject; Node: TTreeNode;
                       var S: string) of object;
```

OnEditing EVENT

Objects Affected   All tree view controls

Purpose   The OnEditing event occurs while a node's text caption is being edited by the user.

Declaration

```
property OnEditing: TTVEditingEvent;
```

Example Syntax

```
// This is the standard handler for the OnEditing event
// Print the caption of the node being edited to a label
procedure TForm1.TreeView1Editing(Sender: TObject; Node: TTreeNode;
  var AllowEdit: Boolean);
begin
  lblEditNode.Caption := Node.Text;
end;
```

Description   OnEditing occurs once while the caption is being edited by the user. It is type TTVEditingEvent, which is declared as

```
TTVEditingEvent = procedure(Sender: TObject; Node: TTreeNode;
                              var AllowEdit: Boolean) of object;
```

OnExpanded EVENT

Objects Affected   All tree view controls

Purpose   The OnExpanded event occurs after a node in the tree view is expanded.

Declaration

```
property OnExpanded: TTVExpandedEvent;
```

Example Syntax

```
// This is the standard handler for the OnExpanded event
procedure TForm1.TreeView1Expanded(Sender: TObject; Node: TTreeNode);
begin
  // Add code here
end;
```

Description   OnExpanded occurs after the node has been expanded. It is type TTVExpandedEvent, which is declared as

```
TTVExpandedEvent = procedure(Sender: TObject; Node: TTreeNode) of object;
```

OnExpanding EVENT

Objects Affected   All tree view controls

Purpose   The OnExpanding event occurs once as a node in the tree view expands.

Declaration

```
property OnExpanding: TTVExpandingEvent;
```

Example Syntax

```
// This is the standard handler for the OnExpanding event
procedure TForm1.TreeView1Expanding(Sender: TObject; Node: TTreeNode;
  var AllowExpansion: Boolean);
begin
  // Add code here
end;
```

Description   OnExpanding is type TTVExpandingEvent, which is declared as

```
TTVExpandingEvent = procedure(Sender: TObject; Node: TTreeNode;
                               var AllowExpansion: Boolean) of object;
```

OnGetImageIndex EVENT

Objects Affected	All tree view controls
Purpose	The OnGetImageIndex event occurs when the ImageIndex property of a tree node is queried by the tree view.
Declaration	

```
property OnGetImageIndex: TTVExpandedEvent;
```

Example Syntax

```
// This is the standard handler for the OnGetImageEvent event
procedure TForm1.TreeView1GetImageIndex(Sender: TObject; Node:
TTreeNode);
begin
  // Add code here
end;
```

Description A tree node contains the index of the icon image used to display itself in the tree view in a property called ImageIndex. Every time ImageIndex is queried or changed, the OnGetImageIndex event is triggered. Handle this event if you need to process a block of code every time the ImageIndex of any tree node in the control is queried. OnGetImageIndex is type TTVExpandedEvent, which is declared as

```
TTVExpandedEvent = procedure(Sender: TObject; Node: TTreeNode)
                   of object;
```

OnGetSelectedIndex EVENT

Objects Affected	All tree view controls
Purpose	The OnGetSelectedIndex event occurs when the SelectedIndex property of a tree node is queried by the tree view.
Declaration	

```
property OnGetSelectedIndex: TTVExpandedEvent;
```

Example Syntax

```
// This is the standard handler for the x event
procedure TForm1.TreeView1GetSelectedIndex(Sender: TObject;
  Node: TTreeNode);
begin
  // Add code here
end;
```

Description A tree node contains the index of the icon image used to display itself when selected in its SelectedIndex property. When SelectedIndex is queried or changed, the OnGetSelectedIndex event occurs. You should handle this event if you want to run a block of code every time the

SelectedIndex property of any tree node in the control is queried. OnGetSelectedIndex is type TTVExpandedEvent, which is declared as

```
TTVExpandedEvent = procedure(Sender: TObject; Node: TTreeNode)
                     of object;
```

ReadOnly PROPERTY

Objects Affected   All tree view controls

Purpose   The ReadOnly property determines whether the user can modify the text captions of tree nodes in the tree view.

Declaration

```
property ReadOnly: Boolean;
```

Example Syntax

```
TreeView1.ReadOnly := True;
```

Description   If ReadOnly is True, the user can edit any tree node text caption in the tree. If ReadOnly is False, the text captions cannot be edited.

ShowButtons PROPERTY

Objects Affected   All tree view controls

Purpose   The ShowButtons property determines whether the plus (+) and minus (-) buttons display next to parent nodes.

Declaration

```
property ShowButtons: Boolean;
```

Example Syntax

```
// Toggle tree view buttons with a menu item
procedure TForm1.DisplayButtons1Click(Sender: TObject);
begin
  if DisplayButtons1.Checked = True then
  begin
    TreeView1.ShowButtons := False;
    DisplayButtons1.Checked := False;
  end
  else begin
    TreeView1.ShowButtons := True;
    DisplayButtons1.Checked := True;
  end
end;
```

Description   If ShowButtons is True, a plus (+) or minus (-) button appears next to each parent node, indicating it can be expanded or collapsed. If ShowButtons is False, no buttons appear, as shown in Figure 60-6. The default value is

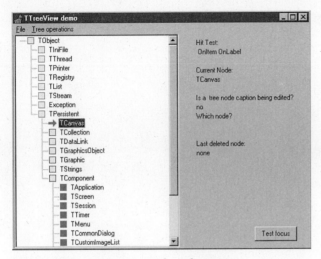

Figure 60-6 A tree view with no buttons

True. We do not suggest disabling the buttons in a tree view, as they provide a valuable visual cue to the user regarding which items can or cannot be expanded and collapsed.

ShowLines PROPERTY

Objects Affected   All tree view controls

Purpose   The ShowLines property determines whether to display the lines connecting parent items with their child nodes.

Declaration

```
property ShowLines: Boolean;
```

Example Syntax

```
// Toggle the tree view lines with a menu item
procedure TForm1.DisplayLines1Click(Sender: TObject);
begin
  if DisplayLines1.Checked = True then
  begin
    TreeView1.ShowLines := False;
    DisplayLines1.Checked := False;
  end
  else begin
    TreeView1.ShowLines := True;
    DisplayLines1.Checked := True;
  end
end;
```

Description   If ShowLines is True, lines connect parent nodes with each of their child nodes, emphasizing the hierarchy. If ShowLines is False, no lines appear,

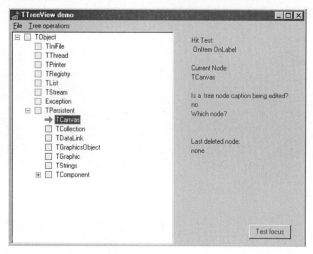

Figure 60-7   A tree view with buttons but no lines

as shown in Figure 60-7. The default value is `True`. As with `ShowButtons`, we do not suggest disabling the lines in a tree view, especially one with many nodes, because they provide a valuable visual cue to the user regarding the hierarchy of items.

ShowRoot PROPERTY

Objects Affected   All tree view controls

Purpose   The `ShowRoot` property determines whether lines and plus (+) or minus (-) buttons connect to the root items in the tree view.

Declaration

```
property ShowRoot: Boolean;
```

Example Syntax

```
procedure TForm1.DisplayRootLines1Click(Sender: TObject);
begin
  if DisplayRootLines1.Checked = True then
  begin
    TreeView1.ShowRoot := False;
    DisplayRootLines1.Checked := False;
  end
  else begin
    TreeView1.ShowRoot := True;
    DisplayRootLines1.Checked := True;
  end
end;
```

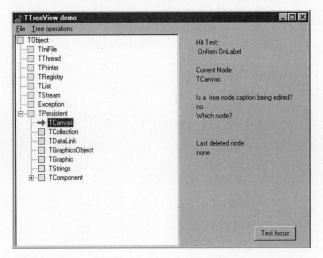

Figure 60-8 When **ShowRoot** is **False**, no line connects to the root item

Description   If **ShowRoot** is **True**, a plus (+) or minus (-) button is connected to each root item with a line. This is the default. If it is **False**, the root items appear flush with the left side of the tree view control, and no buttons or lines are present on the left side of the root items, as shown in Figure 60-8.

SortType PROPERTY

Objects Affected   All tree view controls

Purpose   The **SortType** property determines if and how the items in the tree view are sorted.

Declaration

```
property SortType: TSortType;
```

Example Syntax

```
procedure TForm1.FormCreate(Sender: TObject);
begin
  TreeView1.SortType := stNone;
end;
```

Description   The **SortType** property is type **TSortType**, which defines the values that can be used to determine how the tree view control is sorted. **TSortType** is declared as

```
TSortType = (stNone, stData, stText, stBoth);
```

where the following values have the corresponding effects:

Use This Value...	To Do This...
stBoth	Sort the items when either the data object or item caption is changed.
stData	Sort the items when the data object is changed.
stNone	Do not sort the items.
stText	Sort the items when the item caption is changed.

The default value is **nsNone**.

> **IMPORTANT**
> Once you sort the items, there is no way to return to the previous arrangement, unless it has already been sorted in some way.

StateImages PROPERTY

Objects Affected All tree view controls

Purpose The **StateImages** property determines which image list control contains the images for displaying state images in the tree view.

Declaration

```
property StateImages: TImageList;
```

Example Syntax

```
procedure TForm1.FormCreate(Sender: TObject);
var x: Integer;
begin
  // State images come from ImageList1
  TreeView1.StateImages := ImageList1;

  // set the StateIndex for each node in the tree view
  for x := 0 to TreeView1.Items.Count - 1 do
    TreeView1.Items[x].StateIndex := -1;
end;

// When nodes are double-clicked, toggle the state image
procedure TForm1.TreeView1DblClick(Sender: TObject);
begin
  if TreeView1.Selected <> nil then
    if TreeView1.Selected.StateIndex = -1 then
      TreeView1.Selected.StateIndex := 8
    else TreeView1.Selected.StateIndex := -1;
end;
```

Description **StateImages** determines which image list control is the source for the state images the tree view items use. A state image appears to the left of the item's normal icon. It can appear as a solid bitmap or a mask. In the example above, the state image used for all the items is a custom-made black check mark.

61

TCustomUpDown AND TUpDown

The up-down control was introduced in Winows 95 as a common control although its predecessor, the *spinner* or *spin box control*, has been around since the days of Windows 3.1. The up-down control is like a scroll bar without a scroll box or scroll shaft—it consists of two arrow buttons that can be used to increment and decrement the positional value the control contains. An up-down control can exist as a standalone control, although it would normally be associated with another control (usually an edit box) called, believe it or not, its *buddy control*. A typical up-down control and its associated buddy control are shown in Figure 61-1.

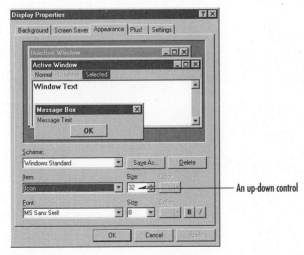

Figure 61-1 An up-down control in the Display Properties dialog box

When an up-down control is associated with a buddy control, the value displayed by the buddy control reflects the value held by the up-down control. Incrementing and decrementing the value held by the up-down control changes the display value of the buddy control accordingly.

Up-down controls can be oriented horizontally, with the arrow buttons pointing left and right, or vertically, with the arrow buttons pointing up and down. They can also align themselves to their buddy control on its left or right side. Up-down controls do not, however, have a caption label, so you may want to add a separate label near your up-down controls.

TCustomUpDown

TCustomUpDown is an abstract base class that provides the base functionality implemented by TUpDown to create up-down controls.

Figure 61-2 shows the derivation of TCustomUpDown and TUpDown. Table 61-1 displays the properties, methods, and events implemented by TCustomUpDown.

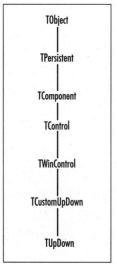

Figure 61-2 Derivation of TCustomUpDown and TUpDown

Table 61-1 Properties, methods, and events implemented by `TCustomUpDown`

Use or Set This...	To Do This...	Inheritance
ALign	Determine how the control is aligned within its parent.	TControl
Assign	Assign one persistent object to another.	TPersistent
BeginDrag	Begin a manual drag operation.	TControl
BoundsRect	Determine the boundary rectangle occupied by the control.	TControl
BringToFront	Bring the control to the front of the z-order.	TControl
Brush	Determine the color and pattern used for the windowed control background.	TComponent
CanFocus	Determine whether the windowed control can receive the focus.	TWinControl
Caption	Label the control with a text string.	TControl
ClassName	Get the name of the object's class.	TObject
ClassParent	Get the object's parent class.	TObject
ClassType	Get the object's actual type.	TObject
ClientHeight	Determine the control's client height.	TControl
ClientOrigin	Determine the upper-left position of the control's client area.	TControl
ClientRect	Determine the rectangle occupied by the control's client area.	TControl
ClientToScreen	Convert control (local) coordinates to screen coordinates.	TControl
ClientWidth	Determine the width of the control's client area.	TControl
Color	Determine the color of the windowed control.	TControl
ComponentCount	Determine the number of owned components.	TComponent
ComponentIndex	Determine the index of the component in its owner's `Components` list.	TComponent
Components	Determine the list of owned components.	TComponent
ComponentState	Determine the state of the current component.	TComponent
ContainsControl	Determine whether the specified control is contained by the windowed control.	TWinControl
ControlAtPos	Determine the control contained at a specified position.	TWinControl
ControlCount	Determine the number of controls contained by the windowed control.	TWinControl
Controls	Access the controls contained by the windowed control using their positions in an array.	TWinControl
ControlState	Determine the state of the control at any given time.	TControl
ControlStyle	Determine what attributes are present in the control.	TControl
Create	Create a new component.	TObject
Ctl3D	Determine whether the windowed control displays in 3D.	TWinControl
Cursor	Determine what image is used for the cursor over the control.	TControl
Destroy	Destroy the component.	TObject
DestroyComponents	Destroy all the components owned by the component.	TComponent
Destroying	Notify the component that it is being destroyed.	TComponent

continued on next page

continued from previous page

Use or Set This...	To Do This...	Inheritance
DragCursor	Determine the shape of the mouse cursor as it drags an object over the control.	TControl
Dragging	Determine whether the control is being dragged.	TControl
DragMode	Determine the drag-and-drop behavior of the control.	TControl
Enabled	Determine whether the control is enabled.	TControl
EndDrag	End or cancel a manual drag operation.	TControl
FindComponent	Find a component in the Components array list.	TComponent
Focused	Determine whether the windowed control has the focus.	TControl
Font	Determine the font used to render text on the control.	TControl
Free	Safely destroy the object.	TObject
GetTextBuf	Copy the text of the control into a buffer.	TControl
GetTextLen	Get the length of the text of the control.	TControl
Handle	Obtain a handle to the windowed control.	TComponent
HandleAllocated	Determine if a handle is allocated for the windowed control.	TWinControl
Height	Determine the height of the control.	TControl
HelpContext	Determine the help context ID of the windowed control.	TComponent
Hide	Make the control invisible.	TControl
Hint	Determine the text that displays in a tooltip for the control.	TControl
InheritsFrom	Determine if the object is descended from a certain class.	TObject
InsertControl	Insert a control into the windowed control's Controls array.	TWinControl
InstanceSize	Determine the amount of memory allocated for the object.	TObject
Invalidate	Force the control to be repainted as soon as possible.	TControl
Left	Determine the left edge of the control within its container.	TControl
Name	Determine the name of the component.	TComponent
OnClick	Handle the event that occurs when a mouse button is clicked.	TControl
OnDblClick	Handle the event that occurs when a mouse button is double-clicked.	TControl
OnDragDrop	Handle the event that occurs when an object is dropped on the control.	TControl
OnDragOver	Handle the event that occurs when an object is dragged over the control.	TControl
OnEndDrag	Handle the event that occurs when a drag-and-drop operation is cancelled.	TControl
OnEnter	Handle the event that occurs when the windowed control receives the focus.	TWinControl
OnExit	Handle the event that occurs when the windowed control loses the focus.	TWinControl
OnKeyDown	Handle the event that occurs when a key is pressed down and not immediately released while the windowed control has the focus.	TWinControl

Use or Set This...	To Do This...	Inheritance
OnKeyPress	Handle the event that occurs when a key is pressed while the windowed control has the focus.	TWinControl
OnKeyUp	Handle the event that occurs when a key is released while the windowed control has the focus.	TWinControl
OnMouseDown	Handle the event that occurs when a mouse button is held down and not immediately released.	TControl
OnMouseMove	Handle the event that occurs when the cursor moves over the control.	TControl
OnMouseUp	Handle the event that occurs when a mouse button is released.	TControl
OnStartDrag	Handle the event that occurs when a drag-and-drop operation is started.	TControl
Owner	Determine the owner of the component.	TComponent
Parent	Determine the parent, or container, of the control.	TControl
ParentColor	Determine whether the Color information of the control's parent is used.	TControl
ParentCtl3D	Determine whether the windowed control uses its parent's Ctl3D settings.	TWinControl
ParentFont	Determine whether the Font information of the control's parent is used.	TControl
ParentShowHint	Determine whether the ShowHint information of the control's parent is used.	TControl
PopupMenu	Determine which pop-up menu is associated with the control.	TControl
Refresh	Erase the control and repaint it.	TControl
RemoveControl	Remove the specified control from the windowed control's Controls array.	TWinControl
Repaint	Repaint the control.	TControl
ScaleBy	Resize the windowed control.	TWinControl
ScreenToClient	Convert screen coordinates to client (control) coordinates.	TControl
SendToBack	Send the control to the end of the z-order.	TControl
SetBounds	Determine the coordinates of the control's bounding rectangle.	TControl
SetFocus	Set the focus to the windowed control.	TWinControl
SetTextBuf	Set the text of the control to the text in a buffer.	TControl
Show	Make the control visible.	Tcontrol
ShowHint	Enable tooltips for the control.	TControl
Showing	Determine whether the windowed control is currently showing on screen.	TComponent
TabOrder	Determine the tab order of the windowed control.	TWinControl
TabStop	Determine whether the windowed control is in the tab order.	TWinControl
Tag	Store an additional integer value with the component.	TComponent

continued on next page

continued from previous page

Use or Set This...	To Do This...	Inheritance
Text	Access the changeable text on the control.	TControl
Top	Determine the upper edge of the control.	TControl
Update	Called automatically by Refresh.	TControl
Visible	Determine whether the control is visible.	TControl
Width	Determine the width of the control.	TControl

TUpDown

Delphi encapsulates the up-down common control with the TUpDown class. TUpDown provides properties that let you manipulate up-down controls in your own programs. TUpDown is available from the Win95 tab of the Component Palette in the Delphi IDE. Table 61-2 displays the properties, methods, and events implemented by TUpDown.

Table 61-2 Properties, methods, and events implemented by TUpDown, in addition to those inherited from TCustomUpDown

Use or Set This...	To Do This...	Inheritance
AlignButton	Determine how the up-down control aligns with its associated control.	None
ArrowKeys	Determine whether the arrow keys on the keyboard can mimic the arrow buttons on the up-down control.	None
Associate	Determine which control is associated with the up-down control.	None
Enabled	Determine whether the up-down control is enabled.	TComponent
Hint	Determine whether the up-down control displays a tooltip.	TComponent
Increment	Determine the amount Position is incremented and decremented when the arrow buttons are clicked.	None
Max	Determine the maximum possible value of Position.	None
Min	Determine the minimum possible value of Position.	None
OnChanging	Handle the event that occurs when the up-down control is changing.	TComponent
OnClick	Handle the event that occurs when the up-down control is clicked.	TComponent
OnEnter	Handle the event that occurs when the up-down control receives the focus.	TComponent
OnExit	Handle the event that occurs when the up-down control loses the focus.	TComponent
OnMouseDown	Handle the event that occurs when a mouse button is clicked and held down.	TComponent
OnMouseMove	Handle the event that occurs when the mouse pointer moves over the up-down control.	TComponent
OnMouseUp	Handle the event that occurs when a mouse button is released.	TComponent
Orientation	Determine whether the up-down control is horizontal or vertical.	None
ParentShowHint	Determine whether the up-down control uses its parent's ShowHint information.	TComponent

Use or Set This...	To Do This...	Inheritance
PopupMenu	Determine which pop-up menu is associated with the up-down control.	TComponent
Position	Determine the value of the up-down control.	None
ShowHint	Determine whether the up-down control displays a tooltip.	TComponent
TabOrder	Determine the position of the up-down control in its parent's tab order.	TComponent
TabStop	Determine whether the up-down control is a tabstop.	TComponent
Thousands	Determine whether the control associated with the up-down control displays a thousands separator.	None
Visible	Determine whether the up-down control is visible.	TComponent
Wrap	Determine whether the up-down control wraps the value of position if the Min or Max values are exceeded.	None

AlignButton PROPERTY

Objects Affected   TUpDown

Purpose   The AlignButton property specifies how the up-down control aligns with the control it is associated with.

Declaration

```
property AlignButton: TUDAlignButton;
```

Example Syntax

```
procedure TForm1.FormCreate(Sender: TObject);
begin
  // Align the up-down control to the right
  UpDown1.AlignButton := udRight;
end;
```

Description   Typically, an up-down control is associated with another control. The AlignButton property specifies how the up-down control is aligned with that control. AlignButton is type TUDAlignButton and can be set to either udLeft or udRight:

```
TUDAlignButton = (udLeft, udRight);
```

If AlignButton is udLeft, the up-down control aligns itself to the left edge of its associate control. If it is udRight, the up-down control aligns itself to the right edge of the control.

The default value is udRight.

ArrowKeys PROPERTY

Objects Affected	`TUpDown`
Purpose	The `ArrowKeys` property determines whether the arrow keys on the keyboard mimic the behavior of the up and down buttons on the up-down control.

Declaration

```
property ArrowKeys: Boolean;
```

Example Syntax

```
procedure TForm1.FormCreate(Sender: TObject);
begin
  // Turn off arrow keys
  UpDown1.ArrowKeys := False;
end;
```

Description   The arrow keys affect the up-down control if it is associated with another control by the `Associate` property. If so, the keys function when that control (say, an edit box) has the focus. If `ArrowKeys` is `True` and the up-down control's associated control has the focus, the arrow keys on the keyboard increment and decrement the up-down control. If `ArrowKeys` is `False`, the keyboard arrow keys have no effect on the up-down control.

Associate PROPERTY

Objects Affected	`TUpDown`
Purpose	The `Associate` property determines which control is associated with the up-down control.

Declaration

```
property Associate: TWinControl;
```

Example Syntax

```
UpDown1.Associate := Edit1;
```

Description   An up-down control can optionally be aligned, or connected, to a companion control, typically an edit box. When the `Associate` property is set, the up-down control aligns itself to the specified control. The control associated with the up-down control reflects the value of the `UpDown` box in its text (or caption) field—the two controls now share this common value.

Typically, it is easiest to associate an up-down control with another control at design time.

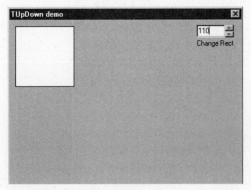

Figure 61-3 An up-down control
associated with an edit box

Increment PROPERTY

Objects Affected	TUpDown
Purpose	The Increment property determines how the up-down control increments and decrements when the arrow buttons are clicked.
Declaration	

```
property Increment: Integer;
```

Example Syntax

```
UpDown1.Increment := 5;
```

Description   By default, up-down controls increment and decrement by 1. You can modify this value by changing the **Increment** property to any valid integer value.

If **ArrowKeys** is **True**, the up-down control also increments and decrements by this amount when the arrow keys are pressed and the up-down control's companion control is selected.

Max PROPERTY

Objects Affected	TUpDown
Purpose	The Max property determines the maximum possible value the up-down control can hold.
Declaration	

```
property Max: SmallInt;
```

Example Syntax

```
procedure TForm1.FormCreate(Sender: TObject);
begin
  UpDown1.Max := 50;
  UpDown1.Min := 0;
  UpDown1.Increment := 5;
  UpDown1.Position := 0;
end;
```

Description   Max essentially determines the maximum possible value for the Position property. This value must be within the range possible for a SmallInt.

Min PROPERTY

Objects Affected   TUpDown

Purpose   The Min property determines the lowest possible value the up-down control can hold.

Declaration

```
property Min: SmallInt;
```

Example Syntax

```
procedure TForm1.FormCreate(Sender: TObject);
begin
  UpDown1.Max := 50;
  UpDown1.Min := 0;
  UpDown1.Increment := 5;
  UpDown1.Position := 0;
end;
```

Description   Min determines the lowest possible value for the Position property. This value must be within the range possible for a SmallInt.

Orientation PROPERTY

Objects Affected   TUpDown

Purpose   The Orientation property determines whether the up-down control is horizontal or vertical.

Declaration

```
property Orientation: TUDOrientation;
```

Example Syntax

```
UpDown1.Orientation := udHorizontal;
```

Description   Up-down control arrows can be oriented so they point left-right or up-down. The Orientation property is type TUDOrientation and can be set to udHorizontal, which makes the arrows point left and right, or udVertical, which makes the arrows point up and down. The default is udVertical.

Position PROPERTY

Objects Affected	TUpDown
Purpose	The Position property indicates the current position of the up-down control.
Declaration	

```
property Position: SmallInt;
```

Example Syntax

```
procedure TForm1.FormCreate(Sender: TObject);
begin
  UpDown1.Max := 50;
  UpDown1.Min := 0;
  UpDown1.Increment := 5;
  UpDown1.Position := 0;
end;
```

Description   The value of Position is within the range specified by the Min and Max properties. If a control is associated with the up-down control, its text displays the value of Position as well. You can, however, write any value to Position you wish. The value does not have to derive from a companion control.

Thousands PROPERTY

Objects Affected	TUpDown
Purpose	The Thousands property determines whether a comma appears as a thousands separator in the text output of Position in the associated control.
Declaration	

```
property Thousands: Boolean;
```

Example Syntax

```
UpDown1.Thousands := False;
```

Description   If Thousands is True and the value of Position exceeds 999, a thousands separator (a comma) appears in the associated control's text output. The value 1000, for example, would print as 1,000. If Thousands is False, no thousands separator appears. The default value is True.

Wrap PROPERTY

Objects Affected   TUpDown

Purpose   The **Wrap** property determines whether the value of **Position** wraps when the maximum or minimum value is reached.

Declaration

```
property Wrap: Boolean;
```

Example Syntax

```
UpDown1.Wrap := True;
```

Description   If **Wrap** is **True** and the user increments **Position** past the value specified by **Max**, the value of **Position** wraps to the value specified by **Min**. If **Wrap** is **False**, the user is unable to increment **Position** past **Max** or decrement it past **Min**.

62

TScrolling-WinControl AND ITS DESCENDANTS

Scrolling windowed controls are those objects that descend from
TScrollingWinControl. *Scrolling windowed controls* are basically windowed controls
whose virtual surface area can be greater than the portion displayed within the visible
client area. They contain scroll bar controls that allow you to scroll the contents of
their windows. This feature sets them apart from standard windowed controls.

TScrollingWinControl

TScrollingWinControl is the abstract base class for scrolling windowed controls. You
will never actually create an instance of **TscrollingWinControl** but it does provide
protected methods and properties that are later published by its ancestors, most
notably **TForm**.

Figure 62-1 shows the hierarchy for **TScrollingWindow** and **TForm**. Table 62-1 displays the properties, methods, and events implemented by **TscrollingWinControl**.

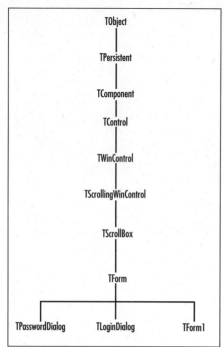

Figure 62-1 Hierarchy for
`TScrollingWindow` and `TForm`

Table 62-1 Properties, methods, and events implemented by `TScrollingWinControl`

Use or Set This...	To Do This...	Inheritance
Align	Determine how the control is aligned within its parent.	TControl
Assign	Assign one persistent object to another.	TPersistent
BeginDrag	Begin a manual drag operation.	TControl
BoundsRect	Determine the boundary rectangle occupied by the control.	TControl
BringToFront	Bring the control to the front of the z-order.	TControl
Brush	Determine the color and pattern used for the windowed control background.	TComponent
CanFocus	Determine whether the windowed control can receive the focus.	TWinControl
Caption	Label the control with a text string.	TControl
ClassName	Get the name of the object's class.	TObject
ClassParent	Get the object's parent class.	TObject
ClassType	Get the object's actual type.	TObject
ClientHeight	Determine the control's client height.	TControl
ClientOrigin	Determine the upper-left position of the control's client area.	TControl
ClientRect	Determine the rectangle occupied by the control's client area.	TControl

Use or Set This...	To Do This...	Inheritance
ClientToScreen	Convert control (local) coordinates to screen coordinates.	TControl
ClientWidth	Determine the width of the control's client area.	TControl
Color	Determine the color of the windowed control.	TControl
ComponentCount	Determines the number of owned components.	TComponent
ComponentIndex	The index of the component in its owner's Components list	TComponent
Components	Determine the list of owned components.	TComponent
ComponentState	Determine the state of the current component.	TComponent
ContainsControl	Determine whether the specified control is contained by the windowed control.	TWinControl
ControlAtPos	Determine the control contained at a specified position.	TWinControl
ControlCount	Determine the number of controls contained by the windowed control.	TWinControl
Controls	Access the controls contained by the windowed control using their positions in an array.	TWinControl
ControlState	Determine the state of the control at any given time.	TControl
ControlStyle	Determine what attributes are present in the control.	TControl
Create	Create a new component.	TObject
Ctl3D	Determine whether the windowed control displays in 3D.	TWinControl
Cursor	Determine what image is used for the cursor over the control.	TControl
Destroy	Destroy the component.	TObject
DestroyComponents	Destroy all of the components owned by the component.	TComponent
Destroying	Notify the component that it is being destroyed.	TComponent
DragCursor	Determine the shape of the mouse cursor as it drags an object over the control.	TControl
Dragging	Determine whether the control is being dragged.	TControl
DragMode	Determine the drag-and-drop behavior of the control.	TControl
Enabled	Determine whether the control is enabled.	TControl
EndDrag	End or cancel a manual drag operation.	TControl
FindComponent	Find a component in the Components array list.	TComponent
Focused	Determine whether the windowed control has the focus.	TControl
Font	Determine the font used to render text on the control.	TControl
Free	Safely destroy the object.	TObject
GetTextBuf	Copy the text of the control into a buffer.	TControl
GetTextLen	Get the length of the text of the control.	TControl
Handle	Obtain a handle to the windowed control.	TComponent
HandleAllocated	Determine if a handle is allocated for the windowed control.	TWinControl
Height	Determine the height of the control.	TControl
HelpContext	Determine the help context ID of the windowed control.	TComponent
Hide	Make the control invisible.	TControl
Hint	Determine the text that displays in a tooltip for the control.	TControl
HorzScrollBar	Access the horizontal scroll bar contained by the control.	None
InheritsFrom	Determine if the object is descended from a certain class.	TObject

continued on next page

continued from previous page

Use or Set This...	To Do This...	Inheritance
InsertControl	Insert a control into the windowed control's Controls array.	TWinControl
InstanceSize	Determine the amount of memory allocated for the object.	TObject
Invalidate	Force the control to be repainted as soon as possible.	TControl
Left	Determine the left edge of the control within its container.	TControl
Name	Determine the name of the component.	Tcomponent
OnClick	Handle the event that occurs when a mouse button is clicked.	TControl
OnDblClick	Handle the event that occurs when a mouse button is double-clicked.	TControl
OnDragDrop	Handle the event that occurs when an object is dropped on the control.	TControl
OnDragOver	Handle the event that occurs when an object is dragged over the control.	TControl
OnEndDrag	Handle the event that occurs when a drag-and-drop operation is cancelled.	TControl
OnEnter	Handle the event that occurs when the windowed control receives the focus.	TWinControl
OnExit	Handle the event that occurs when the windowed control loses the focus.	TWinControl
OnKeyDown	Handle the event that occurs when a key is pressed down and not immediately released while the windowed control has the focus.	TWinControl
OnKeyPress	Handle the event that occurs when a key is pressed while the windowed control has the focus.	TWinControl
OnKeyUp	Handle the event that occurs when a key is released while the windowed control has the focus.	TWinControl
OnMouseDown	Handle the event that occurs when a mouse button is held down and not immediately released.	TControl
OnMouseMove	Handle the event that occurs when the cursor moves over the control.	TControl
OnMouseUp	Handle the event that occurs when a mouse button is released.	TControl
OnStartDrag	Handle the event that occurs when a drag-and-drop operation is started.	TControl
Owner	Determine the owner of the component.	TComponent
Parent	Determine the parent, or container, of the control.	TControl
ParentColor	Determine whether the control's parent's Color information is used.	TControl
ParentCtl3D	Determine whether the windowed control uses its parent's Ctl3D settings.	TWinControl
ParentFont	Determine whether the control's parent's Font information is used.	TControl
ParentShowHint	Determine whether the control's parent's ShowHint information is used.	TControl
PopupMenu	Determine which pop-up menu is associated with the control.	TControl
Refresh	Erase the control and repaint it.	TControl
RemoveControl	Remove the specified control from the windowed control's Controls array.	TWinControl
Repaint	Repaint the control.	TControl
ScaleBy	Resize the windowed control.	TWinControl
ScreenToClient	Convert screen coordinates to client (control) coordinates.	TControl
SendToBack	Send the control to the end of the z-order.	TControl
SetBounds	Determine the coordinates of the control's bounding rectangle.	TControl
SetFocus	Set the focus to the windowed control.	TWinControl
SetTextBuf	Set the text of the control to the text in a buffer.	TControl
Show	Make the control visible.	TControl

Use or Set This...	To Do This...	Inheritance
ShowHint	Enable tooltips for the control.	TControl
Showing	Determine whether the windowed control is currently showing onscreen.	TComponent
TabOrder	Determine the tab order of the windowed control.	TWinControl
TabStop	Determine whether the windowed control is in the tab order.	TWinControl
Tag	Store an additional integer value with the component.	TComponent
Text	Access the changeable text on the control.	TControl
Top	Determine the upper edge of the control.	TControl
Update	Update is called automatically by Refresh.	TControl
VertScrollBar	Access the vertical scroll bar contained by the control.	None
Visible	Determine whether the control is visible.	TControl
Width	Determine the width of the control.	TControl

TForm

TForm is a direct descendant of **TScrollingWinControl** and is perhaps the most common, and famous, of all Delphi VCL objects. Delphi *forms* are a direct encapsulation of the visible *windows* that float on the Windows desktop, the central element of almost all applications you will write with Delphi. Each new application you start automatically creates a blank form window for you. In fact, the words *form* and *window* are completely interchangeable; in this chapter you will encounter both terms many times. They mean the same thing.

It may be worth noting that every visible onscreen element is really a window; command buttons, edit boxes, menus, and icons are all windows to the operating system and to the poor C and C++ programmers forced to program in those environments. The Delphi programmer is sheltered from the intricacies of API programming by the VCL, however, and in most cases the only windows you will need to think about are forms.

The typical form, like the one shown in Figure 62-2, consists of a frame, or *border*, that defines its dimensions. Most windows contain a title bar that presents a title bar icon, caption, and a series of buttons that enable you to minimize, maximize or restore, and close the window. The **TForm** class supplies numerous properties and methods that give you control over the various form elements.

Many forms also contain a menu bar, which is set with the **MainMenu** property, and a status bar, usually located at the bottom of the form. If need be, horizontal and vertical scroll bars can appear so that the contents of the form window can be scrolled. The rest of the window real estate is referred to as the *client area*. This is the area of the form where you can place controls, draw text and graphics, and float child windows.

In Windows, there are two primary types of applications: Single Document Interface (SDI) applications, and Multiple Document Interface (MDI) applications. SDI applications consist of one or more forms that float on the desktop independently of one another. In an SDI application, no window visually contains other windows,

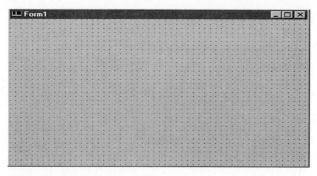

Figure 62-2 Components of a typical form window

even though it is usually clear which window is the parent window. The Delphi IDE uses an SDI interface, for example. Even though the code edit window, Object Inspector, and project windows float freely, it is clear that the main window is the central hub of the IDE.

Microsoft stated, during the development of Windows 95, that it would like to see SDI become the standard application interface for Windows applications. It has yet to follow those rules in-house, however; the best-selling Microsoft Office 97 applications, for example, are MDI applications and are likely to stay that way.

Programming MDI

In an MDI application like Microsoft Word (shown in Figure 62-3), the parent form, or primary window, visually contains one or more child windows. These child windows are considered documents. In Microsoft Word, each child window literally contains a document, in this case a document containing text and graphics.

Although MDI applications visually contain child windows that display documents (perhaps even a single document in different views—one child window for each view), they can also display dialogs in the standard way. It wouldn't make sense for the Print dialog box in Word, for example, to occupy the full client area of the program—it should display as a standard dialog as the user would expect.

MDI programs follow several other conventions that make them unique. Typically, the caption of the active child window is appended to the standard caption in the main form's title bar. MDI child windows can be cascaded, tiled, and arranged if they are in iconic form. MDI applications provide a Window menu that provides menu items for these operations and displays a list of all the child windows (documents) that are currently open so the user can switch between them. A typical Window menu is show in Figure 62-4.

Delphi's support for MDI is fairly extensive, and you will discover in this chapter that many of the properties and methods implemented by `TForm` are designed specifically for MDI applications.

Table 62-2 displays the properties, methods, and events implemented by `TForm`.

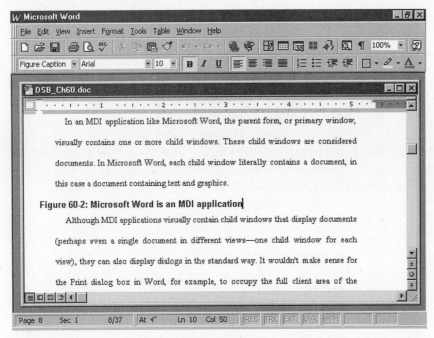

Figure 62-3 Microsoft Word is an MDI application

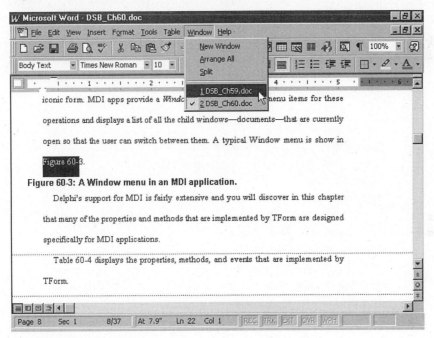

Figure 62-4 A Window menu in an MDI application

Table 62-2 Properties, methods, and events implemented by TForm

Use or Set This...	To Do This...	Inheritance
Active	Determine whether the form is active.	None
ActiveControl	Determine which control receives the focus.	None
ActiveMDIChild	Determine which child window in an MDI application is active.	None
ArrangeIcons	Line up the icons of minimized child windows in an MDI application.	None
AutoScroll	Determine whether scroll bars automatically appear on the form borders.	None
BorderIcons	Determine which buttons appear in the title bar.	None
Canvas	Access the drawing surface of the form.	TComponent
Caption	Determine the caption text in the form title bar.	TComponent
Cascade	Cascade child windows in an MDI application.	None
ClientHandle	Obtain the handle to the form's client area.	None
ClientHeight	Determine the height of the form's client area.	None
ClientWidth	Determine the width of the form's client area.	None
Close	Close the form.	None
Color	Determine the color of the form.	TComponent
Create	Create a new form.	TComponent
Ctl3D	Determine whether the form displays in the newer, 3D style.	TComponent
DefocusControl	Cause the specified control to lose the focus.	None
Destroy	Destroy the form.	TComponent
Enabled	Determine whether the form is enabled.	TComponent
FocusControl	Cause the specified control to receive the focus.	None
Font	Determine the font used to render text on the form.	TComponent
FormStyle	Determine the form style.	None
Height	Determine the height of the form window.	TComponent
Hide	Hide the form.	TControl
HorzScrollBar	Access the form's horizontal scroll bar.	TScrollingWinControl
Icon	Determine the icon image used to represent the form.	None
KeyPreview	Determine whether the form receives keyboard events intended for controls it contains.	None
MDIChildCount	Determine the number of open child windows in an MDI application.	None
MDIChildren	Access the child windows in an MDI application.	None
Menu	Determine which menu is the form's main menu.	None
Next	Activate the next child window in an MDI application.	None
OnActivate	Handle the event that occurs when the form is activated.	TComponent
OnClick	Handle the event that occurs when a mouse button is clicked.	TComponent
OnClose	Handle the event that occurs when the form is closed.	TComponent

Use or Set This...	To Do This...	Inheritance
OnCreate	Handle the event that occurs when the form is created.	TComponent
OnDblClick	Handle the event that occurs when a mouse button is double-clicked.	TComponent
OnDeactivate	Handle the event that occurs when the form is deactivated.	TComponent
OnDestroy	Handle the event that occurs when the form is destroyed.	TComponent
OnDragDrop	Handle the event that occurs when an object is dropped on the form.	TComponent
OnDragOver	Handle the event that occurs when an object is dragged over the form.	TComponent
OnHide	Handle the event that occurs when the form is hidden.	TComponent
OnKeyDown	Handle the event that occurs when a key is pressed and not immediately released.	TComponent
OnKeyPress	Handle the event that occurs when a key is pressed.	TComponent
OnKeyUp	Handle the event that occurs when a key is released.	TComponent
OnMouseDown	Handle the event that occurs when a mouse button is pressed and not immediately released.	TComponent
OnMouseMove	Handle the event that occurs when the mouse pointer moves over the form.	TComponent
OnMouseUp	Handle the event that occurs when a mouse button is released.	TComponent
OnPaint	Handle the event that occurs when the form canvas is painted.	TComponent
OnResize	Handle the event that occurs when the form is resized.	TComponent
OnShow	Handle the event that occurs when the form gains the focus.	TComponent
PopupMenu	Determine which pop-up menu is associated with the form.	TComponent
Position	Determine the placement and size of the form when it initially appears.	None
Previous	Give the focus to the previous child window in an MDI application.	None
Print	Print the form image.	None
PrintScale	Determine how the form is scaled when it is printed.	None
Release	Destroy the form after any pending events have been handled.	None
SetFocus	Give the input focus to the form.	TComponent
Show	Display the form.	None
ShowHint	Determine whether to display a tooltip.	TComponent
ShowModal	Display the form modally.	None
Tile	Tile the child windows in an MDI application.	None
VertScrollBar	Access the form's vertical scroll bar.	TScrollingWinControl
Visible	Determine whether the form is visible.	TComponent
Width	Determine the width of the form.	TComponent
WindowMenu	Determine which menu item is the Window menu item in an MDI application.	None
WindowState	Determine how the form appears when it is initially loaded.	None

Active PROPERTY

Objects Affected	`TForm`
Purpose	The `Active` property determines whether the form is active and has the focus.
Declaration	

```
property Active: Boolean;
```

Example Syntax

```
// Determine whether the form is active
procedure TForm1.Timer1Timer(Sender: TObject);
begin
  if Form1.Active = True then
    lblActive.Caption := 'Yes'
  else lblActive.Caption := 'No';
end;
```

Description   `Active` is a run-time, read-only property that determines whether the form currently is active and has the input focus. If `Active` is `True`, the form is active. If `Active` is `False`, the form is not active.

ActiveControl PROPERTY

Objects Affected	`TForm`
Purpose	The `ActiveControl` property determines which control on the form has the input focus.
Declaration	

```
property ActiveControl: TWinControl;
```

Example Syntax

```
// Determine which control is active
procedure TForm1.Timer1Timer(Sender: TObject);
begin
  lblActiveControl.Caption := Form1.ActiveControl.Name;
end;
```

Description   You can set the `ActiveControl` property before the form loads to specify which control initially has the focus when the form appears. While your application is running, you can check `ActiveControl` to determine which control has the focus. In the above example, the name of the active control is placed in the caption of a label. If you wanted to place the `Text` or `Caption` of the active control in the label's caption, a slightly different approach is necessary:

```
if Form1.ActiveControl is TEdit then
  lblActiveControlText.Caption := TEdit(Form1.ActiveControl).Text
else
  lblActiveControlText.Caption := TLabel(Form1.ActiveControl).Caption;
```

ActiveMDIChild PROPERTY

Objects Affected   TForm

Purpose   The `ActiveMDIChild` property determines which child window has the focus in an MDI application.

Declaration

```
property ActiveMDIChild: Tform;
```

Example Syntax

```
var
  Form1: TForm1;
  strAppName: String;

// . . .

procedure TForm1.FormCreate(Sender: TObject);
begin
  // Set the default main form caption
  strAppName := 'TForm demo — MDI demo';
end;

procedure TForm1.Timer1Timer(Sender: TObject);
begin
  // Construct the full caption of the main form
  Form1.Caption := strAppName + ': ' +
    Form1.ActiveMDIChild.Caption;
end;
```

Description   If your application is an MDI application, the `ActiveMDIChild` property contains the child MDI form that is currently active. Otherwise, this property is invalid. `ActiveMDIChild` is a run-time, read-only property.

ArrangeIcons METHOD

Objects Affected   TForm

Purpose   The `ArrangeIcons` method arranges the icons of minimized child forms neatly within the main MDI form. See Figure 62-5.

Declaration

```
procedure ArrangeIcons;
```

Example Syntax

```
// The menu item Arrange Minimized Icons arranges the icons neatly
procedure TForm1.ArrangeMinizedIcons1Click(Sender: TObject);
begin
  Form1.ArrangeIcons;
end;
```

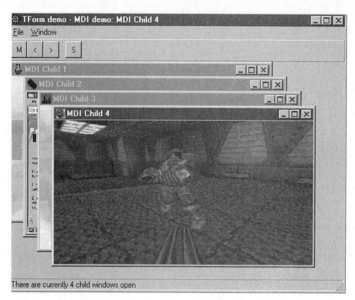

Figure 62-5 The MDI demo adds its child form caption to the
main form caption

Description   If the icons of minimized child forms in an MDI application become jumbled or unorganized, as in Figure 62-6, you can call the `ArrangeIcons` method to arrange them neatly, as in Figure 62-7, so they are lined up near the bottom of the parent window. `ArrangeIcons` has no effect on an SDI application.

AutoScroll PROPERTY

Objects Affected   `TForm`

Purpose   The `AutoScroll` property determines whether scroll bars automatically appear on the left and/or bottom border of the form, if it is not large enough to display all the controls that it contains.

Declaration

```
property AutoScroll stored IsAutoScrollStored;
```

Example Syntax

```
// Disable auto scroll on form1
Form1.AutoScroll := False;
```

Description   If `AutoScroll` is `True`, scroll bars will automatically appear if the form is not large enough to display all its controls. This can happen if the user resizes the form so it is smaller and some of the controls on the form are hidden. If `AutoScroll` is `False`, scroll bars will not automatically appear.

The default value is `True`.

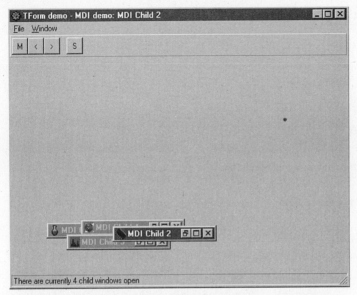

Figure 62-6 Minimized icons that are a mess…

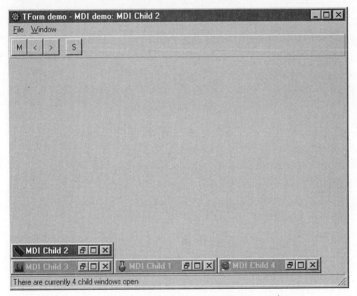

Figure 62-7 …can be arranged neatly with `ArrangeIcons`

BorderIcons PROPERTY

Objects Affected	TForm
Purpose	The BorderIcons property determines which window buttons appear on the title bar of the form.
Declaration	

```
property BorderIcons: TBorderIcons;
```

Example Syntax

```
// Add the standard border icons
procedure TForm1.FormCreate(Sender: TObject);
begin
  Form1.BorderIcons := [biSystemMenu] + [biMinimize] + [biMaximize];
end;
```

Description

BorderIcons is type TBorderIcons, which is a set of possible window buttons. TBorderIcons is declared as

```
TBorderIcons = set of TBorderIcon;
TBorderIcon = (biSystemMenu, biMinimize, biMaximize, biHelp);
```

The following chart describes each border icon.

Use This Icon...	To Do This...
biSystemMenu	Add a system menu to the form (known as a Control menu in Windows 3).
biMinimize	Add a minimize button to the form.
biMaximize	Add a maximize button to the form.
biHelp	Adds a help button to the form.

If minimize and maximize buttons are shown, the help button will not appear. In either case, adding this button will cause help to appear in pop-up windows, rather than using the standard Windows help. The help button looks like a question mark.

Although you can set border icons in code as in the above example, it is easier to do so in the Object Inspector window at design time.

Cascade METHOD

Objects Affected	TForm
Purpose	The Cascade method will cascade the child windows in an MDI application.
Declaration	

```
procedure Cascade;
```

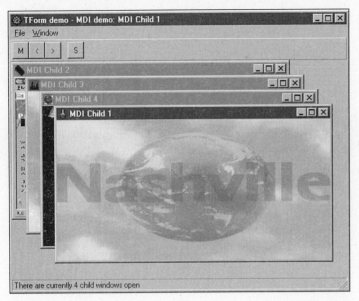

Figure 62-8 Cascading child windows in an MDI application

Example Syntax

```
procedure TForm1.Cascade1Click(Sender: TObject);
begin
  Form1.Cascade;
end;
```

Description

The `Cascade` method will evenly overlap, or cascade, the child windows in an MDI application. By default, child windows in an MDI application are cascaded when the program starts. See Figure 62-8. You can manually call the `Cascade` method to arrange the child windows. Typically, a `Cascade` item appears in the menu of the main window in an MDI application.

ClientHandle PROPERTY

Objects Affected   TForm

Purpose   The `ClientHandle` property contains a Windows handle to the client area of the main form in an MDI application.

Declaration

```
property ClientHandle: HWND;
```

Example Syntax

```
var MyHandle: HWND;
begin
  MyHandle := Form1.ClientHandle;
  // . . .
```

Description ClientHandle is a run-time-only property that applies only to MDI main forms. It contains a handle to the client area of the MDI application's main form. This form must have its **FormStyle** property set to **fsMDIForm**. This property is useful if you need to make API calls that require a handle to the client area of that form.

ClientHeight Property

Objects Affected TForm

Purpose The ClientHeight property contains the height of the form's client area.

Declaration

```
property ClientHeight stored IsClientSizeStored;
```

Example Syntax

```
// Output the height and width of the form and its client area
procedure TForm1.FormResize(Sender: TObject);
begin
  lblClientHeight.Caption := IntToStr(Form1.ClientHeight);
  lblClientWidth.Caption := IntToStr(Form1.ClientWidth);
  lblFormHeight.Caption := IntToStr(Form1.Height);
  lblFormWidth.Caption := IntToStr(Form1.Width);
end;
```

Description ClientHeight is the vertical size of the form's client area, measured in pixels. The client area of a form is the portion of the window found below the title bar and menu bar. See Figure 62-9.

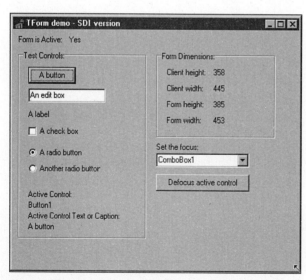

Figure 62-9 Resizing the window automatically updates the metric values

ClientWidth PROPERTY

Objects Affected	TForm
Purpose	The ClientWidth property contains the width of the form's client area.
Declaration	

```
property ClientWidth stored IsClientSizeStored;
```

Example Syntax

```
// Output the height and width of the form and its client area
procedure TForm1.FormResize(Sender: TObject);
begin
  lblClientHeight.Caption := IntToStr(Form1.ClientHeight);
  lblClientWidth.Caption := IntToStr(Form1.ClientWidth);
  lblFormHeight.Caption := IntToStr(Form1.Height);
  lblFormWidth.Caption := IntToStr(Form1.Width);
end;
```

Description   ClientWidth is the horizontal size of the form's client area, measured in pixels. The client area of a form is the portion of the window found below the title bar and menu bar.

Close METHOD

Objects Affected	TForm
Purpose	The Close method closes the form.
Declaration	

```
procedure Close;
```

Example Syntax

```
procedure TForm1.Exit1Click(Sender: TObject);
begin
  Close;
end;
```

Description   The Close method closes the form window if possible. For MDI applications, calling the Close method of the main form will close all child windows as well. If the form can be closed, the OnClose event occurs and any code you have placed in the handler for that event is run.

To terminate a Delphi application, call the Close method for the main form of the application. Typically, an Exit menu item in the file menu is use to close an application, as shown in Figure 62-10.

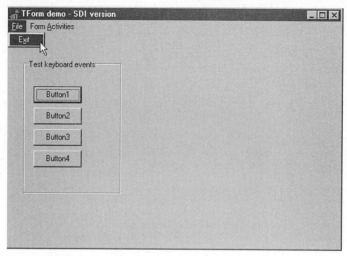

Figure 62-10 Choosing Exit from the File menu triggers this event handler

DefocusControl METHOD

Objects Affected   TForm

Purpose   The **DefocusControl** method removes the focus from the specified control.

Declaration

```
procedure DefocusControl(Control: TWinControl; Removing: Boolean);
```

Parameters

Control   The control that will lose the focus.

Removing   Determines whether to focus the control's parent.

Example Syntax

```
procedure TForm1.Timer1Timer(Sender: TObject);
begin
  if Form1.ActiveControl <> nil then
    lblActiveControl.Caption := Form1.ActiveControl.Name
  else
    lblActiveControl.Caption := 'none';

  if Form1.ActiveControl is TEdit then
    lblActiveControlText.Caption := TEdit(Form1.ActiveControl).Text
  else
    lblActiveControlText.Caption :=TLabel(Form1.ActiveControl).Caption;
end;

procedure TForm1.Button2Click(Sender: TObject);
begin
  Form1.DefocusControl(Form1.ActiveControl, True);
end;
```

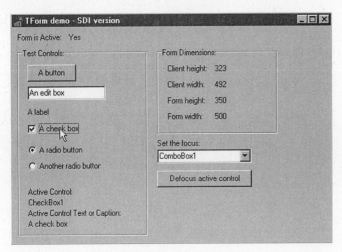

Figure 62-11 Update a label by defocusing the active control

Description

If the control specified by the *Control* parameter has the focus when **DefocusControl** is called, that control will lose the focus. This is demonstrated in Figure 62-11. Figure 62-12 shows the combo box used to focus controls. The *Removing* parameter determines whether to set the focus to the control's parent. If *Removing* is **True**, the focus will be set to the control's parent. Otherwise, no control will have the focus (this will also occur if *Removing* is **True** but the control's parent is the form itself).

FocusControl METHOD

Objects Affected   TForm

Purpose   The **FocusControl** method sets the focus to the specified control.

Declaration

```
procedure FocusControl(Control: TWinControl);
```

Parameter

Control   The control that will gain the focus.

Example Syntax

```
// Load the combo box with the names of the form controls
procedure TForm1.FormCreate(Sender: TObject);
var x: Integer;
begin
  for x := 0 to Form1.ControlCount - 1 do
    ComboBox1.Items.Add(Form1.Controls[x].Name);
  ComboBox1.Text := Form1.ActiveControl.Name;
end;
```

continued on next page

continued from previous page

```
// When the combo box changes, set the focus to the control specified
// in the combo box text
procedure TForm1.ComboBox1Change(Sender: TObject);
begin
  Form1.FocusControl(TWinControl(Form1.Controls[ComboBox1.ItemIndex]));
end;
```

Description   The `FocusControl` property sets the focus to the control specified by the *Control* parameter.

FormStyle PROPERTY

Objects Affected   `TForm`

Purpose   The `FormStyle` property determines the style of the form. See Figure 62-13.

Declaration

```
property FormStyle: TFormStyle;
```

Example Syntax

```
Form1.FormStyle := fsMDIForm;
```

Description   `FormStyle` is a type of `TFormStyle`, which sets the following possible form styles:

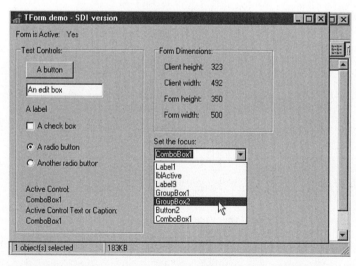

Figure 62-12 The combo box is used to focus any control on the form

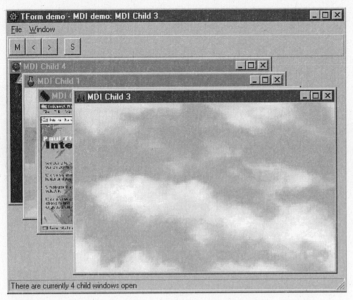

Figure 62-13 In an MDI application, the main form's
`FormStyle` is `fsMDIForm`. The child forms are `fsMDIChild`.

This Form Style...	Has This Effect...
fsMDIChild	The form is an MDI child.
fsMDIForm	The form is a main MDI window.
fsNormal	The form is normal. It is neither an MDI parent window nor an MDI child.
fsStayOnTop	The form is the topmost form in the application unless other forms have their style set to fsStayOnTop.

The default is `fsNormal`.

`HorzScrollBar` PROPERTY

Objects Affected   All scrolling windowed controls

Purpose   The `HorzScrollBar` property represents the form's horizontal scroll bar.

Declaration

```
property HorzScrollBar: TControlScrollBar;
```

Example Syntax

```
// Move the scroll box to the far left of the horizontal scroll bar
Form1.HorzScrollBar.Position := 0;
```

Description   The `HorzScrollBar` property allows you to access the form's horizontal scroll bar properties, like `Increment`, `Margin`, `Position`, `Range`, `Tracking`, and `Visible`. For a horizontal scroll bar to appear on the form, the `Visible` property of `HorzScrollBar` must be set to `True` and its `Range` value must be greater than the value held in the form's `ClientWidth` property. In addition, the form's `AutoScroll` property must be set to `True`.

`HorzScrollBar` is type `TControlScrollBar`. The properties, methods, and events of that class are discussed in Chapter 13, "`TControlScrollBar`."

Icon PROPERTY

Objects Affected   `TForm`

Purpose   The `Icon` property contains the icon that will appear at the left edge of the form's title bar.

Declaration

```
property Icon: TIcon;
```

Example Syntax

```
Form1.Icon := 'factory.ico';
Form2.Icon := 'earth.ico';
```

Description   If no icon is specified, every form in the application will use the icon specified in the `Application` object's `Icon` property. Each form in an application can have its own icon, as shown in Figure 62-14. The icon specified by `Application.Icon` displays in the taskbar button for that application.

KeyPreview PROPERTY

Objects Affected   `TForm`

Purpose   The `KeyPreview` property determines if the form handles keyboard events before the controls it contains handle those events.

Declaration

```
property KeyPreview: Boolean;
```

Example Syntax

```
// If Form1.KeyPreview is False, and a keyboard event is generated
// while a control is focused, this event handler will run
procedure TForm1.Button1KeyPress(Sender: TObject; var Key: Char);
begin
  Application.MessageBox('This dialog was generated by the button',
                        'Control-handled event', MB_OK);
end;

// If Form1.KeyPreview is True, and a keyboard event is generated
// while a control is focused, this event handler will run
```

Figure 62-14 This MDI application used different icons for all its forms

```
procedure TForm1.FormKeyPress(Sender: TObject; var Key: Char);
begin
  Application.MessageBox('This dialog was generated by the form',
                         'Form-handled event', MB_OK);
end;

// This menu item event handler toggles the check mark on the
// menu item and toggles the value for Form1.KeyPreview
procedure TForm1.FormHandlesKeyboardEvents1Click(Sender: TObject);
begin
  if FormHandlesKeyboardEvents1.Checked = True then
  begin
    FormHandlesKeyboardEvents1.Checked := False;
    Form1.KeyPreview := False
  end
  else begin
    FormHandlesKeyboardEvents1.Checked := True;
    Form1.KeyPreview := True;
  end
end;
```

Description   Normally, keyboard events will go to the focused control, but you can use the parent form's **KeyPreview** property to allow the form to handle all keyboard events for the controls it contains by setting the property to **True**. By default, the **KeyPreview** property is **False**. In the example above, a menu item toggles the form **KeyPreview** property so that you can see the effect of keyboard event handling when a control is focused and a key is pressed. Figures 62-15, 62-16, and 62-17 demonstrate the possible effects of **KeyPreview**.

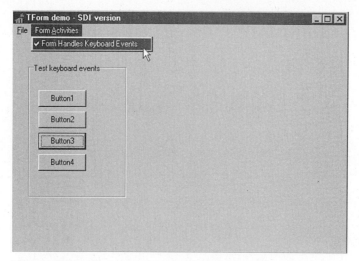

Figure 62-15 The menu item toggles `KeyPreview`

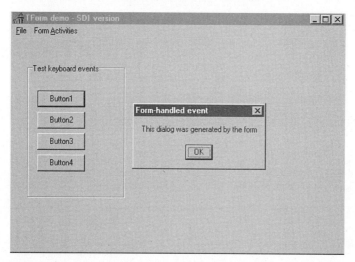

Figure 62-16 A message box created when `KeyPreview` is `True`

MDIChildCount PROPERTY

Objects Affected   TForm

Purpose   The MDIChildCount property contains the number of open MDI child
                        windows.

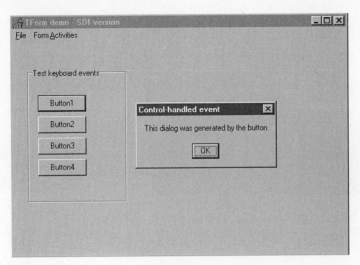

Figure 62-17 A message box created when `KeyPreview` is `False`

Declaration

```
property MDIChildCount: Integer;
```

Example Syntax

```
procedure TForm1.Timer1Timer(Sender: TObject);
begin
  // Output the number of child windows in the status bar
  StatusBar1.SimpleText := 'There are currently ' +
                    IntToStr(Form1.MDIChildCount) +
                    ' child windows open';
end;
```

Description

`MDIChildCount` is a run-time, read-only property that contains the number of open child windows in an MDI application.

MDIChildren PROPERTY

Objects Affected   TForm

Purpose   The `MDIChildren` property allows you to access the child windows in an MDI application.

Declaration

```
property MDIChildren[I: Integer]: TForm;

Example Syntax
procedure TForm1.ShowMDIChildrenbyIndex1Click(Sender: TObject);
var x: Integer;
begin
  for x := 0 to Form1.MDIChildCount - 1 do
    Form1.MDIChildren[x].Caption := 'MDI Child [' +
                        IntToStr(x) + ']';
end;
```

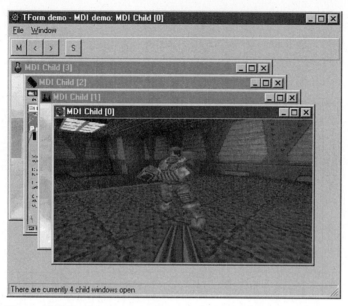

Figure 62-18 A menu item changes the child forms to reflect their MDIChildren index value

Description   MDIChildren is an array that contains the child windows in an MDI application, where the topmost child window is MDIChildren[0], the next lowest is MDIChildren[1], and so on. As the child windows in an MDI application are reordered, their positions in the MDIChildren array change to reflect their logical position. This is shown in Figure 62-18. MDIChildren is a run-time, read-only property.

Menu PROPERTY

Objects Affected   TForm

Purpose   The Menu property specifies the main menu in the form.

Declaration

```
property Menu: TMainMenu;
```

Example Syntax

```
Form1.Menu := MainMenu1;
```

Menu Bar

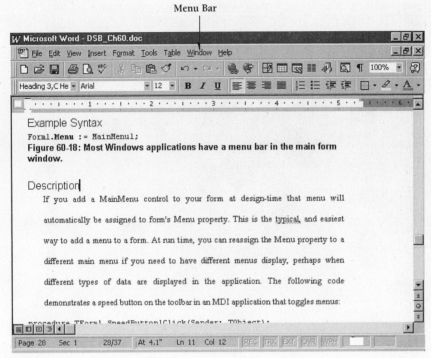

Figure 62-19 Most Windows applications have a menu bar in the main form window

Description

If you add a **MainMenu** control to your form at design time, that menu will automatically be assigned to form's **Menu** property. This is the typical, and easiest way, to add a menu to a form. At run time, you can reassign the **Menu** property to a different main menu if you need to have different menus display, perhaps when different types of data are displayed in the application. A typical main menu is shown in Figure 62-19.

The following code demonstrates a speedbutton on the toolbar in an MDI application that toggles menus as shown in Figure 62-20.

```
procedure TForm1.SpeedButton1Click(Sender: TObject);
begin
  if Form1.Menu = MainMenu1 the
    Form1.Menu := MainMenu2
  else Form1.Menu := MainMenu1;
end;
```

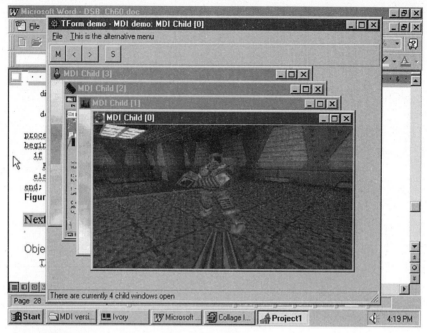

Figure 62-20 Displaying an alternative menu

Next METHOD

Objects Affected	TForm
Purpose	The **Next** method switches the focus to the next child window in an MDI application.
Declaration	

```
procedure Next;
```

Example Syntax

```
procedure TForm1.ActivateNextChildWindow1Click(Sender: TObject);
begin
  Form1.Next;
end;
```

Description   **Next** moves the second-to-topmost child window, making it the current, focused child window. The **Next** method only affects MDI applications, that is, applications that have a main form whose **FormStyle** property is set to **fsMDIForm**.

Position PROPERTY

Objects Affected	TForm
Purpose	The Position property determines the placement and size of the form when it appears.
Declaration	

```
property Position: TPosition;
```

Example Syntax

```
Form1.Position := poScreenCenter;
```

Description   Position is type **TPosition**, which is declared as

```
TPosition = (poDesigned, poDefault, poDefaultPosOnly,
             poDefaultSizeOnly, poScreenCenter);
```

The different position values are described below.

This Position Value...	Does This...
poDefault	Windows determines the form's initial position, width, and height. If you run multiple instances of the application, Windows will cascade the main form of each application as it appears.
poDefaultPosOnly	Windows determines the form's initial position, but the form appears with the width and height it had at design time. Windows will cas-cade multiple instances of the application.
poDefaultSizeOnly	Windows determines the form's initial width and height but places the form in the position used during design time. Windows will cascade multiple instances of the application.
poDesigned	The form appears on the screen in the position in which it was designed with the same width and height.
poScreenCenter	The form is positioned in the center of the screen with the width and height used at design time.

The default is **poDesigned**.

Previous METHOD

Objects Affected	TForm
Purpose	The Previous method switches the focus to the previous child window in an MDI application.
Declaration	

```
procedure Previous;
```

Example Syntax

```
procedure TForm1.ActivePreviousChildWindow1Click(Sender: TObject);
begin
  Form1.Previous;
end;
```

| Description | Previous moves the child window at the bottom of the visual hierarchy of child windows above the topmost child window and into the foreground, making it the current, focused child window. The Previous method affects MDI applications only—applications that have a main form whose FormStyle property is set fsMDIForm. |

Print METHOD

Objects Affected	TForm
Purpose	The Print method prints the form.
Declaration	

```
procedure Print;
```

Example Syntax

```
// Print the main form
procedure TForm1.PrintMainForm1Click(Sender: TObject);
begin
  Form1.Print;
end;

// Print the active child form
procedure TForm1.PrintCurrentChildForm1Click(Sender: TObject);
begin
  Form1.ActiveMDIChild.Print;
end;
```

| Description | The Print method prints the *visual* portion of the client area of the form; the title bar and menu bar (if present) are not printed. |

PrintScale PROPERTY

Objects Affected	TForm
Purpose	The PrintScale property determines how the form is printed.
Declaration	

```
property PrintScale: TPrintScale;
```

Example Syntax

```
procedure TForm6.FormActivate(Sender: TObject);
begin
  if Form1.PrintScale = poNone then
    rbNone.Checked := True
  else if Form1.PrintScale = poProportional then
    rbProportional.Checked := True
  else rbFitToPage.Checked := True;
end;
```

```
procedure TForm6.btnOKClick(Sender: TObject);
begin
  if rbNone.Checked = True then
    Form1.PrintScale := poNone
  else if rbProportional.Checked = True then
    Form1.PrintScale := poProportional
  else Form1.PrintScale := poPrintToFit;
  Close;
end;

procedure TForm6.btnCancelClick(Sender: TObject);
begin
  Close;
end;
```

Description

PrintScale determines the proportions of the form when it is printed.
PrintScale is type TPrintScale, which is declared as

```
TPrintScale = (poNone, poProportional, poPrintToFit);
```

The possible values are described below.

This Print Scale...	Does This...
poNone	The form is not scaled. The results will depend on the printer; the printed form could appear stretched.
poProportional	The form is printed so that it is approximately the same size as it appears on the screen. This is the WYSIWYG printing mode.
poPrintToFit	The form is printed proportionally to the screen and occupies as much of the printed page as possible.

The default value is poProportional.

Release METHOD

Objects Affected	TForm
Purpose	The Release method destroys the form.
Declaration	

```
procedure Release;
```

Example Syntax

```
// Close the MDI child window
procedure TForm3.FormClose(Sender: TObject; var Action: TCloseAction);
begin
  Form3.Release;
end;
```

Description

Release is similar to Free, except that it waits until all the form's event
handlers have finished executing before destroying the form and releasing
any memory associated with the form. Usually, you should just use Close.

Show METHOD

Objects Affected	TForm
Purpose	The Show method displays a form modelessly.
Declaration	

```
procedure Show;
```

Example Syntax

```
// Display the form
Form1.Show;
```

Description A *modeless* form is one you can switch away from without first closing it. Show sets the form's Visible property to True and displays the form by bringing it to the foreground, if possible. This is the preferred method of displaying a modeless form. Forms are closed with the Close method.

ShowModal METHOD

Objects Affected	TForm
Purpose	The ShowModal method displays a modal form.
Declaration	

```
function ShowModal: Integer;
```

Example Syntax

```
// Display the Print Style dialog modally
procedure TForm1.SetPrintStyle1Click(Sender: TObject);
begin
   Form6.ShowModal;
end;
```

Description ShowModal is similar to Show, except that ShowModal makes the form modal. A modal form is one that must be closed before any other form in the application can be accessed. Forms are closed with the Close method.

Tile METHOD

Objects Affected	TForm
Purpose	The Tile method arranges the child windows of an MDI application so that they are tiled and occupy the entire client area of the main form.
Declaration	

```
procedure Tile;
```

Example Syntax

```
procedure TForm1.Tile1Click(Sender: TObject);
begin
  Form1.Tile;
end;
```

Description   Figure 62-21 shows the effect of tiling on child windows. `Tile` has no effect in an SDI application.

WindowMenu PROPERTY

Objects Affected   `TForm`

Purpose   The `WindowMenu` property determines which menu item contains the standard Window menu commands in an MDI application.

Declaration

```
property WindowMenu: TMenuItem;
```

Example Syntax

```
Form1.WindowMenu := Window1;
```

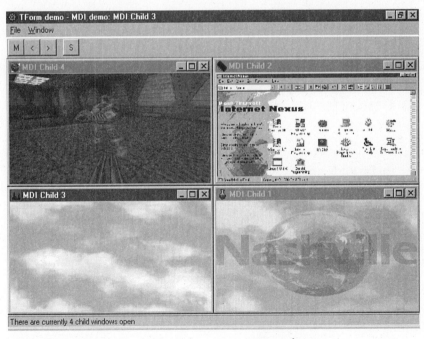

Figure 62-21 Tiling the child windows in an MDI application

Description The main menu of the main form in an MDI application will typically have an item called Window that contains items like Cascade, Arrange Icons, and Tile. These items are designed to allow the user to manipulate the child windows. The `Cascade`, `ArrangeIcons`, and `Tile` methods, respectively, introduced in this chapter, enable you to implement these features. You will need to add these menu items yourself. The examples for these methods include an example `OnClick` event handler for the Window submenu items.

Another feature of a Windows menu in an MDI application is that it will list the open child windows so the user can quickly switch between them. By setting the `WindowMenu` property to a menu item you specify (typically, its caption will, in fact, be Window), Delphi will automatically keep track of the open child windows in your MDI application and list them under the menu item you specify. This is shown in Figure 62-22.

WindowState PROPERTY

Objects Affected TForm

Purpose The `WindowState` property determines how the form displays.

Declaration

```
property WindowState: TWindowState;
```

Example Syntax

```
// Display the window maximized
Form1.WindowState := wsMaximized;
```

Description WindowState is type TWindowState, which is declared as:

```
TWindowState = (wsNormal, wsMinimized, wsMaximized);
```

The possible window states are described below.

This State...	Has This Effect...
wsMaximized	The form is maximized when it is loaded.
wsMinimized	The form is minimized when it is loaded.
wsNormal	The form appears normally, as a window floating on the desktop.

The default value is `wsNormal`.

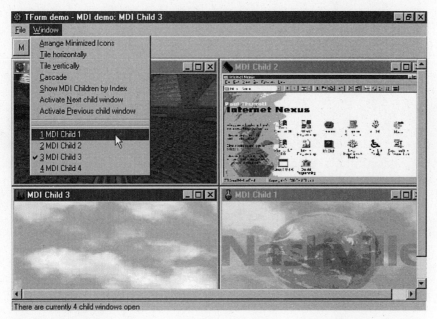

Figure 62-22 Child windows are listed in the Window menu by setting the
WindowMenu property

63

TButtonControl AND ITS DESCENDANTS

Command buttons, check boxes, and radio buttons are common elements found in Windows. They allow the user to select choices, initiate actions, and change properties. In Delphi, these controls are encapsulated by **TButtonControl** and its descendants.

TButtonControl

TButtonControl is a direct descendant of **TWinControl**. It is the abstract base class for all button controls in Delphi.

TButton

The first major descendant of **TButtonControl** is **TButton**, which provides Delphi programmers with command button capabilities. Command buttons are pervasive in the Windows interface, populating Windows and dialogs everywhere. They are typically rectangular in shape, include a text caption, and are used to initiate some sort of action. A typical group of command buttons is shown in Figure 63-1.

The most common command button event you will handle is **OnClick**. The **OnClick** event occurs when the user selects the button by clicking it with the mouse or by pressing (Enter) when the button is focused. Command buttons appear to press in when clicked, giving the user visual feedback that the selection has occured. Statements in the **OnClick** event handler actually occur when the user releases the mouse button.

Figure 63-2 shows the **TButton** branch of the VCL. Table 63-1 displays the properties, methods, and events implemented by **TButton**.

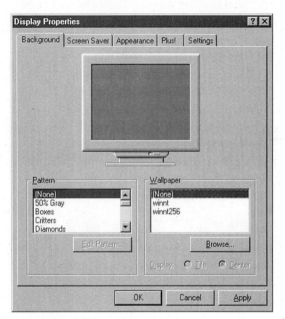

Figure 63-1 Command buttons

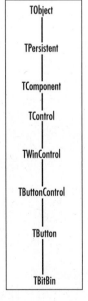

Figure 63-2 The **TButton** branch of the VCL

TObject

TPersistent

TComponent

TControl

TWinControl

TButtonControl

TButton

TBitBin

Table 63-1 Properties, methods, and events implemented by `TButton`

Use or Set This...	To Do This...	Inheritance
Align	Determine how the control is aligned within its parent.	TControl
Assign	Assign one persistent object to another.	TPersistent
BeginDrag	Begin a manual drag operation.	TControl
BoundsRect	Determine the boundary rectangle occupied by the control.	TControl
BringToFront	Bring the control to the front of the z-order.	TControl
Brush	Determine the color and pattern used for the windowed control background.	TComponent
Cancel	Determine whether the button is a Cancel button.	**None**
CanFocus	Determine whether the windowed control can receive the focus.	TWinControl
Caption	Label the control with a text string.	TControl
ClassName	Get the name of the object's class.	TObject
ClassParent	Get the object's parent class.	TObject
ClassType	Get the object's actual type.	TObject
ClientHeight	Determine the control's client height.	TControl
ClientOrigin	Determine the upper-left position of the control's client area.	TControl
ClientRect	Determine the rectangle occupied by the control's client area.	TControl
ClientToScreen	Convert control (local) coordinates to screen coordinates.	TControl
ClientWidth	Determine the width of the control's client area.	TControl
Color	Determine the color of the windowed control.	TControl
ComponentCount	Determine the number of owned components.	TComponent
ComponentIndex	Determine the index of the component in its owner's `Components` list.	TComponent
Components	Determine the list of owned components.	TComponent
ComponentState	Determine the state of the current component.	TComponent
ContainsControl	Determine whether the specified control is contained by the windowed control.	TWinControl
ControlAtPos	Determine the control contained at a specified position.	TWinControl
ControlCount	Determine the number of controls contained by the windowed control.	TWinControl
Controls	Access the controls contained by the windowed control using their positions in an array.	TWinControl
ControlState	Determine the state of the control at any given time.	TControl
ControlStyle	Determine what attributes are present in the control.	TControl
Create	Create a new component.	TObject
Ctl3D	Determine whether the windowed control displays in 3D.	TWinControl
Cursor	Determine what image is used for the cursor over the control.	TControl
Destroy	Destroy the component.	TObject
DestroyComponents	Destroy all of the components owned by the component.	TComponent
Destroying	Notify the component that it is being destroyed.	TComponent
DragCursor	Determine the shape of the mouse cursor as it drags an object over the control.	TControl
Dragging	Determine whether the control is being dragged.	TControl
DragMode	Determine the drag-and-drop behavior of the control.	TControl
Enabled	Determine whether the control is enabled.	TControl

continued on next page

continued from previous page

Use or Set This...	To Do This...	Inheritance
EndDrag	End or cancel a manual drag operation.	TControl
FindComponent	Find a component in the Components array list.	TComponent
Focused	Determine whether the windowed control has the focus.	TControl
Font	Determine the font used to render text on the control.	TControl
Free	Safely destroy the object.	TObject
GetTextBuf	Copy the text of the control into a buffer.	TControl
GetTextLen	Get the length of the text of the control.	TControl
Handle	Obtain a handle to the windowed control.	TComponent
HandleAllocated	Determine if a handle is allocated for the windowed control.	TWinControl
Height	Determine the height of the control.	TControl
HelpContext	Determine the help context ID of the windowed control.	TComponent
Hide	Make the control invisible.	TControl
Hint	Determine the text that displays in a tooltip for the control.	TControl
InheritsFrom	Determine if the object is descended from a certain class.	TObject
InsertControl	Insert a control into the windowed control's Controls array.	TWinControl
InstanceSize	Determine the amount of memory allocated for the object.	TObject
Invalidate	Force the control to be repainted as soon as possible.	TControl
Left	Determine the left edge of the control within its container.	TControl
ModalResult	Determine whether clicking the button closes the form.	None
Name	Determine the name of the component.	TComponent
OnClick	Handle the event that occurs when a mouse button is clicked.	TControl
OnDblClick	Handle the event that occurs when a mouse button is double-clicked.	TControl
OnDragDrop	Handle the event that occurs when an object is dropped on the control.	TControl
OnDragOver	Handle the event that occurs when an object is dragged over the control.	TControl
OnEndDrag	Handle the event that occurs when a drag-and-drop operation is cancelled.	TControl
OnEnter	Handle the event that occurs when the windowed control receives the focus.	TWinControl
OnExit	Handle the event that occurs when the windowed control loses the focus.	TWinControl
OnKeyDown	Handle the event that occurs when a key is pressed down and not immediately released while the windowed control has the focus.	TWinControl
OnKeyPress	Handle the event that occurs when a key is pressed while the windowed control has the focus.	TWinControl
OnKeyUp	Handle the event that occurs when a key is released while the windowed control has the focus.	TWinControl
OnMouseDown	Handle the event that occurs when a mouse button is held down and not immediately released.	TControl
OnMouseMove	Handle the event that occurs when the cursor moves over the control.	TControl
OnMouseUp	Handle the event that occurs when a mouse button is released.	TControl
OnStartDrag	Handle the event that occurs when a drag-and-drop operation is started.	TControl
Owner	Determine the owner of the component.	TComponent
Parent	Determine the parent, or container, of the control.	TControl

Use or Set This...	To Do This...	Inheritance
ParentColor	Determine whether the control's parent's Color information is used.	TControl
ParentCtl	Determine whether the control's parent's ShowHint information is used.	TControl
PopupMenu	Determine which pop-up menu is associated with the control.	TControl
Refresh	Erase the control and repaint it.	TControl
RemoveControl	Remove the specified control from the windowed control's Controls array.	TWinControl
Repaint	Repaint the control.	TControl
ScaleBy	Resize the windowed control.	TWinControl
ScreenToClient	Convert screen coordinates to client (control) coordinates.	TControl
SendToBack	Send the control to the end of the z-order.	TControl
SetBounds	Determine the coordinates of the control's bounding rectangle.	TControl
SetFocus	Set the focus to the windowed control.	TWinControl
SetTextBuf	Set the text of the control to the text in a buffer.	TControl
Show	Make the control visible.	TControl
ShowHint3D	Determine whether the windowed control uses its parent's Ctl3D settings.	TWinControl
ParentFont	Determine whether the control's parent's Font information is used.	TControl
ParentShowHint	Enable tooltips for the control.	TControl
Showing	Determine whether the windowed control is currently showing onscreen.	TComponent
TabOrder	Determine the tab order of the windowed control.	TWinControl
TabStop	Determine whether the windowed control is in the tab order.	TWinControl
Tag	Store an additional integer value with the component.	TComponent
Text	Access the changeable text on the control.	TControl
Top	Determine the upper edge of the control.	TControl
Update	Update is called automatically by Refresh.	TControl
Visible	Determine whether the control is visible.	TControl
Width	Determine the width of the control.	TControl

TBitBtn

TBitBtn is descended from TButton and completes the Delphi implementation of Win32 command buttons by adding the capability to display a glyph. A *glyph* is a small bitmap graphic, typically 16 pixels by 16 pixels, that can appear on the face of a bitmap button. Oddly enough, bitmap buttons and normal command buttons are handled by two (different) classes in Delphi, despite the fact that they are implemented by the same object in the Win32 API. Other programming languages, such as Visual C++ and Visual Basic, treat them as one object as well. Basically, if you want your command button to display a graphic and you are using Delphi, you will need to use TBitBtn. A typical bitmap button is shown in Figure 63-3.

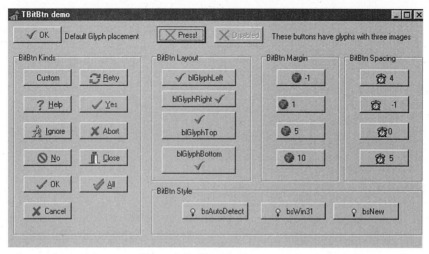

Figure 63-3 A command button with a glyph

A limitation of Delphi bitmap buttons is that the glyph must be a bitmap graphic. In the Win32 API, the button can display icons as well.

As you might expect, most of the new properties implemented by **TBitBtn** deal with the manipulation of glyphs. Table 63-2 displays the properties, methods, and events implemented by **TBitBtn** in addition to the properties, methods, and events it inherits from **TButton**.

Table 63-2 Properties, methods, and events implemented by TBitBtn

Use or Set This...	To Do This...	Inheritance
Cancel	Determine whether the button is a Cancel button.	TButton
Caption	Determine the caption displayed by the button.	TComponent
Click	Simulate a mouse click.	TComponent
Create	Create a new bitmap button.	TComponent
Default	Determine whether the button is the default button.	TComponent
Destroy	Destroy the bitmap button.	TComponent
Enabled	Determine whether the button is enabled.	TComponent
Glyph	Determine which bitmap is displayed on the button.	None
Kind	Determine the kind of bitmap button.	None
Layout	Determine how the glyph and caption are arranged on the button.	None
Margin	Determine the distance between the glyph and the edge of the button.	None
ModalResult	Determine whether clicking the button closes the form.	TButton
NumGlyphs	Determine how many images are contained in the bitmap associated with the glyph.	None
OnEnter	Handle the event that occurs when the component gets the focus.	TComponent
OnExit	Handle the event that occurs when the component loses the focus.	TComponent

Use or Set This...	To Do This...	Inheritance
ParentShowHint	Determine whether to use the button's parent's ShowHint information.	TComponent
ShowHint	Determine whether the button displays a tooltip.	TComponent
Spacing	Determine the spacing between the glyph and the caption.	None
Style	Determine the bitmap button's style.	None
TabOrder	Determine the button's position in its parent's tab order.	TComponent
TabStop	Determine whether the button is a tab stop.	TComponent
Visible	Determine whether the button is visible.	TComponent

TCustomCheckBox

TCustomCheckBox is a direct descendant of **TButtonControl**. It is an abstract base class for check boxes, as implemented by **TCheckBox**. **TCustomCheckBox** introduces many private and protected properties that are later published by **TCheckBox** and provides a way for check boxes to automatically toggle between their possible states when clicked.

Table 63-3 displays the properties, methods, and events implemented by **TCustomCheckBox**.

Table 63-3 Properties, methods, and events implemented by **TCustomCheckBox**

Use or Set This...	To Do This...	Inheritance
Align	Determine how the control is aligned within its parent.	TControl
Assign	Assign one persistent object to another.	TPersistent
BeginDrag	Begin a manual drag operation.	TControl
BoundsRect	Determine the boundary rectangle occupied by the control.	TControl
BringToFront	Bring the control to the front of the z-order.	TControl
Brush	Determine the color and pattern used for the windowed control background.	TComponent
CanFocus	Determine whether the windowed control can receive the focus.	TWinControl
Caption	Label the control with a text string.	TControl
ClassName	Get the name of the object's class.	TObject
ClassParent	Get the object's parent class.	TObject
ClassType	Get the object's actual type.	TObject
ClientHeight	Determine the control's client height.	TControl
ClientOrigin	Determine the upper-left position of the control's client area.	TControl
ClientRect	Determine the rectangle occupied by the control's client area.	TControl
ClientToScreen	Convert control (local) coordinates to screen coordinates.	TControl
ClientWidth	Determine the width of the control's client area.	TControl
Color	Determine the color of the windowed control.	TControl
ComponentCount	Determine the number of owned components.	TComponent
ComponentIndex	The index of the component in its owner's Components list.	TComponent

continued on next page

continued from previous page

Use or Set This...	To Do This...	Inheritance
Components	Determine the list of owned components.	TComponent
ComponentState	Determine the state of the current component.	TComponent
ContainsControl	Determine whether the specified control is contained by the windowed control.	TWinControl
ControlAtPos	Determine the control contained at a specified position.	TWinControl
ControlCount	Determine the number of controls contained by the windowed control.	TWinControl
Controls	Access the controls contained by the windowed control using their positions in an array.	TWinControl
ControlState	Determine the state of the control at any given time.	TControl
ControlStyle	Determine what attributes are present in the control.	TControl
Create	Create a new component.	TObject
Ctl3D	Determine whether the windowed control displays in 3D.	TWinControl
Cursor	Determine what image is used for the cursor over the control.	TControl
Destroy	Destroy the component.	TObject
DestroyComponents	Destroy all of the components owned by the component.	TComponent
Destroying	Notify the component that it is being destroyed.	TComponent
DragCursor	Determine the shape of the mouse cursor as it drags an object over the control.	TControl
Dragging	Determine whether the control is being dragged.	TControl
DragMode	Determine the drag-and-drop behavior of the control.	TControl
Enabled	Determine whether the control is enabled.	TControl
EndDrag	End or cancel a manual drag operation.	TControl
FindComponent	Find a component in the Components array list.	TComponent
Focused	Determine whether the windowed control has the focus.	TControl
Font	Determine the font used to render text on the control.	TControl
Free	Safely destroy the object.	TObject
GetTextBuf	Copy the text of the control into a buffer.	TControl
GetTextLen	Get the length of the text of the control.	TControl
Handle	Obtain a handle to the windowed control.	TComponent
HandleAllocated	Determine if a handle is allocated for the windowed control.	TWinControl
Height	Determine the height of the control.	TControl
HelpContext	Determine the help context ID of the windowed control.	TComponent
Hide	Make the control invisible.	TControl
Hint	Determine the text that displays in a tooltip for the control.	TControl
InheritsFrom	Determine if the object is descended from a certain class.	TObject
InsertControl	Insert a control into the windowed control's Controls array.	TWinControl
InstanceSize	Determine the amount of memory allocated for the object.	TObject
Invalidate	Force the control to be repainted as soon as possible.	TControl
Left	Determine the left edge of the control within its container.	TControl
Name	Determine the name of the component.	TComponent
OnClick	Handle the event that occurs when a mouse button is clicked.	TControl
OnDblClick	Handle the event that occurs when a mouse button is double-clicked.	TControl
OnDragDrop	Handle the event that occurs when an object is dropped on the control.	TControl

Use or Set This...	To Do This...	Inheritance
OnDragOver	Handle the event that occurs when an object is dragged over the control.	TControl
OnEndDrag	Handle the event that occurs when a drag-and-drop operation is cancelled.	TControl
OnEnter	Handle the event that occurs when the windowed control receives the focus.	TWinControl
OnExit	Handle the event that occurs when the windowed control loses the focus.	TWinControl
OnKeyDown	Handle the event that occurs when a key is pressed down and not immediately released while the windowed control has the focus.	TWinControl
OnKeyPress	Handle the event that occurs when a key is pressed while the windowed control has the focus.	TWinControl
OnKeyUp	Handle the event that occurs when a key is released while the windowed control has the focus.	TWinControl
OnMouseDown	Handle the event that occurs when a mouse button is held down and not immediately released.	TControl
OnMouseMove	Handle the event that occurs when the cursor moves over the control.	TControl
OnMouseUp	Handle the event that occurs when a mouse button is released.	TControl
OnStartDrag	Handle the event that occurs when a drag-and-drop operation is started.	TControl
Owner	Determine the owner of the component.	TComponent
Parent	Determine the parent, or container, of the control.	TControl
ParentColor	Determine whether the control's parent's Color information is used.	TControl
ParentCtl3D	Determine whether the windowed control uses its parent's Ctl3D settings.	TWinControl
ParentFont	Determine whether the control's parent's Font information is used.	TControl
ParentShowHint	Determine whether the control's parent's ShowHint information is used.	TControl
PopupMenu	Determine which pop-up menu is associated with the control.	TControl
Refresh	Erase the control and repaint it.	TControl
RemoveControl	Remove the specified control from the windowed control's Controls array.	TWinControl
Repaint	Repaint the control.	TControl
ScaleBy	Resize the windowed control.	TWinControl
ScreenToClient	Convert screen coordinates to client (control) coordinates.	TControl
SendToBack	Send the control to the end of the z-order.	TControl
SetBounds	Determine the coordinates of the control's bounding rectangle.	TControl
SetFocus	Set the focus to the windowed control.	TWinControl
SetTextBuf	Set the text of the control to the text in a buffer.	TControl
Show	Make the control visible.	TControl
ShowHint	Enable tooltips for the control.	TControl
Showing	Determine whether the windowed control is currently showing onscreen.	TComponent
TabOrder	Determine the tab order of the windowed control.	TWinControl
TabStop	Determine whether the windowed control is in the tab order.	TWinControl
Tag	Store an additional integer value with the component.	TComponent
Text	Access the changeable text on the control.	TControl
Top	Determine the upper edge of the control.	TControl
Update	Update is called automatically by Refresh.	TControl
Visible	Determine whether the control is visible.	TControl
Width	Determine the width of the control.	TControl
Create	Create a new custom check box.	TComponent
TabStop	Determine whether the check box is a tab stop.	TComponent

TCheckBox

TCheckBox is a direct implementation of the Win32 check box control, which is used to determine whether an option is selected. Although you sometimes see a group of related check boxes together on a window, perhaps collected in a group box, they are not linked in any way: Each check box operates independently of other check box controls.

A check box appears as a box with a text caption. If the box contains a check mark graphic, the option identified by the check box is set and the check box is said to be *checked*. If the box does not contain a check mark, the option is not set and the check box is said to be *unchecked*. Delphi provides a **Checked** property that allows you to get and set this value.

The user can toggle the check box by clicking it. If the check box is unchecked and the user clicks the check box, it becomes checked and vice versa. This action will not affect any other check boxes. A group of check boxes is shown in Figure 63-4.

Table 63-4 displays the properties, methods, and events implemented by **TCheckBox** in addition to the properties, methods, and events it inherits from **TCustomCheckBox**.

Figure 63-4   Check boxes

Table 63-4 Properties, methods, and events implemented by `TCheckBox`

Use or Set This...	To Do This...	Inheritance
AllowGrayed	Determine whether the check box can be disabled.	None
Caption	Determine the check box caption.	TComponent
Checked	Determine whether the check box is checked.	None
Color	Determine the background color of the check box.	TComponent
Ctl3D	Determine whether the check box displays in a 3D style.	TComponent
DragCursor	Determine the shape of the mouse pointer if it drags an object over the check box.	TComponent
DragMode	Determine the drag-and-drop behavior of the check box.	TComponent
Enabled	Determine whether the check box is enabled.	TComponent
Font	Determine the font used to render the check box caption.	TComponent
OnClick	Handle the event that occurs when the check box is clicked.	TComponent
OnDragDrop	Handle the event that occurs when an object is dropped on the check box.	TComponent
OnDragOver	Handle the event that occurs when an object is dragged over the check box.	TComponent
OnEndDrag	Handle the event that occurs when a drag-and-drop event is cancelled.	TComponent
OnEnter	Handle the event that occurs when the check box receives the focus.	TComponent
OnExit	Handle the event that occurs when the check box loses the focus.	TComponent
OnKeyDown	Handle the event that occurs when a key is pressed down.	TComponent
OnKeyPress	Handle the event that occurs when a key is pressed.	TComponent
OnKeyUp	Handle the event that occurs when a key is released.	TComponent
OnMouseDown	Handle the event that occurs when a mouse button is pressed down.	TComponent
OnMouseMove	Handle the event that occurs when the mouse pointer passes over the check box.	TComponent
OnMouseUp	Handle the event that occurs when a mouse button is released.	TComponent
OnStartDrag	Handle the event that occurs when a drag-and-drop operation begins.	TComponent
ParentColor	Determine whether the check box uses its parent's `Color` information.	TComponent
ParentCtl3D	Determine whether the check box uses its parent's 3D information.	TComponent
ParentFont	Determine whether the check box uses its parent's `Font` information.	TComponent
ParentShowHint	Determine whether the check box uses its parent's `ShowHint` information.	TComponent
PopupMenu	Determine which pop-up menu is associated with the check box.	TComponent
ShowHint	Determine whether the check box displays a tooltip.	TComponent
State	Determine the state of the check box.	None
TabOrder	Determine the position of the check box in its parent's tab order.	TComponent
TabStop	Determine whether the check box is a tab stop.	TComponent
Visible	Determine whether the check box is visible.	TComponent

TRadioButton

TRadioButton is the direct descendant of **TButtonControl** that encapsulates Windows option buttons, sometimes known as radio buttons. Option buttons are very common in Windows and appear as outline circle graphics with text captions. They are typically arranged in a group with other similar option buttons. Choices in the group of option buttons are *mutually exclusive*: If the user selects one option, the other options become unselected.

Delphi supports the grouping of option buttons automatically. Every option button you place on the form surface is automatically in the same group. If you wish to have more than one group of option buttons, you can place groups inside a group control, which also sets off the group visually. In addition, the **TRadioGroup** class, covered in Chapter 65, "**TCustomControl** and Its Descendants," offers yet another way to group radio buttons. A group of radio buttons is shown in Figure 63-5.

It is good practice to ensure that one option button in each group is automatically selected. Unlike check boxes, the state of an option button cannot be changed by successive clicks. Once an option button is selected, the only way to deselect it is to click another option button in the same group.

Table 63-5 displays the properties, methods, and events implemented by **TRadioButton**.

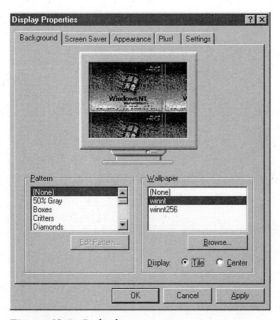

Figure 63-5 Radio buttons

Table 63-5 Properties, methods, and events implemented by `TRadioButton`

Use or Set This...	To Do This...	Inheritance
`Align`	Determine how the control is aligned within its parent.	`TControl`
`Assign`	Assign one persistent object to another.	`TPersistent`
`BeginDrag`	Begin a manual drag operation.	`TControl`
`BoundsRect`	Determine the boundary rectangle occupied by the control.	`TControl`
`BringToFront`	Bring the control to the front of the z-order.	`TControl`
`Brush`	Determine the color and pattern used for the windowed control background.	`TComponent`
`CanFocus`	Determine whether the windowed control can receive the focus.	`TWinControl`
`Caption`	Label the control with a text string.	`TControl`
`ClassName`	Get the name of the object's class.	`TObject`
`ClassParent`	Get the object's parent class.	`TObject`
`ClassType`	Get the object's actual type.	`TObject`
`ClientHeight`	Determine the control's client height.	`TControl`
`ClientOrigin`	Determine the upper-left position of the control's client area.	`TControl`
`ClientRect`	Determine the rectangle occupied by the control's client area.	`TControl`
`ClientToScreen`	Convert control (local) coordinates to screen coordinates.	`TControl`
`ClientWidth`	Determine the width of the control's client area.	`TControl`
`Color`	Determine the color of the windowed control.	`TControl`
`ComponentCount`	Determine the number of owned components.	`TComponent`
`ComponentIndex`	The index of the component in its owner's `Components` list.	`TComponent`
`Components`	Determine the list of owned components.	`TComponent`
`ComponentState`	Determine the state of the current component.	`TComponent`
`ContainsControl`	Determine whether the specified control is contained by windowed control.	`TWinControl`
`ControlAtPos`	Determine the control contained at a specified position.	`TWinControl`
`ControlCount`	Determine the number of controls contained by the windowed control.	`TWinControl`
`Controls`	Access the controls contained by the windowed control using their positions in an array.	`TWinControl`
`ControlState`	Determine the state of the control at any given time.	`TControl`
`ControlStyle`	Determine what attributes are present in the control.	`TControl`
`Create`	Create a new component.	`TObject`
`Ctl3D`	Determine whether the windowed control displays in 3D.	`TWinControl`
`Cursor`	Determine what image is used for the cursor over the control.	`TControl`
`Destroy`	Destroy the component.	`TObject`
`DestroyComponents`	Destroy all of the components owned by the component.	`TComponent`
`Destroying`	Notify the component that it is being destroyed.	`TComponent`
`DragCursor`	Determine the shape of the mouse cursor as it drags an object over the control.	`TControl`
`Dragging`	Determine whether the control is being dragged.	`TControl`
`DragMode`	Determine the drag-and-drop behavior of the control.	`TControl`
`Enabled`	Determine whether the control is enabled.	`TControl`
`EndDrag`	End or cancel a manual drag operation.	`TControl`

continued on next page

continued from previous page

Use or Set This...	To Do This...	Inheritance
FindComponent	Find a component in the `Components` array list.	TComponent
Focused	Determine whether the windowed control has the focus.	TControl
Font	Determine the font used to render text on the control.	TControl
Free	Safely destroy the object.	TObject
GetTextBuf	Copy the text of the control into a buffer.	TControl
GetTextLen	Get the length of the text of the control.	TControl
Handle	Obtain a handle to the windowed control.	TComponent
HandleAllocated	Determine if a handle is allocated for the windowed control.	TWinControl
Height	Determine the height of the control.	TControl
HelpContext	Determine the help context ID of the windowed control.	TComponent
Hide	Make the control invisible.	TControl
Hint	Determine the text that displays in a tooltip for the control.	TControl
InheritsFrom	Determine if the object is descended from a certain class.	TObject
InsertControl	Insert a control into the windowed control's `Controls` array.	TWinControl
InstanceSize	Determine the amount of memory allocated for the object.	TObject
Invalidate	Force the control to be repainted as soon as possible.	TControl
Left	Determine the left edge of the control within its container.	TControl
Name	Determine the name of the component.	TComponent
OnClick	Handle the event that occurs when a mouse button is clicked.	TControl
OnDblClick	Handle the event that occurs when a mouse button is double-clicked.	TControl
OnDragDrop	Handle the event that occurs when an object is dropped on the control.	TControl
OnDragOver	Handle the event that occurs when an object is dragged over the control.	TControl
OnEndDrag	Handle the event that occurs when a drag-and-drop operation is cancelled.	TControl
OnEnter	Handle the event that occurs when the windowed control receives the focus.	TWinControl
OnExit	Handle the event that occurs when the windowed control loses the focus.	TWinControl
OnKeyDown	Handle the event that occurs when a key is pressed down and not immediately released while the windowed control has the focus.	TWinControl
OnKeyPress	Handle the event that occurs when a key is pressed while the windowed control has the focus.	TWinControl
OnKeyUp	Handle the event that occurs when a key is released while the windowed control has the focus.	TWinControl
OnMouseDown	Handle the event that occurs when a mouse button is held down and not immediately released.	TControl
OnMouseMove	Handle the event that occurs when the cursor moves over the control.	TControl
OnMouseUp	Handle the event that occurs when a mouse button is released.	TControl
OnStartDrag	Handle the event that occurs when a drag-and-drop operation is started.	TControl
Owner	Determine the owner of the component.	TComponent
Parent	Determine the parent, or container, of the control.	TControl
ParentColor	Determine whether the control's parent's `Color` information is used.	TControl
ParentCtl3D	Determine whether the windowed control uses its parent's `Ctl3D` settings.	TWinControl

Use or Set This...	To Do This...	Inheritance
ParentFont	Determine whether the control's parent's Font information is used.	TControl
ParentShowHint	Determine whether the control's parent's ShowHint information is used.	TControl
PopupMenu	Determine which pop-up menu is associated with the control.	TControl
Refresh	Erase the control and repaint it.	TControl
RemoveControl	Remove the specified control from the windowed control's Controls array.	TWinControl
Repaint	Repaint the control.	TControl
ScaleBy	Resize the windowed control.	TWinControl
ScreenToClient	Convert screen coordinates to client (control) coordinates.	TControl
SendToBack	Send the control to the end of the z-order.	TControl
SetBounds	Determine the coordinates of the control's bounding rectangle.	TControl
SetFocus	Set the focus to the windowed control.	TWinControl
SetTextBuf	Set the text of the control to the text in a buffer.	TControl
Show	Make the control visible.	TControl
ShowHint	Enable tooltips for the control.	TControl
Showing	Determine whether the windowed control is currently showing onscreen.	TComponent
TabOrder	Determine the tab order of the windowed control.	TWinControl
TabStop	Determine whether the windowed control is in the tab order.	TWinControl
Tag	Store an additional integer value with the component.	TComponent
Text	Access the changeable text on the control.	TControl
Top	Determine the upper edge of the control.	TControl
Update	Update is called automatically by Refresh.	TControl
Visible	Determine whether the control is visible.	TControl
Width	Determine the width of the control.	TControl
Caption	Determine the option button's caption.	TComponent
Checked	Determine whether the option button is selected.	None
Color	Determine the option button's background color.	TComponent
Create	Create a new option button.	TComponent
Ctl3D	Determine whether the option button displays in 3D.	TComponent
DragCursor	Determine the shape of the mouse pointer as it drags an object over the option button.	TComponent
DragMode	Determine the drag-and-drop behavior of the option button.	TComponent
Enabled	Determine whether the option button is enabled.	TComponent
Font	Determine the font used to render the option button's caption.	TComponent
OnClick	Handle the event that occurs when the option button is clicked.	TComponent
OnDblClick	Handle the event that occurs when the option button is double-clicked.	TComponent
OnDragDrop	Handle the event that occurs when an object is dropped on the option button.	TComponent
OnDragOver	Handle the event that occurs when an object is dragged over the option button.	TComponent
OnEndDrag	Handle the event that occurs when a drag-and-drop operation is cancelled.	TComponent
OnEnter	Handle the event that occurs when the option button receives the focus.	TComponent
OnExit	Handle the event that occurs when the option button loses the focus.	TComponent
OnKeyDown	Handle the event that occurs when a key is pressed down.	TComponent

continued on next page

continued from previous page

Use or Set This...	To Do This...	Inheritance
OnKeyPress	Handle the event that occurs when a key is pressed.	TComponent
OnKeyUp	Handle the event that occurs when a key is released.	TComponent
OnMouseDown	Handle the event that occurs when a mouse button is pressed down.	TComponent
OnMouseMove	Handle the event that occurs when the mouse pointer moves over the option button.	TComponent
OnMouseUp	Handle the event that occurs when a mouse button is released.	TComponent
OnStartDrag	Handle the event that occurs when a drag-and-drop operation is started.	TComponent
ParentColor	Determine whether the option button uses its parent's Color information.	TComponent
ParentCtl3D	Deterrmine whether the option button uses its parent's Ctl3D information.	TComponent
ParentFont	Determine whether the option button uses its parent's Font information.	TComponent
ParentShowHint	Determine whether the option button uses its parent's ShowHint information.	TComponent
PopupMenu	Determine which pop-up menu is associated with the option button.	TComponent
ShowHint	Determine whether the option button displays a tooltip.	TComponent
TabOrder	Determine the option button's position in its parent's tab order.	TComponent
TabStop	Determine whether the option button is a tab stop.	TComponent
Visible	Determine whether the option button is visible.	TComponent

AllowGrayed PROPERTY

Objects Affected   TCheckBox

Purpose   The AllowGrayed property determines whether the user can disable the check box.

Declaration

```
property AllowGrayed: Boolean;
```

Example Syntax

```
procedure TForm1.CheckBox4Click(Sender: TObject);
begin
  if CheckBox4.Checked = True then
  begin
    CheckBox1.AllowGrayed := True;
    CheckBox2.AllowGrayed := True;
    CheckBox3.AllowGrayed := True;
  end
  else begin
    CheckBox1.AllowGrayed := False;
    CheckBox2.AllowGrayed := False;
    CheckBox3.AllowGrayed := False;
  end
end;
```

Description   Typically, a check box will cycle between two states when the user clicks it: checked and unchecked. If AllowGrayed is True, the check box will cycle between three states as the user clicks it: checked, unchecked, and disabled. When the check box is in the disabled state, it appears *grayed out*.

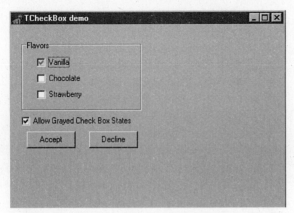

Figure 63-6 A check box toggles the **AllowGrayed** property for the group box check boxes

This effect is shown in Figure 63-6. By convention, a control that is grayed out cannot be enabled by the user—this property allows you to circumvent that behavior with check boxes. The default value is **False**.

Cancel PROPERTY

Objects Affected   TButton, TBitBtn

Purpose   The **Cancel** property determines whether the button is a Cancel button.

Declaration

```
property Cancel: Boolean;
```

Example Syntax

```
procedure TForm1.FormCreate(Sender: TObject);
begin
  btnDecline.Cancel := True;
end;
```

Description   If a button on your form is designated a Cancel button, its **OnClick** event handler will be triggered if the user presses the Esc key. This is commonly used in dialog boxes that have *Yes | No* or *OK | Cancel* buttons, not on the main form of an application. If **Cancel** is **True**, and the user hits Esc, the button's **OnClick** event handler will execute. If **Cancel** is **False**, the Esc key is mapped to the keyboard event handlers for the currently active control.

It is possible for your form to contain more than one Cancel button, although it usually doesn't make sense to do so—the first visible Cancel button in the tab order will execute its **OnClick** event handler.

Checked PROPERTY

Objects Affected	TCheckBox, TRadioButton
Purpose	The Checked property determines whether the control is selected.
Declaration	

```
property Checked: Boolean;
```

Example Syntax

```
procedure TForm1.CheckBox4Click(Sender: TObject);
begin
  if CheckBox4.Checked = True then
  begin
    CheckBox1.AllowGrayed := True;
    CheckBox2.AllowGrayed := True;
    CheckBox3.AllowGrayed := True;
  end
  else begin
    CheckBox1.AllowGrayed := False;
    CheckBox2.AllowGrayed := False;
    CheckBox3.AllowGrayed := False;
  end
end;
```

Description Checked can be True or False: True if the control is selected, and False if it is not.

When a check box is selected, a check mark appears in the check box.

When a radio button is selected, a filled black circle appears in the radio button. Only one radio button in a group can be selected at a time.

The default value is False.

Glyph PROPERTY

Objects Affected	TBitBtn
Purpose	The Glyph property determines which bitmap image appears on the bitmap button.
Declaration	

```
property Glyph: TBitmap;
```

Example Syntax

```
BitBtn1.NumGlyphs := 3;
BitBtn1.Glyph.LoadFromFile('X.bmp');
```

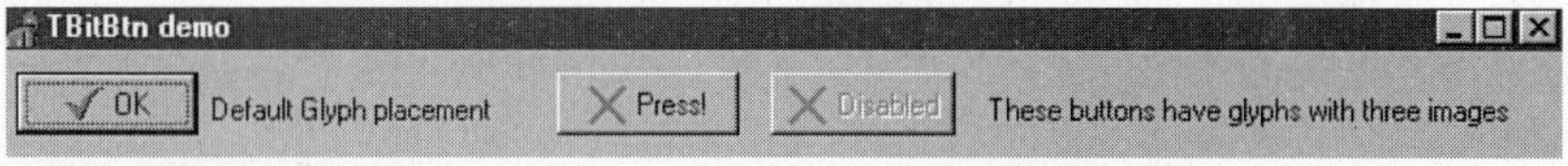

Figure 63-7 Three button states with three different glyphs

Description   Bitmap buttons can display a bitmap image in addition to the standard caption. The bitmap that is displayed is determined by the `Glyph` property. `Glyph` is capable of displaying up to three separate images on the button as long as they are contained within the same bitmap. Each image must be the same height and width (typically 16 pixels by 16 pixels) and ordered in a horizontal row. The image that is displayed is dependent on the current state of the button as shown in Figure 63-7.

This Image Displays...	When the Button Is in This State...
1	Up. The button is unselected. This is the default.
2	Disabled. The button cannot be selected.
3	Down. The button is clicked.

Figure 63-8 shows a button glyph with three images in the Delphi Image Editor.

If you do choose to use multiple images, you must specify the number of images using the `NumGlyphs` property. If only one image is present, Delphi will use it for all states, modifying it automatically.

REMEMBER
The pixel in the lower-left of the image determines which color is transparent when the glyph displays on the button.

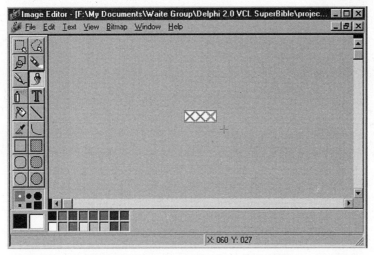

Figure 63-8   Editing a three-image glyph with Delphi's Image Editor

Kind PROPERTY

Objects Affected	TBitBtn
Purpose	The Kind property determines the kind of bitmap button.
Declaration	

```
property Kind: TBitBtnKind;
```

Example Syntax

```
BitBtn1.Kind := bkOK;
```

Description   Delphi supplies several kinds of bitmap buttons. Kind is type TBitBtnKind, which is declared as:

```
TBitBtnKind = (bkCustom, bkOK, bkCancel, bkHelp, bkYes, bkNo, bkClose, ⇐
bkAbort, bkRetry, bkIgnore, bkAll);
```

You can use one of Borland's preset button kinds by setting the bitmap button to one of these kinds, as outlined in the table below. It is not recommended that you change Kind, however, as Borland's non-standard button styles do not visually mix well with the new Windows interface. The different Kind styles are shown in Figure 63-9.

Figure 63-9
The different bitmap
button kinds

Use This Kind...	To Achieve This Effect...
bkCustom	The bitmap button has a glyph of your choosing.
bkOK	The bitmap button has a green check mark and an OK caption. The button's `Default` property is set to `True` and its `ModalResult` value is set to `mrOK`.
bkCancel	The bitmap button has a red X and a Cancel caption. The button's `Cancel` property is set to `True` and its `ModalResult` value is set to `mrCancel`.
bkYes	The bitmap button has a green check mark and a Yes caption. The button's `Default` property is set to `True` and its `ModalResult` value is set to `mrYes`.
bkNo	The bitmap button has a red No symbol (a circle with a line through it) and a No caption. The button's `Cancel` property is set to `True` and its `ModalResult` value is set to `mrNo`.
bkHelp	The bitmap button has a blue-green question mark glyph and a Help caption. When it is clicked, a Help window in the application's help file appears as specified by the application's `HelpFile` property. The button's `HelpContext` property determines which Help window appears.
bkClose	The bitmap button has a glyph showing a door with an exit sign and a Close caption. When the user clicks the button, the form will close.
bkAbort	The bitmap button has a red X and an Abort caption.
bkRetry	The bitmap button has a green retry arrow and a Retry caption.
bkIgnore	The bitmap button displays an ignore glyph and an Ignore caption. This button is used when you want to allow the user to continue after an error has occurred.
bkAll	The bitmap button has a double green check mark and a Yes to All caption.

The default value is `bkCustom`.

Layout PROPERTY

Objects Affected	`TBitBtn`
Purpose	The `Layout` property determines where the glyph appears on the face of the bitmap button.
Declaration	
	`property Layout: TButtonLayout;`
Example Syntax	

```
procedure TForm1.FormCreate(Sender: TObject);
begin
  BitBtn1.Layout := blGlyphLeft;
  BitBtn2.Layout := blGlyphRight;
  BitBtn3.Layout := blGlyphTop;
  BitBtn4.Layout := blGlyphBottom;
end;
```

Figure 63-10 Glyph
layout possibilities

Description   Layout is type TButtonLayout, which is declared as:

TButtonLayout = (blGlyphLeft, blGlyphRight, blGlyphTop, blGlyphBottom);

Layout's possible values are described below.

Use This Value...	To Cause the Glyph to Appear...
blGlyphLeft	To the left of the caption.
blGlyphRight	To the right of the caption.
blGlyphTop	On top of the caption.
blGlyphBottom	Below the caption.

The various glyph layouts are shown in Figure 63-10. The default value is
blGlyphLeft.

Margin PROPERTY

Objects Affected   TBitBtn

Purpose   The Margin property determines the distance between the edge of the button and the glyph.

Declaration

```
property Margin: Integer;
```

Example Syntax

```
procedure TForm1.FormCreate(Sender: TObject);
begin
  BitBtn1.Margin := -1;
  BitBtn2.Margin := 1;
  BitBtn3.Margin := 5;
  BitBtn4.Margin := 10;
end;
```

Figure 63-11
The **Margin** value affects the glyph and caption of a bitmap button

Description

By default, the glyph and caption are centered on the face of the bitmap button. You can use the **Margin** property to manually set the distance, in pixels, between the edge of the button and the glyph, as shown in Figure 63-11. The edge you are aligning with is dependent on the bitmap button's **Layout** property: If **Layout** is **blGlyphLeft**, for example, **Margin** determines the distance between the left edge of the glyph and the left edge of the button. In the code above, the **−1** value indicates that the first bitmap button is set to its default margin: The glyph and caption are centered on the face of the button. The other three bitmap buttons display their glyph and caption at 1, 5, and 10 pixels from the left edge of the button, respectively.

The default value is **−1**, which causes the glyph and caption to be centered on the face of the button.

ModalResult PROPERTY

Objects Affected	`TButton`, `TBitBtn`
Purpose	The **ModalResult** property is used by a button to close its form.
Declaration	

```
property ModalResult: TModalResult;
```

Example Syntax

```
procedure TForm2.FormCreate(Sender: TObject);
begin
  Button1.ModalResult := mrYes;
  Button2.ModalResult := mrNo;
end;
```

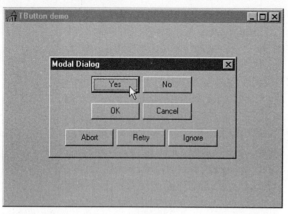

Figure 63-12 This modal dialog can return one of several modal results

```
procedure TForm1.Button1Click(Sender: TObject);
begin
  // Open the modal dialog
  Form2.ShowModal;
  // Use the modal result to determine which button was clicked
  if Form2.ModalResult = idYes then
    Label3.Caption := 'Yes button pressed'
  else if Form2.ModalResult = idNo then
    Label3.Caption := 'No button pressed'
  else if Form2.ModalResult = idOK then
    Label3.Caption := 'OK button pressed'
  else if Form2.ModalResult = idCancel then
    Label3.Caption := 'Cancel button pressed'
  else if Form2.ModalResult = idAbort then
    Label3.Caption := 'Abort button pressed'
  else if Form2.ModalResult = idRetry then
    Label3.Caption := 'Retry button pressed'
  else if Form2.ModalResult = idIgnore then
    Label3.Caption := 'Ignore button pressed';
end;
```

Description

ModalResult determines what value the form's ModalResult property will contain when the form is closed by the button. You can use the button's ModalResult property when you want the user to be able to click it to close the form. In Figure 63-13, various buttons have been created to return typical ModalResult values. ModalResult is type TModalResult, which defines a range of possible integer values. Several of these values are declared as named constants, as shown in the following table:

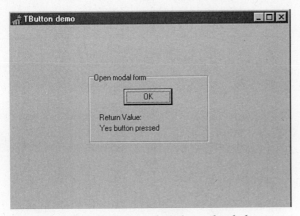

Figure 63-13 The button that closes the dialog is identified with `ModalResult`

Use This Constant...	To Return This Value...
mrAbort	idAbort
mrAll	mrNo + 1
mrCancel	idCancel
mrIgnore	idIgnore
mrNo	idNo
mrNone	0
mrOk	idOK
mrRetry	idRetry
mrYes	idYes

If the `ModalResult` property is a non-zero value, you do not need to explicitly call the form's `Close` method to close the form within the button's `OnClick` event handler. If `ModalResult` is `mrNone` and you wish to use that button to close the form, you must call the `Close` method:

```
procedure TForm1.Button1Click(Sender: TObject);
begin
  Close;
end;
```

In this case, the form's `ModalResult` property would contain `0`. The default value of `ModalResult` is `mrNone`.

NumGlyphs PROPERTY

Objects Affected	TBitBtn
Purpose	The NumGlyphs property determines the number of images contained in the bitmap image used to display a glyph on the bitmap button.
Declaration	

```
property NumGlyphs: TNumGlyphs;
```

Example Syntax

```
BitBtn1.NumGlyphs := 3;
BitBtn1.Glyph.LoadFromFile('X.bmp');
```

Description   If you wish to display different images for each state of the bitmap button, you must create a bitmap image that has three equally sized images arranged horizontally. Then, set the NumGlyphs property to the number of images you wish to use. Refer to the entry for Glyph for details.

Spacing PROPERTY

Objects Affected	TBitBtn
Purpose	The Spacing property determines the size of the space separating the glyph from the caption on the face of the bitmap button.
Declaration	

```
property Spacing: Integer;
```

Example Syntax

```
procedure TForm1.FormCreate(Sender: TObject);
begin
  BitBtn23.Spacing := 4;
  BitBtn24.Spacing := -1;
  BitBtn25.Spacing := 0;
  BitBtn26.Spacing := 5;
end;
```

Description   If Spacing is less than or equal to 0, it determines the number of pixels that separate the glyph from the caption. If Spacing is -1, the button caption is centered between the glyph and the edge of the button furthest from the glyph. In Figure 63-14, various Spacing values are used to demonstrate its effect on the distance between the button's glyph and label.

The default value is 4.

Figure 63-14
Spacing affects
the glyph and
caption of
bitmap buttons

State PROPERTY

Objects Affected   TCheckBox

Purpose   The **State** property determines the state of the check box.

Declaration

```
property State: TCheckBoxState;
```

Example Syntax

```
procedure TForm1.FormCreate(Sender: TObject);
begin
  CheckBox1.State := cbChecked;
  CheckBox2.State := cbUnchecked;
  CheckBox3.State := cbUnchecked;
end;
```

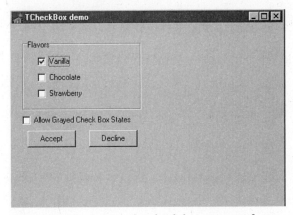

Figure 63-15   Setting the check box states at form
load

Description	State is type TCheckBoxState, which is declared as:
	TCheckBoxState = (cbUnchecked, cbChecked, cbGrayed);
	You can assign the following possible values to State.

This State...	Indicates That...
cbUnchecked	The check box is not selected.
cbChecked	The check box is selected.
cbGrayed	The check box is grayed out and disabled.

State can be used to determine which check box is selected when the form loads. This is shown in Figure 63-15. The default value is cbUnchecked.

Style PROPERTY

Objects Affected	TBitBtn
Purpose	The Style property determines the style of the bitmap button.
Declaration	
	property Style: TButtonStyle;
Example Syntax	
	BitBtn1.Style := bsNew;
Description	Style is provided for backward compatibility: In Windows 95 and Windows NT 3.51/4.0, it has no effect since all controls will automatically adopt the new style. If you are going to be running your application on Windows NT 3.1 or Windows systems with Win32s, you can use the Style property to determine how the bitmap button displays. Style is type TButtonStyle, which is declared as:
	TButtonStyle = (bsAutoDetect, bsWin31, bsNew);
	The possible values are described below.

Use This Style...	To Do This...
bsAutoDetect	Display the button style that is appropriate for the environment you are in.
bsWin31	Display the button using the older style Windows 3.x look.
bsNew	Display the button using the newer bitmap button style, even in older versions of Windows.

The default value is bsAutoDetect.

64

TCustomEdit AND ITS DESCENDANTS

TCustomEdit and its descendants form a complex sub-branch of the VCL encapsulating those text controls the user can edit. The most common control in this group is the simple edit box, but with the releases of Windows 95 and Delphi, the list has grown to include such RTF-compatible controls as the rich edit control.

TCustomEdit

TCustomEdit is the abstract base class for all edit controls in Delphi. This includes the simple edit control, mask edit controls, and all memo controls. All the properties in TCustomEdit are later published in its various child classes. It introduces the concept of *selected text*, in which the user can select a portion of the text the control displays.

Edit controls do not include a descriptive label, so you need to add one using a TLabel control if necessary.

Figure 64-1 displays the TCustomEdit branch of the VCL. Table 64-1 displays the properties, methods, and events implemented by TCustomEdit.

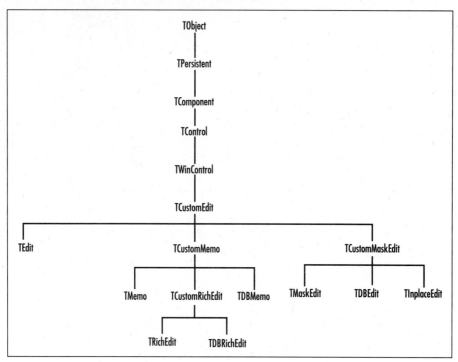

Figure 64-1 The `TCustomEdit` branch of the VCL

Table 64-1 Properties, methods, and events implemented by `TCustomEdit`

Use or Set This...	To Do This...	Inheritance
Align	Determine how the control is aligned within its parent.	TControl
Assign	Assign one persistent object to another.	TPersistent
BeginDrag	Begin a manual drag operation.	TControl
BoundsRect	Determine the boundary rectangle occupied by the control.	TControl
BringToFront	Bring the control to the front of the z-order.	TControl
Brush	Determine the color and pattern used for the windowed control background.	TComponent
CanFocus	Determine whether the windowed control can receive the focus.	TWinControl
Caption	Label the control with a text string.	TControl
ClassName	Get the name of the object's class.	TObject
ClassParent	Get the object's parent class.	TObject
ClassType	Get the object's actual type.	TObject
Clear	Clear the contents of the edit control.	None
ClearSelection	Clear the selected text in the edit control.	None
ClientHeight	Determine the control's client height.	TControl
ClientOrigin	Determine the upper-left position of the control's client area.	TControl

Use or Set This...	To Do This...	Inheritance
ClientRect	Determine the rectangle occupied by the control's client area.	TControl
ClientToScreen	Convert control (local) coordinates to screen coordinates.	TControl
ClientWidth	Determine the width of the control's client area.	TControl
Color	Determine the color of the windowed control.	TControl
ComponentCount	Determine the number of owned components.	TComponent
ComponentIndex	Determine the index of the component in its owner's Components list.	TComponent
Components	Determine the list of owned components.	TComponent
ComponentState	Determine the state of the current component.	TComponent
ContainsControl	Determine whether the specified control is contained by the windowed control.	TWinControl
ControlAtPos	Determine the control contained at a specified position.	TWinControl
ControlCount	Determine the number of controls contained by the windowed control.	TWinControl
Controls	Access the controls contained by the windowed control using their positions in an array.	TWinControl
ControlState	Determine the state of the control at any given time.	TControl
ControlStyle	Determine what attributes are present in the control.	TControl
CopyToClipboard	Copy the text in the control to the clipboard.	None
Create	Create a new component.	TObject
Ctl3D	Determine whether the windowed control displays in 3D.	TWinControl
Cursor	Determine what image is used for the cursor over the control.	TControl
CutToClipboard	Cut the text from the control and copy it to the clipboard.	None
Destroy	Destroy the component.	TObject
DestroyComponents	Destroy all the components owned by the component.	TComponent
Destroying	Notify the component that it is being destroyed.	TComponent
DragCursor	Determine the shape of the mouse cursor as it drags an object over the control.	TControl
Dragging	Determine whether the control is being dragged.	TControl
DragMode	Determine the drag-and-drop behavior of the control.	TControl
Enabled	Determine whether the control is enabled.	TControl
EndDrag	End or cancel a manual drag operation.	TControl
FindComponent	Find a component in the Components array list.	TComponent
Focused	Determine whether the windowed control has the focus.	TControl
Font	Determine the font used to render text on the control.	TControl
Free	Safely destroy the object.	TObject
GetSelTextBuf	Copy the selected text from the control into a buffer.	None
GetTextBuf	Copy the text of the control into a buffer.	TControl
GetTextLen	Get the length of the text of the control.	TControl
Handle	Obtain a handle to the windowed control.	TComponent
HandleAllocated	Determine if a handle is allocated for the windowed control.	TWinControl
Height	Determine the height of the control.	TControl
HelpContext	Determine the help context ID of the windowed control.	TComponent

continued on next page

continued from previous page

Use or Set This...	To Do This...	Inheritance
Hide	Make the control invisible.	TControl
Hint	Determine the text that displays in a tooltip for the control.	TControl
InheritsFrom	Determine if the object is descended from a certain class.	TObject
InsertControl	Insert a control into the windowed control's Controls array.	TWinControl
InstanceSize	Determine the amount of memory allocated for the object.	TObject
Invalidate	Force the control to be repainted as soon as possible.	TControl
Left	Determine the left edge of the control within its container.	TControl
Modified	Determine whether the control was modified.	**None**
Name	Determine the name of the component.	TComponent
OnClick	Handle the event that occurs when a mouse button is clicked.	TControl
OnDblClick	Handle the event that occurs when a mouse button is double-clicked.	TControl
OnDragDrop	Handle the event that occurs when an object is dropped on the control.	TControl
OnDragOver	Handle the event that occurs when an object is dragged over the control.	TControl
OnEndDrag	Handle the event that occurs when a drag-and-drop operation is cancelled.	TControl
OnEnter	Handle the event that occurs when the windowed control receives the focus.	TWinControl
OnExit	Handle the event that occurs when the windowed control loses the focus.	TWinControl
OnKeyDown	Handle the event that occurs when a key is pressed down and not immediately released while the windowed control has the focus.	TWinControl
OnKeyPress	Handle the event that occurs when a key is pressed while the windowed control has the focus.	TWinControl
OnKeyUp	Handle the event that occurs when a key is released while the windowed control has the focus.	TWinControl
OnMouseDown	Handle the event that occurs when a mouse button is held down and not immediately released.	TControl
OnMouseMove	Handle the event that occurs when the cursor moves over the control.	TControl
OnMouseUp	Handle the event that occurs when a mouse button is released.	TControl
OnStartDrag	Handle the event that occurs when a drag-and-drop operation is started.	TControl
Owner	Determine the owner of the component.	TComponent
Parent	Determine the parent, or container, of the control.	TControl
ParentColor	Determine whether the color information of the control's parent is used.	TControl
ParentCtl3D	Determine whether the windowed control uses its parent's Ctl3D settings.	TWinControl
ParentFont	Determine whether the font information of the control's parent is used.	TControl
ParentShowHint	Determine whether the ShowHint information of the control's parent is used.	TControl
PasteFromClipboard	Paste text from the clipboard into the edit control.	**None**
PopupMenu	Determine which pop-up menu is associated with the control.	TControl
Refresh	Erase the control and repaint it.	TControl
RemoveControl	Remove the specified control from the windowed control's Controls array.	TWinControl
Repaint	Repaint the control.	TControl
ScaleBy	Resize the windowed control.	TWinControl

Use or Set This...	To Do This...	Inheritance
ScreenToClient	Convert screen coordinates to client (control) coordinates.	TControl
SelectAll	Select all the text in the control.	None
SelLength	Determine the length of the selected text in the control.	None
SelStart	Determine the starting position of the selected text.	None
SelText	Access the selected text in the edit control.	None
SendToBack	Send the control to the end of the z-order.	TControl
SetBounds	Determine the coordinates of the control's bounding rectangle.	TControl
SetFocus	Set the focus to the windowed control.	TWinControl
SetSelTextBuf	Copy text from a buffer into the edit control, replacing any selected text.	None
SetTextBuf	Set the text of the control to the text in a buffer.	TControl
Show	Make the control visible.	TControl
ShowHint	Enable tooltips for the control.	TControl
Showing	Determine whether the windowed control is currently showing on screen.	TComponent
TabOrder	Determine the tab order of the windowed control.	TWinControl
TabStop	Determine whether the windowed control is in the tab order.	TWinControl
Tag	Store an additional integer value with the component.	TComponent
Text	Access the changeable text on the control.	TControl
Top	Determine the upper edge of the control.	TControl
Update	Called automatically by Refresh.	TControl
Visible	Determine whether the control is visible.	TControl
Width	Determine the width of the control.	TControl

TEdit

TEdit encapsulates most of the features of the standard Win32 edit control, also known as a text box or text field. An *edit control* provides a single line of text inside an optionally-bordered control that the user can edit, or modify. If desired, the text in an edit control can be made read-only so the user cannot modify it.

Figure 64-2 A standard edit control in Windows 95

TEdit provides only the basic functionality of a Win32 edit control. If you need to limit the input that the control accepts, use a mask edit control (TMaskEdit) instead. TEdit is a direct descendant of TCustomEdit.

Table 64-2 displays the properties, methods, and events implemented by TEdit.

Table 64-2 Properties, methods, and events implemented by TEdit, in addition to those inherited from TCustomEdit

Use or Set This...	To Do This...	Inheritance
AutoSelect	Determine whether the text in the edit control is selected automatically when the control receives the focus.	None
AutoSize	Determine whether the control sizes itself automatically.	TComponent
BorderStyle	Determine the border style of the control.	TComponent
CharCase	Determine the case of the text in the control.	None
Color	Determine the background color of the control.	TComponent
Ctl3D	Determine whether the control displays in a 3D style.	TComponent
DragCursor	Determine the shape of the cursor as it drags an object over the control.	TComponent
DragMode	Determine the drag-and-drop behavior of the control.	TComponent
Enabled	Determine whether the control is enabled.	TComponent
Font	Determine the font used to render text in the control.	TComponent
HideSelection	Determine whether selected text in the control remains selected when the control loses the focus.	None
MaxLength	Determine the maximum length of text contained by the control.	None
OnChange	Handle the event that occurs when the text in the control is changed.	TComponent
OnClick	Handle the event that occurs when a mouse button is clicked.	TComponent
OnDblClick	Handle the event that occurs when a mouse button is double-clicked.	TComponent
OnDragDrop	Handle the event that occurs when an object is dropped on the control.	TComponent
OnDragOver	Handle the event that occurs when an object is dragged over the control.	TComponent
OnEndDrag	Handle the event that occurs when a drag-and-drop operation is cancelled.	TComponent
OnEnter	Handle the event that occurs when the control receives the focus.	TComponent
OnExit	Handle the event that occurs when the control loses the focus.	TComponent
OnKeyDown	Handle the event that occurs when a key is pressed and held down.	TComponent
OnKeyPress	Handle the event that occurs when a key is pressed.	TComponent
OnKeyUp	Handle the event that occurs when a key is released.	TComponent
OnMouseDown	Handle the event that occurs when a mouse button is pressed and held down.	TComponent
OnMouseMove	Handle the event that occurs when the mouse pointer passes over the control.	TComponent
OnMouseUp	Handle the event that occurs when a mouse button is released.	TComponent
OnStartDrag	Handle the event that occurs when a drag-and-drop operation is started.	TComponent
ParentColor	Determine whether the control uses its parent's Color information.	TComponent
ParentCtl3D	Determine whether the control uses its parent's Ctl3D information.	TComponent
ParentFont	Determine whether the control uses its parent's Font information.	TComponent

Use or Set This...	To Do This...	Inheritance
ParentShowHint	Determine whether the control uses its parent's ShowHint information.	TComponent
PasswordChar	Determine the character used to hide characters if the control is used for password input.	None
PopupMenu	Determine which pop-up menu is associated with the control.	TComponent
ReadOnly	Determine whether the user can edit text contained by the control.	None
ShowHint	Determine whether the control displays a tooltip.	TComponent
TabOrder	Determine the position of the control in its parent's tab order.	TComponent
TabStop	Determine whether the control is a tab stop.	TComponent
Text	Access the text contained by the edit control.	TCustomEdit
Visible	Determine whether the edit control is visible.	TComponent

TCustomMaskEdit

TCustomMaskEdit descends directly from **TCustomEdit** and is the abstract base class for all mask edit controls. The **MaskEdit** class publishes the properties and methods introduced by **TCustomMaskEdit**.

Table 64-3 displays the properties, methods, and events implemented by **TCustomMaskEdit**.

Table 64-3 Properties, methods, and events implemented by **TCustomMaskEdit**, in addition to those inherited from **TCustomEdit**

Use or Set This...	To Do This...	Inheritance
Clear	Erase the contents of the mask edit control.	TCustomEdit
Create	Create a new custom mask edit control.	TComponent
EditText	Access the value in Text as it appears to the user at run time.	None
IsMasked	Determine whether a mask is used.	None
Text	Access the text contained by the mask edit control.	TCustomEdit

TMaskEdit

TMaskEdit is a descendant of **TCustomMaskEdit** and provides important functionality missing from Delphi's **TEdit** class: the ability to limit user input. Mask edit controls can limit the number of characters the user can enter and the type of characters entered (alphabetic, numeric, and so on), as well as provide input masks for such things as phone numbers and zip codes. Mask edit controls are useful when you need to provide data entry and want the input formatted automatically.

Other than the edit mask capabilities, the mask edit control functions just like a normal edit control.

Table 64-4 displays the properties, methods, and events implemented by TMaskEdit.

Table 64-4 Properties, methods, and events implemented by TMaskEdit, in addition to those inherited from TCustomMaskEdit

Use or Set This...	To Do This...	Inheritance
AutoSelect	Determine whether the text in the mask edit control is selected automatically when the control receives the focus.	TComponent
AutoSize	Determine whether the control sizes itself automatically.	TComponent
BorderStyle	Determine the border style of the control.	TComponent
CharCase	Determine the case of text in the control.	None
Color	Determine the background color of the control.	TComponent
Ctl3D	Determine whether the control displays in a 3D style.	TComponent
DragCursor	Determine the shape of the mouse pointer as it passes over the control.	TComponent
DragMode	Determine the drag-and-drop behavior of the control.	TComponent
EditMask	Determine the mask used to limit user input.	None
Enabled	Determine whether the control is enabled.	TComponent
Font	Determine the font used to render text in the control.	TComponent
MaxLength	Determine the maximum length of text in the control.	None
OnChange	Handle the event that occurs when the text in the control is changed.	TComponent
OnClick	Handle the event that occurs when a mouse button is clicked.	TComponent
OnDblClick	Handle the event that occurs when a mouse button is double-clicked.	TComponent
OnDragDrop	Handle the event that occurs when an object is dropped on the control.	TComponent
OnDragOver	Handle the event that occurs when an object is dragged over the control.	TComponent
OnEndDrag	Handle the event that occurs when a drag-and-drop operation is cancelled.	TComponent
OnEnter	Handle the event that occurs when the control receives the focus.	TComponent
OnExit	Handle the event that occurs when the control loses the focus.	TComponent
OnKeyDown	Handle the event that occurs when a key is pressed and held down.	TComponent
OnKeyPress	Handle the event that occurs when a key is pressed.	TComponent
OnKeyUp	Handle the event that occurs when a key is released.	TComponent
OnMouseDown	Handle the event that occurs when a mouse button is pressed and held down.	TComponent
OnMouseMove	Handle the event that occurs when the mouse pointer passes over the control.	TComponent
OnMouseUpEvent	Handle the event that occurs when a mouse button is released.	TComponent
OnStartDrag	Handle the event that occurs when a drag-and-drop operation is started.	TComponent
ParentColor	Determine whether the control uses its parent's Color information.	TComponent
ParentCtl3D	Determine whether the control uses its parent's Ctl3D information.	TComponent
ParentFont	Determine whether the control uses its parent's Font information.	TComponent
ParentShowHint	Determine whether the control uses its parent's ShowHint information.	TComponent

Use or Set This...	To Do This...	Inheritance
PasswordChar	Determine the character used to hide characters if the control is used for password input.	None
PopupMenu	Determine which pop-up menu is associated with the control.	TComponent
ReadOnly	Determine whether the user can modify the text in the control.	None
ShowHint	Determine whether the control displays a tooltip.	TComponent
TabOrder	Determine the position of the control in its parent's tab order.	TComponent
TabStop	Determine whether the control is a tab stop.	TComponent
Text	Access the text contained by the mask edit control.	TComponent
Visible	Determine whether the control is visible.	TComponent

TCustomMemo

TCustomMemo descends directly from TCustomEdit and is the abstract base class for all memo controls. Memo controls include the older-style memo control and the rich edit control introduced with Windows 95.

Memo controls are multiline edit boxes, combining functionality similar to the standard edit control with the ability to display more than one line of text.

Table 64-5 displays the properties, methods, and events implemented by TCustomMemo.

Table 64-5 Properties, methods, and events implemented by TCustomMemo, in addition to those inherited from TCustomEdit

Use or Set This...	To Do This...	Inheritance
Create	Create a new memo control.	TComponent
Destroy	Destroy the memo control.	TComponent
Lines	Access the lines of text contained by the control.	None

TMemo

TMemo is a direct descendant of TCustomMemo and publishes many of TCustomMemo's protected properties and methods. TMemo can be thought of as a multiline edit control. TMemo's functionality has been largely improved by the rich edit control, which provides extensive font and paragraph formatting.

Table 64-6 displays the properties, methods, and events implemented by TMemo.

Table 64-6 Properties, methods, and events implemented by TMemo, in addition to those inherited from TCustomMemo

Use or Set This...	To Do This...	Inheritance
Align	Determine how the control aligns with its container.	TComponent
Alignment	Determine how text is aligned within the control.	TComponent
BorderStyle	Determine the border style of the control.	TComponent
Color	Determine the background color of the control.	TComponent
Ctl3D	Determine whether the control displays in a 3D style.	TComponent
DragCursor	Determine the shape of the mouse pointer as it drags an object over the control.	TComponent
DragMode	Determine the drag-and-drop behavior of the control.	TComponent
Enabled	Determine whether the control is enabled.	TComponent
Font	Determine which font is used to render text in the control.	TComponent
HideSelection	Determine whether selected text remains selected when the control loses focus.	None
Lines	Access the lines of text in the control.	TCustomMemo
MaxLength	Determine the maximum length of the text contained by the control.	None
OnChange	Handle the event that occurs when the text in the control is changed.	TComponent
OnClick	Handle the event that occurs when a mouse button is clicked.	TComponent
OnDblClick	Handle the event that occurs when a mouse button is double-clicked.	TComponent
OnDragDrop	Handle the event that occurs when an object is dropped on the control.	TComponent
OnDragOver	Handle the event that occurs when an object is dragged over the control.	TComponent
OnEndDrag	Handle the event that occurs when a drag-and-drop operation is cancelled.	TComponent
OnEnter	Handle the event that occurs when the control receives the focus.	TComponent
OnExit	Handle the event that occurs when the control loses the focus.	TComponent
OnKeyDown	Handle the event that occurs when a key is pressed and held down.	TComponent
OnKeyPress	Handle the event that occurs when a key is pressed.	TComponent
OnKeyUp	Handle the event that occurs when a key is released.	TComponent
OnMouseDown	Handle the event that occurs when a mouse button is pressed and held down.	TComponent
OnMouseMove	Handle the event that occurs when the mouse pointer passes over the control.	TComponent
OnMouseUp	Handle the event that occurs when a mouse button is released.	TComponent
OnStartDrag	Handle the event that occurs when a drag-and-drop operation is started.	TComponent
ParentColor	Determine whether the control uses its parent's ParentColor property.	TComponent
ParentCtl3D	Determine whether the control uses its parent's Ctl3D property.	TComponent
ParentFont	Determine whether the control uses its parent's ParentFont property.	TComponent
ParentShowHint	Determine whether the control uses its parent's ParentShowHint property.	TComponent
PopupMenu	Determine which pop-up menu is associated with the control.	TComponent
ReadOnly	Determine whether the user can modify the text in the control.	None
ScrollBars	Determine whether the control displays scroll bars.	TComponent

Use or Set This...	To Do This...	Inheritance
ShowHint	Determine whether the control displays a tooltip.	TComponent
TabOrder	Determine the position of the control in its parent's tab order.	TComponent
TabStop	Determine whether the control is a tab stop.	TComponent
Visible	Determine whether the control is visible.	TComponent
WantReturns	Determine whether the control handles the ENTER key-press.	None
WantTabs	Determine whether the control handles the TAB key-press.	None
WordWrap	Determine whether text in the control automatically wraps.	None

TCustomRichEdit

TCustomRichEdit descends directly from **TCustomMemo** and is the abstract base class for Delphi's implementation of the rich edit control. All the protected properties and methods of **TCustomRichEdit** are later published by **TRichEdit**.

Table 64-7 displays the properties, methods, and events implemented by **TCustomRichEdit**.

Table 64-7 Properties, methods, and events implemented by TCustomRichEdit, in addition to those inherited from TCustomMemo

Use or Set This...	To Do This...	Inheritance
Create	Create a new rich edit control.	TComponent
DefAttributes	Determine the attributes of default text in the control.	None
Paragraph	Access the paragraph formatting information for the paragraph that contains the cursor.	None
Print	Print the text in the rich edit control.	None
SelAttributes	Access the formatting information for the text that is currently selected.	None

TRichEdit

TRichEdit encapsulates the Win32 rich edit control. A rich edit control is a multiline edit control that provides support for such rich-text features as typeface, color, size, and character formatting, in addition to alignment, tabbing, and indenting. The text contained by a rich edit control is compatible with the RTF file type used by the WordPad word processor that comes with Windows. The contents of a rich edit control can also be printed.

Table 64-8 displays the properties, methods, and events implemented by **TRichEdit**.

Table 64-8 Properties, methods, and events implemented by `TRichEdit`, in addition to those inherited from `TCustomRichEdit`

Use or Set This...	To Do This...	Inheritance
Align	Determine how the control aligns with its container.	TComponent
Alignment	Determine how text is aligned within the control.	TComponent
BorderStyle	Determine the border style of the control.	TComponent
Color	Determine the background color of the control.	TComponent
Ctl3D	Determine whether the control displays in a 3D style.	TComponent
DragMode	Determine the drag-and-drop behavior of the control.	TComponent
Enabled	Determine whether the control is enabled.	TComponent
Font	Determine the font used to render text in the control.	TComponent
HideScrollBars	Determine whether the scroll bars used by the control appear when they are needed.	None
HideSelection	Determine whether selected text in the control remains selected when the control loses the focus.	None
Lines	Access the lines of text contained by the control.	None
MaxLength	Determine the maximum number of characters that can be contained by the rich edit control.	None
OnChange	Handle the event that occurs when the text in the control is changed.	TComponent
OnClick	Handle the event that occurs when a mouse button is clicked.	TComponent
OnDblClick	Handle the event that occurs when a mouse button is double-clicked.	TComponent
OnDragDrop	Handle the event that occurs when an object is dropped on the control.	TComponent
OnDragOver	Handle the event that occurs when an object is dragged over the control.	TComponent
OnEndDrag	Handle the event that occurs when a drag-and-drop operation is cancelled.	TComponent
OnEnter	Handle the event that occurs when the control receives the focus.	TComponent
OnExit	Handle the event that occurs when the control loses the focus.	TComponent
OnKeyDown	Handle the event that occurs when a key is pressed and held down.	TComponent
OnKeyPress	Handle the event that occurs when a key is pressed.	TComponent
OnKeyUp	Handle the event that occurs when a key is released.	TComponent
OnMouseDown	Handle the event that occurs when a mouse button is pressed and held down.	TComponent
OnMouseMove	Handle the event that occurs when the mouse pointer passes over the control.	TComponent
OnMouseUp	Handle the event that occurs when a mouse button is released.	TComponent
OnResizeRequest	Handle the event that occurs when the text of the control is too large to fit within the control.	None
OnSelectionChange	Handle the event that occurs when the selected text in the rich edit control changes.	None
OnStartDrag	Handle the event that occurs when a drag-and-drop operation is started.	TComponent
ParentColor	Determine whether the control uses its parent's Color information.	TComponent
ParentCtl3D	Determine whether the control uses its parent's Ctl3D information.	TComponent

Use or Set This...	To Do This...	Inheritance
ParentFont	Determine whether the control uses its parent's Font information.	TComponent
PlainText	Determine whether the text in the control is plain text or rich text.	None
PopupMenu	Determine which pop-up menu is associated with the rich edit control.	TComponent
ReadOnly	Determine whether the user can modify text in the rich edit control.	None
ScrollBars	Determine whether the control displays scroll bars.	None
ShowHint	Determine whether the control displays a tooltip.	TComponent
TabOrder	Determine the position of the control in its parent's tab order.	TComponent
TabStop	Determine whether the control is a tab stop.	TComponent
Visible	Determine whether the control is visible.	TComponent
WantReturns	Determine whether the control handles ENTER key-presses.	None
WantTabs	Determine whether the control handles TAB key-presses.	None
WordWrap	Determine whether text in the control automatically wraps.	None

AutoSelect PROPERTY

Objects Affected	TEdit
Purpose	The AutoSelect property determines if the text in the edit box is automatically selected when the edit box receives the focus.
Declaration	

```
property AutoSelect: Boolean;
```

Example Syntax

```
Edit1.AutoSelect := False;
```

Description If AutoSelect is True, the text in the edit box is automatically selected when the edit box receives the focus, and the cursor is placed after the last character of text. If it is False, the text is not automatically selected, and the cursor appears at the beginning of the text, at the far left of the edit box.

AutoSelect is True by default.

CharCase PROPERTY

Objects Affected	TEdit, TMaskEdit
Purpose	The CharCase property determines the case of the text in the edit box.
Declaration	

```
property CharCase: TEditCharCase;
```

Figure 64-3 Three edit boxes with different `CharCase` values

Example Syntax

```
procedure TForm1.FormCreate(Sender: TObject);
begin
  Edit1.CharCase := ecNormal;
  Edit2.CharCase := ecUpperCase;
  Edit3.CharCase := ecLowerCase;
end;
```

Description

`CharCase` is type `TEditCharCase`, which is declared as:

`TEditCharCase = (ecNormal, ecUpperCase, ecLowerCase);`

The possible values are described below:

Use This Value...	To Display Edit Box Text As...
ecLowerCase	Lowercase
ecNormal	Mixed case
ecUpperCase	Uppercase

If the edit box displays uppercase characters only—that is, if the `CharCase` property is set to `ecUpperCase`—and the user enters mixed case text, the characters the user enters appear in uppercase.

The default value is `ecNormal`.

Clear METHOD

Objects Affected	All edit controls
Purpose	The `Clear` method erases the text in the edit control.
Declaration	

```
procedure Clear;
```

Example Syntax

```
procedure TForm1.sbClearClick(Sender: TObject);
begin
  Edit4.Clear;
end;
```

ClearSelection METHOD

Objects Affected	All edit controls
Purpose	The `ClearSelection` method erases the section of text currently selected in the edit control.
Declaration	

```
procedure ClearSelection;
```

Example Syntax

```
procedure TForm1.sbClearSelClick(Sender: TObject);
begin
  Edit5.ClearSelection;
end;
```

Description `ClearSelection` erases only currently selected text. If no text is selected, nothing happens.

CopyToClipboard METHOD

Objects Affected	All edit controls
Purpose	The `CopyToClipboard` method copies the selected text in the edit control to the clipboard.
Declaration	

```
procedure CopyToClipboard;
```

Example Syntax

```
procedure TForm1.SpeedButton1Click(Sender: TObject);
begin
  RichEdit1.CutToClipboard;
end;

procedure TForm1.SpeedButton2Click(Sender: TObject);
begin
  RichEdit1.CopyToClipboard;
end;

procedure TForm1.SpeedButton3Click(Sender: TObject);
begin
  RichEdit1.PasteFromClipboard;
end;
```

Description If no text is selected, nothing happens.

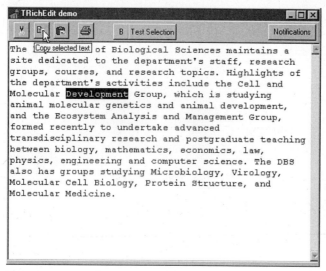

Figure 64-4 In the rich edit demo, three speedbuttons provide cut, copy, and paste facilities

CutToClipboard METHOD

Objects Affected All edit controls

Purpose The CutToClipboard method erases the selected text in the edit control and places it into the clipboard.

Declaration

```
procedure CutToClipboard;
```

Example Syntax

```
procedure TForm1.SpeedButton1Click(Sender: TObject);
begin
  RichEdit1.CutToClipboard;
end;

procedure TForm1.SpeedButton2Click(Sender: TObject);
begin
  RichEdit1.CopyToClipboard;
end;

procedure TForm1.SpeedButton3Click(Sender: TObject);
begin
  RichEdit1.PasteFromClipboard;
end;
```

Description If no text is selected, nothing happens.

DefAttributes PROPERTY

Objects Affected   All rich edit controls

Purpose   The DefAttributes property describes the default attributes of text in the rich edit control.

Declaration

```
property DefAttributes: TTextAttributes;
```

Example Syntax

```
procedure TForm1.FormCreate(Sender: TObject);
begin
  with RichEdit1.DefAttributes do
  begin
    Color := clBlack;
    Name := 'Courier New';
    Size := 9;
  end
end;
```

Description   DefAttributes is type TTextAttributes, which is described in Chapter 18, "TTextAttributes." Basically, DefAttributes has properties such as Color, Name, Style, and Size that determine the default attributes of text in the rich edit control.

EditMask PROPERTY

Objects Affected   TMaskEdit

Purpose   The EditMask property enables you to limit the type of input accepted into a mask edit control.

Declaration

```
property EditMask: string;
```

Example Syntax

```
procedure TForm1.FormCreate(Sender: TObject);
begin
  MaskEdit1.EditMask :='0000000000';
  MaskEdit1.Text := '';
  MaskEdit1.AutoSelect := False;
end;
```

Description   The EditMask property restricts the characters the user can enter into a mask edit control. See Figure 64-5. If the user enters an invalid character, it is not accepted and does not appear. Since EditMask is a string, you assign it to a string of characters representing the valid characters the mask edit accepts. In the above example, the mask edit is told to accept only whole number values.

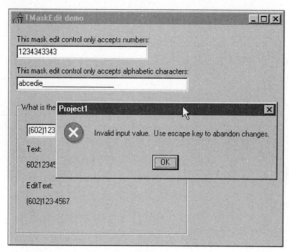

Figure 64-5 The `EditMask` property is used to limit input

A mask consists of three fields. Semicolon characters separate each field. The first field is the mask itself. The second field is a single character that determines whether the literal characters of the mask are considered part of the data. The third field is the character used to represent a blank character in the mask; this is an underscore by default. Default values for the second and third fields are used if none are specified. Creating edit masks is fairly difficult using code. The following table describes the special characters used by `EditMask`:

This Character...	Has This Effect...
!	Leading blanks don't appear in the data. If the ! character is not present, trailing blanks don't appear in the data.
>	Any characters that follow the > character are uppercase until the end of the mask or until a < character is encountered.
<	Any characters that follow the < character are lowercase until the end of the mask or until a > character is encountered.
<>	No case checking occurs.
\	The character that follows a \ character is a literal character.
L	An alphabetic character (A-Z) is required in this position.
l	An alphabetic character (A-Z) is permitted, but not required, in this position.
A	An alphanumeric character (A-Z, a-z, 0-9) is required in this position.
a	An alphanumeric character (A-Z, a-z, 0-9) is permitted, but not required, in this position.
C	A character is required in this position.
c	A character is permitted, but not required, in this position.

This Character...	Has This Effect...
0	A numeric character (0-9) is required in this position.
9	A numeric character (0-9) is permitted, but not required, in this position.
#	A numeric character (0-9) or a plus or minus sign is permitted, but not required, in this position.
:	Used to separate hours, minutes, and seconds in times.
/	Used to separate months, days, and years in dates.
;	Used to separate masks.
_	Inserts a blank space in the edit box that will be automatically skipped over as the user inputs InputMask Editor (see below).

It is easiest to modify the edit mask property in the Delphi IDE. If you double-click the **EditMask** property in the Object Inspector, the InputMask Editor appears, as shown in Figure 64-6.

EditText PROPERTY

Objects Affected   All mask edit controls

Purpose   The **EditText** property is the text the user sees in the mask edit box at run time.

Declaration

```
property EditText: string;
```

Example Syntax

```
procedure TForm1.MaskEdit3Change(Sender: TObject);
begin
  lblTextValue.Caption := MaskEdit3.Text;
  lblEditTextValue.Caption := MaskEdit3.EditText;
end;
```

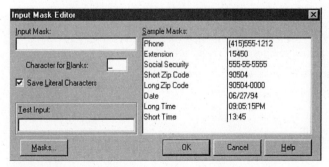

Figure 64-6 The InputMask Editor enables you to easily modify edit masks

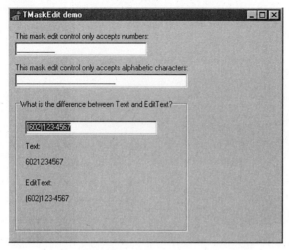

Figure 64-7 The difference between `Text` and `EditText`

Description
`EditText` is a run-time-only property containing the text the user sees in the mask edit box. The `Text` property of a mask edit box contains a different value than `EditText`, if literal mask characters are saved and/or a special character is used to represent blanks (such as an underscore). Otherwise, `Text` and `EditText` contain the same value.

GetSelTextBuf METHOD

Objects Affected All edit controls

Purpose The `GetSelTextBuf` method copies the selected text in the edit control into a text buffer.

Declaration

```
function GetSelTextBuf(Buffer: PChar; BufSize: Integer): Integer;
```

Parameters

Buffer The text buffer to which you are copying the selected text.

BufSize The size of the text buffer.

Example Syntax

```
var
  Form1: TForm1;
  MyBuf: PChar;
  MyBufSize: Integer;

// . . .
```

```
// Copy the selected text in the edit box to a text buffer
procedure TForm1.sbCopyToClick(Sender: TObject);
begin
  MyBufSize := Edit6.SelLength + 1;
  GetMem(MyBuf, MyBufSize);
  Edit6.GetSelTextBuf(MyBuf, MyBufSize);
  lblTextBuf.Caption := StrPas(MyBuf);
end;
```

Description   GetSelTextBuf copies the selected text in the edit box to the text buffer specified by the *Buffer* parameter. The *BufSize* parameter specifies the size of the buffer, which you typically set to the length of the text to copy. If the selected text is larger than the buffer, GetSelTextBuf copies *BufSize* - 1 characters. GetSelTextBuf returns the number of characters copied.

The SetSelTextBuf method copies text from a buffer to an edit control.

HideScrollBars PROPERTY

Objects Affected   TRichEdit

Purpose   The HideScrollBars property determines whether scroll bars automatically appear when the contained text is too long to display in the visible portion of the rich edit control.

Declaration

```
property HideScrollBars: Boolean;
```

Example Syntax

```
procedure TForm1.FormCreate(Sender: TObject);
begin
  RichEdit1.ScrollBars := ssVertical;
  RichEdit1.HideScrollBars := False;
end;
```

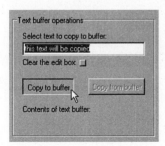

Figure 64-8   Copying text to and from a buffer and edit control

Description   If `HideScrollBars` is `True`, no scroll bars appear if the text in the rich edit control needs to be scrolled. If `HideScrollBars` is `False`, and the `ScrollBars` property is `ssBoth`, `ssHorizontal`, or `ssVertical`, scroll bars appear if the text needs to be scrolled. If `HideScrollBars` is `False` and `ScrollBars` is `ssNone`, no scroll bars appear.

The default value is `True`.

HideSelection PROPERTY

Objects Affected   `TEdit`, `TMemo`, `TRichEdit`

Purpose   The `HideSelection` property determines whether selected text in the control remains selected when the focus shifts to another control.

Declaration

```
property HideSelection: Boolean;
```

Example Syntax

```
Edit1.HideSelection := False;
```

Description   If `HideSelection` is `True`, selected text no longer appears selected when the focus shifts to another control. If it is `False`, selected text remains selected when the focus shifts to another control.

The default value is `True`.

IsMasked PROPERTY

Objects Affected   All mask edit controls

Purpose   The `IsMasked` property determines whether a mask exists for the mask edit control.

Declaration

```
property IsMasked: Boolean;
```

Example Syntax

```
If MaskEdit1.IsMasked = True then
  MaskEdit1.EditMask := '';
```

Description   If `IsMasked` is `True`, a mask exists for the mask edit control, as specified by the `EditMask` property. If `EditMask` has no value, `IsMasked` is `False` and no mask is specified.

Lines PROPERTY

Objects Affected	All memo controls, **TRichEdit**
Purpose	The **Lines** property specifies the lines of text appearing in the memo or rich edit control.
Declaration	

```
property Lines: TStrings;
```

Description	**Lines** is type **TStrings**, which is discussed in Chapter 25.

MaxLength PROPERTY

Objects Affected	All edit controls
Purpose	The **MaxLength** property specifies the maximum number of characters that can be entered in the edit control.
Declaration	

```
property MaxLength: Integer;
```

Example Syntax

```
RichEdit1.MaxLength := 10000;
```

Description MaxLength is an integer, so the theoretical range is **-MaxInt** to **MaxInt**. Realistically, any value from **1** to **MaxInt** results in that value determining the maximum number of allowable characters in the edit control. A value of **0** indicates there is no limit to the number of characters the control can contain.

The default value is 0.

Modified PROPERTY

Objects Affected	All edit controls
Purpose	The **Modified** property determines whether the edit control has been modified.
Declaration	

```
property Modified: Boolean;
```

Example Syntax

```
procedure TForm1.Timer1Timer(Sender: TObject);
begin
if Edit7.Modified = True then
  begin
```

continued on next page

continued from previous page

```
        lblModified.Caption := 'Yes';
        Edit7.Modified := False
      end
    else lblModified.Caption := 'No'
end;
```

Description   `Modified` is a run-time-only property that determines whether the edit control has been modified since it was created or since the `Modified` property was last set to `False`. If `Modified` is `True`, the edit control has been modified. If it is `False`, the control has not been modified.

OnResizeRequest EVENT

Objects Affected   `TRichEdit`

Purpose   The `OnResizeRequest` event occurs when the text in the control has grown larger than the control itself.

Declaration

```
property OnResizeRequest: TRichEditResizeEvent;
```

Example Syntax

```
// Handle the OnResizeRequest event  - when the text in the rich edit
// control exceeds the size of the control, resize the control to
// accommodate the new size of the text
procedure TForm1.RichEdit1ResizeRequest(Sender: TObject; Rect: TRect);
begin
  RichEdit1.BoundsRect := Rect;
end;
```

Description   `OnResizeRequest` is type `TRichEditResizeEvent`, which is declared as:

```
TRichEditResizeEvent = procedure (Sender: TObject; Rect: TRect) of
                                                            object;
```

The *Rect* parameter specifies the size of the rectangle needed to contain the text. In the example above, this rectangle is assigned to the rich edit bounding rectangle, thus resizing the rich edit control.

OnSelectionChange EVENT

Objects Affected   `TRichEdit`

Purpose   The `OnSelectionChange` event occurs when the selected text in the rich edit control changes.

Declaration

```
property OnSelectionChange: TNotifyEvent;
```

Example Syntax

```
var
  Form1: TForm1;
  GetNotifications: Boolean;

implementation

procedure TForm1.FormCreate(Sender: TObject);
begin
  GetNotifications := False;
end;

procedure TForm1.Button1Click(Sender: TObject);
begin
  if GetNotifications = True then
    GetNotifications := False
  else GetNotifications := True;
end;

procedure TForm1.RichEdit1SelectionChange(Sender: TObject);
begin
  if GetNotifications = True then
    Application.MessageBox('Selection text has changed!',
                           'Selection Text Notification',
                           MB_OK);
end;
```

Description

The user can change the selected text by pressing a key on the keyboard or by using the mouse. An example would be deleting the selected text by pressing the DELETE key. If no text is selected, the cursor position is considered the selected text.

OnSelectionChange is type **TNotifyEvent**, the standard event type for events that have no parameters. See Figure 64-9.

It is declared as

```
TNotifyEvent = procedure (Sender: TObject) of object;
```

Paragraph PROPERTY

Objects Affected   All rich edit controls

Purpose   The **Paragraph** property describes the formatting information for the selected paragraph.

Declaration

```
property Paragraph: TParaAttributes;
```

Description   The selected paragraph is the paragraph containing the selected text or, if no text is currently selected, the paragraph containing the cursor. **Paragraph** is type **TParaAttributes**, which is described in Chapter 16.

Paragraph is a run-time, read-only property.

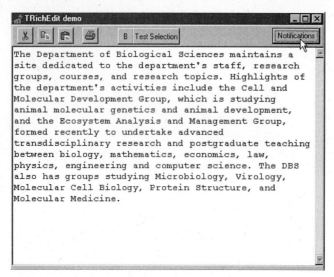

Figure 64-9 The Notifications button toggles whether
`OnSelectionChange` events trigger a message box

PasswordChar PROPERTY

Objects Affected TEdit, TMaskEdit

Purpose The **PasswordChar** property determines what character, if any, is displayed when the edit control is used for password entry.

Declaration

```
property PasswordChar: Char;
```

Example Syntax

```
procedure TForm1.FormCreate(Sender: TObject);
begin
  Edit8.PasswordChar := '*';
end;

procedure TForm1.Edit8KeyPress(Sender: TObject; var Key: Char);
begin
  if Key = #13 then
  begin
    Application.MessageBox('Password Accepted!',
                           'Password Notification', MB_OK);
    Edit8.Clear;
  end
end;
```

Description If **PasswordChar** is the Null character (#0), all text entered in that edit control appears normal, and the edit box functions as you would expect. If

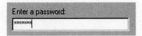

Figure 64-10 When the user types text in the
edit box, each character is replaced by a star.
When ⌈ENTER⌋ is pressed, the password is
evaluated.

you want to use the edit control for password entry, however, you can set
the **PasswordChar** to any valid character value (for instance, the * character). See Figure 64-10. This way, any characters typed appear as the
preselected character, hiding the actual input from anyone looking on.

PasteFromClipboard METHOD

Objects Affected   All edit controls

Purpose   The **PasteFromClipboard** method pastes text in the clipboard to the current cursor location in the edit control.

Declaration

```
procedure PasteFromClipboard;
```

Example Syntax

```
procedure TForm1.SpeedButton1Click(Sender: TObject);
begin
  RichEdit1.CutToClipboard;
end;

procedure TForm1.SpeedButton2Click(Sender: TObject);
begin
  RichEdit1.CopyToClipboard;
end;

procedure TForm1.SpeedButton3Click(Sender: TObject);
begin
  RichEdit1.PasteFromClipboard;
end;
```

Description   If text is selected in the edit control, the pasted text replaces the selected
text. Otherwise, the pasted text appears at the current cursor location. If
there is no text in the clipboard, nothing happens.

PlainText PROPERTY

Objects Affected   TRichEdit

Purpose   The **PlainText** property determines whether text in the rich edit control is
plain or rich text.

Declaration

```
property PlainText: Boolean;
```

Example Syntax

```
RichEdit1.PlainText := True;
```

Description   If `PlainText` is `True`, the rich edit control treats the text it contains as plain text. If it is `False`, the text is treated as rich text and can contain all the formatting features available to RTF.

The default value is `False`.

Print METHOD

Objects Affected	All rich edit controls
Purpose	The `Print` method prints the contents of the rich edit control. Figure 64-11 shows the print button.

Declaration

```
procedure Print(const Caption: string);
```

Parameters

Caption   The title appearing at the top of the printed page.

Example Syntax

```
procedure TForm1.SpeedButton4Click(Sender: TObject);
begin
  RichEdit1.Print('Sample TRichEdit.Print document');
end;
```

ReadOnly PROPERTY

Objects Affected	TEdit, TMaskEdit, TMemo, TRichEdit
Purpose	The `ReadOnly` property determines whether the text contained by the control can be modified by the user.

Declaration

```
property ReadOnly: Boolean;
```

Example Syntax

```
Edit1.ReadOnly := True;
```

Description   If `ReadOnly` is `True`, the user cannot edit the text in the control. If it is `False`, the text can be modified.

The default value is `False`.

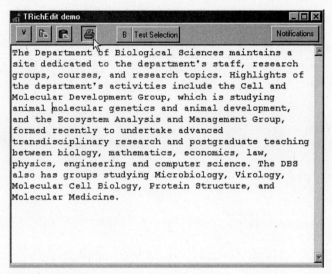

Figure 64-11   Pressing the print button in this demo
TRichEdit program calls the Print method

ScrollBars PROPERTY

Objects Affected   TRichEdit, TMemo

Purpose   The ScrollBars property determines whether the control has scroll bars.

Declaration

```
property ScrollBars: TScrollStyle;
```

Example Syntax

```
procedure TForm1.FormCreate(Sender: TObject);
begin
  RichEdit1.ScrollBars := ssVertical;
  RichEdit1.HideScrollBars := False;
end;
```

Description   ScrollBars is type TScrollStyle, which is declared as:

```
TScrollStyle = (ssNone, ssHorizontal, ssVertical, ssBoth);
```

If ScrollBars is ssNone, there are no scroll bars on the control. To display
horizontal or vertical scroll bars, set ScrollBars to ssHorizontal or
ssVertical, respectively. If you want to display both types of scroll bars,
use ssBoth.

ScrollBars is ssNone by default.

See HideScrollBars for more information.

SelAttributes PROPERTY

Objects Affected	All rich edit controls
Purpose	The `SelAttributes` property determines the attributes of selected text in the rich edit control.
Declaration	

```
property SelAttributes: TTextAttributes;
```

Example Syntax

```
// Change selected text to 12-point red type
procedure TForm1.RichEdit1SelectionChange(Sender: TObject);
begin
  RichEdit1.SelAttributes.Size := 12;
  RichEdit1.SelAttributes.Color := clRed;
end;
```

Description   `SelAttributes` is type `TTextAttributes`, which is described in Chapter 18.

SelectAll METHOD

Objects Affected	All edit controls
Purpose	The `SelectAll` method selects all the text in the edit control.
Declaration	

```
procedure SelectAll;
```

Example Syntax

```
procedure TForm1.sbSelectAllClick(Sender: TObject);
begin
  Form1.FocusControl(Edit9);
  Edit9.SelectAll;
end;
```

Description   You can select portions of the text using the `SelLength` and `SelStart` properties.

SelLength AND SelStart PROPERTIES

Objects Affected	All edit controls
Purpose	The `SelLength` property contains the length, in characters, of the selected text in the edit control. The `SelStart` property determines the starting position of the selected text.
Declaration	

```
property SelLength: Integer;
property SelStart: Integer;
```

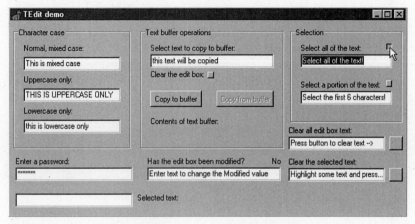

Figure 64-12   Selecting all the text in an edit control

Example Syntax

```
procedure TForm1.sbSelectSomeClick(Sender: TObject);
begin
  Form1.FocusControl(Edit10);
  Edit10.SelStart := 0;
  Edit10.SelLength := 6;
end;
```

Description   You can use the **SelLength** property with **SelStart** to select a portion of the text in the edit control. First, assign the positional value of the character at which you want to start the selection to **SelStart**. Then, assign the number of characters you want selected to **SelLength**. This is demonstrated in the example syntax above. Remember that the first character in a string exists at index position 0.

SelText PROPERTY

Objects Affected   All edit controls

Purpose   The **SelText** property contains the selected text in the edit control. See Figure 64-12.

Declaration

```
property SelText: string;
```

Example Syntax

```
lblSelectedText.Caption := Edit11.SelText;
```

Description   If no text is selected, **SelText** contains an empty string.

SetSelTextBuf METHOD

Objects Affected   All edit controls

Purpose   The `SetSelTextBuf` method copies the text from a buffer into the selected portion of the edit control.

Declaration

```
procedure SetSelTextBuf(Buffer: PChar);
```

Parameters

Buffer   The buffer containing the text to copy.

Example Syntax

```
var
  Form1: TForm1;
  MyBuf: PChar;
  MyBufSize: Integer;

// . . .

// Copy selected text from the edit box to the buffer:
procedure TForm1.sbCopyToClick(Sender: TObject);
begin
  MyBufSize := Edit6.SelLength + 1;
  GetMem(MyBuf, MyBufSize);
  Edit6.GetSelTextBuf(MyBuf, MyBufSize);
  lblTextBuf.Caption := StrPas(MyBuf);
end;

// Copy from the buffer to the edit box:
procedure TForm1.sbCopyFromClick(Sender: TObject);
begin
  Edit6.SetSelTextBuf(MyBuf);
end;
```

Description   `SetSelTextBuf` copies text from the buffer specified by the *Buffer* parameter into the selected region in the edit control. If text is selected in the edit control, the text in the buffer replaces that text. If no text is selected, the text from the buffer is inserted at the cursor position.

WantReturns PROPERTY

Objects Affected   TMemo, TRichEdit

Purpose   The `WantReturns` property determines whether the user can press the ENTER key to begin a new line of text in the memo or rich edit control.

Declaration

```
property WantReturns: Boolean;
```

Example Syntax

```
procedure TForm1.FormCreate(Sender: TObject);
begin
  // Let the form handle enter key presses
  RichEdit1.WantReturns := False;
  // Handle tabs
  RichEdit1.WantTabs := True;
end;
```

Description

If WantReturns is True and the user presses ENTER, a return character is entered in the memo or rich edit control and a new line of text begins. If WantReturns is False, a new line is not started and the key-press is handled by the form containing the control.

The default value is True.

WantTabs PROPERTY

Objects Affected TMemo, TRichEdit

Purpose The WantTabs property determines whether the tab key is enabled while the user enters text in the memo or rich edit control.

Declaration

```
property WantTabs: Boolean;
```

Example Syntax

```
procedure TForm1.FormCreate(Sender: TObject);
begin
  // Let the form handle enter key presses
  RichEdit1.WantReturns := False;
  // Handle tabs
  RichEdit1.WantTabs := True;
end;
```

Description

If WantTabs is True, the tab key functions as it does in any word processing program while the user enters text in the control—it tabs text forward. If it is False, the tab key-press is handled by the form normally containing the control and functions, moving the focus from control to control on the form.

The default value is False.

WordWrap PROPERTY

Objects Affected TMemo, TRichEdit

Purpose The WordWrap property determines if lines of text in the memo or rich edit control wrap at the right edge of the control.

Declaration

```
property WordWrap: Boolean;
```

Example Syntax

```
RichEdit1.WordWrap := False;
```

Description

If `WordWrap` is `True`, lines of text wrap when they encounter the right edge of the control. If `WordWrap` is `False`, lines of text scroll past the edge of the control if they are longer than the control's width. In this event, you can set the `ScrollBars` property to an appropriate value that enables the user to scroll the control so he or she can view all the text.

The default value is `True`.

65

TCustomControl AND ITS DESCENDANTS

Delphi custom controls are specialized windowed controls. They are the most refined group of classes in the VCL hierarchy, and you should derive your own windowed controls from **TCustomControl** or its descendants.

This chapter introduces the final branch of the VCL tree, a hodge-podge collection of classes largely unrelated except for their ability to easily display themselves.

TCustomControl

TCustomControl descends directly from **TWinControl** and is the abstract base class for Delphi custom controls.

Figure 65-1 shows a condensed outline of the **TCustomControl** branch of the VCL. Table 65-1 displays the properties, methods, and events implemented by **TCustomControl**.

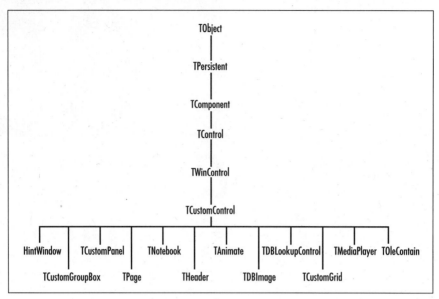

Figure 65-1 The TCustomControl branch of the VCL (condensed)

Table 65-1 Properties, methods, and events implemented by TCustomControl

Use or Set This...	To Do This...	Inheritance
Align	Determine how the control is aligned within its parent.	TControl
Assign	Assign one persistent object to another.	TPersistent
BeginDrag	Begin a manual drag operation.	TControl
BoundsRect	Determine the boundary rectangle occupied by the control.	TControl
BringToFront	Bring the control to the front of the z-order.	TControl
Brush	Determine the color and pattern used for the windowed control background.	TComponent
CanFocus	Determine whether the windowed control can receive the focus.	TWinControl
Caption	Label the control with a text string.	TControl
ClassName	Get the name of the object's class.	TObject
ClassParent	Get the object's parent class.	TObject
ClassType	Get the object's actual type.	TObject
ClientHeight	Determine the control's client height.	TControl
ClientOrigin	Determine the upper-left position of the control's client area.	TControl
ClientRect	Determine the rectangle occupied by the control's client area.	TControl
ClientToScreen	Convert control (local) coordinates to screen coordinates.	TControl
ClientWidth	Determine the width of the control's client area.	TControl
Color	Determine the color of the windowed control.	TControl
ComponentCount	Determine the number of owned components.	TComponent
ComponentIndex	Determine the index of the component in its owner's Components list.	TComponent

Use or Set This...	To Do This...	Inheritance
Components	Determine the list of owned components.	TComponent
ComponentState	Determine the state of the current component.	TComponent
ContainsControl	Determine whether the specified control is contained by windowed control.	TWinControl
ControlAtPos	Determine the control contained at a specified position.	TWinControl
ControlCount	Determine the number of controls contained by the windowed control.	TWinControl
Controls	Access the controls contained by the windowed control using their positions in an array.	TWinControl
ControlState	Determine the state of the control at any given time.	TControl
ControlStyle	Determine what attributes are present in the control.	TControl
Create	Create a new component.	TObject
Ctl3D	Determine whether the windowed control displays in 3D.	TWinControl
Cursor	Determine what image is used for the cursor over the control.	TControl
Destroy	Destroy the component.	TObject
DestroyComponents	Destroy all the components owned by the component.	TComponent
Destroying	Notify the component that it is being destroyed.	TComponent
DragCursor	Determine the shape of the mouse cursor as it drags an object over the control.	TControl
Dragging	Determine whether the control is being dragged.	TControl
DragMode	Determine the drag-and-drop behavior of the control.	TControl
Enabled	Determine whether the control is enabled.	TControl
EndDrag	End or cancel a manual drag operation.	TControl
FindComponent	Find a component in the Components array list.	TComponent
Focused	Determine whether the windowed control has the focus.	TControl
Font	Determine the font used to render text on the control.	TControl
Free	Safely destroy the object.	TObject
GetTextBuf	Copy the text of the control into a buffer.	TControl
GetTextLen	Get the length of the text of the control.	TControl
Handle	Obtain a handle to the windowed control.	TComponent
HandleAllocated	Determine if a handle is allocated for the windowed control.	TWinControl
Height	Determine the height of the control.	TControl
HelpContext	Determine the help context ID of the windowed control.	TComponent
Hide	Make the control invisible.	TControl
Hint	Determine the text that displays in a tooltip for the control.	TControl
InheritsFrom	Determine if the object is descended from a certain class.	TObject
InsertControl	Insert a control into the windowed control's Controls array.	TWinControl
InstanceSize	Determine the amount of memory allocated for the object.	TObject
Invalidate	Force the control to be repainted as soon as possible.	TControl
Left	Determine the left edge of the control within its container.	TControl
Name	Determine the name of the component.	TComponent
OnClick	Handle the event that occurs when a mouse button is clicked.	TControl

continued on next page

continued from previous page

Use or Set This...	To Do This...	Inheritance
OnDblClick	Handle the event that occurs when a mouse button is double-clicked.	TControl
OnDragDrop	Handle the event that occurs when an object is dropped on the control.	TControl
OnDragOver	Handle the event that occurs when an object is dragged over the control.	TControl
OnEndDrag	Handle the event that occurs when a drag-and-drop operation is cancelled.	TControl
OnEnter	Handle the event that occurs when the windowed control receives the focus.	TWinControl
OnExit	Handle the event that occurs when the windowed control loses the focus.	TWinControl
OnKeyDown	Handle the event that occurs when a key is pressed down and not immediately released while the windowed control has the focus.	TWinControl
OnKeyPress	Handle the event that occurs when a key is pressed while the windowed control has the focus.	TWinControl
OnKeyUp	Handle the event that occurs when a key is released while the windowed control has the focus.	TWinControl
OnMouseDown	Handle the event that occurs when a mouse button is held down and not immediately released.	TControl
OnMouseMove	Handle the event that occurs when the cursor moves over the control.	TControl
OnMouseUp	Handle the event that occurs when a mouse button is released.	TControl
OnStartDrag	Handle the event that occurs when a drag-and-drop operation is started.	TControl
Owner	Determine the owner of the component.	TComponent
Parent	Determine the parent, or container, of the control.	TControl
ParentColor	Determine whether the Color information of the control's parent is used.	TControl
ParentCtl3D	Determine whether the windowed control uses its parent's Ctl3D settings.	TWinControl
ParentFont	Determine whether the Font information of the control's parent is used.	TControl
ParentShowHint	Determine whether the ShowHint information of the control's parent is used.	TControl
PopupMenu	Determine which pop-up menu is associated with the control.	TControl
Refresh	Erase the control and repaint it.	TControl
RemoveControl	Remove the specified control from the windowed control's Controls array.	TWinControl
Repaint	Repaint the control.	TControl
ScaleBy	Resize the windowed control.	TWinControl
ScreenToClient	Convert screen coordinates to client (control) coordinates.	TControl
SendToBack	Send the control to the end of the z-order.	TControl
SetBounds	Determine the coordinates of the control's bounding rectangle.	TControl
SetFocus	Set the focus to the windowed control.	TWinControl
SetTextBuf	Set the text of the control to the text in a buffer.	TControl
Show	Make the control visible.	TControl
ShowHint	Enable tooltips for the control.	TControl
Showing	Determine whether the windowed control is currently showing onscreen.	TComponent
TabOrder	Determine the tab order of the windowed control.	TWinControl
TabStop	Determine whether the windowed control is in the tab order.	TWinControl
Tag	Store an additional integer value with the component.	TComponent

Use or Set This...	To Do This...	Inheritance
Text	Access the changeable text on the control.	TControl
Top	Determine the upper edge of the control.	TControl
Update	Called automatically by Refresh.	TControl
Visible	Determine whether the control is visible.	TControl
Width	Determine the width of the control.	TControl

TMediaPlayer

TMediaPlayer descends directly from **TCustomControl** and provides a Delphi interface to the Win32 MCI (Media Control Interface) APIs. The component is a set of buttons providing a control panel for multimedia devices like CD-Audio, AVI movie files, and WAV sound files. The media player is shown in Figure 65-2.

Figure 65-2 The Delphi media player

The media player provides an extensive collection of properties and methods enabling you to manipulate multimedia devices and file formats with support for playing, recording, pausing, stepping and skipping tracks, and requesting device identification.

Table 65-2 displays the properties, methods, and events implemented by **TMediaPlayer**.

Table 65-2 Properties, methods, and events implemented by TMediaPlayer, in addition to the properties and methods introduced by TCustomControl

Use or Set This...	To Do This...	Inheritance
AutoEnable	Determine whether individual buttons on the media player are automatically enabled and disabled.	None
AutoOpen	Determine whether the media player is automatically opened when the application is started.	None
AutoRewind	Determine whether the media player rewinds the medium before playing or recording.	None
Back	Move the position back a number of frames.	None
Capabilities	Determine the capabilities of the open device.	None
Close	Close the open device.	None
ColoredButtons	Determine whether the media player buttons are colored.	None

continued on next page

continued from previous page

Use or Set This...	To Do This...	Inheritance
Create	Create a new media player control.	TComponent
Destroy	Destroy the media player.	TComponent
DeviceID	Determine whether a device is currently open.	None
DeviceType	Determine the type of device that is open.	None
Display	Determine which windowed control is used for output.	None
DisplayRect	Determine which portion of the display control is used for output.	None
Eject	Eject the open medium.	None
Enabled	Determine whether the media player is enabled.	TComponent
EnabledButtons	Determine which buttons on the media player are enabled.	None
EndPos	Specify the position that recording or playing will stop.	None
Error	Determine which MCI error code was returned by the last method call.	None
ErrorMessage	Determine the MCI error message that was returned by the last method call.	None
FileName	Determine the media file that will be opened by the player.	None
Frames	Determine the number of frames used by Step and Back.	None
Length	Determine the length of the medium.	None
Mode	Determine the mode of the open multimedia device.	None
Next	Move the position to the next track.	None
Notify	Determine whether OnNotify events will be handled.	None
NotifyValue	Determine the result of the previously called media method.	None
OnClick	Handle the event that occurs when the media player is clicked.	TComponent
OnEnter	Handle the event that occurs when the media player gains the focus.	TComponent
OnExit	Handle the event that occurs when the media player loses the focus.	TComponent
OnNotify	Handle the event that occurs when a media player method is finished.	None
OnPostClick	Handle the event that occurs when a button on the media player is clicked.	None
Open	Open a new medium.	None
ParentShowHint	Determine whether the control uses its parent's ShowHint information.	TComponent
Pause	Pause the medium or unpause if already paused.	None
PauseOnly	Pause the medium.	None
Play	Play the medium.	None
PopupMenu	Determine which pop-up menu is associated with the player.	TComponent
Position	Determine the current position in the open medium.	None
Previous	Set the current position to the beginning of the previous track.	None
Resume	Resume playing if the medium is paused.	None
Rewind	Set the current position to the beginning of the medium.	None
Save	Save the medium to the file specified by FileName.	None
Shareable	Determine whether more than one application can share the same multimedia device.	None
ShowHint	Determine whether the player displays a tooltip.	TComponent
Start	Determine the starting position in the medium.	None

Use or Set This...	To Do This...	Inheritance
StartPos	Specify a particular starting position in the medium.	None
StartRecording	Start recording at the current position in the medium.	None
Step	Step forward a number of frames.	None
Stop	Stop playing or recording.	None
TabOrder	Determine whether the player is in its parent's tab order.	TComponent
TabStop	Determine whether the player is a tab stop.	TComponent
TimeFormat	Determine the time format used by the player.	None
TrackLength	Determine the length of a specified track.	None
TrackPosition	Determine the current position.	None
Tracks	Determine the number of tracks in the medium.	None
Visible	Determine whether the player is visible.	TComponent
VisibleButtons	Determine which media player buttons are visible.	None
Wait	Determine when media player methods return control to the application.	None

AutoEnable PROPERTY

Objects Affected TMediaPlayer

Purpose The **AutoEnable** property determines whether the media player automatically enables and disables its buttons.

Declaration

```
property AutoEnable: Boolean;
```

Example Syntax

```
MediaPlayer1.AutoEnable := False;
```

Description If **AutoEnable** is **True**, the media player automatically enables or disables its individual buttons. It determines which buttons are appropriate depending on the mode it's in and the device it's manipulating. If **AutoEnable** is **False**, the media player does not automatically enable and disable buttons, so you have to code this manually with the **EnabledButtons** property.

AutoEnable overrides **EnabledButtons** if **AutoEnable** is **True**.

AutoEnable is **True** by default.

AutoOpen PROPERTY

Objects Affected TMediaPlayer

Purpose The **AutoOpen** property determines whether the media player automatically opens when the application runs.

1155

Declaration

```
property AutoOpen: Boolean;
```

Example Syntax

```
MediaPlayer1.AutoOpen := True;
```

Description

If `AutoOpen` is `True`, the media player opens when the application is run, and it tries to open the multimedia device specified by the `DeviceType` property when the form containing it is created at run time. If `AutoOpen` is `False`, the media player does not open, and a multimedia device is not open until the `Open` method is called.

`AutoOpen` is `False` by default.

AutoRewind PROPERTY

Objects Affected	`TMediaPlayer`
Purpose	The `AutoRewind` property determines whether the multimedia device rewinds before playing or recording.

Declaration

```
property AutoRewind: Boolean;
```

Example Syntax

```
MediaPlayer1.AutoRewind := False;
```

Description

If `AutoRewind` is `True`, the position of the multimedia device moves to the beginning when the `Play` or `StartRecording` methods are called. If `AutoRewind` is `False`, playing or recording starts at the current position.

`AutoRewind` has no effect if the `StartPos` or `EndPos` properties are assigned values, or if the multimedia device uses tracks.

The default value is `True`.

Back METHOD

Objects Affected	`TMediaPlayer`
Purpose	The `Back` method steps back a number of frames in the current medium.

Declaration

```
procedure Back;
```

Example Syntax

```
procedure TForm1.sbBackClick(Sender: TObject);
begin
  MediaPlayer1.Back;
end;
```

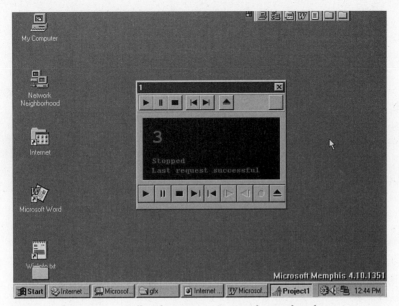

Figure 65-3 Using toolbar buttons to access the media player

Description   The number of frames stepped is determined by the **Frames** property. The
                      Back method is called when the media player's Back button is pressed at
                      run time.

Capabilities PROPERTY

Objects Affected   TMediaPlayer

Purpose   The **Capabilities** property determines the capabilities of the current mul-
                       timedia device.

Declaration

```
property Capabilities: TMPDevCapsSet;
```

Example Syntax

```
procedure TForm1.Capabilities1Click(Sender: TObject);
var Caps: String;
begin
  Caps := 'Capabilities: ';

  if mpCanEject in MediaPlayer1.Capabilities then
    Caps := Caps + 'can eject ';
  if mpCanPlay in MediaPlayer1.Capabilities then
    Caps := Caps + 'can play ';
  if mpCanRecord in MediaPlayer1.Capabilities then
    Caps := Caps + 'can record ';
```

continued on next page

continued from previous page

```
        if mpCanStep in MediaPlayer1.Capabilities then
          Caps := Caps + 'can step ';
        if mpUsesWindow in MediaPlayer1.Capabilities then
          Caps := Caps + 'uses a window for output ';

        Application.MessageBox(PChar(Caps), 'Device Capabilities', MB_OK);
      end;
```

Description The capabilities of the multimedia device are determined when it is opened. `Capabilities` is type `TMPDevCapSet`, which is declared as:

```
TMPDevCapsSet = set of TMPDevCaps;
TMPDevCaps = (mpCanStep, mpCanEject, mpCanPlay, mpCanRecord,
              mpUsesWindows);
```

It is a set of the capabilities described in the following table:

This Capability	Means the Multimedia Device Can...
mpCanEject	Eject media.
mpCanPlay	Play media.
mpCanRecord	Record media.
mpCanStep	Step forward or backward within media.
mpUsesWindow	Use a window for displaying output.

Close METHOD

Objects Affected `TMediaPlayer`

Purpose The `Close` method closes the open multimedia device.

Declaration

```
procedure Close;
```

Description `Close` is automatically called when your application terminates. However, you should call `Close` when you are done using a multimedia resource.

Figure 65-4 This dialog displays when you poll the capabilities of the CD-Audio device

ColoredButtons PROPERTY

Objects Affected	`TMediaPlayer`
Purpose	The `ColoredButtons` property determines which buttons on the media player are colored.
Declaration	

```
property ColoredButtons: TButtonSet;
```

Example Syntax

```
procedure TForm1.FormCreate(Sender: TObject);
begin
  MediaPlayer1.ColoredButtons := [];
end;
```

Description `ColoredButtons` is type `TButtonSet`, which is a set of the buttons in the media control:

```
TButtonSet = set of TMPBtnType;
TMPBtnType = (btPlay, btPause, btStop, btNext, btPrev, btStep, btBack,
              btRecord, btEject);
```

Any buttons not colored appear in black and white. Borland decided, for some reason, to have the buttons colored by default. To make all the buttons black and white, refer to the example code above. If you just want the Play, Pause, and Stop buttons colored, for example, you could use this code:

```
MediaPlayer1.ColoredButtons := [btPlay, btPause, btStop];
```

DeviceID PROPERTY

Objects Affected	`TMediaPlayer`
Purpose	The `DeviceID` property specifies the device ID of the currently open multimedia device.
Declaration	

```
property DeviceID: Word;
```

Description If no device is open, `DeviceID` is 0. Otherwise, the device ID is determined when the device is opened.

DeviceType PROPERTY

Objects Affected	`TMediaPlayer`
Purpose	The `DeviceType` property determines the type of multimedia device opened by the media control.

Declaration

```
property DeviceType: TMPDeviceTypes;
```

Example Syntax

```
procedure TForm1.FormCreate(Sender: TObject);
begin
  // Open the CD
  MediaPlayer1.DeviceType := dtCDAudio;
  MediaPlayer1.AutoRewind := True;
  if MediaPlayer1.AutoOpen = False then
    MediaPlayer1.Open;
end;
```

Description

DeviceType is type TMPDeviceTypes, which is declared as:

```
TMPDeviceTypes = (dtAutoSelect, dtAVIVideo, dtCDAudio, dtDAT,
                  dtDigitalVideo, dtMMMovie, dtOther, dtOverlay,
                  dtScanner, dtSequencer, dtVCR, dtVideodisc,
                  dtWaveAudio);
```

If DeviceType is dtAutoSelect, the type of device opened is determined by the extension of the file name the FileName property specifies. File name extensions are associated with devices in the system registry.

Display PROPERTY

Objects Affected   TMediaPlayer

Purpose   The Display property contains the name of the windowed control the multimedia device uses for output.

Declaration

```
property Display: TWinControl;
```

Example Syntax

```
procedure TForm2.FormCreate(Sender: TObject);
begin
  Form1.MediaPlayer1.Display := TWinControl(TForm2);
  Form1.MediaPlayer1.DisplayRect := Rect(10, 10, 0, 0);
end;
```

Description   The Animation, AVI Video, Digital Video, Overlay, and VCR devices use Display. Display points to a TWinControl object, such as a form or panel, that is the output window for the device. In the case of an AVI Video, for example, you can use the code above to output, or play, the AVI on a form window.

DisplayRect PROPERTY

Objects Affected	TMediaPlayer
Purpose	The DisplayRect property determines the portion of the display control used for output.
Declaration	

```
property DisplayRect: TRect;
```

Example Syntax

```
procedure TForm2.FormCreate(Sender: TObject);
begin
  Form1.MediaPlayer1.Display := TWinControl(TForm2);
  Form1.MediaPlayer1.DisplayRect := Rect(10, 10, 0, 0);
end;
```

Description DisplayRect is a run-time-only property specifying a rectangular area on the control that limits the output of the multimedia device.

To display media in its default size, set the coordinates for the lower-right corner of DisplayRect to 0,0. This is done in the example code above.

Eject METHOD

Objects Affected	TMediaPlayer
Purpose	The Eject method ejects the medium from the currently open multimedia media device.
Declaration	

```
procedure Eject;
```

Example Syntax

```
procedure TForm1.sbEjectClick(Sender: TObject);
begin
  MediaPlayer1.Eject;
end;
```

Description Eject is called when the Eject button on the media control is clicked at run time. In the code above, a speedbutton is used to duplicate the functionality of the media player's Eject button.

EnabledButtons PROPERTY

Objects Affected	TMediaPlayer
Purpose	The EnabledButtons property determines which buttons on the media control are enabled.

Declaration

```
property EnabledButtons: TButtonSet;
```

Example Syntax

```
procedure TForm1.FormCreate(Sender: TObject);
begin
  MediaPlayer1.EnabledButtons := [btPlay, btPause, btStop, btNext,
                                  btPrev, btEject];
end;
```

Description

EnabledButtons is type TButtonSet, which is declared as a set of
TMPBtnType:

```
TButtonSet = set of TMPBtnType;
TMPBtnType = (btPlay, btPause, btStop, btNext, btPrev, btStep, btBack,
              btRecord, btEject);
```

An enabled button is colored (or black) and can be clicked by the user. A
disabled button is grayed-out and cannot be clicked.

By default, all buttons are enabled.

EndPos PROPERTY

Objects Affected   TMediaPlayer

Purpose   The EndPos property specifies the position within the open medium at
which to stop playing or recording.

Declaration

```
property EndPos: Longint;
```

Example Syntax

```
// End recording at the end of track 1
MediaPlayer1.EndPos := MediaPlayer1.TrackLength[1];
```

Description   EndPos is a run-time-only property affecting the first Play or
StartRecording method called after EndPos. EndPos must be called every
time you want it to affect a Play or StartRecording call. It is specified in
the time format determined by the TimeFormat property.

The starting position of recording or playback is set with the StartPos
property.

Error PROPERTY

Objects Affected   TMediaPlayer

Purpose   The Error property contains the most recently returned MCI error code.

Declaration

```
property Error: Longint;
```

Example Syntax

```
procedure TForm1.sbNextClick(Sender: TObject);
begin
  MediaPlayer1.Next;
  if MediaPlayer1.Error = 0 then
    MediaPlayer1.Play
  else
    Application.MessageBox(PChar(MediaPlayer1.ErrorMessage),
              'MCI Error', MB_OK);
end;
```

Description

The Back, Close, Eject, Next, Open, Pause, PauseOnly, Play, Previous, StartRecording, Resume, Rewind, Step, and Stop buttons return MCI error codes assigned to the `Error` property. A message documenting the returned error code is assigned to the `ErrorMessage` property. These error codes and messages are quite extensive. They are documented thoroughly in the Win32 SDK. If you are serious about Win32 programming or MCI programming specifically, it would be worthwhile to get a copy of this SDK.

If the `Error` property contains a zero, the method did not return an error and the media control functioned properly. Any nonzero value indicates an error.

ErrorMessage PROPERTY

Objects Affected   `TMediaPlayer`

Purpose   The `ErrorMessage` property contains a string describing the error whose code is stored in the `Error` property.

Declaration

```
property ErrorMessage: string;
```

Example Syntax

```
procedure TForm1.sbNextClick(Sender: TObject);
begin
  MediaPlayer1.Next;
  if MediaPlayer1.Error = 0 then
    MediaPlayer1.Play
  else
    Application.MessageBox(PChar(MediaPlayer1.ErrorMessage),
              'MCI Error', MB_OK);
end;
```

Description   Just as `Error` contains the error code for the last MCI error, `ErrorMessage` contains a description of the most recent error.

FileName PROPERTY

Objects Affected	TMediaPlayer
Purpose	The FileName property specifies the name of the media file that is opened and/or saved by the media player.
Declaration	

```
property FileName: string;
```

Example Syntax

```
procedure TForm1.FormCreate(Sender: TObject);
begin
  MediaPlayer1.FileName := 'c:\windows\media\skiing.avi';
  MediaPlayer1.Open;
  MediaPlayer1.Display := Form2;
  MediaPlayer1.Play;
end;
```

Description   In the example above, the file name is set when the form is created and is automatically played. If you would like to use a common dialog to open the AVI movie file, you can use code like this:

```
procedure TForm1.sbOpenClick(Sender: TObject);
begin
  if OpenDialog1.Execute then
  begin
    MediaPlayer1.DeviceType := dtAVIVideo;
    MediaPlayer1.FileName := OpenDialog1.FileName;
    MediaPlayer1.Open;
  end;
end;
```

You can also substitute **dtAutoSelect** for **dtAVIVideo** if you want the media player to handle any type of multimedia file.

Frames PROPERTY

Objects Affected	TMediaPlayer
Purpose	The Frames property specifies the number of frames the **Step** and **Back** methods step.
Declaration	

```
property Frames: Longint;
```

Example Syntax

```
// Set AVI stepping to 1 frame
MediaPlayer1.Frames := 1;
```

Description   Frames is a run-time only property specifying the size of the forward step taken by **Step** and the backward step taken by **Back**.

The default is 10 percent of the length of the current medium. Not all mediums support frame stepping, and those that do implement it in different ways.

Length PROPERTY

Objects Affected	TMediaPlayer
Purpose	The Length property determines the length of the currently loaded medium, as specified in the current time format.
Declaration	

```
property Length: Longint;
```

Example Syntax

```
procedure TForm2.FormCreate(Sender: TObject);
begin
  Form1.MediaPlayer1.Display := TWinControl(TForm2);
  Form1.Caption := 'Length: ' + IntToStr(Form1.MediaPlayer1.Length) +
                   ' ms';
end;
```

Description See TimeFormat for information about the various time formats supported by the media player.

Mode PROPERTY

Objects Affected	TMediaPlayer
Purpose	The Mode property determines the media player's current mode.
Declaration	

```
property Mode: TMPModes;
```

Example Syntax

```
procedure TForm1.MediaPlayer1PostClick(Sender: TObject;
                                       Button: TMPBtnType);
begin
  if MediaPlayer1.Mode = mpNotReady then lblMode.Caption := 'Not Ready'
  else
    if MediaPlayer1.Mode = mpStopped then lblMode.Caption := 'Stopped'
  else
    if MediaPlayer1.Mode = mpPlaying then lblMode.Caption := 'Playing'
  else
    if MediaPlayer1.Mode = mpSeeking then lblMode.Caption := 'Seeking'
  else
    if MediaPlayer1.Mode = mpPaused then lblMode.Caption := 'Paused'
  else
    if MediaPlayer1.Mode = mpOpen then lblMode.Caption := 'Open';
end;
```

Figure 65-5 Every time a button is clicked on the media player, a label displays the current mode

Description   Mode is type `TMPModes`, which is declared as:

```
TMPModes = (mpNotReady, mpStopped, mpPlaying, mpRecording, mpSeeking,
            mpPaused, mpOpen);
```

Next METHOD

Objects Affected   `TMediaPlayer`

Purpose   The `Next` method skips to the beginning of the next track in the currently open medium.

Declaration

```
procedure Next;
```

Example Syntax

```
procedure TForm1.sbNextClick(Sender: TObject);
begin
  MediaPlayer1.Next;
  if MediaPlayer1.Error = 0 then
    MediaPlayer1.Play
  else
    Application.MessageBox(PChar(MediaPlayer1.ErrorMessage),
                'MCI Error', MB_OK);
end;
```

Description   `Next` is called when the media player's Next button is pressed. If the current multimedia device doesn't support tracks, calling `Next` steps the current position to the end of the medium. If the last track is the current track, `Next` moves the current position to the beginning of that track.

Notify PROPERTY

Objects Affected   `TMediaPlayer`

Purpose   The `Notify` property determines whether media player button clicks generate `OnNotify` events.

Declaration

```
property Notify: Boolean;
```

Example Syntax

```
procedure TForm1.FormCreate(Sender: TObject);
begin
  MediaPlayer1.DeviceType := dtCDAudio;
  MediaPlayer1.AutoRewind := True;
  MediaPlayer1.Notify := True;
  MediaPlayer1.Wait := False;
  MediaPlayer1.TimeFormat := tfTMSF;

  if MediaPlayer1.AutoOpen = False then
    MediaPlayer1.Open;
end;

procedure TForm1.MediaPlayer1Notify(Sender: TObject);
begin
  if MediaPlayer1.NotifyValue = nvSuccessful then
    lblNotifyValue.Caption := 'Last request successful'
  else if MediaPlayer1.NotifyValue = nvSuperseded then
    lblNotifyValue.Caption := 'Last request superceded'
  else if MediaPlayer1.NotifyValue = nvAborted then
    lblNotifyValue.Caption := 'Last request aborted'
  else if MediaPlayer1.NotifyValue = nvFailure then
    lblNotifyValue.Caption := 'Last request failed';

  MediaPlayer1.Notify := True;
end;
```

Description

If Notify is True, calling the following media player methods generates an OnNotify event: Back, Close, Eject, Next, Open, Pause, PauseOnly, Play, Previous, Resume, Rewind, StartRecording, Step, or Stop. The OnNotify event enables you to handle the event occuring when any media player button is clicked, or when one of the previously mentioned methods is called. A notification message is also generated and stored in the NotifyValue property. Notify must be called every time the OnNotify event occurs, since it only handles the *next* call to one of the media player methods mentioned above. In the code sample above, the Notify property is set to True each time the OnNotify event handler is called.

If Notify is False, the OnNotify event is not generated and no notification messages are stored.

Notify is False by default, but the Play and StartRecording methods trigger an OnNotify event anyway, so you must explicitly set Notify to False if you do not want these methods to generate OnNotify methods.

NotifyValue PROPERTY

Objects Affected	TMediaPlayer
Purpose	The NotifyValue property contains a notification message generated by the last media player method requesting a notification.
Declaration	

```
property NotifyValue: TMPNotifyValues;
```

Example Syntax

```
procedure TForm1.MediaPlayer1Notify(Sender: TObject);
begin
  if MediaPlayer1.NotifyValue = nvSuccessful then
    lblNotifyValue.Caption := 'Last request successful'
  else if MediaPlayer1.NotifyValue = nvSuperseded then
    lblNotifyValue.Caption := 'Last request superceded'
  else if MediaPlayer1.NotifyValue = nvAborted then
    lblNotifyValue.Caption := 'Last request aborted'
  else if MediaPlayer1.NotifyValue = nvFailure then
    lblNotifyValue.Caption := 'Last request failed';

  MediaPlayer1.Notify := True;
end;
```

Description NotifyValue is a run-time, read-only property that is type TMPNotifyValues:

```
TMPNotifyValues = (nvSuccessful, nvSuperseded, nvAborted, nvFailure);
```

When media player methods requesting notifications (**Back**, **Close**, **Eject**, **Next**, **Open**, **Pause**, **PauseOnly**, **Play**, **Previous**, **Resume**, **Rewind**, **StartRecording**, **Step**, or **Stop**) are called, four possible notifications can occur: The call was successful, it was superseded by another command, it was aborted by the user, or it failed. The **NotifyValue** property contains this result.

OnNotify EVENT

Objects Affected	TMediaPlayer
Purpose	The OnNotify event occurs when Notify is True and a media control method is called.
Declaration	

```
property OnNotify: TNotifyEvent;
```

Example Syntax

```
procedure TForm1.MediaPlayer1Notify(Sender: TObject);
begin
  // Standard OnNotify event handler
end;
```

Description   The **OnNotify** event enables you to handle the event occuring when one of the media player methods is called. **OnNotify** occurs by default for every **Play** and **StartRecording** method call, unless **Notify** is explicitly set to **False** just before the call is made. Other media control methods—such as **Back**, **Close**, **Eject**, **Next**, **Open**, **Pause**, **PauseOnly**, **Previous**, **Resume**, **Rewind**, **Step**, or **Stop**—do not trigger this event unless **Notify** is set to **True**. After an **OnNotify** event, **Notify** must be set to **True** or future **OnNotify** events will not occur.

OnPostClick EVENT

Objects Affected   **TMediaPlayer**

Purpose   The media player's **OnPostClick** event occurs after the **OnClick** event handler runs, enabling you to handle individual button clicks.

Declaration

```
property OnPostClick: EMPPostNotify;
```

Example Syntax

```
procedure TForm1.MediaPlayer1PostClick(Sender: TObject;
                                       Button: TMPBtnType);
begin
  if MediaPlayer1.Mode = mpNotReady then lblMode.Caption := 'Not Ready'
  else
    if MediaPlayer1.Mode = mpStopped then lblMode.Caption := 'Stopped'
  else
    if MediaPlayer1.Mode = mpPlaying then lblMode.Caption := 'Playing'
  else
    if MediaPlayer1.Mode = mpSeeking then lblMode.Caption := 'Seeking'
  else
    if MediaPlayer1.Mode = mpPaused then lblMode.Caption := 'Paused'
  else
    if MediaPlayer1.Mode = mpOpen then lblMode.Caption := 'Open';
end;
```

Description   The **OnPostClick** event enables you to handle the event occuring when a button on the media player is clicked. The *Button* parameter specifies which button was pressed and is type **TMPButtonType**:

```
TMPBtnType = (btPlay, btPause, btStop, btNext, btPrev, btStep, btBack,
              btRecord, btEject);
```

If the **Wait** property is **True**, the **OnPostClick** event will not occur until after the **OnClick** event handler is done. If **Wait** is **False**, it is possible the code in the **OnPostClick** event handler will run before the **OnClick** event handler is done.

Open METHOD

Objects Affected	`TMediaPlayer`
Purpose	The `Open` method opens a multimedia device.
Declaration	

```
procedure Open;
```

Example Syntax

```
procedure TForm1.FormCreate(Sender: TObject);
begin
  MediaPlayer1.DeviceType := dtCDAudio;
  if MediaPlayer1.AutoOpen = False then
    MediaPlayer1.Open;
end;
```

Description   Before a multimedia device is opened, the device type must be set with the `DeviceType` property. Once a device is open, you can call other media player methods, such as `Play` or `StartRecording`.

Pause METHOD

Objects Affected	`TMediaPlayer`
Purpose	The `Pause` method pauses the multimedia device currently open in the media player. If it is already paused, it starts playing or recording again.
Declaration	

```
procedure Pause;
```

Example Syntax

```
procedure TForm1.sbPauseClick(Sender: TObject);
begin
  MediaPlayer1.Pause;
end;
```

Description   If the device is already paused when `Pause` is called, it begins playing or recording again. `Pause` does not reset the position, so playing or recording resumes at the position where `Pause` was called. You can also resume playing or recording with the `Resume` method.

`Pause` is called when the Pause button on the media player is clicked.

PauseOnly METHOD

Objects Affected	`TMediaPlayer`
Purpose	The `PauseOnly` method pauses the multimedia device currently open in the media player.

Declaration

```
procedure PauseOnly;
```

Example Syntax

```
procedure TForm1.sbPauseClick(Sender: TObject);
begin
  MediaPlayer1.PauseOnly;
end;
```

Description   Unlike **Pause**, **PauseOnly** does not restart playing or recording if the device is already paused.

PLay METHOD

Objects Affected   TMediaPlayer

Purpose   The **Play** method plays the medium loaded into the open multimedia device.

Declaration

```
procedure Play;
```

Example Syntax

```
procedure TForm1.FormCreate(Sender: TObject);
begin
  MediaPlayer1.DeviceType := dtCDAudio;
  if MediaPlayer1.AutoOpen = False then
  begin
    MediaPlayer1.Open;
    MediaPlayer1.Play
  end
end;

procedure TForm1.sbPlayClick(Sender: TObject);
begin
  MediaPlayer1.Play;
end;
```

Description   If **StartPos** is set, **Play** begins at that position in the medium. Otherwise, it begins at the current position, as determined by the **Position** property. When you first open a device, the current position is set to the beginning of the medium. If **EndPos** is set, **Play** continues until that position. Otherwise, **Play** continues until the length of the medium is reached.

Position PROPERTY

Objects Affected   TMediaPlayer

Purpose   The **Position** property specifies the current position within the open medium.

Declaration

```
property Position: Longint;
```

Example Syntax

```
lblTrack.Caption := IntToStr(lobyte(MediaPlayer1.Position));
```

Description Position is a run-time only property specified in the current time format, which is determined by the **TimeFormat** property. When the medium is first opened, **Position** defaults to its beginning or the position specified by **StartPos** if it is set.

Previous METHOD

Objects Affected TMediaPlayer

Purpose The **Previous** method changes the position to the beginning of the previous or current track, depending on the current position.

Declaration

```
procedure Previous;
```

Example Syntax

```
procedure TForm1.sbPrevClick(Sender: TObject);
begin
  MediaPlayer1.Previous;
end;
```

Description If the current position is the beginning of a track, **Previous** changes the position to the beginning of the previous track. If the position is elsewhere in a track or anywhere within the first track, **Previous** changes the position to the beginning of the current track. If the open device doesn't support tracks, **Previous** sets the current position to the beginning of the medium.

Resume METHOD

Objects Affected TMediaPlayer

Purpose The **Resume** method resumes playing or recording the currently paused medium.

Declaration

```
procedure Resume;
```

Example Syntax

```
procedure TForm1.sbPauseClick(Sender: TObject);
begin
```

```
    if (MediaPlayer1.Mode = mpPaused) or
       (MediaPlayer1.Mode = mpStopped) then
      MediaPlayer1.Resume
    else MediaPlayer1.PauseOnly;
end;
```

Description   The **Resume** method is normally called when the Pause button on the already paused media player is clicked, causing the medium to continue playing from the current position.

Rewind METHOD

Objects Affected   TMediaPlayer

Purpose   The **Rewind** method changes the current position to the beginning of the medium.

Declaration

```
procedure Rewind;
```

Example Syntax

```
procedure TForm1.spPlayFromStartClick(Sender: TObject);
begin
  MediaPlayer1.Rewind;
  MediaPlayer1.Play;
end;
```

Description   The **Rewind** property sets the current position to the beginning of the medium.

Save METHOD

Objects Affected   TMediaPlayer

Purpose   The **Save** method saves the medium to the file specified by the **FileName** property.

Declaration

```
procedure Save;
```

Example Syntax

```
procedure TForm1.sbSaveFileClick(Sender: TObject);
begin
  MediaPlayer1.Save;
end;
```

Description   **Save** is ignored by those devices that do not support saving, such as CD Audio.

Shareable PROPERTY

Objects Affected	TMediaPlayer
Purpose	The `Shareable` property determines whether your application can share a multimedia device with other application programs.
Declaration	

```
property Shareable: Boolean;
```

Example Syntax

```
procedure TForm1.FormCreate(Sender: TObject);
begin
  MediaPlayer1.Shareable := True;
  MediaPlayer1.DeviceType := dtCDAudio;
  if MediaPlayer1.AutoOpen = False then
    MediaPlayer1.Open;
end;
```

Description   If `Shareable` is `True`, more than one application program can access the opened multimedia device at a time. If it is `False`, no other programs can access the device. If you attempt to access the device and it is already in use, you will generate an exception.

The default value of `Shareable` is `False`.

Start PROPERTY

Objects Affected	TMediaPlayer
Purpose	The `Start` property specifies the beginning of the open medium.
Declaration	

```
property Start: Longint;
```

Description   `Start` is a read-only, run-time only property. If the medium supports tracks, `Start` is set to the beginning of the first track. Otherwise, `Start` is set to the beginning of the medium. In either case, `Start` is specified when the medium is opened and is stored in the time format specified by the `TimeFormat` property.

StartPos PROPERTY

Objects Affected	TMediaPlayer
Purpose	The `StartPos` property specifies the position in the open medium to begin playing or recording.

Declaration

```
property StartPos: Longint;
```

Example Syntax

```
// Start recording one-third of the way into track 1
MediaPlayer1.StartPos := MediaPlayer1.TrackLength[1] div 3;
```

Description

StartPos is a run-time-only property specified in the current time format. If StartPos is not specified, the start position for recording or playing is automatically set by the Start property to the beginning of the medium. StartPos affects the next Play or StartRecording method call. You must reset the StartPos value after each call to Play or StartRecording, or it will default to the value specified by Start.

You can set the end position for playback or recording with EndPos.

StartRecording METHOD

Objects Affected   TMediaPlayer

Purpose   The StartRecording method begins recording to the open medium.

Declaration

```
procedure StartRecording;
```

Example Syntax

```
procedure TForm1.sbRecord(Sender: TObject);
begin
  MediaPlayer1.Notify := True;
  MediaPlayer1.StartRecording;
end;
```

Description   StartRecording begins recording at the current position if no StartPos value is specified. If StartPos is specified, StartRecording begins recording at that position. StartRecording is called when the Record button on the media player is clicked.

Step METHOD

Objects Affected   TMediaPlayer

Purpose   The Step method steps the position forward a number of frames in the open medium.

Declaration

```
procedure Step;
```

Example Syntax

```
procedure TForm1.sbForwardClick(Sender: TObject);
begin
  MediaPlayer1.Step;
end;
```

Description   The number of frames stepped is determined by the **Frames** property. The **Step** method is called when the media player's Forward button is pressed at run time.

The **Back** method enables you to step backward.

Stop METHOD

Objects Affected   TMediaPlayer

Purpose   The **Stop** method stops playing or recording.

Declaration

```
procedure Stop;
```

Example Syntax

```
procedure TForm1.sbStopClick(Sender: TObject);
begin
  MediaPlayer1.Stop;
end;
```

Description   **Stop** is called when the **Stop** button on the media player is clicked.

TimeFormat PROPERTY

Objects Affected   TMediaPlayer

Purpose   The **TimeFormat** property determines how time-related property values are formatted.

Declaration

```
property TimeFormat: TMPTimeFormats;
```

Example Syntax

```
procedure TForm1.FormCreate(Sender: TObject);
begin
  MediaPlayer1.DeviceType := dtCDAudio;
  MediaPlayer1.AutoRewind := True;
  MediaPlayer1.Notify := True;
  MediaPlayer1.Wait := False;
  MediaPlayer1.TimeFormat := tfTMSF;

  if MediaPlayer1.AutoOpen = False then
    MediaPlayer1.Open;

end;
```

Description	**TimeFormat** affects the way the values of the **StartPos**, **Length**, **Position**, **Start**, and **EndPos** properties are interpreted and displayed. Not all formats are supported by all devices. **TimeFormat** is stored as a 4-byte integer, although its full size is not used by all formats. It is type **TMPTimeFormats**, which is declared as:

```
TMPTimeFormats = (tfMilliseconds, tfHMS, tfMSF, tfFrames, tfSMPTE24,
                  tfSMPTE25, tfSMPTE30, tfSMPTE30Drop, tfBytes,
                  tfSamples, tfTMSF);
```

The following table describes the various supported time formats:

This Time Format	Stores Data as a...
tfMilliseconds	4-byte integer variable.
tfHMS	4-byte integer that contains hours, minutes, and seconds in order from least significant to most significant byte. The final byte is unused.
tfMSF	4-byte integer that contains minutes, seconds, and frames in order from least significant to most significant byte. The final byte is unused.
tfFrames	4-byte integer variable.
tfSMPTE24	4-byte variable. The values it stores, from least significant to most significant byte, are hours, minutes, seconds, and frames. SMPTE is an acronym for Society of Motion Picture and Television Engineers. In this format, standard division types are 24, 25, and 30 frames per second.
tfSMPTE25	4-byte variable containing 25-frame SMPTE in the same order as 24-frame SMPTE.
tfSMPTE30	4-byte variable containing 30-frame SMPTE in the same order as 24-frame SMPTE.
tfSMPTE30Drop	4-byte variable containing 30-drop-frame SMPTE in the same order as 24-frame SMPTE.
tfBytes	4-byte integer variable.
tfSamples	4-byte integer variable.
tfTMSF	4-byte variable that contains tracks, minutes, seconds, and frames in order from least significant byte most significant byte.

As you can imagine, time formats are quite complex. The Win32 API provides functions that help you decode the 4-byte variables used to store the various time formats. This information is beyond the scope of this book.

TrackLength PROPERTY

Objects Affected	**TMediaPlayer**
Purpose	The **TrackLength** property contains the length of the specified track in the time format determined by the **TimeFormat** property.
Declaration	

```
property TrackLength[TrackNum: Integer]: Longint;
```

Example Syntax

```
procedure TForm1.Timer1Timer(Sender: TObject);
begin
   lblTrackLength.Caption :=
                  IntToStr(TrackLength[StrToInt(lblTrack.Caption)]);
   lblTrack.Caption := IntToStr(lobyte(MediaPlayer1.Position));
   lblTrackPosition.Caption :=
            IntToStr(MediaPlayer1.TrackPosition[MediaPlayer1.Position]);
end;
```

Description   The track is specified by the TrackNum index, in which the first track is 1
and the number of tracks is determined by Tracks.

TrackPosition PROPERTY

Objects Affected   TMediaPlayer

Purpose   The TrackPosition property specifies the starting position of the specified
track.

Declaration

```
property TrackPosition[TrackNum: Integer]: Longint;
```

Example Syntax

```
procedure TForm1.Timer1Timer(Sender: TObject);
begin
   lblTrackLength.Caption :=
                  IntToStr(TrackLength[StrToInt(lblTrack.Caption)]);
   lblTrack.Caption := IntToStr(lobyte(MediaPlayer1.Position));
   lblTrackPosition.Caption :=
            IntToStr(MediaPlayer1.TrackPosition[MediaPlayer1.Position]);
end;
```

Description   TrackPosition is a run-time, read-only property specifying the starting
position of the track specified by the TrackNum index.

Tracks PROPERTY

Objects Affected   TMediaPlayer

Purpose   The Tracks property specifies the number of tracks existing on the open
medium.

Declaration

```
property Tracks: Longint;
```

Example Syntax

```
procedure TForm1.FormCreate(Sender: TObject);
begin
   lblTracks := IntToStr(MediaPlayer1.Tracks);
end;
```

Description   If the device you are using doesn't support tracks, **Tracks** is undefined.
                   Tracks is run-time and read-only.

VisibleButtons PROPERTY

Objects Affected   **TMediaPlayer**

Purpose   The **VisibleButtons** property determines which buttons in the media
                       player are visible.

Declaration

```
property VisibleButtons: TButtonSet;
```

Example Syntax

```
procedure TForm1.FormCreate(Sender: TObject);
begin
  MediaPlayer1.VisibleButtons := [btPlay, btPause, btStop, btNext,
                                  btPrev, btEject];
end
```

Description   **VisibleButtons** is type **TButtonSet**, which is declared as:

```
TButtonSet = set of TMPBtnType;
TMPBtnType = (btPlay, btPause, btStop, btNext, btPrev, btStep, btBack,
              btRecord, btEject);
```

The buttons visible on the media player are accessible to the user.

Wait PROPERTY

Objects Affected   **TMediaPlayer**

Purpose   The **Wait** property determines when media player methods return control
                       to the application.

Declaration

```
property Wait: Boolean;
```

Description   **Wait** is a run-time only property. If **Wait** is **True**, the media player waits
                   until the **Back**, **Close**, **Eject**, **Next**, **Open**, **Pause**, **PauseOnly**, **Play**,
                   Previous, **Resume**, **Rewind**, **StartRecording**, **Step**, or **Stop** method is
                   completed before returning control to the application. If it is **False**, con-
                   trol is returned to the application immediately.

                   Wait only affects the next method call. Every time one of these calls
                   occurs, **Wait** must be reset in order to affect another call.

TCustomPanel

TCustomPanel descends from TCustomControl and is the abstract base class for panel objects. The protected properties and methods in this class are published by TPanel.

Table 65-3 displays the properties, methods, and events implemented by TCustomPanel.

Table 65-3 Properties, methods, and events implemented by TCustomPanel

Use or Set This...	To Do This...	Inheritance
Create	Create a new custom panel.	TComponent

TPanel

TPanel is a direct descendant of TCustomPanel and provides a panel you can place other controls upon. Panels have a dual-beveled edge that can be modified to appear sunken or raised. You can also specify the width of the bevels. Panels are used primarily as visual grouping aids and, in Delphi, as toolbars in combination with speedbuttons.

Table 65-4 displays the properties, methods, and events implemented by TPanel.

Table 65-4 Properties, methods, and events implemented by TPanel

Use or Set This...	To Do This...	Inheritance
Align	Determine how the panel aligns with the form.	TComponent
Alignment	Determine how controls are aligned within the panel.	TComponent
BevelInner	Determine the appearance of the inner bevel.	None
BevelOuter	Determine the appearance of the outer bevel.	None
BevelWidth	Determine the width of the inner and outer bevels.	None
BorderStyle	Determine the border style of the panel.	TComponent
BorderWidth	Determine the width of the panel's border.	TComponent
Caption	Determine the caption that appears on the panel.	TComponent
Color	Determine the background color of the panel.	TComponent
Ctl3D	Determine if the panel displays in a 3D style.	TComponent
DragCursor	Determine the shape of the cursor as it drags an object over the panel.	TComponent
DragMode	Determine the drag-and-drop behavior of the panel.	TComponent
Enabled	Determine whether the panel is enabled.	TComponent
Font	Determine the font used to render the panel caption.	TComponent
Locked	Determine whether a panel that is used as a toolbar is replaced by an OLE object's toolbar when that object is enabled.	None
OnClick	Handle the event that occurs when the panel is clicked.	TComponent

Use or Set This...	To Do This...	Inheritance
OnDblClick	Handle the event that occurs when the panel is double-clicked.	TComponent
OnDragDrop	Handle the event that occurs when the panel is the target of a drag-and-drop operation.	TComponent
OnDragOver	Handle the event that occurs when an object is dragged over the panel.	TComponent
OnEndDrag	Handle the event that occurs when a drag-and-drop operation is cancelled.	TComponent
OnMouseDown	Handle the event that occurs when a mouse button is pressed but not immediately released.	TComponent
OnMouseMove	Handle the event that occurs when the mouse pointer moves over the panel.	TComponent
OnMouseUp	Handle the event that occurs when a mouse button is released.	TComponent
OnStartDrag	Handle the event that occurs when a drag-and-drop operation is started.	TComponent
ParentColor	Determine whether the panel uses its parent's Color information.	TComponent
ParentCtl3D	Determine whether the panel uses its parent's Ctl3D information.	TComponent
ParentFont	Determine whether the panel uses its parent's Font information.	TComponent
ParentShowHint	Determine whether the panel uses its parent's ShowHint information.	TComponent
PopupMenu	Determine which pop-up menu is associated with the panel.	TComponent
ShowHint	Determine whether the panel displays a tooltip.	TComponent
TabOrder	Determine whether the panel is in its parent's tab order.	TComponent
TabStop	Determine whether the panel is a tab stop.	TComponent
Visible	Determine whether the panel is visible.	TComponent

BevelInner PROPERTY

Objects Affected	TPanel
Purpose	The **BevelInner** property determines how the inner bevel of the panel is drawn.
Declaration	

```
property BevelInner: TPanelBevel;
```

Example Syntax

```
Panel1.BevelInner := bvLowered;
```

Description   Panels have two bevels: an outer bevel drawn next to the edge of the control, and an inner bevel just inside the outer bevel. The outer bevel is determined by **BevelOuter**. The width of the space between the bevels is determined by the **BorderWidth** property.

BevelInner is type **TPanelBevel**, which is declared as

```
TPanelBevel = (bvNone, bvLowered, bvRaised);
```

in which **bvNone** is used when no bevel is desired, **bvLowered** draws a bevel that appears to sink into the control, and **bvRaised** draws an inner bevel that seems to visually rise out of the control.

The default value is **bvNone**.

BevelOuter PROPERTY

Objects Affected   TPanel

Purpose   The **BevelOuter** property determines how the outer bevel of the panel is drawn.

Declaration

```
property BevelOuter: TPanelBevel;
```

Example Syntax

```
Panel1.BevelOuter := bvNone;
```

Description   Panels have two bevels: an outer bevel drawn next to the edge of the control, and an inner bevel just inside the outer bevel. The outer bevel is determined by **BevelOuter**. The width of the space between the bevels is determined by the **BorderWidth** property.

BevelOuter is type **TPanelBevel**, which is declared as:

```
TPanelBevel = (bvNone, bvLowered, bvRaised);
```

If you set **BevelOuter** to **bvNone**, no bevel is drawn. **bvLowered** draws a bevel that appears to sink into the control, and **bvRaised** draws an outer bevel that seems to visually rise out of the control. Figure 65-6 illustrates several kinds of bevels.

The default value is **bvRaised**.

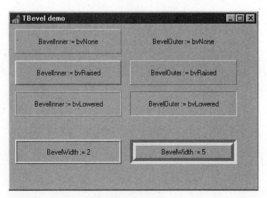

Figure 65-6 Different outer bevels drawn with the standard inner bevel

BevelWidth PROPERTY

Objects Affected	TPanel
Purpose	The **BevelWidth** property determines the width of the inner and outer bevels in the panel control. Refer to Figure 65-7 for examples of bevel widths.
Declaration	

```
property BevelWidth: TBevelWidth;
```

Example Syntax

```
Panel1.BevelWidth := 2;
```

Description   **BevelWidth** determines the width in pixels of the inner and outer bevels. It is type **TBevelWidth**, which is declared as:

```
TBevelWidth: 1..MaxInt;
```

Locked PROPERTY

Objects Affected	TPanel
Purpose	The **Locked** property determines whether a panel being used as a toolbar will be replaced by an OLE container's server toolbar when activated.
Declaration	

```
property Locked: Boolean;
```

Example Syntax

```
// Prevent the Panel1 toolbar from being replaced by the OLE object's
// own toolbars
Panel1.Locked := True;
```

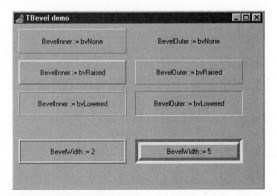

Figure 65-7   Different bevel widths affect the appearance of the panel

Description   If an OLE container is activated in your program, the object's toolbar typically replaces the one in your program. This behavior can be modified
with the `Locked` property. If `Locked` is `True`, the server's toolbars do not
replace your own. If `Locked` is `False`, the server's toolbars replace yours.
See the section on `TOleContainer` for more information about using OLE
containers in your programs.

For a panel to be used as a toolbar, its `Align` property must be set to
`alTop`, `alLeft`, `alRight`, or `alBottom`.

The default value is `False`.

TDBNavigator

`TDBNavigator` is a direct descendant of `TCustomPanel` and provides a media player-
like interface. The database navigator control is unique to Delphi, enabling you to
navigate through records in a dataset. Like the media player, the database navigator
consists of a row of buttons providing record browsing capabilities with first, last,
next, prior, insert, delete, and edit functions.

The buttons perform the following functions:

Use This Button...	To Do This...
First Record	Make the first record the current record.
Prior Record	Make the previous record the current record.
Next Record	Make the next record the current record.
Last Record	Make the last record the current record.
Insert Record	Insert a new record before the current record.
Delete Current Record	Delete the current record.
Edit Current Record	Put the current record in the edit state so it can be modified.
Post Record Edits	Write changes in the current record to the database.
Cancel Record Edits	Cancel changes in the current record to the database.
Refresh Records	Write changes in the current record to the database.

Table 65-5 displays the properties, methods, and events implemented by
`TDBNavigator`.

Table 65-5 Properties, methods, and events implemented by `TDBNavigator`

Use or Set This...	To Do This...	Inheritance
Align	Determine how the control aligns in its container.	TComponent
BtnClick	Simulate a database navigator button click.	None
ConfirmDelete	Determine whether a confirmation dialog box appears when the user attempts to delete the current record.	None
Create	Create a new database navigator control.	TComponent

Use or Set This...	To Do This...	Inheritance
Ctl3D	Determine whether the control displays in a 3D style.	TComponent
DataSource	Determine the source of the data the control manipulates.	None
Destroy	Destroy the database navigator control.	TComponent
DragCursor	Determine the shape of the mouse pointer as it drags an object over the control.	TComponent
DragMode	Determine the drag-and-drop behavior of the control.	TComponent
Enabled	Determine whether the control is enabled.	TComponent
Hints	Specify custom tooltips for each button in the control.	None
OnClick	Handle the event that occurs when the control is clicked.	TComponent
OnDblClick	Handle the event that occurs when the control is double-clicked.	TComponent
OnDragDrop	Handle the event that occurs when an object is dropped on the control.	TComponent
OnDragOver	Handle the event that occurs when an object is dragged over the control.	TComponent
OnEndDrag	Handle the event that occurs when a drag-and-drop operation is cancelled.	TComponent
OnEnter	Handle the event that occurs when the control receives the focus.	TComponent
OnExit	Handle the event that occurs when the control loses the focus.	TComponent
OnResize	Handle the event that occurs when the control is resized.	TComponent
OnStartDrag	Handle the event that occurs when a drag-and-drop operation is started.	TComponent
ParentCtl3D	Determine whether the control uses its parent's Ctl3D information.	TComponent
ParentShowHint	Determine whether the control uses its parent's ShowHint information.	TComponent
PopupMenu	Determine which pop-up menu is associated with the control.	TComponent
SetBounds	Modify the Left, Top, Width, and Height properties.	None
ShowHint	Determine whether the control displays tooltips.	TComponent
TabOrder	Determine the position of the control in its parent's tab order.	TComponent
TabStop	Determine whether the control is a tab stop.	TComponent
Visible	Determine whether the control is visible.	TComponent
VisibleButtons	Determine which buttons on the database navigator are visible.	None

BtnClick METHOD

Objects Affected	TDBNavigator
Purpose	The BtnClick method simulates a button click on the database navigator.
Declaration	

```
procedure BtnClick(Index: TNavigateBtn);
```

Parameters

Index　　　　　　Describes which button click is simulated.

Example Syntax

```
procedure TForm1.DBImage1Click(Sender: TObject);
begin
  DBNavigator1.BtnClick(nbNext);
end;
```

Description When the `BtnClick` method is called, a database navigator button click message is generated. The button clicked is determined by the *Index* parameter, which is type `TNavigateBtn`:

```
TNavigateBtn = (nbFirst, nbPrior, nbNext, nbLast, nbInsert, nbDelete,
nbEdit, nbPost, nbCancel, nbRefresh);
```

Using the code sample

```
DBNavigator1.BtnClick(nbFirst);
```

for example, would simulate the First button pressed.

ConfirmDelete PROPERTY

Objects Affected `TDBNavigator`

Purpose The `ConfirmDelete` property determines whether a confirmation dialog box appears when the user attempts to delete the current record.

Declaration

```
property ConfirmDelete: Boolean;
```

Example Syntax

```
// Allow users to delete records without posting a confirmation dialog
// box.
DBNavigator1.ConfirmDelete := False;
```

Description If `ConfirmDelete` is `True`, a confirmation dialog box appears when the user attempts to delete the current record in the dataset, using the Delete button on the database navigator. If `ConfirmDelete` is `False`, no dialog appears and the record is deleted.

The default value is `True`.

DataSource PROPERTY

Objects Affected `TDBNavigator`

Purpose The `DataSource` property determines where the database navigator ultimately gets its data.

Declaration

```
property DataSource: TDataSource;
```

Example Syntax

```
DBNavigator1.DataSource := DataSource1;
```

Description As with all data-aware controls, the `DataSource` property of the database navigator determines which data source control it uses. The data source control attaches to a dataset, such as a table or query, containing the actual data.

Hints PROPERTY

Objects Affected   TDBNavigator

Purpose   The `Hints` property enables you to specify tooltip text for the database navigator buttons.

Declaration

```
property Hints: TStrings;
```

Example Syntax

```
procedure TForm1.FormCreate(Sender: TObject);
var
  TempStr: TStringList;
begin
  TempStr := TStringList.Create;
  TempStr.Add('Go to first record');
  TempStr.Add('Go to previous record');
  TempStr.Add('Go to next record');
  TempStr.Add('Go to last record');
  TempStr.Add('Add a record');
  TempStr.Add('Delete the current record');
  TempStr.Add('Edit the current record');
  TempStr.Add('');
  TempStr.Add('');
  TempStr.Add('Refresh the data');

  DBNavigator1.Hints := TempStr;
  DBNavigator1.ShowHint := True;
end;
```

Description   The `Hints` property is a strings object. Each string in the `TStrings` object represents a tooltip for a button in the control. The first string in the `Strings` object is the tooltip for the first button, and so on. If you do not specify strings for the `Hints` property and set the control's `ShowHint` property to `True`, default tooltips are displayed. To use a default tooltip, specify " as its string. In the example above, a temporary `Strings` object is created and filled with tooltip strings, then copied to the `Hints` property.

SetBounds METHOD

Objects Affected   TDBNavigator

Purpose   The `SetBounds` method enables you to set the control's `Left`, `Top`, `Width`, and `Height` properties in one call.

Declaration

```
procedure SetBounds(ALeft, ATop, AWidth, AHeight: Integer); override;
```

Parameters

ALeft	Sets the `Left` property of the control.
ATop	Sets the `Top` property of the control.
AWidth	Sets the `Width` property of the control.
AHeight	Sets the `Height` property of the control.

Example Syntax

```
procedure TForm1.FormCreate(Sender: TObject);
begin
  DBNavigator1.SetBounds(16, 160, 410, 25);
end;
```

Description   `SetBounds` enables you to change the four positioning and size properties at one time, so the control is repainted just once.

VisibleButtons PROPERTY

Objects Affected   `TDBNavigator`

Purpose   The `VisibleButtons` property determines which database navigator buttons are visible to the user.

Declaration

```
property VisibleButtons: TButtonSet;
```

Example Syntax

```
procedure TForm1.FormCreate(Sender: TObject);
begin
  // Use all buttons except for Post and Cancel
  DBNavigator1.VisibleButtons := [nbFirst, nbPrior, nbNext,
            nbLast, nbInsert, nbDelete, nbEdit, nbRefresh];
end;
```

Description   `VisibleButtons` is type `TButtonSet`, which is declared as:

```
TButtonSet = set of TNavigateBtn;
TNavigateBtn = (nbFirst, nbPrior, nbNext, nbLast, nbInsert, nbDelete,
            nbEdit, nbPost, nbCancel, nbRefresh);
```

You can modify the set of visible buttons at run time by changing the `VisibleButtons` property.

By default, all buttons in the database navigator are visible.

TCustomGroupBox

`TCustomGroupBox` directly descends from `TCustomControl`. It is the abstract base class for the group box and radio group controls. These group box controls provide more formal control grouping than panels and include properties that enable you to auto-matically align contained controls.

Table 65-8 displays the properties, methods, and events implemented by **TCustomGroupBox**.

Table 65-8 Properties, methods, and events implemented by **TCustomGroupBox**		
Use or Set This...	**To Do This...**	**Inheritance**
AlignControls	Align the group box's child controls.	TWinControl
Create	Create a new custom group box.	TComponent
Paint	Handle the WM_PAINT message.	TControl

TGroupBox

TGroupBox descends from **TCustomGroupBox** and encapsulates the Win32 group box control. Group boxes are used to organize other controls, and they provide a rectangular frame with a descriptive caption.

Generally, group boxes are used to group radio buttons, though Delphi also provides a specialized **TRadioGroup** class. A typical group box is shown in Figure 65-8.

Table 65-9 displays the properties, methods, and events implemented by **TGroupBox**.

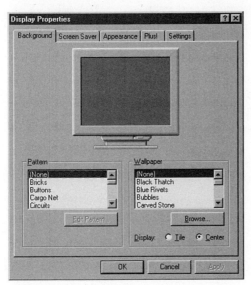

Figure 65-8   A typical group box

Table 65-9 Properties, methods, and events implemented by `TGroupBox`

Use or Set This...	To Do This...	Inheritance
Align	Determine how the group box aligns in its container.	TComponent
Caption	Determine the group box caption.	TComponent
Color	Determine the background color of the group box.	TComponent
Ctl3D	Determine whether the group box displays in a 3D style.	TComponent
DragCursor	Determine the shape of the mouse pointer as it drags an object over the group box.	TComponent
DragMode	Determine the drag-and-drop behavior of the group box.	TComponent
Enabled	Determine whether the group box is enabled.	TComponent
Font	Determine the font used to render the group box caption.	TComponent
OnClick	Handle the event that occurs when the group box is clicked.	Tcomponent
OnDblClick	Handle the event that occurs when the group box is double-clicked.	TComponent
OnDragDrop	Handle the event that occurs when an object is dropped on the group box.	TComponent
OnDragOver	Handle the event that occurs when an object is dragged over the group box.	TComponent
OnEndDrag	Handle the event that occurs when a drag-and-drop operation is cancelled.	TComponent
OnMouseDown	Handle the event that occurs when a mouse button is clicked but not immediately released.	TComponent
OnMouseMove	Handle the event that occurs when the mouse pointer moves over the group box.	TComponent
OnMouseUp	Handle the event that occurs when a mouse button is released.	TComponent
OnStartDrag	Handle the event that occurs when a drag-and-drop operation is started.	TComponent
ParentColor	Determine whether the group box uses its parent's Color information.	TComponent
ParentCtl3D	Determine whether the group box uses its parent's Ctl3D information.	TComponent
ParentFont	Determine whether the group box uses its parent's Font information.	TComponent
ParentShowHint	Determine whether the group box uses its parent's ShowHint information.	TComponent
PopupMenu	Determine which pop-up menu is associated with group box.	TComponent
ShowHint	Determine whether the group box displays a tooltip.	TComponent
TabOrder	Determine the position of the group box in its parent's tab order.	TComponent
TabStop	Determine whether the group box is a tab stop.	TComponent
Visible	Determine whether the group box is visible.	TComponent

TCustomRadioGroup

TCustomRadioGroup descends from **TCustomGroupBox** and is the abstract base class for **TRadioGroup**. The protected properties defined in **TCustomRadioGroup** are later implemented by **TRadioGroup**.

Table 65-10 displays the properties, methods, and events implemented by **TCustomRadioGroup**.

Table 65-10 Properties, methods, and events implemented by TCustomRadioGroup

Use or Set This...	To Do This...	Inheritance
Create	Create a new custom radio group.	TComponent
Destroy	Destroy the custom radio group.	TComponent

TRadioGroup

TRadioGroup is a direct descendant of TCustomRadioGroup and enables you to use radio buttons more easily in a group box. The radio button group box is designed to organize radio buttons and make them work together more easily than if manually added to a regular group box.

Radio buttons are added with the Items property of the radio button group box and can be accessed through the ItemIndex property. They are aligned into one or more columns as specified in the Columns property.

Radio button group boxes can contain other controls as well, although they do not benefit from the automatic alignment and selection features of TRadioGroup.

Table 65-11 displays the properties, methods, and events implemented by TRadioGroup.

Table 65-11 Properties, methods, and events implemented by TRadioGroup

Use or Set This...	To Do This...	Inheritance
Align	Determine how the control aligns within its container.	TComponent
Caption	Determine the caption of the radio button group box.	TComponent
Color	Determine the background color of the control.	TComponent
Columns	Determine how many columns there are in the control.	None
Ctl3D	Determine whether the control displays in a 3D style.	TComponent
DragCursor	Determine the shape of the mouse pointer as it drags an object over the radio button group box.	TComponent
DragMode	Determine the drag-and-drop behavior of the control.	TComponent
Enabled	Determine whether the control is enabled.	TComponent
Font	Determine the font used to render the caption.	TComponent
ItemIndex	Determine which radio button is currently selected.	None
Items	Access the radio buttons in the radio button group box.	None
OnClick	Handle the event that occurs when a mouse button is clicked.	TComponent
OnDragDrop	Handle the event that occurs when an object is dropped on the control.	TComponent
OnDragOver	Handle the event that occurs when an object is dragged over the control.	TComponent
OnEndDrag	Handle the event that occurs when a drag-and-drop operation is cancelled.	TComponent
OnStartDrag	Handle the event that occurs when a drag-and-drop operation is started.	TComponent

continued on next page

continued from previous page

Use or Set This...	To Do This...	Inheritance
ParentColor	Determine whether the control uses its parent's Color information.	TComponent
ParentCtl3D	Determine whether the control uses its parent's Ctl3D information.	TComponent
ParentFont	Determine whether the control uses its parent's Font information.	TComponent
ParentShowHint	Determine whether the control uses its parent's ShowHint information.	TComponent
PopupMenu	Determine which pop-up menu is associated with the control.	TComponent
ShowHint	Determine whether the control displays a tooltip.	TComponent
TabOrder	Determine the position of the control in its parent's tab order.	TComponent
TabStop	Determine whether the control is a tab stop.	TComponent
Visible	Determine whether the control is visible.	TComponent

Columns PROPERTY

Objects Affected TRadioGroup

Purpose The Columns property determines how many columns of radio buttons are in the radio button group box.

Declaration

```
property Columns: Integer;
```

Example Syntax

```
procedure TForm1.FormCreate(Sender: TObject);
begin
  // Display radio buttons in two columns
  RadioGroup1.Columns := 2;
end;
```

Description Columns only affects radio buttons that are part of the radio group's Items array. If you manually add controls to the radio group box—including radio buttons—they will not be included in the sorting that occurs with Columns.

The default value is 1.

ItemIndex PROPERTY

Objects Affected TRadioGroup

Purpose The ItemIndex property contains the positional value of the currently selected radio button in the radio button group. Refer to Figure 65-9.

Declaration

```
property ItemIndex: Integer;
```

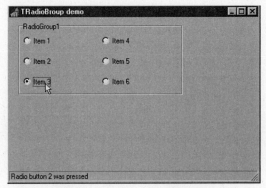

Figure 65-9 Determining which radio button was pressed

Example Syntax

```
procedure TForm1.RadioGroup1Click(Sender: TObject);
begin
  StatusBar1.SimpleText := 'Radio button ' +
           IntToStr(RadioGroup1.ItemIndex) + ' was pressed';
end;
```

Description

You can use **ItemIndex** to select an individual radio button in the group or determine which button is selected. If no radio button is selected, **ItemIndex** is -1. Remember that the first radio button is 0, the second is 1, and so on.

The default value is -1.

Items PROPERTY

Objects Affected   **TRadioGroup**

Purpose   The **Items** property enables you to access the individual radio buttons in the radio button group box.

Declaration

```
property Items: TStrings;
```

Example Syntax

```
procedure TForm1.FormCreate(Sender: TObject);
begin
  RadioGroup1.Items.Add('Item 1');
  RadioGroup1.Items.Add('Item 2');
  RadioGroup1.Items.Add('Item 3');
  RadioGroup1.Items.Add('Item 4');
```

continued on next page

CHAPTER 65

continued from previous page

```
        RadioGroup1.Items.Add('Item 5');
        RadioGroup1.Items.Add('Item 6');

        RadioGroup1.Columns := 2;
end;
```

Description   The **Items** property contains the strings appearing as the radio button captions. It is a zero-based array of strings, in which the first string is
Items[0], the second is **Items[1]**, and so on. **Items** is type **TStrings**, so
you can use **TStrings** methods such as **Add**, **Delete**, and **Insert** to
manipulate the strings.

In the example code above, six items are added to the radio button group
control at run time and organized into two columns.

WHERE TO GO FROM HERE

Cantù, Marco. *Mastering Delphi 2 for Windows 95/NT*. Alameda, CA: Sybex, 1996.

Enstminger, Gary. *The Tao of Objects*. New York: M&T Books, 1995.

Enstminger, Gary. *The Way of Delphi*. New York: M&T Books, 1996.

Konopka, Ray. *Developing Custom Delphi Components*. Scottsdale, AZ: Coriolis Group Books, 1996.

Lischner, Ray. *Secrets of Delphi 2*. Corte Madera, CA: Waite Group Press, 1996.

Wallace, Nathan, et al. *Delphi 2 Developers' Solutions*. Corte Madera, CA: Waite Group Press, 1996.

B

PROJECT CD

Using the CD

The CD contains projects and source code based on the chapter subjects contained within this book, as well as a sample Delphi component, WebHub, that extends your programming capabilities. The project files can be copied to your hard drive or used directly from the CD. This section describes the structure of the CD and explains how to copy files from it to your hard drive.

These instructions assume that your CD-ROM drive is D: and that your hard disk is drive C:. If your system is set up differently, you will need to substitute the correct drive letters for those used in these instructions.

Structure of the CD

The source code on the CD is organized into folders based on the chapter structure found in the book. Please note that some chapters will not have projects associated with them because the subject is an abstract class. For example, Chapter 3, "**TObject**," does not have a project associated with it because **TObject** is an abstract base class. On the other hand, some chapters have more than one project. These will be located in subfolders within the chapter folder.

At the top level of the CD is a folder called SOURCE. This folder contains subfolders for all the chapters that contain projects. For example, a subfolder called Chapter20 contains the **TCanvas** drawing projects for nonwindowed buttons. If individual folders contain more than one project, these projects are divided into their own subfolders within the chapter folders.

Copying the Files

Using My Computer or Explorer, you can create a new folder by displaying the contents of the C: drive, right-clicking the background, and choosing New and then Folder. When the new folder appears, type **DSB** and press ENTER. Now, navigate to the CD-ROM and select the chapter or chapters you would like to copy to your hard disk.

Choose Copy from the Edit menu (or press the Copy button on the taskbar if it is visible). Now, navigate back to your new folder on C:, open it, and select Paste from the Edit menu. The files you selected are copied to your hard disk.

If you want to copy *all* the example files, the simplest thing to do is to navigate to the root of the CD-ROM, Edit→Copy the SOURCE folder, and then Edit→Paste it into the appropriate folder on your hard drive. This copies everything at once and preserves the subfolder structure.

IMPORTANT

When Windows copies files from the CD to the hard drive, the read-only attribute is set. Remove the read only attribute by selecting the file(s). Right-click and select Properties. Uncheck the Read-only box and click on Apply and then OK.

Program Source Code

Each project can be loaded into the Delphi IDE and compiled. They are not designed to work with Delphi 1.0. The executable files on this CD were compiled with a late beta of Delphi 3. If you encounter problems, recompile the programs using the released version of Delphi 3.

The README.TXT File

The CD contains a file named README.TXT that can be read by any text editor (like Notepad) and provides up-to-date information about the projects and source code. To view this file, simply double-click it.

NOTE

The software program WebHub included on the CD is shareware, provided for your evaluation. If you find it useful, you are requested to register it as discussed in its documentation and/or in the About screen of the application. Waite Group Press has not paid the registration fee for this shareware.

INDEX

Symbols

3D effects
    bevel controls (TBevel class), 761-766
    Bevel property, TStatusPanel class, 258
    Beveled property, TSplitter class, 810
    BevelInner property, TPanel class, 1181-1182
    BevelOuter property, TPanel class, 1182
    BevelWidth property, TPanel class, 1183
    Ctl3D property
        TCommonDialog class/descendants, 498
        TWinControl class, 822
    ParentCtl3D property, TWinControl class, 829
16-bit applications, converting to 32-bit, 9-11
    unsupported Delphi 1.0 functions, 11
32-bit optimizing compiler, 5-6
= (equal signs), INI file keys, 36

A

AbsoluteIndex property, TTreeNode class, 183
Abstract directive, 24
accelerator keys, *see* hot keys (TCustomHotKey class)
Active property
    TApplication class, 390
    TDataLink class, 288-289
    TDataSet class, 567
    TForm class, 1060
    TSession class, 459
ActiveBuffer method, TDataSet class, 567-568
ActiveControl property
    TForm class, 1060
    TScreen class, 448-449
ActiveForm property, TScreen class, 449
ActiveMDIChild property, TForm class, 1061
ActivePage property, TPageControl class, 1006
ActiveRecord property, TDataLink class, 289
ActiveX controls, 103-105
Add Fields dialog box, 652

Add method
    TCollection class, 254
    TCustomImageList class/descendants, 521-522
    TList class, 78
    TListItems class, 154
    TMenuItem class, 431
    TPopupList class, 78
    TStrings class/descendants, 343
    TTreeNodes class, 205-206
AddAlias method, TSession class, 459-460
AddChild method, TTreeNodes class, 206-207
AddChildFirst method, TTreeNodes class, 207
AddChildObject method, TTreeNodes class, 208
AddChildObjectFirst method, TTreeNodes class, 208-209
AddFirst method, TTreeNodes class, 209-210
AddIcon method, TCustomImageList/TImageList classes, 522-523
AddImages method, TCustomImageList/TImageList classes, 523-524
AddMapping method, TGridDataLink class, 301
AddMasked method, TCustomImageList class/descendants, 524-525
AddObject method
    TStrings class/descendants, 344
    TTreeNodes class, 210
AddObjectFirst method, TTreeNodes class, 211
AddPassword method, TSession class, 460
AddStandardAlias method, TSession class, 460-461
AddStrings method, TStrings class/descendants, 344-345
AfterCancel event, TDataSet class, 568-569
AfterClose event, TDataSet class, 569
AfterDelete event, TDataSet class, 569-570
AfterEdit event, TDataSet class, 570-571
AfterInsert event, TDataSet class, 571
AfterOpen event, TDataSet class, 571-572
AfterPost event, TDataSet class, 572-573

Align property, TControl class, 720
AlignButton property, TUpDown class, 1045
Alignment property
TColumn class, 255
TColumnTitle class, 124-125
TField/TNumericField class, 662
THeaderSection class, 255
TListColumn class, 255
TParaAttributes class, 162
TPopupMenu class, 480-481
TStatusPanel class, 255
AllocBy property
TCustomImageList/TImageList classes, 525
TListView/TCustomListView classes, 964-965
AllowAllUp property, TSpeedButton class, 799-800
AllowClick property, THeaderSection class, 255-256
AllowDelete property, TDBCtrlGrid class, 840
AllowGrayed property, TCheckBox class, 1102-1103
AllowInsert property, TDBCtrlGrid class, 840-841
AlphaSort method
TCustomTreeView/TTreeView classes, 1022
TListView/TCustomListView classes, 965-966
TTreeNode class, 184
Append method, TDataSet class, 573-574
AppendRecord method, TDataSet class, 574-576
applications, see TApplication class
ApplyUpdates method, TDataSet class, 576-577
Arc method, TCanvas class, 221
Arrange method, TListView/TCustomListView classes, 966-967
ArrangeIcons method, TForm class, 1061-1063
Arrangement property, TIconsOptions class, 138
ArrowKeys property, TUpDown class, 1046
AsBoolean property, TField class/descendants, 662-663
AsCurrency property, TField class/descendants, 663-664
AsDateTime property, TField class/descendants, 664-665
AsFloat property, TField class/descendants, 665
AsInteger property, TField class/descendants, 665-666
Assign method
TCollection class, 256
TCustomImageList/TImageList classes, 526-527

Assign method (continued)
TField class/descendants, 666
TPersistent class, 109-110
TStrings class/descendants, 345-346
AssignedValues property, TColumn class, 257
AssignValue method, TField class/descendants, 667
Associate property, TUpDown class, 1046
AsString property, TField class/descendants, 667-668
AsText property, TClipboard class, 113
AsVariant property, TField class/descendants, 668
AttributeSet property, TField class/descendants, 669
AutoArrange property, TIconsOptions class, 138
AutoCalcFields property, TDataSet class, 577
AutoEdit property, TDataSource class, 424
AutoEnable property, TMediaPlayer class, 1155
AutoMerge property, TMainMenu class, 481-482
AutoOpen property, TMediaPlayer class, 1155-1156
AutoPopup property, TPopupMenu class, 482
AutoRewind property, TMediaPlayer class, 1156
AutoScroll property, TForm class, 1062
AutoSelect property, TEdit class, 1127
AutoSize property, TImage class, 770-771

B

Back method, TMediaPlayer class, 1156-1157
BDE (Borland Database Engine), 9
BeforeCancel event, TDataSet class, 578-579
BeforeClose event, TDataSet class, 579-580
BeforeDelete event, TDataSet class, 580-581
BeforeEdit event, TDataSet class, 581
BeforeInsert event, TDataSet class, 582-583
BeforeOpen event, TDataSet class, 583-584
BeforePost event, TDataSet class, 584-585
BeginDrag method
TControl class, 720-721
TCustomImageList/TImageList classes, 527
BeginUpdate method
TCollection class, 257-258
TListItems class, 154-155
TStrings class/descendants, 346
TTreeNodes class, 212
bevel controls (TBevel class), 761-766

Bevel property, TStatusPanel class, 258
Beveled property, TSplitter class, 810
BevelInner property, TPanel class, 1181-1182
BevelOuter property, TPanel class, 1182
BevelWidth property, TPanel class, 1183
Bitmap property
    TBrush class, 308
    TPicture class, 168
bitmaps (TBitmap class), 319-320
    Canvas property, 320
    Handle property, 323
    TBitmap class, 324, 327-328
    TBitmap/TIcon/TMetafile classes, 323, 329
    IgnorePalette property, 324
    Monochrome, 327-328
    Palette property, 329
    see also glyph images; graphics
BkColor property, TCustomImageList/TImageList classes, 527-528
BlendColor property, TCustomImageList/TImageList classes, 528-529
BlobType property, TBlobField class, 658, 669-670
BOF property, TDataSet class, 577-578
Bookmark property, TDataSet class, 585
bookmarks
    FreeBookmark method, TDataSet class, 608
    GetBookmark method, TDataSet class, 608-609
    GotoBookmark method, TDataSet class, 611-612
boolean values
    ReadBool method, TRegistry class, 71
    ReadBool property, TIniFile class, 39-40
    WriteBool method
        TIniFile class, 45-46
        TRegistry class, 73-74
BorderIcons property, TForm class, 1064
BorderStyle property, TCustomListBox class/descendants, 942-943
Borland Database Engine (BDE), 9
BoundingRect property, TListView/TCustomListView classes, 967
BoundsRect property, TControl class, 721
Break property, TMenuItem class, 431-432

BringToFront method
    TApplication class, 391
    TControl class, 721-722
brush object, *see* TBrush class
Brush property
    TCanvas class, 222
    TShape class, 782-783
BtnClick method, TDBNavigator class, 1185-1186
buddy controls, 1039-1040
BufferCount property, TDataLink class, 289-290
buttons
    ButtonStyle property, TColumn class, 258-259
    ColoredButtons property, TMediaPlayer class, 1159
    EnabledButtons property, TMediaPlayer class, 1161
    glyphs, 1092
        Glyph property (TBitBtn class), 1104-1105
        image number, 1112
        layout, 1107-1108
        margins, 1108-1109
        spacing, 1112-1113
    speedbuttons, *see* TSpeedButton class
    TButtonControl class, *see* TButtonControl class
    VisibleButtons property,
        TDBNavigator class, 1188
        TMediaPlayer class, 1179

C

CachedUpdates property, TDataSet class, 585-586
Calculated property, TField class/descendants, 670-671
Cancel method, TDataSet class, 587
Cancel property, TButton/TBitBtn classes, 1103
CancelEdit method, TListItem class, 142-143
CancelUpdates method, TDataSet class, 588
CanModify property
    TDataSet class, 586-587
    TField class/descendants, 671
    TFieldDataLink class, 294
canvas objects, 217-220
    events, 218
        OnChange, 233-234
        OnChanging, 234-235

canvas objects (*continued*)
  handles, 217
    CreateHandle method (TPrinterCanvas objects), 220
    LineTo method, 232
  metafile canvas objects, 219-220
  methods, 218-219
    Arc, 221
    Chord, 223
    CopyRect, 225-226
    Draw, 226
    DrawFocusRect, 227
    Ellipse, 228
    FillRect, 228-229
    FloodFill, 229
    FrameRect, 231
    LineTo, 232
    MoveTo, 232
    Pie, 237-238
    Polygon, 239
    Polyline, 240
    Rectangle, 240-241
    Refresh, 241
    RoundRect, 241-242
    StretchDraw, 242-243
    TextHeight, 243
    TextOut, 244
    TextRect, 244-245
    TextWidth, 245
  properties, 218
    Brush, 222
    CopyMode, 224
    Font, 230
    Handle, 231
    Pen, 235-236
    PenPos, 237
  printer canvas objects, 220
Canvas property
  TBitmap class, 320
  TGraphicControl class, 758-759
Capabilities property, TMediaPlayer class, 1157-1158
Capacity method, TList class, 79

Capacity property, TStrings class/descendants, 346-347
Caption property
  TColumnTitle class, 125
  TControl class, 722
  TListItem class, 143
  TMenuItem class, 432-433
Cascade method, TForm class, 1064-1065
CD-ROM included with book, 1197-1198
  Delphi 3 SuperBible Help System, 26
Center property, Image class, 771-772
character types, 6-7
CharCase property, TEdit/TMaskEdit classes, 1127-1128
check boxes
  TCheckBox class, 1096-1097
    AllowGrayed property, 1102-1103
    Checked property, 1104
    State property, 1113-1114
  TCustomCheckBox, 1093-1095
CheckBrowseMode method, TDataSet class, 588-589
Checked property
  TCheckBox/TRadioButton classes, 1104
  TMenuItem class, 433-434
CheckRange property, TBCDField class, 671-672
child windows
  MDI applications, 1056
  see also TForm class
Chord method, TCanvas class, 223
classes
  Exception, 89, 91-92, 96-97
    Create method, 97
    CreateFmt method, 97
    CreateFmtHelp method, 97-98
    CreateHelp method, 98
    CreateRes method, 98-99
    CreateResFmt method, 99
    CreateResFmtHelp method, 99-100
    HelpContext property, 100
    Message property, 100-101
    see also exceptions
  Metafile, 319
  TApplication, 387-390

classes (*continued*)

    Active property, 390

    BringToFront method, 391

    CreateForm method, 391-392

    ExeName property, 392

    Handle property, 392-393

    HelpCommand method, 393-395

    HelpContext method, 395

    HelpFile property, 396

    HelpJump method, 396

    HintColor property, 397

    HintHidePause property, 397

    HintPause property, 398

    HintShortPause property, 398-399

    Icon property, 399

    Initialize method, 400

    MainForm property, 400-401

    MessageBox method, 402-404

    Minimize method, 404

    OnActivate event, 404-405

    OnDeActivate event, 406-407

    OnException event, 407-408

    OnHelp event, 408

    OnHint event, 409-410

    OnIdle event, 410-411

    OnMessage event, 411-412

    OnMinimize event, 413-414

    OnRestore event, 414-415

    OnShowHint event, 415-417

    Restore method, 417-418

    Run method, 418-419

    ShowHint property, 419

    ShowMainForm property, 419-420

    Terminate method, 420

    Title property, 420-421

TAutoIncField, 657

    see also TField class

TBCDField, 657-658

    CheckRange property, 671-672

    Currency property, 674-675

    DisplayFormat property, 678

    MaxValue function, 696

    MinValue function, 696-697

    Precision property, 702

    SetCurrency method, 706

    Size property, 707

classes (*continued*)

TBevel, 761-766

TBinaryField, 658

    Size property, 707

TBitBtn, 1091-1093

    Cancel property, 1103

    Glyph property, 1104-1105

    Kind property, 1106-1107

    Layout property, 1107-1108

    Margin property, 1108-1109

    ModalResult property, 1109-1111

    NumGlyphs property, 1112

    Spacing property, 1112-1113

    Style property, 1114

    see also TSpeedButton class

TBitmap, 319-320

    Canvas property, 320

    Handle property, 323

    IgnorePalette property, 324

    Monochrome, 327-328

    Palette property, 329

    see also TGraphics class

TBlobField

    BlobType property, 658-670

    LoadFromFile function, 690-691

    LoadFromStream function, 691

    SaveToFile method, 704

    SaveToStream method, 705

    SetFieldType method, 707

    Size property, 707

TBoolean, 658

    see also TField class

TBrush, 306, 315

    Bitmap property, 308

    Color property, 309

    Handle property, 309-310

    OnChange event, 312-313

    Style property, 314-315

TButton, 1087-1091

    Cancel property, 1103

    ModalResult property, 1109-1111

TButtonControl, 1087

    see also TButton class; TSpeedButton class

TBytesField, 659

    see also TField class

classes (*continued*)

TCanvas, 217-220
  Arc method, 221
  Brush property, 222
  Chord method, 223
  CopyMode property, 224
  CopyRect method, 225-226
  derivation, 217
  Draw method, 226
  DrawFocusRect method, 227
  Ellipse method, 228
  FillRect method, 228-229
  FloodFill method, 229
  Font property, 230
  FrameRect method, 231
  Handle property, 231
  LineTo method, 232
  MoveTo method, 232
  OnChange event, 233-234
  OnChanging event, 234-235
  Pen property, 235-236
  PenPos property, 237
  Pie method, 237-238
  Polygon method, 239
  Polyline method, 240
  Rectangle method, 240-241
  Refresh method, 241
  RoundRect method, 241-242
  StretchDraw method, 242-243
  TextHeight method, 243
  TextOut method, 244
  TextRect method, 244-245
  TextWidth method, 245
  TMetaFileCanvas child class, 219-220
  TPrinter child class, 220
TCheckBox, 1096-1097
  AllowGrayed property, 1102-1103
  Checked property, 1104
  State property, 1113-1114
TClipboard, 111-112
  AsText property, 113
  Clear method, 113
  Close method, 114
  FormatCount property, 114
  Formats property, 115

classes (*continued*)

  GetAsHandle method, 116
  GetComponent method, 116-117
  GetTextBuf method, 117-118
  HasFormat method, 118-119
  Open method, 119
  SetAsHandle method, 119-120
  SetComponent method, 120
  SetTextBuf method, 121
TCollection, 247-254
  Add method, 254
  Assign method, 256
  BeginUpdate method, 257-258
  Clear method, 260
  Count property, 262-263
  Create method, 262-263
  Destroy method, 266
  EndUpdate method, 267
  example project, 282-285
  FindItemID method, 269
  GetItem method, 272
  Items property, 273-274
  TDBGridColumns class, see
    TDBGridColumns class
  THeaderSection class, 251
  THeaderSections class, 250
  TListColumns class, 249
  TStatusPanels class, 251, 282-285
TCollectionItem, 247-254
  Collection property, 260-261
  Create method, 262-263
  Destroy method, 266
  example project, 282-285
  Index property, 273
  SetIndex method, 278-279
  TColumn class, see TColumn class
  THeaderSection class, see THeaderSection
    class
  TListColumn class, see TListColumn class
  TStatusPanel class, see TStatusPanel class
TColorDialog, 489
  Color property, 497
  Ctl3D property, 498
  CustomColors property, 499
  Execute method, 501

classes (*continued*)

    HelpContext property, 505-506

    Options property, 510-511

  TColumn

    Alignment property, 255

    AssignedValues property, 257

    ButtonStyle property, 258-259

    Color property, 261

    CreateTitle method, 263

    DefaultAlignment method, 264

    DefaultColor method, 264

    DefaultFont method, 265

    DefaultReadOnly method, 265

    DefaultWidth method, 266

    DropDownRows property, 267

    Field property, 268

    Fieldname property, 268

    Font property, 269-270

    GetGrid method, 271

    PickList property, 276

    ReadOnly property, 277

    RestoreDefaults method, 278

    Title property, 281

    Width property, 281

  TColumnTitle, 123-124

    Alignment property, 124-125

    Caption property, 125

    Color property, 125

    DefaultAlignment method, 126

    DefaultCaption method, 126-127

    DefaultColor method, 127

    DefaultFont method, 127-128

    Font property, 128-129

    RestoreDefaults method, 129

  TComboBox, 914-915

    Clear method, 916-917

    DropDownCount property, 918

    DroppedDown property, 918

    ItemHeight property, 920

    ItemIndex property, 920-921

    Items property, 921-922

    OnDrawItem event, 922-923

    OnDropDown event, 922

    OnMeasureItem event, 923

    Sorted property, 924

classes (*continued*)

    Style property, 924-925

    see also TCustomComboBox class;

      TDBComboBox class

  TComboBoxStrings, 336

    Add method, 343

    see also TStrings class

  TCommonDialog, 487-488

    Ctl3D property, 498

    HelpContext property, 505-506

  TComponent, 379-380

    ComponentCount property, 381

    ComponentIndex property, 381

    Components property, 382

    ComponentState property, 382-383

    DestroyComponents method, 383

    Destroying method, 383

    FindComponent method, 383-384

    Name property, 384-385

    Owner property, 385

    Tag property, 385-386

  TControl, 717-719

    Align property, 720

    BeginDrag method, 720-721

    BoundsRect property, 721

    BringToFront method, 721-722

    Caption property, 722

    ClientHeight property, 722-723

    ClientOrigin property, 723

    ClientRect property, 723-724

    ClientToScreen method, 724

    ClientWidth property, 724-725

    Color property, 725

    ControlState property, 725

    ControlStyle property, 726

    Cursor property, 726

    DragCursor property, 727

    Dragging method, 727

    DragMode property, 728

    Enabled property, 728

    EndDrag method, 728-729

    Font property, 729

    GetTextBuf method, 729

    GetTextLen method, 730

    Height property, 730

classes (*continued*)

    Hide method, 731

    Hint property, 731-732

    Invalidate method, 733

    Left property, 733

    OnClick event, 733-734

    OnDblClick event, 734-735

    OnDragDrop event, 735-736

    OnDragOver event, 736-738

    OnEndDrag event, 738-739

    OnMouseDown event, 739-740

    OnMouseEvent event, 740-741

    OnMouseUp event, 741-742

    OnStartDrag event, 742-743

    Parent property, 743-744

    ParentColor property, 744

    ParentFont property, 744

    ParentShowHint property, 745

    PopupMenu property, 745

    Refresh method, 746

    Repaint method, 746

    ScreenToClient method, 746-747

    SendToBack method, 747

    SetBounds method, 747-748

    SetTextBuf method, 748

    Show method, 748-749

    ShowHint property, 749

    Text property, 749-750

    Top property, 750

    Update method, 750

    Visible property, 751

    Width property, 751

  TControlScrollBar, 131-132

    Increment property, 132-133

    Kind property, 133

    Margin property, 133

    methods, 132

    Position property, 134

    Range property, 134

    ScrollPos property, 135

    Visible property, 135

  TCurrencyField, 659

    Currency property, 674-675

    DisplayFormat property, 678

    MaxValue function, 696

classes (*continued*)

    MinValue function, 696-697

    Precision property, 702

    see also TField class

  TCustomCheckBox, 1093-1095

  TCustomComboBox, 909-913

    Clear method, 916-917

    DropDownCount property, 918

    DroppedDown property, 918

    ItemIndex property, 920-921

    Items property, 921-922

    TComboBox, 914-915

    TDBComboBox, 915-916

    TDriveComboBox, 910

    TFilterComboBox, 910

    see also TComboBox; TDBComboBox

  TCustomControl, see TCustomControl class

  TCustomEdit, 1115-1119

    Clear method, 1128

    ClearSelection method, 1129

    CopyToClipboard method, 1129-1130

    CutToClipboard method, 1130

    GetSelectTextBuf method, 1134-1135

    MaxLength property, 1137

    Modified property, 1137-1138

    PasteFromClipboard method, 1141

    SelectAll method, 1144

    SelLength property, 1144-1145

    SelStart property, 1144-1145

    SelText property, 1145

    SetSelTextBuf method, 1146

    TCustomMemo class,

      see TCustomMemo class

    see also edit controls

  TCustomGroupBox, 1188-1189

    TCustomRadioGroup class, 1190-1191

    TGroupBox class, 1189-1190

    TRadioGroup class, 1191-1194

    see also TCustomControl class

  TCustomHotKey, 927-931

    THotKey class, 931-933

  TCustomImageList, 517-520

    Add method, 521-522

    AddIcon method, 522-523

    AddImages method, 523-524

classes (*continued*)

    AddMasked method, 524-525

    AllocBy property, 525

    Assign method, 526-527

    BeginDrag method, 527

    BkColor property, 527-528

    BlendColor property, 528-529

    Clear method, 529

    Count property, 529

    Create method, 530

    CreateSize method, 530-531

    Delete method, 531-532

    Destroy method, 532

    DragCursor property, 533

    Dragging property, 533-534

    DragLock method, 534

    DragMove method, 534-535

    DragUnlock method, 535

    Draw method, 535

    DrawingStyle property, 536

    DrawOverlay method, 537-538

    EFireLoad method, 538-539

    EndDrag method, 538

    GetBitmap method, 539-540

    GetHotSpot method, 540

    GetIcon method, 540-541

    GetImageBitmap method, 541

    GetInstRes method, 542

    GetMaskBitmap method, 542

    GetResource method, 543

    Handle property, 544

    HandleAllocated property, 544-545

    Height property, 545

    HideDragImage method, 545

    ImageType property, 545-546

    Insert method, 546-547

    InsertIcon method, 547-548

    InsertMasked method, 548-549

    Masked property, 549

    Move method, 549-550

    OnChange event, 550

    Overlay method, 550-551

    RegisterChanges method, 551-554

    Replace method, 554-555

    ReplaceIcon method, 555

classes (*continued*)

    ReplaceMasked method, 555-556

    ResInstLoad method, 556

    ResourceLoad method, 556-557

    SetDragImage method, 557

    ShareImages property, 557-558

    ShowDragImage method, 558

    TGlyphList, see TGlyphList class

    TImageList, see TImageList class

    UnRegisterChanges method, 558-559

    Width property, 559

  TCustomLabel, 787-791, 793

    properties/method/events, 788-790

    TDBText class, 790

    TLabel class, 791-792

  TCustomListBox, 935-939

    BorderStyle property, 942-943

    Clear method, 943

    ExtendedSelect property, 945

    IntegralHeight property, 946

    ItemAtPos method, 947-948

    ItemHeight property, 948

    ItemIndex property, 948-949

    ItemRect method, 949-950

    Items property, 950

    MultiSelect property, 951

    OnMeasureItem event, 951-952

    SelCount property, 952-953

    Selected property, 953

    Sorted property, 954

    TDBListBox, 939-941, 944, 952

    TListBox, 941-942

    TopIndex property, 954-955

  TCustomListView, 957-962

    AllocBy property, 964-965

    AlphaSort method, 965-966

    Arrange method, 966-967

    BoundingRect property, 967

    Column property, 968

    ColumnClick property, 968-969

    Columns property, 969-970

    ColumnSort method, 970-971

    DropTarget property, 971-972

    FindCaption method, 972-974

    FindData method, 974-975

classes (*continued*)

GetItemAt method, 976
GetNearestItem method, 976-977
GetNextItem method, 978-979
IconOptions property, 979-980
IsEditing method, 980
ItemFocused property, 980-981
Items property, 981-982
LargeImages property, 982-983
MultiSelect property, 983
OnChange event, 983
OnChanging event, 984
OnColumnClick event, 984-985
OnCompare event, 985
OnDeletion event, 985-986
OnEdited event, 986
OnEditing event, 986-987
OnInsert event, 987
ReadOnly property, 988
Scroll method, 988
SelCount property, 988-989
Selected property, 989
ShowColumnHeaders property, 989-990
SmallImages property, 990
SortTypes property, 990-991
StateImages property, 991-992
StringWidth method, 992-993
UpdateItems method, 993-994
ViewOrigin property, 994
VisibleRowCount property, 995
TCustomMaskEdit, 1121
TMaskEdit class, 1121-1123
see also TCustomEdit class
TCustomMemo, 1123
Lines property, 1137
TCustomRichEdit,
see TCustomRichEdit class
TMemo class, 1123-1125, 1136,
1142-1143, 1146-1148
see also TCustomEdit class
TCustomPanel, 1180
TDBNavigator class, 1184-1188
TPanel class, 1180-1184
see also TCustomControl class

classes (*continued*)

TCustomRadioGroup, 1190-1191
methods, 1191
TRadioGroup class, 1191-1194
TCustomRichEdit, 1125
DefAttributes property, 1131
Paragraph property, 1139-1140
Print property, 1142
SelAttributes property, 1144
TRichEdit class, see TRichEdit class
see also TCustomMemo class
TCustomTabControl, 997-1002
TPageControl class, see TPageControl class
TCustomTreeView, 1015-1019
AlphaSort method, 1022
FullCollapse method, 1022-1023
FullExpand method, 1023
GetHitTestInfoAt method, 1023-1025
GetNodeAt method, 1025-1026
HideSelection property, 1026
Images property, 1026-1027
IsEditing method, 1027
Items property, 1028
OnChanging event, 1028-1029
OnCollapsed event, 1029
OnCollapsing event, 1029-1030
OnCompare event, 1030
OnDeletion event, 1030-1031
OnEdited event, 1031
OnEditing event, 1031-1032
OnExpanded event, 1032
OnExpanding event, 1032
OnGetImageIndex event, 1033
OnSelectedIndex event, 1033
ReadOnly property, 1034
ShowButtons property, 1034-1035
ShowLines property, 1035-1036
ShowRoot property, 1036-1037
SortImages property, 1038
SortType property, 1037-1038
TCustomUpDown, 1039-1044
TUpDown class, 1044-1050
TDataLink, 287-288
Active property, 288-289
ActiveRecord property, 289

classes (*continued*)

    BufferCount property, 289-290

    DataSet property, 290

    DataSource property, 290

    DataSourceFixed property, 291

    Edit method, 291-292

    Editing property, 291

    ReadOnly property, 292

    RecordCount property, 292

    UpdateRecord method, 293

    TDataSourceLink class, 299

    TDBCtrlGridLink class, 304

    TFieldDataLink class, 293-299

    TGridDataLink class, 300-304

    TListSourceLink class, 300

    TNavDataLink class, 299

    TQueryDataLink class, 299

    TTableDataLink class, 293

  TDataSet, 563-566

    Active property, 567

    ActiveBuffer method, 567-568

    AfterCancel event, 568-569

    AfterClose event, 569

    AfterDelete event, 569-570

    AfterEdit event, 570-571

    AfterInsert event, 571

    AfterOpen event, 571-572

    AfterPost event, 572-573

    Append method, 573-574

    AppendRecord method, 574-576

    ApplyUpdates method, 576-577

    AutoCalcFields property, 577

    BeforeCancel event, 578-579

    BeforeClose event, 579-580

    BeforeDelete event, 580-581

    BeforeEdit event, 581

    BeforeInsert event, 582-583

    BeforeOpen event, 583-584

    BeforePost event, 584-585

    BOF property, 577-578

    Bookmark property, 585

    CachedUpdates property, 585-586

    Cancel method, 587

    CancelUpdates method, 588

    CanModify property, 586-587

classes (*continued*)

    CheckBrowseMode method, 588-589

    ClearFields method, 589

    Close method, 589-590

    CommitUpdates method, 590-591

    ControlsDisabled method, 591

    CursorPosChanged method, 591-592

    DataSource property, 592

    DefaultFields property, 592-593

    Delete method, 593

    DisableControls method, 594

    Edit method, 594-595

    EnableControls method, 595-596

    EOF property, 596

    ExpIndex property, 597

    FetchAll method, 597

    FieldByName method, 597-598

    FieldCount property, 598-599

    FieldDefs property, 599-600

    Fields property, 601

    FieldValues property, 600-601

    Filter property, 602

    Filtered property, 603

    FilterOptions property, 603

    FindField method, 604-606

    FindFirst/FindLast/FindNext/FindPrior methods, 605-606

    First method, 606-607

    Found property, 607-608

    FreeBookmark method, 608

    GetBookmark method, 608-609

    GetCurrentRecord method, 609

    GetFieldList method, 610

    GetFieldNames method, 610-611

    GotoBookmark method, 611-612

    Handle property, 612

    Insert method, 612-613

    InsertRecord method, 613-616

    IsLinkedTo method, 616

    KeySize property, 616-617

    Last method, 617-618

    Locale property, 618

    Locate method, 618-619

    Lookup method, 619-621

    Modified property, 621

classes (*continued*)

    MoveBy method, 621-622

    Next method, 622-623

    OnCalcFields event, 623-624

    OnDeleteError event, 624-625

    OnEditError event, 625-627

    OnFilterRecord event, 627-628

    OnNewRecord event, 628-629

    OnPostError event, 629-630

    OnServerYield event, 630-631

    OnUpdateError event, 631-632

    OnUpdateRecord event, 633-634

    Open method, 634-635

    Post method, 635

    Prior method, 635-636

    RecNo property, 636

    RecordCount property, 637

    RecordSize property, 637-638

    Refresh method, 638-639

    Resync method, 639

    RevertRecord method, 640

    SetDetailFields method, 640-641

    SetFields method, 641-642

    State property, 642

    TDBDataSet, 563-564, 646

    TQuery, 563-564, 647

    TStoredProc, 563-564, 646-647

    TTable, 563-564, 646-647

    UpdateCursorPos method, 643

    UpdateObject property, 643-644

    UpdateRecord method, 644

    UpdateRecordTypes property, 644-645

    UpdatesPending property, 645

    UpdateStatus method, 645

  TDataSource, 423-424

    AutoEdit property, 424

    DataSet property, 424-425

    Edit method, 425

    Enabled property, 425-426

    IsLinkedTo method, 426

    OnDataChange event, 426-427

    OnStateChange event, 427

    OnUpdateData event, 427

    State property, 428

classes (*continued*)

  TDataSourceLink, 299

  TDateField, 659

    DisplayFormat property, 678

    see also TField class

  TDateTimeField, 659

    DisplayFormat property, 678

    see also TField class

  TDBComboBox, 915-916

    Clear method, 916-917

    DataField property, 917

    DataSource property, 917

    DropDownCount property, 918

    DroppedDown property, 918

    Field property, 919-920

    ItemHeight property, 920

    ItemIndex property, 920-921

    Items property, 921-922

    OnDrawItem event, 922-923

    OnDropDown event, 922

    OnMeasureItem event, 923

    ReadOnly property, 923-924

    Sorted property, 924

    Style property, 924-925

    see also TCustomComboBox class;

      TComboBox class

  TDBCtrlGrid, 835-840

    AllowDelete property, 840

    AllowInsert property, 840-841

    ColCount property, 841

    DataSource property, 841

    DoKey method, 842-843

    EditMode property, 843

    OnPaintPanel event, 843-845

    Orientation property, 845

    PanelBorder property, 846

    PanelCount property, 847

    PanelHeight property, 847

    PanelIndex property, 847

    PanelWidth property, 848

    RowCount property, 848

    ShowFocus property, 848-849

  TDBCtrlGridLink, 304

classes (*continued*)

TDBDataSet, 563-564, 646
    see also TDataSet class
TDBEdit, *see TCustomMaskEdit class*
TDBGridColumns
    Grid property, 272-273
    Rebuild Columns method, 277
    RestoreDefaults method, 278
    State property, 279
TDBListBox, 939-941
    DataField property, 944
    DataSource property, 944
    ReadOnly property, 952
    see also TCustomListBox class
TDBMemo, *see TCustomMemo class*
TDBNavigator, 1184-1185
    BtnClick method, 1185-1186
    ConfirmDelete property, 1186
    DataSource property, 1186-1187
    Hints property, 1187
    SetBounds method, 1187-1188
    VisibleButtons property, 1188
    see also TCustomControl class
TDBRichEdit, *see TCustomRichEdit class*
TDBText class, 790-791
    DataField/DataSource properties, 793
TDirectoryListBox, 935
TDriveComboBox, 910
    see also TCustomComboBox class
TEdit, 1119-1121
    AutoSelect property, 1127
    CharCase property, 1127-1128
    HideSelection property, 1136
    PasswordChar property, 1140-1141
    ReadOnly property, 1142-1143
    see also TCustomEdit class
TField, 649-651, 653-657
    Alignment property, 662
    AsBoolean property, 662-663
    AsCurrency property, 663-664
    AsDateTime property, 664-665
    AsFloat property, 665
    AsInteger property, 665-666
    Assign method, 666

classes (*continued*)

    AssignValue method, 667
    AsString property, 667-668
    AsVariant property, 668
    AttributeSet property, 669
    Calculated property, 670-671
    CanModify property, 671
    Clear method, 672
    Create constructor, 673-674
    DataSet property, 675
    DataSize property, 675-676
    DataType property, 676-677
    Destroy destructor, 677
    DisplayLabel property, 678-679
    DisplayName property, 679
    DisplayText property, 680
    DisplayValues property, 680-681
    DisplayWidth property, 681
    EditFormat property, 681-682
    EditMask property, 682
    EditMaskPtr property, 683
    FieldKind property, 683-684
    FieldName property, 684-685
    FieldNo property, 685
    FocusControl method, 685-686
    GetData function, 686
    Index property, 687
    IsBlob function, 687-688
    IsIndexField function, 688
    IsNull property, 689
    IsValidChar function, 689
    KeyFields property, 690
    Lookup property, 691-692
    LookupCache property, 692-693
    LookupDataSet property, 693
    LookupKeyFields function, 693-694
    LookupList function, 694-695
    LookupResultField function, 695
    NewValue property, 697
    Offset function, 698
    OldValue property, 698-699
    OnChange event, 699
    OnGetText event, 700
    OnSetText event, 700

classes (*continued*)

    OnValidate event, 701
    ReadOnly property, 702-703
    RefreshLookupList method, 703
    Required property, 703-704
    ServerCalcField property, 705-706
    SetData method, 706
    SetFieldType method, 707
    Size property, 707
    TAutoIncField class, 657
    TBCDField class, see TBCDField class
    TBinaryField class, 658, 707
    TBlobField class, see TBlobField class
    TBoolean class, 658
    TBytesField class, 659
    TCurrencyField class,
       see TCurrencyField class
    TDateField class, 678
    TDateTimeField class, 678
    Text property, 708
    TFloatField class, see TFloatField class
    TGraphicField class, 660, 690-691,
       704-705
    TIntegerField class, 660, 678, 696-697
    TMemoField class, 690-691, 704-705, 708
    TNumericField class, 660
    Transliterate property, 709
    TSmallIntField class, 661, 678, 696-697
    TStringField class, 661, 707-708
    TTimeField class, 661, 678
    TVarBytesField class, 661
    TWordField class, 661, 678, 696-697
    Validate property, 709
    ValidChars property, 709
    Value property, 710
    Visible property, 711-712
    see also fields
  TFieldDataLink, 293-294
    CanModify property, 294
    Control property, 294-295
    Edit method, 295
    Editing property, 295
    Field property, 296
    FieldName property, 296-297

classes (*continued*)

    Modified method, 297
    OnActiveChange event, 297
    OnDataChange event, 298
    OnEditingChange event, 298
    OnUpdateData event, 298-299
    Reset method, 299
  TFileListBox, 935
  TFilterComboBox, 910
    see also TCustomComboBox class
  TFindDialog, 489-490
    Ctl3D property, 498
    Execute method, 501
    FindText property, 504
    Handle property, 505
    HelpContext property, 505
    Left property, 506-507
    OnFind event, 509
    Options property, 510-512
    Position property, 513-514
    Top property, 516
    see also TReplace class
  TFloatField, 659-660
    Currency property, 674-675
    DisplayFormat property, 678
    MaxValue function, 696
    MinValue function, 696-697
    Precision property, 702
    see also TField class
  TFont, 307, 315-316
    Color property, 309
    Handle property, 309-310
    Height property, 310
    Name property, 312
    OnChange event, 312-313
    Pitch property, 313
    Size property, 314
    Style property, 314-316
  TFontDialog, 490-491
    Ctl3D property, 498
    Device property, 500
    Execute method, 501
    Font property, 504-505
    HelpContext property, 505-506

classes (*continued*)

      MaxFontSize property, 507

      MinFontSize property, 507-508

      OnApply event, 508

      Options property, 510, 512

   TForm, 1051-1052, 1055-1059

      Active property, 1060

      ActiveControl property, 1060

      ActiveMDIChild property, 1061

      ArrangeIcons method, 1061-1063

      AutoScroll property, 1062

      BorderIcons property, 1064

      Cascade method, 1064-1065

      ClientHandle property, 1065-1066

      ClientHeight property, 1066

      ClientWidth property, 1067

      Close method, 1067-1068

      DefocusControl method, 1068-1069

      FocusControl method, 1069-1070

      FormStyle property, 1070-1071

      Icon property, 1072

      KeyPreview property, 1072-1074

      MDI applications, 1056-1057

      MDIChildCount property, 1074-1075

      MDIChildren property, 1075-1076

      Menu property, 1076-1078

      Next method, 1078

      Position property, 1079

      Previous method, 1079-1080

      Print method, 1080-1081

      PrintScale property, 1080-1081

      Show method, 1082

      ShowModal method, 1082

      Tile method, 1082-1083

      WindowMenu property, 1083-1084

      WindowState property, 1084-1085

      see also TScrollingWinControl class

   TGlyphList, 517, 521

      Add method, 521-522

      AddMasked method, 524-525

      Count property, 529

      Create method, 530

      Delete method, 531-532

      Destroy method, 532

classes (*continued*)

   TGraphic, 317-318

      Empty property, 322

      Height property, 323

      LoadFromClipboardFormat method, 324-325

      LoadFromFile method, 325-326

      Modified property, 327

      OnChange event, 328-329

      SaveToClipboardFormat method, 329-330

      SaveToFile method, 330-331

      TBitmap class, 319-320, 323-324, 327-329

      TIcon class, 318-319, 323

      TMetafile class, 319, 321-323, 326, 329

      Width property, 331

   TGraphicControl, 755-759

      events, 756-758

      methods, 756-758

      properties, 756-758

      see also nowindowed controls

   TGraphicField, 660

      LoadFromFile function, 690-691

      LoadFromStream function, 691

      SaveToFile method, 704

      SaveToStream method, 705

      see also TField class

   TGraphicsObject, 305-306

      properties/methods/events, 306

      TBrush class, 306, 308-309, 312-315

      TFont class, 307, 309-310, 312-316

      TPen class, 306-307, 309-316

   TGridDataLink, 300

      AddMapping method, 301

      ClearMapping method, 301

      DefaultFields property, 302

      FieldCount property, 302

      Fields property, 302-303

      Modified method, 303

      Reset method, 303

      SparseMap property, 303-304

   TGroupBox, 1189-1190

   THeaderControl, 851-855

      methods, 852-855

      OnDrawSection event, 855

classes (*continued*)

    OnResize event, 855
    OnSectionClick event, 856-857
    OnSectionResize event, 857-858
    OnSectionTrack event, 858-859
    Sections property, 859
  THeaderSection
    Alignment property, 255
    AllowClick property, 255-256
    Left property, 274-275
    MaxWidth property, 275
    MinWidth property, 275-276
    Right property, 278
    Style property, 280
    Text property, 280
    Width property, 281
  THeaderStrings, 336-337
    see also TStrings class
  THotKey, 927-928, 931-932
    HotKey property, 932-933
    InvalidKeys property, 933-934
    Modifiers property, 934
    see also TCustomHotKey class
  TIcon, 318-319
    Handle property, 323
    see also TGraphic class
  TIconOptions, 137-139
    Arrangement property, 138
    AutoArrange property, 138
    WrapText property, 139
  TImage, 767-773
    AutoSize property, 770-771
    Center property, 771-772
    Picture property, 772
    Stretch property, 773
  TImageList, 517, 520
    Add method, 521-522
    AddIcon method, 522-523
    AddImages method, 523-524
    AddMasked method, 524-525
    AllocBy property, 525
    Assign method, 526-527
    BeginDrag method, 527
    BkColor property, 527-528

classes (*continued*)

    BlendColor property, 528-529
    Clear method, 529
    Count property, 529
    Create method, 530
    CreateSize method, 530-531
    Delete method, 531-532
    Destroy method, 532
    DragCursor property, 533
    Dragging property, 533-534
    DragLock method, 534
    DragMove method, 534-535
    DragUnlock method, 535
    Draw method, 535
    DrawingStyle property, 536
    DrawOverlay method, 537-538
    EndDrag method, 538
    example project, 559-561
    FireLoad method, 538-539
    GetBitmap method, 539-540
    GetHotSpot method, 540
    GetIcon method, 540-541
    GetImageBitmap method, 541
    GetInstRes method, 542
    GetMaskBitmap method, 542
    GetResource method, 543
    Handle property, 544
    HandleAllocated property, 544-545
    Height property, 545
    HideDragImage method, 545
    ImageType property, 545-546
    Insert method, 546-547
    InsertIcon method, 547-548
    InsertMasked method, 548-549
    Masked property, 549
    Move method, 549-550
    OnChange event, 550
    Overlay method, 550-551
    RegisterChanges method, 551-554
    Replace method, 554-555
    ReplaceIcon method, 555
    ReplaceMasked method, 555-556
    ResInstLoad method, 556
    ResourceLoad method, 556-557

classes (*continued*)

    SetDragImage method, 557

    ShareImages property, 557-558

    ShowDragImage method, 558

    UnRegisterChanges method, 558-559

    Width property, 559

TIndexFiles, 337

    Add method, 343

    see also TStrings class

TIniFile, 35-37

    Create method, 37

    DeleteKey method, 37-38

    EraseSection method, 38-39

    FileName property, 39

    ReadBool property, 39-40

    ReadInteger method, 40-41

    ReadSection method, 41-42

    ReadSections method, 42

    ReadSectionValues method, 43-44

    ReadString method, 45

    WriteBool method, 45-46

    WriteInteger method, 46-47

    WriteString method, 47-48

TInplaceEdit, *see TCustomMaskEdit class*

TIntegerField, 660

    DisplayFormat property, 678

    MaxValue function, 696

    MinValue function, 696-697

    see also TField class

TLabel, 791-792

TList, 75-77

    Add method, 78

    Capacity method, 79

    Clear method, 79-80

    Count method, 80

    Delete method, 81

    Exchange method, 81-82

    Expand method, 82

    First method, 82-83

    IndexOf method, 83

    Insert method, 83-84

    Item property, 84

    Last method, 84-85

    List property, 85

classes (*continued*)

    Move method, 85-86

    Pack method, 86

    Remove method, 86-87

    Sort method, 87-88

TListBox, 941-942

    see also TCustomListBox class

TListBoxStrings, 338

    Add method, 343

    see also TStrings class

TListColumn, 249

    Alignment property, 255

    Width property, 281

    WidthType property, 282

TListColumns, 249

    Owner property, 276

TListItem, 141-142

    CancelEdit method, 142-143

    Caption property, 143

    Create method, 143-144

    Cut property, 144

    Data property, 145

    Delete method, 145-146

    DropTarget property, 146

    EditCaption method, 146-147

    Focused property, 147

    Handle property, 147-148

    ImageIndex property, 148

    Index property, 148-149

    ListView property, 149

    MakeVisible method, 149-150

    OverlayIndex property, 150

    Owner property, 150-151

    Selected property, 151

    StateIndex property, 151-152

    SubItems property, 152

    Update method, 152-153

TListItems, 153

    Add method, 154

    BeginUpdate method, 154-155

    Clear method, 155

    Count property, 155-156

    Delete method, 156

    EndUpdate method, 156-157

classes (*continued*)

>Handle property, 157
>
>IndexOf method, 158
>
>Insert method, 158-159
>
>Item property, 159
>
>Owner property, 160

TListSourceLink, 300

TListView, 957-958, 962-964

>AllocBy property, 964-965
>
>AlphaSort method, 965-966
>
>Arrange method, 966-967
>
>BoundingRect property, 967
>
>Column property, 968
>
>ColumnClick property, 968-969
>
>Columns property, 969-970
>
>ColumnSort method, 970-971
>
>DropTarget property, 971-972
>
>FindCaption method, 972-974
>
>FindData method, 974-975
>
>GetItemAt method, 976
>
>GetNearestItem method, 976-977
>
>GetNextItem method, 978-979
>
>IconOptions property, 979-980
>
>IsEditing method, 980
>
>ItemFocused property, 980-981
>
>Items property, 981-982
>
>LargeImages property, 982-983
>
>MultiSelect property, 983
>
>OnChange event, 983
>
>OnChanging event, 984
>
>OnColumnClick event, 984-985
>
>OnCompare event, 985
>
>OnDeletion event, 985-986
>
>OnEdited event, 986
>
>OnEditing event, 986-987
>
>OnInsert event, 987
>
>ReadOnly property, 988
>
>Scroll method, 988
>
>SelCount property, 988-989
>
>Selected property, 989
>
>ShowColumnHeaders property, 989-990
>
>SmallImages property, 990
>
>SortTypes property, 990-991
>
>StateImages property, 991-992

classes (*continued*)

>StringWidth method, 992-993
>
>TIconOptions class, 137-139
>
>UpdateItems method, 993-994
>
>ViewOrigin property, 994
>
>VisibleRowCount property, 995

TLoginDialog, *see* TForm class

TMainMenu, 479

>AutoMerge property, 481-482
>
>FindItem method, 482
>
>Handle property, 483
>
>Merge method, 484
>
>Unmerge method, 486

TMaskEdit, 1121-1123

>CharCase property, 1127-1128
>
>EditMask property, 1131-1133
>
>EditText property, 1133-1134
>
>IsMasked property, 1136
>
>PasswordChar property, 1140-1141
>
>ReadOnly property, 1142-1143

TMediaPlayer, 1153-1155

>AutoEnable property, 1155
>
>AutoOpen property, 1155-1156
>
>AutoRewind property, 1156
>
>Back method, 1156-1157
>
>Capabilities property, 1157-1158
>
>Close method, 1158
>
>ColoredButtons property, 1159
>
>DeviceID property, 1159
>
>DeviceType property, 1159-1160
>
>Display property, 1160
>
>DisplayRect property, 1161
>
>Eject method, 1161
>
>EnabledButtons property, 1161-1162
>
>EndPos property, 1162
>
>Error property, 1162-1163
>
>ErrorMessage property, 1163
>
>events, 1153-1154
>
>FileName property, 1164
>
>Frames property, 1164-1165
>
>Length property, 1165
>
>methods, 1153-1154
>
>Mode property, 1165-1166
>
>Next method, 1166

classes (*continued*)

    Notify property, 1166-1167

    NotifyValue property, 1168

    OnNotify event, 1168-1169

    OnPostClick event, 1169

    Open method, 1170

    Pause method, 1170

    PauseOnly method, 1170-1171

    Play method, 1171

    Position property, 1171-1172

    Previous method, 1172

    properties, 1153-1154

    Resume method, 1172-1173

    Rewind method, 1173

    Save method, 1173

    Shareable property, 1174

    Start property, 1174

    StartPos property, 1174-1175

    StartRecording method, 1175

    Step method, 1175

    Stop method, 1176

    TimeFormat property, 1176-1177

    TrackLength property, 1177-1178

    TrackPosition property, 1178

    Tracks property, 1178-1179

    VisibleButtons property, 1179

    Wait property, 1179

    see also TCustomControl class

  TMemo, 660, 1123-1125

    HideSelection property, 1136

    LoadFromFile function, 690-691

    LoadFromStream function, 691

    ReadOnly property, 1142-1143

    SaveToFile method, 704

    SaveToStream method, 705

    ScrollBars property, 1143

    WantReturns property, 1146-1147

    WantTabs property, 1147

    WordWrap property, 1147-1148

    see also TCustomMemo class

  TMemoField, Transliterate property, 708

  TMemoStrings, 338

    see also TStrings class

  TMenu, 477-479

    FindItem method, 482-483

    Handle property, 483

classes (*continued*)

  TMenuItem, 429-430

    Add method, 431

    Break property, 431-432

    Caption property, 432-433

    Checked property, 433-434

    Click method, 434

    Count property, 434-435

    Default property, 435-436

    Delete method, 436

    Enabled property, 436-437

    GroupIndex property, 437

    Handle property, 438

    HelpContext property, 438

    IndexOf method, 438

    Insert method, 439

    Items property, 440

    MenuIndex property, 440

    OnClick event, 441

    Parent property, 441

    RadioItem property, 442

    Remove method, 443

    ShortCut property, 443-444

    Visible property, 444-445

  TMetafile

    CreatedBy property, 321-322

    Description property, 321

    Enhanced property, 322

    Handle property, 323

    MMHeight property, 326

    MMWidth property, 326

    Palette property, 329

    see also TGraphic class

  TNavDataLink, 299

  TNotebook, 998

  TNumericField, 660

    Alignment property, 662

    see also TField class

  TObject, 29-33

    Class Type, 31

    ClassName method, 30

    ClassParent method, 30-31

    Create method, 31-32

    Destroy method, 32

    Free method, 32-33

classes (*continued*)

      InheritsFrom method, 33
      InstanceSize method, 33
   TOpenDialog, 491-493
      Ctl3D property, 498
      DefaultExt property, 499-500
      Execute method, 501
      FileName property, 501-502
      Files property, 502
      Filter property, 503
      FilterIndex property, 503-504
      filters, 492
      HelpContext property, 505-506
      InitialDir property, 506
      Options property, 510, 512-513
      Title property, 515
      see also TSave class
   TOutlineStrings, 339
      Add method, 343
      GetObject method, 354
      PutObject method, 366
      see also TStrings class
   TPageAccess, 339
      see also TStrings class
   TPageControl, 1002-1004
      ActivePage property, 1006
      FindNextPage method, 1007-1008
      MultiLine property, 1008-1009
      PageCount property, 1009-1010
      Pages property, 1010
      TabHeight property, 1012
      TabWidth property, 1012-1013
      SelectNextPage property, 1010-1011
      see also TCustomTabControl class
   TPaintBox, 775-777
   TPanel, 1180-1181
      BevelInner property, 1181-1182
      BevelOuter property, 1182
      BevelWidth property, 1183
      Locked property, 1183-1184
   TParaAttributes, 161-166
      Alignment property, 162
      FirstIndent property, 163
      LeftIndent property, 164
      methods, 161

classes (*continued*)

      Numbering property, 164
      RightIndent property, 165
      Tab property, 165
      TabCount property, 166
   TPasswordDialog, *see TForm class*
   TPen, 306-307, 315
      Color property, 309
      Handle property, 309-310
      Mode property, 310-311
      OnChange event, 312-313
      Style property, 314-316
      Width property, 316
   TPersistent, 109-110
   TPicture, 167-170, 172-173
      ancestry, 167
      Bitmap property, 168
      Graphic property, 169
      Height property, 169-170
      Icon property, 170
      LoadFromFile method, 170
      OnChange event, 171
      SaveToFile method, 173
      Width property, 173
   TPopupList, 76-77
      Add method, 78
      Remove method, 86-87
   TPopupMenu, 479-480
      Alignment property, 480-481
      AutoPopup property, 482
      FindItem method, 482
      Handle property, 483
      HelpContext property, 483-484
      OnPopup event, 484
      Popup method, 485
      PopupComponent property, 485-486
   TPrintDialog, 493-494
      Collate property, 497
      Copies property, 498
      Ctl3D property, 498
      Execute method, 501
      MaxPage property, 507
      MinPage property, 508
      Options property, 510, 513
      PrintRange property, 514

classes (*continued*)

    PrintToFile property, 514-515
    ToPage property, 516
TPrinterSetupDialog, 494-495
    Ctl3D property, 498
    Execute method, 501
    HelpContext property, 505-506
    ReplaceText property, 515
TProgressBar, 861-865
    Max property, 865
    Min property, 865-866
    Position property, 866
    Step property, 866
    StepBy method, 867
    StepIt method, 867-868
TQuery, 563-564, 647
    see also TDataSet class
TQueryDataLink, 299
TRadioButton, 1098-1102
    Checked property, 1104
TRadioGroup, 1191-1192
    Columns property, 1192
    ItemIndex property, 1192-1193
    Items property, 1193-1194
TRegistry
    CloseKey property, 60-61
    CreateKey property, 61
    CurrentKey property, 62
    CurrentPath property, 62
    DeleteKey property, 62-63
    DeleteValue method, 63-64
    GetDataInfo method, 64-65
    GetDataSize method, 65
    GetDataType method, 65-66
    GetKeyInfo method, 66-67
    GetKeyNames method, 67
    GetValueNames method, 68
    HasSubKeys method, 68-69
    KeyExists method, 69
    LazyWrite property, 69-70
    OpenKey method, 70
    Read methods, 71
    RenameValue method, 71-72
    RootKey property, 72

classes (*continued*)

    ValueExists method, 72-73
    Write methods, 73-74
TReplaceDialog, 495-496
    Ctl3D property, 498
    Execute method, 501
    FindText property, 504
    Handle property, 505
    HelpContext property, 505-506
    Left property, 506-507
    OnFind event, 509
    OnReplace event, 509-510
    Options property, 510-512
    Position property, 513-514
    Top property, 516
    see also TFind class
TRichEdit, 1125-1127
    HideScrollBars property, 1135-1136
    HideSelection property, 1136
    Lines property, 1137
    OnResizeRequest event, 1138
    OnSelectionChange event, 1138-1139
    PlainText property, 1141-1142
    ReadOnly property, 1142-1143
    ScrollBars property, 1143
    WantReturns property, 1146-1147
    WantTabs property, 1147
    WordWrap property, 1147-1148
    see also TCustomRichEdit class
TRichEditStrings, 339-340
    PlainText property, 365-366
    see also TStrings class
TSaveDialog, 496
    Ctl3D property, 498
    DefaultExt property, 499-500
    Execute method, 501
    FileName property, 501-502
    Files property, 502
    Filter property, 503
    FilterIndex property, 503-504
    filters, 492
    HelpContext property, 505-506
    InitialDir property, 506
    Options property, 510, 512-513

classes (*continued*)

  Title property, 515
  see also TOpen class
 TScreen, 447-448
  ActiveControl property, 448-449
  ActiveForm property, 449
  Cursor property, 449-450
  Cursors property, 450-451
  Fonts property, 451-452
  FormCount property, 452
  Forms property, 452
  Height property, 452-453
  methods, 448
  OnActiveControlChange event, 453-454
  OnActiveFormChange event, 454-455
  Width property, 455-456
 TScrollBar, 869-872
  Kind property, 873
  LargeChange property, 873
  Max property, 873-874
  Min property, 874
  OnScroll event, 874-876
  Position property, 876
  SetParams method, 876-877
  SmallChange property, 877
 TScrollingWinControl, 1051-1055
  HorzScrollBar property, 1071-1072
 TSession, 457-459
  Active property, 459
  AddAlias method, 459-460
  AddPassword method, 460
  AddStandardAlias method, 460-461
  Close method, 461
  ConfigMode property, 461-462
  Databases property, 462
  DeleteAlias method, 462-463
  DropConnections method, 463
  FindDatabase method, 463-464
  GetAliasDriverName method, 464
  GetAliasNames method, 464
  GetAliasParams method, 465
  GetDatabaseNames method, 465
  GetDriverNames method, 465-466
  GetDriverParams method, 466
  GetPassword method, 466

classes (*continued*)

  KeepConnections property, 467
  OnPassword event, 467-468
  OnStartUp event, 468-469
  Open method, 469
  PrivateDir property, 469
  RemoveAllPasswords method, 470
  RemovePassword method, 470
  SaveConfigFile method, 470
  SessionName property, 470-471
 TShape, 779-782
  Brush property, 782-783
  Pen property, 783
  Shape property, 784
  StyleChanged method, 785
 TSmallIntField, 661
  DisplayFormat property, 678
  MaxValue function, 696
  MinValue function, 696-697
  see also TField class
 TSpeedButton, 795-799
  AllowAllUp property, 799-800
  Down property, 801
  Glyph property, 801-802
  GroupIndex property, 802-803
  Layout property, 803
  Margin property, 804
  methods/events, 797-799
  NumGlyphs property, 804
  Spacing property, 805
  see also TButtonControl class
 TSplitter class, 807-810
  Beveled property, 810
  MinSize property, 810-811
  OnMoved event, 811-812
 TStatusBar, 879-883
  Panels property, 883-884
  SimplePanel property, 884-885
  SimpleText property, 885
  SizeGrip property, 886
 TStatusPanel
  Alignment property, 255
  Bevel property, 258
  GetDisplayName method, 270
  GetDisplayName property, 280

classes (*continued*)

    Text property, 280
    Width property, 281
TStoredProc, 563-564, 646-647
    see also TDataSet class
TStringField, 661
    Size property, 707
    Transliterate property, 708
    see also TField class
TStringGridStrings, 340
    see also TStrings class
TStringList, 340-341
    Add method, 343
    Duplicates property, 351-352
    Find property, 353-354
    OnChange event, 361-363
    OnChanging event, 363-364
    Sort method, 368-369
    Sorted property, 369
    see also TStrings class
TStrings, 333-336
    Add method, 343
    AddObject method, 344
    AddStrings method, 344-345
    Assign method, 345-346
    BeginUpdate method, 346
    Capacity property, 346-347
    Clear method, 347
    CommaText property, 347-348
    Count property, 348-349
    Create method, 349-350
    Delete method, 350-351
    Destroy method, 351
    EndUpdate method, 352
    Equals method, 352-353
    example project, 371-375
    Exchange method, 353
    IndexOf method, 356
    IndexOfName method, 356
    IndexOfObject method, 357
    Insert method, 357-358
    InsertObject method, 358-359
    LoadFromFile method, 359
    LoadFromStream method, 359
    Move method, 360

classes (*continued*)

    Names property, 360
    Objects property, 361
    SaveToFile method, 366-367
    SaveToStream method, 367
    SetText method, 367-368
    Strings property, 369-370
    TComboBoxStrings class, 336
    Text property, 370
    THeaderStrings class, 336-337
    TIndexFiles class, 337
    TListBoxStrings class, 338
    TMemoStrings class, 338
    TOutlineStrings class, 339, 354, 366
    TPageAccess class, 339
    TRichEditStrings class, 339-340
    TStringGridStrings class, 340
    TStringList class, see TStringList class
    TSubItems class, 341, 343, 355, 364-365
    TTabPageAccess class, 342
    TTabStrings class, 342
    TTreeStrings class, 343, 364-365, 370-371
TSubItems, 341
    Add method, 343
    Handle property, 355
    Owner property, 364-365
    see also TStrings class
TTabbedNotebook, 998
TTabControl, 1004-1005
    DisplayRect property, 1007
    MultiLine property, 1008-1009
    TabHeight property, 1012
    Tabs property, 1011-1012
    TabWidth property, 1012-1013
    see also TCustomTabControl class
TTable, 563-564, 646-647
    see also TDataSet class
TTableDataLink, 293
TTabPageAccess, 342
    see also TStrings class
TTabSet, 998
TTabSheet, 887-891
    PageControl method, 892
    PageIndex property, 892
    TabVisible property, 893

classes (*continued*)

TTabStrings, 342
    see also TStrings class
TTextAttributes, 175, 177-180
    Color property, 176
    ConsistentAttributes property, 177
    Height property, 177-178
    lineage, 176
    Name property, 178
    Pitch property, 178-179
    Protected property, 179
    Size property, 179-180
    Style property, 180
TThread, 49-51
    Create method, 52
    OnTerminate event, 52-53
    Priority property, 53
    Resume method, 54
    Suspend method, 54
    Suspended property, 55
    Terminate method, 55
TTimeField, 661
    DisplayFormat property, 678
    see also TField class
TTimer, 473-475
TTrackBar, 895-899
    Frequency property, 900
    LineSize property, 900-901
    Max property, 901
    Min property, 902
    Orientation property, 902-903
    PageSize property, 903
    Position property, 904
    SelEnd property, 904-905
    SelStart property, 905-906
    SetTick method, 906
    TickMarks property, 906-907
    TickStyle property, 907-908
TTreeNode, 181-183
    AbsoluteIndex property, 183
    AlphaSort method, 184
    Collapse method, 185
    Count property, 185
    Cut property, 186
    Data property, 186-187

classes (*continued*)

    Delete method, 187
    DeleteChildren method, 187
    Deleting property, 188
    DropTarget property, 188
    EditText method, 189
    EndEdit method, 189
    Expand method, 190
    Expanded property, 190-191
    Focused property, 191
    GetFirstChild method, 191
    GetLastChild method, 192
    GetNext method, 192
    GetNextChild method, 193
    GetNextSibling method, 193
    GetNextVisible method, 194
    GetPrev method, 194
    GetPrevChild method, 195
    GetPrevSibling method, 195
    Handle property, 196
    HasAsParent method, 196
    HasChildren property, 197
    ImageIndex property, 197
    Index property, 198
    IndexOf property, 198-199
    IsVisible property, 199
    Item property, 199
    Level property, 200
    MakeVisible method, 200
    MoveTo method, 200-201
    OverLayIndex property, 201-202
    Parent property, 202
    SelectedIndex property, 202-203
    StateIndex property, 203
    Text property, 203
    TreeView property, 204
TTreeNodes, 181, 204
    Add method, 205-206
    AddChild method, 206-207
    AddChildFirst method, 207
    AddChildObject method, 208
    AddChildObjectFirst method, 208-209
    AddFirst method, 209-210
    AddObject method, 210
    AddObjectFirst method, 211

classes (*continued*)

    BeginUpdate method, 212

    Clear method, 212

    Count property, 213

    Delete method, 213

    EndUpdate method, 214

    GetFirstNode method, 214

    Handle property, 215

    Insert method, 215

    InsertObject method, 216

    Owner property, 216

  TTreeStrings, 343

    Add method, 343

    Owner property, 364-365

    see also TStrings class

  TTreeView, 1015-1016, 1020-1021

    AlphaSort method, 1022

    FullCollapse method, 1022-1023

    FullExpand method, 1023

    GetHitTestInfoAt method, 1023-1025

    GetNodeAt method, 1025-1026

    HideSelection property, 1026

    Images property, 1026-1027

    IsEditing method, 1027

    Items property, 1028

    OnChanging event, 1028-1029

    OnCollapsed event, 1029

    OnCollapsing event, 1029-1030

    OnCompare event, 1030

    OnDeletion event, 1030-1031

    OnEdited event, 1031

    OnEditing event, 1031-1032

    OnExpanded event, 1032

    OnExpanding event, 1032

    OnGetImageIndex event, 1033

    OnSelectedIndex event, 1033

    ReadOnly property, 1034

    ShowButtons property, 1034-1035

    ShowLines property, 1035-1036

    ShowRoot property, 1036-1037

    SortImages property, 1038

    SortType property, 1037-1038

  TUpDown, 1044-1045

  TVarBytesField, 661

    see also TField class

classes (*continued*)

  TWinControl, 815-818

    ContainsControl method, 818-820

    ControlAtPos method, 820

    ControlCount property, 820-821

    Controls method, 821-822

    Ctl3D property, 822

    HandleAllocated method, 823

    InsertControl method, 823-824

    OnEnter event, 824-825

    OnExit event, 825-826

    OnKeyDown event, 826-827

    OnKeyPress event, 827-828

    OnKeyUp event, 828-829

    ParentCtl3D property, 829

    RemoveControl method, 830

    ScaleBy method, 830-831

    SetFocus method, 832

    TabOrder property, 832-833

    TabStop property, 833

  TWordField, 661

    DisplayFormat property, 678

    MaxValue function, 696

    MinValue function, 696-697

    see also TField class

  visibility specifiers, 19-21

  see also objects

ClassName method, TObject class, 30

ClassParent method, TObject class, 30-31

ClassType method, TObject class, 31

Clear method

  TClipboard class, 113

  TCollection class, 260

  TCustomComboBox class/descendants, 916-917

  TCustomEdit class/descendants, 1128

  TCustomImageList/TImageList classes, 529

  TCustomListBox class/descendants, 943

  TField class/descendants, 672

  TList class, 79-80

  TListItems class, 155

  TStrings class, 347

  TTreeNodes class, 212

ClearFields method, TDataSet class, 589

ClearMapping method, TGridDataLink class, 301

ClearSelection method, TCustomEdit class/ descendants, 1129

Click method, TMenuItem class, 434

ClientHandle property, TForm class, 1065-1066

ClientHeight property

    TControl class, 722-723

    TForm class, 1066

ClientOrigin property, TControl class, 723

ClientRect property, TControl class, 723-724

ClientToScreen method, TControl class, 724

ClientWidth property

    TControl class, 724-725

    TForm class, 1067

Clipboard, 111-112

    CopyToClipboard method, TCustomEdit class/descendants, 1129-1130

    CutToClipboard method, TCustomEdit class, 1130

    formats, 115-116

    LoadFromClipboardFormat method, TGraphic class, 324-325

    PasteFromClipboard method, TCustomEdit class/descendants, 1141

    SaveToClipboardFormat method, TGraphic class, 329

    see also edit controls; TClipboard class

Close method

    TClipboard class, 114

    TDataSet class, 589-590

    TForm class, 1067-1068

    TMediaPlayer class, 1158

    TSession class, 461

CloseKey method, TRegistry class, 60-61

code, viewing source code, 388

code listings

    BlobType property settings, 658

    CD-ROM code, 1198

    demAlignment field method function, 714-715

    Field properties pushbutton event handler, 712

    forms

        application with two forms, 401

        basic Delphi form, 16

    interrogateField method, 713-714

    lists, creating and organizing objects in, 75-76

code listings (*continued*)

    metafile creation (TMetaFileCanvas), 219

    new project source code, 388

    new thread object, instantiating, 51

    new thread unit, 50

    Registry, accessing, 59

        determining operating system, 58-59

    speedbutton event handler, 796

    TCollection class example project, 282-285

    TCollectionItem class example project, 282-285

    TCustomImageList enumerated types, 518

    Tflddlg dialog Examine pushbutton event handler, 713

    Tflddlg form creation handler, 712

    TImageList class example project, 560

    try-except code block (exception handling), 90

    try-finally code block (exception handling), 90-91

    unit file sections, 18-19

    WIN.INI file section, 35

ColCount property, TDBCtrlGrid class, 841

Collapse method, TTreeNode class, 185

Collate property, TPrintDialog class, 497

Collection property, TCollectionItem class, 260-261

color

    BkColor property, TCustomImageList/ TImageList classes, 527-528

    BlendColor property, TCustomImageList/ TImageList classes, 528-529

    Canvas property, TGraphicControl class, 759

    color dialog boxes, 489

        Color property, 497

        Ctl3D property, 498

        CustomColors property, 499

        Execute method, 501

        HelpContext property, 505-506

        Options property, 510-511

    HintColor property, TApplication class, 397

    ParentColor property, TControl class, 744

Color property

    TBrush/TPen/TFont classes, 309

    TColorDialog class, 497

    TColumn class, 261

Color property (*continued*)
    TColumnTitle class, 125
    TControl class, 725
    TTextAttributes object, 176
**ColoredButtons property, TMediaPlayer
    class, 1159**
**Column property, TListView/TCustomListView
    classes, 968**
column titles, 123-124
    see also TColumnTitle class
**ColumnClick property,
    TListView/TCustomListView classes, 968-969**
Columns property
    TListView/TCustomListView classes, 969-970
    TRadioGroup class, 1192
**ColumnSort method, TListView/TCustomListView
    classes, 970-971**
COM (Common Object Model)
    programming, 103
        Internet controls, 103-105
    support, 8
combo boxes (TCustomComboBox class), 909-911
    events, 911-913
    methods, 911-913
        Clear, 916-917
    properties, 911-913
        DropDownCount, 918
        DroppedDown, 918
        ItemIndex, 920-921
        Items, 921-922
    TComboBox class, 914-915
        ItemHeight property, 920
        OnDrawItem event, 922-923
        OnDropDown event, 922
        OnMeasureItem event, 923
        Sorted property, 924
        Style property, 924-925
    TComboBoxStrings class, 336
    TDBComboBox class, 915-916
        DataField property, 917
        DataSource property, 917
        Field property, 919-920
        ItemHeight property, 920
        OnDrawItem event, 922-923
        OnDropDown event, 922

combo boxes (*continued*)
    OnMeasureItem event, 923
    ReadOnly property, 923-924
    Sorted property, 924
    Style property, 924-925
    TDriveComboBox class, 910
    TFilterComboBox class, 910
    see also list boxes
commands
    buttons, *see* TButton class
    HelpCommand method, TApplication class,
      394-395
**CommaText property, TStrings class/descendants,
    347-348**
CommitUpdates method, TDataSet class, 590-591
common dialog boxes
    TColorDialog class, 489
        Color property, 497
        Ctl3D property, 498
        CustomColors property, 499
        Execute method, 501
        HelpContext property, 505-506
        Options property, 510-511
    TCommonDialog class, 487-488
        Ctl3D property, 498
        HelpContext property, 505-506
    TFindDialog class, 489-490
        Ctl3D property, 498
        Execute method, 501
        FindText property, 504
        Handle property, 505
        HelpContext property, 505
        Left property, 506-507
        OnFind event, 509
        Options property, 510-512
        Position property, 513-514
        Top property, 516
        see also TFind class
    TFontDialog class, 490-491
        Ctl3D property, 498
        Device property, 500
        Execute method, 501
        Font property, 504-505
        HelpContext property, 505-506
        MaxFontSize property, 507

common dialog boxes (*continued*)

    MinFontSize property, 507-508

    OnApply event, 508

    Options property, 510, 512

    TOpenDialog class, 491-493

        Ctl3D property, 498

        DefaultExt property, 499-500

        Execute method, 501

        FileName property, 501-502

        Files property, 502

        Filter property, 503

        FilterIndex property, 503-504

        filters, 492

        HelpContext property, 505-506

        InitialDir property, 506

        Options property, 510, 512-513

        Title property, 515

        see also TSave class

    TPrintDialog class, 493-494

        Collate property, 497

        Copies property, 498

        Ctl3D property, 498

        Execute method, 501

        MaxPage property, 507

        MinPage property, 508

        Options property, 510, 513

        PrintRange property, 514

        PrintToFile property, 514-515

        ToPage property, 516

    TPrinterSetupDialog class, 494-495

        Ctl3D property, 498

        Execute method, 501

        HelpContext property, 505-506

        ReplaceText property, 515

    TReplaceDialog class, 495-496

        Ctl3D property, 498

        Execute method, 501

        FindText property, 504

        Handle property, 505

        HelpContext property, 505-506

        Left property, 506-507

        OnFind event, 509

        OnReplace event, 509-510

        Options property, 510-512

common dialog boxes (*continued*)

    Position property, 513-514

    Top property, 516

    see also TFind class

    TSaveDialog class, 496

        Ctl3D property, 498

        DefaultExt property, 499-500

        Execute method, 501

        FileName property, 501-502

        Files property, 502

        Filter property, 503

        FilterIndex property, 503-504

        filters, 492

        HelpContext property, 505-506

        InitialDir property, 506

        Options property, 510, 512-513

        Title property, 515

        see also TOpen class

Component Palette, 379

    Data Access page, 423

    System page, 473-475

ComponentCount property, TComponent class, 381

ComponentIndex property, TComponent class, 381

components, 4, 21, 379-380

    controls, *see* controls

    fields, *see* fields

    GetComponent method, TClipboard class, 116-117

    HasFormat method, TClipboard class, 119

    SetComponent method, TClipboard class, 120

    SetTextBuf method, TClipboard class, 121

    TApplication class, 387-390

        Active property, 390

        BringToFront method, 391

        CreateForm method, 391-392

        ExeName property, 392

        Handle property, 392-393

        HelpCommand method, 393-395

        HelpContext method, 395

        HelpFile property, 396

        HelpJump method, 396

        HintColor property, 397

        HintHidePause property, 397

components (*continued*)

    HintPause property, 398
    HintShortPause property, 398-399
    Icon property, 399
    Initialize method, 400
    MainForm property, 400-401
    MessageBox method, 402-404
    Minimize method, 404
    OnActivate event, 404-405
    OnDeActivate event, 406-407
    OnException event, 407-408
    OnHelp event, 408
    OnHint event, 409-410
    OnIdle event, 410-411
    OnMessage event, 411-412
    OnMinimize event, 413-414
    OnRestore event, 414-415
    OnShowHint event, 415-417
    Restore method, 417-418
    Run method, 418-419
    ShowHint property, 419
    ShowMainForm property, 419-420
    Terminate method, 420
    Title property, 420-421
  TCommonDialog class, 487-488
    see also common dialog boxes
  TComponent class, 379-380
    ComponentCount property, 381
    ComponentIndex property, 381
    Components property, 382
    ComponentState property, 382-383
    DestroyComponents method, 383
    Destroying method, 383
    FindComponent method, 383-384
    Name property, 384-385
    Owner property, 385
    Tag property, 385-386
  TControl class, *see* TControl class
  TCustomImageList class,
    see TCustomImageList class
  TDataSet class, *see* TDataSet class
  TDataSource class, 423-424
    AutoEdit property, 424
    DataSet property, 424-425
    Edit method, 425

components (*continued*)

    Enabled property, 425-426
    IsLinkedTo method, 426
    OnDataChange event, 426-427
    OnStateChange event, 427
    OnUpdateData event, 427
    State property, 428
  TGlyphList class, *see* TGlyphList class
  TImageList class, *see* TImageList class
  TMainMenu class, 479
    AutoMerge property, 481-482
    FindItem method, 482
    Handle property, 483
    Merge method, 484
    Unmerge method, 486
  TMenu class, 477-479
    FindItem method, 482-483
    Handle property, 483
  TMenuItem class, *see* TMenuItem class
  TPopupMenu class, 479-480
    Alignment property, 480-481
    AutoPopup property, 482
    FindItem method, 482
    Handle property, 483
    HelpContext property, 483-484
    OnPopup event, 484
    Popup method, 485
    PopupComponent property, 485-486
  TScreen class, 447-448
    ActiveControl property, 448-449
    ActiveForm property, 449
    Cursor property, 449-450
    Cursors property, 450-451
    Fonts property, 451-452
    FormCount property, 452
    Forms property, 452
    Height property, 452-453
    methods, 448
    OnActiveControlChange event, 453-454
    OnActiveFormChange event, 454-455
    Width property, 455-456
  TSession class, 457-459
    Active property, 459
    AddAlias method, 459-460
    AddPassword method, 460

components (*continued*)

AddStandardAlias method, 460-461

Close method, 461

ConfigMode property, 461-462

Databases property, 462

DeleteAlias method, 462-463

DropConnections method, 463

FindDatabase method, 463-464

GetAliasDriverName method, 464

GetAliasNames method, 464

GetAliasParams method, 465

GetDatabaseNames method, 465

GetDriverNames method, 465-466

GetDriverParams method, 466

GetPassword method, 466

KeepConnections property, 467

OnPassword event, 467-468

OnStartUp event, 468-469

Open method, 469

PrivateDir property, 469

RemoveAllPasswords method, 470

RemovePassword method, 470

SaveConfigFile method, 470

SessionName property, 470-471

TTimer class, 473-475

visual/nonvisual, 379

Components property, TComponent class, 382

ComponentState property, TComponent class, 382-383

config files,

ConfigMode property, TSession class, 461-462

SaveConfigFile method, TSession class, 470

ConfirmDelete property, TDBNavigator class, 1186

ConsistentAttributes property, TTextAttributes object, 177

constructors, *see* Create method

ContainsControl method, TWinControl class, 818-820

Control property, TFieldDataLink class, 294-295

ControlAtPos method, TWinControl class, 820

ControlCount property, TWinControl class, 820-821

controls, 10, 21

ActiveX controls, 103-105

buddy controls, 1039-1040

controls (*continued*)

custom controls, *see* Custom controls (TCustomControl class)

event handlers, 22

speedbuttons, 796

nonwindowed, 755

TBevel class, 761-766

TCustomLabel class, 787-790

TDBText class, 790-791, 793

TGraphicControl class, 755-759

TImage class, 767-773

TLabel class, 791-792

TPaintBox class, 775-777

TShape class, 779-782

TSpeedButton class, *see* TSpeedButton class

TSplitter class, 807-811

scroll bars/boxes, 131

see also TControlScrollBar class

TControl class, *see* TControl class

VBXs (Visual Basic custom controls), 10

see also Custom controls (TCustomControl class)

windowed, *see* windowed controls

Controls method, TWinControl class, 821-822

ControlsDisabled method, TDataSet class, 591

ControlState property, TControl class, 725

ControlStyle property, TControl class, 726

converting 16-bit applications to 32-bit, 9-11

unsupported Delphi 1.0 functions, 11

Copies property, TPrintDialog class, 498

CopyMode property, TCanvas class, 224

CopyRect method, TCanvas class, 225-226

CopyToClipboard method, TCustomEdit class/descendants, 1129-1130

Count method, TList class, 80

Count property

TCollection class, 262-263

TCustomImageList class/descendants, 529

TListItems class, 155-156

TMenuItem class, 434-435

TStrings class/descendants, 348-349

TTreeNode class, 185

TTreeNodes class, 213

Create method, 29
    Exception class, 97
    TCollection class, 262-263
    TCollectionItem class, 262-263
    TCustomImageList class/descendants, 530
    TField class/descendants, 673-674
    TIniFile class, 37
    TListItem class, 143-144
    TMetaFileCanvas objects, 220
    TObject class, 31-32
    TPrinterCanvas objects, 220
    TStrings class/descendants, 349-350
    TThread class, 52
CreatedBy property, TMetafile class, 321-322
CreateFmt method, Exception class, 97
CreateFmtHelp method, Exception class, 97-98
CreateForm method, TApplication class, 391-392
CreateHandle method, TPrinterCanvas
    objects, 220
CreateHelp method, Exception class, 98
CreateKey method, TRegistry class, 61
CreateRes method, Exception class, 98-99
CreateResFmt method, Exception class, 99
CreateResFmtHelp method, Exception class,
    99-100
CreateSize method, TCustomImageList/TImageList
    classes, 530-531
CreateTitle method, TColumn class, 263
Ctl3D property
    ParentCtl3D property, TWinControl class, 829
    TCommonDialog class/descendants, 498
    TWinControl class, 822
currency
    currency type, 7
    ReadCurrency method, TRegistry class, 71
    WriteCurrency method, TRegistry class, 73-74
Currency property,
    BCDField/TCurrencyField/TFloatField classes,
    674-675
CurrentKey property, TRegistry class, 62
CurrentPath property, TRegistry class, 62
• Cursor property
    TControl class, 726
    TScreen class, 449-450

CursorPosChanged method, TDataSet class,
    591-592
Cursors property, TScreen class, 450-451
Custom controls (TCustomControl class),
    1149-1153
    events, 1150-1153
    methods, 1150-1153
    properties, 1150-1153
    TCustomGroupBox, 1188-1189
        TCustomRadioGroup, 1190-1191
        TGroupBox, 1189-1190
        TRadioGroup, 1191-1194
    TCustomPanel class, 1180
        TDBNavigator, 1184-1188
        TPanel, 1180-1184
    TMediaPlayer class, 1153-1155
        AutoEnable property, 1155
        AutoOpen property, 1155-1156
        AutoRewind property, 1156
        Back method, 1156-1157
        Capabilities property, 1157-1158
        Close method, 1158
        ColoredButtons property, 1159
        DeviceID property, 1159
        DeviceType property, 1159-1160
        Display property, 1160
        DisplayRect property, 1161
        Eject method, 1161
        EnabledButtons property, 1161-1162
        EndPos property, 1162
        Error property, 1162-1163
        ErrorMessage property, 1163
        FileName property, 1164
        Frames property, 1164-1165
        Length property, 1165
        Mode property, 1165-1166
        Next method, 1166
        Notify property, 1166-1167
        NotifyValue property, 1168
        OnNotify event, 1168-1169
        OnPostClick event, 1169
        Open method, 1170
        Pause method, 1170
        PauseOnly method, 1170-1171

Custom controls (*continued*)

Play method, 1171

Position property, 1171-1172

Previous method, 1172

Resume method, 1172-1173

Rewind method, 1173

Save method, 1173

Shareable property, 1174

Start property, 1174

StartPos property, 1174-1175

StartRecording method, 1175

Step method, 1175

Stop method, 1176

TimeFormat property, 1176-1177

TrackLength property, 1177-1178

TrackPosition property, 1178

Tracks property, 1178-1179

VisibleButtons property, 1179

Wait property, 1179

custom labels, *see* **TCustomLabel class**

CustomColors property, TColorDialog class, 499

Cut property

TListItem class, 144

TTreeNode class, 186

CutToClipboard method, TCustomEdit class, 1130

D

data

GetDataInfo method, TRegistry class, 64-65

GetDataSize method, TRegistry class, 65

links, *see* TDataLink class

modules, 8

source components, 423-424

see also TDataSource class

types, GetDataType method, TRegistry class, 65-66

Data property

TListItem class, 145

TTreeNode class, 186-187

databases

grids (control), *see* TDBCtrlGrid class

list boxes, *see* TDBListBox class

TDBDataSet class, 563-564, 646

see also TDataSet class

Databases property, TSession class, 462

DataField property

TDBComboBox class, 917

TDBListBox class, 944

TDBText class, 793

DataSet property

TDataLink class, 290

TDataSource class, 424-425

TField class/descendants, 675

datasets

fields, *see* TField class

TDataSet class, *see* TDataSet class

TDBDataSet class, 563-564, 646

see also TDataSet class

TQuery class, 563-564, 647

see also TDataSet class

TStoredProc class, 563-564, 646-647

see also TDataSet class

TTable class, 563-564, 646-647

see also TDataSet class

DataSize property, TField class/descendants, 675-676

DataSource property

TDataLink class, 290

TDataSet class, 592

TDBComboBox class, 917

TDBCtrlGrid class, 841

TDBListBox class, 944

TDBNavigator class, 1186-1187

TDBText class, 793

DataSourceFixed property, TDataLink class, 291

DataType property, TField class/descendants, 676-677

date

ReadDate method, TRegistry class, 71

ReadDateTime method, TRegistry class, 71

WriteDate method, TRegistry class, 73-74

WriteDateTime method, TRegistry class, 73-74

DBGrid Columns Editor, 123

DC (Device Context), *see* **canvas objects**

debugger, 8-9

DefAttributes property, TCustomRichEdit class/descendants, 1131

Default property, TMenuItem class, 435-436

DefaultAlignment method
    TColumn class, 264
    TColumnTitle class, 126
DefaultCaption method, TColumnTitle class, 126-127
DefaultColor method
    TColumn class, 264
    TColumnTitle class, 127
DefaultExt property, TOpenDialog/TSaveDialog classes, 499-500
DefaultFields property
    TDataSet class, 592-593
    TGridDataLink class, 302
DefaultFont method
    TColumn class, 265
    TColumnTitle class, 127-128
DefaultReadOnly method, TColumn class, 265
DefaultWidth method, TColumn class, 266
DefocusControl method, TForm class, 1068-1069
Delete method
    TCustomImageList class/descendants, 531-532
    TDataSet class, 593
    TList class, 81
    TListItem class, 145-146
    TListItems class, 156
    TMenuItem class, 436
    TStrings class/descendants, 350-351
    TTreeNode class, 187
    TTreeNodes class, 213
DeleteAlias method, TSession class, 462-463
DeleteChildren method, TTreeNode class, 187
DeleteKey method
    TIniFile class, 37-38
    TRegistry class, 62-63
DeleteValue method, TRegistry class, 63-64
Deleting property, TTreeNode class, 188
Delphi, 3-4
    new features, 4-9
        32-Bit optimizing compiler, 5-6
        Borland Database Engine (BDE), 9
        character types, 6-7
        COM support, 8
        currency type, 7
        data modules, 8
        debugger, 8-9

Delphi (*continued***)**
    Object Repository, 9
    string types, 7
    variant type, 8
    VCL (Visual Component Library), 9
    versions
        control equivalents, 10
        converting 16-bit applications to 32-bit, 9-11
        unsupported 1.0 RTL functions, 11
Delphi 3 SuperBible, 11-14
    CD-ROM in book, 1197-1198
    Help System, 26
DemAlignment method, code listing, 714-715
Description property, TMetafile class, 321
Destroy method, 29
    TCollection class, 266
    TCollectionItem class, 266
    TCustomImageList class/descendants, 532
    TField class/descendants, 677
    TMetaFileCanvas objects, 220
    TObject class, 32
    TStrings class/descendants, 351
DestroyComponents method, TComponent class, 383
Destroying method, TComponent class, 383
destructors, *see* **Destroy method**
device context (DC), *see* **canvas objects**
Device property, TFontDialog class, 500
DeviceID property, TMediaPlayer class, 1159
DeviceType property, TMediaPlayer class, 1159-1160
dialog boxes
    Add Fields, 652
    check boxes, *see* check boxes
    combo boxes, *see* combo boxes
    list boxes, *see* list boxes
    list view, *see* list view
    New Thread, 50
    NewField, 655
    progress bars (TProgressBar class), 861-865
        Max property, 865
        Min property, 865-866
        Position property, 866

dialog boxes (*continued*)

    Step property, 866
    StepBy method, 867-868
  Project Options dialog box
    Application page, 387, 399
    Forms page, 401
  radio buttons (TRadioButton class),
    1098-1102, 1104
  scroll bars (TScrollBar class), 870-872
    Kind property, 873
    LargeChange property, 873
    Max property, 873-874
    Min property, 874
    OnScroll event, 874-876
    Position property, 876
    SetParams method, 876-877
    SmallChange property, 877
  sliders, *see* track bars (TTrackBar class)
  status bars (TStatusBar class), 879-883
    Panels property, 883-884
    SimplePanel property, 884-885
    SimpleText property, 885
    SizeGrip property, 886
  tab sheets (TTabSheet class), 888-891
    PageControl method, 892
    PageIndex property, 892
    TabVisible property, 893
  TColorDialog class, 189
    Color property, 497
    Ctl3D property, 498
    CustomColors property, 499
    Execute method, 501
    HelpContext property, 505-506
    Options property, 510-511
  TCommonDialog class, 487-488
    Ctl3D property, 498
    HelpContext property, 505-506
  TCustomTabControl class, 997-1002
    TPageControl, see TPageControl class
  TFindDialog class, 489-490
    Ctl3D property, 498
    Execute method, 501
    FindText property, 504
    Handle property, 505
    HelpContext property, 505

dialog boxes (*continued*)

    Left property, 506-507
    OnFind event, 509
    Options property, 510-512
    Position property, 513-514
    Top property, 516
    see also TReplace class
  TFontDialog class, 490-491
    Ctl3D property, 498
    Device property, 500
    Execute method, 501
    Font property, 504-506
    HelpContext property, 505
    MaxFontSize property, 507
    MinFontSize property, 507-508
    OnApply event, 508
    Options property, 510, 512
  TLoginDialog class, *see* TForm class
  TNotebook class, 998
  TOpenDialog class, 491-493
    Ctl3D property, 498
    DefaultExt property, 499-500
    Execute method, 501
    FileName property, 501-502
    Files property, 502
    Filter property, 503
    FilterIndex property, 503-504
    filters, 492
    HelpContext property, 505-506
    InitialDir property, 506
    Options property, 510, 512-513
    Title property, 515
    see also TSave class
  TPageControl class, 1002-1004
    ActivePage property, 1006
    FindNextPage method, 1007-1008
    MultiLine property, 1008-1009
    PageCount property, 1009-1010
    Pages property, 1010
    SelectNextPage property, 1010-1011
    TabHeight property, 1012
    TabWidth property, 1012-1013
    see also TCustomTabControl class
  TPasswordDialog class, *see* TForm class

dialog boxes (*continued*)

    TPrintDialog class, 493-494

        Collate property, 497

        Copies property, 498

        Ctl3D property, 498

        Execute method, 501

        MaxPage property, 507

        MinPage property, 508

        Options property, 510, 513

        PrintRange property, 514

        PrintToFile property, 514-515

        ToPage property, 516

    TPrinterSetupDialog class, 494-495

        Ctl3D property, 498

        Execute method, 501

        HelpContext property, 505-506

        ReplaceText property, 515

    track bars (TTrackBar class), 895-899

        Frequency property, 900

        LineSize property, 900-901

        Max property, 901

        Min property, 902

        Orientation property, 902-903

        PageSize property, 903

        Position property, 904

        SelEnd property, 904-905

        SelStart property, 905-906

        SetTick method, 906

        TickMarks property, 906-907

        TickStyle property, 907-908

    TReplaceDialog class, 495-496

        Ctl3D property, 498

        Execute method, 501

        FindText property, 504

        Handle property, 505

        HelpContext property, 505-506

        Left property, 506-507

        OnFind event, 509

        OnReplace event, 509-510

        Options property, 510-512

        Position property, 513-514

        Top property, 516

        see also TFind class

    TSaveDialog class, 496

        Ctl3D property, 498

        DefaultExt property, 499-500

dialog boxes (*continued*)

        Execute method, 501

        FileName property, 501-502

        Files property, 502

        Filter property, 503

        FilterIndex property, 503-504

        filters, 492

        HelpContext property, 505-506

        InitialDir property, 506

        Options property, 510, 512-513

        Title property, 515

        see also TOpen class

    TTabbedNotebook class, 998

    TTabControl class, 1004-1005

        DisplayRect property, 1007

        MultiLine property, 1008-1009

        TabHeight property, 1012

        Tabs property, 1011-1012

        TabWidth property, 1012-1013

        see also TCustomTabControl class

    TTabSet class, 998

directives, 23-24

    see also methods

DisableControls method, TDataSet class, 594

Display property, TMediaPlayer class, 1160

DisplayFormat property, TField class descendants, 678

DisplayLabel property, TField class/descendants, 678-679

DisplayName property, TField class/ descendants, 679

DisplayRect property

    TMediaPlayer class, 1161

    TTabControl class, 1007

DisplayText property, TField class/descendants, 680

DisplayValues property, TField class/descendants, 680-681

DisplayWidth property, TField class/ descendants, 681

DoKey method, TDBCtrlGrid class, 842-843

Down property, TSpeedButton class, 801

DragCursor property

    TControl class, 727

    TCustomImageList/TImageList classes, 533

Dragging method, TControl class, 727

Dragging property, TCustomImageList/TImageList classes, 533-534

DragLock method, TCustomImageList/TImageList classes, 534

DragMode property, TControl class, 728

DragMove method, TCustomImageList/TImageList classes, 534-535

DragUnlock method, TCustomImageList/TImageList classes, 535

Draw method
    TCanvas class, 226
    TCustomImageList/TImageList classes, 535

DrawFocusRect method, TCanvas class, 227

drawing, *see* graphics

DrawingStyle property, TCustomImageList/TImageList classes, 536

DrawOverlay method, TCustomImageList/TImageList classes, 537-538

DropConnections method, TSession class, 463

DropDownCount property, TCustomComboBox class/descendants, 918

DropDownRows property, TColumn class, 267

DroppedDown property, TCustomComboBox class/descendants, 918

DropTarget property
    TListItem class, 146
    TListView/TCustomListView classes, 971-972
    TTreeNode class, 188

Duplicates property, TStringList class, 351-352

dynamic methods, 23

E

edit controls (TCustomEdit class), 1116-1119
    Clear method, 1128
    ClearSelection method, 1129
    CopyToClipboard method, 1129-1130
    CutToClipboard method, 1130
    GetSelectTextBuf method, 1134-1135
    mask edit controls (TCustomMaskEdit class), 1121
        TMaskEdit class, 1121-1123
    MaxLength property, 1137
    memo controls (TCustomMemo class), *see* memo controls
    Modified property, 1137-1138

edit controls (*continued*)
    PasteFromClipboard method, 1141
    rich edit controls, 1125
        DefAttributes property, 1131
        Paragraph property, 1139-1140
        Print property, 1142
        SelAttributes property, 1144
        TRichEdit class, 1125-1127
        TRichEdit class, see TRichEdit class
    SelectAll method, 1144
    selected text, 1115
    SelLength property, 1144-1145
    SelStart property, 1144-1145
    SelText property, 1145
    SetSelTextBuf method, 1146
    TEdit class, 1119-1121
        AutoSelect property, 1127
        CharCase property, 1127-1128
        HideSelection property, 1136
        PasswordChar property, 1140-1141
        ReadOnly property, 1142-1143

Edit method
    TDataLink class, 291-292
    TDataSet class, 594-595
    TDataSource class, 425
    TFieldDataLink class, 295

EditCaption method, TListItem class, 146-147

EditFormat property, TField class/descendants, 681-682

Editing property
    TDataLink class, 291
    TFieldDataLink class, 295

EditMask property
    TField class/descendants, 682
    TMaskEdit class, 1131-1133

EditMaskPtr property, TField class/descendants, 683

EditMode property, TDBCtrlGrid class, 843

EditText method, TTreeNode class, 189

EditText property, TMaskEdit class, 1133-1134

EndEdit method, TTreeNode class, 189

Eject method, TMediaPlayer class, 1161

Ellipse method, TCanvas class, 228

Empty property, TGraphic class, 322

EnableControls method, TDataSet class, 595-596

Enabled property
TControl class, 728
TDataSource class, 425-426
TMenuItem class, 436-437
TTimer class, 474-475
EnabledButtons property, TMediaPlayer class,
1161-1162
EndDrag method, TControl class, 728-729
TCustomImageList/TImageList classes, 538
EndPos property, TMediaPlayer class, 1162
EndUpdate method
TCollection class, 267
TListItems class, 156-157
TStrings class/descendants, 352
TTreeNodes class, 214
Enhanced property, TMetafile class, 322
EOF property, TDataSet class, 596
equal signs (=), INI file keys, 36
Equals method, TStrings class/descendants,
352-353
EraseSection method, TIniFile class, 38-39
Error property, TMediaPlayer class, 1162-1163
ErrorMessage property, TMediaPlayer class, 1163
errors, *see* **exceptions**
events
AfterCancel, TDataSet class, 568-569
AfterClose, TDataSet class, 569
AfterDelete, TDataSet class, 569-570
AfterEdit, TDataSet class, 570-571
AfterInsert, TDataSet class, 571
AfterOpen, TDataSet class, 571-572
AfterPost, TDataSet class, 572-573
BeforeCancel, TDataSet class, 578-579
BeforeClose, TDataSet class, 579-580
BeforeDelete, TDataSet class, 580-581
BeforeEdit, TDataSet class, 581
BeforeInsert, TDataSet class, 582-583
BeforeOpen, TDataSet class, 583-584
BeforePost, TDataSet class, 584-585
handlers, 22
speedbuttons, 796
see also methods
OnActivate, TApplication class, 404-405
OnActiveChange, TFieldDataLink class, 297

events (*continued*)
OnActiveControlChange, TScreen class,
453-454
OnActiveFormChange, TScreen class, 454-455
OnApply, TFontDialog class, 508
OnCalcFields, TDataSet class, 623-624
OnChange
TBrush/TPen/TFont classes, 312-313
TCanvas class, 233-234
TCustomImageList/TImageList classes, 550
TField class/descendants, 699
TGraphic class, 328-329
TListView/TCustomListView classes, 983
TPicture class, 171
TStringList class, 361-363
OnChanging
TCanvas class, 234-235
TCustomTreeView/TTreeView classes,
1028-1029
TListView/TCustomListView classes, 984
TStringList class, 363-364
OnClick
TControl class, 733-734
TMenuItem class, 441
OnCollapsed, TCustomTreeView/TTreeView
classes, 1029
OnCollapsing, TCustomTreeView/TTreeView
classes, 1029-1030
OnColumnClick, TListView/TCustomListView
classes, 984-985
OnCompare
TCustomTreeView/TTreeView classes, 1030
TListView/TCustomListView classes, 985
OnDataChange
TDataSource class, 426-427
TFieldDataLink class, 298
OnDblClick, TControl class, 734-735
OnDeActivate, TApplication class, 406-407
OnDeleteError, TDataSet class, 624-625
OnDeletion
TCustomTreeView/TTreeView classes,
1030-1031
TListView/TCustomListView classes,
985-986

events (*continued*)

OnDragDrop, TControl class, 735-736

OnDragOver, TControl class, 736-738

OnDrawItem, TComboBox/TDBComboBox classes, 922-923

OnDrawSection, THeaderControl class, 855

OnDropDown, TComboBox/TDBComboBox classes, 922

OnEdited

    TCustomTreeView/TTreeView classes, 1031

    TListView/TCustomListView classes, 986

OnEditError, TDataSet class, 625-627

OnEditing

    TCustomTreeView/TTreeView classes, 1031-1032

    TListView/TCustomListView classes, 986-987

OnEditingChange, TFieldDataLink class, 298

OnEndDrag, TControl class, 738-739

OnEnter, TWinControl class, 824-825

OnException, TApplication class, 407-408

OnExit, TWinControl class, 825-826

OnExpanded, TCustomTreeView/TTreeView classes, 1032

OnExpanding, TCustomTreeView/TTreeView classes, 1032

OnFilterRecord, TDataSet class, 627-628

OnFind

    TFindDialog class, 509

    TReplaceDialog class, 509

OnGetImageIndex, TCustomTreeView/TTreeView classes, 1033

OnGetText, TField class/descendants, 700

OnHelp, TApplication class, 408

OnHint, TApplication class, 409-410

OnIdle, TApplication class, 410-411

OnInsert, TListView/TCustomListView classes, 987

OnKeyDown, TWinControl class, 826-827

OnKeyPress, TWinControl class, 827-828

OnKeyUp, TWinControl class, 828-829

OnMeasureItem

    TComboBox/TDBComboBox classes, 923

    TCustomListBox class/descendants, 951-952

OnMessage, TApplication class, 411-412

events (*continued*)

OnMinimize, TApplication class, 413-414

OnMouseDown, TControl class, 739-740

OnMouseEvent, TControl class, 740-741

OnMouseUp, TControl class, 741-742

OnMoved, TSplitter class, 811-812

OnNewRecord, TDataSet class, 628-629

OnNotify, TMediaPlayer class, 1168-1169

OnPaintPanel, TDBCtrlGrid class, 843-845

OnPassword, TSession class, 467-468

OnPopup, TPopupMenu class, 484

OnPostClick, TMediaPlayer class, 1169

OnPostError, TDataSet class, 629-630

OnReplace, TReplaceDialog class, 509-510

OnResize, THeaderControl class, 855

OnResizeRequest, TRichEdit class, 1138

OnRestore, TApplication class, 414-415

OnScroll, TScrollBar class, 874-876

OnSectionClick, THeaderControl class, 856-857

OnSectionResize, THeaderControl class, 857-858

OnSectionTrack, THeaderControl class, 858-859

OnSelectedIndex, TCustomTreeView/TTreeView classes, 1033

OnSelectionChange, TRichEdit class, 1138-1139

OnServerYield, TDataSet class, 630-631

OnSetText, TField class/descendants, 700

OnShowHint, TApplication class, 415-417

OnStartDrag, TControl class, 742-743

OnStartUp, TSession class, 468-469

OnStateChange, TDataSource class, 427

OnTerminate, TThread class, 52-53

OnTimer, TTimer class, 475

OnUpdateData

    TDataSource class, 427

    TFieldDataLink class, 298-299

OnUpdateError, TDataSet class, 631-632

OnUpdateRecord, TDataSet class, 633-634

OnValidate, TField class/descendants, 701

example projects

TCollection class, 282-285

TCollectionItem class, 282-285

example projects (*continued*)
TImageList class, 559-561
TStatusPanel, 282-285
TStatusPanels class, 282-285
TStringList class, 371
TStrings class, 371-375
Exception class, 89
methods, 96-97
Create, 97
CreateFmt, 97
CreateFmtHelp, 97-98
CreateHelp, 98
CreateRes, 98-99
CreateResFmt, 99
CreateResFmtHelp, 99-100
properties, 96-97
HelpContext, 100
Message, 100-101
exceptions, 89-96
handling, 90-91
OnException event, TApplication class, 407
see also Exception class
Exchange method
TList class, 81-82
TStrings class/descendants, 353
Execute method, 501
ExeName property, TApplication class, 392
Expand method
TList class, 82
TTreeNode class, 190
Expanded property, TTreeNode class, 190-191
ExpIndex property, TDataSet class, 597
ExtendedSelect property, TCustomListBox
class/descendants, 945

F

FetchAll method, TDataSet class, 597
Field property
TColumn class, 268
TDBComboBox class, 919-920
TFieldDataLink class, 296
FieldByName method, TDataSet class, 597-598
FieldCount property
TDataSet class, 599
TGridDataLink class, 302

FieldDefs property, TDataSet class, 599-600
FieldKind property, TField class/descendants,
683-684
FieldName property
TColumn class, 268
TField class/descendants, 684-685
TFieldDataLink class, 296-297
FieldNo property, TField class/descendants, 685
fields, 649-655
DataField property, TDBComboBox class, 917
DefaultFields property, TGridDataLink
class, 302
Field editor, 651-652
FindField method, TDataSet class, 604-606
GetFieldList method, TDataSet class, 610
GetFieldNames method, TDataSet class,
610-611
persistent field components, 651-653
arranging order, 653-654
creating, 654-655
defining, 654
deleting, 653
SetDetailFields method, TDataSet class,
640-641
SetFields method, TDataSet class, 641-642
TField class, 649-651
see also TField class
TFieldDataLink class, 293-294
Fields property
TDataSet class, 601
TGridDataLink class, 302-303
FieldValues property
TDataSet class, 600-601
FileName property
TIniFile class, 39
TMediaPlayer class, 1164
TOpenDialog/TSaveDialog classes, 501-502
files
HelpFile property, TApplication class, 396
LoadFromFile method
TGraphic class, 325-326
TStrings class, 359
SaveConfigFile method, TSession class, 470
SaveToFile method, TStrings class, 366

Files property, TOpenDialog/TSaveDialog classes, 502
FillRect method, TCanvas class, 228-229
Filter Editor, 492
Filter property
    TDataSet class, 602
    TOpenDialog/TSaveDialog classes, 503
Filtered property, TDataSet class, 603
FilterIndex property, TOpenDialog/TSaveDialog classes, 503-504
FilterOptions property, TDataSet class, 603
filters
    OnFilterRecord event, TDataSet class, 627-628
    TFilterComboBox class, 910
Find dialog boxes, 489-490
    Execute method, 501
    OnFind event, 509
    properties, 490
        Ctl3D, 498
        FindText, 504
        Handle, 505
        HelpContext, 505
        Left, 506-507
        Options, 510-512
        Position, 513-514
        Top, 516
    see also Replace dialog boxes
Find property, TStringList class, 353-354
FindCaption method, TListView/TCustomListView classes, 972-974
FindComponent method, TComponent class, 383-384
FindData method, TListView/TCustomListView classes, 974-975
FindDatabase method, TSession class, 463-464
FindField method, TDataSet class, 604-606
FindFirst method, TDataSet class, 605-606
FindItem method, TMenu class/descendants, 482-483
FindItemID method, TCollection class, 269
FindLast method, TDataSet class, 605-606
FindNext method, TDataSet class, 605-606
FindNextPage method, TPageControl class, 1007-1008
FindPrior method, TDataSet class, 605-606

FindText property
    TFindDialog class, 504
    TReplaceDialog class, 504
FireLoad method, TCustomImageList/TImageList classes, 538-539
First method
    TDataSet class, 606-607
    TList class, 82-83
FirstIndent property, TParaAttributes class, 163
FloodFill method, TCanvas class, 229
focus, setting, 832
FocusControl method
    TField class/descendants, 685-686
    TForm class, 1069-1070
Focused property
    TListItem class, 147
    TTreeNode class, 191
Font property
    TCanvas class, 230
    TColumn class, 269-270
    TColumnTitle class, 128-129
    TControl class, 729
    TFontDialog class, 504-505
fonts
    Font dialog boxes, 490-491
    ParentFont property, TControl class, 744
    TFontDialog class
        Ctl3D property, 498
        Device property, 500
        Execute method, 501
        Font property, 504-505
        HelpContext property, 505-506
        MaxFontSize property, 507
        MinFontSize property, 507-508
        OnApply event, 508
        Options property, 510, 512
    see also TFont class
Fonts property, TScreen class, 451-452
FormatCount property, TClipboard class, 114
Formats property, TClipboard class, 115
FormCount property, TScreen class, 452
forms
    CreateForm method, TApplication class, 391
    MainForm property, TApplication class, 400-401

forms (*continued*)

    Project Options dialog box, Forms page, 401

    ShowMainForm property, TApplication class, 419-420

    TForm class, *see* TForm class

    see also TScrollingWinControl class

Forms property, TScreen class, 452

FormStyle property, TForm class, 1070-1071

Found property, TDataSet class, 607-608

FrameRect method, TCanvas class, 231

Frames property, TMediaPlayer class, 1164-1165

Free method, TObject class, 32-33

FreeBookmark method, TDataSet class, 608

Frequency property, TTrackBar class, 900

FTP (File Transfer Protocol) control, 104

FullCollapse method,
    TCustomTreeView/TTreeView classes,
    1022-1023

FullExpand method, TCustomTreeView/TTreeView
    classes, 1023

functions

    GetData, TField class/descendants, 686

    IsBlob, TField class/descendants, 687-688

    IsIndexField, TField class/descendants, 688

    IsValidChar, TField class/descendants, 689

    LoadFromFile,
        TBlobField/TGraphicField/TMemoField
        class, 690-691

    LoadFromStream,
        TBlobField/TGraphicField/TMemoField
        class, 691

    LookupKeyFields, TField class/descendants,
        693-694

    LookupList, TField class/descendants, 694-695

    LookupResultField, TField class/
        descendants, 695

    MaxValue, TField class/descendants, 696

    MinValue, TField class/descendants, 696-697

    Offset, TField class/descendants, 698

    see also methods

G

GetAliasDriverName method, TSession class, 464

GetAliasNames method, TSession class, 464

GetAliasParams method, TSession class, 465

GetAsHandle method, TClipboard class, 116

GetBitmap method, TCustomImageList/TImageList
    classes, 539-540

GetBookmark method, TDataSet class, 608-609

GetComponent method, TClipboard class, 116-117

GetCurrentRecord method, TDataSet class, 609

GetData function, TField class/descendants, 686

GetDatabaseNames method, TSession class, 465

GetDataInfo method, TRegistry class, 64-65

GetDataSize method, TRegistry class, 65

GetDataType method, TRegistry class, 65-66

GetDisplayName method, TStatusPanel class, 270

GetDisplayName property, TStatusPanel class, 280

GetDriverNames method, TSession class, 465-466

GetDriverParams method, TSession class, 466

GetFieldList method, TDataSet class, 610

GetFieldNames method, TDataSet class, 610-611

GetFirstChild method, TTreeNode class, 191

GetFirstNode method, TTreeNodes class, 214

GetGrid method, TColumn class, 271

GetHitTestInfoAt method,
    TCustomTreeView/TTreeView classes,
    1023-1025

GetHotSpot method,
    TCustomImageList/TImageList classes, 540

GetIcon method, TCustomImageList/TImageList
    classes, 540-541

GetImageBitmap method,
    TCustomImageList/TImageList classes, 541

GetInstRes method,
    TCustomImageList/TImageList classes, 542

GetItem method, TCollection class, 272

GetItemAt method, TListView/TCustomListView
    classes, 976

GetKeyInfo method, TRegistry class, 66-67

GetKeyNames method, TRegistry class, 67

GetLastChild method, TTreeNode class, 192

GetMaskBitmap method,
    TCustomImageList/TImageList classes, 542

GetNearestItem method,
    TListView/TCustomListView classes, 976-977

GetNext method, TTreeNode class, 192

GetNextChild method, TTreeNode class, 193

GetNextItem method, TListView/TCustomListView
    classes, 978-979

GetNextSibling method, TTreeNode class, 193

GetNextVisible method, TTreeNode class, 194

GetNodeAt method, TCustomTreeView/TTreeView classes, 1025-1026

GetPassword method, TSession class, 466

GetPrev method, TTreeNode class, 194

GetPrevChild method, TTreeNode class, 195

GetPrevSibling method, TTreeNode class, 195

GetResource method, TCustomImageList/TImageList classes, 543

GetSelectTextBuf method, TCustomEdit class/descendants, 1134-1135

GetTextBuf method
    TClipboard class, 117-118
    TControl class, 729

GetTextLen method, TControl class, 730

GetValueNames method, TRegistry class, 68

Glyph property
    TBitBtn class, 1104-1105
    TSpeedButton class, 801-802

glyph images, buttons, 1092
    image number, 1112
    layout, 1107-1108
    margins, 1108-1109
    spacing, 1112-1113
    see also TGlyphList class

GotoBookmark method, TDataSet class, 611-612

Graphic property, TPicture class, 169

graphics, 305, 317
    EInvalidGraphic exception, 96
    EInvalidGraphicOperation exception, 96
    glyphs, *see* glyph images, buttons
    graphic controls (nonwindowed), 755
        TBevel class, 761-766
        TCustomLabel class, 787-790
        TDBText class, 790-791, 793
        TGraphicControl class, 755-759
        TImage class, 770, 767-769, 771-773
        TLabel class, 791-792
        TPaintBox class, 775-777
        TShape class, 779-782
        TSpeedButton class, see TSpeedButton class
        TSplitter class class, 807-811

graphics (*continued*)
    list views
        Arrange method, 966-967
        LargeImages property, 982-983
        SmallImages property, 990
        StateImages property, 991-992
        ViewOrigin property, 994
        VisibleRowCount property, 995
    TCustomImageList class, *see* TCustomImageList class
    TGlyphList class, *see* TGlyphList class
    TGraphic class, 317-318
        Empty property, 322
        Height property, 323
        LoadFromClipboardFormat methods, 324-325
        LoadFromFile methods, 325-326
        Modified property, 327
        OnChange event, 328-329
        SaveToClipboardFormat methods, 329-330
        SaveToFile methods, 330-331
        TBitmap, 319-320, 323-324, 327-329
        TIcon, 318-319, 323
        TMetafile, 319, 321-323, 326, 329
        Width property, 331
    TGraphicField class, *see* TGraphicField class
    TGraphicsObject class, 305-306
        properties/methods/events, 306
        TBrush, 306, 308-309, 312-315
        TFont, 307, 309-310, 312-316
        TPen, 306-307, 309-316
    TImageList class, *see* TImageList class
    TPicture class, 167-170, 172-173
        Bitmap property, 168
        Graphic property, 169
        Height property, 169-170
        Icon property, 170
        LoadFromFile method, 170
        OnChangeevent, 171
        SaveToFile method, 173
        Width property, 173
    see also canvas objects

Grid property, TDBGridColumns class, 272-273

Group boxes, *see* TCustomGroupBox class
GroupIndex property
    TMenuItem class, 437
    TSpeedButton class, 802-803

H

Handle property
    TApplication class, 392-393
    TBrush/TPen/TFont classes, 309
    TCanvas class, 231
    TCustomImageList/TImageList classes, 544
    TDataSet class, 612
    TFindDialog class, 505
    TGraphicsObject class, 310
    TIcon class, 323
    TListItem class, 147-148
    TListItems class, 157
    TMenu class/descendants, 483
    TMenuItem class, 438
    TReplaceDialog class, 505
    TSubItems class, 355
    TTreeNode class, 196
    TTreeNodes class, 215
HandleAllocated method, TWinControl class, 823
HandleAllocated property,
    TCustomImageList/TImageList classes, 544-545
handles, windowed controls, 815
handling
    events, 22
    exceptions, 90-91
HasAsParent method, TTreeNode class, 196
HasChildren property, TTreeNode class, 197
HasFormat method, TClipboard class, 118-119
HasSubKeys method, TRegistry class, 68-69
header controls (THeaderControl class), 851-855
    events, 852-855
        OnDrawSection, 855
        OnResize, 855
        OnSectionClick, 856-857
        OnSectionResize, 857-858
        OnSectionTrack, 858-859
    methods, 852-855
    properties, 852-855
        Sections, 859

Height property
    TControl class, 730
    TCustomImageList/TImageList classes, 545
    TFont class, 310
    TGraphic class, 323
    TPicture class, 169-170
    TScreen class, 452-453
    TTextAttributes object, 177-178
help
    Delphi 3 SuperBible Help System, 26
    OnHelp event, TApplication class, 408
HelpCommand method, TApplication class,
    393-395
HelpContext method, TApplication class, 395
HelpContext property
    Exception class, 100
    TColorDialog class, 506
    TCommonDialog class/descendants, 505-506
    TFontDialog class, 505-506
    TMenuItem class, 438
    TPopupMenu class, 483-484
    TPrinterSetupDialog class, 505-506
HelpFile property, TApplication class, 396
HelpJump method, TApplication class, 396
Hide method, TControl class, 731
HideDragImage method,
    TCustomImageList/TImageList classes, 545
HideScrollBars property, TRichEdit class,
    1135-1136
HideSelection property
    TCustomTreeView/TTreeView classes, 1026
    TEdit/TMemo/TRichEdit classes, 1136
Hint property, TControl class, 731-732
HintColor property, TApplication class, 397
HintHidePause property, TApplication class, 397
HintPause property, TApplication class, 398
hints
    OnHint event, TApplication class, 409-410
    OnShowHint event, TApplication class, 415
    ParentShowHint property, TControl class, 745
    ShowHint property
        TApplication class, 419
        TControl class, 749
    see also tooltips
Hints property, TDBNavigator class, 1187

HintShortPause property, TApplication class,
398-399
HorzScrollBar property, TScrollingWinControl
class, 1071-1072
hot keys (TCustomHotKey class), 927-931
    methods, 928-931
    THotKey class, 931-932
        HotKey property, 932-933
        InvalidKeys property, 933-934
        Modifiers property, 934
HotKey property, THotKey class, 932-933
HTML (Hypertext Markup Language) control, 104
HTTP (Hypertext Transfer Protocol) control, 104

I

Icon property
    TApplication class, 399
    TForm class, 1072
    TPicture class, 170
IconOptions property,
    TListView/TCustomListView classes, 979-980
icons
    AddIcon method,
        TCustomImageList/TImageList classes,
        522-523
    ArrangeIcons method, TForm class, 1061-1063
    BorderIcons property, TForm class, 1064
    Cascade method, TForm class, 1064-1065
    ClientHandle property, TForm class, 1065-1066
    ClientHeight property, TForm class, 1066
    ClientWidth property, TForm class, 1067
    Close method, TForm class, 1067-1068
    DefocusControl method, TForm class,
        1068-1069
    FocusControl method, TForm class, 1069-1070
    FormStyle property, TForm class, 1070-1071
    GetIcon method,
        TCustomImageList/TImageList classes,
        540-541
    InsertIcon method,
        TCustomImageList/TImageList classes,
        547-548
    KeyPreview property, TForm class, 1072-1074
    MDIChildCount property, TForm class, 1075

icons (*continued*)
    MDIChildren property, TForm class, 1076
    Next method, TForm class, 1078
    Previous method, TForm class, 1079-1080
    Print method, TForm class, 1080-1081
    ReplaceIcon method,
        TCustomImageList/TImageList classes, 555
    Show method, TForm class, 1082
    ShowModal method, TForm class, 1082
    TIcon class, 318-319
    TIconOptions class, 137-139
    Tile method, TForm class, 1082-1083
IDE (Integrated Development Environment)
    Component Palette, 379
    viewing project source, Application object, 388
image controls (TImage class), 767-769
    AutoSize property, 770
    Center property, 771
    Picture property, 772
    Stretch property, 773
Image editor, editing glyphs, 1105
image lists, *see* **TCustomImageList class;**
    TGlyphList class; TImageList class
ImageIndex property
    TListItem class, 148
    TTreeNode class, 197
Images property, TCustomTreeView/TTreeView
    classes, 1026-1027
ImageType property,
    TCustomImageList/TImageList classes, 545-546
Increment property
    TControlScrollBar class, 132-133
    TUpDown class, 1047
indenting, TParaAttributes class
    FirstIndent property, 163
    LeftIndent property, 164
    RightIndent property, 165
Index property
    TCollectionItem class, 273
    TField class/descendants, 687
    TListItem class, 148-149
    TTreeNode class, 198
IndexOf method
    TList class, 83
    TListItems class, 158

icons (*continued*)
TMenuItem class, 438
TStrings class/descendants, 356
IndexOf property, TTreeNode class, 198-199
IndexOfName method, TStrings class/
descendants, 356
IndexOfObject method, TStrings class/
descendants, 357
InheritsFrom method, TObject class, 33
INI files, 35-36
see also TIniFile class
InitialDir property, TOpenDialog/TSaveDialog
classes, 506
Initialize method, TApplication class, 400
Insert method
TCustomImageList/TImageList classes, 546-547
TDataSet class, 612-613
TList class, 83-84
TListItems class, 158-159
TMenuItem class, 439
TStrings class/descendants, 357-358
TTreeNodes class, 215
InsertControl method, TWinControl class, 823-824
InsertIcon method, TCustomImageList/TImageList
classes, 547-548
InsertMasked method,
TCustomImageList/TImageList classes, 548-549
InsertObject method
TStrings class/descendants, 358-359
TTreeNodes class, 216
InsertRecord method, TDataSet class, 613-616
instances, 16
InstanceSize method, TObject class, 33
instantiating threads, 51
integers
EInIntError exception, 93
ReadInteger method
TIniFile class, 40
TRegistry class, 71
WriteInteger method
TIniFile class, 46-47
TRegistry class, 73-74
IntegralHeight property, TCustomListBox
class/descendants, 946
Internet controls, 103-105

Interval property, TTimer class, 475
Invalidate method, TControl class, 733
InvalidKeys property, THotKey class, 933-934
Is keyword, 24
IsBlob function, TField class/descendants, 687-688
IsEditing method
TCustomTreeView/TTreeView classes, 1027
TListView/TCustomListView classes, 980
IsIndexField function, TField class/
descendants, 688
IsLinkedTo method
TDataSet class, 616
TDataSource class, 426
IsMasked property, TMaskEdit class, 1136
IsNull property, TField class/descendants, 689
IsValidChar function, TField class/
descendants, 689
IsVisible property, TTreeNode class, 199
Item property
TList class, 84
TListItems class, 159
TTreeNode class, 199
ItemAtPos method, TCustomListBox class/
descendants, 947-948
ItemFocused property,
TListView/TCustomListView classes, 980-981
ItemHeight property
TComboBox/TDBComboBox classes, 920
TCustomListBox class/descendants, 948
ItemIndex property
TCustomComboBox class/descendants,
920-921
TCustomListBox class/descendants, 948-949
TRadioGroup class, 1192-1193
ItemRect method, TCustomListBox class/
descendants, 949-950
Items property
TCollection class, 273-274
TCustomComboBox class/descendants,
921-922
TCustomListBox class/descendants, 950
TCustomTreeView/TTreeView classes, 1028
TListView/TCustomListView classes, 981-982
TMenuItem class, 440
TRadioGroup class, 1193-1194

J-K

KeepConnections property, TSession class, 467

keyboard shortcut keys, *see* hot keys
(TCustomHotKey class)

KeyExists method, TRegistry class, 69

KeyFields property, TField class/descendants, 690

KeyPreview property, TForm class, 1072-1074

keys

    CloseKey method, TRegistry class, 60-61

    CreateKey method, TRegistry class, 61

    CurrentKey property, TRegistry class, 62

    DeleteKey method, TRegistry class, 62-63

    GetKeyInfo method, TRegistry class, 66-67

    GetKeyNames method, TRegistry class, 67

    HasSubKeys method, TRegistry class, 68-69

    INI files, 36

        DeleteKey method, 37-38

    KeyExists method, TRegistry class, 69

    OpenKey method, TRegistry class, 70

    Registry, 57

    RootKey property, TRegistry class, 72

KeySize property, TDataSet class, 616-617

keywords

    abstract, 24

    dynamic, 23

    is, 24

    override, 23

    virtual, 23

Kind property

    TBitBtn class, 1106-1107

    TControlScrollBar class, 133

L

labels (TCustomLabel class), 787-790

    TDBText class, 790-791, 793

    TLabel class, 791-792

LargeImages property,
TListView/TCustomListView classes, 982-983

Last method

    TDataSet class, 617-618

    TList class, 84-85

Layout property

    TBitBtn class, 1107-1108

    TSpeedButton class, 803

LazyWrite property, TRegistry class, 69-70

Left property

    TControl class, 733

    TFindDialog class, 506-507

    THeaderSection class, 274-275

    TReplaceDialog class, 506-507

LeftIndent property, TParaAttributes class, 164

Length property, TMediaPlayer class, 1165

Level property, TTreeNode class, 200

Lines property, TRichEdit/TCustomMemo
classes, 1137

LineSize property, TTrackBar class, 900-901

LineTo method, TCanvas class, 232

links

    IsLinkedTo method, TDataSet class, 616

    TDataLink class, 287-293

    TDataSourceLink class, 299

    TDBCtrlGridLink class, 304

    TFieldDataLink class, 293-299

    TGridDataLink class, 300-304

    TListSourceLink class, 300

    TNavDataLink class, 299

    TQueryDataLink class, 299

list boxes (TCustomListBox class), 935-939

    events, 936-939

        OnMeasureItem, 951-952

    methods, 936-939

        Clear, 943

        ItemAtPos, 947-948

        ItemRect, 949-950

    properties, 936-939

        BorderStyle, 942-943

        ExtendedSelect, 945

        IntegralHeight, 946

        ItemHeight, 948

        ItemIndex, 948-949

        Items, 950

        MultiSelect, 951

        SelCount, 952-953

        Selected, 953

        Sorted, 954

        TopIndex, 954-955

    TDBListBox class, 939-942

        DataField property, 944

        DataSource property, 944

        ReadOnly property, 952

list boxes (*continued*)

    TDirectoryListBox class, 935

    TFileListBox class, 935

    see also combo boxes

List property, TList class, 85

List view

    TCustomListView class, 957-962

        AllocBy property, 964-965

        AlphaSort method, 965-966

        Arrange method, 966-967

        BoundingRect property, 967

        Column property, 968

        ColumnClick property, 968-969

        Columns property, 969-970

        ColumnSort method, 970-971

        DropTarget property, 971-972

        FindCaption method, 972-974

        FindData method, 974-975

        GetItemAt method, 976

        GetNearestItem method, 976-977

        GetNextItem method, 978-979

        IconOptions property, 979-980

        IsEditing method, 980

        ItemFocused property, 980-981

        Items property, 981-982

        LargeImages property, 982-983

        MultiSelect property, 983

        OnChange event, 983

        OnChanging event, 984

        OnColumnClick event, 984-985

        OnCompare event, 985

        OnDeletion event, 985-986

        OnEdited event, 986

        OnEditing event, 986-987

        OnInsert event, 987

        ReadOnly property, 988

        Scroll method, 988

        SelCount property, 988-989

        Selected property, 989

        ShowColumnHeaders property, 989-990

        SmallImages property, 990

        SortTypes property, 990-991

        StateImages property, 991-992

        StringWidth method, 992-993

        UpdateItems method, 993-994

List view (*continued*)

        ViewOrigin property, 994

        VisibleRowCount property, 995

    TListView class, 957-958, 962-964

        AllocBy property, 964-965

        AlphaSort method, 965-966

        Arrange method, 966-967

        BoundingRect property, 967

        Column property, 968

        ColumnClick property, 968-969

        Columns property, 969-970

        ColumnSort method, 970-971

        DropTarget property, 971-972

        FindCaption method, 972-974

        FindData method, 974-975

        GetItemAt method, 976

        GetNearestItem method, 976-977

        GetNextItem method, 978-979

        IconOptions property, 979-980

        IsEditing method, 980

        ItemFocused property, 980-981

        Items property, 981-982

        LargeImages property, 982-983

        MultiSelect property, 983

        OnChange event, 983

        OnChanging event, 984

        OnColumnClick event, 984-985

        OnCompare event, 985

        OnDeletion event, 985-986

        OnEdited event, 986

        OnEditing event, 986-987

        OnInsert event, 987

        ReadOnly property, 988

        Scroll method, 988

        SelCount property, 988-989

        Selected property, 989

        ShowColumnHeaders property, 989-990

        SmallImages property, 990

        SortTypes property, 990-991

        StateImages property, 991-992

        StringWidth method, 992-993

        UpdateItems method, 993-994

        ViewOrigin property, 994

        VisibleRowCount property, 995

listings, *see* **code listings**

lists, 75-77
    EListError exception, 95
    GetFieldList method, TDataSet class, 610
    persistent field lists, *see* fields, persistent field
        components
    TCustomImageList class, *see* TCustomImageList
        class
    TGlyphList class, *see* TGlyphList class
    TImageList class, *see* TImageList class
    TList class, *see* TList class
    TListBoxStrings class, 338
    TListItem class, 141-142
        CancelEdit method, 142-143
        Caption property, 143
        Create method, 143-144
        Cut property, 144
        Data property, 145
        Delete method, 145-146
        DropTarget property, 146
        EditCaption method, 146-147
        Focused property, 147
        Handle property, 147-148
        ImageIndex property, 148
        Index property, 148-149
        ListView property, 149
        MakeVisible method, 149-150
        OverlayIndex property, 150
        Owner property, 150-151
        Selected property, 151
        StateIndex property, 151-152
        SubItems property, 152
        Update method, 152-153
    TListItems class, 153
        Add method, 154
        BeginUpdate method, 154-155
        Clear method, 155
        Count property, 155-156
        Delete method, 156
        EndUpdate method, 156-157
        Handle property, 157
        IndexOf method, 158
        Insert method, 158-159
        Item property, 159
        Owner property, 160
    TListSourceLink class, 300

lists (*continued*)
    TPopupList class, *see* TPopupList class
    TStringList class, 340-341
        Add method, 343
        Duplicates property, 351-352
        example project, 371
        Find property, 353-354
        OnChange event, 361-363
        OnChanging event, 363-364
        Sort method, 368-369
        Sorted property, 369
ListView Columns Editor, 970
ListView Items Editor, 144
ListView property, TListItem class, 149
LoadFromClipboardFormat method, TGraphic
    class, 324-325
LoadFromFile function,
    TBlobField/TGraphicField/TMemoField classes,
    690-691
LoadFromFile method
    TGraphic class, 325-326
    TPicture class, 170
    TStrings class/descendants, 359
LoadFromStream function,
    TBlobField/TGraphicField/TMemoField
    classes, 691
LoadFromStream method, TStrings class/
    descendants, 359
Locale property, TDataSet class, 618
Locate method, TDataSet class, 618-619
Locked property, TPanel class, 1183-1184
logins, TLoginDialog class, *see* TForm class
Lookup method, TDataSet class, 619-621
Lookup property, TField class/descendants,
    691-692
LookupCache property, TField class/descendants,
    692-693
LookupDataSet property, TField class/
    descendants, 693
LookupKeyFields function, TField class/
    descendants, 693-694
LookupList function, TField class/descendants,
    694-695
LookupResultField function, TField class/
    descendants, 695

M

MainForm property, TApplication class, 400-401
MakeVisible method
TListItem class, 149-150
TTreeNode class, 200
Margin property
TBitBtn class, 1108-1109
TControlScrollBar class, 133
TSpeedButton class, 804
Mask edit controls (TCustomMaskEdit class), 1121
events, 1121
methods, 1121
properties, 1121
TMaskEdit class, 1121-1123
CharCase property, 1127-1128
EditMask property, 1131-1133
EditText property, 1133-1134
IsMasked property, 1136
PasswordChar property, 1140-1141
ReadOnly property, 1142-1143
see also TCustomEdit class
Masked property, TCustomImageList/TImageList classes, 549
Max property
TProgressBar class, 865
TTrackBar class, 901
TUpDown class, 1047-1048
MaxFontSize property, TFontDialog class, 507
MaxLength property, TCustomEdit class/descendants, 1137
MaxPage property, TPrintDialog class, 507
MaxValue function, TField class/descendants, 696
MaxWidth property, THeaderSection class, 275
MCI (Media Control Interface), *see* TMediaPlayer class
MDI applications (Multiple Document Interface), 1055-1057
see also TForm class
MDIChildCount property, TForm class, 1074-1075
MDIChildren property, TForm class, 1075-1076
Media Control Interface (MCI), *see* TMediaPlayer class
Media player, *see* TMediaPlayer class

memo controls (TCustomMemo class), 1123
Lines property, 1137
TCustomRichEdit class, 1125
DefAttributes property, 1131
Paragraph property, 1139-1140
Print property, 1142
SelAttributes property, 1144
TRichEdit, 1125-1127
TMemo class, 1123-1125
HideSelection property, 1136
ReadOnly property, 1142-1143
ScrollBars property, 1143
WantReturns property, 1146-1147
WantTabs property, 1147
WordWrap property, 1147-1148
see also TCustomEdit class
memory, EInOutError exception, 92
Menu Designer, 477-478
Menu property, TForm class, 1076-1078
MenuIndex property, TMenuItem class, 440
menus, 477-478
EMenuError exception, 96
TMainMenu class, 479
AutoMerge property, 481-482
FindItem method, 482
Handle property, 483
Merge method, 484
Unmerge method, 486
TMenu class, 477-479
FindItem method, 482-483
Handle property, 483
TMenuItem class, 429-430
Add method, 431
Break property, 431-432
Caption property, 432-433
Checked property, 433-434
Click method, 434
Count property, 434-435
Default property, 435-436
Delete method, 436
Enabled property, 436-437
GroupIndex property, 437
Handle property, 438
HelpContext property, 438

menus (*continued*)

> IndexOf method, 438
> Insert method, 439
> Items property, 440
> MenuIndex property, 440
> OnClick event, 441
> Parent property, 441
> RadioItem property, 442
> Remove method, 443
> ShortCut property, 443-444
> Visible property, 444-445

> TPopupMenu class, 479-480
>> Alignment property, 480-481
>> AutoPopup property, 482
>> FindItem method, 482
>> Handle property, 483
>> HelpContext property, 483-484
>> OnPopup event, 484
>> Popup method, 485
>> PopupComponent property, 485-486

Merge method, TMainMenu class, 484

messages

> Message property, Exception class, 100-101
> MessageBox method, TApplication class, 402-404
> OnMessage event, TApplication class, 411-412

metafiles

> metafile canvas objects, 219-220
>> see also canvas objects
> TMetafile class, 319, 321-323, 326, 329
>> see also TGraphic class

methods, 16, 23

> ActiveBuffer, TDataSet class, 567-568
> Add
>> TCollection class, 254
>> TCustomImageList class/descendants, 521-522
>> TList class, 78
>> TListItems class, 154
>> TMenuItem class, 431
>> TPopupList class, 78
>> TStrings class/descendants, 343
>> TTreeNodes class, 205-206
> AddAlias, TSession class, 459-460
> AddChild, TTreeNodes class, 206-207

methods (*continued*)

> AddChildFirst, TTreeNodes class, 207
> AddChildObject, TTreeNodes class, 208
> AddChildObjectFirst, TTreeNodes class, 208-209
> AddFirst, TTreeNodes class, 209-210
> AddIcon, TCustomImageList/TImageList classes, 522-523
> AddImages, TCustomImageList/TImageList classes, 523-524
> AddMapping, TGridDataLink class, 301
> AddMasked, TCustomImageList class/descendants, 524-525
> AddObject,
>> TStrings class/descendants, 344
>> TTreeNodes class, 210
> AddObjectFirst, TTreeNodes class, 211
> AddPassword, TSession class, 460
> AddStandardAlias, TSession class, 460-461
> AddStrings, TStrings class/descendants, 344-345
> AlphaSort
>> TCustomTreeView/TTreeView classes, 1022
>> TListView/TCustomListView classes, 965-966
>> TTreeNode class, 184
> Append, TDataSet class, 573-574
> AppendRecord, TDataSet class, 574-576
> ApplyUpdates, TDataSet class, 576-577
> Arc, TCanvas class, 221
> Arrange, TListView/TCustomListView classes, 966-967
> ArrangeIcons, TForm class, 1061-1063
> Assign
>> TCollection class, 256
>> TCustomImageList/TImageList classes, 526-527
>> TField class/descendants, 666
>> TPersistent class, 109-110
>> TStrings class/descendants, 345-346
> AssignValue, TField class/descendants, 667
> Back, TMediaPlayer class, 1156-1157
> BeginDrag
>> TControl class, 720-721
>> TCustomImageList/TImageList classes, 527

methods (*continued*)

BeginUpdate

TCollection class, 257-258

TListItems class, 154-155

TStrings class/descendants, 346

TTreeNodes class, 212

BringToFront

TApplication class, 391

TControl class, 721-722

BtnClick, TDBNavigator class, 1185-1186

Cancel, TDataSet class, 587

CancelEdit, TListItem class, 142-143

CancelUpdates, TDataSet class, 588

Capacity, TList class, 79

Cascade, TForm class, 1064-1065

CheckBrowseMode, TDataSet class, 588-589

Chord, TCanvas class, 223

ClassName, TObject class, 30

ClassParent, TObject class, 30-31

ClassType, TObject class, 31

Clear

TClipboard class, 113

TCollection class, 260

TCustomComboBox class/descendants,
916-917

TCustomEdit class/descendants, 1128

TCustomImageList/TImageList classes, 529

TCustomListBox class/descendants, 943

TField class/descendants, 672

TList class, 79-80

TListItems class, 155

TStrings class, 347

TTreeNodes class, 212

ClearFields, TDataSet class, 589

ClearMapping, TGridDataLink class, 301

ClearSelection, TCustomEdit class/
descendants, 1129

Click, TMenuItem class, 434

ClientToScreen, TControl class, 724

Close

TClipboard class, 114

TDataSet class, 589-590

TForm class, 1067-1068

TMediaPlayer class, 1158

TSession class, 461

methods (*continued*)

CloseKey, TRegistry, 60-61

Collapse, TTreeNode class, 185

ColumnSort, TListView/TCustomListView
classes, 970-971

CommitUpdates, TDataSet class, 590-591

ContainsControl, TWinControl class, 818-820

ControlAtPos, TWinControl class, 820

Controls, TWinControl class, 821-822

ControlsDisabled, TDataSet class, 591

CopyRect, TCanvas class, 225-226

CopyToClipboard

TCustomEdit class, 1130

TCustomEdit class/descendants, 1129

Count, TList class, 80

Create, 29

Exception class, 97

TCollection class, 262-263

TCollectionItem class, 262-263

TCustomImageList class/descendants, 530

TField class/descendants, 673-674

TIniFile, 37

TListItem class, 143-144

TObject class, 31-32

TStrings class/descendants, 349-350

TThread class, 52

CreateForm, TApplication class, 391-392

CreateFmt, Exception class, 97

CreateFmtHelp, Exception class, 97-98

CreateHelp, Exception class, 98

CreateKey, TRegistry, 61

CreateRes, Exception class, 98-99

CreateResFmt, Exception class, 99

CreateResFmtHelp, Exception class, 99-100

CreateSize, TCustomImageList/TImageList
classes, 530-531

CreateTitle, TColumn class, 263

CursorPosChanged, TDataSet class, 591-592

CutToClipboard, TCustomEdit class, 1130

DefaultAlignment, TColumn class, 264

DefaultAlignment, TColumnTitle class, 126

DefaultCaption, TColumnTitle class, 126-127

DefaultColor, TColumn class, 264

DefaultColor, TColumnTitle class, 127

DefaultFont, TColumn class, 265

DefaultFont, TColumnTitle class, 127-128

methods (*continued*)

DefaultReadOnly, TColumn class, 265

DefaultWidth, TColumn class, 266

DefocusControl, TForm class, 1068-1069

Delete

TCustomImageList class/descendants,
531-532

TDataSet class, 593

TList class, 81

TListItem class, 145-146

TListItems class, 156

TMenuItem class, 436

TStrings class/descendants, 350-351

TTreeNode class, 187

TTreeNodes class, 213

DeleteAlias, TSession class, 462-463

DeleteChildren, TTreeNode class, 187

DeleteKey

TIniFile, 37-38

TRegistry, 62-63

DeleteValue, TRegistry, 63-64

Destroy, 29

TCollection class, 266

TCollectionItem class, 266

TCustomImageList class/descendants, 532

TField class/descendants, 677

TObject class, 32

TStrings class/descendants, 351

DestroyComponents, TComponent class, 383

Destroying, TComponent class, 383

directives, 23-24

DisableControls, TDataSet class, 594

DoKey, TDBCtrlGrid class, 842-843

Dragging, TControl class, 727

DragLock, TCustomImageList/TImageList
classes, 534

DragMove, TCustomImageList/TImageList
classes, 534-535

DragUnlock, TCustomImageList/TImageList
classes, 535

Draw

TCanvas class, 226

TCustomImageList/TImageList classes, 535

DrawFocusRect, TCanvas class, 227

methods (*continued*)

DrawOverlay, TCustomImageList/TImageList
classes, 537-538

DropConnections, TSession class, 463

Edit

TDataLink class, 291-292

TDataSet class, 594-595

TDataSource class, 425

TFieldDataLink class, 295

EditCaption, TListItem class, 146-147

EditText, TTreeNode class, 189

Eject, TMediaPlayer class, 1161

Ellipse, TCanvas class, 228

EnableControls, TDataSet class, 595-596

EndDrag

TControl class, 728-729

TCustomImageList/TImageList classes, 538

EndEdit, TTreeNode class, 189

EndUpdate,

TCollection class, 267

TListItems class, 156-157

TStrings class/descendants, 352

TTreeNodes class, 214

Equals, TStrings class/descendants, 352-353

EraseSection, TIniFile, 38-39

event handlers, 22

see also events, handlers

Exchange

TList class, 81-82

TStrings class/descendants, 353

Execute

TColorDialog class, 501

TFindDialog class, 501

TFontDialog class, 501

TOpenDialog class, 501

TPrintDialog class, 501

TPrinterSetupDialog class, 501

TReplaceDialog class, 501

TSaveDialog class, 501

Expand

TList class, 82

TTreeNode class, 190

FetchAll, TDataSet class, 597

FieldByName, TDataSet class, 597-598

FillRect, TCanvas class, 228-229

methods (*continued*)

FindCaption, TListView/TCustomListView classes, 972-974

FindComponent, TComponent class, 383-384

FindData, TListView/TCustomListView classes, 974-975

FindDatabase, TSession class, 463-464

FindField, TDataSet class, 604-606

FindFirst, TDataSet class, 605-606

FindItemID, TCollection class, 269

FindLast, TDataSet class, 605-606

FindNext, TDataSet class, 605-606

FindNextPage, TPageControl class, 1007-1008

FindPrior, TDataSet class, 605-606

FireLoad, TCustomImageList/TImageList classes, 538-539

First, TDataSet class, 606-607

First, TList class, 82-83

FirstItem, TMenu class/descendants, 482-483

FloodFill, TCanvas class, 229

FocusControl
TField class/descendants, 685-686
TForm class, 1069-1070

FrameRect, TCanvas class, 231

Free, TObject class, 32-33

FreeBookmark, TDataSet class, 608

FullCollapse, TCustomTreeView/TTreeView classes, 1022-1023

FullExpand, TCustomTreeView/TTreeView classes, 1023

GetAliasDriverName, TSession class, 464

GetAliasNames, TSession class, 464

GetAliasParams, TSession class, 465

GetAsHandle, TClipboard class, 116

GetBitmap, TCustomImageList/TImageList classes, 539-540

GetBookmark, TDataSet class, 608-609

GetComponent, TClipboard class, 116-117

GetCurrentRecord, TDataSet class, 609

GetData function, TField class/descendants, 686

GetDatabaseNames, TSession class, 465

GetDataInfo, TRegistry, 64-65

GetDataSize, TRegistry, 65

GetDataType, TRegistry, 65-66

GetDisplayName,TStatusPanel class, 270

methods (*continued*)

GetDriverNames, TSession class, 465-466

GetDriverParams, TSession class, 466

GetFieldList, TDataSet class, 610

GetFieldNames, TDataSet class, 610-611

GetFirstChild, TTreeNode class, 191

GetFirstNode, TTreeNodes class, 214

GetGrid, TColumn class, 271

GetHitTestInfoAt, TCustomTreeView/TTreeView classes, 1023-1025

GetHotSpot, TCustomImageList/TImageList classes, 540

GetIcon, TCustomImageList/TImageList classes, 540-541

GetImageBitmap, TCustomImageList/TImageList classes, 541

GetInstRes, TCustomImageList/TImageList classes, 542

GetItem, TCollection class, 272

GetItemAt, TListView/TCustomListView classes, 976

GetKeyInfo, TRegistry, 66-67

GetKeyNames, TRegistry, 67

GetLastChild, TTreeNode class, 192

GetMaskBitmap, TCustomImageList/TImageList classes, 542

GetNearestItem, TListView/TCustomListView classes, 976-977

GetNext, TTreeNode class, 192

GetNextChild, TTreeNode class, 193

GetNextItem, TListView/TCustomListView classes, 978-979

GetNextSibling, TTreeNode class, 193

GetNextVisible, TTreeNode class, 194

GetNodeAt, TCustomTreeView/TTreeView classes, 1025-1026

GetPassword, TSession class, 466

GetPrev, TTreeNode class, 194

GetPrevChild, TTreeNode class, 195

GetPrevSibling, TTreeNode class, 195

GetResource, TCustomImageList/TImageList classes, 543

GetSelectTextBuf, TCustomEdit class/descendants, 1134-1135

methods (*continued*)

GetTextBuf

    TClipboard class, 117-118

    TControl class, 729

GetTextLen, TControl class, 730

GetValueNames, TRegistry, 68

GotoBookmark, TDataSet class, 611-612

HandleAllocated, TWinControl class, 823

HasAsParent, TTreeNode class, 196

HasFormat, TClipboard class, 118-119

HasSubKeys, TRegistry, 68-69

HelpCommand, TApplication class, 393-395

HelpContext, TApplication class, 395

HelpJump, TApplication class, 396

Hide, TControl class, 731

HideDragImage, TCustomImageList/TImageList classes, 545

IndexOf

    TList class, 83

    TListItems class, 158

    TMenuItem class, 438

    TStrings class/descendants, 356

IndexOfName, TStrings class/descendants, 356

IndexOfObject, TStrings class/descendants, 357

InheritsFrom, TObject class, 33

Initialize, TApplication class, 400

Insert

    TCustomImageList/TImageList classes, 546-547

    TDataSet class, 612-613

    TList class, 83-84

    TListItems class, 158-159

    TMenuItem class, 439

    TStrings class/descendants, 357-358

    TTreeNodes class, 215

InsertControl, TWinControl class, 823-824

InsertIcon, TCustomImageList/TImageList classes, 547-548

InsertMasked, TCustomImageList/TImageList classes, 548-549

InsertObject

    TStrings class/descendants, 358-359

    TTreeNodes class, 216

InsertRecord, TDataSet class, 613-616

InstanceSize, TObject class, 33

methods (*continued*)

interrogateField code listing, 713-714

Invalidate, TControl class, 733

IsBlob function, TField class/descendants, 687-688

IsEditing

    TCustomTreeView/TTreeView classes, 1027

    TListView/TCustomListView classes, 980

IsIndexField function, TField class/descendants, 688

IsLinkedTo

    TDataSet class, 616

    TDataSource class, 426

IsValidChar function, TField class/descendants, 689

ItemAtPos, TCustomListBox class/descendants, 947-948

ItemRect, TCustomListBox class/descendants, 949-950

KeyExists, TRegistry, 69

Last

    TDataSet class, 617-618

    TList class, 84-85

LineTo, TCanvas class, 232

LoadFromClipboardFormat, TGraphic class, 324-325

LoadFromFile

    TGraphic class, 325-326

    TPicture class, 170

    TStrings class/descendants, 359

LoadFromFile function, TBlobField/TGraphicField/TMemoField class, 690-691

LoadFromStream, TStrings class/descendants, 359

LoadFromStream function, TBlobField/TGraphicField/TMemoField class, 691

Locate, TDataSet class, 618-619

Lookup, TDataSet class, 619-621

LookupKeyFields function, TField class/descendants, 693-694

LookupList function, TField class/descendants, 694-695

methods (*continued*)

LookupResultField function, TField class/descendants, 695

MakeVisible,
> *TListItem class, 149-150*
> *TTreeNode class, 200*

MaxValue, TField class/descendants, 696

Merge, TMainMenu class, 484

MessageBox, TApplication class, 402-404

Minimize, TApplication class, 404

MinValue, TField class/descendants, 696-697

Modified
> *TFieldDataLink class, 297*
> *TGridDataLink class, 303*

Move
> *TCustomImageList/TImageList classes, 549-550*
> *TList class, 85-86*
> *TStrings class/descendants, 360*

MoveBy, TDataSet class, 621-622

MoveTo
> *TCanvas class, 232*
> *TTreeNode class, 200-201*

Next
> *TDataSet class, 622-623*
> *TForm class, 1078*
> *TMediaPlayer class, 1166*

Offset function, TField class/descendants, 698

Open
> *TClipboard class, 119*
> *TDataSet class, 634-635*
> *TMediaPlayer class, 1170*
> *TSession class, 469*

OpenKey, TRegistry, 70

Overlay, TCustomImageList/TImageList classes, 550-551

Pack, TList class, 86

PageControl
> *TTabSheeGetPassword method*
> *TSession class, 466*

Pie, TCanvas class, 237-238

Polygon, TCanvas class, 239

Polyline, TCanvas class, 240

Read methods, TRegistry, 71

ReadInteger, TIniFile class, 40-41

methods (*continued*)

ReadSection, TIniFile class, 41-42

ReadSections, TIniFile class, 42

ReadSectionValues, TIniFile class, 43-44

ReadString, TIniFile class, 45

Rebuild Columns, TDBGridColumns class, 277

Rectangle, TCanvas class, 240-241

Refresh, TCanvas class, 241

Remove
> *TList class, 86-87*
> *TPopupList class, 86-87*

RenameValue, TRegistry, 71-72

RestoreDefaults
> *TColumn class, 278*
> *TColumnTitle class, 129*
> *TDBGridColumns class, 278*

Resume, TThread class, 54

RoundRect, TCanvas class, 241-242

SaveToStream
> *TBlobField/TGraphicField/TMemoField class, 705*
> *TStrings class/descendants, 367*

SaveToFile, TPicture class, 173

ScaleBy, TWinControl class, 830-831

ScreenToClient, TControl class, 746-747

Scroll, TListView/TCustomListView classes, 988

SelectAll, TCustomEdit class/descendants, 1144

SendToBack, TControl class, 747

SetAsHandle, TClipboard class, 119-120

SetBounds
> *TControl class, 747-748*
> *TDBNavigator class, 1187-1188*

SetComponent, TClipboard class, 120

SetCurrency, TBCDField class, 706

SetData, TField class/descendants, 706

SetDetailFields, TDataSet class, 640-641

SetDragImage, TCustomImageList/TImageList classes, 557

SetFields, TDataSet class, 641-642

SetFieldType, TBlobField/TField classes, 707

SetFocus, TWinControl class, 832

SetIndex TCollectionItem class, 278-279

SetParams, TScrollBar class, 876-877

SetSelTextBuf, TCustomEdit class/descendants, 1146

methods (*continued*)

SetText, TStrings class/descendants, 367-368

SetTextBuf

    TClipboard class, 121

    TControl class, 748

SetTick, TTrackBar class, 906

Show

    TControl class, 748-749

    TForm class, 1082

ShowDragImage,

    TCustomImageList/TImageList classes, 558

ShowModal, TForm class, 1082

Sort

    TList class, 87-88

    TStringList class, 368-369

StartRecording, TMediaPlayer class, 1175

Step, TMediaPlayer class, 1175

StepBy, TProgressBar class, 867

StepIt, TProgressBar class, 867-868

Stop, TMediaPlayer class, 1176

StretchDraw, TCanvas class, 242-243

StringWidth, TListView/TCustomListView

    classes, 992-993

StyleChanged, TShape class, 785

Suspend, TThread class, 54

Terminate

    TApplication class, 420

    TThread class, 55

TextHeight, TCanvas class, 243

TextOut, TCanvas class, 244

TextRect, TCanvas class, 244-245

TextWidth, TCanvas class, 245

Tile, Form class, 1082-1083

Unmerge, TMainMenu class, 486

UnRegisterChanges,

    TCustomImageList/TImageList classes,

    558-559

Update

    TControl class, 750

    TListItem class, 152-153

UpdateCursorPos, TDataSet class, 643

UpdateItems, TListView/TCustomListView

    classes, 993-994

UpdateRecord

    TDataLink class, 293

    TDataSet class, 644

methods (*continued*)

UpdateStatus, TDataSet class, 645

ValueExists, TRegistry, 72-73

Write methods, TRegistry, 73-74

WriteBool, TIniFile class, 45-46

WriteInteger, TIniFile class, 46-47

WriteString, TIniFile class, 47-48

Microsoft Word (MDI application), 1056-1057

Min property

TProgressBar class, 865-866

TTrackBar class, 902

TUpDown class, 1048

MinFontSize property, TFontDialog class, 507-508

Minimize method, TApplication class, 404

MinPage property, TPrintDialog class, 508

MinSize property, TSplitter class, 810-811

MinValue function, TField clas/descendants,
696-697

MinWidth property, THeaderSection class, 275-276

MMHeight property, TMetafile class, 326

MMWidth property, TMetafile class, 326

ModalResult property, TButton/TBitBtn classes,
1109-1111

Mode property

TMediaPlayer class, 1165-1166

TPen class, 310-311

Modified method

TFieldDataLink class, 297

TGridDataLink class, 303

Modified property

TCustomEdit class/descendants, 1137-1138

TDataSet class, 621

TGraphic class, 327

Modifiers property, THotKey class, 934

Move method

TCustomImageList/TImageList classes, 549-550

TList class, 85-86

TStrings class/descendants, 360

MoveBy method, TDataSet class, 621-622

MoveTo method

TCanvas class, 232

TTreeNode class, 200-201

MultiLine property, TTabControl/TPageControl
classes, 1008-1009

multimedia, *see* **TMediaPlayer**

Multiple Document Interface, *see* MDI applications
MultiSelect property
    TCustomListBox class/descendants, 951
    TListView/TCustomListView classes, 983

N

Name property
    TComponent class, 384-385
    TFont class, 312
    TTextAttributes object, 178
Names property, TStrings class/descendants, 360
naming threads, 50
New Thread dialog box, 50
NewField dialog box, 655
NewValue property, TField class/descendants, 697
Next method
    TDataSet class, 622-623
    TForm class, 1078
    TMediaPlayer class, 1166
NNTP (Network News Transfer Protocol)
  control, 104
nonwindowed controls, 755
    TBevel class, 761-766
    TCustomLabel class, 787-790
        TDBText class, 790-791, 793
        TLabel class, 791-792
    TGraphicControl class, 755-759
    TImage class, 767-769
        AutoSize property, 770
        Center property, 771
        Picture property, 772
        Stretch property, 773
    TPaintBox class, 775-777
    TShape class, 779-782
        Brush property, 782-783
        Pen property, 783
        Shape property, 784
        StyleChanged method, 785
    TSpeedButton class, 795-799
        AllowAllUp property, 799-800
        Down property, 801
        Glyph property, 801-802
        GroupIndex property, 802-803
        Layout property, 803
        Margin property, 804

nonwindowed controls (*continued*)
    methods/events, 797-799
    NumGlyphs property, 804
    Spacing property, 805
    TSplitter class, 807-810
        Beveled property, 810
        MinSize property, 810-811
        OnMoved event, 811-812
Notify property, TMediaPlayer class, 1166-1167
NotifyValue property, TMediaPlayer class, 1168
Numbering property, TParaAttributes class, 164
NumGlyphs property
    TBitBtn class, 1112
    TSpeedButton class, 804

O

Object Browser, 25-26
Object Repository, 9
Object-Oriented Programming, (OOP), 15-18
    encapsulation, 17-18
    inheritance, 17
    polymorphism, 17
    pure/hybrid languages, 15-16
objects
    applications, *see* TApplication class
    event handlers, 22
        speedbuttons, 796
        see also methods
    exception objects, *see* exceptions
    instances, 16
    lists, *see* TList class, TPopupList class
    menus, *see* menus
    methods, 16, 23
        directives, 23-24
        see also methods
    persistent, 109-110
        canvas, see TCanvas class
        column titles, 123-124
        components, see components
        pictures, 167-168
        scroll bars, 131-132
        TCollection class, see TCollection class
        TDataLink, see TDataLink class
        TGraphic class, see TGraphic class
        TGraphicsObject class, 305

objects (*continued*)

> *TListItem, see TListItem*
> *TListItems, see TListItems*
> *TStrings class, see TStrings class*
> *TTextAttributes, 175, 177-180*
> *TTreeNode, see TTreeNode class*
> *TTreeNodes, see TTreeNodes class*

> properties, 16, 22-23
> > *see also properties*
> RTTI (Run-Time Type Information), 24-25
> session, *see TSession class*
> threads, adding, 49
> > *see also TThread class*
> timers, TTimer class, 473-475
> TIniFile class, *see TIniFile class*
> TObject class, *see TObject class*
> TRegistry class, *see TRegistry class*
> types, 16
> UpdateObject property, TDataSet class, 643
> *see also classes*

Objects property, TStrings class/descendants, 361
Offset function, TField class/descendants, 698
OldValue property, TField class/descendants, 698-699
OnActivate event, TApplication class, 404-405
OnActiveChange event, TFieldDataLink class, 297
OnActiveControlChange event, TScreen class, 453-454
OnActiveFormChange event, TScreen class, 454-455
OnApply event, TFontDialog class, 508
OnCalcFields event, TDataSet class, 623-624
OnChange event

> TBrush/TPen/TFont classes, 312-313
> TCanvas class, 233-234
> TField class/descendants, 699
> TGraphic class, 328-329
> TListView/TCustomListView classes, 983
> TPicture class, 171
> TStringList class, 361-363

OnChanging event

> TCanvas class, 234-235
> TCustomTreeView/TTreeView classes, 1028-1029
> TListView/TCustomListView classes, 984
> TStringList class, 363-364

OnClick event

> TControl class, 733-734
> TMenuItem class, 441

OnCollapsed event, TCustomTreeView/TTreeView classes, 1029
OnCollapsing event, TCustomTreeView/TTreeView classes, 1029-1030
OnColumnClick event, TListView/TCustomListView classes, 984-985
OnCompare event

> TCustomTreeView/TTreeView classes, 1030
> TListView/TCustomListView classes, 985

OnDataChange event

> TDataSource class, 426-427
> TFieldDataLink class, 298

OnDblClick event, TControl class, 734-735
OnDeActivate event, TApplication class, 406-407
OnDeleteError event, TDataSet class, 624-625
OnDeletion event

> TCustomTreeView/TTreeView classes, 1030-1031
> TListView/TCustomListView classes, 985-986

OnDragDrop event, TControl class, 735-736
OnDragOver event, TControl class, 736-738
OnDrawItem event, TComboBox/TDBComboBox classes, 922-923
OnDrawSection event, THeaderControl class, 855
OnDropDown event, TComboBox/TDBComboBox classes, 922
OnEdited event

> TCustomTreeView/TTreeView classes, 1031
> TListView/TCustomListView classes, 986

OnEditError event, TDataSet class, 625-627
OnEditing event

> TCustomTreeView/TTreeView classes, 1031-1032
> TListView/TCustomListView classes, 986-987

OnEditingChange event, TFieldDataLink class, 298
OnEndDrag event, TControl class, 738-739
OnEnter event, TWinControl class, 824-825
OnException event, TApplication class, 407-408
OnExit event, TWinControl class, 825-826
OnExpanded event, TCustomTreeView/TTreeView classes, 1032
OnExpanding event, TCustomTreeView/TTreeView classes, 1032

OnFilterRecord event, TDataSet class, 627-628

OnFind event
TFindDialog class, 509
TReplaceDialog class, 509

OnGetImageIndex event,
TCustomTreeView/TTreeView classes, 1033

OnGetText event, TField class/descendants, 700

OnHelp event, TApplication class, 408

OnHint event, TApplication class, 409-410

OnIdle event, TApplication class, 410-411

OnInsert event, TListView/TCustomListView
classes, 987

OnKeyDown event, TWinControl class, 826-827

OnKeyPress event, TWinControl class, 827-828

OnKeyUp event, TWinControl class, 828-829

OnMeasureItem event
TComboBox/TDBComboBox classes, 923
TCustomListBox class/descendants, 951-952

OnMessage event, TApplication class, 411-412

OnMinimize event, TApplication class, 413-414

OnMouseDown event, TControl class, 739-740

OnMouseEvent event, TControl class, 740-741

OnMouseUp event, TControl class, 741-742

OnMoved event, TSplitter class, 811-812

OnNewRecord event, TDataSet class, 628-629

OnNotify event, TMediaPlayer class, 1168-1169

OnPaintPanel event, TDBCtrlGrid class, 843-845

OnPassword event, TSession class, 467-468

OnPostClick event, TMediaPlayer class, 1169

OnPostError event, TDataSet class, 629-630

OnReplace event, TReplaceDialog class, 509-510

OnResize event, THeaderControl class, 855

OnResizeRequest event, TRichEdit class, 1138

OnRestore event, TApplication class, 414-415

OnSectionClick event, THeaderControl class,
856-857

OnSectionResize event, THeaderControl class,
857-858

OnSectionTrack event, THeaderControl class,
858-859

OnSelectedIndex event,
TCustomTreeView/TTreeView classes, 1033

OnSelectionChange event, TRichEdit classes,
1138-1139

OnServerYield event, TDataSet class, 630-631

OnSetText event, TField class/descendants, 700

OnShowHint event, TApplication class, 415-417

OnStartDrag event, TControl class, 742-743

OnStartUp event, TSession class, 468-469

OnStateChange events, TDataSource class, 427

OnTerminate event, TThread class, 52-53

OnTimer event, TTimer class, 475

OnUpdateData event, TFieldDataLink class,
298-299

OnUpdateData events, TDataSource class, 427

OnUpdateError event, TDataSet class, 631-632

OnUpdateRecord event, TDataSet class, 633-634

OnValidate event, TField class/descendants, 701

OOP (Object-Oriented Programming), 15-18
encapsulation, 17-18
inheritance, 17
polymorphism, 17
pure/hybrid languages, 15-16

Open dialog boxes, 491-492
filters, 492
methods, 493
Execute method, 501
properties, 493
Ctl3D, 498
DefaultExt, 499-500
FileName, 501-502
Files, 502
Filter, 503
FilterIndex, 503-504
HelpContext, 505-506
InitialDir, 506
Options, 510, 512-513
Title, 515
see also Save dialog boxes

Open method
TClipboard class, 119
TDataSet class, 634-635
TMediaPlayer class, 1170
TSession class, 469

OpenKey method, TRegistry class, 70

Optimizing compiler, 5-6

Options property
TColorDialog class, 510-511
TFindDialog class, 510-512
TFontDialog class, 510, 512

Options property (*continued*)
TOpenDialog/TSaveDialog classes, 510, 512-513
TPrintDialog class, 510, 513
TReplaceDialog class, 510-512
Orientation property
TDBCtrlGrid class, 845
TTrackBar class, 902-903
TUpDown class, 1048
Overlay method, TCustomImageList/TImageList classes, 550-551
OverlayIndex property, TListItem class, 150
OverLayIndex property, TTreeNode class, 201-202
Override directive, 23
Owner property
TComponent class, 385
TListColumns class, 276
TListItem class, 150-151
TListItems class, 160
TSubitems/TTreeStrings classes, 364
TTreeNodes class, 216

P

Pack method, TList class, 86
page controls, *see* TTabSheet class
PageControl method, TTabSheet class, 892
PageCount property, TPageControl class, 1009-1010
Pages property, TPageControl class, 1010
PageSize property, TTrackBar class, 903
paint box controls (TImage class), 775-777
Palette property, TBitmap/TMetafile classes, 329
PanelBorder property, TDBCtrlGrid class, 846
PanelCount property, TDBCtrlGrid class, 847
PanelHeight property, TDBCtrlGrid class, 847
PanelIndex property, TDBCtrlGrid class, 847
panels
TDBCtrlGrid class, *see* TDBCtrlGrid class
TPanel class, *see* TPanel class
Panels property, TStatusBar class, 883-884
PanelWidth property, TDBCtrlGrid class, 848
panes, *see* splitter controls
Paradox tables, TDataSet class Refresh method, 639

Paragraph property, TCustomRichEdit class/descendants, 1139-1140
paragraphs, TParaAttributes class, 161-166
Alignment property, 162
FirstIndent property, 163
LeftIndent property, 164
Numbering property, 164
RightIndent property, 165
Tab property, 165
TabCount property, 166
Parent property
TControl class, 743-744
TMenuItem class, 441
TTreeNode class, 202
ParentColor property, TControl class, 744
ParentCtl3D property, TWinControl class, 829
ParentFont property, TControl class, 744
ParentShowHint property, TControl class, 745
PasswordChar property
TEdit/TMaskEdit classes, 1140-1141
TMaskEdit class, 1140-1141
passwords
AddPassword method, TSession class, 460
GetPassword method, TSession class, 466
OnPassword event, TSession class, 467-468
RemoveAllPasswords method, TSession class, 470
RemovePassword method, TSession class, 470
TPasswordDialog, *see* TForm class
PasteFromClipboard method, TCustomEdit class/descendants, 1141
Pause method, TMediaPlayer class, 1170
PauseOnly method, TMediaPlayer class, 1170-1171
pen object, *see* TPen class
Pen property
TCanvas class, 235-236
TShape class, 783
PenPos property, TCanvas class, 237
persistent objects, 109-110
column titles, 123-124
see also TColumnTitle class
components, *see* components
persistent field components, creating, 651-655
pictures, *see* TPicture class
scroll bars, 131
see also TControlScrollBar class

persistent objects (*continued*)

    TCanvas class, 217-220

        Arc method, 221

        Brush property, 222

        Chord method, 223

        CopyMode property, 224

        CopyRect method, 225-226

        derivation, 217

        Draw method, 226

        DrawFocusRect method, 227

        Ellipse method, 228

        FillRect method, 228-229

        FloodFill method, 229

        Font property, 230

        FrameRect method, 231

        Handle property, 231

        LineTo method, 232

        metafile canvas objects, 219-220

        MoveTo method, 232

        OnChange event, 233-234

        OnChanging event, 234-235

        Pen property, 235-236

        PenPos property, 237

        Pie method, 237-238

        Polygon method, 239

        Polyline method, 240

        printer canvas objects, 220

        Rectangle method, 240-241

        Refresh method, 241

        RoundRect method, 241-242

        StretchDraw method, 242-243

        TextHeight method, 243

        TextOut method, 244

        TextRect method, 244-245

        TextWidth method, 245

    TClipboardclass, *see* TClipboard class

    TCollection class, *see* TCollection class

    TDataLink class, 287-288

        Active property, 288-289

        ActiveRecord property, 289

        BufferCount property, 289-290

        DataSet property, 290

        DataSource property, 290

        DataSourceFixed property, 291

        Edit method, 291-292

persistent objects (*continued*)

        Editing property, 291

        ReadOnly property, 292

        RecordCount property, 292

        TDataSourceLink, 299

        TDBCtrlGridLink, 304

        TFieldDataLink, 293-299

        TGridDataLink, 300-304

        TListSourceLink, 300

        TNavDataLink, 299

        TQueryDataLink, 299

        TTableDataLink, 293

        UpdateRecord method, 293

    TGraphic class, 317-318

        Empty property, 322

        Height property, 323

        LoadFromClipboardFormat method, 324-325

        LoadFromFile method, 325-326

        Modified property, 327

        OnChange event, 328-329

        SaveToClipboardFormat method, 329-330

        SaveToFile method, 330-331

        TBitmap, 319-320, 323-324, 327-329

        TIcon, 318-319, 323

        TMetafile, 319, 321-323, 326, 329

        Width property, 331

    TGraphicsObject class, 305-306

        properties/methods/events, 306

        TBrush, 306, 308-309, 312-315

        TFont, 307, 309-310, 312-316

        TPen, 306-307, 309-316

    TListItem, 141-142

        CancelEdit method, 142-143

        Caption property, 143

        Create method, 143-144

        Cut property, 144

        Data property, 145

        Delete method, 145-146

        DropTarget property, 146

        EditCaption method, 146-147

        Focused property, 147

        Handle property, 147-148

        ImageIndex property, 148

        Index property, 148-149

persistent objects (*continued*)

    ListView property, 149

    MakeVisible method, 149-150

    OverlayIndex property, 150

    Owner property, 150-151

    Selected property, 151

    StateIndex property, 151-152

    SubItems property, 152

    Update method, 152-153

  TListItems, 153

    Add method, 154

    BeginUpdate method, 154-155

    Clear method, 155

    Count property, 155-156

    Delete method, 156

    EndUpdate method, 156-157

    Handle property, 157

    IndexOf method, 158

    Insert method, 158-159

    Item property, 159

    Owner property, 160

  TPicture class, 167-170, 172-173

    Bitmap property, 168

    Graphic property, 169

    Height property, 169-170

    Icon property, 170

    LoadFromFile method, 170

    OnChange event, 171

    SaveToFile method, 173

    Width property, 173

  TStrings class, 333-336

    Add method, 343

    AddObject method, 344

    AddStrings method, 344-345

    Assign method, 345-346

    BeginUpdate method, 346

    Capacity property, 346-347

    Clear method, 347

    CommaText property, 347-348

    Count property, 348-349

    Create method, 349-350

    Delete method, 350-351

    Destroy method, 351

persistent objects (*continued*)

    Duplicates property, 351-352

    EndUpdate method, 352

    Equals method, 352-353

    example project, 371-375

    Exchange method, 353

    Find property, 353-354

    Handle property, 355

    IndexOf method, 356

    IndexOfName method, 356

    IndexOfObject method, 357

    Insert method, 357-358

    InsertObject method, 358-359

    LoadFromFile method, 359

    LoadFromStream method, 359

    Move method, 360

    Names property, 360

    Objects property, 361

    OnChange event, 361-363

    OnChanging event, 363-364

    Owner property, 364-365

    SaveToFile method, 366-367

    SaveToStream method, 367

    SetText method, 367-368

    Sort method, 368-369

    Sorted property, 369

    Strings property, 369-370

    TComboBoxStrings, 336

    Text property, 370

    THeaderStrings, 336-337

    TIndexFiles, 337

    TListBoxStrings, 338

    TMemoStrings, 338

    TOutlineStrings, 339, 354, 366

    TPageAccess, 339

    TRichEditStrings, 339-340

    TStringGridStrings, 340

    TStringList, 340-341

    TSubItems, 341

    TTabPageAccess, 342

    TTabStrings, 342

    TTreeStrings, 343

    Values property, 370-371

persistent objects (*continued*)

TTextAttribute

    Color property, 176

    ConsistentAttributes property, 177

    Height property, 177-178

    Name property, 178

    Pitch property, 178-179

    Protected property, 179

    Size property, 179-180

    Style property, 180

TTextAttributes, 175-180

TTreeNode, 181-183

    AbsoluteIndex property, 183

    AlphaSort method, 184

    Collapse method, 185

    Count property, 185

    Cut property, 186

    Data property, 186-187

    Delete method, 187

    DeleteChildren method, 187

    Deleting property, 188

    DropTarget property, 188

    EditText method, 189

    EndEdit method, 189

    Expand method, 190

    Expanded property, 190-191

    Focused property, 191

    GetFirstChild method, 191

    GetLastChild method, 192

    GetNext method, 192

    GetNextChild method, 193

    GetNextSibling method, 193

    GetNextVisible method, 194

    GetPrev method, 194

    GetPrevChild method, 195

    GetPrevSibling method, 195

    Handle property, 196

    HasAsParento method, 196

    HasChildren property, 197

    ImageIndex property, 197

    Index property, 198

    IndexOf property, 198-199

    IsVisible property, 199

    Item property, 199

    Level property, 200

    MoveTo method, 200-201

persistent objects (*continued*)

    OverLayIndex property, 201-202

    Parent property, 202

    SelectedIndex property, 202-203

    StateIndex property, 203

    Text property, 203

    TreeView property, 204

TTreeNodes, 181, 204

    Add method, 205-206

    AddChild method, 206-207

    AddChildFirst method, 207

    AddChildObject method, 208

    AddChildObjectFirst method, 208-209

    AddFirst method, 209-210

    AddObject method, 210

    AddObjectFirst method, 211

    BeginUpdate method, 212

    Clear method, 212

    Count property, 213

    Delete method, 213

    EndUpdate method, 214

    GetFirstNode method, 214

    Handle property, 215

    Insert method, 215

    InsertObject method, 216

    Owner property, 216

PickList property, TColumn class, **276**

picture objects (TPicture class), **167**

    Bitmap property, 168

    Graphic property, 169

    Height property, 169-170

    Icon property, 170

    LoadFromFile method, 170

    OnChange event, 171

    SaveToFile method, 173

    Width property, 173

    see also graphics

Picture property, TImage class, **772**

Pie method, TCanvas class, **237-238**

Pitch property

    TFont class, 313

    TTextAttributes object, 178-179

PlainText property

    TRichEdit class, 1141-1142

    TStrings class, 365-366

Play method, TMediaPlayer class, **1171**

Polygon method, TCanvas class, 239

Polyline method, TCanvas class, 240

POP (Post Office Protocol) control, 105

popup menus

TPopupMenu class, 479-480

Alignment property, 480-481

AutoPopup property, 482

FindItem method, 482

Handle property, 483

HelpContext property, 483

OnPopup event, 484

Popup method, 485

PopupComponent property, 485-486

Popup method, TPopupMenu class, 484-485

PopupComponent property, TPopupMenu class, 485-486

PopupMenu property, TControl class, 745

Position property

TControlScrollBar class, 134

TFindDialog class, 513-514

TForm class, 1079

TMediaPlayer class, 1171-1172

TProgressBar class, 866

TReplaceDialog class, 513-514

TTrackBar class, 904

Position property, TUpDown class, 1049

Post method, TDataSet class, 635

Precision property,
BCDField/TCurrencyField/TFloatField classes, 702

Previous method

TForm class, 1079-1080

TMediaPlayer class, 1172

Print dialog boxes, 493-494

methods, 494

Execute, 501

properties, 494

Collate, 497

Copies, 498

Ctl3D, 498

MaxPage, 507

MinPage, 508

Options, 510, 513

PrintRange, 514

PrintToFile, 514-515

ToPage, 516

Print method, TForm class, 1080-1081

Print property, TCustomRichEdit class/
descendants, 1142

Printer Setup dialog boxes, 494-495

Execute method, 501

properties

Ctl3D, 498

HelpContext, 505-506

ReplaceText, 515

printing

EPrinter exception, 96

printer canvas objects, 220

see also canvas objects

PrintRange property, TPrintDialog class, 514

PrintScale property, TForm class, 1080-1081

PrintToFile property, TPrintDialog class, 514-515

Prior method, TDataSet class, 635-636

Priority property, TThread class, 53

Private visibility specifier, 20-21

PrivateDir property, TSession class, 469

progress bars, (TProgressBar class), 861-865

events, 862-865

methods, 862-865

StepBy, 867

StepIt, 867-868

properties, 862-865

Max, 865

Min, 865-866

Position, 866

Step, 866

Project Options dialog box

Application page, 387

changing icons, 399

Forms page, 401

properties, 16, 22-23

AbsoluteIndex, TTreeNode class, 183

Active

TApplication class, 390

TDataLink class, 288-289

TDataSet class, 567

TForm class, 1060

TSession class, 459

ActiveControl

TForm class, 1060

TScreen class, 448-449

ActiveForm, TScreen class, 449

properties (*continued*)

    ActiveMDIChild, TForm class, 1061

    ActivePage, TPageControl class, 1006

    ActiveRecord, TDataLink class, 289

    Align, TControl, 720

    AlignButton, TUpDown class, 1045

    Alignment

        TColumn class, 255

        TColumnTitle class, 124-125

        TField/TNumericField class, 662

        THeaderSection class, 255

        TListColumn class, 255

        TParaAttributes class, 162

        TPopupMenu class, 480-481

        TStatusPanel class, 255

    AllocBy

        TCustomImageList/TImageList classes, 525

        TListView/TCustomListView classes, 964-965

    AllowAllUp, TSpeedButton class, 799-800

    AllowClick, THeaderSection class, 255-256

    AllowDelete property, TDBCtrlGrid class, 840

    AllowGrayed, TCheckBox class, 1102-1103

    AllowInsert property, TDBCtrlGrid class, 840-841

    Arrangement, TIconOptions class, 138

    ArrowKeys, TUpDown class, 1046

    AsBoolean, TField class/descendants, 662-663

    AsCurrency, TField class/descendants, 663-664

    AsDateTime, TField class/descendants, 664-665

    AsFloat, TField class/descendants, 665

    AsInteger, TField class/descendants, 665-666

    AssignedValues, TColumn class, 257

    Associate, TUpDown class, 1046

    AsString, TField class/descendants, 667-668

    AsText, TClipboard class, 113

    AsVariant, TField class/descendants, 668

    AttributeSet, TField class/descendants, 669

    AutoArrange, TIconOptions class, 138

    AutoCalcFields, TDataSet class, 577

    AutoEdit, TDataSource class, 424

    AutoEnable, TMediaPlayer class, 1155

    AutoMerge, TMainMenu class, 481-482

    AutoOpen, TMediaPlayer class, 1155-1156

    AutoPopup, TPopupMenu class, 482

properties (*continued*)

    AutoRewind, TMediaPlayer class, 1156

    AutoScroll, TForm class, 1062

    AutoSelect, TEdit class, 1127

    AutoSize, TImage class, 770-771

    Bevel, TStatusPanel class, 258

    Beveled, TSplitter class, 810

    BevelInner, TPanel class, 1181-1182

    BevelOuter, TPanel class, 1182

    BevelWidth, TPanel class, 1183

    Bitmap, TPicture class, 168

    BkColor, TCustomImageList/TImageList classes, 527-528

    BlendColor, TCustomImageList/TImageList classes, 528-529

    BlobType, TBlobField class, 658, 669-670

    BOF, TDataSet class, 577-578

    Bookmark, TDataSet class, 585

    BorderIcons, TForm class, 1064

    BorderStyle, TCustomListBox class/descendants, 942-943

    BoundingRect, TListView/TCustomListView classes, 967

    BoundsRect, TControl, 721

    Break, TMenuItem class, 431-432

    Brush

        TCanvas class, 222

        TShape class, 782-783

    BufferCount, TDataLink class, 289-290

    ButtonStyle, TColumn class, 258-259

    CachedUpdates, TDataSet class, 585-586

    Calculated, TField class/descendants, 670-671

    Cancel, TButton/TBitBtn classes, 1103

    CanModify

        TDataSet class, 586-587

        TField class/descendants, 671

        TFieldDataLink class, 294

    Canvas

        TBitmap class, 320

        TGraphicControl, 758-759

    Capabilities, TMediaPlayer class, 1157-1158

    Capacity, TStrings class/descendants, 346-347

    Caption

        TColumnTitle class, 125

        TControl, 722

properties (*continued*)

    TListItem class, 143
    TMenuItem class, 432-433
Center, TImage class, 771-772
CharCase, TEdit/TMaskEdit classes, 1127-1128
Checked
    TCheckBox/TRadioButton classes, 1104
    TMenuItem class, 433-434
CheckRange, TBCDField class, 671-672
ClientHandle, TForm class, 1065-1066
ClientHeight
    TControl, 722-723
    TForm class, 1066
ClientOrigin, TControl, 723
ClientRect, TControl, 723-724
ClientWidth
    TControl, 724-725
    TForm class, 1067
ColCount property, TDBCtrlGrid class, 841
Collate, TPrintDialog class, 497
Collection, TCollectionItem class, 260-261
Color
    TBrush/TPen/TFont classes, 309
    TColorDialog class, 497
    TColumn class, 261
    TColumnTitle class, 125
    TControl, 725
    TTextAtributes class, 176
ColoredButtons, TMediaPlayer class, 1159
Column, TListView/TCustomListView classes, 968
ColumnClick, TListView/TCustomListView classes, 968-969
Columns
    TListView/TCustomListView classes, 969-970
    TRadioGroup class, 1192
CommaText, TStrings class/descendants, 347-348
ComponentCount, TComponent class, 381
ComponentIndex, TComponent class, 381
Components, TComponent class, 382
ComponentState, TComponent class, 382-383
ConfigMode, TSession class, 461-462
ConfirmDelete, TDBNavigator class, 1186

properties (*continued*)

ConsistentAttributes, TTextAtributes class, 177
Control, TFieldDataLink class, 294-295
ControlCount, TWinControl class, 820-821
ControlState, TControl, 725
ControlStyle, TControl, 726
Copies, TPrintDialog class, 498
CopyMode, TCanvas class, 224
Count
    TCollection class, 262-263
    TCustomImageList class/descendants, 529
    TListItems class, 155-156
    TMenuItem class, 434-435
    TStrings class/descendants, 348-349
    TTreeNode class, 185
    TTreeNodes class, 213
CreatedBy, TMetafile class, 321-322
Ctl3D
    TCommonDialog class/descendants, 498
    TWinControl class, 822
Currency, TBCDField/TCurrencyField/TFloatField classes, 674-675
CurrentKey, TRegistry class, 62
CurrentPath, TRegistry class, 62
Cursor
    TControl, 726
    TScreen class, 449-450
Cursors, TScreen class, 450-451
CustomColors, TColorDialog class, 499
Cut
    TListItem class, 144
    TTreeNode class, 186
Data
    TListItem class, 145
    TTreeNode class, 186-187
Databases, TSession class, 462
DataField
    TDBComboBox class, 917
    TDBListBox class, 944
    TDBText class, 793
DataSet
    TDataLink class, 290
    TDataSource class, 424-425
    TField class/descendants, 675

properties (*continued*)

DataSize, TField class/descendants, 675-676

DataSource

    TDataLink class, 290

    TDataSet class, 592

    TDBComboBox class, 917

    TDBListBox class, 944

    TDBNavigator class, 1186-1187

    TDBText class, 793

DataSource property, TDBCtrlGrid class, 841

DataSourceFixed, TDataLink class, 291

DataType, TField class/descendants, 676-677

DefAttributes, TCustomRichEdit class/
descendants, 1131

Default, TMenuItem class, 435-436

DefaultExt, TOpenDialog/TSaveDialog class,
499-500

DefaultFields

    TDataSet class, 592-593

    TGridDataLink class, 302

Deleting, TTreeNode class, 188

Description, TMetafile class, 321

Device, TFontDialog class, 500

DeviceID, TMediaPlayer class, 1159

DeviceType, TMediaPlayer class, 1159-1160

Display, TMediaPlayer class, 1160

DisplayFormat, TField class descendants, 678

DisplayLabel, TField class/descendants, 678-
679

DisplayName, TField class/descendants, 679

DisplayRect

    TMediaPlayer class, 1161

    TTabControl class, 1007

DisplayText, TField class/descendants, 680

DisplayValues, TField class/descendants,
680-681

DisplayWidth, TField class/descendants, 681

Down, TSpeedButton class, 801

DragCursor

    TControl, 727

    TCustomImageList/TImageList classes, 533

Dragging, TCustomImageList/TImageList
classes, 533-534

DragMode, TControl, 728

DrawingStyle, TCustomImageList/TImageList
classes, 536

properties (*continued*)

DropDownCount, TCustomComboBox
class/descendants, 918

DropDownRows, TColumn class, 267

DroppedDown, TCustomComboBox
class/descendants, 918

DropTarget

    TListItem class, 146

    *TListView/TCustomListView classes,
971-972*

    TTreeNode class, 188

Duplicates, TStringList class, 351-352

EditFormat, TField class/descendants, 681-682

Editing

    TDataLink class, 291

    TFieldDataLink class, 295

EditMask

    TField class/descendants, 682

    TMaskEdit class, 1131-1133

EditMaskPtr, TField class/descendants, 683

EditMode property, TDBCtrlGrid class, 843

EditText, TMaskEdit class, 1133-1134

Empty, TGraphic class, 322

Enabled

    TControl, 728

    TDataSource class, 425-426

    TMenuItem class, 436-437

    TTimer class, 474-475

EnabledButtons, TMediaPlayer class,
1161-1162

EndPos, TMediaPlayer class, 1162

Enhanced, TMetafile class, 322

EOF, TDataSet class, 596

Error, TMediaPlayer class, 1162-1163

ErrorMessage, TMediaPlayer class, 1163

ExeName, TApplication class, 392

Expanded, TTreeNode class, 190-191

ExpIndex, TDataSet class, 597

ExtendedSelect, TCustomListBox class/
descendants, 945

Field

    TColumn class, 268

    TDBComboBox class, 919-920

    TFieldDataLink class, 296

properties (*continued*)

FieldCount

    TDataSet class, 598-599

    TGridDataLink class, 302

FieldDefs, TDataSet class, 599-600

FieldKind, TField class/descendants, 683-684

FieldName

    TColumn class, 268

    TField class/descendants, 684-685

    TFieldDataLink class, 296-297

FieldNo, TField class/descendants, 685

Fields

    TDataSet class, 601

    TGridDataLink class, 302-303

FieldValues, TDataSet class, 600-601

FileName

    TIniFile, 39

    TMediaPlayer class, 1164

    TOpenDialog/TSaveDialog class, 501-502

Files, TOpenDialog/TSaveDialog class, 502

Filter

    TDataSet class, 602

    TOpenDialog/TSaveDialog class, 503

Filtered, TDataSet class, 603

FilterIndex, TOpenDialog/TSaveDialog class, 503-504

FilterOptions, TDataSet class, 603

Find, TStringList class, 353-354

FindText

    TFindDialog class, 504

    TReplaceDialog class, 504

FirstIndent, TParaAttributes class, 163

Focused,

    TListItem class, 147

    TTreeNode class, 191

Font

    TCanvas class, 230

    TColumn class, 269-270

    TColumnTitle class, 128-129

    TControl, 729

    TFontDialog class, 504-505

Fonts, TScreen class, 451-452

FormatCount, TClipboard class, 114

Formats, TClipboard class, 115

FormCount, TScreen class, 452

properties (*continued*)

Forms, TScreen class, 452

FormStyle, TForm class, 1070-1071

Found, TDataSet class, 607-608

Frames, TMediaPlayer class, 1164-1165

Frequency, TTrackBar class, 900

GetDisplayName, TStatusPanel class, 280

Glyph

    TBitBtn class, 1104-1105

    TSpeedButton class, 801-802

    Graphic, TPicture class, 169

    Grid, TDBGridColumns class, 272-273

GroupIndex

    TMenuItem class, 437

    TSpeedButton class, 802-803

Handle

    TApplication class, 392-393

    TBitmap/TMetafile/TBitmap classes, 323

    TBrush/TPen/TFont classes, 309

    TCanvas class, 231

    TCustomImageList/TImageList classes, 544

    TDataSet class, 612

    TFindDialog class, 505

    TGraphicsObject class, 310

    TIcon class, 323

    TListItem class, 147-148

    TListItems class, 157

    TMenu class/descendants, 483

    TMenuItem class, 438

    TReplaceDialog class, 505

    TSubItems class, 355

    TTreeNode class, 196

    TTreeNodes class, 215

HandleAllocated,

    TCustomImageList/TImageList classes, 544-545

HasChildren, TTreeNode class, 197

Height

    TControl, 730

    TCustomImageList/TImageList classes, 545

    TFont class, 310

    TGraphic class, 323

    TPicture class, 169-170

    TScreen class, 452-453

    TTextAttributes class, 177-178

properties (*continued*)

HelpContext
- *Exception class, 100*
- *TColorDialog class, 506*
- *TCommonDialog class/descendants, 505-506*
- *TFontDialog class, 505-506*
- *TMenuItem class, 438*
- *TPopupMenu class, 483-484*
- *TPrinterSetupDialog class, 505-506*

HelpFile, TApplication class, 396

HideScrollBars, TRichEdit class, 1135-1136

HideSelection
- *TCustomTreeView/TTreeView classes, 1026*
- *TEdit/TMemo/TRichEdit classes, 1136*

Hint, TControl class, 731-732

HintColor, TApplication class, 397

HintHidePause, TApplication class, 397

HintPause, TApplication class, 398

Hints, TDBNavigator class, 1187

HintShortPause, TApplication class, 398-399

HorzScrollBar, TScrollingWinControl class, 1071-1072

HotKey, THotKey class, 932-933

Icon
- *TApplication class, 399*
- *TForm class, 1072*
- *TPicture class, 170*

IconOptions, TListView/TCustomListView classes, 979-980

IgnorePalette, TBitmap class, 324

ImageIndex,
- *TListItem class, 148*
- *TTreeNode class, 197*

Images, TCustomTreeView/TTreeView classes, 1026-1027

ImageType, TCustomImageList/TImageList classes, 545-546

Increment
- *TControlScrollBar class, 132-133*
- *TUpDown class, 1047*

Index
- *TCollectionItem class, 273*
- *TField class/descendants, 687*
- *TListItem class, 148-149*
- *TTreeNode class, 198*

properties (*continued*)

IndexOf, TTreeNode class, 198-199

InitialDir, TOpenDialog/TSaveDialog class, 506

IntegralHeight, TCustomListBox class/descendants, 946

Interval, TTimer class, 475

InvalidKeys, THotKey class, 933-934

IsMasked, TMaskEdit class, 1136

IsNull, TField class/descendants, 689

IsVisible, TTreeNode class, 199

Item
- *TList class, 84*
- *TListItems class, 159*
- *TTreeNode class, 199*

ItemFocused, TListView/TCustomListView classes, 980-981

ItemHeight
- *TComboBox/TDBComboBox classes, 920*
- *TCustomListBox class/descendants, 948*

ItemIndex
- *TCustomComboBox class/descendants, 920-921*
- *TCustomListBox class/descendants, 948-949*
- *TRadioGroup class, 1192-1193*

Items
- *TCollection class, 273-274*
- *TCustomComboBox class/descendants, 921-922*
- *TCustomListBox class/descendants, 950*
- *TCustomTreeView/TTreeView classes, 1028*
- *TListView/TCustomListView classes, 981-982*
- *TMenuItem class, 440*
- *TRadioGroup class, 1193-1194*

KeepConnections, TSession class, 467

KeyFields, TField class/descendants, 690

KeyPreview, TForm class, 1072-1074

KeySize, TDataSet class, 616-617

Kind
- *TBitBtn class, 1106-1107*
- *TControlScrollBar class, 133*
- *TScrollBar class, 873*

LargeChange, TScrollBar class, 873

LargeImages, TListView/TCustomListView classes, 982-983

properties (*continued*)

    Layout
        TBitBtn class, 1107-1108
        TSpeedButton class, 803
    LazyWrite, TRegistry class, 69-70
    Left
        TControl, 733
        TFindDialog class, 506-507
        THeaderSection class, 274-275
        TReplaceDialog class, 506-507
    LeftIndent, TParaAttributes class, 164
    Length, TMediaPlayer class, 1165
    Level, TTreeNode class, 200
    Lines, TRichEdit/TCustomMemo classes, 1137
    LineSize, TTrackBar class, 900-901
    List, TList class, 85
    ListView, TListItem class, 149
    Locale, TDataSet class, 618
    Locked, TPanel class, 1183-1184
    Lookup, TField class/descendants, 691-692
    LookupCache, TField class/descendants,
      692-693
    LookupDataSet, TField class/descendants, 693
    MainForm, TApplication class, 400-401
    Margin
        TBitBtn class, 1108-1109
        TControlScrollBar class, 133
        TSpeedButton class, 804
    Masked, TCustomImageList/TImageList
      classes, 549
    Max
        TProgressBar class, 865
        TScrollBar class, 873-874
        TTrackBar class, 901
        TUpDown class, 1047-1048
    MaxFontSize, TFontDialog class, 507
    MaxLength, TCustomEdit class/
      descendants, 1137
    MaxPage, TPrintDialog class, 507
    MaxWidth, THeaderSection class, 275
    MDIChildCount, TForm class, 1074-1075
    MDIChildren, TForm class, 1075-1076
    Menu, TForm class, 1076-1078
    MenuIndex, TMenuItem class, 440
    Message, Exception class, 100-101

properties (*continued*)

    Min
        TProgressBar class, 865-866
        TScrollBar class, 874
        TTrackBar class, 902
        TUpDown class, 1048
    MinFontSize, TFontDialog class, 507-508
    MinPage, TPrintDialog class, 508
    MinSize, TSplitter class, 810-811
    MinWidth, THeaderSection class, 275-276
    MMHeight, TMetafile class, 326
    MMWidth, TMetafile class, 326
    ModalResult, TButton/TBitBtn classes,
      1109-1111
    Mode
        TMediaPlayer class, 1165-1166
        TPen class, 310-311
    Modified
        TCustomEdit class/descendants, 1137-1138
        TDataSet class, 621
        TGraphic class, 327
    Modifiers, THotKey class, 934
    Monochrome, TBitmap class, 327-328
    MultiLine, TTabControl/TPageControl classes,
      1008-1009
    MultiSelect
        TCustomListBox class/descendants, 951
        TListView/TCustomListView classes, 983
    Name
        TComponent class, 384-385
        TFont class, 312
        TTextAtributes class, 178
    Names, TStrings class/descendants, 360
    NewValue, TField class/descendants, 697
    Notify, TMediaPlayer class, 1166-1167
    NotifyValue, TMediaPlayer class, 1168
    Numbering, TParaAttributes class, 164
    NumGlyphs
        TBitBtn class, 1112
        TSpeedButton class, 804
    Objects, TStrings class/descendants, 361
    OldValue, TField class/descendants, 698-699
    Options
        TColorDialog class, 510-511
        TFindDialog class, 510-512

properties (*continued*)

    TFontDialog class, 510, 512

    TOpenDialog/TSaveDialog class, 510,
       512-513

    TPrintDialog class, 510, 513

    TReplaceDialog class, 510-512

    Orientation

       TTrackBar class, 902-903

       TUpDown class, 1048

    Orientation property, TDBCtrlGrid class, 845

    OverlayIndex

       TListItem class, 150

       TTreeNode class, 201-202

    Owner

       TComponent class, 385

       TListColumns class, 276

       TListItem class, 150-151

       TListItems class, 160

       TSubitems/TTreeStrings classes, 364

       TTreeNodes class, 216

    PageCount, TPageControl class, 1009-1010

    PageIndex, TTabSheet class, 892

    Pages, TPageControl class, 1010

    PageSize, TTrackBar class, 903

    Palette, TBitmap/TMetafile classes, 329

    PanelBorder property, TDBCtrlGrid class, 846

    PanelCount property, TDBCtrlGrid class, 847

    PanelHeight property, TDBCtrlGrid class, 847

    PanelIndex property, TDBCtrlGrid class, 847

    Panels, TStatusBar class, 883-884

    PanelWidth property, TDBCtrlGrid class, 848

    Paragraph, TCustomRichEdit class/descendants,
      1139-1140

    Parent

       TControl, 743-744

       TMenuItem class, 441

       TTreeNode class, 202

    ParentColor, TControl, 744

    ParentCtl3D, TWinControl class, 829

    ParentFont, TControl, 744

    ParentShowHint, TControl, 745

    PasswordChar

       TEdit/TMaskEdit classes, 1140-1141

       TMaskEdit class, 1140-1141

properties (*continued*)

    Pen

       TCanvas class, 235-236

       TShape class, 783

    PenPos, TCanvas class, 237

    PickList, TColumn class, 276

    Picture, TImage class, 772

    Pitch

       TFont class, 313

       TTextAttributes class, 178-179

    PlainText

       TRichEdit class, 1141-1142

       TStrings class, 365-366

    PopupComponent, TPopupMenu class,
      485-486

    PopupMenu, TControl, 745

    Position

       TControlScrollBar class, 134

       TFindDialog class, 513-514

       TForm class, 1079

       TMediaPlayer class, 1171-1172

       TProgressBar class, 866

       TReplaceDialog class, 513-514

       TScrollBar class, 876

       TTrackBar class, 904

    Position, TUpDown class, 1049

    Precision,
      TBCDField/TCurrencyField/TFloatField
      classes, 702

    Print, TCustomRichEdit class/descendants,
      1142

    PrintRange, TPrintDialog class, 514

    PrintScale, TForm class, 1080-1081

    PrintToFile, TPrintDialog class, 514-515

    Priority, TTextAttributes class, TThread class, 53

    PrivateDir, TSession class, 469

    Protected, TTextAttributes class, 179

    RadioItem, TMenuItem class, 442

    Range,TControlScrollBar class, 134

    ReadBool, TIniFile class, 39-40

    ReadOnly

       TColumn class, 277

       TCustomTreeView/TTreeView classes, 1034

       TDataLink class, 292

properties (*continued*)

    TDBComboBox class, 923-924

    TDBListBox class, 952

    TEdit class, 1142-1143

    TField class/descendants, 702-703

    TListView/TCustomListView classes, 988

    TMaskEdit class, 1142-1143

    TMemo class, 1142-1143

    TRichEdit class, 1142-1143

RecNo, TDataSet class, 636

RecordCount

    TDataLink class, 292

    TDataSet class, 637

RecordSize, TDataSet class, 637-638

ReplaceText, TPrinterSetupDialog class, 515

Required, TField class/descendants, 703-704

Right, THeaderSection class, 278

RightIndent, TParaAttributes class, 165

Rootkey, TRegistry class, 72

RowCount property, TDBCtrlGrid class, 848

ScrollBars, TRichEdit/TMemo classes, 1143

ScrollPos, TControlScrollBar class, 135

Sections, THeaderControl class, 859

SelAttributes, TCustomRichEdit class/
    descendants, 1144

SelCount

    TCustomListBox class/descendants, 952-953

    TListView/TCustomListView classes, 988-989

Selected

    TCustomListBox class/descendants, 953

    TListItem class, 151

    TListView/TCustomListView classes, 989

SelectedIndex, TTreeNode class, 202-203

SelectNextPage, TPageControl class, 1010-1011

SelEnd, TTrackBar class, 904-905

SelLength

    TCustomEdit class, 1145

    TCustomEdit class/descendants, 1144

SelStart

    TCustomEdit class, 1145

    TCustomEdit class/descendants, 1144

    TTrackBar class, 905-906

SelText, TCustomEdit class, 1145

properties (*continued*)

ServerCalcField, TField class/descendants, 705-706

SessionName, TSession class, 470-471

Shape

    TBevel class, 764-765

    TShape class, 784

Shareable, TMediaPlayer class, 1174

ShareImages, TCustomImageList/TImageList classes, 557-558

ShortCut, TMenuItem class, 443-444

ShowButtons, TCustomTreeView/TTreeView classes, 1034-1035

ShowColumnHeaders, TListView/TCustomListView classes, 989-990

ShowFocus property, TDBCtrlGrid class, 848-849

ShowHint

    TApplication class, 419

    TControl, 749

ShowLines, TCustomTreeView/TTreeView classes, 1035-1036

ShowMainForm, TApplication class, 419-420

ShowRoot, TCustomTreeView/TTreeView classes, 1036-1037

SimplePanel, TStatusBar class, 884-885

SimpleText, TStatusBar class, 885

Size

    TField class/descendants, 707

    TFont class, 314

    TTextAttributes class, 179-180

SizeGrip, TStatusBar class, 886

SmallChange, TScrollBar class, 877

SmallImages, TListView/TCustomListView classes, 990

Sorted

    TComboBox/TDBComboBox classes, 924

    TCustomListBox class/descendants, 954

    TStringList class, 369

SortImages, TCustomTreeView/TTreeView classes, 1038

SortType, TCustomTreeView/TTreeView classes, 1037-1038

properties (*continued*)

SortTypes, TListView/TCustomListView classes, 990-991

Spacing

 TBitBtn class, 1112-1113

 TSpeedButton class, 805

SparseMap, TGridDataLink class, 303-304

Start, TMediaPlayer class, 1174

StartPos, TMediaPlayer class, 1174-1175

State

 TCheckBox class, 1113-1114

 TDataSet class, 642

 TDataSource class, 428

 TDBGridColumns class, 279

StateImages, TListView/TCustomListView classes, 991-992

StateIndex,

 TListItem class, 151-152

 TTreeNode class, 203

Step, TProgressBar class, 866

Stretch, TImage class, 773

Strings, TStrings class/descendants, 369-370

Style

 TBevel class, 765-766

 TBitBtn class, 1114

 TBrush/TPen/TFont classes, 314-316

 TComboBox/TDBComboBox classes, 924-925

 THeaderSection class, 280

 TTextAttributes class, 180

SubItems, TListItem class, 152

Suspended, TTextAttributes/TThread classes, 55

Tab, TParaAttributes class, 165

TabCount, TParaAttributes class, 166

TabHeight, TTabControl/TPageControl classes, 1012

TabOrder, TWinControl class, 832-833

Tabs, TTabControl class, 1011-1012

TabStop, TWinControl class, 833

TabVisible, TTabSheet class, 893

TabWidth, TTabControl/TPageControl classes, 1012-1013

Tag, TComponent class, 385-386

properties (*continued*)

Text

 TControl, 749-750

 TField class/descendants, 708

 THeaderSection class, 280

 TStrings class/descendants, 370

 TStatusPanel class, 280

 TTreeNode class, 203

Thousands, TUpDown class, 1049

TickMarks, TTrackBar class, 906-907

TickStyle, TTrackBar class, 907-908

TimeFormat, TMediaPlayer class, 1176-1177

Title

 TApplication class, 420-421

 TColumn class, 281

 TOpenDialog/TSaveDialog class, 515

Top

 TControl, 750

 TFindDialog class, 516

 TReplaceDialog class, 516

ToPage, TPrintDialog class, 516

TopIndex, TCustomListBox class/descendants, 954-955

TrackLength, TMediaPlayer class, 1177-1178

TrackPosition, TMediaPlayer class, 1178

Tracks, TMediaPlayer class, 1178-1179

Transliterate

 TField class/descendants, 709

 TMemoField/TStringField classes, 708

TreeView, TTreeNode class, 204

UpdateObject, TDataSet class, 643-644

UpdateRecordTypes, TDataSet class, 644-645

UpdatesPending, TDataSet class, 645

Validate, TField class/descendants, 709

ValidChars, TField class/descendants, 709

Value, TField class/descendants, 710

Values, TStrings class/descendants, 370-371

ViewOrigin, TListView/TCustomListView classes, 994

Visible

 TControl, 751

 TControlScrollBar class, 135

properties (*continued*)

    TField class/descendants, 711-712

    TMenuItem class, 444-445

    VisibleButtons

        TDBNavigator class, 1188

        TMediaPlayer class, 1179

    VisibleRowCount, TListView/TCustomListView

        classes, 995

    Wait, TMediaPlayer class, 1179

    WantReturns, TRichEdit/TMemo classes,

        1146-1147

    WantTabs, TRichEdit/TMemo classes, 1147

    Width

        TColumn class, 281

        TControl, 751

        TCustomImageList/TImageList classes, 559

        TGraphic class, 331

        THeaderSection class, 281

        TListColumn class, 281

        TPen, 316

        TPicture class, 173

        TScreen class, 455-456

        TStatusPanel class, 281

    WidthType, TListColumn class, 282

    WindowMenu, TForm class, 1083-1084

    WindowState, TForm class, 1084-1085

    WordWrap, TRichEdit/TMemo classes,

        1147-1148

    Wrap, TUpDown class, 1050

    WrapText, TIconOptions class, 139

property sheet dialog boxes, 887

    tab sheets, 887-891

        PageControl method, 892

        PageIndex property, 892

        TabVisible property, 893

    TCustomTabControl class, 997-1002

    TPageControl class, 1002-1004

        ActivePage property, 1006

        FindNextPage method, 1007-1008

        MultiLine property, 1008-1009

        PageCount property, 1009-1010

        Pages property, 1010

        SelectNextPage property, 1010-1011

        TabHeight property, 1012

property sheet dialog boxes (*continued*)

        TabWidth property, 1012-1013

        see also TCustomTabControl class

    TTabControl class, 1004-1005

        DisplayRect property, 1007

        MultiLine property, 1008-1009

        TabHeight property, 1012

        Tabs property, 1011-1012

        TabWidth property, 1012-1013

        see also TCustomTabControl class

Protected property, TTextAttributes object, 179

protected visibility specifier, 20-21

protocols, Internet controls, 104-105

public visibility specifier, 20-21

published visibility specifier, 20-21

Q-R

queries

    TQueryDataLink class, 299

    TQuery class, 563-564, 647

        see also TDataSet class

RAD, (Rapid Application Development), 3

radio buttons (TRadioButton class), 1098-1102

    Checked property, 1104

RadioItem property, TMenuItem class, 442

Range property, TControlScrollBar class, 134

ReadBinaryData method, TRegistry class, 71

ReadBool method, TRegistry class, 71

ReadBool property, TIniFile class, 39-40

ReadCurrency method, TRegistry class, 71

ReadDate method, TRegistry class, 71

ReadDateTime method, TRegistry class, 71

ReadFloat method, TRegistry class, 71

ReadInteger method

    TIniFile class, 40-41

    TRegistry class, 71

ReadOnly property

    TColumn class, 277

    TCustomTreeView/TTreeView classes, 1034

    TDataLink class, 292

    TDBComboBox class, 923-924

    TDBListBox class, 952

    TEdit class, 1142-1143

ReadOnly property (*continued*)
TField class/descendants, 702-703
TListView/TCustomListView classes, 988
TMaskEdit class, 1142-1143
TMemo class, 1142-1143
TRichEdit class, 1142-1143
ReadSection method, TIniFile class, 41-42
ReadSections method, TIniFile class, 42
ReadSectionValues method, TIniFile class, 43-44
ReadString method
TIniFile class, 45
TRegistry class, 71
ReadTime method, TRegistry class, 71
Rebuild Columns method, TDBGridColumns class, 277
RecNo property, TDataSet class, 636
RecordCount property
TDataLink class, 292
TDataSet class, 637
records
InsertRecord method, TDataSet class, 613-616
OnFilterRecord event, TDataSet class, 627-628
OnNewRecord event, TDataSet class, 628-629
OnPostError event, TDataSet class, 629-630
OnServerYield event, TDataSet class, 630-631
OnUpdateError event, TDataSet class, 631-632
OnUpdateRecord event, TDataSet class, 633-634
RevertRecord method, TDataSet class, 640
RecordSize property, TDataSet class, 637-638
Rectangle method, TCanvas class, 240-241
Refresh method
TCanvas class, 241
TControl class, 746
TDataSet class, 638-639
RefreshLookupList methods, TField class/ descendants, 703
RegisterChanges method, TCustomImageList/TImageList classes, 551-554
Registry, 57-59
accessing, 59
INI files, *see* TIniFile class
keys, 57

Registry (*continued*)
operating systems, 57-59
see also TRegistry class
Remove method
TMenuItem class, 443
TPopupList/TList classes, 86-87
RemoveAllPasswords method, TSession class, 470
RemoveControl method, TWinControl class, 830
RemovePassword method, TSession class, 470
RenameValue method, TRegistry class, 71-72
Repaint method, TControl class, 746
Replace dialog boxes, 495
events
OnFind event, 509
OnReplace event, 509-510
methods, 496
Execute, 501
properties, 496
Ctl3D, 498
FindText, 504
Handle, 505
HelpContext, 505-506
Left, 506-507
Options, 510-512
Position, 513-514
Top, 516
see also Find dialog boxes
Replace method, TCustomImageList/TImageList classes, 554-555
ReplaceIcon method, TCustomImageList/TImageList classes, 555
ReplaceMasked method, TCustomImageList/TImageList classes, 555-556
ReplaceText property, TPrinterSetupDialog class, 515
Required property, TField class/descendants, 703-704
Reset method
TFieldDataLink class, 299
TGridDataLink class, 303
ResInstLoad method, TCustomImageList/TImageList classes, 556

ResourceLoad method,
TCustomImageList/TImageList classes, 556-557
Resources, exception handling, 91
Restore method, TApplication class, 417-418
RestoreDefaults method
TColumn class, 278
TColumnTitle class, 129
TDBGridColumns class, 278
Resume method
TMediaPlayer class, 1172-1173
TThread class, 54
Resync method, TDataSet class, 639
RevertRecord method, TDataSet class, 640
Rewind method, TMediaPlayer class, 1173
rich edit controls (TCustomRichEdit class), 1125
events, 1125
methods, 1125
paragraphs, TParaAttributes class, 161-166
properties, 1125
DefAttributes, 1131
Paragraph, 1139-1140
Print, 1142
SelAttributes, 1144
TRichEdit class, 1125-1127
HideScrollBars property, 1135-1136
HideSelection property, 1136
Lines property, 1137
OnResizeRequest event, 1138
OnSelectionChange event, 1138-1139
PlainText property, 1141-1142
ReadOnly property, 1142-1143
ScrollBars property, 1143
WantReturns property, 1146-1147
WantTabs property, 1147
WordWrap property, 1147-1148
TRichEditStrings class, 339-340
PlainText property, 365-366
see also TCustomMemo class
Right property, THeaderSection class, 278
RightIndent property, TParaAttributes class, 165
RootKey property, TRegistry class, 72
RoundRect method, TCanvas class, 241-242
RowCount property, TDBCtrlGrid class, 848
RTL (Run-Time Library) functions, 11
RTTI (Run-Time Type Information), 24-25
Run method, TApplication class, 418-419

S

Save dialog boxes, 496
Execute method, 501
filters, 492
properties
Ctl3D, 498
DefaultExt, 499-500
FileName, 501-502
Files, 502
Filter, 503
FilterIndex, 503-504
HelpContext, 505-506
InitialDir, 506
Options, 510, 512-513
Title, 515
see also Open dialog boxes
Save method, TMediaPlayer class, 1173
SaveConfigFile method, TSession class, 470
SaveToClipboardFormat method, TGraphic class, 329-330
SaveToFile method
TBlobField/TGraphicField/TMemoField classes, 704
TGraphic class, 330-331
TPicture class, 173
TStrings class/descendants, 366-367
SaveToStream method
TBlobField/TGraphicField/TMemoField classes, 705
TStrings class/descendants, 367
ScaleBy method, TWinControl class, 830-831
screens (TScreen class), 447-448
ActiveControl property, 448-449
ActiveForm property, 449
Cursor property, 449-450
Cursors property, 450-451
Fonts property, 451-452
FormCount property, 452
Forms property, 452
Height property, 452-453
methods, 448
OnActiveControlChange event, 453-454
OnActiveFormChange event, 454-455
Width property, 455-456
ScreenToClient method, TControl class, 746-747

scroll bars, 131

    HideScrollBars property, TRichEdit class, 1135-1136

    TScrollBar class, 869-872

        Kind property, 873

        LargeChange property, 873

        Max property, 873-874

        Min property, 874

        OnScroll event, 874-876

        Position property, 876

        SetParams method, 876-877

        SmallChange property, 877

    see also scrolling window controls; TControlScrollBar class

scroll box objects, 131

    see also TControlScrollBar class

Scroll method, TListView/TCustomListView classes, 988

ScrollBars property, TRichEdit/TMemo classes, 1143

scrolling windowed controls (TScrollingWinControl class), 1051-1055

    events, 1052-1055

    HorzScrollBar property, 1071-1072

    methods, 1052-1055

    properties, 1052-1055

        HorzScrollBar, 1071-1072

    TForm class, 1051-1052, 1055-1059

        Active property, 1060

        ActiveControl property, 1060

        ActiveMDIChild property, 1061

        ArrangeIcons method, 1061-1063

        AutoScroll property, 1062

        BorderIcons property, 1064

        Cascade method, 1064-1065

        ClientHandle property, 1065-1066

        ClientHeight property, 1066

        ClientWidth property, 1067

        Close method, 1067-1068

        DefocusControl method, 1068-1069

        FocusControl method, 1069-1070

        FormStyle property, 1070-1071

        Icon property, 1072

        KeyPreview property, 1072-1074

        MDI applications, 1056-1057

scrolling windowed controls (*continued*)

        MDIChildCount property, 1074-1075

        MDIChildren property, 1075-1076

        Menu property, 1076-1078

        Next method, 1078

        Position property, 1079

        Previous method, 1079-1080

        Print method, 1080-1081

        PrintScale property, 1080-1081

        Show method, 1082

        ShowModal method, 1082

        Tile method, 1082-1083

        WindowMenu property, 1083-1084

        WindowState property, 1084-1085

ScrollPos property, TControlScrollBar class, 135

SDI applications (Single Document Interface), 1055-1056

sections (unit files), 18-19

    INI files, 35

        EraseSection method, 38-39

        ReadSection method, 41

        ReadSections method, 42

        ReadSectionsValues method, 43-44

Sections property, THeaderControl class, 859

SelAttributes property, TCustomRichEdit class/dscendants, 1144

SelCount property

    TCustomListBox class/descendants, 952-953

    TListView/TCustomListView classes, 988-989

SelectAll method, TCustomEdit class/ descendants, 1144

Selected property

    TCustomListBox class/descendants, 953

    TListItem class, 151

    TListView/TCustomListView classes, 989

selected text, edit controls, 1115

    see also edit controls

SelectedIndex property, TTreeNode class, 202-203

SelectNextPage property, TPageControl class, 1010-1011

SelEnd property, TTrackBar class, 904-906

SelLength property

    TCustomEdit class, 1145

    TCustomEdit class/descendants, 1144

SelStart property
  TCustomEdit class, 1145
  TCustomEdit class/descendants, 1144
SelText property, TCustomEdit class, 1145
SendToBack method, TControl class, 747
ServerCalcField property, TField class/
  descendants, 705-706
SessionName property, TSession class, 470-471
SetAsHandle method, TClipboard class, 119-120
SetBounds method
  TControl class, 747-748
  TDBNavigator class, 1187-1188
SetComponent method, TClipboard class, 120
SetCurrency method, TBCDField class, 706
SetData method, TField class/descendants, 706
SetDetailFields method, TDataSet class, 640-641
SetDragImage method,
  TCustomImageList/TImageList classes, 557
SetFields method, TDataSet class, 641-642
SetFieldType method, TBlobField/TField
  classes, 707
SetFocus method, TWinControl class, 832
SetIndex method, TCollectionItem class, 278-279
SetSelTextBuf method, TCustomEdit class/
  descendants, 1146
SetText method, TStrings class/descendants,
  367-368
SetTextBuf method
  TClipboard class, 121
  TControl class, 748
SetTick method, TTrackBar class, 906
Shape property
  TBevel class, 764-765
  TShape class, 784
shapes (TShape class), 779-782
  Brush property, 782-783
  Pen property, 783
  Shape property, 784
  StyleChanged method, 785
Shareable property, TMediaPlayer class, 1174
ShareImages property,
  TCustomImageList/TImageList classes, 557-558
shortcut keys, see hot keys (TCustomHotKey class)
ShortCut property, TMenuItem class, 443-444

Show method
  TControl class, 748-749
  TForm class, 1082
ShowButtons property, TCustomTreeView/
  TTreeView classes, 1034-1035
ShowColumnHeaders property,
  TListView/TCustomListView classes, 989-990
ShowDragImage method,
  TCustomImageList/TImageList classes, 558
ShowFocus property, TDBCtrlGrid class, 848-849
ShowHint property
  TApplication class, 419
  TControl class, 749
ShowLines property, TCustomTreeView/TTreeView
  classes, 1035-1036
ShowMainForm property, TApplication class,
  419-420
ShowModal method, TForm class, 1082
ShowRoot property, TCustomTreeView/TTreeView
  classes, 1036-1037
SimplePanel property, TStatusBar class, 884-885
SimpleText property, TStatusBar class, 885
Single Document Interface (SDI) applications,
  1055-1056
Size property
  TField class/descendants, 707
  TFont class, 314
  TTextAttributes object, 179-180
SizeGrip property, TStatusBar class, 886
SmallImages property,
  TListView/TCustomListView classes, 990
SMTP (Simple Mail Transport Protocol)
  control, 105
Sort method
  TList class, 87-88
  TStringList class, 368-369
Sorted property
  TComboBox/TDBComboBox classes, 924
  TCustomListBox class/descendants, 954
  TStringList class, 369
SortImages property,
  TCustomTreeView/TTreeView classes, 1038
SortType property, TCustomTreeView/TTreeView
  classes, 1037-1038

SortTypes property, TListView/TCustomListView classes, 990-991

source code

CD-ROM in book, 1198

viewing, 388

see also code listings

Spacing property

TBitBtn class, 1112-1113

TSpeedButton class, 805

SparseMap property, TGridDataLink class, 303-304

speedbuttons, *see* TSpeedButton class

splitter controls (TSplitter class), 807-810

Beveled property, 810

MinSize property, 810-811

OnMoved event, 811-812

Start property, TMediaPlayer class, 1174

StartPos property, TMediaPlayer class, 1174-1175

StartRecording method, TMediaPlayer class, 1175

State property

TCheckBox class, 1113-1114

TDataSet class, 642

TDataSource class, 428

TDBGridColumns class, 279

StateImages property, TListView/TCustomListView classes, 991-992

StateIndex property

TListItem class, 151-152

TTreeNode class, 203

status bars (TStatusBar class), 879-883

events, 880-883

methods, 880-883

properties, 880-883

Panels, 883-884

SimplePanel, 884-885

SimpleText, 885

SizeGrip, 886

see also TStatusPanel class; TStatusPanels class

StatusBar Panels Editor, 884

Step method, TMediaPlayer class, 1175

Step property, TProgressBar class, 866

StepBy method, TProgressBar class, 867

StepIt method, TProgressBar class, 867-868

Stop method, TMediaPlayer class, 1176

Stretch property, TImage class, 773

StretchDraw method, TCanvas class, 242-243

String list editor, 1012

strings

EStringListError exception, 96

ReadString method

TIniFile class, 45

TRegistry class, 71

types, 7

WriteString method

TIniFile class, 47-48

TRegistry class, 73-74

see also TStrings class

Strings property, TStrings class/descendants, 369-370

StringWidth method, TListView/TCustomListView classes, 992-993

Style property

TBevel class, 765-766

TBitBtn class, 1114

TBrush/TPen/TFont classes, 314-316

TComboBox/TDBComboBox classes, 924-925

THeaderSection class, 280

TTextAttributes object, 180

StyleChanged method, TShape class, 785

SubItems property, TListItem class, 152

support, Delphi 3 SuperBible Help System, 26

Suspend method, TThread class, 54

Suspended property, TThread class, 55

symbols, *see* character types

T

Tab property, TParaAttributes class, 165

TabCount property, TParaAttributes class, 166

TabHeight property, TTabControl/TPageControl classes, 1012

tables

Paradox tables, TDataSet class Refresh method, 639

TTable class, 563-564, 646-647

see also TDataSet class

TTableDataLink class, 293

TabOrder property, TWinControl class, 832-833

Delphi 3 SuperBible

tabs
  sheets (TTabSheet class), 887-891
    PageControl method, 892
    PageIndex property, 892
    TabVisible property, 893
  TCustomTabControl class, 997-1002
  TPageControl class, 1002-1004
    ActivePage property, 1006
    FindNextPage method, 1007-1008
    MultiLine property, 1008-1009
    PageCount property, 1009-1010
    Pages property, 1010
    SelectNextPage property, 1010-1011
    TabHeight property, 1012
    TabWidth property, 1012-1013
    see also TCustomTabControl class
  TTabbedNotebook class, 998
  TTabControl class, 1004-1005
    DisplayRect property, 1007
    MultiLine property, 1008-1009
    TabHeight property, 1012
    Tabs property, 1011-1012
    TabWidth property, 1012-1013
    see also TCustomTabControl class
  TTabSet class, 998
Tabs property, TTabControl class, 1011-1012
TabStop property, TWinControl class, 833
TabWidth property, TTabControl/TPageControl classes, 1012-1013
Tag property, TComponent class, 385-386
TApplication class, 387-390
  events, 389-390
    OnActivate, 404-405
    OnDeActivate, 406-407
    OnException, 407-408
    OnHelp, 408
    OnHint, 409-410
    OnIdle, 410-411
    OnMessage, 411-412
    OnMinimize, 413-414
    OnRestore, 414-415
    OnShowHint, 415-417
  methods, 389-390
    BringToFront, 391
    CreateForm, 391-392

TApplication class (*continued*)
    HelpCommand, 393-395
    HelpContext, 395
    HelpJump, 396
    Initialize, 400
    MessageBox, 402-404
    Minimize, 404
    Restore, 417-418
    Run, 418-419
    Terminate, 420
  properties, 389-390
    Active, 390
    ExeName, 392
    Handle, 392-393
    HelpFile, 396
    HintColor, 397
    HintHidePause, 397
    HintPause, 398
    HintShortPause, 398-399
    Icon, 399
    MainForm, 400-401
    ShowHint, 419
    ShowMainForm, 419-420
    Title, 420-421
TAutoIncField class, 657
  see also TField class
TBCDField class, 657-658
  methods
    MaxValue function, 696
    MinValue function, 696-697
    SetCurrency, 706
  properties
    CheckRange, 671-672
    Currency, 674-675
    DisplayFormat, 678
    Precision, 702
    Size, 707
  see also TField class
TBevel class, 761-766
  methods/events, 762-764
  properties, 762-764
    Shape, 764-765
    Style, 765-766
TBinaryField class, 658
  Size property, 707
  see also TField class

TBitBtn class, 1091-1093
    events, 1092-1093
    methods, 1092-1093
    properties, 1092-1093
        Cancel, 1103
        Glyph, 1104-1105
        Kind, 1106-1107
        Layout, 1107-1108
        Margin, 1108-1109
        ModalResult, 1109-1111
        NumGlyphs, 1112
        Spacing, 1112-1113
        Style, 1114
    see also TSpeedButton class
TBitmap class, 319-320
    events, 320
    methods, 320
    properties, 320
        Canvas, 320
        Handle, 323
        IgnorePalette, 324
        Monochrome, 327-328
        Palette, 329
    see also TGraphic class
TBlobField
    methods
        LoadFromFile function, 690-691
        LoadFromStream function, 691
        SaveToFile, 704
        SaveToStream, 705
        SetFieldType, 707
    properties
        BlobType, 658, 669-670
        Size, 707
TBoolean class, 658
    see also TField class
TBrush class, 306, 315
    OnChange event, 312-313
    properties
        Bitmap, 308
        Color, 309
        Handle, 309-310
        Style, 314-315
TButton class, 1087-1091
    events, 1089-1091
    methods, 1089-1091

TButton class (*continued*)
    properties, 1089-1091
        Cancel, 1103
        ModalResult, 1109-1111
    TBitBtn class, 1091-1093
        Cancel property, 1103
        Glyph property, 1104-1105
        Kind property, 1106-1107
        Layout property, 1107-1108
        Margin property, 1108-1109
        ModalResult property, 1109-1111
        NumGlyphs property, 1112
        Spacing property, 1112-1113
        Style property, 1114
    TCheckBox class, 1096-1097
        AllowGrayed property, 1102-1103
        Checked property, 1104
        State property, 1113-1114
    TCustomCheckBox class, 1093-1095
    TRadioButton class, 1098-1102
        Checked property, 1104
TButtonControl class, 1087
    TBitBtn class, 1091-1093
        Cancel property, 1103
        Glyph property, 1104-1105
        Kind property, 1106-1107
        Layout property, 1107-1108
        Margin property, 1108-1109
        ModalResult property, 1109-1111
        NumGlyphs property, 1112
        Spacing property, 1112-1113
        Style property, 1114
    TButton class, 1087-1091
        Cancel property, 1103
        ModalResult property, 1109-1111
    TCustomCheckBox class, 1093
    see also TSpeedButton class
TBytesField class, 659
    see also TField class
TCanvas class, 217-220
    derivation, 217
    events, 218
        OnChange, 233-234
        OnChanging, 234-235
    handles, 217
        CreateHandle method (TPrinterCanvas
            objects), 220

TCanvas class (*continued*)

    methods, 218-219

        Arc, 221

        Chord, 223

        CopyRect, 225-226

        Draw, 226

        DrawFocusRect, 227

        Ellipse, 228

        FillRect, 228-229

        FloodFill, 229

        FrameRect, 231

        LineTo, 232

        MoveTo, 232

        Pie, 237-238

        Polygon, 239

        Polyline, 240

        Rectangle, 240-241

        Refresh, 241

        RoundRect, 241-242

        StretchDraw, 242-243

        TextHeight, 243

        TextOut, 244

        TextRect, 244-245

        TextWidth, 245

    properties, 218

        Brush, 222

        CopyMode, 224

        Font, 230

        Handle, 231

        Pen, 235-236

        PenPos, 237

    TMetaFileCanvas child class, 219-220

    TPrinter child class, 220

TCheckBox class, 1096-1097

    events, 1097

    methods, 1097

    properties, 1097

        AllowGrayed, 1102-1103

        Checked, 1104

        State, 1113-1114

TClipboard class, 111-112

    methods, 112

        Clear, 113

        Close, 114

        GetAsHandle, 116

        GetComponent, 116-117

        GetTextBuf, 117-118

TClipboard class (*continued*)

        HasFormat, 118-119

        Open, 119

        SetAsHandle, 119-120

        SetComponent, 120

        SetTextBuf, 121

    properties, 112

        AsText, 113

        FormatCount, 114

        Formats, 115

TCollection class, 247-254

    example project, 282-285

    methods, 248

        Add, 254

        Assign, 256

        BeginUpdate, 257-258

        Clear, 260

        Create, 262-263

        Destroy, 266

        EndUpdate, 267

        FindItemID, 269

        GetItem, 272

    properties, 248

        Count, 262-263

        Items, 273-274

    TDBGridColumns, 252-253

        see also TDBGridColumns class

    THeaderSection, 251

    THeaderSections, 250

    TListColumns, 249

    TStatusPanels, 251

        example project, 282-285

TCollectionItem class, 247-254

    example project, 282-285

    methods, 249

        Create, 262-263

        Destroy, 266

        SetIndex, 278-279

    properties, 249

        Collection, 260-261

        Index, 273

    TColumn, 253-254

        see also TColumn class

    THeaderSection, 250

        see also THeaderSection class

TCollectionItem class (*continued*)

    TListColumn, 249-250

        see also TCollectionItem class

    TStatusPanel, 252

        example project, 282-285

        see also TStatusPanel class

    see also TCollection class

TColorDialog class, 489

    methods, 489

        Execute, 501

    properties, 489

        Color, 497

        Ctl3D, 498

        CustomColors, 499

        HelpContext, 505-506

        Options, 510-511

TColumn class, 253-254

    methods

        CreateTitle, 263

        DefaultAlignment, 264

        DefaultColor, 264

        DefaultFont, 265

        DefaultReadOnly, 265

        DefaultWidth, 266

        GetGrid, 271

        RestoreDefaults, 278

    properties

        Alignment, 255

        AssignedValues, 257

        ButtonStyle, 258-259

        Color, 261

        DropDownRows, 267

        Field, 268

        Fieldname, 268

        Font, 269-270

        PickList, 276

        ReadOnly, 277

        Title, 281

        Width, 281

    see also TCollectionItem class

TColumnTitle class, 123-124

    methods, 124

        DefaultAlignment, 126

        DefaultCaption, 126-127

        DefaultColor, 127

TColumnTitle class (*continued*)

    DefaultFont, 127-128

    RestoreDefaults, 129

    properties, 124

        Alignment, 124-125

        Caption, 125

        Color, 125

        Font, 128-129

TComboBox class, 914-915

    events, 914-915

        OnDrawItem, 922-923

        OnDropDown, 922

        OnMeasureItem, 923

    methods, 914-915

        Clear, 916-917

    properties, 914-915

        DropDownCount, 918

        DroppedDown, 918

        ItemHeight, 920

        ItemIndex, 920-921

        Items, 921-922

        Sorted, 924

        Style, 924-925

    see also TCustomComboBox class;

        TDBComboBox class

TComboBoxStrings class, 336

    Add method, 343

    see also TStrings class

TCommonDialog class, 487-488

    methods, 488

    properties, 488

        Ctl3D, 498

        HelpContext, 505-506

    TColor, *see* TColor class

    TFind, *see* TFind class

    TFont, *see* TFont class

    TOpen, *see* TOpen class

    TPrint, *see* TPrint class

    TPrinterSetup, *see* TPrinterSetup class

    TReplace, *see* TReplace class

    TSaveDialog, *see* TSaveDialog class

TComponent class, 21, 379-380

    methods, 380

        DestroyComponents, 383

        Destroying, 383

        FindComponent, 383-384

TComponent class (*continued*)

properties, 380

ComponentCount, 381

ComponentIndex, 381

Components, 382

ComponentState, 382-383

Name, 384-385

Owner, 385

Tag, 385-386

TControl class, 21, 717-719

events, 718-719

OnClick, 733-734

OnDblClick, 734-735

OnDragDrop, 735-736

OnDragOver, 736-738

OnEndDrag, 738-739

OnMouseDown, 739-740

OnMouseEvent, 740-741

OnMouseUp, 741-742

OnStartDrag, 742-743

methods, 718-719

BeginDrag, 720-721

BringToFront, 721-722

ClientToScreen, 724

Dragging, 727

EndDrag, 728-729

GetTextBuf, 729

GetTextLen, 730

Hide, 731

Invalidate, 733

Refresh, 746

Repaint, 746

ScreenToClient, 746-747

SendToBack, 717

SetBounds, 747-748

SetTextBuf, 748

Show, 748-749

Update, 750

properties, 718-719

Align, 720

BoundsRect, 721

Caption, 722

ClientHeight, 722-723

ClientOrigin, 723

ClientRect, 723-724

ClientWidth, 724-725

TControl class (*continued*)

Color, 725

ControlState, 725

ControlStyle, 726

Cursor, 726

DragCursor, 727

DragMode, 728

Enabled, 728

Font, 729

Height, 730

Hint, 731-732

Left, 733

Parent, 743-744

ParentColor, 744

ParentFont, 744

ParentShowHint, 745

PopupMenu, 745

ShowHint, 749

Text, 749-750

Top, 750

Visible, 751

Width, 751

TControlScrollBar class, 131-132

methods, 132

properties, 132

Increment, 132-133

Kind, 133

Margin, 133

Position, 134

Range, 134

ScrollPos, 135

Visible, 135

TCP (Transmission Control Protocol) control, 105

TCurrencyField class, 659

methods

MaxValue function, 696

MinValue function, 696-697

properties

Currency, 674-675

DisplayFormat, 678

Precision, 702

TCustomCheckBox class, 1093-1095

events, 1093-1095

methods, 1093-1095

properties, 1093-1095

TCustomComboBox class, 909-911
    events, 911-913
    methods, 911-913
        Clear, 916-917
    properties, 911-913
        DropDownCount, 918
        DroppedDown, 918
        ItemIndex, 920-921
        Items, 921-922
    TComboBox, 914-915
        see also TComboBox
    TDBComboBox, 915-916
        see also TDBComboBox
    TDriveComboBox, 910
    TFilterComboBox, 910
    see also TCustomListBox class
TCustomControl class, 1149-1153
    events, 1150-1153
    methods, 1150-1153
    properties, 1150-1153
    TCustomGroupBox, 1188-1189
        TCustomRadioGroup, 1190-1191
        TGroupBox, 1189-1190
        TRadioGroup, 1191-1194
    TCustomPanel, 1180
        TDBNavigator, 1184-1188
        TPanel, 1180-1184
    TMediaPlayer, 1153-1155
        AutoEnable property, 1155
        AutoOpen property, 1155-1156
        AutoRewind property, 1156
        Back method, 1156-1157
        Capabilities property, 1157-1158
        Close method, 1158
        ColoredButtons property, 1159
        DeviceID property, 1159
        DeviceType property, 1159-1160
        Display property, 1160
        DisplayRect property, 1161
        Eject method, 1161
        EnabledButtons property, 1161-1162
        EndPos property, 1162
        Error property, 1162-1163
        ErrorMessage property, 1163
        FileName property, 1164

TCustomControl class (*continued*)
        Frames property, 1164-1165
        Length property, 1165
        Mode property, 1165-1166
        Next method, 1166
        Notify property, 1166-1167
        NotifyValue property, 1168
        OnNotify event, 1168-1169
        OnPostClick event, 1169
        Open method, 1170
        Pause method, 1170
        PauseOnly method, 1170-1171
        Play method, 1171
        Position property, 1171-1172
        Previous method, 1172
        Resume method, 1172-1173
        Rewind method, 1173
        Save method, 1173
        Shareable property, 1174
        Start property, 1174
        StartPos property, 1174-1175
        StartRecording method, 1175
        Step method, 1175
        Stop method, 1176
        TimeFormat property, 1176-1177
        TrackLength property, 1177-1178
        TrackPosition property, 1178
        Tracks property, 1178-1179
        VisibleButtons property, 1179
        Wait property, 1179
TCustomEdit class, 1115-1119
    events, 1116-1119
    methods, 1116-1119
        Clear, 1128
        ClearSelection, 1129
        CopyToClipboard, 1129-1130
        CutToClipboard, 1130
        GetSelectTextBuf, 1134-1135
        PasteFromClipboard, 1141
        SelectAll, 1144
        SetSelTextBuf, 1146
    properties, 1116-1119
        MaxLength, 1137
        Modified, 1137-1138
        SelLength, 1144-1145

TCustomEdit class (*continued*)

    SelStart, 1144-1145

    SelText, 1145

  TCustomMaskEdit class, 1121

  TCustomMemo class, 1123

    Lines property, 1137

    TCustomRichEdit, see TCustomRichEdit

      class

    TMemo class, 1123-1125, 1136,

      1142-1143, 1146-1148

    see also memo controls

  TEdit class, 1119-1121

    AutoSelect property, 1127

    CharCase property, 1127-1128

    HideSelection property, 1136

    PasswordChar property, 1140-1141

    ReadOnly property, 1142-1143

  TMaskEdit class, 1121-1123

    CharCase property, 1127-1128

    EditMask property, 1131-1133

    EditText property, 1133-1134

    IsMasked property, 1136

    PasswordChar property, 1140-1141

    ReadOnly property, 1142-1143

TCustomGroupBox class, 1188-1189

  events, 1189

  methods, 1189

  properties, 1189

  TCustomRadioGroup, 1190-1191

    TRadioGroup, 1191-1194

  TGroupBox, 1189-1190

  see also TCustomControl

TCustomHotKey class, 927-931

  methods, 928-931

  THotKey, 931-932

    HotKey property, 932-933

    InvalidKeys property, 933-934

    Modifiers property, 934

TCustomImageList class, 517-520

  events, 518-520

    OnChange, 550

  methods, 518-520

    Add, 521-522

    AddIcon, 522-523

    AddImages, 523-524

TCustomImageList class (*continued*)

    AddMasked, 524-525

    Assign, 526-527

    BeginDrag, 527

    Clear, 529

    Create, 530

    CreateSize, 530-531

    Delete, 531-532

    Destroy, 532

    DragLock, 534

    DragMove, 534-535

    DragUnlock, 535

    Draw, 535

    DrawOverlay, 537-538

    EndDrag, 538

    FireLoad, 538-539

    GetBitmap, 539-540

    GetHotSpot, 540

    GetIcon, 540-541

    GetImageBitmap, 541

    GetInstRes, 542

    GetMaskBitmap, 542

    GetResource, 543

    HideDragImage, 545

    Insert, 546-547

    InsertIcon, 547-548

    InsertMasked, 548-549

    Move, 549-550

    Overlay, 550-551

    RegisterChanges, 551-554

    Replace, 554-555

    ReplaceIcon, 555

    ReplaceMasked, 555-556

    ResInstLoad, 556

    ResourceLoad, 556-557

    SetDragImage, 557

    ShowDragImage, 558

    UnRegisterChanges, 558-559

  properties, 518-520

    AllocBy, 525

    BkColor, 527-528

    BlendColor, 528-529

    Count, 529

    DragCursor, 533

    Dragging, 533-534

TCustomImageList class (*continued*)
    DrawingStyle, 536
    Handle, 544
    HandleAllocated, 544-545
    Height, 545
    ImageType, 545-546
    Masked, 549
    ShareImages, 557-558
    Width, 559
  TGlyphList, 521
    see also TGlyphList class
  TImageList, 520
    example project, 559-561
    see also TImageList class
TCustomLabel class, 787-791, 793
  properties/method/events, 788-790
  TDBText class, 790
  TLabel class, 791-792
TCustomList class, TListColumns, 249
TCustomListBox class, 935-939
  events, 936-939
    OnMeasureItem, 951-952
  methods, 936-939
    Clear, 943
    ItemAtPos, 947-948
    ItemRect, 949-950
  properties, 936-939
    BorderStyle, 942-943
    ExtendedSelect, 945
    IntegralHeight, 946
    ItemHeight, 948
    ItemIndex, 948-949
    Items, 950
    MultiSelect, 951
    SelCount, 952-953
    Selected, 953
    Sorted, 954
    TopIndex, 954-955
  TDBListBox, 939-941
    DataField property, 944
    DataSource property, 944
    ReadOnly property, 952
  TListBox, 941-942
  see also TCustomComboBox class

TCustomListView class, 957-962
  events, 958-962
    OnChange, 983
    OnChanging, 984
    OnColumnClick, 984-985
    OnCompare, 985
    OnDeletion, 985-986
    OnEdited, 986
    OnEditing, 986-987
    OnInsert, 987
  methods, 958-962
    AlphaSort, 965-966
    Arrange, 966-967
    ColumnSort, 970-971
    FindCaption, 972-974
    FindData, 974-975
    GetItemAt, 976
    GetNearestItem, 976-977
    GetNextItem, 978-979
    IsEditing, 980
    Scroll, 988
    StringWidth, 992-993
    UpdateItems, 993-994
  properties, 958-962
    AllocBy, 964-965
    BoundingRect, 967
    Column, 968
    ColumnClick, 968-969
    Columns, 969-970
    DropTarget, 971-972
    IconOptions, 979-980
    ItemFocused, 980-981
    Items, 981-982
    LargeImages, 982-983
    MultiSelect, 983
    ReadOnly, 988
    SelCount, 988-989
    Selected, 989
    ShowColumnHeaders, 989-990
    SmallImages, 990
    SortTypes, 990-991
    StateImages, 991-992
    ViewOrigin, 994
    VisibleRowCount, 995

TCustomMaskEdit class, 1121
  events, 1121
  methods, 1121
  properties, 1121
  TMaskEdit class, 1121-1123
    CharCase property, 1127-1128
    EditMask property, 1131-1133
    EditText property, 1133-1134
    IsMasked property, 1136
    PasswordChar property, 1140-1141
    ReadOnly property, 1142-1143
  see also TCustomEdit class
TCustomMemo class, 1123
  events, 1123
  methods, 1123
  properties, 1123
    Lines, 1137
  TCustomRichEdit, 1125
    DefAttributes property, 1131
    Paragraph property, 1139-1140
    Print property, 1142
    SelAttributes property, 1144
    TRichEdit, 1125-1127
  see also TCustomRichEdit class, 1125
  TMemo, 1123-1125
    HideSelection property, 1136
    ReadOnly property, 1142-1143
    ScrollBars property, 1143
    WantReturns property, 1146-1147
    WantTabs property, 1147
    WordWrap property, 1147-1148
  see also TCustomEdit class
TCustomPanel class, 1180
  see also TCustomControl class
  TDBNavigator, 1184-1185
    BtnClick method, 1185-1186
    ConfirmDelete property, 1186
    DataSource property, 1186-1187
    Hints property, 1187
    SetBounds method, 1187-1188
    VisibleButtons property, 1188
  TPanel, 1180-1184

TCustomRadioGroup class, 1190-1191
  methods, 1191
  TRadioGroup, 1191-1192
    Columns property, 1192
    ItemIndex property, 1192-1193
    Items property, 1193-1194
TCustomRichEdit class, 1125
  events, 1125
  methods, 1125
  properties, 1125
    DefAttributes, 1131
    Paragraph, 1139-1140
    Print, 1142
    SelAttributes, 1144
  TRichEdit, 1125-1127
    HideScrollBars property, 1135-1136
    HideSelection property, 1136
    Lines property, 1137
    OnResizeRequest event, 1138
    OnSelectionChange event, 1138-1139
    PlainText property, 1141-1142
    ReadOnly property, 1142-1143
    ScrollBars property, 1143
    WantReturns property, 1146-1147
    WantTabs property, 1147
    WordWrap property, 1147-1148
  see also TCustomMemo class
TCustomTabControl class, 997-1002
  events, 999-1002
  methods, 999-1002
  properties, 999-1002
  TPageControl, 1002-1004
    ActivePage property, 1006
    FindNextPage method, 1007-1008
    MultiLine property, 1008-1009
    PageCount property, 1009-1010
    Pages property, 1010
    SelectNextPage property, 1010-1011
    TabHeight property, 1012
    TabWidth property, 1012-1013
  TTabControl, 1004-1005
    DisplayRect property, 1007
    MultiLine property, 1008-1009

TCustomTabControl class (*continued*)
    TabHeight property, 1012
    Tabs property, 1011-1012
    TabWidth property, 1012-1013
  see also TTabSheet class
TCustomTreeView class, 1015-1019
  events, 1017-1019
    OnChanging, 1028-1029
    OnCollapsed, 1029
    OnCollapsing, 1029-1030
    OnCompare, 1030
    OnDeletion, 1030-1031
    OnEdited, 1031
    OnEditing, 1031-1032
    OnExpanded, 1032
    OnExpanding, 1032
    OnGetImageIndex, 1033
    OnSelectedIndex, 1033
  methods, 1017-1019
    AlphaSort, 1022
    FullCollapse, 1022-1023
    FullExpand, 1023
    GetHitTestInfoAt, 1023-1025
    GetNodeAt, 1025-1026
    IsEditing, 1027
  properties, 1017-1019
    HideSelection, 1026
    Images, 1026-1027
    Items, 1028
    ReadOnly, 1034
    ShowButtons, 1034-1035
    ShowLines, 1035-1036
    ShowRoot, 1036-1037
    SortImages, 1038
    SortType, 1037-1038
TCustomUpDown class, 1039-1044
  events, 1041-1044
  methods, 1041-1044
  properties, 1041-1044
  TUpDown class, 1044-1045
    AlignButton property, 1045
    ArrowKeys property, 1046
    Associate property, 1046
    Increment property, 1047

TCustomUpDown class (*continued*)
    Max property, 1047-1048
    Min property, 1048
    Orientation property, 1048
    Position property, 1049
    Thousands property, 1049
    Wrap property, 1050
TDataLink class, 287-288
  methods, 288
    Edit, 291-292
    UpdateRecord, 293
  properties, 288
    Active, 288-289
    ActiveRecord, 289
    BufferCount, 289-290
    DataSet, 290
    DataSource, 290
    DataSourceFixed, 291
    Editing, 291
    ReadOnly, 292
    RecordCount, 292
  TDataSourceLink, 299
  TDBCtrlGridLink, 304
  TFieldDataLink, 293-294
    CanModify property, 294
    Control property, 294-295
    Edit method, 295
    Editing property, 295
    Field property, 296
    FieldName property, 296-297
    Modified method, 297
    OnActiveChange event, 297
    OnDataChange event, 298
    OnEditingChange event, 298
    OnUpdateData event, 298-299
    Reset method, 299
  TGridDataLink, 300
    AddMapping method, 301
    ClearMapping method, 301
    DefaultFields property, 302
    FieldCount property, 302
    Fields property, 302-303
    Modified method, 303
    Reset method, 303
    SparseMap property, 303-304

TDataLink class (*continued*)

    TListSourceLink, 300

    TNavDataLink, 299

    TQueryDataLink, 299

    TTableDataLink, 293

TDataSet class, 563-566

    events, 564-566

        AfterCancel, 568-569

        AfterClose, 569

        AfterDelete, 569-570

        AfterEdit, 570-571

        AfterInsert, 571

        AfterOpen, 571-572

        AfterPost, 572-573

        BeforeCancel, 578-579

        BeforeClose, 579-580

        BeforeDelete, 580-581

        BeforeEdit, 581

        BeforeInsert, 582-583

        BeforeOpen, 583-584

        BeforePost, 584-585

        OnCalcFields, 623-624

        OnDeleteError, 624-625

        OnEditError, 625-627

        OnFilterRecord, 627-628

        OnNewRecord, 628-629

        OnPostError, 629-630

        OnServerYield, 630-631

        OnUpdateError, 631-632

        OnUpdateRecord, 633-634

    methods, 564-566

        ActiveBuffer, 567-568

        Append, 573-574

        AppendRecord, 574-576

        ApplyUpdates, 576-577

        Cancel, 587

        CancelUpdates, 588

        CheckBrowseMode, 588-589

        ClearFields, 589

        Close, 589-590

        CommitUpdates, 590-591

        ControlsDisabled, 591

        CursorPosChanged, 591-592

        Delete, 593

        DisableControls, 594

TDataSet class (*continued*)

    Edit, 594-595

    EnableControls, 595-596

    FetchAll, 597

    FieldByName, 597-598

    FindField, 604-606

    FindFirst/FindLast/FindNext/FindPrior,
        605-606

    First, 606-607

    FreeBookmark, 608

    GetBookmark, 608-609

    GetCurrentRecord, 609

    GetFieldList, 610

    GetFieldNames, 610-611

    GotoBookmark, 611-612

    Insert, 612-613

    InsertRecord, 613-616

    IsLinkedTo, 616

    Last, 617-618

    Locate, 618-619

    Lookup, 619-621

    MoveBy, 621-622

    Next, 622-623

    Open, 634-635

    Post, 635

    Prior, 635-636

    Refresh, 638-639

    Resync, 639

    RevertRecord, 640

    SetDetailFields, 640-641

    SetFields, 641-642

    UpdateCursorPos, 643

    UpdateRecord, 644

    UpdateStatus, 645

    properties, 564-566

    Active, 567

    AutoCalcFields, 577

    BOF, 577-578

    Bookmark, 585

    CachedUpdates, 585-586

    CanModify, 586-587

    DataSource, 592

    DefaultFields, 592-593

    EOF, 596

    ExpIndex, 597

TDataSet class (*continued*)
    FieldCount, 598-599
    FieldDefs, 599-600
    Fields, 601
    FieldValues, 600-601
    Filter, 602
    Filtered, 603
    FilterOptions, 603
    Found, 607-608
    Handle, 612
    KeySize, 616-617
    Locale, 618
    Modified, 621
    RecNo, 636
    RecordCount, 637
    RecordSize, 637-638
    State, 642
    UpdateObject, 643-644
    UpdateRecordTypes, 644-645
    UpdatesPending, 645
  TDBDataSet, 563-564, 646
  TQuery, 563-564, 647
  TStoredProc, 563-564, 646-647
  TTable, 563-564, 646-647
TDataSource class, 423-424
  events, 424
    OnDataChange, 426-427
    OnStateChange, 427
    OnUpdateData, 427
  methods, 424
  properties, 424
    AutoEdit, 424
    DataSet, 424-425
    Edit, 425
    Enabled, 425-426
    IsLinkedTo, 426
    State, 428
TDataSourceLink class, 299
TDateField class, 659
  DisplayFormat property, 678
TDateTimeField class, 659
  DisplayFormat property, 678
TDBComboBox class, 915-916
  events, 915-916
    OnDrawItem, 922-923
    OnDropDown, 922
    OnMeasureItem, 923

TDBComboBox class (*continued*)
  methods, 915-916
    Clear, 916-917
  properties, 915-916
    DataField, 917
    DataSource, 917
    DropDownCount, 918
    DroppedDown, 918
    Field, 919-920
    ItemHeight, 920
    ItemIndex, 920-921
    Items, 921-922
    ReadOnly, 923-924
    Sorted, 924
    Style, 924-925
  see also TCustomComboBox class;
    TComboBox class
TDBCtrlGrid class, 835-840
  events, 837-840
    OnPaintPanel, 843-845
  methods, 837-840
    DoKey, 842-843
  properties, 837-840
    AllowDelete, 840
    AllowInsert, 840-841
    ColCount, 841
    DataSource, 841
    EditMode, 843
    Orientation, 845
    PanelBorder, 846
    PanelCount, 847
    PanelHeight, 847
    PanelIndex, 847
    PanelWidth, 848
    RowCount, 848
    ShowFocus, 848-849
TDBCtrlGridLink class, 304
TDBDataSet class, 563-564, 646
  see also TDataSet class
TDBEdit class, *see* **TCustomMaskEdit class**
TDBGridColumns class, 252-253
  methods
    Rebuild Columns, 277
    RestoreDefaults, 278
  property
    Grid, 272-273
    State, 279
  see also TCollection class

Delphi 3 SuperBible

TDBListBox class, 939-941
- properties
  - *DataField, 944*
  - *DataSource, 944*
  - *ReadOnly, 952*
  - see also TCustomListBox class

TDBMemo class, see **TCustomMemo class**

TDBNavigator class, 1184-1185
- events, 1184-1185
- methods, 1184-1185
  - *BtnClick, 1185-1186*
  - *SetBounds, 1187-1188*
- properties, 1184-1185
  - *ConfirmDelete, 1186*
  - *DataSource, 1186-1187*
  - *Hints, 1187*
  - *VisibleButtons, 1188*
  - see also TCustomControl class

TDBRichEdit class, see **TCustomRichEdit class**

TDBText class, 790-791
- DataField/DataSource properties, 793

TDirectoryListBox class, 935

TDriveComboBox class, 910
- see also TCustomComboBox class

TEdit class, 1119-1121
- events, 1120-1121
- methods, 1120-1121
- properties, 1120-1121
  - *AutoSelect, 1127*
  - *CharCase, 1127-1128*
  - *HideSelection, 1136*
  - *PasswordChar, 1140-1141*
  - *ReadOnly, 1142-1143*
  - see also TCustomEdit class

Terminate method
- TApplication class, 420
- TThread class, 55

text labels (TCustomLabel class), 787-790
- database labels (TDBText class), 790-791, 793
- labels (TLabel class), 791-792

Text property
- TControl class, 749-750
- TField class/descendants, 708
- THeaderSection class, 280
- TStatusPanel class, 280

Text property (*continued*)
- TStrings class/descendants, 370
- TTreeNode class, 203

TextHeight method, TCanvas class, 243

TextOut method, TCanvas class, 244

TextRect method, TCanvas class, 244-245

TextWidth method, TCanvas class, 245

TField class, 649-651, 653-657
- events, 657
  - *OnChange, 699*
  - *OnGetText, 700*
  - *OnSetText, 700*
  - *OnValidate, 701*
- functions
  - *GetData, 686*
  - *IsBlob, 687-688*
  - *LookupKeyFields, 693-694*
  - *LookupList, 694-695*
  - *LookupResultField, 695*
  - *Offset, 698*
- methods, 656-657
  - *Assign, 666*
  - *AssignValue, 667*
  - *Clear, 672*
  - *Create constructor, 673-674*
  - *Destroy destructor, 677*
  - *FocusControl, 685-686*
  - *GetData function, 686*
  - *IsBlob function, 687-688*
  - *IsIndexField function, 688*
  - *IsValidChar function, 689*
  - *RefreshLookupList, 703*
  - *SetData, 706*
  - *SetFieldType, 707*
- properties, 655-657
  - *Alignment, 662*
  - *AsBoolean, 662-663*
  - *AsCurrency, 663-664*
  - *AsDateTime, 664-665*
  - *AsFloat, 665*
  - *AsInteger, 665-666*
  - *AsString, 667-668*
  - *AsVariant, 668*
  - *AttributeSet, 669*
  - *Calculated, 670-671*

TField class (*continued*)

    CanModify, 671

    DataSet, 675

    DataSize, 675-676

    DataType, 676-677

    DisplayLabel, 678-679

    DisplayName, 679

    DisplayText, 680

    DisplayValues, 680-681

    DisplayWidth, 681

    EditFormat, 681-682

    EditMask, 682

    EditMaskPtr, 683

    FieldKind, 683-684

    FieldName, 684-685

    FieldNo, 685

    Index, 687

    IsNull, 689

    KeyFields, 690

    Lookup, 691-692

    LookupCache, 692-693

    LookupDataSet, 693

    NewValue, 697

    OldValue, 698-699

    ReadOnly, 702-703

    Required, 703-704

    ServerCalcField, 705-706

    Size, 707

    Text, 708

    Transliterate, 709

    Validate, 709

    ValidChars, 709

    Value, 710

    Visible, 711-712

  TAutoIncField, 657

  TBCDField, 657-658

    CheckRange property, 671-672

    Currency method, 706

    Currency property, 674-675, 702

    DisplayFormat property, 678

    MaxValue function, 696

    MinValue function, 696-697

    Size property, 707

  TBinaryField, 658

    Size property, 707

TField class (*continued*)

  TBlobField

    BlobType property, 658, 669-670

    LoadFromFile function, 690-691

    LoadFromStream function, 691

    SaveToFile method, 704

    SaveToStream method, 705

    SetFieldType method, 707

    Size property, 707

  TBoolean, 658

  TBytesField, 659

  TCurrencyField, 659

    Currency property, 674-675

    DisplayFormat property, 678

    MaxValue function, 696

    MinValue function, 696-697

    Precision property, 702

  TDateField, 659

    DisplayFormat property, 678

  TDateTimeField, 659

    DisplayFormat property, 678

  TFloatField, 659-660

    Currency property, 674-675

    DisplayFormat property, 678

    MaxValue function, 696

    MinValue function, 696-697

    Precision property, 702

  TGraphicField, 660

    LoadFromFile function, 690-691

    LoadFromStream function, 691

    SaveToFile method, 704

    SaveToStream method, 705

  TIntegerField, 660

    DisplayFormat property, 678

    MaxValue function, 696

    MinValue function, 696-697

  TMemoField

    LoadFromFile function, 690-691

    LoadFromStream function, 691

    SaveToFile method, 704

    SaveToStream method, 705

    Transliterate property, 708

    see also TField class

  TNumericField, 660

TField class (*continued*)
TSmallIntField, 661
DisplayFormat property, 678
MaxValue function, 696
MinValue function, 696-697
TStringField, 661
Size property, 707
Transliterate property, 708
TTimeField, 661
DisplayFormat property, 678
TVarBytesField, 661
TWordField, 661
DisplayFormat property, 678
MaxValue function, 696
MinValue function, 696-697
see also fields
TFieldDataLink class, 293-294
events, 294
OnActiveChange, 297
OnDataChange, 298
OnEditingChange, 298
OnUpdateData, 298-299
methods, 294
Edit, 295
Modified, 297
Reset, 299
properties, 294
CanModify, 294
Control, 294-295
Editing, 295
Field, 296
FieldName, 296-297
TFileListBox class, 935
TFilterComboBox class, 910
see also TCustomComboBox class
TFindDialog class, 489-490
methods, 490
Execute, 501
OnFind event, 509
properties, 490
Ctl3D, 498
FindText, 504
Handle, 505
HelpContext, 505
Left, 506-507

TFindDialog class (*continued*)
Options, 510-512
Position, 513-514
Top, 516
see also TReplace class
TFloatField class, 659-660
methods
MaxValue function, 696
MinValue function, 696-697
properties
Currency, 674-675
DisplayFormat, 678
Precision, 702
TFont class, 307, 315-316
OnChange event, 312-313
properties
Color, 309
Handle, 309-310
Height, 310
Name, 312
Pitch, 313
Size, 314
Style, 314-316
TFontDialog class, 490-491
methods, 491
Execute, 501
OnApply event, 508
properties, 491
Ctl3D, 498
Device, 500
events, 491
Font, 504-505
HelpContext, 505-506
MaxFontSize, 507
MinFontSize, 507-508
Options, 510, 512
TForm class, 1051-1052, 1055-1059
events, 1058-1059
MDI applications, 1056-1057
methods, 1058-1059
ArrangeIcons, 1061-1063
Cascade, 1064-1065
Close, 1067-1068
DefocusControl, 1068-1069
FocusControl, 1069-1070

TForm class (*continued*)
    Next, 1078
    Previous, 1079-1080
    Print, 1080-1081
    Show, 1082
    ShowModal, 1082
    Tile, 1082-1083
  properties, 1058-1059
    Active, 1060
    ActiveControl, 1060
    ActiveMDIChild, 1061
    AutoScroll, 1062
    BorderIcons, 1064
    ClientHandle, 1065-1066
    ClientHeight, 1066
    ClientWidth, 1067
    FormStyle, 1070-1071
    Icon, 1072
    KeyPreview, 1072-1074
    MDIChildCount, 1074-1075
    MDIChildren, 1075-1076
    Menu, 1076-1078
    Position, 1079
    PrintScale, 1080-1081
    WindowMenu, 1083-1084
    WindowState, 1084-1085
  see also TScrollingWinControl class
TGlyphList class, 517, 521
  Count property, 529
  methods, 521
    Add, 521-522
    AddMasked, 524-525
    Create, 530
    Delete, 531-532
    Destroy, 532
TGraphic class, 317-318
  events, 318
    OnChange, 328-329
  methods, 318
    LoadFromClipboardFormat, 324-325
    LoadFromFile, 325-326
    SaveToClipboardFormat, 329-330
    SaveToFile, 330-331
  properties, 318
    Empty, 322
    Height, 323

TGraphic class (*continued*)
    Modified, 327
    Width, 331
  TBitmap, 319-320
    Canvas property, 320
    Handle property, 323
    IgnorePalette property, 324
    Monochrome property, 327-328
    Palette property, 329
  TIcon, 318-319
    Handle property, 323
  TMetafile, 319
    CreatedBy property, 321-322
    Description property, 321
    Enhanced property, 322
    Handle property, 323
    MMHeight property, 326
    MMWidth property, 326
    Palette property, 329
TGraphicControl class, 21, 755-759
  events, 756-758
  methods, 756-758
  properties, 756-757
    Canvas, 758-759
  see also nonwindowed controls
TGraphicField, 660
  methods
    LoadFromFile function, 690-691
    LoadFromStream function, 691
    SaveToFile, 704
    SaveToStream, 705
  see also TField class
TGraphicsObject class, 305-306
  properties/methods/events, 306
  TBrush, 306, 308-309, 312-315
  TFont, 307, 309-310, 312-316
  TPen, 306-307, 309-316
TGridDataLink class, 300
  methods, 300
    AddMapping, 301
    ClearMapping, 301
    Modified, 303
    Reset, 303
  properties, 300
    DefaultFields, 302
    FieldCount, 302

TGridDataLink class (*continued*)
    Fields, 302-303
    SparseMap, 303-304
TGroupBox class, 1189-1190
THeaderControl class, 851-855
    events, 852-855
        OnDrawSection, 855
        OnResize, 855
        OnSectionClick, 856-857
        OnSectionResize, 857-858
        OnSectionTrack, 858-859
    methods, 852-855
    properties, 852-855
        Sections, 859
THeaderSection
    properties
        Alignment, 255
        AllowClick, 255-256
        Left, 274-275
        MaxWidth, 275
        MinWidth, 275-276
        Right, 278
        Style, 280
        Text, 280
        Width, 281
THeaderSection class, 250-251
    see also TCollectionItem class
THeaderSections class, 250
    see also TCollection class
THeaderStrings class, 336-337
    see also TStrings class
THotKey class, 927-928, 931-932
    events, 932
    ●methods, 932
    properties, 932
        HotKey, 932-933
        InvalidKeys, 933-934
        Modifiers, 934
    see also TCustomHotKey class
Thousands property, TUpDown class, 1049
threads, 49-51
    adding to objects, 49
    instantiating, 51
    naming, 50
    see also TThread class

three-dimesional effects
    Ctl3D property
        TCommonDialog class/descendants, 498
        TWinControl class, 822
    ParentCtl3D property, TWinControl class, 829
    TBevel class, 761-766
TickMarks property, TTrackBar class, 906-907
TickStyle property, TTrackBar class, 907-908
TIcon class, 318-319
    Handle property, 323
    see also TGraphic class
TIconOptions class, 137-139
    methods, 137
    properties, 137
        Arrangement, 138
        AutoArrange, 138
        WrapText, 139
Tile method, TForm class, 1082-1083
TImage class, 767-773
    methods/events, 768-770
    properties, 768-770
        AutoSize, 770-771
        Center, 771-772
        Picture, 772
        Stretch, 773
TImageList class, 517, 520
    events, 520
        OnChange, 550
    example project, 559-561
    methods, 520
        Add, 521-522
        AddIcon, 522-523
        AddImages, 523-524
        AddMasked, 524-525
        Assign, 526-527
        BeginDrag, 527
        Clear, 529
        Create, 530
        CreateSize, 530-531
        Delete, 531-532
        Destroy, 532
        DragLock, 534
        DragMove, 534-535
        DragUnlock, 535
        Draw, 535

TImageList class (*continued*)
  DrawOverlay, 537-538
  EndDrag, 538
  FireLoad, 538-539
  GetBitmap, 539-540
  GetHotSpot, 540
  GetIcon, 540-541
  GetImageBitmap, 541
  GetInstRes, 542
  GetMaskBitmap, 542
  GetResource, 543
  HideDragImage, 545
  Insert, 546-547
  InsertIcon, 547-548
  InsertMasked, 548-549
  Move, 549-550
  Overlay, 550-551
  RegisterChanges, 551-554
  Replace, 554-555
  ReplaceIcon, 555
  ReplaceMasked, 555-556
  ResInstLoad, 556
  ResourceLoad, 556-557
  SetDragImage, 557
  ShowDragImage, 558
  UnRegisterChanges, 558-559
properties, 520
  AllocBy, 525
  BkColor, 527-528
  BlendColor, 528-529
  Count, 529
  DragCursor, 533
  Dragging, 533-534
  DrawingStyle, 536
  Handle, 544
  HandleAllocated, 544-545
  Height, 545
  ImageType, 545-546
  Masked, 549
  ShareImages, 557-558
  Width, 559
time
  ReadDateTime method, TRegistry class, 71
  ReadTime method, TRegistry class, 71

time (*continued*)
  WriteDateTime method, TRegistry class, 73-74
  WriteTime method, TRegistry class, 73-74
TimeFormat property, TMediaPlayer class,
  1176-1177
timers, TTimer class, 473-475
TIndexFiles class, 337
  Add method, 343
  see also TStrings class
TIniFile class, 35-36
  methods, 36-37
    Create, 37
    DeleteKey, 37-38
    EraseSection, 38-39
    ReadInteger, 40-41
    ReadSection, 41-42
    ReadSections, 42
    ReadSectionValues, 43-44
    ReadString, 45
    WriteBool, 45-46
    WriteInteger, 46-47
    WriteString, 47-48
  properties
    FileName, 39
    ReadBool, 39-40
TInplaceEdit class, *see* **TCustomMaskEdit class**
TIntegerField class, 660
  DisplayFormat property, 678
  methods
    MaxValue function, 696
    MinValue function, 696-697
Title property
  TApplication class, 420-421
  TColumn class, 281
  TOpenDialog/TSaveDialog classes, 515
TLabel class, 791-792
TList class, 75-77
  methods, 77
    Add, 78
    Capacity, 79
    Clear, 79-80
    Count, 80
    Delete, 81
    Exchange, 81-82
    Expand, 82
    First, 82-83

TList class (*continued*)
  IndexOf, 83
  Insert, 83-84
  Last, 84-85
  Move, 85-86
  Pack, 86
  Remove, 86-87
  Sort, 87-88
 properties, 77
  Item, 84
  List, 85
TListBox class, 941-942
 see also TCustomListBox class
TListBoxStrings class, 338
 Add method, 343
 see also TStrings class
TListColumn class, 249-250
 properties
  Alignment, 255
  Width, 281
  WidthType, 282
TListColumns class, 249
 Owner property, 276
 see also TCollection class
TListItem class, 141-142
 methods, 142
  CancelEdit, 142-143
  Create, 143-144
  Delete, 145-146
  EditCaption, 146-147
  MakeVisible, 149-150
  Update, 152-153
 properties, 142
  Caption, 143
  Cut, 144
  Data, 145
  DropTarget, 146
  Focused, 147
  Handle, 147-148
  ImageIndex, 148
  Index, 148-149
  ListView, 149
  OverlayIndex, 150
  Owner, 150-151
  Selected, 151

TListItem class(*continued*)
  StateIndex, 151-152
  SubItems, 152
TListItems class, 153
 methods, 153
  Add, 154
  BeginUpdate, 154-155
  Clear, 155
  Delete, 156
  EndUpdate, 156-157
  IndexOf, 158
  Insert, 158-159
 properties, 153
  Count, 155-156
  Handle, 157
  Item, 159
  Owner, 160
TListSourceLink class, 300
TListView class, 957-958, 962-964
 events, 963-964
  OnChange, 983
  OnChanging, 984
  OnColumnClick, 984-985
  OnCompare, 985
  OnDeletion, 985-986
  OnEdited, 986
  OnEditing, 986-987
  OnInsert, 987
 methods, 963-964
  AlphaSort, 965-966
  Arrange, 966-967
  ColumnSort, 970-971
  FindCaption, 972-974
  FindData, 974-975
  GetItemAt, 976
  GetNearestItem, 976-977
  GetNextItem, 978-979
  IsEditing, 980
  Scroll, 988
  StringWidth, 992-993
  UpdateItems, 993-994
 properties, 963-964
  AllocBy, 964-965
  BoundingRect, 967
  Column, 968

TListView class (*continued*)
>   *ColumnClick, 968-969*
>   *Columns, 969-970*
>   *DropTarget, 971-972*
>   *IconOptions, 979-980*
>   *ItemFocused, 980-981*
>   *Items, 981-982*
>   *LargeImages, 982-983*
>   *MultiSelect, 983*
>   *ReadOnly, 988*
>   *SelCount, 988-989*
>   *Selected, 989*
>   *ShowColumnHeaders, 989-990*
>   *SmallImages, 990*
>   *SortTypes, 990-991*
>   *StateImages, 991-992*
>   *ViewOrigin, 994*
>   *VisibleRowCount, 995*
> TIconOptions class, 137-139

TLoginDialog class, *see* **TForm class**

TMainMenu class, 479, 481-483
> methods
>   *FindItem, 482*
>   *Merge, 484*
>   *Unmerge, 486*
> properties
>   *AutoMerge, 481-482*
>   *Handle, 483*

TMaskEdit class, 1121-1123
> properties
>   *CharCase, 1127-1128*
>   *EditMask, 1131-1133*
>   *EditText, 1133-1134*
>   *IsMasked, 1136*
>   *PasswordChar, 1140-1141*
>   *ReadOnly, 1142-1143*
> *see also* TCustomMaskEdit class

TMediaPlayer class, 1153-1155
> events, 1153-1155
>   *OnNotify, 1168-1169*
>   *OnPostClick, 1169*
> methods, 1153-1155
>   *Back, 1156-1157*
>   *Close, 1158*
>   *Eject, 1161*

TMediaPlayer class (*continued*)
>   *Next, 1166*
>   *Open, 1170*
>   *Pause, 1170*
>   *PauseOnly, 1170-1171*
>   *Play, 1171*
>   *Previous, 1172*
>   *Resume, 1172-1173*
>   *Rewind, 1173*
>   *Save, 1173*
>   *StartRecording, 1175*
>   *Step, 1175*
>   *Stop, 1176*
> properties, 1153-1155
>   *AutoEnable, 1155*
>   *AutoOpen, 1155-1156*
>   *AutoRewind, 1156*
>   *Capabilities, 1157-1158*
>   *ColoredButtons, 1159*
>   *DeviceID, 1159*
>   *DeviceType, 1159-1160*
>   *Display, 1160*
>   *DisplayRect, 1161*
>   *EnabledButtons, 1161-1162*
>   *EndPos, 1162*
>   *Error, 1162-1163*
>   *ErrorMessage, 1163*
>   *FileName, 1164*
>   *Frames, 1164-1165*
>   *Length, 1165*
>   *Mode, 1165-1166*
>   *Notify, 1166-1167*
>   *NotifyValue, 1168*
>   *Position, 1171-1172*
>   *Shareable, 1174*
>   *Start, 1174*
>   *StartPos, 1174-1175*
>   *TimeFormat, 1176-1177*
>   *TrackLength, 1177-1178*
>   *TrackPosition, 1178*
>   *Tracks, 1178-1179*
>   *VisibleButtons, 1179*
>   *Wait, 1179*
> *see also* TCustomControl class

TMemo class, 1123-1125
    events, 1124-1125
    methods, 1124-1125
    properties, 1124-1125
        HideSelection, 1136
        ReadOnly, 1142-1143
        ScrollBars, 1143
        WantReturns, 1146-1147
        WantTabs, 1147
        WordWrap, 1147-1148
    see also TCustomMemo class
TMemoField class, 660
    methods
        LoadFromFile function, 690-691
        LoadFromStream function, 691
        SaveToFile, 704
        SaveToStream, 705
    Transliterate property, 708
TMemoStrings class, 338
    see also TStrings class
TMenu class, 477-479, 482-483
    methods, 478
        FirstItem, 482-483
    properties, 478-479
        Handle, 483
TMenuItem class, 429-430
    events, 430
        OnClick, 441
    methods, 430
        Add, 431
        Click, 434
        Delete, 436
        IndexOf, 438
        Insert, 439
        Remove, 443
    properties, 430
        Break, 431-432
        Caption, 432-433
        Checked, 433-434
        Count, 434-435
        Default, 435-436
        Enabled, 436-437
        GroupIndex, 437
        Handle, 438
        HelpContext, 438
        Items, 440
        MenuIndex, 440

TMenuItem class (*continued*)
        Parent, 441
        RadioItem, 442
        ShortCut, 443-444
        Visible, 444-445
TMetafile class, 319
    methods, 319
    properties, 319
        CreatedBy, 321-322
        Description, 321
        Enhanced, 322
        Handle, 323
        MMHeight, 326
        MMWidth, 326
        Palette, 329
        see also TGraphic class, properties
TMetaFileCanvas objects, 219-220
    see also TCanvas class
TNavDataLink class, 299
TNotebook class, 998
TNumericField class, 660
    Alignment property, 662
TObject class, 21, 29
    methods, 29-30
        ClassName, 30
        ClassParent, 30-31
        ClassType, 31
        Create, 31-32
        Destroy, 32
        Free, 32-33
        InheritsFrom, 33
        InstanceSize, 33
toolbars, creating, 795-796
    see also TSpeedButton class
Tooltips
    HintColor property, TApplication class, 397
    HintHidePause property, TApplication
        class, 397
    HintPause property, TApplication class, 398
    HintShortPause property, TApplication class,
        398-399
    OnShowHint event, TApplication class, 415
    ShowHint property, TApplication class, 419
Top property
    TControl class, 750
    TFindDialog class, 516
    TReplaceDialog class, 516
ToPage property, TPrintDialog class, 516

TOpenDialog class, 491-492
    Execute method, 501
    filters, 492
    methods, 493
    properties, 493
        Ctl3D, 498
        DefaultExt, 499-500
        FileName, 501-502
        Files, 502
        Filter, 503
        FilterIndex, 503-504
        HelpContext, 505-506
        InitialDir, 506
        Options, 510, 512-513
        Title, 515
    see also TSave class
TopIndex property, TCustomListBox class/
    descendants, 954-955
TOutlineStrings class, 339
    methods
        Add, 343
        GetObject, 354
        PutObject, 366
    see also TStrings class
TPageAccess class, 339
    see also TStrings class
TPageControl class, 1002-1004
    events, 1003-1004
    methods, 1003-1004
        FindNextPage, 1007-1008
    properties, 1003-1004
        ActivePage, 1006
        MultiLine, 1008-1009
        PageCount, 1009-1010
        Pages, 1010
        SelectNextPage, 1010-1011
        TabHeight, 1012
        TabWidth, 1012-1013
    see also TTabSheet class; TCustomTabControl
    class
TPaintBox class, 775-777
TPanel class, 1180-1181
    events, 1180-1181
    methods, 1180-1181
    properties, 1180-1181
        BevelInner, 1181-1182
        BevelOuter, 1182

TPanel class (*continued*)
        BevelWidth, 1183
        Locked, 1183-1184
TParaAttributes class, 161-166
    methods, 161
    properties
        Alignment, 162
        FirstIndent, 163
        LeftIndent, 164
        Numbering, 164
        RightIndent, 165
        Tab, 165
        TabCount, 166
TPasswordDialog class, *see* **TForm class, 1052**
TPen class, 306-307, 315
    OnChange event, 312-313
    properties
        Color, 309
        Handle, 309-310
        Mode, 310-311
        Style, 314-316
        Width, 316
TPersistent class, 21, 109-110
    Assign method, 109-110
TPicture class, 167-173
    events, 168
        OnChange, 171
    methods, 168
        LoadFromFile, 170
        SaveToFile, 173
    properties, 168
        Bitmap, 168
        Graphic, 169
        Height, 169-170
        Icon, 170
        Width, 173
TPopupList class, 76-77
    methods, 77
        Add, 78
        Remove, 86-87
TPopupMenu class, 479-486
    OnPopup event, 484
    methods
        FindItem, 482
        Popup, 485

TPopupMenu class (*continued*)
properties
Alignment, 480-481
AutoPopup, 482
Handle, 483
HelpContext, 483-484
PopupComponent, 485-486
TPrintDialog class, 493-494
methods, 494
Execute, 501
properties, 494
Collate, 497
Copies, 498
Ctl3D, 498
MaxPage, 507
MinPage, 508
Options, 510, 513
PrintRange, 514
PrintToFile, 514-515
ToPage, 516
TPrinterCanvas objects, 220
see also TCanvas class
TPrinterSetupDialog class, 494-495
Execute method, 501
properties
Ctl3D, 498
HelpContext, 505-506
ReplaceText, 515
TProgressBar class, 861-865
events, 862-865
methods, 862-865
StepBy, 867
StepIt, 867-868
properties, 862-865
Max, 865
Min, 865-866
Position, 866
Step, 866
TQuery class, 563-564, 647
see also TDataSet class
TQueryDataLink class, 299
Track bars (TTrackBar class), 896-899
events, 896-899
methods, 896-899
SetTick, 906

Track bars (*continued*)
properties, 896-899
Frequency, 900
LineSize, 900-901
Max, 901
Min, 902
Orientation, 902-903
PageSize, 903
Position, 904
SelEnd, 904-905
SelStart, 905-906
TickMarks, 906-907
TickStyle, 907-908
TrackLength property, TMediaPlayer class, 1177-1178
TrackPosition property, TMediaPlayer class, 1178
Tracks property, TMediaPlayer class, 1178-1179
TRadioButton class, 1098-1102, 1104
events, 1099-1102
methods, 1099-1102
properties, 1099-1102
Checked, 1104
TRadioGroup class, 1191-1192
events, 1191-1192
methods, 1191-1192
properties, 1191-1192
Columns, 1192
ItemIndex, 1192-1193
Items, 1193-1194
Transliterate property
TField class/descendants, 709
TMemoField/TStringField classes, 708
Tree view
TCustomTreeView class, 1015-1019
AlphaSort method, 1022
FullCollapse method, 1022-1023
FullExpand method, 1023
GetHitTestInfoAt method, 1023-1025
GetNodeAt method, 1025-1026
HideSelection property, 1026
Images property, 1026-1027
IsEditing method, 1027
Items property, 1028
OnChanging event, 1028-1029
OnCollapsed event, 1029

Tree view (*continued*)

    OnCollapsing event, 1029-1030

    OnCompare event, 1030

    OnDeletion event, 1030-1031

    OnEdited event, 1031

    OnEditing event, 1031-1032

    OnExpanded event, 1032

    OnExpanding event, 1032

    OnGetImageIndex event, 1033

    OnSelectedIndex event, 1033

    ReadOnly property, 1034

    ShowButtons property, 1034-1035

    ShowLines property, 1035-1036

    ShowRoot property, 1036-1037

    SortImages property, 1038

    SortType property, 1037-1038

  TTreeNode class, 181-183

    AbsoluteIndex property, 183

    AlphaSort method, 184

    Collapse method, 185

    Count property, 185

    Cut property, 186

    Data property, 186-187

    Delete method, 187

    DeleteChildren method, 187

    Deleting property, 188

    DropTarget property, 188

    EditText method, 189

    EndEdit method, 189

    Expand method, 190

    Expanded property, 190-191

    Focused property, 191

    GetFirstChild method, 191

    GetLastChild method, 192

    GetNext method, 192

    GetNextChild method, 193

    GetNextSibling method, 193

    GetNextVisible method, 194

    GetPrev method, 194

    GetPrevChild method, 195

    GetPrevSibling method, 195

    Handle property, 196

    HasAsParent method, 196

    HasChildren property, 197

    ImageIndex property, 197

Tree view (*continued*)

    Index property, 198

    IndexOf property, 198-199

    IsVisible property, 199

    Item property, 199

    Level property, 200

    MakeVisible method, 200

    MoveTo method, 200-201

    OverLayIndex property, 201-202

    Parent property, 202

    SelectedIndex property, 202-203

    StateIndex property, 203

    Text property, 203

    TreeView property, 204

  TTreeNodes class, 181, 204

    Add method, 205-206

    AddChild method, 206-207

    AddChildFirst method, 207

    AddChildObject method, 208

    AddChildObjectFirst method, 208-209

    AddFirst method, 209-210

    AddObject method, 210

    AddObjectFirst method, 211

    BeginUpdate method, 212

    Clear method, 212

    Count property, 213

    Delete method, 213

    EndUpdate method, 214

    GetFirstNode method, 214

    Handle property, 215

    Insert method, 215

    InsertObject method, 216

    Owner property, 216

  TTreeStrings class, 343

    Add method, 343

    Owner property, 364-365

  TTreeView class, 1015-1016, 1020-1021

    AlphaSort method, 1022

    FullCollapse method, 1022-1023

    FullExpand method, 1023

    GetHitTestInfoAt method, 1023-1025

    GetNodeAt method, 1025-1026

    HideSelection property, 1026

    Images property, 1026-1027

    IsEditing method, 1027

Tree view (*continued*)

    Items property, 1028
    OnChanging event, 1028-1029
    OnCollapsed event, 1029
    OnCollapsing event, 1029-1030
    OnCompare event, 1030
    OnDeletion event, 1030-1031
    OnEdited event, 1031
    OnEditing event, 1031-1032
    OnExpanded event, 1032
    OnExpanding event, 1032
    OnGetImageIndex event, 1033
    OnSelectedIndex event, 1033
    ReadOnly property, 1034
    ShowButtons property, 1034-1035
    ShowLines property, 1035-1036
    ShowRoot property, 1036-1037
    SortImages property, 1038
    SortType property, 1037-1038

TreeView property, TTreeNode class, 204

TRegistry class

  methods, 59-60
    CloseKey, 60-61
    CreateKey, 61
    DeleteKey, 62-63
    DeleteValue, 63-64
    GetDataInfo, 64-65
    GetDataSize, 65
    GetDataType, 65-66
    GetKeyInfo, 66-67
    GetKeyNames, 67
    GetValueNames, 68
    HasSubKeys, 68-69
    KeyExists, 69
    OpenKey, 70
    Read, 71
    RenameValue, 71-72
    ValueExists, 72-73
    Write, 73-74
  properties, 59-60
    CurrentKey, 62
    CurrentPath, 62
    LazyWrite, 69-70
    RootKey, 72

TReplaceDialog class, 495-496

  events
    OnFind event, 509
    OnReplace event, 509-510
  methods, 496
    Execute, 501
  properties, 496
    Ctl3D, 498
    FindText, 504
    Handle, 505
    HelpContext, 505-506
    Left, 506-507
    Options, 510-512
    Position, 513-514
    Top, 516
  see also TFind class

TRichEdit class, 1125-1127

  events, 1126-1127
    OnResizeRequest, 1138
    OnSelectionChange, 1138-1139
  methods, 1126-1127
  PlainText property, 1141-1142
  properties, 1126-1127
    HideScrollBars, 1135-1136
    HideSelection, 1136
    Lines, 1137
    ReadOnly, 1142-1143
    ScrollBars, 1143
    WantReturns, 1146-1147
    WantTabs, 1147
    WordWrap, 1147-1148
  TTextAttributes class, 175, 177-180
    Color property, 176
    ConsistentAttributes property, 177
    Height property, 177-178
    Name property, 178
    Pitch property, 178-179
    Protected property, 179
    Size property, 179-180
    Style property, 180
  see also rich edit controls; TCustomRichEdit class

TRichEditStrings class, 339-340
    PlainText property, 365-366
    see also TStrings class
try-except code block (exception handling), 90
try-finally code block (exception handling), 90-91
TSaveDialog class, 496
    Execute method, 501
    filters, 492
    properties
        Ctl3D, 498
        DefaultExt, 499-500
        FileName, 501-502
        Files, 502
        Filter, 503
        FilterIndex, 503-504
        HelpContext, 505-506
        InitialDir, 506
        Options, 510, 512-513
        Title, 515
    see also TOpen class
TScreen class, 447-448
    events, 448
        OnActiveControlChange, 453-454
        OnActiveFormChange, 454-455
    methods, 448
    properties, 448
        ActiveControl, 448-449
        ActiveForm, 449
        Cursor, 449-450
        Cursors, 450-451
        Fonts, 451-452
        FormCount, 452
        Forms, 452
        Height, 452-453
        Width, 455-456
TScrollBar class, 869-872
    methods, 870-872
        SetParams, 876-877
    OnScroll event, 874-876
    properties, 870-872
        Kind, 873
        LargeChange, 873
        Max, 873-874
        Min, 874

TScrollBar class (*continued*)
    Position, 876
    SmallChange, 877
    see TScrollingWinControl class
TScrollingWinControl class, 1051-1055
    events, 1052-1055
    methods, 1052-1055
    properties, 1052-1055
        HorzScrollBar, 1071-1072
TSession class, 457-459
    events, 458-459
        OnPassword, 467-468
        OnStartUp, 468-469
    methods, 458-459
        AddAlias, 459-460
        AddPassword, 460
        AddStandardAlias, 460-461
        Close, 461
        DeleteAlias, 462-463
        DropConnections, 463
        FindDatabase, 463-464
        GetAliasDriverName, 464
        GetAliasNames, 464
        GetAliasParams, 465
        GetDatabaseNames, 465
        GetDriverNames, 465-466
        GetDriverParams, 466
        GetPassword, 466
        Open, 469
        RemoveAllPasswords, 470
        RemovePassword, 470
        SaveConfigFile, 470
    properties, 458-459
        Active, 459
        ConfigMode, 461-462
        Databases, 462
        KeepConnections, 467
        PrivateDir, 469
        SessionName, 470-471
TShape class, 779
    events, 780-782
    methods, 780-782
        StyleChanged, 785
    properties, 780-782

TShape class (*continued*)
    Brush, 782-783
    Pen, 783
    Shape, 784
TSmallIntField class, 661
  DisplayFormat property, 678
  methods
    MaxValue function, 696
    MinValue function, 696-697
TSpeedButton class, 795-799
  methods/events, 797-799
  properties, 797-799
    AllowAllUp, 799-800
    Down, 801
    Glyph, 801-802
    GroupIndex, 802-803
    Layout, 803
    Margin, 804
    NumGlyphs, 804
    Spacing, 805
  see also TButtonControl class
TSplitter class, 807-810
  events, 808-810
    OnMoved, 811-812
  methods, 808-810
  properties, 808-810
    Beveled, 810
    MinSize, 810-811
TStatusBar class, 879 883
  events, 880-883
  methods, 880-883
  properties, 880-883
    Panels, 883-884
    SimplePanel, 884-885
    SimpleText, 885
    SizeGrip, 886
TStatusPanel
  GetDisplayName method, 270
  properties
    Alignment, 255
    Bevel, 258
    GetDisplayName, 280
    Text, 280
    Width, 281

TStatusPanel class, 252
  example project, 282-285
  see also TCollectionItem class
TStatusPanels class, 251
  example project, 282-285
  see also TCollection class
TStoredProc class, 563-564, 646-647
  see also TDataSet class
TString class, 334
TStringField class, 661
  properties
    Size, 707
    Transliterate, 708
TStringGridStrings class, 340
  see also TStrings class
TStringList class, 340-341
  events
    OnChange, 361-363
    OnChanging, 363-364
  methods
    Sort, 343, 368-369
  properties
    Duplicates, 351-352
    Find, 353-354
    Sorted, 369
  see also TStrings class
TStrings class, 333-335
  example project, 371-375
  methods, 335
    Add, 343
    AddObject, 344
    AddStrings, 344-345
    Assign, 345-346
    BeginUpdate, 346
    Clear, 347
    Create, 349-350
    Delete, 350-351
    Destroy, 351
    EndUpdate, 352
    Equals, 352-353
    Exchange, 353
    IndexOf, 356
    IndexOfName, 356
    IndexOfObject, 357

TStrings class (*continued*)
    Insert, 357-358
    InsertObject, 358-359
    LoadFromFile, 359
    LoadFromStream, 359
    Move, 360
    SaveToFile, 366-367
    SaveToStream, 367
    SetText, 367-368
  properties, 335-336
    Capacity, 346-347
    CommaText, 347-348
    Count, 348-349
    Names, 360
    Objects, 361
    Strings, 369-370
    Text, 370
    Values, 370-371
  TComboBoxStrings, 336
    Add method, 343
  THeaderStrings, 336-337
  TIndexFiles, 337
    Add method, 343
  TListBoxStrings, 338
    Add method, 343
  TMemoStrings, 338
  TOutlineStrings, 339
    Add method, 343
    GetObject method, 354
    PutObject method, 366
  TPageAccess, 339
  TRichEditStrings, 339-340
    PlainText property, 365-366
  TStringGridStrings, 340
  TStringList, 340-341
    Add method, 343
    Duplicates property, 351-352
    Find property, 353-354
    OnChange event, 361-363
    OnChanging event, 363-364
    Sort method, 368-369
    Sorted property, 369
  TSubItems, 341
    Add method, 343
    Handle property, 355
    Owner property, 364-365
  TTabPageAccess, 342

TStrings class (*continued*)
  TTabStrings, 342
  TTreeStrings, 343
    Add method, 343
    Owner property, 364-365
TSubItems class, 341
  Add method, 343
  Handle property, 355
  Owner property, 364-365
  see also TStrings class
TTabbedNotebook class, 998
TTabControl class, 1004-1005
  events, 1005
  methods, 1005
  properties, 1005
    DisplayRect, 1007
    MultiLine, 1008-1009
    TabHeight, 1012
    Tabs, 1011-1012
    TabWidth, 1012-1013
  see also TCustomTabControl class
TTable class, 563-564, 646-647
  see also TDataSet class
TTableDataLink class, 293
TTabPageAccess class, 342
  see also TStrings class
TTabSet class, 998
TTabSheet class, 887-891
  events, 889-891
  methods, 889-891
    PageControl, 892
  properties, 889-891
    PageIndex, 892
    TabVisible, 893

TTabStrings class, 342
  see also TStrings class
TTextAtributes class, 175, 177-180
  properties, 175
    Color, 176
    ConsistentAttributes, 177
    Height, 177-178
    Name, 178
    Pitch, 178-179
    Protected, 179
    Size, 179-180
    Style, 180

TThread class, 49-51
  events, 51
    OnTerminate, 52-53
  methods, 51
    Create, 52
    Resume, 54
    Suspend, 54
    Terminate, 55
  properties, 51
    Priority, 53
    Suspended, 55
TTimeField class, 661
  DisplayFormat property, 678
TTimer class, 473-475
TTrackBar class, 895-899
  events, 896-899
  methods, 896-899
    SetTick, 906
  properties, 896-899
    Frequency, 900
    LineSize, 900-901
    Max, 901
    Min, 902
    Orientation, 902-903
    PageSize, 903
    Position, 904
    SelEnd, 904-905
    SelStart, 905-906
    TickMarks, 906-907
    TickStyle, 907-908
TTreeNode class, 181-183
  methods, 182-183
    AlphaSort, 184
    Collapse, 185
    Delete, 187
    DeleteChildren, 187
    EditText, 189
    EndEdit, 189
    Expand, 190
    GetFirstChild, 191
    GetLastChild, 192
    GetNext, 192
    GetNextChild, 193
    GetNextSibling, 193
    GetNextVisible, 194
    GetPrev, 194

TTreeNode class (*continued*)
    GetPrevChild, 195
    GetPrevSibling, 195
    HasAsParent, 196
    MakeVisible, 200
    MoveTo, 200-201
  properties, 182-183
    AbsoluteIndex, 183
    Count, 185
    Cut, 186
    Data, 186-187
    Deleting, 188
    DropTarget, 188
    Expanded, 190-191
    Focused, 191
    Handle, 196
    HasChildren, 197
    ImageIndex property, 197
    Index, 198
    IndexOf, 198-199
    IsVisible, 199
    Item, 199
    Level, 200
    OverLayIndex property, 201-202
    Parent property, 202
    SelectedIndex property, 202-203
    StateIndex property, 203
    Text property, 203
    TreeView, 204
  see also TCustomTreeView
TTreeNodes class, 181
  methods, 204-205
    Add, 205-206
    AddChild, 206-207
    AddChildFirst, 207
    AddChildObject, 208
    AddChildObjectFirst, 208-209
    AddFirst, 209-210
    AddObject, 210
    AddObjectFirst, 211
    BeginUpdate, 212
    Clear, 212
    Delete, 213
    EndUpdate, 214
    GetFirstNode, 214
    Insert, 215
    InsertObject, 216

TTreeNodes class (*continued*)
    properties, 204-205
        Count property, 213
        Handle, 215
        Owner property, 216
    see also TCustomTreeView
TTreeStrings class, 343
    Add method, 343
    Owner property, 364-365
    see also TStrings class
TTreeView class, 1015-1016, 1020-1021
    events, 1020-1021
        OnChanging, 1028-1029
        OnCollapsed, 1029
        OnCollapsing, 1029-1030
        OnCompare, 1030
        OnDeletion, 1030-1031
        OnEdited, 1031
        OnEditing, 1031-1032
        OnExpanded, 1032
        OnExpanding, 1032
        OnGetImageIndex, 1033
        OnSelectedIndex, 1033
    methods, 1020-1021
        AlphaSort, 1022
        FullCollapse, 1022-1023
        FullExpand, 1023
        GetHitTestInfoAt, 1023-1025
        GetNodeAt, 1025-1026
        IsEditing, 1027
    properties, 1020-1021
        HideSelection, 1026
        Images, 1026-1027
        Items, 1028
        ReadOnly, 1034
        ShowButtons, 1034-1035
        ShowLines, 1035-1036
        ShowRoot, 1036-1037
        SortImages, 1038
        SortType, 1037-1038
TTreeView control
    see also TTreeNode class, TTreeNodes class
TUpDown class, 1044-1045
    events, 1044-1045
    methods, 1044-1045
    properties, 1044-1045

TUpDown class (*continued*)
    AlignButton, 1045
    ArrowKeys, 1046
    Associate, 1046
    Increment, 1047
    Max, 1047-1048
    Min, 1048
    Orientation, 1048
    Position, 1049
    Thousands, 1049
    Wrap, 1050
TVarBytesField class, 661
TWinControl class, 21, 815-818
    events, 816-818
        OnEnter, 824-825
        OnExit, 825-826
        OnKeyDown, 826-827
        OnKeyPress, 827-828
        OnKeyUp, 828-829
    methods, 816-818
        ContainsControl, 818-820
        ControlAtPos, 820
        Controls, 821-822
        HandleAllocated, 823
        InsertControl, 823-824
        RemoveControl, 830
        ScaleBy, 830-831
        SetFocus, 832
    properties, 816-818
        ControlCount, 820-821
        Ctl3D, 822
        ParentCtl3D, 829
        TabOrder, 832-833
        TabStop, 833
    see also windowed controls
TWordField class, 661
    DisplayFormat property, 678
    methods
        MaxValue function, 696
        MinValue function, 696-697
types
    characters, 6
    currency, 7
    defined, 16
    sizes, 10
    string, 7
    variant, 8

U

UDP (User Datagram Protocol) control, 105
Unicode, 6
units, 18-19
    finalization sections, 18-19
    implementation sections, 18-19
    initialization sections, 18-19
    interface sections, 18-19
    statements, 18-19
    visibility specifiers, 19-21
Unmerge method, TMainMenu class, 486
UnRegisterChanges method,
    TCustomImageList/TImageList classes, 558-559
up-down controls (TCustomUpDown class),
    1039-1045
    AlignButton property, 1045
    ArrowKeys property, 1046
    Associate property, 1046
    Increment property, 1047
    Max property, 1047-1048
    Min property, 1048
    Orientation property, 1048
    Position property, 1049
    Thousands property, 1049
    Wrap property, 1050
Update method
    TControl class, 750
    TListItem class, 152-153
UpdateCursorPos method, TDataSet class, 643
UpdateItems method, TListView/TCustomListView
    classes, 993-994
UpdateObject property, TDataSet class, 643-644
UpdateRecord method
    TDataLink class, 293
    TDataSet class, 644
UpdateRecordTypes property, TDataSet class,
    644-645
UpdatesPending property, TDataSet class, 645
UpdateStatus method, TDataSet class, 645

V

Validate property, TField class/descendants, 709
ValidChars property, TField class/descendants, 709
Value property, TField class/descendants, 710

ValueExists method, TRegistry class, 72-73
values
    DeleteValue method, TRegistry class, 63-64
    GetValueNames method, TRegistry class, 68
Values property, TStrings class/descendants,
    370-371
variant type, 8
VBXs (Visual Basic custom controls), 10
VCL (Visual Component Library), 3-4, 9, 21-26
    branches, 21-22
    classes, 21
    components, 21
        controls, 21
    event-handling, 22-23
    methods, 23
        directives, 23-24
    Object Browser, 25-26
    OOP (Object-Oriented Programming), 1-18
        encapsulation, 17-18
        inheritance, 17
        polymorphism, 17
        pure/hybrid languages, 15-16
    properties, 22-23
    RTTI (Run-Time Type Information), 24-25
    TComponent class, *see* TComponent class
        TControl class, see TControl class
    TGraphicControl class, *see* TGraphicControl
        class
    TObject class, *see* TObject class
    TPersistent class, *see* TPersistent class
    tree, 21
    TWinControl class, *see* TWinControl class
viewing source code, 388
ViewOrigin property, TListView/TCustomListView
    classes, 994
virtual methods, 23
Visible property
    TControl class, 751
    TControlScrollBar class, 135
    TField class/descendants, 711-712
    TMenuItem class, 444-445
VisibleButtons property
    TDBNavigator class, 1188
    TMediaPlayer class, 1179

VisibleRowCount property,
 TListView/TCustomListView classes, 995
Visual Component Library, *see* VCL

W-X-Y-Z

Wait property, TMediaPlayer class, 1179
WantReturns property, TRichEdit/TMemo classes,
 1146-1147
WantTabs property, TRichEdit/TMemo
 classes, 1147
WebHub program (included on CD), 1198
Width property
 TColumn class, 281
 TControl class, 751
 TCustomImageList/TImageList classes, 559
 TGraphic class, 331
 THeaderSection class, 281
 TListColumn class, 281
 TPen, 316
 TPicture class, 173
 TScreen class, 455-456
 TStatusPanel class, 281
WidthType property, TListColumn class, 282
WIN.INI files, *see* TIniFile class
windowed controls, 815-818
 edit controls (TCustomEdit class), 1115-1119
  Clear method, 1128
  ClearSelection method, 1129
  CopyToClipboard method, 1129-1130
  CutToClipboard method, 1130
  GetSelTextBuf method, 1134-1135
  MaxLength property, 1137
  memo controls, see memo controls, 1123
  Modified property, 1137-1138
  PasteFromClipboard method, 1141
  rich edit controls, 1125
  SelectAll method, 1144
  selected text, 1115
  SelLength property, 1144-1145
  SelStart property, 1144-1145
  SelText property, 1145
  SetSelTextBuf method, 1146
  TCustomMaskEdit class, 1121
  TEdit class, 1119-1121
  TMaskEdit class, 1121-1123
 see also edit controls

windowed controls (*continued*)
 events, 816-818
  OnEnter, 824-825
  OnExit, 825-826
  OnKeyDown, 826-827
  OnKeyPress, 827-828
  OnKeyUp, 828-829
 forms, *see* TForms class
 handles, 815
 methods, 816-818
  ContainsControl, 818-820
  ControlAtPos, 820
  Controls, 821-822
  HandleAllocated, 823
  InsertControl, 823-824
  RemoveControl, 830
  ScaleBy, 830-831
  SetFocus, 832
 properties, 816-818
  ControlCount, 820-821
  Ctl3D, 822
  ParentCtl3D, 829
  TabOrder, 832-833
  TabStop, 833
 TButtonControl class, 1087
  TButton, see TButton class
 TCustomComboBox class, 909-913
  Clear method, 916-917
  DropDownCount property, 918
  DroppedDown property, 918
  ItemIndex property, 920-921
  Items property, 921-922
  TComboBox, 914-915
  TDBComboBox, 915-916
  TDriveComboBox, 910
  TFilterComboBox, 910
  see also TComboBox, TDBComboBox
 TCustomControl class, *see* TCustomControl
  class
 TCustomHotKey class, 927-931
  THotKey, 931-933
 TCustomListBox class, 935-939
  BorderStyle property, 942-943
  Clear method, 943
  ExtendedSelect property, 945
  IntegralHeight property, 946

windowed controls (*continued*)

      ItemAtPos method, 947-948

      ItemHeight property, 948

      ItemIndex property, 948-949

      ItemRect method, 949-950

      Items property, 950

      MultiSelect property, 951

      OnMeasureItem event, 951-952

      SelCount property, 952-953

      Selected property, 953

      Sorted property, 954

      TDBListBox, 939-941, 944, 952

      TListBox, 941-942

      TopIndex property, 954-955

  TCustomListView class, 957-962

      AllocBy property, 964-965

      AlphaSort method, 965-966

      Arrange method, 966-967

      BoundingRect property, 967

      Column property, 968

      ColumnClick property, 968-969

      Columns property, 969-970

      ColumnSort method, 970-971

      DropTarget property, 971-972

      FindCaption method, 972-974

      FindData method, 974-975

      GetItemAt method, 976

      GetNearestItem method, 976-977

      GetNextItem method, 978-979

      IconOptions property, 979-980

      IsEditing method, 980

      ItemFocused property, 980-981

      Items property, 981-982

      LargeImages property, 982-983

      MultiSelect property, 983

      OnChange event, 983

      OnChanging event, 984

      OnColumnClick event, 984-985

      OnCompare event, 985

      OnDeletion event, 985-986

      OnEdited event, 986

      OnEditing event, 986-987

      OnInsert event, 987

      ReadOnly property, 988

      Scroll method, 988

windowed controls (*continued*)

      SelCount property, 988-989

      Selected property, 989

      ShowColumnHeaders property, 989-990

      SmallImages property, 990

      SortTypes property, 990-991

      StateImages property, 991-992

      StringWidth method, 992-993

      UpdateItems method, 993-994

      ViewOrigin property, 994

      VisibleRowCount property, 995

  TCustomTabControl class, 997-1002

      TPageControl, see TPageControl class

  TCustomTreeView class, 1015-1019

      AlphaSort method, 1022

      FullCollapse method, 1022-1023

      FullExpand method, 1023

      GetHitTestInfoAt method, 1023-1025

      GetNodeAt method, 1025-1026

      HideSelection property, 1026

      Images property, 1026-1027

      IsEditing method, 1027

      Items property, 1028

      OnChanging event, 1028-1029

      OnCollapsed event, 1029

      OnCollapsing event, 1029-1030

      OnCompare event, 1030

      OnDeletion event, 1030-1031

      OnEdited event, 1031

      OnEditing event, 1031-1032

      OnExpanded event, 1032

      OnExpanding event, 1032

      OnGetImageIndex event, 1033

      OnSelectedIndex event, 1033

      ReadOnly property, 1034

      ShowButtons property, 1034-1035

      ShowLines property, 1035-1036

      ShowRoot property, 1036-1037

      SortImages property, 1038

      SortType property, 1037-1038

  TCustomUpDown class, 1039-1044

      TUpDown, 1044-1050

  TDBCtrlGrid class, 835-840

      AllowDelete property, 840

      AllowInsert property, 840-841

windowed controls (*continued*)

    ColCount property, 841

    DataSource property, 841

    DoKey method, 842-843

    EditMode property, 843

    OnPaintPanel event, 843-845

    Orientation property, 845

    PanelBorder property, 846

    PanelCount property, 847

    PanelHeight property, 847

    PanelIndex property, 847

    PanelWidth property, 848

    RowCount property, 848

    ShowFocus property, 848-849

  THeaderControl class, 851-855

    methods, 852-855

    OnDrawSection event, 855

    OnResize event, 855

    OnSectionClick event, 856-858

    OnSectionTrack event, 858-859

    Sections property, 859

  TListView class, 957-958, 962-964

    AllocBy property, 964-965

    AlphaSort method, 965-966

    Arrange method, 966-967

    BoundingRect property, 967

    Column property, 968

    ColumnClick property, 968-969

    Columns property, 969-970

    ColumnSort method, 970-971

    DropTarget property, 971-972

    FindCaption method, 972-974

    FindData method, 974-975

    GetItemAt method, 976

    GetNearestItem method, 976-977

    GetNextItem method, 978-979

    IconOptions property, 979-980

    IsEditing method, 980

    ItemFocused property, 980-981

    Items property, 981-982

    LargeImages property, 982-983

    MultiSelect property, 983

    OnChange event, 983

    OnChanging event, 984

    OnColumnClick event, 984-985

    OnCompare event, 985

windowed controls (*continued*)

    OnDeletion event, 985-986

    OnEdited event, 986

    OnEditing event, 986-987

    OnInsert event, 987

    ReadOnly property, 988

    Scroll method, 988

    SelCount property, 988-989

    Selected property, 989

    ShowColumnHeaders property, 989-990

    SmallImages property, 990

    SortTypes property, 990-991

    StateImages property, 991-992

    StringWidth method, 992-993

    UpdateItems method, 993-994

    ViewOrigin property, 994

    VisibleRowCount property, 995

  TLoginDialog class, *see* TForm class

  TPageControl class, 1002-1004

    ActivePage property, 1006

    FindNextPage method, 1007-1008

    MultiLine property, 1008-1009

    PageCount property, 1009-1010

    Pages property, 1010

    SelectNextPage property, 1010-1011

    TabHeight property, 1012

    TabWidth property, 1012-1013

  TPasswordDialog class, *see* TForm class

  TProgressBar class, 861-865

    Max property, 865

    Min property, 865-866

    Position property, 866

    Step property, 866

    StepBy method, 867

    StepIt method, 867-868

  TScrollBar class, 869-872

    Kind property, 873

    LargeChange property, 873

    Max property, 873-874

    Min property, 874

    OnScroll event, 874-876

    Position property, 876

    SetParams method, 876-877

    SmallChange property, 877

  TScrollingWinControl class, 1051-1055

    HorzScrollBar property, 1071-1072

    TForm class, see TForm class

windowed controls (*continued*)

TStatusBar class, 879-883
Panels property, 883-884
SimplePanel property, 884-885
SimpleText property, 885
SizeGrip property, 886

TTabControl class, 1004-1005
DisplayRect property, 1007
MultiLine property, 1008-1009
TabHeight property, 1012
Tabs property, 1011-1012
TabWidth property, 1012-1013

TTabSheet class, 887-891
PageControl method, 892
PageIndex property, 892
TabVisible property, 893

TTrackBar class, 895-899
Frequency property, 900
LineSize property, 900-901
Max property, 901
Min property, 902
Orientation property, 902-903
PageSize property, 903
Position property, 904
SelEnd property, 904-905
SelStart property, 905-906
SetTick method, 906
TickMarks property, 906-907
TickStyle property, 907-908

TTreeView class, 1015-1016, 1020-1021
AlphaSort method, 1022
FullCollapse method, 1022-1023
FullExpand method, 1023
GetHitTestInfoAt method, 1023-1025
GetNodeAt method, 1025-1026
HideSelection property, 1026
Images property, 1026-1027
IsEditing method, 1027
Items property, 1028
OnChanging event, 1028-1029
OnCollapsed event, 1029
OnCollapsing event, 1029-1030
OnCompare event, 1030

windowed controls (*continued*)

OnDeletion event, 1030-1031
OnEdited event, 1031
OnEditing event, 1031-1032
OnExpanded event, 1032
OnExpanding event, 1032
OnGetImageIndex event, 1033
OnSelectedIndex event, 1033
ReadOnly property, 1034
ShowButtons property, 1034-1035
ShowLines property, 1035-1036
ShowRoot property, 1036-1037
SortImages property, 1038
SortType property, 1037-1038

TWinControl class, 815

WindowMenu property, TForm class, 1083-1084

windows
data modules, 8
see also forms

Windows 95/NT Registry, 57-59

WindowState property, TForm class, 1084-1085

WordWrap property, TRichEdit/TMemo classes, 1147-1148

Wrap property, TUpDown class, 1050

WrapText property, TIconsOptions class, 139

WriteBool method
TIniFile class, 45-46
TRegistry class, 73-74

WriteCurrency method, TRegistry class, 73-74

WriteDate method, TRegistry class, 73-74

WriteDateTime method, TRegistry class, 73-74

WriteFloat method, TRegistry class, 73-74

WriteInteger method
TIniFile class, 46-47
TRegistry class, 73-74

WriteString method
TIniFile class, 47-48
TRegistry class, 73-74

WriteTime method, TRegistry class, 73-74

ENVIRONMENTAL AWARENESS

Books have a substantial influence on the destruction of the forests of the Earth. For example, it takes 17 trees to produce one ton of paper. A first printing of 30,000 copies of a typical 480-page book consumes 108,000 pounds of paper, which will require 918 trees!

Waite Group Press™ is against the clear-cutting of forests and supports refor-estation of the Pacific Northwest of the United States and Canada, where most of this paper comes from. As a publisher with several hundred thousand books sold each year, we feel an obligation to give back to the planet. We will therefore support organi-zations that seek to preserve the forests of planet Earth.

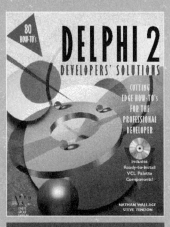

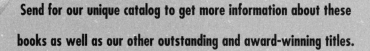

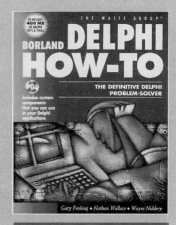

Message from the
Publisher

WELCOME TO OUR NERVOUS SYSTEM

Some people say that the World Wide Web is a graphical extension of the information superhighway, just a network of humans and machines sending each other long lists of the equivalent of digital junk mail.

I think it is much more than that. To me, the Web is nothing less than the nervous system of the entire planet—not just a collection of computer brains connected together, but more like a billion silicon neurons entangled and recirculating electro-chemical signals of information and data, each contributing to the birth of another CPU and another Web site.

Think of each person's hard disk connected at once to every other hard disk on earth, driven by human navigators searching like Columbus for the New World. Seen this way the Web is more of a super entity, a growing, living thing, controlled by the universal human will to expand, to be more. Yet, unlike a purposeful business plan with rigid rules, the Web expands in a nonlinear, unpredictable, creative way that echoes natural evolution.

We created our Web site not just to extend the reach of our computer book products but to be part of this synaptic neural network, to experience, like a nerve in the body, the flow of ideas and then to pass those ideas up the food chain of the mind. Your mind. Even more, we wanted to pump some of our own creative juices into this rich wine of technology.

TASTE OUR DIGITAL WINE

And so we ask you to taste our wine by visiting the body of our business. Begin by understanding the metaphor we have created for our Web site—a universal learning center, situated in outer space in the form of a space station. A place where you can journey to study any topic from the convenience of your own screen. Right now we are focusing on computer topics, but the stars are the limit on the Web.

If you are interested in discussing this Web site or finding out more about the Waite Group, please send me email with your comments, and I will be happy to respond. Being a programmer myself, I love to talk about technology and find out what our readers are looking for.

Sincerely,

Mitchell Waite

Mitchell Waite, C.E.O. and Publisher

200 Tamal Plaza
Corte Madera, CA 94925
415-924-2575
415-924-2576 fax

Website:
http://www.waite.com/waite

CREATING THE HIGHEST QUALITY COMPUTER BOOKS IN THE INDUSTRY

Waite Group Press

Come Visit
WAITE.COM
Waite Group Press
World Wide Web Site

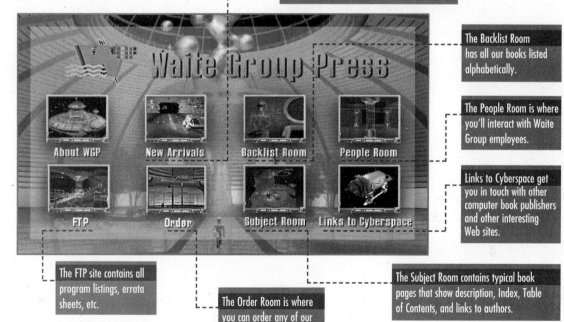

Now find all the latest information on Waite Group books at our new Web site, **http://www.waite.com/waite.** You'll find an online catalog where you can examine and order any title, review upcoming books, and send email to our authors and editors. Our FTP site has all you need to update your book: the latest program listings, errata sheets, most recent versions of Fractint, POV Ray, Polyray, DMorph, and all the programs featured in our books. So download, talk to us, ask questions, on **http://www.waite.com/waite.**

The New Arrivals Room has all our new books listed by month. Just click for a description, Index, Table of Contents, and links to authors.

The Backlist Room has all our books listed alphabetically.

The People Room is where you'll interact with Waite Group employees.

Links to Cyberspace get you in touch with other computer book publishers and other interesting Web sites.

About WGP

New Arrivals

Backlist Room

People Room

FTP

Order

Subject Room

Links to Cyberspace

The FTP site contains all program listings, errata sheets, etc.

The Order Room is where you can order any of our books online.

The Subject Room contains typical book pages that show description, Index, Table of Contents, and links to authors.

World Wide Web:

COME SURF OUR TURF—THE WAITE GROUP WEB

http://www.waite.com/waite
Gopher: gopher.waite.com
FTP: ftp.waite.com

LIMITED WARRANTY

The following warranties shall be effective for 90 days from the date of purchase: (i) The Waite Group, Inc. warrants the enclosed disk to be free of defects in materials and workmanship under normal use; and (ii) The Waite Group, Inc. warrants that the programs, unless modified by the purchaser, will substantially perform the functions described in the documentation provided by The Waite Group, Inc. when operated on the designated hardware and operating system. The Waite Group, Inc. does not warrant that the programs will meet purchaser's requirements or that operation of a program will be uninterrupted or error-free. The program warranty does not cover any program that has been altered or changed in any way by anyone other than The Waite Group, Inc. The Waite Group, Inc. is not responsible for problems caused by changes in the operating characteristics of computer hardware or computer operating systems that are made after the release of the programs, nor for problems in the interaction of the programs with each other or other software.

THESE WARRANTIES ARE EXCLUSIVE AND IN LIEU OF ALL OTHER WARRANTIES OF MERCHANTABILITY OR FITNESS FOR A PARTICULAR PURPOSE OR OF ANY OTHER WARRANTY, WHETHER EXPRESS OR IMPLIED.

EXCLUSIVE REMEDY

The Waite Group, Inc. will replace any defective disk without charge if the defective disk is returned to The Waite Group, Inc. within 90 days from date of purchase.

This is Purchaser's sole and exclusive remedy for any breach of warranty or claim for contract, tort, or damages.

LIMITATION OF LIABILITY

THE WAITE GROUP, INC. AND THE AUTHORS OF THE PROGRAMS SHALL NOT IN ANY CASE BE LIABLE FOR SPECIAL, INCIDENTAL, CONSEQUENTIAL, INDIRECT, OR OTHER SIMILAR DAMAGES ARISING FROM ANY BREACH OF THESE WARRANTIES EVEN IF THE WAITE GROUP, INC. OR ITS AGENT HAS BEEN ADVISED OF THE POSSIBILITY OF SUCH DAMAGES.

THE LIABILITY FOR DAMAGES OF THE WAITE GROUP, INC. AND THE AUTHORS OF THE PROGRAMS UNDER THIS AGREEMENT SHALL IN NO EVENT EXCEED THE PURCHASE PRICE PAID.

COMPLETE AGREEMENT

This Agreement constitutes the complete agreement between The Waite Group, Inc. and the authors of the programs, and you, the purchaser.

Some states do not allow the exclusion or limitation of implied warranties or liability for incidental or consequential damages, so the above exclusions or limitations may not apply to you. This limited warranty gives you specific legal rights; you may have others, which vary from state to state.

SATISFACTION REPORT CARD

Please fill out this card if you wish to know of future updates to
Delphi 3 SuperBible, or to receive our catalog.

First Name: **Last Name:**

Street Address:

City: **State:**   **Zip:**

E-Mail Address

Daytime Telephone: (   )

Date product was acquired: Month   **Day**   **Year**   **Your Occupation:**

Overall, how would you rate *Delphi 3 SuperBible*?

☐ Excellent   ☐ Very Good   ☐ Good
☐ Fair   ☐ Below Average   ☐ Poor

What did you like MOST about this book?

What did you like LEAST about this book?

Please describe any problems you may have encountered with installing or using the disk:

How did you use this book (problem-solver, tutorial, reference...)?

What is your level of computer expertise?

☐ New   ☐ Dabbler   ☐ Hacker
☐ Power User   ☐ Programmer   ☐ Experienced Professional

What computer languages are you familiar with?

Please describe your computer hardware:

Computer _____ Hard disk _____
5.25" disk drives _____ 3.5" disk drives _____
Video card _____ Monitor _____
Printer _____ Peripherals _____
Sound Board _____ CD-ROM _____

Where did you buy this book?

☐ Bookstore (name):
☐ Discount store (name):
☐ Computer store (name):
☐ Catalog (name):
☐ Direct from WGP   ☐ Other

What price did you pay for this book?

What influenced your purchase of this book?

☐ Recommendation   ☐ Advertisement
☐ Magazine review   ☐ Store display
☐ Mailing   ☐ Book's format
☐ Reputation of Waite Group Press   ☐ Other

How many computer books do you buy each year?

How many other Waite Group books do you own?

What is your favorite Waite Group book?

Is there any program or subject you would like to see Waite Group Press cover in a similar approach?

Additional comments?

Please send to: **Waite Group Press**
               200 Tamal Plaza
               Corte Madera, CA 94925

☐ **Check here for a free Waite Group catalog**

BEFORE YOU OPEN THE DISK OR CD-ROM PACKAGE ON THE FACING PAGE, CAREFULLY READ THE LICENSE AGREEMENT.

Opening this package indicates that you agree to abide by the license agreement found in the back of this book. If you do not agree with it, promptly return the unopened disk package (including the related book) to the place you obtained them for a refund.